Preface

Forgotten Veterans UK (FVUK) was set up as a charity to support service veterans ~~~~~~ out the UK. This is done through selfless commitment to others by a small team of volunteers located around the UK. FVUK was formally recognised as a charity in November, 2017, by the Charity Commission of England and Wales.

One of the founding principles of FVUK is to remember the past, alongside helping with the future, for veterans. Following on from the success of the Charity's first book, For Your Tomorrow – 100 Years of War Poetry, it was decided by the Trustees and Management to produce a second book, this time based around the Second World War, to commemorate the 75th Anniversary of the D-Day Landings on 6th June, 1944. Like the first book, all the proceeds from the sale of this book will go directly to providing support for service veterans.

We should remember the past and by doing so we are remembering those who gave service to their country, in many cases also their lives. This book is called 'They Gave Their Today - A Book of Heroes'. Within the pages, whilst looking at important events that shaped the war, we also look in detail at a number of heroes from the six-year conflict. In reality everyone who took part in the Second World War is a hero. But, as we discovered whilst researching and writing this book, heroes come in many shapes and sizes. We have a real selection, some well known, and many not so well known, male, female and some animal heroes. The most difficult part for the Team was choosing who to include; we decided to include heroes from many different countries of the world, including Germany, to give thanks for their actions and often self-sacrifice, without which the war may have had a very different outcome.

The book cover was designed by Glyn Macey and uses a famous World War II photograph which Glyn re-illustrated to create the haunting silhouette effect. The font, Gill Sans, designed by Eric Gill in 1918, was used on virtually all war propaganda posters from the end of the Great War and throughout the Second World War in Britain.

I would like to thank all the FVUK Management and the Team involved in the production of this book, with particular thanks to our team of proof-readers for their patience and understanding; to Mark Mason for his guidance and support, and to Douglas Miller and Thomas Fairley for their research in specific areas. Finally a very special thank you goes to my good friend and Co-Editor Christina Drummond without whose assistance and never-ending input we could not have completed this book. Her total support from the concept, as well as her writing, research and sound advice and guidance at all stages was invaluable.

We, at FVUK, hope you enjoy this book and see it as a suitable gesture to our chosen heroes to mark this important event in history. As well as the book playing a part in the history of war, it also forms part of the history of Forgotten Veterans UK. The heroes we have featured will now never be forgotten.

May all those who suffered, or are still suffering, having given service in defence of their country be at peace.

Peter Macey
Editor-in-Chief
Trustee Forgotten Veterans UK

Release

William Noel Hodgson

A leaping wind from England,
The skies without a stain,
Clean cut against the morning
Slim poplars after rain,
The foolish noise of sparrows –
And starlings in the wood,
After the grime of battle
We know what these are good.

Death whining down from Heaven,
Death roaring from the ground,
Death stinking in the nostrils,
Death shrill in every sound,
Doubting we charged and conquered –
Hopeless we struck and stood.
Now when the fight is ended
We know that is was good.

We that have been the strongest
Cry like a beaten child,
The sanest eyes unholy,
The cleanest hands defiled,
We that have known the heartblood
Less than the lees of wine,
We that have seen men broken
We know man is divine.

Lieutenant William Hodgson M.C. composed these words in October, 1915, whilst marching to a rest camp after severe fighting during the Battle of Loos. His words are revered as being factual and often tender but vivid in reality. Whatever subject he considered, he wrote about aptly, with felicitous phrase and real emotion. It was at war that his best writing is considered to have come about, in the stir of the fight, with emotions high. It was during battle that he was awarded a Military Cross for his actions. It was also in war that he died instantly when cut down by a German machine gun at the start of the Battle of the Somme.

This poem was written during the Great War, commonly referred to at the time as……..

'The War To End All Wars'

A Rise to Power

The Treaty of Versailles was a Peace Treaty. Signed on 29th June, 1919, five years after the assassination of the Archduke Ferdinand, the Treaty officially ended the state of war between Germany and the Allies. Article 231 of the Treaty required Germany to accept the responsibility of itself and its allies for causing all the loss and damage during the war and a requirement for Germany to disarm, make territorial concessions and pay reparations.

The Deutsche Arbeiterpartie, German Workers Party, known as the DAP, was a political group that had emerged at the end of the Great War and established its headquarters in a Bierkeller, at Hofbräuhaus am Platzl in Munich. The Party would meet regularly in the Festsaal, the Feast Hall, on the third floor of the building.

It was at one such meeting, just eight months after the Treaty of Versailles had been accepted and signed, on 24th February, 1920, that a 31-year-old Corporal, who was at the time attached to the political unit of the Bavarian Reichswehr, and had been tasked with spying on the DAP, entered the Bierkeller. He had become a member of the DAP in October, 1919, and had got to know the DAP leader, Anton Drexler. On this night he entered the building with the intention of speaking at the party meeting. Drexler was aware of his intentions and had allied himself with the newcomer. Finally the man stood up to give a speech. Three hours later, after much shouting with arms swinging, fists clenched and the table beside him being banged several times, the orator received tumultuous applause and cheering from the hundreds of men within the Festival Hall.

By the end of the evening the DAP had changed its name to the Nationalsozialistische Deutsche Arbeiterpartie, the National Socialist German Workers Party or NSDAP, which would be better known as the Nazi party. The apparently angry and volatile speaker had outlined a twenty-five point plan that was in his opinion inalienable and unalterable. This was in effect a political manifesto and included many items that we would expect these days: better education for children, better healthcare and employment for all German citizens. The main criterion of all the points was to establish once and for all what defined a citizen of Germany. Many of these twenty-five points were quickly forgotten but four would remain as a cornerstone to the new political party:

There would be a Union of all German speaking people.

Only Germans would be classed as citizens of Germany.

There would be a complete repudiation of the Treaty of Versailles.

There would be 'a settlement with the Jews' – who, the orator berated, were the source of all Germany's ills. All Jews would be deprived of German status, none would hold official office, none would be allowed to write for any newspapers and any Jew who arrived in Germany after the start of 1914 would be deported.

The crowd roared approval. Germany in 1920 was in an economic meltdown with high unemployment and rationing due to the outcome of the Great War and through the stipulations of the Treaty of Versailles. Here, finally, was someone telling the assembled group why they had lost the war and more importantly, who was to blame. The Nazi Party came into being on 24th February, 1920. The unknown man, Adolf Hitler was unanimously elected leader of the Nazi party in July the following year and took the title Führer.

In November, 1921, the Sturm Abteilung, SA, was formed, known as Stormtroopers, they were the party militia and also known as brownshirts because of their uniform. Two years later, led by Hitler, two thousand NSDAP and SA members marched on Munich in an attempt to overthrow the Bavarian Government. They were met by one hundred police. There were fatalities on both sides and the coup failed. The leaders were arrested and charged with treason. Hitler was found guilty and given a five-year prison sentence although he only served ten months, during which time he wrote his book, Mein Kampf.

In 1924, four years after the party had started, the NSDAP achieved 4% of the national vote. Despite its poor performance in the voting the party was evolving. The Schutzstaffel formed in 1925. Commonly known as SS, the elite group wore black shirts to distinguish themselves from the SA. Initially formed as Hitler's personal bodyguard, they later took over as the party militia. The following year the Hitler Youth, League of German Worker Youth, was formed and became integrated into the SA. The first annual party conference for the NSDAP took place at Nuremberg on 20th August, 1927. Known as the Nuremberg Rally, all subsequent annual meetings would take place at the same location. Despite Hitler's best efforts in the political ring, by 1928 the NSDAP only received 2.6% of the national vote.

Then on 29th October, 1929, the largest stock market crash in history happened in Wall Street, New York. This was, at least in part, instrumental in the NSDAP rise to power in Germany. The United States had bankrolled Germany to assist with the country's recovery after the Great War, but after the crash the U.S. demanded all of their loans back in full. The crash created havoc around the world and the years that followed became known as the Great Depression. Germany was just starting to find its footing, but the U.S. action led to companies collapsing, unemployment and poverty rising and no one had any idea how to deal with the problem. No one, that was, other than Hitler, who reverted to his original twenty-five point plan, concentrating all his efforts on what he termed as 'real' German citizens. By 1930, NSDAP had achieved 18% of the national vote making them the second largest political party, and in 1932 they won the elections with over 37% of the national vote.

In January of the following year Adolf Hitler was elected Chancellor of Germany. By the end of 1933 the Nazi party were in total control of local Government. Hitler was in a position where he could make laws without consulting the Reichstag, having banned all other political parties from the Country.

The years of 1934 to 1938 saw Hitler's popularity grow whilst the Nazi party started to eradicate everything that was not considered German. Non-German books were burnt, German citizens who were unsupportive to the Nazi regime were killed, including members of the SA, during what was called the Night of the Long Knives. Relationships between German citizens and Jews were outlawed, Jewish shops and synagogues were destroyed on Kristallnacht, the Night of Broken Glass, the status of all Jews was removed, and Hitler took Germany out of the League of Nations and banned all trade unions.

Adolf Hitler was named Man of the Year in the 1938 issue of Time Magazine.

15th March, 1939, saw Germany invade Czechoslovakia, then on 1st September, Poland.

A Declaration of War

At 11.15 a.m. on 3rd September, 1939, the British Prime Minister, Mr. Neville Chamberlain, broadcast to the nation announcing that a state of war existed between Britain and Germany:

"This morning the British Ambassador in Berlin handed the German Government a final note stating that, unless we heard from them by 11 o'clock they were prepared at once to withdraw their troops from Poland, a state of war would exist between us. I have to tell you now that no such undertaking has been received, and that consequently this country is at war with Germany.

"You can imagine what a bitter blow it is to me that all my long struggle to win peace has failed. Yet I cannot believe that there is anything more or anything different that I could have done and that would have been more successful.

"Up to the very last it would have been quite possible to have arranged a peaceful and honourable settlement between Germany and Poland, but Hitler would not have it. He had evidently made up his mind to attack Poland whatever happened, and although He now says he put forward reasonable proposals which were rejected by the Poles, that is not a true statement. The proposals were never shown to the Poles, nor to us, and, although they were announced in a German broadcast on Thursday night, Hitler did not wait to hear comments on them, but ordered his troops to cross the Polish frontier. His action shows convincingly that there is no chance of expecting that this man will ever give up his practice of using force to gain his will. He can only be stopped by force.

"We and France are today, in fulfilment of our obligations, going to the aid of Poland, who is so bravely resisting this wicked and unprovoked attack on her people. We have a clear conscience. We have done all that any country could do to establish peace. The situation in which no word given by Germany's ruler could be trusted and no people or country could feel themselves safe has become intolerable. And now that we have resolved to finish it, I know that you will all play your part with calmness and courage.

"At such a moment as this the assurances of support that we have received from the Empire are a source of profound encouragement to us.

"The Government have made plans under which it will be possible to carry on the work of the nation in the days of stress and strain that may be ahead. But these plans need your help. You may be taking your part in the fighting services or as a volunteer in one of the branches of Civil Defence. If so you will report for duty in accordance with the instructions you have received. You may be engaged in work essential to the prosecution of war for the maintenance of the life of the people - in factories, in transport, in public utility concerns, or in the supply of other necessaries of life. If so, it is of vital importance that you should carry on with your jobs.

"Now may God bless you all. May He defend the right. It is the evil things that we shall be fighting against - brute force, bad faith, injustice, oppression and persecution - and against them I am certain that the right will prevail."

On 10th May, 1940, Neville Chamberlain stood down as Prime Minister and Winston Churchill took over the role.

A Call to Fight

At the start of the Great War it seemed that everyone wanted to volunteer their services for their country, although by 1915 this eagerness to go into battle had diminished considerably. Whereas at the start of the Second World War very few volunteered for service in comparison to what had happened in 1914.

In 1939 the British Army comprised just under 900,000 officers and soldiers; considered relatively small in comparison to some other countries. Whereas the Royal Navy was the largest naval force in the world with over three hundred warships included fifteen battleships, seven aircraft carriers, sixty six cruisers, one hundred and eighty-four destroyers, forty-five patrol vessels, and sixty submarines. The Royal Air Force had around two thousand aircraft.

Due to the situation in Europe with rising tensions, Leslie Hore-Belisha, the Secretary of State for War, persuaded the Government to re-introduce a form of conscription, the Military Training Act, at the end of April, 1939. Conscription had been used during the Great War but had been stopped in 1920. Initially limited to only single men from the age of 20 to 22 years old, they would be known as 'militiamen' to distinguish them from the regular army. To emphasise this distinction, each man was issued with a suit in addition to his uniform. The intention was that all those conscripted would undergo six months basic training before being discharged into an active reserve.

At the outbreak of war, on 3rd September, 1939, the Military Training Act was superseded by the National Service (Armed Forces) Act. This imposed a liability to conscription for all men between the ages of 18 and 41 years old. Some could be rejected for medical reasons and any who were engaged in what were considered vital industries or occupations.

However, due to the heavy toll that war takes on human life, three years later, in 1942, all males between the ages 18 and 51 years old and all females from 20 to 30 years old who were resident in Britain were liable to be called up. Again there were specific exemptions which included married women, women with children of certain ages and those who would not be suitable due to health problems, amongst others. Pregnant women were not exempted but were usually not called up. Men under 20 years old were initially not liable to be sent overseas, but this exemption was lifted by 1942.

Britain did not completely demobilise in 1945, conscription continued after the war had finished. Those already in the armed forces were given a release clause, determined by the length of service and age. Releases from all three services began in June, 1945, and the last of the conscripts for the war had all been released by 1949. All women were released at the end of the war.

All Day It Has Rained

Alun Lewis

All day it has rained, and we on the edge of the moors
Have sprawled in our bell-tents, moody and dull as boors,
Groundsheets and blankets spread on the muddy ground
And from the first grey wakening we have found
No refuge from the skirmishing fine rain
And the wind that made the canvas heave and flap
And the taut wet guy-ropes ravel out and snap.
All day the rain has glided, wave and mist and dream,
Drenching the gorse and heather, a gossamer stream
Too light to stir the acorns that suddenly
Snatched from their cups by the wild south-westerly
Pattered against the tent and our upturned dreaming faces.
And we stretched out, unbuttoning our braces,
Smoking a Woodbine, darning dirty socks,
Reading the Sunday papers – I saw a fox
And mentioned it in the note I scribbled home; –
And we talked of girls and dropping bombs on Rome,
And thought of the quiet dead and the loud celebrities
Exhorting us to slaughter, and the herded refugees:
Yet thought softly, morosely of them, and as indifferently
As of ourselves or those whom we
For years have loved, and will again
Tomorrow maybe love; but now it is the rain
Possesses us entirely, the twilight and the rain.

And I can remember nothing dearer or more to my heart
Than the children I watched in the woods on Saturday
Shaking down burning chestnuts for the schoolyard's merry play,
Or the shaggy patient dog who followed me
By Sheet and Steep and up the wooded scree
To the Shoulder o' Mutton where Edward Thomas Edward brooded long
On death and beauty – till a bullet stopped his song.

A hero's Tale - Alun Lewis

 Alun Lewis was born on the 1ˢᵗ July, 1915, in Cwmaman, in Cynon Valley, Wales. One of four sons of school-teacher parents, he attended Cowbridge Grammar school, and obtained scholarships to Aberystwyth University and the University of Manchester. His dream of being a journalist did not materialise, so he worked as a teacher, and continued with the poetry he had been writing since quite young.

He announced his pacifism in a newspaper article: 'If War Comes, Will I Fight?' In May, 1939, he wrote: 'The army, the bloody, silly, ridiculous, red-faced army – in its bloody boring khaki – God save me from joining up.' A few months later he said that he would join up, that he had a 'deep sort of fatalist feeling' about it. He wanted to experience life, but not kill, although perhaps be killed. After the outbreak of the Second World War, he joined the Royal Engineers, and later obtained a commission.

In 1942, the year in which he was sent to India with the South Wales Borderers, Alun's first collection of poems was published: 'Raiders' Dawn and Other Poems', followed soon after by a volume of stories, 'The Last Inspection'. His other works were published posthumously. The second collection of poems entitled 'Ha! Ha! Among the Trumpets', featured a forward by Robert Graves, with whom he had corresponded, and whose son David was killed in 1942, in the same location as Alun was to die a year later.

He longed to be home, away from what he saw as the futility of military life; he had suffered from depression for quite some time, and found it easy to describe disorientation and emptiness. Yet he refused a post of instructor in Intelligence: "I will not lecture until I have fought". He wrote that to find out the 'secret knowledge' of soldiers he would have to go into action with them, saying it was "instinctive and categorical in me, the need to experience".

The critic Ian Hamilton wrote that Alun Lewis' poetry reflects his attempts 'to catch and hold some vision that would illuminate its desolation with meaning'. Marriage to his wife, Gweno, gave him stability, some shelter from what he said was his 'strange enemy', yet he struggled with self-hatred and despondency to the end. Gweno Lewis wrote that he managed to get everything under control by the time he had washed and shaved: "I don't think others noticed. If he appeared silent and withdrawn, wasn't he after all the Battalion poet?"

In Alun's last letter to Gweno, he wrote that his long self-torture was resolving itself 'into a discipline of the emotions and hopes of you and me', that his grasp was broader and steadier than it had been for a long time. Offered a safe position in headquarters, he repeatedly requested to go into action.

On the 5ᵗʰ March, 1944, he prepared to go out on patrol, washed and shaved, and then he discharged his pistol.

The Regiment's official report was that it was an accident.

A Hero's Tale - Kenneth Campbell

 Kenneth Campbell was born on 21st April, 1917, in Saltcoats, Ayrshire in Scotland. The youngest of six children, he attended Sedbergh School and Clare College, Cambridge, from which he obtained a degree in Chemistry and joined the Cambridge University Air Squadron.

In 1938 he was commissioned into the Royal Air Force Volunteer Reserve as a Pilot Officer, and mobilised on 25th September, 1939. After training he was based on R.A.F. Abbotsinch in Scotland. The following April he had been promoted to Flying Officer, and in September he joined 22 Squadron, who were engaged in attacking enemy shipping during the Battle of the Atlantic.

His actions on 6th April, 1941, earned him the posthumous award of the Victoria Cross. Detailed to attack the enemy battle cruiser Gneisenau in Brest Harbour, he flew his Bristol Beaufort through concentrated anti-aircraft fire from approximately 1,000 weapons in order to launch a torpedo at the battle cruiser with impeccable precision. Such precision was required as the Gneisenau was moored 500 yards from the mole in Brest's inner harbour.

Flying Officer Campbell's citation tells the story:

'In recognition of most conspicuous bravery. The battle cruiser was secured alongside the wall on the north shore of the harbour, protected by a stone mole bending around it from the west. On rising ground behind the ship stood protective batteries of guns. Other batteries were clustered thickly round the two arms of land which encircle the outer harbour. In this outer harbour were moored three heavily-armed anti-aircraft ships, guarding the battle cruiser. Even if an aircraft succeeded in penetrating these formidable defences, it would be almost impossible, after delivering a low-level attack, to avoid crashing into the rising ground beyond. This was well known to Flying Officer Campbell who, despising the heavy odds went cheerfully and resolutely to the task. He ran the gauntlet of the defences. Coming in at almost sea level, he passed the anti-aircraft ships at less than mast-height in the very mouths of their guns and skimming over the mole launched a torpedo at point-blank range. The battle cruiser was severely damaged below the water-line and was obliged to return to the dock whence she had come only the day before. By pressing home his attack at close quarters in the face of withering fire on a course fraught with extreme peril, Flying Officer Campbell displayed valour of the highest order."

Following the attack he was forced to make a steep banking turn, revealing his aircraft to the enemy gunners, he was hit and crashed into the harbour. The aircraft was salvaged and the crew members were buried in Brest Cemetery. Members of the French Resistance were witnesses on the day and the details were passed on until they reached England. They told of his courage in the face of impossible odds.

There is a memorial to Flying Officer Campbell in Sedburgh School, and a memorial plaque and bench in his home-town of Saltcoats. The R.A.F. named one of their original Vickers VC10 aircraft in his honour.

A Hero's Tale – Richard Jolly

Richard Frank Jolly was born on 28th August, 1896, in Wandsworth, London, the son of an auctioneer and estate agent. He was educated at Bedford School, where he was Company Sergeant Major in the Officer Training Corps, and joined the Royal Navy in September of 1914 with a special entry cadetship. During training at the Royal Naval Engineer College in Plymouth, he was awarded first prize in gunnery and torpedo. During the Great War, Commander Jolly served as a midshipman on the battle cruiser Princess Royal, then later on the destroyer Foxhound and the minesweeper Penarth.

He married Brenda Bowring Wimble in 1919, and they had a son, Martin. Between the wars Commander Jolly served on various ships, including Valiant, Walpole, Viscount and Vivien, his first command being on HMS Rowena. By 1932 he had been promoted to the rank of Commander, and was appointed Training Commander at Chatham.

He was given command of HMS Mohawk in October of 1939. On the 16th of that month, HMS Mohawk was patrolling the Firth of Forth, near Edinburgh, when she came under attack by enemy aircraft. These details were provided in a subsequent report: 'After arrival in Forth came under air attacks by Ju 88 aircraft and straddled by two bombs which on explosion scattered splinters causing extensive casualties to personnel on the bridge and upper decks. Fifteen of the ship's company were killed and thirty were injured'.

Among those injured was Commander Jolly; he was wounded in the stomach, but refused medical attention and also refused to leave his post, saying: "Leave me, go and look after the others." Assisted by his Navigating Officer, who was also wounded, he directed his ship for the next hour and twenty minutes, and succumbed to his injuries a few hours after bringing her safely into port.

The Captain of his flotilla reported: 'Commander Jolly was an imperturbable Commander of careful judgement who devoted his energies to perfecting his ship and ship's company for battle. His fearlessness and honesty in counsel were remarkable, and he proved his bravery and devotion to his wounded men when for a long period he manoeuvred his ship despite a mortal wound'. Sadly, HMS Mohawk was sunk in April, 1941, by an Italian destroyer which it had attacked, the destroyer managing to launch torpedoes before it in turn sank.

For his actions that day Commander Jolly was posthumously awarded the Medal of the Military Division of the Most Excellent Division of the British Empire for Gallantry in bringing his ship into harbour when he was mortally wounded. A year later, in September, 1940, the medal was exchanged by his family for the George Cross upon its inauguration; it is privately held with his other medals: 1914-15 Star, British War Medal 1914-20, Victory Medal 1914-19, 1939-45 Star, Atlantic Star, War Medal 1939-45, 1935 George V Silver Jubilee Medal, and 1937 Edward VIII Coronation Medal.

Commander Jolly is buried at St. Peter's Church, Boughton Monchelsea, Kent.

A Hero's Tale - Sophie Magdalena Scholl

As Sophie Scholl was led to the guillotine her last words were:

"How can we expect righteousness to prevail when there is hardly anyone willing to give himself up individually to a righteous cause. Such a fine, sunny day, and I have to go, but what does my death matter, if through us, thousands of people are awakened and stirred to action."

Sophie was born on 9th May, 1921, in Forchtenberg, Germany, one of four children of the town's Mayor. When she was twelve years old, Sophie joined the League of German Girls. While enthusiastic at first, she was unhappy about the Nazi ideology that was affecting the group. After the Nuremberg Laws of 1935, two of her friends who were Jewish were not allowed to join the League. Sophie complained, and also insisted that Heinrich Heine, a Jewish writer, was essential reading for students of literature.

Her father and brothers were already critical of the Nazi regime; her brother, Hans had joined the Hitler Youth programme in 1933 but became disillusioned. By the time he and some friends were arrested in 1937 for participation in the German Youth Movement, Sophie's opposition to the Nazi regime was absolute.

After graduating from school in 1940, Sophie began working as a kindergarten teacher. She was well-read in philosophy and theology, and had developed a strong Christian faith along with a talent for art. In 1941, she was conscripted into the Auxiliary War Service as a nursery teacher. She felt it was unacceptably militarised and became involved in passive resistance. Such service was required for university entrance, so after six months she was able to enrol in the University of Munich to study philosophy and biology.

In 1942 Hans Scholl founded the White Rose, with Willia Graf and Christoph Probst. They produced anti-Nazi leaflets to distribute around Munich, and Sophie began to distribute the leaflets - as a woman, it was less likely that she would be stopped and questioned. The leaflets contained exhortations such as 'Nothing is so unworthy of a nation as allowing itself to be governed without opposition by a clique that has yielded to base instinct…Western civilisation must defend itself against fascism and offer passive resistance, before the nation's last young man has given his blood on some battlefield.'

In February, 1943, Sophie, Hans and other members of the White Rose were arrested for distributing the leaflets. Their trial was presided over by Roland Freisler, an ardent Nazi and Chief Justice of the People's Court of the Greater German Reich. With a broken leg, a direct result of her interrogation, Sophie said:

"Somebody, after all, had to make a start. What we wrote and said is also believed by many others. They just don't dare express themselves as we did. You know the war is lost. Why don't you have the courage to face it?"

The trial was short with no defence witnesses. Sophie, Hans and Christoph Probst were found guilty and sentenced to death.

Rationed Britain

In 1939, Britain was importing in the region of 20,000,000 tons of food per year, including about 70% of its cheese and sugar, nearly 80% of fruit and about 70% of cereals and fats. More than half of the meat industry relied on imported feed to support its domestic meat production.

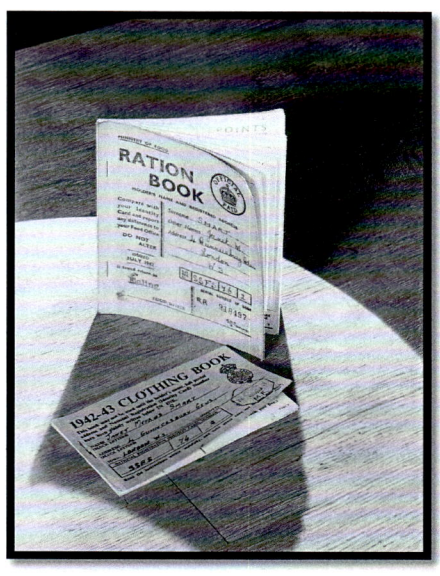

One of the strategies of Germany was to prevent imports into Britain, one of the main target areas being convoys crossing the Atlantic. By restricting the British industry, particularly of food supplies could, it was believed, potentially starve the nation into submission.

The Ministry of Food introduced a system of rationing. In order to purchase rationed items, each person had to register at chosen shops and in turn was provided with a ration book containing coupons. The shopkeeper was provided with enough food only for registered customers. Customers had to take their ration book with them when shopping, and the relevant coupon or coupons would be cancelled.

The first commodity to be rationed was petrol. In January, 1940, bacon, butter and sugar were rationed. This was followed by successive ration schemes for meat, tea, jam, biscuits, cereals, cheese, eggs, lard, milk, canned and dried fruit. In June, 1942, the Combined Food Board was set up by Britain and the United States to co-ordinate the world supply of food to the Allies, with special attention to flows from the U.S. and Canada to Britain. Almost all types of food, apart from vegetables and bread, were rationed by August, 1942.

Vegetables and fruit were not rationed but supplies were limited. Some types of imported fruit such as lemons and bananas virtually disappeared from shops. Oranges continued to be sold, however most greengrocers reserved them for children and pregnant women. Domestically grown fruit such as apples still appeared from time to time, but sellers imposed their own restrictions due to the shortage. Many people grew their own vegetables, greatly encouraged by the highly successful 'Dig for Victory' campaign. Game meat like rabbit and pigeon was not rationed but often only available through the black market.

In June, 1941, clothing became a rationed commodity by a points system. As no clothing coupons had been issued it was decided that the unused margarine coupons in ration books would be valid for clothing. The initial allowance was for one new outfit per year but as the war progressed the points were reduced until buying a coat used almost a year's clothing coupons.

From 1st July, 1942, the use of public civilian petrol was banned. Thereafter, vehicle fuel was only available to what was termed official use and included emergency services, public transport and the armed forces. Fuel supplied to approved users was dyed, and use of this fuel for non-essential purposes was considered a crime.

A Hero's Tale - Gerard Broadmead Roope

Gerard Roope was born on 13th March 1903, in Hillbrook Trull, Somerset. Once he had completed his education in 1927, he chose to join the Royal Navy. He married and had a son, Michael, who went on to become a Commander in the Royal Navy.

Lieutenant-Commander Roope was the first person to be awarded the Victoria Cross in the Second World War, and had also been Mentioned in Despatches for 'courage, resource, zeal and devotion to duty while serving with the Home Fleet in Norwegian waters and elsewhere.'

Well-liked and respected, he had taken command of H.M.S. Glowworm on 22nd July, 1938. A 'G' class destroyer, she had been launched three years earlier.

On the 5th April, 1940, H.M.S. Glowworm left for Norway as one of the escorts for the battle cruiser Renown, which had been dispatched to intercept the anticipated German invasion force. Three days later they encountered the German Heavy Cruiser Admiral Von Hipper. Using a smoke screen they fired ten torpedoes, but none found their mark, and they were hit by the cruiser's guns. Lieutenant Commander Roope ordered a sharp turn and headed straight for the cruiser with the intention of ramming it. They tore into its starboard side, tearing away armoured plating and damaging the torpedo tubes. They then drew clear and fired again, with Glowworm's only gun that was still firing. Before long she started to sink, her bows wrecked, and Lieutenant Commander Roope gave the order to abandon ship. As she went down, the crew climbed on to her bow, some diving into the sea; then her depth charges blew, killing some of the crew. The captain of the German cruiser began to pick up the survivors.

Lieutenant Commander Roope drowned after helping members of his crew don life-jackets, enabling them to be rescued by the German cruiser. An eye-witness reported that he could have saved himself but stayed in the water helping his men until exhaustion and the cold overcame him. Only thirty-one of his crew survived. The Germans treated them well, telling them they put up a good fight and that their captain was a very brave man. The only surviving officer, Lieutenant Robert Ramsey, told the story after the war; he received the Distinguished Service Order, and Engine Room Artificer Henry Gregg, Petty Officer Walter Scott and Able Seaman Reginald Merritt were awarded the Conspicuous Gallantry Medal.

The commander of Admiral Von Hipper, Captain Helmuth Heye, wrote to the British authorities recommending that Lieutenant-Commander Roope be awarded the Victoria Cross for his courage in engaging what was clearly a vastly superior warship. He acknowledged that his own crew and vessel had been placed in danger, but nevertheless hoped that he would have had the courage to act in the same way, had the positions been reversed: 'In my opinion, the bearing of the commander and crew of the Glowworm was excellent.'

It was the only time that an enemy recommended the Victoria Cross.

A Hero's Tale – Albert Matthew Osborne

Matt Osborne was born on 19th October, 1906, in Grimsby, Lincolnshire. His parents' only son, he went to boarding school in Blackpool and then enlisted in the Royal Air Force Reserves in July, 1940. After what was considered to be very basic training he was put to work as an aircraft mechanic. It is not known what work he had done before enlisting, but he was a competent mechanic, serving at various bases around the United Kingdom before being posted to Malta, upon which the Luftwaffe were making regular attacks.

He was awarded the posthumous George Cross for his 'unsurpassed courage and devotion to duty' during German air attacks and the citation details his many acts of valour:

'During a period of fierce enemy air attacks on Malta, Leading Aircraftman Osborne has displayed unsurpassed courage and devotion to duty. In circumstances of the greatest danger he was always first at hand to deal with emergencies, whether in fire fighting operations or in rescue work. This airman's fearless courage and great leadership on all occasions have been beyond praise.'

The citation goes on to list the many reasons for the award, given as examples of 'his promptitude and gallantry': he made safe the torpedo of a burning aircraft, as for ten minutes he worked three feet from the main petrol tank; extinguished a burning aircraft during a heavy bombing attack; attempted to save a burning aircraft and subsequently removed torpedoes from the area; assisted in saving the pilot of a burning aircraft and extinguishing the fire; saved another aircraft from being destroyed by fire; for six hours attempted to extricate airmen from a bombed shelter, despite continued heavy bombing as well as the danger of falling stone-work; and in the course of one day he fought fires in two aircraft, his efforts resulting in the saving of one, freed a burning flare caught in an aircraft thereby enabling the pilot to proceed, and checked the fire in a burning aircraft, ensuring the greater part of it remained undamaged.'

Leading Aircraftman Osborne was killed on 2nd April, 1942. During an intense air attack he led a party to put out the flames of a burning aircraft. A petrol tank exploded and he was injured; he recovered somewhat and returned to fight the fire but was killed by the explosion of an air vessel as he attempted to pour water over torpedoes which were in danger of exploding. The Air Officer Commanding, R.A.F. Mediterranean, stated that "Leading Aircraftman Osborne was one of the bravest airmen it has been my privilege to meet."

He is buried in the Malta (Capuccini) Naval Cemetery, where his gravestone does not mention his name; it is merely carved with the number 96. At R.A.F. Halton in Buckinghamshire, the Reserves basic recruitment course was renamed the 'Osborne Course' in his honour.

Matt Osborne's name is on the Cleethorpes War Memorial as well as the R.A.F. Memorial in St. Clement Danes Church in Aldwych.

A Hero's Tale - Violette Szabo

Violette Szabo was born on 26th June, 1921, in Paris, to an English father and French mother. Much of her childhood was spent between the two countries, but at the age of eleven her family settled in London. She left school at the age of fourteen and was working as a shop assistant at the outbreak of the Second World War.

In 1940, Violette married Etienne Szabo, who was serving with de Gaulle's Free French forces. The following year she enlisted with the Auxiliary Territorial Service, and a year later gave birth to their daughter. Four months afterwards Etienne was killed during the battle of El Alamein.

In July, 1943, Violette met Special Operations Executive Recruiting Officer Selwyn Jepson, to whom she was recommended. He stressed that volunteering brought great risks. Violette, anxious to avenge her husband's death, accepted and went through intensive physical and psychological examinations. The board, while impressed by her 'plucky and persistent' efforts, were not impressed by her average intelligence and lack of initiative. She scraped through with a 'D' grade and was sent to join a paramilitary and commando training group in Scotland, where she proved to be a crack shot. She was, however, judged to be too temperamental and lacking 'the ruse, stability and the finesse' for clandestine work.

With D-Day just months away, female couriers were urgently required, and she was offered her first mission, a dangerous assignment which would last for several weeks. She proved herself to be a capable and resourceful agent and was promoted to the rank of Ensign in the First Aid Nursing Yeomanry, which was a cover used by female S.O.E. agents.

She volunteered for another mission, which involved parachuting into France, close to Limoges. She was travelling with another agent by car when they encountered a road-block and she was captured, although the agent escaped. She was taken to Paris where she was interrogated at the infamous headquarters of the Sicherheitsdienst, the SS security service. There is no evidence that she gave anything away, or that she was tortured.

In August, 1944, Violette was sent to the Saarbrücken transit camp in Germany. After ten days she was transferred to the Ravensbrück concentration camp and from there to a smaller camp at Torgau. In October she was taken to a derelict camp south of Königsberg where she and others were put to work under dreadful conditions, building a new runway.

In January, 1945, Violette was returned to Ravensbrück. The SS were executing agents, knowing defeat was looming, and at the end of January she was executed in the crematorium yard. In the chaos at the end of the war, her fate was unsure. In March, 1946, the Daily Express produced an article, 'Chute Girl Missing'. Several weeks later an S.O.E. officer reported an eyewitness testimony of her execution.

Later that year Violette was posthumously awarded the George Cross; she was also awarded the French Croix de Guerre and the Médaille de la Résistance.

Operation Pied Piper

Operation Pipe Piper officially started on 1ˢᵗ September, 1939, when the Government announced its intention to evacuate all non-essential people, particularly children, from areas that were seen as being at risk from aerial bombardment, and moved to what were considered safer, or less targeted areas of the country.

Throughout the war more than 3.5 million people were evacuated from cities around Britain. There were further waves of official evacuations and re-evacuations from the south and east coasts during June, 1940, when it was suspected that a seaborne invasion might occur. Affected cities from the months of the Blitz up to September, 1940, were seen as all those of strategic importance and included London, Plymouth, Liverpool, Bristol, Coventry, Manchester and Birmingham to name but a few in England; Cardiff in Wales; Glasgow, Aberdeen and Edinburgh in Scotland; and Belfast in Northern Ireland, amongst others.

The Evacuation Scheme was developed during the Summer of 1938 by the Anderson Committee and implemented by the Ministry of Health. The country was divided into zones classified as 'Evacuation', 'Neutral' or 'Reception'. Priority evacuees were moved from the urban centres and billeted in any available private housing in more rural areas. Each zone covered roughly a third of the population, although several areas that were later bombed had not been classified for evacuation.

Evacuees leaving Bristol to travel to Devon in 1940

Designated reception areas compiled lists of available housing. Space was found for around two thousand people and the government also constructed camps which provided a few thousand additional spaces.

Almost 3.75 million people were displaced. In the first three days of official evacuation, 1.5 million people were moved, of which 827,000 were children of school age; 524,000 were mothers with children under the age of 5; there were 13,000 pregnant women, 70,000 disabled people and over 103,000 teachers and other 'helpers'.

Some strained areas took the children into local schools by adopting the approach used during the Great War called 'double shift education', taking twice as long but doubling the number taught. But the movement of teachers also meant that almost a million children that had been kept at home for one reason or another had no source of education.

Many children were parted from their parents. As well as the residential camps, many children were sent to stay with strangers and families, with mixed results. And many children returned home, when it was considered safe to do so, only to find their homes and their families were no longer where they had left them, or in some cases even still alive.

A Hero's Tale – George Ward Gunn

 George Ward Gunn was born on 26th July, 1912, in Neston, Cheshire. The eldest of four sons of a general practitioner, he was educated at Mostyn House School, where his father was the school's medical officer, and at Sedburgh School before going to London to train as an articled accountant. At the outbreak of the Second World War he was working as a chartered accountant with Messrs. Sissons & Co. in London. He immediately volunteered to enlist, and was called up in December, 1939, when he became a gunner in the Royal Horse Artillery. One of his brothers served with the Royal Artillery, and another with the Royal Army Medical Corps, his third brother remained at home to continue his studies.

In August, 1940, Second Lieutenant Gunn received his commission after attending the Officers' Training Corps camp. In May, 1941, for his service in Libya, he was awarded the Military Cross for 'gallantry and coolness' and for inspiring his garrison in January of that year at the Battle of Tobruk.

On the day of his death, 21st November, 1941, Second Lieutenant Gunn was in command of A Troop, J Battery, when the Germans were counter-attacking with sixty tanks near the airfield of Sidi Rezegh. There were four QF 2 pounder anti-tank guns under his command, mounted on trucks – he drove between them in an unarmoured vehicle, encouraging his men and reorganising them when necessary. The guns and their crews were knocked out one by one, the last one having been set alight with only the Sergeant having survived. Second Lieutenant Gunn aided the Battery Commander in attacking the flames, then took over the gun, with the Sergeant acting as his loader. He ignored the enemy fire and the threat of the flames exploding the ammunition as he fired approximately four dozen rounds, setting two of the German tanks alight, before being killed by a shot to the head.

Major Pinney, the Battery Commander, regained charge of the gun and continued on; as a result of their combined actions, the battery was given the honour title of 'Sidi Rezegh'. Second Lieutenant Gunn's Victoria Cross citation reads:

'Second-Lieutenant Gunn showed the most conspicuous courage in attacking this large number of enemy tanks with a single unarmoured gun, and his utter disregard for extreme danger was an example which inspired all who saw it. He remained undismayed by intense fire and overwhelming odds, and his gallant resistance only ceased with his death. But for this very gallant action the enemy tanks would undoubtedly have over-run our position.'

There is a memorial to Gunn at both of his schools, Mostyn House and Sedbergh School, and in his parish church of St. Mary & St. Helen's. A street in his home town, Neston, was named in his honour. His Victoria Cross medal is in storage. Second Lieutenant Gunn is buried in the Knightsbridge War Cemetery at Tobruk in Libya.

A Hero's Tale - Anton Schmid

Anton Schmid was born on 9th January, 1900, in Vienna, Austria. His parents were devout Roman Catholics from Moravia, and his father worked as a baker. After being educated in a Catholic school, Anton served an apprenticeship as an electrician. He was drafted into the Austro-Hungarian army in 1918, and saw action during the retreat from Italy. After the war he qualified as an electrician, opened a radio shop, married and had a daughter.

At the outbreak of the Second World War he was drafted into the German army, Austria having become part of Germany in 1938. He served at first in Poland, then in August, 1941, he was transferred to Vilnius, part of the German occupation zone after the invasion of the Soviet Union. His job was to interrogate soldiers who had become separated from their units. Based on the results of his interrogation, the soldiers could be reassigned or charged with desertion or cowardice in the face of the enemy, and if found guilty would be executed. Anton's level of compassion was already evident, as he showed kindness to the soldiers, recognising that many suffered from trauma and exhaustion, and tried to think of ways to avoid charging them with possible offences.

As his office was located in the railway station, he saw first-hand the enforced movement of Jews. From the start, whilst moved by the scenes he witnessed he did not originally intend to save them, but he responded to pleas for help, and gained a reputation for showing compassion similar to that which he had shown the battle-weary soldiers. Word spread quickly that there was a friendly soldier. He was aided in his emancipatory work by his assistant, a Jewish woman who had seen him on the street and asked for his help; she was proficient at office work and spoke several languages.

His help took many forms: employment in his unit, transportation to safer locations, releases from prison, new documentation and even shelter in his own home, when it was necessary. After meeting the Jewish Zionist activist Mordechai Tenenbaum-Tamarof, he began to work with the Jewish underground and was able to liaise with its various groups. People were provided with special passes as expert workers, and others were smuggled out in military vehicles, the alternative being certain death at the hands of the Nazis.

On New Year's Eve, 1941, Anton invited leaders of the Jewish underground to his home; Mordechai Tenenbaum-Tamarof was present and promised Anton that when the Jewish state came about he would be honoured for his humanitarian work. Less than a year later, during the Byalistok ghetto uprising, Mordechai would die by his own hand rather than be captured. He warned Anton to be careful, that he was in grave danger as word of his rescue work was spreading fast.

The following month Anton was arrested, court-martialled for high treason and found guilty. He was executed on 13th April, 1942.

In 1964, Mordechai Tenenbaum-Tamarof's promise to the German soldier was fulfilled, as Yad Vashem, Israel's official memorial to the victims of the Holocaust, bestowed on Anton Schmid the title of "Righteous among the Nations".

Dawn After The Raid

Timothy Corsellis

As a whisper in the darkness
As the hushing of the wind
As the rising of a salmon
When the water rims with ripples
Life moved laboriously over death.
As the programme seller in the audience
Blind to the passion on the stage
As the swimmer in a surging sea
As the Britisher in a foreign country
Life busied itself with death.
The blue overalls and metal helmets
The lorries, one time used for coal,
The worried warden and the rescue worker
Hovered and hurried among the ruins.
Under this pile of fallen masonry
Under those spillikins of beams
Where number thirty two lies shattered
There may be a body
Dig
For there may be a body.
Distorted corpse once breathed slum air
Lived in the grey dust where it died;
Is it for this that bending we strived
And fought in other's blood and other's sorrow
To reach these wretched mangled remains?
Is it for this that we ached in the darkness
Not knowing that nearby
Another house had fallen
To the blast of that same bomb.
Sweat fell, we were not the strong and young
They were out training, preparing,
We are the best of those remaining
We are the mellow and the hardened
And though our backs are hard of bending
Under aloofness our souls bend rending
The sorrow out of the bereaved father's breast
Tearing it out and holding it in our own hands
Adopting it to our own bodies
Caring for the children we had never seen
Sometimes we pray to be hardened and callous
But God turns a deaf ear
And we know hate and sorrow,
Intimately
And we do not mind dying tomorrow.

A Hero's Tale - Timothy John Manley Corsellis

Timothy Corsellis was born on 27th January, 1921, in Eltham, London. He was one of four children of a barrister who had fought at Gallipoli in the Great War. Despite having lost part of his arm during that war, he learned to fly but died in a plane crash when Timothy was nine years old.

Timothy attended St. Clare Preparatory School in Walmer, Kent, and Winchester College, where he was a voracious reader, the library archives showing that he borrowed a total of fifty-six books in less than three months. He also wrote almost eighty poems during his time there; it was an agreeable circumstance that nearby was the meadow where John Keats had composed "*Ode to Autumn*".

Unlike so many of his friends, he did not go to university. After leaving school he became an articled clerk in Wandsworth Town Hall, but his deepest desire was to be a poet.

In April, 1939, Timothy registered as a Conscientious Objector on religious grounds, and at the outbreak of the Second World War he became an Air Raid Precautions Warden. The poetry he wrote during that year was described as transitional. But after Dunkirk and the fall of France, and after hearing Churchill's empowering speeches, Timothy asked to be removed from the Conscientious Objectors' list and volunteered for training as a fighter pilot. During a six-month training period he continued to write and produced many of his better-known poems.

In January, 1941, Timothy was assigned to Bomber Command. He asked for a transfer to a fighter squadron or the Fleet Air Arm, explaining that his conscience would not permit him to take part in what he believed would be the indiscriminate bombing of civilians. The following month he was given an honourable discharge, after which he successfully applied to the Air Transport Auxiliary. As his right eye required medical treatment, he had to return to his previous position as an Air Raid Precautions worker until August.

Over Easter, during the Blitz, Timothy wrote three of his most salient poems: 'Real Despair', 'Repression' and 'Dawn After the Raid', reflecting the most important holy day in the Christian calendar. He had taken a renewed interest in religion after meeting a young woman at a Christian discussion group. They corresponded for several months and he wrote the poem 'Amethyst Crucifix' after being disappointed when she did not return his feelings.

By August, his eye condition had healed and he took up his post at the Air Transport Auxiliary headquarters in Maidenhead. It was at that time that he met the poet Stephen Spender, one of whose last poems was dedicated to Timothy, such an impression had he made.

On 10th October, 1941, at the age of twenty, Timothy was killed instantly when the plane he was flying stalled and crashed. The poet Oscar Williams wrote of him: "…he had written some verse that indicated a brilliant talent, a talent that was never permitted to flower; death in action does not nourish poetry".

A Hero's Tale - John Thompson McKellar "Jock" Anderson

John Anderson was born on 12th January, 1918, in Hampstead, London. He was educated at Stowe School and Trinity College, Cambridge, from which he received a Bachelor of Arts (Honours) degree in Modern Languages and History. One of his close friends was fellow Victoria Cross recipient, Geoffrey Leonard Cheshire, Baron Cheshire, who became a highly decorated Royal Air Force pilot.

While still at university he married, and he and his wife had a son. After university he joined the 8th Battalion, Argyll and Sutherland Highlanders (Princess Louise's), serving at first in North Africa and being awarded the Distinguished Service Order 'in recognition of gallant and distinguished services in North Africa', after which he was promoted from Lieutenant to Acting Major.

On the 23rd April, 1943, he saw action during the Battle of Longstop Hill, at Djebel el Ahmera, Djebel Rhar, in Tunisia. His Battalion had dug in the night before, wherever they could find cover on the open ground, in preparation for the battle the next day. As soon as they began the advance the next morning, heavy enemy gunfire began to take its toll and they suffered heavy casualties. For his actions on that day, for being such an inspiration to his men, and for eliminating strong points during the fighting around Djebel Ahmera, Major Anderson was awarded the Victoria Cross.

The citation refers to his 'conspicuous gallantry and outstanding devotion to duty', as over a period of five hours he and his men endured intense and relentless enemy machine-gun and mortar fire. It was during daylight hours and they were on a lengthy expanse of open hillside with only intermittent periods of smoke cover. Before the first objective had been reached they had sustained heavy casualties from the enemy opposition, with all the other rifle company commanders either having been killed or seriously wounded. While under heavy and continuous enemy fire, Major Anderson reorganised the Battalion, took command, and led the assault on the second objective. Despite receiving a leg wound, he carried on and eventually captured Longstop Hill with approximately forty men, which included four officers. Major Anderson had personally led attacks on three enemy machine-gun nests as well as an enemy mortar position of four mortars which had been held by over thirty Germans. His men captured two hundred prisoners and had killed many more. The citation stated that, 'It is largely due to this officer's bravery and daring that 'Longstop' Hill was captured, and it was the inspiration of his example which encouraged leaderless men to continue the advance'.

Several weeks later Major Anderson left North Africa to take part in the assault on Italy but he was killed in action at Termoli on 5th October 1943, at the age of twenty-five. He is buried in the Sangro River War Cemetery in Abruzzo, Italy.

His Victoria Cross medal was donated by his family to the Argyll and Sutherland Highlanders Museum at Stirling Castle in Scotland.

Operation Dynamo – The Miracle of Dunkirk

Just after his appointment as Prime Minister in May, 1940, Winston Churchill gave a speech to the House of Commons in which he said the events unfolding at Dunkirk were a colossal military disaster, and that the whole root and core and brain of the British Army had been stranded and seemed about to perish or be captured.

The Battle of Dunkirk took place at Dunkerque, France, between 26th May, and 4th June, 1940. From the start of the War in September, 1939, until May, 1940, the time that lapsed became known as the Phoney War, on the grounds that very little had happened in terms of fighting, but by mid-May, 1940, everything was about to change.

On 10th May, to the East, the German Army Group B invaded the Netherlands and advanced at speed to the west. In response, the Supreme Allied Commander, French General Gamelin initiated his 'Plan D' by entering into Belgium to engage the Germans. This plan relied on the Maginot Line fortifications along the French-German border holding up. However, the German Army had already crossed through most of the Netherlands before the General's French forces arrived. As a result Gamelin committed the forces under his command, three French mechanised armies and the British Expeditionary Force, towards the River Dyle. Then on 14th May, German Army Group A advanced through the Ardennes and moved rapidly to the west before turning north towards the English Channel which in effect outflanked the Allied forces. A series of Allied counter-attacks failed to sever the German spearhead, which reached the coast on 20th May, separating the British, French and Belgian forces. After reaching the Channel, the German forces swung north along the coast, threatening to capture the ports and trap the British and French before they could evacuate to Britain. The plan was to drive the Allied forces into the sea with no escape possible.

Then in one of the most debated decisions of the war, the Germans halted their advance at Dunkirk. It is debated because it was rumoured that Hitler himself had made the order to stop, but in reality the decision was made by the local commanders, although possibly sanctioned by Hitler. The army was ordered to halt for three days, which gave the Allies a vital window of opportunity to plan their escape. Unbeknown to the Germans, the Allies put Operation Dynamo into action. Also known as the Miracle of Dunkirk, over 330,000 troops were evacuated from the beach at Dunkirk. An order was put out in Britain to commandeer all seaworthy vessels along the South coast for use by the Royal Navy, in order rescue the soldiers on the beach at Dunkirk. Some even from as far west as Cornwall volunteered their boats, provided they could crew them. On the first day just over only seven and a half thousand Allied soldiers were evacuated but by the end of the eighth day the figure had risen to over 338,000 in total by over eight hundred vessels, which were a mix of Royal Naval ships and privately owned vessels including fishing boats, yachts, pleasure cruisers, lifeboats and tugs. Over two hundred and forty private boats were sunk during the Operation along with eight Royal Navy ships.

In his famous 'we shall fight them on the beaches' speech on 4th June, Winston Churchill hailed the rescue at Dunkirk as a miracle of deliverance.

A Hero's Tale - Rawdon Hume Middleton

Rawdon Hume Middleton was born in New South Wales, Australia, on 22nd July, 1916, the son of a station-manager. After leaving school he worked as a jackaroo on a grazing property, and was described as 'Slightly built, a good-looking young man, very quiet and a little moody with a strong streak of honest determination'. His great-uncle was the colonial explorer, Hamilton Hume.

Pilot Officer Middleton enlisted in the Royal Australian Air Force under the Empire Air Training Scheme, and learned to fly in Australia and Canada. He arrived in England in September, 1941, and by November, 1942, he was serving with No. 149 Squadron, Royal Air Force, having completed twenty-eight operational flights.

On the 29th November, 1942, he took off from R.A.F. Lakenheath in Suffolk, having been detailed to bomb the Fiat aircraft works in Turin. It was his twenty-ninth combat sortie, one short of the thirty required for completion of a tour and mandatory rotation off combat operations. Over the target area he had to make three low-level passes and on the third was hit by heavy anti-aircraft fire - he suffered many grievous wounds, including shrapnel in his arms, legs and body, his right eye was torn from its socket and his jaw shattered. He passed out and his seriously-wounded second pilot managed to regain control of the plunging plane at 800 feet and drop the bombs before receiving first aid from other crew members.

Middleton regained consciousness in time to help recover control, but although he knew his chances of survival were slim he was determined to fly his crippled aircraft home and return his crew to safety. During the return flight he frequently said over the intercom "I'll make the English Coast. I'll get you home." After four hours, and further damage by flak over France, he reached the coast of England with five minutes of fuel reserves. He then turned the aircraft parallel to the coast and ordered his crew to bail out. Five did so and landed safely, but two remained to try to talk him into a forced landing on the coast, which he must have known would risk extensive casualties on the ground. He steered the aircraft out over the sea off Dymchurch and the two crew members bailed out but did not survive - they were Sergeant James Ernest Jeffery, age nineteen, and Sergeant John William Mackie, age thirty-three. Both were Mentioned in Dispatches.

The plane crashed into the Channel and Pilot Officer Middleton's body was washed ashore two months later; he was 26 years old. His was the first Victoria Cross, only one of a few awarded to a member of the R.A.A.F. in the Second World War. The last line of his citation reads:

'His devotion to duty in the face of overwhelming odds is unsurpassed in the annals of the Royal Air Force."

Pilot Officer Middleton is buried at Beck Row, Mildenhall, Suffolk, and his Victoria Cross and uniform are displayed at the Australian War Memorial in Canberra.

A Hero's Tale - Inayat Khan (Alias Madeleine) – The Spy Princess

Princess Inayat-un-nisa Inayat Khan was born in Russia on 1ˢᵗ January, 1914, to a distinguished background. Her father was an Indian Sufi master and musician; her mother was American Ora Ray Baker, the niece of Christian Science founder Mary Baker Eddy, and her paternal great-great-grandfather was the ruler of ancient Kingdom of Mysore. The family were living in France when Germany invaded and they escaped to Bordeaux before boarding a boat to Falmouth in Cornwall.

Although Inayat was deeply influenced by pacifist teachings, she and her brother Vilayat decided to help defeat the Nazi tyranny: Inayat joined the Women's Auxiliary Air Force and trained as a wireless operator. She was posted to the bomber training school; however, due to her language skills, she was recruited by the British Intelligence Agency, SOE and moved to F (France) Section for specialist training. Her SOE training team reported about her, 'Not overburdened with brains but has worked hard and shown keenness, apart from some dislike of the security side of the course. She has an unstable and temperamental personality and it is very doubtful whether she is really suited to work in the field.'

Nevertheless, in June, 1943, Inayat became the first woman to be sent to France. Under the codename 'Madeleine' her role was wireless operator, transmitting messages using Morse code, a particularly dangerous occupation. Operators would hide themselves, with aerials strung up in attics or disguised as washing lines. Tapping out Morse on the key of transmitters they would often wait hours alone for a signal back just to say the message was received. If transmissions went for more than 20 minutes, the signals could be picked up by the Germans, and detection vans could trace the source. If operators moved location, the bulky transmitter had to be carried, often concealed in a suitcase. If stopped and searched the operator would have no way out. In 1943, an operator's life expectancy was six weeks.

Despite any shortcomings she might have had, her proficiency of the French language and her operating skills were excellent, and she had a determined attitude to her work, refusing to quit, even as other operators were arrested around her. But in October, 1943, she was caught by the Gestapo following a tip-off by one of the senior members of the group she had been operating with. At the time of the arrest she fought them so fiercely she was classified as an extremely dangerous prisoner. A month of interrogation yielded no information about her SOE activities, and she even sent a coded message about her compromised position whilst incarcerated, although the SOE ignored it.

The Germans finally found her notebooks, which gave them enough information to send false messages, luring more British spies to France for immediate arrest. In November, Inayat escaped from custody, but was caught and held in shackles for ten months. On 11ᵗʰ September, 1944, she was transferred with three other female prisoners to Dachau. The following morning all four were executed.

Inayat Khan was Britain's first Muslim war heroine and has no known grave. She was posthumously awarded the George Medal. A memorial bust was erected in her honour in Gordon Square Gardens, London, and she featured on a postage stamp in 2014 as part of the Royal Mail's Remarkable Lives series.

Animal and Human Hero Tales
Olga and Constable Thwaites, Regal and Constable Poole, Upstart and Inspector Morley

Olga, Regal and Upstart were horses belonging to the Metropolitan Police Service who were the only horses to be awarded the Dickin Medal on 11th April, 1947, to honour their service during the Second World War. The ceremony took place in Hyde Park. They were recognised for the courage they exhibited during the London Blitz; police horses were trained to remain calm during stressful situations while the authorities aided civilians during the bombings and aftermath.

The Metropolitan Police Mounted Branch was formed in 1760, making it the oldest part of the Metropolitan Police, and at that time it was known as the Bow Street Horse Patrol. They patrolled the turnpikes approaching London, and in later years, being stationed throughout London, they were used for traffic control and official duties. During the Second World War there were 186 horses in the division, each having a handler who usually stayed with the horse during the horse's entire career.

Olga, a bay mare with a narrow white right front coronet marking, was used in crowd control and rescue operations in South London. On 3rd July, 1944, Olga's usual handler could not be present, so she was taken out on patrol by Constable J. Thwaites. They were on Besley Street near the railway line when a bomb exploded 300 feet in front of them, destroying four houses and killing four people. Olga was startled by debris falling close to her, but she allowed Constable Thwaites to calm her down and take her to the site of the devastation. They were able to help the survivors and discourage people who may be a hindrance from coming into the area.

Regal, a bay gelding with a small white star on his forehead and socks on his hind legs, was based in Muswell Hill in North London. His handler was Constable Hector Poole. On 19th April, 1941, incendiary bombs dropped near the Muswell Hill police stables. A fire broke out in the forage room and spread quickly to the area close to Regal's stall. Regal was not injured and did not panic, allowing himself to be led out of the burning stable. Just over three years later, Regal suffered an injury when the stable was again hit by a bomb. A V-1 flying bomb caused the station roof to partially collapse over the stable area.

Upstart, a chestnut gelding with four white feet and a small star and narrow strip on his face, was originally based near Hyde Park. The stable there was damaged by enemy fire, so Upstart was relocated to East London. He was patrolling in Bethnal Green with his handler, Detective Inspector J. Morley, when a bomb landed about seventy-five feet in front of them. Both were showered in glass and shrapnel, but Upstart remained calm as D.I. Morley directed both traffic and crowds afterwards.

Olga, Regal and Upstart are buried at the Metropolitan Police Mounted Training Establishment at Thames Ditton, which also houses a museum in which their Dickin Medals are displayed.

The Battle of Britain

The Battle of Britain takes its name from a speech given by Winston Churchill on 18th June, 1940, in which he said:

> "What General Weygand called the 'Battle of France' is over. I expect that the Battle of Britain is about to begin"

The Battle of Britain was a time when the Royal Air Force came to the rescue of the country and over the short period of time it took place, during the months of July through to October, 1940, the R.A.F. defended Britain's mainland from a major air attack by the Luftwaffe. The battle has been described as the first major military campaign fought entirely by air forces.

The primary objective of the German forces was to compel Britain into agreeing to a negotiated peace settlement. In July, 1940, Germany began to develop air and sea blockades,

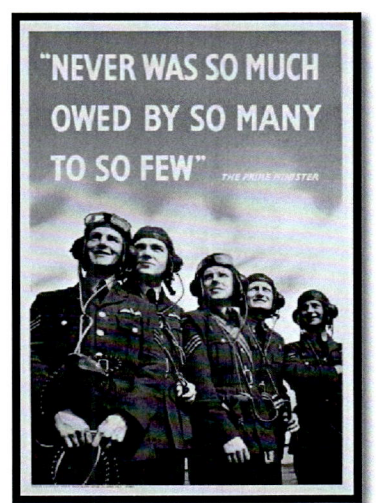

the Luftwaffe mainly targeting coastal-shipping convoys, ports and shipping centres. The plan was to starve the British nation of supplies. On 1st August, the Luftwaffe was directed to achieve air superiority over the R.A.F. with the primary aim of incapacitating British Fighter Command. Just under two weeks later the objective changed to attack airfields and the accompanying infrastructure. As the battle progressed, the Luftwaffe also started targeting factories involved in the production of aircraft. Then they moved the objective to what became known as 'terror bombing' – hitting areas of political significance or civilian targets.

Since the events of Dunkirk had unfolded, Britain still faced the threat of invasion by sea. The German High Command understood the difficulties of a seaborne attack and were fully aware that the Royal Navy had control over both the English Channel and North Sea. This was no surprise since the concentration of German sea warfare was based around its submarine fleet with only a handful of battleships. On 16th July, Hitler, determined to conquer Britain, ordered the preparation of a potential amphibious and airborne assault on Britain, known as Operation Sea Lion. This would be put into place once the Luftwaffe had established full air superiority in the skies above Britain.

However in September, R.A.F. Bomber Command's night raids over France and Germany disrupted the German preparations of converting barges. And, primarily during September, the Luftwaffe failed to overwhelm the R.A.F. fighters along the British coastline. The Luftwaffe proved unable to sustain daylight raids due to the ferocity of the British fighter crews, flying mainly Hurricane and Spitfire aircraft. This forced Germany to postpone and later cancel the planned invasion, although the Luftwaffe continued night-bombing operations on strategic targets, which became known as the Blitz, and which continued until mid-1941.

The result of the Battle of Britain was the first major defeat for Germany in the Second World War and a crucial turning point in the conflict in the defence of Britain.

A Hero's Tale - John Wallace Linton

John Linton was born on 15th October, 1904, in Newport in Monmouthshire. The son of an architect, he was educated at the Royal Navy's colleges at Osborne House on the Isle of Wight, and Dartmouth in Devon. He joined the Royal Navy on leaving school and served on H.M.S. Dauntless in the Mediterranean, then joined Submarines in 1927, being appointed to H.M.S. Dolphin and promoted to Sub-Lieutenant. By 1936 he had been promoted to Lieutenant-Commander, and in 1940 was appointed Commander of the submarine, Pandora which was destroyed by the Luftwaffe in Malta in1942. In 1941 he was awarded the Distinguished Service Cross for courage and determination in sinking two Italian supply ships and then in 1942 was appointed a Companion of the Distinguished Service Order for courage and skill in successful submarine patrols in H.M.S. Turbulent.

In February, 1943, Commander Linton died when H.M.S. Turbulent sank near the harbour of Maddelina, Italy. In February of that year, she had sailed from Algiers for a patrol in the Tyrrhenian Sea. Her movements were known until the 12th of March after which no further messages were received, and she did not return on the 23rd when expected, which is why that date is generally used as the day of her loss. As she has never been recovered, it is not known if she fell victim to an attack or a mine.

Commander Linton was awarded the posthumous Victoria Cross for valour. His citation reads:

'From the outbreak of War until H.M.S. Turbulent's last patrol, Commander Linton was constantly in command of submarines, and inflicted great damage on the Enemy. He sank one Cruiser, one Destroyer, one U-boat, twenty-eight Supply Ships, and destroyed three trains by gun-fire. In his last year he spent 255 days at sea, submerged for half the time, and his ship was hunted thirteen times and had 250 depth charges aimed at her. His many brilliant successes were due to his constant activity and skill, and the daring which never failed him when there was an Enemy to be attacked. On one occasion he sighted a convoy of two Merchantmen and two Destroyers in mist and moonlight. He worked round ahead of them and dived to attack as it passed through the moon's rays. On bringing his sights to bear he found himself right ahead of a Destroyer. He held his course till the Destroyer was almost on top of him, and, when his sights came on the convoy, he fired. His great courage and determination were rewarded. He sank one Merchantman and one Destroyer outright, and set the other Merchantman on fire so that she blew up. His career has been one of conspicuous gallantry and extreme devotion to duty in the presence of the enemy.'

Commander Linton's body was never recovered. A public house in Newport was renamed in his honour; his name appears on the Portsmouth Naval Memorial in Hampshire, and his Victoria Cross is on display at the Imperial War Museum in London.

A Hero's Tale – Cyril Joe Barton

In his last letter home to his younger brother, Kenneth, Cyril Joe Barton wrote:

"I am quite prepared to die, death hold no terrors for me. I have done nothing to merit glory."

Cyril was born on 5ᵗʰ June, 1921, in Elveden, Suffolk. He attended the Beverley Boys' School in New Maldon, Surrey, and went on to study at the Kingston-upon-Thames Technical College. He was then apprenticed as a draughtsman at the Parnall Air Factory Works in Tolworth.

At the age of nineteen, in April, 1941, Cyril joined the Royal Air Force. He was promoted to Leading Aircraftman in November of that year, and was then sent to the United States for pilot training. A year later he returned to England after graduating as a Sergeant Pilot. He joined No. 19 Operational Training Unit at Kinloss in Morayshire in May of 1943 and began making selections for his future bomber crew. They soon moved on to No. 1663 Heavy Conversion Unit at Rufforth in Yorkshire. While there, Cyril undertook his first two operational sorties over Germany. He was second pilot on two attacks on Hamburg and in August he made his first conversion flight in a Halifax with his complete crew, after which they began to train to operational standard.

In September they moved to Breighton Airfield in Yorkshire and joined 78 Squadron, their first operational unit. By then, having undertaken several operational sorties over Germany, Cyril was promoted to Flight Sergeant and then commissioned as a Pilot Officer. The following January he and his crew moved to Snaith Airfield, near Pollington in Yorkshire, to join 578 Squadron, which had just been formed from C Flight of 51 Squadron. In March Cyril made his fourth raid on Berlin, another raid on Essen and then on the night of the 30th January, 1944, the crew set out for an attack on Nuremberg – the nineteenth sortie of his career, and for which he would be awarded the Victoria Cross, posthumously.

Seventy miles from the target, his Handley Page Halifax bomber was attacked by two night fighters – the radio and rear turret were disabled, intercom lines cut, two fuel tanks punctured, and the starboard inner engine was on fire. Three of his crew bailed out, a signal having been misinterpreted, so Cyril was left without a navigator, bombardier and wireless operator. He nevertheless carried on with the remaining three crew members and released the bombs himself.

As they reached the coast of England on the journey home, they ran out of fuel. Determined not to crash onto the houses and pit head workings of the village of Ryhope, near Sunderland, Cyril made a forced landing. The three crew members survived the crash, but he died from his injuries soon after being pulled from the wreckage.

Cyril is buried in the Bonner Hill Road Cemetery in Kingston-upon-Thames. His Victoria Cross medial was donated to the Royal Air Force Museum in London, located in the former Hendon Aerodrome.

Heroes Tales – Jacques Stosskopf, Alan Turing and Gordon Welchman

Submarine Warfare and the Enigma Machine

In 1946, Winston Churchill said:

"The only thing that frightened me during the war was the U-Boat peril."

The Iron Cross is a familiar award given to many German servicemen during the Great War and Second World War, and for those who showed even greater determination in the face of

the enemy, the Knight's Cross was awarded. But superseding these awards and at the top of the German award chain, was the Knight's Cross with Oak Leaves, the highest award in the Nazi military world during the Second World War.

One such recipient was a U-Boat Commander by the name of Günther Prien who showed exceptional valour and daring during his relatively short-lived career in the German Navy, much to the detriment of the Allied sea-going services and particularly the Atlantic convoys.

By December, 1940, the German U-Boat became some of the most feared weaponry facing the Allies. Having spent many years in development by German scientists, a new design was hit upon and a mass construction programme followed to build the new Unterseeboot, Undersea boat. They became known in the West as U-Boats, following an order by Churchill, that only Allied forces would have Submarines, whereas enemy forces would all be known as U-Boats.

Attempts to develop underwater technology for use in combat have been around since the 5th century. The first American military submarine, called the Turtle, was built at the start of the War of Independence in 1776. It was the first submersible that was capable of independent operation and movement and designed to attack British warships, but was unsuccessful. Further developments were made in France in the early 1800s, but again were unsuccessful and the French and British gave up the idea. All the submarines up until then had been propelled by man-power and it wasn't until the mid-1800s that different propulsion methods were designed and tested.

The first U-Boat was commissioned into the German Navy in 1906. It had a double hull and single torpedo tube. Two years later all the U-Boats were larger in capacity and contained as least two tubes for torpedoes. The U19 class of German submarine was the first to have a diesel engine installed, and by the start of the Great War the German Navy possessed a total of forty eight U-Boats, with thirteen different classes of vessel either in service or under construction.

In September, 1935, Admiral Carl Donitz became the head of the U-Boat fleet. With the lead up to hostilities and by the start of the Second World War the German fleet of U-Boats was seen as the dominant force under the sea. The plan Donitz had put in place was for the U-Boats to move in groups, known as 'wolf packs' and attack convoys with a target of 750,000 tons of British merchant shipping being sunk per year. The German Navy had concentrated their efforts underwater instead of above and the surface ships were limited to only six battleships, many small in design to give them better manoeuvrability and firepower. These included the Bismarck and her sister ship, Tirpitz.

By December, 1940, the U-Boats were wreaking havoc with allied shipping and the Atlantic convoys. In late November convoy HX 90 left Nova Scotia in Canada bound for Liverpool, all cargo ships carrying essential war materials. The convoy comprised forty-one ships with five escorts. Fighting ships were limited due to their other duties, and as such all convoys would meet up with further escorts just south of Iceland to be escorted into British waters. At the time there were seven U-Boats on the convoy route along with three Italian submarines. They were deployed in a line on the edge of the western approach, hoping to intercept eastbound convoys. On 1st December, 1940, the incoming convoy was spotted and marked as a target by the U-Boat patrol commander. The Captain of U101 was told to shadow and report, but could not resist the temptation and fired all twelve of his torpedoes, sinking three of the convoy ships and damaging another. Just after midnight Gunther Prien turned up in his boat, U47, and sank another of the convoy ships. With more Navy ships appearing, the U-Boats disappeared, long enough to allow the convoy to escape the attack. One more ship was lost to a German bomber but the remaining twenty-nine cargo ships with heavy escort limped into Liverpool. This was the greatest success the U-Boat Command had achieved and rear Admiral Dönitz, the senior commander, was delighted. The attack on Convoy HX 90 was a big setback for the Allies and one of the most serious convoy losses of the Atlantic Campaign.

German U-Boats were held at Lorient, on the French coast in specially designed reinforced concrete pens, designed by Jacques Stosskopf, a French marine engineer who appeared to be collaborating with the Nazis with his expertise in creating impenetrable structures that still exist today. But at the same time Stosskopf was acting as a spy for the resistance, passing on information about the pens' activities with numbers and types of U-Boats held at Lorient.

The major breakthrough came on 9th May, 1941, when the Royal Navy destroyer, HMS Bulldog, captured the U-boat U-110 in the North Atlantic. On board they discovered an Enigma machine, its cipher keys and code books. This capture would lead to British code-breakers deciphering the code and identifying where the wolf-packs were patrolling.

The Enigma machine was invented by Dr. Arthur Scherbius towards the end of the Great War. Enigma means 'Riddle' in Greek and was designed as such to set codes. The military Enigma has nearly 159 quintillion different settings. The German authorities believed the Enigma code to be unbreakable.

They had not heard of British mathematicians Alan Turing and Gordon Welchman. Turing, educated at Cambridge and Princeton, worked at the British Government's Code and Cypher School before the outbreak of the Second World War. He took up a role at Bletchley Park in Buckinghamshire, deciphering the military codes used by the Germans. Along with his colleague Welchman, a mathematician, university professor and author, the pair invented the Bombe, following the work of three Polish mathematicians, which would reduce the number of combinations that they had to examine in the Enigma. The code-breakers work was significantly reduced and within a year German air force signals were being read at Bletchley Park; the following year German navy signals could be read and passed on to British Intelligence. The Bombe could crack 3,000 German messages each day, thereby providing invaluable information to the Allies about German strategy and movements.

Günther Prien won his Knight's Cross with Oak Leaves in 1939 when he audaciously took U47 directly into the British naval stronghold of Scapa Flow in Scotland. Completely undetected, he navigated into the secure area and sank the British Battleship, the Royal Oak, before escaping as easily as he has entered the area. Thereafter he was known as one of the greatest submariners ever, and his vessel U47 became famous too. In total Prien sank thirty-one Allied ships and seriously damaged another eight. Prien is believed to have died when U47 was sunk on 8th March, 1941. So much was the mystery around his death that the German High Command denied it for days whilst the British Government propaganda went wild with celebration, taunting the German Command with media messages demanding to know where Prien was. The Germans eventually conceded they had lost one of their greatest submariners. The German statement was made after Winston Churchill had personally announced his death in the House of Commons to tumultuous applause.

Gunther Prien was given the nickname 'Der Stier von Scapa Flow', The Bull of Scapa Flow.

Jacques Stosskopf was arrested when his resistance activities were exposed. He was tortured by the Gestapo and executed on 1st September, 1944.

Following the war, Welchman moved to the United States and took up U.S. Citizenship. He died in 1982.

Alan Turing worked at the National Physical Laboratory where he designed the Automatic Computing Machine, one of the first designs for a stored-programme computer. In 1952 he was arrested for attempting a homosexual act in a public house with an undercover policeman. He accepted chemical castration treatment as an alternative to a prison sentence. He died in 1954, 16 days before his 42nd birthday, from cyanide poisoning. An inquest determined his death to be suicide. In 2019, Alan Turing was named the ultimate Icon of the 20th Century, following a BBC programme which invited votes from across the UK.

A Hero's Tale – Arthur Louis Aaron

Arthur Aaron was born in Leeds on 5th March, 1922, the son of a Russian father and Scottish mother. He was educated at Roundhay School and the Leeds College of Architecture, to which he won a scholarship, and he joined the Air Defence Cadet Corps, being set on learning to fly.

In 1941 after he enlisted into the R.A.F. he was sent to the British Flying Training School in Texas and graduated in June, 1942. He continued instruction on his return to England, learning to fly the Short Stirling bomber. In April, 1943, he joined 218 Gold Coast Squadron at R.A.F. Downham Market, and in May was promoted to flight sergeant. He bombed many targets in Germany over the following three months, and his actions on one sortie, during which his Stirling was badly damaged, earned him the Distinguished Flying Medal.

On 12th August, 1943, Flight Sergeant Aaron set off for a raid on Turin in Italy. His aircraft was badly damaged by gunfire, either friendly fire or by a night fighter. Three engines and the front and rear turrets were hit, making the aircraft unstable and nearly impossible to control. The navigator was killed and other crew members injured. Flight Sergeant Aaron was hit in the face, lung and right arm. Despite those injuries he levelled the aircraft out; unable to speak because of his facial injuries, he gestured for his bomb aimer to take over, the course being set for Sicily and North Africa.

After being treated with morphia he insisted on returning to the cockpit, where he had to be lifted into his seat. He made two attempts to take control but was in too much pain and exhausted, so he wrote instructions with his left hand. After five hours, the flare path at Bone airfield was sighted, he gave directions for the hazardous landing in the darkness. Nine hours after landing he died. It is believed that had he conserved his strength and not exerted himself, he could have survived. For his actions that day he was awarded the Victoria Cross, the citation including:

'He saw it as his duty to exert himself to the utmost, to ensure his aircraft and crew did not fall into enemy hands. In appalling conditions he showed the greatest qualities of courage, determination and leadership and, though wounded and dying, he set an example of devotion to duty which has seldom been equalled and never surpassed.'

In a letter to his parents, Air Chief Marshal Sir Arthur Harris wrote:

"In my opinion never, even in the annals of the Royal Air Force, has the Victoria Cross been awarded for skill, determination and courage in the face of the enemy of a higher order than that displayed by your son on his last flight".

Flight Sergeant Aaron is commemorated at the Jewish Military Museum in Hendon, and there is a statue in his honour in Leeds. He is buried in the Bone War Cemetery in Algeria.

A Hero's Tale - Dennis Donnini

 Dennis Donnini was born on 17th November, 1925, in Easington in County Durham, the youngest of five children. His father, Alfredo, was an Italian immigrant who had moved to England in 1899, and married a Scottish woman. Together they sold ice cream as well as running a billiards establishment.

Dennis attended Corby Grammar School (now St. Aidan's) in Sunderland, and enlisted in the 4th/5th Battalion of the Royal Scots Fusiliers, in 1944, when he was eighteen years old. He was 4'10" in height, which at the time was just acceptable in the British Army.

Dennis Donnini was the youngest soldier in the Second World War to be awarded the Victoria Cross.

Fusilier Donnini was killed during Operation Blackcock when his platoon was ordered to attack the small village of Stein in Selfkant, Germany, close to the Dutch border. They came under heavy fire from the enemy hiding out in one of the houses, and Fusilier Donnini was wounded in the head. After recovering consciousness, and although bleeding profusely, he charged 30 yards down the open road and hurled a grenade into the house, from which the enemy fled, pursued by the survivors of the platoon.

Fuslier Donnini was wounded a second time, but continued firing his Bren gun until he was killed after the grenade he was carrying was hit by a bullet and exploded. His courage and selflessness enabled his outnumbered comrades to overcome the enemy consisting of thirty German soldiers and two machine guns. His Victoria Cross citation states

> 'The superb gallantry and self-sacrifice of Fusilier Donnini [which] drew the enemy fire away from his companions on to himself. Throughout this action, fought from beginning to end at point blank range, the dash, determination and magnificent courage of Fusilier Donnini enabled his comrades to overcome an enemy more than twice their own number.'

One of Fusilier Donnini's brothers, Alfred, had been a prisoner of war since 1940, having been captured at Dunkirk. His other brother Louis had been killed in May, 1944, while serving as a driver in the Royal Army Service Corps. His two sisters, Corrina and Sylvia, served with the Auxiliary Territorial Service. Meanwhile Fusilier Donnini's father, as an Italian, had been interned as an enemy alien even though he had lived in England with his wife for more than forty years - he remained detained until being released at the behest of King George VI, whom he met after he was granted leave to receive his son's posthumous Victoria Cross at Buckingham Palace. There is a memorial to Fusilier Donnini at the Easington Colliery in his home town – a wall painting featuring his portrait in the sky over a field of poppies, flanked by his Victoria Cross medal and gravestone, with the words 'Local Hero Dennis Donnini VC', underneath.

Dennis was nineteen years old at the time of his death, and is buried in the Commonwealth Cemetery, at Sittard in Limburg in the Netherlands.

A Hero's Tale - Andrée de Jongh

 One of the most successful Second World War rescue operations for the Allies was initiated by a 23-year-old woman named Andrée de Jongh.

Andrée was born in 1916 in German-occupied Belgium and was raised in the shadow of the Great War. Long before she reached adulthood, De Jongh's father, a schoolmaster, made certain his daughter was well-versed in Belgium's wartime history, its villains and its heroes. Topping the list for her were two women, executed in Brussels by the Germans: the Belgian spy Gabrielle Petit and British nurse Edith Cavell.

Andrée's admiration for Cavell was so great that after becoming a commercial artist, she also trained as a first-aid worker. When the Nazis invaded and occupied Belgium in the spring of 1940, Andrée became motivated to emulate Cavell in an additional way: resistance work, specifically the rescue of Allied servicemen.

Cavell had facilitated the escape of Allied servicemen from German-occupied Belgium and France by hiding them in her Brussels clinic, then arranging their escape across the guarded border between Belgium and the neutral Netherlands during the Great War. Andrée had a more difficult task. Belgium was now surrounded on all sides by German-occupied territory. She, along with her father and several others, decided to commence an enormously ambitious project, a 1,200 mile escape line that would take trapped servicemen from Belgium through occupied France, by way of safe houses along the route and then across the Pyrenees Mountain range into neutral Spain.

The trial run for the audacious effort ended in failure but Andrée refused to quit. Instead she asked for British assistance when she appeared at the British consulate in Balboa, Spain, with three rescued Allied servicemen. The official refused to believe that petite, youthful, neatly-dressed young woman was a resister who had just traversed the wintery Pyrenees peaks. Instead he suspected her of being a German spy. Andrée eventually won him over before gaining the support of the British Military Intelligence Service.

There were many Belgians involved in Andrée's operation, eventually termed the 'Comet Line' for its unusual swiftness. Andrée made thirty-two round-trips, personally guiding 118 servicemen to freedom. But on 15th January, 1943, during her thirty-third trip, Andrée was betrayed into the hands of the Germans. She admitted responsibility for the entire operation but because of her youthful appearance they didn't believe her. However, because she would not betray anyone else, they sent her to the Ravensbruck concentration camp.

The Comet Line continued to run in Andrée's absence, ultimately rescuing approximately 700 Allied airmen. Andrée managed to survive the war and received multiple awards from Belgium, France, Great Britain, and the United States. After regaining her health, she became a nurse and worked in various leper colonies in the Belgian Congo and Ethiopia. In later life, when her sight started to fail, she returned to Brussels.

She died in 2007 at the age of 90.

El Alamein

John Jarmain

There are flowers now, they say, at Alamein;
Yes, flowers in the minefields now.
So those that come to view that vacant scene,
Where death remains and agony has been
Will find the lilies grow –
Flowers, and nothing that we know.
So they rang the bells for us and Alamein,
Bells which we could not hear:
And to those that heard the bells what could it mean,
That name of loss and pride, El Alamein?
– Not the murk and harm of war,
But their hope, their own warm prayer.
It will become a staid historic name,
That crazy sea of sand!
Like Troy or Agincourt its single fame
Will be the garland for our brow, our claim,
On us a fleck of glory to the end:
And there our dead will keep their holy ground.
But this is not the place that we recall,
The crowded desert crossed with foaming tracks,
The one blotched building, lacking half a wall,
The grey-faced men, sand powdered over all;
The tanks, the guns, the trucks,
The black, dark-smoking wrecks.
So be it: none but us has known that land:
El Alamein will still be only ours
And those ten days of chaos in the sand.
Others will come who cannot understand,
Will halt beside the rusty minefield wires
And find there – flowers.

A Hero's Tale - John Jarmain

John Jarmain was born in 1911, in Shrewsbury. He won a scholarship to Shrewsbury School and went on to attend Queen's College, Cambridge, at which he read mathematics and won a blue for gymnastics. After graduating he married, and he and his wife moved to West Pennard, near Glastonbury in Somerset. To supplement the income from his poetry, he began working as a schoolmaster, teaching mathematics, English, literature and Italian at Millfield School in Street. Always having been a private person, he became known as something of a recluse.

In September, 1939, he enlisted in the Royal Artillery, serving with 242 Oban Battery, 61st Anti-Tank Regiment who were attached to the 51st Highland Division. Two years later, after hard training in Scotland, he was sent to Egypt and saw action at the Battle of El Alamein in October and November of 1942. He also saw action in a number of battles until the surrender of Tunis in May of 1943, being in exposed positions on the front line: Tobruk, Mersa Brega, Misurata, Leptis Magna, Tripoli, the Mareth Line, Wadi Akrit and Enfidaville.

During this time he wrote what was considered to be his best poetry - he wrote wherever he found himself, in dugouts, living rough in the desert, on the move, and at night in the moonlight. These poems he sent to his second wife, whom he had married in Salisbury on 10th May, 1940, the same day the Nazi regime invaded Belgium. He was a pacifist who had the word 'atheist' on his dog tags.

"I don't suppose God will take a blind bit of notice," he would say to those who thought he was being disrespectful.

Having been promoted to the rank of Major, and commanding 193 Battery, John took part in the invasion of Sicily in July, 1943, and saw action at Vizzini, Ramacca, Gerbini and the Sferro Hills, after which he returned to England in preparation for D-Day. He landed in Normandy on 7th June, 1944, and ended up in an exposed salient to the east of Caen in the Calvados region. But just under three weeks later, the of 26th June, 1944, he was killed at dawn, in the village of St. Honorine-la-Chardonorette, by a fragment of mortar shell while he was driving down to inspect his troops.

Major John Jermain is buried in the 6th Airborne Cemetery at Ranville, ten kilometres north-east of Caen in Normandy. John left behind five children.

Professor Tim Kendall, Director of the University of Exeter's Centre for Literature and Archives, said:

"The poets of the Second World War are less well-known than their First World War predecessors, but at their best, they were just as powerful. In Jarmain's work, the mud of the Somme is replaced by desert landscape. Jarmain becomes a connoisseur of sand as he studies its shapes and shifting colours under different climatic conditions. He is a landscape poet inspired by some of the most hostile and forbidding landscapes ever endured."

A Hero's Tale - Edwin Essery Swales

 Edwin Swales was born on 3rd July, 1915, in Inanda, Natal, South Africa. His father, a farmer, died during the influenza epidemic of 1918, so his mother moved her children to Durban, where he attended school and later was employed by Barclays Bank.

In 1935 he joined the Natal Mounted Rifles, serving in Kenya, Abyssinia, Somalia and Eritrea. He joined the South African Air Force in 1942 and was seconded to the Royal Air Force in 1943. In December, 1944, he was awarded the Distinguished Flying Cross following a bombing raid on Cologne, during which he outmanoeuvred five enemy aircraft. The citation references his 'spirited action' and 'exceptional coolness.'

On the 23rd February, 1945, while serving with the elite R.A.F. Pathfinders, Major Swales was killed when his aircraft was disabled and crash-landed near Valenciennes in northern France. It was his forty-third operational flight, for which he was awarded the posthumous Victoria Cross. As Master Bomber of a force which attacked Pforzheim in Germany, it was his role to locate the target area and give the bombers precise aiming instructions. After reaching the target one of his engines was damaged by a German fighter, and even though his rear guns failed he proceeded with the mission. The German fighter closed in, firing again, damaging Major Swales' second engine. He managed to stay over the target area, continuing to issue instructions until the mission, one of the most concentrated and successful of the war, was complete.

Major Swales then started for home, determined to keep his aircraft and crew out of enemy hands. His aircraft was so badly damaged it was difficult to keep in the air, its speed being reduced and the blind-flying instruments not functioning. By the time he reached France he was flying in heavy clouds with turbulence, losing height and the aircraft becoming more difficult to control. In this desperate situation he ordered his crew to bail out, and was alone when his aircraft plunged to earth. His Victoria Cross citation states:

'Intrepid in the attack, courageous in the face of danger, he did his duty to the last, giving his life that his comrades might live.'

Air Chief Marshal Sir Arthur 'Bomber' Harris wrote to Major Swales' mother: 'On every occasion your son proved himself to be a determined fighter and resolute captain of his crew. His devotion to duty and complete disregard for his own safety will remain an example and inspiration to us all.'

In Durban a street was named after him, but was later renamed after an operative of the African National Congress militant wing. One opponent of this change stated that there should be no sacrifice of Major Swales' legacy: "One whose extremely brave deeds were awarded in a war which was to liberate the entire western world of tyrannical and rather deadly racial political philosophy as well as dictatorial megalomaniacs supporting such ideology."

Major Swales is buried in the War Cemetery at Leopoldsburg in Belgium.

A Hero's Tale – Jans Baalsrud

Jan Sigurd Baalsrud was born on 13th December, 1917, in Kristiana, now Oslo, in Norway. He trained as an instrument-maker, and in 1938 completed military service.

Germany invaded Norway on 9th April, 1940, after intercepting British plans to prevent them taking Norway and Sweden. Norway was unprepared for war, hoping to maintain the neutrality that kept it safe during the Great War. Thus began the unsuccessful two-month Norwegian Campaign, with which Jan Baalsrud was involved. The royal family had fled to the United Kingdom, and government members went into exile; they were replaced by Vidkun Quisling, whose name has become a noun, meaning a traitor who collaborates with an occupying regime.

Baalsrud escaped to Sweden where he was trained as a spy by the British legation. Caught by the Swedes during his fourth trip to Norway, he was tried as a spy, imprisoned for three months and then expelled from the country. He travelled through several countries for the next few months, then arrived in Scotland where he was recruited by the Special Operations Executive and trained in intelligence and sabotage operations in the Scottish highlands.

Around that time, the small fishing boats that were travelling between Scotland and Norway came to the attention of those needing to transport agents, radio equipment, munitions and fugitives between the two countries. The Shetland Islands were ideal, and thus began the operation known as The Shetland Bus. Jan Baalsrud set off for Norway aboard one of the fishing boats, the Brattholm, on 24th March, 1943, on a mission with eleven others to recruit resistance fighters and destroy the air control tower at Bardufoss.

Their contact had died and the man replacing him reported them to the Germans. A gunship was sent to ambush them, but Jan escaped and reached the shore. He was shot in the foot yet managed to kill the two Germans who chased him. He travelled for nearly a week, through heavy snow, managing to avoid German search parties. Farmers helped him with food and shelter. During a storm an avalanche carried him three hundred feet down into a valley. Concussed and snow blind, he made his way to the settlement of Furuflaten and was taken in by a resistance group. After recovering somewhat, they took him up the Revdal mountain to a group of Lapps who took him across the Swedish border by reindeer, in exchange for brandy, coffee and tobacco.

It was two months after the ambush of the Brattholm - he was barely alive, weighing less than six stone, and missing his toes, which he had amputated himself due to frostbite. His recovery was slow and he had to learn to walk again, after which he returned to Scotland to train resistance fighters.

He returned to Norway to continue the fight, until Norway was liberated in 1945. For his service, Jan was awarded the St. Olav's Medal with Oak Branch.

He passed away on 30th December, 1988.

A Peace Proposal

In May, 1941, one of the most intriguing stories of the Second World War happened. It began with a Messerschmitt Bf 110 crashing in a field at Floors Farm, Eaglesham, on the south side of Glasgow, Scotland. The date was 10th May. The pilot was discovered struggling with his parachute by a ploughman, David McLean. Identifying himself as 'Hauptmann Alfred Horn', the pilot said he had an important message for the Duke of Hamilton.

McLean helped him to his nearby cottage and contacted the local Home Guard unit, who escorted the captive to their headquarters in Busby, East Renfrewshire. He was taken from there to the Police station at Giffnock arriving just after midnight. He was searched and his possessions confiscated. Horn, the name he was going by, repeatedly requested to meet with the Duke of Hamilton whilst being questioned with the aid of an interpreter, Major Donald, the area commandant of Royal Observer Corps. After the interview, he was taken under guard to Maryhill Barracks on the north side of Glasgow where his injuries were treated. By this time some of his captors suspected the German's true identity, though he continued to insist his name was Horn.

The true identity of the pilot was Rudolf Hess, a German politician and second-in-command of the Nazi party. Hess wanted to speak with the Duke of Hamilton as he believed he was prominent in the British Government, and being on the opposition was against Britain's involvement in the War. Hess had a peace proposal to offer. His view was that while the war was progressing, Hitler's attention had become focused on foreign affairs and the conduct of the war. Hess was not directly engaged in these endeavours and was becoming increasingly sidelined from the affairs of the nation and from Hitler's attention; Martin Bormann had successfully ousted Hess in many of his duties and usurped his position at Hitler's side. Hess was concerned that Germany would face a war on two fronts, the West and East, as plans progressed for Operation Barbarossa, the invasion of the Soviet Union, which was scheduled to take place in 1941.

Hess had decided to attempt to bring Britain to the negotiating table by travelling himself to seek meetings with the British Government. He asked the advice of his friend Albrecht Haushofer, who suggested several potential contacts in Britain including a friend of Haushofer, the Duke of Hamilton. Hess settled on Hamilton as his main contact point. On his instructions, Haushofer wrote to Hamilton in September, 1940, but the letter was intercepted by MI5 and the Duke did not see it until March of the following year.

Before his departure from Germany, Hess gave his adjutant a letter addressed to Hitler that detailed his intentions to open peace negotiations with the British. He planned to initially do so with the Duke of Hamilton, believing the Duke was willing to negotiate peace with the Nazis on terms that would be acceptable to Hitler. The letter was delivered to Hitler at the Berghof on 11th May.

The Duke of Hamilton arrived at Maryhill Barracks the next morning, and after examining the prisoner's effects, he met alone with Hess who immediately admitted his true identity and outlined the reason for his flight. Hess could speak English well, but was having trouble understanding Hamilton. He told Hamilton that he was on a 'mission of humanity' and that Hitler 'wished to stop the fighting' with Britain. Hess, who had prepared extensive notes, spoke to Hamilton and a representative from the Foreign Office at length about Hitler's expansionary plans and the need for Britain to let the Nazis have free rein in Europe, in exchange for Britain being allowed to keep its overseas possessions and be free from attack.

On receipt of the letter from Hess, Hitler stripped him of all of his party and state offices, and secretly ordered him shot on sight if he ever returned to Germany.

An American journalist who met both Hitler and Hess believed that Hess was sent to Britain by Hitler to deliver the message to Churchill himself. However, the Soviet leader Joseph Stalin believed the flight had been engineered by the British, and challenged Churchill with this fact at a meeting in 1944. Churchill denied any involvement.

Despite flying directly from Germany to Britain, his plane was detected and two spitfires were sent up to intercept it, they never found him. Another spitfire was sent up and again Hess eluded them. This, in his own words, was one of his greatest flying achievements.

Rudolf Hess remained under arrest until the end of the war. He was tried at the Nuremburg Trials; he escaped the death penalty but was sentenced to life imprisonment and sent to Spandau Prison in Berlin. Hess remained in Spandau until his death on 17th August, 1987, suspected as suicide.

Spandau Prison, Berlin

A Hero's Tale – Patrick Reid

Patrick Reid was born on 13th November, 1910, in Ranchi, India. He was educated in England and Ireland before being sent to Clongowes Wood College in County Kildare, studying later at Wimbledon College and King's College, in London. After graduating in 1932 he trained as a civil engineer.

Patrick was commissioned into the Territorial Army in 1933, and two years later served with the Royal Army Service Corps (Supplementary Reserve). By the outbreak of the Second World War he had been promoted to the rank of Lieutenant and was mobilised for active duty. On the 27th May, 1940, he was taken prisoner and sent to Laufen Castle in Bavaria, whereupon he began to plan an escape. A tunnel was dug to a shed on a nearby property, and on the 5th September he and five other prisoners escaped. They planned to head to Yugoslavia, but after five days were captured in Radstadt, Austria. They were punished with solitary confinement for a month, with only bread and water for sustenance.

Colditz Castle was considered out of all the German prisons to be the most escape-proof, and Major Reid was sent there in November, 1940, and was soon planning an escape. At the end of May, 1941, after bribing a guard, he and eleven other prisoners crawled through a sewer pipe, the first step of a plan which would end with a climb over a twelve-foot barbed-wire-topped wall. The bribed guard betrayed them and once again Major Reid found himself in solitary confinement.

He became the Escape Officer until April, 1942, when he was replaced by Captain Richard Howe, who had been one of the other captured escapees from Laufen Castle. In October, 1942, he planned and achieved his own successful escape with three other prisoners, Flight Lieutenant Howard Wardle, Major Ronald Littledale and Lieutenant Commander William Stephens. Having cut through bars on a window, they were able to cross an outer yard without being seen by any guards, then went through the cellar under the Commandant's headquarters and crawled through an air shaft into the moat, finally escaping through the park. Separating into pairs, they travelled to Tuttlingen near the Swiss border, with Major Reid and Flight Lieutenant Wardle crossing the border on the 20th October.

Major Reid worked for MI6 in Switzerland gathering information from arriving escapees, from March, 1943, for three years, while he was an Assistant Military Attaché. He left the army in March, 1947, then served as First Secretary (Commercial) in the British Embassy in Ankara, Turkey, for three years. From then until 1953, he was Chief Administrator for the Organisation for European Economic Co-operation in Paris.

For his 'gallant and distinguished services in the field', Major Reid was awarded the Military Cross on 4th May, 1939 and in December, 1945, he became a Member of the Order of the British Empire (Military Division).

He passed away at the Frenchay Hospital in Bristol on 22nd May, 1990, at the age of seventy-nine.

War in the Desert

The North African Campaign took place from 10th June, 1940, to 13th May, 1943. Campaigns were fought in both the Libyan and Egyptian deserts and in Morocco, Algeria and Tunisia.

Fighting started when Italy joined the war in support of Germany on 10th June, 1940. The initial stages were successful for the Allies with the 11th Hussars and 1st Royal Tank Regiment crossing into Libya from Egypt and taking the Italian Fort Capusso. This was followed by various counter-offensives from both the Italians and Allies, finally resulting in the Italian 10th Army being destroyed by the Allies in December, 1940. Then in February, 1941, the German Afrika Corps arrived, in order to support the beleaguered Italians and to avoid complete defeat in the region. Germany's top General, Field Marshal Erwin Rommel, was in command.

A series of battles for control of Libya and regions of Egypt followed which reached a climax in the second battle of El Alamein when the British Commander, Lieutenant General Bernard Montgomery, with the additional assistance of the United States forces who arrived in theatre on 11th May, 1942, inflicted a decisive defeat on the Afrika Corps in October, 1942, forcing the Corps' remnants into Tunisia before forcing their surrender in May, 1943.

Information gleaned using the British 'Ultra' code-breaking intelligence was critical to the Allied success in North Africa, and the victory led directly to the Italian Campaign, the successes of which culminated in the downfall of the fascist government in Italy and eliminated Hitler's main European ally.

Johannes Erwin Eugen Rommel

Rommel is widely considered one of the greatest military minds and strategists that Germany had. Popularly known as the 'Der Wüstenfuchs' – 'Desert Fox' - he served as Field Marshal during the Second World War. He had been a highly decorated officer in the Great War.

He distinguished himself as the commander of the 7th Panzer Division during the invasion of France in 1940. His leadership of German and Italian forces in the North African Campaign established his reputation as one of the most able tank commanders. Among his British adversaries he earned a strong reputation for chivalry, and the North African Campaign has often been referred to as a 'war without hate'.

However, in 1944 Rommel was implicated as one of the leading supporters in the '29th July, Plot' to assassinate Hitler, which failed. Due to Rommel's status as a national hero, Hitler decided to remove him quietly as opposed to a public execution. He was given a choice between taking his own life in return for assurances that his reputation would remain intact and that his family would not be persecuted following his death, or to face a trial that would result in his disgrace and execution; he chose the former, committing suicide using a cyanide tablet.

Rommel was given a full state funeral.

A Hero's Tale - Alan Mitchell

George Allan Mitchell was born in Highgate in London on 30th August, 1911. He attended Farmer Road Boys' School in Leyton, and enlisted in the army before the outbreak of the second world war, serving with 1st Battalion, the London Scottish (Gordon Highlanders) Regiment. He went to Italy with his battalion in late 1942 as part of the invasion, and in the early hours of 24th January, 1944, his actions gained him the Victoria Cross.

Private Mitchell's company had been ordered to carry out an attack on Damiano Ridge; the only two officers were wounded early on, the platoon commander was killed right after ordering a movement against enemy machine guns, and there was no platoon sergeant. As they advanced, they were met with point-blank range heavy machine gun fire. Private Mitchell charged alone up the hill with a rifle and bayonet, through intense fire, and killed the machine-gun crew, enabling his platoon to continue.

Again they came under heavy fire by the enemy and he went forward followed by what remained of his section; they killed six Germans and took twelve prisoners. They were again fired upon shortly afterwards. Private Mitchell went forward, alone again and killed the crew. For his actions that day he was posthumously awarded the Victoria Cross.

Allan's citation reads:

'The section now found itself immediately below the crest of the hill from which heavy small arms fire was being directed and grenades were being thrown. Private Mitchell's ammunition was exhausted, but in spite of this he called on the men for one further effort and again led the assault up the steep and rocky hillside. Dashing to the front, he was again the first man to reach the enemy position and was mainly instrumental in forcing the remainder of the enemy to surrender. A few minutes later, a German who had surrendered, picked up a rifle and shot Private Mitchell through the head. Throughout this operation, carried out on a very dark night, up a steep hillside covered in rocks and scrub, Private Mitchell displayed courage and devotion to duty of the very highest order. His complete disregard of the enemy fire, the fearless way in which he continually exposed himself, and his refusal to accept defeat, so inspired his comrades, that together they succeeded in overcoming and defeating an enemy superior in numbers, and helped by all the advantages of the ground.'

Private Mitchell's Victoria Cross medal was held by his family until 1949, when it was put in safe-keeping at his school, which had been renamed after him. In 2006, his Regiment purchased the medal, at which time it was handed over to the Regimental Museum. The funds enabled the school to install a mobile classroom for computer training and job searching.

Private Mitchell is buried in the Commonwealth War Graves Commission Minturno War Cemetery at Sessa Arunca, overlooking the Garigliano River and Damiano Mountains.

A Hero's Tale - Wilhelm Hosenfeld

 Wilhelm Hosenfeld was born on 2nd May, 1895, in Hesse, Prussia. He was one of six children of a Catholic schoolteacher, who raised them with patriotism and piety. When the Great War broke out he joined the infantry. Seriously wounded in 1917, he was awarded the Second Class Iron Cross. At the end of the war he worked as a teacher, married the daughter of an artist, and they had five children.

Although he eschewed anti-Jewish and anti-Catholic sentiment, he was interested in national-socialism, and joined the Workers' Party in 1935, believing they would aid Germany in recovering from post-war austerity and the 1918 defeat. Called up in 1939, he was sent to Poland to aid in the construction of a prison camp. Taking pity on a pregnant woman he met outside the camp, he arranged for her husband's release, and then saved the life of a soon-to-be-executed man, convincing the Gestapo that he needed the prisoner for some essential work.

By December 1939, he had witnessed enough atrocities to turn him against the Nazi ideology. He wrote:
"Have they freed criminals and disturbed people from psychiatric hospitals that function like rabid dogs? Unfortunately, no, these are the people who occupy high positions in our country."

He gained strength from his faith and went to mass where he learnt Polish, and began providing false documents in order to save the lives of priests, Jews and members of the Polish resistance. In 1943 he wrote:
"Innumerable Jews have been killed, without any reason, without meaning. It is beyond understanding. These brutes think we will win the war that way. But we have lost the war with this frightful mass murder. It is impossible to believe these things, although they are true. By allowing these actions, we are partakers of the guilt."

After the Warsaw Uprising in 1944, Wilhelm served in German counter-intelligence, where he demanded that prisoners were to be treated in accordance with the Geneva Convention, against the orders of Heinrich Himmler. During the winter of 1944 he encountered the pianist, Wladyslaw Szpilman; he kept him hidden and brought him food and clothing. Wladyslaw described Wilhelm in his memoirs as 'the only human being in German uniform' – the story of their relationship is told in the 2002 film, The Pianist.

In 1945, Wilhelm was imprisoned by the Soviets, and in 1950, he was sentenced to twenty-five years for war crimes simply because he was a German officer. Władysław Szpilman asked for his release but the Soviets refused. Wilhelm suffered brutal interrogation, and died in August, 1953, of a ruptured thoracic aorta, a direct result of the torture he received.

After his widow's death, hundreds of letters and several notebooks were found and published in 2004. Władysław Szpilman asked Yad Vashem, at the Holocaust Remembrance Centre, to recognise him as 'Righteous among the Nations', the highest distinction Israel can bestow on non-Jews. In 2009, this was finally given. He was posthumously awarded the Commander's Cross of the Order of Poland Restituta, and a plaque marks the building where he and Wladyslaw met – its installation was attended by their children.

The Bouncing Bomb

In July 2017, divers from the British Diving Association were deep in the waters of Loch Striven, in Scotland, recovering two remnants that had not been seen since the Second World War. The pieces they brought up from the bed of the Loch were spherical in shape with flattened sides. Three feet in diameter, they weighed 1,200lbs. They were dummy bombs. At the time of their invention they were given the name The Highball. The bombs retrieved in 2017 had not been seen since 1943.

Loch Striven is a sea loch extending off the Firth of Clyde and forms part of the Cowal Peninsula in Argyll and Bute, on the West of Scotland. Nowadays it is a popular tourist spot for sightseers, fishing and hill climbers around the Loch. But in the lead up to 1943 the Loch was off limits to all, except those involved in a top secret mission; testing a newly designed bomb. So much so was the secrecy that smoke machines were used, to deploy thick white smoke all around the Loch, to prevent anyone from witnessing the tests. Over the test period around two hundred dummy Highballs were dropped onto the Loch.

Designed by one of the most famous scientists of the war years, Sir Barnes Wallis, the Highball was part of the bouncing bomb programme. It was a uniquely different design to the Dambuster and as such was surrounded by a very high level of secrecy during the testing phase. Prior to launch, the bombs were spun up by the opening of an air duct under the aircraft, after which they had to be dropped at a set speed, altitude, and precise distance from a target to be effective. Once the design had been perfected, the flights over the Loch were used for crew training, as exact precision was required to get the bombs to bounce effectively up to their specific target - instead of hitting it, the Highball would sink beside the target and become a depth charge to explode at a specific depth alongside its target.

The Highball was designed with only one target in mind, the German battleship, the Tirpitz, a sister ship to one of the most feared of the German fleet, the Bismarck. The battleship which had been used to attack the North Atlantic convoys was holed-up in a secret mooring in Norwegian waters, so access was very limited. All battleships have their maximum strength of armour around the sides, whereas the hull is less well-protected. A depth-charge bomb going off near the hull would, it was believed, cause in most cases irreparable damage to a ship. Highball was never used operationally but Wallis' other bouncing bomb, known as Upkeep, and weighing in at nearly 10,000lbs had been designed for a totally different purpose. Nineteen of them were used during Operation Chastise in May, 1943. The Dambuster Mission, as it became known, led to the destruction of the Mohne and Edersee Dams, which when destroyed caused catastrophic flooding of the Ruhr valley and villages in the Eder Valley, one of the prime industrial locations of Germany.

On 12th November, 1944, during Operation Catechism, Lancaster Bombers carrying Tallboy bombs sank their target, the Tirpitz, and although other targets were planned for Highball. which included the Italian Navy and German u-boat pens at Lorient, they were never used in anger.

A Hero's Tale – Guy Gibson

Guy Penrose Gibson was born in India on 12th August, 1918. He was taken to England as a child and educated in Oxford. In order to fulfill his desire to become a test pilot, he joined the R.A.F., being commissioned on 31st January, 1937, gaining his pilot's wings in May, and was promoted to Pilot Officer in November.

After training, Pilot Officer Gibson was posted to 85 Squadron. From April to September of 1940 where he completed thirty-four operations, acquired a reputation for being fearless, and was promoted to Flight Lieutenant. In November 1940 he was sent to 29 Squadron, and experienced a lull in operations until March, 1941, when he destroyed a German bomber near Skegness. Promotion to Squadron Leader followed and by September he had completed ninety-nine operational sorties. He was awarded the Distinguished Flying Cross in 1940, and in 1941 received the Bar to the D.F.C. for 'utmost courage and devotion to duty'.

He spent a short time as Chief Flying Instructor, returning to operations in April, 1942, joining 106 Squadron for eleven months and taking part in most of their major raids. During that time he was awarded the Distinguished Service Order for many sorties, including the raids on Danzig, Genoa and Milan – the citation referring to his skill and courage. The following year he was awarded the Bar to the D.S.O. by which time he had completed one hundred and seventy-two sorties, including attacks on Berlin and Stuttgart – the citation for the Bar referred to his 'skilful leadership and contempt for danger'. He was then asked to form a new squadron for a special operation.

The operation for which 617 Squadron was formed was an attack on six dams in Germany - the Dambusters raid. Much consideration was given to the choice of crews for the specially-modified Lancasters, carrying Barnes Wallis' 'bouncing bomb', nicknamed 'Upkeep'. Gibson made the first attack on the Mohne Dam on the night of 16th May, 1943, drawing fire on himself so that those following could attack the dam in turn – he repeated this procedure at the Eder dam, showing complete disregard for his own safety. For his actions he was awarded the Victoria Cross, and thirty-three men from his crews received gallantry awards. Afterwards, along with Winston Churchill, Gibson visited Canada and the United States, where he received the U.S. Legion of Merit.

In 1944, Gibson was given the opportunity to run for Parliament, but he wanted only to return to flying. The Air Officer Commander in Chief, Arthur 'Bomber' Harris, arranged for one last sortie: an attack on the Rheydt and the Monchengladbach railway and industrial centres on 19th September.

During the flight, he and his navigator Squadron Leader James Warwick D.F.C. were seen to have engine trouble over Steenburgen in the Netherlands, just before the aircraft crashed in a ball of flames.

Wing Commander Gibson and Squadron Leader Warwick are buried in the Kruisland Cemetery in Steenburgen.

A Hero's Tale - Dr Aiden MacCarthy

 Aidan MacCarthy was born in Castletownbere on the Beara Peninsula in County Cork, Ireland, in 1914. He was educated at Clongowes Wood School and University College, Cork, from which he graduated in 1938, with a medical degree. To find employment as a doctor, he moved first to Wales, and then to London, where on the eve of the Second World War he joined the Royal Air Force. He enlisted on a short-service commission, but remained for thirty years.

Among those evacuated from Dunkirk in June, 1940, for three days he tended to wounded and dying soldiers while under fire from enemy aircraft. The ship he was on was torpedoed in the Channel, but he made it safely back to England. He was promoted to the rank of flight lieutenant and in 1941 at R.A.F. Honington, he helped to rescue two crewmen from a burning crashed Wellington bomber, sustaining burn injuries as he dragged them from the aircraft and for his actions he was awarded the George Medal.

In 1942, Dr. MacCarthy was serving in the Far East when he was taken prisoner by the Japanese in Sumatra. He was sent to a prison camp in Java where he was tortured and beaten, but despite this he did what he could for his fellow prisoners who were in need of medical care. Two years later he was being taken to Japan to work as a slave when the ship he was being transported on was sunk by the U.S. Navy. Other prison ships were torpedoed and sunk, causing the deaths of hundreds of prisoners of war as well as their captors.

Dr. MacCarthy was rescued by a Japanese destroyer, but suffered such brutality at the hands of the crew that he jumped overboard to escape, to be rescued thereafter from the water by a Japanese fishing boat. The crew took him to Japan, where he was sent to a prisoner-of-war camp in Nagasaki. After having been warned by a secret radio message, he and other prisoners hid in an air-raid shelter when the city was bombed. He was a witness to the devastation caused by the atomic bomb. At the time of the Japanese surrender he was the most senior allied serviceman in Japan.

Dr. MacCarthy was one of some 70,000 Irish people who served in the British armed forces during the Second World War, with another 50,000 from Northern Ireland. Many, regardless of their political beliefs or attitude to Irish nationality, believed that they had no choice but to support Great Britain in the fight against Hitler and the Nazi regime.

After the war, Dr. MacCarthy was appointed an Officer of the Order of the British Empire, and in 1948, was promoted to the rank of Squadron Leader. After leaving the Royal Air Force, he practiced as a doctor in England, and in 1979, he published an account of his wartime experiences in a book titled, 'A Doctor's War'.

Dr. MacCarthy passed away in London on 11th October, 1995.

A Hero's Tale - Krystyna Skarbek alias Jacqueline Almand and Christine Granville

 Krystyna Skarbek was the daughter of a Polish Count and the granddaughter of a wealthy Jewish banker. She was born in Warsaw in 1908, and had a comfortable upbringing in Poland. When she was 22 her Father died and the financial empire that he controlled collapsed. To ease the strain on the family Krystyna moved out and got a job in a car factory, but due to ill-health caused by the exhaust fumes she gave it up, but she was compensated by the factory.

A marriage in 1930 proved incompatible and ended. This was followed by a love affair that came to nothing. To clear her mind and improve her health Krystyna taught herself to ski. It was at one session on the Zakopane ski slope that she lost control and was saved when a man stepped into her path and stopped her descent. Her rescuer was Jerzy Giżycki, a brilliant eccentric who came from a wealthy family in Podolski. At fourteen, he had run away from home, and worked in the United States as a cowboy and gold prospector. He eventually became an author and travelled the world in search of material for his books and articles. He also knew Africa well and liked the country.

On 2nd November, 1938, Krystyna and Giżycki married. He was offered a diplomatic posting to Ethiopia where he served as the Consul General for Poland until September, 1939, when the war broke out. Krystyna signed up with Britain's Section D to return to Poland through Hungary and assisted communications with the Allies. Impressed with what they described as the 'flaming Polish patriot', the British Intelligence Service accepted her plan and weeks later she was working to organise Polish resistance groups in order to smuggle Polish pilots out of the occupied nation. Under the guise of Jacqueline Almand, she was arrested by the Gestapo in 1941, but by biting her tongue until it bled she convinced her captures she had the highly epidemic tuberculosis and they eventually released her. Krystyna and her partner Andrzej Kowerski went to the British embassy and received new identities as Christine Granville and Andrew Kennedy. They were smuggled out of Poland through Yugoslavia to Turkey where they were welcomed by the British.

The resistance group they had been working with had been compromised by German spies and she could not return to Poland, so Krystyna trained as a radio operator and paratrooper. After D-Day she parachuted into France to continue her resistance work, but her assigned area was overrun by Germans so she escaped, hiking over seventy miles to safety. She worked in the Alps attempting to turn Axis fighters, taking extraordinary risks to pull off further capers. On one occasion she outed herself as a spy to French officials working for the Gestapo and arranged a prisoner's release by promises of money. Both she and the prisoner made it out alive. This feat alone secured her reputation as a legendary spy.

After the war Krystyna was awarded the Croix de Guerre and the George Medal and made a Member of the Order of the British Empire. She lived in Britain and Africa then Australia. Krystyna Skarbek alias Jacqueline Almand and Christine Granville was murdered in 1952, by a stalker who was obsessed with her fame and legendary status.

It was rumoured she had an affair with the James Bond author Ian Fleming. Whilst there is no evidence to prove this, it is widely believed that at least two of his 'Bond Girls' were based on Krystyna Skarbek.

Aristocrats: 'I Think I Am Becoming A God'

Keith Douglas

The noble horse with courage in his eye,
clean in the bone, looks up at a shellburst:
away fly the images of the shires
but he puts the pipe back in his mouth.
Peter was unfortunately killed by an 88;
it took his leg away, he died in the ambulance.
I saw him crawling on the sand, he said
It's most unfair, they've shot my foot off.

How can I live among this gentle
obsolescent breed of heroes, and not weep?
Unicorns, almost,
for they are fading into two legends
in which their stupidity and chivalry
are celebrated. Each, fool and hero, will be an immortal.
These plains were their cricket pitch
and in the mountains the tremendous drop fences
brought down some of the runners. Here then
under the stones and earth they dispose themselves,
I think with their famous unconcern.
It is not gunfire I hear, but a hunting horn.

A Hero's Tale - Keith Castellain Douglas

Keith Douglas was born on 24th January, 1920, in Tunbridge Wells, Kent, the son of Captain Keith Sholto Douglas M.C. He was educated at Edgeborough School in Guildford, and at Christ's Hospital, a charity school in Horsham in Sussex, which numbered among its former pupils Samuel Taylor Coleridge and Charles Lamb. His literary and artistic talents were noticeable at a young age; he was writing poetry, sketching and producing pen-and-ink drawings in his mid-teens.

During his time at Christ's Hospital he joined the Officers' Training Corps where he excelled. He attended Merton College, Oxford, reading History and English, the Great War poet Edmund Blunden was one of his tutors. He edited the Oxford University student newspaper 'The Cherwell', which had been founded the year he was born.

In July, 1940, Douglas entered the Royal Military College at Sandhurst, and seven months later was commissioned into the 2nd Derbyshire Yeomanry. He wrote ten of his renowned poems between then and when he was sent to North Africa in June, 1941, attached to the Nottinghamshire (Sherwood Rangers) Yeomanry, in Cairo and Palestine. From then until November of 1943 he wrote thirty-seven more poems, which form the bulk of the work that made him one of the foremost of the Second World War poets. He wrote, 'Hell cannot be let loose twice; it was let loose in the Great War and it is the same old hell now'.

Douglas was serving as a camouflage officer when the Second Battle of El Alamein began on 23rd October, 1942. Desperately wanting to abandon his office job and gain combat experience, he defied orders the following day and drove to Regimental Headquarters stating that he had was being sent to the front. He was posted to A Squadron, which was in need of reinforcements, to assume command of a tank troop. He recorded his experiences in his memoir 'Alamein to Zem Zem', which he also illustrated.

Captain Douglas remained with his Regiment until he was wounded by a land mine near Tripoli, in January, 1943. It was while he was recuperating that he wrote some of his most famous poems based on his combat experiences. He returned to England towards the end of that year as his Regiment was preparing to participate in the D-Day landings. He sailed with the invasion fleet for Normandy on 6th June, 1944.

Three days later, as his Regiment was advancing from Bayeux, he was killed near Caen by enemy mortar fire. He was buried close to where he died but after the war his remains were moved to the Tilly-sur-Seulles War Cemetery, twelve kilometres from Bayeux.

Critic Desmond Graham stated, "Perhaps the only poet of his generation to build successfully on the achievement of WWI soldier-poets Wilfred Owen and Isaac Rosenberg, he is regarded as the finest British poet of the Second World War and, by many, the finest poet of his generation."

Operation Overlord – The D-Day Landings

Operation Overlord, the Allied invasion of the Normandy coastline commenced on Tuesday, 6th June, 1944. Codenamed Operation Neptune, it would become the largest seaborne invasion in history.

Planning for the invasion began in 1943. In the months leading up to the invasion, the Allies conducted a substantial military deception. Under the codename Operation Bodyguard, it was designed to mislead German intelligence as to the date and location of the Allied landings. D-Day was meant to start on 5th June, but due to weather conditions the attack was put back 24 hours. Although the weather was still not ideal the following day, any further postponement would have meant a delay of at least two weeks. This was due to the invasion planners' requirements for the phase of the moon, the tides, and the time of day, meaning only a few days each month were deemed suitable.

At the time of the invasion, Hitler had placed his top commander, Field Marshal Erwin Rommel, in command of the German forces on the Western Front. He was responsible for the development of fortifications along the Atlantic wall, in anticipation of an Allied attack. But on 6th June, 1944, Rommel was on leave, so Hitler himself took command of the military and strategic decisions that lay ahead.

Under a careful deception plan the Allies conducted several subsidiary operations designed to mislead the Germans. This included a misinformation campaign using fake radio traffic to lead the Germans into expecting an attack on Norway, known as Fortitude North. Fortitude South was another part of the deception involving the creation of a fictitious U.S Army Group supposedly located in Kent and Sussex. Designed to deceive the Germans into believing the main attack would take place at Calais, genuine radio messages from 21st Army Group were first routed to Kent via landline and then broadcast, to give German intelligence the impression that most of the Allied troops were stationed there. General Patton was stationed in England until 6th July, reinforcing the deceit that Calais was the second target.

German radar stations on the French coast were destroyed in preparation for the landings and on the night before the invasion, a small group of the newly-formed Special Air Service operators deployed dummy paratroopers over Le Havre and Isigny. This led the Germans to believe that an additional airborne landing had occurred. On that same night, as part of Operation Taxable, 617 Squadron dropped strips of metal foil which were mistakenly interpreted by German radar operators as a naval convoy near Le Havre. The illusion was bolstered by a group of small vessels towing barrage balloons. A similar deception was undertaken in the Pas-de-Calais area.

By the start of the invasion thousands of paratroopers were already behind enemy lines. securing bridges and roads. The amphibious landings were preceded by extensive aerial and naval bombardment, and an airborne assault. The beach landings began at 6.30 a.m. Paris time when British and Canadian troops overcame light opposition and landed, capturing the beaches codenamed Gold, Juno and Sword. The U.S. forces did the same at Utah beach but met much fiercer opposition at Omaha and suffered heavy casualties. The men landed under heavy fire from gun emplacements overlooking the beach, the shore was mined and covered with wooden stakes, metal tripods and barbed wire. This made the work of the beach-clearing teams difficult and dangerous.

By the end of the first day, approximately 156,000 Allied troops had successfully stormed the beaches at Normandy. According to estimates around 4,000 Allied troops were lost on the first day of Operation Overlord, with thousands more missing or injured. However, despite the successes of the landings themselves the Allies failed to achieve any of their goals on the first day. The targets of Carentan and Bayeux remained in German hands, and the major objective, Caen, was not captured until 21st July. Only two beaches, Juno and Gold, were linked on the first day, with all five beachheads not being connected until 12th June. The operation had gained an important foothold which the Allies expanded over the coming months. German losses on the first day were estimated between 4,000 and 9,000.

When the news reached Hitler about the invasion he still believed, rather naively but thanks to the deceptions that had been put in place, that the main invasion would still take place north of the River Seine. so he refused to send troops south to counter any attack. Whether Rommel would have done the same will never be known, but this decision was critical to the success of the Allies in those first few days.

5,000 landing and assault craft, 289 escort vessels, and 277 minesweepers were used as part of Operation Overlord.

The victory at Normandy can be put down to a number of factors: German preparations along the Atlantic Wall were only partially completed; the deceptions undertaken were successful leaving the Germans obliged to defend a huge stretch of coastline; the Allies achieved and maintained air supremacy, making Germans aerial observations out of the question; the transport infrastructure in France was severely disrupted by Allied bombers and by the work of the French Resistance, making the German supply chain very difficult; and ultimately the indecisiveness of the German High Command at a critical time were also factors that led to success for the Allies.

Operation Overlord led to the liberation of German-occupied France and at a later stage, Europe from Nazi control, and laid the foundations for the Allied victory on the Western Front.

SUPREME HEADQUARTERS
ALLIED EXPEDITIONARY FORCE

Soldiers, Sailors and Airmen of the Allied Expeditionary Force!

You are about to embark upon the Great Crusade, toward which we have striven these many months. The eyes of the world are upon you. The hopes and prayers of liberty-loving people everywhere march with you. In company with our brave Allies and brothers-in-arms on other Fronts, you will bring about the destruction of the German war machine, the elimination of Nazi tyranny over the oppressed peoples of Europe, and security for ourselves in a free world.

Your task will not be an easy one. Your enemy is well trained, well equipped and battle-hardened. He will fight savagely.

But this is the year 1944 ! Much has happened since the Nazi triumphs of 1940-41. The United Nations have inflicted upon the Germans great defeats, in open battle, man-to-man. Our air offensive has seriously reduced their strength in the air and their capacity to wage war on the ground. Our Home Fronts have given us an overwhelming superiority in weapons and munitions of war, and placed at our disposal great reserves of trained fighting men. The tide has turned ! The free men of the world are marching together to Victory !

I have full confidence in your courage, devotion to duty and skill in battle. We will accept nothing less than full Victory !

Good Luck ! And let us all beseech the blessing of Almighty God upon this great and noble undertaking.

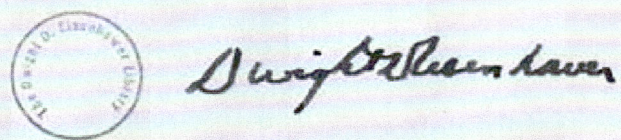

The letter from General Eisenhower to all Allies participating in the D-Day Landings

Heroes Tales – Gustav the Pigeon and Jozef the Priest

The first report received in Britain on the success of the beach landings following the D-Day invasions came courtesy of a member of the Royal Air Force's Homing Pigeon Division, by the name of Gustav. The message read:

"We are just 20 miles or so off the beaches. First assault troops landed 0750. Signal says no interference from enemy gunfire on beach. Steaming steadily information. Lightnings, Typhoons, Fortresses, crossing since 0545. No enemy aircraft seen."

Gustav was a carrier pigeon who had been trained by Frederick Jackson of Cosham in Hampshire. Pigeons were often transported in wicker baskets on the backs of servicemen in order to be set free later with vital information.

Pigeons were first used 3,000 years ago when they were sent out to proclaim the winners of the original Olympic Games, and their use as messengers can be traced back to the twelfth century.

During the early years of the war Gustav carried messages for the Belgian Resistance. Belgium was invaded on 10th May, 1940, along with Luxembourg and the Netherlands, and surrendered to the Germans after eighteen days of fighting. However, pockets of resistance throughout Belgium appeared, believed to have grown to 5% of the population at their peak.

A Catholic Priest, Jozef Raskin, whose codename was Leopold Vindictive 200, was prominent in the Belgian Resistance movement. Formerly a missionary, he was an accomplished artist and had served in the Great War. At the outbreak of the Second World War he was drafted into the Belgian military as a chaplain; he was knowledgeable about radiography, had a good grasp of languages and was able to listen in on the German occupiers and by doing so located their positions on the Belgian coast. Part of his work in the Great War had been as an observer, drawing finely-detailed maps, a skill that would came into play again, along with his skill for being able to produce extraordinarily small handwriting.

It was Raskin who was prominent in using R.A.F. pigeons for communication. One 3-millimetre cylinder attached to a bird's leg would contain a piece of thin paper folded to the size of a postage stamp, and would be covered with detailed drawings and up to 5,000 words. In 1942 he was betrayed by a German spy and executed the following year.

Gustav was one of six carrier pigeons who were given to the Reuters war correspondent Montague Taylor to take with him when he travelled with Allied forces across the English Channel in advance of D-Day. Following the landings, Taylor released him with his cylinder containing the critical news of success in Normandy. Gustav had flown 150 miles from where he was released to his loft at R.A.F. Thorney Island, facing a headwind of around 30 miles per hour. His journey took him five hours and sixteen minutes, and it was his message that was the first to reach Britain.

Gustav was awarded the Dickin Medal for bravery, his citation read:

'For delivering the first message from the Normandy beaches from a ship off the beachhead while serving with the R.A.F. on June 6, 1944'.

Gustav's medal is on display at the D-Day Museum in Portsmouth, Hampshire.

The Story of the Dickin Medal

Mrs. Maria Dickin founded the People's Dispensary for Sick Animals of the Poor in 1917, provide a free service for those in need. She had been shocked by the extreme poverty in the East End of London and the appalling condition of the animals living there. Mrs. Dickin devoted her life to caring for animals, and she became known as a tireless campaigner for animal welfare.

It was Maria who instituted the Dickin Medal in December, 1943, to recognise outstanding acts of bravery shown by animals in wartime, and honour their remarkable contribution in the saving of countless lives. It stands for the qualities of diligence, fearlessness, relentlessness and resolution, and is awarded to animals who displayed 'conspicuous gallantry or devotion to duty while serving or associated with any branch of the Armed Forces or Civil Defence Units'.

The large bronze medallion is inscribed with the words 'For Gallantry' and 'We Also Serve' within a laurel wreath. The ribbon's green, brown and blue stripes symbolise the armed forces of sea, land and air. It has been awarded over seventy times, many of the recipients having served during the Second World War.

The largest recipients by type are pigeons. As well as Gustav were Pigeon G.I. Joe who was credited with making the most outstanding flight by a U.S. Army pigeon; he flew twenty miles in twenty minutes, taking a message that saved one hundred soldiers from being bombed by their own planes. Pigeon Kenley Lass was the first to deliver intelligence from an agent in enemy-occupied France; she had been parachuted in with the agent and flew three hundred miles home in less than seven hours. Pigeon Scotch Lass, although injured, flew across the North Sea from the Netherlands to deliver thirty-eight micro-photographs.

Rob the collie made over twenty parachute descents during the North African campaign and later with a Special Air Unit in Italy; numerous times he saved his human comrades from discovery and capture. Beauty the terrier, Rip the stray mongrel, and Rex the Alsatian located people trapped in bombed buildings. While Sergeant Gander, a Newfoundland saved the lives of infantrymen in Hong Kong by snatching up a grenade and running away with it, he had previously saved many lives by halting the enemy's advance and protecting wounded soldiers.

The medal was awarded a total of fifty-four times between 1943 and 1949. Thirty-two recipients were pigeons alongside eighteen dogs, three horses and a ship's cat.

A Hero's Tale – James Stokes

James Stokes was born in the Gorbals, Glasgow, on 6th February, 1915. One of four children, his parents both died while he was young and he was sent to work on a farm belonging to relatives in Ireland. He later returned to Scotland, married, and in 1943 enlisted with the Royal Artillery.

While home on leave he got into an altercation with a man who insulted his wife, putting the man in hospital. James was given the choice of either military prison for eight years or taking part in the Normandy landings. He landed in France on 6th June, 1944, with the 2nd Battalion, King's Shropshire Light Infantry, a unit which sustained heavy losses that day. They became part of the line that made up the allied front and saw action at Caen, Manneville and the Seine. For his actions on 1st March, 1945, during the attack on Kervenheim in the Rheinland, Private James Stokes was posthumously awarded the Victoria Cross.

As the platoon was being re-organised after coming under heavy enemy rifle and machine gun fire from nearby farm buildings, James took it upon himself to dash forward alone through the enemy fire without waiting for orders. He fired as he ran into the buildings, able to change the magazine with lightning speed; he was seen to take his fighting knife from his belt, and a short while later emerged shepherding twelve prisoners. As the platoon prepared to move on, he was ordered to attend the Regimental Aid Post due to the wound he has sustained on his neck, but he refused, saying, "I'll be alright, sir!"

When the platoon came under fire again, this time from a house, he again rushed forward by himself, fell to the ground wounded, then got up and continued on despite the intense enemy fire. He entered the house, and once again appeared with prisoners, five on this occasion.

His company then prepared for a further assault on what was considered the enemy strong point. Despite being severely wounded, Private Stokes yet again dashed forward through intense fire until he fell close to the enemy position. As he lay on the ground he continued to fire his rifle until he died from the eight wounds in his upper body. Small in stature, but with immense courage, his solo charges surprised his comrades as well as the Germans, as he drew fire upon himself to distract the enemy from the advancing Shropshires.

Private Stokes' Victoria Cross citation states:

"His magnificent courage, devotion to duty and splendid example, inspired all those round him and ensured the success of the attack at a critical moment; moreover, his self-sacrifice saved his Platoon and Company many serious casualties".

James is buried in the Reichswald Forest War Cemetery, at Kleve in Germany.

In 1976, the James Stokes V.C. Celtic Supporters Club came into being; members of the club had grown up with him and so took great pride in commemorating his bravery.

A Hero's Tale – Nancy Wake – The White Mouse

Nancy Grace Augusta Wake was born in New Zealand on 30th August, 1912, and raised in Australia. She worked as a journalist in New York and London before marrying a wealthy French industrialist and moving to France. The couple were living in Marseilles when the war broke out.

Wake immediately went to work for the French Resistance, hiding and smuggling men out of France and ferrying contraband supplies and falsified documents. She later joined an escape network set up by a British officer, Ian Garrow, assisting the escape of Allied troops from France. Wake was captured at least once and interrogated but never gave any secrets away. Wake soon became a leading figure in the Maquis groups of the French Resistance and by 1943, Wake was the declared the Gestapo's most wanted person with a 5-million-franc price on her head.

With the Nazis in hot pursuit, Wake managed to escape to Britain in 1943, and joined the Special Operations Executive, a British intelligence agency. After training with weapons and parachutes, she was dropped back into France on 1st March, 1944, near to Auvergne, becoming a liaison between London and the local Maquis group headed by Captain Henri Tardivat.

She had no trouble shooting Nazis or blowing up buildings with the French guerrilla fighters in the service of the resistance. She was even reported as once killing a SS sentry with her bare hands. At one point the Germans sent 22,000 soldiers to wipe out Wake's resistance group. However, due to her extraordinary organisational abilities her Maquisards defeated the Germans, causing around 1,400 German deaths, while suffering only around 100 fatalities themselves. Wake's Maquisards accounted for around 70% of an estimated 2,000 Germans that were killed by the French Resistance during the liberation of France.

After the war, Nancy Wake was awarded the George Medal by the British Government, the Medal of Freedom by the United States, and the Médaille de la Résistance and three Croix de Guerre by France, among other honours. She was one of the most decorated Allied servicewomen.

She later found out that her husband had died in 1943, when the Gestapo had tortured him to find out his wife's whereabouts. He refused to co-operate, to the point of his death.

Wake published her biography, 'The White Mouse', in 1988. This was the nickname the Gestapo gave her due to her talent of sneaking by them undetected.

Nancy Wake died on 7th August, 2011, aged 98.

The Stories of Burma and Singapore

February, 1942, saw the Battle of Singapore, fought in the South-East Asian theatre when Japan invaded the British stronghold. Singapore was the major British military base in South-East Asia, and was the key to British imperial inter-war defence planning for South-East Asia and the South-West Pacific. The fighting in Singapore lasted one week, starting on 8th February. During the short takeover of the island by the Japanese forces, 5,000 Allies were killed or wounded and in the region of 80,000 taken prisoner of war. This was the largest surrender of British-led forces in history. Churchill called the surrender the worst disaster in British military history.

The Burma Campaign was a series of battles fought in the British colony of Burma and involved Allied forces supported by the Chinese fighting against the invading forces of Japan. The British Empire forces peaked at around one million land and air forces, drawn primarily from India which was under British control, including the Chindits, a special operations group of the British and Indian armies. The British Army in India was equivalent to eight regular infantry divisions and six tank regiments. In addition around one hundred thousand East and West African colonial troops were involved.

The Burma Independence Army was trained by the Japanese and spearheaded the initial attacks against British Empire forces. But it was a very difficult campaign from start to finish. Its geographical characteristics in the region meant weather, diseases and terrain had a major effect on operations.

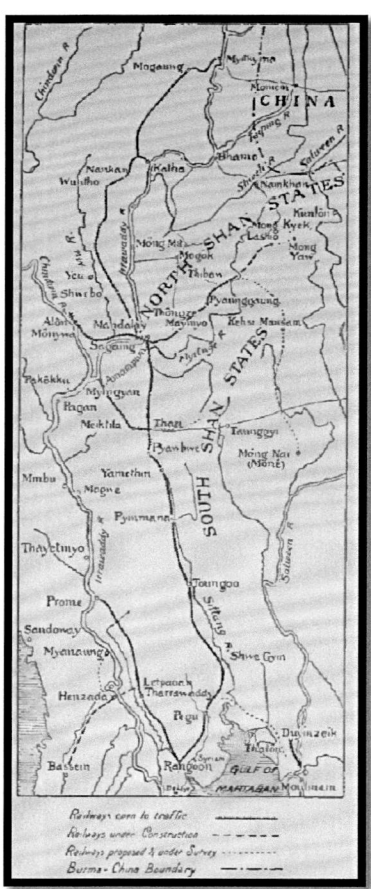

The campaign was also politically complex, the British, U.S. and Chinese all had different strategic priorities. Probably more notably it was the only land campaign by the Allies in the Pacific Theatre which ran continuously from the start of hostilities to the end of the war. The climate of the region was dominated by the seasonal monsoon rains, which allowed effective campaigning for just over half of each year. In addition the Allies had given priority to the defeat of the Nazi regime in Europe, so the Burma Campaign took second place in terms of support.

The Campaign itself was broken down into four phases: Japanese invasion in 1942; failed attempts by the Allies to mount offensives into Burma from late 1942 to early 1944; the 1944 Japanese invasion of India which ultimately failed; then, finally the successful Allied offensive which reoccupied Burma from late 1944 to mid 1945.

Probably one of the more famous of the Campaign's events was what would be known as the Burma railway. Also known as the Death Railway, it was designed to run two hundred and fifty-eight miles between Ban Pong in Thailand and Thanbyuzayat in Burma. Built entirely by hand, by 60,000 prisoners of war and around 200,000 labourers, it was forced labour and a living hell for those involved.

Following the successful invasion of Burma by Japan in 1942, logistical routes to supply the Japanese forces in Burma had to be established. Japan was dependent upon the sea, bringing supplies and troops to Burma around the Malay Peninsula. However, this route was becoming more vulnerable to attack by Allied submarines, particularly following the Allied successes in the Battle of Midway. Therefore to avoid the hazardous 2,000-mile sea journey, a railway to run from Bangkok to Rangoon appeared the best solution.

The movement of prisoners of war northward from Changi Prison in Singapore and other prisons began in May, 1942. Construction of the railway began in Burma on 15th September, 1942, and in Thailand in November. The completion date was set for December 1943, but the railway was completed ahead of schedule. On 17th October, 1943, construction gangs originating in Burma working south met up with gangs who had started in Thailand, working north.

The first prisoners of war, 3,000 Australians, to go to Burma worked on airfields and other infrastructure initially before beginning construction of the northern terminus of the railway in October, 1942. The first prisoners of war to work in Thailand, 3,000 British soldiers, left Changi in June, 1942, to start work on the southern terminus. More prisoners of war were imported from Singapore and the Dutch East Indies as construction advanced. Construction camps housed around one thousand workers and were established every five to ten miles along the route. Workers were moved up and down the railway line as needed.

The construction camps consisted of open-sided barracks built of bamboo poles with thatched roofs. The barracks were about sixty metres long with sleeping platforms raised above the ground on each side of an earthen floor. Two hundred men were housed in each barracks, giving each man a two-foot wide space in which to live and sleep.

The prisoners of war found themselves at the bottom of a social system. Their guards were harsh, fanatical, and deadly at times. The living and working conditions on the Railway were described as 'horrific', with mistreatment, sickness, and starvation. The estimated number of prisoners who died during construction varies considerably, but it is estimated that between twelve and sixteen thousand perished.

A Hero's Tale, in his own words – Fred Cox

Private Hugh Frederick Cox, 2nd battalion, East Surrey Regiment, was a driver. He enlisted in 1937, and was already out in the Far East when war broke out in 1939. The East Surreys were in Malaya when Japan invaded in late 1941, and were pushed back to Singapore. The Battalion suffered heavy casualties and those who survived were taken prisoner in February, 1942. Fred was in Changi prisoner of war camp then other smaller camps in Singapore before being sent to the railway construction in March, 1943. The extract relates to the following few months on the Railway at Kanburi (Kanchanaburi).

An extract from the book, 'Faith, Hope and Rice' written by Fred's daughter Ellie Taylor, from Fred's notes written in 1946/47 and verified by the timeline of his experiences, through research with the Thai-Burma Railway Centre.

'The beginning of the monsoon season had a huge impact on the progress of work on the railway. From our first days at Kanburi, we had been working for six to eight hours a day, often in intense heat and with most, if not all, of us suffering from malnutrition and a variety of deficiency diseases. Occasionally, if the Japanese considered us to have finished a particular task in good time, we would be given a day off, and those days were so welcome; a chance to rest our aching arms and legs and our sore feet. Then heavy rain began to hamper progress, embankments were washed away and had to be rebuilt, and as every surface became slippery underfoot - especially as many of us had nothing on our feet - it became much more difficult to move around. As a result, we were told that we had to work for longer each day and, against a great deal of opposition from our doctors, the Japanese began to demand that even those who were very sick should contribute to work on the railway.'

'From then on, our days began earlier. We had to have our breakfast and be on parade shortly after dawn broke. After we had been detailed to various working parties and drawn our tools from the tool shed, we would begin what was often a twelve hour day's work and there were very few days off. We no longer went back to the camp for our meal at lunch time; rather, it would be brought out to us, so that we could resume work again as soon as our break was finished. Whichever kind of work we were doing, we were pushed to do it faster, and beaten if we were considered to be slacking. No allowances were made for those who were suffering with blistered hands or feet, or were weakened by repeated bouts of dysentery, or for those in pain from bad leg ulcers. Such things made no difference whatsoever to the guards, who delivered a whack with a bamboo pole to anyone they felt wasn't working hard enough. We were given to understand that Japanese powers on high had decreed that the railway had to be finished sooner than had initially been planned for.'

'The guards were under pressure to see that this was achieved, and it was of no concern to them how many of us died in the process… The increased workload meant that sickness claimed more and more of us. I doubt any of us would have been passed as fit for work under normal circumstances and most of us would have been hospitalised. As it was, the Japanese were reluctant to class anyone as unfit for work. As far as they were concerned, if you couldn't stand upright, then you could sit down and work, but you would work and this sort of callousness had ceased to shock us.'

A Hero's Tale - Bruce Steel Kingsbury

 Bruce Kingsbury was born on 8th January, 1918, in Preston, near Melbourne, Australia, of British parents. He attended Melbourne Technical College and then joined his father's real estate firm. Not finding office work satisfying he did farm work for a while, returning to real estate until May, 1940, when he enlisted in the Second Australian Imperial Force.

Private Kingsbury was posted to the 2nd/2nd Pioneer Battalion then transferred to the 2nd/14th Battalion. They left Sydney on 19th of October, 1940, aboard H.M.T. Aquitania, bound for the Middle East. After training in Palestine and being stationed at Mersa Matruh in Egypt, they took part in the invasion of Syria in June, 1941. Operation Exporter's aim was to prevent Germany from using the territory as a staging ground from which to attack the allied forces. It was under the control of the Vichy High Commissioner, who had allowed the Luftwaffe to refuel there. The 2nd/14th Battalion took part in the attack on Hill 1284, held by the Vichy French. Afterwards the French commander described the courage and endurance of the Australians as 'incomparable'. They then set up training camp at Hill 69, outside Jerusalem, and six months later left for Australia due to the outbreak of war in the Pacific.

After undergoing training in Queensland, they sailed to Port Moresby, their objective being to halt the Japanese on the Kokoda Track. The Japanese had landed with 1,500 troops and had another 4,000 following. Private Kingsbury's Battalion suffered heavy losses in August when the enemy repeatedly attacked their positions and their headquarters came under threat. Volunteering with other survivors to launch a counter-attack, Private Kingsbury, in the words of his friend, Private Allen Avery, 'came forward with this Bren and he just mowed them down. He was an inspiration to everybody else around him'. Before his comrades could catch up with him, he continued forward towards the heavy machine-gun fire of the Japanese, but was then cut down by a sniper's bullet.

For his actions that day, Bruce Kingsbury was awarded the posthumous Victoria Cross. The Battalion's second-in-command Major P. E. Rhoden recorded that "his valour had demonstrated that the previously undefeated Japanese could be beaten".

Part of the Victoria Cross citation reads:

'The Battalion to which Private Kingsbury belonged had been holding a position in the Isurava area for two days against continuous and fierce enemy attacks. Private Kingsbury, who was one of the few survivors of a Platoon which had been overrun and severely cut about by the enemy, immediately volunteered to join a different platoon which had been ordered to counterattack. Private Kingsbury displayed a complete disregard for his own safety. His initiative and superb courage made possible the recapture of a position, which undoubtedly saved Battalion Headquarters, as well as causing heavy casualties amongst the enemy. His coolness, determination and devotion to duty in the face of great odds were an inspiration to his comrades.'

Private Kingsbury is buried in the Bomana War Cemetery at Port Moresby.

The Foreign Gate
(an extract)

Sidney Keyes

'At Dunkirk I
Rolled in the shallows, and the living trod
Across me for a bridge ...'
               'Let me speak out
Against this sham of policy, for pain
Alone is true. I was a general
Who fought the cunning Africans, returned
Crowned with harsh laurel, frantically cheered
Through Roman streets. I spoke of fame and glory.
Women grabbed at my robe. Great poets praised me.
I died of cancer, screaming, in a year.'
'I fell on a black Spanish hillside
Under the thorn-hedge, fighting for a dream
That troubled me in Paris; vomited
My faith and courage out among the stones ...'
'I was a barb of light, a burning cross
Of wood and canvas, falling through the night.'
'I was shot down at morning, in a yard.'

The moon regards them without shame. The wind
Rises and twitters through the wreck of bone ...
               'It is so hard to be alone
Continually, watching the great stars march
Their circular unending route; sharp sand
Straying about the eyes, blinding the quick-eyed spirit.'
A soldier's death is hard;
There's no prescribed or easy word
For dissolution in the Army books.
The uniform of pain with pain put on is straiter
Than any lover's garment; yet the death
Of these is different, and their glory greater.
Once men, then moving figures on a map,
Patiently giving time and strength and vision
Even identity
Into the future's keeping;

A Hero's Tale - Sidney Keyes

Sidney Keyes was born on 27th May, 1922, in Dartford, Kent. His mother contracted peritonitis when he was a few weeks old and died. His father was absent during much his childhood, so he was raised by his aunts and his paternal grandfather. His father and grandfather each married three times, and his family life was deemed to be unhappy and contentious. A solitary and studious boy in frail health, he spent his time reading about mythology, legends and history, becoming fascinated by the macabre, death and metamorphosis.

Sidney began writing poetry at a young age, and was educated at Dartford Grammar School, Tonbridge School, and Queen's College, Oxford, to which he won a history scholarship. A poem he wrote at the age of sixteen for his grandfather was described as 'of a quite astonishing precocity'. Sidney continued to write poetry while at university, as well as editing the *Cherwell* magazine. While at Oxford, he also formed a dramatic society.

In April, 1942, Sidney left Oxford and joined the army. Being of a somewhat dreamy nature, he was considered to be a hopeless soldier to the despair of the training officers, yet he was commissioned into his father's old regiment, the Queen's Own Royal West Kent Regiment, in October, 1942. His first volume of poetry, 'The Iron Laurel', was published that year, and contains the poem, 'The Foreign Gate', prophetic in the foretelling of his own death in battle.

In March, 1943, his battalion was sent to North Africa, by which time he had earned the respect of his men for his courage and steadfastness. He kept a notebook and wrote letters, showing that he calmly accepted his fate. In the early hours of the morning of the 29th April, in the attack on Hill 133, near Sidi Abdulla in the Tunisian mountains, he was last seen fighting back-to-back with a comrade in their efforts to fend off a German counter-attack. The exact circumstances of his death are unclear; there is a belief that he was taken prisoner and killed by the Germans during captivity. He is buried in the Massicault War Cemetery, at Manouba, Tunisia.

Sidney's second volume, 'The Cruel Solstice', was published posthumously in 1944. He had been writing poems up until the day of his death, but these were unfortunately lost, although his notebook and his letters survived. He was awarded the Hawthornden Prize for The Cruel Solstice and The Iron Laurel. Simon Jenner, writing for The Recusant, said: "Keyes was a master of blank verse, of deft metonymic manipulation, disturbed pastoral".

To the poet Owen Lowery he was 'an exiled lover in harmony with nature and at odds with the violence of his time'. His own image of himself was of 'a candle flame rising up and burning the more brightly just as it was on the point of extinction'.

Sidney Keyes is considered to be one of the most outstanding poets of the Second World War, and his work surely presaged greater things.

A Hero's Tale – Virginia Hall

Virginia Hall was born on 6ᵗʰ April, 1906, in Baltimore, Maryland, into a wealthy family. At school she had been an exceptional student, was editor-in-chief of the school newspaper and also the elected class president. She went on to attend two prestigious colleges, Radliffe and Barnard, followed by extensive studying and travelling in Europe – while there she earned a diploma in economics and international law, and learned to speak French, German and Italian.

After completing her studies, Virginia worked as a clerk at the U.S. embassy in Warsaw, Poland, and then in Izmir in Turkey. In 1932, while hunting in Turkey, she accidentally shot herself in the left leg; it turned gangrenous and had to be amputated below the knee. She had wanted to join the diplomatic corps, but they did not accept people with disabilities, even though she learned to walk with a prosthetic leg.

Virginia travelled to Paris before the German invasion in 1940, and worked as a driver with the French ambulance service. As Paris fell to the Germans, she fled to London, where she volunteered for service with the Special Operations Executive. After training, she was sent to France to aid the French Resistance and to collect intelligence on German operations while posing as a New York Post reporter.

Within three months Virginia had established a secret network codenamed Heckler, which provided information to the allies and helped downed British pilots escape to safety. She was known to the Germans as the 'Limping Lady' and was on the Nazi's most-wanted list. As they succeeded in seizing all of France by November, 1942, she fled to Spain, but was arrested for entering the country illegally. After being imprisoned for six weeks she was released when a fellow-inmate notified American officials in Barcelona, and Virginia joined the U.S. Office of Strategic Services' Special Operations Branch.

In May, 1944, Virginia was sent back to France, working undercover as a farm-hand, to report on German troop movements, act as a radio operator, co-ordinate supply drops for Allied forces and more. According to the Smithsonian: 'In her final report to headquarters, Hall stated that her team had destroyed four bridges, derailed freight trains, severed a key rail line in multiple places and downed telephone lines. They were also credited with killing some 150 Germans and capturing 500 more.' By this time she was no longer required as the Allied troops who had landed at Normandy began to move into the area and take it over.

Virginia had been considered the Gestapo's most dangerous of all the Allied spies.

After the end of the war, Virginia received three awards: the Croix de Guerre avec Palme from the French government, the Member of the Order of the British Empire, and the United States' Distinguished Service Cross. She continued to work for the Special Activities Division of the Central Intelligence Agency as an analyst until retirement in 1966 at the age of sixty.

She then returned home to Maryland, and passed away in 1982.

A Hero's Tale - Claud Raymond

Claud Raymond was born on 2nd October, 1923, in Mottistone on the Isle of Wight, one of four children of Lieutenant Colonel Maurice Claud Raymond C.I.E., M.C. Claud grew up in Seaford in Sussex and was educated at Wellington College and Trinity Hall, Cambridge, then was commissioned into the Corps of Royal Engineers in May of 1943. Showing great keenness early in 1945, he became involved in the fierce fighting in the Burma jungle.

His actions on the day before his death earned him the posthumous award of the Victoria Cross. He had been second-in-command of a small patrol, part of a larger detachment of a special force, sent to obtain information and create a diversion by attacking and destroying enemy posts forty miles in advance of an Indian Infantry Brigade. They landed on the bank of the Thinganet Chaung, known to be strongly held by the enemy. As they neared the village of Talaku they had to cross open ground and were heavily fired on by an enemy detachment from the nearby jungle area.

Lieutenant Raymond immediately charged in the direction of the fire. Although wounded in the right shoulder, he continued on, firing his rifle from the hip. A few yards on a Japanese grenade was thrown at him and he fell to the ground. Although severely wounded and bleeding heavily he got up and led his men under intense fire. He was hit again, his wrist shattered, but again he did not waver and proceeded into the enemy position, killing two Japanese and wounding a third. The remaining Japanese fled back into the jungle, leaving behind much of their equipment. Without what was described as the courageous leadership and great determination of Lieutenant Raymond, the attack would most likely not have been successful, the position having been strongly fortified and formidable.

Lieutenant Raymond refused medical treatment until the other injured men had been attended to, and he insisted on walking back to the landing craft without being treated in order to avoid delay. However, after having walked for a mile he collapsed and had to be carried the rest of the way on a stretcher, all the time encouraging the other wounded and attempting to keep them cheerful. He passed away within a few hours.

His Victoria Cross citation reads in part:

'The outstanding gallantry, remarkable endurance and fortitude of Lieutenant Raymond, which refused to allow him to collapse, although mortally wounded, was an inspiration to everyone and a major factor in the capture of the strong point. His self-sacrifice in refusing attention to his wounds undoubtedly saved the patrol, by allowing it to withdraw in time before the Japanese could bring up fresh forces from neighbouring positions for a counter attack.'

Because he belonged to an old family from County Kerry in Ireland, he is also considered an Irish Victoria Cross winner. Lieutenant Raymond is buried in the Taukkyan War Cemetery near Rangoon in what is now Myanmar, and is remembered on the town memorial in Seaford.

A Hero's Tale – Judy the Dog

Judy, a pure-bred English pointer, was born in 1936 in Shanghai. She was purchased as a mascot for the gunboat H.M.S. Gnat. The crew intended to train her as a gun-dog, pointers being a popular choice, but Judy did not show any aptitude to the task but she was to prove to have other talents. Judy would alert the crew to pirates, and any approaching aircraft. In 1939 some of the crew along with Judy transferred to H.M.S. Grasshopper, which deployed to Singapore after war was declared. During the Battle of Singapore, they were taking evacuees to Batavia when they were attacked by Japanese aircraft. Abandoning ship, the crew made it ashore where Judy dug to locate a fresh-water spring. They were rescued and taken to Sumatra, for a 200-mile trek to Padang; Judy warned of predators, and even survived a crocodile attack en route. But on their arrival they were captured by the Japanese, having missed the last evacuation ship.

One of the crew, L.A.C. Frank Williams adopted Judy, sharing his rations with her and ensuring she was officially registered as a P.O.W. She alerted the prisoners to guards approaching as well as any snakes and scorpions. When some stolen rice was about to be discovered, Judy dashed into the room with a human skull in her mouth, petrifying the superstitious guards, then fled into the jungle. Prisoner Les Searle said: "Animals have a built-in system which picks up all radiations of different sensations such as fear, happiness, panic and sorrow. Judy sensed the danger in that room and she knew what to do about it."

The living conditions in the camp were appalling and Judy protected the prisoners and was in turn protected by Frank. Another prisoner commented: "I was fascinated at the complete understanding between Frank and Judy…her eyes only softened when Frank touched her or spoke to her". In June, 1944, the prisoners were returning to Singapore when their ship was hit by Allied torpedoes. Judy saved lives and a witness commented that she was 'like an aquatic version of a Saint Bernard'. She let four survivors use her as a float. Only when all were safe, did she allow herself to be rescued. The survivors were returned to Sumatra to work on the railway. Judy caught snakes and rats to feed the men and herself.

In 1945, Frank caught malaria; one of the guards ordered that Judy be cooked and fed to him. She disappeared into the jungle; when she returned Frank considered killing her himself humanely, but looked into her eyes and decided she must live.

After liberation Judy's received the Dickin Medal inscribed: 'For magnificent courage and endurance in Japanese prison camps, which helped maintain morale among her fellow prisoners and also for saving many lives through her intelligence and watchfulness'.

Frank and Judy stayed together and when she died, Frank built a marble monument with a plaque containing the words: 'A gallant old girl who…gave more in companionship than she ever received…and was in her short lifetime an inspiration of courage, hope and a will to live, to many who would have given up in their time of trial, had it not been for her example and fortitude'.

A Hero's Tale – Albert Rothwell

Albert Rothwell was born in December in 1918, in Haslingden, Lancashire. He was educated at Haslingden Central Council School and attended Trinity Baptist Church, and after leaving school he worked with his father in the family business as a house furnisher.

Albert enlisted after the outbreak of the second world war, joining the 1st/5th Battalion of the Sherwood Foresters (Nottinghamshire and Derbyshire Regiment). The battalion was a first line Territorial Army formation. The unit saw service in 1940, with the British Expeditionary Force in France and Belgium, and were among those evacuated at Dunkirk. Later that year they were ordered out to Malaya in to defend the peninsula and Singapore against the Japanese. Albert's parents received a postcard from him, sent from Bombay and presumably posted as he was on his way to Singapore.

On the 8th December in 1941, the Japanese invaded Malaya, and crossed the Straits of Johore to invade Singapore on 8th February, 1942. Singapore fell a week later, and Albert's battalion was pushed back but continued to fight on until they were captured. They were taken to the prisoner of war camp at Changi, and then were among the thousands of prisoners of war who were sent to work on the infamous Burma railway.

A combination of overwork, malnutrition, sickness and cruelty took many lives. Men were literally worked to death, received no medical treatment, and were often brutalized, tortured and starved. Under such conditions, Albert died on 2nd April, 1943. His father had written to him in May of that year, not knowing that his son had died. The letter was returned marked as undeliverable due to the addressee being reported as deceased. Mr. Rothwell wrote to the War Office, and on 20th June 1944, an official at the War Office wrote back to him:

"I am directed to state, with regret, that there is, unfortunately, no reason to doubt the report which was received from the Japanese authorities through the International Red Cross Committee, to the effect that No. 4981465 Private A. Rothwell, the Sherwood Foresters, died on 2nd April, 1943. It is confirmed that your son's name was broadcast by the Vatican Radio on 27th August, 1943, but it can only be assumed that the news of Private Rothwell's death had not reached the Vatican at that date. I am to convey to you an expression of the sincere sympathy of the Department in the great loss which you have sustained."

Albert is buried in the Kanchanaburi War Cemetery in Thailand, which contains the graves or commemorations of over 5,000 Commonwealth casualties, and is looked after by the Commonwealth War Graves Commission. The Cemetery is on the site of a former base camp that many Japanese prisoners of war would have passed through, as they were taken to the railway.

Albert's gravestone bears the words: 'A life given that we might live in peace'.

Operation Market Garden

There is a scene in the film, 'A Bridge Too Far', when the actor Elliott Gould, playing the part of U.S. Colonel Robert Stout, approaches Lieutenant Colonel Joe Vandeleur, commanding 3rd Battalion, the Irish Guards, played by Michael Caine, and asks whether the Battalion had any bridging equipment, after the bridge on the Son had been blown minutes before the U.S. unit was about to cross the river. Caine came out with a classic reply when he said,

"When you refer to Bailey crap, I take it you mean that glorious, precision-made, British-built bridge which is the envy of the civilized world? Yes we have some."

Whether the conversation ever took place no one knows, Hollywood does like to exaggerate its artistic license. In reality it took 14 Squadron, Royal Engineers, just over twelve hours to construct the Bailey bridge, in excess of 190 feet, under cover of complete darkness the bridge crossed the span of the river Son near Valkenswaard in Holland.

The date of the bridge build was 17th September, 1944. The Irish Guards were part of the lead for the advancing XXX Corps on the fateful mission, known as Operation Market Garden. 17th September was a dark moon night, the night before the appearance of a new moon. The bridge build was carried out in almost complete darkness, which as any Sappers will know this type of build, particularly with the Bailey, was no mean feat. The bridge was completed by 14 Squadron and the Allies advanced, albeit way behind what had been a very tight schedule.

And due to the fact that 17th September was a dark night, the general rule was that airborne operations would not be carried out when no natural light of any kind existed. It was therefore decided to carry out the drop of paratroopers into the Dutch countryside during broad daylight. With a mixture of C47 aircraft, carrying paratroopers or tugging gliders filled with more troops and equipment vital to the mission, the biggest airborne operation ever to take place had started. This operation was repeated over the next few days with wave after wave of paratroopers being deployed into the battle zone.

Market Garden was the brainchild of the senior British Commander, Field Marshall Montgomery. As time was going on, it was becoming apparent that just north of Normandy the advancing troops, following the successful D-Day Landings in June the same year, were becoming bogged down with heavy fighting. Montgomery wanted a broad attack from all Allied forces pushing directly for the Rhine. His U.S. counterpart, and senior commander, General Dwight D Eisenhower, disagreed. In truth, there was never much that the two Commanders ever agreed upon, nor unsurprisingly Monty with the other U.S. General, Patton. Eisenhower finally agreed following pressure from both the British and U.S. Governments to try to pacify his British counterpart.

Although Attenborough's film does show heroics on all sides, it also highlights the failures and lack of planning that was Operation Market Garden. Market, the codename for the airborne forces, and Garden, the land forces. The aim was simple, to capture the main bridges at Eindhoven and Nijmegen leading up to and including Arnhem. Once the bridges were controlled, the allies could establish clear supply routes towards Germany for the fight ahead to Berlin. This would be carried out with a massive air drop in various areas around the Netherlands in order to clear a path for the armoured XXX Corps to barge its way through what was perceived as very little resistance from the retreating German Army.

The reality was that nothing is that simple in war and much of the intelligence that appeared to suggest otherwise was ignored. But the intelligence presented to the Command Team was spot on. What lay ahead of the Allied invasion was the II Panzer Corps, including two panzer units, in and around Arnhem and Nijmegen, under the leadership of Field Marshall Model. Model was one of Germany's greatest generals and was particularly well-known for his defensive tactics.

Paratroopers are classed as Special Forces; designed to travel relatively lightly, be able to move in and out of areas quickly and hold positions for short periods of time. They cannot carry the right amount of ammunition for long engagements and in turn are reliant on ground

forces for replenishment. But a prolonged engagement was precisely the position the British, American, Canadian and Polish paratroopers were put into, due to the slow progress of the advancing Allied forces to reach their final destinations. In addition much of the equipment, including vehicles that were meant to be transported by glider, didn't arrive or were damaged, whilst the radio equipment they were using to communicate either had limited use due to distances between the units, or just failed to work.

The Operation opened with Allied successes all round. But greater resistance was just around the corner. Despite initial gains by U.S. troops, the bridge at Son was blown by the Germans, hence the reason for requesting the Bailey from the Royal Engineers.

Nijmegen Bridge and that of Eindhoven were captured successfully by the Allies, but none of the other objectives were met as successfully, with the British taking heavy casualties during the week-long operation. Completely due to the substantial forces of the German armoured units and the defensive tactics of Field Marshall Model, the British and Americans found it very slow going and failed to reach Arnhem in order to support the British Paratroopers there. Under the command of Colonel John Frost, 2nd Parachute Battalion, comprising of 745 lightly armed men, landed near Oosterbeek and marched into Arnhem, only be met by far superior forces in the form of the Second SS Panzercorps. They found themselves completely cut off from the rest of 1st Airborne. Despite a brave effort and losses of 250 men either killed or injured, Frost and his unit gave up the fight on 24th September, and were taken prisoners of war.

The only possible tactical error that Model made was his decision not to blow the bridges at Nijmegen and Arnhem. Had he done so, the Allied Operation would have immediately failed. In all, nearly 42,000 paratroopers from the four nationalities dropped into the Netherlands during Operation Market Garden, to be supported by one Armoured Division as well as an Armoured Brigade and two Infantry Divisions.

The operation suffered nearly 18,000 casualties, the heaviest casualties being lost in and around Arnhem. Operation Market Garden was later classed as a failure from the point of view of its main architect Field Marshall Montgomery.

A Hero's Tale – Lachhiman Gurung

Lachhiman Gurung was born on 30th December, 1917, in Dakhani, Nepal. In December, 1940, he joined the Indian Army (later known as the British Indian Army to distinguish it from the army of India). After basic training he joined the 8th Gurkha Rifles and served with the 4th Battalion.

For his actions in May, 1945, he was awarded the Victoria Cross. The 89th Indian Brigade of the 7th Division had been ordered across the Irrawaddy River to destroy the enemy north of the Prome to Taungup road. Two companies of the 4th/8th Gurkha Rifles were in place to block the retreating Japanese at the village of Taungdaw. In the early hours of the morning of the 13th May, over two hundred Japanese soldiers attacked their position, cutting off communication. Rifleman Gurung and two comrades had been manning their post on the jungle track which led to his platoon's position approximately a hundred yards away. Twice grenades landed near him, and twice he was able to hurl them back. When he picked up the third one, it exploded and he suffered severe wounds to his right arm and leg, face and body, as well as the loss of his fingers. His comrades also suffered serious wounds.

As the Japanese rushed forward, Rifleman Gurung, despite his wounds, loaded and fired his rifle steadily at them. His comrades, lying wounded close by, reported that he shouted, "Come and fight a Gurkha!" as he fired at the enemy. The Japanese advanced in waves, with Rifleman Gurung at times firing at point blank range, for a period of over four hours. When it was finally daylight, it was discovered that he had killed thirty-one Japanese soldiers, while alone and with only one hand and in pain from his many other serious wounds. He said later: "I had to fight because there was no other way. I felt I was going to die anyway, so I might as well die standing on my feet. All I knew was that I had to go on and hold them back. I am glad that helped the other soldiers in my platoon, but they would have all done the same thing."

Rifleman Gurung's platoon held the Japanese at bay, killing another fifty-six, for another two days until they were relieved. He was taken to hospital, where it was discovered that he had lost the use of his right eye as well as his right hand. He remained serving with the Gurkha Rifles, transferring to the Indian Army after Independence in 1947, and retired that year to become a farmer.

In 2008, he was living in Hounslow and became involved in the successful campaign to allow Gurkhas to settle in the United Kingdom; he was made a Freeman of the borough, and later honorary vice-president of the Chiswick branch of the Royal British Legion.

Rifleman Gurung passed away on 12th December, 2010, at the age of ninety-two, and is buried in Chiswick New Cemetery.

Epitaph

Robert Desnos

I lived in those times. For a thousand years
I have been dead. Not fallen, but hunted;
When all human decency was imprisoned,
I was free amongst the masked slaves.

I lived in those times, yet I was free.
I watched the river, the earth, the sky,
Turning around me, keeping their balance,
The seasons provided their birds and their honey.

You who live, what have you made of your luck?
Do you regret the time when I struggled?
Have you cultivated for the common harvest?
Have you enriched the town I lived in?

Living men, think nothing of me. I am dead.
Nothing survives of my spirit or my body

Robert Desnos (alias Pierre Andier and Lucken Gallois)

Robert Desnos was born on 4th July, 1900, in Paris. He attended a commercial college and was then employed as a clerk before securing a post at the Paris-Soir newspaper, writing a literary column. When he was nineteen years old he published some of his work in the Dadaist magazine 'Litterature', and three years later published a collection of surrealistic aphorisms, 'Prose Selavy'. Two years' military service was mandatory, and it was during this time that he met the poet Andre Breton. Together they worked on automatic writing, defined as 'writing said to be produced by a spiritual, occult, or subconscious agency rather than by the conscious intention of the writer'.

Robert went on to publish much of his work up to 1930, including 'Deuil pour deuil' (Mourning for Mourning), 'La Liberté ou l'amour!' (Liberty or Love!), 'The Night of Loveless Nights', 'Corps et biens' (Body and Goods), as well as the play, 'La Place de l'étoile', and the film script 'L'Étoile de mer'. He also wrote for radio and television until the outbreak of the Second World War, his style then being described as lighter and at times musical.

During the occupation of Paris by the Nazis he used various pseudonyms to write articles in the Paris newspapers and magazines. He had by that time begun serving again with the French Army and had become involved with the French Resistance. The Gestapo did not appreciate his subtle mocking of the Nazis and sought to uncover the writer behind the names Pierre Andier and Lucken Gallois, among others. He continued to write for magazines, wrote cinema reviews and became more involved with politics.

Robert knew he was in danger but refused to leave Paris. In February, 1944, his identity and activities were uncovered and he was arrested by the Gestapo and imprisoned. He was sent to Auschwitz in Poland, then to Buchenwald, near Weimar in Germany, and from there to Flossenburg in Germany. His final place of incarceration was at Theresienstadt in occupied Czechoslovakia, a hybrid concentration camp and ghetto, where he was kept in a special section reserved for political prisoners. The poetry that he wrote while imprisoned was destroyed, reportedly by accident, after his death. He wrote constantly to his wife, Lucie Badoud, nicknamed Youkie.

On 8th May, 1945, Soviet troops liberated the camp, many of the SS had already fled some days before. There was a typhoid epidemic, with more than 1,500 prisoners and 43 medical staff dying around the time of liberation, including Robert Desnos.

His contemporary, Paul Eluard, said: "Until death, Desnos struggled. Throughout his poems the idea of freedom runs like a terrible fire…Desnos' poetry is a poetry of courage. It has every possible audacity of thought and expression…He is the prodigal son of a people subject to prudence, economy, patience, but nevertheless always astonished the world by his sudden anger, the desire for emancipation and unforeseen surges".

Robert is buried in the Montparnasse Cemetery in Paris.

The Horror of Auschwitz

27th January marks International Holocaust Memorial Day. It was on that date in 1945 when the Soviet Army entered and liberated Auschwitz ll-Birkenau.

In truth the Russians would have had no idea what to expect as they entered the camp, although rumours had been rife, around the world, and publicised in London since 1942, of what was happening in the concentration camps in Poland, much of which was ignored. What the Soviet Army found were around seven thousand people, near death or dying, and evidence to suggest many hundreds of thousands more had been killed.

The original camp at Auschwitz was first constructed to hold Polish political prisoners who arrived in May, 1940. But the camp was quickly expanded as the war progressed. Auschwitz II–Birkenau became a major site to carry out what would become known as the Nazi's Final Solution to the Jewish Question. In simple terms, the final solution was designed and intended to exterminate the Jewish race. The first mass execution at Auschwitz happened in September, 1941, although not primarily involving Jews as the main target. But from early 1942 until late 1944, packed train loads of Jewish prisoners of all ages arrived at the camp from all over Europe. An estimated 1.3 million people were sent to the camp, of whom around 1.1 million died.

Approximately ninety percent of those killed at Auschwitz were Jews. Other prisoners, made up of Polish, Russian, Romani, homosexuals and Jehovah's Witnesses, were amongst the other ten percent. Many not killed in the gas chambers died of starvation, or through forced labour, infectious diseases, individual executions or as a result of medical experimentation carried out at the hand of Josef Mengele, known as the Angel of Death.

The Allied powers did not act on early reports of atrocities at the camp, and indeed their failure to attempt to bomb the camp and its railway infrastructure remains controversial today. Over eight hundred prisoners attempted to escape from Auschwitz with just over one hundred and forty being successful.

As Soviet troops approached Auschwitz in January, 1945, prior to their imminent arrival, most of the camps' population was sent west on what would become known as a death march. Executions took place all along the route with the bodies being put into mass graves that many of the other prisoners on the March were forced to dig by hand.

The Polish Government-in-exile in London first reported the gassing of prisoners on 21st July, 1942. These reports were disregarded as exaggerated or unreliable by the Allied powers. The attitude of the Allies only changed with receipt of the detailed 32-page Vrba–Wetzler report, compiled by two Jewish prisoners, Rudolf Vrba and Alfréd Wetzler, who both escaped on 7th April, 1944. This report finally convinced the Allied leaders that mass killings were and had been taking place in Auschwitz for years.

On 31st July, 1941, the primary architect of the exterminations, Hermann Göring, gave written authorisation to Heydrich, Chief of the Reich Main Security Office (RSHA), to prepare and submit a plan for Die Endlösung der Judenfrage, the Final Solution of the Jewish question, in territories under German control, and he was to coordinate the participation of all involved government organisations.

The first mass exterminations at Auschwitz took place in early September, 1941, when nine hundred Soviet prisoners of war and ill inmates were killed. They were gathered in the sealed basement of a building and gassed with Zyklon B. The prisoners were ordered to undress outside and then were locked in the building, before the gas was released. By July 1942, the SS were conducting 'selections'. Incoming Jewish prisoners were segregated; those deemed able to work were sent to the Selection Officer's right and admitted into the camp, those deemed unfit for labour were sent to the Selection Officer's left and immediately executed, by gassing. The group selected to die, about three-quarters of the total that arrived, included all children, and women with small children, elderly and all those who appeared not to be completely fit, either mentally or physically.

After the selection process was complete, those too ill or too young to walk to the chamber were transported there on trucks, or killed on the spot with a bullet to the head. Latterly the train line that ran into Auschwitz was extended to run directly to the gas chambers. The belongings of new arrivals were seized by the SS. The uniformed officers told the victims they were to take a shower and undergo delousing. The victims undressed in an outer chamber and walked into the gas chamber, which had been disguised as a shower facility. Some prisoners were even issued soap and a towel. Once the doors were shut, the guards released Zyklon B pellets through vents in the roof or holes in the side of the chamber. Those inside would be dead within 20 minutes.

Following the exterminations, any spectacles, artificial limbs, jewellery and hair were removed from the corpses along with any dental work which was extracted so the gold could be melted down. The bodies were burnt in the nearby incinerators with the ashes buried, thrown in the river or used as fertilizer in the camp. It really depended how much time the guards wished to spend on this process as to how the ashes were disposed of.

From May, until July, 1944, just under half a million Hungarian Jews, half of the pre-war population, were deported to Auschwitz. The incoming volume was so great that the SS resorted to burning corpses in open-air pits as well as in the crematoria. The last mass transports to arrive in Auschwitz were 60,000–70,000 Jews from the Łódź Ghetto, along with around 2,000 from Theresienstadt, and then 8,000 from Slovakia in October, 1944. The exact number of victims at Auschwitz is difficult to fix with certainty, because many prisoners were never registered and much evidence was destroyed by the SS.

Letter To My Wife

Miklós Radnóti

Beneath, the nether worlds, deep, still, and mute.
Silence howls in my ears, and I cry out.
No answer could come back, it is so far
From that sad Serbia swooned into war.
And you're so distant. But my heart redeems
Your voice all day, entangled in my dreams.
So I am still, while close about me sough
The great cold ferns, that slowly stir and bow.

When I'll see you, I don't know. You whose calm
Is as the weight and sureness of a psalm,
Whose beauty's like the shadow and the light,
Whom I could find if I were blind and mute,
Hide in the landscape now, and from within
Leap to my eye, as if cast by my brain.
You were real once; now you have fallen in
To that deep well of teenage dreams again.
Jealous interrogations: tell me; speak.
Do you still love me? Will you on that peak
Of my past youth become my future wife?
– but now I fall awake to real life
And know that's what you are: wife, friend of years
– just far away. Beyond three wild frontiers.
And Fall comes. Will it also leave with me?
Kisses are sharper in the memory.

Daylight and miracles seemed different things.
Above, the echelons of bombers' wings:
Skies once amazing blue with your eyes' glow
Are darkened now. Tight with desire to blow,
The bombs must fall. I live in spite of these,
A prisoner. All of my fantasies
I measure out. And I will find you still;
For you I've walked the full length of the soul,

A Hero's Tale - Miklós Radnóti

 Miklós Radnóti was born Miklós Glatter on 5th May, 1909, in Budapest to Jewish parents. His mother died shortly after his birth, and his twin brother was stillborn. His aunt took him into her family and raised him while his father worked in the textile business owned by her husband. After leaving school Miklós trained in his uncle's company for a while, then worked for literary magazines, writing poetry and publishing his first collection of verse, 'Pagan Statue', in 1930. He then spent five years at the University of Szeged, studying philosophy as well as Hungarian and French literature, earning his Ph.D., his thesis being on 'The Artistic Development of Margit Kaffka'.

During that time he published his second book, 'Song of New-Fashioned Shepherds', which was banned for indecency and led to a short prison sentence. He also began translating African stories and folk stories into Hungarian. After graduation he changed his surname to Radnóti, Radnót having been the birthplace of his paternal grandfather. He married in 1935, and began teaching at the Zsigmond Kemeny School in Budapest. In 1937 his book 'Walk on, Condemned', won the coveted Baumgarten Prize.

Miklós was conscripted into the Hungarian Army, serving with a Jewish labour battalion from September to October, 1940, and from July, 1942, to April, 1943. In May, 1943, he and his wife converted to Catholicism, not because he considered it to be advantageous, but because he had held a long-standing fascination with Catholicism, inspired by the priest Sandor Silk, who was his professor of literature at university. The conversion made no difference as he was still considered a Jew and was drafted into forced labour in May, 1944. Miklós continued to write poetry as he armed and disarmed explosives on the Ukrainian front, and laboured in the copper mines in Yugoslavia, being incarcerated in the Bor concentration camp.

As the German army retreated from the approaching Russian army, the concentration camp was evacuated and the prisoners were forced to march through Yugoslavia and Hungary. During March, Miklós wrote not only poems but also told of his experiences. He was badly beaten at one time by a soldier who was irritated with him for constantly writing. Eventually, on 6th November, exhausted, starved and badly treated, he collapsed. Twenty-one of his fellow prisoners were also in such conditions as to be unable to continue walking. They were all shot by the Hungarian guards and dumped into a mass grave.

A year after the end of the Second World War, the grave was exhumed. On Miklós' body was discovered the notebook in which he had been writing during the march. It contained his last poems including 'Letter To My Wife'. His collected work, 'Clouded Sky', was published in 1946, and his writings – poems, letters, fragments, observations – continue to be translated, published, and widely read.

The Hungarian poet and award-winning foreign correspondent Thomas Orszag-Land describes Miklós Radnóti as 'the greatest among the mature writers of the period to witness and record the Holocaust'.

A Hero's Tale – Witold Pilecki

 Witold Pilecki was born on 13th May, 1901, in Olonets in Russia, the son of a civil servant, and grandson of a Polish aristocrat whose estate had been confiscated by the Russian government for supporting the uprising of 1863-1864. As a teenager he became a member of the ZHP Scouts, a secret organisation which had sections in the partisan forces after the outbreak of the Russian Revolution. Witold saw action with the Lithuanian and Belarusian Self-Defence Militia before enlisting in the Polish Volunteer Army. He fought in the Polish-Soviet War, Kiev Offensive, Battle of Warsaw, and Polish-Lithuanian War. For gallantry, he was twice awarded the Cross of Valour.

In 1921, he transferred to the army reserve, was promoted to corporal and enrolled in university but could not afford to complete his studies. After attending the Cavalry Reserve Officers' Training School in Grudziadz in 1926, he was assigned to the 26th Lancer Regiment. The following year he reclaimed his ancestral estate, and in 1938 received the Silver Cross of Merit for his community work.

He was appointed Commander of the 1st Lidsky Squadron, which suffered heavy losses during the German invasion of Poland. After the government surrendered to Germany in September, 1939, he and thousands of others continued to fight, founding the Secret Polish Army. By summer of 1940, several of his comrades were in Auschwitz. He volunteered to infiltrate the camp on an intelligence-gathering mission, obtained false papers and allowed himself to be picked up in Warsaw and sent on the train to Auschwitz. On arrival he was selected to be a worker. A resistance organisation was created within the camp to provide news, obtain food and medicine, pass on messages and assist with escapes. In March, 1941, a message Witold sent reached London, which detailed conditions in the camp and of prisoners not going through the registration process which meant there were far more victims than had been documented. The message was never reacted to in London. In 1942, prisoners built a radio transmitter and broadcast details of arrivals, conditions and details of exterminations. Again anyone receiving the transmissions never responded to them. In April, 1943, Witold escaped from Auschwitz; he crossed the Sola and Vistula rivers, reaching Nowy Wisnicz, where contacted the Home Army and presented detailed reports on everything about Auschwitz.

In 1944, Witold fought in the Warsaw uprising, was captured and sent to a Bavarian prison camp. After 1945, he provided intelligence for the Polish Second Corps, but in 1947, he was arrested by the Polish Secret Police and tortured. In March, 1948, he was charged with illegal border crossing, forging documents, carrying illegal arms, espionage, and planning to assassinate officials. Witold denied the assassination and espionage charges, but admitted passing information to the Polish Second Corps. He pleaded guilty, claiming that he did not break any laws. Jozef Cyrankiewicz, an Auschwitz survivor and future Polish prime minister, testified against him. On 25th May, he was executed.

Witold Pilecki is considered to be one of the greatest wartime heroes. Poland's Chief Rabbi Michael Schudrich wrote: 'When God created the human being, God had in mind that we should all be like Captain Witold Pilecki, of blessed memory.'

A Hero's Tale - Michael Allmand

Michael Allmand was born on 22nd August, 1923, in Golders Green, London. The son of the Professor of Chemistry at King's College, London, he was educated at Ampleforth College in Yorkshire, and Oriel College, Oxford, where he read history and was the founder of a literary review journal.

A year after beginning his university studies and being involved in Officer Cadet Training, he was commissioned into the Indian Army Corps, and joined the 6th Duke of Connaught's Own Lancers. Working as an instructor, he was keen to be on active service. When GHQ India called for volunteers to serve in the Second Chindit Expedition, he responded immediately, and was attached to the 3rd Battalion, 6th Gurkha Rifles part of 77th Infantry Brigade. The Commander was Brigadier J.M. Calvert, known as Mad Mike.

On the 6th June, 1944, the 77th Brigade advanced towards Mogaung in Burma. They fought over 4,000 Japanese through monsoon weather, with torrential rain and swampy terrain, suffering casualties not only from combat but disease – by the end of the week their number was reduced from over 2,000 to 550. Michael Allmand had proved himself as a capable leader, and by this time, at the age of twenty, he had been promoted to Captain.

For his actions up until the day of his death on 24th June, he was posthumously awarded the Victoria Cross, part of his citation tells the story of his courage:

'The Battalion was ordered to attack the Pin Hmi Road Bridge. The approach was narrow, the road banked up, land on either side was swampy and densely covered in jungle. The Japanese, dug in along the banks and in the jungle with machine guns and small arms, were putting up the most desperate resistance. As the platoon come within twenty yards, the enemy opened heavy fire, inflicting severe casualties. Captain Allmand with the utmost gallantry charged on by himself, hurling grenades into enemy gun positions and killing three Japanese with his kukri. Inspired by [this] splendid example the surviving men followed and captured their objective. Two days later Captain Allmand, owing to casualties among the officers, took command and, dashing ahead through long grass and marshy ground, swept by machine gun fire, killed a number of enemy machine gunners and led his men onto the ridge that they had been ordered to seize. In the final attack, Captain Allmand...moved forward alone through deep mud and shell-holes and charged a Japanese machine gun nest single-handed, but he was mortally wounded and died shortly afterwards. The superb gallantry, outstanding leadership and protracted heroism of this very brave officer were a wonderful example to the whole Battalion and in the highest traditions of his regiment.'

Captain Allmand lies buried in the Taukkyan War Cemetery in Burma, and there is a memorial window in his honour in the St. Edward the Confessor Catholic Church in Golders Green. His medals are displayed in the Gurkha Regimental Museum in Winchester, Hampshire.

A Hero's Tale – Lyudmila Mikhailovna Pavlichenko

Lyudmila Pavlichenko was born on 12th July, 1916, in Bila Tserkva, in the Russian Empire. Her family moved to Kiev when she was a teenager, where she found work as a metal grinder at the Kiev Arsenal Factory and joined a shooting club. She married at the age of sixteen and had a son, divorcing soon afterwards. In 1937, she began attending Kiev University, studying history.

When German troops poured into the Soviet Union in June, 1941, Lyudmila wanted to join the army. She was described as looking like a model with manicured nails, fashionable clothes and styled hair, and was laughed at by the recruiter when she told him she wanted to fight. He told her that they didn't take 'girls', and suggested she take up nursing. Lyudmila produced her marksman certificate and sharpshooter badge, and was later given a rifle and shown two Romanian soldiers in the distance. She shot them with two single rounds and was accepted into the Red Army's 25th Chapayev Rifle Division.

After being sent to the battle lines in Greece and Moldova, Lyudmila killed over 180 Germans in her first seventy-five days. She distinguished herself as a fearsome sniper, capable of remaining still for hours on end behind enemy lines, in extremely dangerous circumstances. She fought in the Battle of Sevastopol and during the eight months there, she was wounded several times including being hit in the face by shrapnel. Her position was bombed, it is believed, primarily due to her high kill count.

Lyudmila often faced enemy snipers, and killed thirty-six of them, some of whom were highly decorated soldiers. According to Russian sources she earned the reputation as the scourge of the German army on the Eastern front. The Germans called to her through loud-speakers, offering her comfort and sweets if she would defect.

In 1942, Lyudmila was the first Soviet citizen to be received by a U.S. President. Franklin D. Roosevelt welcomed her to the White House. At the time she met with Washington reporters, who annoyed her with their comments when one reporter criticized the length of the skirt of her uniform, saying that in America women wore shorter skirts and besides her uniform made her look fat. Her response was firm; "I wear my uniform with honour. It has the Order of Lenin on it. It has been covered with blood in battle. It is plain to see that with American women what is important is whether they wear silk underwear under their uniforms. What the uniform stands for, they have yet to learn." She was later asked if she wore make-up to battle!

Lyudmila was one of 2,000 female Red Army snipers who fought in the Second World War and one of only 500 who survived. It is believed she had many more kills than her official score of 309, as kills must be confirmed by a third party and snipers often work alone.

After the war, Lyudmila went back to university to finish her degree. Her wounds did not fully heal, which affected her health. She passed away in her son's arms at the age of fifty-eight.

Heroes Tales – Glen the Para Dog and Private Emile Servais Corteil

Glen the Alsatian shepherd was a Para-Dog who took part in the D-Day Landings in Normandy on 6th June, 1944. His role in A Company, 9th (Essex) Parachute Regiment, was to assist with guard and patrol duties, and on D-Day he completed the parachute descent with his handler, Private Emile "Jack" Servais Corteil, from Watford in Hertfordshire, who was nineteen years old. Glen's job, once they landed, would have been to stand stock still to warn of anyone approaching or being nearby.

Para-Dogs were trained to jump alone before their handlers. They had small parachutes with special harnesses, which enabled them to land with their stronger rear legs; on landing they were to lie on their parachute and wait for their handler, a small red light being attached to their harness. During training, Glen took to jumping with great enthusiasm, and would wait patiently for Private Corteil to land, the private being the only person from whom Glen took orders.

In the early hours of 6th June, 1944, over 700 parachutists were taken into action in Dakota C47 aircraft for the drop into the target area. One of the 9th Battalion's objectives was to take the German battery at Merville-Franceville, the site of guns large enough to be used against the Allied troops on the landing beaches. They were also to block the roads to the village of Le Plein, and capture the village as well as the German Navy Headquarters at Sallenelles.

Strong winds, poor visibility of the dropping zones due to the design of the aircraft, and deliberate flooding by the Germans of the area from the River Dives, were to prove catastrophic. The 9th Battalion suffered the loss of 192 men, most of them drowning in the flood waters; many others came down far from the landing site, which left approximately 150 to storm the battery before the landings began.

Private Corteil and Glen landed a few miles from the target area, along with Brigadier James Hill of 3rd Parachute Brigade, and over three dozen of his men. The Brigadier marched them towards the target area but on the way they were hit by a Royal Air Force aerial bombardment intended for the Germans, who they anticipated would be waiting for the beach landings. All but the Brigadier and a couple of his men were killed, including Glen and Private Corteil; the Brigadier and the survivors pushed on to their destination.

Glen and Private Corteil were found several days later by a search party of 9th Battalion survivors with their chaplain. Lying together in a bomb crater, Private Corteil was still holding Glen's leash. Those who knew them spoke of the strong trust and affection between them, and of their inseparable bond. Glen and Private Corteil are buried together in the Ranville War Cemetery in Normandy.

On their headstone are the words,
'Had you known our boy you would have loved him too, 'Glen' his paratroop dog was killed with him'.

The Big Bang

In August, 1945, one of the biggest events in history took place. This event would change the world; leading to the almost complete annihilation of two major cities and many of their peoples. It was an event that would start and prove to be one the longest disputes between what would become known as the two main super power countries of the world.

Colonel Paul W Tibbets, U.S.A.F., had been briefed on a top secret mission in 1945. He was the lead pilot and even selected his own plane whilst it was still on the assembly line. A giant of the skies, made by Boeing for the United States Air Force, the B-29-45-MO Superfortress, more commonly known as the B29 Bomber, was commissioned into the hands of the U.S. Air Force on 18th May, 1945. The B-29 Paul Tibbets had selected was for a specific mission and had a specific target. As soon as it was ready for operation, Tibbets named the plane after his Mother. Her name was Enola Gay Tibbets.

During the 1930s and 1940s Germany led the world in science and so it was no accident that the race to produce the first atomic bomb had started in Germany in 1939. It was in December the year before that a German scientist, Otto Hahn, discovered nuclear fission, a way to split atoms and separate neutrons and gamma photons, which by doing so, he found the reaction would release huge amounts of energy. In 1939, German scientists and engineers, realising the enormity of what had been discovered, started to work on their own nuclear weapons programme which they planned to use during the Second World War.

However, due to the impending invasion of Poland in September, 1939, a few months after the programme had started it was stopped. This was primarily due to the fact that many of the scientists involved in the atomic project were drafted into the Wehrmacht. Another German nuclear weapons programme was restarted on 1st September, 1939, with the scientist who had not been selected for front line duty. It was also the same day German tanks drove across the Polish border. However, by 1942, it was assessed by the German high command that nuclear fission would not significantly contribute to winning the war and the science and development behind such a project was proving expensive. An order was received to stop the programme; it was never restarted in Germany.

In the same year that the Germans abandoned their attempts to create a nuclear bomb, the United States were carrying out their own scientific tests into nuclear fission and fusion – the ability to make atomic nuclei come very close and then collide at a very high speed and join to form a new nucleus. Within New Mexico, United States, Canadian and British scientists were working on what would become known as the Manhattan Project. Under Professor J. Robert Oppenheimer, an American theoretical physicist and professor of physics, the project would lead to the creation of an atomic bomb.

On 6th August, 1945, with Paul Tibbets piloting the Enola Gay, three B-29s took off from the Mariana Islands located in the Pacific Ocean with their target of Hiroshima, six hours flight from their airfield. The accompanying B-29s, one with scientific instruments and the other to take photographs of what was to come, all took off within minutes of each other but then separated, flying different courses towards the island of Iwo Jima. There they met up again at over 8,000 feet and plotted a direct course for Japan.

The single load Enola Gay was carrying was codenamed 'Little Boy'. A 9,700lb atomic bomb, 10 feet long and over 2 feet in diameter, it had been set with a predetermined detonation height of 600 metres above land. The bomb was armed whilst in flight and around 30 minutes prior to reaching the target site all safety mechanisms were removed. At a height of around 31,000 feet, directly above Hiroshima, the bomb was released from Enola Gay.

Little Boy took 45 seconds to fall to its detonation height before it exploded. The resulting blast and aftershocks destroyed approximately one square mile of the city below, with resulting fires destroying nearly five square miles.

It is estimated over 70,000 people died instantly with around another 80,000 seriously injured. This number represents a third of the population of Hiroshima in 1945.

Only 20,000 of those that died or were injured were believed to have been military personnel.

The atomic bombing of Hiroshima failed to force Japan Government into submission, so three days later, on 9th August, 1945, the U.S. dropped another atomic bomb, this time on the City of Nagasaki. It was only then that Japan surrendered. It is estimated the two bombings resulted in the deaths of around 200,000 people, mainly civilians.

When asked about the bomb, its chief scientist, Professor J. Robert Oppenheimer, is quoted as saying,

"I remembered the line from the Hindu scripture the Bhagavad Gita; Vishnu is trying to persuade the prince that he should do his duty, and to impress him takes on his multi-armed form, and say.....

"Now I am become death, the destroyer of worlds"

A Hero's Tale – Lord Leonard Cheshire

Geoffrey Leonard Cheshire was born on 7th September, 1917, in Chester, the son of barrister, Dr. Geoffrey Chevalier Cheshire. He was educated at the Dragon School in Oxford, Chatham House in Stowe, and studied law at Merton College, Oxford.

In 1937 he joined the University Air Squadron, and was commissioned into the R.A.F. Volunteer Reserve that November. He mobilised for War in October, 1939, receiving his wings in December. Two months later he was promoted to Flying Officer in April, 1940, he joined 102 Squadron. He spent the next five months on bombing raids on Germany, targeting Berlin, Bremen, Cologne and Essen. His actions on 12th November, 1940, earned him the Distinguished Service Order: his target had been an oil refinery near Cologne, but due to the cloud conditions and wind he chose to attack the railway yards at Cologne instead. His plane was heavily damaged from two anti-aircraft shells, but he managed to release the bombs and fly home.

Early in 1941, he joined 35 Squadron. He was awarded the Distinguished Flying Cross, and a month later received a Bar to his D.S.O. for 'outstanding leadership and skill on operations'. He was promoted to Flight Lieutenant soon afterwards then promotion to Squadron Leader came in October. In January, 1942, Leonard was posted to No. 1652 Heavy Conversion Unit at Marston Moor as an instructor. He nevertheless flew four operational missions, including the first of 'Bomber' Harris's 1,000-bomber raids. Soon came another promotion, to Wing Commander and a second Bar to his D.S.O. This was followed in April, 1943, by the appointment to Station Commander and promotion to Group Captain, the youngest ever at only twenty-five years old.

He returned to operational flying in command of 617 Squadron, known for the 'Dambusters' raid. Leonard led a mission to destroy the Saumur railway tunnel, three days after D-Day, designed to block Germany's main rail supply between Normandy and the south. On 6th July he flew his 100th operational mission, an attack on a missile site at Marquise. For the very rare citation of 'sustained courage and outstanding effort', he was awarded the Victoria Cross. Leonard was the British observer for the second atomic bomb raid against Japan, on 9th August, 1945. He was situated in the third B-29 that flew over Nagasaki.

Discharge from the R.A.F. came five months later when he was diagnosed with psycho-neurosis. He founded the Leonard Cheshire Charity for disabled people, establishing Cheshire Homes which is one of the U.K.'s top thirty charities.

Sir Max Hastings, military historian, said of him: "Cheshire was a legend in Bomber Command, a remarkable man with an almost mystical air about him…but without affectation or pretension. He inspired great loyalty in his men. Rather than have his own crew, he flew with inexperienced people to give them confidence. When at a new base, he made sure to learn the name of every person there."

Leonard Cheshire passed away in July, 1992, and is buried at St. Mary's Church, Cavendish in Suffolk.

A Hero's Tale - Nadezhda Vasilyevna Popova

Nedezhda Popova was born on the December, 1921, in Dolgoye in the Ukraine. Growing up, she thought of becoming a doctor or teacher, but meeting a pilot who landed his plane near her home one day changed her mind. "I thought only gods could fly. It was amazing that a simple man could get in a plane and fly away". She joined a flying club, later graduating from the Kherson aviation school and becoming an instructor.

After the outbreak of the Second World War, she volunteered as a fighter pilot, but was turned down as women were not accepted for combat. In 1941 Marina Raskova, who became a much-decorated pilot, was allowed to found three Russian all-female air regiments.

Nadezhda's brother, Leonid, had been killed at the front. His death, along with how she saw the invading Germans treating her people, spurred her on: "I saw the German aircraft flying along our roads filled with people who were leaving their homes, firing at them with their machine guns. Seeing this gave me feelings inside that made me want to fight them".

Nadezhda trained as a military pilot and then joined a night bombing regiment. She was soon in command of the 2nd Women's Regiment, the members of which ranged in age from seventeen to twenty-six. They flew only at night in planes that had been used as crop-dusters before the war and were not equipped with radar, radio, guns nor parachutes. The women who flew them became known as 'Night Witches', because the sound their canvas-and-plywood planes made was to the Germans like that of broomsticks swishing.

The Regiment grew famous as they terrorised the enemy, shutting down their engines in the last stages of their bombing runs. They flew over 30,000 sorties, and counted among their ranks thirty Heroes of the Soviet Union and three fighter aces. No other countries sent their female pilots on bombing raids, as the Soviets did.

During the war, Nadezhda served in Belorussia, Poland and Germany, her missions totalling 852 including eighteen in one night. In 1942, she was shot down in the North Caucasus and met the man she would marry, decorated pilot Semyon Kharlamov. After the war she spoke of her missions: "At night sometimes, I look up into the dark sky, close my eyes and picture myself as a girl at the controls of my bomber, and think, 'Nadya, how on earth did you do it?' When the wind was strong it would toss the plane. In winter when you'd look out to see your target better, you got frostbite, our feet froze in our boots, but we carried on. If you give up nothing is done and you are not a hero. Those who gave in were gunned down and burned alive as they had no parachutes".

Nadezhda Popova passed away on 8th July, 2013, at the age of ninety-one. Ukrainian President Viktor Yanukovych called her life 'an example of selfless service to Motherland'.

A Hero's Tale - George Albert Cairns

George Cairns was born on 12th December, 1913, in Tooting, London. After completing his schooling, he moved to Sidcup to work in the Belgian Bank. At the outbreak of the Second World War, he was commissioned into the Somerset Light Infantry (Prince Albert's), which was attached to the South Staffordshire Regiment in Burma; they were a Chindit Battalion, part of the 77th Indian Infantry Brigade.

In March, 1944, they had been dug in close to a hill near Henu and Mawlu, an area known as the White City; unknown to them at the time they were close to a small Japanese force who did not know of the British presence. On the 16th March the fighting began. The British were under the command of General Michael Calvert who led the attack in person, and he reported that "at the top of the hill, about fifty yards square, an extraordinary mêlée took place, everyone shooting, bayoneting, kicking at everyone else, rather like an officers' guest night."

Lieutenant Cairns died on the 19th March, weakened due to his left arm having been hacked off the previous day by a Japanese soldier. Despite being so grievously wounded he killed his attacker, picked up the fallen Japanese sword which had taken his arm and continued fighting. For his actions that day he was awarded the Victoria Cross, the citation stating that the Japanese were completely routed, a rare occurrence at that time.

Lieutenant Norman Durant, commanding one of the South Staffordshire Regiment's machine gun platoons, described the action in a letter to his family: 'The first thing I saw on reaching the path was horrible hand-to-hand struggle going on up the hill. George Cairns and a Jap were struggling on the ground, I saw George break free and stab the Jap again and again like a madman. It was only when I got near that I saw he himself had already been bayoneted twice through the side and that his left arm was hanging on by a few strips of muscle. How he had found the strength to fight was a miracle, but the effort had been too much and he died the next morning. After a brief intermission, Calvert's forces broke the Japanese resistance, driving them from the area. In spite of our casualties, we had all that elation of winners of a good battle.'

Lieutenant Cairns, lying injured, asked:
"Have we won, sir? Did we do our stuff? Don't worry about me."

His wife approached her Member of Parliament in 1949 to make representations to the War Office for the Victoria Cross; she had been listening to a radio broadcast and heard of her husband's bravery. The original recommendation was lost due to an aircraft crash, and further delay was caused as two of the required three witnesses had been killed.

Lieutenant Cairns is buried in the Taukkyan War Cemetery in Burma, and there is memorial to him at St. Mary the Virgin Church at Brighstone on the Isle of Wight.

A Hero's Tale – Aleksey Maresyev

Aleksey Maresyev was born on 20th May, 1916, in Kamyshin, on the banks of the Volga. It was at the local cinema that Aleksey watched a film about aviation, and was inspired to learn to fly. The local branch of the Communist party were seeking vocational school students to build a new city, Komsomolsk-on-Amur. Aleksey was reluctant to go, but his teachers told him refusal would jeopardise his future.

Once that work was completed, in 1937, Aleksey joined the Red Army and served in the border patrol aviation unit as a technician. He said his job was to "put the tail of the plane into the proper parking position." Eighteen months later he went to the Military School of Aviation where he earned his wings, graduating in 1940, a year before Russia entered the war.

The Russian fighter planes could not compare to those flown by the Germans. Aleksey made his first flight as a fighter pilot in one such plane in 1941, and within a few months had shot down four Luftwaffe aces. In April, 1942, he was downed by two German planes in a forest near Staraya; he crashed into snow in Nazi-occupied territory, and although wounded he made his way through the dense forest for eighteen days before reaching the village of Plavni. He was cared for by a peasant family until another Soviet plane arrived and he was taken to hospital. His condition was poor and both his legs had to be amputated.

Aleksey was inspired by the Russian pilot Prokofyev-Seversky who continued to fly despite having lost a foot. Aleksey was so determined that he not only learned how to walk using prosthetics, he learned to dance. When he applied to fly again, the military doctors did not even realize he had prosthetics, and were so impressed that they accepted his request to resume flying. He returned to his squadron, where he was supervised until the commander felt he was safe to fly alone. On his first solo flight, he downed three Luftwaffe planes, bringing his total to eleven enemy planes downed during eighty-six combat flights.

In 1943, he received the Golden Star, 'Hero of the Soviet Union', the highest military award. War correspondent Boris Polevoy wrote an article about him, and in 1944, the story was made into a film. In an interview he said, "There's nothing extraordinary in what I have done. The fact that I've been turned into a legend irritates me."

He became a flying instructor and then resigned from the military in 1946. He spent years helping his fellow veterans and in 1983 was elected Chairman of the Soviet War Veterans Committee. He also became a member of the Soviet parliament.

In May, 2001, he was taken to hospital with a heart complaint, and passed away an hour before he was to be honoured in the Central Russian Army Theatre where the Russian Armed Forces orchestra were playing; they stood for a minute of silence in his honour.

A Hero's Tale – Ronald Thomas Stewart MacPherson

Tommy Macpherson was born on 4th October, 1920, in Edinburgh. He was one of seven children of Sir Thomas Stewart MacPherson, a High Court Judge. Tommy was educated at Edinburgh Academy Prep School and Fettes College, where he joined the Officers' Training Corps. He attended Trinity College, Oxford, but his studies were interrupted by the outbreak of the Second World War.

Tommy was commissioned into the Queen's Own Cameron Highlanders (Territorial). In 1940, he volunteered to serve with the Commandos and became an assistant to Lord Lovat, who was the fieldcraft instructor. By March, 1941, he had arrived in Suez with 11th (Scottish) Commando, and three months later was fighting the Vichy French, the objective being to take the Kafr Badda bridge on the Litani River in Palestine; the mission proved successful, but the unit sustained heavy casualties.

On his return to Cyprus, Tommy was appointed Military Governor of the north-east part of the island, was promoted to Captain, and then ordered to carry out a reconnaissance of the beach in advance of Operation Flipper, the raid on Rommel's headquarters in Cyrenaica, but he and his comrades were captured by the Italians. After trying to escape, Tommy was sent to Campo 41 and later to Campo 5, a fortress built on a rock near Genoa. The prison was taken over by the Germans in September, 1943. Tommy later escaped from a Gestapo camp on the Polish-Lithuanian border; he and others were helped by the Polish Resistance and smuggled aboard a Swedish ship. Once in international waters, they gave themselves up to the captain and were taken to Stockholm to be released to the British Embassy. He arrived home in November, 1943, and was awarded the Military Cross.

Tommy was then recruited by the Special Operations Executive, promoted to the rank of Major, and flew on one of the first Jedburgh missions into France. In June, 1944, on Operation Quinine, with a French officer and a radio operator, he was dropped into France to organise Maquis resistance groups. They led them against the Das Reich Panzer division, organised raids on road and railway lines, ambushed enemy convoys, demolished a bridge and co-ordinated large-scale guerilla operations. There was a price of 300,000 francs on Tommy's head by then, and he was awarded the first Bar to his Military Cross.

At the end of the war in Europe Tommy was awarded a second Bar to his Military Cross, and also received the Medaglio d'Argento, the Italian Resistance Medal, the Croix de Guerre and the Légion d'Honneur. He was demobilised and rejoined the Territorial Army. Tommy returned to Oxford to complete his studies and obtained a First in Philosophy, Politics and Economics.

He retired from the army in 1968, the year of his appointment as Commander of the Most Excellent Order of the British Empire, and he was knighted in 1992. Tommy published his autobiography, 'Behind Enemy Lines', in 2010.

He passed away on 6th November, 2014, at the age of 94.

A Hero's Tale – Billy Strachan

William Arthur Watkin Strachan was born in Kingston, Jamaica, on 16th April, 1921. He left school in December, 1939, with a burning ambition to get to Britain, join the R.A.F. and learn to fly. To raise his boat fare he sold his trumpet and other belongings and hitched a ride on a boat across the Atlantic. With only £2 10 shilling in his pocket and a suitcase containing one change of clothes, Billy arrived in England in March, 1940. After a night in the YMCA he went straight to the Air Ministry in Kingsway to try to join up.

Up until the 1939, in Britain, a colour bar was in place for entry into the services, and in London at that time, signs such as 'No dogs and no blacks' were common in many rental premises.

An R.A.F. sergeant met Billy at the Ministry and told him 'he and his sort should go back where they came from and join up there'. A young officer came by and asked Billy where he was from. "Kingston." He replied to which the officer said, "I am from Richmond."

Billy was given strict medical, education and intelligence tests and by the next morning he was wearing his R.A.F. uniform. After 12 weeks' basic training as a wireless operator and air gunner, he was promoted to sergeant. He joined a Bombers Squadron flying out of Waterbeach in Cambridge. making nightly raids over German industrial targets. His first crew were from various countries of what was still the British Empire. They flew a bomber named Vizagapatam, from the people of the Indian district who paid for the plane. When Billy had completed 30 operations he was entitled to a job on the ground. But when asked what he wanted to do, he asked to retrain as a pilot. He learned quickly and was allowed to fly solo after only seven hours' training.

In 1942, Billy Strachan became a bomber pilot. He was famous for his hair-raising but clever way of escaping German fighters. The trick, he explained, was to wait until the enemy was right on your tail and, at the last minute, cut the engine, sending your lumbering Lancaster into a plunging dive, letting the fighter overshoot harmlessly above. Billy Strachan gained two more promotions to become Flying Officer and then Flight Lieutenant. But on his fifteenth trip as a bomber pilot his nerve snapped:

"I remember so clearly. I was carrying a 12,000 pound bomb destined for some German shipping. It was a foggy night, with visibility about 100 yards. I asked my engineer to make sure we were on course to get over the top of the cathedral tower. He replied: 'We've just passed it.' I looked out and suddenly realised that it was just beyond our wingtips. This was the last straw. I knew I simply couldn't go on – that this was the end of me as a pilot!"

Strachan, served as an R.A.F. Liaison Officer sorting out racial tensions on bases and sometimes advocated for black servicemen in Courts Martial, he was only too willing to help. Suave and genial but possessing a steely determination to fight social injustice in all its manifestations, he was soon addressing meetings all over London on behalf of West Indian migrants. He later became Secretary of the London arm of the Trinidad-based Caribbean Labour Congress, working closely with leaders of Caribbean independence movements.

Billy Strachan died in 1998

The End of the War

In April, 1945, massive gains in land and territory were made by the Allies on the Western Front and by the Soviet Forces on the Eastern Front. But with the military successes came some startling discoveries; Russian forces discovered Auschwitz and the British found Bergen-Belsen, to name but a few.

Captured SS guards were subsequently tried at Allied war crimes tribunals at Nuremberg where many were sentenced to death or life imprisonment. It is estimated up to 10,000 Nazi war criminals eventually fled Europe, mostly to the South American continent.

On 28th April, 1945, Mussolini was executed along with other known fascists after Italian partisans, in support of the Allies, liberated Milan and Turin. He had been found trying to escape to Switzerland under the cover of a German military unit.

On 30th April, as the Battles of Nuremberg and Hamburg were nearing their ends, with Allied successes the Battle of Berlin was in full swing as the Soviet Army attacked the city. All escape routes for Hitler, who was in his bunker, were cut off. Realising that all was lost and no doubt not wishing to suffer the fate of execution Hitler committed suicide, along with his wife, Eva Braun. In his last letter, Hitler appointed his successors: Admiral Dönitz to be the new President of Germany, and Joseph Goebbels as the new Chancellor. Goebbels took his own life the day after, leaving Dönitz in sole charge.

The Battle of Berlin ended in German surrender to the Soviet Army on 2nd May, and on 4th May, German forces in Bavaria and North West Germany, as well as those in Denmark and the Netherlands, surrendered.

An unconditional surrender by Germany was negotiated between 6th and 7th May, then on 8th May, Winston Churchill made a radio broadcast at 3pm announcing:

"Hostilities will end officially at one minute after midnight tonight, but in the interests of saving lives the 'cease fire' began yesterday to be sounded all along the front, and our dear Channel Islands are also to be freed today."

The war in the Pacific was still going with no sign of surrender and so for the only time in world warfare history, during August, 1945, the United States used two nuclear bombs, dropped within a few days of each other on the Japanese cities of Hiroshima and Nagasaki, in order to force Japan into submission. Japan finally announced their surrender on 15th August, 1945, and this was formally signed on 2nd September, 1945, bringing about a complete cessation of hostilities from that date and effectively ending the Second World War.

During the six years of the Second World War it is estimated that the total death toll in the world, directly due to the war, was between 70–85 million people, of which around 55 million were either military of civilians who died as a result of military actions, with around another 23 million who died from war-related disease or famine.

Memories Page

This page is made up of memories of what parents or grandparents of FVUK members mentioned about the Second World War:

'I remember my Mum saying that her and her sister Meg were told to be quiet and sit still as the family huddled around the wireless and heard the Prime Minister declare War on Germany'. Peter

'My Mum told me about the time she narrowly missed being killed in early 1940. She was in a playground with her sister when a lone plane flew over, it would have been using the estuary as a guide. It wasn't until bullets started raining down on them that she realised it must have been a German plane. The only safe place was under the metal sea-saw. Mum said she grabbed her sister and pushed her under the sea-saw before going under herself. She said the sounds of bullets pinged off the sea-saw and her and her sister cuddled together crying and screaming, until the plane passed over and they ran home'. Julie

Two doors down from where we lived a young couple moved into the house and when they went up into the attic, the Police and MOD were called to find the discovery of a crystal radio set and coding machine. It was never discovered who had used it, nor whether it was used to spy and send messages to Germany. JS

'My Dad told me that in 1945 a soldier still in uniform walked up a lane looking for the house where his wife had moved to. He saw a little girl and asked her if she knew Mrs Blackburn. "That's my Mummy", she replied to the Dad she had never met. John Blackburn had served in the desert with the 8th Army before being taken prisoner of war. His daughter was born on 1940, two months after he went to war. PM

'My Dad's tank suffered a petrol stoppage and as he jumped out to fix it, he was engaged by a Japanese bunker and automatic fire broke out all around him. With his sten gun and grenades my Dad organised his Bombay Grenadier escort and some of the 4/15 th Punjab to the hit the bunker hard while his crew got the tank going again. He was awarded the Military Medal for his actions and featured in the book, 'The Life of a Regiment 1919 – 1945'. Haggis

'My Dad was in the Navy under command on Peter Scott, the Son of Scott, of the Antarctic. He was a gunner on a Motor Torpedo Boat. When they reached India he decided to buy something to bring home to his Mum, and purchased an Indian Rug. The rug was wrapped in brown paper and placed under his bunk. The boat then proceeded to fight in the Far East. After VJ Day one night the crew were allowed to go ashore in Changi. Only a skeleton crew was left on-board the boat. A Japanese fighter pilot, who clearly was not aware of, or was ignoring the fact that VJ Day had happened, attacked the harbour and sank my Dad's MTB sending the rug to the depths of the sea.' John

"My Mum, Auntie and Uncle were evacuated with mixed results. My Uncle lived with a family on a farm and the family wanted to adopt him, although that never happened. My Mum and Auntie went to stay with a family but were not cared for and returned home in a dirty state, with nits." Angie

CW01500379

Contents

Preface, Introduction, Thanks & Entry Format

The Shows

The People

The launch of ITV on 22 September 1955, brought something new to British television - commercials [*'It's tingling fresh. It's as fresh as ice. It's Gibbs SR toothpaste'*] and the genesis of the Independent Television Corporation [ITC] - *The Adventures of Robin Hood*.

The abolition of viewers watching dramas produced in dusty BBC TV studios was swift. Within the time it takes to cast, rehearse and film new programming, ITC provided the network with an inexorable mix of quality programming - shows which continue to delight millions of viewers today, decades *after* they were first transmitted, courtesy of the satellite/cable companies *UK Gold* and *Bravo* [not to mention recent outings on *BBC TV 1/2* and *C4*] - all of whom sure know a good thing when they see one.

That said, the question begs why?

The answer isn't really that surprising. Streets ahead of today's nose-in-the-gutter, effing and blinding, sex-laden TV shows, viewers tune into them time after time after time because they deliver the goods - they *entertain*.

No-one grasped this better than Lew [now Lord Lew] Grade.

In 1954, when he formed the Independent Television Corporation with Prince Littler and Val Parnell and signed his name to a cheque financing the company's first-ever TV production, he was but months away from etching his name indelibly on the entertainment industry role of honour as *the* single most dominating personality in British television. Throughout the formative years of ITV and on through the Sixties and early Seventies, his name became inextricably linked to the single biggest outpouring of quality television programming produced by a UK company - a plethora of delights held in fond regard and viewed as classics of the genre.

It began with a chance meeting with a woman called Hannah Weinstein. Head of a company making TV commercials and eager to break into TV production, she suggested that the legendary English hero Robin Hood would be ideal subject material. Convinced that he was backing a winner, Grade put up the money to finance *The Adventures of Robin Hood* - the first of many historical costumed series to be made by Weinstein's company, Sapphire Films. [Incidentally, though Sapphire Films had already filmed the Boris Karloff thriller series *Colonel Marsh of Scotland Yard*, the series was NOT financed by ITC].

A resounding success on the CBS American television network and extremely popular in the UK, *Robin Hood* showed a huge profit and paved the way for further historical dramas: *The Buccaneers*, *The Adventures of Sir Lancelot* and, co-financed by ITC, *The Count of Monte Cristo* and *The Adventures of the Scarlet Pimpernel*.

After *William Tell*, the company turned it's eye to the thriller genre with *H.G. Wells' Invisible Man*, *The New Adventures of Charlie Chan*, *O.S.S.* and *The Four Just Men*, Sapphire Films' last co-production. The world premiere of Patrick McGoohan's *Danger Man* - the first [arguably the best] of the British TV secret agents - came next. Thereafter things moved along at spectacular pace.

The Saint, with Roger Moore [four seasons, 114 episodes], *Danger Man* [three seasons of hour-long episodes, two of which were filmed in colour, as was ITC's custom from 1962], *The Prisoner*, *The Baron*, *Man in a Suitcase*, *The Champions*, *Department S*, *The Persuaders* ..... the list goes on.

True to say the Sixties, affectionately viewed as 'the Golden Years' of British television, simply wouldn't have been the treasure house it was *without* ITC's line up of creative, entertaining, star-laden shows - and TV viewers everywhere owe a debt of gratitude to the man who was blessed with the Midas touch.

Swift to recognise that the 'little black box' would turn us into a nation of couch potatoes, Lord Grade has a lot to answer for - all of it good. Thank you, Sir, for a lifetime of happy viewing. May your Havana's never extinguish.

We offer this book as our mark of respect.

Dave Rogers

Preface   by S. J. Gillis

It was around 3 AM on Christmas morning and, obviously, just the right time to have a sneak preview of the Gillis presents. Therefore I skulked down the stairs carefully avoiding the squeaky ones and, in deference to the sleeping household, refrained from illuminating the journey.

I was horrified at the scene before me: a life sized robot with antennas! How could my parents be so out of tune with the real me? I was ten years old and above such childish things. Thoughts raced through my mind on how I was to deal with the situation, how I would pretend to enjoy playing with the monstrosity.

Suddenly, the light was switched on and the robot revealed its real guise: it was a television on its own stand and the antennas turned into an indoor aerial. My extremely annoyed mother sent me back to bed.

The television was duly installed in my room and afforded me the sheer luxury of lying on the bed watching *The Flintstones*, *Scooby-Doo*, *Jackanory* and other equally important programmes.

On Sundays I ate my dinner whilst sat watching the flickering black and white box - such flickering could be halted by the careful throwing of an assortment of items at the right hand side of the screen, such items would include slippers, teddy bears and finally my pillow. After these were exhausted one had to go through the laborious process of gathering up said missiles and, returning them to the armaments depot [the bed] in preparation for repeat manoeuvres - anyway, on Sundays, the local ITV station - ATV - would broadcast repeat showings of such programmes as *The Champions*, *Department S* and, my favourites, *Randall and Hopkirk [Deceased]* and *The Prisoner*.

This was my introduction to the world of ITC. I was thrilled by all of the shows and looked forward to each weekly instalment. Growing up in the sixties and seventies I was treated to shows such as *The Saint*, *UFO* and *Space 1999* and, looking back, all of my favourites, with the exception of *Doctor Who* and *Star Trek*, were ITC shows. At the time I was indifferent to this fact. To me the significance of the programmes hung on more important matters: *UFO*: Ed Straker lived down the road from my mate; *Man in a Suitcase*: kids at school called me McGill and I was infuriated that every time I watched it we didn't see him shrink to 12 inches high and return to his house in a case; *Joe 90*: I had all the stuff - including the secret compartment case and the mug; *Captain Scarlet*: he was cool; *The Saint*: I got it into my head that he was a wimp because he didn't carry a gun and *The Champions*: they had secret powers.

In adulthood these shows were a fond memory and I was yet to find out that many felt the same way.

In the 1980s these classics became available on video and I eagerly went out and bought the likes of *The Prisoner* as soon as they were released. As the years have gone by these small screen masterpieces have simply refused to end up in a dusty vault. Repeat showings have now become common and most of the output is freely available on video. It is amazing to see their continuing popularity and the shows attracting new fans. Hollywood too has been captivated by them with movie versions of *The Persuaders!*, *The Prisoner* and *Thunderbirds* in the works.

The tremendous output of ITC is chronicled within this book and it serves as a testament as to what the British entertainment industry can be capable of. It remains to be seen if a single company can ever equal the achievements made by Lew Grade's organisation.

The wealth of talent herein is amazing. We have Peter O'Toole as a spear carrier, Anthony Hopkins as a crazed germ warfare expert, Gene Roddenberry concerned with the Australian Gold Rush and John Schlesinger in Sherwood Forest. We have swashbucklers, spies, agents, ghosts, men in tights and space aliens. Who could ask for anything more?

So, *The Rogers & Gillis Guide to ITC*, has been a labour of love for Dave & I and it has afforded me with the perfect excuse for watching and enjoying the shows all over again.
I do this lying on my bed.......

S J Gillis

Introduction   by Dave Rogers

Research for this book began in earnest in October 1986, when Boxtree Books [then Baker and Mahaffy Pub.] commissioned me to write *The ITV Encyclopaedia of Adventure* [Boxtree/TV Times 1988].

Little did I know the hardships involved in pulling the information together. Despite hands on response to my requests for listings info from several of the company's responsible for producing the series to be covered in the book [the majority of whom had been gobbled-up by the 'big boys' and were no longer making programmes], just two had comprehensive written records, the remainder excusing themselves by laying the blame for their 'sparse' paperwork on the new management [how little things change!].

Friends and colleagues played their part. The *TV Times* provided an additional source [in this instance, archived by research libraries] - but some clown had been busy with the razor blade! Things started well, with entry after entry being transcribed, then - slice, cut and slice again, whole entries [sometimes pages] lost at the stoke of a scalpel!

The consequence. Errors crept into the listings [not just from the despoiled listing magazine but also in some of the paperwork I received from the production companies!] making what was seen as *the* definitive listing to ITV programming, a valuable first time reference guide but not, by any stretch of the imagination, the book I had originally set out to achieve.

This volume redresses the balance - in so far as the ITC series are concerned.

Never catalogued in their entirety, but spread piecemeal across a half-dozen books or so, this volume contains the first comprehensive production listings to programmes produced, or co-financed, by ITC from 1955 to when, to all intents and purposes, the company ceased making television shows. Indeed, as we accommodate some of the more popular thriller/adventure shows produced directly by, or for, ATV [as ITC became], we venture to say that *The Rogers & Gillis Guide to ITC* is *the* single most *definitive* guide ever published under one cover.

It would be impossible, of course, to include everything produced under the ITC/ATV banner. If you were looking for *Jesus of Nazareth*, despite its estimated cumulative world audience of 90 million viewers [!] you wont find it here. Nor, say, *Hammer House of Horror*, or Brian Clemens', brilliant and inventive, *Thriller* [aside from anything else, Brian Clemens has more than enough credits in these pages!]. Our theme is one of *spies*, *superguys* [and *gals*], *detectives*, *excitement* and *ADVENTURE*!

Thanks

While every effort has been made to verify the listings format for gaffes, we'd be fools to imagine that a boo-boo or two hasn't made it to the printed page. Spot anything you disagree with - <u>and have documentary evidence to prove it</u> - and we'll be delighted to correct any false information in the next volume.

Books of this nature don't write themselves. Several people deserve acknowledgement for their help and support.

Thanks then to [in alphabetical order]: Colin Bailey, Roger Clark, Jeremy Guy, Henry Holland, Barrie MacDonald, Tony Mechele, Dave Watkins, Alison Wiggin & Graham Williams. [To those who promised info but sat on their hands - perhaps with the intention of seeing the project grind to a halt? - Hey guys, we made it anyway!].

On the day that the original *ITV Encyclopaedia* was published, I met with friends - all knowledgeable TV buffs - and invited them to scour the listings for errors and send me chapter and verse re any incorrect entries. Their comprehensive and well-founded comments [nothing, but nothing gets by these guys] served as the first source for revisions and corrections to the listings contained herein. It's several years down the road, but - sincere thanks to Neal Alsop, Simon Coward and Andrew Pixley. Without whom we'd be less the wiser.

Dave Rogers & S J Gillis

Entries are listed in alphabetical order. To facilitate easy reference, each entry spans one programme in its entirety as denoted by the following, stylised, example:

Series Title: **The Adventures of Robin Hood**
Followed by a format appraisal and a regular cast list:
Robin Hood: **Richard Greene**
Little John: **Archie Duncan, Rufus Cruikshank**
***
season one
39 monochrome 30 - minute episodes
The total number of seasons and episodes, colour or monochrome, and time duration [based upon a network time slot of 30/60 minutes] that cover one programme in its entirety. Note: To avoid regional variations - some series played in different areas on different dates, with some episodes being omitted from the run - all episodes are listed in chronological order *as they appear in ITC synopsis brochures.*
***
Episode Title, author and director:
<u>The Coming of Robin Hood</u>
w **Eric Heath**
d **Ralph Smart**
Followed by a story synopsis and supporting cast.
Whenever a character is introduced, we have noted their appearance: for example:
Little John: **Archie Duncan** [intro]
***
After the final entry for each series you will find the production credits:
Series Title: **The Adventures of Robin Hood:**
Devised by: [where known]
Producer: **Sidney Cole**
Executive Producer: **Hannah Weinstein**
Associate Producer: **Sidney Cole, Thelma Connell**
Music by: **Edwin Astley, Albert Elms**
Production Supervisor: **George Mills**
Script Supervisor/Consultant: **Albert G. Ruben**
Creative Consultant: [where known]
Production Manager: [where known]
Casting Director: [where known]
Assistant Director: **Christopher Noble**
Stunt Arranger: [where known]
Music Editor: [where known]
Make-up: **Walter Schneiderman**
Hairdressing: **Eileen Bates, Bill Griffiths**
Wardrobe: **Brenda Gardner**
Production Company: **A Sapphire Films Production** for Sapphire Films, for the **Incorporated Television Programme Co.**
Production Venue: **Filmed at Nettlefold Studios**
The total number of episodes that made up the *entire* series: **143 monochrome 30-minute episodes**
The year[s] of production: **1955 - 1958**

<u>Addenda</u>
Where relevant, we have denoted made-for-television feature films [compiled from episodes] and listed their content source: for example, from **The Champions:**

🎞 A 'feature' *Legend of The Champions* was issued, being a compilation of *The Beginning* and *The Interrogation.*

[Where known] we have listed paperback book tie-ins and listed the year of publication, author, publisher, and source of the story: for example, from **The Champions:**

📖 *The Champions: The Sixth Sense is Death* [1969: John Garforth: Hodder Paperbacks: novelisation of *The Experiment* and *The Beginning*].

The Shows

The Adventurer

Gene Barry, star of *Burke's Law*, stars as Gene Bradley, a US Government agent working undercover in the guise of a globe-trotting film star and tycoon.

Billed as "Everybody's pin-up - nobody's fool", the actor failed to lift the series out of the ordinary. Asked to "travel the world with *The Adventurer*, in a series of vital, new and dynamic situations in which every turn brings the zing of danger, drama and originality", viewers might well have been forgiven for believing that they had seen it all before.

Sad to say the series squandered the talent of actor Barry Morse.

Injected into the proceedings as Mr Parminter, Bradley's secret service contact posing as the film star's manager-cum-producer, he was given little to do beyond carry a total look of disbelief at the entire proceedings. Stuart Damon [one of the better things about the series], disappeared without explanation after 2 episodes!

Regular cast:
Gene Bradley: **Gene Barry**
Mr Parminter: **Barry Morse**
Diane [Bradley's agency contact]: **Catherine Schell**
Gavin Jones [Bradley's companion, also an agent]: **Garrick Hagon**
Brandon: **Dennis Price**

The Good Book
w **Lou Shaw**
d **Cyril Frankel**

Sowing the seeds of distrust is easy for the jet-setting espionage agent, Gene Bradley. But sometimes things have a tendency to backfire in your face. Has Bradley overplayed his hand this time? Parminter believes he has - and sets out to prove it.

Diane: **Catherine Schell** [intro]
Vince: **Stuart Damon** [intro]
Nita: **Adrienne Corri**
Armand: **John Moffatt**
Marian: **Gabrielle Drake**
Pierre: **Ben Kingsley**
Gigilo: **Perry Soblosky**

Poor Little Rich Girl
w **Donald James**
d **Cyril Frankel**

With a little help from Bradley and Diane, a spoiled heiress learns the hard way how to live with her millions.

Diane: **Catherine Schell**
Vince: **Stuart Damon**
Suzy Dolman: **Judy Geeson**
Consul: **John Savident**
Zavar: **Maurice Browning**
Kanarek: **Marc Zuber**
Charolais: **Nik Zaran**
Cafe Proprietor: **John Serret**
Marco: **Sean Hewitt**
Driver: **Aharon Ipale**

Return to Sender
w **Marty Roth**
d **Cyril Frankel**

Requested by Mr Parminter 'to be ready for action' while visiting the French Riviera, Bradley's holiday plans take on sinister implications when he discovers a dead girl in his hotel room.

Gavin: **Garrick Hagon** [intro]
Fleming: **Patrick Mower**
Gorman: **Donald Burton**
Valerie Green: **Sharon Gurney**
Michele: **Pamela Salem**
Mr Pinter: **Brian Hewitt-Jones**
Hotel Clerk: **Franco Derosa**
Debbie: **Debbie Russ**

Double Exposure
w **Marty Roth**
d **Cyril Frankel**

When Mr Parminter hears that Bradley's friend, multi-millionaire industrialist Jan de Groote, has been replaced by an impostor, the Adventurer is sent to Amsterdam to investigate who is behind the attempt to take over De Groot's industrial empire.

Diane: **Catherine Schell**
Gavin: **Garrick Hagon**
Jan De Groot: **Donald Houston**
Colonel Kazan: **Carl Duering**
Elayna: **Ingrid Pitt**

Thrust and Counter Thrust
w **Frank Telford**
d **Paul Dickson**

A consulate party in Nice has some unexpected guests - and gives Bradley's romantic interlude with Countess Marie a touch of intrigue and danger.

Diane: **Catherine Schell**
Gavin: **Garrick Hagon**
Baron Drovotkin: **Clifford Evans**
Countess Marie: **Eunice Gayson**
Colonel Andreyev: **Simon Lack**
Nicholas: **Wensley Pithey**
Stephen: **Stephen Sheppard**
Guard: **Stanley Lebor**
Anton Juryck: **David Lawton**

Miss Me Once, Miss Me Twice and Miss Me Once Again
w **Marty Roth**
d **Cyril Frankel**

An agent expects to put his life on the line. But why should Parminter ask Bradley to play the most dangerous role of his career - as a stand in for a potential murder victim?

Diane: **Catherine Schell**
Wayne: **Ed Bishop**
Gregory Varna: **Alex Scott**
Vladimir Horvic: **John Barrie**
Micholos Zentner: **Bernard Kay**
Lady Hargrom: **Margaretta Scott**
Hotel Clerk: **Ray Chiarella**
Aide: **Paul Greaves**
Manservant: **Keith Ashley**
Woman Delegate: **Elaine Montgomerie**
Man in Corridor: **Stuart Nichol**

Counterstrike
w **Tony Williamson**
d **Paul Dickson**

When scientist Andrei Korony tries to defect to the West, but makes a navigational error and lands in Central Europe, Bradley hatches a clever plot to engineer his escape.

Diane: **Catherine Schell**

Gavin: **Garrick Hagon**
Karen Voriska: **Kara Wilson**
Lanik: **George Mikell**
Prokov: **Martin Wyldeck**
Jansen: **John Malcolm**
Korony: **John Herrington**
Woodsman: **Frederick Schiller**
Waitress: **Anna Kilpinen**

The Bradley Way
w **Gerald Kelsey**
d **Val Guest**

Bradley plays on a husband's jealousy to help save an elderly general from foreign agents, who are forcibly keeping the man drugged.

Diane: **Catherine Schell**
Werner Von Beck: **Richard Marner**
Virginia Douglas: **Janey Key**
Josef Kerston: **Anthony Ainley**
Brett: **Warren Stanhope**
Gerda Hoffman: **Joanna Dunham**
Borislav: **Sean Caffrey**
General Schlessen: **Norman Caro**

Love Always, Magda
w **Philip Broadley**
d **Cyril Frankel**

When he receives a cable from his friend Don Fleming, saying that he has met Magda, the girl whom Bradley loved, but who walked out on him suddenly, the Adventurer flies to Beirut to learn the truth about her departure.

Nessim: **Kieron Moore**
Magda: **Cyd Hayman**
Don Fleming: **Paul Maxwell**
Narouz: **David Cargill**
Maurice: **Stefan Kalipha**
Al Graham: **Jerry Stovin**
Simone Laforque: **Vera Fusek**
Jane: **Sue Gerrard**
John Burdett: **John Horseley**
Angelo: **Larry Taylor**
Belly Dancer: **Kerima**

Nearly the End of the Picture
w **Philip Broadley**
d **Cyril Frankel**

Two lovely girls and a beautiful painting involve Bradley in an adventure which leads him into danger and intrigue in the South of France.

Brandon: **Dennis Price** [intro]
Dorinda: **Angela Scoular**
Martin: **David Buck**
Clarissa De Vere Allan: **Fiona Lewis**
Alden: **Mark Jones**
Alex: **Milton Johns**

Has Anyone Here Seen Kelly?
w **Tony Williamson**
d **Val Guest**

When his good friend, Mike Kelly, fails to keep an appointment in Switzerland, Bradley visits Mike's office in Geneva. He finds that Mike hasn't been seen for several weeks...and his apartment has a new occupant - a beautiful young girl.

Gerard Laroche: **Sandor Eles**
Milena Corri: **Anouska Hempel**

Luigi: **Eric Pohlmann**
Dino: **Michael Forrest**
Mike Kelly: **Rio Fanning**
Carl: **Barrie Cookson**
Beavis: **Robert Raglan**
Chris Jefford: **Lionel Murton**
Edwards: **Ronald Chenery**
Lanik: **Christopher Sandford**
Janitor: **Norman Chappell**
Jane: **Sue Gerrard**
Co-Star: **Laraine Humphrys**

Deadlock
w **Donald James**
d **Val Guest**

Bradley's friendship with scientist Franz Kolmar leads him into danger when Kolmar's plans for a new project are stolen. The ransom for their return? One million dollars to be paid in cash to a mysterious man in Istanbul.

Sakuma: **Wolfe Morris**
Franz Kolmar: **Mervyn Johns**
Kay Masterson: **Jennie Linden**
Johnny Morrison: **Burt Kwouk**
Bank Director: **Robert Rietty**
Police Inspector: **Al Garcia**
Hotel Clerk: **Howard Goorney**

Skeleton in the Cupboard
w **Donald James**
d **Cyril Frankel**

The Adventurer finds himself involved in a bizarre mystery. Why should a respected university professor turn thief, fake his own death and place his whole future in jeopardy?

Karen Ballard: **Sylvia Syms**
John Ballard: **Basil Dignam**
Sir Richard McKenzie: **Richard Vernon**
Marks: **Roy Kinnear**
Carl Gardner: **Lance Percival**
Johnson: **Johnny Wade**
Farmer: **Edwin Brown**

Target!
w **Philip Broadley**
d **Cyril Frankel**

Realising that he is too well known not to be recognised when claiming to be an illegal arms dealer, Bradley, anxious to expose Dutch dealer Mosselman, dons the disguise of Mr Cotton.

Willet Mosselman: **Guy Deghy**
Harry Venner: **George Sewell**
Astrid: **Astrid Frank**
Captain Arilla: **Michael Godfrey**
Police Inspector: **Alan Downer**
Porter: **Dennis McCarthy**
Jan: **Leslie Crawford**
Dieter: **Tristan Rogers**

Action!
w **Brian Clemens**
d **Barry Morse**

Why should Bradley deliberately avoid a group of his fans when arriving in Scotland? Why should the film star also miss an important appointment with General McCready, whose life is in danger? The answer spells death for someone. Bradley has been 'programmed' to kill.

Ann Somerby: **Natasha Pyne**

John Campbell: **John Collin**
Carl Bruner: **David Lampson**
Lola Wells: **Alexandra Bastedo**
Peter Maller: **Bob Cartland**
General McCready: **Cec Linder**
Major: **Karl Held**
Pestrade: **Hugh Walters**
Zenn: **Paddy Ryan**
Police Inspector: **John Dunbar**
Driver: **Stuart Sherwin**
Shopkeeper: **Norman Atkyns**

I'll Get There Sometime
w **Tony Williamson**
d **Val Guest**

When Bradley goes to the aid of a man being attacked in an hotel room he finds himself in more trouble than he bargained for. Meanwhile Mr Parminter plays the role of knight errant to help a damsel in distress.

Diane: **Catherine Schell**
Gavin: **Garrick Hagon**
Ryker: **Patrick Jordan**
Karen Dorron: **Pippa Steel**
Werner: **Frank Barrie**
Tony: **John Levene**
Max: **Andrew Bradford**

The Solid Gold Hearse
w **Tony Williamson**
d **Val Guest**

Mr Parminter has a problem on his hands: how to prevent a huge amount of gold bullion leaving the country. Bradley cannot help. He's busy making a Western - but he can offer a solution to Parminter's dilemma.

Diane: **Catherine Schell**
Gavin: **Garrick Hagon**
Wyvern: **Sydney Tafler**
Miesner: **Kevin Stoney**
Farley: **David Weston**
Riener: **Janos Kurucz**
Assistant Director: **Peter Birrel**
Director: **Ken Wayne**

To the Lowest Bidder
w **Donald James**
d **Val Guest**

The Adventurer finds himself taking sides when a crooked business combine makes the competing bids for a new highway a contract - or death - issue.

Samuel Cookson: **Anthony Nicholls**
Sarah Cookson: **Jane Asher**
Laura: **Sheila Gish**
Forrester: **Carl Rigg**
Lizzy: **Gillian Bailey**
Carlson: **David Kelly**
Johnny: **John York**
Gaston: **Alf Joint**
Milkman: **David Pugh**

Full Fathom Five
w **Donald James**
d **Val Guest**

A modern-day bunch of brigands give Bradley and his friend, Father Antonius, a run for their money when they try to retrieve some priceless stained glass windows.

Diane: **Catherine Schell**

Gavin: **Garrick Hagon**
Father Antonius: **Andre Morrell**
Maria Gustave: **Prunella Ransome**
Rymans: **Peter Jeffrey**
Sir Richard: **Michael Gwynn**
Nurse: **Rona Newton-John**
Claire Adams: **Judy Matheson**
Andre Gustave: **Donald Eccles**

Going, Going...
w **Gerald Kelsey**
d **Val Guest**

When a foreign scientist, given asylum in Britain, disappears, Mr Parminter suspects Bradley of playing a double game. Can Bradley prove his innocence in time to allay further suspicion and arrest?

Diane: **Catherine Schell**
Gavin: **Garrick Hagon**
Eisen: **Arnold Diamond**
Taiho: **Burt Kwouk**
Brooks: **Norman Bird**
Yvette: **Bridget Armstrong**
Lynsky: **Norman Ettlinger**
Rostov: **George Little**
Auctioneer: **Robert James**
Bolton: **Mischa De La Motte**

The Not-So-Merry Widow
w **Marty Roth**
d **Cyril Frankel**

When a beautiful woman claims to be his girlfriend, Bradley has every reason to be confused - he's never seen her before! What is she up to? The Adventurer digs deeper - and lands himself in a cartload of trouble.

Lady Diana Battersley: **Barbara Murray**
Brandon: **Dennis Price**
Inspector Chilton: **Charles Kay**
Vanessa: **Angela Douglas**
Geoffrey Gains: **Maurice Kaufmann**
Hotel Manager: **Geoffrey Russell**
Sir Walter Battersley: **Alan Judd**
Reporter: **David Rayner**
Reporter: **Nicholas Evans**

The Case of the Poisoned Pawn
w **Philip Broadley**
d **Cyril Frankel**

The stakes are high when Bradley faces Brian Hamilton, a young gambler, across the gambling table. Parminter has ordered Bradley to thrash Hamilton in the hope that he will then divulge the secret source of his money.

Brandon: **Dennis Price**
Lord Franklin: **Cyril Luckham**
Brian Hamilton: **Stuart Wilson**
Lady Anne Benson: **Dawn Addams**
Nicky Asteri: **Martin Benson**
Julia Franklin: **Jenny Handley**
Superintendent: **Paul Williamson**
Max: **Max Latimer**
Secretary: **Christine Donna**
Grant: **David Blagden**
Bank Official: **Michael Martin**

Icons Are Forever
w **Tony Williamson**
d **Cyril Frankel**

Gene Bradley has personal reasons for helping a lovely young Contessa to elope - and for discovering what secret lies behind the closely-guarded Russian icon in an Italian castle.

Contessa Maria: **Stephanie Beacham**
Holvera: **Noel Willman**
Darron: **Alfred Marks**
Carlo: **Alan Lake**
Miguel: **Marc Boyle**
Security Man: **Richardson Morgan**

Mr Calloway is a Very Cautious Man
w **Donald James**
d **Barry Morse**

Bradley deliberately allows himself to be arrested and face a jail sentence to learn the truth behind the mysterious case of a dead man who appears to be very much alive.

Stopford: **Paul Daneman**
Ingrid Shore: **Toby Robins**
Calloway: **Freddie Jones**
Inspector Tribe: **Victor Lucas**
Russell: **David Hargreaves**
Laura Darnley: **Anne Sharp**
Soames: **Anthony Rowlands**
Records Clerk: **John Stuart**
Customs Officer: **Robert Gillespie**
Secretary: **Nancie Wait**

Make it a Million
w **Tony Williamson**
d **Barry Morse**

Returning from location work in India, Bradley discovers that he is being impersonated as part of a clever confidence trick. The answer appears simple: he'll beat his double at his own game - but there are difficulties when you impersonate yourself.

Gavin: **Garrick Hagon**
Charlesworth: **Paul Eddington**
Hilverston: **Ronald Radd**
Merrick: **Doug Fisher**
Julia: **Joanna Jones**
Newburg: **George Pravda**
Butler: **Geoffrey Reed**
Lawson: **Anthony Dawes**
Winters: **Paul Hardwick**
First Businessman: **Bernard Severn**
Second Businessman: **Martin Carroll**
Stewardess: **Gail Galih**

Somebody Doesn't Like Me
w **Donald James**
d **Cyril Frankel**

Someone clearly doesn't like Gene Bradley: a big reward is offered to whoever kills him. Mr Parminter believes that 'con' girl Krista Magnus is behind the plot, but the Adventurer isn't so sure. Then his private jet is sabotaged...

Gavin: **Garrick Hagon**
Krista: **Penelope Horner**
Roberts: **Peter Vaughan**
Sorenson: **Reginald Marsh**
Buckley: **Robin Hawdon**
Morgan: **Jim Norton**
Co-Pilot: **William Abney**
Reynolds: **James Ware**
Barman: **Jeremy Higgins**
Commissionaire: **Edward Dentith**

📖

The Adventurer [1973: Robert Miall aka John Burke: Pan Books: novelisations of *Return to Sender, Thrust and Counter Thrust* & *Poor Little Rich Girl*].

The Adventurer:

Series created by: **Monty Berman** and **Dennis Spooner**
Producer: **Monty Berman**
Associate Producer: **Barry Delmaine**
Title Theme by: **John Barry**
Music by: **Paul Clay**
Music Supervision: **Don Kirshner**
Executive Story Consultant: **Dennis Spooner**
Creative Consultant: **Cyril Frankel**
Production Manager: **Ian Goddard**
Casting Director: **Ann Donne**
Assistant Director: **Ken Baker, Albert Withrick**
Stunt Co-ordinator: **Alf Joint, John Sullivan**
Make-up: **Colin Garde**
Hairdresser: **Michael Jones, Eithne Fennell**
Wardrobe Supervisor: **Laura Nightingale**

A Scoton Production for ITC World Wide Distribution
Made on location and at EMI Elstree Studios.

26 colour thirty-minute episodes
1972

The Adventures of Robin Hood

When King Richard I of England departed on his Crusade to the Holy Land, he left his son, Arthur, in the care of his brother, Prince John, a man who schemed to rid himself of the young Prince and thus declare himself heir to the throne. To help him achieve this aim, Prince John gathered around him the powerful Norman lords and placed the shire of Nottingham under the 'protection' of his friend, the Sheriff. It wasn't long before the poor people of England were reeling under the harsh taxes imposed by the Prince. But there was a young nobleman remained faithful to King Richard - Robin of Locksley, who, as leader of a band of freedom fighters, outlawed by Prince John, robbed the rich and gave to the poor. Robin and his men became a constant thorn in the Sheriff's side and an unwelcome threat to Prince John's plans.

The adventures of England's legendary hero were brought vividly to life in this popular fifties series which, primarily aimed at the younger viewer, quickly established itself as a firm favourite with viewers of all ages. It went on to become one of the longest-running television shows of all time and made its stars among the best known faces on television.

Robin, played throughout by Richard Greene, cut a dashing figure as he and his men thwarted the Sheriff's plans at every turn, helped, more often than not, by the lovely Lady Marian Fitzwalter [although she did not appear in every story]. Known to Robin and his men as Maid Marian, two actresses became associated with the role. Bernadette O'Farrell and Patricia Driscoll. A Childhood friend of the outlaw leader, she helped Robin and his men in every way possible to defeat the plotting and intrigue of their common enemy. A fact frequently overlooked by television historians is that although Archie Duncan is credited as playing Robin's second-in-command, the gentle giant, Little John, the role was actually shared by two actors: Duncan broke his leg during the production while attempting to halt a bolting horse which threatened to trample two child actors underfoot - a feat which earned him the Queen's Medal of Bravery - and in ten of the stories he was replaced by actor Rufus Cruikshank. Other notable roles shared by two or more actors were: Prince John, played on various occasions by Donald Pleasence, Hubert Gregg and, in one story, Brian Haines. Will Scarlett, a travelling minstrel who was 'adopted' by Robin's men, was played on two occasions by actor Ronald Howard, before the part was taken over permanently by Paul Eddington for the final season. Young Prince Arthur was portrayed by three actors: Peter Asher, Richard O'Sullivan and Jonathan Bailey.

The series holds a second claim to fame: it spawned a million-selling signature tune which entered the top twenty in January 1956, and remained there for a lengthy stay. Written and recorded by Dick James, the song became one of the most successful television themes of all time. Few of us could resist the temptation to sing along when the opening bars informed us that:

'Robin Hood, Robin Hood, is riding through the glen;
Robin Hood, Robin Hood, with his band of men.
Feared by the bad, loved by the good,
Robin Hood, Robin Hood, Robin Hood.'

A technicolor cinema version of the legend, *Sword of Sherwood Forest*, was filmed in 1960. Produced by Hammer Films, in conjunction with Columbia Productions, this lacked the appeal of the television series. Though Richard Greene reprised his role as Robin, his outlaws - faces we'd come to know so well on television - were played by new actors. The film wasn't a success.

Regular cast:
Robin Hood: **Richard Greene**

Maid Marian: **Bernadette O'Farrell, Paricia Driscoll**
Little John: **Archie Duncan, Rufus Cruikshank**
Friar Tuck: **Alexander Gauge**
Will Scarlett: **Ronald Howard, Paul Eddington**
Derwent: **Victor Woolf**
Sheriff: **Alan Wheatley**
Deputy Sheriff: **John Arnatt** [from season 4]
Joan: **Simone Lovell**

season one
39 monochrome 30-minute episodes. 1955

The Coming of Robin Hood
w **Eric Heath**
d **Ralph Smart**

After several years fighting in the Holy Land with King Richard, young Robin of Locksley returns to England to find that his estates have been seized by a Norman knight, Roger de Lisle. Unable to gain justice at the court of the newly-elected Sheriff of Nottingham, Robin is forced to turn outlaw.

The Sheriff: **Alan Wheatley**
Sir Roger de Lisle: **Leo McKern**
Count de Severne: **Gerard Heinz**
Edgar: **Alfie Bass**
Gate Keeper: **Norman Mac Owen**
Gate Keeper's Wife: **Susan Richards**
Gilbert: **Willoughby Gray**
Sheriff's Clerk: **Gabriel Toyne**
Will Scatlock: **Bruce Seton** [uncredited]

The Moneylender
w **Ian Larkin & Eric Heath**
d **Ralph Smart**

Forced to retreat to Sherwood Forest, Robin joins Scatlock's outlaw band. To prove his worth, he is sent to deal with an unscrupulous moneylender who is charging 100 per cent interest on money he has lent to the poor. Robin's handling of the affair leads to conflict with Scatlock, who sees the newcomer as a threat to his leadership.

The Sheriff: **Alan Wheatley**
Edgar: **Alfie Bass**
Herbert of Doncaster: **Leo McKern**
Hawkins: **Kenneth Edwards**
Howard: **John Drake**
Nailer: **Willoughby Gray**
Old Man Driver: **Gabriel Toyne**
Will Scatlock: **Bruce Seton** [uncredited]

Dead or Alive
w **Eric Heath**
d **Dan Birt**

Little John, a serf at Rutland Court, is ordered by his master to capture Robin Hood. Discovering the outlaw's camp, and finding sympathy with Robin's cause, Little John joins the band of outlaws and is appointed Robin's second-in-command.

Little John: **Archie Duncan** [intro]
The Earl: **John Rutland**
The Countess: **Agnes Bernelle**
Joan: **Simone Lovell** [intro]
Eric: **Gabriel Toyne**
Alfred: **Victor Woolf**

Friar Tuck
w Eric Heath
d Ralph Smart

Disguised as a monk, Robin visits Friar Tuck, a jovial, fat, holy man, and together they organise the escape of Mildred from the clutches of the evil Lord Germaine and the Sheriff. Though his church is in Nottingham, the friar becomes a close ally of the outlaw and begins to pay frequent visits to Sherwood.

Friar Tuck: **Alexander Gauge** [intro]
The Sheriff: **Alan Wheatley**
Sir William: **Leslie Phillips**
Lord Germain: **Douglas Wilmer**
Mildred: **Faith Bailey**
Joan: **Simone Lovell**
Harold: **John Drake**

Maid Marian
w Anne Rodney
d Ralph Smart

Having ambushed the Sheriff's courier, Robin's life is placed in peril: he is arrested by the Sheriff and Lady Marian Fitzwalter, his childhood companion, is accused of being in league with the outlaws.

Maid Marian: **Bernadette O'Farrell** [intro]
The Sheriff: **Alan Wheatley**
Ned: **John Drake**
Nanny: **Marie Burke**
Cedric: **Victor Woolf**
Much: **Willoughby Gray**
Edgar: **Shaun Noble**
Lieutenant: **David Edwards**
Eric: **Gabriel Toyne**

A Guest for the Gallows
w Eric Heath
d Ralph Smart

For obvious reasons, Robin and the Sheriff are sworn enemies. Why then should the Sheriff seek the outlaw's help? With no love lost between them, Robin is on his guard for treachery.

The Sheriff: **Alan Wheatley**
Little John: **Archie Duncan**
Friar Tuck: **Alexander Gauge**
Butcher: **Dennis Shaw**
Will Stutely: **Robert Desmond**
Lass: **Jan Miller**

The Inquisitor
w Anne Rodney
d Ralph Smart

When Friar Tuck is arrested by the Abbot of a nearby abbey, Robin and Little John secretly enter the abbey in wine barrels. Overhearing their friend confess to crimes he did not commit, Robin overpowers Tuck's inquisitor and, in disguise, pleads the Friar's innocence to the Archbishop.

Maid Marian: **Bernadette O'Farrell**
Friar Tuck: **Alexander Gauge**
Little John: **Archie Duncan**
Archbishop: **Carl Bernard**
Chef: **Wolf Morris**
Inquisitor: **Willougby Gray**
Ploughman: **David Edwards**
Monk: **Victor Woolf**
Scullery Boy: **Timothy Brooking**

The Knight Who Came To Dinner
w Eric Heath
d Ralph Smart

The outlaws lend Sir Richard of the Lea, a penniless knight, the money he needs to pay off his debts. To ensure that the debts are repaid, Robin sends Friar Tuck along disguised as Sir Richard's squire - the Friar and the knight soon find themselves up to their necks in trouble.

The Sheriff: **Alan Wheatley**
Sir Richard: **Ian Hunter** [intro]
Friar Tuck: **Alexander Gauge**
Little John: **Archie Duncan**
Maid Marian: **Bernadette O'Farrell**
Sir Bertram: **Robin Bailey**
The Abbot: **Frank Royd**
Aubrey: **Willoughby Gray**
Cedric: **Victor Woolf**

The Challenge
w Eric Heath
d Ralph Smart

Believing that one of his troops can outshoot anyone in England with the longbow, the Sheriff organises an archery contest. Sir Richard of the Lea, a gambler at heart, enters Robin's name for the contest.

The Sheriff: **Alan Wheatley**
Maid Marian: **Bernadette O'Farrell**
Friar Tuck: **Alexander Gauge**
Little John: **Archie Duncan**
Sir Richard: **Ian Hunter**
Leonia: **Patricia Burke**
Simon: **John Drake**

Queen Eleanor
w Eric Heath
d Dan Birt

When the Queen Mother, Eleanor of Aquitaine, departs from Nottingham castle with a large donation she has collected for King Richard's campaign, the Sheriff arranges to have her entourage ambushed and steal her gold - but he has reckoned without Robin Hood.

Maid Marian: **Bernadette O'Farrell**
Queen Eleanor: **Jill Esmond** [intro]
Friar Tuck: **Alexander Gauge**
Little John: **Archie Duncan**
The Sheriff: **Alan Wheatley**
Count de Waldern: **Ballard Berkley**
Bruno: **Gerald Cross**
Sir Giles: **John Drake**

Checkmate
w Peter Lambda
d Ralph Smart

Hearing that the Count de Waldern is planning to conscript 3,000 recruits to terrorise the community, Robin hatches a plan to thwart the Count's evil scheme.

Friar Tuck: **Alexander Gauge**
Count de Waldern: **Leslie Phillips**
Little John: **Archie Duncan**
Maid Marian: **Bernadette O'Farrell**
Armourer: **Alastair Hunter**
Major Domo: **Willoughby Gray**
Granny: **Marie Burke**
Cedric: **Victor Woolf**

The Ordeal
w Eric Heath
d Dan Birt

When Edgar, a member of Robin's band, is falsely accused by the Sheriff of murdering Jack the Waggoner and is ordered to submit to trial by ordeal - plucking an iron bar from a boiling cauldron - Robin decides to intervene.

Friar Tuck: **Alexander Gauge**
Little John: **Archie Duncan**
Maid Marian: **Bernadette O'Farrell**
The Sheriff: **Alan Wheatley**
Edgar: **Alfie Bass**
Matilda: **Dorothy Allison**
Humphrey: **Willoughby Gray**
Alvin: **John Drake**

Husband for Marian
w John Dyson
d Bernard Knowles

When Marian's hand is promised in marriage to an unpleasant and untrustworthy knight, Robin, disguised as a German knight, needs all his powers of persuasion to halt the wedding ceremony.

Maid Marian: **Bernadette O'Farrell**
Friar Tuck: **Alexander Gauge**
Little John: **Rufus Cruickshank** [intro]
Sir Hubert: **Brian Worth**
Ada: **Thora Hird**
Uncle George: **A. J. Brown**
Derwent: **Victor Woolf**
Manservant: **Paul Connell**

The Highlander
w Eric Heath
d Ralph Smart

Duncan, a highland visitor to the outlaw camp, is viewed with suspicion by Little John. Robin, however, pays no heed to his friend's observation - until one morning Duncan is discovered trying to burgle the outlaw's treasure cave.

Duncan: **Hugh McDermott**
Maid Marian: **Bernadette O'Farrell**
Friar Tuck: **Alexander Gauge**
Little John: **Rufus Cruickshank**
Otto: **Willoughby Gray**
Derwent: **Victor Woolf**

The Youngest Outlaw
w John Dyson
d Bernard Knowles

While out hunting, Robin and Little John find a boy who claims he has run away from Waldern Castle, to join Robin's outlaws. Unknown to them the lad is really Prince Arthur, son of King Richard - and Prince John has issued orders to have the boy killed.

Friar Tuck: **Alexander Gauge**
Little John: **Rufus Cruickshank**
Marian: **Bernadette O'Farrell**
Lord Terrence: **Bruce Seton**
Lady Torrence: **Patricia Burke**
Arthur: **Peter Asher**
Joan: **Simone Lovell**
Alfred: **Victor Woolf**
Cedric: **Willoughby Gray**

The Betrothal
w Paul Symonds
d Ralph Smart

Once again Sir Richard of the Lea has financial troubles due to his heavy gambling. Robin has a solution to the knight's problem: Sir Richard's son should marry the daughter of a wealthy knight. But will Sir Richard agree to Robin's proposition?

Sir Richard: **Ian Hunter**
Friar Tuck: **Alexander Gauge**
Little John: **Rufus Cruickshank**
Maid Marian: **Bernadette O'Farrell**
Lady Leonia: **Patricia Burke**
Sir Claude: **Phillip Guard**
Gladys: **Jennifer Jayne**
Hugh: **Charles Lloyd Pack**
Sir Blaise: **John Dearth**
Sir Miles: **Charles Stapley**

The Alchemist
w Eric Heath
d Ralph Smart

When a village woman is accused of dabbling in witchcraft and is sentenced to be burned at the stake, Robin must find a way of postponing the sentence until he can prove her innocence.

Friar Tuck: **Alexander Gauge**
The Sheriff: **Alan Wheatley**
Little John: **Rufus Cruickshank**
The Earl: **Anthony Sharp**
The Countess: **Harriette John**
Ethelreda: **Dorothy Blythe**
Millicent: **Joyce Blair**
Rolf: **Charles Stapley**

The Jongleur
w John Dyson
d Bernard Knowles

A travelling minstrel finds out the hard way that it doesn't pay to take the sheriff's word on trust. Having led Robin and Little John into a well-prepared trap devised by the Sheriff, the vagabond soon finds himself singing a different tune.

Friar Tuck: **Alexander Gauge**
The Sheriff: **Alan Wheatley**
Little John: **Rufus Cruickshank**
Bartholomew: **Peter Hammond**
Count de Waldern: **Willoughby Gray**
Physician: **John Dearth**
Informer: **Charles Lamb**

The Brothers
w Eric Heath
d Bernard Knowles

Robin has his work cut out when trying to decide which of two brothers, rescued by the outlaws when fleeing from the Sheriff, wishes to take his vows as a priest. Is it David or Guy? Robin seeks the help of an Abbot - who provides a startling solution.

Friar Tuck: **Alexander Gauge**
Maid Marian: **Bernadette O'Farrell**
The Sheriff: **Alan Wheatley**
David / Guy: **Michael Brill**
The Abbott: **A J Brown**
Stationarius: **Willoughby Gray**
Clerk: **Victor Woolf**

The Intruders
w **Paul Symonds**
d **Ralph Smart**

Robin and Little John come to the aid of two pilgrims who have been robbed as they strolled through Sherwood Forest. Their story intrigues the outlaws - the robbers called themselves Robin Hood's men.

Maid Marian: **Bernadette O'Farrell**
Little John: **Rufus Cruickshank**
The Abbot: **John Longden**
Jules: **Michael McKeag**
Godric: **Ian Whittaker**
Hildebrand: **Willoughby Gray**
First Pilgrim: **Victor Woolf**
Second Pilgrim: **John Dearth**

The Sheriff's Boots
w **James Aldridge & Ralph Smart**
d **Ralph Smart**

The Sheriff is well known for priding himself on being well dressed, but when he orders a new pair of boots, what would he say if he knew the one's he'd received were outlaw boots - supplied by his arch enemy, Robin Hood!

The Sheriff: **Alan Wheatley**
Friar Tuck: **Alexander Gauge**
Maid Marian: **Bernadette O'Farrell**
Little John: **Rufus Cruickshank**
Nell: **Joan Sims**
Master Higgs: **John Dearth**
Blackbeard: **Charles Stapley**
Will: **Arthur Skinner**
Villager: **Kenneth Edwards**
Old Woman: **Elsie Wagstaff**

Errand of Mercy
w **John Dyson**
d **Ralph Smart**

Nottingham village is stricken with a disease called St Anthony's Fire. Robin and his outlaws give their services to the local apothecary to find herbs to combat the outbreak, but trouble of a different kind plagues the outlaws when Robin is recognised by a beggar.

The Sheriff: **Alan Wheatley**
Little John: **Rufus Cruickshank**
Anselem: **Hal Osmond**
The Informer: **John Dearth**
Master Giles: **Willoughby Gray**
Ethel: **Paula Byrne**
Lieutenant: **Charles Stapley**
Sergeant: **Arthur Skinner**

The Vandals
w **C. Douglas Phipps**
d **Arthur Crabtree**

A village is pillaged and Robin's men get the blame. Then a dead man is found with an arrow in his back - supposedly fired by Robin. The outlaw leader must act swiftly if he is to bring the perpetrator to justice and clear his name.

The Sheriff: **Alan Wheatley**
Friar Tuck: **Alexander Gauge**
Little John: **Rufus Cruickshank**
Lady Irina: **Ingeborg Wells**
Baron Hubert: **John Dearth**
Charles the Hunter: **Charles Stapley**
Limpus: **Victor Woolf**
Lady Jane: **Miriam McCormick**

First Citizen: **Gabriel Toyne**

Richard the Lionheart
w **Paul Symonds**
d **Bernard Knowles**

Everyone knows that Robin Hood is one of King Richard's most faithful subjects. Why then should Robin have so much trouble proving his loyalty to Peregrinus, a heavily hooded visitor to the outlaw camp?

Peregrinus: **Patrick Barr** [intro]
Friar Tuck: **Alexander Gauge**
Maid Marian: **Bernadette O'Farrell**
Little John: **Archie Duncan**
The Sheriff: **Alan Wheatley**
De Belvoir: **John Dearth**
Lady Coulchaud: **Muriel Young**
Hubert: **Willoughby Gray**

Ladies of Sherwood
w **Ralph Smart**
d **Ralph Smart**

Arthur of Tetsbury, an ally of the outlaws, is sentenced to be hanged for supposedly holding back money meant for King Richard's Crusade. Aware that Robin will try to rescue his friend, the Sheriff lays a trap - but women's clothes can hide many things, including outlaws.

The Sheriff: **Alan Wheatley**
Arthur of Tetsbury: **Willoughby Gray**
Joan: **Simone Lovell**
Will: **John Dearth**
Lame Ned: **Victor Woolf**
Captain: **Charles Stapley**
Cook: **Laurence Maine**

Will Scarlet
w **John Dyson**
d **Ralph Smart**

Will Scarlet's eye for the ladies, and his habit of trusting everyone readily, leads Robin and his men into a load of trouble between two lovely ladies and the Sheriff.

Will Scarlet: **Ronald Howard** [intro]
Little John: **Archie Duncan**
Tuck: **Alexander Gauge**
The Sheriff: **Alan Wheatley**
Joan: **Simone Lovell**
Olivia: **Jennifer Jayne**
Captain Lash: **John Dearth**
Sergeant: **Willoughby Gray**

The Deserted Castle
w **Eric Heath**
d **Bernard Knowles**

When the Sheriff leads an attack on a deserted castle in which 'something is going on', what he finds there only increases his hatred for Robin Hood. To add insult to injury, it also severely dents his pride in front of his men-at-arms.

Queen Eleanor: **Jill Esmond**
Little John: **Archie Duncan**
Maid Marian: **Bernadette O'Farrell**
Friar Tuck: **Alexander Gauge**
The Sheriff: **Alan Wheatley**
Will Scarlet: **Ronald Howard**
Pinot: **John Stuart**
Chamberlin: **John Longden**
Sir Gaillard: **Charles Stapley**
Joan: **Simone Lovell**

The Miser
w Ralph Smart
d Bernard Knowles

Robin's nature is such that he trusts everyone - until they give him cause to think otherwise. It follows, then, that a miser stands little chance of gaining the outlaw's friendship - and this leads to complications of a very strange variety.

Little John: **Archie Duncan**
Friar Tuck: **Alexander Gauge**
The Sheriff: **Alan Wheatley**
Sir William de Courcier: **Laurence Naismith**
Lady de Courcier: **Patricia Marmont**
Seneschal: **Charles Stapley**
Lt. Howard: **Paul Connell**
Hodge: **Willoughby Gray**
Arthur: **John Dearth**
Skinner: **Arthur Skinner**

Trial by Battle
w Arthur Behr
d Terence Fisher

The Sheriff's vendetta against Robin Hood erupts into his most villainous scheme yet. Lady Marian is arrested and sent for trial, suspected of murder. To prove her innocence, two men must battle for her life - and only if her defender wins is she proved innocent.

Maid Marian: **Bernadette O'Farrell**
Friar Tuck: **Alexander Gauge**
The Sheriff: **Alan Wheatley**
Little John: **Archie Duncan**
King's Commissioner: **Hal Osmond**
Sir Gyles: **John Longden**
Sir Walter: **Nicholas Parsons**
Sir Hubert: **Barry Shawzin**
Earl of Drune: **Willoughby Gray**

Children of the Greenwood
w John Cousins
d Ralph Smart

Arthur a Bland stands accused of a murder he didn't commit. Overpowering his guard, he flees to Sherwood, leaving his children behind. They in turn are held as hostages, unless A'Bland gives himself up - and Robin feels obliged to rescue them.

Little John: **Archie Duncan**
Friar Tuck: **Alexander Gauge**
Maid Marian: **Bernadette O'Farrell**
Alice: **Jane Asher**
Oswald: **Peter Asher**
Arthur a Bland: **Arthur Skinner**
Walter Fitzurse: **John Longden**
Sergeant: **Willoughby Gray**
Dick the Smith: **Charles Stapley**
Cook: **John Dearth**

The May Queen
w Ralph Smart
d Bernard Knowles

It is the May Queen's prerogative to signal the start of the May Day tournament. Robin and his men use this to their advantage: it is difficult to see exactly who is contesting what under thick tournament armour - as the Sheriff finds out to his cost.

Little John: **Archie Duncan**
The Sheriff: **Alan Wheatley**
Friar Tuck: **Alexander Gauge**

Genevieve: **Gillian Sterrett**
Sir Walter: **Ian Bannen**
Lady Donnington: **Dulcie Bowman**
Blackstone: **John Longden**
De Clifford: **John Dearth**
Stranger: **Charles Stapley**

The Wanderer
w Albert G. Ruben
d Bernard Knowles

When Joseph, a healer, cures Sir Walter by unconventional means, it annoys the other Nottingham healers - and Joseph's flight into Sherwood brings an annoyance that the outlaws find hard to dismiss.

Joseph: **Karel Stepanek**
Friar Tuck: **Alexander Gauge**
Sheriff: **Alan Wheatley**
Sir Walter: **John Longden**
First Healer: **Willoughby Gray**
Second Healer: **John Dearth**
Edward: **Victor Woolf**
Reveller: **Arthur Skinner**
Edward's Wife: **Paula Byrne**

The Byzantine Treasure
w Paul Symonds
d Terence Fisher

Discovering that two gold plates taken from an entourage travelling through Sherwood belong to the Queen Mother, Robin asks Sir Richard of the Lea to return them: such treasures could prove 'too hot to handle' - but can Sir Richard be trusted?

Sir Richard: **Ian Hunter**
Lady Leonia: **Patricia Burke**
Maid Marian: **Bernadette O'Farrell**
Friar Tuck: **Alexander Gauge**
Little John: **Archie Duncan**
Stationarius: **John Stuart**
Vef: **William Squire**
Archbishop: **John Longden**
Goldsmith: **John Dearth**
Nicholas: **Willoughby Gray**
Armourer: **Victor Woolf**
Vintner: **Arthur Skinner**
Mercer: **Paul Connell**
Spicer: **Charles Stapley**

Secret Mission
w Ralph Smart
d Lindsay Anderson

Peregrinus returns to the Greenwood. Having displayed his prowess with the bow and sword, he continues to cast doubts on Robin's allegiance to King Richard. What's his motive? And why is the stranger so protective of his identity?

Peregrinus: **Patrick Barr**
The Sheriff: **Alan Wheatley**
Friar Tuck: **Alexander Gauge**
Little John: **Archie Duncan**
Wulfrie: **John Longden**
Will: **Charles Stapley**
Innkeeper: **Paul Connell**
Derwent: **Victor Woolf**

Table's Turned
w Anne Rodney
d Bernard Knowles

9

Derwent and Much are conned into accepting some loot they believe to be gold. When it turns out that the prize is two young children, who prove to be a thorn in the outlaw's side, Robin must find a way of turning the tables on the con men.

Little John: **Archie Duncan**
Maid Marian: **Bernadette O'Farrell**
Count Leger: **John Longden**
Suzette: **Anne Davey**
Francoise: **Andrew de la Motte**
Nurse: **Norah Gordon**
Derwent: **Victor Woolf**
Joan: **Helen Forrest**
Much: **Arthur Skinner**
Hubert: **John Dearth**
William: **Charles Stapley**

The Traitor
w **Norma Shannon** and **Ralph Smart**
d **Terence Fisher**

Robin must find out which one of the three men entrusted with carrying the ransom money for King Richard's release is a traitor. All three men have taken a knight's oath of innocence, and Robin must discover the libertine.

Maid Marian: **Bernadette O'Farrell**
Friar Tuck: **Alexander Gauge**
Little John: **Archie Duncan**
Westmorland: **Hugh Latimer**
High Constable: **Willoughby Gray**
Exeter: **Charles Stapley**
Faversham: **John Dearth**
Tailor: **John Longden**
Nurse: **Marie Burke**
Joan: **Helen Forrest**
Rolf: **Arthur Skinner**

The Thorkill Ghost
w **Arthur Behr**
d **Terence Fisher**

Harold, its tenant, believes that Thorkill Castle is haunted. Robin doesn't, so he sets out to lay the spectre of a long-dead knight once and for all - but before you can exorcise a spirit, you must first of all find it and that, as Robin discovers, isn't the easiest of tasks.

Elsbeth: **Barbara Mullen**
Maid Marian: **Bernadette O'Farrell**
Harold: **Ian Whittaker**
Edmund: **Charles Stapley**
Ned: **John Longden**
Derwent: **Victor Woolf**
Quentin: **Arthur Skinner**
Bodo: **John Dearth**
Page: **Sandy Lyle**
Noel: **Michael McKeag**

The Wager
w **Warren Howard**
d **Bernard Knowles**

Betting Friar Tuck that he can collect more by begging than the Friar can by prayer, the two men separate, each determined to win the bet - and each to their own troubles, which arrive very quickly indeed.

Friar Tuck: **Alexander Gauge**
Blind Beggar: **Geoffrey Keen**
Beggar: **George Rose**
Dumb Beggar: **Leonard Sharp**
Lame Beggar: **John Watson**
Deaf Beggar: **Gabriel Toyne**

Feeble Beggar: **John Dearth**
Tall Monk: **Willoughby Gray**
Short Monk: **Victor Woolf**
Lt. Howard: **Charles Stapley**
Mistress Rawlins: **Ann Gudrun**

The Prisoner
w **Anne Rodney**
d **Bernard Knowles**

Robin believes that a courier sent by Prince John to the Sheriff bears news that is of importance to the outlaws. Rumour has it that the messenger brings news of King Richard's death, but Robin refuses to believe this and sets out to find the truth.

Maid Marian: **Bernadette O'Farrell**
Prince John: **Donald Pleasence**
Jaques, the Jester: **Donald Bradley**
Archbishop: **Jack Melford**
Sally: **Valerie Cardew**
Blondel: **Willoughby Gray**
Prince John's Wife: **Doris Nolan**
Capt. of Guard: **Arthur Skinner**

season two
39 monochrome 30-minute episodes
1955-56

A Village Wooing
w **Neil R. Collins**
d **Bernard Knowles**

No one really needs a reason to join Robin's band. They just ask. But Wat Longfellow's request is most unusual: he loves the Widow Winifred, and asks Robin and Marian to play the role of Cupid on his behalf.

Friar Tuck: **Alexander Gauge**
Maid Marian: **Bernadette O'Farrell**
Little John: **Archie Duncan**
Bailiff Baldwin: **Donald Pleasnece**
Widow Winifred: **Betty Impey**
Wat Longfellow: **Leslie Phillips**
Guard Commander: **Peter Bennett**
Sir Godfrey: **Willoughby Gray**
Derwent: **Victor Woolf**
Quentin: **Paul Hansard**

The Scientist
w **Neil R. Collins**
d **Terry Bishop**

Anxious to lay his hands on a new discovery from Albertus, the scientist, Prince John forces Albertus to retreat to Sherwood where, deep in the dense foliage, the scientist seeks refuge to continue to work to aid King Richard.

Friar Tuck: **Alexander Gauge**
The Sheriff: **Alan Wheatley**
Little John: **Archie Duncan**
Albertus: **Miles Malleson**
The Abbott: **Charles Lloyd Pack**
Gervaise: **Paul Hansard**
Roger of Danby: **Willoughby Gray**
Librarian: **Peter Bennett**
Derwent: **Victor Woolf**
Hugh: **Andrew Crawford**
First Soldier: **Edward Mulhare**

Blackmail
w **Paul Symonds**
d **Bernard Knowles**

When a stranger overhears a conversation between Marian and the outlaw leader, it spells trouble for Robin: he is soon the victim of a blackmail attempt. But a pendulum swings two ways, and Robin has a stroke of good fortune.

Friar Tuck: **Alexander Gauge**
Maid Marian: **Bernadette O'Farrell**
Sir Richard of Lea: **Ian Hunter**
The Sheriff: **Alan Wheatley**
Little John: **Archie Duncan**
Lucas: **Anthony Dawson**
Lady Leonia: **Patricia Burke**
Ulf : **Edward Mulhare**
Bafe: **Willoughby Gray**
Derwent: **Victor Woolf**
Lescaux: **Paul Hansard**
Steward: **Peter Bennett**
Guard: **Shaun O'Riordan**

A Year and a Day
w **Neil R. Collins**
d **Bernard Knowles**

Surgeon Calend, a runaway serf, is being pursued by the Sheriff's men when Robin and his men find him. If the runaway can stay at large for a year and a day, the law states that he will be declared a freeman. Robin decides that there is no better place to hide than Sherwood Forest.

Friar Tuck: **Alexander Gauge**
Maid Marian: **Bernadette O'Farrell**
The Sheriff: **Alan Wheatley**
Little John: **Archie Duncan**
Surgeon Calend: **Shaun O'Riordan**
Lord Quincy: **Martin Lane**
Lawyer: **Peter Bennett**
Ben: **Dervis Ward**
Constable: **Paul Hansard**
Clerk: **Victor Woolf**
Tinker: **Willoughby Gray**
Child: **Amanda Coxell**

The Goldmaker
w **Paul Symonds**
d **Terry Bishop**

Easily led astray by any moneymaking opportunity, Sir Richard of the Lea turns to Robin for help when Lepidus, an alchemist who says he can turn pewter into gold, offers to do so to Sir Richard's family plate.

The Sheriff: **Alan Wheatley**
Maid Marian: **Bernadette O'Farrell**
Lepidus: **Alfie Bass**
Sir Richard of the Lea: **Ian Hunter**
Lieutenant: **Anthony Baird**
Mercer: **Peter Bennett**
Goldsmith: **Victor Woolf**
Ned: **Paul Hansard**
Will: **Shaun O'Riordan**
Man-at-Arms: **Edward Mulhare**
Forester: **Willoughby Gray**

The Impostor
w **Norman Best**
d **Lindsay Anderson**

Robin must devise a plan to test his theory that Lady Pomfret has found a way around the law which states that, after an absence of seven years, a person is deemed to be dead and his property forfeit: Robin believes Lady Pomfret's husband is much alive.

Friar Tuck: **Alexandre Gauge**

Maid Marian: **Bernadette O'Farrell**
Little John: **Archie Duncan**
Lady Pomfret: **Brenda de Banzie**
Prival: **Nigel Green**
Lord Pomfret: **Jack Melford**
Le Blond: **Edward Mulhare**
Notarius: **Victor Woolf**
Rolf: **Paul Hansard**
Quentin: **Shaun O'Riordan**
Tom: **Martin Lane**

Ransom
w **John Dyson**
d **Terence Fisher**

The poor and ill-used villagers of Nottingham are ordered to pay 500 crowns each in taxes. But where can such a price be found among the needy? Robin provides the answer - much to the Sheriff's annoyance.

Friar Tuck: **Alexander Gauge**
The Sheriff: **Alan Wheatley**
Little John: **Archie Duncan**
Sir Guy: **Paul Daneman**
Count Beaumont: **Robert Raglan**
Count of Severne: **Philip Ashley**
Senechal: **Martin Lane**
Edwin: **Peter Bennett**
Lieutenant: **Edward Mulhare**
Joan: **Simone Lovell**
Derwent: **Victor Woolf**

Isabella
w **Neil R. Collins**
d **Lindsay Anderson**

A girlhood friend of Marian's, Avice, now the wife of Prince John, calls on Marian to ask her to enlist Robin's help: her husband is planning to divorce her so that he can marry Isabella, a French princess, thus getting the support of France. Robin's dilemma - can the woman be trusted?

Maid Marian: **Bernadette O'Farrell**
Little John: **Archie Duncan**
Isabella: **Zena Walker**
Avice: **Helen Cherry**
Prince John: **Donald Pleasence**
Pembroke: **Alan Edwards**
Sir Damon: **Martin Lane**
Landlord: **Howard Lang**
Page: **Shaun O'Riordan**
Tavern Keeper: **Peter Bennett**
Old Woman: **Noel Hood**
Chambermaid: **Lynette Mills**
Will: **Nicholas Brady**
Maid in Waiting: **Isobel Crieg**

The Hero
w **John Dyson**
d **Terence Fisher**

Mark, a cunning vagrant, is acclaimed a hero when he kills the Sheriff's brother. But when he retreats to Sherwood for safety from the Sheriff's men, his 'heroics' lead the outlaws into a greater danger than they've thus far experienced.

The Sheriff: **Alan Wheatley**
Little John: **Archie Duncan**
Mark: **Bill Owen**
Sorel: **John Dearth**
Montfichet: **Ralph Michael**
Mother Agnes: **Susan Richmond**
Woodman: **Peter Bennett**
Woodman's Wife: **Mona Lilian**

Jack: **Shaun O'Riordan**
First Villager: **Victor Woolf**
Second Villager: **Paul Eddington**
First Man-at-Arms: **Howard Greene**
Second Man-at-Arms: **Martin Lane**

The Haunted Mill
w **Paul Symonds**
d **Lindsay Anderson**

Sir William is trying to buy an old mill so that he can charge whatever he wishes for grading flour. To strengthen his claim, he lets it be known that the mill is haunted but Robin, who doesn't believe in ghosts, sets out to frustrate Sir William's plans.

Friar Tuck: **Alexander Gauge**
Maid Marian: **Bernadette O'Farrell**
The Sheriff: **Alan Wheatley**
Little John: **Archie Duncan**
Tom the Miller: **James Hayter**
Sir William: **Laurence Hardy**
Hale: **John Schlesinger**
Abbot of Whitby: **Victor Woolf**
Baron Mornay: **Edward Mulhare**
Edward: **Peter Bennett**
Seneschal: **Shaun O'Riordan**
Page: **Martin Lane**

Outlaw Money
w **John Dyson**
d **Terry Bishop**

To help the overtaxed villagers of Lotham, Robin asks Master Henry, a silversmith, to melt down tableware into coin. Unknown to the outlaw, Henry, suspected of being sympathetic to King Richard, is being watched by the Sheriff's men.

Friar Tuck: **Alexander Gauge**
Master Henry: **Sidney James**
Sheriff: **Alan Wheatley**
Little John: **Archie Duncan**
Minter: **Leonard Sachs**
Count William: **Paul Eddington**
Sheriff's Lieutenant: **Martin Lane**
Derwent: **Victor Woolf**
Quentin: **Shaun O'Riordan**
Rufus: **Richard Pascoe**
Marketmaster: **Elster Kay**
Bishop: **Walter Horsburgh**

The Black Patch
w **John Dyson**
d **Terry Bishop**

Sir Dunstan, a guest of Lady Marian, discloses to her his vow to the Sheriff to wear a black eye patch until he has captured Robin Hood and claimed the reward. On her way to deliver this news to Robin, Marian falls victim to a well-laid trap.

Friar Tuck: **Alexander Gauge**
Maid Marian: **Bernadette O'Farrell**
Little John: **Archie Duncan**
Sheriff: **Alan Wheatley**
Sir Dunstan: **Duncan Lamont**
Fitzrobert: **Colin Croft**
Agnes: **Gwenda Williams**
Eldred: **Peter Bennett**
Steward: **Edward Mulhard**
Lady Beth: **Diana Beaumont**
Sir Henry Beaulieu: **Victor Woolf**
Sir Dunstan's Captain: **Bernard Bresslaw**

Sheriff's Captain: **Martin Lane**
Lieutenant: **Shaun O'Riordan**

The Friar's Pilgrimage
w **Peter Key**
d **Arthur Crabtree**

When Friar Tuck decides to visit Canterbury to learn bee-keeping, Robin decides to join him. The Friar is soon glad he did so: their adventure is less straightforward than expected and the holy man learns more than he bargained for.

Friar Tuck: **Alexander Gauge**
Lady Matilda: **Greta Gynt**
Little John: **Archie Duncan**
Count Duprez: **Paul Eddington**
Alice: **Maureen Davis**
Edward: **Shaun O'Riordan**
Blacksmith: **Dervis Ward**
Constable: **Patrick Troughton**
First Soldier: **Peter Retey**
Second Soldier: **Mark Hashfield**

The Trap
w **Charles Early**
d **Terry Bishop**

The Sheriff's feud with the outlaws takes on a new turn when he asks Sir Simon, a trusted ally to Prince John, to capture Robin Hood. Simon advises a clever scheme and, posing as a cobbler, he is admitted into the outlaw band.

Sir Simon: **Alfred Burke**
Sheriff: **Alan Wheatley**
Little John: **Archie Duncan**
Derwent: **Victor Woolf**
Eldred: **Peter Bennett**
Tom O'Gaunt: **Andrew Downie**
Monk: **Alastair Hunter**
Helen: **Helen Forrest**
Sheriff's Guard: **George Murcell**
Man-at-Arms: **Michael Collins**
Archer: **Shaun O'Riordan**
Foppish Lord: **Edward Mulhare**

Hubert
w **Ralph Smart** and **Anne Rodney**
d **Terence Fisher**

Forced into marrying a man she does not love, Rowena is imprisoned in her husband's castle. When her true love, Sir Hubert, is captured while trying to free her, the task of saving the lovers falls to Robin and his men.

Friar Tuck: **Alexander Gauge**
Rowena: **Dorothy Bromiley**
Little John: **Archie Duncan**
Sir Hubert: **William Greene**
Thomas: **William Mervyn**
De Vere: **Richard Pasco**
Friar Dennis: **Graham Crowden**
Derwent: **Victor Woolf**
De Vere's cook: **Sidney Vivian**
Seneschal: **Martin Lane**
Sir Walter: **Paul Eddington**
First Groom: **Shaun O'Riordan**

The Dream
w **Anne Rodney**
d **Terence Fisher**

When Lady Marian's cousin, Sir William, arrives at the outlaw camp bearing a message from the Queen Mother asking for help, Robin instantly agrees to do so. But his plans

are soon changed when Marian dreams that the outlaw is walking into a trap.

Maid Marian: **Bernadette O'Farrell**
Sheriff: **Alan Wheatley**
Little John: **Archie Duncan**
Sir William: **Patrick Troughton**
Nanny: **Marie Burke**
Derwent: **Victor Woolf**
Sailor: **Shaun O'Riordan**
Look-out: **Paul Eddington**

The Blackbird
w **Francis Nesbitt**
d **Terence Fisher**

When Little John storms off into the forest, after losing his temper during a friendly game with the outlaws, he is immediately captured by the Sheriff - who then offers a handsome reward to anyone willing to hang the outlaw.

Friar Tuck: **Alexander Gauge**
Maid Marian: **Bernadette O'Farrell**
Sheriff: **Alan Wheatley**
Little John: **Archie Duncan**
Seneschal: **Patrick Troughton**
Derwent: **Victor Woolf**
Joan: **Simone Lovell**
Bishop: **Walter Horsburgh**
Quentin: **Shaun O'Riordan**
Sergeant: **Fred Goddard**
Man-at-Arms: **Paul Eddington**
Jailer: **Bernard Goldman**

The Shell Game
w **Anne Rodney**
d **Terry Bishop**

Annoyed when their leader gives shelter to Pick, a confidence trickster, Robin's men become even more alarmed when he asks Pick to steal some jewels for King Richard's campaign. Robin believes the man is trustworthy - his men do not.

Friar Tuck: **Alexander Gauge**
Pick: **Sam Kydd**
Little John: **Archie Duncan**
Polly: **Irene Handl**
April: **Myrtle Reed**
Traveller: **Patrick Troughton**
Derwent: **Victor Woolf**
Sad Simon: **Paul Eddington**
Wall Eye: **Shaun O'Riordan**
Soldier: **Conrad Phillips**
Barmaid: **Sylvia Kay**

The Final Tax
w **Paul Symonds**
d **Terry Bishop**

Friar Tuck plans to thwart a rascally bailiff who intends to collect taxes from Tom Joyner, a dying man. Though the bailiff is legally entitled to do so, with Robin's help, the Friar has other ideas.

Friar Tuck: **Alexander Gauge**
Little John: **Archie Duncan**
Sir Charles: **Paul Eddington**
Bailiff: **Dennis Edwards**
Tom: **Fred Goddard**
Donia: **Patricia Burke**
Simon: **Barry Fennell**
The Reeve: **Alan Edwards**
Derwent: **Victor Woolf**

Retainer: **Jefferson Clifford**
Ned: **Wilfred Brambell**

Ambush
w **Ernest Borneman & Ralph Smart**
d **Lindsay Anderson**

To pave the way for his own ambitions, Prince John orders the Sheriff to kill Prince Arthur and leave evidence which will lay the boy's assassination at Robin's door. When the outlaw gets him of the Sheriff's plans, he decides to ambush the ambushers.

Friar Tuck: **Alexander Gauge**
Maid Marian: **Bernadette O'Farrell**
Little John: **Archie Duncan**
Sheriff: **Alan Wheatley**
Prince John: **Donald Pleasence**
Prince Arthur: **Peter Asher**
Constance: **Dorothy Alison**
Derwent: **Victor Woolf**
Edwin: **Peter Bennett**
Prince John's Captain: **Shaun O'Riordan**
Courtier: **Edward Mulhare**
Spy: **Martin Lane**

The Bandit of Brittany
w **Milton S. Schlesinger**
d **Terry Bishop**

While escorting Prince Arthur to the safety of France, Robin and Friar Tuck discover there is a French 'Robin Hood' - Jacques - who captures them and refuses to release the Friar until Robin embarks on a special mission for him.

Friar Tuck: **Alexander Gauge**
Jacques: **Harold Kasket**
Duchess Constance: **Dorothy Alison**
Prince Arthur: **Peter Asher**
Raoul: **Patrick Troughton**
Warden: **Charles Farrell**
Blind Man: **Shaun O'Riordan**
Leborgne: **Paul Eddington**
Cressy: **Tony Thawnton**
Guard: **Patrick Bedford**

The Goldmaker's Return
w **Alan Moreland**
d **Terry Bishop**

Lepidus the alchemist returns to Nottingham - and immediately falls foul of the Sheriff, who sentences him to be hanged unless he produces gold within a week. Feeling responsible for the man's plight, Robin decides to rescue the goldmaker. ✍ Robin does not appear in this episode.

Maid Marian: **Bernadette O'Farrell**
Little John: **Archie Duncan**
Sheriff: **Alan Wheatley**
Lepidus: **Alfie Bass**
Sir Peter : **Brian Coleman**
Sir Paul: **Paul Eddington**
Derwent: **Victor Woolf**
Will: **Tony Thawnton**
Howard: **Alan Edwards**
Guard: **Terry Yorke**

Flight from France
w **Milton S. Schlesinger**
d **Terry Bishop**

While waiting for a boat to take them back to England, Robin and Friar Tuck see Sir Roderick, an emissary of

Prince John, collecting gold for his master. Overpowering Sir Roderick, Robin decides to impersonate him and claim the gold for the outlaws.

Friar Tuck: **Alexander Gauge**
Michele: **Ingeborg Wells**
Duc de Mirancy: **Alec Mango**
Emile: **Michael Barrington**
Duc de Guise: **Paul Eddington**
Old Duke: **Roy Russell**
Fat Duke: **Bryan Coleman**
Sir Roderick Gascon: **Alan Edwards**
Servant: **Edmund Warwick**

Fair Play
w **Sidney Wells**
d **Terry Bishop**

'The Flying Four', a troupe of travelling acrobats, are waylaid by Robin's men as they pass through Sherwood. They plead for mercy, but Robin's men mean them no harm - in fact their arrival is very fortuitous indeed.

Little John: **Archie Duncan**
Sheriff: **Alan Wheatley**
Herr Mielke: **Thomas Gallagher**
Owen: **Colin Broadley**
Tom: **Paul Eddington**
Harry: **Robert Raikes**
Will: **Tony Thawnton**
Derwent: **Victor Woolf**
Quentin: **Alan Edwards**
Madame Zsa Zsa: **Selma Vaz Dias**
Agatha: **Isobel Grieg**
"The Flying Four": **The Volants**

The Secret Pool
w **John Dyson**
d **Don Chaffey**

Robin and Marian are fishing in a pool that lies on Sir Cedric's estate - although it appears that the knight is unaware of its existence. When Robin shares dinner with Cedric that evening, the outlaw has an unusual tale to impart.

Maid Marian: **Bernadette O'Farrell**
Sheriff: **Alan Wheatley**
Sir Cedric: **George Benson**
Henry: **Paul Eddington**
Howard: **Alan Edwards**
Warden: **Victor Woolf**
Man-at-Arms: **Basil Beale**

The Path of True Love
aka **Locksley Hall [in USA]**
w **Alan Moreland** and **Basil Dawson**
d **Terence Fisher**

When Robin and Marian decide to visit Locksley Hall - a place which holds sentimental attachments for both of them - neither is prepared for the reception they receive from its present owner, Sir Charles.

Maid Marian: **Bernadette O'Farrell**
Sheriff: **Alan Wheatley**
Sir Charles: **Lionel Jeffries**
Master Ricardo: **Hal Osmond**
Hereward: **Ronald Hines**
Old Martin: **Max Faulkner**
Barty: **Nigel Davenport**
Town Crier: **Graham Stewart**

The Dowry
w **Neil R. Collins**
d **Anthony Squire**

A prosperous London merchant and his daughter Bess are on their way to Nottingham with a dowry of 1,000 gold crowns. Garth, a recent recruit to Robin's band, decides to relieve them of the money - a crime which incurs the Sheriff's wrath and spells further trouble for outlaws.

Little John: **Archie Duncan**
Sheriff: **Alan Wheatley**
Bess: **Jeanette Hutchinson**
Garth: **David Cameron**
Sir Harold: **Paul Eddington**
Judd: **William Mervyn**
Alan-a-Dale: **John Schlesinger**
Man-at-Arms: **Edmund Warwick**

The York Treasure
w **Clare Thorne**
d **Terry Bishop**

When Robin hears that someone is plotting to steal gold meant for refugees, he and Little John set out to waylay the brigands and return the money to its intended recipients - but danger of a different kind marks their every move.

Little John: **Archie Duncan**
Sheriff: **Alan Wheatley**
Esther: **Helena de Crespo**
Joseph of Cordoba: **Karel Stepanek**
Malbete: **Allan Cuthbertson**
Alfred: **Emrys Leyshon**
Aaron: **Paul Eddington**
Fisherman: **Wilfred Brambell**
Large Man: **Desmond Roberts**
Drinker: **Edmund Warwick**

The Borrowed Baby
w **Aileen Hamilton**
d **Don Chaffey**

Suspecting that Lady Marian is an accomplice of the outlaws, the Count of Severne devises a plan to expose her. Though an unwilling pawn in the game, the Sheriff agrees to the plan - providing Robin Hood is brought in for 'questioning'.

Friar Tuck: **Alexander Gauge**
Sheriff: **Alan Wheatley**
Little John: **Archie Duncan**
Count of Severne: **Guy Verney**
Kate: **Dorothy Gordon**
Giles: **Graham Stewart**
Alison: **Sylvia Kay**
Molly: **Megan Williams**
Derwent: **Victor Woolf**
Man-at-Arms: **Paul Eddington**

Food for Thought
w **Sidney Wells**
d **Terry Bishop**

Count Olivier's tenants are starving. He has instructed his tax officer to take the food ration and place it in storage. Robin's dilemma? How to steal the food and return it to the villagers without the Count's knowledge.

Little John: **Archie Duncan**
Count Olivier: **John Sharplin**
Seneschal: **Patrick Troughton**
Sam Ludlow: **Meredith Edwards**
Tom Barker: **Duncan Lamont**

Master Weylin: **Emrys Leyshon**
Derwent: **Victor Woolf**
Maurice: **Charles Lloyd Pack**
Scullion: **Bruce Sharman**
Villager: **Dervis Ward**

Too Many Earls
w **Milton S. Schlesinger**
d **Robert Day**

Marian's uncle, the Earl of Rochdale, begins quarrelling with the Earl of Northgate. The outcome is stalemate, so Marian suggests that they settle their differences with an archery contest. But who is the mysterious archer chosen by the Sheriff to shoot for Northgate?

Maid Marian: **Bernadette O'Farrell**
Sheriff: **Alan Wheatley**
Little John: **Archie Duncan**
Earl of Rochdale: **Arthur Howard**
Earl of Northgate: **Victor Platt**
Derwent: **Victor Woolf**
Lord Lawrence: **Nigel Davenport**
Sheriff's Captain: **Peter Johnson**
Sheriff's Servant: **Peter Welch**
Horatio: **Clive Revill**
Judge: **Arthur Lawrence**

Highland Fling
w **Leighton Reynolds**
d **Terry Bishop**

Robin and Friar Tuck are on a mission for King Richard: they are to visit Scotland and collect 500 gold crowns owed to Richard by King William of Scotland - but why should the Scottish King be so reluctant to hand over the gold?

Friar Tuck: **Alexander Gauge**
Duncan: **Hugh McDermott**
Meg: **Hilary Paterson**
Davy: **Andrew Faulds**
Malcolm: **Graham Stewart**
King William: **Duncan McIntyre**
Treasurer: **Jock McKay**
Hermit: **Raymond Ray**
Baron Mornay: **Paul Eddington**
Landlord: **Victor Woolf**

The Mystery of Ireland's Eye
w **James Carhartt** and **Nicolas Winter**
d **Terry Bishop**

Suspecting that her uncle is being held prisoner on an island off the Irish coast, Marian, together with Robin and Friar Tuck, hire a boat to take them there. Their arrival is greeted with alarm - and Marian receives the fright of her life.

Friar Tuck: **Alexander Gauge**
Maid Marian: **Bernadette O'Farrell**
Rolf: **Eddie Byrne**
Sir Edward: **A. J. Brown**
Brigid: **Concepta Fennell**
Malloy: **Diarmuid Kelly**
Captain: **Nigel Davenport**
Seaman: **Ronald Hines**
Dickon: **Jefferson Clifford**
Serf: **Graham Stewart**

The Little People
w **James Carhartt** and **Nicolas Winter**
d **Don Chaffey**

Escorting Marian back home from Ireland after rescuing her uncle, Robin and Friar Tuck hear the legend of the little people. Robin scoffs at the tale, but Tuck is not so sceptical.

Friar Tuck: **Alexander Gauge**
Maid Marian: **Bernadette O'Farrell**
Patrick Nolan: **Barry Keegan**
Maeve Nolan: **Peggy Marshall**
Brian: **Colin Broadley**
Deidre: **Carole Lorimer**
Tim: **Claude Kingston**
Connor: **Paul Eddington**

The Infidel
w **John Dyson** and **Basil Dawson**
d **Terence Fisher**

Sir James devises a plot to inherit his uncle's fortune. Blame for the crime will point at an innocent man - Ali Ben Azra - and the Sheriff has been informed. Can Robin teach Sir James a lesson in sportsmanship - and clip the Sheriff's wings at the same time?

Maid Marian: **Bernadette O'Farrell**
Little John: **Archie Duncan**
Ali: **Francis Matthews**
Sir James: **Nigel Davenport**
Lucas: **Alex Scott**
Baron Mark: **Noel Coleman**
Father Justin: **Roland Bartrop**
William: **Graham Stewart**
Edgar: **Ronald Hines**
Simon: **Edmund Warwick**

The Frightened Tailor
w **Michael Connor**
d **Anthony Squire**

When a list of people loyal to King Richard comes into the Sheriff's possession, Robin, with a little help from his friend the tailor, retrieves the list before his enemy can put it to wrongful use.

The Tailor: **Hugh Burden**
Maid Marian: **Bernadette O'Farrell**
Little John: **Archie Duncan**
Sheriff: **Alan Wheatley**
Waldo: **Graham Stewart**
Lieutenant: **David William**
Seneschal: **Michael Peake**
Ned Carter: **Ronald Hines**
Sentry: **Nigel Davenport**

The Black Five
w **Michael Connor**
d **Anthony Squire**

When the Sheriff receives threats to his life, what could be more natural than to send for his 'friend' Robin Hood! Robin's interest is aroused by his enemy's change of tune, but what has caused this reversal of thought?

Maid Marian: **Bernadette O'Farrell**
Sheriff: **Alan Wheatley**
Little John: **Archie Duncan**
Earl de Moreville: **Patrick Cargill**
de Moreville's Seneschal: **Manning Wilson**
Sheriff's Seneschal: **Dennis Edwards**
Derwent: **Victor Woolf**
Wounded Man : **Peter Welch**
Sheriff's Lieutenant: **Peter Retey**
Messenger: **Graham Stewart**
Man-at-Arms: **Gordon Whiting**

The Road in the Air
w **Carol Warner Gluck** and **Albert A Dorner**
d **Robert Day**

Robin must think of a way to cross the land approaching Tom's mill: Sir William, Tom's landlord, has imposed an import duty on grain taken from the mill and his guards are gathered to repel intruders. An ingenious device provides Robin with the answer.

Tom the Miller: **James Hayter**
Maid Marian: **Bernadette O'Farrell**
Sheriff: **Alan Wheatley**
Little John: **Archie Duncan**
Sir William: **Laurence Hardy**
Claud: **Nigel Davenport**
Notary: **Ronald Hines**
Hugh: **Arthur Skinner**
Andrew: **Graham Stewart**
Derwent: **Victor Woolf**

Carlotta
w **Michael Connor** and **Basil Dawson**
d **Anthony Squire**

Robin and his band have set a date to steal a gold shipment planned for Prince John's coffers, but Little John is nowhere to be found. Has the gentle giant finally been smitten by the love of a fair lady?

Maid Marian: **Bernadette O'Farrell**
Carlotta: **Jennifer Jayne**
Little John: **Archie Duncan**
Sheriff: **Alan Wheatley**
Joan: **Simone Lovell**
Derwent: **Victor Woolf**
Sheriff's Lieutenant: **Max Faulkner**
Outlaw: **Ronald Hines**
Man-at-Arms: **Terry Yorke**

---

season three
39 monochrome 30-minute episodes
1957-58

The Salt King
w **Carey Wilber**
d **Don Chaffey**

Certain lords are maintaining a monopoly on essential goods: one such commodity is salt, and Lord Guthrie has formed an alliance with the Sheriff to hold back supplies. Robin gets to hear of this, and things get very spicy indeed.

Friar Tuck: **Alexander Gauge**
Maid Marian: **Patricia Driscoll** [intro]
Little John: **Archie Duncan**
Sheriff: **Alan Wheatley**
Lord Guthrie: **Manning Wilson**
Derwent: **Victor Woolf**
Wilfrid: **Paul Eddington**
Captain: **Tony Thawnton**
First Lord: **Max Faulkner**

A Tuck in Time
w **James Carhartt** and **Nicolas Winter**
d **Terry Bishop**

Edgar, Tuck's brother, returns home from overseas. With him, he's brought a deadly machine and he's prepared to sell it the highest bidder - Prince John. Tuck must attempt to lead his brother back into the fold before the deal is completed.

Friar Tuck: **Alexander Gauge**
Edgar: **Alexander Gauge**
Maid Marian: **Patricia Driscoll**
Sheriff: **Alan Wheatley**
Prince John: **Hubert Gregg** [intro]
Little John: **Archie Duncan**
Sir Reginald: **Paul Eddington**
Jeremy: **Wilfrid Downing**

Pepper
w **Michael Connor**
d **Robert Day**

Robin and his men become involved in the affairs of a Byzantine Princess, Irene, who is being held hostage by Prince John. Their dilemma? How does one enter a heavily guarded castle without being seen?

Maid Marian: **Patricia Driscoll**
Prince John: **Hubert Gregg**
Princess Irene: **Monica Stevenson**
Little John: **Archie Duncan**
Ambassador: **Peter Welch**
Derwent: **Victor Woolf**
Chloe: **Norma Parnell**
Iris: **Lesley Parry**
Troubadour: **Paul Hansard**

The Charter
w **John Dyson**
d **Terry Bishop**

The only person who knows the hiding place of a charter which will limit Prince John's power should he become King is Lord Greenwald, who is seriously ill. Marian discovers where the charter is hidden, but can Robin retrieve it before the Sheriff?

Friar Tuck: **Alexander Gauge**
Maid Marian: **Patricia Driscoll**
Sheriff: **Alan Wheatley**
Sir Bascom: **Harry H. Corbett**
Sir Eustace: **Paul Eddington**
Squire: **Sean Lynch**
Hulm: **Philip Ray**
The Boy: **Michael Ellison**
The Girl: **Ann Hughes**
Guard: **Max Faulkner**

Change of Heart
w **Basil Dawson**
d **Terry Bishop**

Having heard that Lord Humphrey intends to expel the Celts from the Forest of Dean, Friar Tuck seeks Robin's advice and together they force the knight to rethink his motives.

Friar Tuck: **Alexander Gauge**
Lord Humphrey: **Eddie Byrne**
Little John: **Archie Duncan**
Brack: **Michael Ripper**
Derwent: **Victor Woolf**
Colin: **Paul Eddington**
Meg: **Sally Travers**

Brother Battle
w **Leslie Poynton**
d **Robert Day**

When Brother Wootan starts a school in Sherwood, much to the outlaw's amusement, Little John becomes a somewhat unwilling pupil. What are his motives? The answer sets the Greenwood alive with laughter.

Friar Tuck: **Alexander Gauge**
Brother Wootan: **Francis De Wolff**
Little John: **Archie Duncan**
Sheriff: **Alan Wheatley**
Mark: **Claude Kingston**
Derwent: **Victor Woolf**
Howard: **Paul Eddington**
Guard: **Fred Goddard**
Man-at-Arms: **Terry Yorke**

My Brother's Keeper
w **Neil R. Collins**
d **Don Chaffey**

Abelard lies dead - slain by his brother Loren, who lays the killing at Robin's door. Anxious to clear his friend's name, Friar Tuck arranges a play - starring the dead man's corpse!

Friar Tuck: **Alexander Gauge**
Maid Marian: **Patricia Driscoll**
Little John: **Archie Duncan**
Sheriff: **Alan Wheatley**
Sir Loren: **Maurice Kaufmann**
Lord Duquesne: **Carl Bernard**
Sir Abelard: **David Cameron**
Satan: **Paul Eddington**
Derwent: **Victor Woolf**
Adam: **Keith Anderson**
Eve: **Virginia Maskell**

An Apple for the Archer
w **James Aldridge**
d **Terry Bishop**

Ordered by her father's will to marry the finest bowman in England, Mary Quartermaine must choose between family loyalty and her love for Pierre of Bordeaux. Robin pulls a few strings to help her dilemma.

Little John: **Archie Duncan**
Mary Quartermaine: **Ann Firbank**
Timothy Cox: **Kenneth Cope**
Pierre of Bordeaux: **Paul Eddington**
Uncle Robert: **John Gatrell**
Count Percy: **Robert Bernal**
Ben Bradley: **Charles Lamb**
Derwent: **Victor Woolf**

The Angry Village
w **Shirl Hendryx**
d **Terry Bishop**

A drought hits Sherwood, and Robin and Little John have to leave the safety of the forest to search for water. During their travels, they meet some villagers hiding grain to avoid paying their taxes. The next day, the grain disappears and suspicion falls on the strangers.

Little John: **Archie Duncan**
Jason: **Harry H. Corbett**
Hogarth: **Rowland Bartrop**
Cal: **Geoffrey Bayldon**
Older Man: **Leonard Sharp**
Davey: **Clive Parritt**
Captain: **Paul Eddington**
Derwent: **Victor Woolf**
Woman: **Susan Westerby**

The Mark
w **Robert Newman**
d **Robert Day**

Sir Blaise, a Norman lord, plans to build a fortress on his land. To dupe the community, he lets it be known that the new building is to be a church in honour of St Barnaby. Enter Robin Hood and Friar Tuck, and the knight is soon given a very heavy cross to bear.

Friar Tuck: **Alexander Gauge**
Little John: **Archie Duncan**
Derwent: **Victor Woolf**
Sir Blaise: **Charles Gray**
Walter: **Philip Ray**
Diccon: **Kenneth Cope**
Bishop: **Llewellyn Rees**

The Bride of Robin Hood
w **Oliver Skene**
d **Anthony Squire**

To escape a forced marriage to Walter, Brenda runs away from home. Having proved herself a gallant archer by saving Robin's life, in return she asks a favour - she wishes to become Robin's wife!

Friar Tuck: **Alexander Gauge**
Marian: **Patricia Driscoll**
Little John: **Archie Duncan**
Brenda: **Billie Whitelaw**
Walter: **Ronald Allan**
Joan: **Simone Lovell**
Alfred: **Peter Halliday**
Derwent: **Victor Woolf**
Quentin: **John Baker**

To Be a Student
w **Sidney Wells**
d **Robert Day**

When Prince John tries to recruit young children for troops, Peter Larkin flees to the Greenwood to join Robin and his outlaws. But his arrival is a portent of doom for Robin's men, and they soon have reason to regret his presence.

Friar Tuck: **Alexander Gauge**
Little John: **Archie Duncan**
Peter Larkin: **Derek Waring**
Agnes: **Maureen Davis**
Bement: **Hugh Moxey**
Rolfe: **Paul Eddington**
Sir William: **Alan Rowe**
Count Eger: **John H. Watson**
Jack: **Roger Bizley**
Abbot: **Walter Horsburgh**

The Christmas Goose
w **Oliver Skene**
d **Don Chaffey**

Davy, an 11-year old boy caught stealing mistletoe on Sir Leon's estate, is sentenced to be flogged. Robin, however, gives the boy his own kind of Christmas present - one which helps to cook the bailiff's goose.

Friar Tuck: **Alexander Gauge**
Davy: **Jon Whiteley**
Sir Leon: **Jack Watling**
Bailiff: **Paul Eddington**
Susan: **Jane Asher**
Little John: **Archie Duncan**
Quentin: **John Baker**
Derwent: **Victor Woolf**
Stella: **Anne Firth**

The Challenge of the Black Knight
w **Leon Griffiths**
d **Anthony Squire**

As a special birthday treat to his son, Will, Ned Dale, an outlaw, takes him hunting with Little John. But things go terribly wrong when they are challenged by a knight dressed entirely in black armour, and Will decides to prove his manhood.

Little John: **Archie Duncan**
Sheriff: **Alan Wheatley**
Sir Roger: **John Arnatt**
Will: **Richard O'Sullivan**
Ned: **Dervis Ward**
Lieutenant: **Ronald Ibbs**
Tom: **Paul Eddinton**
Servant: **Terry Yorke**
Derwent: **Victor Woolf**

The Rivals
w **Leslie Poynton**
d **Robert Day**

When ordered to increase the taxes, the Sheriff's lieutenant proposes an alternative plan to raise money - one which will benefit both men. Why not form a rival gang of outlaws and steal from the rich like Robin Hood!

Friar Tuck: **Alexander Gauge**
Sheriff: **Alan Wheatley**
Little John: **Archie Duncan**
Derwent: **Victor Woolf**
Dick Banks: **Carl Bernard**
Seneschal: **Paul Eddington**
Edward: **Michael Ashwin**
Willie Steele: **Colin Broadley**
Rich Merchant: **Basil Dignam**

The Profiteer
w **Samuel B. West**
d **Terry Bishop**

When the Lord of the Manor refuses to help people of Lothan village after their crops have failed, Robin Hood comes to their rescue by sending Andrew, a serf, to buy food from London. But the Sheriff gets wind of Robin's plan and hatches a scheme of his own.

Friar Tuck: **Alexander Gauge**
Little John: **Archie Duncan**
Andrew: **Gordon Jackson**
Hodges: **John Longden**
Pamela: **Barbara Archer**
Rypon: **Paul Eddington**
Joan: **Simone Lovell**
Martha: **Catherine Finn**
Village Elder: **Leonard Sharp**

Knight Errant
w **Michael Connor**
d **Anthony Squire**

Engrossed in his archery practice, Robin ignores Marian's pleas to speak with him on a matter of urgency. Furious, she storms off alone, and that's when the trouble starts - for Marian, Robin and Sir Jack of Southwork.

Maid Marian: **Patricia Driscoll**
Sheriff: **Alan Wheatley**
Little John: **Archie Duncan**
Sir Jack: **William Lucas**
Derwent: **Victor Woolf**
Captain: **Paul Eddington**

The Healing Hand
w **Leon Griffiths**
d **Bernard Knowles**

Viewed by his friends as large of frame and small of mind, Little John is the ideal victim for Oswald of the Healing Hand, a 'quack' doctor, who finds it an easy task to dupe the outlaw - but things have a way of turning out for the best.

Oswald: **Michael Ripper**
Baron Barclay: **Bryan Coleman**
Little John: **Archie Duncan**
Captain: **Paul Eddington**
Joan: **Simone Lovell**
Derwent: **Victor Woolf**
Thin Man: **James Ellis**
First Soldier: **Desmond Jordan**
Villager: **Robert Hunter**

One Man's Meat
w **George** and **Gertrude Fass**
d **Don Chaffey**

Squire Woodstock has discovered a new kind of bran which he dubs his 'universal food'. Believing that it will replace all other food, he arranges for Robin and Friar Tuck to taste the 'wonder' bran, with comical results.

Friar Tuck: **Alexander Gauge**
Edmund Woodstock: **Robin Bailey**
Thaddeus Goldfinch: **Kevin Stoney**
Patrick: **Paul Eddington**
Henry: **Gary Raymond**
Betsey: **Ann Reid**
Derwent: **Victor Woolf**

Too Many Robins
w **John Dyson**
d **Robert Day**

One Robin in Sherwood is one too many for the Sheriff - now there are two! Tom the Thatcher is impersonating the outlaw to impress his girlfriend, Alma. But as Tom soon discovers, playing outlaw has its serious side.

Maid Marian: **Patricia Driscoll**
Little John: **Archie Duncan**
Alma: **Susan Stephen**
Tom: **Derek Waring**
Bart: **Jack Lambert**
Lieutenant: **Edward Judd**
Derwent: **Victor Woolf**

The Crusaders
w **Samuel B. West**
d **Gerry Bryant**

Robin, keeping a rendezvous with four knights with whom he fought in the Crusades, does not know he's walking into a trap hatched by the Sheriff. Can his enemy win this time? Or has Robin an ace up his sleeve?

Friar Tuck: **Alexander Gauge**
Sheriff: **Alan Wheatley**
Beaumont: **Bryan Coleman**
Little John: **Archie Duncan**
Lieutenant: **Roy Purcell**
Sir Hugh: **Paul Eddington**
Sir Charles: **Manning Wilson**
Sir Paul: **Julian Somers**
Derwent: **Victor Woolf**

Castle in the Air
w **Oliver Skene**
d **Peter Maxwell**

Once again on the losing end of a gambling game, Sir Richard of the Lea turns to Robin for help. His opponent in

the game is Sir Adrian, a man who believes in winning at any cost - and Robin suspects the game was crooked.

Maid Marian: **Patricia Driscoll**
Sir Adrian: **David Oxley**
Sir Richard of the Lea: **Ian Hunter**
Lady Leonia: **Patricia Burke**
Sheriff: **Alan Wheatley**
Little John: **Archie Duncan**
Outlaw: **David Hart**

The Double
w **Basil Dawson**
d **Gerry Bryant**

When Bolbec, sworn enemy of Robin Hood, arrives at Nottingham Castle, he bears news of interest to the Sheriff. He has a foolproof plan to rid the forest of the outlaw. He then introduces his hooded guest - Robin's double.

Luke Tanner: **Richard Greene**
Friar Tuck: **Alexander Gauge**
Sheriff: **Alan Wheatley**
Little John: **Archie Duncan**
Bolbec: **John Gabriel**
Prince Arthur: **Richard O'Sullivan**
Constance: **Pamela Alan**
Sir Humphrey: **Richard Thorp**
Lieutenant: **Max Faulkner**

Roman Gold
w **Basil Dawson**
d **Peter Maxwell**

Out hunting, Robin and his men unearth some ancient Roman gold, which the outlaw leader plans to distribute to the needy. The Sheriff, however, content that his need is the greatest, lays claim to the treasure in the crown's name.

Friar Tuck: **Alexander Gauge**
Sheriff: **Alan Wheatley**
Dr. Quince: **George A. Cooper**
Little John: **Archie Duncan**
Tybalt: **Ballard Berkeley**
Derwent: **Victor Woolf**
Landlord: **Edmund Warwick**
Howard: **Peter Welch**
Man-at-Arms: **David Davenport**

The Ghost that Failed
w **Leon Griffiths**
d **Peter Maxwell**

Believing that the land belonging to Simon Dexter is haunted, local farmers seek advice from Friar Tuck. He is sceptical but agrees to accompany Robin to Dexter's estate. What they find astonishes both men.

Friar Tuck: **Alexander Gauge**
Maid Marian: **Patricia Driscoll**
Little John: **Archie Duncan**
Simon Dexter: **Rupert Davies**
Jenny: **Barbara Lott**
Ralph: **Kevin Stoney**
Yeoman: **John Barrie**
Derwent: **Victor Woolf**

The Minstrel
w **Leslie Poynton**
d **Peter Seabourne**

A minstrel's song can prove very handy, particularly when it helps Robin and his outlaws foil a dastardly plot by Prince

John, who is conspiring to form an alliance with the Prince of Aragon.

Friar Tuck: **Alexander Gauge**
Maid Marian: **Patricia Driscoll**
Sheriff: **Alan Wheatley**
Roland: **Francis Matthews**
Little John: **Archie Duncan**
Prince John: **Brian Haines**
Ambassador: **Roger Delgado**
Lieutenant: **John Harvey**
Prison Guard: **Graham Stewart**
First Small Girl: **Jane Asher**

The Doctor
w **Leslie Poynton**
d **Peter Seabourne**

When Little John breaks his leg while escaping from the Sheriff, Robin and Friar Tuck take him to the home of Sir George Woodley, a specialist in broken limbs. While the doctor attends Little John, his servant reports their visit to the Sheriff!

Friar Tuck: **Alexander Gauge**
Sheriff: **Alan Wheatley**
Little John: **Archie Duncan**
Benvolio: **Henry Vidon**
Sir George Woodley: **John Harvey**
Howard: **Paul Eddington**
Sheriff's Doctor: **Noel Davis**
Derwent: **Victor Woolf**

The Fire
w **Philip Bolsover**
d **Robert Day**

Having cornered Little John and Derwent in a cave, the Sheriff orders his men to smoke them out. From the flames of defeat appears new hope - and the Sheriff will eventually have to seek Robin's help.

Friar Tuck: **Alexander Gauge**
Sheriff: **Alan Wheatley**
Little John: **Archie Duncan**
Derwent: **Victor Woolf**
Forester: **Neil Hallett**
Lieutenant: **Paul Eddington**
First Man-at-Arms: **Arthur Skinner**
Second Man-at-Arms: **Jack Taylor**
Third Man-at-Arms: **Jeremy White**

At the Sign of the Blue Boar
w **Sidney B. Wells**
d **Ernest Borneman**

Master Blount, a miserly tailor, is jealous of Ulrich, the landlord of the Blue Boar Inn which Robin and his men frequent. To implicate the innkeeper, Blount informs the Sheriff, who employs the tailor to spy for him.

Sheriff: **Alan Wheatley**
Little John: **Archie Duncan**
William Blount: **Geoffrey Chater**
Saunders: **Harold Goodwin**
Ulrich: **Martin Wyldeck**
Alison: **Anne Reid**
Derwent: **Victor Woolf**

Quickness of the Hand
w **R. W. Bogany**
d **Robert Day**

The tournament over, three knights decide to earn some money by claiming the reward for Robin's capture. Disguised as strolling players, they enter the outlaws' camp and await their opportunity to strike.

Friar Tuck: **Alexander Gauge**
Sheriff: **Alan Wheatley**
Little John: **Archie Duncan**
Sir Laurence: **Richard Pasco**
Sir John: **Brian Oulton**
Sir Ralph: **Richard Caldicot**
Lieutenant: **John Dearth**
Squire: **Terry Yorke**

Elixir of Youth
w **Samuel B. West**
d **Terry Bishop**

In desperate need of money, Sir Boland has promised the hand of his ward, Melissa, to Sir Louis, an elderly Norman. When Tuck, a friend of the girl's, hears this news, he and Robin make arrangements of their own.

Friar Tuck: **Alexander Gauge**
Maid Marian: **Patricia Driscoll**
Sir Louis: **Reginald Beckwith**
Little John: **Archie Duncan**
Sir Boland: **Patrick Troughton**
Melissa: **Anne Reid**
Alwyn: **Kenneth Cope**
Will: **David Hart**
Arnulf: **Alex Seton**

The Genius
w **Oliver Skene**
d **Peter Seabourne**

Nicodemus, a master mathematician, seeks entrance to the Abbey of Southwall to escape Prince John - who is anxious to use the scholar's genius to construct a deadly weapon. refused entrance, Nicodemus seeks refuge in Sherwood.

Friar Tuck: **Alexander Gauge**
Nicodemus: **Harry H. Corbett**
Little John: **Archie Duncan**
Count de Severne: **Geoffrey Bayldon**
Abbot: **Charles Lloyd Pack**
Augustine: **Paul Hansard**
Abelard: **Tommy Rose**
Lieutenant: **Alex Scott**
First Sentry: **Arthur Skinner**
Second Sentry: **Keith Anderson**

The Youthful Menace
w **Arthur Dales**
d **Robert Day**

Edwin, Marian's nephew, is scornful of her claims about Robin's allegiance to King Richard. To confirm her knowledge, Marian takes him to the outlaw camp. A mistake: Edwin's presence there becomes a threat to the outlaws freedom.

Maid Marian: **Patricia Driscoll**
Edwin: **Peter Kerr**
Little John: **Archie Duncan**
Derwent: **Victor Woolf**
Peasant: **John Gatrell**
Guard: **Graham Stewart**

The Lottery
w **Peter Yeldham**
d **Peter Seabourne**

The Sheriff plans to raise some money for Prince John by using a clever variation on an old theme. His plan seems foolproof - but as always, he has reckoned without Robin's intervention.

Friar Tuck: **Alexander Gauge**
Maid Marian: **Patricia Driscoll**
Sheriff: **Alan Wheatley**
Little John: **Archie Duncan**
Will Sharpe: **Alfred Burke**
Frisby: **Ian Whittaker**
Lieutenant: **John Harvey**
Cook: **Edmund Warwick**

Lincoln Green
w **Neil R. Collins**
d **Terry Bishop**

Forewarned that Robin Hood and Maid Marian will visit Nottingham Fair to buy new supplies of Lincoln Green cloth, the Sheriff stations his men-at-arms in the town square - but a tailor's scissors provide Robin with an unusual escape route.

Maid Marian: **Patricia Driscoll**
Sheriff: **Alan Wheatley**
Little John: **Archie Duncan**
Shanks: **Charles Houston**
David: **Geoffrey Chater**
Dyer: **Arthur Lawrence**
Spinner: **Hal Osmond**
Weaver: **Leonard Sharp**
Clerk: **Max Faulkner**

Woman's War
w **Philip Bolsover**
d **Peter Seabourne**

After she has been rescued by the Sheriff's men, Robin agrees to allow two of his men to escort Ann de Brisac, a noblewoman, to a place where where she claims to have hidden gold: after their departure, Marian arrives with news that the woman is a spy.

Maid Marian: **Patricia Driscoll**
Sheriff: **Alan Wheatley**
Ann de Brissac: **Zena Walker**
Little John: **Archie Duncan**
Michael: **Neil Hallett**
Derwent: **Victor Woolf**
Guard: **Tony Thawnton**
Second Guard: **Graham Stewart**

Little Mother
w **Philip Bolsover**
d **Terry Bishop**

Seeing an elderly woman being abused by two of the Sheriff's men-at-arms, Marian and Little John intervene: to his surprise, Robin's second-in-command discovers that the woman is his mother!

Friar Tuck : **Alexander Gauge**
Maid Marian: **Patricia Driscoll**
Little John: **Archie Duncan**
Little Mother: **Renee Houston**
Duke: **Charles Houston**
Derwent: **Victor Woolf**
First Man-at-Arms: **Lawrence James**
Second Man-at-Arms: **Arthur Skinner**
Peasant Boy: **Anthony Green**
'Two Fingers': **Desmond Llewellyn**

Marian's Prize
w **Louis Marks**
d **Peter Seabourne**

Robin's name has been entered for an archery contest. The problem, he's away visiting friends. Can Marian, selected in his absence, fool the Sheriff and win the shooting tournament?

Friar Tuck: **Alexander Gauge**
Maid Marian: **Patricia Driscoll**
Prince John: **Donald Pleasence**
Little John: **Archie Duncan**
Lord Northeave: **Jack Melford**
Derwent: **Victor Woolf**
Walter: **Paul Eddington**
Will: **Brian Alexis**
Stephen: **Graham Stewart**
Herald: **Arthur Lawrence**

Farewell to Tuck
w **Arthur Dales**
d **Terry Bishop**

When the Archbishop of Canterbury visits Nottingham, the Sheriff sees a way of depleting Robin's band by one: he'll get rid of the troublesome Friar Tuck once and for all. As usual, the outlaws have the last laugh.

Friar Tuck: **Alexander Gauge**
Sheriff: **Alan Wheatley**
Little John: **Archie Duncan**
Archbishop: **Carl Bernard**
Alison: **Anne Reid**
Jack: **Harold Goodwin**
Lieutenant: **Paul Eddington**
Michael: **Edmund Warwick**
Catherine: **Catherine Finn**

---

season four
26 Monochrome 30-minute episodes.
1959

Sybella
w **Michael Connor**
d **Terry Bishop**

A nobleman is attacked while on his way to join King Richard in the Holy Land. His murderer, Baron Onslow, changes clothes with the dead man and rides to Nottingham Castle in his place. But will his disguise fool Robin Hood?

Maid Marian: **Patricia Driscoll**
Sheriff: **Alan Wheatley**
Sybella: **Soraya Rafat**
Baron Onslow: **David Davies**
Derwent: **Victor Woolf**
Ralph: **Geoffrey Taylor**
Juggler: **Michael Peake**
Earl of Steyne: **Norman Mitchell**
Attendant: **Graham Stewart**

The Lady Killer
w **Jan Read**
d **Terry Bishop**

Robin and Derwent, out hunting, are recalled to their camp on a matter of great urgency: Will Scarlett has been arrested for poaching! Their plan to rescue him from the Sheriff's clutches has a most unusual outcome.

Maid Marian: **Patricia Driscoll**

Sheriff: **Alan Wheatley**
Will Scarlett: **Paul Eddington** [intro]
Maud: **Geraldine Hagan**
Derwent: **Victor Woolf**
De Sarigny: **Derek Birch**
Lieutenant: **Ronald Hines**
First Forester: **Keith Rawlings**
Harold: **Gordon Whiting**
Edgar: **Brian Alexis**

A Touch of Fever
w **Leon Griffiths**
d **Peter Seabourne**

Difficulties for Marian when she recognises one of three knights captured by the outlaws as her cousin. Before she can beg for his release, she must first of all discover why he is in the company of rogues.

Maid Marian: **Patricia Driscoll**
Sheriff: **Alan Wheatley**
Will Scarlett: **Paul Eddington**
Sir Nigel Fitzhulme: **John Carson**
Sir John Hanley: **Ronald Hines**
Sir Gerald Fullerton: **Humphrey Lestocq**
Derwent: **Victor Woolf**

Tuck's Love Day
w **Alan Hackney**
d **Terry Bishop**

Always in trouble with his Abbot, Friar Tuck is unusually concerned when he is unable to collect his share of the church money. In despair, he turns to the outlaws - and Robin finds a very unusual cure for his friend's ailment.

Friar Tuck: **Alexander Gauge**
Sheriff: **Alan Wheatley**
Will Scarlett: **Paul Eddington**
Sir Geoffrey: **Basil Dignam**
Roger: **Peter Torquill**
Derwent: **Victor Woolf**
Abbot: **Walter Horsburgh**
Lieutenant: **Morton Lowry**

The Flying Sorcerer
w **Palmer Thompson**
d **Bernard Knowles**

Lord Giles of Richmond, in Nottingham to collect taxes, sees an opportunity to misuse his position by robbing the needy. With Friar Tuck's help, Robin teaches him a lesson.

Maid Marian: **Patricia Driscoll**
Lord Eilmar: **Arthur Howard**
Lord Giles: **Anthony Jacobs**
Harold: **Gordon Whiting**
Mauger: **Terry Yorke**
Lieutenant: **Morton Lowry**
Tradesman: **Arthur Skinner**
Merchant: **Middleton Woods**

The Loaf
w **Philip Bolsover**
d **Peter Seabourne**

If there is money to be made, the Sheriff seldom worries about the plight of others. However, when he decides to make a fat profit by selling off flour grain belonging to the villagers, Robin teaches him some table manners.

Friar Tuck: **Alexander Gauge**
Sheriff: **Alan Wheatley**
Will Scarlett: **Paul Eddington**

Derwent: **Victor Woolf**
Boy: **Michael Lewis**
Girl: **Angela White**
Mother: **Anne Firth**
Commander: **Neil Hallett**
First Soldier: **Keith Rawlings**
Second Soldier: **Keith Anderson**

Six Strings to his Bow
w **Richard Bowers**
d **Terry Bishop**

Unaware that he is wanted for murder by Prince John, Alan-a-Dale returns to Sherwood. His arrival serves to increase the already tension-filled feud between Robin and the Sheriff, who is hot on the minstrel's trail.

Marian: **Patricia Driscoll**
Sheriff: **Alan Wheatley**
Alan-a-Dale: **Richard Coleman**
Will Scarlett: **Paul Eddington**
Derwent: **Victor Woolf**
Joan: **Simone Lovell**
Lieutenant: **Morton Lowry**

The Devil You Don't Know
w **Owen Holder**
d **Peter Seabourne**

When Robin and Will Scarlett are out searching for Alan-a-Dale, who has failed to return to camp, they see a group of soldiers escorting a man shackled in irons. Their intervention on the man's behalf leads to surprising results.

Marian: **Patricial Driscoll**
Sheriff: **Alan Wheatley**
Ralph [Deputy Sheriff] - **John Arnatt** [intro]
Will Scarlett: **Paul Eddington**
Alan-a-Dale: **Richard Coleman**
Derwent: **Victor Woolf**
Lieutenant: **Ronald Hines**
Bault: **Keith Rawlings**

Goodbye, Little John
w **Raymond Bowers**
d **Robert Day**

Little John is concerned that Will Scarlett has taken his place - in all but name - as Robin's lieutenant. Robin denies this is true, but his friend angrily storms out of Sherwood, swearing never to return.

Friar Tuck: **Alexander Gauge**
Little John: **Archie Duncan**
Deputy Sheriff: **John Arnatt**
Will Scarlett: **Paul Eddington**
Joan: **Simone Lovell**
Derwent: **Victor Woolf**
Lieutenant: **Morton Lowry**
Bault: **Graham Stewart**
Sturdy Man: **Denis Holmes**

Hostage for a Hangman
w **Arthur Dales**
d **Peter Seabourne**

No stranger to trouble, Robin faces the Sheriff's latest threat with grave concern: his enemy has threatened to hang one serf a day until the outlaw gives himself up.

Maid Marian: **Patricia Driscoll**
Deputy Sheriff: **John Arnatt**
Little John: **Archie Duncan**
Will Scarlett: **Paul Eddington**

Alan-a-Dale: **Richard Coleman**
Lord Orford: **Humphrey Lestocq**
Lord Beaumont: **Jack Melford**
Lieutenant: **Ronald Hines**
Bault: **Terry Yorke**

Hue and Cry
w **Alan Hackney**
d **Compton Bennett**

Set upon and robbed of his chain of office by a masked man, the Deputy Sheriff wrongly suspects the outlaws of the crime. What follows places Robin's life under threat - and provides unwanted troubles for Little John and Maid Marian.

Maid Marian: **Patricia Driscoll**
Deputy Sheriff: **John Arnatt**
Little John: **Archie Duncan**
Will Scarlett: **Paul Eddington**
Dick: **Ronald Hines**
Jenny: **Geraldine Hagan**
Smith: **Kevin Stoney**
Lieutenant: **Graham Stewart**

The Reluctant Rebel
w **Leon Griffiths**
d **Peter Seabourne**

In order to gather first-hand knowledge of life in the Greenwood, Sir Geoffrey, a writer, and his manservant, Herbert, pose as outlaws and join Robin's band. What they discover - if they live long enough to write about it - would fill a book.

Little John: **Archie Duncan**
Herbert: **Leslie Phillips**
Sir Geoffrey: **John Carson**
Will Scarlett: **Paul Eddington**
Jim Stark: **Hugh Cross**

The Oath
w **Arthur Dales**
d **Compton Bennett**

It doesn't pay to underestimate Friar Tuck - as the Deputy Sheriff finds out when he hatches a plot to have the Friar take an oath that he doesn't consort with the outlaws.

Friar Tuck: **Alexander Gauge**
Deputy Sheriff: **John Arnatt**
Little John: **Archie Duncan**
Archbishop: **Carl Bernard**
Will Scarlett: **Paul Eddington**
Joan: **Simone Lovell**
Courier: **Roy Purcell**
Lieutenant: **Morton Lowry**

The Charm Pedlar
w **Alan Hackney**
d **Peter Seabourne**

To Robin, a man willing to trust his fellow man in most things, Issac, the charm pedlar recently arrived in Sherwood, appears to be a harmless quack. So why should Tuck be so suspicious of the newcomer?

Friar Tuck: **Alexander Gauge**
Maid Marian: **Patricia Driscoll**
Deputy Sheriff: **John Arnatt**
Hugo: **Victor Maddern**
Little John: **Archie Duncan**
Will Scarlett: **Paul Eddington**
Lieutenant: **Morton Lowry**
First Villager: **Keith Rawlings**

The Bagpiper
w **Jan Read**
d **Terry Bishop**

Duncan, the wild Highland clansman, returns to the outlaw camp and reeks havoc among Robin's men. This time he has a plan to overthrone the Sheriff. Robin's dilemma? How to oppose the clansman without incurring his wrath.

Maid Marian: **Patricia Driscoll**
Duncan: **Hugh McDermott**
Little John: **Archie Duncan**
Will Scarlett: **Paul Eddington**
Sir Fulke: **Patrick Troughton**
Tam: **Andrew Downie**

The Parting Guest
w **Louis Marks**
d **Terry Bishop**

Duncan, a wild Highland clansman, is hardly a welcome guest in Robin's camp - particularly when his interest appears to be solely in the Lady Marian. A worried outlaw leader seeks Friar Tuck's advice.

Maid Marian: **Patricia Driscoll**
Duncan: **Hugh McDermott**
Little John: **Archie Duncan**
Jessie: **Ellen McIntosh**
Will Scarlett: **Paul Eddington**
Derwent: **Victor Woolf**

The Debt
w **Leon Griffiths**
d **Anthony Squire**

Posing as one of Robin's outlaws, a foreigner attacks and robs several people as they wander through Sherwood. The man's capture brings Robin a dilemma: seven years earlier, the man had saved his life in the Crusades.

Friar Tuck: **Alexander Gauge**
Maid Marian: **Patricia Driscoll**
Deputy Sheriff: **John Arnatt**
Little John: **Archie Duncan**
Martin: **Brian Rawlinson**
Will Scarlett: **Paul Eddington**
Alice Dale: **Maureen Davis**
John Dale: **Terry Yorke**

Bride for an Outlaw
w **Louis Marks**
d **Gordon Parry**

Sir Bligh, a wealthy merchant, learns that his daughter's suitor plans to visit her. Robin, escaping from the Sheriff's men, enters the house and is mistaken for the man - an event which leads the outlaw leader into treachery.

Friar Tuck: **Alexander Gauge**
Deputy Sheriff: **John Arnatt**
Judith Denton: **Mary Manson**
Sir Peter: **Nigel Davenport**
Bligh Denton: **John Horsley**
Ann: **Camilla Hasse**
Will Scarlett: **Paul Eddington**
Lieutenant: **Morton Lowry**

Race Against Time
w **Arthur Dales**
d **Terry Bishop**

The Duchess of Britanny is taking Prince Arthur to safety in the North, and Robin is asked to provide an escort. The outlaw leader offers to lead the entourage himself - and finds some surprising adventures along the way.

Little John: **Archie Duncan**
Wilfred: **Michael Ripper**
Sir Hartley: **David Davies**
Will Scarlet: **Paul Eddington**
Duchess Constance: **Patricia Marmont**
Prince Arthur: **Jonathan Bailey**
Clerk: **Max Faulkner**
Joan: **Simone Lovell**
Serving Girl: **Susan Travers**
Sir Nedrick: **Arthur Lawrence**

A Bushel of Apples
w **Jan Read**
d **Terry Bishop**

When he hears that Sir Watkyn's men-at-arms have extorted livestock and wages from the peasants, Friar Tuck turns to the church for help. Sir Watkyn has denied the charge, but Father Ignatius - abetted by Robin - has a solution to the problem.

Friar Tuck: **Alexander Gauge**
Maid Marian: **Patricia Driscoll**
Deputy Sheriff: **John Arnatt**
Little John: **Archie Duncan**
Will Scarlett: **Paul Eddington**
Sir Watkyn: **Harry H. Corbett**
Father Ignatius: **Philip Latham**
First Man-at-Arms: **Ivor Collin**
Peasant: **Paddy Joyce**

The Pharaoh Stones
w **William Templeton**
d **Gordon Parry**

Little John is given three dice-stones by a pedlar, which he claims once belonged to the Ancient Egyptian Kings. Truth or not, the stones bring more than their fair share of trouble to the Greenwood.

Maid Marian: **Patricia Driscoll**
Little John: **Archie Duncan**
Will Scarlett: **Paul Eddington**
Derwent: **Victor Woolf**
Edgar: **John Forrest**
Pedlar: **Carl Bernard**
Tax Collector: **Donald Bissett**
Lieutenant: **Morton Lowry**

Double Trouble
w **Louis Marks**
d **Terry Bishop**

Edgar, Friar Tuck's identical twin brother, arrives in Nottingham and brings mayhem in his wake: he has agreed to lead the Sheriff to the outlaw camp - little realising that by doing so, he places his brother's life in peril.

Friar Tuck: **Alexander Gauge**
Edgar: **Alexander Gauge**
Maid Marian: **Patricia Driscoll**
Deputy Sheriff: **John Arnatt**
Little John: **Archie Duncan**
Will Scarlett: **Paul Eddington**
Bishop: **Charles Lloyd Pack**
Lieutenant: **Morton Lowry**
Old Man: **Edmund Warwick**

The Champion
w **Leon Griffiths**
d **Gordon Parry**

When Marian tells Robin that, following the death of her father, her estate is to be taken over by Sir Quentin, Robin has other ideas - particularly when he suspects the Sheriff is behind the scheme.

Friar Tuck: **Alexander Gauge**
Maid Marian: **Patricia Driscoll**
Deputy Sheriff: **John Arnatt**
Sir Perry: **Jack Allen**
Little John: **Archie Duncan**
Will Scarlett: **Paul Eddington**
Sir Guy: **John Horsley**
Surveyor: **Keith Rawlings**

Trapped
w **Wilton Schiller**
d **Terry Bishop**

Sir Marmot, a Norman knight, seizes travellers and then places them on trial on trumped up charges. If they refuse to pay the fine he imposes, he sentences them to work on his estate. One of his victims is Little John - which proves to be a very costly mistake!

Friar Tuck: **Alexander Gauge**
Maid Marian: **Patricia Driscoll**
Deputy Sheriff : **John Arnatt**
Little John: **Archie Duncan**
Sir Marmot: **Laurence Hardy**
William: **Maurice Kaufman**
Peter: **Ronald Hines**

The Edge and the Point
w **Raymond Bowers**
d **Gordon Parry**

Former Crusader Boland decides to make some money by capturing the outlaw leader, and demanding payment from the Sheriff. He soon discovers that you must first capture your prey - and Robin has ideas of his own.

Friar Tuck: **Alexander Gauge**
Maid Marian: **Patricia Driscoll**
Deputy Sheriff: **John Arnatt**
Boland: **Michael Gough**
Little John: **Archie Duncan**
Will Scarlett: **Paul Eddington**
Lieutenant: **Morton Lowry**
Sergeant: **Terry Yorke**

The Truce
w **Leon Griffiths**
d **Gordon Parry**

The Deputy Sheriff, usually hostile to Robin Hood, sends a message to Sherwood declaring a truce. Out of necessity, he requires the outlaws' help. Robin, suspecting treachery, formulates a plan of campaign.

Friar Tuck: **Alexander Gauge**
Maid Marian: **Patricia Driscoll**
Deputy Sheriff: **John Arnatt**
Little John: **Archie Duncan**
Will Scarlett: **Paul Eddington**
Lord Repton: **Richard Caldicot**
Crispin: **Derek Tansley**
Lieutenant: **Morton Lowry**
Marshall: **Kevin Stoney**

✍ Three colorised 'features' were issued in the nineties, each being a compilation of episodes from the series: *Robin Hood's Greatest Adventure*, *Quest for the Crown* and unknown.

The Adventures of Robin Hood:

Season one:
Producer: **Sidney Cole**
Executive Producer: **Hannah Weinstein**
Associate Producer: **Sidney Cole, Thelma Connell**
Music by: **Edwin Astley, Albert Elms**
Production Supervisor: **George Mills**
Script Supervisor: **Albert G. Ruben**
Assistant Director: **Christopher Noble**
Make-up: **Walter Schneiderman**
Hairdresser: **Eileen Bates, Bill Griffiths**
Wardrobe: **Brenda Gardner**
A Sapphire Films Production for the Incorporated Television Programme Co.
Filmed at Nettlefold Studios.
39 monochrome 30 minute episodes
1955

Season two:
Producer: **Sidney Cole**
Executive Producer: **Hannah Weinstein**
Associate Producer: **Thelma Connell**
Music by: **Edwin Astley, Albert Elms**
Production Supervisor: **Harold Buck**
Script Supervisor: **Albert G. Ruben**
Make-up: **Walter Schneiderman**
A Weinstein Production for Sapphire Films, for the Incorporated Television Programme Co.
Filmed at Nettlefold Studios.
39 monochrome 30 minute episodes
1955-56

Season three:
Producer: **Sidney Cole**
Associate Producer: **Thelma Connell**
Music by: **Albert Elms**
Production Supervisor: **Harold Buck**
Script Supervisor: **Albert G. Ruben**
Make-up: **Walter Schneiderman**
A Hannah Weinstein Production for Sapphire Films, for the Incorporated Television Programme Co.
Filmed at Walton Studios.
39 monochrome 30 minute episodes
1957-58

Season four:
Producer: **Sidney Cole**
Music by: **Albert Elms**
Production Supervisor: **Harold Buck**
Script Supervisor: **Raymond Bowers**
Make-up: **Walter Schneiderman**
A Hannah Fisher Production for Sapphire Films, for the Incorporated Television Programme Co.
Filmed at Walton Studios.
26 monochrome 30 minute episodes
1959

The Adventures of Sir Lancelot

The classic deeds of King Arthur and his Knights of the Round Table, as depicted by the adventures of Sir Lancelot du Lac, a chivalrous, devil-may-care knight and the brightest star at King Arthur's Court. The stories concerned themselves mainly with Lancelot's calling as the Queen Champion to stave off threats to the throne by marauding invaders. Though seen, Excalibur, Arthur's legendary sword, was almost entirely forgotten. Not so the powers of Merlin, the court magician, whose 'spells' and 'potions' were treated with reverence - by all save the youngest member of the court.

An animated and thoroughly enjoyable - though sometimes unintentionally amusing - version of the Camelot legend. The series is best remembered for its spirited action sequences and the performance of its star, William Russell.

'Now listen to my story, listen while I sing.
Of days of old in England when Arthur was the King.
Of Merlin the Magician and Guinevere the Queen and
Lancelot, the bravest knight the world has ever seen.
In days of old, when knights were bold, the story's told of
Lancelot.
He rode the wilds of England, adventures for to seek. To
rescue maidens in distress and help the poor and weak.
If anyone oppressed you, he'd be your champion; he
fought a million battles and never lost a one.
In days of old, when knights were bold, the story's told of
Lancelot.'

Regular cast:
Sir Lancelot: **William Russell**
King Arthur: **Bruce Seton** [episodes 1 to 3 only]
King Arthur: **Ronald Leigh-Hunt**
Queen Guinevere: **Jane Hylton**
Merlin: **Cyril Smith**
Brian: **Robert Scroggins**

The Knight with the Red Plume
w **Leighton Reynolds**
d **Ralph Smart**

Riding to Camelot to join King Arthur's knights, Sir Lancelot du Lac is challenged by three armed knights. Having defeated them, he proceeds to Camelot where, after proving his worth in a duel, he is appointed Champion to Queen Guinevere.

Queen Guinevere: **Jane Hylton**
King Arthur: **Bruce Seton**
Merlin: **Cyril Smith**
Sir Gawaine: **Andrew Crawford**
Leonides: **Peter Bennett**
Sir Kay: **Brian Worth**
Sir Lionel: **Paul Hansard**
Sir Christopher: **Edwin Richfield**

The Ferocious Fathers
w **Leighton Reynolds**
d **Ralph Smart**

His master's castle under siege, Brian, a kitchen boy for Sir Ugan, races to Camelot to seek King Arthur's help. Sir Lancelot is given the task of helping Sir Ugan, and in return, the knight allows young Brian to serve as Lancelot's squire.

Brian: **Robert Scroggins** [intro]
Sir Melias: **George Woodbridge**
Sir Urgan: **Ballard Berkley**

Helen: **Norah Gorsen**
Enid: **Pauline Olsen**
Clodion: **David Morrell**
Andred: **Derry Nesbitt**
Rolf: **Frederick Treves**

The Queen's Knight
w **Leighton Reynolds**
d **Ralph Smart**

When Queen Guinevere is abducted by King Arthur's cousin, Sir Modred, who wishes to exchange her for Arthur's kingdom of Northumbria. Disguised as a cartier, Lancelot endeavours to rescue her - but is captured and thrown into a dungeon.

Queen Guinevere: **Jane Hylton**
King Arthur: **Bruce Seton**
Merlin: **Cyril Smith**
Sir Modred: **Brian Worth**
King Pell: **John Dearth**
Leonides: **Peter Bennett**
Brian: **Robert Scroggins**
Sir Cebus: **Shaun O'Riordan**
Sir Tor: **Edwin Richfield**
Sir Gawaine: **Andrew Crawford**
Lionel: **Paul Hansard**
Isobel: **Caroline Denzil**

The Outcast
w **Leslie Poynton**
d **Bernard Knowles**

When Brian takes up training to become a knight, the other boys show resentment. One of them, Osbert, accuses Brian of stealing the Queen's ring, and it takes the combined efforts of Sir Lancelot and Mary, the Queen's ward, to clear his name.

King Arthur: **Ronald Leigh-Hunt**
Queen Guinevere: **Jane Hylton**
Brian: **Robert Scroggins**
Merlin: **Cyril Smith**
Sir Glavin: **Patrick McGoohan**
Sir Kay: **David Morrell**
Mary: **Simone McQueen**
Hugh: **Douglas Argent**
Osbert: **Paul Williamson**
Will: **John Dale**
First Maiden: **Sally Deane**
Clerk: **Frederick Treves**
First Boy: **Anthony Toller**
Guard: **Derry Nesbitt**

Winged Victory
w **John Ridgely**
d **Arthur Crabtree**

Prince Boudwin's castle is besieged by King Mark and his men. Lancelot, leading a party of King Arthur's knights to repel the invaders, is captured. The wily old Merlin has a rescue plan - involving his pet pigeons!

King Mark: **Nigel Green**
Prince Boudwin: **Douglas Argent**
Queen Isolt: **Mary Laura Wood**
Brian: **Robert Scroggins**
Merlin: **Cyril Smith**
King Arthur: **Ronald Leigh-Hunt**
Emissary: **Garry Thorne**
Sir Tristran: **Derry Nesbitt**
Sir Claud: **David Morrell**
Torture Master: **John Gale**

Sir Bliant
w **John Ridgely**
d **Bernard Knowles**

When Sir Bliant's three sons kidnap the three daughters of their neighbour, Sir Rolf, the distressed knight seeks King Arthur's help. Merlin's magic is called for - Sir Bliant receives 'double' retribution from 'himself'.

King Arthur: **Ronald Leigh-Hunt**
Brian: **Robert Scroggins**
Katherine: **Gillian Owen**
Bart: **Nigel Green**
Breuse: **Derry Nesbitt**
Bartelot: **David Morell**
Sir Bliant: **William Russell**
Merlin: **Cyril Smith**
Old Retainer: **Garry Thorne**
Foppish Man: **Douglas Argent**
Sir Rolf: **Frederick Treves**
First Sister: **Evelyn Cordeau**
Second Sister: **Yvonne Warren**

The Magic Sword
w **Leighton Reynolds**
d **Arthur Crabtree**

When he announces that Sir Lancelot's sword has magical powers, Merlin courts trouble of his own making. Sir Bernard puts the magician's claim to test - with surprising results for both Lancelot and Merlin.

Merlin: **Cyril Smith**
Brian: **Robert Scroggins**
Sir Bernard: **Dan Cunningham**
Lydia: **Nora Cheyney**
Leonides: **George Woodbridge**
Sir Kay: **David Morrell**
Sir Hugh: **Douglas Argent**
Dion: **Derry Nesbitt**
Guard: **Garry Thorne**
First Peasant: **Frederick Treves**
Second Peasant: **Nigel Green**
First Knight: **John Gale**
Second Knight: **Paul Williamson**
Third Knight: **Michael Scott**
Damas: **David King**

Lancelot's Banishment
w **Peggy Philips**
d **Anthony Squire**

Learning that King Marhaus, an ambitious foreigner, plans to kill King Arthur during a 'friendly' jousting tournament, Lancelot informs his sovereign. Unwilling to accept his friend's guilt, the King banishes Lancelot from his court!

Lady Angela: **Zena Walker**
King Marhaus: **Derek Aylward**
King Arthur: **Ronald Leigh-Hunt**
Queen Guinevere: **Jane Hylton**
Merlin: **Cyril Smith**
Firth: **Derry Nesbitt**
Harpist: **Robert Crewdson**
Sir Grint: **Nigel Green**
First Guard: **Frederick Treves**
Second Guard: **John Gale**

Roman Wall
w **Harold Kent**
d **Arthur Crabtree**

At the invitation of King Boltan, who tells them that his daughter, Iolta, has been abducted by ghostly warriors

dressed in Roman attire, Lancelot and Brian scale a high boundary wall and discovers a sign which says 'Rome - 1,200 miles'!

Brian: **Robert Scroggins**
Trullus: **Gerald Cross**
Probus: **Nigel Green**
Gogus: **Derry Nesbitt**
Boltan: **David Morrell**
Lady Iolta: **Yvonne Warren**
Amadeus: **John Gale**

Caledon
w **Leighton Reynolds**
d **Terry Bishop**

On a lone mission of friendship to a distant Northern ally, and carrying a priceless gift from his King, Sir Lancelot is attacked, robbed and left for dead by brigands. Help arrives in a strange form - a wonder horse named Caledon.

King Arthur: **Ronald Leigh-Hunt**
Merlin: **Cyril Smith**
Queen Guinevere: **Jane Hylton**
Jaggyd: **George Murcell**
Farmer: **Nigel Green**
Sir Kay: **David Morrell**
Sir Lionel: **Paul Williamson**
Farmer's Son: **John Gale**
First Brigante: **Derry Nesbitt**
Guard: **Garry Thorne**

Shepherd's War
w **Leslie Poynton**
d **Bernard Knowles**

Hearing that friendly shepherds are under attack by plundering knights, Sir Lancelot volunteers to help. But first he must teach the shepherds the importance of self-defence - a task complicated by their loathing of combat.

King Arthur: **Ronald Leigh-Hunt**
Merlin: **Cyril Smith**
Elsa: **Jennifer Jayne**
Chad: **Derry Nesbitt**
Aidan: **Meadows White**
Lloyd: **George Merritt**
Matt: **Edmund Warwick**
Petroc: **James Grout**
Colman: **Frederick Treves**
Mador: **Douglas Argent**
Sir Lionel: **Paul Williamson**
Sir Christopher: **John Gale**
Sir Kay: **David Morrell**

The Pirates
w **Leighton Reynolds**
d **Bernard Knowles**

When a pirate ship beaches near Camelot and King Arthur receives news that the pirates intend to rob the tomb of his father, Uther Pendragon, Sir Lancelot and his knights are faced with the task of guarding Pendragon's vault.

Llian: **Noel Purcell**
Queen Guinevere: **Jane Hylton**
King Arthur: **Ronald Leigh-Hunt**
Merlin: **Cyril Smith**
Sir Kay: **David Morrell**
Mac Kevin: **Derry Nesbitt**
Villager: **Frederick Treves**
Sir Lionel: **Paul Williamson**
Old Man: **Douglas Argent**
Man-at-Arms: **Garry Thorne**
Captain: **John Gale**

The Black Castle
w **Peggy Phillips**
d **Anthony Squire**

Torwald, a knight, holds Lord Trebizond to ransom in the Black Castle. Lorraine, Trebizond's daughter, rides to Camelot to seek the help of her betrothed, Sir Cedric. Meanwhile, Lancelot and Brian find themselves outside Torwald's castle.

Queen Guinevere: **Jane Hylton**
King Arthur: **Ronald Leigh-Hunt**
Torwald: **Peter Coke**
Cedric: **Michael Blakemore**
Lorraine: **Hermene French**
Robert: **Paul Williamson**
Brian: **Robert Scroggins**
Magnus: **Derry Nesbitt**
Welshman: **Kenneth Luckman**
Peasant: **John Gale**
Porter: **David Morrell**
Sir Trebizond: **Douglas Argent**
Bearer: **Frederick Treves**

Double Identity
w **Harold Kent**
d **Laurence Huntington**

Sir Richard, on his way to Taunton to be married, is kidnapped by his cousin, Alfred, who takes his place. Attending the wedding ceremony, Sir Lancelot sees through Alfred's disguise and lays a plot to unmask the impostor.

King Arthur: **Ronald Leigh-Hunt**
Merlin: **Cyril Smith**
Brian: **Robert Scroggins**
Richard/ Alfred: **Howard Pays**
John: **John Bailey**
Lady Margaret: **Diana Fairfax**
Gloria: **June Sylvaine**
Cedric: **Reginald Hearne**
Priest: **Edward Judd**
Lord Mayor: **Philip Lennard**
Peasant: **Eric Corrie**

The Bridge
w **Peter Key**
d **Peter Maxwell**

By an ancient treaty, the bridge connecting the village of Pontifax with the kingdom of King Marhaus must be kept free of taxes. When Arthur's enemy threatens to close the bridge, the King sends two of his knights to help the villagers.

King Arthur: **Ronald Leigh-Hunt**
Queen Guinevere: **Jane Hylton**
Brian: **Robert Scroggins**
Angela: **Zena Walker**
King Marhaus: **Derek Aylward**
Caradoc: **Jack May**
Priest: **Eric Corrie**
Sir Grint: **Edward Judd**
Sir Eustace: **Reginald Herne**
Peasant: **Max Faulkner**
Traveller: **Noel Davis**

The Witch's Brew
w **Peggy Phillips**
d **Terry Bishop**

News reaches Camelot that King Rolf has imprisoned his own son for treason. Disturbed by such unlikely behaviour from his peace-loving ally, King Arthur sends Sir Lancelot to investigate.

Merlin: **Cyril Smith**
King Arthur: **Ronald Leigh-Hunt**
Brian: **Robert Scroggins**
Eunice: **Maxine Audley**
King Rolf: **Leonard Sachs**
Damien: **Graham Stewart**
Hedrick: **Reginald Hearne**
Alan: **Brian Roper**
Soldier: **Edward Judd**
Jailer: **Eric Corrie**

Ruby of Radnor
w **Hamish Hamilton Burns**
d **Laurence Huntington**

King Arthur has a dilemma. Despite providing extra guards, the crown jewels have been stolen from Radnor Abbey. Lancelot and his knights must recover them within 24 hours - but they must first discover who stole them!

King Arthur: **Ronald Leigh-Hunt**
Guinevere: **Jane Hylton**
Merlin: **Cyril Smith**
Brian: **Robert Scroggins**
Sir Kay: **David Morrell**
Everard: **Colin Tapley**
Garth: **Edward Judd**
Robert: **Eric Corrie**
Hugo: **Reginald Hearne**
Peasant: **Harold Goodwin**
Jailer: **Desmond Raynor**

The Lesser Breed
w **Peggy Phillips**
d **Terry Bishop**

When Lancelot and Brian set forth to dispel the rumour of a three-headed sea monster terrorising the district, they find more than they at first bargained for: a stunningly beautiful girl, and a very dangerous situation.

King Arthur: **Ronald Leigh-Hunt**
Merlin: **Cyril Smith**
Brian: **Robert Scroggins**
Sella: **Ann Stephens**
Eck: **Gerald Heinz**
Horg: **Fred Goddard**
Sir Kay: **David Morrell**
Fisherman: **Wilfred Brambell**
Overseer: **Eric Corrie**
Guard: **Brian Moorehead**
Auctioneer: **Edward Judd**

The Magic Book
w **Leslie Poynton**
d **Terry Bishop**

Fearing that the Danes will attack Tyning Abbey and steal valuable documents, King Arthur sends Lancelot and Merlin to defend the Abbot. But how can two stave off an attack by many? Merlin provides the answer.

King Arthur: **Ronald Leigh-Hunt**
Merlin: **Cyril Smith**
Brian: **Robert Scroggins**
Sir Kay: **David Morrell**
Telmah: **Norman Mitchell**
Father Till: **Eddie Malin**
Father Telford: **John Cazabon**
Sir Paddagore: **Douglas Argent**
Sir Exeter: **Frederick Treves**
Cook-monk: **Derry Nesbitt**

Knight Errant
w **Peggy Phillips** and **Selwyn Jepson**
d **Bernard Knowles**

Helen and Bragwaine have inherited their father's kingdom, but their wicked guardian, Kafan, is determined to marry Helen off to an aged King. When she refuses to agree to his request, Sir Lancelot and Sir Kay are sent to her aid.

King Arthur: **Ronald Leigh-Hunt**
Sir Kay: **David Morrell**
Merlin: **Cyril Smith**
Kafan: **Julian Somers**
Lady Helen: **Margaret Anderson**
Lady Bragwaine: **Hazel Penwarden**
Sir Christopher: **John Gale**
Sir Lionel: **Paul Williamson**
Jailer: **Nigel Green**
First Knight: **Douglas Argent**
Handmaiden: **Maureen Davis**
Sir Oringle: **Derry Nesbitt**

The Theft of Excalibur
w **Hamish Hamilton Burns** and **Peggy Philips**
d **Bernard Knowles**

A knight is held for ransom. The price for his release - King Arthur's sword, Excalibur. With Merlin's help, Lancelot and Brian engage the kidnappers in battle in order to retrieve the sword before it can be used for misdeeds.

Barney Brandygore: **Alfie Bass**
King Arthur: **Ronald Leigh-Hunt**
Guinevere: **Jane Hylton**
Brian: **Robert Scroggins**
Merlin: **Cyril Smith**
Michael: **David Bough**
Robert: **John Charlesworth**
Sir Kay: **David Morrell**
Tristram: **Derry Nesbitt**
First Thief: **Frederick Treves**
Second Thief: **Nigel Green**
Squire: **Garry Thorne**

The Mortaise Fair
w **Leslie Poynton**
d **Laurence Huntington**

The Madras Pearl, given to Queen Guinevere by the Rajah of Kaipur, is lost during a fire. Aware that its loss could jeopardise relations between King Arthur and his ally, Lancelot swears to find it.

Guinevere: **Jane Hylton**
Brian: **Robert Scroggins**
Hassim: **Martin Benson**
Zuleika: **Chin Yu**
Baron Mortaise: **William Franklyn**
Osbert: **Eric Corrie**
Ronk: **Edward Judd**
Man-at-Arms: **Terence Yorke**
Merchant: **Robert Robinson**
Rajah: **Richard Hearne**
Chinese Dice Player: **Paul Way**

Maid of Somerset
w **Peggy Phillips**
d **Peter Maxwell**

When the Maid of Somerset arrives at Camelot seeking King Arthur's help against an oppressor of her village, the King nominates Sir Lancelot to handle the affair. During his journey to Somerset, the knight and his ward are attacked and taken prisoner.

Merlin: **Cyril Smith**
Brian: **Robert Scroggins**
Ellen: **Patricia Kneale**
John: **Brown Derby**
King Meliot: **Duncan Lewis**
Richard: **Barry Fennell**
James: **Edward Judd**
Paul: **Eddie Malin**
The Saracen: **Eric Corrie**
Chamberlain: **Reginald Hearne**

Sir Crustabread
w **Leslie Poynton**
d **Laurence Huntingdon**

A visit from the Lady Lynette plunges Sir Lancelot into a danger-fraught mission. Disguised as a disreputable baker, he must save her daughter from a bigamous marriage to Baron Braynor.

King Arthur: **Ronald Leigh-Hunt**
Merlin: **Cyril Smith**
Sir Kay: **David Morrell**
Lynette: **Virginia Vernon**
Baron Braynor: **Hector Ross**
Lady Eleanor: **Roma Denville**
Sir Gringamore: **Alan Edwards**
Sir Gawaine: **Brian Nissen**
Sir Christopher: **Frederick Jaeger**
Captain: **Reginald Hearne**
Baker: **Sidney Vivian**

The Ugly Duckling
w **Leslie Poynton**
d **George More O'Ferrall**

Sir Lancelot and Brian try to help a young girl who has put her life in danger to attract attention to herself. Having been rejected by her suitors, they find the girl suspicious of their motives - until Brian has a bright idea.

King Arthur: **Ronald Leigh-Hunt**
Merlin: **Cyril Smith**
Sybil: **Carol Marsh**
Amora: **Jeannette Hutchinson**
Sir Egbert: **Hector Ross**
Lady Lamorak: **Avice Landone**
Gault: **Ian Whittaker**
Sir Kay: **David Morrell**
Sir Christopher: **Edward Judd**

The Prince of Limerick
w **Leslie Poynton**
d **Laurence Huntington**

In Ireland, on a mission for their king, Lancelot and Brian find that the Emerald Isle holds a special fascination of its own - particularly if you're a friend of the Prince of Limerick.

Brian: **Robert Scroggins**
Prince of Limerick: **Jerome Willis**
Baron Wicklaw: **Thomas R. Duggan**
Princess Kathleen: **Lynne Furlong**
King Anguish: **Tony Quinn**

The Lady Lilith
w **Leslie Poynton**
d **Laurence Huntington**

When Sir Liones's claim to an inheritance is disputed by the Lady Lilith, King Arthur must find a way to end the dispute without offending either party. Requested to help, Sir Lancelot offers a novel solution to the King's delemma.

King Arthur: **Ronald Leigh-Hunt**
Merlin: **Cyril Smith**
Brian: **Robert Scroggins**
Lady Lilith: **Shirley Cooklin**
Sir Liones: **Richard Leech**
Abel: **Edward Judd**
Sir Kay: **David Morrell**
Seneschal: **Eric Corrie**
Blacksmith: **Reginald Hearne**

Knights' Choice
w **Peggy Phillips**
d **Peter Maxwell**

There is a vacant seat at the Round Table, and King Arthur decides to hold a contest to find the bravest knight in England. Morgana le Fay enters - but she's a woman ...isn't she?

King Arthur: **Ronald Leigh-Hunt**
Merlin: **Cyril Smith**
Morgana le Fay: **Alison Leggatt**
Rupert: **Robert Hardy**
Balin: **Derek Waring**
Sir Kay: **David Morrell**
Sir Julian: **Reginald Hearne**
Sentry: **Edward Judd**
Herald: **Eric Corrie**

The Missing Princess
w **Leslie Poynton**
d **Desmond Davis**

What has happened to Princess Anne? That's the dilemma facing Sir Lancelot when King Arthur pleads with him to find her - but sometimes people have no wish to be found, and who should question their motives?

King Arthur: **Ronald Leigh-Hunt**
Anne: **Mary Steele**
Marta: **Linda Gray**
Athelred: **John Horsley**
Evanston: **Reginald Hearne**
Helga: **Mary Manson**
First Woman: **Catherine Ellison**
Second Woman: **Jeannette Hutchinson**

Thieves
w **Hamish Hamilton Burns**
d **Bernard Knowles**

Attempting to show King Arthur how difficult it is to get honest employment once a man has been branded a thief, Lancelot persuades the King to join him in the streets. Disguised as robbers, they enter a den of thieves - and find trouble in abundance!

King Arthur: **Ronald Leigh-Hunt**
Merlin: **Cyril Smith**
Norrin: **Jack Melford**
Lord Vanton: **Colin Tapley**
Sir Kay: **David Morrell**
Happy Thief: **Peter Assinder**
Wooden Leg: **Sidney Head**
Leader of the King's men: **Edward Judd**
Piggott: **John Dearth**
Woman: **Anarose Carrigan**
Bartender: **Noel Davis**

The Adventures of Sir Lancelot:

Producers: **Sidney Cole, Dallas Bower** and **Bernard Knowles**
Executive Producer: **Hannah Weinstein**
Music by: **Edwin Astley** and **Albert Elms**
Production Supervisor: **George Mills**
Script Supervision: **Albert G. Ruben**
Production Manager: **E.S. Laurie**
Assistant Director: **Peter Weingreen**
Make-up Supervision: **Walter Schneiderman**
Hairdresser: **Betty Sherriff**
Wardrobe: **Brenda Gardner**

A Weinstein Production for Sapphire Films Limited., for the Independent Television Programme Co. Ltd.

Filmed at Nettlefold Studios, Walton-on-Thames

30 b/w and colour 30-minute episodes
1957

The Baron

Inspired by the character created by John Creasey [writing as Anthony Morton], whose novels described the Baron as a gentleman jewel thief until love changed his ways and he became a reformed character and Scotland Yard confidant, readers of the books would have had a tough time recognising the hero of this ITC-produced series as Creasey's loveable rogue. In the hands of producer Monty Berman, the character was translated into that of London-based American antiques dealer, John Mannering, a trouble shooter for the antiques industry. Better known as the Baron - a nickname he's acquired because the cattle on his American ranch sported the Baron brand - the stories depicted his investigations into crimes associated with the art world and his attempts to recover stolen art treasures, or expose the perpetrators behind a cleverly-executed art swindle.

Aware that such material had limited dramatic appeal, Berman introduced several other new factors into the proceedings by making Mannering, a man with exclusive antiques shops in London, Paris and Washington, a character who was not above using these establishments as a front for undercover activities. On several occasions during the series, the hero found himself working for the head concho of British Intelligence - John Templeton-Green. To assist Mannering during these adventures, Berman introduced another character you'd be hard-pressed to find on the printed page - Cordelia Winfield, a bubbly, attractive agent working for the Special Branch Diplomatic Service. She swiftly became Mannering's full-time assistant, and appeared in virtually every story. Also featured in several adventures was David Marlowe, the Baron's business associate.

When likened to Simon Templar [aka The Saint] - the Baron's nearest contemporary - the series fared favourably in the action department [Mannering packed a mean punch], but it suffered on occassion from pedestrian scripts. It nevertheless proved popular with the public, and though the series was originally scheduled for 26 episodes, 30 were produced.

Regular cast:
The Baron: **Steve Forrest**
Cordelia: **Sue Lloyd**
Templeton-Green: **Colin Gordon**
David Marlowe: **Paul Ferris**

Diplomatic Immunity
w **Dennis Spooner**
d **Leslie Norman**

Victim of a series of large-scale art robberies, the Baron and Cordelia go behind the Iron Curtain to recover the stolen loot. But they have reckoned without international diplomacy which, as they discover, can present unseen problems.

David Marlowe: **Paul Ferris** [intro]
Cordelia: **Sue Lloyd** [intro]
Templeton-Green: **Colin Gordon** [intro]
Eva Dumel: **Dora Reisser**
Georges Sforza: **Frank Gatliff**
Laslo Polk: **Robert Crewdson**
Kimitz: **Michael Wolf**
Swann: **Jolyon Booth**
Anna Lobovitch: **Claire Davenport**
Latticia: **Maggie Wright**
Gill: **Patrick Durkin**
Lovegrove: **Frederick Abbott**

Red Horse, Red Rider
w **Terry Nation**
d **John Moxey**

The Baron puts his life and reputation on the line to help a patriot sell a million-dollar antique to raise funds for a rebel cause. When intrigue and murder enter the picture, Mannering must plan his next move with caution.

Savannah: **Jane Merrow**
Miros: **Frank Wolff**
David Marlowe: **Paul Ferris**
Salan: **John Bennett**
Shamir: **Edward Brayshaw**
Olmira: **Harold Goldblatt**
Alifa: **Sandor Eles**
Arko: **John Bryans**
Verdon: **Bruce Montague**
Ruth Parke: **Jane Blackburn**

The Persuaders
w **Dennis Spooner**
d **Leslie Norman**

In an effort to persuade the Baron to act as their front man in a major art swindle, a gang of ruthless art thieves kidnap his assistant, David Marlowe, and hold him hostage under the threat of his life.

Roddy Harrington: **James Villiers**
Verity Montand: **Georgina Ward**
Templeton-Green: **Colin Gordon**
Upton: **Ronald Hines**
Hollins: **Charles Houston**
David Marlowe: **Paul Ferris**
Sara: **Virginia Stride**
Sir Robert Ellacott: **Martin Wyldeck**
Markham: **Reginald Jessup**
The Scientist: **Derek Benfield**
Scott: **Zeph Gladstone**
Lowery: **Tony Thawnton**
Ann: **Jennifer Clulow**

Epitath for a Hero
w **Terry Nation**
d **John Moxey**

Though it means betraying the trust of a man who saved his life, the Baron takes part in a well-organised jewel robbery. But as the thieves soon discover, even the best-laid plans are prone to Murphy's Law.

Cordelia: **Sue Lloyd**
Helga Sorenson: **Patricia Haines**
Jim Carey: **Paul Maxwell**
Templeton-Green: **Colin Gordon**
Owen Davies: **Artro Morris**
Charlie: **Nosher Powell**
David Marlowe: **Paul Ferris**
The Gaunt Man: **William Lyon Brown**

Something for a Rainy Day
w **Terry Nation**
d **Cyril Frankel**

The Baron has to ask himself: is a jewel thief entitled to the rewards of his crime after he has served a long prison sentence? The insurance company says no, but Mannering has other ideas.

Cordelia: **Sue Lloyd**
Max Holder: **Patrick Allen**
Mark Seldon: **Michael Gwynn**
Ann Seldon: **Ann Lynn**
Charlotte Russell: **Lois Maxwell**
Lucas: **Derek Newark**
The French Truck Driver: **Julian Sherrier**
Benson: **Billy Milton**

Enemy of the State
w **Dennis Spooner**
d **Jeremy Summers**

When Cordelia, standing in for him at an appointment behind the Iron Curtain, is arrested by State Security, Mannering instigates a daring plan to obtain her release - a plan which involves placing himself in the firing line.

Jadwiga Szoblik: **Anton Diffring**
Colonel Bucholz: **Joseph Furst**
Cordelia: **Sue Lloyd**
Templeton-Green: **Colin Gordon**
Spinoza: **John Abineri**
Albrecht: **Michael Wolf**
Ernst Rishner: **Brian Phelan**
Ronald Bell: **Richard Carpenter**
Colin Bradfield: **Gary Watson**
Claire Bradfield: **Veronica Strong**
Heinman: **Terence Lodge**

And Suddenly You're Dead
w **Terry Nation** and **Dennis Spooner**
d **Cyril Frankel**

The Baron and Cordelia find themselves faced with a terrifying enemy - a group of people will stop at nothing to achieve their aims ... including the threat to open up new horrors in germ warfare!

Cordelia: **Sue Lloyd**
Ingar Sorenson: **Kay Walsh**
Larry Holmes: **Alan MacNaughton**
Reiner: **Vladek Sheybal**
Kruger: **Bernard Kay**
Bishop: **John Collin**
Insp. Strauss: **George Pravda**
Peter Franklin: **Jerry Stovin**
Neuman: **Ernst Walder**
Garage Attendant: **Conrad Monk**

The Legions of Ammak
w **Michael Cramoy**
d **John Moxey**

When the Baron transacts a deal for an eccentric millionaire who wishes to purchase a fabulous treasure from a foreign king, he uncovers a fantastic plot to swindle a foreign President of his country's art treasures.

King Ibrahim/Roland Noyes: **Peter Wyngarde**
Ofeg Cossackian: **George Murcell**
David Marlowe: **Paul Ferris**
Colonel Ahmed Bey: **Michael Godfrey**
Mira Cossackian: **Isa Miranda**
Sirocco: **Valli Newby**
Dinny Brand: **Kenneth Colley**
Katherine Vale: **Kerry Marsh**
Hargraves: **Arthur Hewlett**
Bank Cashier: **John Barcroft**
Betty Francis: **Angela Lovell**
Abdullah: **Jim Bolton**

Samurai West
w **Brian Degas**
d **John Moxey**

When he buys a valuable Samurai sword from a Japanese dealer, the Baron incurs the wrath of several people seeking to bring the Japanese gentleman - a former commandant of a prisoner-of-war camp - to justice.

Asano: **Lee Montague**
Norman Sterling: **Raymond Huntley**

David Marlowe: **Paul Ferris**
Samantha: **Jeanne Roland**
Yasugi: **Larry Taylor**
Tom Sterling: **Colin Jeavons**
Miss Chanter: **Hal Dyer**
Nurse: **Sidonie Bond**
Simpson: **Royston Tickner**
Det. Sgt: **Clifford Earl**

Masquerade [Part 1 of 2: Masquerade]
w **Terry Nation** and **Dennis Spooner**
d **Cyril Frankel**

An audacious scheme to murder the Baron and replace him with a double, helped by plastic surgery, places the lives of Mannering and Cordelia in great danger. Their dilemma is increased when Mannering 'disappears', and Cordelia sees double.

Cordelia: **Sue Lloyd**
Morgan Travis: **Bernard Lee**
Selina Travis: **Yvonne Furneaux**
Revell: **John Carson**
Fox-Stuart: **Kenneth J. Warren**
Anstruther: **Geoffrey Palmer**
Ministry Clerk: **John Barrett**
Receptionist: **Lisa Thomas**
Chauffeur [Reynolds]: **Peter Thomas**

Masquerade [Part 2 of 2: The Killing]
w **Terry Nation** and **Dennis Spooner**
d **Cyril Frankel**

The Baron faces the greatest test of his career - how to foil a plan to steal the Crown Jewels, and lay the blame at Mannering's door? His life depends on his ability to impersonate himself.

Cordelia: **Sue Lloyd**
Morgan Travis: **Bernard Lee**
Selina Travis: **Yvonne Furneaux**
Revell: **John Carson**
Frank Martin: **Frank Wolff**
Fox-Stuart: **Kenneth J. Warren**
Anstruther: **Geoffrey Palmer**
Castle: **John Gabriel**
Brooks: **John Gill**
Reynolds: **Peter Thomas**
Security Guard: **Anthony Blackshaw**

The Maze
w **Tony O'Grady** [aka **Brian Clemens**]
d **Jeremy Summers**

The Baron 'loses' 24 hours of his life. Tracing back the path of events for that missing day brings him into contact with a deadly enemy - and leads him through a maze of remarkable events.

Cordelia: **Sue Lloyd**
Gaydon: **Alan MacNaughton**
Walter Farrow: **Don Borisenko**
Det. Insp. Walsh: **Glynn Edwards**
Det. Sgt. Miller: **David Morrell**
Jill Prentice: **Judith Arthy**
Marvin: **John Orchard**
Landlord: **Arthur Pentelow**
Griffiths: **Royston Tickner**
Marsh: **Patrick Durkin**
Mark Prentice: **Richard Mathews**

Portrait of Louisa
w **Terry Nation**
d **John Moxey**

When a woman asks him to buy her some valuable miniatures, the Baron is drawn into a web of blackmail and murder - with himself as the fall guy of the plot.

Louisa Trenton: **Moira Redmond**
Jane Benson: **Jo Rowbottom**
Sutton: **Brian Wilde**
Inspector Powell: **Meredith Edwards**
Nigel Brockhurst: **Terence Alexander**
Peter Langley: **Mark Burns**
David Marlowe: **Paul Ferris**
Sgt. Richards: **Richard Owens**
Beth: **Lisa Thomas**
The Barman: **Leo Kayne**

There's Someone Close Behind You
w **Terry Nation** and **Dennis Spooner**
d **Roy Baker**

Mannering's nose for trouble sniffs out a big-scale robbery attempt - which leads to the smell of death when a gang boss orders the Baron to be eliminated.

Cordelia: **Sue Lloyd**
Gregg Wilde: **Richard Wyler**
Det. Insp. Thomson: **Jerome Willis**
Frank Oddy: **Philip Madoc**
Sheldon: **Mike Pratt**
Alan Jordan: **Michael Robbins**
Marty Cranwell: **Ken Parry**
Stanley Merrick: **Norman Scace**
Insp. Bob Weston: **Raymond Adamson**
Yeldham: **Peter Forbes-Robertson**
Wayne: **Paul Harris**

Storm Warning [Part 1 of 2: StormWarning]
w **Terry Nation**
d **Gordon Flemyng**

When Cordelia witnesses a murder on board a cruise line, Mannering finds himself victim of an unusual hijack attempt.

Cordelia: **Sue Lloyd**
Brian Carlton: **Dudley Sutton**
Captain Brenner: **Reginald Marsh**
John Garvey: **John Woodvine**
Calvin Baggio: **Derek Newark**
Coleman: **Roland Brand**
Peters: **Terry Mountain**
Tang: **Andy Ho**
Chee: **Michael Chow**
Policeman No 1: **Dennis Chin**

Storm Warning [Part 2 of 2: The Island]
w **Terry Nation**
d **Gordon Flemyng**

Victims of a gang of hijackers, the Baron and Cordelia must find a way of defeating a fantastic plot to steal a manned space capsule.

Cordelia: **Sue Lloyd**
Brian Carlton: **Dudley Sutton**
Captain Brenner: **Reginald Marsh**
Calvin Baggio: **Derek Newark**
David Laver: **David Healy**
Insp. Ralph Nelson: **Michael Hawkins**
Willis: **Warren Stanhope**
Coleman: **Roland Brand**
Peters: **Terry Mountain**
Paul Millett: **Jeffry Wickham**
Lt. Lang: **William Buck**

Time to Kill
w **Dennis Spooner**
d **Robert Asher**

The Baron has to decide whether the curse on a valuable cameo is mere superstition. Several people have already given their lives to possess it, and the trail of tragedy looks like continuing when Mannering is asked to buy it.

Cordelia: **Sue Lloyd**
Vincente Carreras: **David Garth**
Menendez: **Peter Bowles**
Captain Sereda: **George Murcell**
Justo Vitale: **Hamilton Dyce**
Christina Vitale: **Geraldine Moffatt**
Carlos Lamas: **Edward Brayshaw**
Gardo: **Steven Scott**
Josefina: **Frieda Knorr**
Hotel Clerk: **David Calderisi**
Taxi Driver: **David Lander**

A Memory of Evil
w **Terry Nation** and **Dennis Spooner**
d **Don Chaffey**

When Nazi art treasures appear on the British antiques market, Mannering finds himself making a trip overseas - to find murder and treachery in a mountain retreat.

Cordelia: **Sue Lloyd**
Curt Hoffman: **Robert Hardy**
Nikki Holtz: **Anne Bell**
Heller: **Edwin Richfield**
Templeton-Greene: **Colin Gordon**
Lucien Holz: **Frederick Bartman**
Oscar Dancer: **Jon Rollason**
Josef Holz: **John Tate**
Rudi Gemmel: **Danvers Walker**
Hein: **Mark Peterson**
Granger: **John Cazabon**

You Can't Win Them All
w **Dennis Spooner**
d **Don Chaffey**

Mannering stakes his life to expose a big time gambler he knows to be a ruthless killer. Though the odds are stacked against him, the Baron has an ace up his sleeve.

Cordelia: **Sue Lloyd**
Sefton Folkard: **Sam Wannamaker**
Chief Insp. Filmer: **Reginald Marsh**
Whetlor: **David Burke**
Tredgett: **John Bown**
Jim Gaynor: **Peter Bowles**
Ronnie Osborne: **John Cater**
Coburn: **Mark Dignam**
Darby: **Tony Caunter**
Sgt. Copley: **Douglas Livingstone**
Warders 1 & 2: **Edwin Brown & Ken Haward**

The High Terrace
w **Dennis Spooner**
d **Robert Asher**

A phoney religious order and a trail of treachery lead the Baron to suspect that the mystery surrounding the disappearance of two wealthy women bears closer investigation.

Cordelia: **Sue Lloyd**
The Chosen One: **Max Adrian**
Sara Knight: **Jan Holden**

Inspector Summers: **John Collin**
Phyllis Thornton: **Veronica Hurst**
Johnny Haswell: **Donald Webster**
Rhys Brown: **Dell Baker**
Madame Bregonzi: **Phyllis Montefiore**
Clifford Thornton: **Robert Bridges**
Reynolds: **John Crocker**
Porter: **Joe Ritchie**

The Seven Eyes of Night
w **Terry Nation**
d **Robert Asher**

A valuable necklace, bought from a beautiful French widow, leads Mannering into an ingenious plot to steal a valuable art treasure.

Cordelia: **Sue Lloyd**
Jeff Walker: **Jeremy Brett**
Madame Devereaux: **Patricia English**
Nancy Cummings: **Hilary Tindall**
Insp. Lamille: **Arnold Diamond**
Verel: **Christopher Benjamin**
Carre: **Michael Segal**

Night of the Hunter
w **Terry Nation**
d **Roy Baker**

Aware that money raised by him from the sale of antiques belonging to the wife of a foreign President will be used to finance a revolution, the Baron decides to deliver the money himself - and finds himself face to face with a ruthless dictator.

Cordelia: **Sue Lloyd**
The General: **Derek Godfrey**
Madame Nicharos: **Katharine Blake**
Daniella: **Zeph Gladstone**
Capt. Brandt: **Walter Gotell**
Stavaros: **Garfield Morgan**
Nicholas: **David Garfield**
Cravos: **David Nettheim**
Peter: **Peter Bourne**
Mikos: **Clive Cazes**
Seaman: **Eric Mason**

The Edge of Fear
w **Dennis Spooner**
d **Quentin Lawrence**

When a painting is stolen from the Louvre in Paris, the criminal fraternity ask the question: is it the Mona Lisa? To confirm their suspicions, they consult the one man who can confirm its authenticity - the Baron.

Cordelia: **Sue Lloyd**
Kent Jordan: **William Franklyn**
Colbert: **Willoughby Goddard**
Lord Mountford: **Alan Wheatley**
Cerdan: **John Abineri**
Foster: **Gerald Sim**
Richards: **David Cargill**
Dr Poulton: **Paul Dawkins**
Sr Summers: **David Beale**
Air Hostess: **Dafna Dan**
Coleman: **John Gatrell**

Long Ago and Far Away
w **Dennis Spooner**
d **Robert Tronson**

When Cordelia disappears while visiting South America, The Baron's quest to find her is met with a hostile reception from the natives and places him on an unexpected collision course with rebel forces led by a would-be dictator, Raphael Saumarez.

Cordelia: **Sue Lloyd**
Roland Haswell: **Barrie Ingham**
Raphael: **Douglas Wilmer**
Ramon Petrarca: **Alex Scott**
Captain Heifetz: **Eric Pohlmann**
Joaquin Salvador: **Paul Stassino**
Gautler: **Michael Forrest**
Phillips: **David Swift**
Eleanor Saumarez: **Annette Carell**
Gambler in El Hamra Bar: **Barry Lineham**
Bartender: **Peter Hutchins**
Lieutenant: **Jonathan Elsom**
First Policeman: **Conrad Monk**
Second Policeman: **George Zenios**
Airline Hostess: **Janna Hill**

So Dark the Night
w **Terry Nation** and **Dennis Spooner**
d **Robert Tronson**

Two young girls lead the Baron and Cordelia into a web of intrigue, murder and revenge. Mannering must find out what lies behind the shuttered windows of a mysterious country house.

Cordelia: **Sue Lloyd**
Frank Ashton: **George Baker**
Dr Richard Thornton: **John Franklyn-Robbins**
Joyce Grant: **Gillian Lewis**
Ben Cross: **John Garrie**
Landlord: **Freddie Jones**
Felicia Talbot: **Caroline Blakiston**
Carl Grant: **Brown Derby**
Policeman: **Colin Rix**

The Long, Long Day
w **Tony O'Grady** [aka **Brian Clemens**]
d **Roy Baker**

While visiting a friend in Italy, the Baron finds himself protecting a murder witness - a young girl who can expose the leader behind a spate of killings. Mannering's dilemma: the Mafia boss knows their whereabouts, and is closing in for the kill.

Cordelia: **Sue Lloyd**
Marco Navini: **Peter Arne**
Maria Pullerno: **Dallia Penn**
Murphy: **Eddie Byrne**
Guiseppe Borzo: **John Bluthal**
Vee: **Derrick Sherwin**
Bruno Navini: **Brian Rawlinson**
Vittoria Guardy: **Richard Warner**
Barman: **John Bryans**
Pantoni: **Neil Robinson**
Pia Vallachio: **Sue Donovan**

Roundabout
w **Terry Nation**
d **Robert Tronson**

Informed that his own Paris office is being used as a cover for a dope-smuggling racket, the Baron sets out to trace the leader of the gang - a vicious mobster who will let nothing stand in the way of get-rich schemes.

Jeanne Varda: **June Ritchie**
Georges Delair: **Edwin Richfield**
Samantha Ballard: **Annette Andre**
Lisa Declair: **Lisa Daniely**

Insp. Macaulay: **Norman Bird**
Peter Savel: **Sandor Eles**
Richard Bates: **Ewan Roberts**
Heuer: **Victor Beaumont**
Caron: **Charles Thomas**
Doctor: **Frederick Treves**
Claudine: **Lisa Thomas**

The Man Outside
w **Terry Nation**
d **Roy Baker**

The loss of a valuable ring leads Mannering to Scotland where, together with Cordelia, he uncovers an astonishing plan to wreck Britain's economy. It isn't long before he and his colleague find themselves up to their necks in trouble.

Cordelia: **Sue Lloyd**
Bruno Orsini: **David Bauer**
Dino Rossi: **Paul Maxwell**
Vince Florio: **Michael Coles**
Phillip Tremayne: **Jeremy Burnham**
Douglas Macrae: **Donald Douglas**
Inspector Duncan: **John Ringham**
Jean Henderson: **Anne Sharp**
Fergus: **Joseph Greig**
Landlord: **Harry Littlewood**
Policeman: **Roy Hanlon**

Countdown
w **Terry Nation**
d **Robert Asher**

Unaware of the reason why they have been asked to keep a rendezvous with a stranger, Mannering and Cordelia arrive at the designated meeting point - and find themselves facing a countdown to death.

Cordelia: **Sue Lloyd**
Arkin Morley: **Edward Woodward**
Compton: **Philip Locke**
Stanley White: **Harold Lang**
"Fats" Logan: **Michael Wynne**
Hamilton: **Peter Brace**
Yates: **Leslie White**
Police Inspector: **David King**
Film director: **Malcolm Farquhar**
Film Actress: **Valerie Leon**

Farewell to Yesterday
w **Harry H. Junkin**
d **Leslie Norman**

Working undercover, the Baron investigates claims that a dead airline steward had been working for one of the largest art smuggling rings of the century. His enquiries bring startling results.

Cathy Dorne: **Sylvia Syms**
Nick: **William Sylvester**
Templeton-Green: **Colin Gordon**
David Marlowe: **Paul Ferris**
Dino: **Victor Maddern**
John Cavendish: **Patrick Bedford**
Marko: **Barry Shawzin**
Train Steward: **Arnold Diamond**
Air Steward: **Peter Brett**
Air Stewardess: **Christine Child**
Police Captain: **Clive Cazes**
English Woman: **Totte Truman Taylor**
English Man: **Walter Horsbrugh**

Two features were issued, being a compilation of the episodes listed: *Man In a Looking Glass* [*Masquerade* Parts 1 & 2] and *Mystery Island* [*Storm Warning* Parts 1 & 2].

The Baron:

Based on the character created by **John Creasey**
Producer: **Monty Berman**
Production Supervisor: **Johnny Goodman**
Music: **Edwin Astley**
Script Editor: **Terry Nation**
Assistant Director: **Ken Baker, Pat Kelly**
Second Unit Director: **Johnny Hough**
Music Editor: **Deveril Goodman**
Casting Director: **Anthony Arnell**
Make-up: **Michael Morris**
Hairdressing: **Mervyn Medalie, Helen Penfold**
Wardrobe Supervisor: **Laura Nightingale**
[Miss Lloyd's Wardrobe by Wallis]

An ITC Production for ITC World Wide Distribution
Made on location and at Associated British Elstree Studios

30 colour 60-minute episodes
1966

The Buccaneers

aka Dan Tempest

Promoted as 'television's first ever pirate series', this swashbuckling adventure series presented the exploits of Captain Dan Tempest, a pardoned ex-pirate turned King's man, and his friendly rival Lieutenant Beamish, the newly-appointed deputy governor of New Providence - a Caribbean pirate stronghold, which had recently been taken back from the buccaneers.

Prior to the arrival of the King's men, Tempest had virtually ruled the island with his followers - a hearty crew of lovable rogues who, if the occasion demanded, would have followed their leader to the ends of the Earth. The arrival of the King's troops changed all that, and Tempest and his men became 'good guys' - their swords and allegiances sworn to the King, the rivalry with the new governor forgotten as side by side with Beamish they faced their common enemies, the Spaniards: sea-going rogues who refused to bow to the new authority and were the scourge of all free men.

Breaking with tradition, the producers used the first two stories to record the events surrounding the purging of the pirates from the colony and Tempest - the series 'lead character - didn't appear until the third episode.

> *"Let's go a rovin', a rovin' across the ocean.*
> *Oh let's go a rovin' and join the Buccaneers.*
> *We'll find adventure, adventure across the ocean.*
> *We'll find adventure and join the Buccaneers.*
> *He's the greatest man we know, say he's not and*
> *you'll be walkin' the plank, sir.*
> *"Let's go a rovin', a rovin' across the ocean.*
> *Oh let's go a rovin' and join the Buccaneers."*

Regular cast:
Dan Tempest: **Robert Shaw** [from episode .3]
Lieutenant Beamish: **Peter Hammond** [episodes 1 to 29]
Armando: **Edwin Richfield**
Alfie [later Taffy]: **Paul Hansard**
Gaff: **Brian Rawlinson** [from episode 4]
Bassett: **Neil Hallett** [episodes 4 to 29]
Dickon: **Wilfred Downing** [from episode 6]
Pop: **Willoughby Gray** [from episode 6]

Blackbeard
w **Thomas A. Stockwell**
d **Ralph Smart**

Woodes Rogers arrives at New Providence and takes up his position as Governor. His first task: free the island from buccaneers, and offer a pardon to those who swear allegiance to the King.

Blackbeard: **George Margo**
Lieutenant Beamish: **Peter Hammond**
Benjy: **Hugh David**
Sawney: **Alfie Bass**
Captain Hornigold: **Andrew Crawford**
Rackam: **Brian Worth**
Armando: **Edwin Richfield**
Costellaux: **Peter Bennett**
Alfie: **Paul Hansard**
Morgan: **Patrick Jordan**

The Raiders
w **Terence Moore**
d **Ralph Smart**

Worried that New Providence will be left undefended when he sets out to chase a pirate ship which has attacked the island, Governor Rogers leaves Lieutenant Beamish in command of the garrison.

Woodes Rogers: **Alec Clunes**
Ivy: **Jane Griffiths**
Van Brugh: **Alec Mango**
Lieut. Beamish: **Peter Hammond**
Benjy: **Hugh David**
Capt. Hornigold: **Andrew Crawford**
Charles Vane: **Brian Worth**
Sikes: **Peter Bennett**
Alfie: **Paul Hansard**
Armando: **Edwin Richfield**
Jamie: **Patrick Jordan**

Captain Dan Tempest
w **Terence Moore**
d **Ralph Smart**

Governor Rogers continues to offer free pardons to those pirates who reform. His main target is Dan Tempest - a man previously looked upon as uncrowned leader of New Providence. To convert him would be a triumph indeed.

Woodes Rogers: **Alec Clunes**
Dan Tempest: **Robert Shaw** [intro]
Lieutenant Beamish: **Peter Hammond**
Benjy: **Hugh David**
Capt. Hornigold: **Andrew Crawford**
Blackbeard: **George Margo**
Lolita: **Judith Wyler**
Armando: **Edwin Richfield**
Rackam: **Brian Worth**
Alfie: **Paul Hansard**
Murchison: **Peter Bennett**

Dan Tempest's War with Spain
w **Zachary Weiss**
d **Leslie Arliss**

Displeased because Lolita, his girlfriend, has deserted him, Tempest is distracted by more important matters - the Spaniards have launched an attack on the island.

Armando: **Edwin Richfield**
Lieut. Beamish: **Peter Hammond**
Guernsey: **Brian Rawlinson**
Taffy: **Paul Hansard**
Van Brugh: **Alec Mango**
Costellaux: **Terence Cooper**
Lieut. Mendez: **Denis Lacey**
Capt. Catalan: **Robert Rietty**
Petty Officer: **Roy Purcell**
Spanish speaking sailor: **Tony Thawnton**
Sam Bassett: **Neil Hallett**

The Wasp
w **Peter C. Hodgkins**
d **Terry Bishop**

Young Dickon, a stowaway aboard Tempest's ship, The Sultana, provides the captain and his crew with a major headache. But trouble of a different kind is brewing out at sea - Blackbeard is organising a campaign of attack.

Beamish: **Peter Hammond**
Gaff Guernsey: **Brian Rawlinson**
Pop: **Willoughby Gray**
Blackbeard: **Terence Cooper**
Bassett: **Neil Hallett**
The Boy [Dickon]: **Wilfred Downing**

Whale Gold
w **Zachary Weiss**
d **Leslie Arliss**

When ambergris - a valuable substance found in the sperm whale, and used in expensive perfume - is found by Pat, a colonist, it spells trouble for Tempest and his crew. Men have been known to kill for it - and it appears that someone has plans to do just that.

Gaff Guernsey: **Brian Rawlinson**
Pat: **Noel Purcell**
Dickon: **Wilfred Downing**
Grimes: **Terence Cooper**
Armando: **Edwin Richfield**
Sykes: **Tony Thawnton**
Taffy: **Paul Hansard**
Old Pop: **Willoughby Gray**

Slave Ship
w **John Cousins**
d **Terry Bishop**

A deserted galleon and three escaped prisoners lead Tempest and his crew into mayhem and intrigue. The buccaneer faces race against time to rescue the three fugitives from their own foolhardiness.

Trevallion: **Roy Purcell**
Deacon: **Eynon Evans**
Sam: **Earl Cameron**
Van Brugh: **Alec Mango**
Beamish: **Peter Hammond**
Harris: **Willoughby Gray**
Hornigold: **Neil Hallett**
Captain Scobie: **Tony Thawnton**
Davies: **Brian Rawlinson**
Guard: **Denis Lacey**

Gunpowder Plot
w **Terence Moore**
d **Leslie Arliss**

When Blackbeard steals the garrison's gunpowder supply, Tempest is faced with finding a new supplier. But the naval authorities refuse to condone his departure - so the wily ex-pirate resorts to his former ways to cut through the red tape.

Governor: **Andre Morell**
Beamish: **Peter Hammond**
Governor's Daughter: **Pamela Wright**
Armando: **Edwin Richfield**
Governor's wife: **Noel Hood**
Gaff: **Brian Rawlinson**
Dickon: **Wilfred Downing**
Taffy: **Paul Hansard**
Bassett: **Neil Hallett**

The Articles of War
w **Peggy Philips** and **Alan Moreland**
d **Leslie Arliss**

Witnessing the slow starvation of several families, Tempest must find a way to ignore the Articles of War - which state that only children of the sick and needy may have meat.

Hernandez: **Eric Pohlmann**
Beamish: **Peter Hammond**
Gaff: **Brian Rawlinson**
Taffy: **Paul Hansard**
Armando: **Edwin Richfield**
Count Pedro Alfonso: **Denis Lacey**
Sailor: **Rupert Evans**
Jamieson: **Tony Thawnton**
Pop: **Willoughby Gray**
Bassett: **Neil Hallett**

Ghost Ship
w **Peter C. Hodgkins**
d **Robert Day**

Becalmed in the Sargasso Sea, The Sultana has not moved for three days. The crew are growing restless and the situation worsens by the hour. Then Tempest sees a ship which apparently has no one on board - and all hell breaks loose.

Taffy: **Paul Hansard**
De Groot: **Colin Douglas**
Mate: **Alfred Burke**
Jenkins: **Eddie Malin**
Armando: **Edwin Richfield**
Dickon: **Wilfred Downing**
Gaff: **Brian Rawlinson**
Martin: **Rupert Evans**

Conquest of New Providence
w **Terence Moore**
d **Leslie Arliss** and **Robert Day**

Returning from a mission abroad, Tempest and his crew find that New Providence has been taken over by Estaban. The Spanish flag is flying over the fortress, and Beamish and his troops are kicking their heels in a dungeon.

Beamish: **Peter Hammond**
Estaban: **Roger Delgado**
Armando: **Edwin Richfield**
Taffy: **Paul Hansard**
Maria: **Gillian Owen**
Bessie: **Diana Potter**
Gaff: **Brian Rawlinson**
Bassett: **Neil Hallett**
Costellaux: **Terence Cooper**
Thompson: **Roy Purcell**
Phelps: **John Gatrell**

Mother Doughty's Crew
w **Zachary Weiss**
d **Pennington Richards**

When Mother Doughty and her daughter, Betsy, announce the latter's forthcoming marriage to Gaff, no one is more surprised than Gaff himself - who knows nothing of the affair! Engaged to be married to another girl, Gaff pleads with Tempest to help.

Beamish: **Peter Hammond**
Mother Doughty: **Ena Burrill**
Betsy: **Anna Walmsley**
Armando: **Edwin Richfield**
Taffy: **Paul Hansard**
Gaff: **Brian Rawlinson**
Captain: **John Gatrell**
Son: **Roy Purcell**
Son: **John Sullivan**
Son: **Dermot McMahon**
Son: **Denis Lacey**

Blood will Tell
w **Zachary Weiss**
d **Robert Day**

Tempest is faced with a mission of the utmost urgency: he must locate the real owner of Gresham Island. Unless he does so, the island Will be made a free port - one that will offer a safe stronghold for the Spanish fleet.

Beamish: **Peter Hammond**
Piggott: **Dawson France**
Dickon: **Wilfred Downing**

Gaff: **Brian Rawlinson**
Bassett: **Neil Hallett**
Costellaux: **Terence Cooper**
Van Brugh: **Alec Mango**
Pym: **Willoughby Goddard**
Bellows: **John Dearth**
Pym's Slave: **Serge Lemince**
Nan Y Macao: **Pearl Prescod**

Hurricane
w **Terence Moore** and **Peggy Philips**
d **Leslie Arliss**

The hurricane which is sweeping across New Providence blows good fortune in its wake. Tempest hears that a Spanish pirate ship is grounded on the rocks - an opportunity too good to miss.

Beamish: **Peter Hammond**
Taffy: **Paul Hansard**
Armando: **Edwin Richfield**
Bassett: **Neil Hallett**
Gaff: **Brian Rawlinson**
Van Brugh : **Alec Mango**
Spanish Lieutenant: **Derek Sydney**
The Chief: **Frank Singuinea**
Spanish Admiral: **Ewan Solon**
Spanish Aide: **David Ritch**
Maria: **Gillian Owen**

Dead Man's Rock
w **Peter C. Hodgkins**
d **Robert Day**

With The Sultana being overhauled, Tempest can offer no resistance when Lieutenant Beamish surrenders New Providence to the Spaniards, and is taken prisoner to the fortress known as El Morre - Dead Man's Rock.

Beamish: **Peter Hammond**
Rodrigues: **Richard Pasco**
Bassett: **Neil Hallett**
Gaff: **Brian Rawlinson**
Dickon: **Wilfred Downing**
Armando: **Edwin Richfield**
Woman with baby: **Anne Padwick**
Spanish soldier: **Roy Purcell**
Spanish prisoner: **Peter Garstin**
Spanish jailer: **Terence Cooper**
Canteyo: **Rajah Chaudhuri**

Dangerous Cargo
w **Zachary Weiss**
d **Leslie Arliss**

Keeping a secret rendezvous with British warship captain, Steele, offers no threat to Tempest's peace of mind. But the sealed orders Steele is carrying will prove to be a nightmare for the buccaneer - even when they involve a beautiful woman.

Lady Hilary Winrod: **Sarah Lawson**
Captain Steele: **Ivan Craig**
Beamish: **Peter Hammond**
Dickon: **Wilfred Downing**
Taffy: **Paul Hansard**
Gaff: **Brian Rawlinson**
Captain Mendoza: **Roger Delgado**
Merchant Skipper: **Roy Purcell**
Spanish Mate: **Denis Lacey**
Merchant Mate: **Rupert Evans**
Tavern Keeper: **John Gatrell**
Pirate: **Neil Hallett**
Lord Winrod: **Derek Nimmo**

Hand of the Hawk
w **Peter C. Hodgkins**
d **Robert Day**

If Tempest is to avert tragedy for himself and his crew, he must find a way of converting certain defeat into victory. His chance to do just that arrives from a very unexpected source.

Captain Flash: **Anthony Dawson**
Chantey Jack: **Sidney James**
Beamish: **Peter Hammond**
Armando: **Edwin Richfield**
Costellaux: **Terence Cooper**
Dickon: **Wilfred Downing**
Gaff: **Brian Rawlinson**
Taffy: **Paul Hansard**
Sailor: **Roy Purcell**
Mate: **Julian Strange**

Gentleman Jack and the Lady
w **Zachary Weiss**
d **Leslie Arliss**

When his plans to board a Spanish warship are thwarted by a French galleon, Tempest encounters trouble of a very strange variety indeed - Gentleman Jack, the French ship's captain, wears skirts..., but is certainly no lady.

Anne "Gentleman Jack" Bonny : **Hazel Court**
Beamish: **Peter Hammond**
Gaff: **Brian Rawlinson**
Taffy: **Paul Hansard**
Dickon: **Wilfred Downing**
William: **John Gatrell**
Bassett: **Neil Hallett**
Spanish Captain: **Denis Lacey**
Costellaux: **Terence Cooper**
Spanish Gunner: **Rupert Evans**

Mr Beamish and the Hangman's Noose
w **Terence Moore**
d **Pennington Richards**

Lieutenant Beamish rarely makes mistakes. But this time Tempest feels he has gone to far. When the buccaneer receives word that Beamish has ordered his men to hang two lawbreakers, Tempest decides to oppose his ally.

Beamish: **Peter Hammond**
Taffy: **Paul Hansard**
Armando: **Edwin Richfield**
Dickon: **Wilfred Downing**
Gaff: **Brian Rawlinson**
Bassett: **Neil Hallett**
Van Brugh: **Alec Mango**
Mainwaring: **Lewis Gedge**
Sergeant: **Terence Cooper**
Marine: **Rupert Evans**
Admiral Bingham: **Stringer Davis**
Captain Harding: **Roy Purcell**

Marooned
w **Peter C. Hodgkins**
d **Leslie Arliss**

While everyone is attending the Queen's birthday festivities, someone breaks into the garrison's armoury and steals a powder magazine. Dan Tempest has his work cut out finding the guilty party.

Clip West: **Bill Owen**
Beamish: **Peter Hammond**
Gaff: **Brian Rawlinson**
Taffy: **Paul Hansard**

Pop: **Willoughby Gray**
Dickon: **Wilfred Downing**
Phineas Bunch: **Willoughby Goddard**
Macarty: **Terence Cooper**
Cunningham: **Denis Lacey**
Sam One-Eye: **Tony Thawnton**
Sentry: **Roy Purcell**
Second Sentry: **Rupert Evans**
Bassett: **Neil Hallett**
Look-out: **Michael Rathborne**

Before the Mast
w **Roger MacDougall**
d **Ralph Smart**

Tempest and his crew leave New Providence at daybreak. Their mission: to upset the carefully laid plans of El Supremo - a Spaniard who is waging war on Beamish's supply ships.

El Supremo: **Ferdy Mayne**
Rodriguez: **Roger Snowden**
One Eye: **Salvin Stewart**
Bosun: **Willoughby Gray**
Dickon: **Wilfred Downing**
Jose: **Denis Lacey**
Gaff Guernsey: **Brian Rawlinson**
Beamish: **Peter Hammond**
Taffy: **Paul Hansard**
Barman: **Neil Hallett**

Dan Tempest and the Amazons
w **Zachary Weiss**
d **Pennington Richards**

A new kind of trouble plagues Tempest and his crew - women. Their arrival has placed the swashbuckler's life in jeopardy. With the Spaniards hot on his trail, the buccaneer seems doomed - but help is at hand.

Beamish: **Peter Hammond**
Abigail: **Joan Sims**
Armando: **Edwin Richfield**
Dickon: **Wilfred Downing**
Taffy: **Paul Hansard**
Captain Delacour: **Roy Purcell**
Bassett: **Neil Hallett**
Gaff Guernsey: **Brian Rawlinson**
Costellaux: **Terence Cooper**
Look-out: **Rupert Evans**
Mollie: **Anna Walmsley**
First Mate: **Tony Thawnton**
Bo'sun: **Denis Lacey**
Second Woman: **Diana Potter**
Third Woman: **Merrill Colebrook**

The Ladies
w **Roger MacDougall**
d **Pennington Richards**

Hearing that The Caroline carries a very precious cargo - women - Blackbeard makes plans to board the vessel under a flag of 'truce'. Tempest, however, has other plans.

Beamish: **Peter Hammond**
Christine: **Petra Davies**
Captain Hawkins: **Roy Purcell**
Juanita: **Dalia Penn**
Blackbeard: **Terence Cooper**
Armando: **Edwin Richfield**
Bassett: **Neil Hallett**
Cranstone: **Tony Thawnton**
Gaff: **Brian Rawlinson**
Taffy: **Paul Hansard**

Dawson: **Eddie Malin**
Posford: **Denis Lacey**
First Man Shaving: **Willoughby Gray**
Second Man Shaving: **Rupert Evans**

The Surgeon of Sangra Rojo
w **Thomas A. Stockwell**
d **Pennington Richards**

An epidemic sweeps the province. Tempest, assigned to bring the only surgeon available to administer aid, must run the gauntlet of Spanish guns waiting for any ship daring to leave New Providence island.

Francisco: **Dino Galvani**
Beamis: **Peter Hammond**
Van Brugh: **Alec Mango**
Armando: **Edwin Richfield**
Dickon: **Wilfred Downing**
First Spanish Sailor: **Denis Lacey**
First Spanish Guard: **Roy Purcell**
Spanish Officer: **Philip Ashley**
Gaff: **Brian Rawlinson**
Fish Peddler: **Tony Thawnton**
Old Woman: **Jane Eccles**
Jack: **Rupert Evans**
Bassett: **Neil Hallett**
Pop: **Willoughby Gray**
Taffy: **Paul Hansard**
Pigtail: **John Schlesinger**
Maria: **Yvonne Warren**
Old Indian: **Frank Olegario**

The Return of Calico Jack
w **Zachary Weiss** and **Basil Dawson**
d **Pennington Richards**

With Tempest away on a mission, Calico Jack's arrival on New Providence is given a less than enthusiastic welcome. The newcomer appears unmovable - until Dan's crew come up with a foolproof method of defence.

Calico Jack: **Brian Worth**
Beamish: **Peter Hammond**
Gaff: **Brian Rawlinson**
Taffy: **Paul Hansard**
Armando: **Edwin Richfield**
Costellaux: **Terence Cooper**
Groggins: **Meadows White**
Racquel: **Jan Miller**
Mrs. Wainwright: **Anne Blake**
Van Brugh: **Alec Mango**
Bassett: **Neil Hallett**
Pop: **Willoughby Gray**

Conquistador
w **Terence Moore** and **Basil Dawson**
d **Robert Day**

Why should The Sultana leave New Providence sporting the Jolly Roger? Has Tempest reverted to his old ways? The answer surprises everyone, including Dan's crew - and an astonished Lieutenant Beamish.

Beamish: **Peter Hammond**
Estaban: **Roger Delgado**
Van Brugh: **Alec Mango**
Juan: **Roger Gage**
Charlie: **Larry Hoodekoff**
Maria: **Gillian Owen**
Armando: **Edwin Richfield**
Bassett: **Neil Hallett**
Taffy: **Paul Hansard**
Gaff: **Brian Rawlinson**
Pop: **Willoughby Gray**

The Aztec Treasure
w Terence Moore
d Pennington Richards

Martin, a man rescued by Tempest during a brawl in Port Royal, proposes a business proposition in thanks. If Tempest will finance the journey, Martin will lead him to the hiding place of a fabulous treasure. Tempest's dilemma - can the stranger be trusted?

Martin: **Thomas G. Duggan**
Tazco: **Michael Ritterman**
Quetzl: **Frederick Treves**
Barmaid: **Sally Pearce**
Armando: **Edwin Richfield**
Gaff: **Brian Rawlinson**
Taffy: **Paul Hansard**

Prize of Andalusia
w Basil Dawson and Zachary Weiss
d Peter Maxwell

Out to capture a large consignment of gold being transported by a Spanish galleon, Tempest comes face to face with a new enemy - the Marquesa, an opponent the buccaneer is hard pressed to ignore.

Marquesa: **Jean Cadell**
Sebastian: **Conrad Phillips**
Gomez: **Bruno Barnabe**
Blasco: **David Ritch**
Gaff: **Brian Rawlinson**
Taffy: **Paul Hansard**
Armando: **Edwin Richfield**
Pop: **Willoughby Gray**
Merchant officer: **John Gatrell**
Spanish Sailor: **Denis Lacey**
Servant: **Frank Pendlebury**

Cutlass Wedding
w Thomas A. Stockwell
d Robert Day

Tempest and his crew are making preparations for Taffy's wedding to Emily - the first marriage to be performed in New Providence. But someone appears to bear the sweethearts a grudge - and the couple turn to Tempest for help.

Abigail: **Joan Sims**
Beamish: **Peter Hammond**
Emily: **Maureen Davis**
Bassett: **Neil Hallett**
Taffy: **Paul Hansard**
Armando: **Edwin Richfield**
Gaff: **Brian Rawlinson**
Molly: **Eileen Elton**
La Forte: **Paul Eddington**
Old Tom: **Raymond Ray**
Pirate: **Roy Purcell**

Dan Tempest Holds an Auction
w Alan Moreland
d Peter Maxwell

Handing over the command of the 'Sultana' to Gaff Guernsey, Tempest visits South Carolina to sell cargo for the Governor. Content that he's acquired the best deal possible. Tempest is taken aback when he discovers that he has been duped. Somehow he must find a way of repaying such treachery.

✍
This episode signifies a slight change in the show's format.

Gaff: **Brian Rawlinson**
Sir Charles Johnson: **Robert Perceval**
Rafton: **Ballard Berkeley**
Paula Meadows: **Jane Griffiths**
Lawyer Knox: **John Harvey**
Chris: **Bernard Brown**
Taffy: **Paul Hansard**
Armando: **Edwin Richfield**
Hicks: **Roy Purcell**
Auctioneer: **Peter Retey**
Guard: **Max Faulkner**

Flip and Jenny
w Neil R. Collins
d Peter Maxwell

Stowaways are trouble at any time. But when Tempest and his crew discover two young children hidden below decks, they have no inkling of the troubles that will beset them - or their ally, Lord Hinch.

Flip: **Peter Soule**
Jenny: **Jane Asher**
Lord Hinch: **Robert Hardy**
Gaff: **Brian Rawlinson**
Armando: **Edwin Richfield**
Taffy: **Paul Hansard**
Dickon: **Wilfred Downin**
Purdy: **Colin Douglas**
Constable Herridge: **Seymour Green**
Sylvester: **Derek Tansley**
Guard: **Roy Purcell**

To the Rescue
w Phillis Miller
d Peter Maxwell

On an errand of mercy to the port of Savannah, Tempest finds that several traders have been swindled. Never one to condone trickery or deceit, the buccaneer decides to turn the tables on the thieves by employing some trickery of his own making.

Paula: **Jane Griffiths**
Major Percy: **Ewan Solon**
Louis Brion: **Andre Charisse**
Sarah Brion: **Norma Parnell**
Captain Barker: **Michael Golden**
Armando: **Edwin Richfield**
Gaff: **Brian Rawlinson**
Taffy: **Paul Hansard**
Bowles: **Roy Purcell**
Jenks: **Noel Davis**
Pop: **Willoughby Gray**

Indian Fighters
w Neil R. Collins
d Peter Maxwell

If Perkins, said to be a great Indian fighter, is as brave as he makes out, why should he run to Tempest for help when confronted by two police constables on the occasion of his triumphant return to New Providence?

Perkins: **Ronan O'Casey**
Paula: **Jane Griffiths**
Johnson: **Robert Perceval**
Gaff: **Brian Rawlinson**
Armande: **Edwin Richfield**
Taffy: **Paul Hansard**
Constable: **Roy Purcell**
Magistrate: **Edmund Warwick**
Captain: **Denis Lacey**
Servant: **Max Faulkner**

Mistress Higgins' Treasure
w **Thomas A. Stockwell**
d **Pennington Richards**

It's the old treasure story again - and Tempest and his crew are always interested in buried treasure, no matter how strange the source of information. But can they believe the story circulated by Mistress Higgins - a school teacher?

Mistress Higgins: **Adrienne Corri**
Pennington: **Howard Pays**
Armando: **Edwin Richfield**
Gaff: **Brian Rawlinson**
Taffy: **Paul Hansard**
Mingo: **Roy Purcell**
Boy: **Barry Fennell**
Second Boy: **Claude Kingston**
Girl: **Jane Asher**

The Spy Aboard
w **Neil R. Collins**
d **Robert Day**

Everyone knows that Captain Tempest trusts his fellow men, but lately, odd things have been happening. When it becomes apparent that one of his crew is spying for the enemy, the buccaneer's confidence reaches an all-time low.

Pegleg: **Richard Johnson**
Cookie: **John Salew**
Noah: **Danny Green**
Armando: **Edwin Richfield**
Taffy: **Paul Hansard**
Gaff: **Brian Rawlinson**
Raikes: **Jack Hedley**
Jordan: **Denis Lacey**
Landlord: **Roy Purcell**
Old Man: **Wilfred Brambell**
Noll: **Oliver McGreevy**

The Decoy
w **Albert G. Ruben**
d **Pennington Richards**

A young girl's story provides Tempest and his crew with plenty of surprises - all of them bad. She claims to have escaped from pirates, who took her husband prisoner. But is the girl telling the truth?

Rebecca: **Virginia Maskell**
Turk: **Marne Maitland**
George: **Derek Waring**
Gaff: **Brian Rawlinson**
Armando: **Edwin Richfield**
Taffy: **Paul Hansard**
Mate: **Roy Purcell**
Pirate: **Denis Lacey**

Pirate Honour
w **Marion Myers**
d **Peter Maxwell**

Though Tempest has resolved to sidestep any trouble while visiting Savannah, when he comes across a young boy being ill-treated his resolution is put severely to the test. His change of mind comes swiftly - and causes trouble for all concerned.

Edwin: **Michael Caridia**
Black Bart: **Alex Scott**
Mrs. Drewitt: **Ilona Ference**
Gaff: **Brian Rawlinson**
Armando: **Edwin Richfield**
Taffy: **Paul Hansard**
Dickon: **Wilfred Downing**

Pop: **Willoughby Gray**
Major Langley: **Brian Oulton**
Officer: **Roy Purcell**
Sergeant: **Patrick Connor**

Instrument of War
w **Peter Rossano**
d **Bernard Knowles**

With The Sultana anchored off the Carolina coastline, Tempest - on a secret mission to Andrewsville, where a number of Scots are unjustly imprisoned - must plan his rescue attempt carefully. Should he fail, it could cost the lives of everyone aboard.

Dougal: **John Harvey**
Marsh: **Alfred Burke**
Laird: **Andrew Keir**
Gaff: **Brian Rawlinson**
Armando: **Edwin Richfield**
Taffy: **Paul Hansard**
David Ramsey: **Charles Houston**
Sheila McLellan: **Gay Cameron**
First Guard: **Roy Purcell**
Second Guard: **Dennis Edwards**

Printer's Devil
w **Terence Moore**
d **Bernard Knowles**

When Tempest arranges the rescue of Josiah Parkerhouse - a man arrested for printing a series of articles criticising the state - his troubles are only just beginning, and his friendship with the man will be put under severe pressure.

Josiah Parkerhouse: **Miles Malleson**
Sir Joplin James: **Noel Coleman**
Sharp: **Maxwell Shaw**
Taffy: **Paul Hansard**
Armando: **Edwin Richfield**
Pop: **Willoughby Gray**
Mrs. Miles: **Jean Eloor**
Constable: **Denis Lacey**
Harkness: **Roy Purcell**
Magistrate: **Walter Horsburgh**
Officer: **Dennis Edwards**

The Buccaneers:

Producers: **Sidney Cole, Ralph Smart and Pennington Richards**
Executive Producer: **Hannah Weinstein**
Music by: **Albert Elms, Edwin Astley and Kenneth V. Jones**
Script Supervision: **Kathryn Dawes, Albert G. Ruben**
Production Manager: **Roy Parkinson**
Assistant Director: **Frank Hollands**
Make-up: **Charles Nash**
Hairdresser: **Jayne Seymour**
Wardrobe: **Jim Donlevy**

A Weinstein Production for Sapphire Films Ltd., for The Incorporated Television Programme Co. Ltd.

Filmed at Twickenham Studios.

39 monochrome 30-minute episodes
1956

Captain Scarlet and the Mysterons

A lavishly-mounted action-packed offering from the Gerry Anderson 'Supermarionation' stable, this came close to being the definitive Anderson product.

Set in the year 2068, the first story told how, during a Mars exploration mission, Captain Black, an agent of Spectrum [a world security network organisation whose agents were named after the colours in the spectrum] misinterpreted the intentions of the Martian inhabitants, the Mysterons, as hostile, and annihilated their city - leaving the Mysterons to retaliate by waging a war of attrition on Earth. Using their ability to recreate any object or person which has been destroyed, the Mysterons took control of Captain Black and used him to act as their agent on Earth. They later decide to kill and restore Spectrum agent, Captain Scarlet, by the same process, but their plan backfires and Scarlet becomes their indestructible enemy. Thereafter, the episodes depicted Spectrum's battle against the Mysterons and their attempts to discover a way of detecting their presence. The Mysterons themselves were never seen.

Character voices:
Captain Scarlet: **Francis Matthews**
Colonel White: **Donald Gray**
Captain Blue: **Ed Bishop**
Captain Grey: **Paul Maxwell**
Captain Magenta: **Gary Files**
Lieutenant Green: **Cy Grant**
Dr Fawn: **Charles Tingwell**
Melody Angel: **Sylvia Anderson**
Rhapsody/Destiny Angel: **Liz Morgan**
Symphony Angel: **Janna Hill**
Harmony Angel: **Lian Shin**
Additional characters: **Jeremy Wilkin**
Voice of Mysterons: **Donald Gray**

Pilot: The Mysterons
w **Gerry Anderson** and **Sylvia Anderson**
d **Desmond Saunders**

The inhabitants of an alien city on Mars turn their cameras on the human explorers. Captain Black, mistaking these for weapons, destroys the alien city. The Mysterons swear revenge, and the war of nerves begins.

Winged Assassin
w **Tony Barwick**
d **David Lane**

Captain Scarlet - now indestructible after his fatal fall - is sent to protect the General of the United Asian Republic, who is believed to be the Mysterons' next target.

Big Ben Strikes Again
w **Tony Barwick**
d **Brian Burgess**

Pursuing the latest Mysteron threat - a plan to destroy London with a nuclear device - Captains Scarlet and Blue become interested when they hear from a transport driver that he heard Big Ben strike thirteen before he was knocked out.

Manhunt
w **Tony Barwick**
d **Alan Perry**

When a break-in at an Atomic Research Centre goes wrong and video film is developed which shows that Captain Black is a Mysteron agent, Captain Scarlet is sent to hunt him down.

Avalanche
w **Shane Rimmer**
d **Brian Burgess**

A dead Mysteron agent pumps liquid oxygen from his tanker into the control domes of the Outer Space defence system. Captain Scarlet and Lieutenant Green attempt to stop him.

White as Snow
w **Peter Curran** and **David Williams**
d **Robert Lynn**

Having threatened to destroy Colonel White, the Mysterons use their powers to recreate the man ordered to protect him - a steward on board a submarine in which Colonel White takes refuge.

The Trap
w **Alan Pattillo**
d **Alan Perry**

When the Mysterons plan to clip the Wings of the World by destroying the World Air Conference, Captain Scarlet and Symphony Angel are assigned to repel the attack.

Operation Time
w **Richard Conway** and **Stephen Mattick**
d **Ken Turner**

When Captain Magenta solves the latest Mysteron riddle - 'kill time' - and Spectrum reach the conclusion that it points to an attempt being made on the life of General Tiempo, a man about to undergo surgery, the operation venue is changed. But is it too late?

Spectrum Strikes Back
w **Tony Barwick**
d **Ken Turner**

Spectrum demonstrate their latest devices in their war against the enemy: an X-ray machine to detect the aliens, and a gun to destroy them. As they do so, the Mysterons attack.

Special Assignment
w **Tony Barwick**
d **Bob Lynn**

In debt after gambling on roulette, Captain Scarlet resigns his post. He is then approached by two strangers who promise to clear his debts if he steals a Spectrum Pursuit Vehicle - for Captain Black.

The Heart of New York
w **Tony Barwick**
d **Alan Perry**

When the Mysterons threaten to destroy Manhattan and Spectrum has the city evacuated, three crooks seize their opportunity to rob the Second National Bank - but Captain Black locks them in a vault.

Lunarville 7
w **Tony Barwick**
d **Bob Lynn**

Receiving a message that the Controller of Lunarville 7, the Moon's largest colony, claims to have made peace with the Mysterons, Captains Scarlet and Blue are sent to investigate.

Point 783
w **Peter Curran** and **David Williams**
d **Bob Lynn**

Discovering that Commander of Supreme Headquarters Earth Forces [SHEF] is to be the Mysterons' next target, Colonel White sends agents Scarlet and Blue to protect him - and guard SHEF's ultimate new weapon, the Unitron.

Model Spy
w **Bill Hedley**
d **Ken Turner**

Andre Verdain, a fashion designer, is marked for death by the Mysterons. Though agents Destiny, Symphony, Scarlet and Blue are sent to protect him, they must first overcome another Mysteron threat.

Seek and Destroy
w **Peter Curran** and **David Williams**
d **Alan Perry**

Scarlet and Blue go to the rescue of Destiny Angel when an attempt is made on her life. Meanwhile the Mysterons announce that they will destroy the newly-built Angel Interceptors.

The Traitor
w **Tony Barwick**
d **Alan Perry**

When Spectrum Hovercrafts start crashing in Australia without reason, agents Scarlet and Blue investigate - but Scarlet finds himself held responsible for the accidents.

Renegade Rocket
w **Ralph Hart**
d **Brian Burgess**

After undergoing the Mysterons recreation treatment, a rocket technician launches a rocket at Spectrum HQ. Scarlet and Blue must decipher the destruct code before the rocket hits its target.

Crater 101
w **Tony Barwick**
d **Ken Turner**

When Scarlet, Blue and Green are sent to the Moon to destroy a Mysteron city, they have no way of knowing that the driver of the lunar tank bringing them an atomic device to do this is an agent for their enemy.

Shadow of Fear
w **Tony Barwick**
d **Bob Lynn**

Spectrum plan to observe the Mysteron city on Mars by planting a camera satellite on Phobos. Scarlet and Blue are given the task of guarding the astronomers - one of them is a Mysteron agent.

Dangerous Rendezvous
w **Tony Barwick**
d **Brian Burgess**

Returning to Cloudbase with the pulsator device taken from the Mysteron city on the Moon - which has been adapted to allow Colonel White to speak to the aliens - Captain Scarlet is suspicious when the enemy agrees to meet for peace talks.

Fire at Rig 15
w **Bryan Cooper**
d **Ken Turner**

Smith, a drilling expert, is attacked and given the 'treatment' by the Mysterons while capping a bore at Rig 15. Under Captain Black's orders, he sets out to destroy Spectrum's fuel supply complex.

Treble Cross
w **Tony Barwick**
d **Alan Perry**

The Mysterons plan to destroy Futura City by replacing Air Force Major Gravener with an alien double. Unaware that he's walking into a trap, Captain Scarlet enters the scene.

Flight 104
w **Tony Barwick**
d **Bob Lynn**

Agents Blue and Scarlet are assigned to escort a leading astrophysicist by plane to a conference in Geneva. During their flight, the plane comes under the control of the Mysterons.

Place of Angels
w **Leo Eaton**
d **Leo Eaton**

When the Mysterons threaten to destroy 'the place of Angels', they take over research biochemist Judy Chapman - who then takes a deadly culture to contaminate the Los Angeles water supply.

Noose of Ice
w **Tony Barwick**
d **Ken Turner**

Captain Scarlet and agent Blue go to a North Pole Tritonium mine, where the walls of ice are held back by elements powered by a generator substation - an establishment now under Mysteron control.

Expo 2068
w **Shane Rimmer**
d **Leo Eaton**

The Mysterons threaten to destroy the North Atlantic Sea Board with a nuclear device stolen by Captain Black. Agents Scarlet and Blue are sent to intervene.

The Launching
w **Peter Curran** and **David Williams**
d **Brian Burgess**

When a newspaper reporter is killed on his way to visit President Roberts, the Mysterons' next target, and his body undergoes the alien recreation treatment, it spells trouble for Spectrum agent Captain Scarlet.

Codename Europa
w **David Lee**
d **Alan Perry**

Mysteron agent Captain Black shoots electronics expert Carney, then sets out to destroy the Congress of Europe by killing its three main members.

Inferno
w **Shane Rimmer** and **Tony Barwick**
d **Alan Perry**

After it has been destroyed by asteroids, the Mysterons plan to use an SKR4 Space Recovery Ship to destroy a desalinisation plant in South America. Spectrum agents are sent to thwart their plans.

Flight to Atlantica
w **Tony Barwick**
d **Leo Eaton**

When the Mysterons announce their plans to destroy the Atlantica World Navy complex, Colonel White sends agents Ochre and Blue to protect the base. But the two men suddenly begin to attack Atlantica - why?

Attack on Cloudbase
w **Tony Barwick**
d **Ken Turner**

The Mysterons continue to mount raids against Spectrum-held strongholds. During an attack by alien flying saucers, the Angels are launched but Destiny is killed. In the ensuing chaos, Captain Scarlet loses his powers of indestructibility!.

The Inquisition
w **Tony Barwick**
d **Ken Turner**

When Captain Blue is knocked out after a meal with agent Scarlet and regains consciousness on Cloudbase, deserted but for Colgan, a security agent who suspects Blue of being a traitor, Blue finds himself in a very tense situation - one that could have far-reaching consequences for the entire Spectrum network.

✍

Two 'features' were issued, each being a compilation of episodes:
Revenge of the Mysterons from Mars [Made up from *The Mysterons, Winged Assassin, Seek & Destroy* and *Attack on Cloudbase*].
Captain Scarlet & The Mysterons [Made up from *Shadow of Fear, Lunarville, Crater 101* and *Dangerous Rendezvous*].

📖 All three original stories, Armada Paperbacks [May Fair Books] Century 21 Publishing Ltd.:
Captain Scarlet and The Mysterons #1 Spectrum File [1967: John Theydon];
Captain Scarlet and the Silent Saboteur #2 Spectrum File [1967: John Theydon];
The Angels and the Creeping Enemy #3 Spectrum File [1968: John Theydon].

Captain Scarlet and the Mysterons:

Created by: **Gerry Anderson** and **Sylvia Anderson**
Producer: **Reg Hill**
Associate Producer: **John Read**
Executive Producer: **Gerry Anderson**
Music by: **Barry Gray**
Note: The song 'The Spectrum' does not appear in all episodes
Script Editor: **Tony Barwick**
Visual Effects Supervisor: **Desmond Saunders**
Special Effects: **Derek Meddings**

An ITC/Century 21 Television Production

32 colour 30-minute episodes
1967

The Champions

Craig Sterling, Sharron Macready and Richard Barrett - The Champions - agents for Nemesis, a Geneva based crimefighting agency formed to combat situations that might lead to international incident and destroy the delicate balance of power between the great nations. Given powers which raise their bodies, their minds and senses to fantastic level, they become super human - but they are not immortal. They can be killed. The greater the risks, the greater the danger to themselves. Their uncanny powers place them into situations no others could face.

"Craig Sterling, Sharron Macready and Richard Barrett.... The Champions.
Endowed with the qualities and skills of superhumans - qualities and skills, both physical and mental, to the peak of human performance. Gifts given to them by the unknown race of people, when their plane crashed near a lost civilisation in Tibet. Now, with their secret known only to them, they are able to use their fantastic powers to their best advantage ...
as - The Champions of Law, Order and Justice.
Operators of the International Agency, Nemesis!"

One of the most popular Monty Berman/Dennis Spooner shows, this became a firm favourite with fans of the genre.

Regular cast:
Craig Sterling: **Stuart Damon**
Sharron Macready: **Alexandra Bastedo**
Richard Barrett: **William Gaunt**
Tremayne: **Anthony Nicholls**
Voice-over narration: **David Bauer** [uncredited]

The Beginning
w **Dennis Spooner**
d **Cyril Frankel**

When Nemesis agents Sterling, Macready and Barrett set out on a dangerous mission to Tibet, they have no idea that 'death' awaits their arrival - or that they will be 'reborn' and return to their base as superhumans.

Old Man: **Felix Aylmer**
Whittaker: **Kenneth J Warren**
Chislenka: **Joseph Furst**
Ho Ling: **Eric Young**
Chinese Major: **Burt Kwouk**

The Invisible Man
w **Donald James**
d **Cyril Frankel**

Tipped off that the proceeds from a large bank robbery are to be placed in a Swiss bank, the Nemesis agents must find out from which bank the money is to be stolen. Somewhat surprisingly, noises in Craig's head reveal the answer.

Hallam: **Peter Wyngarde**
Sir Frederick: **Basil Dignam**
Van Velden: **Aubrey Morris**
Culliford: **Sumner James**
Bowsin: **Steve Plytas**

Reply Box No: 666
w **Philip Broadley**
d **Cyril Frankel**

Sent to the Caribbean to investigate a mysterious ad placed in a newspaper's personal column - 'Wanted, a parrot that speaks German' - the Champions find themselves facing a dangerous enemy who specialises in explosives.

Semenkin: **George Roubicek**
Jules: **Anton Rodgers**
Cleo: **Imogen Hassall**
Nikko: **George Murcell**
Bourges: **Brian Worth**
Corinne: **Nike Arrighi**
Clive: **Linbert Spencer**

The Experiment
w **Tony Williamson**
d **Cyril Frankel**

A scientist tries to create superhumans to equal the Nemesis team. Sharron Macready is tricked into taking part in the experiment, and Craig Sterling and Richard Barrett are faced with their toughest opponent yet.

Cranmore: **Allan Cuthbertson**
Marianne Grant: **Caroline Blakiston**
Chrissie: **Madelena Nichol**
David Bauer: **Doctor Glind**
Officer: **Philip Bond**
Barman: **Russell Waters**
Doctor Farley: **Nicholas Courtney**
Susan: **Nita Lorraine**
Jean: **Jonathan Burn**
Paul: **Peter J. Elliott**

Happening
w **Brian Clemens**
d **Cyril Frankel**

When three men find themselves isolated in an atom test area with a bomb due to go off at any moment, Champion Richard Barrett, one of the trio, must face deadly peril by trying to disarm the device.

Joss: **Michael Gough**
Banner: **Jack MacGowran**
Winters: **Grant Taylor**
Aston: **Bill Cummings**

Operation Deep-freeze
w **Gerald Kelsey**
d **Paul Dickson**

The leader of a small country attempts to force the United Nations to recognise his despotic power by establishing a secret missile base in Antarctica. The outcome has The Champions undergoing the deep-freeze treatment.

General Gomez: **Patrick Wymark**
Hemmings: **Robert Urquhart**
Margoli: **Peter Arne**
Jost: **Walter Gotell**
Ship's Captain: **Dallas Cavell**
Colonel Santos: **George Pastell**
Mendoza: **Michael Godfrey**
Gregson: **Martin Boddey**
Zerrilli: **Derek Sydney**
Heffner: **Alan White**

The Survivors
w **Donald James**
d **Cyril Frankel**

What lies behind the murder of three students in the Austrian Alps? The Champions are assigned to discover what or who is behind several killings in the same lakeside vicinity.

Franz/Colonel Reitz: **Clifford Evans**
Richter: **Donald Houston**
Emil: **Bernard Kay**
Schmeltz: **John Tate**

Mine Attendant: **Frederick Schiller**
Hans Davison: **John Porter**
Pieter: **Stephen Yardley**
Heinz: **Hugo Panczak**

To Trap a Rat
w **Ralph Smart**
d **Sam Wanamaker**

Tainted drugs are being offered for sale in London, and drug addicts are becoming victims. The Champions are asked to find the suppliers behind the lethal consignments before any further damage is done.

Walter Pelham: **Guy Rolf**
Jane Purcell: **Kate O'Mara**
Sandra: **Edina Ronay**
Edwards: **Michael Standing**
Peanut vendor: **Toke Townley**
Ambulance Doctor: **John Lee**
Ambulanceman: **Michael Guest**

The Iron Man
w **Philip Broadley**
d **John Moxey**

When asked to protect the life of a former dictator, the superhumans take on a very unusual role - as domestic staff at his home. Before long, domestic duties gives way to far more dangerous considerations.

El Caudillo: **George Murcell**
Pedraza: **Patrick Magee**
Carlos: **Stephen Berkoff**
Gallezan: **Robert Crewdson**
General Tornes: **Michael Mellinger**
Cabello: **Norman Florence**

The Ghost Plane
w **Donald James**
d **John Gilling**

Asked to investigate the movements of Dr Newman, a man whose plans for a revolutionary new aircraft have been shelved, the Champions find themselves hot on the trail of a secret's broker.

Doctor John Newman: **Andrew Keir**
Coates: **Michael Wynne**
Hardwick: **Tony Steedman**
Hilary: **Vanessa Lindall**
Bridges: **Dennis Chinnery**
Admiral: **Derek Murcott**
Pilot: **Paul Grist**
Crolic: **John Bryans**

The Dark Island
w **Tony Williamson**
d **Cyril Frankel**

When three agents fail to return from a tropical island, The Champions are sent to investigate. Richard lands by parachute, Sharron and Craig arrive posing as husband and wife. All three face instant danger.

Kellor: **Vladek Sheybal**
Admiral: **Alan Gifford**
Perango: **Benito Carruthers**
Controller: **Bill Nagy**
Kai Min: **Andy Ho**
Radio operator: **Richard Bond**
Tsi Chang: **Robert Lee**

The Fanatics
w **Terry Nation**
d **John Gilling**

Assigned to infiltrate a group of fanatical assassins, Richard Barrett joins the gang - and learns that Tremayne is to be their next victim. But can one man stop a determined group of killers - perhaps, when you're superhuman.

Croft: **Gerald Harper**
Anderson: **Julian Glover**
Colonel Banks: **Donald Pickering**
Roger Carson: **David Burke**
Krasner: **David Morrell**
Faber: **Barry Stanton**
Collings: **John Robinson**

Twelve Hours
w **Donald James**
d **Paul Dickson**

Having seen a visiting President safely aboard a waiting submarine, the Nemesis agents believe their troubles to be over. But an unknown assassination attempt waits around the corner, and they'll soon require their special powers.

Drobnic: **Henry Gilbert**
Raven: **Mike Pratt**
Admiral Cox: **Peter Howell**
Lt. Commander. Street: **John Turner**
Naval Captain: **John Stone**
Madame Drobnic: **Viola Keats**
Jackson: **Laurie Asprey**
Telegraphist: **Rio Fanning**

The Search
w **Dennis Spooner**
d **Leslie Norman**

When an atomic submarine, loaded with four nuclear weapons, is stolen by a new Nazi regime, The Champions find themselves racing against time to thwart the enemy plans to hold London hostage under nuclear threat!

Kruger Haller: **John Woodvine**
Dr Mueller: **Joseph Furst**
Conrad Schultz: **Reginald Marsh**
Suzanne Taylor: **Patricia English**
Allbrecht: **Ernst Walder**
Innkeeper: **Gabor Baraker**

The Gilded Cage
w **Philip Broadley**
d **Cyril Frankel**

When intruders break into Nemesis headquarters and steal Richard Barrett's file, Tremayne is worried that someone will attempt to wipe out Nemesis agents. To investigate further, Barrett allows himself to be kidnapped by the thieves.

Symond: **John Carson**
Samantha: **Jennie Linden**
Lovegrove: **Clinton Greyn**
Orley: **Charles Houston**
Brandon: **Tony Caunter**
Haswell: **Sebastian Breaks**
Manager: **Vernon Dobtcheff**

Shadow of the Panther
w **Tony Williamson**
d **Freddie Francis**

Is the death of a Nemesis doctor the result of voodoo magic - or something more easily explained? The Champions' investigations lead them into danger against a throbbing background of voodoo drums.

Prengo: **Zia Mohyeddin**
David Crayley: **Donald Sutherland**
Charters: **Hedger Wallace**
Riley: **Tony Wall**
Doctor: **Christopher Carlos**
Girl in Red: **Tania**
Waiter: **Kenneth Gardiner**

A Case of Lemmings
w **Philip Broadley**
d **Paul Dickson**

When several Interpol agents take their own lives, Nemesis agents Barrett, Sterling and Macready go to Italy to investigate. What they discover leads them to a daring plot to infiltrate the entire Interpol network.

Umberto: **John Bailey**
Claudine: **Jeanne Roland**
Del Marco: **Edward Brayshaw**
Jacquet: **Michael Graham**
Pillet: **Michael Slater**
Madame Carnot: **Olive McFarland**
Frenchman: **Jacques Cey**
Frenchwoman: **Madge Brindley**

The Mission
w **Donald James**
d **Robert Asher**

Craig and Sharron pose as a Mafiosa gangster and his girlfriend in an attempt to infiltrate an organisation which provides escape routes for criminals, who have had their faces altered by plastic surgery. Sharron finds herself booked for a facelift!

Dr Pederson: **Anthony Bate**
Hogan: **Dermot Kelly**
George: **Harry Towb**
Sophia: **Patricia Haines**
Maltman: **Robert Russell**
Emil Boder: **Paul Hansard**

The Interrogation
w **Dennis Spooner**
d **Cyril Frankel**

Agents Barrett and Macready are worried that their partner hasn't returned after his latest mission. Sensing that he is in trouble, they seek Tremayne's help - but he appears unconcerned. Meanwhile, Craig is in deadly danger.

The Interrogator: **Colin Blakely**

The Silent Enemy
w **Donald James**
d **Robert Asher**

Assigned to reconstruct the voyage of a nuclear submarine which has been found with all its crew dead, The Champions find themselves on a macabre voyage - which results in terrifying consequences.

Captain Baxter: **Paul Maxwell**
Admiral Parker: **Warren Stanhope**
Minoes: **Marne Maitland**
Stanton: **James Maxwell**
The Minister: **Esmond Knight**
Lighthouse Keeper: **David Blake Kelly**

Lighthouse Keeper: **Rio Fannnig**

The Bodysnatchers
w **Terry Nation**
d **Paul Dickson**

What hidden meaning is contained in a letter received from a journalist in Wales? The trio of Nemesis agents find themselves involved in a macabre espionage plot in their attempt to find out.

Squires: **Bernard Lee**
Yeats: **Philip Locke**
Inge Kalmutt: **Ann Lynn**
Frank Nicholls: **J. G. Devlin**
David Fenton: **Gregory Phillips**
Lee Rogers: **Christina Taylor**
White: **Frederic Abbott**

Get Me Out of Here!
w **Ralph Smart**
d **Cyril Frankel**

Sent to a Caribbean island to rescue Anna Maria Martes, a world famous doctor being held against her will, The Champions need all their combined powers to stave off the unwanted attention they attract on their arrival.

Anna Maria Martes: **Frances Cuka**
Commandante: **Ronald Radd**
Angel Martes: **Philip Madoc**
Minister: **Eric Pohlmann**
Cuevos: **Anthony Newlands**
Josef: **Godfrey Quigley**
Police Captain: **Norman Florence**
Detective: **Richard Montez**

The Night People
w **Donald James**
d **Robert Asher**

Unaware that she is heading into danger, Sharron Macready travels to Cornwall for a few days' well-earned rest. After receiving a phone call from her, Craig Sterling and Richard Barrett go to join her - but find that she has disappeared.

Douglas Trennick: **Terence Alexander**
Mrs Trennick: **Adrienne Corri**
Porth: **David Lodge**
Jane Soames: **Anne Sharp**
Dan: **Michael Bilton**
George Whetlor: **Walter Sparrow**
Hoad: **Jerold Wells**
Clerk: **Frank Thornton**

Project Zero
w **Tony Williamson**
d **Don Sharp**

The murder of Travis, a scientist, culminates in a series of strange disappearances among people working on a top secret experiment. The Champions, masquerading as boffins, set out to solve the case - and end up in deadly danger.

Voss: **Rupert Davies**
Antrobus: **Peter Copley**
Grayson: **Reginald Jessup**
Forster: **Geoffrey Chater**
Miss Davies: **Jan Holden**
Postmaster: **Nicholas Smith**
Sloane: **Donald Morley**
Travis: **John Moore**
Wittering: **Maurice Browning**
Chairman: **John Horsley**

Hedges: **Eric Lander**
Stewardess: **Jill Curzon**
Pilot: **Bruce Beeby**

Desert Journey
w **Ian Stuart Black**
d **Paul Dickson**

Attempting to escort a reluctant Bey to his strife-torn North African state, the Nemesis agents face a dangerous journey through the desert - a place where danger lies hidden among the swirling sand dunes.

The Bey: **Jeremy Brett**
Yussef: **Roger Delgado**
Sheikh: **Peter Madden**
Said: **Nik Zaran**
Curtis: **Reg Lye**
Branco: **Henry Soskin**
Major Tuat: **Tony Cyrus**
Sonia: **Yole Marinelli**

Full Circle
w **Donald James**
d **John Gilling**

Craig Sterling poses as a prisoner to plug a clever escape route. He and a fellow inmate make good their freedom, but the Nemesis agent finds more than he bargained for at their journey's end.

Westerman: **Patrick Allen**
Garcian: **Martin Benson**
Sara: **Gabrielle Drake**
Booker: **John Nettleton**
Carrington: **Jack Gwillim**
Pickering: **James Donnelly**
Sergeant Fairfax: **Lawrence James**
Collins: **Victor Brooks**

Nutcracker
w **Philip Broadley**
d **Roy Ward Baker**

After attempts are made to break into a vault containing top secret NATO documents. The Champions are assigned to test if the vault really is impregnable. Their mission is a dangerous one - the vault's safety device is programmed to kill any intruder!

Duncan: **William Squire**
Lord Mauncey: **David Langton**
Warren: **John Frankn-Robbins**
Manager: **Michael Barrington**
Walcott: **John Brown**
Travers: **David Kelsey**
Guard: **Dervis Ward**
Assistant: **Robert Mill**

The Final Countdown
w **Gerald Kelsey**
d **John Gilling**

What at first appears a simple task to three people endowed with unusual powers - locating an unexploded bomb - culminates in a mission fraught with danger for the Nemesis agents.

Kruger: **Derek Newark**
Von Splitz: **Alan MacNaughton**
Neinmann: **Wolf Frees**
Wolf Eisen: **Basil Henson**
Schultz: **Morris Perry**
Anna: **Hannah Gordon**

Helden: **Norman Jones**
Tom Brooks: **Michael Lees**

The Gun-Runners
w **Dennis Spooner**
d **Robert Asher**

Assigned to track down a gang of ruthless gun-runners, the Nemesis agents find themselves faced with intrigue and murder in a Burmese jungle. Their opponents will stop at nothing to prevent them, and their lives are in deadly peril.

Hartington: **William Franklyn**
Selvameni: **Paul Stassino**
Filmer: **David Lodge**
Schroeder: **Guy Deghy**
Burmese Police Captain: **Eric Young**
Nadkarni: **Wolfe Morris**
Ministry Clerk: **Nicolas Chagrin**

Autokill
w **Brian Clemens**
d **Roy Ward Baker**

The Champions find themselves facing an unbeatable enemy - themselves! Someone has programmed one of the team to kill his colleagues, and the Nemesis agents face danger from all sides as they try to discover their real enemy.

Barkar: **Eric Pohlmann**
Klein: **Paul Eddington**
Doctor Amis: **Harold Innocent**
George Brading: **Richard Owens**
Vanessa Brading: **Rachel Herbert**
Mechanic: **Conrad Monk**
American Colonel: **Bruce Boa**

✍ A 'feature' *Legend of The Champions*, was issued, being a compilation of *The Begining* and *The Interrogation*.

📖 *The Champions: The Sixth Sense is Death* [1969: John Garforth: Hodder Paperbacks: novelisation of *The Experiment* and *The Beginning*].

The Champions:

Created by: **Monty Berman** and **Dennis Spooner**
Producer: **Monty Berman**
Associate Producer: **Johnny Goodman**
[All episodes except 3,5,7,16,25,27,28,30]
Music by: **Edwin Astley, Albert Elms** and **Robert Farnon**
Theme tune by: **Tony Hatch**
Script Supervision: **Dennis Spooner**
Production Manager: **Malcolm Christopher**
Casting by: **Judith Jourd**
Stunt Arranger: **Bill Sawyer**
Music Editor: **Deveril Goodman**
Make-up Supervisor: **Gerry Fletcher**
Wardrobe Supervisor: **Laura Nightingale**
Special Effects: **Sid Pearson**

An ITC Production for ITC World Wide Distribution
Filmed on location and at Associated British Elstree Studios

30 colour 60-minute episodes
1968

The Count of Monte Cristo

Loosely [very!] based on the classic Alexandre Dumas adventure story, this swashbuckler retold how Edmund Dantes was falsely convicted of crimes against the state and sentenced to life imprisonment in the dreaded Chateau d'If. Having learned of the existence of a fabulous treasure from a dying prisoner, Dantes escaped to the island of Monte Cristo, found the lost treasure and returned to France.

What happened to him afterwards provides the theme for the series. His fabulous wealth allows him to do as he wishes with his life. He takes his revenge on those who treated him so cruelly and devotes himself to righting the wrong that others have suffered and to helping the poor.

Its star, George Dolenz [father of 'Monkee' Mickey] had more buckle than swash, while his co-star, Nick Cravat, came pretty close to repeating the role he had played in the Burt Lancaster film, *The Flame and the Arrow.*

Regular cast:
Edmund Dantes
[The Count of Monte Cristo]: **George Dolenz**
Jacopo: **Nick Cravat**
Mario: **Fortunio Bonanova** [episodes 1 - 3]
Carlo: **Henry Corden** [episodes 5 - 7]
Rico: **Robert Cawdron** [episodes 8 - 39]

✍

writer and director credits for episodes 2 - 39 unknown
episodes 1 - 8 and 17 - 21 were told in serialised format

The Affair of the Three Napoleons
w **Sidney Marshall**
d **Bud Boetticher**

Renee Morell, daughter of one of the Count's oldest friends, seeks help. Her father has been brutally murdered. The only clue to his killer consists of three gold coins which she found clutched in her dying father's hand. The Count of Monte Cristo sets out to avenge his friend's death.

Renee Morrell: **Faith Domergue**
De Villefort: **John Sutton**
Morrell: **Paul Cavanaugh**

The Pen and the Sword

The Count of Monte Cristo uncovers the theft of two million in Army funds and settles his account with General Beauclair, one of those responsible. Now, using the alias Veritas, his prime target is Minister of Justice Bonjean, the mastermind behind the theft.

Minister of Justice Bonjean: **Leslie Bradley**
Charmaine: **Mary Ellen Kay**
Henrietta: **Pat Wright**
Dubois: **John Bleifer**

The De Berry Affair

The Count of Monte Cristo foils an attempt to assassinate King Louis Phillipe. The would-be assassin claims to have been hired by the Duchess De Berry - the king's niece, and daughter of the ex-king of France. The woman is arrested and sentenced to death. Then King Louis asks the Count to rescue her from prison?

Duchess De Berry: **Susan Cummings**
Louis: **Walter Kingsford**
Thiers: **Anthony Caruso**
Sevier: **Peter Gray**
Dubois: **Peter Brocco**
Lieutenant: **Robert Human**

The Black Death

The plague has struck Paris. When it becomes obvious that Malherb, the Minister of Health, is fattening his own purse at the expense of the sick, the Count of Monte Cristo determines to expose Malherb - but assassins have been sent on his trail.

Dr Rousse: **Herbert Tudley**
Malherb: **Tom Browne**
Perrier: **Lewis Martin**
Gautier: **David Leonard**
Madame Rousse: **Ruth Swanson**

Affair of Honour

When a duelist is killed.. not by a deadly sword thrust, but by poison on the blade of his adversary, the Count uncovers evidence to convince him that the young man accused of murder is innocent. As a result of his efforts, he finds himself threatened by the law for helping the man escape.

Ferrar: **Bob Clarke**
Debray: **John Warburton**
Marie: **Yvette Dugay**
Beaumont: **Frank Wilcox**
Susan: **Maxine Cooper**
Von Humbolt: **Charles Meredity**

First Train to Paris

The advent of the first steam locomotive brings tremendous public excitement in France, its trial run being eagerly awaited by the nation. Then the Count of Monte Cristo is apprised of a news story which states that the locomotive exploded in route - a story printed some six hours before the explosion is set to take place!

Gerald: **John Elderedge**
Elise: **Adrienne Marden**
Cordot: **John Hoyt**
Verdis: **Paul Shepherd**

The Sardinia Affair

Arriving on the island of Sardinia in response to an urgent message from his friend Mario, the Count of Monte Cristo finds Mario dead, shot through the back by an arrow. Aldo Patrini has been charged with his murder. The Count launches a private investigation - and finds dirty work afoot.

Patrini: **Paul Picerni**
Teresa: **Lita Milan**
D'Alba: **Carleton G . Young**
Madroff: **Jack Kruschen**

A Toy for the Infanta

The King of Spain is dying. By his death bed await Queen Maria and her 4-year old daughter, the Infanta Isabella. Not far away is Don Carlos, the King's ruthless and ambitious brother who plots for the throne. Don Feliz, the Spanish Ambassador enlists the help of the Count of Monte Cristo.

Queen Maria: **Margaret Whiting**
Don Carlos: **Noel Willman**
Don Feliz: **Austin Trevor**
The Infanta: **Gay Emma**
The Abbot: **Richard Caldicot**
The Nurse: **Olivia Irving**
The Ambassador: **Gerard Heinz**

Marseilles

Dismissed from his post as French Consul because Spanish merchant ships have been attacked by French pirate vessels. De Breve visits his friend the Count of Monte Cristo. Can he find the real culprits?. Joined by Albert, who wants to help clear his father's name, the Count and his friends go to sea to uncover a traitor.

Albert: **Conrad Phillips**
Rousse: **Andre Mikhelson**
Marcel: **Patrick Troughton**
Yvonne: **Simone Lovell**

The Talleyrand Affair

Entrusted to carry a message from the King of France to England, the Count of Monte Cristo and his companions Jacopo and Rico, are waylaid at an inn but fight their way free. Reaching London, the Count finds himself the victim of the treacherous Duchess of Maastricht.

Palmerstone: **Finlay Currie**
Duchess of Maastricht: **Patricia Laffan**
Talleyrand: **Malcolm Keen**
Baron Garonne: **Ferdy Mayne**
Paul: **Patrick Morgan**

The Texas Affair

In a lone coach, speeding towards Paris, John Crane and his daughter, Martha, are set upon by horsemen led by Soult, who kill the coach driver and turn their pistols on the occupants. Fortune smiles when the Count of Monte Cristo and his friends send the brigands flying - a turn of events that leads them into deadly danger.

John Crane: **Macdonald Parke**
Martha Crane: **Betta St John**
Andre Soult: **Reed De Rouen**
Henri Mate: **Henry Oscar**
French Prime Minister: **Stanley Van Beers**

The Luxembourg Affair

The Duke of Luxembourg is dead. His daughter, Therese, arrives to take over her duties to the realm - but General Ludovic seeks regal power himself. Therese finds herself a prisoner in her own home - her salvation resting on the intervention of the Count of Monte Cristo, from whom Ludovic has arranged a loan to further his evil plans.

General Ludovic: **Lloyd Lamble**
Duchess Therese: **Maureen O'Reilly**
Madeleine: **Mary Laura Wood**
Petrov: **Alexis Bobrinskey**
Captain of the Guard: **Joseph Ryan**
Marianne: **Ann Lynn**

The Mazzini Affair

Mazzini, a brave Italian leader and national hero, is being held prisoner by ruthless Austrian freedom fighters, Reiker and Freidrich, who interrogate Mazzini and order his execution. At a secret rendezvous, the Count of Monte Cristo and Jacopo meet Carla, Mazzini's fiancee, whose rescue plan swings into well-oiled action.

Mazzini: **Michael Aldridge**
Carla: **Maureen Connell**
Reiker: **John Chandos**
Freidrich: **Andrew Faulds**
Father Pietro: **Milton Rosmer**

The Carbonari

When Louis Fauntello is murdered by the Carbonari, they leave their sign of death on his forehead, a charcoal cross. The Count of Monte Cristo, Jacopo and Rico take an interest in the notorious gang of conspirators, thieves and murderers who are plaguing France with their reign of terror.

Henri Fauntello: **Percy Marmont**
Dubroc: **William Franklyn**
Annette Fauntello: **Patricia Marmont**
Villon: **Arnold Bell**

The Devil's Emissary

Diabolo, a dealer in 'black magic' has set up residence in the peaceful valley of St. Falaise in the French Alps. Demanding money, Diabolo threatens the Baron's daughter, Marie with death. In the face of great odds, the Count of Monte Cristo determines to vanquish Diabolo's deadly power.

Diabolo: **John Sherman**
Marie: **Jan Holden**
Louis Martell: **Ian Fleming**
Moray: **Leslie Weston**
Revel: **Rupert White**
Dupre: **Peter Garstine**
Dardelle: **Anthony Baird**
Abbe: **Oliver Burt**

Bordeaux

When the Count de Morcef is imprisoned on a false charge of robbery and taken prisoner by Florian. Morcef's wife, Mercedes, is forced to sell her treasured ruby ring to buy her husband's freedom, a ring which at one time marked her engagement to Edmund Dantes - who, buying the ring in a jeweller's shop, sets out to discover why she sold it.

Mercedes: **Betty McDowell**
Bonnet: **Alan Wheatley**
Florian: **Walter Gotell**
Count de Morcef: **Noel Willman**
Jeweller: **Billy Milton**

Return to the Chateau d'If

When the young Duke of Renoldi, en route to his wedding with his finance, Marguerite, is abducted and thrown anonymously into the dungeons of the Chateau d'If, the Count of Monte Cristo effects his reinstatement to the dungeon where he was once held prisoner for twelve long years.

Marguerite: **Nancy Hale**
Renoldi: **Lian Sullivan**
Charcot: **Pierre Watkin**
Rabat: **Ken Gibbs**
Borden: **Ian MacDonald**
Abbe Faria: **Cyril Delavanti**
Lantini: **Allen Pinson**

The Golden Blade

The Count becomes interested when the Army Paymaster's gold shipment is stolen by bandits, and Lassino, a young Sergeant is accused of the theft. Monte Cristo knows the man and is far from convinced by what seems to be overwhelming evidence - but he has just five days to prove the man's innocence.

Lassino: **Glenn Langan**
Cecile: **Patricia Hardy**
D'Avril: **Alan Wells**

Prosecutor: **Phil Van Zandt**
Esco: **Kim Spalding**

Andorra

Responding to a request for help from his old friend, the Duke of Andorra, the Count arrives too late. The Duke is dead, murdered by his ambitious brother and his children gone, having fled in fear of their lives. The Count must find the children before their uncle's troops hunt them down and slay them.

Victor: **Peter Namkos**
Renee: **Susan Seaforth**
Gerard: **John Ernest Crawford**
Louis: **Nestor Paiva**
Bouchet: **Harry Lauter**
Porello: **Nolan Leary**

The Duel

Four men have been marked for death. One by one, provoked by insults made in public, they have fought and succumbed to a deadly, cold-blooded duellist. Determined to learn the cause of the duels, the Count of Monte Cristo allows himself to be branded a coward to avert the death of a fifth victim - a friend.

Rolla: **Stacy Harris**
Odette: **Claudia Barrett**
Marnet: **Gar Moore**
Balbec: **Michael Whalen**
Vicomte de Combray: **John Hamilton**
Michaud: **David Hoffman**

Victor Hugo

A one-time gallery slave, suspected of attempting to assassinate playwright Victor Hugo, is seized by the police. Only the Count of Monte Cristo is convinced of his innocence. Single-handed , he attempts to uncover the guilty party. An ironic twist of fate sees Victor Hugo, himself, brought before the bar, accused of murder.

Victor Hugo: **Keith Richards**
Cambrai: **Leonard Mudie**
Du Chablon: **Paul Kavanaugh**
De Crissac: **Britt Lomand**
Polineaux: **Ian Wolfe**
Tirelle: **Rick Vallin**
Gendarme: **Pierce Lyden**

Flight to Calais

Accompanied by Duchess Mathilde, and the Count of Monte Cristo, entrusted with ensuring her safe passage to London, Princess Anne of France travels to England, to cement the relationship between the two countries. Taking quarters at an inn, they retire for the night - then the Princess disappears!

Anne: **Ann Stephens**
Simone: **Andrienne Corri**
Duchess: **Elaine Inescourt**
Paul: **John Trevor**
Milet: **Hugh Williams**
Brentano: **May Brimmel**
Inn Keeper: **Sidney Vivian**

Naples

When a wounded man appears on board his yacht, but dies before he can speak, the Count of Monte Cristo finds a document on his body which shows the dead man was an emissary from the firm of Savini, the Count's bankers.

Suspecting foul play, the Count sails to Naples - to unravel a web of intrigue and treachery.

Bianca: **Hildy Christian**
Savini: **Maurice Kaufmann**
Brosa/Questore: **Phillip Leaver**
Durracq: **Raf De La Torre**
Lackey: **Patrick Jordan**
Stranger : **Nigel Davenport**
Bardo: **Halstan Crimmins**
Assassin: **Terence O'Regan**

Albania

An assassin is sent to murder the Count of Monte Cristo. A shot from Jacopo brings the assassin down but he dies before they can question him. learning that a man calling himself 'Monte Cristo' gave the order for his demise, the Count and Jacopo determine that an impostor is at large - but who is he. And what's his evil purpose?

Bogus Cristo: **Ralph Michael**
Gabrier: **Christopher Steele**
Maritza: **Jean Quick**
Hassan Ben Ali: **Peter Stephens**
Landlord: **Leslie Kyle**
Jailer: **David Lander**
Baron Lhota: **John Garside**
Assassin: **Lee Montague**
Sentry: **Murray Kash**

The Art of Terror

The Count of Monte Cristo receives a visit from, Jeanine. Terror stricken, she tells how her brother, Victor, and numerous other sailors have been abducted by a gang of thugs who are terrorising anyone boarding the Monte Cristo line. Together with Jacopo and Nico the Count sets out to solve the mystery.

Saveau: **Andrew Faulds**
Pierre Duval: **Julian Sommers**
Captain: **Alistair Hunter**
Victor Gaulte: **Vivian Matalon**
Corteau: **Anthony Baird**
Marat: **Stanley Groome**
Jeanine: **Elvi Hall**
Bergere: **George Skillan**

The Experiment

Research chemist Pierre Fresnay, and his wife, Suzanne, expect that the Academy of Science will reward Pierre for his discovery of a new use for oxygen. To their horror Pierre is arrested, charged with treason and sent to the Bastille. Suzanne seeks help from the Count of Monte Cristo.

Suzanne: **Diana Fairfax**
Pierre: **Conrad Phillips**
Resson: **Andre Van Gyseghem**
Honore: **Harriette Johns**
Marne: **Desmond Roberts**
Bonar: **Joseph Ryan**
Attendant: **Randall Kinkead**
Guard: **Richard Grant**

Mecklenburg

Crown Princess Helena of Mecklenburg loves Prince Ferdinand of France, but she is being urged to marry Frederick, Prince of Prussia. When the sinister Baron Reimer has Ferdinand arrested, the Queen of France turns to the Count of Monte Cristo for help.

Helena: **Mary Steele**
Ferdinand: **John Fabian**
Reimer: **Raymond Huntley**
Frederick: **Anthony Newlands**
Julia: **Julie Sommers**
Hesse: **Carl Bernard**
The Queen: **Margaretta Scott**
Secretary: **Peter Fontaine**

The Portuguese Affair

Dennis Dodge, a young British naval officer, is on his way to marry Teresa. Minutes after he arrives at her home in Lisbon, Dodge is placed under arrest for murder. One of the guests is the Count of Monte Cristo, there to fulfil his promise to the girl's father to give Teresa away when she married. It takes a resourceful Count to unravel the mystery.

Branza: **Patrick Troughton**
Cuevos: **Bill Nagy**
Teresa: **Mercy Haystead**
Cobbler: **Ben Williams**
Ruiz: **Barry Keegan**
Cavalo: **Leslie Perrins**
Lopes: **Philip Lennard**
Dodge: **Richard Bebb**

Lichtenburg

Visiting Lichtenburg, the Count of Monte Cristo and his companions go to the aid of a young nobleman who is being assailed by three swordsmen. The Count recognises the man as a friend of his - Baron Franz Wilhelm. Told by Franz that Prince Gustav, the King's nephew has branded him a traitor, the Count decides to act.

Franz: **Roderick Lovell**
Steiger: **Stanley Van Beers**
Anna: **Margaret Whiting**
Metz: **Allan Cuthbertson**
Farmer: **Howell Davies**
Doctor: **Reginald Atkinson**
Gustav: **Esmond Knight**
Landlord: **Jack Cuningham**

Burgundy

The grape-growers of Burgundy are forced to pay 'protection money' to Citizen Borner. Phillipe Porter refuses to pay, a situation made dangerous because he loves Josette, daughter of Cadeaux, a member of Borner's gang. Brutally forced into payment by Le Drue, Phillipe seeks the help of the Count of Monte Cristo.

Josette: **Simone Lovell**
Little Girl: **Donna Andrews**
Phillipe: **William Franklyn**
Le Drue: **Walter Gotell**
Borner: **Charles Lloyd Pack**
Cadeaux: **Charles Farrell**
Neighbour: **Ian Ainsley**

Majorca

Visiting Majorca, the Count is disturbed to find that newspapers carry reports of his death. Visiting the cathedral where the body is awaiting burial he meets Eugenie, the dead man's widow. When his life is threatened Monte Cristo decides to investigate the mystery - and plunges headlong into a web of intrigue and danger.

Eugenie: **Maureen Connell**
Concierge: **John Barrard**

Rossi: **Philip Vickers**
Felipe: **Ian Bannen**
Priest: **Paul Hardwicke**
Newsvendor: **Tony Sympson**

Monaco

Years before, the Count had financed the printing shop of Menard, an ex-counterfeiter. since then he has followed an honest profession. Now counterfeit money is circulating and the police are closing in - their prime suspect, Menard. The Count of Monte Cristo decides to ensure that justice prevails.

Menard: **Charles Lamb**
Mdme. Sablon: **Patricia Laffan**
Armand: **Lloyd Lamble**
Villon: **Lee Montague**
Gabrielle: **Adrienne Corri**
Croupier: **Michael Alexander**
Gendarme: **Stratford Johns**
Dukas: **Arthur Young**

Sicily

The Count is stunned. Antonio Cavalcanti, one of the men who had vowed to seek out and kill Edmund Dantes soon after he had escaped the Chateau d'If, begs an audience with the Count of Monte Cristo. The Count's predicament: Will his enemy recognise him as being one and the same?

Monevido: **Alexander Gauge**
Benedetto: **Eddie Byrne**
Cavalcanti: **Guy Verney**
Alfredo: **Maurice Kaufmann**
Jailer: **Victor Platt**
Secchi: **Max Brimmel**
Eugentia: **June Rodney**

A Matter of Justice

Lieutenant Albert Lenz is charged with treason. Held in secret, the trial is bogus, Lenz the victim of evil intrigue. Given no chance to defend himself, Lenz must rely on his mother to recruit the services of the Count of Monte Cristo in defence of an innocent man.

Lt. Lenz: **Michael Anderson**
Madame Lenz: **Beverly Gregg**
Major Du Valle: **John Phillips**
Gen. Le Claire: **Ronald Adam**
Col. Michelle: **Alan Wheatley**
Maurine Ronda: **Charles Carson**
Capt. Bodine: **Colin Douglas**

Point Counter Point

Baron Danglers and his niece, Simone, live in Toulon under the assumed names of Hugo and Sacia de Rollin. A bitter enemy of the Count of Monte Cristo, Danglers is particularly excited when he finds a way of severely embarrassing the Count - a ruse that could easily lead to the Count's arrest and execution.

Simone: **Betty McDowell**
Danglers: **John Loder**
Vittorio: **Frank Carriello**
Marat: **John Longden**
Armand: **Raymond Young**
Innkeeper: **Leo Franklyn**
Capt. Joubert: **Frank Barnes**
Renault: **Stuart Mitchell**

The Island

Abducted by the Count's old antagonist, the Duchess Maastricht, and tortured for information about the island where Monte Cristo's fortune lies hidden. Nico faces grave danger unless the Count and Jacopo can engineer his release and settle an old account.

Duchess: **Patricia Laffan**
Valpezzo: **Robert Brown**
Bonaparte: **Michael Mellinger**
Dubois: **Max Brimmel**
The Ferret: **Patrick Troughton**
Fishwoman: **Rita Webb**
First Corsican: **Garry Thorne**

Athens

The Count of Monte Cristo visits Athens on a tour of the Greek ruins. While there his guide, Zorba, is murdered. The culprit is Baron Von Hanstein, who wishes to acquire a priceless piece of sculpture. The dead man's son seeks justice and the Count opens his investigations - unaware that Hanstein plots to murder him as well.

Constantine: **Diarmuid Kelly**
Von Hanstein: **Reed De Rouen**
Elena: **Louis Gainsborough**
Zorba: **Cyril Shaps**
Demetrios: **Reginald Jessup**
Niki: **Michael Brooke**
Palamas: **Elwyn Brook Jones**

The Barefoot Empress

Travelling incognito, Anna, Empress of Austria, is unaware that her progress through France is being watched by Baron Buray, a man ordered to assassinate her. But three other people know of Buray's intentions, the Count of Monte Cristo and his companions, Jacopo and Rico - who elect to follow the Empress at a safe distance.

Anna: **Jane Griffiths**
Baron Buray: **Robert Brown**
Latoure: **Carl Bernard**
Equerry: **Brian Rawlinson**
Tall Man: **Ewan Solon**
Eugenia: **Moira Lynd**

The Grecian Gift [aka The Brothers]

Antoine Gizet rides to Paris on a mission to the Count of Monte Cristo. He carries a new invention of his father's which, if intercepted by the government, will revolutionize the French Navy. En route he is waylaid by his twin brother, Francois. Leaving Antoine for dead, Francois intends to pass himself off as his brother. Can the Count of Mont Cristo see through the deception?

Antoine/Francois: **Conrad Phillips**
Suzanne: **Mary Steele**
Phillipe: **Noel Howlett**
Marrat: **Douglas Wilmer**
Secretary: **Peter Halliday**
Woodcutter: **Frank Pemberton**
Groom: **Frederick Tripp**

The Count of Monte Cristo:

Adapted from the novel by **Alexandre Dumas**
Producer: **Sidney Marshall**
Executive Producer: **Leon Fromkess**
Production Supervisor: **Rudolph Flothow**
Directors: **Charles Bennett, Dennis Vance, David MacDonald, Sidney Salkow**
Director of Photography: **Sam Leavitt A.S.C.**
Assistant Director: **Bruce Fowler Jnr.**
Make-up: **Lee Greenway**
Wardrobe: **Einar Bourman**

A Television Programmes of America Presentation for ITC World Wide Distribution.

Filmed in Hollywood and at Associated Television's Elstree Studios.

39 monochrome 30 minute episodes
1956

Danger Man I

The exploits of John Drake, a special security operative for the North Atlantic Treaty Organisation [NATO], who went wherever duty called in his unending crusade to rid the world of subversive elements. Handsome, athletic, fearless, Drake frequently took risks to achieve his aim, but they were calculated risks in the cause of world peace. A man who detested any form of physical violence [yet faced danger every day of his life], he was often forced to fight his unscrupulous enemies with whatever means were available to him.

International in both outlook and setting, no two stories found Drake in the same location. One week he'd be in Paris, the next, Brazil. One week later he'd be trudging through dense African undergrowth; Drake went wherever his own particular brand of justice could be used to best effect.

The stories themselves provided more than their fair share of thrills, but always remained logical and realistic and never went 'over-the-top' or insulted the viewers' intelligence.

Fans of the series will no doubt recall the opening sequence that introduced the 30-minute stories: a tall figure emerged from a federal building in Washington DC, crossed to a sleek white sports car, threw his mackintosh into the rear seat and drove away at speed. Throughout this sequence a voice-over narration informed us that:

> 'Every government has its Secret Service branch.
> America, the CIA; France, the Deuxieme Bureau
> and England, MI5.
> NATO also has its own.
> A messy job. That's when they call on me
> - or someone like me.
> Oh yes, my name is Drake,
> John Drake.'

The best of its genre, the series made an international name of its star, Patrick McGoohan.

Regular cast:
John Drake: **Patrick McGoohan**
Hardy: **Richard Wattis**
Col. Keller: **Lionel Murton**

---

season one

39 monochrome 30-minute episodes
1960-61

View from the Villa
w **Brian Clemens** and **Ralph Smart**
d **Terry Bishop**

An American banker in Rome in charge of gold worth $5 million is found dead, and the gold - which represented part of America's NATO contribution - is missing. Drake investigates, but is hampered by the attention of a woman who deals in murder.

Gina Scarlotti: **Barbara Shelley**
Stella Delroym: **Delphi Lawrence**
Mayne: **John Lee**
Mego: **Colin Douglas**
Delroy: **Philip Latham**
Finch: **Court Benson**
Waiter: **Andreas Malandrinos**
Cafe Artist: **Charles Houston**
Marine Officer: **Raymond Young**
Housekeeper: **Marie Burke**
Taxi Driver: **David Ritch**
Maid: **June Rodney**

Time to Kill
w **Brian Clemens** and **Ian Stuart Black**
[from a story by **Brian Clemens**]
d **Ralph Smart**

Despite being handcuffed to a beautiful woman, Drake succeeds in his mission to capture a vicious international killer. But first he has to prove himself innocent of a murder charge!

Lisa Orin: **Sarah Lawson**
Colonel Keller: **Lionel Murton**
Hans Vogeler: **Derren Nesbitt**
Professor Barkoff: **Carl Jaffe**
Sally Raymond: **Louise Collins**
Waiter: **Anthony Jacobs**
Patrolman: **Endre Muller**
Frontier Guard: **Edward Hardwicke**
Frontier Guard: **Harvey Hall**

Josetta
w **Ralph Smart**
d **Michael Truman**

Drake is assigned to protect a blind girl who heard her brother being shot and can recognise the killer's voice. When the girl's evidence proves insufficient to convict the killer, Drake is forced into tricking him into admitting his guilt.

Juan: **Kenneth Haigh**
Josetta: **Julia Arnall**
Colonel Segur: **Campbell Singer**
Olot: **Randall Kinkead**
Sandra: **Claire Gordon**
Motril: **Glenn Beck**
Miguel: **Robert Bernal**
Head Waiter: **Cecil Brock**
Policeman: **Anthony Viccars**

The Blue Veil
w **Don Ingalis** and **Ralph Smart**
d **Charles Frend**

Drake is sent to the Arabian desert where, posing as a hard-drinking deadbeat, he gains access to a mine and finds the evidence he needs to help a stranded showgirl return to England.

Spooner: **Laurence Naismith**
Clare: **Lisa Gastoni**
The Moukta: **Ferdy Mayne**
Hassan: **Joseph Cuby**
The Pilot: **Peter Thornton**

The Lovers
w **Jo Eisinger** and **Doreen Montgomery**
d **Peter Graham Scott**

Drake receives a surprise telephone call from an old enemy, Miguel Torres. He requests Drake to work with him to guard 'The Lovers', a president and his wife visiting England.

Maria: **Maxine Audley**
Stavros: **Martin Miller**
Miguel Torres: **Michael Ripper**
President Pablo Gomez: **Ewen Solon**
Leonido: **Carl Bernard**
Rosa: **Hermione Gregory**

The Girl in Pink Pyjamas
w **Ian Stuart Black** and **Ralph Smart**
[from a story by **Brian Clemens**]
d **Peter Graham Scott**

When a beautiful girl, wearing pink pyjamas, is found wandering in a dazed condition along a lonely road in a Balkan state, it provides Drake with a clue to an attempted assassination plot.

The Girl: **Angela Browne**
Dr. Keller: **John Crawford**
Major Minos: **Alan Tilvern**
Dr. Stanifors: **Robert Raglan**
Hospital Director: **Richard Warner**
President Varnold: **Robert Cawdron**
Farmer's Wife: **Colette Wilde**
Country Doctor: **Frederick Schiller**
Franz: **Harvey Hall**
Anaesthetist: **Richard Marner**
Nurse: **Janine Gray**
Telephone Operator: **Marian Diamond**

Position of Trust
w **Jo Eisinger** [from a story by **Ralph Smart**]
d **Ralph Smart**

Drake is assigned to track down and destroy a Middle East drug syndicate who are supplying opium on a world-wide scale. He becomes as much involved in the human tragedy as he does in the syndicate members.

Captain Aldrich: **Donald Pleasence**
Sandi Lewis: **Lois Maxwell**
Paul: **John Phillips**
Alison: **Gilbert Winfield**
Mrs Aldrich: **Irene Prador**
Fawzi: **Martin Benson**
Mrs Fawzi: **Madeleine Kasket**
Casino Manager: **Derek Godfrey**
Aly: **Derrich Sherwin**

The Lonely Chair
w **John Roddick** and **Ralph Smart**
d **Charles Frend**

Called in to tackle a politically sensitive case, Drake takes the place of a wealthy crippled industrialist to crack down on a gang who are holding his daughter ransom in exchange for secret designs plans.

Noelle Laurence: **Hazel Court**
Patrick Laurence: **Sam Wanamaker**
Hardy: **Richard Wattis**
Brenner: **Patrick Troughton**
Holst: **Howard Pays**
Caldwell: **Jack Melford**
Fordyce: **Alexander Archdale**
Rolf: **Robert Harbin**
Mrs Hardy: **Dorothy Hersee**
Porter: **Clifford Earl**
Sally: **Liz Lanchbury**

The Sanctuary
w **John Roddick** and **Ralph Smart**
d **Charles Frend**

Suspecting that a terrorist, about to be released from a prison, has similar work awaiting him, the authorities assign Drake to impersonate him. Travelling to a remote part of Scotland, he discovers that a bird sanctuary hides a sinister secret.

Crawford: **Kieron Moore**
Kathy: **Wendy Williams**
Liamond: **Barry Keegan**
Anders: **Charles Farrell**
Brannigan: **Shay Gorman**
Neil: **John Rae**

Hamish: **Ewen MacDuff**
Mullins: **Peter Murray**

An Affair of State
w **Oscar Brodny**
d **Peter Graham Scott**

Drake flies to a small Caribbean island where an American economics expert is reported to have committed suicide. British Intelligence have their doubts about the claim, and Drake must discover the true cause of the man's death.

Ortiz: **Patrick Wymark**
Alvarado: **John Le Mesurier**
Raquel Vargas: **Dorothy White**
Jose Santiago: **Warren Mitchell**
Mr Hartley: **Alan Gifford**
Airport Official: **Victor Baring**
Barman: **Michael Hitchman**
Groupier: **Andre Charise**
Police Sergeant: **Anthony Viccars**
Hostess: **Fenella Fielding**

The Key
w **Jack Whittingham** [from a story by **Ralph Smart**]
d **Seth Holt**

Called in by the American ambassador in Vienna to investigate how confidential information is being passed from the Embassy, Drake's enquiries bring him into contact with a fellow agent, posing as a newspaper man.

Logan: **Robert Flemyng**
Maria: **Monique Ahrens**
Ambassador: **Charles Carson**
Alex: **Charles Gray**
Joe: **Peter Swanwick**
Police Superintendent: **Charles Lloyd Pack**
Detective: **Martin Sterndale**

The Sisters
w **Jo Eisinger** [from a story by **Brian Clemens**]
d **Seth Holt**

A beautiful girl flees to England to seek political asylum. Drake is assigned to vet her request - but when a second girl arrives also seeking asylum, and claiming to be the sister of the first, he begins to suspect their identities.

Nadia: **Mai Zetterling**
Gerda: **Barbara Murray**
Hardy: **Richard Wattis**
Radek: **Sydney Tafler**
Security Officer: **Anthony Dawson**
Nagor: **Martin Wyldeck**
Embassy Secretary: **Hedger Wallace**
Parsinski: **Michael Hunt**
Glazanov: **Michael Jacques**
Maria: **Antonia Gilpin**
Lena: **Margo Mayne**

The Prisoner
w **Ralph Smart** and **Robert Stewart**
d **Terry Bishop**

An American citizen in the Caribbean is accused of espionage and takes refuge in the American Embassy, which he cannot leave for fear of being arrested. Drake is assigned to help- and does so with the aid of a classical pianist.

James Carpenter and Oscar Schumak: **William Sylvester**
Sue Carpenter: **June Thorburn**
Colonel Vasco: **William Lucas**
President: **Michael Peake**

Passport Officer: **Keith Goodman**
Policeman: **John Slavid**

The Traitor
w **John Roddick**
d **Terry Bishop**

Drake must find out what makes a man a traitor. When an English agent and his wife suddenly flee the country and head for Kashmir, Drake follows a known foreign courier to their destination. But danger shadows his every move.

Noel Goddard: **Ronald Howard**
Louise Goddard: **Barbara Shelley**
Rollo Waters: **Jack Watling**
Banarji: **Warren Mitchell**
Panah: **Derek Sydney**
Blatta: **George A. Cooper**
Guard on Train: **Guy Deghy**

Deadline
w **Jo Eisinger** [from a story by **Ian Stuart Black**]
d **Peter Graham Scott**

When an unsolved murder gives rise to a wave of terrorism in an African country, Drake plunges into the jungle to find an attractive native woman who can tell him the truth about the murder.

Khano: **William Marshall**
Thompson: **Edric Connor**
Mai: **Barbara Chilcott**
Ajali: **Christopher Carlos**
Professor Moma: **Earl Cameron**
Moses Amadu: **Lionel Ngakane**
Sir Aaron Nelson: **Andre Dakar**
Daniels: **John Harrison**
Bartender: **Lloyd Reckord**
Officer: **Harcourt Curacao**
Native Woman: **Pearl Prescod**

Colonel Rodriguez
w **Ralph Smart**
d **Julian Aymes**

An American reporter is arrested for allegedly spying in a Caribbean country, and Drake is sent out as another journalist - but he too is arrested by a crooked police chief who tries to frame him for murder.

Colonel Rodriguez: **Noel Willman**
Martine: **Maxine Audley**
Joan Bernard: **Honor Blackman**
Walter Bernard: **Ronald Allen**
General Abeijon: **Campbell Singer**
Pietro: **Cyril Shaps**
Chloe: **Pearl Prescod**
Danny: **Neville Becker**
Barman: **Lloyd Reckford**
Policeman: **Brian Jackson**

The Island
w **Ralph Smart** and **Brian Clemens**
d **R. Pennington Richards**

Stranded on a remote island after a plane crash with three other survivors - a beautiful heiress and two contract hit-men whom Drake had been taking for trial - the agent needs all his ingenuity to stay alive.

Mr Wilson: **Allan Cuthbertson**
Mr Jones: **Peter Stephens**
Bobby: **Ann Firbank**
Kane: **Michael Ripper**

Pilot: **Ronan O'Casey**
Bobby: **Richard Thorp**
Airport Official: **Charles Irwin**
Stewardess: **Nyree Dawn Porter**

Find and Return
w **Jo Eisinger**
d **Seth Holt**

Drake has to find a woman wanted for espionage - and possibly high treason. It means a trip to the Middle East and certain danger - other agents are interested in the woman and are closing in fast.

Vanessa: **Moira Lister**
Nikolides: **Donald Pleasence**
Hardy: **Richard Wattis**
Ramfi: **Paul Stassino**
Mrs Ramfi: **Zena Marshall**
Mrs Nikolides: **Nancy Seabrooke**
Detective: **Keith Rawlings**
Airport Official: **Frank Thornton**
Shashig: **Warren Mitchell**

The Girl who Liked GIs
w **Marc Brandel** and **Ralph Smart**
d **Michael Truman**

Was the death of an American soldier in Munich an accident or murder? Posing as a GI, Drake visits the soldier's girlfriend and father, but he cannot find definite proof - until he discovers a photograph the dead man had left to be developed.

Vicki: **Anna Gaylor**
Lotsbeyer: **Anthony Bushell**
Wetzel: **Nigel Green**
Doyle: **Paul Maxwell**
Krug: **Charles Farrell**
Sgt. Peter Ross: **Graydon Gould**
Sgt. Poole: **Bill Edwards**
Manservant: **Rudolf Offenbach**
Receptionist: **Betty Le Beau**

Name, Date and Place
w **Ralph Smart** and **John Roddick**
d **Charles Frend**

When three state officials are all murdered in an identical way, Drake is assigned to discover who is behind their deaths. He uncovers a very beautiful murderess and commissions her to murder someone - himself?

Nash: **Cyril Raymond**
Hardy: **Richard Wattis**
Deirdre: **Kathleen Byron**
Rosemary: **Patricia Marmont**
Kim Russell: **Jean Marsh**
Nita: **Susan Travers**
Franky: **Delena Kidd**
Chambermaid: **Olive McFarland**
Vogel: **Guy Deghy**
Small Man: **Frederick Piper**
Butler: **Beaufoy Milton**
Det. Ins. Marks: **Frank Sieman**
Bank Clerk: **John Gardiner**
Gambler: **Jimmy Lomas**
Det. Sgt. Davis: **Peter Hutton**
Servant: **Howard Greene**

Vacation
w **Ralph Smart**
d **Patrick McGoohan**

On a vacation to the Riviera, Drake recognises a notorious professional assassin. He changes places with the killer in order to discover his intended victim, but once he has done so, he finds the victim isn't so innocent as he makes out.

Andrew Amory: **Hugh McDermott**
Baron: **Esmond Knight**
Veronica: **Jacqueline Ellis**
Georges: **Barrie Ingham**
Gautier: **Lawrence Davidson**
Butler: **John Wynyard**
Ricki: **Richard Clarke**
Gunsmith: **Charles Lloyd Pack**

The Conspirators
w **Ralph Smart** and **John Roddick**
d **Michael Truman**

A British diplomat is murdered to prevent him giving evidence at an inquiry into maladministration in Africa. Drake is sent to protect the man's wife but she refuses to concede that she's in danger - until someone tries to kill her.

Lady Lindsay: **Patricia Driscoll**
Saunders: **Terence Longdon**
Sir Arthur Lindsay: **Hugh Moxey**
Craven: **Alfred Burke**
Innkeeper: **Percy Herbert**
Burke: **Rory McDermot**
Skipper: **Neil McCarthy**
George: **Michael Sands**
Kip: **Ian Ellis**
Tim: **Timothy Benke**

The Honeymooners
w **Ralph Smart** and **Lewis Davidson**
d **Charles Frend**

A Chinese businessman is found dead in the hotel bedroom of an English couple honeymooning on an island in the Far East, and the husband is arrested for murder. Drake must take desperate action to obtain the man's release from prison.

Mr. Chung Sun-Minister of Justice: **Lee Montague**
Ted Baker: **Ronald Allen**
Joan Baker: **Sally Bazely**
President: **Michael Peake**
Reporter: **Kerrigan Prescott**
Williams: **Sheldon Lawrence**
Mitchu: **Anthony Chin**
Police Lieutenant: **Eric Young**
Gate-Keeper: **Nyo Toon**
Maid: **Barbara Lee**
Receptionist: **Jimmy Fung**

The Gallows Tree
w **Ralph Smart** and **Marc Brandel**
d **Michael Truman**

A car stolen in the Scottish highland bears the fingerprints of the organiser of a spy ring who was reported dead ten years previously. Drake traces him to a remote island and finds a quite unexpected surprise.

Laing: **Paul Rogers**
Jean: **Wendy Craig**
Clements: **Raymond Huntley**
Craig: **Ewan Roberts**
Mackenzie: **Andrew Crawford**
Hamish: **John Glyn-Jones**
Shepherd: **John Rae**
Hawkes: **Reginald Hearne**
Duncan: **Gareth Tandy**
Conductor: **Michael Bird**

"Jock": **Finlay Currie**

The Relaxed Informer
w **Ralph Smart** and **Robert Stewart**
d **Anthony Bushell**

To Drake, a drastic situation [a top security leak] calls for drastic action. So he carries out an audacious hold-up in Bavaria. The recording wire he steals from a courier leads him into dangerous waters.

Joseph Brenner: **Duncan Lamont**
Ruth: **Moira Redmond**
Colonel Doyle: **Paul Maxwell**
Frederick: **Brian Rawlinson**
Benedict: **Stanley Van Beers**
Captain Brandt: **Tom Gill**
Greta: **Pauline Letts**
French Delegate: **Henry Vidon**
Sergeant: **Charles Vance**

The Brothers
w **Ralph Smart**
d **Charles Frend**

When a plane crashes off the coast of Sicily and its occupants are shot and robbed by bandits, who make off with a diplomatic pouch, Drake is assigned to retrieve the secret documents - at any cost.

Lita Rossi: **Lisa Gastoni**
Police Commissioner: **George Coulouris**
Guiseppe: **Ronald Fraser**
Hugo: **Derren Nesbitt**
Luigi: **John Woodvine**
Housekeeper: **Nancy Beckh**
Policeman: **Gino Melvazzi**
First Airman: **Rodney Burice**
Second Airman: **Wesley Murphy**

The Journey Ends Halfway
w **Ian Stuart Black**
d **Clive Donner**

Drake becomes involved in oriental intrigue when, in the guise of a Czech engineer, he travels to China to investigate the disappearance of an eminent doctor who had been trying to escape from the Communist regime.

Dr. Bakalter: **Paul Daneman**
McFadden: **Willoughby Goddard**
Miss Lee: **Anna May Wong**
Senor Paterno: **Paul Hardtmuth**
Masseur: **Martin Boddey**
Tai: **Burt Kwouk**
Police Sergeant: **R. Bobby Naidoo**
Ming: **Eric Young**
Police Officer: **Gerry Lee**
Chang: **Anthony Chin**
Miss Shoo: **Lian-Shin Yang**

Bury the Dead
w **Ralph Smart** [from a story by **Brian Clemens**]
d **Clive Donner**

A ticket for the opera in Palermo, received by Drake in Washington, whirls the agent into a dangerous adventure in Sicily. The ticket contains a coded message that a NATO agent has been killed: Drake is to take over the dead man's mission.

Jo Harris: **Beverly Garland**
Hugo Delano: **Dermot Walsh**
Police Captain: **Paul Stassino**

Bart: **Patrick Troughton**
Bruno: **George Murcell**
Barman: **George Eugeniou**
Tony Costello: **Robert Shaw**

Sabotage
w **Michael Pertwee** and **Ian Stuart Black**
d **Peter Graham Scott**

When a transport plane on its way from Singapore to New Guinea suddenly breaks radio contact with its base, and an explosion sends it to its doom. Drake, posing as a hard-drinking pilot, flies out to investigate.

Peta: **Maggie Fitzgibbon**
Giselle: **Yvonne Romain**
Meisener: **Oliver Burt**
Benson: **Alex Scott**
Chin Lee: **R. Bobby Naidoo**
Ann: **Lyn Ashley**
Taxi-Driver: **Jimmy Fung**
Pilot: **John Sterland**
Co-Pilot: **Peter Dolphin**

The Contessa
w **John Roddick** and **Ralph Smart**
d **Terry Bishop**

Cocaine found hidden in the jacket of an injured longshoreman in the New York dock sends Drake on a hectic chase to Genoa to await the return of the man's ship.
Posing as a down-at-heel dockhand, he discovers a huge drug-smuggling operation.

Francesca: **Hazel Court**
Julio: **John Wyse**
Keller: **Lionel Murton**
Minister: **Ralph Truman**
Mario: **Bill Nagy**
Rosa: **Jennifer Jayne**
Maria: **Irene Prador**
Giorgio: **Dudley Foster**
Rossi: **Edward Cast**
Lucia: **Jackie Collins**
Intern: **Glenn Beck**
Singer: **Terence Cooper**

The Leak
w **Ralph Smart** and **Brian Clemens**
d **Anthony Bushell**

Drake is sent to North Africa to investigate the frequency with which employees at an atomic energy plant are being taken ill - apparently suffering from radiation. He discovers the source of the leak, but needs proof that it is sabotage.

Doctor Leclair: **Zena Marshall**
Doctor Bryant: **Bernard Archard**
Sheik Ahmed: **Marne Maitland**
Martin: **Anthony Dawson**
Finch: **Lawrence Davidson**
Colonel Perar: **Walter Gotell**
Secretary: **William Peacock**
Salah: **Barry Shawzin**
Mrs Parkes: **Patsy Smart**
Sadi: **Joseph Cuby**
Moham: **Eric Pohlman**

The Trap
w **Ralph Smart** and **John Roddick**
d **R. Pennington Richards**

When a clerk in the cipher office of the American Embassy walks out of her job and flies to Venice, Drake must discover

if she is a willing or unwilling dupe in a game of international spying activities.

Beth: **Jeanne Moody**
Gino: **Noel Trevarthen**
Carla: **Marie Burke**
Whitmore: **Alan Gifford**
Liz: **Louise Collins**
Miss Bishop: **Georgina Cookson**
Papa: **Victor Rietty**
Mama: **Miki Iveria**
Stashig: **John Bonney**
Officer: **Patrick Maynard**
Pilot: **Graham Stewart**
A Neighbour: **Charles Mansell**
A Servant: **Norman Lapedus**

The Actor
w **Marc Brandel**
d **Michael Truman**

A security information leak takes Drake to a Hong Kong broadcasting station as a member of a team transmitting English lessons. He discovers that a code is being used to pass secrets to the Chinese - but the discovery almost costs him his life.

Colonel Graves: **Rupert Davies**
Al Jason: **Gary Cockrell**
Suzan: **Julie Allan**
Mrs Harkness: **Patsy Rowlands**
Chen Tung: **Burt Kwouk**
General Chu Yee: **Andy Ho**
Mr Toy: **Eric Young**
Karibz: **Sam Chowdhary**
Receptionist: **Chin-Yu**
Secretary: **Soo-Bee Lee**

Hired Assassin
w **Ralph Smart** and **John Roddick**
d **Charles Frend**

Hearing that an attempt is to be made to assassinate a foreign president when he visits a South American country, Drake infiltrates the terrorist group - and is immediately assigned the task of leading the assassination attempt.

Alexis: **Alan Wheatley**
Luis: **Cyril Shaps**
Edouardo: **Nyall Florenz**
Juanita: **Judy Carne**
Senor Lazar: **Wensley Pithey**
Col. Fernandez: **Bill Nagy**
Pietro: **Harry Lockart**
Viccenti: **J. Leslie Erith**
Kovac: **Charles Hill**
Pepe: **Frank Thorton**
Girl in Florists: **Camilla Hasse**

The Deputy Coyannis Story
w **Jo Eisinger**
d **Peter Graham Scott**

Funds sent to a mid-European country for rehabilitation purposes do not appear to be reaching those in need, so Drake is assigned to find out who has misappropriated the funds and to put a stop to their activities.

Coyannis: **John Phillips**
Zameda: **Charles Gray**
Lorain Zameda: **Heather Chasen**
Captain Achard: **Liam Gaffney**
Marco: **Stuart Hutchison**
Salcito: **Peter Welch**

Medana: **Julie Hopkins**
Storch: **Robert Raglan**
Finance Minister: **Leonard Sachs**
Acardi: **Bartlett Mullins**

Find and Destroy
w **Ralph Smart** and **John Roddick**
d **Charles Frend**

When a prototype intelligence submarine is wrecked off the coast of South America, Drake is assigned to blow up the vessel before anyone can examine the sophisticated equipment on board - but foreign agents are already on their way.

Major Hassler: **Peter Arne**
Melina: **Nadja Regin**
John Gordon: **Peter Sallis**
Helen: **Helen Morton**
Commander Ford: **Ronald Leigh-Hunt**
Enrico: **Alec Mango**
Fedor: **Richard Clarke**
Corto: **Brad Dancy**
Pia: **Rebecca Dignam**

Under the Lake
w **Jack Whittingham**
d **Seth Holt**

A train journey to Vienna affords Drake the opportunity to form a friendship with an attractive young woman whose father he believes to be behind a world-wide forgery syndicate.

Gunther Klaus: **Christopher Rhodes**
Mrs Grahame: **Hermione Baddeley**
Mitzi: **Moira Redmond**
Colonel Keller: **Lionel Murton**
Von Golling: **Roger Delgado**
Receptionist: **Walter Gotell**
Attendant: **Norman Florence**
Driver: **Jack Cunningham**
Porter: **Andrew Downie**
Cable Car Attendant: **Reginald Jessup**

The Nurse
w **Ralph Smart** and **Brian Clemens**
d **Peter Graham Scott**

A dramatic meeting with a Scots nurse in the heart of an Arabian desert plunges Drake into a mission to save the son and heir of an Arabian king who has been assassinated.

Mary MacPherson: **Eileen Moore**
Prior: **Jack MacGowran**
The Innkeeper: **Eric Pohlmann**
Hamilton: **Robert Ayres**
Helen Hamilton: **Heather Chasen**
Moukta: **Harold Kasket**
Idris: **Harry Lockart**
Ahmed: **David Oxley**
General Khan: **Andrew Faulds**
Ghazi: **Maxwell Shaw**
Pilot: **Harold Siddons**

Dead Man Walks
w **Ralph Smart** and **Brian Clemens**
d **Charles Frend**

When all the members of a research team experimenting in tropical plant diseases are believed to have died in suspicious circumstances, Drake is sent to Kashmir where crops are being devastated by a new strain of virus.

Hardy: **Richard Wattis**
Sita Shapadi: **Marla Landi**
Natalie Smith: **Julia Arnall**
Keith Smith: **Richard Pearson**
Rangit Pal: **Michael Ripper**
Professor Hanbury: **Bryan Coleman**
Nawi: **Joanna Dunham**
Azad: **William Peacock**
Wasing: **Zia Mohyeddin**

Danger Man II
aka Secret Agent

Three years after the 30-minute series ceased production, John Drake reappeared in a new series of adventures. However, changes had been made. Each episode was now of 60-minutes duration. Whereas the previous series had found Drake assigned as special investigator to an undesignated NATO department based in an American government building, he now found himself a fully-fledged member of Her Majesty's Secret Service and assigned as a Special Security Agent to a London-based ministry department designated M9. He also had a new boss and was seen receiving his assignments directly from a deskbound 'M'-type superior. [In a former series Drake was seen receiving orders from government ministers of all nationalities.]
Unchanged were the keynotes of each story: Drake was still a loner, and continued to enter each new adventure with as much zeal and determination to succeed as he had shown previously. Action and suspense were still the order of the day, and no expense was spared to inject each story with a liberal sprinkling of nailbiting suspense. [Highlights of each story were the further development of Drake's 'software gadgets': tiepins that served as cameras; cherries containing miniature microphones; electric shavers which doubled as a tape-recorder/transmitter - all were housed in the agent's gimmick-ridden attache case.]
✍ Seasons 2 - 4 syndicated in the USA as *Secret Agent*.

Regular cast:
John Drake: **Patrick McGoohan**
Hobbs [his superior]: **Peter Madden**

season two
32 monochrome 60-minute episodes.
1964-65

Yesterday's Enemies
w **Donald Jonson**
d **Charles Crichton**

When a former British agent appears to have set up his own network of double agents in the Lebanon, Drake is assigned to bring the man to heel. He must first penetrate his opponent's control headquarters - and that proves a dangerous task.

Jo Dutton: **Maureen Connell**
Archer: **Howard Marion Crawford**
Attala : **Anton Rodgers**
Mrs Curtis: **Joan Hickson**
Brett: **Peter Copeley**
Mrs Archer: **Patricia Driscoll**
Harris: **Aubrey Morris**
Hobbs: **Peter Madden**
Bertrand: **Ivor Salter**
Mary Wilson: **April Wilding**
Stewardess: **Lynn Taylor**
Immigration Officer: **George Eugeniou**
Barman: **George Zenios**

Nickolaou: **Nadim Sawalha**
Kemal: **Raul Alkazzi**

The Professionals
w **Wilfred Greatorex** and **Louis Marks**
d **Michael Truman**

A British businessman disappears, and to discover his whereabouts Drake is appointed to the Embassy staff in Prague. Learning from the man's wife that he had money problems and had left her for the exotic Ira Frankel, Drake sets out to find the woman - when he does so, he discovers more than he bargained for.

Mrs Pearson: **Helen Cherry**
Ira: **Nadja Regin**
Desmond Pearson: **Jerry Stovin**
Milos Kaldor: **Alex Scott**
Rhodes: **John Welsh**
Ambassador: **Noel Johnson**
Miss Burnham: **Joan Young**
Interrogator: **Steve Plytas**
Czech Receptionist: **Hana Pravda**
Landlord: **Jan Conrad**
Nadia: **Stella Courtney**
Czech Policeman: **John G. Heller**
Secretary: **Brenda Dunrich**
Police Motorcyclist: **Charles Laszlo**

Colony Three
w **Donald Jonson**
d **Don Chaffey**

Drake takes the place of a defector and discovers a special camp in Europe, which is a reconstruction of an English village known as Hamden. His assignment leads him into dangerous waters.

Randall: **Glen Owen**
Donovan: **Niall MacGinnis**
Richardson: **Peter Arne**
Janet: **Catherine Woodville**
Student: **George Mikell**
Admiral Hobbs: **Peter Madden**
Lord Denby: **Edward Underdown**
Lady Denby: **Cicely Paget-Bowen**
Fuller: **Peter Jesson**
Soldier: **Laurence Herder**
Agent: **Charles Laszlo**

The Galloping Major
w **David Stone**
d **Peter Maxwell**

After an unsuccessful assassination attempt on the life of the Prime Minister of a newly independent African state, Drake is sent out to investigate the situation and to help shape the man's destiny.

Prime Minister: **William Marshall**
Colonel Nyboto: **Errol John**
Kassawan: **Earl Cameron**
Dr Manudu: **Edric Connor**
Lasalle: **Arnold Diamond**
Suzanne: **Jill Melford**
General Powers: **Geoffrey Lumsden**
Mrs Manningham: **Nora Nicholson**
Barman: **Lloyd Reckford**
Personal Asst: **Zakes Mokae**
Adjutant: **Danny Daniels**
Girl: **Heather Emanuel**
NCO: **Ron Blackman**
Attendant: **Jimmy Falana**
Sergeant: **Willie Payne**

Fair Exchange
w **Wilfred Greatorex** and **Marc Brandel**
d **Charles Crichton**

A British agent, who was captured and tortured in East Germany, discharges herself from hospital and returns to kill the man who tortured her. Drake, posing as her husband, has his hands full when she refuses to forget the past.

Lisa: **Lelia Goldoni**
Pieter: **James Maxwell**
Wilhelm Berg: **George Mikell**
Otto Berg: **Andre Van Gyseghem**
Foster: **Barry Linehan**
Mumford: **Edwin Apps**
Gorton: **Raymond Adamson**
Dr McKenna: **Noel Howlett**
Sustri: **Kenneth Adams**
German Farmer: **Thomas Gallagher**
German Guard: **John Kirby**
Servant: **Hugo De Vernier**
East German Guard: **Jerry Tunnicliffe**
German Taxi Driver: **Bernard Davies**
Pohlman: **Ernest Lindsay**
English Taxi Driver: **Bruce Whightman**

Fish on the Hook
w **John Roddick** and **Michael Pertwee**
d **Robert Day**

The name 'Fish' hides the identity of the controller of the British agents in the Middle East. When his identity is in danger of being exposed, Drake is sent to bring the man to safety - but he must first discover 'Fish's' identity.

Gerdi: **Dawn Addams**
Nadia: **Zena Marshall**
Rowland: **Terence Longdon**
Dr Zoren: **Martin Miller**
Gamal: **Peter Bowles**
Tewflick: **Vladek Sheybal**
Abdul: **Michael Godfrey**
Maxwell: **Harvey Hall**
Albert: **Robert Henderson**
G's Secretary: **Clive Russell**
Cockney Soldier: **Walter Randall**
Arab Girl: **Durra**
Captain: **Prem Bakshi**
Dr Zoren's Nurse: **Karen Clare**

The Colonel's Daughter
w **David Weir**
d **Philip Leacock**

Drake goes to India to investigate a leakage of military secrets. The Chief of Police proves to be an old friend, and the two men are soon involved in investigating a series of suspicious deaths.

Joanna: **Virginia Maskell**
Colonel Blakeley: **Michael Trubshawe**
Chopra: **Warren Mitchell**
Khan: **Zia Mohyeddin**
Minister: **John Bennett**
Petel: **George Pastell**
Interrogator: **Kenneth Adams**
Plainclothes Man: **Frank Olegario**
Picton Jones: **Michael Nightingale**
Gumta: **Kumar Ranji**
Personal Asst to Minister: **Balu Patel**
Barman: **Dean Francis**
Margaret: **Zoe Zephyr**
Subra: **Jaron Yaltan**

The Battle of the Cameras
w Philip Broadley
d Don Chaffey

Secret documents which could be used in chemical warfare have been stolen and Drake traces them to a millionaire industrialist living in a heavily guarded villa. But all is not what it at first appears.

Martine: **Dawn Addams**
Kent: **Niall MacGinnis**
Genicot: **Frederick Bartman**
Hobbs: **Peter Madden**
Alex: **Patrick Newell**
Barman: **Jose Berlinka**
Croupier: **Gilbert France**
Senior Executive: **John Serret**
Chief Chemist: **Henry De Bray**
Night Manager: **Hugo De Vernier**

No Marks for Servility
w Ralph Smart
d Don Chaffey

Drake poses as a manservant to investigate a man suspected of being a big-time swindler. His 'master' is an arrogant and ill-mannered oaf and the open hostility between them makes life difficult for Drake.

Armstrong: **Mervyn Johns**
Judy: **Francesca Annis**
Gregori: **Howard Marion Crawford**
Helen: **Suzan Farmer**
Avraam: **Peter Illing**
Hobbs: **Peter Madden**
Strotti: **John Cazabon**
Lady Fielding: **Elizabeth Ashley**
Sir Charles Fielding: **Frederick Piper**
Joseph: **John G. Heller**

A Man to be Trusted
w Raymond Bowers
d Peter Maxwell

Sent to Haiti to discover if two M9 agents talked under torture - and subsequently death - Drake is suspicious that one of the local contacts he has been given is a traitor - but which one?

Mora: **Harvey Ashby**
Lorna Corlander: **Patricia Donahue**
Dorset: **Ralph Michael**
Louise Bancroft: **Eunice Gayson**
Stella Dorset: **Wanda Ventham**
Papa Camille: **Christopher Carlos**
Customs Officer: **Alvaro Fontana**
Carlos: **Harry Baird**
Manservant: **Tracy Connell**
and
The Boscoe Holder Dancers

Don't Nail Him Yet
w Philip Broadley
d Michael Truman
Drake dons the disguise of a teacher in order to investigate claims that agent Rawson is handing over naval secrets. Wanting to trap the organisation behind Rawson, Drake plays a waiting game and follows him.

Rawson: **John Fraser**
Diana: **Sheila Allen**
Lucus: **Anthony Dawson**
Gorton: **Raymond Adamson**
Mumford: **Edwin Apps**

Sir Ralph: **Edward Chapman**
Bennett: **Edward Cast**
Sue: **Wendy Richard**
Lennie: **Leonard Monaghan**
Bill: **Keith Bell**
Jeannie: **Jackie Pearce**
Waiter: **Nicholas Hawtrey**
Pub Landlord: **Ian Collin**

A Date with Doris
w Philip Broadley
d Quentin Lawrence

When a British agent is framed for the murder of an actress, and the frame-up appears to be part of a revolution attempt, Drake travels to the Caribbean with orders to bring the man to safety.

Juana Romero: **Jane Merrow**
Joaquin Paratore: **Ronald Radd**
Eduardo: **Eric Pohlmann**
Peter Miller: **James Maxwell**
Plain Clothes Man: **Marne Maitland**
Major Casado: **Richard Bebb**
Chemist: **David Lander**
Van Driver: **David Cargill**
Reception Clerk: **Carlos Douglas**
Bell Boy: **Micky Ventura**
Police Officer: **Alvaro Fontana**
Segeant: **David Charlesworth**
Jose: **Guido Adorni**
Doorman: **Donald Tandy**
Tavern Keeper: **Charles Hill**
Conchita: **Magda Konopke**
Naval Lieutenant: **Richard Owens**
First Assassin : **Juan Ilinares**
Second Assassin: **Michael Martin**
Soldier: **Roy Vincente**
Sergeant's Man: **Peter Brayham**
Policeman: **Michael Maten**

That's Two of Us Sorry
w Jan Read
d Quentin Lawrence

When fingerprints are found on a briefcase from which valuable documents have been stolen, Drake finds himself in Scotland searching for a man believed dead for 20 years - and ducking the amorous advances of a beautiful girl.

Sheila: **Francesca Annis**
Landlord: **Finlay Currie**
Magnus Sutherland: **Nigel Green**
Angus McKinnon: **Duncan Lamont**
Donald McKinnon: **Brian Phelan**
Braithwaite: **Graham Crowden**
Mrs Braithwaite: **Barbara Lott**
Mrs McKinnon: **Julie Wallace**
Mackay: **Duncan McIntyre**
Security Man: **Rory McDermot**
Miss Montgomery: **Sara Branch**
Dr Hutchins: **Stephen Jack**
Todd: **John Southworth**
Nikita: **Ian Flintoff**

Such Men are Dangerous
w Ralph Smart
d Don Chaffey

Drake masquerades as an ex-prisoner to penetrate an organisation that recruits and trains potential terrorist to eliminate political leaders. His first mission brings him into contact with deadly danger.

Major Latour: **Lee Montague**
Shorty Pratt: **Jack McGowran**
Mr Sen: **Zia Mohyeddin**
General: **Jack Gwillam**
Jack Taylor: **John Cairney**
Solicitor: **Alan Wheatley**
Diana: **Georgina Ward**
Hobbs: **Peter Madden**
Red Johnson: **Robert O'Neil**
Odzala: **Thomas Baptiste**
Tweedy Gentleman: **Roger Maxwell**
Edwin Bowden: **Tom Gill**
Williams: **Ivor Salter**
Butler: **Eric Chitty**
Miss Jackson: **Dorinda Stevens**
Gateman: **Patrick Connor**
Harry Hutchinson: **David Cargill**
Inspector: **Henry Kay**
Girl: **Martine Beswick**
Girl: **Judy Huxstable**
Girl: **Ann Colston**

Whatever Happened to George Foster?
w **David Stone**
d **Don Chaffey**

A wealthy British industrialist is involved in a plot to overthrow a Latin American government. Drake draws the matters to the attention of his superior - but is promptly told to forget about it!

Pauline: **Adrienne Corri**
Lord Ammanford: **Bernard Lee**
Certhia: **Jill Medford**
Lady Ammanford: **Joyce Carey**
The Stranger: **Colin Douglas**
Nanny: **Patsy Smart**
Sir Joseph Manton: **Richard Caldicot**
Secretary: **Redmond Phillips**
Charlie Hewitt: **Jack Bligh**
Police Sergeant: **Michael Collins**
Miss Jones: **Dorothea Phillips**
Airport Clerk: **Sonia Fox**
Ginger: **Jeremy Ranchev**
Mrs Foster: **Barbara Leake**
Garage Attendant: **Bill Corlett**
Schoolmaster: **Eynon Evans**
Landlord: **Dafydd Havard**
Vicar: **Evan Thomas**
Jones the Boat: **Norman Wynne**
Farmer: **Roderick Jones**
Garage Manager: **Brian Anderson**

A Room in the Basement
w **Ralph Smart**
d **Don Chaffey**

When the British Government finds its hands tied by diplomatic red tape, Drake gathers together a group of mercenaries to rescue a colleague being held prisoner in an Embassy building in Switzerland.

Susan: **Jane Merrow**
Bernhard: **William Lucas**
Military Attache: **Michael Gwynn**
British Ambassador: **Mark Dignam**
Dr Huber: **Gerard Heinz**
Keith Turnbull: **John Breslin**
Luke: **Edward Cast**
British First Secretary: **John Welsh**
Third Secretary: **Jack May**
Sister Rousseau: **Margo Johns**
Annette: **Kate O'Mara**
Man Receptionist: **John Cater**

Servant: **Jose Berlinka**
Sergeant: **Peter Elliott**

The Affair at Castelevara
w **James Foster**
d **Quentin Lawrence**

When a defeated ex-leader returns to his country after a revolution, and is sentenced to death, Drake joins forces with an American agent on a mission to rescue him. But they must first defeat the threat of General Ventura.

Carlos Bisbal: **Eric Pohlmann**
Ramon Torres: **Harold Goldblatt**
General Ventura: **Martin Benson**
Sir Duncan: **Andre Morell**
Van Horn: **Alan Gifford**
Fortunato Santos: **Aubrey Morris**
El Ferro: **Brian Worth**
Maite: **Sonia Fox**
Kemp: **Charles Tingwell**
Colonel Montes: **Richard Leech**
Manual: **David Saire**
Detective: **David Graham**
Immigration Oficer: **David Ritch**
Prison Guard: **Clive Cazes**
Policeman in Cafe: **Paul Armstrong**

The Ubiquitous Mr Lovegrove
w **David Stone**
d **Don Chaffey**

A treasury official accuses Drake of running up high gambling debts [a security risk for any agent]; Drake denies the charge and visits the casino - where he is greeted as a long-standing client!

Elaine: **Adrienne Corri**
Mr Lovegrove: **Eric Barker**
Mr Alexander: **Francis De Wolff**
Mrs Fairbrother: **Patsy Rowlands**
'Umbrella': **Peter Butterworth**
Morgan: **Edward Underdown**
'Briefcase': **Mike Pratt**
Man in Black: **John Cazabon**
Doorman: **Desmond Llewelyn**
Receptionist: **Patrick Connor**
Fletcher: **Peter Gill**
Croupier: **Terrance Hooper**

It's Up to the Lady
w **Philip Broadley** [from a story by **John Roddick**]
d **Michael Truman**

When a British Government official defects and shortly afterwards his wife leaves the country, Drake follows her to Greece to persuade her husband to return. But where should a wife's loyalty lie when her husband is accused of being a traitor?

Paula: **Sylvia Syms**
Charles: **Robert Urquhart**
Nicos: **Maxwell Shaw**
Hobbs: **Peter Madden**
Paula's Mother: **Vera Cook**
Mimiko: **Harry Tardios**
Customs Man: **Meadows White**
Secretary: **Sarah Brackett**
Greek Policeman: **Andreas Lysandrou**
Greek Boy: **George Zenios**
British Agent: **Anthony Baird**
Plainclothes Man: **John Bryans**
Truck Driver: **William Hurndell**
Girl: **Sally Douglas**

Have a Glass of Wine
w **David Stone**
d **Peter Maxwell**

A government employee photographs secret papers and then takes a 'holiday' in France with the documents in her luggage. Drake is assigned to follow her and discover her contacts - a trail which leads him to a French Chateau.

Suzanne: **Ann Lynn**
Lamaze: **Warren Mitchell**
Police Chief: **George Benson**
Zelda: **Kathleen Breck**
Jules: **Victor Brookes**
Gaston: **Michael Balfour**
Henri: **Larry Taylor**
Duty Officer: **Brian Weske**
Old Lady: **Anita Sharp Bolster**
Madame Lafleur: **Ann Heffernan**
Annette: **Sarah Brackett**
Chateau Guide: **Roger Avon**
Pierre: **Michael Coccoran**

The Mirror's New
w **Philip Broadley**
d **Michael Truman**

Drake finds Paris far from gay when he is asked to investigate the disappearance of a British Embassy official. When Drake finds him, he claims to have amnesia and no memory of past events - but Drake thinks otherwise.

Bierce: **Donald Houston**
Sir Jeremy: **David Hutcheson**
Penny: **Wanda Ventham**
Nicola: **Nicola Pagett**
George Murgia: **Bill Nagy**
Virginia Bierce: **Mary Yeomans**
Esser: **Ernst Walder**
Frances: **Alison Seebohm**
Second Pursuer: **Jerome Willis**
Diana: **Yvonne Marquand**
First Pursuer: **Frank Maher**

Parallel Lines Sometimes Meet
w **Malcolm Hulke** [additional dialogue by **Ralph Smart**]
d **Don Chaffey**

When a couple employed at a top secret weapons research station are kidnapped while on holiday in Devon, Drake finds himself teamed with a beautiful Russian agent who has been assigned to the case.

Nicola Tarasova: **Moira Redmond**
Dessiles: **Errol John**
Darcy: **Earl Cameron**
Lieutenant Labaste: **Clifton Jones**
James Owen: **Paul Danquah**
Victor N'Dias: **Christopher Carlos**
Madame Celeste: **Pearl Prescod**
David Elliot: **Robert Dean**
Vernon Brooks: **Edward Brayshaw**
Mrs Elliot: **Margaret Nolan**
Nero: **Boscoe Holder**
Eirlys Brooks: **Janet Hargreaves**
Guard: **Louis Mahoney**
Anarchist: **Joseph Layode**

You're Not in Any Trouble, Are You?
w **Philip Broadley**
d **Don Chaffey**

In order to infiltrate a murder organisation and expose its leaders, Drake commissions a murder - his own ! But matters are complicated when he befriends a young girl holidaying in Rome.

Lena: **Susan Hampshire**
Enzo Bandone: **Andre Van Gyseghem**
Ernesto: **John Cazabon**
Dave: **Bill Edwards**
Ellis: **Jeremy Burnham**
Emmerson: **John Welsh**
Receptionist: **Robert Rietty**
Old Man: **Andreas Malandrinos**
Barman: **Frank Coda**
Fausto: **Tony Baron**
Left Luggage Clerk: **Harry Tardios**
Boy in the Bar: **Ray Barron**
Bell Boy: **Paul Layton**
Masan: **Burt Kwouk**

The Black Book
w **Philip Broadley**
d **Michael Truman**

The brother of a high-ranking official at the British Embassy in Paris is being blackmailed and Drake is sent to discover why and by whom. His French contact is an unusual one - a husky-voiced girl on the telephone.

Simone: **Georgina Ward**
Sir Noel Blanchard: **Griffith Jones**
General Carteret: **Jack Gwillim**
Lady Blanchard: **Patricia Haines**
Serge: **Mike Pratt**
James: **Richard Owens**
First Counter Agent: **Frederic Abbot**
Second Counter Agent: **Ray Roberts**
Business Man: **Edward Sinclair**
Politician: **Beresford Williams**

A Very Dangerous Game
w **Ralph Smart** and **David Stone**
d **Don Chaffey**

Posing as a defector in order to infiltrate a spy ring in Singapore, Drake is approached by the Chinese who wants him to spy on British Intelligence! Faced with exposure, he offers to do so.

Lisa Lee: **Yvonne Furneaux**
Chi Ling: **Peter Arne**
Suzy: **Poulet Tu**
Simpson: **Anthony Dawson**
Khim: **Burt Kwouk**
Dickinson: **Geoffrey Bayldon**
Comdr Corbett: **Dennis Ramsden**
George: **Charles Carson**
British Controller: **Mike Pratt**
Pauline: **Norma West**
Questioner: **Anthony Chinn**
Wardrobe Master: **Cyril Chamberlain**
Arthur: **Christopher Sandford**
Watcher: **Cecil Cheng**
Gunman: **Paul Tann**
Hostess: **Mona Chong**
Young Man in Bar: **Harry Brookes**
Second Hostess: **Yu-Ling**
Barman: **Tommy Yap**
Manservant: **Donald Chan**

Sting in the Tail
w **Philip Broadley**
d **Peter Yates**

Drake takes a calculated risk in provoking the jealousy of Noureddine, a political assassin wanted by the Paris police, as a means of getting the man to leave the safety of Beirut.

Alexandros: **Ronald Radd**
Noureddine: **Derren Nesbitt**
James: **John Standing**
Marie Valedon: **Jeanne Roland**
Stephen Miller: **David Collings**
Shah of Assini: **Jeremy Spenser**
Police Inspector: **Julian Somers**
Sir Alan: **Andrew Laurence**
Daphne Miller: **Mary Webster**
Bulack: **Ernst Ulman**
Michele: **Juliet Harmer**
Model: **Christine Child**
Messadi: **Neville Becker**
Cafe Owner: **Jose Berlinka**
Airport Clerk: **Zeynep Tarimer**

English Lady Takes Lodgers
w **David Stone**
d **Michael Truman**

Drake heads for Lisbon to trace an agency suspected of exchanging stolen secrets - some of them British. He turns up a dead agent, and a landlady with a convenient sideline in forged passports.

Emma: **Gabriella Licudi**
Pilkington: **Robert Urquhart**
Commander Collinson: **Howard Marion Crawford**
Philippe Granville: **Frederick Bartman**
Colonel Torres: **Gary Hope**
Customs Official: **Jerome Willis**
Rosalind Fielding: **Judy Huxtable**
Taxi Driver: **Clive Cazes**
Porter: **Roger Worrod**

Loyalty Always Pays
w **David Stone**
d **Peter Yates**

The last message a British agent made before his sudden death confirms M9's suspicions that the Chinese are about to gain a foothold in an African country in which Britain has financial interests. Drake is sent to Africa to discredit the Chinese and restore the status quo.

Beyla: **Johnny Sekka**
Enugu: **Errol John**
Prime Minister: **Earl Cameron**
Major Barrington: **Nigel Stock**
Lucas: **Ray Brooks**
Miss Sefadu: **Dolores Mantez**
Colonel M'Bota: **Mark Heath**
Mrs Barrington: **Joan Newell**
Susy: **Joan Hooley**
Kanda: **Lloyd Reckord**
Doorman: **Dan Jackson**
Vickers: **Edward Jewesbury**
Chin Lee: **Robert Lee**
Lieut Kankana: **Bari Jonson**
First Removal Man: **Harry Baird**
Second Removal Man: **Benny Nightingale**
Barman: **Yemi Ajibade**
Third Removal Man: **Harcourt Curacao**
Secretary: **George A. Saunders**
Affluent Man: **Joseph Layode**

The Mercenaries
w **Ralph Smart**
d **Don Chaffey**

When an M9 agent is murdered while investigating the activities of a mercenary army in Africa, Drake is sent to complete his murdered colleague's assignment - and uncovers a plot to dispose of an African premier.

Caroline Winter: **Patricia Donahue**
Prime Minister: **John Slater**
Sergeant Bates: **Percy Herbert**
General G'Niore: **Peter Arne**
Dr Winter: **Frederick Peisley**
General White: **Jack Gwillim**
Pierre Deschamps: **John Gabriel**
Colonel Coote: **Derrick DeMarney**
Sinclair Jones: **Zia Mohyeddin**
Hawkinson: **Dervis Ward**
Buchanan: **Shane Rimmer**
Brewster: **Patrick Jordan**
Cleaner: **Paul Danquah**
Receptionist: **Zorenia Osborne**
PM's Secretary: **Christopher Carlos**
Police Officer: **David Lander**
Lab Assistant: **Heather Emmanuel**
Boscoe Holder: **Boscoe Holder**

Judgement Day
w **Donald Jonson** [from a story by **Michael Bird**]
d **Don Chaffey**

Sent to the Middle East to bring back a German scientist accused of having committed atrocities against prisoners of war, Drake finds himself acting as defending counsel in a bid to save the man's life.

Jessica: **Alexandra Stewart**
Shimon: **John Woodvine**
Pilot: **Maurice Kaufmann**
Garriga: **Guy Deghy**
Ygal: **David Saire**
James: **Peter Halliday**
Airport Official: **Neville Becker**
Hotel Landlord: **Harold Berens**
David: **Ben-Ari**
Carrier: **Mohhammad Moosa Shamsi**
Driver: **Yashar Adem**
Bookseller: **Bakshi Prem**

The Outcast
w **Donald Jonson**
d **Michael Truman**

Assigned to investigate whether there is any connection between the murder of a Wren illegally found in possession of secret papers and the disappearance of her boyfriend, Drake finds himself pursuing a suspect to Spain.

Leo Perrins: **Bernard Bresslaw**
Nora Cazalet: **Patricia Haines**
Xavier: **Brian Worth**
Helen Cazalet: **Judy Geeson**
Commander Marsden: **Richard Caldicott**
The Stranger: **Stephen Yardley**
Sandra: **Anita West**
'Dead' man: **Frederic Abbott**
Lieutenant Barrington: **Caron Gardner**
Spanish Bus Official: **Paul Armstrong**
Ramon: **Tony Lee**
Flamenco Dancer: **Marina Vasquez**

Are You Going to Be More Permanent?
w **Philip Broadley**
d **Don Chaffey**

Which of three agents stationed in Switzerland is a traitor? Drake must discover the answer before any further M9 agents are murdered. His plan involves putting himself in the firing line - a move which could cost him his life.

Lesley Arden: **Susan Hampshire**
Kronenberg: **Maxwell Shaw**

Joseph Laclos: **Howard Goorney**
Colonel Salmson: **John Miller**
Man in Museum: **George Cormack**
American: **Murray Cash**
Estate Agent: **Denis Shaw**
French Customer: **Cameron Miller**
Jordon: **Desmond Cullum-Jones**
First Agent: **Brian Gilmar**
Second Agent: **Frank Maher**
Vladimir: **Tony Thawnton**
Girl in Taxi: **Lesley Allen**

---

season three
13 monochrome 60-minute episodes
1965-66

To Our Best Friend
w **Ralph Smart**
d **Patrick McGoohan**

Drake is reluctant to investigate M9's allegations that a fellow agent and close personal friend is a traitor; nevertheless he does so - and finds himself faced with a dilemma between personal loyalties and duty.

Bill Vincent: **Donald Houston**
Leslie Vincent: **Ann Bell**
Ivan: **T. P. McKenna**
Colonel: **Jack Allen**
Rutledge: **John Gabriel**
Betrand: **Roderick Lovell**
First Secretary: **Charles Lloyd Pack**
Translator: **Robert Rietty**
Natalie: **Gita Denise**
Sayyed: **Julian Sherrier**
Phelps: **Christopher Sandford**
Solomin: **Frederick Farley**
Poltyev: **Cyril Cross**
Watcher: **Simon Brent**
Simpson: **Brian Weske**
Girl in Phone Box: **Rhonda Ryan**

The Man on the Beach
w **Philip Broadley**
d **Peter Yates**

Drake's mission to identify a double agent in the M9 network operating from a luxury hotel in Jamaica leads to difficulties when he finds himself being accused of being in the pay of the enemy.

Cleo: **Barbara Steele**
Wykes: **Glyn Houston**
Sir Alan Grose: **David Hutcheson**
Howes: **Peter Hughes**
Lyle: **Clifton Jones**
Callaghan: **Fredric Abbott**
Lady Kilrush: **Juliet Harmer**
Mary Ann: **Dolores Mantez**
Rafael: **Gary Hope**
Calypso Singer: **Tommy Eytle**
Cellar Man: **Harry Baird**
Barman: **Paul Danquah**
Millie: **Pearl Prescod**

Say It with Flowers
w **Ralph Smart** and **Jacques Gilles**
d **Peter Yates**

When money is drawn from the account of a man reported to have died at an exclusive clinic in Switzerland, Drake investigates and finds that the establishment is a cover for selling secret information.

Wallace / Hagen: **Ian Hendry**
Dr Brajanska: **John Phillips**
Caroline: **Jemma Hyde**
Krummenacher: **Harold Kasket**
Kasser: **Martin Wyldeck**
Meyer: **William Dexter**
Verena: **Rachel Herbert**
Man in Taxi: **Basil Dignam**
Buchler: **Kevin Stoney**
Miss Wallace: **Gretchen Franklin**
Carl: **Frank Maher**
Wilhelm: **Les White**

The Man Who wouldn't Talk
w **Donald Jonson** and **Ralph Smart**
d **Michael Truman**

When an M9 agent operating in Europe is captured, Drake is assigned to ensure that the man doesn't reveal the names of his colleagues under torture. But other people are interested in the man - and Drake, as usual, finds trouble.

Lydia Greshnova: **Jane Merrow**
Meredith: **Norman Rodway**
Interrogator: **Ralph Michael**
Forbes: **Brian Worth**
Peter: **Simon Brent**
Policeman at Garage: **Murray Hayne**
Garage Manager: **Mike Pratt**
Doctor Radev: **Frank Gatliff**
HQ Policeman: **Roy Marsden**
Night Porter: **John Herrington**
Second Security Man: **David Orchard**
Third Security Man: **Ken Haward**
Girl in Bath: **Angela Lovell**

Someone Is Liable to Get Hurt
w **Philip Broadley** and **Ralph Smart**
d **Michael Truman**

Drake is on a double mission: he's to investigate reports that a Caribbean country's pending election is threatened by illegal arms deal, and he must solve the mystery of an agent's disappearance.

Volos: **Maurice Denham**
Dr Sawari: **Zia Mohyeddin**
Magda Kallai: **Geraldine Moffat**
Chand: **Earl Cameron**
Manuel: **John G. Heller**
Colonel Maturin: **Jerome Willis**
Holst: **Roy Herrick**
Adam: **George Baisley**

Dangerous Secret
w **Ralph Smart** and **Donald Jonson**
d **Stuart Burge**

A leading scientist has disappeared, taking with him the secret of a lethal mutant virus. Drake traces him to France where another scientist, a woman, has promised him work of a peaceful nature.

Louise Carron: **Elizabeth Shepherd**
Colin Ashby: **Lyndon Brook**
Fenton: **Derek Francis**
Mather: **John Brooking**
Dark Glasses: **Gordon Whiting**
Barbier: **Reginald Barrat**
Barjou: **Michael Anthony**
Jill Preston: **Sheila Steafel**
Barjou's Secretary: **Maureen Davis**
Receptionist: **Nicole Shelby**
Girl: **Jacqueline Hall**

Mark Lester: **Mark Lester**
Alex: **Peter Brace**
Stefan: **Peter Brayham**
Leon: **Derek Baker**
Carl: **Alf Joint**

I Can Only Offer You Sherry
w **Ralph Smart**
d **George Pollock**

When a young girl, Jean Smith, is suspected of leaking security secrets from her embassy in the Middle East, Drake, posing as a visiting journalist, is sent to find out what's behind her motives.

Jean Smith: **Wendy Craig**
Ma'Suud: **Anthony Newlands**
Nubar: **Bernard Archard**
Seghir: **Henry Gilbert**
Police Sergeant: **Tony Jason**
First Watcher: **Ben Ari**
Second Watcher: **Alan Chuntz**
First Thug: **Bob Anderson**
Second Thug: **Eddie Powell**
Military Attache / Fortune Teller: **Warren Mitchell**

The Hunting Party
w **Philip Broadley**
d **Pat Jackson**

When a wealthy landowner is suspected of leaking confidential information to foreign newspapers, Drake becomes his butler to investigate the leak. He soon finds himself the human prey in a deadly hunt.

Claudia Jordan: **Moira Lister**
Basil Jordan: **Denholm Elliott**
Max Dell: **Edward Underdown**
Ross: **John Welsh**
Edwards: **Alan White**
Coleman: **William Ingram**
Peer: **Oliver Johnston**
Vernon: **John Barcroft**
Gandon: **Michael Godfrey**
Zepos: **Michael Peake**
Annette: **Jean Shaw**
Martine: **Barbara Graley**
House of Lords Messenger: **John Dunbar**
French Postman: **Wilfred Grove**

Two Birds with One Bullet
w **Jesse Lasky Jr** and **Pat Silver**
d **Peter Yates**

Having discovered that one of the parties in a forthcoming election plans to murder their own candidates and lay the blame at Britain's door, Drake is sent to the Caribbean to prevent the killing.

Commissioner Winlow: **Geoffrey Keen**
Pilar Lin: **Lelia Goldoni**
Dr Shargis: **Paul Curran**
Singri Rhamin: **John Woodvine**
Aldo Shargis: **Richard O'Sullivan**
Jose: **Guido Adorni**
Censor: **Anne Blake**
First Prison Guard: **Albert Shepherd**
Police Officer: **Malcolm Rogers**
Guard: **Clive Cazes**
Second Prison Guard: **Reuben Elvy**

I'm Afraid You Have the Wrong Number
w **Ralph Smart**
d **George Pollock**

Convinced that the betrayal of an organiser of one of M9's networks in Switzerland could only have been accomplished by one of his own agents, Drake plays a deadly game of Russian roulette to discover the traitor.

Captain Schulman: **Paul Eddington**
Leanka: **Jeanne Moody**
Leontine: **Guy Deghy**
Aurel: **John Cazabon**
Stoian: **Frederic Abbott**
Standfast: **Vincent Harding**
Corbu: **Les White**
Police Sergeant: **Grantham Ashley**

The Man with the Foot
w **Raymond Bowers**
d **Jeremy Summers**

When a freelance agent discovers his identity, Drake is ordered take a holiday. But even in an isolated Spanish hotel he cannot shake off his pursuers - until he devises a clever scheme to 'disappear'.

Derringham: **Bernard Lee**
Monckton: **Robert Urquhart**
Gomez: **Paul Curran**
Maruja: **Isobel Black**
Soleby: **Hugh McDermott**
Abelardo: **Michael Forest**
Reever: **Charles Houston**
Hencke: **Gert Klauber**

The Paper Chase
w **Philip Broadley** and **Ralph Smart**
d **Patrick McGoohan**

When a briefcase containing confidential papers is stolen from a friend, Drake is asked to recover them. Following their trail leads the agent into acute danger in Rome.

Nandina: **Joan Greenwood**
Eddie Gelb: **Kenneth J. Warren**
Tamasio: **Aubrey Morris**
Laprade: **Ferdy Mayne**
Gordon Symonds: **Simon Lack**
Joe: **Peter Swanwick**
Frankie: **Peter Stephens**
Sam: **Oliver MacGreevy**
Canesi: **Sandor Eles**
Gloria: **Clair Gordon**
Paula: **Hanja Kochansky**
Constantine: **Steve Plytas**
Waiter: **Andreas Malandrinos**
Agent: **Ben Ari**

Not So Jolly Roger
w **Tony Williamson**
d **Don Chaffey**

Drake is assigned to investigate the seaborne pirate radio station, Radio Jolly Roger, which is suspected of transmitting coded messages to Europe. When Andrews, an M9 contact there, dies mysteriously, Drake takes his place in the guise of a disc jockey.

Marco Janson: **Edwin Richfield**
Corrigan: **Wilfred Lawson**
Linda Janson: **Lisa Daniely**
Susan Wade: **Patsy Ann Noble**
Mullins: **Andrew Faulds**
Summers: **Jon Rollason**
Andrews: **Christopher Sandford**
Fisherman: **John Tate**

65

season four
2 colour 60-minute episodes
1966

Koroshi
w **Norman Hudis**
d **Michael Truman**

An M9 Japanese girl agent meets sudden death while transmitting a message from Tokyo, warning that a leading United Nation's mediator will be assassinated within hours of his arrival in New York. Drake is assigned to ensure the man's safety, and to discover how the girl's identity was blown.

Ako Nakamura: **Yoko Tani**
Rosemary: **Amanda Barrie**
Sanders: **Ronald Howard**
Tanaka: **Burt Kwouk**
Old Japanese Man: **John Garrie**
Fortune: **Jeremy Longhurst**
Potter: **Christopher Benjamin**
Japanese Granddaughter: **Lilani Young**

Shinda Shima
w **Norman Hudis**
d **Peter Yates** and **Michael Truman**

Assigned to take the place of an electronics expert arrested by Japanese customs men for being in possession of secret circuit designs, Drake follows a trail to Shinda Shima ['the murdered island'] and finds himself up against a Japanese murder brotherhood.

Miho: **Yoko Tani**
Richards: **Kenneth Griffith**
Controller: **George Coulouris**
Pauline: **Maxine Audley**
Commander Yamada: **David Toguri**
Contact Man: **Tommy Yapp**
Edward Sharp: **Edward Ogden**
First Girl Islander: **Mona Chong**
Manager of Two-Tailed Dragon: **Robert Lee**
Second Girl Islander: **Paula Li Shiu**
Passport Official: **Kristopher Kum**
Airline Clerk: **Anna Mai**
Hostess: **Barbara Yu Ling**

✍ *Koroshi* and *Shinda Shima* - shot as a project fourth series, were the only two stories made in colour. These were subsequently edited together [in reverse order, and with an added 'linking' sequence] and shown in the USA in 1968 as a full-length TV Movie entitled *Koroshi*.

📖 All five, original stories:
Departure Deferred [1965: W Howard Baker: Consul Books]; *Storm Over Rockall* [1965: W Howard Baker: Macfadden-Bartell Books]; *Hell for Tomorrow* [1966: Peter Leslie: Macfadden-Bartell Books]; No Way Out [1966: Wilfred McNeilly: Macfadden-Bartell Books]; *The Exterminator* [1967: W A Ballinger: Macfadden-Bartell Books and re-released by Zenith Books in 1988].

Danger Man I:

Season one:
Series Created by **Ralph Smart**
Produced by **Ralph Smart**
Associate Producer: **Ian Stuart Black** [episodes 1-12] **Aida Young** [episodes 13 - 39]
Music by: **Edwin Astley**
Production Manager: **Douglas Twiddy**
Casting Director: **Harry Fine**
Assistant Director: **David Tomblin**
Art Director: **Frank White**
Editors: **Derek Hyde Chambers, David Hawkins, Peter Pitt**
Director of Photography: **Brendan J Stafford**
Second Unit Director: **John Schlesinger** [episodes 1, 2, 27 & 37]

Filmed at MGM Studios, Boreham Wood
An ITC Production for ITC World Wide Distribution

39 monochrome 30-minute episodes
1960-61

Danger Man II:
[aka **Secret Agent**]

Season two:
Producers: **Sidney Cole, Aida Young**
Executive Producer: **Ralph Smart**
Associate Producer: **Barry Delmaine**
Music by: **Edwin Astley**
Production Supervisor: **Barry Delmaine**
Script Editor: **Wilfred Greatorex**
Casting Director: **Rose Tobias-Shaw**
Assistant Directors: **David Tomblin, Gino Marotta, Peter Price, Tony Way, Doug Hermes**
Art Directors: **Jack Shampan, Seamus Flannery, Lionel Couch**
Editors: **Ann Chegwidden, Lee Doig, John Glen, Gordon Pilkington**
Director of Photography: **Brendan J Stafford**
Music Editor: **Allan Killick**
Make-up: **Eddie Knight**
Hairdressing: **Pat Mc Dermott**
Wardrobe: **Masada Wilmot**

Filmed at MGM Studios, Boreham Wood [episodes 1 - 26] and Shepperton Studios [episodes 27 - 32]
An ITC Production for ITC World Wide Distribution

32 monochrome 60-minute episodes
1964-65

Season three:
Producer: **Sidney Cole**
Executive Producer: **Ralph Smart**
Associate Producer: **Barry Delmaine**
Music by: **Edwin Astley**
Script Editor: **Wilfred Greatorex**
Script Consultant: **George Markstein**
Casting Director: **Rose Tobias-Shaw**
Assistant Directors: **Doug Hermes, Peter Price**
Art Director: **Lionel Couch**
Editors: **Lee Doig, John Glen, Bill Lenny**
Director of Photography: **Brendan J Stafford**
Music Editor: **Allan Killick**
Make-up: **Eddie Knight**
Hairdressing: **Betty Sherriff**
Wardrobe: **Masada Wilmot**

Filmed at Shepperton Studios
An ITC Production for ITC World Wide Distribution
13 monochrome 60-minute episodes
1965-66

Season four:
Producer: **Sidney Cole**
Executive Producer: **Ralph Smart**
Associate Producer: **Barry Delmaine**
Music by: **Edwin Astley**
Script Editor: **George Markstein**
Casting Director: **Rose Tobias-Shaw**
Assistant Director: **Peter Price**
Art Director: **Albert Witherick**
Editors: **Lee Doig, John Glen**
Director of Photography: **Brendan J Stafford**

Filmed at Shepperton Studios
An ITC Production for ITC World Wide Distribution

2 colour 60-minute episodes
1966

Department S

A tremendously popular series about the world's most unusual police department and its team of equally unusual investigators.

Department S, an offshoot of Interpol, was asked to solve the sort of cases which had baffled everyone else: those connected either with natural calamities or crimes that through their complexity or illogicality had left the best brains of Interpol scratching their heads in puzzlement.

Principal investigator for Department S was Jason King ... witty, flamboyantly dressed, romantic, King was the successful author with a vivid imagination. He viewed each case as if it were a plot he'd devised for one of his books, then asked himself what his detective hero, Mark Caine, would do or think in the same circumstances. His opinions and knowledge of the criminal mind never ceased to amaze [sometimes amuse] his shrewd, athletic, practical colleague, Stewart Sullivan, a man with a down-to-earth approach to detection, who tended to shoot down King's ideas [while storing away those he thought as being practical]. The third member of the team, Annabelle Hurst, approached each case from a scientific viewpoint, combining glamour with laboratory and computer.

Working together towards a common end, all were interested only in the unorthodox, bringing logic where none was apparent, adding sense to the senseless and explaining the inexplicable. Their divergent approaches to each case did not always bring an individual solution but, combined, they lead to success.

Never far away from the action was department Head, Sir Curtis Seretse, who was seen giving the team their assignments and occasionally joined them in the field. Devised by Monty Berman and Dennis Spooner, this highly inventive series was their shining hour.

Regular cast:
Jason King: **Peter Wyngarde**
Stewart Sullivan: **Joel Fabiani**
Annabelle Hurst: **Rosemary Nicols**
Sir Curtis Seretse: **Dennis Alaba Peters**

Six Days
w **Gerald Kelsey**
d **Cyril Frankel**

When an airliner goes missing for six days, then suddenly reappears - but the crew and passengers have no recollection of what has happened, or indeed that they were reported missing - the Department S team are asked to solve the mystery.

Captain Carter: **Bernard Horsfall**
Walsham: **Peter Bromilow**
Hallet: **Tony Steedman**
Janet: **Geraldine Moffatt**
Borowitsch: **Peter Bowles**
Air Traffic Controller: **John Gabriel**
Lady Hallett: **Marion Mathie**
Durres: **Al Mancini**
Peck: **Geoffrey Chater**
Stevens: **Charles Houston**

The Trojan Tanker
w **Philip Broadley**
d **Ray Austin**

What mystery lies behind a crashed tanker decked out like a luxury yacht, with only one occupant - a beautiful unconscious girl, who disappears before an ambulance arrives. Jason King arrives on the scene with an astonishing theory.

Veronica Bray: **Patricia Haines**
Mike Taylor: **Simon Oates**
Paolo Cortoli: **Bill Nagy**
Johnson: **Fredric Abbott**
Eccles: **Michael Balfour**
Croupier: **John Serret**
Fausta: **Monika Dietrich**
French Driver: **Larry Taylor**
Eccles' Girlfriend: **Penny Bird**

A Cellar Full of Silence
w **Terry Nation**
d **John Gilling**

The department S team are called in to unravel the intriguing puzzle behind the discovery of four bodies, all in fancy dress, found in the cellar of a deserted house.

Martin Kyle: **Paul Whitsun-Jones**
Libby Spear: **Denise Buckley**
Walter Pally: **Robin Hawdon**
Tronson: **Brandon Brady**
Vic Kent: **Edward Brayshaw**
Doctor Davis: **Brian Oulton**
Norman Fowler: **Frank Forsyth**

The Pied Piper of Hambledown
w **Donald James**
d **Roy Ward Baker**

When it appears that all Hambledown's inhabitants have been kidnapped - save one, a young girl - the department S investigators travel there to seek an answer to the baffling mystery doing so leads them into intrigue and danger.

Colonel Loring: **Richard Vernon**
Susan Lewis: **Gina Warwick**
Doctor Brogan: **Jeremy Young**
Harry Lewis: **Peter Lawrence**
Yates: **Stanley Beard**
Young Doctor: **John Kelland**
Typist: **Susan Broderick**
The Farmer: **Raymond Armstrong**

One of Our Aircraft is Empty
w **Tony Williamson**
d **Paul Dickson**

When a pilotless aircraft makes a perfect landing at London Airport, King, Sullivan and Hurst find the solution to the mystery in Ireland - but the outcome is far from what they expected.

Terrell: **Anton Rodgers**
Howard Finch: **Basil Dignam**
Julia Howarth: **Gillian Lewis**
Jane Kilverton: **Angela Lovell**
George Grant: **John Gabriel**
Miss Simms: **Edina Ronay**
Chalmers: **Robert Russell**
Jean: **Janet Key**
Waiter: **Andre Charise**
Mechanic: **Alan Hockey**
First Maintenance Man: **Roger Avon**

The Man in the Elegant Room
w **Terry Nation**
d **Cyril Frankel**

When a dead girl and a gibbering demented young man are found in a beautiful room built inside a disused factory, the Department S team investigate a very unusual case of murder.

Paul Trenton: **Stratford Johns**
Selina Trenton: **Toby Robins**
Doug Martin: **John Hallam**
Trish: **Juliet Harmer**
Danny Terrill: **Clive Colin Bowler**
Burton: **Michael Robbins**
Police Inspector: **Frank Gatliff**
Steven Radlett: **Peter Reynolds**
Harry Finch: **Martin Boddey**
Professor Bryant: **Anne Blake**
Secretary to Seretse: **Peter Brett**
Male Nurse: **Tony Caunter**
Jason King's Companion: **Maggie Kimberley**

Handicap Dead
w **Philip Broadley**
d **John Gilling**

The Department S sleuths are assigned to discover the facts behind the deaths of several golfers - and find that the solution to the mystery lies a very long way from the lush, but deadly, playing green.

Eddie Curtis: **Neil McCallum**
Diane Lynne: **Dawn Addams**
Sonny: **Dudley Sutton**
Kruger: **John Bailey**
Red: **Norman Eshley**
Don: **Brian McDermott**
Julie: **Jennifer Clulow**
Commentator: **Neal Arden**
Lady Croupier: **Dawn Beret**
Official: **Tony Thawnton**
Bill: **James Drake**

Black Out
w **Philip Broadley**
d **Ray Austin**

The connection between the kidnapping of a writer of food books and a new space product leads the team into a mystery fraught with danger and intrigue. Jason loses his cool, and Annabelle nearly loses her life.

Doctor Lang: **Neil Hallett**
Brigitte: **Sue Lloyd**
Robin Skelton/Peter Sinclair: **Richard Caldicot**
Wolf: **David Sumner**
Flores: **Paul Stassino**
Billie: **Caron Gardner**
Psychiatrist: **Mark Singleton**
Strobel: **Michael Mellinger**
Colin Whetlor: **David Beale**

Who Plays the Dummy?
w **Tony Williamson**
d **John Gilling**

Everyone knows that a dummy can't drive a car. So why should a crashed car have only a tailor's dummy at the wheel? The Department S team are assigned to find the answer - and place themselves in an explosive situation.

Gilford: **Alan MacNaughtan**
Pietra: **Kate O'Mara**
Sarrat: **George Pastell**
Greer: **John Bindon**
N.A.T.O. General: **Patrick Waddington**
Sir Wilfred: **William Kendall**
Lorio: **David Lander**
Colonel Barfield: **Peter Myers**
Spanish Colonel: **Raymond Young**
Spanish Mechanic: **Ray Marioni**

The Treasure of the Costa del Sol
w **Philip Broadley**
d **John Gilling**

The Department S team take a well-earned break and immediately land themselves in hot water. They net some very strange fish indeed - a catch which plunges them into intrigue and mayhem.

Camilo Garria: **George Pastell**
Elaine: **Isla Blair**
Maxime: **John Louis Mansi**
Achille: **Peter Thomas**
Adolfo: **David Prowse**
Estelle: **June Abbott**
Anita: **Olivia Hamnett**
Thorn: **Peter J. Elliott**
Cal: **David Gregory**

The Man Who Got a New Face
w **Philip Broadley**
d **Cyril Frankel**

The team of investigators find themselves faced with the strange mystery of a dead man found with a clown's mask on his face - a clue, perhaps, to a vicious vendetta between two millionaires' love for a beautiful film star?

Nicole: **Alexandra Bastedo**
Monique: **Adrienne Corri**
Emilio Andre: **Eric Pohlmann**
Kolliatis: **Arnold Diamond**
French Cabaret Artiste: **Angela Lovell**
Film Director: **David Kelsey**
Gerhard: **William Wilde**
Jean: **Nik Zaran**
Dave: **Clifford Earl**

Les Fleurs du Mal
w **Philip Broadley**
d **Cyril Frankel**

Three plastic flowers hold the secret of a grim robbery with murder. The Department S team must sniff out the clues to expose an extraordinary chain of events which leads them to a not-so-appealing crime.

Stacey: **Donal Donnelly**
Weber: **Michael Gothard**
Enzo Brandini: **Alex Scott**
Henri Rachou: **John Tate**
Danielle: **Edina Ronay**
Gina: **Joanna Jones**
Johnnie: **John Porter-Davison**
Boy: **Ricardo Campos**
Commandante: **Dennis Bernard**

The Shift That Never was
w **Donald James**
d **John Gilling**

Why should an entire factory take the day off - and what connects a beauty parlour with an atomic generating station? The Department S investigators find themselves faced with an intriguing mystery.

Johnny: **James Kerry**
Kate Mortimer: **Caroline Blakiston**
Douglas Stayte: **Eric Lander**
Bellman: **Eddie Byrne**
Parsons: **Toke Townley**
The Detective: **John Horsley**
Frank: **Anthony Dutton**
Sam: **Leslie Schofield**
The Photographer: **Laurie Asprey**

A Ticket to Nowhere
w Tony Williamson
d Cyril Frankel

The Department S sleuths investigate the strange disappearance of a Swedish scientist and the equally strange death of a financier. But how can they complete their investigations when they repeatedly forget everything they've discovered!

Lisa Crane: **Fiona Lewis**
Drieker: **Michael Gwynn**
Carter: **Alan Wheatley**
Susan Blain: **Bridget Brice**
Black: **Griffith Davies**
Hershall: **John Steiner**
Quince: **Neil McCarthy**
Paula: **Juliet Harmer**
Supervisor: **Anthony Ainley**
Co-Pilot: **Brian Harrison**

The Man from X
w Tony Williamson
d Gill Taylor

When a man wearing a spacesuit is found wandering through the streets of London and then dies before he can be questioned, the Department S team have only one clue to act upon - the man had recently been in a vacuum and has slight radiation burns.

Carter: **John Nettleton**
Leila: **Wanda Ventham**
Lowery: **Duncan Lamont**
Mallin: **Tony Selby**
Fraser: **Stanley Lebor**
Max Rinston: **Norman Chancer**
Travers: **Brian Badcoe**
Danvers: **Godfrey James**
Young Girl in Car: **Sally-Jane Spencer**
Young Boy in Car: **Robin John**
Girl in Discotheque: **Carol Rochelle**
Receptionist: **Rosemary Donnelly**

Dead Men Die Twice
w Philip Broadley
d Ray Austin

A man dies. Three years later, his unfortunate double is murdered - twice, just to make sure. A strange case for the investigative talents of the team from Department S, who find that 'dead' men really do die twice.

Lomax/Reeves: **Kieron Moore**
Tania: **Barbara Murray**
The Dandy: **Alan Lake**
Harlan: **David Bauer**
Charles Barjou: **John Cater**
Alain: **Edward Caddick**
Lizardos: **Steve Plytas**
Brunette: **Anna Matisse**
Mortuary Attendant: **John Serret**
Hotel Receptionist: **Mary Mitchell**
Machet: **Roy Hanlon**
Taxi Driver: **Jacques Cey**

The Perfect Operation
w Leslie Darbon
d Cyril Frankel

When a surgeon is interrupted during a brain operation - and another man takes over - the Department S team uncover an ingenious plot by a group of mysterious villains to infiltrate a spy network.

Walker: **Cyril Luckham**
Allison: **Ronald Radd**
Agatha Pollen: **Jean Marsh**
Smith: **Basil Dignam**
Dutrov: **Martin Miller**
Turkish Caretaker: **Marne Maitland**
Korlandt: **Harold Kasket**
Haslet-Wood: **Ronald Leigh-Hunt**
Turkish Nurse: **Francisca Tu**
Topek: **Philip Locke**
Balik: **George Roubicek**

The Duplicated Man
w Harry W. Junkin
d Paul Dickson

It has taken double agent Anthony James ten years to build up a double identity, and the Department S team must uncover his new face within days - the Russians have shown their interest and they want to kill him.

AnthonyJamesHarvey/AndrewHeywood: **Robert Urquhart**
May Heywood: **Ann Bell**
Kirov: **Guy Deghy**
Miss Wexler: **Sarah Lawson**
Henry Smith: **Basil Dignam**
Mrs. Harvey: **Winifred Evans**
Karnack: **Oliver MacGreevey**
Volodin: **Constantin de Goguel**
Hallam: **Edward Cast**
Gerald: **James Donnelly**
Parkinson: **Patrick Westwood**
Cranmore: **Robert Mill**

The Mysterious Man in the Flying Machine
w Philip Broadley
d Cyril Frankel

When the body of a murdered man is found inside a mock-up aircraft in a Paris warehouse, the Department S sleuth ask themselves why anyone should go to so much trouble to simulate a real flight? A message scrawled in lipstick provides the answer.

Lucky Le Beau: **Hans Meyer**
Gerard: **Clinton Greyn**
Francoise: **Virginia North**
Veronica: **Sue Gerrard**
Carl: **Anthony Scott**
Masiol: **Hal Galili**
Durand: **Michel Faure**
Gendarme: **Makki Marseilles**

The Double Death of Charlie Crippen
w Leslie Darbon
d John Gilling

The Department S team find themselves in Naples to investigate an unusual assassination attempt in which the 'victim' was a dummy. A trail of clues leads them to uncover a sinister cold-hearted plot.

Slovik: **Peter Arne**
Paul Dupont: **Edward de Souza**
Captain Svenoski: **John Savident**
Countess Von Streicher: **Yolande Turner**
Gina: **Veronica Carlson**
Stanic: **Michael Godfrey**
Nurse: **Edwina Carroll**
Maria Pilic: **Hana-Maria Pravda**
Car Salesman: **Earl Green**
Count Von Streicher: **George Pravda**
Petrangeli: **Nicholas Chagrin**
Antonio Mardi: **Gertan Klauber**

Death on Reflection
w Philip Broadley
d Ray Austin

When an antique mirror sells for four times its value at an auction and the buyer is murdered shortly afterwards, Jason, Stewart and Annabelle have their work cut out sifting through the countless clues they uncover.

Yves: **Guy Rolfe**
The Comtesse: **Jennifer Hilary**
The Auctioneer: **Peter Copeley**
Gresford: **Paul Whitsun-Jones**
Heppel: **Michael Barrington**
Terry Mitchell: **Harvey Sokoloff**
Cynthia: **Susan Denny**
Joanna: **Vicki Graham**
Moira: **Cathy Graham**
Marie: **Vivienne Cohen**

Last Train to Redbridge
w Gerald Kelsey
d John Gilling

Multiple murders on a tube train involve the Department S team in a case in which they uncover a devious espionage network behind the facade of a quiet country village in Sussex.

Draper: **Leslie Sands**
Mrs Taylor: **Patricia English**
Clark: **Derek Newark**
Rogers: **Harvey Hall**
Taxi Driver: **Tommy Godfrey**
Bray: **Inigo Jackson**
The Doctor: **Neal Arden**
Sawyer: **Frank Forsyth**
The Policeman: **Victor Brooks**
The Porter: **Reginald Barratt**
Hooper: **Roger Avon**
Police Driver: **Lionel Wheeler**

A Small War of Nerves
w Harry W. Junkin
d Leslie Norman

Informed that a scientist has invented a poison gas which could kill a million people - and he intends to use it to hold England hostage - the department S sleuths find themselves racing against time to prevent the man from doing so.

Greg Halliday: **Anthony Hopkins**
Major Harwood: **Frederick Jaeger**
Doctor Stickney: **Colin Gordon**
Mrs Evans: **Eleanor Summerfield**
Ruckert: **Bryan Wyman**
Corbett: **Mark Elweg**
Reggie: **Peter Graves**
Mechanic: **Larry Martin**
The Porter: **Charles Lamb**
Policeman.: **David Renolds**
Carl Young: **Nosher Powell**

The Bones of Byrom Blain
w Tony Williamson
d Paul Dickson

An intriguing mystery faces the investigative talents of the department S sleuths: on his arrival at a Ministry of Defence establishment, Byrom Blain disintegrated into a skeleton! The team must find out why.

Byrom Blain: **John Barron**
Crawley: **Patrick Barr**

Eldon: **Gerald Campion**
Superintendent Collins: **Michael Griffiths**
Head Waiter: **Richard Durden**
Logan: **Davyd Harries**
Lomax: **Albert Shepherd**
Police Sergeant: **Julian Herrington**
Miss Garwood: **Katharine Schofield**
Special Branch Man: **Ian Cullen**
Stewardess: **Anoushka Hempel**
Delivery Man: **Ben Howard**
Captain of Aircraft: **John Acheson**
Train Steward: **Andre Charise**

Spencer Bodily is 60 Years Old
w Harry W. Junkin
d Leslie Norman

Despite looking no more than 20, an autopsy on Spencer Bodily's dead body proves he must have been at least 60 - an event that has startling repercussions for the Department S team, sent to investigate the crime.

Kendall: **Iain Cuthbertson**
Ingrid Von Elzdorf: **Patricia Donahue**
Graves: **Warren Stanhope**
Martin: **Robert Sessions**
Mendham: **Garfield Morgan**
Green: **Arthur Cox**
Gadden: **Barry Andrews**
Hughes: **Richard Heffer**
Lydia: **Hilary Pritchard**
Guido Volponi: **Leonardo Pieroni**
Spencer Bodily: **Gavin Campbell**
Gerald: **Reginald Jessup**
Arab: **Milton Reid**

The Ghost of Mary Burnham
w Harry W. Junkin
d Cyril Frankel

Is it the ghost of his wife that John Burnham keeps seeing and hearing, or just a clever plot to mentally unbalance the brilliant economist? That's the question facing the Department S team when they are asked to solve the mystery.

John Burnham: **Donald Houston**
Mary Burnham: **Lois Maxwell**
Drayton: **Norman Bird**
Dr Grant: **Anthony Nicholls**
Novack: **Weston Gavin**
Miss Bronson: **Susan Fleetwood**
Taxi Driver: **Ron Pember**
The Priest: **Ellis Dale**
Telephone Operator: **Suzanne Vasey**
Young Boy: **Gustav Henry**
The Nurse: **Michelle Karli**
The Blonde: **Christine Pryor**

A Fish Out of Water
w Philip Broadley
d Cyril Frankel

When the body of an Interpol agent is found drowned in Beirut, Jason King is sent to take over his mission, to crack an international smuggling ring. The agent immediately finds his life threatened by a beautiful girl.

Rafic: **Lee Montague**
Michele Duplay: **Magda Konopka**
Esplin: **Cyril Shaps**
Takla: **Wolfe Morris**
Chemist: **John Cazabon**
Bridge Player: **Alex Gallier**

Bridge Player: **Elma Soiron**
Sandra: **Maggie Wright**
Nazib: **John Keston**
Kazime: **Paul Tamarin**
Filipo: **Yuri Borienko**
Dancer: **Angel Melek**
Girl: **Beverley Winn**
Boy: **Richard Essame**

The Soup of the Day
w **Leslie Darbon**
d **Leslie Norman**

Why should anyone wish to break into a bombed warehouse and steal dozens of cases of tinned soup? The Department S team investigate the break-in and discover that the soup contained some very strange ingredients indeed.

Rupert Fallon: **Michael Coles**
Gregory: **Anthony Valentine**
Jeremy Standish: **Ronald Lacey**
Villiers: **John Ronane**
Greene: **Patrick Mower**
Maria: **Isobel Black**
Segres: **Peter Arne**
Ramos: **David Healy**
Lavinia: **Ann Holloway**
Trish: **Pippa Steel**
Melissa: **Pamela Ann Davy**
Dominic: **Sandor Eles**
Albert: **Patrick Durkin**
Police Inspector: **Robert Cawdron**
Finlay: **Ellis Dale**
Driver: **David Morrell**
Rogers: **Michael Guest**
The Waiter: **Cecil Cheng**

Department S:

Series created by: **Monty Berman** and **Dennis Spooner**
Producer: **Monty Berman**
Music by: **Edwin Astley**
Production Supervisor: **Ronald Liles**
Executive Story Consultant: **Dennis Spooner**
Creative Consultant: **Cyril Frankel**
Production Manager: **Ray Frift**
Casting Director: **Judith Jourd**
Assistant Director: **Ken Baker**
Second Unit Director: **Jack Lowin**
Stunt Co-ordinator: **Frank Maher**
Editor: **Philip Barnikel**
Art Director: **Robert Jones**
Director of Photography: **Frank Watts**
Continuity: **Elizabeth Wilcox**
Music Editor: **Deveril Goodman**
Make-up: **Gerry Fletcher**
Hairdressing: **Mike Jones, Hilda Fox**
Wardrobe: **Laura Nightingale**

Made on location and at Associated British Elstree Studios
An ITC Production

28 colour 60-minute episodes
1969

Espionage

The most dangerous jobs in the world! They're spies, secret agents, saboteurs, undercover men. Detection means disaster - they will be disowned by the countries that employ them. Sometimes, they're patriots. Sometimes, they're traitors. Whichever they are, they are in demand both in times of peace and war....men and women of daring courage.

The Incurable One
w Halstead Welles & Sidney Carroll
d Stuart Rosenberg

Featured: Steven Hill, Ingrid Thulin, Michael Gwynn

The Weakling
w Arnold Pearl
d Stuart Rosenberg

Featured: John Gregson, Dennis Hopper, Patricia Neal

He Rises On Sunday, and We On Monday
w Alvin Sapinsley
d David Greene

Featured: Billie Whitelaw, Patrick Troughton, Andrew Keir

Covenant With Death
w Peter Stone
d Stuart Rosenberg

Featured: Bradford Dillman, David Kossoff, Allan Cuthbertson

The Gentle Spies
w Ernest Kinoy
d David Greene

Featured: Barry Foster, Michael Hordern, Angela Douglas

The Dragon Slayer
w Halstead Welles & Albert Ruben
d William T. Kotcheff

Featured: Lee Montague, Patrick Cargill, Thorley Walters

To the Very End
w Norman Borisoff & David Greene
[from a story by N. Borisoff]
d David Greene

Featured: Clifford Evans, David Buck, James Fox

A Camel to Ride
w John Furia Jr
d Fielder Cook

Featured: Bill Travers, Marne Maitland, Roger Delgado

The Whistling Shrimp
w Leon Tokatyan
d Stuart Rosenberg

Featured: Arthur Kennedy, Larry Gates, David J. Stewart

The Light of the Friendly Star
w John Gay
d James Sheldon

Featured: Carl Schell, Ronald Howard, Loretta Parry

A Tiny Drop of Poison
w John D. Hess
d Herbert Hirschman

Featured: Jim Backus, Donald Harron, William Smithers

Festival of Pawns
w Raymond Bowers [from a story by Robert Dozier]
d James Sheldon

Featured: George Grizzard, Sam Wannamaker, Maxwell Shaw
Special Guest Star: Diane Cilento

Never Turn Your Back On a Friend
w Mel Davenport
d Michael Powell

Featured: George Voskovec, Donald Madden, Mark Eden
Special Guest Star: Pamela Brown

Medal For a Turned Coat
w Larry Cohen
d David Greene

Featured: Fritz Weaver, Joseph Furst, Nigel Stock

Final Decision
w Donald Jonson
d Ray Herbert

Featured: Ann Lynn, Alan Gifford, James Maxwell
Special Guest Star: Martin Balsam

Do You Remember Leo Winters?
w Art Wallace
d Robert Butler

Featured: George A. Cooper, Peter Madden, Rhoda Lewis

We, the Hunted
w Peter Yeldham
d Kenneth Hughes

Featured: Joe Campanella, Madlyn Rhue, Al Mulock

The Frantic Rebel
w Ernest Kinoy
d Michael Powell

Featured: Roger Livesey, Stanley Baxter, Jill Bennett

Castles In Spain
w Raymond Bowers [from a story by Norman Borisoff]
d Anton M. Leader

Featured: Roland Culver, Neil McCallum, Anne Lawson
Special Guest Star: Chester Morris

Snow on Mount Kama
w Allan Prior, Donald Jonson & Kenneth Hughes
[from a story by Allan Prior]
d Kenneth Hughes

Featured: **Bernard Lee, Nigel Davenport, Maureen Connell**

Once a Spy
w **Julian Bond**
d **David Greene**

Featured: **Millicent Martin, William Lucas, Peter Vaughan**

The Liberators
w **John Furia Jr**
d **Seth Holt**

Featured: **Robert Webber, Michael Tolan, Lelia Goldoni**
Special Guest Star: **Donald Pleasence**

A Free Agent
w **Leo Marks**
d **Michael Powell**

Featured: **Anthony Quayle, Sian Phillips, Norman Foster**

Some Other Kind of World
w **Joseph Liss**
d **Herbert Hirschman**

Featured: **Tom Stern, Dora Reisser, Alan Tilvern**
Special Guest Star: **Ron Randell**

Espionage:

Producer: **George Justin**
Executive Producer: **Herbert Hirschman**

24 colour 60-minute episodes
1963

Father Brown

G. K. Chesterton's classic clergyman-detective, brought vividly to life. Father Brown's involvement with crime brings him into contact with every strata of society, his individual approach to detection ['through the mind and soul'] and his understanding of the darker side of human nature, keen observation and intelligent deduction, providing the solution to many unusual mysteries. Motto 'Have Bible ...Will Travel' he enjoys the challenge of solving crime, but his interest is more in those concerned than the crime itself.

A short-lived, though fondly-remembered series. Kenneth More was a perfect choice for the quiet and retiring detective and the entire proceeding reeked of class.

Regular cast:
Father Brown: **Kenneth More**
Flambeau [episodes 2,3,5,6,8]: **Dennis Burgess**

The Hammer of God
d **Robert Tronson**

A village scandal leads to the murder of Colonel Bohun, the Squire. No human hand, it seems, could have been responsible, and the police are puzzled. Enter Father Brown, whose scientific knowledge of the laws of nature and the human soul solves the mystery.

Rev. Wilfred Bohun: **William Russell**
Colonel Bohun: **Graham Crowden**
Elizabeth Barnes: **Geraldine Moffatt**
Simeon Barnes: **John Forgeham**
Mrs Bohun: **Anna Steele**
Mrs Deveraux: **Anna Wing**
Mallory: **Harry Walker**
Gibbs: **Peter Hawkins**
Landlord: **Frederick Hall**
Joe: **Alun Armstrong**
Inspector Palmer: **Roger Hume**
Doctor Wynn: **Robert James**

The Mirror of the Magistrate
d **Peter Jefferies**

Sir Humphrey Gwynne, a retired Judge, is found dead in his garden summerhouse. Suspicion falls upon Irish journalist, Michael Flood and anarchist-playwright, Osric Orm - who name Father Brown as their guarantor. When Orm is arrested, Father Brown uses logic to prove Orm's innocence.

Flambeau: **Dennis Burgess**
Sir Arthur Travers KC: **Philip Stone**
Sir Humphrey Gwynne: **Paul Curran**
Sir Wilfred Underhill KC: **David King**
Inspector James Bagshaw: **Mark Kingston**
Osric Orm: **David Pinner**
Carstairs K.C.: **Roger Rowland**
Sir Matthew Blake KC: **Michael Logan**
Buller: **Bruno Barnabe**
Michael Flood: **Michael O'Hagan**
Green: **Artro Morris**
Doctor: **Dennis Edwards**
Police Constable: **Philip Trewinnard**
Firearms Expert: **Richard Aylen**
Florrie: **Lynne Furlong**

The Quick One
d **Ian Fordyce**

Spending the weekend with his friend Flambeau, Father Brown crosses the path of Raggley, a cantankerous local trouble-maker. When Raggley is murdered, Father Brown must uncover the murderer and deduce why anyone would stab a man who had already been poisoned.

Flambeau: **Dennis Burgess**
Raggley: **Bernard Lee**
Edith: **Penelope Horner**
Inspector Greenwood: **Brian Hawksley**
Rev. David Pryce-Jones: **Frederick Treves**
Akbar: **Tariq Yunus**
Wills: **Geoffrey Russell**
Jukes: **Christopher Benjamin**
Vance: **Paul Williamson**
Leeds: **Anthony Langdon**
Grant: **William Dysart**
Ashley: **Maxwell Shaw**
Beatrice: **Mary Ann Severne**
Miss Parvant: **Charlotte Mitchell**
Constable: **Alexander John**
Constable: **Robert Walker**
Commercial Travellers: **Ron Musgrove, Colin Thomas, Fred Davis**
Barman: **James Haswell**
Reading Police Constable: **Barry Summerford**
Boy: **Geoff Blundell**

The Dagger With Wings
d **Peter Jefferies**

Father Brown has an encounter with black magic - or is it a more straightforward case of multiple murders? It isn't long before people are receiving letters containing drawings of a winged dagger - a weapon of death, and Father Brown becomes conscious of his own danger.

John Strake: **David Buck**
Augustus Aylmer: **A.J. Brown**
Philip Aylmer: **Michael Sheard**
Stephen Aylmer: **David Swift**
Daphne Aylmer: **April Walker**
Arnold Aylmer: **Nicholas Evans**
Simon Vesty: **Vernon Dobtcheff**
Inspector Boyne: **T.P. McKenna**
Blacker: **Alan Hockey**
Nurse: **Zara Jaber**
Judge: **Norman Scace**
Police Constable: **Desmond Cullum-Jones**
Hazel: **Sarah Golding**

The Actor and the Alibi
d **Robert Tronson**

Father Brown ventures into the back-stage world of the theatre at the request of his friend Flambeau, who has been engaged to trace a missing girl. Flambeau has found her and believes Father Brown can persuade her to return home. Then Mandeville, the theatre manager, is murdered.

Flambeau: **Dennis Burgess**
Margaret Mandeville: **Rachel Gurney**
Mundon Mandeville: **John Stratton**
Norman Knight: **David Savile**
Detective Insp. Forbush: **Richard Warner**
Ashton Jarvis: **Oliver Maguire**
Ralph Randall: **Michael Hall**
Mrs Sands: **Sheila Keith**
Irene Maroni: **Rita Giovannini**
Doris Jennings: **Roberta Tovey**
Aubrey Vernon: **John Levitt**
Miss Theresa Talbot: **Julia Sutton**
Lady Miriam Marden: **Ellen Sheean**
Sam-Stage Doorkeeper: **Frederick Radley**
Police Sgt.: **Wally Thomas**

The Eye of Apollo
d **Peter Jefferies**

Not for the first time, the criminal-turned detective Flambeau, is responsible for placing Father Brown at the centre of a strange mystery - the murder of a sun-worshipper, and a will that turns out to be a sheet of blank paper, except for a sentence and some scratches.

Flambeau: **Dennis Burgess**
Kalon: **Ronald Pickup**
Pauline Stacey: **Alison Key**
Joan Stacey: **Emily Richard**
Thurston: **Dudley Jones**
Miss Ammerley: **Rosamund Greenwood**
Gerald Lloyd: **Christopher Good**
Corliss: **Oliver Ford-Davies**
Police Constable: **Ken Halliwell**

The Head of Caesar
d **Robert Tronson**

Father Brown goes to the help of a frightened, guilt-stricken girl who has stolen from her brother and is being blackmailed by a mysterious figure wearing a false nose. Hearing that the girl and her friends are to attend the Fine Arts Ball in fancy dress. Father Brown sees a way of exposing the blackmailer.

Flambeau: **Dennis Burgess**
Christabel Carstairs: **Rosalind Ayres**
Arthur Carstairs: **John Normington**
Philip Hawker: **Brian Anthony**
Giles Carstairs: **Christian Rodska**
Colonel Carstairs: **Graham Leaman**
Miss Oliphant: **Elsie Randolph**
Mr. Truslove: **Robin Meredith**
Max: **John Rutland**
Madge: **Michelle Newell**
Hector: **Stephen Marsh**
Mrs Gow: **Betty Alberge**
Fisher: **Lala Lloyd**
Art Student: **Jacky Bristow**
Art Student: **Sue Bishop**
Art Student: **Silvia Lane**
Art Student: **Audrey Searle**
Art Student: **David Wilde**
Art Student: **John Cash**
Priest: **Stuart Myers**
Priest: **Tony Lang**
Police Sgt.: **Ron Musgrove**
Police Constable: **Les Conrad**

The Secret Garden
d **Peter Jefferies**

In Paris as a guest of Aristide Valentin, the Chief of Police, Father Brown has a heady problem to solve. The decapitated body of a man has been found in the garden - a body still warm, so the murder has obviously only just taken place. But who is responsible for the heinous crime?

Aristide Valentin: **Ferdy Mayne**
Julius K. Brayne: **Peter Dyneley**
Lord Galloway: **Cyril Luckham**
Lady Galloway: **Joan Benham**
Lady Margaret Graham: **Eileen Waugh**
Commandant Neil O'Brien: **Charles Dance**
Dr. Bernard Simon: **Rowland Davies**
Duchess of Mont.St. Michel: **Rosemarie Dunham**
Beaumont: **Stefan Gryff**
Ivan: **Athol Coats**

The Curse of the Golden Cross
d **Robert Tronson**

Vengeance from the grave or a murder plot? Father Brown must channel his detective powers into finding the solution to a curse which jeopardises the life of archaeologist, Professor Smaill.

Professor Gerald Smaill: **James Maxwell**
Rev. John Walters: **Peter Copley**
Lady Diana Wales: **Sarah Lawson**
Helen Smaill: **Gwyneth Powell**
Leonard Smyth: **Geoffrey Chater**
Boon: **Stanley Lebor**
John Godfrey: **Peter Penry-Jones**
Paul Tarrant: **Lawrence Trimble**
Doctor: **Hector Ross**
Landlord: **Ronald Mayer**
Passengers: **Victor Harrington, Eileen Matthews, Anet Peters, Sally Foulger, Tony Snell, Michael Musgrave**
Stewards: **Ali Baba, Oscar Charles**
Barman: **Douglas Rowe**

The Man with Two Beards
d **Peter Jefferies**

Father Brown becomes involved in the mystery of a daring jewel thief known as Michael Moonshine. But is the thief a murderer? Father Brown thinks not. He has grounds for suspecting that another man is guilty of the crimes being attributed to the robber - a man with a red beard and moustache.

Carver: **Bill Maynard**
Mrs Banks: **Megs Jenkins**
John Banks: **Anthony Allen**
Lady Pulman: **Fabia Drake**
Sir Leopold Pulman: **Peter Graves**
Michael Smith: **Larry Noble**
Mr Banks: **David Lodge**
Opal Banks: **Freda Dowie**
Daniel Devine: **Brian Croucher**
Barnard: **Eric Longworth**
Grocer: **Alan Gerrard**

Three Tools of Death
d **Robert Tronson**

A well-known philanthropist is found dead and suspicion falls on his daughter. But her fiance steps forward to confess to the crime. Called in by the police, Father Brown is shown three instruments of death found at the scene: a revolver, a knife and a rope - but he has a knotty time travelling the problem.

Patrick Royce: **John Flanagan**
Sir Aaron Armstrong: **James Hayter**
Alice Armstrong: **Nina Thomas**
Magnus: **Jacob Witkin**
Chief Insp. Gilder: **Anthony Dutton**
Det. Sergeant Merton: **David Morton**
Milkman: **Keith James**
Sir Aaron's Double: **Billy Hughes**
Prof. Edmond Gailbraith: **John Moore**
Technician/Policeman: **Les Conrad**
Technician: **Ken Tracy**
Policeman: **John Cannon**

The Oracle of the Dog
d **Peter Jefferies**

Like so many ex-Army officers, Colonel Druce doesn't suffer fools gladly. The fact that he decides to change his will causes considerable concern to his family - and one of them

commits murder to retain the status quo. Father Brown seeks the help of a dog to expose the guilty party.

Colonel Druce: **Rupert Davies**
Donald Druce: **Guy Slater**
Harry Druce: **Richard Hesser**
Janet Druce: **Mel Martin**
Patrick Floyd: **Bob Sherman**
Henri Valentine: **Garard Paquis**
Mr Aubrey Traill: **John Atkinson**
Inspector Cole: **Edward Evans**
Police Constable: **Michael Stock**
Dog Trainer: **John Holmes**

The Arrow of Heaven
d **Robert Tronson**

A millionaire collector risks a curse when he buys a gold chalice which has brought death to its previous owners. When the man receives letters signed 'Daniel Doom' warning that his life is in danger, Father Brown is asked if he can help.

Brander Merton: **John Phillips**
Colonel Hector Merton: **Mike Pratt**
Petra Merton: **Angela Douglas**
John Wilton: **George Roubicek**
Norman Drage: **David Healy**
Bernard Blake: **Julian Somers**
Father Superior: **Richard Hurndall**
Harris: **Antony Scott**
First Guard: **Christopher Crooks**
Second Guard: **Mike Lewin**
Auctioneer: **Eric Dodson**
Guard/Auction Client: **David Melbourne**
Guard/Auction Client: **James Muir**
Guard/Auction Client: **Clive Rogers**
Guard/Auction Client: **Robert Davies**
Auction Client: **Donald Stratford**
Auction Client: **Gordon Christie**
Guard/Porter: **Ronald Goodale**
Auction Client: **Audrey Kirby**
Auction Client: **Lisa Bergmayer**
Auction Client: **Melinda Tracey**
Auction Client: **Maureen Purkis**
Auction Client: **Chantal Gray**

ITC produced a two-hour television feature film *Father Brown Detective*. Starring Bernard Hughes as the detective, this is not part of the Kenneth More canon.

Father Brown:

Stories adapted from the G. K. Chesterton *Father Brown* stories by: **Hugh Leonard**
Story Advisor: **Michael Voysey**
Producer: **Ian Fordyce**
Music: **Jack Parnell**
Editor: **Stanley Staffe**
Designer: **Michael Eve**

An ATV Network Production for ITC World Wide Distribution.

13 colour 60-minute episodes
1974

Fireball XL5

Fireball XL5 - one of a fleet of rockets used by the twenty-first-century World Space Patrol to monitor and protect Sector 25 of the Solar System from alien invaders - was Gerry Anderson's second 'Supermarionation' outing.

Commanded by Colonel Steve Zodiac, 'a brave and fearless hero', and his crew - Venus, a Doctor of Space Medicine [and Zodiac's romantic interest!]; Professor 'Matt' Matic, Fireball's science officer and navigator; co-pilot Robert the Robot [a transparent 'brain']; and Zoonie, Venus's pet Lazoon - Fireball zoomed around the galaxy confronting all kinds of strange alien creatures [armed with equally strange weapons] and making contact with new civilisations.

Assigned to their missions by Commander Zero and his aide, Lieutenant 90, the crew's main opponents were, believe it or not - Mr and Mrs Space Spy!

More popular today than when it was first transmitted, the series was a path-leader in puppet animation.

Character voices:
Steve Zodiac: **Paul Maxwell**
Prof. Matic: **David Graham**
Venus: **Sylvia Anderson**
Robert the Robot: **Gerry Anderson**
Commander Zero: **John Bluthal**
Lieut 90/Zoonie: **David Graham**

Planet 46
w **Gerry Anderson** and **Sylvia Anderson**
d **Gerry Anderson**

A missile capable of destroying the whole world has been fired at Earth by Planet 46. The crew of Fireball XL5 are assigned to stop the missile reaching its target. They do so - but find themselves captives of the Subterraneans.

Hypnotic Sphere
w **Alan Fennell**
d **Alan Pattillo**

When several space tankers are put out of action and their crews hypnotised, Steve Zodiac and his crew escort another tanker and find themselves hypnotised by a strange light beam and an equally strange voice.

Planet of Platonia
w **Alan Fennell**
d **David Elliott**

Landing on the Platinum Planet, to take its king to Earth for trade talks, Steve and his team have no way of knowing that Volvo, the King's aide, has planted a bomb inside Robert the Robot.

Space Magnet
w **Anthony Marriott**
d **Bill Harris**

Sent to investigate the disappearance of Fireball XL7, Steve and his crew discover that the remains of FBXL7 are being used to feed a giant power house, whose electromagnet is being used to pull the Moon out of its orbit.

The Doomed Planet
w **Alan Fennell**
D **Alan Pattillo**

When a flying saucer leads the crew of Fireball XL5 to Membrono - a planet doomed to be destroyed by another planet which has come out of its orbit - Steve Zodiac and Robert the Robot help an old man to save the planet from destruction.

Plant Man from Space
w **Anthony Marriott**
d **John Kelly**

A missile lands on Earth, but fails to explode. Soon, a giant plant begins to threaten Space City and Steve and his crew become involved with a new enemy - Dr Rootes, a man possessed with growing plants.

The Sun Temple
w **Anthony Marriott**
d **John Kelly**

Believing that missiles from Space City, being used to destroy rogue meteorites, will anger their God, the Rejuscans destroy the Space City launching site. When Zodiac and his crew investigate, Venus is captured - and sentenced to death.

Space Immigrants
w **Anthony Marriott**
d **Alan Pattillo**

Flying to New Earth in Mayflower III, to set up equipment to make the new planet suitable for human life, Venus and engineer Jock are threatened with extinction by Lillispations. Becoming suspicious, Zodiac jets off to investigate.

Space Monster
w **Gerry Anderson**
d **John Kelly**

Trying to solve the disappearance of Fireball XL2, Zodiac and his crew receive a distress call from the planet Monotane. Landing on the planet in Fireball Junior, they discover the crew of FBXL2 - guarded by a giant space creature.

Flying Zodiac
w **Anthony Marriott**
d **Bill Harris**

When a circus visits space City, the clowns Madame Mivia and Cosmo - in reality Mr and Mrs Space Spy - plan to use the big top to allow the Nomadians to take over Earth. Zodiac has other ideas.

XL5 to H_2O
w **Alan Fennell**
d **John Kelly**

Sent to give aid to two survivors of a planet who are being attacked by a fish man, the crew of Fireball XL5 arrive to find the glass city of the planet destroyed and that the survivors have disappeared.

Spies in Space
w **Alan Fennell**
d **Alan Pattillo**

When Fireball XL9 is attacked and damaged, Zodiac and his crew are assigned to take over its patrol duties - an event which leads them into a trap laid by Mr and Mrs Space Spy, who plan to steal Fireball XL5.

Space Pirates
w **Anthony Marriott**
d **Bill Harris**

Hearing that Space Pirates from the planet Aridan are holding up freighters from planet Minera, Zodiac decides to take a spacecraft and trick the pirates into thinking it is helpless, but the pirates get to hear of his plans.

Convict in Space
w **Alan Fennell**
d **Bill Harris**

Captured by Steve Zodiac after stealing some top secret documents, the spy Deblis is sentenced to 20 years imprisonment on the prison planet Conva. Flying there, Fireball and its crew are captured by Mr and Mrs Space Spy.

Space Pen
w **Dennis Spooner**
d **John Kelly**

After two crooks manage to steal some isotopes from the Space City vault, Zodiac and his crew chase them to the planet Conva, where Steve tricks the crooks into thinking he is a space pirate who has stolen Fireball XL5.

The Last of the Zanadus
w **Anthony Marriott**
d **Alan Pattillo**

Kudos, the last inhabitant of the planet Zanadu, plans to kill all Lazoons and gives Zoonie a deadly virus. Steve and Venus face a race against time to take possession of an antidote from Zanadu's fountain of life .

Wings of Danger
w **Alan Fennell**
d **David Elliott**

Two Subterraneans plan to kill Zodiac by using a robot bird, fitted with deadly radium capsules. Luring the Fireball XL5 crew to their planet, the bird begins to attack - and Zodiac receives a direct hit.

The Triads
w **Alan Fennell**
d **David Elliott**

The crew of Fireball XL5 are sent to investigate why nuclear explosions have taken place on the planet Triad. Crash-landing on the planet, Steve and his crew find themselves under attack by a giant tiger, but rescue is on the way in the shape of two giants, Graff and Snaff.

Prisoner on the Lost Planet
w **Anthony Marriott**
d **Bill Harris**

Landing on a strange planet in response to a distress call, Steve and his crew find a beautiful woman who tells them she has been exiled there, but wants to go to Earth. When Steve tells her that isn't possible, she threatens to activate a nearby volcano and destroy the entire planet.

Flight to Danger
w **Alan Fennell**
d **David Elliott**

Trying to gain his astronaut wings, Lieutenant 90 attempts a solo orbit of the Moon, but something goes wrong and his capsule explodes. Steve and his crew attempt to find him, but fail to do so.

Sabotage
w **Anthony Marriott**
d **John Kelly**

A bomb, planted by two Arcon warriors aboard XL5, explodes and puts the rocket out of control and the two warriors use their Gamma ray to transport Steve and his crew to their spaceship, where they are taken prisoner.

Space Vacation
w **Dennis Spooner**
d **Alan Pattillo**

Zodiac, Venus and the Professor land on the planet Olympus for a holiday. At a party given in their honour, Venus is taken hostage in an attempt to get Steve to take on a secret mission.

Robert to the Rescue
w **Dennis Spooner**
d **Bill Harris**

Sent to investigate a new planet, which suddenly appears then disappears, Fireball XL5 is brought down by unseen forces. Leaving the craft, Zodiac and his crew find themselves in total blackness - and Robert the Robot disappears.

Mystery of the TA2
w **Dennis Spooner**
d **John Kelly**

Having discovered the wreckage of TA2, a spaceship which disappeared 48 years ago, Steve and his crew find a map which proves that Colonel Denton, the pilot of TA2, intended to reach the planet Arctan. Zodiac sets out to find him.

The Forbidden Planet
w **Anthony Marriott**
d **David Elliott**

Having discovered the planet Nutopia by using an ultrascope which can look into deep space, Zodiac and his crew are unaware that the Nutopians plan to use their transmission device to kidnap Venus - as their eternal companion.

Dangerous Cargo
w **Dennis Spooner**
d **John Kelly**

After surveying a derelict planet, Steve and his crew return to Space City and are told to return to the planet with Vesuvium Nine - the most powerful explosive known to man - and destroy it.

The Granatoid Tanks
w **Alan Fennell**
d **Alan Pattillo**

About to leave the glass-surfaced Planet 73, two scientists see hostile Granatoid tanks coming towards them. In panic, they send a message to Space City for help, and Fireball XL5 is assigned to rescue them.

1875
w **Anthony Marriott**
d **Bill Harris**

Steve, Venus and Commander Zero enter Professor Matic's time machine - and find themselves back in 1875, in a western town. Steve is elected Sheriff and Venus become French Lil, a bandit, with Commander Zero as her accomplice.

The Robot Freighter Mystery
w **Alan Fennell**
d **David Elliott**

Suspecting that the Biggs Brothers are behind a spate of recent robot freighter sabotage, Steve is assigned to check that the brothers really are responsible for collecting 'space salvage' by dubious means.

Drama at Space City
w **Anthony Marriott**
d **Alan Pattillo**

Looking after Zoonie, while Steve and Venus take a well-earned holiday, Commander Zero goes into the cabin of Fireball XL5 with the Lazoon, who gives the order 'Full Power' - which Robert the Robot takes literally, and launches the spacecraft!

Whistle for Danger
w **Dennis Spooner**
d **John Kelly**

Sent to the planet Floran, to launch a bomb in the atmosphere to destroy the plant disease Planetoid 3, the crew of Fireball XL5 are taken prisoner by two Florans, drugged and imprisoned in a tall tower.

The Day the Earth Froze
w **Alan Fennell**
d **David Elliott**

A note found in the hand of an unconscious patrol crewman leads Zodiac and his crew to a distant planet. The crew are captured by two icemen, who inform them that they plan to destroy the Earth by reflecting the Sun's rays.

Faster than Light
w **Anthony Marriott**
d **Bill Harris**

The supply line to Space City is placed in jeopardy when Fireball XL5's stabilisers break down. In this condition, Fireball - which travels faster than light - could prove highly dangerous for its crew.

Invasion Earth
w **Dennis Spooner**
d **Alan Pattillo**

When two Fireball patrol ships, sent to investigate a strange cloud in space, explode, and strange alien spaceships emerge from the cloud and land at Space City, Zodiac and his crew face mortal danger.

Ghosts of Space
w **Alan Fennell**
d **John Kelly**

When Earth geologist Frazer, discovers electronic rock on the planet Electron, he asks Zodiac to take it back to Space City. The astronaut refuses - and strange things begin to happen to Steve and his crew.

A Day in the Life of a Space General
w **Alan Fennell**
d **David Elliott**

When Lieutenant 90 becomes General 90, things begin to go wrong. Steve Zodiac falls into a swamp while on holiday and General 90 orders a red alert to intercept an alien invasion. What can lie behind the strange events?

Trial by Robot
w **Alan Fennell**
d **Alan Pattillo**

The only clue to the disappearance of Robots from several planets points to the fact that wherever Professor Himber - the world's greatest authority on robots - gave lectures, robots disappeared. Zodiac must discover why.

Space City Special
w **Dennis Spooner**
d **Alan Pattillo**

Returning to Space City on one of the new supersonic airlines, Venus, in the company of General Rossiter, has no idea that the vehicle's pilot, Major Todd, has been brainwashed by the Subterraneans - and intends to crash the airliner.

The Fire Fighters
w **Alan Fennell**
d **John Kelly**

When balls of fire begin to fall on Earth from a cloud in space, the crew of Fireball XL5 are assigned to avert the threat - a mission that ends with Zodiac risking all to save Earth from total destruction.

Fireball XL5:

Created by: **Gerry Anderson & Sylvia Anderson**
Producer: **Gerry Anderson**
Associate Producer: **Reg Hill**
Production Supervisor: **David Elliott**
Art Direction: **Bob Bell**
Music by: **Barry Gray**
[Title music by: **Charles Blackwell**
 Vocal by **Don Spencer**]
Special Effects: **Derek Meddings**
Script Supervisors: **Gerry Anderson & Sylvia Anderson**
Puppetry Supervision: **Christine Glanville** and **Mary Turner**

An AP Films Production in association with ATV for ITC World Wide Dist.
Filmed in Supermarionation

39 monochrome 30-minute episodes
1962

The Four Just Men

Based on the word famous novel by Edgar Wallace, the series told how Ben Manfred MP, called together three ex-World War II comrades to form a secret union to provide justice in a world where injustice was rife. Calling themselves The Four Just Men, Manfred and his colleagues - Tim Collier, top line American journalist based in Paris, Jeff Ryder, brilliant freelance lawyer at Columbia University, and Ricco Poccari, a celebrated Rome hotelier - set out to administer their own brand of law wherever injustice spread its ugly tentacles. They do not seek revenge but a fair deal for the oppressed. No problem proved too large or too small to warrant their involvement - providing the cause was worthy. In seeking justice for others, they face danger for themselves.

Overseen by Manfred, each of the team share their adventures with their personal secretary/assistant: Collier placed his trust [and sometimes his life] in the hands of the beautiful Nicole; Ryder's confidant was Vicky; Italian beauty, Guilia, was never far from Poccari's side, and Manfred sometimes sought the aide of Jock, an ex-O.S.S. agent.

"Throughout time, there have been men to whom justice is more important than life itself.
From these ranks come
four men prepared to fight valiantly on the side of justice
wherever the need may be.
Joined together in this cause, they are
The Four Just Men."

Regular cast:
Ben Manfred: **Jack Hawkins**
Tim Collier: **Dan Dailey**
Jeff Ryder: **Richard Conte**
Ricco Poccari: **Vittorio de Sica**
Nicole: **Honor Blackman**
Vicky: **June Thorburn**
Guilia: **Lisa Gastoni**
Jock: **Andrew Keir**

✍

Filmed in four separate blocks [the four stars actually appearing together in the pilot story only] Collier and Ryder were each allocated ten episodes, and Manfred and Poccari appeared in nine episodes respectively - the series being screened on a rotational basis to allow each actor to star in their own weekly adventure.

The Battle of the Bridge
w **Gene Coon** [from a story by **Miriam Geiger & Don Castle**]
d **Basil Dearden**

Four men who last met in battle during the Allied Invasion of Italy in 1943 are summoned to Foxgrove Manor, to hear a message recorded shortly before his death by Colonel Bacon, their wartime commanding officer. He appeals to them to band together in combating injustice, and says he has left a substantial amount of money for them to use in pursuit of their work. They all agree and hereby become the Four Just Men.

Manfred: **Jack Hawkins** [intro]
Collier: **Dan Dailey** [intro]
Ryder: **Richard Conte** [intro]
Poccari: **Vottorio de Sica** [intro]
Cyril Bacon: **Anthony Bushell**
Guido [as a boy]: **Joseph Cuby**
Guido [as a man]: **Vivian Matalon**
Priest: **Jack May**
German Officer: **Ernst Walder**

First Sentry: **George Mikell**
Second Sentry: **John Karlsen**
Butler: **Henry de Bray**

The Prime Minister
w **Oliver Skene** [from a story by **Alec Coppel**]
d **Don Chaffey**

Tim Collier is appointed to protect the life of the Prime Minister of a Middle Eastern country, in Paris to address the UN Security Council. Assisted by his secretary Nicole, Collier must outwit the PM's enemies - men determined to assassinate him.

Nicole: **Honor Blackman** [intro]
Mozek: **Peter Illing**
Alem: **Maurice Kaufmann**
Chairman: **Robert Ayres**
Middle East Delegate: **Michael Ritterman**
Stout Man: **Arthur Gomez**
Akbal: **David Ritch**
Airline Man: **Desmond Jordan**
Gendarme: **Robert Robinson**
Newspaperman: **Clive Baxter**

Village of Shame
w **Lindsay Galloway**
d **Basil Dearden**

Crusading MP Ben Manfred, takes on an entire village when they band together to stop him getting at the truth behind the murder of a former friend. The dead man had uncovered a German sympathiser in the village - Manfred determines to unmask the traitor and avenge the murder.

Jock: **Andrew Keir** [intro]
Cabane: **Leo Britt**
Janine: **Malou Pantera**
Cesar: **George Pastell**
Edmond: **Paul Stassino**
Albert: **Hugh Manning**
Cure: **John Gabriel**
Gendarme: **Arthur Gomez**
Fisherman: **Andre Charisse**
Farmer: **Robert Cawdron**
Boy: **Kurt Siegenberg**

The Judge
w **Marc Brandel**
d **Harry Watt**

When a young woman is charged with poisoning her husband, lawyer Jeff Ryder finds himself at the mercy of an angry mob and faced with the popularity of a local doctor, whose evidence implicating the girl is accepted without question.

Dr. Chase: **James Dyrenforth**
Mrs Chase: **Estelle Brody**
Helen: **Naomi Chance**
Jean Lawson: **Kay Callard**
Hill: **Robert Robinson**
Police Chief: **Peter Dyneley**
Joann: **Ruda Michelle**
District Attorney: **Robert Ayres**
Cop: **Bruce Boa**
Reporter: **Mark Baker**
Clerk: **Denis Holmes**
Woman: **Virginia Bedard**

The Crying Jester
w **William Fairchild**
d **William Fairchild**

Hotelier, Ricco Poccari buys a fascinating painting, not knowing its history. Two men die as a result, and Poccari is faced with a race against time to solve the mystery and clear the name of an innocent man.

Betty Green: **Betty McDowell**
Harry Green: **Morton Lowry**
Berto: **Lee Montague**
Rapelli: **George Pravda**
Luigi: **Dudley Foster**
Thin Man: **Keith Smith**
Art Dealer: **Leonard Sachs**
Anselmo: **David Cole**
Coroner: **Frank Thornton**
Inspector Nardi: **Max Brimmell**

The Beatniques
w **Wilton Schiller** [from a story by **Alec Coppel**]
d **Don Chaffey**

In Cannes to cover the film festival, Tim Collier is approached by a famous film actress who is being blackmailed. Some incriminating love letters have been stolen from her room. Collier has 12 hours in which to unmask the culprit.

Nedra: **Delphi Lawrence**
Bannon: **Cec Linder**
Mouche: **Malou Pantera**
Pantin: **David Graham**
Amant: **Oscar Quitak**
Youth: **David Ritch**
Bob: **Max Faulkner**
Journalist: **Denis Edwards**
Photographer: **Tony Thawnton**
Clerk: **Frank Thornton**
Gendarmes: **Arthur Gomez & Keith Rawlings**

The Deserter
w **John Baines**
d **Basil Dearden**

When a young British army officer, on active duty in the Mediterranean, is sent for court-martial for desertion, the boy's mother enlists the aid of Ben Manfred to stand for the defence and establish his innocence.

Captain Bannion: **Richard Johnson**
Colonel Parkes: **Ronald Howard**
Mrs Bannon: **Melissa Stribling**
Judge Advocate: **Basil Dignam**
President: **Noel Howlett**
Clerk: **Arthur Gomez**
Security Officer: **Clive Baxter**
Sergeant: **Neil Hallett**
Corporal Bates: **Michael Bates**
Corporal Jeavons: **Harold Goodwin**
Woman: **Anne Padwick**
Stavro: **Thomas Hare**

Dead Man's Switch
w **Wilton Schiller**
d **Harry Watt**

When the father of a young Puerto Rican, injured in a brawl in a New York night club and branded a racist, decides to take the law into his own hands, Jeff Ryder finds himself risking his life to prevent further tragedy.

Rivera: **Richard Pascoe**
Garnes: **Bill Nagy**
Mrs Garnes: **Mary Barclay**
Doctor: **Robert Henderson**
Flynn: **Gordon Tanner**

Andy: **John McLaren**
Father Martin: **Lee Hamilton**
Maria: **Margaret Wolfit**
Mac: **Robert Gallico**
Gus: **Charles Irwin**
Demolition Officer: **Jim Anderson**

The Night of the Precious Stones
w **Guy Morgan**
d **William Fairchild**

A daring jewel robbery takes place at a charity ball held at Poccari's hotel and the priceless Empress Diamonds disappear. The police are able to arrest every member of the gang - except one, whose identity is unknown. Who is he? Poccari must find out.

Duchess Della Riviero: **Brenda de Banzie**
Giulia: **Lisa Gastoni** [intro]
Connolly: **Bruce Boa**
Kubek: **Michael Ritterman**
Inspector Nardi: **Patrick Troughton**
Renzino: **Sean Lynch**
Watkins: **Norton Lowry**
Crandall: **Brian Worth**
Franconi: **Gordon Sterne**
Le Bon: **Oreste Orloff**

The Deadly Capsule
w **Jan Read** [from a story by **Oliver Skene & Samuel B. West**]
d **Compton Bennett**

Tim Collier investigates the peculiar circumstances surrounding the death of a famous atomic scientist. In addition to establishing the cause, he must also find a deadly radioactive capsule - a mission which becomes all the more urgent when a group of young children take possession of the capsule.

Nicole: **Honor Blackman**
Scheye: **Elwyn Brook Jones**
Mrs Weiss: **Lily Kann**
Weiss: **Frederick Schrecker**
Technician: **Paul Martin**
Phillipe: **John Sterling**
Pierre: **Kurt Siegenberg**
Father: **Newton Blick**
Wife: **Joan Haythorne**
Cure: **Andre Charisse**

Their Man in London
w **Leon Griffiths**
d **Basil Dearden**

Ben Manfred's aid is sought by a girl student. Her fiance has been kidnapped by a corrupt South American political regime, bent on murdering its opponents in London. Can Manfred succeed in rescuing the young patriot and exposing the kidnappers?

Hilary Colson: **June Thorburn**
Falworth: **Mark Dignam**
Dos Petros: **Ralph Truman**
Rosanna Lopez: **Eira Heath**
Jock: **Andrew Keir**
Hernandez: **Maurice Kaufmann**
Jose Pereza: **Paul Stassino**

Maya
w **William Fairchild**
d **William Fairchild**

Assigned to persuade a murdered king's self-exiled, pleasure-loving sister, Maya, to renounce her life of ease in

Italy and return to her own country, Poccari makes headway - until the girl's enemies show their murderous hand.

Maya: **Mai Zetterling**
Giulia: **Lisa Gastoni**
Gathis: **Peter Illing**
Bruno: **Raymond Young**
Zolta: **Michael Peake**

National Treasure
w **Owen Holder** [from a story by **Janet Green**]
d **Basil Dearden**

When a dying millionaire confesses to Ben Manfred that a Rembrant in a London art gallery is a copy and the original, obtained by dubious means, is in his possession. Manfred agrees to replace the fake with the original - little realising that he will become involved in intrigue and murder.

Paul: **William Lucas**
Curator: **Richard Wordsworth**
Jock: **Andrew Keir**
Seers: **Toke Townley**
Lord Eastleigh: **Charles Cullum**
Bowles Jr: **Michael Atkinson**
Bowles Sr: **Kenneth Edwards**
Miss Lee: **Patricia Hayes**
Auctioneer: **Frank Thornton**
Gentleman: **David Waller**
Taxi Driver: **Arthur Gomez**
Doctor: **Denis Holmes**

Panic Button
w **Marianne Foster** & **Samuel B. West**
d **Anthony Bushell**

After a research scientist is exposed to a small, harmless amount of radiation, Jeff Ryder has the seemingly hopeless task of convincing a town rife with suspicion and ignorance that the danger to the scientist or the community is minimal.

Ray Pearson: **Paul Carpenter**
Sue Pearson: **Sheila Gallagher**
Val Pearson: **Louise Hayward**
Norma Willett: **Tucker McGuire**
Carl Willett: **Jess Conrad**
George Rudley: **Warren Mitchell**
Sheriff: **Ewan Solon**
Walter: **Richard Wordsworth**
First Man: **Mark Baker**
Milkman: **Jonathan White**
Student: **Tom Gerard**
Madame Hubert: **Valerie Craig**

The Man With the Golden Touch
w **Louis Marks** [from a story by **Jan Read**]
d **Basil Dearden**

A millionaire's antique urn, sold to provide funds for a private home for the poor of Naples, is stolen, and former juvenile delinquent, Pietro, is arrested for the crime. Believing the boy innocent, Poccari sets out to expose the real thieves.

Pietro: **Richard O'Sullivan**
Valio: **Philip Latham**
Clemente: **Brewster Mason**
Mother: **Gillian Owen**
Terranti: **Bruno Barnabe**
Inspector: **Ewan Solon**
Bellboy: **Paul Cole**
Auctioneer: **Frank Thornton**
Dealer: **Joseph Attard**

Marie
w **Gene Levitt** & **Louis Marks**
d **Don Chaffey**

Tim Collier stops a young girl from committing suicide, but before he can question her she disappears. Certain that she will try again to take her life, he sets out to find her - and a dramatic secret is unfolded in the alleys of Paris.

Nicole: **Honor Blackman**
Marie: **Perlita Neilson**
Dr Fawzil: **Alex Mango**
Madame Susa: **Peggy Ann Clifford**
Azin: **Frank Thornton**
Travel Agent: **Harry Tardios**
Rene: **Julian Sherrier**
Plainclothesman: **Keith Rawlings**
Phillipe: **Michael Peake**

The Survivor
w **Marc Brandel**
d **Basil Dearden**

Given a list of names of persons known to be Nazi sympathisers by a one-time concentration camp inmate, Ben Manfred is anxious that the men be brought to justice. But the police will not help and Manfred is left to risk his life by unmasking the guilty.

Paul Koster: **Donald Pleasence**
Ann: **Patricia Burke**
Cowen: **Allan Cuthbertson**
Jock: **Andrew Keir**
Stoyen Matchek: **Arthur Gomez**
Sir Harold Tyler: **Kevin Stoney**
Announcer: **Frank Thornton**
M.I.5 Man: **Denis Holmes**
Landlady: **Dorothy Darke**

The Discovery
w **Marc Brandel**
d **Don Chaffey**

An elderly invalid dies after being injected with a rare and possibly dangerous drug. The doctor in attendance is arrested and charged with murder. The DA is determined to secure a conviction, but Jeff Ryder believes implicitly in his client's innocence.

Legari: **John Gabriel**
Dr Hart: **Bud Knapp**
District Attorney: **Lionel Murton**
Marie Trescal: **Helena Hughes**
Vicky: **June Thorburn** [intro]
Judge: **Robert Henderson**
Andy Winters: **Craig Adams**
Bond: **Timothy Grey**
Mrs Fellows: **Vivienne Drummond**
Linden: **Gary Thorne**
Dr. Wayne: **Gordon Sterne**

The Rietti Group
w **William Fairchild**
d **William Fairchild**

Joining his former comrades for a reunion dinner, one-time partisan, Ricco Poccari has the thankless task of informing his friends that one of their number is a traitor. Poccari is faced with unmasking the guilty man and pronouncing sentence - death.

Giulia: **Lisa Gastoni**
Count Montesco: **Geoffrey Keen**
Jim: **Simon Lack**

Joe: **Ronan O'Casey**
Lorenzo: **Olaf Pooley**
Bianchi: **Denis Holmes**
Rodrigo: **Arthur Gomez**
Francesco: **Robert Rietty**
Maid: **Madeleine Leon**

The Man in the Road
w **George Slavin & Samuel B. West**
d **Don Chaffey**

When attempting to clear an American Ambassador's wife of a hit-and-run traffic charge, Tim Collier and his secretary Nicole uncover a heinous blackmail plot set in motion by the ambassador's opponents to discredit his work.

Nicole: **Honor Blackman**
Mark Richmond: **Patrick Barr**
Marcia Richmond: **Simone Lovell**
Robert: **Richard Clarke**
Paul Lederer: **Charles Gray**
Frank Appleby: **James Dyrenforth**
Gendarme: **Frank Thornton**
Proprietor: **Denis Holmes**
Sam Brady: **Gordon Tanner**
Yvonne: **Jane Asher**

Money To Burn
w **Jan Read**
d **Basil Dearden**

Suspicious that a large consignment of bank notes intended for a South American republic have been printed as part of a plot to undermine the currency of the country and establish a dictatorship, Ben Manfred investigates.

Sir Walter Barling: **Ian Hunter**
Lady Barling: **Helena Pickard**
Jock: **Andrew Keir**
Doninguez: **Charles Gray**
Colonel Gomez: **Alan Tilbern**
General de Santos: **Wolf Frees**
Enrique Vidal: **Frank Thornton**
Receptionist: **Susan Travers**
Secretary: **Bee Duffell**
Ambassador: **Andre Michelson**
Postman: **Denis Holmes**

Crack-Up
w **Louis Marks** [from a story by **Lee Loeb**]
d **Anthony Bushell**

Five years after a plane carrying a half-million dollars in bullion is lost over Canada, lawyer Jeff Ryder finds himself involved in a drama of avarice, opportunism and treachery that threatens to explode into murder.

Stuart: **Robert Shaw**
Vicky: **June Thorburn**
Ingrid Brandt: **Delena Kidd**
Flynn: **Charles Irwin**
Rustie: **Paul Eddington**
Krager: **Richard Clarke**

The Miracle of St. Philippe
w **Jan Read** and **Louis Marks** [from a story by **Barbara Hammer**]
d **Don Chaffey**

The theft from a local village of a sacred relic which is believed to have magical healing powers, comes under the scrutiny of journalist Tim Collier - a task made difficult when he discovers that every member of the Town Council stood to gain by the theft.

Nicole: **Honor Blackman**
Dante: **Paul Daneman**
Captain: **Manning Wilson**
Briand: **Richard Caldicott**
Leclerc: **John Gabriel**
Mayor: **Jacques Brunius**
Lucie: **Maureen Davis**
Wife: **Margaret Tyzack**

The Slaver
w **Lindsay Galloway**
d **Harry Watt**

A young American journalist disappears when investigating a story. Asked to find her, Ricco Poccari stumbles upon an insidious market in white slavery run by ruthless Arab racketeers - a mission of mercy with danger around every corner.

Guilia: **Lisa Gastoni**
Sadik Bey: **Charles Gray**
Rosalina: **June Rodney**
Insp. Russo: **Roger Delgado**
Dexter: **Ronan O'Casey**
Elderly negro: **Orlando Martins**
Menardi: **Anthony Jacobs**
Capt. Abdul: **Edric Connor**
Officer: **Tony Thawnton**

The Princess
w **Frank Tarloff** and **Louis Marks** [from a story by **Louis Marks**]
d **Don Chaffey**

Visiting Europe, Princess Toma is dogged by a number of inexplicable incidents, one of which might easily have cost her her life. Is someone trying to murder her? Tim Collier and Nicole must find the truth behind the series of 'accidents'.

Nicole: **Honor Blackman**
Princess Toma: **Betta St John**
Amishar: **Leonard Sachs**
Mendri: **Lee Montague**
Lady-in-Waiting: **Madeleine Leon**
Hotel Manager: **Manning Wilson**
Train conductor: **Arthur Gomez**

The Protector
w **Alan Moreland & Leon Griffiths** [from a story by **Alan Moreland & Samuel B. West**]
d **Don Chaffey**

Janis Bannerman believes she is slowly going insane. Is she suffering from tragic delusions or, as Jeff Ryder suspects, the victim of a dangerous conspiracy to rob her of her considerable fortune?

Vicky: **June Thorburn**
Janis: **Maureen Connell**
Bannerman: **Ferdy Mayne**
Meadows: **Larry Cross**
Moffat: **John Welsh**
Wilson: **Charles de Temple**

The Man in the Royal Suite
w **John Collier** and **Samuel B. West** [from an idea by **Alec Coppel**]
d **William Fairchild**

A clerk, deported from America to Rome, finds himself at the mercy of a racketeer. He seeks help from Ricco Poccari, who decides to hide the man in his hotel's lavish royal suite,

disguised as a millionaire. But the racketeer is not so easily fooled.

Giulia: **Lisa Gastoni**
Milotti: **Kenneth Connor**
Ponta: **Eric Pohlmann**
Zizi: **Susan Marryott**
Francesco: **Robert Rietty**
Tony: **Barry Shawzin**
Max: **Oliver MacGreevy**
Barber: **Edward Evans**
Pietro: **Thomas Hare**

The Grandmother
w **Marc Brandel**
d **Don Chaffey**

Reporting on a scandal involving the supply of faulty ammunition, Tim Collier finds that the reputation of one of the most honoured families in France will be ruined if the facts are made known - a truth that the family is determined to keep secret.

Nicole: **Honor Blackman**
Madame de Seiberd: **Marie Ney**
Colonel de Seiberd: **Fred Kitchen**
Guy de Seiberd: **Trader Faulkner**
Madeleine de Seiberd: **Joanna Dunham**
Raoul: **John Van Eyssen**
Waiter: **John Dearth**
Manservant: **Arthur Gomez**

The Man Who Wasn't There
w **Lindsay Galloway**
d **Basil Dearden**

An eminent metallurgist engaged on top secret work goes missing. His daughter believes that the government have hidden him away for his own safety. Ben Manfred thinks otherwise - and uncovers an elaborate plot involving kidnapping and treachery.

Arkwright: **Lionel Jeffries**
Menger: **Gerard Heinz**
Ilse: **Sheila Allen**
Under Secretary: **William Mervyn**
Barker: **Michael Ripper**
Rice: **Anthony Sharp**
Jock: **Andrew Keir**
Fiona: **Ellen MacIntosh**
Officer: **Richard Thorp**

The Bystanders
w **Francis Rosenwald**
d **Don Chaffey**

Twenty-year old United States tennis ace, Ted Forrest, is tipped as a hopeful in the forthcoming Wimbledon Championships. Then scandal enters his life when a 12-year old girl accuses him of attacking her. Can Jeff Ryder discover the truth?

Ted: **Ronald Allen**
Katy: **Jeanette Bradbury**
Mrs Fennimore: **Margaret Vines**
Albert Peterson: **Phil Brown**
Mrs Peterson: **Mary Kenton**
Ed Forrest: **Robert Gallico**
Sue Forrest: **Nancy Bacall**
District Attorney: **Patrick Holt**
Romano: **Catharina Ferraz**
Tony Romano: **David Franks**
Frank Kleng: **Errol McKinnon**
Dan Reeves: **Robert Perceval**

Rogue's Harvest
w **T.E.V. Clarke**
d **Basil Dearden**

Ricco Poccari is faced with a problem. How to save an embittered young criminal from returning to crime now that he has left jail. Poccari's unconventional method of teaching the youth a lesson has hilarious and romantic results.

Enrico Baldini: **Richard Pasco**
Maria: **Elizabeth Wallace**
Inspector Russo: **Roger Delgado**
Coralie Marlow: **Vera Fusek**
Berto Fellini: **George Pastell**
Girgio Rizzi: **William Peacock**
Hotel Clerk: **Victor Baring**

The Godfather
w **Wilton Schiller** [based on a story by **Wilton Schiller & William Fairchild**]
d **Don Chaffey**

When Collier's friend Ernst Frenke arrives in Paris to buy arms from black market racketeers, the reporter and his secretary, Nicole, finds themselves solving a kidnap plot in a most unusual manner.

Nicole: **Honor Blackman**
Ernst Frenke: **George Murcell**
Martha Frenke: **Cecile Chevreau**
Marie Clement: **Sheila Allen**
Joshua: **Michael Lewis**
Trenet: **Eric Pohlmann**
Skovic: **Laurence Payne**
Doran: **Manning Wilson**
Kalmar: **Arthur Gomez**
Hugo: **Tom Clegg**
Mark: **Bruno Barnabe**

Riot
w **Leon Griffiths** [from a story by **Louis Marks**]
d **Anthony Bushell**

Called to a State Prison, where resentment among the inmates has flared into violence, bloodshed and murder, lawyer Jeff Ryder finds himself at the mercy of desperate convicts who hold him hostage during a pitched battle with State Troopers.

Nelson: **Neil McCullum**
Dougan: **Peter Dyneley**
Minelli: **Mark Baker**
Brady: **Percy Herbert**
Whiting: **Sheldon Lawrence**
Captain: **Morton Lowry**
Warden: **Larry Cross**
Guard: **Max Faulkner**

The Heritage
w **Louis Marks**
d **Basil Dearden**

A plot to blow up a police station in Ireland is foiled by a young nationalist who is strongly opposed to violence. Now wanted by both sides, he seeks the help of Ben Manfred to resolve the problem of divided loyalties.

Kevan Malone: **Barry Keegan**
O'Rorke: **Shay Gorman**
Cathy O'Shaughnessy: **Concepta Fennell**
Captain Davies: **Ronald Leigh-Hunt**
Plomer M.P.: **Jack Melford**
Shamus: **Desmond Jordan**
Sean: **Cecil Brock**

The Last Days of Nick Pompey
w **Jackson Gillis**
d **Don Chaffey**

When gangster Nick Pompey finds that his wife and child have mysteriously disappeared in Italy, he pleads for help from lawyer Jeff Ryder. Agreeing to help, Ryder arrives in Italy and locates the couple. But bringing them home requires an ingenious line of thought.

Nick Pompey: **Reed de Rouen**
Maria: **Betty McDowell**
Santolla: **Eddie Byrne**
Lita: **Yvette Hesler**
John: **Terence Cooper**
Customs man: **Lee Hamilton**
Passport man: **Arthur Gross**
Stewardess: **Madeleine Leon**
Man: **Peter La Trobe**
Policeman: **Oliver MacGreevy**
Salesgirl: **Norma Parnell**

The Moment of Truth
w **Francis Rosenwald**
d **Don Chaffey**

Young bullfighter Cesarito Arenos has a secret fear which not even Vito, his trainer, can cure. Cesarito is frightened to enter the ring! Concerned, Vito enlists the aid of Tim Collier. But can Collier avert tragedy at Cesarito's next bull fight?

Nicole: **Honor Blackman**
Cesarito: **Jeremy Spenser**
Vito: **Patrick Troughton**
Bartender: **Arthur Gomez**
Impresario: **Cecil Brock**

Justice For Gino
w **Lindsay Galloway** [from a story by **Michael Connor**]
d **Harry Watt**

Jeff Ryder is troubled, his childhood friend Gino plans to avenge his gangster brother's death by any means disposable - including murder! Can Ryder convince his friend to allow courtroom justice to prevail?

Vicky: **June Thorburn**
Arthur Vivian: **Vivian Matalon**
Gino: **Alan Gifford**
Inga: **Louise Collins**
Zoldi: **Alan Tilvern**
Andy: **John McLaren**
Louise: **Mavis Villiers**
Lieutenant: **Al Mulock**
Little man: **Redmond Phillips**
First man: **Sean Kelly**
Priest: **Edward Evans**

The Boy Without a Country
w **Marc Brandel**
d **Basil Dearden**

A young stateless orphan, becomes the victim of a cruel captain when employed as a cabin boy. When the ship docks in London, the youth runs away. His plight attracts the attention of Ben Manfred MP., who determines to right an injustice.

Captain Renald: **Martin Benson**
Jock: **Andrew Keir**
Vito: **Joseph Cuby**
Dr Cramer: **Peter Illing**
Sergeant: **Victor Brooks**
Policeman: **Frank Thornton**

First Tart: **Rosemary Dunham**
Second Tart: **Myrtle Reed**
Helper: **Graham Stewart**
Tramp: **Wilfred Fletcher**

Treviso Dam
w **Lindsay Galloway**
d **Basil Dearden**

Ricco Poccari is drawn into the mysterious death of a young man working on the building of a large dam. The question to be asked: was the man killed by a colleague who had eyes on his girlfriend, or is the truth more complicated and sinister?

Giulia: **Lisa Gastoni**
Contessa: **Fenella Fielding**
Giorgio: **Alan Bates**
Anna: **Judi Dench**
Mazza: **George Pastell**
Carlo: **Brian McDermott**
Enrico: **John Brown**

The Four Just Men:

Based on the best-selling novel by **Edgar Wallace**
Producer: **Sidney Cole** [Pilot - Hawkins, de Sica episodes]
Jud Kinberg [Dailey, Conte episodes]
Executive Producer: **Hannah Weinstein**
Associate Producer: **Basil Appleby**
Music by: **Francis Chagrin**
Script Supervision: **Louis Marks**
Production Supervisor: **Harold Buck**
Production Manager: **Eddie Pike**
Assistant Director: **George Pollard**
Make-up Supervisor: **Walter Scheiderman**
Wardrobe Supervisor: **Brenda Gardner**

A Hannah Fisher Production for Sapphire Films Ltd., for Associated TeleVision
An ITC Presentation
Made at Walton Studios, Walton-on-Thames

39 monochrome 30-minute episodes
1959

Ghost Squad

"In the world-wide war against crime, there are men and women trained to sink their own identity in the international underworld. They work alone, in danger and in shadow, unrecognised by friend and enemy alike. They are the operators of the almost legendary Ghost Squad".

So began each episode of this suspense-filled, and infinitely watchable, detective/spy drama series, inspired by the real-life exploits of the men and women of Scotland Yard's legendary undercover unit [dubbed by ex-Detective John Gosling as the 'Ghost Squad' in his book of that name].

Distinguished by two formats [*Ghost Squad* and *GS5*], the series documented the adventures of a team of crimebusting agents whose brief is to infiltrate their way into the inner sanctums of major underworld gangs and international espionage agencies, and snuff out their activities by whatever means are available to them - including assassination. Masters of convincing disguise, they live a thousand lives, masquerading as jewel thieves, smugglers, swindlers, racketeers, even murderers, their safety depending on their own wits. Known only to their immediate superiors, there is nothing to identify them with the governing body they represent.

The cop on the beat doesn't know who they are. He might even arrest them. Though working with the co-operation of the world's police, they have no protection. There is no-one to stand by them if they are caught. They are on their own. Their missions a closely guarded secret between themselves and their controllers [a GS agent could work side by side with other members of the unit without knowing his or her identity] Often working alone, they share a common bond - hazardous missions, in which the mortality rate is high.

The man in charge is Sir Andrew Wilson, who operates from his apartment in the centre of London. To all intents and purposes a private flat, from here priority telephone lines keep him in touch with the top brass of police forces on five continents. From here go the instructions to the body of highly-trained, courageous operatives who belong to the unit. Indispensable to the organisation's administrative centre is Helen Winters, Sir Andrew's confidential secretary [who has aspirations herself to become a GS field operative].

Series one recounted the assignments of principal operator, Nick Craig, whose expertise in the field of deception, explosives, electronics and knowledge of theatrical make-up techniques [Nick's parents were seasoned thespians] made him a natural for the post. Four new characters were introduced in the second series. Agent Tony Miller, a two-fisted, merciless defender of justice; Geoffrey Stock, the department's new chief administrator [Sir Andrew and his secretary Helen having been posted to a new unit]; Jean Carter, primarily Stock's secretary, but later a fully-fledged GS operative, and agent Sally Lomax. It was in this series that Nick Craig met his death [by an explosive device - the tragedy being referred to, but never witnessed on screen], but a new series was just around the corner and the show continued for a third series of 13 episodes under the title GS5.

A notable point: the series gave rise to one of the more memorable television theme tunes, a haunting piece [whistled throughout] by composer Philip Green.

Regular cast:
Nick Craig: **Michael Quinn**
Sir Andrew Wilson: **Donald Wolfit**
Helen Winters: **Angela Browne**
Tony Miller: **Neil Hallett**
Geoffrey Stock: **Anthony Marlowe**
Jean Carter: **Claire Nielson**
Sally Lomax: **Patricia Mort**
Peter Clarke: **Ray Barrett** [intro GS5]
Billy Clay: **Ray Austin** [intro GS5]

---

season one
13 monochrome 60-minute episodes
1961

Ticket for Blackmail
w **Lindsay Galloway**
d **Norman Harrison**

Newly-appointed Ghost Squad operative Nick Craig is assigned to expose an illicit diamond smuggling gang. To do so he travels to the South of France as a passenger on a holiday coach tour.

Suzanne: **Petra Davies**
Karolides: **Paul Stassino**
Joe Tobias: **Ronald Leigh Hunt**
Graham Tobias: **Alex Scott**
Charley: **Donald Morley**
Florian: **Neil Arden**
Degrange: **Edwin Richfield**

Bullet With My Name on it
w **Tony O'Grady** [aka **Brian Clemens**]
d **Don Sharp**

Investigating a murder-for-sale bureau in Rome, Nick Craig, impersonating an American criminal lawyer, plays his role too well - and finds his life threatened by professional assassins.

Chris Charles: **Peter Williams**
Kane: **Alfred Burke**
Gina: **Catherine Feller**
Frank O'Hara: **William Greene**
Poppa: **Guy Deghy**
Tony: **Sheldon Lawrence**

Hong Kong Story
w **Anthony Marriott & Connery Chappell**
d **Don Sharp**

When an assassin's bullet misses its target, a VIP, and kills an airline steward standing next to him, Sir Andrew Wilson, responsible for the dignitary's safety, assigns Nick Craig to investigate the incident.

Wacker Dawson: **Bill Kerr**
Suzie: **Julie Allan**
Wang : **George Pastell**
Dr Siligi: **Leonard Sachs**
Robert E. Lee: **Eric Young**
Airline Captain: **Norman Johns**
Khan: **Frank Olegario**

High Wire
w **Lewis Davidson**
d **Norman Harrison**

Craig dons the disguise of a wall of death motorcycle rider to infiltrate a gang responsible for a series of audacious robberies. His ability to ride the machines leads to him being offered the role of look-out on the gang's next job.

Fred Rice: **William Hartnell**
Rita: **Anne Wakefield**
Moker: **John Cairney**
Pauline: **Colette Wilde**
Simon: **Tom Adams**
Fairground Barker: **Vic Wise**

The Broken Doll
w **Patrick Campbell**
d **Don Sharp**

Three things link the deaths of four British girls murdered in Marseilles, all worked at the same nightclub, all were blonde, and all were beautiful. Nick Craig finds a fourth clue - and sets out to solve the murders.

Julie: **Julia Arnall**
Federoff: **Simon Lack**
Tante Marie: **Jean Anderson**
Greg: **Harry Locke**
Hortense: **Gabriella Licudi**
Duclos: **Richard Leech**
Gold: **Richard Bebb**
Joffe: **John G. Heller**

Eyes of the Bat
w **Robert Stewart**
d **Don Sharp**

Craig's latest assignment could cost him his life: impersonating a safe blower, he must infiltrate a gang planning a major bank robbery and blackmailing fashion models for their secrets.

Ambrose Jerome: **William Lucas**
Simone: **Jean Clarke**
Birdie: **Lionel Murton**
Peter: **Edward Cast**
Joe Kenton: **Donald Churchill**
Vic Diamond: **Dudley Foster**
Doctor: **Iris Russell**

Still Waters
w **Max Marquis**
d **Robert Lynn**

Masquerading as a crooked Dutch diamond merchant, Craig attempts to infiltrate a worldwide smuggling racket and expose the head man. His disguise is penetrated - and he barely escapes with his life.

Arny Long: **John Carson**
Captain Starr: **Stratford Johns**
Wim Harmsen: **Victor Beaumont**
Paula: **Juliet Winsor**
Herd: **Max Butterfield**
Inspector Lothar: **Raymond Adamson**
Dr Smits: **Patricia Marmont**

Assassin
w **Dick Sharples & Gerald Kelsey**
d **Robert Lynn**

Called in to help save the life of a young American framed for the killing of Kubitz, a mid-European Prime Minister, Nick Craig finds himself facing a task as difficult as any he has previously encountered.

Anna: **Jill Ireland**
Koster: **Joseph Furst**
Kowska: **George Coulouris**
Frank Maine: **Paul Maxwell**
Jacobi: **John Salew**
Gunsmith: **Norman Bird**
Kubitz: **Garard Green**
Grunther: **Roland Brand**
Ricci: **Christopher Witty**

Death from a Distance
w **Lindsay Galloway & Connery Chappell**
d **Robert Lynn**

Recruited into the GS team on a special mission to ensure the safety of a visiting president, Det. Insp. Brett's methods raise a few eyebrows - none higher than Craig's, who asks if the newcomer is all that he seems.

Stephen Brett: **William Sylvester**
Jackie: **Hazel Court**
Ronter: **Anton Diffring**
Volgu: **John Le Mesurier**
Pavelich: **John Crawford**
Holgar: **Roger Delgado**
Kartalis: **Douglas Wilmer**
Susie: **Moira Redmond**
Michaelis: **Harold Kasket**
Sonia: **Angela White**

Million Dollar Ransom
w **Dick Sharples & Gerald Kelsey**
d **Don Sharp**

Craig is sent to Sweden to thwart the plans of a ruthless gang of kidnappers who intend to use the Monte Carlo motor rally as a cover to smuggle a kidnapped scientist out of the country.

Bob Royston: **Bruce Beeby**
Phil Slade: **Peter Dyneley**
Helen Winters: **Angela Browne**
Pat Miller: **Jennifer Jayne**
Dr. Cookson: **John McLaren**
Mrs Cookson: **Jenny Laird**
Colonel Karlen: **Barry Keegan**
Carlsen: **Keith Pyott**
Dr. Lundquist: **Olaf Pooley**

Catspaw *
w **Bill Craig**
d **Robert Lynn**

When a man's body is discovered in a crate unloaded from a boat at a Baltimore Dock, Craig flies to South America with orders to infiltrate a 'hit' squad, a team of assassins prepared to kill anyone for money.

Torres: **Paul Stassino**
Roblez: **Bill Nagy**
Ribas: **Michael Goodliffe**
Anita: **Moira Redmond**
Forbes: **Walter Brown**
Mendoza: **George Pastell**
Rosendo: **Guy Deghy**
Badillo: **Alec Mango**

The Green Shoes *
w **Robert Holmes**
d **Don Sharp**

Hearing that an attempt will be made to kidnap a research scientist, Nick Craig visits a Nuclear Research Centre with orders to protect the man. Strange things begin to happen - and the GS operative faces a deadly enemy.

Rev. Anthony Felling: **Ewan Solon**
Tamara Luchovak: **Joyce Blair**
Professor Wallace: **John Welsh**
Braune: **Martin Miller**
Bream: **Glyn Houston**
Snaith: **Neil Hallett**
Stage Manager: **Edward Cast**
Salesman: **Bernard Hunter**

Princess *
w **Dick Sharples & Gerald Kelsey**
d **Robert Lynn**

Craig finds himself in an unexpected but pleasurable location - a girl's finishing school in Switzerland. His mission: to chaperone a princess whose life has been threatened after her betrothal to the crown prince.

Nadia: **Barbara Evans**
Laura: **Honor Blackman**
Decker: **Robert Rietty**
Sabri: **Marne Maitland**
Affiat: **Warren Mitchell**
Leeser: **Maxwell Shaw**
Cannack: **Richard Marner**

✍

Episodes denoted by an asterisk were filmed for the first series, but held back [due to an actors' strike] and tagged on to the beginning of series two.

season two
26 monochrom 60-minute episode
1962/63

Interrupted Requiem
w **Bill Craig**
d **John Nelson Burton**

When his daughter is reported dead in a plane crash, scientist Anton Brissac informs the GS team that he believes that she is being held hostage. New GS chief Geoffrey Stock assigns Nick Craig to find out why.

Geoffrey Stock: **Anthony Marlowe** [intro]
Jean Carter: **Claire Nielson** [intro]
Jan Kupra: **Richard Dare**
Kristyna: **Ellen McIntosh**
Anton Brissac: **Leonard Sachs**
Bowles: **Frederick Peisley**
Prior: **Derek Nimmo**
Beyla: **Norman Scace**
Melchek: **John Barrett**
Security Officer: **Henry Longhurst**
Air Hostess: **Erica Houen**
Air Captain: **Patrick Carter**

East of Mandalay
w **Bill Craig**
d **Dennis Vance**

Staggered by information he receives, GS chief Stock sends his new operator, Tony Miller, to investigate the sale of illegal arms. Posing as a mercenary, Miller uncovers a plot to overthrow a foreign country.

Tony Miller: **Neil Hallett** [intro]
Sir Charles Thorne: **Ian Fleming**
Suratmo: **Barry Shawzin**
Burton: **Brian Haines**
Sara Van Neikerk: **Jacqui Chan**
Hoyoto: **Wolfe Morris**
Captain Hann: **Christopher Carlos**
U Toke: **Denis Shaw**
Barman: **Eric Young**
Foreman Miner: **Donald Chinn**
Native Policeman: **Melan Mitchell**
Native Guard: **Peter Diamond**

Sentences of Death
w **Geoffrey Bellman & John Whitney**
d **Peter Sasdy**

Investigating the activities of a dope-smuggling ring in Trieste, Craig's cover is blown. Tortured and injected with a truth drug, he passes on information which will endanger the life of GS operator Tony Miller, who has followed Craig to Trieste.

Geoffrey Stock: **Anthony Marlowe**

Jean Carter: **Claire Nielson**
Paul: **Ronald Leigh Hunt**
Philippa: **Ann Lynn**
Barman: **Bernard Spear**
Night Watchman: **Reg Lye**
Dr Roach: **John Rae**
Beavis: **Stuart Saunders**
Ticket Inspector: **Michael Beint**
Preston: **Tom Chatto**
Police Officer: **John Boyd Brent**

The Golden Silence
w **John Lucarotti**
d **John Nelson Burton**

The murder of a GS operative and a car with excessive pressure in its front tyres leads Tony Miller to Holland. The dead man was following a travel agency courier when he died. Miller takes his place.

Jean Carter: **Claire Nielson**
Mike Ferrers: **Gordon Jackson**
Blakestone: **David Garth**
Midge Carberry: **Myrtle Reed**
Tom Didcot: **Patrick Blackwell**
Max Leach: **David Lodge**
Waiter: **Richard Klee**
Customs Man: **Doel Luscombe**
Mechanic: **Frank Seton**
Foreman: **Charles Farrell**
Secretary: **June Shaw**
Dave Welford: **Robin Hughes**

The Retirement of Gentle Dove
w **Philip Levene**
d **Dennis Vance**

GS chief Geoffrey Stock enters an old people's home to investigate the death of a notorious wartime Intelligence Department head known only as the Gentle Dove. Nick Craig will maintain contact by visiting him in the guise of his nephew.

Siegfried: **Mia Karam**
Sir Kenneth Ingram: **Maxwell Foster**
Lady M. Ingram: **Helen Goss**
Mrs Lister: **Valarie White**
Major Stone: **Carl Bernard**
Mr Tresilian: **Philip Ray**
Miss Reeves: **Olwen Brookes**
Anna: **Ilona Ference**
Mrs Every: **Margaret Vines**
Lieber: **Ballard Berkeley**

The Missing People
w **Peter Yeldham**
d **Antony Kearey**

A hideous traffic in refugees and the murder of a nightclub hostess provides the link to one of the most callous cases Tony Miller has handled. The GS agent finds more that he bargained for - and danger lurking in the shadows.

Geoffrey Stock: **Anthony Marlowe**
Jean Carter: **Claire Nielson**
Cresswell: **Nigel Green**
Rose: **Patricia Mort**
Slim Salmon: **Willoughby Goddard**
Smith: **Rio Fanning**
Mrs Weisnevsky: **Hana Pravda**
Diane: **Majie Lawrence**
Jeans: **Peter Fraser**
Leather Jacket: **Glyn Dearman**
Wolkowsky: **Anthony Morton**

Josie: **Pamela Ann Davy**
Inspector Collins: **Peter Hughes**
Doctor: **Ian Clark**
Tadeusz: **Michael Ritterman**
Sally: **Patricia Clapton**
Czech Official: **Theodore Wilhelm**

Lost In Transit
w **Basil Dawson**
d **Phil Brown**

Investigating the upsurge of a new Nazi party, GS operator Tony Miller finds himself up against a modern-day Fuhrer who plans to overthrow the British Government and take over the country.

Geoffrey Stock: **Anthony Marlowe**
Jean Carter: **Claire Nielson**
Karl Epper: **John Woodvine**
Lise: **Delphi Lawrence**
Van Tempel: **Anthony Jacobs**
Jimmy Rice: **Jeremy Young**
Meeker: **Walter Randall**
Lefty: **Tom Busby**
Heinrich: **Charles Hill**
Desmoulins: **Andre Maranne**
Nicholas Mayer: **Arnold Diamond**
Berlin Policeman: **Wilfred Carter**
Air Hostess: **Mary Abbott**
Passport Officer: **Michael Oxley**
Mortuary Attendant: **John Scott Martin**
Hans: **Vincent Harding**
Haakman-Dutch Tough: **Brian Vaughan**

The Man With the Delicate Hands
w **Philip Levene**
d **Peter Sasdy**

A body found in a burnt out car is identified as that of interpreter Paul Lambert. When the evidence shows that the body may not have been Lambert's after all, Tony Miller is assigned to the case - for Lambert possessed information of vital importance.

Henry Dickenson: **Basil Dignam**
Jean Carter: **Claire Nielson**
Helen Lambert: **Rosemary Dorken**
Peter Brenner: **Derek Francis**
Dr Arne: **Anne Blake**
Hans Delarge: **Eric Chitty**
Paul Lambert: **Brian Nissen**
Vaughan: **Patrick Boxill**
Jan: **Lee Richardson**
Hotel Porter: **Keith Marsh**
Police Inspector: **Brian Dent**
Superintendent: **Grenville Eves**
Bell Boy: **Christian Holder**
Shultz: **Endre Muller**

Hot Money
w **Louis Marks**
d **John Nelson Burton**

Giuseppe del Piazzo, includes a forged note in the money he pays into his bank. The Ghost Squad is informed. The note bears a serial number which corresponds to a genuine note stolen in a bank robbery. Nick Craig is assigned to uncover the link.

Geoffrey Stock: **Anthony Marlowe**
Jean Carter: **Claire Nielson**
del Piazzo: **Andreas Malandrinos**
Mina: **Samantha Eggar**
Granger: **Lloyd Lamble**

Sam: **Max Bacon**
Police Inspector: **John Scott**
Detective: **David Davenport**
Doctor: **Frederick Farley**
Bank Teller: **Kenneth Colley**
Second Bank Teller: **John Simpson**

The Grand Duchess
w **Julian Bond**
d **Christopher Morahan**

A valuable Goya painting disappears, but causes no surprise to the Ghost Squad. The robbery was carried out by agent Tony Miller - part of a carefully planned operation to uncover the man behind a series of audacious art robberies.

Geoffrey Stock: **Anthony Marlowe**
Jean Carter: **Claire Nielson**
Truloff: **Peter Elliott**
Lazenger: **John Barron**
Oregin: **Arnold Marle**
Caterer: **Cameron Hall**
Farley: **John Ringham**
Waiter: **Michael Robbins**
First Security Man: **Clifford Cox**
Second Security Man: **Roger Avon**
Downs: **Garfield Morgan**
Voyce: **William Gaunt**
Barron: **Colin Douglas**

A First Class Way to Die
w **John Lucarotti**
d **Peter Sasdy**

Assigned to keep an eye on the distinguished scientist, Professor Nesterenko, during a luxury cruise, Nick Craig has lots of questions to answer. Why is Anya, the professor's niece, carrying a gun? Why is a steward taking such interest in her? And who is the mysterious figure known as "The Kondor?"

Geoffrey Stock: **Anthony Marlowe**
Jean Carter: **Claire Nielson**
Tony Miller: **Neil Hallett**
Professor Nesterenko: **Laurence Hardy**
Anya Krovchuk: **Jennifer Daniel**
Larry Arnell: **Peter Dyneley**
Ettore Scaccia: **Peter Halliday**
Nils: **Anthony Sagar**
Clavik: **Jerry Stovin**
The Captain: **Charles Morgan**
Deck Officer: **Richard Burrell**
Steward: **Michael Browning**
Ella Gante: **Pamela Conway**
The Boy: **Keith Anderson**
The Girl: **Mitzi Rogers**

Quarantine at Kavar
w **Basil Dawson**
d **Geoffrey Nethercott**

Sent to the Middle East to find out what has happened to members of an archaeological dig, GS operatives Nick Craig and Jean Carter find themselves involved with terrorists and threatened with an outbreak of plague.

Sazi Keller: **Elvi Hale**
Dr Hussein Rasul: **Maurice Kaufmann**
The Emir of Kavar: **Martin Wlydeck**
Tim Casey: **John Carlin**
Dwight Sherman: **Al Mulock**
Major Sayid: **Roger Delgado**
Clive Jessell-Cave: **David King**
Beni: **Ralph Nossek**

Hassan: **George Eugeniou**
Ali: **Patrick Carter**
Gholam: **Dallas Cavell**
Dr Morrow: **Gerald Lawson**
Tel. Operator: **Julian Sherrier**
Lawton V/O: **David King**
Policeman: **John Hatton**

The Desperate Diplomat
w **Joshua Adam [aka Lewis Griefer]**
d **Peter Sasdy**

Nick Craig, set the task of sorting out the problems of a diplomat who is being threatened, finds himself investigating a drug-running racket. His enquiries lead him to Anna, whose late husband ran the Rome end of the operation.

Geoffrey Stock: **Anthony Marlowe**
Jean Carter: **Claire Nielson**
Clive Errington: **Derek De Marney**
Margaret Errington: **Barbara Shelley**
Neville Shand: **Ferdy Mayne**
Sir Thomas Glanville: **Richard Caldicott**
Anna: **Naomi Chance**
Jocko: **Tom Bowman**
Jack Harris: **Edgar K. Bruce**
Joe: **Ivor Salter**
Maid: **Anne Carroll**

The Big Time
w **Leon Griffiths**
d **Peter Sasdy**

When a small-time crook steals a handbag belonging to Jane Sinclair-Morley, but the woman denies losing her bag, the crime attracts the attention of the Ghost Squad. Nick Craig investigates - and murder and diamond-smuggling are soon part of the equation.

Geoffrey Stock: **Anthony Marlowe**
Jane Sinclair-Morley: **Pauline Stroud**
Floor Walker: **Henry McGee**
Rooney: **Paul Farrell**
Peter Welcome: **Derek Waring**
Barrow: **Edwin Brown**
Mrs Cheavers: **Betty Henderson**
Slattery: **George Murcell**
Mr Wheedon: **Toke Townley**
Father Huggins: **Vincent Ball**
Policeman: **Stanley Walsh**
Doctor: **Dennis Edwards**
Mr Jason: **Geoffrey Chater**
Barbara Keogh: **Maya Sorell**
Joe Baker: **Tom Payne**

The Last Jump
w **Richard Harris**
d **Dennis Vance**

When a paratrooper's chute fails to open during a training exercise, Stock and Miller join the parachute regiment to expose a murderer and find the secret behind the disappearance of vital secret equipment for the design of a new guided missile.

Marks: **Harry Ross**
Dr. Weltmann: **Rudolph Offenback**
Lt. Colonel Trent: **Thomas Heathcote**
Capt. Roly Horstead: **Jack Watling**
Lt. Keith Blanford: **John Bonney**
Major Jack Naismith: **Denis Thorne**
Ft. Officer Sarah Glindon: **Margaret Courtenay**
Ft. Lt. Ward: **David Davenport**
Jean Carter: **Claire Nielson**

Escape Route
w **Peter Yeldham**
d **Antony Kearey**

Agents Nick Craig and Jean Carter pursue a wealthy embezzler to Sydney, Australia. Suspected of being behind an organisation that helps people on the run to disappear, the fugitive has absconded with £100,000 and has undergone plastic surgery to change his appearance.

Detective: **John Frawley**
Sergeant: **Edward Ogden**
Insp. Munroe: **John Scott**
Club Member: **Roger Maxwell**
Elliott Chapman: **Terence Alexander**
Steward: **Joe Gibbons**
Julia Wilson: **Harriette Johns**
Mr Hathwin: **Bill Shine**
Johnson: **John Junkin**
Carlo: **Harry Tardios**
Captain: **Alan White**
Swede: **Steven Scott**
Rockworth: **Hugh Burden**

Mr Five Per Cent
w **Louis Marks**
d **Phil Brown**

When a large consignments of illegal arms threaten to destroy the uneasy truce in a foreign state, GS agent Tony Miller enlists the services of a known dope-pedlar in order to discover the secret of a new Canadian automatic rifle, so far supplied only to NATO troops.

Anton Dukavic: **Guy Deghy**
Tony Esposito: **Edwin Richfield**
Liz Esposito: **Naomi Chance**
Yvette: **Julia Allan**
Pettorosso: **George Roderick**
Willi: **Thomas Gallagher**
Fisherman: **Tony Sympson**
Carlo: **William Marlowe**
First Detective: **Frank Tregear**
First American: **Philip Oxman**
Second Detective: **Bud Strait**
Second American: **Cyril Cross**
Giovanni: **Frank Wheatley**
Afredo: **Steve Kirby**

The Heir Apparent
w **Julian Bond**
d **Dennis Vance**

GS operator Nick Craig becomes a games master at a school in order to protect the heir apparent to a friendly Middle East oil state. Much to his discomfort, Nick must master Rugby football in a hurry - then further discomfort arrives in the shape of a man called Ben Ali.

Geoffrey Stock: **Anthony Marlowe**
Jean Carter: **Claire Nielson**
The Commander: **Frank Middlemas**
Ben Ali: **Roger Delgado**
Roger Belcher: **Arnold Diamond**
Gavin Riordan: **David Blake Kelly**
Philip Pearson: **Bill Horsley**
Jim: **Donald Oliver**
Karim: **Julian Sherrier**
Arab: **James Gill**
Manager of Nightclub: **Michael Forest**
The Ruler: **Henry Oscar**
Sarah Pearson: **Carolyn Pertwee**

Death of a Sportsman
w **Basil Dawson**
d **James Ferman**

In Cairo on a stolen diamonds investigation, Tony Miller sees a man he thinks he recognise, a man presumed dead - an observation which leads him to adopt the identity of Peters, a prospective buyer of illicit stones. Aided by new GS recruit Sally Lomax, Miller almost bites off more than he can chew.

Geoffrey Stock: **Anthony Marlowe**
Spencer Deeds: **John Longden**
Sally Lomax: **Patricia Mort** [intro]
Beni: **Peter Diamond**
Hotel Clerk: **Thor Pierres**
Major Mahmoud: **Warren Mitchell**
Operator: **Alexander Browne**
Akbar: **Frank Olegario**
Rev. J. Crichton: **Noel Howlett**
Dr. Malik: **Arnold Yarrow**
Rahman: **Leo Carera**
Mrs Mason: **Helen Sessions**
Caroline Deeds: **Patricia Haines**
Zervas: **Martin Benson**

P.G. 7
w **Basil Dawson**
d **Phil Brown**

P.G.7, a new form of air-borne inhalant gas, is lethal. When a burglary takes place at the laboratory where it has been developed and there is every indication that, Ginger Todd, the thief is unaware of the danger, GS agents Nick Craig and Jean Carter are assigned to solve the crisis.

Todd: **Alistair Williamson**
Owen: **Ross Hutchinson**
Diana Heeley: **Pauline Yates**
Geoffrey Haydon: **Frank Gatliff**
Det. Insp. Russell: **Ewan Thomas**
Sebastian Boone: **Michael Gwynn**
Barman: **John Dunbar**
Rocco: **Cec Montgomery**
Sullivan: **Gordon Tanner**
Faria: **George Pastell**
Clerk: **Roger Jenkinson**
Silva: **Derek Sydney**
Second Clerk: **Richard Klee**

Polsky
w **Tudor Gates**
d **Dennis Vance**

A series of big payroll robberies follow a pattern similar to that of a crime-wave in France - the work of an extremist right-wing organisation. The Ghost Squad is called in and Tony Miller is told to infiltrate the gang. He does so by assuming the identity of a former safe-breaker known as Polsky.

Geoffrey Stock: **Anthony Marlowe**
Jean Carter: **Claire Nielson**
Mr Hicks: **Ray Barrett**
Jack Berg: **Tom Bowman**
Joe Dunning: **Ray Austin**
Magistrate: **Gabriel Toyne**
Constable: **Alex Ross**
Probation Officer: **Denis Holmes**
Maisie: **Pamela Gale**
Girl in phone box: **Fernanda Marlowe**
Mr Minto: **Gerald Cross**
Butler: **Henry Kay**
Nyziad Senior: **Frederick Schiller**

The Magic Bullet
w **Maurice Wiltshire**
d **James Ferman**

Assigned to protect the life - and secrets - of an eminent metallurgist attending a science conference at a country retreat, Nick Craig springs an elaborate trap on a group of foreign spies - but murder takes a hand and almost ruins his chance of success.

Jean Carter: **Claire Nielson**
Professor Baker: **David Markham**
Dr Ibanez: **Mary Morris**
Sir William Hallows: **Maurice Hedley**
Sir David Andrews: **Norman Claridge**
Professor Brodny: **Alexis Chesnakov**
Dr Sanchez: **Dan Jackson**
Dr. Diaz: **George Eugeniou**
Lady Caroline Andrews: **Clare Kelly**
Doctor: **David King**
Airport Security Officer: **Peter Wyatt**
Monsieur Roget: **Dennis Bernard**
Hotel Clerk: **Michael Oxley**

The Menacing Mazurka
w **John Lucarotti**
d **Hugh Rennie**

Ghost Squad chief Stock thinks it wise to have someone close at hand when the Bassari State Dancers visit London. Tony Miller is given the job of arranging their publicity - and ends up foiling a sordid game of diplomatic blackmail.

Jean Carter: **Claire Nielson**
Kobelik: **Olaf Pooley**
Linka: **Penny Whittam**
Ilse Virany: **Jacqueline Ellis**
Feyer: **Harry Towb**
Photographer: **Desmond Davies**
Reporter: **Mark Kelly**
Andret: **Ray Austin**
Laslo Radiv: **George Pravda**
Ambassador: **Michael Ritterman**
Mrs Marquand-Forster: **Ruth Lodge**
Barman: **Colin Cresswell**
Chauffeur: **Dixon Adams**
Inspector: **Clement McCallin**
Police Sgt: **Rex Robinson**

Gertrude
w **Bill MacIllwraith**
d **Antony Kearey**

Ghost Squad operator Nick Craig takes a wife - all in the call of business, of course. And what a wife, Gertrude is a cabaret artist who dabbles in subversive activities. Flamboyant and unpredictable, her colourful outlook on life lands Craig and fellow agent, Jean Carter, in deep, deep trouble.

Henry Cameron: **Archie Duncan**
Gertrude: **Mary Mackenzie**
Sir Thomas Glanville: **Richard Caldicot**
Arab father: **Steve Plytas**
Arab son: **James Gill**
Inspector: **Douglas Wilmer**
First Guard: **Tony Lawrence**
Second Guard: **Jerry Elboz**
Abdul: **Henry Soskin**
Ali: **Raf De La Torre**
Landlord: **Louis Raynes**

The Thirteenth Girl
w **Joshua Adam** [aka **Lewis Griefer**]
d **Peter Sasdy**

Ten Swiss au pair girls, working in England, have disappeared: two have been found - murdered. The Ghost Squad enlists agent Sally Lomax, who travels to Switzerland and, provided with a Swiss background, returns to London - aware that she could become the killer's next victim!

Geoffrey Stock: **Anthony Marlowe**
Franz Hartmann: **John Carson**
Connie Amherst: **Peggy Marshall**
Ray Evans: **John Ronane**
Mrs Henderson: **Molly Weir**
Bodil Henderson: **Edina Ronay**
Mr Whitehead: **John Wentworth**
Johnny De Souza: **Simon Oates**
Miss Carew: **Margaret John**
W.P.C.: **Rita Davies**
Reg Cross: **John Atkinson**
Pinto: **Peter Diamond**
Annalisa: **Ingrid Benning**
Sullivan: **Willie Payne**

Sabotage
w **Reed De Rouen**
d **Hugh Rennie**

A notorious Dutch saboteur is intercepted on his way to a trouble spot in the Indian Ocean. Assigned to impersonate him, Tony Miller must carry out the function the man was supposed to perform - to blow-up the newly-developed facilities of the island's only deep water harbour.

Geoffrey Stock: **Anthony Marlowe**
Ali: **Ray Austin**
Sir Ian Rand-Fuller: **Maurice Colbourne**
Lt. Nigel Brookes: **Philip Guard**
Emil Zadeck: **Eric Pohlmann**
Nancy Rand-Fuller: **Jill Medford**
Edmund Wilson: **John Paul**
Miss Brown: **Elizabeth Zinn**
Maria: **Aliza Gur**
Hotel Barmaid: **Lucille Soong**
John Mallory: **Maurice Durant**
Tom: **Raoul Alkazzi**

G.S.5

13 monochrome 60-minute episodes
1964

GS5 began with the introduction of another new character, Peter Clarke, a soft-spoken agent who abhorred violence [until aroused] and preferred to get his quarry through slow, methodical investigation - which, to Miller's mind, made him a soft' replacement for his dead friend Nick Craig. Deeply upset by Nick's death, Miller became more merciless with the crooks he encountered and showed open disdain for Clarke's nonchalant ways. Nevertheless, the partnership worked and the final outing by the GS team was among the best of the entire series - helped in large order by the scriptwriting/editing attributes of Brian Clemens, who was only months away from his successful association with *The Avengers*.
Another newcomer joined the team a few weeks later, Billy Clay. Played by [then] stuntman, Ray Austin, Clay owned the gym frequented by the squad's agents, his job being to harden them up for their dangerous undercover activities.

An Eye for An Eye
w **Kenneth Hayles**
d **Eric Price**

Mourning the death of his fellow agent and friend Nick Craig, Miller, and new GS5 operator Peter Clarke, are sent

to check out the explosion at sea. Their investigations bring surprising - and to Miller - highly satisfactory results.

Peter Clarke: **Ray Barrett** [intro]
Geoffrey Stock: **Anthony Marlowe**
Jean Carter: **Claire Nielson**
Laura Adams: **Dilys Laye**
Dixon: **Brian Oulton**
Roo: **Lloyd Lamble**
Policewoman: **Carol Mauray**
Grant: **Ken Parry**
Smithy: **Frederic Abbott**
Maisie: **Joy Stewart**
McKay: **William Marlowe**

A Cast of Thousands
w **Larry Forrester**
d **Peter Sasdy**

Working undercover, GS5 agent Sally Lomax discovers that an elusive typewriter holds the key to her investigations into 'accidents' on a film set. Suspecting sabotage, she uncovers a murder cartel.

Geoffrey Stock: **Anthony Marlowe**
Jean Carter: **Claire Nielson**
Nelson Rador: **Steven Berkoff**
Teresa Pantera: **Isa Miranda**
Josef Farago: **George Pravda**
Jodie: **Frank Lieberman**
Royston Lambert: **Edwin Richfield**
Jensen: **George Mikall**
Dave Sherman: **Richard Easton**
Sammy: **Christian Holder**
Betty McQuaig: **Joy Owen**
Bovic: **John Wentworth**

Death of a Cop
w **Roger Marshall**
d **Dennis Vance**

Masquerading as a new reporter, Tony Miller investigates the death of a policeman suspected of being 'on the take' from gamblers. His search for the cop killer leads him into the world of high finance.

Geoffrey Stock: **Anthony Marlowe**
Jean Carter: **Claire Nielson**
PC Brown: **Barry Wilsher**
Smart: **Terry Richards**
Kauffman: **Robert Brown**
Costa: **Arnold Diamond**
De Souza: **Roger Delgado**
Betty Asher: **Betty McDowall**
Asst. Commissioner: **Geoffrey Denton**
Anne Brown: **Patricia Heneghan**
Larry Montague: **Michael Golden**
Ambassador: **Denis Shaw**
Policewoman: **Carol Mauray**
Cleaning Woman: **Gladys Dawson**
Vice President: **Sydney Arnold**

Party for Murder
w **Nicholas Palmer**
d **Dennis Vance**

Assigned to investigate a series of sabotage incidents involving a new machine being designed for South America, Clarke 'defects' to the Fascist party responsible for the crime - with dangerous results.

Tony Miller: **Neil Hallett**
Geoffrey Stock: **Anthony Marlowe**
Jean Carter: **Claire Nielson**

Creasey: **John Robinson**
Elisabeth Creasey: **Lois Maxwell**
Graves: **Barry Letts**
Jose: **Michael Mellinger**
Withers: **Brian Haines**
Scarb: **Jack Philips**
Walter: **Larry Taylor**
Billy Clay: **Ray Austin** [intro]

Dead Men Don't Drive
w **Tudor Gates**
d **Peter Sasdy**

GS5 operative Tony Miller finds himself facing a tough problem: how could a man be seen driving a car through a village and yet, when the vehicle crashed, the man is found to have been dead for several hours?

Grinley: **Edwin Brown**
Doctor: **Colin Douglas**
Geoffrey Stock: **Anthony Marlowe**
Jean Carter: **Claire Nielson**
Billy Clay: **Ray Austin**
Sandy: **Kenneth Watson**
Hart: **Ronald Leigh-Hunt**
Mrs Benning: **Joan Phillips**
Yvonne Marsden: **Zena Marshall**
Mrs Kerman: **Amy Dalby**

Pay Up or Else
w **Dave Cummin**
d **Eric Price**

When a protection racket gang declare war on innocent people, GS5 agent Tony Miller is assigned to infiltrate the gang and force the opposing sides into a showdown. He achieves this - with startling results.

Berger: **Bernard Barnsley**
Kurnitz: **Brian Weske**
Marty Evans: **Micky Dillon**
Demaris: **Felix Felton**
Harry Mason: **Harry Towb**
Jean Carter: **Claire Nielson**
Geoffrey Stock: **Anthony Marlowe**
Supt. Finder: **Terence Longden** [intro]
Lewis: **Alan Browning**
Milo: **John Barrard**
Gina: **Shusha Assar**
Billy Clay: **Ray Austin**

Dr. Ayre
w **Brian Clemens**
d **Eric Price**

Stock's disbelief that a 'master criminal' is behind a series of brilliantly executed robberies is severely shaken when operative Peter Clarke brings him conclusive proof that successful criminal Dr. Ayre is masterminding further audacious crimes.

Sidney Grafton: **Gerry Duggan**
Paul Morris: **Garfield Morgan**
Geoffrey Stock: **Anthony Marlowe**
Jean Carter: **Claire Nielson**
Supt. Finder: **Terence Longden**
Sara Harvey: **Tamara Hinchco**
Bank Manager: **Dennis Edwards**
Hotel Receptionist: **Betty England**
Jill Norman: **Jennifer Wilson**
Tommy Farrell: **Freddie Earle**
Little Man: **Leonard Russell**
Barman: **David Lander**

Airport Official: **Colin Rix**
Stewardess: **Gloria Best**

Scorpion Rock
w **Guy Morgan**
d **Bill Stewart**

The island of Baleric hides a sinister secret which GS5 operator Tony Miller must solve if he is to have any chance of locating the whereabouts of a fellow undercover agent believed kidnapped by dictator Zafra.

Pip Jago: **Mike Sands**
Nicola Webb: **Catherine Woodville**
Emilio Zafra: **Paul Whitsun-Jones**
Pepe: **Walter Randall**
Charles Swinburne: **Norman Pitt**
Geoffrey Stock: **Anthony Marlowe**
Jean Carter: **Claire Nielson**
Stripey Hoskins: **Michael Robbins**
Barman: **Victor Baring**
Adml. Makepeace: **Arthur Hewlett**
Police Captain: **Peter Allenby**
Pablo: **Lee Richardson**
Flamenco Dancer: **Pepita Ramirez**

The Goldfish Bowl
w **Tudor Gates**
d **Bill Stewart**

Sent to check out the strange goings on at a secret missile base, GS5 operatives Clarke and Miller find their cover blown and the enemy awaiting their arrival - a dangerous situation when you're seeking a sadistic killer.

Geoffrey Stock: **Anthony Marlowe**
Jean Carter: **Claire Nielson**
Col. Havis: **John Stuart**
Policeman: **Donald McKillop**
Mortuary Attendant: **Rory McDermott**
Smart: **Talfryn Thomas**
Mr Bigley: **Walter Swash**
Mrs Bigley: **Winifred Dennis**
Crawford: **Gerald Sim**
Secretary: **Clare Owen**
Martin: **John Pike**
Gross: **Arnold Marle**
Mara: **Erika Brand**
Smithers: **Kenneth Edwards**
Whitmarsh: **Brian Hankins**
Bentall: **James Urquhart**
Officer: **Peter Hagar**

Seven Sisters of Wong
w **Brian Clemens**
d **Bill Stewart**

Masquerading as a dope-peddler, agent Tony Miller meets a beautiful Chinese girl and finds himself involved with a secret patriot army, who intend to use his services - whether he likes it or not!

Doctor: **Shane Rimmer**
Nurse: **Anne Murray**
Geoffrey Stock: **Anthony Marlowe**
Bassett: **Reed de Rouen**
Jean Carter: **Claire Nielson**
Harris: **Frank Seton**
Masie: **Carole Boyer**
Freddie Moran: **Donald Morley**
Mary Sin Chui: **Maureen Beck**
Deprae: **Leonard Sachs**
Floyd: **Bari Johnson**

Rich Ruby Wine
w **Joshua Adam** [aka **Lewis Griefer**]
d **Eric Price**

Stock assigns his entire department to locate Franz Rudolph Gruber, a former Nazi chief in Hungary. Gruber is known to have in his possession the Howarth jewel collection - which Stock suspects will be used to finance a new Nazi regime.

Tom: **Anthony Broughton**
Wally: **Joe Ritchie**
Peter Clarke: **Ray Barrett**
Jean Carter: **Claire Nielson**
Billy Clay: **Ray Austin**
Geoffrey Stock: **Anthony Marlowe**
Tony Miller: **Neil Hallett**
Mayer: **Harold Goldblatt**
Mears: **Terence Soall**
Anna: **Adina Mandlova**
Dutch: **Tutte Lemkow**
Ernst Hartmann: **Geoffrey Bayldon**

Hideout
w **Malcolm Hulke**
d **Peter Sasdy**

Undercover operative Sally Lomax is assigned to delve into the past of a man whom Stock believes to be a murderer. The man, Dawson, is now managing a holiday camp - at which several 'accidents' have taken place. Sally books in - but her holiday is far from peaceful.

Shirley Simpson: **Julie Samuel**
Leslie Dawson: **Emrys Jones**
Insp. Bates: **Edward Burnham**
Geoffrey Stock: **Anthony Marlowe**
Jean Carter: **Claire Nielson**
Rita: **Lilian Grassom**
Freddie Maguire: **Gerald Harper**
Johnny Pitt: **Norman Chappell**
Larry Woods: **John Boyd Brent**
Jim Johnson: **Lee Richardson**
Harry Simpson: **David Blake Kelly**
Billy Clay: **Ray Austin**
Cleaner: **Vi Stevens**

It Won't be a Stylish Marriage
w **Brad Ashton**
d **Bill Stewart**

After a whirlwind courtship on the French Riviera, GS5 agent Peter Clarke, posing as a shy businessman, 'marries' Yvette, an attractive French Girl - in order to discover the secret behind another French girl's mysterious death.

Police Sergeant: **Geoffrey Alexander**
George Redmond: **Peter Hughes**
Police Inspector: **John Otway**
Geoffrey Stock: **Anthony Marlowe**
Police Inspector: **Robert Raglan**
Croupier: **Norman Bennett**
Heppie: **George A. Cooper**
Duval: **David Garth**
Sally Lomax: **Patricia Mort**
Yvette: **Nyree Dawn Porter**
Jean Carter: **Claire Nielson**
Policewoman: **Carol Mauray**
Fulroy: **Ian Clark**
Thompson: **David King**
Count Marrais: **Carl Duering**

Ghost Squad:

Season one:
Producer: **Connery Chappell**
Associate Producer: **Denis Holt**
Music by: **Philip Green**
Production Manager: **Donald Toms**
Assistant Director: **Frank Ernst**
Make-up: **Trevor Crole-Rees**

An ATV Production for ITC World Wide Distribution

13 monochrome 60 - minute episodes
1961

Season two:
Producer: **Anthony Kearey**
Associate Producer: **Denis Holt**
Music by: **Philip Green**

A Rank Organisation Television Film in Association with Associated Television Ltd. for ITC World Wide Distribution.

26 monochrome 60 - minute episodes
1962-63

G.S.5:

Producer: **Dennis Vance**
Music by: **Philip Green**
Script Editor: **Brian Clemens**
Fights arranged by: **Ray Austin**

A Rank Organisation Television Film in Association with Associated Television Ltd. for ITC World Wide Distribution.

13 monochrome 60 - minute episodes
1964

Gideon's Way

Based on the character created by John Creasey, this superior mid-'60s 'documentary' - style police series [the last joint production between Robert S. Baker and Monty Berman], centred around the criminal investigations of Commander George Gideon of Scotland Yard, a solid hard-working policeman with a nose for sniffing out crime. With his second-in-command, Chief Inspector David Keen, the two men formed a formidable crimebusting team. Both had come up through the ranks, and both men worked towards the same objective: solving [and wherever possible] preventing serious crime.

Remembered for its extensive use of location photography [almost every story was filmed in and around London], the series drew critical acclaim for its depiction of crime as an unglamourous business and policemen a human beings - men and women who had private lives, homes, personal interests. Noteable in all departments.

Regular cast:
Commander George Gideon: **John Gregson**
Det. Chief Inspector David Keen: **Alexander Davion**
Kate Gideon: **Daphne Anderson**

State Visit
w **Jim O'Connolly**
d **John Moxey**

Commander Gideon and Inspector Keen are assigned to protect the life of a visiting German statesman who has received threats to his life from Max Fischer, a former victim of Nazi persecution.

Max Fischer: **Alfie Bass**
Sarah Fischer: **Catharine Lacey**
Comm. Scott-Marle: **Basil Dignam** [intro]
Dep. Comm. Rae Cox: **Gerald Harper**
Jean Cox: **Patricia English**
Morris: **David Lodge**
Jim Richards: **Julian Holloway**
Warner: **Norman Scace**
Commander Ripple: **Jack Gwillim**
Chief Supt. Joe Bell: **Ian Rossiter** [intro]
Matthew Gideon: **Richard James** [intro]
Malcolm Gideon: **Giles Watling** [intro]

The 'V' Men
w **Alan Falconer**
d **Cyril Frankel**

When Sir Arthur Vane's neo-fascist activities begin to prove a thorn in Scotland Yard's side, and Vane complains that his life has been threatened, Commander Gideon and Inspector Keen are instructed to protect Vane from danger.

Sir Arthur Vane: **Ronald Culver**
Geoffrey Miles: **Keith Baxter**
Cathy Miller: **Angela Douglas**
Chief Supt. Bill Parsons: **Allan Cuthbertson**
Commissioner Scott-Marle: **Basil Dignam**
Det. Chief Supt. Joe Bell: **Ian Rossiter**
Keith Smith: **Dervis Ward**
Leo Samson: **Inigo Jackson**
Majorie Bennett: **Christine Finn**
John Hamilton: **Peter Russell**
Peter Bennett: **Dyson Lovell**

The Firebug
w **David Chandler**
d **Roy Baker**

An outbreak of fires in old buildings leads Gideon and Keen to a man motivated by circumstances not of his own making. But if he is really an arsonist, shouldn't Gideon arrest him? Why then does he fail to do so?

Bishop: **George Cole**
Mrs Tennison: **Avril Elgar**
Chief Officer Carmichael: **Martin Boddey**
Det. Sgt. Steve Brady: **Aubrey Richards**
Matthew Gideon: **Richard James**
Malcolm Gideon: **Giles Watling**
Mrs Critchley: **Hilda Barry**
Mr Gilliat: **Norman Wynne**
Scooter Salesman: **Peter Reeves**
Bill White: **Joby Blanshard**
Det. Insp. Dillon: **Edward Dentith**
Det. Chief. Supt. Joe Bell: **Ian Rossiter**

The Big Fix
w **Jack Whittingham**
d **James Hill**

Gideon and Keen enter the world of horse-racing - a world in which money can save a man's life or lead him to lose it, suddenly - particularly if the man owes a fortune in gambling debts.

Joe Short: **Michael Ripper**
Janet Middleton: **Penelope Horner**
Col. Alec Middleton: **Maurice Hedley**
Bill Campbell: **Robert Brown**
Dandy Johnson: **Brian Phelan**
Mabel Short: **Margery Mason**
Percy Knox: **John Glyn-Jones**
Bookie Thompson: **Max Bacon**
Jimmy: **Griffith Davies**
Ron Short: **Michael Goodman**
Alice Short: **Sandra Payne**
The Veterinarian: **Tom Gill**

The Housekeeper
w **David Chantler**
d **Leslie Norman**

Gideon faces a race against time to unmask a shrewd, calculating opponent - a killer who dares him to attempt to halt his next crime. Gideon's dilemma: which of two potential victims is the next on the madman's hit list?

Martha Maricut: **Kay Walsh**
Ralph Maricut: **Harry Fowler**
Percy Whitehead: **Oliver Johnson**
Della Maricut: **Marjie Lawrence**
Det. Supt. Warr: **John Dearth**
Jean Anderson: **Barbara Couper**
Geoffrey Carr: **Middleton Woods**
Det. Insp. Marsham: **John Martin**
P.C. Farley: **Mark Powell**
Doctor Wren: **Lloyd Pearson**
Matthew Gideon: **Richard James**
The Postman: **Richard Davies**

The Lady Killer
w **David Chantler**
d **Leslie Norman**

A killer stalks the streets murdering pretty young girls. Inspector Keen, aroused by the intuition of his girlfriend, leads the search for the mysterious modern-day Bluebeard - and lands himself in great danger.

Robert Carne: **Ray Barrett**
Marion Grove: **Rosemary Leach**
Rina: **Justine Lord**

Bert Macey: **John Tate**
Parker: **Timothy Bateson**
Sergeant Fowler: **Harold Lang**
P.C. Awkwright: **Graham Curnow**
Mrs Harrow: **Nora Gordon**
Mr Baker: **Ronald Adam**
The Coroner: **Kenneth Edwards**
Harry: **Howard Douglas**

To Catch a Tiger
w **Iain MacCormick**
d **Leslie Norman**

Words whispered by a dying nurse lead Commander Gideon and Inspector Keen to re-open an old case. By doing so, they unwittingly unleash a new chain of tragic events on an old Scotland Yard colleague.

John Borgman: **Walter Brown**
Supt. Fred Lee: **Norman Bird**
Sir Percy Richmond: **Raymond Huntley**
Charlotte Borgman: **Vanda Godsell**
Clare Selby: **Erica Rogers**
Jane Kennet: **Delphi Lawrence**
Paul Samuels: **Meredith Edwards**
Mrs Samuels: **Patsy Smart**
Cuthbertson: **John Gabriel**
Sergeant Carmichael: **Glyn Houston** [intro]

Big Fish, Little Fish
w **Alan Falconer**
d **Cyril Frankel**

When a young pickpocket plies his tracks on the London streets, it begins a chain of events that leads Commander Gideon to the existence of a well-organised group of thieves intent on pulling off a major crime.

Mrs Clark: **Angela Baddeley**
'Happy' Roden: **Jack McGowran**
Mark 'Frisky' Lee: **Maxwell Shaw**
Gabriel Lyon: **Sydney Tafler**
Bessie Cowan: **Avis Bunnage**
Supt. Bill Hemmingway: **Wensley Pithey**
Ada Lee: **Suzan Farmer**
Mrs Wray: **Carmel McSharry**
Peter Wray: **Alan Baulch**
Tod Cowan: **Harry Tomb**

The White Rat
w **Harry W. Junkin**
d **Roy Baker**

When a robbery case turns to a murder enquiry, Commander Gideon and Inspector Keen are assigned to the case. Hearing that his old friend Syd Taylor is heading the enquiry, Gideon expects fast results - but events prove him wrong.

Rose Lenman: **Virginia Maskell**
Mickey Keston: **Ray McAnnally**
Fingers: **Dermot Kelly**
Sergeant Syd Taylor: **David Davies**
Mary Henderson: **Susan Lloyd**
Yob: **David Gregory**
Alf: **Michael Wynne**
Det. Chief Supt. Joe Bell: **Ian Rossitter**
Jock: **Roy Hanlon**
Supt. Hopkinson: **John Horsley**
Jean: **Maggie Wright**
Captain Vanner: **Richard Beale**

How to Retire Without Really Working
w **Norman Hudis**
d **George Pollock**

Outwardly the epitome of middle class respectability, Robert Gresham actually lives on the proceeds of petty crime. The crime he's planning now is far from petty and will cause Commander Gideon much aggravation.

Robert Gresham: **Eric Barker**
Margaret Gresham: **Joyce Grant**
Mr Pater: **William Mervyn**
Shorty Fleming: **Jack Rodney**
Mr Hunter: **Charles Lloyd Pack**
The Contact Man: **Oliver McGreevy**
Hotel Manager: **Tom Gill**
Mack Martinson: **Henry McGhee**
Div. Insp. Marsh: **Michael Beint**
The Barrow Boy: **Brian Weske**
Matthew Gideon: **Richard James**
Malcolm Gideon: **Giles Watling**

Subway to Revenge
w **Norman Hudis**
d **Roy Baker**

A vicious murder on the London Underground brings Commander Giedeon an investigation he'd rather be without - and his enquiries lead him to question his department's methods of investigation.

Ellen Winters: **Anne Lawson**
James Lane: **Donald Churchill**
John Stewart: **Bryan Pringle**
Robson: **Esmond Knight**
Mrs Lane: **Noel Dyson**
Wilson: **Alan Browning**
Det. Supt. Lemaitre: **Reginald Jessup** [intro]
Matthew Gideon: **Richard James**
Malcolm Gideon: **Giles Watling**
Duty Sergeant: **Brian Rawlinson**
Sir Edwin: **Kenneth Hanny**
Foreman: **Donald McKillop**

The Great Plane Robbery
w **Alan Falconer**
d **Leslie Norman**

It's one of the most audacious crimes of the century - the theft of gold bullion from an aircraft in flight! Commander Gideon has few days left to discover who is behind the robbery - and how it was achieved.

Bailey: **George Baker**
Frank Dobson: **Edwin Richfield**
Len: **Gary Miller**
Kautsky: **George Murcell**
Mrs Kautsky: **Freda Ramford**
Harold: **Jeremy Burnham**
Doctor Hill: **Reg Lye**
Phyllis: **Pamela Conway**
Ace: **David Orchard**
Cameron: **Julian Somers**
Control Tower Supervisor: **Peter Williams**
Sid Kautsky: **John Hall**

Gang War
w **David Chandler**
d **Quentin Lawrence**

No copper likes to have a gang war break out on his patch, but that's what could happen if Gideon cannot stave off the plans of an ambitious, scheming woman who plans to pull off a major crime.

Lollo Romano: **Jane Merrow**
Frank Romano: **Ray Brooks**
Jerry Blake: **Ronald Lacey**

97

Henry Waldo: **Frederick Bartman**
Supt. Browning: **Donald Morley**
Duke: **Clive Colin Bowler**
Cowboy: **James Chase**
Lefty: **Patrick Durkin**
Weasel: **Louis Mansi**
Sammy: **Keith Bell**
Tony Mazzo: **Will Stampe**
Sideman: **James Ottaway**

The Tin God
w **Harry W. Junkin**
d **John Gilling**

Alerted to the fact that two dangerous prisoners have broken out of jail, Commander Gideon spreads a wide net over London to catch them - but they give him the slip and take refuge in the home of a young mother.

John 'Benny' Benson: **Derren Nesbitt**
Ruby Benson: **Jennifer Wilson**
Freddy Tinsdale: **John Hurt**
Uncle Charley: **Arthur Lovegrove**
Syd Benson: **Michael Cashman**
Det. Chief Supt. Joe Bell: **Ian Rossiter**
Danny: **Sydney Vivian**
'Taffy' Jones: **Jack Rodney**
PC Lashbrook: **Vincent Harding**
Malcolm Gideon: **Giles Watling**

The Alibi Man
w **Iain MacCormick**
d **Cyril Frankel**

Convinced that he knows the identity of a murderer, Gideon must find sufficient proof to arrest him - a task made doubly difficult when a professional alibi-seller gives the man a new identity.

Bruce Carroway: **Jack Hedley**
Majorie Bellman: **Jennifer Daniel**
Eric Little: **James Culliford**
Mary Calloway: **Sheila Allen**
Cathy Bellman: **Nicola Pagett**
Det. Supt. Le Maitre: **Reginald Jessup**
Jeff Grant: **Geoffrey Palmer**
Det. Insp. Elmhurst: **Keith Anderson**
Det. Supt. Brown: **Michael Collins**
The Pathologist: **John Rae**
Malcolm Gideon: **Giles Watling**
Veronica Kendal: **Elizabeth Counsell**

Fall High, Fall Hard
w **Malcolm Hulke**
d **Leslie Norman**

A two-year-old unsolved murder mystery attracts the attention of Gideon and Keen. Reopening the case, they find that history appears to be repeating itself - with murderous effect.

Tony Erickson: **Donald Houston**
Joan Erickson: **Sarah Lawson**
Charles Randle: **Victor Maddern**
Det. Sgt. Carmichael: **Glyn Houston**
Thompson: **Gordon Gostelow**
Jenson: **Mike Pratt**
Smith: **Michael Robbins**
Doctor Cooper: **Gordon Whiting**
Jerome: **Walter Horsbrugh**
Sylvia: **Dilys Rosser**
Sgt. Bailey: **Clifford Earl**

The Wall
w **David Chandler**
d **Leslie Norman**

Everyday domestic affairs are not usually brought to Gideon's attention, but when a husband disappears without trace the policeman takes an interest in the circumstances surrounding the case.

Will Rikker: **John Barrie**
Netta Penn: **Ann Bell**
Liz Rikker: **Megs Jenkins**
Michael Penn: **Richard Carpenter**
Mary Mason: **Pauline Yates**
Ralph Mason: **Bernard Brown**
Sally: **Toni Palmer**
Tom Jenkins: **John F. Landry**
Langley: **Philip Ray**
Supt. Ridgeway: **Victor Brooks**
Sergeant Greenwood: **Ian McNaughton**
'Skipper' trained by **John Holmes**

The Prowler
w **Harry W. Junkin**
d **Robert Tronson**

When a mentally disturbed young man brings terror to the streets of London by clipping young girls' hair, Commander Gideon and Inspector Keen begin an extensive search to trap him - before the pranks turn into murder.

Alan Campbell-Gore: **David Collins**
Lady Campbell-Gore: **Fanny Rowe**
Marjorie Hayling: **Gillian Lewis**
Sophie Murdoch: **Rosemary Dunham**
Det. Chief Supt. Appleby: **Thomas Heathcote**
Det. Supt. Lemaitre: **Reginald Jessup**
Matthew Gideon: **Richard James**
Det. Sgt Doug Brown: **Richard Burrell**
Jack: **Peter Jesson**
Muriel: **Carol Gardner**
Jennifer Lewis: **Gillian French**
Mr Lewis: **Arthur Pentelow**

The Thin Red Line
w **Iain MacCormick**
d **Cyril Frankel**

The theft of silver trophies commemorating past glories of an army regiment involve Gideon and Keen in a search for a man's past memories - memories which may [or may not] hold a clue to the crime.

General Sir Hector McGregor: **Finlay Currie**
Major Donald Ross: **Allan Cuthbertson**
Captain Robbie McGregor: **John Cairney**
Colonel McAlpine: **David Hutcheson**
Sergeant McKinnon: **Gordon Jackson**
Comm. Scott-Marle: **Basil Dignam**
'Bookie' Barton-Smith: **Donald Pickering**
Captain James Murray: **Michael Meacham**
Ann Ross: **Mary Yeomans**
The Owner of Krootnings: **Guy Deghy**
Antoine Dubec: **John Serret**
Det. Supt. Lemaitre: **Reginald Jessup**

A Perfect Crime
w **Alan Falconer**
d **Leslie Norman**

What appears to be the perfect crime - a major robbery of jewels which were never recovered - points Commander Gideon to a man who has led a very successful double life - until the detective deflates the man's ego.

Spender 'Todd': **Patrick Allen**
Ann Beaumont: **Ann Lynn**
Casey: **Patrick Bedford**
Sandra Casey: **Jean Marsh**
Hartz: **Alec Mango**
Commissioner Scott-Marle: **Basil Dignam**
Det. Supt. Lemaitre: **Reginald Jessup**
Mr Barnes: **Anthony Baird**
The Magistrate: **Robert Sansom**
The Taxi Driver: **Richard Davies**
The Janitor: **George Merritt**

The Millionaire's Daughter
w **Norman Hudis**
d **Cyril Frankel**

The arrival in London of an American millionaire with his wife and daughter involves Gideon in a very unusual kidnapping - one which isn't all it appears to be, and one that disastrously misfires.

Alan Blake: **Don Borisenko**
Elliott Henderson: **David Bauer**
Felissa Henderson: **Lois Maxwell**
Erica Townsend: **Georgina Ward**
Nina Henderson: **Lans Traverse**
Philip Guest: **Donald Sutherland**
The Professor: **Charles Carson**
Gerry Adams: **Brian Weske**
Frank Simmons: **Alec Ross**
Det. Supt. Lemaitre: **Reginald Jessup**
Matthew Gideon: **Richard James**

Morna
w **Alan Falconer**
d **Cyril Frankel**

Commander Gideon faces a severe test of his investigative abilities when asked to discover the identity of a killer who has murdered a beautiful young girl without apparent motive.

Harriet Bright: **Kay Walsh**
Morna: **Angela Douglas**
Chay: **Johnny Sekka**
Leonard Bright: **John Junkin**
Michael Usher: **Norman Bowler**
Commissioner Scott-Marle: **Basil Dignam**
Sir Ribert Copthorne: **Ronald Adams**
Lady Copthorne: **Shelagh Fraser**
Chief Insp. Budd: **Victor Platt**
Lydia Merritt: **Alita Naughton**
Matthew Gideon: **Richard James**
Keston: **Barry Lowe**

Boy With a Gun
w **Iain MacCormick**
d **Jeremy Summers**

Threatened by three bullies, Chris, the son of an eminent police surgeon working in Gideon's department, pulls a gun and shoots one of the boys. The outcome brings unexpected friends for Chris, and a tough case for Gideon.

Doctor Kirk: **Anthony Bate**
Tim Murphy: **George Sewell**
Vince Kelly: **Michael Craze**
Chez Kelly: **Michael Standing**
Helen Kirk: **Ruth Trouncer**
Chris Kirk: **Howard Knight**
Mary Murphy: **Mary Quin**
Finny: **Joe Gladwin**
Charlie Berry: **Royston Tickner**
Det. Insp. Smith: **Tony Thawnton**

Mick: **Roger Foss**
Daisy: **Carol Gardner**

The Reluctant Witness
w **Norman Hudis**
d **Jeremy Summers**

Gideon discovers that a man found dead is Tony Bray, a police informer whom he wrongly convicted and who consequently spent four years in jail. Gideon determines to find his killer - at any price.

Red Carter: **Mike Pratt**
Syd Carter: **David Gregory**
PC John Moss: **Trevor Bannister**
Rachel Gully: **Audrey Nicholson**
Mrs Gully: **Patricia Burke**
Mrs Moss: **Madeleine Christie**
Det. Supt. Lemaitre: **Reginald Jessup**
Tony Bray: **Frederick Peisley**
Martha Bray: **Gretchen Franklin**
Larry Larkin: **Dervis Ward**
Lucy Sansetti: **Gloria Paul**
Radio Man: **Jolyon Booth**

The Rhyme and the Reason
w **Jack Whittingham**
d **John Gilling**

When the sister of a boy suspected of murder comes to him for help, Commander Gideon politely refuses. But later that day a tragic event causes him to rethink his position - with dreadful results for all concerned.

Mary Rose: **Jo Rowbottom**
Bill Rose: **Alan Rothwell**
Fred Norton: **Edward Evans**
Mrs Norton: **Clare Kelly**
Winifred Norton: **Carol White**
Divisional Supt. Smedd: **Duncan Lamont**
Rod Jenkins: **Clive Colin Bowler**
Pru Gideon: **Andrea Allan**
Matthew Gideon: **Richard James**
Malcolm Gideon: **Giles Watling**

The Nightlifers
w **Iain MacCormick**
d **John Moxey**

Young people who live for 'kicks' and have an irresponsible outlook on life present Commander Gideon with a problem. Which one of them is responsible for a selfish crime? Or can it be all three?

Peta Sloane: **Anton Rodgers**
Tim Coles: **Derek Fowlds**
Elspeth McRae: **Jean Marsh**
Sue Young: **Annette Andre**
Alison Clifton: **Pauline Munro**
Tony King: **James Hunter**
Det. Insp. Caldwell: **Roddy McMillan**
Doctor Coles: **Laurence Hardy**
Mrs Coles: **Joyce Carey**
Mr King: **Richard Hurndall**
Mrs King: **Viola Keats**
Joe Moss: **Harry Locke**

Gideon's Way:

Producer: **Robert S. Baker** and **Monty Berman**
Production Supervisor: **Ernest Holding**
Music: **Edwin Astley**
Script Supervision: **Harry W. Junkin**
Assistant Director: **Dennis Robertson, Bill Snaith, Derek Parr**
Music Editor: **John Beaton**
Casting Director: **David Booth**
Make-up Supervision: **Dick Bonnor-Moris, Bill Lodge**
Hairdressing Supervision: **Helen Penfold, Hilda Fox**
Wardrobe Supervision: **Laura Nightingale**

A New World Production for ITC World Wide Distribution
Made on location and at Associated British Elstree Studios

26 monochrome 60-minute episodes
1965

H.G. Wells' Invisible Man

'A man who can investigate crimes without being seen.
A man who can go where no ordinary man
could hope to enter.
A man searching for the answer to his invisibility
... The Invisible Man.'

The story of how scientist Peter Brady tested his theory of optical density, discovered how to render any matter invisible - then become invisible himself when further experiments misfired [an optical conductor fused and showered him with chemicals mixed with oxygen].

Thereafter the series followed his adventures as he tried to discover a formula that would restore him to visible form - while staving off the forces of evil who attempted to discover the secret of his invisibility. [During the first story, Brady was hunted down and imprisoned by British ministry scientists who saw him as a national menace - before being convinced otherwise and releasing him to continue his research. In consideration of this, Brady elected to use his strange power for 'the benefit of mankind' and undertook many hazardous missions for the British Government.]

On screen, Brady appeared swathed in bandages, overcoat or Laboratory overall, and sunglasses! Oddly enough, the actor who played the role was never credited - though his voice belonged to actor Tim Turner [who appears in *Man in Disguise*].

✍ We can confirm the existence of an episode from this series which contains a different original scenario of how Peter Brady came to be The Invisible Man to that given in the story *Secret Experiment*!

The story, usually transmitted with its o/s title blanked out, closely follows the storyline of *Bank Raid*, but contains several differences in the o/s action - the most notable being that the first eight minutes or so retells how, by accident, Brady became the-man-who-wasn't-there, in a totally different scenario to that contained in the first story!

In this episode, the actor playing the bandage-swathed scientist is not the thespian who played the role in all other stories! He is of smaller statute and the voice used to convey Brady's dialogue sounds suspiciously like Canadian actor Robert Beatty![?] Viewing the story compels uncalled-for amusement. The actor playing The Invisible Man bumps into furniture and doors, his 'headless' shoulder-padding is clearly visible, and the 'special effects' are far removed from the technical expertise of the other stories.

Conclusion: two pilot stories were filmed, of which this was the first. One look at the results and the producers decided to think again and call for a remake.

Regular cast:
Peter Brady: **?**
Diane 'Dee' [his sister]: **Lisa Daniely**
Sally [his niece]: **Deborah Watling**

Secret Experiment
w **Michael Connor** and **Michael Cramoy**
d **Pennington Richards**

A secret experiment has dramatic results for scientist Peter Brady - he vanishes into thin air! Or does he? He's just a man who isn't there - an invisible man! Accepting his fate, he decides to use his newly-found power to aid others.

Diane Brady: **Lisa Daniely**
Sally: **Deborah Watling**
Dr Hanning: **Lloyd Lamble**
Kemp: **Bruce Seton**
Sir Charles Anderson: **Ernest Clark**
Crompton: **Michael Goodliffe**

Crisis in the Desert
w **Ralph Smart**
d **Pennington Richards**

Colonel Warren, of British Military Intelligence, seeks Brady's aid. His mission: to rescue a British agent from the secret police of a foreign country. Sans clothes, the Invisible Man flies into danger.

Yolanda: **Adrienne Corri**
Hassan: **Eric Pohlmann**
Omar: **Martin Benson**
Nesib: **Peter Sallis**
Jack Howard: **Howard Pays**
Col. Warren: **Douglas Wilmer**
Corporal: **Derren Nesbitt**
Surgeon: **Derek Sydney**

The Locked Room
w **Lindsay Galloway** [from a story by **Ralph Smart**]
d **Pennington Richards**

Tania, a scientist from behind the Iron Curtain working in London, is ordered to return home for criticising her government. Brady, believing she can help him to regain his visibility, gives her some unseen assistance.

Diane: **Lisa Daniely**
Sally: **Deborah Watling**
Tania: **Zena Marshall**
Dr. Hanning: **Lloyd Lamble**
Dushkin: **Rupert Davies**
Clerk: **Emrys Leyshow**
Phillips: **Noel Coleman**
Porter: **Alexander Dore**

Behind the Mask
w **Stanley Mann** and **Leslie Arliss** [from a story by **Stanley Mann**]
d **Pennington Richards**

Tricked into visiting the home of the disfigured Raphael Constantine, Peter Brady receives a strange request. He is asked to use his invisibility to recover a secret document which incriminates his host in a crime he didn't commit.

Constantine: **Dennis Price**
Max: **Edwin Richfield**
Maria: **Barbara Chilcott**
Josef: **David Ritch**
Juan: **Michael Jacques**
President Domecq: **Arthur Gomez**
Official: **John Wynn Jones**

Play to Kill
w **Leslie Arliss** [from a story by **Robert Westerby**]
d **Peter Maxwell**

Was actress Barbara Crane really responsible for a cliff-top accident which cost a hobo his life? She believes she was - the Invisible Man thinks otherwise and sets out to prove her innocence.

Barbara Crane: **Helen Cherry**
Diane: **Lisa Daniely**
Colonel: **Colin Gordon**
Tom: **Hugh Tatimer**
Simon: **Garry Thorne**
Manton: **Ballard Berkeley**
Arthurson: **Vincent Holman**

The Mink Coat
w **Ian Stuart Black** [from a story by **Leonore Coffee**]
d **Pennington Richards**

Unknown to Penny Page, the mink coat she is carrying to France contains vital stolen documents hidden in its lining. Fortunately for her, her fellow passengers include Diane and Peter Brady - The Invisible Man.

Penny Page: **Hazel Court**
Diane: **Lisa Daniely**
Walker: **Derek Godfrey**
Bunny: **Harold Berens**
Marcel: **Murray Kash**
Custom Officer: **Keith Rawlings**
Madame Dupont: **Joan Hickson**
Photographer: **John Ruddock**

Picnic with Death
w **Leonard Fincham** and **Leslie Arliss** [from a story by **Leonard Fincham**]
d **Pennington Richards**

Through the friendship of his niece Sally, Brady becomes involved with a woman whose husband and sister-in-law are plotting to murder her. However, Brady's invisibility allows him to stay one jump ahead of their plans.

Diane: **Lisa Daniely**
Sally: **Deborah Watling**
John Norton: **Derek Bond**
Carol Norton: **Faith Brook**
Linda Norton: **Margaret McCourt**
Janet Norton: **Maureen Pryor**
Sir Charles: **Ernest Clark**
Stableman: **Michael Ripper**

Blind Justice
w **Ralph Smart**
d **Pennington Richards**

The Invisible Man becomes a blind woman's eyes to help her find the gang of cut-throats responsible for her husband's death. The woman's blindness allows her to 'see' Brady, which makes his task that much easier.

Diane: **Lisa Daniely**
Arthur Hold: **Philip Friend**
Sandy Mason: **Jack Watling**
Simmons: **Julian Somers**
Katherine: **Honor Blackman**
Sparrow: **Leslie Phillips**
Det. Insp. Heath: **Robert Raglan**
Det. Sergeant: **Desmond Llewelyn**

Strange Partners
w **Michael Cramoy**
d **Pennington Richards**

Being invisible is a defence against detection from any human being. But when Brady accepts a new mission, he discovers that invisibility is no protection against man's canine friends.

Diane: **Lisa Daniely**
Sally: **Deborah Watling**
Inspector Quillan: **Victor Platt**
Collins: **Jack Melford**
Vickers: **Patrick Troughton**
Ryan: **Robert Cawdron**
Doctor: **Reginald Hearne**
Lucian Currie: **Griffith Jones**

The Gun Runners
w **Ian Stuart Black**
d **Peter Maxwell**

When the pocket-sized Mediterranean state of Bay Akim looks like becoming a trouble spot and a haven for gun-runners, the British Government asks Brady to help it rid the state of Sardi, a ruthless dictator.

Zena Fleming: **Louise Allbritton**
Col. Grahame: **Bruce Seton**
Sardi: **Paul Stassino**
Arosa: **Charles Hill**
Hotel Manager: **Josef Attard**
Milia: **Lawrence Taylor**
Ali: **James Booth**
Airport Clerk: **Morris Sweden**
Receptionist: **Ann Dimitri**

Odds Against Death
w **Ian Stuart Black** [from a story idea by **Stanley Mann**]
d **Pennington Richards**

To save the daughter of brilliant scientist, Professor Owens, from danger, Brady uses his invisibility to manipulate the casino tables in Italy in Owens' favour. Unknowingly, the scientist is gambling his daughter's life away.

Professor Owens: **Walter Fitzgerald**
Diane: **Lisa Daniely**
Lucia: **Colette Wilde**
Suzy Owens: **Julia Lockwood**
Caletta: **Alan Tilvern**
Bruno: **Peter Taylor**
Croupier: **Peter Elliott**
Manager: **Olaf Pooley**

Jailbreak
w **Ian Stuart Black**
d **Pennington Richards**

Convinced that Joe Green, a man sentenced for robbery, was falsely accused, Peter Brady strips off his clothes and helps Green to locate a blonde who can prove his alibi and bring the real criminal to justice.

Joe Green: **Dermot Walsh**
Diane : **Lisa Daniely**
Sally: **Deborah Watling**
Doris: **Denny Dayvis**
Brenner: **Michael Brennan**
Governor: **Ralph Michael**
Sharp: **Ronald Fraser**
Taylor: **Charles Farrell**
Robson: **Maurice Kaufman**

Bank Raid
w **Doreen Montgomery** and **Ralph Smart**
d **Ralph Smart**

When his niece, Sally, is kidnapped and held hostage by a gang of criminals, Brady has to rob a bank to save her life - but the Invisible Man has a trump card up his unseen sleeve.

Diane: **Lisa Daniely**
Sally: **Deborah Watling**
Crowther: **Willoughby Goddard**
Williams: **Brian Rawlinson**
Headmistress: **Patricia Marmont**

Death Cell
w **Michael Connor**
d **Peter Maxwell**

A beautiful woman escapes from a mental home and appeals to Brady to help her prove her fiance innocent of the murder of a policeman. Brady pays an unseen visit to the man - and receives a surprise.

Diane: **Lisa Daniely**
Ellen Summers: **Lana Morris**
Dr. Trevor: **Ian Wallace**
George Wilson: **William Lucas**
Sir Charles: **Bruce Seton**
Prison Governor: **Jack Lambert**
Miss Beck: **Bettina Dickson**
Mrs Willis: **Patricia Burke**

Point of Destruction
w **Ian Stuart Black**
d **Quentin Lawrence**

When three test pilots lose their lives in identical plane crashes, then a fourth narrowly escapes death, Peter Brady investigates the failure of a top secret fuel diffuser which is suspected of causing the accidents.

Scott: **Duncan Lamont**
Diane: **Lisa Daniely**
Sally: **Deborah Watling**
Dr. Court: **John Rudling**
Katrina: **Patricia Jessel**
Stephan: **Derren Nesbitt**
Jenny: **Jane Barrett**
Control Officer: **Barry Letts**

The Vanishing Evidence
w **Ian Stuart Black**
d **Peter Maxwell**

Peter Thal, an international spy, murders Professor Harper and steals vital secrets on which he had been working. Colonel Ward seeks out the Invisible Man's help to follow Thal to Holland.

Professor Harper: **James Raglan**
Peter Thal: **Charles Gray**
Colonel Ward: **Ernest Clark**
Jenny Reyden: **Sarah Lawson**
Porter: **Michael Ripper**
Inspector Strang: **Peter Illing**
Superintendent: **Ewan Solon**

The Prize
w **Ian Stuart Black**
d **Quentin Lawrence**

Arriving in Scandinavia to collect a prize for his contribution to science, Brady becomes involved in the strange affair of Tania Roskoff, a brilliant Soviet writer who has been arrested while crossing the border.

Tania: **Mai Zetterling**
Gunzi: **Anton Differing**
Diane: **Lisa Daniely**
Professor Kenig: **Tony Church**
General: **Tom Gill**
Sentry: **Clive Baxter**
Capt. Bera: **Richard Clarke**
Agasha: **Ruth Lodge**

Flight into Darkness
w **Ian Stuart Black** [from a story by **W. H. Altman**]
d **Peter Maxwell**

Believing that his discovery in the field of anti-gravity will endanger mankind, Dr Stephens destroys all his papers and

disappears. Sans clothes, the Invisible Man is asked to bring him to England.

Wade: **John Harvey**
Sir Jasper: **Michael Shepley**
Pat Stephens: **Joanna Dunham**
Sewell: **Colin Douglas**
Fisher: **Alex Scott**
Dr. Stephens: **Geoffrey Keen**
Wilson: **Esmond Knight**

The Decoy
w **Brenda Blackmore**
d **Quentin Lawrence**

When one of two identical twins, Terry and Toni Trent, a musical act touring Britain, disappears, the Invisible Man volunteers to help. Terry disappeared at a Soho hotel - at which Brady arrives as an unseen guest.

Capt. Rubens: **Robert Gallico**
Starvos: **Philip Leaver**
Andraes: **Wolf Morris**
Giorgio: **Barry Shawzin**
General: **Lionel Murton**
First Secretary: **Bruno Barnabe**
Toni Trent: **Betta St. John**
Terry Trent: **Betta St. John**

The White Rabbit
w **Ian Stuart Black**
d **Quentin Lawrence**

When a young woman doctor in France sees a white rabbit materialise out of thin air, and her evidence points to a Fascist plot to use the discovery of making things invisible to launch a revolt, Peter Brady is soon on the scene.

Suzanne Dumasse: **Marla Landi**
Hugo: **Austin Trevor**
Rocher: **Paul Daneman**
Valois: **Arnold Marle**
Professor Blaire: **Arnold Diamond**
Max: **Reed De Rouen**
Louise: **Myrtle Reed**
Dr. Dumasse: **Keith Pyott**
Colette: **Isobel Black**
Brun: **Andre Charise**
Chauffeur: **Andre Muller**

Man in Disguise
w **Brenda Blackmore** [from a story by **Leslie Arliss**]
d **Quentin Lawrence** and **Peter Maxwell**

Tricked into handing over his passport to a beautiful girl in Paris, enabling the girl's accomplice to impersonate him and smuggle dope into England, Brady finds himself involved in an international drugs racket.

Nick: **Tim Turner**
Sally: **Deborah Watling**
Madeleine: **Leigh Madison**
Matt: **Lee Montague**
Det. Inspector : **Robert Raglan**
Sgt. Day: **Howard Pays**
Sgt. Winter: **Jeanette Sterke**
Victor: **Robert Rietty**
Club Manager: **Denis Shaw**
Aylmer: **Felix Felton**

Man in Power
w **Ian Stuart Black**
d **Peter Maxwell**

A Middle East king is murdered by his power-crazy army chief. The Invisible Man finds himself involved in helping the king's sister and brother regain their father's throne.

King Rashid: **Vivian Matalon**
Princess Taima: **Nadia Regin**
Prince Jonetta: **Gary Raymond**
Hassan: **Andre Keir**
Col. Fayid: **Derek Sydney**
Ambassador: **Ivan Craig**
General Shafari: **Andre Morell**

The Rocket
w **Michael Pertwee**
d **Quentin Lawrence**

When gambling losses lead one of Brady's ex-colleagues into selling off secret information to a foreign power, the scientist's invisibility proves a very valuable asset in retrieving the documents.

Smith: **Glyn Owen**
Reitter: **Russell Waters**
Prof. Howard: **Robert Brown**
Det. Inspector: **Robert Raglan**
Mrs Smith: **Jennifer Wright**
Driver Evans: **Harold Goodwin**
Sergeant: **Maurice Durant**
Bill: **Colin Croft**

Shadow Bomb
w **Tony O'Grady** [aka **Brian Clemens**] and **Ian Stuart Black** [from a story by **Tony O'Grady**]
d **Peter Maxwell**

When his friend risks being blown up by a new type of bomb detonator, Brady steps into danger as his replacement. Should even a shadow fall across the new device, the bomb will explode - instantly.

Captain Finch: **Conrad Phillips**
Betty: **Jennifer Jayne**
Lloyd: **Walter Gotell**
Lieutenant Daniels: **Ian Hendry**
General Martin: **Anthony Bushell**

The Big Plot
w - **Ian Stuart Black** [from a story by **Tony O'Grady** - aka **Brian Clemens** and **Ralph Smart**]
d **Peter Maxwell**

When a plane crash reveals that someone was smuggling into England a canister of Uranium 235, used in the manufacture of atomic weapons, The Invisible Man needs all his guile to smash a plot to start World War III.

Waring: **William Squire**
Helen: **Barbara Shelley**
Lord Peversham: **John Arnatt**
First Officer: **Richard Warner**
Second Officer: **Derrick Sheerwin**
Macbane: **Edward Hardwicke**
Minister: **Basil Dignam**
Sir Charles: **Ewen Macduff**
Hanstra: **Terence Cooper**

Shadow on the Screen
w **Ian Stuart Black** [from a story by **Ralph Smart** and **Philip Levene**]
d **Pennington Richards**

In the belief that he's helping the wife of a refugee to get her scientist husband from behind the Iron Curtain, Brady finds himself the victim of a clever trap. The woman is a communist spy who intends to learn the Invisible Man's secret.

Sonia Vasa: **Greta Gynt**
Diane: **Lisa Daniely**
Stephen Vasa: **Edward Judd**
Bratski: **Redmond Phillips**
Captain: **Andre Mikhelson**
Commissar: **Anthony Newlands**
Sir Charles: **Ernest Clark**
Woman in Lift: **Irene Handle**

H. G. Wells' Invisible Man:

Based on characters created by **H. G. Wells**
Suggested and developed for television by **Larry White**
Producer: **Ralph Smart**
Production Supervisor: **Aida Young**
Music by: **Sydney John Kay**
Assistant Director: **David Tomblin**

An Incorporated Television Programme Co. Ltd Production
Made at National Studios, Elstree

26 monochrome 30-minute episodes
1959

Interpol Calling

Interpol! A word that stirs the imagination. The world-wide police organisation spreads its net far and wide, linking police efforts of every country ... the dramas on the Interpol files providing unlimited scope for international action.
The series showed how the organisation's detectives never let up on criminals. When the call is for Interpol, there is no escape for the guilty.

"Set in a dignified building in Paris, lies the headquarters of the International Criminal Police Organisation (Interpol for short).
Some of the most extraordinary stories in the annals of crime have happened here.
Interpol Calling tells just some of those stories."

Regular cast:
Inspector Paul Duval: **Charles Korvin**
Inspector Mornay: **Edwin Richfield**

The Angola Brights
w **Larry Forrester**
d **Pennington Richards**

Martin Bekker, a Dutchman employed in a diamond mine in Angola, steals four uncut matched stones. To decoy his getaway, he blows up the mine. Many employees are killed. Inspector Duval is assigned to the case.

Coetzee: **Rupert Davies**
Bekker: **Alfred Burke**
Meyer: **Phillip Ray**
Costa: **Arthur Gomez**
De Silva: **Julian Sherrier**

You Can't Die Twice
w **Barbara Hammer** [from a story by **Leonard Fincham**]
d **Pennington Richards**

When a sailor is killed after he disembarks from a freighter at New York, and his passport is found to be a stolen one, Inspector Duval discovers that the dead man's real name was Szarek - a refugee, who was illegally smuggled into the USA.

Captain Tully: **Cec Linder**
Mr Dorner: **Gerard Heinz**
Insp. Krantz: **Arnold Diamond**
Anna Grauber: **Colette Wilde**
Muller: **Leonard Sachs**
Marston: **Robert Arden**
Carter: **Philo Hauser**
Creedy: **George Margo**

The Money Game
w **Lewis Davidson**
d **Pennington Richards**

A gang trick financial columnist, Brownley, into believing that the financier, Untermeyer, is dead. Stock-markets are thrown into confusion. The con-men make a fortune. Then Brownley is murdered....

The Baron: **Walter Rilla**
Castillon: **Ferdy Mayne**
Marie Webber: **Delphi Lawrence**
Brownley: **Phil Brown**
Zeist: **Walter Gotell**

No Flowers for Onno
w **Robert Stewart**
d **Pennington Richards**

When author Andrew Slater decided to write a book about war heroes, Onno Van Veer and Peter Grenville, believed to have been executed in 1943 by the German S.S., Inspector Duval of Interpol unearths a tale of treachery and murder.

Esler: **Victor Beaumont**
Onno: **Kevin Stoney**
Emmy: **Leigh Madison**
Dekker: **Bruno Barnabe**
Slater: **Edward Jewesbury**

Private View
w **Robert Stewart**
d **Pennington Richards**

Thieves steal half a million pounds worth of Old Masters from the collection of Sir Isaac Spendler. Checking the Interpol files for suspects, Duval narrows his search to Art Dealer, Wolf Barstrom.

Wolf Barstrom: **Michael Goodliffe**
Nina: **Moria Redmond**
Mac Andrew: **Ernest Clark**
Pimm: **Leslie French**
Sir Isaac Spendler: **Frederick Leister**

Air Switch
w **Gil Winfield** and **Leonard Fincham**
d **Pennington Richards**

Investigating the disappearance of a valuable anti-biotic called Tetracycline, Duval discovers that supplies of the drug meant for the World Health Organisation, contain water. The switch must have been made in transit. But how - and by whom?

Pat Adams: **Colin Croft**
Capt. Flormann: **John Van Eyssen**
Insp. Holt: **Trevor Reid**
Capt. Merrick: **Lloyd Lamble**
Helen: **Dorinda Stevens**

The Sleeping Giant
w **Larry Forrester**
d **Pennington Richards**

Bomb disposable officers are called in when a huge unexploded bomb is found against the side of the Glengowrie Dam, Scotland. Dropped in a wartime raid, the bomb is of an unknown type - Inspector Duval is asked to trace its makers.

Kustrinski: **John Crawford**
David: **David Cameron**
Von Schriber: **Esmond Knight**
Von Stegger: **Oliver Burt**
MacLelland: **Jack Stewart**
Sgt. Logie: **Rufus Cruickshank**

The Chinese Mask
w **Lewis Davidson**
d **Pennington Richards**

A cargo of valuable platinum is stolen during a flight from Rangoon to Hong Kong. The method used is unique. Someone explodes a tear-gas bomb and forces the aircraft down. Inspector Duval discovers that similar robberies have taken place.

Bill Grant: **Bill Nagy**
Jane Grant: **Jan Holden**
Reg Couts: **Howard Marion Crawford**
Insp. Angus: **Brown Derby**
Ti Sung: **Zed Zakari**
Mr Burton: **Derek Tansley**

Slave Ship
w **Gil Winfield, Geoffrey Orme** and **Edwin Richfield**
d **Pennington Richards**

Duval is confronted by the mysterious disappearance of many thousands of natives from East Africa. Many investigations have been made into slave trading in the past - with only a handful of convictions. Duval determines to change that.

Colonel Briggs: **David Davies**
Doctor Gorman: **Meredith Edwards**
Leooir: **Harold Kasket**
Gamel: **Cyril Shaps**
Abdul: **Oscar Quitak**
Sgt. Hamid: **Errol John**
Commander Siddons: **Howard Lang**

The Long Weekend
w **David Chantler**
d **Charles Frend**

A merchant seaman has been washed up on the South Coast of England - with a bullet in his head. Seven days earlier the same man had been reported lost overboard from his ship - in the Mediterranean, 2,000 miles away! Duval is intrigued...

Prof. Renee: **David Kossoff**
Capt. Gallard: **Francis de Wolff**
Monsieur Lamprou: **John Le Mesurier**
Margie: **Balbina**
Georges: **Andre Maranne**

The Thirteen Innocents
w **David Chantler**
d **Pennington Richards**

The trading company run by Sukru in Istanbul serves as a perfect cover for his real trade: dope-smuggling. He has evaded detection and arrest by a foolproof method - 13 carrier pigeons, who carry the dope fixed to their legs. But Duval is closing in...

Capt. Omar: **Peter Illing**
Sukru: **Patrick Troughton**
Ritter: **Guy Deghy**
Franz: **Larry Burns**

The Two-Headed Monster
w **David Chantler**
d **Pennington Richards**

Johnny Stefano, an Italian crook, is deported back to Naples after serving a prison sentence in the USA. Three months later, news reaches Duval that Stefano has invited a group of protection racketeers to join him in Naples. Duval decides to investigate.

Maria: **Maria Landi**
Stefano: **Alan Tilvern**
Capt. Pagano: **George Pastell**
Debre: **Robert Cawdron**

Last Man Lucky
w **Neville Dasey**
d **Pennington Richards**

A gang member is killed by his colleagues in Paris. Among his papers, police find a list with initials and dates. Duval discovers that the paper is a murder list - a lead to the existence of a Murder Incorporated gang - an outfit that is paid to kill?

Amy: **Annabel Maule**

Helen Mills: **Sandra Dorne**
Roberts: **Ewen MacDuff**
Steve Taylor: **Donald Stewart**
Victor Perrot: **Michael Brennan**

Diamond S.O.S.
w **Tony O'Grady [Brian Clemens] & Leonard Fincham**
d **Charles Frend**

A girl posing as a wealthy celebrity, and her accomplices, posing as detectives, have staged several daring robberies of top-quality gems. Details of this ingenious confidence trick come to the ears of Inspector Duval.

Helene: **Lisa Daniely**
Grimond: **Rowland Bartrop**
Pinelli: **Robert Rietty**
Inspector Grimond: **Peter Vaughan**
Parker: **Hugh Morton**

Dead On Arrival
w **Max Marquis** and **Philip Chambers** [from a story by **Leonard Fincham**]
d **Max Varnel**

When the body of a NATO courier is found in a sleeping compartment of the Black Sea Express, there appears to be no apparent motive for the murder. So Duval flies to Istanbul to duplicate the courier's last journey.

Suzy: **Jane Hylton**
Attendant : **Robert Brown**
Amiel: **Rowland Bartrop**
Dikalos: **Lee Montague**
Captain Omar: **Gamel Fares**
Second Lieut.: **Harry Landis**

The Man's Clown
w **Robert Stewart**
d **Charles Frend**

Duval is on the track of forger, Eddie Keflik. He knows that his quarry is in Europe, Keflik has blackmailed Willi, a clown in a travelling circus, into working for him. The Big Top might well provide a lead.

Helene: **Lisa Daniely**
Willi: **Warren Mitchell**
Keflik: **John Crawford**
Lisa: **Waverly Lee**
Capt. Pagano: **George Pastell**
Nun: **Jean Anderson**

The Thousand Mile Alibi
w **John Kruse** [from a story by **Leonard Fincham**]
d **George Pollock**

Cliff McGrath couldn't have murdered his wife. Television cameras pictured him leading the Italian Mille Migla motor race at the time of her death - or did they? Duval investigates the crime and comes up with a startling conclusion.

Cliff McGrath: **William Lucas**
Capt. Pagano: **George Pastell**
Mike McGrath: **Paul Eddington**
Grimond: **Rowland Bartrop**
Zita McGrath: **Margaret Diamond**

The Girl with Grey Hair
w **Leonard Fincham, Michael Hankinson** and **Robert Stewart**
d **Charles Frend**

After reports of his death in Italy, the price of paintings by artist Hugo Ballard began to soar. So why would, Anita, slash one of her husband's paintings with a knife? Questioned by Duval, the woman says the picture is a fake.

Anita: **Mary Laura Wood**
Michelle: **Elisabeth Wilson**
Hugo: **Ronald Leigh-Hunt**
Culotta: **George Pastell**
Mario: **Stanley Van Beers**

Mr George
w **David Chantler**
d **Charles Frend**

Warned by 'George' that a warehouse is about to burn down, a London insurance firm are too late to act and pay out £100,000. 'George' now demands a further £100,000 in American dollars. Enter Inspector Duval....

Carol: **Susan Travers**
Hanson: **Richard Leech**
Ahmed: **Martin Benson**
Johnny: **Brian Nash**

Checkmate
w **Sam Newman**
d **Bill Lewthwaite**

David Baker successfully robs a Tel Aviv bank, using a girlfriend's threat to commit suicide as a diversion. Both evade the police and reach Madrid. Duval must find them and their illegally obtained fortune.

Baker: **Gaylord Cavallaro**
Diane: **Barbara Shelley**
Antigas: **Arnold Bell**
Luis: **David Lander**

The Heiress
w **Leonard Fincham and Max Marquis** [from a story by **Philip Chambers**]
d **Pennington Richards**

Ronald Millais is known to the police. But he has committed no crime, just simply lived on women who fall for his easy charm. But this time Millais is accused of kidnapping a millionaire's daughter. Duval must determine the truth.

Louisa: **Julia Lockwood**
Millais: **Maurice Kaufmann**
Carlotta: **Betty McDowell**
Lebrun: **Donald Morley**
Howard: **Christopher Rhodes**
Dr. Martin: **Austin Trevor**

Game for Three Hands
w **Robert Stewart**
d **Pennington Richards**

In Montreal for Interpol's annual conference, Duval expects to stay in lecture rooms and at conference tables. Instead, he ends up catching a wanted murderer - a man who escaped his clutches way back in 1939!

Leroy: **Peter Dyneley**
Bonnier: **Alan Gifford**
Blanche: **Paula Byrne**
MacPherson: **Russell Waters**
Doctor: **Charles Richardson**

Act of Piracy
w **Edwin Richfield** [from a story by **John Kruse**]
d **Pennington Richards**

Three men pose as a US Navy Patrol, board the S.S. Jensen and make off with a million dollars worth of platinum - leaving behind the bodies of the captain and the crew. Duval flies to Mexico to interview one of seven men who knew of the consignment.

Ember: **Richard Gale**
Simms: **Reed de Rouen**
Gonzales: **Steve Plytas**
Gomiero: **Alex Mango**

The Collector
w **Wilton Schiller** and **David Chantler**
d **Pennington Richards**

Gangster Mike Marko amassed a fortune from the rackets, but did not live to spend it. Pavone, his lieutenant, stepped in to help himself. "...The Collector.." the last words muttered a lottery-ticket seller put Duval on Pavone's trail.

Carlo: **Leonard Sachs**
Pavone: **Paul Stassino**
Maria: **Christina Gregg**
Finn: **Richard Leech**

Payment in Advance
w **Larry Forrester**
d **Pennington Richards**

Mistakenly jailed for the 'murder' of Kaltmann, his business partner, Schroeder, hints that he intends to commit the crime for which he has already been punished. Realising that Schroeder is a man of his word, Duval gives orders for the ex-convict to be watched.

Schroeder: **Raymond Huntley**
Dr. Berger: **Carl Duering**
Fischer: **Walter Gotell**
Eva: **Wendy Williams**

Fingers of Guilt
w **Robert Stewart** [from a story by **Tom Hutchinson and Ernie Player**]
d **Robert Lynn**

Diamond dealer, Jacob Moltz, and his accomplice, girl magician, Frankie Silver, devise a foolproof plan to rob the biggest diamond house in Amsterdam - and lay the blame at safebreaker Sash Morran's door. The crime takes place, leaving the police and Duval baffled.

Sash: **Bill Nagy**
Moltz: **John Salew**
Frankie: **June Merlin**

Eight Days Inclusive
w **Robert Stewart**
d **Robert Lynn**

Gill and Lena, employed as driver and hostess by a coach firm, have a profitable sideline - armed hold-ups in the towns they visit. Duval enters the case after a Paris jeweller is murdered.

Gill: **Glyn Owen**
Lena: **Rona Anderson**
Capt. Fehr: **Robert Hunter**

Trial at Cranby's Creek
w **Larry Forrester**
d **Pennington Richards**

When a policeman is shot in the back in the opal mining settlement of Cranby's Creek, in the Australian outback, the

towns people allege the shooting was done by Emil Brock - a man wanted for murder by Interpol.

Cranby: **Thomas Duggan**
Brock: **Rowland Bartrop**
Doc Carson: **Leslie Weston**
Ruth: **Felicity Young**
Graham: **Charles Houston**
Russ: **Michael Balfour**

White Blackmail
w **Robert Stewart**
d **Robert Lynn**

Tipped-off by an American newspaper man about a possible organised blackmail racket in a Swiss ski resort, posing as his Paris banker friend, Count de Regny, Duval arrives in Switzerland and realises that he has been set-up as the next victim.

Ingrid Hoffman: **Mary Morris**
Hannah: **Nanette Newman**
Steinitz: **Douglas Wilmer**
Fawley: **Francis Matthews**
Hunter: **Robert Gallico**

Pipeline
w **Larry Forrester**
d **David MacDonald**

In South America to pick up, Carson, a man wanted for murder, Duval discovers that he has walked into the middle of a revolution - a turn of events which leads to Duval and his quarry working side by side in the interests of others.

Dave Carson: **John Bentley**
Garetta: **Richard Leech**
Vicenta: **Elisabeth Wilson**
Colonel: **Dervis Ward**

Ascent to Murder
w **Larry Forrester**
d **Robert Lynn**

American financier, Pearce Clyde, is wanted for questioning by the US Treasury. Ordered to bring the man back to face justice, Duval arrives at Clyde's hotel in the Himalayas. When searching Clyde's room, Duval sets off a booby-trap.

Miki: **Ursula Howells**
Clouston: **Anthony Dawson**
Peters: **Howard Marion Crawford**
Clyde: **Gordon Tanner**
Baratopi: **Julian Sherrier**
Lt. Gupta: **John Cairney**

Desert Hi-Jack
w **Robert Stewart** and **Harold Orton**
d **Jeremy Summers**

When the Foreign Legion report that shipments of arms have gone astray, Duval flies out to investigate - gun-running is a profitable business for the racketeers. He immediately suspects archaeologist, Professor Velard, of being an impostor.

Fake Professor: **John Salew**
Corporal Kahn: **Patrick Jordan**
Shana: **Colette Wilde**
Renoir: **Henry Oscar**
Commandant: **Neal Arden**

Dressed To Kill
w **David Chantler** and **Robert Stewart**
d **Robert Lynn**

Duval agrees to help his old friend, Bernarde, owner of a Paris salon, to keep his latest creations secret until the big fashion show. But Harry Grayson and Mamie Byant have other ideas.

Harry: **David Knight**
Carol: **Hazel Court**
Bernarde: **Frederick Jaeger**
Monique: **Caroline Leigh**
Mamie: **Paula Byrne**

The Absent Assassin
w **Larry Forrester**
d **Robert Lynn**

Karl Haussman, a former Nazi, is released from Spandau and plans a terrible revenge against the four men who gave evidence against him at the Nuremberg trials. Inspector Duval must out-think the fiendishly-clever killer.

Haussman: **Donald Pleasence**
Insp. Malcolm: **Frederick Piper**
Zelnikov: **Russell Waters**
Lord Ruskington: **John Longden**
Mottier: **William Thorp Deveraux**

Cargo of Death
w **Michael Connor** and **Leonard Fincham**
d **Pennington Richards**

Thieves have stolen a consignment of live cholera vaccine from the Chandra Laboratories in Karachi - enough to infect 50,000 people and start an epidemic. Duval flies to Delhi to try to locate the deadline vaccine.

Bhandari: **Marne Maitland**
Porton: **Laurence Payne**
Doctor : **Surya Kumari**
Buchanan: **John Gatrell**

Slow Boat to Amsterdam
w **Lindsay Galloway**
d **Bill Lewthwaite**

A piece of platinum found on the body of a girl fished out of a canal in Northern France, leads Inspector Duval to a diamond robbery in the South of France - and murder in Cannes.

Nevil: **William Franklyn**
Blink: **Francis de Woolf**
Sid: **Bernard Cribbins**
Commissaire: **Stanley Van Beers**
Thibault: **Harold Kasket**

A Foreign Body
w **Robert Stewart**
d **Norman Harrison**

When the police find the body of a French girl in the boot of an American car, Interpol is called in. Although everything points to Ben Stack, as the murderer, Duval is not convinced.

Ben Stack: **John Crawford**
Insp. Hill: **Michael Balfour**
Chaublin: **Stratford Johns**
D'Ambrosio: **Carl Duering**
Landau: **John Chandos**

In the Swim
w **Connery Chappell** and **Robert Stewart**
d **Robert Lynn**

Lars Lukas, a Finnish swimmer, is shot after completing the swim from France. It appears to be a murder without a motive - until Duval hears a tape-recording of Lukas' last words - a lead to a smuggling ring.

Montell: **John Horsley**
Millicent: **Dorinda Stevens**
Cummings: **Trevor Reid**
Commander Smith: **Jack Lambert**
Hotel Manager: **Arthur Lawrence**
Johnny: **Robert McKenzie**

The Three Keys
w **Connery Chappell** and **Robert Stewart** [from a story by **Paul Erickson**]
d **Robert Lynn**

Thackeray, an international forger, believes he has a fool-proof system of circulating counterfeit money. He robs safes and substitutes forged bills for the real thing. But Inspector Duval is hot on his trail.

Thackeray: **Lionel Murton**
Slade: **Cyril Shaps**
Artigas: **Anthony Jacobs**
Lambert: **Arnold Diamond**
Insp. Hopkins: **Basil Dignam**

Interpol Calling:

Producer:
Anthony Perry [episodes 1 to 19, 21 to 26, 35]
Connery Chappell [episodes 20, 27 to 34, 36 to 39]
Executive Producer: **F. Sherwin Green**

Produced by Rank/ Wrather
An ATV Presentation

39 monochrome 30-minute episodes
1959-60

Jason King

The return of the urbane, extravagant, dandy sleuth from *Department S* [see entry under that name]. Television's most way-out character, this time King has no attachments [the elite organisation known as Department S being presumably disbanded?]. He is Jason King, author. The world is his oyster. A man on his own, he's always on the move. Anything can happen whenever he goes in search of material for his Mark Caine books - and usually does. He encounters greater danger, deeper intrigue, amusing situations and [much] more beautiful girls than ever before.

There are drawbacks to being a freelance, of course, like being coerced into dabbling in espionage on behalf of HM Government by Sir Brian, a British civil servant who threatens to shop him to the Inland Revenue for unpaid taxes!

Great fun - but one wishes that Jason could make up his mind about the length and thickness of his moustache and sideburns!?

Regular cast:
Jason King: **Peter Wyngarde**
Nicola Harvester [his publisher]: **Ann Sharp**
Sir Brian: **Dennis Price**
Ryland [Sir Brian's assistant]: **Ronald Lacey**

Wanna Buy a Television Series [aka A Face I Used to Know]
w **Dennis Spooner**
d **Jeremy Summers**

Deciding that it's time for Mark Caine to reach a wider audience, Jason tries to sell his character to a TV producer by telling him the story of his greatest adventure.

Harry Carmel: **David Bauer**
Umberto Bellini: **Derek Francis**
Michelle Andre: **Anna Palk**
Gerard: **George Innes**
Frank Calder: **James Donnelly**
Litchfield: **James Warwick**
Insp. Rosseau: **Andre Maranne**
Dr Stayman: **Nicholas Courtney**
Nurse: **Anne Aston**
Cafe Owner: **Nicholas Kaminos**
American assistant: **Richard Pendry**
Negro assistant: **Willie Jonah**
Chinese assistant: **Geoff Chono**
Kyriascu: **Ronald Chenery**

A Page Before Dying
w **Tony Williamson**
d **Jeremy Summers**

Everyone is reading the new Mark Caine novel: the British, the Americans, and the West Germans. It's from the latter that Jason receives an invitation to sell the film rights - and the next thing he knows, he is in a safe, in East Berlin!

Sir Brian: **Dennis Price** [intro]
Ryland: **Ronald Lacey** [intro]
Lanik: **Carl Duering**
Versch: **Harry Landis**
Jenson: **Richard Wyler**
Ingrid: **Madeline Hinde**
Schulz: **Henry G. Gilbert**
Hoffman: **Philip Madoc**
The Electrician: **Michael Sheard**
Gorini: **Olaf Pooley**
Hotel Clerk: **Frans Van Norde**
German Police Officer: **Roy Patrick**
First Girl: **Jennie Lee-Wright**

Buried in the Cold, Cold Ground
w **Philip Broadley**
d **Jeremy Summers**

Jason really should have known better than to give a lift to a pretty young girl. This one turns out to be a newly-released prisoner - and she leads him a not-so-merry chase through the South of France.

Felicity: **Michele Dotrice**
Dacre: **Frederick Jaeger**
Sandro: **Gary Raymond**
Lanz: **Lewis Fiander**
Mistral: **Reg Lye**
Zoe Ballard: **Lyn Ashley**
Marie Mercier: **Irena Mayeska**
Inspector Maziol: **Simon Lack** [intro]
French Maid: **Jane Lapotaire**
Sister of Mercy: **Violetta**
Man in Saloon Car: **Peter King**
Gendarme: **Michael McStay**
Dana: **Maggie Wright**

A Deadly Line in Digits
w **Tony Williamson**
d **Jeremy Summers**

It's a case of 'anything you can do, a computer can do better' when Jason gets involved with several large-scale robberies, which must have had inside information. Jason's problem: the info was known only to Scotland Yard's computer!

Sir Brian: **Dennis Price**
Kenworthy: **Donald Houston**
Ryland: **Ronald Lacey**
Julia Marsh: **Joanna Jones**
Mr Quirly: **Freddie Jones**
Jan Rose: **Jan Waters**
Supt Landon: **Philip Stone**
Lemmy: **Barry Lowe**
Charlie: **Leonard Trolley**
Count De Ville: **Michael Anthony**
Miranda: **Monika Dietrich**
Constance: **Davina Taylor**
Messenger: **Robin Ford**
Signor Cabor: **Richard Marner**
Stretfield: **John Forbes Robertson**
Tanfield: **Peter Forbes Robertson**

Variations on a Theme
w **Philip Broadley**
d **Cyril Frankel**

Jason has little time to enjoy the splendours of Vienna, when rival gangs try to use him as bait to snare double agent Alan Keeble - whom Jason believed dead, until he received a message asking him to visit Vienna.

Alan Keeble: **Ralph Bates**
John: **Julian Glover**
Kelkov: **Eric Pohlmann**
Hoffman: **Walter Hertner**
Viney: **Basil Dignam**
Hazell: **Sebastian Breaks**
Alexandra: **Alexandra Bastedo**
Greta Weiss: **Magda Konopka**
Dischev: **Michael David**
Balenkov: **Janus Kurucz**
Croupier: **Colin Vancao**
Waiter: **Will Knightly**
Bell Boy: **Adrian Hall**

As Easy as A B C
w **Tony Williamson**
d **Jeremy Summers**

The fact that every Mark Caine novel is the subject of thorough research by Jason hasn't escaped Charles and Edward, two petty crooks. They pull off a job by copying the plot of Jason's latest book - and leave the author to carry the can.

Charles: **Nigel Green**
Edward: **Michael Bates**
Mireille: **Ayshea Brough**
Arlene: **Yutte Stensgaard**
Chief Inspector Poron: **Hamilton Dyce**
Capitano Rizio: **Paul Stassino** [intro]
German Police Officer: **Peter Hager**
Luigi: **Larry Taylor**
Dino: **Ray Marioni**

To Russia With ....Panache
w **Tony Williamson**
d **Paul Dickson**

An honour indeed. Believing that Jason is the only man alive capable of solving a mystery which is baffling them, the Russians engage his service - by abducting him and transporting him to Moscow in a wooden crate!

Alexandra Lamova: **Pamela Salem**
Anna Brenskaja: **Elizabeth Counsell**
Colonel Kelkov: **John Malcolm**
Perekev: **Jeffry Wickham**
Kivich: **Tutte Lemkow**
Krosnic: **Stefan Oryff**
Stavalov: **Michael Poole**
The Tall Girl: **Andrea Allan**
Jania: **Milton Reid**
Hotel Maid: **Anna Kilpinen**
Strong-arm Man: **Marcus Mariner**
Joseph: **Wally Michaels**
Mavitch: **Timothy Craven**
Markevitch: **Richard Marner**
Danik: **Mark Malioz**
Skirnof: **Gaeor Vernon**

A Red, Red Rose Forever
w **Donald James**
d **Cyril Frankel**

When a fellow passenger on a flight to Switzerland collapses en route, with a bunch of roses in his hand, Jason helps him into an ambulance and is left holding the roses. Before he knows it, the flowers are swapped for a rifle with the comment that instructions will follow ...

Ryland: **Ronald Lacey**
Simone: **Barbara Murray**
Anne Winters: **Isla Blair**
Dr Claudel: **Alan MacNaughton**
Professor D'Arblay: **Tony Steedman**
Carson: **Mike Pratt**
Hartman: **Derek Newark**
The Police Inspector: **Christopher Benjamin**
The Nurse: **Fanny Sugg**
Stevens: **Ralph Truman**
The Receptionist: **Angela Richards**
The Motor Cyclist: **Carl Bohun**
Swiss Policeman: **Greg Palmer**
The Bank Guard: **Kenton Moore**

All that Glisters [part 1 of 2]
w **Philip Broadley**
d **Cyril Frankel**

Jason becomes involved in a complicated game of bluff and counter-bluff when he is asked to introduce adventurer John Mallen to Phillipe de Brion - a man who wishes to buy a golden antique for a cool half a million dollars...

Frankie Luca: **Lee Patterson**
John Mallen: **Clinton Greyn**
Phillipe de Brion: **Anton Rodgers**
Martine: **Joanna Dunham**
Jonquil: **Madeline Smith**
Deshfield: **Leslie French**
Vaturia: **Michael Gwynn**
Well: **Paul Humpoletz**
Enzio: **Tony Vogel**
Emilie: **Michael Petrovitch**
Lyman: **William Kearns**
Strebel: **Theodore Wilhelm**
Risk: **John Rumney**
Xanthe: **Me Me Lay**

All that Glisters [part 2 of 2]
w **Philip Broadley**
d **Cyril Frankel**

Jason finds himself a pawn in a deadly game when the search for the stolen antique switches from Paris to Rome and the author finds that chasing gold can lead to certain death.

Frankie Luca: **Lee Patterson**
John Mallen: **Clinton Greyn**
Phillipe de Brion: **Anton Rodgers**
Martine: **Joanna Dunham**
Jonquil: **Madeline Smith**
Vaturia: **Michael Gwynn**
Angelo: **Hans Meyer**
Enzio: **Tony Vogel**
Deshfield: **Leslie French**
Well: **Paul Humpoletz**
Waiter: **Reginald Peters**
Girl in cafe: **Celestine Burden**
Mia: **Valerie Stanton**
Xanthe: **Me Me Lay**

Flamingos Only Fly on Tuesdays
w **Tony Williamson**
d **Jeremy Summers**

Opposition parties may be essential in a democracy, but as Jason finds out during a trip to the Caribbean, in a state of revolution they only get in the way - particularly if you're mistaken for a gun-runner.

Pelli: **Hugh McDermott**
Lyra Delon: **Hildegard Neil**
Drakin: **David Healy**
Jaevert: **Philip Bond**
Sebastian: **Clifton Jones**
Mareen: **Nik Zaran**
Benny: **Neville Aurelius**
Female Clerk: **Marcia Fox**
Hector: **Louis Mahoney**
Waiter in Cafe: **Bloke Modisane**
Karen: **Siobhan Quinlan**

Toki
w **Philip Broadley**
d **Jeremy Summers**

Seeking inspiration to finish his latest novel and meet his publisher's deadline, Jason visits a Paris cafe and meets Toki, a girl for whom King would abdicate. But Toki already has a leader - Le Grand, a ruthless gangster - and that's when Jason's troubles begin.

Jean le Grand: **Kieron Moore**
Toki: **Felicity Kendall**
Giorgio: **Tony Beckley**
Oliver: **David Buck**
Nicola Harvester: **Anne Sharp** [intro]
Inspector Maziol: **Simon Lack**
Jules: **Oliver MacGreevy**
Maurice: **Yuri Borienko**
Cafe Waiter: **George Camiller**
Plainclothes Insp.: **Neville Barber**

The Constance Missal
w **Harry W. Junkin**
d **Jeremy Summers**

Jason has girl trouble again. This time two beautiful females hypnotise him and steal the only copy of a film manuscript he's written. But the girls have more than film scripts on their mind - as their unwilling accomplice Jason soon discovers.

Claudia: **Geraldine Moffatt**
Elaine: **Janey Key**
Lord Barnes: **Clive Revill**
Howard: **Charles Lloyd Pack**
Collingwood: **Richard Hurndall**
Sir Richard: **David Hutchenson**
Nicola Harvester: **Anne Sharp**
Hal: **Jurgen Andersen**
Jenkins: **Arthur Brough**
Isabella: **Jane Cardew**

Uneasy Lies the Head
w **Donald James**
d **Cyril Frankel**

Jason is concerned and confused when a friend shows him newspaper cuttings with pictures of him in Istanbul - but he is in Paris! Who is impersonating him, and why? Jason determines to find out - and steps straight into danger.

Alfred Trim: **Lance Percival**
Shelley Blackman: **Juliet Harmer**
Ryland: **Ronald Lacey**
Colonel Davat: **Harold Kasket**
Sonja: **Kara Wilson**
Shimoon: **Sandor Eles**
Nicola Harvester: **Anne Sharp**
The Lieutenant: **Anthony Stamboulier**
The Chairman: **Geoffrey Denton**
American Delegate: **J. M. Ray**
Russian Delegate: **Steve Plytas**
French Delegate: **Andre Charisse**
Engineer: **Denis Duval**
Hotel Clerk: **Tony Thawnton**
Receptionist: **Susan Brodrick**
Kemal: **Kievork Malikyan**
Airport Stewardess: **Jasmina Hilton**

Nadine
w **Philip Broadley**
d **Cyril Frankel**

Always seeking inspiration for his Mark Caine novels, Jason meets Nadine, a girl who seems to provide all the inspiration he needs. But the girl is playing her own deadly game - with Jason as the joker in the pack.

Nadine: **Ingrid Pitt**
Ringo: **Alfred Marks**
Achille: **Patrick Mower**
Placide: **Al Mancini**
Nicola: **Anne Sharp**
Kim: **Stacey Gregg**
Chuck: **John Hamill**

Male Secretary: **Walter Randall**
Tony Mussoni: **Al Garcia**
Kyriacon: **Clive Cazes**
Gerard Reder: **Harry Brooks Jun.**

A Kiss for a Beautiful Killer
w **Gerald Kelsey**
d **Cyril Frankel**

Does Jason really hold the key to the secret that both sides of a South American revolution are seeking so desperately? He thinks not. They think otherwise - and are prepared to go to any lengths to extract his information.

Cordoba: **Clifford Evans**
Delphi: **Kate O'Mara**
Rodriguez: **Alex Scott**
Rigmera: **Maurice Roeves**
Miguel: **Stanley Lebor**
Menendez: **Patrick Westwood**
Pedro: **Aharon Ipale**
Garcia: **Richard Montez**
Ramon: **Ricardo Hermanny**
Phillipe: **Damien Thomas**
Radio Operator: **Roger Lloyd Pack**
Estelle: **Hylette Adolphe**
Policeman: **Marc Zuber**

If it's Got to Go - It's Got to Go
w **Tony Williamson**
d **Cyril Frankel**

Why has Jason been tricked into visiting a German health farm? Whatever the reason, his stay at the establishment proves far from healthy - someone keeps trying to help him lose weight, with a diet of bullets.

Myra Bergen: **Jennifer Hilary**
Doctor Litz: **John Le Mesurier**
Doctor Wilstein: **Felix Aylmer**
Sister Dryker: **Yootha Joyce**
Inspector Gruman: **Guy Deghy**
Nylene: **Natasha Pyne**
Young Nurse: **Bridget Armstrong**
Gym Instructor: **George Benson**
Hotel Manager: **Gerard Heinz**
Suzanne: **Anna Brett**
Attendant: **John Sullivan**
Morgan: **Jon Croft**
Lerik: **Ivor Salter**

A Thin Band of Air
w **Harry W. Junkin**
d **Cyril Frankel**

Accompanied by a beautiful young photographer, Lee Bailey, who is working on the publicity for the author's new book, Jason visits Paris - where a dead man's Russian accent and a ten-year old kidnapping endanger both their lives.

Lee Bailey: **Francesca Tu**
John Hewlett: **John Hallam**
Rene Chenard: **T.P. McKenna**
Jean Cazette: **Cyril Shaps**
Irene Culver: **Edina Ronay**
Mrs Zaleski: **Patience Collier**
Gregoire: **Dawn Grainger**
Armand: **Tony Anholt**
Doctor Lucenet: **John Serret**
Gervais: **James Mellor**

It's Too Bad about Auntie
w **Harry W. Junkin**
d **Jeremy Summers**

A little old lady who accuses a young girl of murder. An extraordinary surplus of vacuum cleaners. Two links in an unusual puzzle which Jason finally clears up - but only after some daring undercover work.

Mary Trevor: **Sarah Lawson**
Geoffrey Winters: **Jack Watling**
Andrew Bishop: **Allen Rickford**
Det. Sgt Roddick: **Dinsdale Landen**
Det. Insp. Fields: **Norman Bird**
Lady Pamela Radfield: **Fiona Lewis**
Mr Horner: **Geoffrey Chater**
Mrs Bishop: **Sylvia Coleridge**
Robert Trevor: **Basil Henson**
Miss Howe: **Margot Field**
Mrs Edwards: **Dorothea Phillips**
The Police Doctor: **Clifford Earl**
The Photographer: **David Firth**

The Stones of Venice
w **Donald James**
d **Jeremy Summers**

Arriving in Venice for a holiday, Jason is surprised to find he's been awarded a special prize for his latest Mark Caine novel The Stones of Venice - a book he hasn't written! Further surprises arrive in the shape of two thugs carrying guns.

Capitano Garozzo: **Roger Delgado**
Ingrid and Teresa Bonival: **Anna Gael**
Colonel Gardner: **William Squire**
Tomasi: **John Lorane**
Anna: **Irene Prador**
Marco: **John Cazabon**
Fausto: **Ray Chiarella**
Gina: **Imogen Hassall**
Secretary: **Heather Barbour**
Kitchen Porter: **Mario Zoppellini**

A Royal Flush
w **Philip Broadley**
d **Roy Ward Baker**

Nothing appeals to Jason's vanity more than a beautiful girl seeking his help. But he soon finds trouble when he arrives at a suite she booked for him at a Capri hotel - and the girl fails to keep the rendezvous.

Karen: **Elaine Taylor**
Princess Vania: **Penelope Horner**
Vitorio: **Wolfe Morris**
Euzio: **Anthony Corlan**
Hazell: **Sebastian Breaks**
Corso: **Inigo Jackson**
Ludwig: **Richard Heffer**
Boris: **Terence Lodge**
Nurse: **Georgina Simpson**
Teresa: **Donna Reading**
Pietro: **David Janson**
Vladimir: **Chris Cunningham**
Stanislav: **Peter Whitting**
Crew Member: **Simon Gough**
Waiter: **Paul Greenhalgh**

Every Picture Tells a Story
w **Robert Banks Stewart**
d **Cyril Frankel**

Having your character presented to a wider audience is all very well - providing you agree to the promotion. But an unauthorised strip cartoon based on his Mark Caine character has sinister implications for Jason when it is translated into Chinese.

✍ A 30-minute version also exists

Arthur Tsumg: **Clifford Evans**
Sam Finnigin: **Neil McCullum**
Lucy Cameron: **Kara Wilson**
Rutledge: **Allan Cuthbertson**
Lee Chung: **Bert Kwouk**
Jimmy Foy: **John A. Pinn**
F. J. Wing: **Robert Lee**
Airport Barman: **Eric Young**
Nicola Harvester: **Anne Sharp**
Stewardess: **Cheryl Kennedy**
Pearl Yenn: **Mona Chong**
Teller: **Cecil Cheng**
Inspector Kee: **Andy Ho**
Fisherman: **Ken Nazarin**
Ming Finnigin: **Kathleen Eu**

Chapter One: The Company I Keep
w **Donald James**
d **Cyril Frankel**

Has Jason become clairvoyant? When all the ingredients of his latest Mark Caine novel actually start to happen, the author believes he has. But sinister forces are behind the puzzling affair.

Contessa Di Magiere: **Tony Robins**
Alfred Thistle: **Ronald Radd**
Giorgie: **Paul Whitsun-Jones**
Capitano Rizio: **Paul Stassino**
Simpson: **Stephanie Beacham**
Nicola Harvester: **Anne Sharp**
Anne Wilcox: **Sarah Atkinson**
Renata: **Marianne Benet**
Karl: **Martin Wyldeck**
Sven: **George Selway**
Hotel Clerk: **Franco Derosa**

Zenia
w **Philip Broadley**
d **Roy Ward Baker**

When the young daughter of a foreign president is kidnapped by revolutionaries, Jason is asked to find her. Finding her is one thing, obtaining her freedom another. But Jason has a plan in mind - one based on a Mark Caine adventure.

Leila: **Patricia English**
President: **Michael Goodliffe**
Oran: **Donald Burton**
Dana: **Angela Douglas**
Zenia: **Zienia Merton**
Nerine: **Sharon Gurney**
Marko: **Stuart Wilson**
Nicolas: **Philip Donaghy**
Nicoyram: **Carlos Douglas**
Male Revolutionary: **Paul Freeman**
Girl Revolutionary: **Janey Edis**
Patron: **Phil Ryan**
Tala: **Harry Burgess-Wall**
Kazakov: **Dave Carter**

An Author in Search of Two Characters
w **Dennis Spooner**
d **Cyril Frankel**

A stranger runs towards Jason, a shot rings out and the man dies. A Frankenstein-like monster beats the author unconscious. Dreams? Hardly, these are just two of the events in Jason's new film script - and they are taking place around him!

Ackroyd: **Dudley Foster**
Chief Inspector Hughes: **Ivor Dean**
Claire: **Liz Fraser**
Eve: **Sue Lloyd**

Tredgett: **Neil McCarthy**
Robbins: **Roy Kinnear**
Det. Sgt Watkins: **Brian Grellis**
Griffin: **Brian Oulton**
Commissionaire: **Alan Curtis**
Bernard: **Hugh Walters**
Film Director: **Janes Grout**
The Hero: **Stanley McGeagh**
Reynolds: **John Sullivan**

That Isn't Me, It's Somebody Else
w **Dennis Spooner**
d **Roy Ward Baker**

A bogus Jason King sets a problem for the adventure-loving author. The double has set out to kill a gangland boss. But Jason seems unconcerned - until, to escape from marriage, he takes refuge in the Italian villa of the big-time gangster.

Bonisalvi: **George Murcell**
Bennett: **Patrick Troughton**
Martine: **Toby Robins**
Broggi: **Simon Oates**
Malazza: **George Margo**
Nicola Harvester: **Anne Sharp**
Capitano Jaseheroni: **John Junkin**
Mayer: **William Abney**
Escatore: **Victor Baring**
Falpiaz: **Tommy Godfrey**
Luigi: **Louis Raynes**
Jean: **Hugh Fletcher**
First Oilman: **Hal Galili**
Air Hostess: **Julie Crosthwait**
First Fan: **Juliet Kempson**
Second Fan: **Linda Cunningham**
Third Fan: **Heather Wright**

Jason King [1972: Robert Miall aka John Burke: Pan Books novelisations of *A Deadly Line in Digits* and *Chapter One: The Company I Keep*]; *Kill Jason King* [1972: Robert Miall: Pan Books: novelisation of *As Easy as ABC*].

Jason King:

Created by: **Dennis Spooner** and **Monty Berman**
Producer: **Monty Berman**
Executive Story Consultant: **Dennis Spooner**
Music by: **Laurie Johnson**
Music Co-ordinator: **Paul Clay**
Creative Consultant: **Cyril Frankel**
Production Supervisor: **Ronald Liles**
Assistant Director: **Ken Baker, Gino Marotta**
Stunt Co-ordinator: **John Sullivan**
Casting: **Ann Donne**
Make-up: **Basil Newell, George Blackler, Eddie Knight**
Hairdresser: **Mibs Parker, Alice Holmes**
Costume Supervisor: **Laura Nightingale**

A Scoton Production for ITC World Wide Distribution
Filmed on location and at EMI/MGM Elstree Studios

26 colour 60-minute episodes
1971

Joe 90

The tenth of Gerry Anderson's unique television puppet creations - but this time with less emphasis on machinery and space-type action, and a nine-year old star character.

The first episode [untitled on screen, but widely known as Most Special Agent] told how Professor Ian McClaine gave his adopted son, Joe, amazing powers provided by a pair of special glasses which fused the boy's brain impulse to his own. Called the BIG RAT [Brain Impulse Galvanascope, Record and Transfer], Joe could then assume the skills and personality of whoever's brain pattern was entered into the machine. As a result he became a brilliant scientist who worked for and with Commander Shane Weston of the World Intelligence Network [WIN] and his deputy Sam Loover, and undertook dangerous missions on their behalf.

With the reduction of special effects and gadgetry [the only major item of hardware was Professor McClaine's Jet Car], and the first ever location work used for an Anderson puppet series [Episode 13, *The Unorthodox Shepherd*], the series should have been every bit as successful as Anderson's earlier work, but failed to capture the viewers' attention.

Character voices:
Joe 90: **Len Jones**
Prof. McClaine: **Rupert Davies**
Shane Weston: **David Healey**
Sam Loover: **Keith Alexander**
Ada Harris: **Sylvia Anderson**

The Most Special Agent
w **Gerry Anderson** and **Sylvia Anderson**
d **Desmond Saunders**

Persuaded that by using his new invention BIG RAT on his nine-year old adopted son, Joe, he could become an invaluable agent for WIN, Commander Weston tells Joe a story of what might happen if he did become an agent; he could steal a new Russian prototype plane. Joe does just that, and becomes WIN's youngest 'Most Special Agent'.

Most Special Astronaut
w **Tony Barwick**
d **Peter Anderson**

With the aid of a top astronaut's brain pattern, Joe is able to save two astronauts from extinction.

Project 90
w **Tony Barwick**
d **Peter Anderson**

The only way Joe can save his kidnapped father is to acquire the brain patterns of a balloonist.

Hi-jacked
w **Tony Barwick**
d **Alan Perry**

Joe must devise a plan to stop the world's most dangerous gun-runner and smuggler from achieving his aims.

Colonel McClaine
w **Tony Barwick**
d **Ken Turner**

Using the brain patterns of an explosives expert and a top Army driver, Joe transports a dangerous cargo across Africa.

The Fortress
w **Shane Rimmer**
d **Leo Eaton**

Joe is assigned to rescue a fellow WIN agent from a San Marino jail, before the man can tell his WIN secrets.

King for a Day
w **Shane Rimmer**
d **Leo Eaton**

To prevent a Middle Eastern heir to the throne being kidnapped, Joe impersonates him - and gets kidnapped himself.

International Concerto
w **Tony Barwick**
d **Alan Perry**

A world famous pianist needs a replacement for a broadcast recital. With the aid of BIG RAT, Joe plays a lively tune.

Splashdown
w **Tony Barwick**
d **Leo Eaton**

When two electronics experts are killed, Joe assumes the persona of a crack test pilot to investigate their deaths.

Big Fish
w **Shane Rimmer**
d **Alan Perry**

Joe must find a way to gain access and retrieve a secret submarine stranded at the bottom of the sea - in enemy waters.

Relative Danger
w **Shane Rimmer**
d **Peter Anderson**

Using the brain patterns of a leading underground explorer, Joe must save three men trapped deep in a cavern.

Operation McClaine
w **Gerry Anderson** and **David Lane**
d **Ken Turner**

When a famous writer needs brain surgery, and the leading specialist is injured in a plane crash, Joe performs the operation - but gives someone else the credit.

The Unorthodox Shepherd
w **Tony Barwick**
d **Ken Turner**

Joe, his father and Sam Loover investigate a supposedly haunted church that is being used as a cover for dubious activities.

Business Holiday
w **Tony Barwick**
d **Alan Perry**

Sam wants to steal a tank and repel a military force, so Joe is given the brain pattern of an Army Colonel.

Arctic Adventure
w **Tony Barwick**
d **Alan Perry**

A nuclear bomb is lost somewhere in the Arctic wasteland. Joe is sent to recover it and secure its time mechanism.

Double Agent
w **Tony Barwick**
d **Ken Turner**

By accident, Joe gains the brain pattern of a double agent. WIN have to find him before he can cause mischief.

Three's a Crowd
w **Tony Barwick**
d **Peter Anderson**

Joe has to step in when his father's new girlfriend appears to have more on her mind than a romantic interlude.

The Professional
w **Gerry Anderson** and **Sylvia Anderson**
d **Desmond Saunders**

Joe's liable to end up in trouble - unless he can avoid it. Someone is plying a deadly game of cat and mouse - a very dangerous game.

The Race
w **Tony Barwick**
d **Alan Perry**

Joe is given the brain pattern of a Monte Carlo rally driver after WIN receives a challenge they dare not refuse.

Talkdown
w **Tony Barwick**
d **Alan Perry**

Joe becomes a test pilot to discover why a hypersonic fighter plane crashed in mysterious circumstances.

Breakout
w **Shane Rimmer**
d **Leo Eaton**

Two escaped convicts capture a canon and destroy the track carrying a prime minister's train. Using the brain pattern of a bobsleigh champion, Joe saves the day.

Child of the Sun God
w **John Lucarotti**
d **Peter Anderson**

In order to take receipt of an antidote to a deadly poison, Joe must convince a lost Indian tribe that he is their legendary sun god.

See You Down There
w **Tony Barwick**
d **Leo Eaton**

Being a WIN agent can have its drawbacks, as Joe and his father find out when they are asked to convince a man that he is losing his mind!

Lone Handed 90
w **Des Saunders** and **Keith Wilson**
d **Ken Turner**

Joe dreams of becoming a western sheriff, and finds himself involved in shoot-outs and a life on the open range.

Attack of the Tiger
w **Tony Barwick**
d **Peter Anderson**

Joe finds himself one step away from danger - and two steps behind his enemy - when asked to undertake a mission for WIN.

Viva Cordova
w **Tony Barwick**
d **Peter Anderson**

When a Mexican president's life is threatened, Joe enters the scene - and finds himself in the firing line.

Mission X-41
w **Pat Dunlop**
d **Ken Turner**

The formula for a new antibody has to be learned. Joe adopts the brain pattern of a top scientist to gain its secrets for WIN.

Test Flight
w **Donald James**
d **Peter Anderson**

Joe stops a sabotage threat with the aid of a computer specialist and an explosives expert's brain patterns.

Trial at Sea
w **Donald James**
d **Leo Eaton**

Joe finds himself held hostage aboard a transatlantic super liner - and only he can prevent a major disaster.

The Birthday
w **Tony Barwick**
d **Leo Eaton**
Format by **Gerry Anderson** and **Sylvia Anderson**

As a special birthday treat for Joe, Professor McClaine and his friends recall some of his son's greatest adventures.

✍ A 'feature' version was issued, *Amazing Adventures of Joe 90*, being a compilation of: *The Most Special Agent, Splash Down, Attack of the Tiger & Arctic Adventure.*

📖 original stories:
Joe 90 and the Raiders [1968: Tod Sullivan: Armada Paperbacks (May Fair Books) Century 21 Publishing Ltd.];
Joe 90 in Revenge [1969: Howard Elson: Armada Paperbacks (May Fair Books) Century 21 Publishing Ltd.].

Joe 90:

Format by: **Gerry Anderson** and **Sylvia Anderson**
Characters created by: **Sylvia Anderson**
Producer: **David Lane**
Executive Producer: **Reg Hill**
Music by: **Barry Gray**
Visual Effects: **Derek Meddings**
Senior Visual Effects Director: **Jimmy Elliott**
Script Editor: **Tony Barwick**
Production Manager: **Frank Hollands**
Puppet Co-ordinator: **Mary Turner**
Puppet Operators: **Charmaine Wood, Wanda Webb, Rowena White**
Big Rat by: **Century 21 Film Props**

A Century 21 Production for ITC World Wide Distribution.
Filmed in Supermarionation

30 colour 30-minute episodes
1969

Man in a Suitcase

A rough and tumble adventure series in the Danger Man mould, this portrayed the adventures of ex-CIA man, turned freelance investigator, McGill.

Kicked out of American Intelligence through no fault of his own [he was framed by his superiors in the cause of international intrigue], his career in ruins, his reputation lost. McGill was forced to start life anew. He became the 'Man in a Suitcase' - a bounty hunter working for anyone who would hire him ['$500 a day - plus expenses'], using the experience he'd gained in the espionage jungle to earn a living. He's a modern bounty-hunter, working for money, but believing that what he is doing is worthwhile. Intolerant of injustice, he doesn't seek danger, it seeks him.

The tools of his trade were few. A leather suitcase containing a change of clothes and a gun. Sometimes he found himself acting as a private eye in order to save a wrecked marriage. One week later he'd be hired to protect the life of a threatened man. But because of his past, McGill could claim no protection from the authorities - even when cheated by clients, which he was, on several occasions.

He made mistakes and was always aware that hidden in the shadows were those who knew of his former CIA background and who wouldn't think twice about using their knowledge to obtain his help or discredit him.

They didn't come any tougher than McGill - but how he managed to work his way through a no-holds-barred fight, say, across a garage forecourt, down subway steps and onto a station platform, without ever once removing his cigarette from his mouth, is beyond the author!

Originally produced under the title *McGill*, the series adopted the title [*Man in a Suitcase*] prior to commission.

Regular cast:
McGill: **Richard Bradford**

Man from the Dead
w **Stanley R. Greenberg**
d **Pat Jackson**

News of vital interest to McGill appears in a newspaper - the sighting by Rachel Thyssen of her supposedly dead father - and McGill determines to find Harry Thyssen by shadowing the girl when she visits him.

Harry Thyssen: **John Barrie**
Rachel Thyssen: **Angela Browne**
Coughlin: **Lionel Murton**
Williams: **Stuart Damon**
Receptionist: **Fabia Drake**
Pfeiffer: **Timothy Bateson**
Landlady: **Dandy Nichols**
Leader: **David Nettheim**
Cap: **Gerry Wain**
Moustache: **Arthur Howell**
Policeman: **Clifford Earl**
Agent: **Fred Haggerty**

Brainwash
w **Frances Megahy** and **Bernie Cooper**
d **Charles Crichton**

Kicked out of American Intelligence, McGill begins his life anew as a freelance trouble-shooter. But always at the back of his mind is the suffering he faced as a result of someone else's treachery - a man he'll meet again, one day.

John: **Colin Blakely**
Colonel Davies: **Howard Marion Crawford**
Judy: **Suzan Farmer**
Doctor Gwabe: **Edric Connor**
First Guard: **Bill Brandon**
Second Guard: **George Leech**

The Sitting Pigeon
w **Edmund Ward**
d **Gerry O'Hara**

Hired to guard a crook who has ideas of grandeur and is willing to sell out his brothers, McGill finds himself facing a ruthless enemy - one who is prepared to kill to achieve his ambitions.

Rudyard: **Robin Bailey**
Rufus Blake: **George Sewell**
Valerie: **Lois Daine**
Jackson: **Mark Eden**
Olsen: **Joe Melia**
Geordie: **Sean Lynch**
Franklin: **James Grout**
Baxter: **David Garfield**
Gilley: **Garfield Morgan**
Miss Dinsdale: **Carol Cleveland**
Anderson: **Peter Burton**
Prison Officer: **Tom Bowman**
Female Singer: **Grace Arnold**
Male singer: **Humphrey Heathcote**
First Model: **Merrill Colebrook**
Second Model: **Julie Bevan**

Day of Execution
w **Philip Broadley**
d **Charles Crichton**

Will a threat to kill him be carried out? That's the dilemma facing McGill as he whiles away the time wondering if every tick of the clock will bring him closer to his unknown assassin.

Jarvis: **Robert Urquhart**
Moria: **Rosemary Nicols**
Willard: **Donald Sutherland**
Peter: **T.P. McKenna**
Bradshaw: **Jeremy Spencer**
Carman: **Brian Peck**
Anita: **Maggie Wright**
Caretaker: **Jimmy Gardner**
Girl at Cleaners: **Sally Geeson**
Announcer: **Brenda Lawrence**
Messenger Boy: **Richard James**

Variation on a Million Bucks [part 1 of 2]
w **Stanley R. Greenberg**
d **Pat Jackson**

A million dollars has been hidden away in a Lisbon Bank. Believing that he is the only man with the key to the safe deposit, McGill travels to Lisbon. But he is not the only man after the money - as he finds to his cost...

Michaels: **Ron Randell**
Taiko: **Yoko Tani**
Max Stein: **Anton Rodgers**
Kenneth: **Aubrey Morris**
Bert: **Simon Brent**
Johnson: **Warren Stanhope**
Harrassed Man: **Arthur Howell**
Guard: **Richard Montez**
Detective Sergeant Peters: **Mike Pratt**
Killer: **John Lee**
Charles: **Alan White**
Bob: **David Baxter**
Lionel: **David Scheur**
Girl in Cafe: **Gundel Sargent**
First Model: **Marie-Lise Gres**
Second Model: **Penny Spicer**

Variation on a Million Bucks [part 2 of 2]
w **Stanley R. Greenberg**
d **Robert Tronson**

Blackmailed and under escort, McGill reaches the safe deposit box containing the answer to his prayers. But his troubles are far from over: someone else has plans for the loot - and McGill.

Michaels: **Ron Randell**
Taiko: **Yoko Tani**
Max Stein: **Anton Rodgers**
Kenneth: **Aubrey Morris**
Bert: **Simon Brent**
Johnson: **Warren Stanhope**
Harrassed Man: **Arthur Howell**
Guard: **Richard Montez**
Captain: **Norman Rosington**
Lucia: **Gay Hamilton**
Ryan: **Harry Landis**
Manny: **Jeremy Wilkin**
Steward: **Harry Tardios**
First Seaman: **George Zenios**
Second Seaman: **Agath Angelos**
Third Seaman: **Maki Marseilles**
Pharmacist's Mate: **Andreas Lysandrou**

✍ A 'feature', *To Chase a Million*, was issued, being a compilation of *Variation on a Million Bucks*, Parts 1 and 2.

Sweet Sue
w **Philip Broadley**
d **Robert Tronson**

An apparently straightforward case concerning a wealthy man's wayward daughter takes a decidedly nasty turn when McGill digs too deep into the man's business affairs.

Sue: **Judy Geeson**
Mandel: **George A. Cooper**
Charles: **David Cole**
Kemp: **Ian McCulloch**
Miss Brown: **Jacqueline Pearce**
Brent: **Terence Donovan**
Waiter: **Lewis Teasdale**
Clerk: **John Clive**

Essay in Evil
w **Kevin B. Laffan**
d **Freddie Francis**

When three respectable businessmen take it upon themselves to remove the opposition, McGill finds himself involved in a business arrangement with a very nasty sting in its tail.

George Masters: **Donald Houston**
Felix De Burg: **Peter Vaughan**
Peters: **John Cairney**
Lucinda Masters: **Wendy Hall**
Harris: **Maurice Good**
Lorry Driver: **Frank Forsyth**
Lorry Driver's Mate: **Richard Owens**
Receptionist: **Angela Lovell**
Naval Guard: **Darryl Kavana**
Hairdresser: **Marianne Stone**
Crick: **Peter Brace**

The Girl Who Never Was
w **Donald Jonson**
d **Robert Tronson**

Hired to trace a missing painting, McGill enters the shady world of art dealers. He discovers that the ownership of a

masterpiece brings out the best in some, the worst in others - and McGill is dealing with one of the latter.

Kershaw: **Bernard Lee**
Todd: **Basil Dignam**
Mavis: **Priscilla Morgan**
Foley: **Harold Goodwin**
Gilchrist: **Annette Caroll**
Bateson: **David Garfield**
Manager of Aladdin's Cave: **Derek Smee**
Henry: **Raymond Smith**
French: **Jack Bligh**
Francis: **Vicki Woolf**
Martin: **Charles Lawrence**
German Soldier: **Roy Vincente**
British Soldier: **Bill Dean**

All That Glitters
w **Stanley R. Greenberg**
d **Herbert Wise**

Called to investigate the disappearance of a little boy, McGill finds that in place of the usual distraught parents, two apparently unconnected people are faced with a joint emotional crisis.

Dolores Hornsby: **Barbara Shelley**
Michael Hornsby: **Michael Goodliffe**
George Hornsby: **Eric Thompson**
Tommy: **Duncan Lamont**
Mason: **Norman Wynne**
Mrs Hart: **Dorothy Edwards**
Rankin: **Edward Underdown**
Rudy: **Derek Newark**
Steve: **Alan Baulch**
Doctor: **Peter Bennett**
Barman: **Kevin Stoney**
Sergeant Jones: **Dickie Owen**
General Denmayer: **Larry Cross**
Dowager: **Kathleen St.John**

Dead Man's Shoes
w **Edmund Ward**
d **Peter Duffell**

Danger looms its ugly head in a peaceful village. McGill, asked to undertake a straightforward case, suddenly finds himself the target for a group of vicious gangsters waiting to kill him. But why?

Lucas Guardino: **Derren Nesbitt**
John Gilsen: **John Carson**
Peters: **James Villiers**
Juliet Crowther: **Jayne Sofiano**
Van Ruys: **Murray Evans**
Reverend Simon Blanding: **Noel Howlett**
James Hedley: **Gerald Sim**
William: **Laurie Asprey**
Joe Mason: **David Saire**
Philip Kane: **John Brandon**
Roberts: **Norman Mitchell**
Jackie: **Harry Brooks**
Harry: **Larry Martin**

Find the Lady
w **Philip Broadley**
d **Robert Tronson**

'Find the Signora', a dying man's last words provides McGill with a puzzle. Who is the Signora? The answer leads him to a hotel room in Rome - and a man who has vowed to kill him on sight.

Commandante: **Patrick Cargill**

Guilio: **Maxwell Shaw**
Francesca: **Jeanne Roland**
Mori: **John Garrie**
Insurance Executive: **Robert Rietty**
Angela: **Norma Foster**
Giuseppe: **Clive Cazes**
Barman: **Guido Adorni**
Receptionist: **Carlos Douglas**

The Bridge
w **Robert Muller**
d **Pat Jackson**

Engaged to discover the truth behind a young man's attempt suicide, McGill uncovers more trouble than he bargained for in the shape of Annabelle Fenchurch.

Lord Gormond: **Bill Owen**
Annabelle Fenchurch: **Jane Merrow**
Sir Walter Fenchurch: **Anthony Nicholls**
Tim Gormond: **Rodney Bewes**
Danny: **Michael Culver**
Lady Gormond: **Maureen Pryor**
Rossiter: **Peter Birrel**
Lestrange: **Simon Williams**
Model Girl: **Judith Arthy**
Second Yobbo: **Christopher Coll**

The Man Who Stood Still
w **Raymond Bowers**
d **Peter Duffell**

Tricked into arranging a meeting between two old war comrades, McGill has a problem on his hands. One betrayed the other and seeks revenge - but which is which?

Gomez: **Rupert Davies**
Palma: **Cyril Shaps**
Teniente: **Alex Scott**
Luis: **Philip Bond**
Leocadia: **Jeanna L'Esty**
Paco: **Neville Becker**
Senora Gomez: **Hira Talfrey**
Spanish Taxi Driver: **Richard Montez**

Burden of Proof
w **Edmund Ward**
d **Peter Duffell**

Harry Faversham, the English adviser to a Central American republic, is accused of stealing the country's gold reserves. McGill is assigned to watch his movements - unobserved.

Harry Faversham: **John Gregson**
Carla Faversham: **Nicola Pagett**
Ambassador: **Roger Delgado**
Colonel Filipe Garcia: **Wolfe Morris**
Sir Charles Grainger: **Charles Lloyd Pack**
Detective Inspector Hedley: **Gerald Sim**
Captain Roman Guzman: **Oscar Quitak**
Porter: **Alistair Hunter**
Les: **John Railton**
Charlie: **Richard Coe**
Getulio: **Larry Taylor**
Croupier: **Allan Watts**
Club Manager: **John Chandos**

The Whisper
w **Morris Farhi**
d **Charles Crichton**

A difficult and, if he gets it wrong, unrewarding case for McGill. He must decide if Father Loyola, a Jesuit priest in Africa, is genuine - or a crook using his religion as a means to benefit himself.

Marcus Spencer : **Patrick Allen**
Father Loyola: **Colin Blakely**
Penelope Spencer: **Sheila Brennan**
Detective Inspector Samuels: **Wallace Eaton**
Corporal Salinge: **Clifton Jones**
Major Anderson: **Patrick Jordan**
Alfred Porter: **Jerold Wells**
Father General: **Brian Hawksley**
Alex: **Didi Sullivan**
Tchumbu: **Tommy Ansah**
Masekela: **Michael Williamson**
Memba: **Dick Offor**

Why They Killed Nolan
w **Donald Jonson**
d **Charles Crichton**

Framed for the murder of a seedy private investigator who came to him for advice, McGill has one chance to save himself and stay alive. He must find out why the man was killed - and by whom.

Nolan: **Sam Kydd**
Mrs Arnoldson: **Ursula Howells**
Arnoldson: **Griffith Jones**
Mrs Nolan: **Paula Byrne**
Taxi Driver: **Harold Goodwin**
Chauffeur: **Duncan Lamont**
Inspector George: **Russell Napier**
Angela: **Nike Arrighi**
Inspector Glenn: **John Lee**
Lodger: **Trevor Peacock**
Manageress: **Denise Buckley**
Librarian: **Myvanny Jenn**
P.C. Martin: **Norman Hartley**
Cashier: **Mark Elwes**

The Boston Square
w **Wilfred Greatorex**
d **Don Chaffey**

When a noted oceanographer disappears with secret information - the results of his research into commercial sea farming - his employers ask McGill to find out why. He ends up by fishing in murky and dangerous waters.

Packard: **Rex Everhart**
Rudnik: **Peter Arne**
Dalby: **Vincent Ball**
Sir Edric Coulsdon: **Basil Dignam**
Professor Leros: **Howard Goorney**
Desk Clerk: **Jose Berlinka**
American Official: **Robert Perceval**
Greek Airline Hostess: **Jeanna L'Esty**
Miss Lamb: **Alexandra Stevenson**
American Agent: **Edward Bishop**

Somebody Loses, Somebody ...Wins?
w **Jan Read**
d **John Glen**

McGill takes on a strange assignment in East Berlin - and finds himself back in the world of espionage, with the dormant embers of an almost-forgotten romance about to burst into flame again.

Johann Liebkind: **Godfrey Quigley**
Ruth: **Jacqueline Pearce**
Kommandant: **Philip Madoc**
MfS Colonel: **Carl Duering**

Oberfeld: **Paul Hansard**
Karl Braun: **Carl Bernard**
Ernst Liebkind: **Gordon Sterne**
Fedora: **Peter Hagar**
Official in Airport: **David Scheur**
Doorkeeper: **Derek Prentice**
Receptionist: **Wendy Hall**
Old Crone: **Gerda Koeppler**
Young German Woman: **Maria Warburg**
Singer: **Bettina Jonic**

Blind Spot
w **Victor Canning**
d **Jeremy Summers**

McGill is hired to protect a blind girl, the innocent victim of circumstances whose presence at the scene of a murder she could not see has brought threats to her life from a killer who has no knowledge of her handicap.

Henry Thibaud: **Marius Goring**
Marcelle: **Felicity Kendall**
Maurice: **Derek Newark**
Inspector Banard: **William Dexter**
Stephane: **Inigo Jackson**
Delucroix: **Michael Bates**
Leon: **Keith Marsh**
Madame Robart: **Gillian Lind**
Arlette: **Nina Haby**
Jeweller: **Constantinde Goguel**
First Thug: **Frank Maher**
Second Thug: **Terence Yorke**

No Friend of Mine
w **John Stanton**
d **Charles Crichton**

McGill finds himself a job in Africa as a mercenary and becomes involved in intrigue between white settlers and natives whose concept is 'Let the blood come, because after the blood comes freedom.'

Garfield Cameron: **Clive Morton**
Masuto: **Errol John**
Turner: **Allan Cuthbertson**
Governor: **Ralph Michael**
Patricia Baldwin: **Philippa Gail**
James Baldwin: **Peter Halliday**
Bates: **Harvey Hall**
Ringleader: **Danny Daniels**
Second African: **Horace James**
Smith: **Patrick Connell**

Jigsaw Man
w **Stanley R. Greenberg** and **Reed de Rouen**
d **Charles Frend**

McGill has the difficult task of piecing together two parts of a human jigsaw - two brothers, one of whom keeps running away from the huge family fortune. Why should this be? McGill seeks the answer.

Silvio: **Paul Bertroya**
Tony: **Michael Sarne**
Ugo: **Maurice Kaufmann**
Berger: **John Bluthal**
Ciro: **John Collin**
Louise: **Bridget Armstrong**
Francine: **Shivaun O'Casey**
Ivanna: **Nike Arrighi**
Marcia: **Brenda Lawrence**

Web With Four Spiders
w **Edmund Ward**
d **Robert Tronson**

Dr James Norbert, a brilliant American lawyer, receives photographs of himself in the arms of a girl. He assigns McGill to track down the person who took them - and discover why. Blackmail seems unlikely, Norbert has received no demands.

Doctor James Norbet: **Ray McAnally**
Martha: **Jacqueline Ellis**
Simon Croft: **Simon Oates**
Sir Giles Watkins: **Ralph Michael**
Joe Gulliver: **John Savident**
Johnson: **Warren Stanhope**
Lew Geraghty: **Lawrence James**
Frederick: **Edward Evans**
Philip Oliver: **Philip Bond**
Digby Haynes: **Edward Rhodes**
Jamieson: **Robert Macleod**
Commissionaire: **Frank Forsyth**
Taxi Driver: **Geoffrey Reed**
Tout: **David Cargill**
Johnny: **Anthony Doonan**
Girl: **Katie Fitzroy**
Pageboy: **Douglas Jones**

Which Way Did He Go, McGill?
w **Frances Megahy and Bernie Cooper**
d **Freddie Francis**

When a released prisoner searches for his share of the loot stolen in a major crime, McGill finds himself the unwilling pawn in a deadly treasure hunt - a game with danger on all sides.

Earle: **Donald Sutherland**
Joy: **Jennifer Jayne**
Soames: **Hugh McDermott**
Eddy: **J.G. Devlin**
Fulton: **Tom Criddle**
Norman: **Hedger Wallace**
Mrs Norman: **Veronica Hurst**
Detective Inspector Stoke: **Michael Hawkins**
Managing Director: **Frank Gatliff**
Douglas: **Henry Soskin**
Model: **Rachelle Miller**
Steward: **Frank Forsyth**
Detective Constable: **Kenneth Cowan**
Porter: **Basil Clarke**
Plainclothes Man: **Robert Pitt**
Helper in Stables: **Mary Maude**

Property of a Gentleman
w **Wilfred Greatorex**
d **Peter Duffell**

When a veteran actor gets carried away with the role he is playing and reveals the truth about a bizarre plot, McGill finds cause to have his gun ready to repel any emergency that springs to the fore.

Gerald Farson: **Terence Alexander**
Jane Farson: **Justine Lord**
Doctor James Vance: **Derek Francis**
Chester Farson/Gray: **Gordon Gostelow**
Auctioneer: **Frank Gatliff**
Porter: **Frederic Abbott**
Logan: **Victor Brooks**
Charles Farson: **Charles Hodgson**

The Revolutionaries
w **Jan Read** and **Peter Duffell** [from a story by **Kevin B. Laffan**]
d **Peter Duffell**

Seeking to help a political exile's campaign to restore his North African country to rightful rule, McGill takes on the

role of peace-maker - but finds himself up against ruthless men who wish to see him dead.

Dr Maza: **Hugh Burden**
Haider: **Ferdy Mayne**
Chantal: **Sonia Fox**
Nuri: **David Sumner**
Malouf: **Barry Shawzin**
Inspector Bergson: **Bruce Boa**
Tonia Colsen: **Marga Roche**
Amin: **Louis Negin**
Yuseef: **David Cargill**
Casim: **Nik Zaran**
Police Sergeant: **Hal Hamilton**
Pilot: **Mark Peterson**

Who's Mad Now?
w **Roger Parkes**
d **Freddie Francis**

Called in to help an old friend, McGill begins to wonder who is telling the truth. She says she is being followed, her husband says she's neurotic - who is right?

Jason: **Robert Hutton**
Joan: **Audine Leith**
Doctor Forsythe: **Philip Madoc**
Toby: **John Harvey**
Mrs Cuggen: **Harriette Johns**
Diana: **Luanshya Greer**
Williams: **Hedger Wallace**

Three Blinks of the Eyes
w **Vincent Tilsley**
d **Charles Crichton**

McGill has trouble on his hands - but that's nothing new. This time, however, he's been accused of murder, and faces the guillotine, unless he can find the wealthy woman who hired him to bring her playboy husband to heel.

Eleanor: **Faith Brook**
Bernard: **Drew Henley**
Examining Magistrate: **Charles Lloyd Pack**
Janine: **Dora Reisser**
Inspector Lamotte: **John Gabriel**
Gaoler: **Colin Jeavons**
Comere: **Yvette Herries**
Barman: **Hans De Vries**
Dancers: **Tony Kemp, Maggie Victer, Sandra Burville, Ann Chapman, Marlene Domanske, Cheryl St.Clair, Rene Satoris, Micheal Tye-Walker**

Castle in the Clouds
w **Jan Read**
d **Peter Duffell**

A senior servant's entanglement with a beautiful - but dangerous - adventures leads McGill into a delicate case with murder as the outcome. McGill finds himself chased by foreign agents seeking to right an injustice.

Sir Dennis Salt: **Gerald Flood**
Magda: **Gay Hamilton**
Ezard: **Edward Fox**
Reynolds: **Sydney Tafler**
Lady Carol Salt: **Rachel Herbert**
Senior Official: **Joseph Wise**
Saleslady: **Faith Kent**
Porter: **Will Stampe**
Girl Cleaner: **Jan Williams**
Newspaper Seller: **Arthur Griffiths**

Night Flight to Andora
w **Jan Read** and **Reed de Rouen**
d **Freddie Francis**

McGill takes on a desperate mission to engineer the release of an innocent victim held in a fortified mansion in the Pyrenees. But things begin to go wrong almost from the start. Why? Is there a traitor in his team?

Radek: **Peter Woodthorpe**
Rafael: **Zia Mohyeddin**
Anne Weeks: **Luanshya Greer**
Eddy: **Ewan Hooper**
Maxted: **Edward Underdown**
Buck: **Reed de Rouen**
Tomas: **Carlos Pierre**
Luis: **Robert Crewdson**
Butler: **Peter Swanwick**
Hotel Proprietor: **Frederick Beauman**
Police Officer: **Richard Montez**
Van Driver: **Charles Laurence**
Radek's Girl Friend: **Nita Lorraine**

📖

The Sleeping Cupid [1967: E.G Whitney: Daily Mirror Books: original story].

Man in a Suitcase:

Series created by: **Richard Harris** and **Dennis Spooner** [from an idea by **Stanley R. Greenberg**]
Producer: **Sidney Cole**
Associate Producer: **Barry Delmaine**
Music by: **Albert Elms**
Title Theme composed by: **Ron Grainer**
Executive Story Consultant: **Stanley R. Greenberg**
Script Editor: **Jan Read**
Production Manager: **Bert Pearl**
Casting Director: **Rose Tobias-Shaw**
Assistant Director: **Richard Kilburn, Doug Hermes**
Second Unit Director: **John Glen**
Stunt Arranger: **Roy Vincente**
Music Editor: **Alan Willis**
Make-up: **Jim Evans, Sylvia Croft**
Hairdressing: **Frieda Steiger, Blanche Arden**
Wardrobe Supervisor: **Kay Gilbert**

An ITC Production for ITC World Wide Distribution
Filmed on location and at Pinewood Studios

30 colour 60-minute episodes
1967

Man of the World

The photographic assignments of freelance photographer-cum-journalist-cum adventurer, Mike Strait. He's suave. He's debonair. He's a seasoned professional - 'a man with the world in his lens'. From the streets of Paris, to the sands of Egypt, he takes aim with his camera and shoots for adventure. In a world of beautiful women, ruthless criminals and international action, he's a Man of the World.

Mike Strait's assignments for the world's leading fashion magazines takes him all over the globe - and he is seldom far from trouble. Cameras are the tools of his trade, but intrigue and danger follow him like a magnet and he finds himself drawn into all kinds of exciting adventures.

A so-so adventure series that had lots of snap, but very little crackle or pop.

Regular cast:
Mike Strait: **Craig Stevens**
Maggie: **Tracey Reed**
Hank: **Graham Stark**

---

season one
13 monochrome 60-minute episodes
1962

Death of a Conference
w **Tudor Gates** and **Robert E. Thompson**
d **David Greene**

When a man falls dead from an assassin's bullet, with him die the hope for peace in a South American country. Mike Strait covers a peace conference - and becomes entangled in violence and double-dealing.

Maggie: **Tracey Reed** [intro]
Alex: **Warren Mitchell**
General Montreaux: **John Phillips**
Thiboeuf: **Patrick Troughton**
Madame Thiboeuf: **Zena Marshall**
Haddi: **Carl Jaffe**
Said: **John Carson**
Dolguib: **Mark Dignam**
Duchamp: **Gerald Flood**
Guard Captain: **Alan Rowe**
Hafiz: **David Graham**

Masquerade in Spain
w **Lindsay Hardy**
d **David Greene**

Assigned to take exclusive pictures of one of the world's richest women, Strait plunges deep into a web of kidnapping and murder - a fantastic plot involving himself and the girl as hostages.

Maggie: **Tracey Reed**
Hank: **Graham Stark** [intro]
Denzo: **Clifford Evans**
Cleo: **Marie France**
Melissa: **Christina Gregg**
Gomez: **George Coulouris**
Sebastian: **George Pastell**
Stavros: **Noel Coleman**
Martin: Guy **Kingsley Poynter**
Miguel: **Andreas Malandrinos**
Beauty Shop girl: **Malou Pantera**

Blaze of Glory
w **John Roddick**
d **Harry Booth**

When Strait meets an ace racing driver whose eyesight is failing, he sees a way to help the young man achieve his aim of winning a top racing rally - but someone waits in the background to spell disaster to their noble ambition.

Maggie: **Tracey Reed**
Kim: **Patricia Donahue**
Tony Gardner: **Peter Dyneley**
Mario Cirrano: **Eric Pohlmann**
Ricky Cirrano: **Norman Florence**
Dr Stelitz: **Martin Miller**
Shorty: **Dermot Kelly**
His friend: **Sheree Winton**
Policeman: **Victor Baring**
Nurse: **Jane Merrow**

The Runaways
w **Michael Pertwee**
d **Charles Crichton**

Strait's problem. How to ward off the overtures of a lovely runaway, a girl who falls in love with every man she meets - including Strait, who must solve the dilemma while staying romantically unattached.

Maggie: **Tracey Reed**
Hank: **Graham Stark**
Joanne: **Erica Rogers** [intro]
Mrs Van Kempson: **Renee Houston** [intro]
Martin: **Leon Peers**
Smedley: **Harvey Hall**
Lord Allwood: **Noel Harrison**
Johnson: **Gary Marsh**
Van Kempson: **Donald Stewart** [intro]

The Frontier
w **Lindsay Galloway**
d **Anthony Bushell**

On a photographic assignment close to the Indian-Chinese border, Strait becomes entangled in an Indian doctor's sacrifice to bring peace to a village threatened by a group of would-be dictators - a drama he would rather do without.

Hossari: **Gary Raymond**
Chang: **Peter Arne**
Dr Bahandi: **Leela Naidu**
High Lama: **Alfred Burke**
Liu: **Burt Kwouk**
Chou: **Eric Young**
Headman: **Bobby Naidoo**
Indian Sgt: **George Little**
Indian Medical Officer: **Mellan Mitchell**
Chinese Doctor: **Donald Chinn**

The Sentimental Agent
w **Jack Davies**
d **Charles Frend**

With Strait imprisoned for taking unauthorised pictures in a South American State, Maggie enlists the help of Carlos Borella, an import merchant, and rogue, to secure his release. Borella will help - for a price.

Borella: **Carlos Thompson**
Lee: **Shirley Eaton**
The Minister: **Peter Jones**
Maggie: **Tracey Reed**
Zapata: **Cyril Shaps**
Lopez: **John Hollis**
Driver: **Richard Montez**
Customs officer: **Steve Plytas**
Stefano: **George Eugeniou**
Consulate official: **Neville Becker**

Ramon: **Wilfred Grove**
Officer: **Ray Patrick**
Receptionist: **Liane Aukin**
Page: **Michael Caspi**
Guard: **Brian Hawkins**

✍ With a name change to Varela, Carlos Thompson starred in his own series *The Sentimental Agent*. [See entry under that name].

The Highland Story
w **Lindsay Galloway**
d **Charles Frend**

Assigned to report on the Scottish highland clan system, Strait finds the residents of a Scottish village, less than friendly to his cause. Why won't they talk about their 'sacred' highland traditions?

Maggie: **Tracey Reed**
Donald: **Finlay Currie**
Fiona: **Noelle Middleton**
The MacGillie: **John Laurie**
Charlie West: **Ray Barrett**
Alastair: **Andrew Downie**
Elspeth: **Ruth Lodge**
Archie, the piper: **Peter Sinclair**
Lachy: **John Rae**
Willie: **Kenneth Watson**
An Australian: **Barry Linehan**
His wife: **Patsy Smart**

The Nature of Justice
w **Tudor Gates**
d **Harry Booth**

Professor O'Connor has discovered a stone tablet with ancient engravings providing a possible link with one of the earliest civilisations. Assigned to cover the story, Strait finds himself entangled in a deadly web of suspicion and deceit.

O'Connor: **Robert Flemyng**
Sheikh Ibrahim Ben Said: **Bernard Archard**
Jane: **Jacqueline Ellis**
Gault: **Ewen Solon**
Ali: **Michael Mellinger**
Martin: **Glenn Beck**

The Mindreader
w **Ian Stuart Black**
d **David Greene**

Carla is believed to possess an uncanny telepathic power - one which enables her to read other people's minds. But does she? Mike Strait must seek out the truth - Carla's life, and sanity, depend on the outcome.

Carla: **Juliet Mills**
Linda: **Moira Redmond**
Downing: **Patrick Wymark**
Prof. Harding: **Charles Heslop**
Blyvus: **Leslie French**
Paul: **David Sumner**
Inspector Melton: **Jack Watson**
Policeman: **Alec Rose**
Galvano: **Ray Lewis**

Portrait of a Girl
w **Lindsay Galloway**
d **Charles Frend**

It's an ingenious scheme, to extract money from rich Americans by selling them fake Gainsborough paintings of

their 'ancestors'. Strait's investigations lead him to a fashion house with more than haute couture in its vaults.

Langford: **Colin Gordon**
Joanne: **Erica Rogers**
Van Kempson: **Donald Stewart**
Galworth: **Michael Goodliffe**
Sir Hugo Kempson: **Oliver Jonstone**
Landy Kempson: **Joyce Barbour**
Casey: **Neil McCarthy**

Specialist for the Kill
w **Lindsay Hardy**
d **Jeremy Summers**

It was meant to be a casual assignment in Berlin. But when Strait stumbles across an assassination attempt, the trip turns into a nightmare that cannot end until the photographer has unmasked a group of would-be killers.

Colonel Cutler: **Paul Maxwell** [intro]
Polikoff: **Derren Nesbitt**
Maggie: **Tracey Reed**
The Croat: **Ken Baker**
Nina: **Didi Sullivan**
General Oliver: **Gordon Tanner**
President Majcek: **George Pravda**
Frau Dorfer: **Marianne Deeming**
Stoll: **Oscar Quitak**
Abramov: **Gabor Baraker**
Guzik: **Frank Olegario**
Collins: **Sean Kelly**
Gretchen: **Audrey Wilson**
Hedi: **Maxine Spyrou**

A Family Affair
w **Norman Borisoff** and **Robert Thompson**
d **Anthony Bushell**

In Paris to photograph models, Strait's assignment begins with a bang when a fashion salon is rocked by an explosion. Someone is set upon wiping the competition off the fashion map. But whom? And Why?

Corbett: **Eugene Decker**
Inspector Sanglett: **Richard Warner**
Hele: **Lisa Page**
Duval: **Richard Leech**
Baron De Charlot: **Keith Pyott**
Henry Burton: **Alan Gifford**
Madame Duclos: **Hira Talfrey**
Mlle Danois: **Maria Corvin**
Midwesterner: **Paul Whitsun-Jones**
Monique: **Clemence Bettany**
Directrice: **Ruth Lodge**

Shadow of the Wall
w **Ian Stuart Black**
d **Harry Booth**

When his friend is arrested and charged with espionage in West Berlin, Strait finds himself the target of crossfire from a group of of terrorists plotting to overthrow a government minister.

Wilhelm: **Joseph Furst**
Colonel Cutler: **Paul Maxwell**
Linda: **Suzanne Neve**
Vesper: **Scott Finch**
Jorgens: **Charles Lloyd-Pack**
Bertha: **Sheila Raynor**
Director: **Nancy Nevinson**
Captain Wells: **Benedicta Leigh**
Policeman: **Steven Scott**
Driver: **Terence Fallon**

```
┌─────────────────────────────────┐
│           season two            │
└─────────────────────────────────┘
```
7 monochrome 60-minute episodes
1962

The Bandit
w John Pudney
d Charles Crichton

Working in Mexico, Strait becomes involved when a tempestuous film actress, kidnapped by a Sicilian bandit, shows apparent disregard to her plight - or the threats to her life. Why? Mike must 'rescue' the girl and snap out the truth.

Nicko: **Sam Wannamaker**
Maria: **Natasha Parry**
Gioti: **John Woodvine**
Polo: **John MacCarthy**
Tonio: **Peter Kriss**
Arturo: **Gertan Klauber**
Chivaro: **Robert Rietty**
Captain: **Michael Ritterman**
Peasant: **Raymond Ray**
Assistant Director: **Nigel Hawthorne**

The Enemy
w Julian Bond
d John Moxey

When an Italian doctor rejects 'civilisation' to work in the African jungle, Strait is handed the task of locating the doctor. The man was working on a new virus when he upped and left. Mike must confirm that the virus still exists.

Dr Moetti: **Anthony Quayle**
Souen: **Tai Chin**
Major Teong: **John Meillon**
Lt Hang: **John Hollis**
Nurse: **Dolores Dickon**
Orderly: **Pat Goh**

Double Exposure
w Jack Davies
d Jeremy Summers

It's a holiday - of sorts - behind the Iron Curtain. But trouble has a way of getting photographed by Mike's camera lens. This time to the aid of an eccentric woman to solve the mystery surrounding her missing son.

Mrs Rosewall: **Cecily Courtneidge**
Trina: **Erika Remberg**
Grabowsky: **Nigel Davenport**
Washington official: **John Tate**
Hotel manager: **Philo Hauser**
Karinski: **Dorothea Philips**
Night club singer: **Honora Burke**
Communist officer: **Marshall Jones**
Austrian officer: **Michael Segal**
Motorcyclist: **Brian Wright**
Cigarette girl: **Sally Douglas**

Jungle Mission
w Lindsay Galloway
d Harry Booth

Covering the story of a rebel leader in the Amazon, Strait encounters an order of nuns who run a jungle mission - one that has been the victim of several raids by guerrillas. Mike determines to help them - but how?

Perez: **Paul Maxwell**
Mother Superior: **Noelle Middleton**
Padrone: **Alexander Davion**

Luis: **George Eugeniou**
Garcia: **Alan Rowe**
Ananga: **Leo Carera**
Simon: **Frank Singuineau**
Acquilina: **Isobel Black**

In the Picture
w Brian Clemens
d John Moxey

Though he does not realise it at the time, a picture Strait has taken reveals the secret behind a plot to assassinate a mid-European president. When the would-be killers gain this knowledge, the villains move in - and a killer has Strait in his sights!

Maria: **Nadja Regin**
Troyan: **Albert Lieven**
President: **Wensley Pithey**
Klos: **Michael Shaw**
Debar: **Peter Madden**
Pec: **Edward Cast**
Lecha: **Maurice Kaufmann**
Chamacy: **Bartlett Mullins**
Sphela: **Andre Maranne**
Van driver: **Harry De Bray**
House servant: **Max Faulkner**
Gallery assistant: **Jean Rollins**
Security guard: **Brandon Brady**
Hotel receptionist: **Earl Greene**

The Bullfighter
w Marc Brandel
d Harry Booth

In Spain to take pictures of a promising young bullfighter, Strait cannot fathom why an air of mystery surrounds the man. Supplied with the answer, he realises that this time he will need more than a camera lens to ensure that he completes his assignment.

Carmen: **Maria Landi**
Luiz: **Joseph Cuby**
Catrina: **Eileen Way**
Garcia: **Richard Montez**
Rivera: **John Bailey**
Ramos: **Ferdy Mayne**
Dr Sanchez: **Michael Peake**
Rodriguez: **George Street**
General: **Reginald Jarman**
Flamenco dancer: **Juanita Brunnel**
Flamenco dancer: **Ramon Tillar**
Flamenco singer: **Carlos Basillsco**
Guitarist: **Enrique Bejerano**

The Prince
w Arthur Berlin
d Charles Crichton

Strait helps to establish the true identity of a young boy who, kidnapped seven years earlier, reappears and claims to be the heir to the throne. But is he? And how will Mike prove it to people disinclined to accept the results of his investigations?

Count Maximillian Korvin: **Geoffrey Keen**
Tulan: **Michael Sirr**
Susan Forrester: **Ann Gillis**
Forrester: **Warren Stanhope**
Miss Bentley: **Enid Lorrimer**
Anna: **Sylva Langova**
Burton: **Larry Cross**
Carter: **Robert Arden**
Sergeant: **Bill Edwards**
Asian girl: **Marie Yang**

Man of the World:

Produced by: **Harry Fine**
Executive Producer: **Leslie Harris**
Theme   music 'Man of the World' by: **Henry Mancini**
Director of music: **Ivor Slaney**
Production Supervisor: **Barry Delmaine**
Script Editor: **Ian Stuart Black**
Production Manager: **Raymond Kerba**
Casting Director: **Irene Lamb**
Assistant Director: **Ron Jackson**
Location Director: **Harry Booth**
Make-up: **Colin Garde**
Hairdressing: **Helene Bevan**
Wardrobe: **Larry Stewart**
Clothes created by members of the **Fashion Group of London**

An ATV Production for ITC Presentation
Made on location and at Shepperton Studios

20 monochrome 60-minute episodes
1962

O.S.S.

A series of spy adventures with a difference - each story related to actual events which took place in the tense atmosphere of World War II.

This well-made collection of espionage adventures told the story of the O.S.S. [Office of Strategic Services, America's counter-espionage organisation - a forerunner of the CIA and wartime equivalent of Britain's MI5], and in particular, the exploits of ace spy-smasher, Major Frank Hawthorne.

The series showed how its members operated in the most hazardous conditions possible ...how they infiltrated enemy lines... and the assistance they gave to the members of the Resistance Movements who fought to disrupt Hitler's intelligence system.

'This is an agent of the O.S.S., one of the faceless,
nameless enemy who fought the lonely war,
the silent war on the fighting fronts and behind enemy
lines - until now, stories untold of heroes unknown.
This is a mission from the annals of the O.S.S. -
the Office of Strategic Services'.

Regular cast:
Major Frank Hawthorne: **Ron Randell**
Chief: **Lionel Murton**
Sgt O'Brien [not all episodes]: **Robert Gallico**

Operation Foulball
w **Paul Dudley**
d **Robert Siodmak**

Posing as an army deserter, Major Frank Hawthorne joins a resistance movement. Captured, he learns the story of two brothers who have mounted a successful campaign by feeding false information on V.1 rockets to the Germans.

James: **Lyndon Brook**
Bill: **Patrick Holt**
Sheila: **Naomi Chance**
MI5 agent: **Frank Hawkins**
General: **Robert Henderson**

Operation Big House
w **Manning O'Brine** and **Paul Dudley**
d **Laurence Huntington**

The O.S.S. want some documents from a safe in the Germany Embassy in Rome. Rafferty cracked a safe of the same model in 1938. Trouble is, he's serving time in Dartmoor. Frank Hawthorne is put in prison to convince the man to help - and engineer Rafferty's escape!

Rafferty: **Leonard Sharp**
Luigi: **Roger Delgado**
German Ambassador: **Patrick Waddington**
Secretary: **John Van Eyssen**
U.S.S. Driver: **Gilbert Winfield**
Prison guard: **Alan Rolfe**
Fascist: **Derek Sydney**
Prison Governor: **John Stuart**

Operation Flint Axe
w **Paul Dudley**
d **Robert Siodmak**

Frank's mission is to find some important papers hidden in Paris by one of his O.S.S. colleagues who is missing and believed to have turned traitor. Arriving in Paris, Frank narrowly escapes capture. Who tipped off the Germans?

Joe Hinds: **Robert Rietty**
Lucille: **Zena Marshall**

Colonel Williams: **Barry Keegan**
Doctor: **Donald Stewart**
Ann Hinds: **Patricia Plunkett**
German Officer: **Carl Duering**

Operation Lovebird
w **Paul Dudley**
d **Pennington Richards**

In order to free his wife who is being held captive, German agent Van Kuhl, offers to work for the English and supply Major Hawthorne with a briefcase containing German Documents of interest to the O.S.S. But Van Kuhl's love for his wife carries a sting in its tail.

Van Kuhl: **Edwin Richfield**
Carla: **Jan Holden**
Courier: **Cyril Chamberlain**
Nazi Officer: **Theodore Wilheim**
Crewman: **Tom Watson**

Operation Tulip
w **Paul Dudley**
d **Peter Maxwell**

Frank joins the Dutch underground to sabotage a German submarine that's nearing completion. The first attempt at blowing up the submarine fails. Prompted by the first incident, the Germans place a number of hostages aboard to forestall a second attempt.

Karger: **Dennis Shaw**
Kimmel: **Frederick Piper**
Ilse: **Sandra Dorne**
Favermann: **Donald Masters**
Van Groot: **William Thorpe Devereaux**
Bruehl: **Howard Lang**
Sentry: **Peter Taylor**
Hendrick: **Peter Swanwick**
Otto Weiner: **Thomas Foulkes**
Kommandant: **Walter Gotell**

Operation Sweet Talk
w **Paul Dudley**
d **Pennington Richards**

Frank must convince a young dancer, Kyro Caro, to do a job for the O.S.S. and protect her while she is doing it. German agents, Klaus and Fischer have other ideas and plant a bomb in Caro's apartment.

Kyro Caro: **Laya Raki**
Fischer: **Edwin Richfield**
General: **Robert Perceval**
Oliver: **Charles Irwin**
Klaus: **Jerome Wells**

Operation Fracture
w **Paul Dudley**
d **Peter Maxwell**

Ordered to Schweinfort to find out who is leaking information to the enemy, Frank bails out during a raid over the city with a faked head wound. Regaining consciousness, he finds himself in an American army hospital - but is everything as it appears?

Nurse: **Rene Goddard**
US Doctor: **James Dyrenforth**
Corporal: **Ryck Rydon**
Batman: **Oscar Quitak**
Co-pilot: **Bob O'Neal**
Doctor: **Arthur Bentley**
Kellerman: **Brian Haines**

Hill Billy: **John Turner**
US Sergeant : **Robert Gallico**
Franz: **Graham Stewart**
Pilot: **Murray Cash**

Operation Death Trap
w **Paul Dudley** and **Robert Spafford**
d **Laurence Huntington**

Josette, a Parisian underground agent, has been caught by the Nazis and is being tortured in an effort to force her to divulge the identity of other French agents. Frank's mission is to arrange her escape - or kill her - before the Germans force a confession.

Kolonel: **Gerard Heinz**
Simon: **Guy Deghy**
Jean Pierre: **Michael David**
Doctor: **Stanley Van Beers**
Nazi guard: **Ronald Fraser**
Josette: **Jeanette Sterke**
Pillette: **Richard Molinas**
Raoul: **Patrick Jordan**
Claude: **Jacques Cey**
Labourdet: **Rudolf Offenbach**
Soldier: **David Williams**

Operation Orange Blossom
w **Paul Dudley**
d **Laurence Huntington**

Frank and Virginia, another O.S.S. agent, journey to Casablanca. Posing as newly-weds, they must find and capture an enemy agent called Rolo. Their mission is dangerous: to flush out the enemy, the Chief has circulated rumours that the newly-weds are working for the O.S.S.!

Virginia: **Lois Maxwell**
Loder: **Lloyd Lamble**
Marina: **Irene Prador**
French girl: **Yvonne Warren**
Hotel Clerk: **John Gabriel**
Shelley: **Derek Prentice**
Matthews: **Morris Sweden**
Petty Officer: **Ronald Brand**
Sailor: **Edward Ballard**

Operation Meatball
w **Paul Dudley**
d **Peter Maxwell** and **Peter Wrestler**

Frank joins three Canadian special force members to blow up the Vonhelmet Experimental Laboratory in Germany. They accomplish their mission, but their plan backfires when the only man who knew their escape route is found dead.

Mike: **Ryck Rydon**
Patsy: **Franklyn Fox**
Frenchy: **Gaylord Cavallaro**
Ilse: **Leslie Dudley**
Kommandant: **Richard Shaw**
Kapitan: **Tom Bowman**
Nazi officer: **John Unicomb**
Brig. General: **Robert Henderson**

Operation Powder Puff
w **Paul Dudley**
d **Robert Siodmak**

Frank, with the help of MI5 agent Foxie, travels to France to blow up a bridge which provides the Germans with a supply line for the German army. Joined by Gabrielle, a member of the French underground, they successfully blow up the bridge - with a little help from 'Hitler'!

Peter Fox: **Francis Matthews**
Gabrielle: **Sheila Brennan**
Max: **Patrick Jordan**
Jean: **Howard Lang**
German guard: **John Heller**
Nun: **John Cazabon**
Brig. Bosville: **Arnold Diamond**
Madam Mureax: **Enid Lorimer**
Suzy: **Caroline Sheldon Williams**
Kommandant: **Carl Jaffe**
Navy Lt.: **John Crowest**
Children from the **Aida Foster School**

Operation Payday
w **Paul Dudley**
d **Pennington Richards**

Replacing another agent killed in action, Frank travels to Italy carrying several thousand lira for the Italian troops - unaware that Cesare, his contact, has been forced by a gang of black marketeers to reveal when the money is expected. A game of cat and mouse ensues, and Frank is captured.

Cesare: **Thomas Duggan**
Marco: **Clive Carson**
Maria: **Sandra Francis**
Tullio: **Martin Benson**
Guido: **Victor Baring**

Operation Yodel
w **Paul Dudley**
d **Laurence Huntington**

American turncoats are being smuggled into Germany from Switzerland to act as spies. Posing as an American, Frank joins the traitors to find out why and unmask the man heading the operation. Met by Suzanne, a German agent, they board a plane - for London!

Suzanne: **Paula Byrne**
Schneider: **Jimmy Karoubi**
Doctor: **Alastair Hunter**
Creman: **Max Faulkner**
Rawston: **Reginald Hearne**

Operation Blue Eyes
w **Paul Dudley**
d **Pennington Richards**

Frank's mission: to blow up a factory in Milan. Joined by "Blue Eyes," an Italian agent, they travel to Italy posing as doctor and nurse. En route, they are stopped by a German officer and forced to perform an appendectomy on his commander.

Blue Eyes: **Lisa Gastoni**
Radio Sgt.: **John Valentine**
Nazi officer: **Bernard Hunter**
Ober-Lieut.: **Peter Reynolds**
Pietro: **Bill Fraser**

Operation Chopping Block
w **Paul Dudley**
d **Robert Day**

Dropped over Germany to blow up a factory which manufactures booby traps, Frank and O.S.S. operative, Foxie, are captured when the Germans set up a drag net to catch a man named Schuster, whose family has been killed by the Germans. Insane, and bent on vengeance, Schuster has wired up the surrounding area to explode!

Foxie: **Leslie Phillips**
Zero: **Morris Sweden**

Kommandant: **Wolf Frees**
Eckler: **Tony Doonan**
Schuster: **John Gabriel**
Cabbie: **George Tovey**
Nazi officer: **Max Faulkner**
M.I.5 agent: **Frank Hawkins**
Zero's sister: **Anita Sharpe-Bolster**

Operation Dagger
w **Paul Dudley**
d **Pennington Richards**

Sent to France to bring back a lone wolf French patriot whose activities are embarrassing the organised Maquis, Frank meets Le Couteau, but they are attacked by Germans and Frank takes a wound in the leg. They take refuge in a large country house owned by a retired French General - which the Germans attack in force.

Le Couteau: **Michael Ripper**
General Latour: **Esmond Knight**
Madame Latour: **Nora Swinburne**
Abwehr Lieut: **Geoffrey Bayldon**
Abwehr Oberst von Bloch: **Ferdy Mayne**
Gendarme: **Reginald Hearne**
German Officer: **Tom Naylor**

Operation Jingle Bells
w **Paul Dudley**
d **Allan Davis**

It's Christmas, but Frank has to leave on a mission to Europe to rescue two O.S.S. agents before they are interrogated by the Gestapo. Helped by a member of the resistance and his two young sons, Frank's mission is placed in jeopardy when the boys find a bar of chocolate in his ration bag - chocolate that is poisoned!

Rene: **Stuart Guidotti**
Jean: **George Howell**
Eilers: **Tom Busby**
McGaffery: **Vivian Matalon**
Nazi leader: **Cyril Wheeler**
First Nazi: **Tony Shepherd**
Second Nazi: **John Cronin**
First Nazi Patrol: **Alan Wilson**
Second Nazi Patrol: **Reginald Hearne**
Waitress: **Pauline Winter**
Flt. Sgt. : **Robin Gammel**
Papa: **Billy Milton**
US General: **Robert Percival**

Operation Post Office
w **Paul Dudley**
d **Laurence Huntington**

Matelon, a French, scientist, is rescued from the Germans and brought to London where it is hoped he will co-operate with the Allies. He will not - until his wife is brought to join him and they can go to America. Frank, sent to Paris to bring back Matelon's wife, finds that she has been poisoned.

Matelon: **Richard Bebb**
Gizi: **Sandra Dorne**
Hartley: **Reed de Rouen**
Schneider: **Gerard Heinz**
Doctor: **Charles Stapley**
Mireaux: **Conrad Phillips**
Junior officer: **George Mikell**

Operation Eel
w **Paul Dudley**
d **Robert Siodmak**

Frank is sent to North Africa to find a pilot who knows the location of the mines in a channel leading to Port Lyauty so that a force can capture it. Contacted by another O.S.S. agent, they arrange to smuggle the pilot over the French border in an oil drum.

US Capt: **Robert Ayres**
Jones: **James Hayter**
Schneider: **Anton Diffring**
German Minister: **Neal Arden**
Dancer: **Jane Dore**
Spahi Major: **Peter Burton**
Club Manager: **Arthur Brander**
Aran Vendor: **Richard Golding**
Dupont: **Rupert Davies**
Doctor: **Frank Sieman**
Girl at Bar: **Joy Webster**
French officer: **Tony Thawnton**
French soldier: **John Dearth**

Operation Sardine
w **Paul Dudley**
d **Allan Davis**

Frank travels to Begen in a two-man submarine. His mission: to sabotage the Athletic Club which is used by the Gestapo to keep their shipping records. Frank will be helped by Dr Henri, the method to be used, an explosive charge concealed in a thermos flask. But the doctor is betrayed and taken prisoner.

Lt. Patrick: **Gerald Harper**
Dr. Henri: **Gerik Schjelderup**
Inga: **Ellen Blueth**
Kurt: **Carl Conway**
Neilson: **Brian Sheeny**
Kommandant: **Arthur Lawrence**
Voice: **Raymond Lulham**
German: **Charles Stapley**

Operation Yo Yo
w **Paul Dudley**
d **Pennington Richards**

Sent as a replacement to the U.S. Third Army in Germany to find a German agent, Frank is accompanied by Captain Crawford. Fired at when they parachute into Germany, Frank manages to fight the enemy off, but Crawford refuses to use his gun. He then has to reveal to Frank, that he is an army Chaplain.

Crawford: **John Crawford**
U.S. Sgt.: **Bill Edwards**
Pilot: **David Graham**
Co-pilot: **Don Mason**
Mike: **Franklyn Fox**
Field Comm.: **Cyril Chamberlain**
Junior officer: **Timothy Grey**
Sergeant : **Ryck Rydon**

Operation Barbecue
w **Paul Dudley**
d **Allan Davis**

Four ships carrying cargoes of magnesium, vital for making aircraft metal, have been blown up under cover of air raids. It is believed that the ships were sabotaged by a member of the crew. Equipped with a bomb detector, Frank signs on as a replacement member of the crew.

Bosville: **Basil Dignam**
Whitey Svensson: **Christopher Rhodes**
Joe Sammis: **Robert Arden**

Bull Hoolahan: **Thomas Gallagher**
Sam: **Lionel Ngakane**
Girl Singer: **Diane Todd**
First Seaman: **Michael Kelly**
Second Seaman: **Robin Gamel**
M.I.5 Man: **John Witty**
Music Shop Proprietor: **James Hayter**

Operation Blackbird
w **Paul Dudley**
d **Laurence Huntington**

Posing as a medical orderly, Frank joins some wounded airmen, who are being flown back to the States. One of the airmen has been supplying the Germans with information about bombing raids. Frank must expose him and bring the man to justice - but his mission has been sabotaged.

Olson: **Sheldon Lawrence**
Sammartino: **Gaylord Cavallaro**
Tex Norton: **Kerrigan Prescott**
Kolinski: **Murray Kash**
Karl Wagner: **Franklyn Fox**
Flight Medic: **Gordon Stern**
First Pilot: **Gerry Stovin**
Nurse: **Joanne Dainton**
Military Policeman: **Roland Brand**
Intruder: **Kenneth Midwood**
Second Pilot: **John Bay**
Radio Officer: **Harry Moor**
Navigator: **Bill Edwards**

Operation Newsboy
w **Paul Dudley**
d **Laurence Huntington**

Frank thinks up an idea whereby pictures of Buchenwald Prison Camp can be dropped into Germany to make the troops see what their leaders are capable of and, it is hoped, will stop fighting in disgust.

Editor: **Lloyd Lamble**
Falkenburg: **Neil Hallett**
Gunther: **Ronald Leigh-Hunt**
Ella: **Sarah Lawson**
Flight Sgt.: **Donald Aulds**

Operation Firefly
w **Paul Dudley**
d **Pennington Richards**

American agent Bob Ferry has been captured in Brussels while in possession of a valuable piece of microfilm. Someone betrayed him and Frank is sent to Belgium with a bomb concealed in a pencil. His mission: to expose the informer, bring Ferry home and destroy the microfilm before the German's discover its secrets.

Dessinger: **Christopher Lee**
Ferry: **Gordon Tanner**
Emil: **Esmond Knight**
First Nazi: **Edward Judd**
General Kroll: **Carl Jaffe**
First Farmer: **Howard Lang**
Second Farmer: **Clifford Buckton**
Peasant: **Antony Sheppard**

Operation Buried Alive

sans info

O.S.S.:

Producer: **Jules Buck**
Associate Producer: **Robert Pik**
Executive Producers: **Joseph Harris** and **William Eliscu**
Production Supervisor: **Ted Lloyd**

A Robert Siodmak Production in Association with LSQ
An ITC and Buckeye Enterprises Production

26 monochrome 30-minute episodes
1957

The Persuaders!

Take Daniel Wilde, an irrepressible, fun-loving American who had dragged his way out of the New York slums, and made [and lost] his first million before his thirtieth birthday. A man with a remarkable talent for making money - but who used that gift solely to squander away his riches pursuing the life of an international thrill-seeking playboy. Team him with Lord Brett Sinclair, a 'flower of the British aristocracy', a man born to a family motto of honour, justice and fair play - but who had side-stepped his pedigree in favour of womanising, fast cars and an easy lifestyle; and add Judge Fulton, a retired lawkeeper who had spent his life defending the innocent and punishing the guilty, while watching the justice he served to allow others not worthy of its mercy to slip through the net to continue their life of crime.

Put them together and you had The Persuaders, two daredevil playboys seeking adventure who were blackmailed into becoming the lawman's 'instrument of justice' - defenders of the law as dispensed by Judge in his campaign to rid the world of villainy.

Projected to run for five seasons of 26 episodes, the series was cancelled when it failed to attract an audience in the US [it was beaten to the punch by *Mission Impossible* - then at the height of its success] and only 24 episodes were produced.

A glossy, lively comedy/suspense adventure series which earned its stars a fortune - for playing themselves!

Regular cast:
Danny Wilde: **Tony Curtis**
Lord Brett Sinclair: **Roger Moore**
Judge Fulton: **Laurence Naismith**

Overture
w **Brian Clemens**
d **Basil Dearden**

Danny and Brett set out on their first assignment - to find a brunette whose heart-shaped birthmark could prove her real identity. An exciting prospect, but one that leads them into danger and intrigue.

Judge Fulton: **Laurence Naismith**
Maria: **Imogen Hassall**
Coley: **Alex Scott**
Dupont: **Michael Godfrey**
Maitre D: **Bruno Barnabe**
Inspector Flavel: **Neal Arden**
Triver: **John Acheson**

The Gold Napoleon
w **Val Guest**
d **Roy Ward Baker**

Is there gold beneath the bronze of Napoleon gold replicas? That's what Danny and Brett must find out - providing someone allows them do so - after setting up Danny as a real live [but almost dead] target.

Michelle Devigne: **Susan George**
Pullicino: **Alfred Marks**
Judge Fulton: **Laurence Naismith**
Devigne: **Harold Goldblatt**
Vernier: **Michael McStay**
Chief of Police: **Hugh Manning**
Jacoby: **Charles Houston**
Sister: **Balbina**
Hospital Porter: **Hugo De Vernier**
Douane: **Jean Driant**

Take Seven
w **Terry Nation**
d **Sidney Hayers**

The mysterious reappearance of a 'long lost brother' seeking his share of a rich estate finds the Persuaders in the firing line when they try to help a young girl with family problems on her mind.

Jenny Lindley: **Sinead Cusack**
Judge Fulton: **Laurence Naismith**
Mark Lindley: **Christian Roberts**
Maggie: **Sue Lloyd**
The Farmer: **Victor Platt**
Peter Hayward: **Garfield Morgan**
David Conron: **Richard Hurndall**
Harvester: **John Kelland**
The Secretary: **Veronica Hurst**
Mandy: **Julie Crossthwait**
The Major: **Colin Vancao**

Greensleeves
w **Terence Feely**
d **David Greene**

When a derelict old mansion suddenly reopens its doors without the knowledge of its owner, Brett Sinclair, Danny finds new employment - as butler to Brett, who impersonates himself to uncover the mystery.

Melanie Sadler: **Rosemary Nicols**
Richard Congoto: **Cy Grant**
Sir John Hassocks: **Andrew Keir**
Piers Emerson: **Tom Adams**
Carmen Congoto: **Carmen Munroe**
Dr. Kibu: **Clifton Jones**
Jackson: **Michael Martin**
Gregory Ward: **George Woodbridge**
Benny Ryan: **Tommy Godfrey**
Moorehead: **Arthur Brough**
Leyland: **Robert Cawdron**

Powerswitch
w **John Kruse**
d **Basil Dearden**

A dead girl found floating in a Cote d'Azur bay. Her beautiful flatmate with something to hide. Two pieces of a puzzle that plunge Danny and Brett into dangerous waters - inhabited by human sharks.

Pekoe: **Annette Andre**
Judge Fulton: **Laurence Naismith**
Crane: **Terence Alexander**
Lisa: **Melissa Stribling**
Koestler: **John Phillips**
Quinn Travis: **Lionel Blair**
Inspector Blanchard: **Paul Whitsun-Jones**
Ravel: **Les Crawford**
Rent-A-Car Girl: **Vicki Woolf**

The Time and the Place
w **Michael Pertwee**
d **Roger Moore**

Beautiful girls and the Persuaders go hand in hand. But when the playboys offer to help a young girl stranded on a country road, the 'damsel in distress' proves quite incapable of keeping her honour.

Lord Croxley: **Ian Hendry**
Marie: **Anna Palk**
Ryder: **Patrick O'Connell**
Sir George: **Robert Flemyng**
T.V. Interviewer: **David Rees**
Prime Minister: **Basil Dignam**
Benton: **Duncan Lamont**
Marsden: **Terence Sewards**

Porter: **Campbell Singer**
The General: **Geoffrey Toone**
Traffic Warden: **Olga Lowe**

Someone Like Me
w **Terry Nation**
d **Roy Ward Baker**

One Brett Sinclair is almost too much for Danny to handle, but two prove unbearable - particularly when Danny finds himself on the receiving end of the fake Brett's activities. Danny's dilemma: who is the real one and who is the impostor?

Dr. Fowler: **Reginald Marsh**
Nurse Crane: **Anne De Vigier**
Sam Milford: **Bernard Lee**
Miss Lindsay: **Joanne Dainton**
Scott Maskell: **Jeremy Burnham**
David Alton: **Tony Wright**
Dr. Gordon: **Gerald Sim**
Charlie: **Johnny Briggs**
Danny's Girl: **Vivien Neves**
Brett's Girl: **Diana Terry**

Anyone Can Play
w **Tony Williamson**
d **Leslie Norman**

Danny discovers a gold mine. Gambling in a Brighton casino and finding he isn't allowed to lose, he plays for high stakes - and finds that he has difficulty in disposing of his winnings. Until death plays its hand.

Lyn: **Cyd Hayman**
Heather: **Dudley Foster**
Ryker: **Ed Devereaux**
Sir Maxwell Dean: **Richard Vernon**
Webster: **Tim Goodman**
Pelli: **Patrick Jordan**
Train Guard: **Patrick Connor**
London Agent: **Christopher Coll**
Northern Agent: **Graham Weston**
Inspector Langford: **Peter Forbes-Robertson**
Croupier: **Kit Taylor**

The Old, the New and the Deadly
w **Brian Clemens**
d **Leslie Norman**

Birds have always been Danny's weakness - the female variety of course. But when he becomes involved with a fanatical ex-Nazi, a girl who is trying to clear her father's name, and a statuette of a bird, he's guaranteed to make the feathers fly.

Suzy: **Anna Gael**
Groski: **Derren Nesbitt**
Verner: **Kenneth J. Warren**
Prue: **Juliet Harmer**
Marceau: **Patrick Troughton**
Frank: **Gary Cockrell**
Serena: **Jasmina Hilton**
Luther: **Frederick Jaeger**
Denton: **Michael Segal**
Hotel Desk Clerk: **Michael Anthony**

Angie. . . Angie
w **Milton S. Gelman**
d **Val Guest**

A weekend of fun and champagne at the Cannes Film Festival turns into a deadly life-taking scenario, when Danny meets up with Angie, a boyhood friend from the Bronx - a man with murder on his mind.

Angie: **Larry Storch**
Judge Fulton: **Laurence Naismith**
Ben: **Lionel Murton**
Marissa: **Kirsten Lindholm**
Kyle Sandor: **John Alderson**
Bank Secretary: **Anna Brett**
Madame La Gata: **Rose Alba**

Chain of Events
w **Terry Nation**
d **Peter Hunt**

Life under canvas for Brett means deep freezers and feather beds, while Danny makes do with roughing it. So while Brett digests his ready-made breakfast, Danny casts a fishing line to catch his - and hooks a load of trouble for both of them.

Emily: **Suzanna Leigh**
Schubert: **Peter Vaughan**
Britten: **George Baker**
Dr. Rogers: **John Glyn-Jones**
Beecham-Bennett: **Morris Perry**
Police Constable: **Neil Wilson**
Previn: **James Beckett**
Carlton: **Jeremy Child**
Bill Wilton: **James Bree**

That's Me Over There
w **Brian Clemens**
d **Leslie Norman**

Thaddeus Krane has grown fat on famine and wealthy on war. Someone is out to expose him for the crook he is - which results in the informer being killed, Brett being kidnapped and Danny posing as a not-so-likely English Lord!

Thaddeus Krane: **Geoffrey Keen**
Ann Summers: **Suzan Farmer**
Judge Fulton: **Laurence Naismith**
Colonel Wright: **Allan Cuthbertson**
Prue: **Juliet Harmer**
Cliff Turner: **Terence Edmond**
Prentice: **Neil Hallett**
Mather: **Peter Gilmore**
Lloyd: **Derek Newark**
Auctioneer: **John Stone**
Fat Man: **Patrick Newell**

The Long Goodbye
w **Michael Pertwee**
d **Roger Moore**

The discovery by Danny and Brett of a skeleton in a crashed plane in the Scottish Highlands leads the two thrill-seekers into an adventure from which they emerge smelling ever-so-slightly from murder.

Sir Hugo Chalmers: **Leo Genn**
Carla Wilks: **Nicola Pagett**
Judge Fulton: **Laurence Naismith**
Theopolos: **Noel Willman**
Carla I: **Madeline Smith**
Carla II: **Anouska Hempel**
Jenson: **Brian Jackson**
Boris: **Glynn Edwards**
Piper: **Peter Sallis**
Space Queen: **Valerie Leon**
Little Girl: **Deborah Moore**

The Man in the Middle
w **Donald James**
d **Leslie Norman**

When Brett is captured while trying to trap a British traitor and Danny has to rescue him before his cover is blown, who better to help him than another noble Sinclair - Archibald Sinclair Beauchamp. A mistake - as Danny discovers to his cost.

Archie: **Terry Thomas**
Kay: **Suzy Kendall**
Krilov: **Stephen Greif**
Jones: **Frank Maher**
Gregor: **John Orchard**
Donkey Cart Driver: **Michael Balfour**
David Price: **Stanley Meadows**
Senka: **Geraldine Moffatt**
Smith: **Richard Burrell**

Element of Risk
w **Tony Barwick**
d **Gerald Mayer**

When someone mistakes Danny for the undisputed mastermind of crime, a planner of pure genius, Danny is prepared to play along - even though his life depends on the outcome. Brett meanwhile has troubles of his own.

Charlie: **June Ritchie**
Mitchell: **Peter Bowles**
Judge Fulton: **Laurence Naismith**
Carl: **William Marlowe**
Lomax: **Shane Rimmer**
Anderson: **J. M. Bay**
Joan: **Karen Kessey**
Jean: **Katherine Kessey**
The Farmer: **Victor Platt**
The Lieutenant: **Bob Sherman**
Colonel Adler: **David Healy**
Grant: **Anthony Doonan**
Inspector Williams: **James Cosmo**
Sophie: **Margaret Nolan**
Girl at Airport: **Carol Cleveland**
Radio Operator: **Michael Sloan**
Kramer: **George Fisher**

A Home of One's Own
w **Terry Nation**
d **James Hill**

When Danny buys a 'little piece of England' - a cottage in the country - and the locals turn nasty, his dreams of becoming an English squire end up in ashes. Brett meanwhile meets a lady birdwatcher - who carries a gun!

Lucy: **Hannah Gordon**
Rupert Hathaway: **John Ronane**
Abel Gaunt: **Leon Greene**
Policeman: **Michael Wynne**
The Poacher: **Talfryn Thomas**
Walden: **Michael Sheard**

Five Miles to Midnight
w **Terry Nation**
d **Val Guest**

Opening a travel business can have its drawbacks, as Danny and Brett discover when their first customer turns up to be Frank Rocco, a New York hoodlum on the run from a gang of Italian mobsters.

Sidonie: **Joan Collins**

Frank Rocco: **Robert Hutton**
Judge Fulton: **Laurence Naismith**
Torino: **Robert Rietty**
Sangallo: **Ferdy Mayne**
Nicola: **Jean Marsh**
Brusati: **Arnold Diamond**
Vasile: **Ian Thompson**
Manny Howard: **Robert Gallico**

Nuisance Value
w **David Rolfe** and **Tony Barwick**
d **Leslie Norman**

When someone forcibly takes away Danny's latest girlfriend, heiress to a fantastic fortune, the Bronx-born playboy and his partner Lord Brett Sinclair decide to nip their adversary's passion-flower in the bud - with somewhat unexpected results.

Lisa: **Viviane Ventura**
Zorakin: **George Murcell**
Mary: **Sarah Lawson**
Michel: **Ralph Bates**
Kurt: **Michael Culver**
Patterson: **David Cargill**
Inspector Santos: **Ricardo Montez**
Matra: **Clive Cazes**
Bodega Landlord: **George Roderick**

The Morning After
w **Walter Black**
d **Leslie Norman**

When Brett awakens after a heavy night's drinking party and finds he has a wife - a very glamorous one, too - it takes more than Danny's friendship to untangle the surrounding web of intrigue.

Kristin: **Catherine Schell**
Judge Fulton: **Laurence Naismith**
Jon: **Tony Bonner**
Bibi: **Yutte Stensgaard**
Christianson: **Bernard Horsfall**
Lars Seelman: **Griffith Jones**
Anderson: **Frank Gatliff**
Liv: **Penny Sugg**
The Butler: **Walter Horsbrugh**
Chambermaid: **Marianne Stone**

Read and Destroy
w **Peter Yeldham**
d **Roy Ward Baker**

When Felix Meadows, a man wanted after an audacious East-West double cross, turns to Brett for sanctuary, Sinclair sends him to his safety home in Berkshire - but someone watches their every move and things don't turn out as planned.

Felix Meadowes: **Joss Ackland**
Cavendish: **Nigel Green**
Heidi: **Kate O'Mara**
Ingrid: **Magda Konopka**
Chivers: **George Merritt**
Pfeiffer: **Elliott Sullivan**
Sir Charles Worthington: **William Mervyn**
Ivanov: **Harvey Hall**
Dieter Schultz: **Carl Bohun**
Benson: **Brian Hayes**

A Death in the Family
w **Terry Nation**
d **Sidney Hayers**

The Sinclair clan is shrinking. Some distant relative is playing out his own game of 'Kind Hearts and Coronets' by killing off everyone who stands between him and the Sinclair title. Will Brett be the next to die? Whose face lies behind the killer's smile?

Kate: **Diane Cilento**
Roland: **Denholm Elliott**
Duke of Caith: **Roland Culver**
Lance: **William Rushton**
Sir Angus: **Moultrie Kelsall**
Onslow: **Christopher Sandford**
Mr Beebe: **Ivor Dean**
The General: **Roger Moore**
The Admiral: **Roger Moore**
Lady Agatha: **Roger Moore**

The Ozerov Inheritance
w **Harry W. Junkin**
d **Roy Ward Baker**

The Grand Duchess Ozerov requires Brett and Danny's help. Someone has laid claim to ownership of the family jewels and they must prove the Duchess's right. Doing so leads them to uncover a death in the past - and one in the present.

Grand Duchess Ozerov: **Gladys Cooper**
Princess Alexandra: **Prunella Ransome**
Sergei: **Gary Raymond**
Yelker: **Joseph Furst**
Magda: **Georgina Simpson**
Walther: **Timothy Parkes**
Dante: **Denys Peek**
Inspector Mansour: **Raymond Young**
Professor Ganguin: **Cyril Shaps**
Stewardess: **Anouska Hempel**
Uncle Rodney: **Arnold Ridley**
Nikolai: **Yuri Borienko**

To the Death, Baby
w **Donald James**
d **Basil Dearden**

Hired to break up the friendship between Shelley Masterson, a beautiful heiress and her dubious boyfriend, Danny and Brett find that a bit of soft soap can make anyone slip - right into the dirty money laundry business.

Shelley Masterson: **Jennie Linden**
Foster: **Terence Morgan**
Hatton: **Thorley Walters**
Coady: **Harold Innocent**
Ramon: **Robert Russell**
Estoban: **Roger Delgado**
Waiter: **Juan Moreno**

Someone Waiting
w **Terry Nation**
d **Peter Medak**

The victim, Lord Brett Sinclair - the suspect, Danny Wilde? When Danny gets whiff that someone is out to sabotage his friend's dreams of becoming a world-beating motor-racing driver, his efforts to avoid disaster leave Brett at the starting gate.

Carrie: **Penelope Horner**
Jenkins Brothers: **John Cairney**
Lyndon: **Donald Pickering**
Louise: **Lois Maxwell**
Vine: **Maxwell Shaw**
John Radcliffe: **Tim Barrett**
Dwyer: **Sam Kydd**

Jerry Sandford: **David Neal**
Magda: **Jenny Hanley**
Yates: **Sean Lynch**
Joe: **Helena Ross**
Sam: **Russ Henderson**

Four features were released being compilations of episodes: *London Conspiracy* [*Greensleeves* and *A Home of One's Own*]; *Mission - Monte Carlo* [*Powerswitch* and *The Gold Napoleon*]; *Sporting Chance* [*To Death, Baby, Someone Waiting* and *Anyone Can Play*] and *The Switch* [*Angie, Angie* and *The Ozerov Inheritance*].
A fifth, *Overture* [*Overture* and *Man in the Middle*], was prepared but never issued.

The Persuaders Book I [1971: Frederick E. Smith: Pan Books: novelisations of *Overture* and *Angie, Angie*]; *The Persuaders Book II* [1972: Frederick E. Smith: Pan Books: novelisations of *Five Miles to Midnight* and *Someone Like Me*]; *The Persuaders Book III* [1973: Frederick E. Smith: Pan Books: novelisations of *The Gold Napoleon, Greensleeves* and *The Old, The New and The Deadly*].

The Persuaders!:

Series Devised and Produced by: **Robert S. Baker**
In Charge of Production: **Johnny Goodman**
Story Consultant and Associate Producer: **Terry Nation**
Co-story Consultant: **Milton S. Gelman**
"The Persuaders" Theme by: **John Barry**
Music by: **Ken Thorne**
Musical Supervision by: **Don Kirshner**
Production Manager: **Malcolm Christopher**
Assistant Director: **Peter Price**
Music Editor: **Deveril Goodman**
Make-up: **Gerry Fletcher**
Hairdressing: **Mike Jones**
Wardrobe Supervision: **Johnny Briggs**
[Lord Sinclair's clothes designed by: **Roger Moore**]

Filmed on location and at Pinewood Studios
A Television Reporters / International Tribune Production for ITC World Wide Distribution.

Made on location and at Pinewood Studios

24 colour 60-minute episodes
1971

The Prisoner

The series that elevated television adventure series to the pinnacle of success and aroused so much interest that even today, thirty years after its first transmission, it remains one of the oddest and most thought-provoking television experiences of all time. A series so stunningly different that it became a major cult and spawned a worldwide appreciation society [*Six of One*] which is viewed as the frontrunner among the many television-related fan clubs which have sprung up to commemorate what many believe to be television's Golden years - the decade between 1960 and 1970.

Following closely on the heels of Patrick McGoohan's successful *Danger Man* [see entry under that name], viewers who expected a continuation of the exploits of the super-cool agent John Drake were in for a rude awakening. With few exceptions, viewers all over the world were totally bemused by what they saw; the surrealistic adventures of a man with no name - only a number. An ex-spy known only as Number Six. A man marooned in a mysterious village from which he would never escape - but spent each waking hour attempting to do so.

Imprisoned in his cottage/cell, watched on every side by close circuit television cameras, he determined to outwit his chief adversary Number Two, and discover the identity of Number One - a man set on brainwashing the secrets from the mind of his tormented captive.

> *'Where am I?'*
> *'In the village.'*
> *'What do you want?'*
> *'Information.'*
> *'You won't get it!'*

Without debating the longevity of the programme, or trying to qualify its lasting appeal, it's enough to say this was Patrick McGoohan's personal tour de force. He thought up the idea, wrote and directed some of the episodes, was executive producer for the entire series - and starred in the title role.

Like it or hate it, the programme was, and remains, a slice of television history. There has been nothing like it before or since, and it remains a challenging, inventive tribute to its creator.

Regular cast:
Number Six: **Patrick McGoohan**
The Butler: **Angelo Muscat**
Number Two: **Leo McKern**

✍ This episode guide is in production order.

Arrival
w **George Markstein** and **David Tomblin**
d **Don Chaffey**

A menacing roll of thunder. A tiny sports car zooming through the streets of London. Doors that are flung back to the sound of thunderclaps as an unnamed man slams down his resignation on his superior's desk. A return drive home to pack for a holiday. An omnimus black hearse parked outside his window. A cloud of billowing gas and the man falls unconscious.... to awaken in a strange and mysterious village. The man has become... The Prisoner, a man with no name, just a number. The reason for his abduction - his resignation. 'They' wish to know why he resigned. He won't tell. He attempts to escape. But there is no escape. He has become Number Six - a man who can trust no one but himself.

Number Two: **Guy Doleman**
Cobb: **Paul Eddington**
The Woman: **Virginia Maskell**

The New Number Two: **George Baker**
The Butler: **Angelo Muscat**
Taxi Driver: **Barbara Yu Ling**
Maid: Stephanie Randall
Doctor: **Jack Allen**
Welfare Worker: **Fabia Drake**
Shopkeeper: **Denis Shaw**
Gardener/Electrician: **Oliver MacGreevey**
Ex-Admiral: **Frederick Piper**
Waitress: **Patsy Smart**
Labour Exchange Manager: **Christopher Benjamin**
Supervisor: **Peter Swanwick**
Hospital Attendant: **David Garfield**
First Croquet player: **Peter Brace**
Second Croquet player: **Keith Peacock**

Free for All
w **Paddy Fitz** [Patrick McGoohan]
d **Patrick McGoohan**

The Prisoner stands for election as the new Number two, but finds that his rights are just limited as before. Is the election genuine or just another trick? And why should the current Number Two appear to greet his election speech with enthusiastic applause?

Number Two: **Eric Portman**
Number Fifty Eight: **Rachel Herbert**
Labour Exchange Manager: **George Benson**
The Butler: **Angelo Muscat**
Reporter: **Harold Berens**
Man in Cave: **John Cazabon**
Photographer: **Dene Cooper**
Supervisor: **Kenneth Benda**
Waitress: **Holly Doone**
First Mechanic: **Peter Brace**
Second Merchant: **Alf Joint**

Checkmate
w **Gerald Kelsey**
d **Don Chaffey**

The Prisoner plays a dangerous game when invited to take part in an unusual game of chess: the board is a lawn, the chess pieces people. Unknown to the Prisoner, the Queen has been brainwashed by Number Two, who intends to use her attraction to Number Six to destroy him.

Number Two: **Peter Wyngarde**
The Rook: **Ronald Radd**
The Queen: **Rosalie Crutchley**
Man with the Stick: **George Coulouris**
First Psychiatrist: **Patricia Jessel**
The Butler: **Angelo Muscat**
Second Psychiatrist: **Bee Duffell**
Supervisor: **Basil Dignam**
Painter: **Danvers Walker**
Shopkeeper: **Denis Shaw**
Ass. Supervisor: **Victor Platt**
Nurse: **Shivaun O'Casey**
Skipper: **Geoffrey Reed**
Sailor: **Terence Donovan**
First Tower Guard: **Joe Dunne**
Second Tower Guard: **Romo Gorrara**

Dance of the Dead
w **Anthony Skene**
d **Don Chaffey**

Having discovered a body washed up on the shore and removed the dead man's wallet and a radio which works but emits only quotations, Number Six puts his own identification on the body and refloats it in the barren hope

that it will be found and a search initiated. Returning to the Village he discovers the drowned man - and is placed on trial.

Number Two: **Mary Morris**
The Doctor: **Duncan Macrae**
Girl Bo-Peep / The Observer: **Norma West**
The Butler: **Angelo Muscat**
Town Crier: **Aubrey Morris**
Psychiatrist: **Bee Duffell**
Day Supervisor: **Camilla Hasse**
Dutton: **Alan White**
Night Supervisor: **Michael Nightingale**
Night Maid: **Patsy Smart**
Maid: **Denise Buckley**
Postman: **George Merritt**
Flowerman: **John Frawley**
Lady in Corridor: **Lucy Griffiths**
Second Doctor: **William Lyon Brown**

The Chimes of Big Ben
w **Vincent Tilsley**
d **Don Chaffey**

Nadia, a new arrival in the village, is moved into the cottage next to Number Six. She too has recently resigned her job. She too tries to escape - alone, before accepting her neighbour's help. Using her contacts they escape to London - or do they?

Number Two: **Leo McKern**
The General: **Finlay Currie**
Nadia: **Nadia Grey**
Fotheringay: **Richard Wattis**
The Butler: **Angelo Muscat**
Colonel J: **Kevin Stoney**
Number 2 Asst: **Christopher Benjamin**
Karel: **David Arlen**
Supervisor: **Peter Swanwick**
Number 38: **Hilda Barry**
First Judge: **Jack Le-White**
Second Judge: **John Maxim**
Third Judge: **Lucy Griffiths**

The Schizoid Man
w **Terence Feely**
d **Pat Jackson**

Number Two puts into operation his latest ploy to break the Prisoner - his exact double and a girl who claims a telepathic link with Number Six. While he sleeps, a form of brainwashing reverses his brain pattern - but not his instinct for survival or his determination to escape!

Number Two: **Anton Rodgers**
Alison: **Jane Merrow**
Supervisor: **Earl Cameron**
The Butler: **Angelo Muscat**
Number 36: **Gay Cameron**
Doctor: **David Nettheim**
Nurse: **Pat Green**
First Guardian: **Gerry Crampton**
Second Guardian: **Dinny Powell**

It's Your Funeral
w **Michael Cramoy**
d **Robert Asher**

Number Two promotes his latest weapon in the fight to gain information from Number Six - misinformation. In order to stop the Prisoner foiling an assassination attempt, Number Six is fed incorrect information which leads him to cry 'wolf' just once too often.

Watchmaker's Daughter: **Annette Andre**
Number One Hundred: **Mark Eden**
New Number 2: **Derren Nesbitt**
Retiring Number 2: **Andre Van Gyseghem**
Watchmaker: **Martin Miller**
Computer Attendant: **Wanda Ventham**
The Butler: **Angelo Muscat**
Number 2's Assistant: **Mark Burns**
Supervisor: **Peter Swanwick**
Artist: **Charles Lloyd Pack**
Number 36: **Grace Arnold**
Stall Holder: **Arthur White**
M. C. Councillor: **Michael Bilton**
Kosho Opponent: **Gerry Crampton**

A Change of Mind
w **Roger Parkes**
d **Joseph Serf [Patrick McGoohan]**

The Prisoner falls foul of further attempts to gain his secrets - he becomes the latest victim of an instant social conversion process designed to change the villager's attitudes. The attractive Number Eighty-Six is the bait - but will the Prisoner bite?

Number Two: **John Sharpe**
Number Eighty-Six: **Angela Browne**
The Doctor: **George Pravda**
The Butler: **Angelo Muscat**
Number 42: **Kathleen Breck**
Supervisor: **Peter Swanwick**
Lobo Man: **Thomas Heathcote**
Committe Chairman: **Bartlett Mullins**
Number 93: **Michael Miller**
First member of Social Group: **Joseph Cuby**
Second member of Social Group: **Michael Chow**
Number 48: **June Ellis**
First Woodland Man: **John Hamilton**
Second Woodland Man: **Michael Billington**

A, B and C
w **Anthony Skene**
d **Pat Jackson**

In a bid to discover why the Prisoner resigned, Number Two decides to risk subjecting him to a new experimental process in which his dreams can be penetrated. Under its influence, Number Six must relay the truth - or is he playing a game of cat and mouse with his captors?

Number Two: **Colin Gordon**
Engadine: **Katherine Kath**
Number Fourteen: **Sheila Allen**
'A': **Peter Bowles**
The Butler: **Angelo Muscat**
Blonde Lady: **Georgina Cookson**
'B': **Annette Carel**
Flower Girl: **Lucille Soong**
Maid at Party: **Bettine Le Beau**
Thug: **Terry Yorke**
Thug: **Peter Brayham**
Henchman: **Bill Cummings**

The General
w **Lewis Greifer [aka Joshua Adam]**
d **Peter Graham Scott**

'Speedlearn' and a sublimator device. The latest process to keep the village occupants subservient. Both are distrusted by Number Six who, with the help of Number Twelve, a young man, manages to thwart Number Two's latest project - though not without loss of life.

Number Two: **Colin Gordon**

Number Twelve: **John Castle**
The Professor: **Peter Howell**
The Butler: **Angelo Muscat**
The Announcer: **Al Mancini**
Professor's Wife: **Betty McDowall**
Supervisor: **Peter Swanwick**
Doctor: **Conrad Phillips**
Man in Buggy: **Michael Miller**
Waiter: **Keith Pyott**
Cafe and First Top Hat: **Ian Fleming**
Mechanic: **Norman Mitchell**
Projection Operator: **Peter Bourne**
First Corridor Guard: **George Leech**
Second Corridor Guard: **Jackie Cooper**

Hammer into Anvil
w **Roger Woddis**
d **Pat Jackson**

Swearing to avenge the death of a girl whose appeals for help when being persecuted by Number Two go unheard, Number Six attempts to trick Number Two into believing that he is a decoy sent from the outside world to spy on him.

Number Two: **Patrick Cargill**
Number Fourteen: **Basil Hoskins**
Psychiatrist: **Norman Scace**
Band Master: **Victor Maddern**
New Supervisor: **Derek Aylward**
The Butler: **Angelo Muscat**
Number 73: **Hilary Dwyer**
Control Room Operator: **Arthur Gross**
Supervisor: **Peter Swanwick**
Shop Assistant: **Victor Woolf**
Laboratory Technician: **Michael Segal**
Shop Kiosk Girl: **Margo Andrew**
Female Code Expert: **Susan Sheers**
First Guardian: **Jackie Cooper**
Second Guardian: **Fred Haggerty**
Third Guardian: **Eddie Powell**
Fourth Guardian: **George Leach**

Many Happy Returns
w **Anthony Skene**
d **Joseph Serf [Patrick McGoohan]**

When the Village appears abandoned - so far as he can tell, the Prisoner is alone - Number Six sees the chance to escape. Building a raft he does so, but finds himself a prisoner once more - this time in the hands of his friends and colleagues in London.

The Colonel: **Donald Sinden**
Thorpe: **Patrick Cargill**
Mrs Butterworth: **Georgina Cookson**
Group Captain: **Brian Worth**
Commander: **Richard Caldicott**
Gunther: **Dennis Chinnery**
Ernst: **Jon Laurimore**
Gypsy Girl: **Nike Arrighi**
Maid: **Grace Arnold**
Gypsy Man: **Larry Taylor**

Do Not Forsake Me, Oh My Darling
w **Vincent Tilsley**
d **Pat Jackson**

The Prisoner's nightmare continues. Awaking in his own London flat - but with the body of a stranger and his memory tampered with - he finds that no one recognises him - not his fiancee, her father, nor even Sir Charles, one of his former employers. Has Number Two finally won the game?

Number Two: **Clifford Evans**

Janet: **Zena Walker**
The Colonel: **Nigel Stock**
The Butler: **Angelo Muscat**
Seltzman: **Hugo Schuster**
Sir Charles: **John Wentworth**
Villiers: **James Bree**
Minister: **Kynaston Reeves**
Danvers: **Lloyd Lamble**
Camera Shop Manager: **Lockwood West**
Potter: **Frederic Abbott**
Cafe Waiter: **Gertan Klauber**
Old Guest: **Henry Longhurst**
First Young Man: **Danvers Walker**
Young Guest: **John Nolan**

Living in Harmony
w **David Tomblin**
[from a story by **David Tomblin** and **Ian L. Rakoff**]
d **David Tomblin**

When the Prisoner suddenly finds himself in a Western town where he has been appointed sheriff, he faces mental conflict when he refuses to wear guns - even though a gunfight is unavoidable.
✍ This instalment was never transmitted during the series' network schedule, but reappeared in syndication.

The Kid: **Alexis Kanner**
The Judge: **David Bauer**
Kathy: **Valerie French**
Town Elder: **Gordon Tanner**
Bystander: **Gordon Sterne**
Will: **Michael Balfour**
Mexican Sam: **Larry Taylor**
Town Dignitary: **Monti De Lyle**
Horse dealer: **Douglas Jones**
First Gunman: **Bill Nick**
Second Gunman: **Les Crawford**
Third Gunman: **Frank Maher**
First Horseman: **Max Faulkner**
Second Horseman: **Bill Cummings**
Third Horseman: **Eddie Eddon**

The Girl Who Was Death
w **Terence Feely** [from an idea by **David Tomblin**]
d **David Tomblin**

She calls herself Death. A worthy opponent for Number Six - the Survivor. When the two meet something must give. But who will remain when the two pit themselves in a head-to-head battle? A bedtime story with a difference, or the Prisoner's flight of fantasy?

Sonia: **Justine Lord**
Schnipps: **Kenneth Griffith**
Potter: **Christopher Benjamin**
Killer Karminski: **Michael Brennan**
Boxing M.C.: **Harold Berens**
Barmaid: **Sheena Marsh**
Marshall Scots Napoleon: **Max Faulkner**
Marshall Welsh Napoleon: **John Rees**
Marshall Yorkshire Napoleon: **Joe Gladwin**
Bowler: **John Drake**
Little Girl: **Gaynor Steward**
First Little Boy: **Graham Steward**
Second Little Boy: **Stephen Howe**
Young Man with Camera: **Alexis Kanner**

Once Upon a Time
w **Patrick McGoohan**
d **Patrick McGoohan**

When the Prisoner and Number Two face a deadly conflict of wills, one man must break. For the loser it spells the end,

but Number Six is well aware of the risks he's undertaking. Prepared for the ordeal he faces relentless interrogation to discover why he resigned - but will his secrets be known when the challenge is over?

Number Two: **Leo McKern**
Supervisor: **Peter Swanwick**
Umbrella Man: **John Cazabon**
The Butler: **Angelo Muscat**
Number 86: **John Maxim**

Fall Out
w **Patrick McGoohan**
d **Patrick McGoohan**

The final trial begins. It's outcome will decide the prisoner's fate. Will he remain entombed in the village or finally win the right to be treated as a free man? Will he escape to begin life anew? Will Number One finally be unmasked? The question is resolved when, together with Number Forty-Eight and the Butler they engineer their freedom and return to London...
... A menacing roll of thunder. a tiny sports car zooming through the streets of London. We see the driver's face. His expression is grim...
The end - or the beginning?

Number Two: **Leo McKern**
Number Forty-Eight: **Alexis Kanner**
The President: **Kenneth Griffith**
The Butler: **Angelo Muscat**
The Supervisor: **Peter Swanwick**
The Delegate: **Michael Miller**

All three, original stories: *The Prisoner* [1969: Thomas M. Disch: Ace Books: re-issued 1979 by Dobson Books and 1980 by New English Library]; *The Prisoner #2: Number Two* [1969: David McDaniel: Ace Books: re-issued 1981, as *Who is Number Two*, by Dobson Books and 1982, also as *Who is Number Two*, by New English Library]; *The Prisoner #3: A Day in the Life* [1970: Hank Stein: Ace Books: re-issued 1979, as *The Prisoner 2: A Day in the Life*, by Dobson Books and 1981 by New English Library].

The Prisoner:

Executive Producer: **Patrick McGoohan**
Produced by: **David Tomblin**
Script Editor: **George Markstein**
Production Manager: **Bernard Williams, Ronald Liles**
Director of Photography: **Brendan J. Stafford, B.S.C.**
Art Director: **Jack Shampan**
Editor: **Lee Doig, Spencer Reeve, Geoffrey Foot GBFE, John S. Smith, Eric Boyd-Perkins, Noreen Ackland GBFE**
Theme by: **Ron Grainer**
Musical Director / Incidental music: **Albert Elms**
Assistant Director: **Gino Marotta, Ernie Lewis**
Sound Editor: **Ken Rolls, Wilfred Thompson, Peter Elliott, Stanley Smith, Clive Smith**
Sound Recordist: **John Bramall, Cyril Swern**
Music Editor: **Bob Dearberg, Eric Mival**
Casting Director: **Rose Tobias-Shaw**
Continuity: **Ann Besserman, Phyllis Townshend, Doris Martin, Josie Fulford**
Set Dresser: **John Lageu, Kenneth Bridgeman, Colin Southcott**
Make-up: **Eddie Knight, Frank Turner**
Hairdressing: **Pat McDermot, Olive Mills**
Wardrobe: **Dora Lloyd, Masada Wilmot**

An ITC Production by Everyman Films Limited Made on location in the grounds of The Hotel Portmeirion, Penrhyndeudraeth, North Wales By courtesy of Mr Clough Williams-Ellis and at Metro-Goldwyn-Mayer Studios, Borehamwood, England

17 colour 60-minute episodes
1967 - 1968

The Protectors

A glossy but much over-used cops and robbers format which chronicled the activities of Harry Rule, Paul Buchet and Caroline, the glamorous Contessa di Contini - collectively known as The Protectors, three experts at protecting those in peril, who came together to battle evil from their international crimefighting agency.

No risk was too great. No assignment too challenging. The team handled dangerous and highly sensitive investigations across the world.

Head of the agency was Harry Rule, an ice-cool professional whose ultra-modern office is based in London. [He could just as easily be found cavorting around his luxury Tudor-style country home which he shared his au pair Suki, and his Irish wolfhound 'Gus'] Wealthy to the point of being crass, Lady Caroline Oglivie [aka the Contessa], lived in a lavishly furnished villa in Rome. Like her partners she, too, operated a detective agency - although her speciality was seeking out art and antiques fakes. Buchet, a baby-faced French-born intellectual, operated from his Paris apartment - at least he did so whenever he wasn't otherwise occupied by the attention of a seemingly endless stream of beautiful girlfriends! The youngest member of the trio, his bland exterior concealed a tough and sophisticated alertness whenever he was called in to partner his colleagues.

Regular cast:
Harry Rule: **Robert Vaughan**
Contessa di Contini: **Nyree Dawn Porter**
Paul Buchet: **Tony Anholt**
Suki: **Yasuko Nasagumi** [season one only]
Chino: **Anthony Chinn** [season one only]

---
season one
---
26 Colour 30-minute episodes

2,000ft to Die
w **Terence Feely**
d **Johnny Hough**

Freddie Reiwald, a daredevil film stuntman, has good reason to be frightened - someone is out to kill him. Enter Harry Rule.

Reiwald: **Harvey Hall**
Ransome: **Nicholas Jones**
Susan: **Jacqueline Stanbury**
Carozza: **Paul Stassino**
Civil Servant: **John Scott**

Brother Hood
w **John Goldsmith**
d **Don Chaffey**

At the request of industrial tycoon Bela Karoleon, the Protectors engineer an audacious prison escape for his brother.

Sandor Karoleon: **Vladek Sheybal**
Bela Karoleon: **Patrick Troughton**
Maria Karoleon: **Jill Balcon**
Heller: **John Cazabon**
Governor: **Robert Brown**
Pannides: **Leon Lissek**
Yanos: **Antony Stamboulieh**

See No Evil
w **Donald Johnson**
d **Jeremy Summers**

The Protectors become involved with a blackmailed senator, a ruthless gang of cut-throats and a sinister blind man in Rome.

Max: **James Bolam**
The Blind Man: **Alan Webb**
Waiter: **Al Mancini**
Senator: **Leonard Sachs**
Mario: **Phillip Hinton**
Driver: **Anthony Haygarth**

Disappearing Trick
w **Brian Clemens**
d **Jeremy Summers**

The Contessa di Contini finds herself in deep trouble when she tries to help her friend Brad Huron win a wager.

Carl Huron: **David Bauer**
Brad Huron: **Derren Nesbitt**
Malloy: **Chris Malcolm**
Walters: **Don Henderson**
Cafe Owner: **Michael De Costa**
Garage Mechanic: **David Calderisi**

Ceremony for the Dead
w **Donald James**
d **Jeremy Summers**

A game of bluff and counter-bluff with a gang of kidnappers places the Contessa di Contini's life in danger.

Medina: **Stanley Lebor**
Madame Rue: **Toby Robins**
Police Inspector: **Charles Thake**
Skipper: **Robert Sessions**
Julie: **Jenny Lee Wright**

It was All Over in Leipzig
w **Donald James**
d **Don Chaffey**

When the Contessa meets up with two men from her past, the Protectors find themselves investigating a plot to overthrow a government.

Jim Palmer: **Ron Randell**
Girl with Pram: **Tanya Bayona**
Lintar: **Paul Weston**
Markos: **Phil Brown**
Maria: **Diane Mercer**

The Quick Brown Fox
w **Donald James**
d **Don Chaffey**

A wrongly-dated typewritten note helps the Protectors expose the mastermind behind a new Nazi organisation.

Keller: **Morris Petty**
Osuna: **Mark Malicz**
Helga: **Anna Matisse**
Monica: **Angie Grant**
Banker: **Christopher Benjamin**
Spanish Official: **Kenneth Hendel**

King Con
w **Tony Barwick**
d **Jeremy Summers**

When Alan Sutherland swindles Irena Gleskova out of a 12th-century icon, the Protectors decide the time is ripe to con a conman.

Sutherland: **Anton Rodgers**
Auctioneer: **Peter Cellier**
Emil: **Michael Da Costa**
Irena: **Izabella Telezynska**
Cribbs: **Ronald Lacey**
Salesman: **Brian Worth**

Thinkback
w **Brian Clemens**
d **Cyril Frankel**

When Harry Rule wakes up in a hospital bed, his first thought is for his passenger, the Contessa - but the doctor swears that there was no one else in the crashed car!

Inspector Wilson: **Ian Hendry**
Nurse: **Penny Sugg**
Doctor: **Donald Burton**
Sergeant Peters: **Keith Bell**
Ginter: **James Culliford**
Dilling: **Geoffrey Morris**

A Kind of Wild Justice
w **Donald James**
d **Jeremy Summers**

Savage justice against Harry Rule. A girl first of all shoots him - then poisons him for jailing her father.

Jill: **Kubi Chaza**
Kate: **Anna Palk**
Reagan: **Patrick O'Connell**
Soaper: **Barry Stanton**
Mechanic: **Paul Freeman**
Turf Accountant: **Brian Jackson**
Health Clinic Proprietor: **Lewis Jones**

Balance of Terror
w **John Goldsmith**
d **Don Chaffey**

When a Russian scientist goes missing in London armed with a phial of toxin which could wipe out the entire city, the Russians call in Harry Rule.

Krassinkov: **Nigel Green**
Schelpin: **Laurence Naismith**
KGB Man: **Janos Kurucz**
Grodny: **Angus Lennie**
Russian Delegate: **Milos Kirek**
Hotel Receptionist: **Barry Warren**

Triple Cross
w **Lew Davidson**
d **John Hough**

Framed for the theft of some rare jewels, Harry Rule and the Contessa find themselves involved with murder and bombs as they try to get them back.

Charlie: **John Neville**
Garage Attendant: **Bill Stewart**
Charlie's Girlfriend: **Angharad Rees**
Kofax: **Peter Bowles**
Gem Setter: **John Barrard**
Detective: **Del Henney**

The Numbers Game
w **Ralph Smart**
d **Don Chaffey**

A letter in code opens up new avenues and alleyways when Harry Rule and the Contessa set out to crack a dope smuggling gang.

Susan: **Margareta Lee**
Frank: **Henry McGee**
Sir Walter: **Frederick Treves**
Luigi: **George Innes**
Savage: **Richard Easton**
Giocovetti: **Peter Arne**

For the Rest of your Natural ...
w **Tony Barwick**
d **Johnny Hough**

The Countess finds herself on trial for her life - with a grotesque jury of cut-outs, and a psychopathic killer as prosecutor!

Colin Grant: **Norman Rodway**
Visitor: **Damien Thomas**
Detective: **Kenneth Gilbert**
Girlfriend: **Susan Travers**

The Bodyguards
w **Dennis Spooner**
d **Don Chaffey**

Why would a dead man need protection? And why did someone fire several bullets into his coffin to ensure he remained so? The Protectors find the answer.

Robard: **Freddie Jones**
Mason: **Manning Redwood**
Butler: **Harry Hutchinson**
Inspector Newman: **Ken Watson**

A Matter of Life and Death
w **Donald James**
d **Don Chaffey**

When Harry Rule is cunningly lured to Africa, his colleagues find themselves involved in a strange smuggling racket.

Goran: **Barrie Houghton**
Mallory: **Patrick Allen**
Mallory's Girl: **Julie Crossthwaite**
Baruna: **Maxwell Shaw**
Doctor: **Cyril Shapps**

The Big Hit
w **Donald James**
d **Roy Ward Baker**

When a pretty girl slips a drug into Paul Buchet's drink and attempts are made on Harry's life, the Protectors go underground to unmask the enemy.

Jason Howard: **Derek Smith**
Fencing Master: **Arthur Howell**
'Assassin': **Bob Anderson**
Suzanne: **Morag Hood**
Barman: **Tony Bateman**
Howard's Henchman: **Carl Rigg**
Howard's Henchman: **Phil Woods**

One and One Makes One
w **Jesse Lasky** and **Pat Lasky**
d **Don Chaffey**

The Protectors find themselves faced with finding a foreign agent who has killed and replaced a top Canadian spy.

Shkoder: **Michael Gough**
Maria Ghardala: **Georgia Brown**
Yanos: **Anthony Stamboulieh**
Bennett: **Neil McCallum**
Kramer: **Christopher Dunham**

Talkdown
w **Pat Lasky** and **Jesse Lasky**
d **Jeremy Summers**

Someone with a vendetta against Harry Rule lures the detective into a deadly trap - a speeding plane which Harry has no idea how to control.

Foster: **Derren Nesbitt**
Air Traffic Control: **John Joyce**
Inspector Hill: **John Nettleton**
Rifle Range Supervisor: **William Moore**

Vocal
w **Brian Clemens**
d **Cyril Frankel**

Paul Butler and the Contessa find themselves in desperate situation when they are held prisoner by a mysterious man called Azon.

Azon: **David Buck**
Gregg: **Ian Hogg**
Vickers: **Shane Rimmer**

With a Little Help from my Friends
w **Sylvia Anderson**
d **Jeremy Summers**

Assigned to protect a president during his stay in London, Harry Rule finds, to his cost, that his involvement brings a threat to his family.

Kahan: **Jeremy Brett**
Laura: **Hannah Gordon**
Pursuer: **Roshan Seth**
Kahan's Henchmen: **Julian Sherrier**
Kahan's Henchmen: **Marc Zuber**
Butler: **John Gatrell**
Boy: **Daron Barnham**
President: **Martin Benson**
President's Aide: **Saeed Jaffrey**
Doctor: **Desmond Jordan**

Chase
w **Brian Clemens**
d **Harry Booth**

When the Contessa gives Harry a new shotgun for his birthday, the detective soon has need to put it to good use.

Garder: **Patrick Magee**
Kurt: **Keith Buckley**
Perston: **Donald Eccles**
Vent: **Tom Chadbon**
Gromeld: **Gertan Klauber**
Second Tracker: **Graham Mallard**
Garder's Secretary: **Izabella Telezynska**

Your Witness
w **Donald James**
d **Jeremy Summers**

Christie is the key witness in a murder investigation. The Protectors are hired to protect her - but she protests, and then disappears.

Dixon: **George Baker**
Christie: **Stephanie Beacham**
Monique: **Judith Arthy**
Bayard: **Georges Lambert**
Barman: **Gordon Sterne**
Croupier: **Hugo De Vernier**

It Could be Practically Anywhere on the Island
w **Tony Barwick**
d **Robert Vaughan**

When Linda McCall's poodle Muffin is stolen, Harry Rule finds himself racing around the island searching for - er, dog droppings!

Felix Costa: **Sherwood Price**
Linda McCall: **Linda Staab**
Mary Laroche: **Madeline Hinde**
Hotel Manager: **Michael Da Costa**
Bartender: **Peter Fontaine**
Jonathan P. Hacket: **Dervis Ward**
Joe Flynn: **Vernon Dobtcheff**
Mrs Jonathan P. Hacket: **Wendy Hutchinson**
Doctor: **David Glover**

The First Circle
w **Tony Barwick**
d **Don Chaffey**

Called in to protect Colonel John Hunter, a Vietnam war veteran whose life is filled with nightmares of war horrors, Harry Rule finds himself in the firing line.

Hunter: **Ed Bishop**
Slade: **John Collin**
Security Man: **Frederick Bennett**
Policeman: **George Roubicek**
Mrs Hunter: **Sally Bazely**

A Case for the Right
w **Jesse Lasky** and **Pat Lasky**
d **Michael Lindsay-Hogg**

When they gatecrash a prince's party, the Protectors find themselves involved in a sinister affair amid some Roman tombs.

Carpiano: **Milo O'Shea**
Fabrizzio: **Jacques Sernas**
Extremist Officer: **Jeffrey Segal**

season two
26 colour 30-minute episodes

Quin
w **Trevor Preston**
d **Don Leaver**

The Protectors become involved in a grim search for Quin, one of the most dangerous men in the world.

Quin: **Peter Vaughan**
Allen: **Brian Glover**
Paco: **Henry Woolf**
Garcia: **Anthony Langdon**
Maxwell: **Tristan Rogers**
Waiter: **Jesus Suzman**
Taxi Driver: **Luis Bar Boo**

Bagman
w **Terry Nation**
d **Johnny Hough**

The Protectors play a game of hunt the criminal when a ransom demand in Copenhagen leads them to an abandoned fort.

Christian: **Stephan Chase**

Mrs Andersen: **Patricia Haines**
Evi Andersen: **Lalla Ward**
Hansen: **Oliver Ford-Davies**
Davidson: **Paul Dawkins**
Beck: **Karl Ahlefeldt**
Waiter: **Gert Thynov**

Fighting Fund
w **John Kruse**
d **Jeremy Summers**

Supported by the river police, Harry Rule leads the hunt for a gang of terrorists who have stolen valuable treasures to auction for arms.

Marquesa Visconti: **Lisa Daniely**
Dr Bianco: **Mischa De La Motte**
Bishop: **Hugh Morton**
Professor Williams: **Jack Lynn**
Principessa Lilli: **Gladys Spencer**
Leo: **David Suchet**
Vincenzo: **Ben Howard**
Police Captain: **Gino Melvazzi**
Bank Manager: **Sal Pantelone**

The Last Frontier
w **Tony Barwick**
d **Charles Crichton**

The Protectors are assigned to smuggle a beautiful Russian scientist into England - but their plan is exposed and the enemy is out to stop them.

Irina Gayevska: **Hildegard Neil**
Eastbrook: **William Lucas**
Khukov: **Yuri Borienko**
Jones: **Peter Cellier**
British Delegate: **Dennis Clinton**
Girl at Anif: **Manuela Renard**

Baubles, Bangles and Beads
w **Terry Nation**
d **Jeremy Summers**

A doublecross in Denmark leads the Protectors face to face with danger - with the Contessa's life depending on the outcome.

Bergen: **Frederick Jaegar**
Katis Bergen: **Yvonne Antrobus**
Insurance Executive: **John Barron**
Motor Cyclist: **Andrew Bradford**
Gang: **Peter Porteous**
Gang: **Martin Grace**
Gang: **Robert Russell**
Car Hire Receptionist: **Jacqueline Stanbury**
Miss Hansen: **Paula Patterson**

Petard
w **Tony Barwick**
d **Cyril Frankel**

Espionage rears its ugly head when Harry Rule gets involved in the cut-throat world of international business.

Wyatt: **Iain Cuthbertson**
Alec Weston: **Cyril Luckham**
Linda: **Angela Douglas**
David Lee: **Ralph Bates**
David Cameron: **Clinton Greyn**
Ludo Jones: **John Kane**
Conway: **Milton Johns**
Scudder: **Mark Jones**
Engleton: **Basil Dignam**

Night Security Man: **Lewis Wilson**
Cleaner: **Carmel McSharry**

Goodbye George
w **Brian Clemens**
d **Michael Lindsay-Hogg**

Intent on discovering what has happened to George, the Contessa di Contini finds herself surrounded by macabre and strange events.

Caspar: **Paul Jones**
Maria: **Geraldine Moffatt**
Barney Mailer: **Barry Keegan**
Cedric Parton: **Lionel Murton**
Policeman: **Arnold Diamond**
Bank Teller: **Paul McDowell**
Intruder: **Malcolm Hayes**

Wam [Part 1 of 2]
w **Tony Barwick**
d **Jeremy Summers**

Why should Monica Davies write to her father, who has cut her out of his will, that she will soon be rich without his help...?

William Arthur Mackay: **Prentis Hancock**
Monica Davies: **Jill Townsend**
Attendant: **Rudolf Barry**
Davies: **Michael Glover**
Official: **John Herrington**
Manager: **Bert Fortell**

Wam [Part 2 of 2]
w **Tony Barwick**
d **Jeremy Summers**

... The Protectors are hired to find the answer - and find themselves involved in a drama on a mountain top in Salzburg, where holiday-makers are being held to ransom.

William Arthur Mackay: **Prentis Hancock**
Monica Davies: **Jill Townsend**
Inspector Luhrs: **Michael Sheard**
Attendant/Official: **John Herrington**
Commissioner Braun: **Olaf Pooley**

Implicado
w **Tony Barwick**
d **Jeremy Summers**

Harry Rule and Paul Buchet are assigned to investigate the case of an English boy arrested in Spain on drug-smuggling charges.

Raphael Santana: **Patrick Mower**
Stephen Douglas: **Peter Firth**
Jacques: **Aldo Sanbrell**
Patron: **Pat La Touche**
Waiter: **Carl Forgione**
Policeman at Cafe: **Stephen Greif**
Mrs Douglas: **Ruth Trouncer**
Doctor Dove: **Neil Hallett**
Assassin: **Ron Eagleton**

Dragon Chase
w **John Kruse**
d **Charles Crichton**

The Protectors find that protecting a Russian they have smuggled into Britain offers the greatest challenge of their career.

Lockier: **Donald Houston**
Nickolai: **William Dexter**
Devlin: **Kenneth Colley**
Peter: **Bruce Robinson**
Jenny [Student]: **Mary Larkin**
Jasper [Student]: **Jack Galloway**
Mike [Student]: **Gary Hamilton**
First Russian: **Richard Marner**
Stage Door Keeper: **Norman Atkyns**

Decoy
w **Brian Clemens**
d **Michael Lindsay-Hogg**

When a 'dead' man steps out of Harry Rule's past, it spells danger for the detective - and intrigue for the Contessa di Contini.

Jerry Butler: **Ronald Radd**
Nick Archer: **Mark Damon**
Marcus: **George Innes**
Police Captain: **Bruce Montague**
Conyapepi: **Stephen Sheppard**
Hotel Porter: **Pierre Bedenes**
Desk Clerk: **George Little**
Airline Steward: **George Von Moos**
Girlfriend: **Erika Bergmann**

Border Line
w **Anthony Terpiloff**
d **Charles Crichton**

The Protectors are asked to help an Hungarian-born actress to smuggle her father's body across the border.

Ilona Tabori: **Georgia Brown**
Zoltan Kolas: **Oscar Homolka**
Press Reporter: **Jon Laurimore**
Customs Official: **David Allister**
[Hungarian] Border Guard: **Gabor Vernon**
[Hungarian] Border Guard: **Petar Vidovic**
[Hungarian] Peasant Woman: **Elizabeth Balogh**

Zeke's Blues
w **Shane Rimmer**
d **Jeremy Summers**

When Harry Rule meets up with an old adversary he finds little comfort in a drama played out to music.

Zeke: **Shane Rimmer**
Kasankas: **Paul Curran**
Patrick: **Ray Lonnen**
Fred: **Jackie Leapman**
George: **Donald Webster**
Max: **Graham Weston**
Bradley: **James Ottaway**

Lena
w **Trevor Preston**
d **Don Leaver**

When a young female journalist faces danger while seeking to expose a politician in Venice, the Protectors lend a hand.

Lena: **Judy Parfitt**
Pursuer: **Mario Depita**
Russi: **Roger Lloyd Pack**
Gunman: **Terry Plummer**
Maria Russi: **Judi Bloom**
Vendor: **Alexander Borin**
Mauro Carpiano: **John Thaw**
Helene Morleiter: **Miki Iveria**

Barman: **Leo Dolan**
Paolo Morleiter: **Frederick Peisley**

The Bridge
w **Tony Barwick**
d **Jeremy Summers**

A kidnapped girl leads Harry Rule into an explosive situation when he is charged with handing over her ransom.

David Mitchell: **Richard Morant**
De Santos: **Michael Goodliffe**
Mitchell: **James Maxwell**
Anna De Santos: **Diana Quick**
Juan: **Christopher Mitchell**
Carlos: **David Mayberry**

Sugar and Spice
w **David Butler**
d **Charles Crichton**

Threats to an industrialist's schoolgirl daughter lead to Harry Rule and the Contessa mounting counter-abduction plans.

Vicky Standish: **Debbie Russ**
Manning: **Derek Anders**
Colson: **Phil Woods**
Sir Charles Standish: **Norman Ettlinger**
Brian Dukes: **John Normington**
Headmistress: **Cicely Paget-Bowman**
Kruger: **Shane Shelton**
Barnes: **Gerry Crampton**

Burning Bush
w **Trevor Preston**
d **Don Leaver**

Harry Rule finds himself involved with the strange world of the supernatural when a Canadian heiress disappears in London.

Anne Ferris: **Sinead Cusack**
Mark Jenner: **Ken Hutchison**
Mrs Apsimon: **Madge Ryan**
Adam Ferris: **Anthony Steel**

The Tiger and the Goat
w **Trevor Preston**
d **Jeremy Summers**

Paul Buchet finds himself racing against time to save the Contessa's life - she is being used as bait to lure an assassin into the open.

Commander Whiting: **Douglas Wilmer**
David Barsella: **Derek Godfrey**
Reece: **Derek Newark**
Clarke: **Drewe Henley**
Ibbett: **Neville Hughes**
Jarman: **Max Faulkner**
Tom Watt: **Doug Fisher**

Route 27
w **Terry Nation**
d **Don Leaver**

Working alone, Harry Rule finds himself following the trail of a drug-smuggling gang, operating from a brewery.

Sandven: **Michael Coles**
Inspector Lars Bergen: **Jeremy Wilkin**
Nurse: **Virginia Wetherell**
Doctor: **Christopher Masters**

Revell: **Carl Bohun**
Lendrop: **Dan Meaden**
Detective: **Terry Richards**
Chauffeur: **Norman Beaton**
Bell Boy: **Andrew Burleigh**

Trial
w **Robert Banks Stewart**
d **Charles Crichton**

When someone attempts to interfere with the course of justice by threatening a judge, the Protectors enter the scene.

Arthur Gordon: **Joss Ackland**
Anne Gordon: **Gwen Cherrell**
Justice Cronin: **Richard Hurndall**
Prosecuting Counsel: **John Ringham**
John Gordon: **Paul Kelly**
Nurse: **Margaret John**
Gardener: **Fred McNaughton**
Secretary: **Sally James**
Police Inspector: **Graham Ashley**

Shadbolt
w **Tony Barwick**
d **Johnny Hough**

Shadbolt is a cruel, professional assassin. He doesn't mind who he kills - providing it pays well. Shadbolt's next victim is Harry Rule!

Shadbolt: **Tom Bell**
Girl: **Georgina Hale**
Police Inspector: **Stanley Stewart**
Attendant: **Neville Barber**

A Pocketful of Posies
w **Terry Nation**
d **Cyril Frankel**

Is cabaret singer Carrie Blaine losing her mind, or is she really being haunted? The Protectors become ghost-busters to save her sanity.

Carrie Blaine: **Eartha Kitt**
Mario Toza: **Kieron Moore**
Joe: **Terry Cantor**
Philip Bentley: **Bernard Kay**
Sara Trent: **Kate O'Mara**
Nelly Baxter: **Gretchen Franklin**
Theatre Doctor: **John Law**
Consultant: **Michael Lees**
Reporter: **John Croft**

Wheels
w **Tony Barwick**
d **David Tomblin**

Attempting to stop a daring Swiss bank robbery, Harry Rule finds himself running circles around the thieves.

Manning: **Dinsdale Landen**
Sneider: **George Pravda**
Anton: **Robert Coleby**

The Insider
w **Trevor Preston**
d **Don Leaver**

The Protectors take positive action to lay their hands on a stolen film - but receive a negative response from its owner.

Smith: **Stuart Wilson**

Editor: **Tim Pearce**
Chambers: **Donald Hewlett**
Secretary: **Alison Griffin**
Chauffeur: **Alf Costa**
Taxi Driver: **Alf Joint**

Blockbuster
w **Shane Rimmer**
d **Jeremy Summers**

The Protectors are assigned to probe a series of plutonium robberies and discover how a convoy of it disappeared.

Police Inspector: **Peter Jeffrey**
Birch: **Stanley Meadows**
Bailey: **Christopher Neame**
Slater: **Maurice O'Connell**
Doyle: **Eric Dodson**
Barney: **Raymond Skipp**
Workman: **Ron Pember**
Policeman: **Paul Antrim**

The Protectors [1973: Robert Miall aka John Burke: Pan Books: novelisations of *The Bodyguards*, *Disappearing Trick* and *The Numbers Game*].

The Protectors:

Producers: **Gerry Anderson** and **Reg Hill**
Executive in charge of Ferdporqui Productions: **Sherwood Price**
Music by: **John Cameron**
[Theme *'Avenues and Alleyways'* by **Mitch Murray** and **Peter Callander**, sung by **Tony Christie**]
Script Editor: **Tony Barwick**
Production Manager: **Norman Foster**
Casting Director: **Mary Selway, Michael Barnes**
Assistant Director: **David Bracknell, Gino Marotta**
Stunt Director: **Roy Vincente**
Music Editor: **Alan Willis**
Make-up: **Eddie Knight**
Hairdresing: **Betty Sherriff**
Wardrobe: **James Smith, Frank Vinalli**

A Group Three Production for ITC World Wide Distribution
Filmed on location and at EMI/MGM Studios, Elstree.

52 colour 30-minute episodes.
1972

Randall and Hopkirk [Deceased]

'There's something different about this pair of private eyes... one of them is dead!' So ran the billing for this oddball entry into the sixties cops and robbers stakes, which starred a different kind of investigative duo: private eye Jeff Randall and his partner Marty Hopkirk - a ghost!

Partners in a private enquiry agency, Jeff and Marty appeared to have everything going for them - until the day when Marty was run down and killed by a car. Thus began one of the most unusual partnerships in television detective fiction. Barely minutes after his death, Marty returned as a ghost to help his partner to track down his killer [his death had been arranged to keep him silent regarding a divorce enquiry] - and by so doing, has outstayed his welcome in heaven [or wherever detectives lay down their guns], by invoking an ancient curse which stated that:

*'Before the sun shall rise
each ghost unto his grave must go.
Cursed be the ghost who dares to stay
and face the awful light of day.'*

Ergo, Marty was fated to remain on earth as a ghost - but one seen only by his partner Jeff, to whom he quickly became a welcome [sometimes unwelcome] spiritual adviser.

With lots of high-speed action, some better-than-most plots [plus some stinkers], the show was guaranteed success - in all save the most profitable market of all, the USA. Syndicated there under the title *My Partner the Ghost* [with a redone title sequence], it failed to find an audience and disappeared almost as fast as Marty's spectre.

Regular cast:
Jeff Randall: **Mike Pratt**
Marty Hopkirk: **Kenneth Cope**
Jean Hopkirk: **Annette Andre**
Jennifer: **Judith Arthy**
Inspector Large: **Ivor Dean**

My Late Lamented Friend and Partner
w **Ralph Smart**
d **Cyril Frankel**

The enquiry team of Randall and Hopkirk loses a partner, but not its spirit. Jeff goes hunting for shadows, while Marty plays peek-a-boo with people who'd rather he remained unseen and unheard.

John Sorrensen: **Frank Windsor**
Fay Sorrensen: **Anne Sharp**
Beatnik: **Ronald Lacey**
Night Porter: **Harry Locke**
Happy Lee: **Dolores Mantez**
Assassin: **Harold Innocent**
Electrician: **Dave Carter**
Hotel proprietor: **Anthony Sagar**
Detective: **James Donnelly**
Doctor: **Tom Chatto**
Manservant: **Mikki Marseilles**

A Disturbing Case
w **Mike Pratt** and **Ian Wilson**
d **Ray Austin**

Talking to 'himself' lands Jeff in hospital and further trouble when a hypnotist who is using patients to rob their homes takes on Marty who, though unseen, gives the doctor a sight to remember.

Jennifer: **Judith Arthy**
Dr. Conrad: **David Bauer**
Dr. Lambert: **Gerald Flood**
Inspector Nelson: **Michael Griffiths**
Whitty: **William Mervyn**
Arthur Phillips: **Charles Morgan**
Smart: **Patrick Jordan**
The Sergeant: **Adrian Ropes**
First male nurse: **Geoffrey Reed**
Second male nurse: **Max Faulkner**
Hales: **Les White**

That's How Murder Snowballs
w **Ray Austin**
d **Paul Dickson**

Jeff discovers that an ability to read minds doesn't always pay the rent. It can in fact get you into an awful lot of trouble - and it does. But when Marty's around, anything can happen.

Gloria Marsh: **Grazina Frame**
Snowy: **Arthur Brough**
Barry Jones: **Patrick Holt**
Tony Lang: **Harold Berens**
Kay: **Valerie Leon**
Inspector Nelson: **Michael Griffiths**
Mark: **James Bellchamber**
Fernandez: **Tony Thawnton**
Abel: **David Jason**
Kim: **Stuart Hoyle**
Old Lady: **Marie Makino**
Doctor: **John Cazabon**
Ventriloquist: **John Styles**
Man with cards: **Simon Barnes**

Never Trust a Ghost
w **Tony Williamson**
d **Leslie Norman**

Why should Marty continue to report that people have been murdered when no bodies are found to confirm his accusations? Jeff knows that something is going on - but what? Has Marty started seeing things?

James Howarth: **Peter Vaughan**
Karen Howarth: **Caroline Blakiston**
Inspector Clayton: **Donald Morley**
Rawlins: **Philip Madoc**
Dr. Plevitt: **Brian Oulton**
Sandra: **Edina Ronay**

Who Ever Heard of a Ghost Dying?
w **Tony Williamson**
d **Ray Austin**

Marty in danger of being exorcised! Jeff has his work cut out protecting his ghostly partner from the overzealous attentions of Hellingworth and Purley - two ghostbusters, who want Marty out of the way to further their own plans.

Hellingworth: **John Fraser**
Carol Latimer: **Alexandra Bastedo**
Inspector Large: **Ivor Dean**
Cecil Purley: **Charles Lloyd Pack**
Doctor: **Richard Caldicot**
The Butler: **Peter Hughes**
Lord Manning: **John Richmond**
Ray: **Romo Gorrara**
Pete: **Terry Plummer**
Larry: **Paddy Ryan**
Constable: **Robin John**
Second Constable: **Philip Weston**

The House on Haunted Hill
w Tony Williamson
d Ray Austin

Who ever heard of a ghost being scared of - ghosts? Jeff Randall did. Far from helping Jeff to get to the bottom of the secret of a haunted house, Marty's white suit develops goosebumps.

Jennifer: **Judith Arthy**
Walter Previss: **Jeremy Burnham**
Frederick P. Waller: **Peter Jones**
Henry Mace Horsfall: **Dermot Kelly**
Langford: **Duncan Lamont**
Lattimer: **Keith Buckley**
Webster: **George A. Cooper**
Carlson: **Garfield Morgan**
Colonel Jarrett: **William Kendall**
Miss James: **Carol Rachelle**
Smith: **David Sinclair**
Simpson: **John Kidd**
Jackson: **Terry Duggan**

When Did you Start to Stop Seeing Things?
w Tony Williamson
d Jeremy Summers

Is Jeff free of his spiritual helper? When Marty fails to make contact with his partner, it appears so. Bad timing. If ever Jeff needed a partner to help him crack a case, this is it!

Inspector Large: **Ivor Dean**
Sir Oliver Norenton: **Clifford Evans**
Jarvis: **Keith Barron**
James Laker: **Reginald Marsh**
Mrs Trotter: **Bessie Love**
Hepple: **Basil Dignam**
Holly: **Philip James**
Tully: **John Garvin**
Hinch: **David Downer**
Sir Timothy Grange: **Peter Stephens**
Diana: **Rosemary Donnelly**
Tilvers: **David Stoll**

Just for the Record
w Donald James
d Jeremy Summers

Jeff and Jean are hired to look after two beauty contestants. Jeff's task is an agreeable one - looking after Miss Russia. Language proves a problem - and the involvement of a ghost certainly does!

Pargiter: **Ronald Radd**
Anne Soames: **Olivia Hamnett**
Lord Dorking: **Nosher Powell**
Lord Surrey: **Danny Green**
Miss Moscow: **Jan Rossini**
Senior official: **Michael Beint**
Old man: **Jack Woolgar**
Miss Budapest: **Kathja Wyeth**
Attendant: **Clifford Cox**
Police Sergeant: **Ken Watson**
Photographer: **Kevin Smith**

Murder Ain't What It Used to Be!
w Tony Williamson
d Jeremy Summers

A vendetta between a notorious Chicago gangster and a ghost proves to be a somewhat difficult case for Jeff Randall. It appears that the gangster's rival is reaching out from the grave to settle old accounts - and Marty is the unwilling third party!

Paul Kirstner: **Alan Gifford**
Bugsy Spanio: **David Healy**
Susan Kirstner: **Sue Gerrard**
Mrs. Maddox: **Joyce Carey**
Jack Lacey: **Raymond Adamson**
Harry: **Patrick Connor**
Hotel Porter: **Charles Lamb**

But What a Sweet Little Room
w Ralph Smart
d Roy Ward Baker

When his client dies in an 'accidental' car crash. Jeff seeks Marty's help to expose a phoney medium who makes her living by duping her clients into believing that she can contact the deceased.

Arthur de Crecy: **Michael Goodliffe**
Madame Hanska: **Doris Hare**
Elliot: **Norman Bird**
Julia Fenwick: **Anne De Vigier**
Anne Fenwick: **Frances Bennett**
Rawlings: **Raymond Young**
Salesman: **Chris Gannon**
Andrews: **Cyril Renison**
Martha: **Betty Woolfe**
Police Inspector: **Joby Blanshard**

Who Killed Cock Robin
w Tony Williamson
d Roy Ward Baker

Hired to guard a tropical bird aviary, Jeff finds himself investigating a complicated plot to strip his friends of their feathers. But birds can be killed - not murdered ... can't they?

Laverick: **Cyril Luckham**
Sandra Joyce: **Jane Merrow**
Mrs. Howe: **Gabrielle Brune**
Beeches: **David Lodge**
Colonel Chalmers: **Maurice Hedley**
James Howe: **Tenniel Evans**
Gimbal: **Michael Goldie**
Police Sergeant: **David Webb**
Johns: **Philip Lennard**
Carol: **Susan Broderick**
Peter: **Leslie Schofield**

The Ghost Who Saved the Bank at Monte Carlo
w Tony Williamson
d Jeremy Summers

She has perfected a gambling system that will win her a fortune. So why doesn't her number come up? Because Marty's spectral hand is operating the roulette wheel, that's why - and the ghost has even more games up his sleeve.

Clara Faringham: **Mary Merrall**
Lawsey: **Brian Blessed**
Suzanne: **Veronica Carlson**
Sagran: **John Sharp**
Tapiro: **Roger Delgado**
Max: **Nicholas Courtney**
Terry: **Roger Croucher**
Andre: **Nicholas Chagrin**
Claude: **Clive Cazes**
Verrier: **Michael Forrest**
Hibert: **Hans De Vries**
French Croupier: **Colin Vancao**
Young Lady: **Eva Enger**
Hotel Receptionist: **Richard Pescud**
Bell Boy: **Christopher Eedy**

For the Girl Who Has Everything
w Donald James
d Cyril Frankel

When death strikes in a haunted castle. Jeff finds himself investigating a weird mystery, and Marty discovers that a ghost-hunter and a psychic can see him - and seeing is believing, isn't it?

Kim Wentworth: **Lois Maxwell**
Mrs. Pleasance: **Marjorie Rhodes**
James McAllister: **Freddie Jones**
Larry Wentworth: **Michael Coles**
Jean-Claude: **Paul Bertroya**
Laura Slade: **Carol Cleveland**
Vicar: **Eric Dodson**
Girl: **Carol Dilworth**
Police Sergeant: **George Lee**
Coroner: **Basil Clarke**

You Can Always Find a Fall Guy
w Donald James
d Ray Austin

You don't expect a nun, of all people, to doublecross you - unless she turns out to be something quite different. Jeff is held prisoner, and Marty tries to break the habit of a lifetime.

Miss Holliday: **Juliet Harmer**
Yateman: **Patrick Barr**
Edwards: **Garfield Morgan**
Douglas Kershaw: **Jeremy Young**
Surgeon: **Tony Steedman**
First detective: **Clifford Earl**
Patient: **Edward Caddick**
Receptionist: **Ingrid Sylvester**
Nurse: **Maggie London**
Anaesthetist: **Michael Graham**
Mechanic: **John Walker**

The Smile Behind the Veil
w Gerald Kelsey
d Jeremy Summers

Whose face hides behind the veil of a funeral mourner - and why is she smiling? Jeff finds himself looking for the answer - and Marty performs miracles to wipe the smile off the face of a murderer.

Seaton: **Alex Scott**
Cynthia: **Hilary Tindall**
Donald Seaton: **Gary Watson**
Mrs Evans: **Freda Jackson**
Hooper: **Peter Jesson**
Grant: **Robin Hawdon**
Brooks: **George Howe**
Dyson: **John Bott**
Male hiker: **Michael Radford**
Girl hiker: **Clare Jenkins**
Police Constable: **David Forbes**
Policeman: **Peter Lawrence**

A Sentimental Journey
w Donald James
d Leslie Norman

When consignment of 'goods' worth £10,000 turns out to be an attractive blonde, Jeff concedes that the assignment is to his liking - until trying to escort her from Glasgow to London takes on murderous implications.

Sam Seymour: **William Squire**
Dandy Garrison: **Tracey Crisp**

Tony: **Drewe Henley**
Det. Sgt. Watts: **Victor Maddern**
Hamilton: **Antony Baird**
Alexander: **John Rae**
Man in phone booth: **Larry Taylor**
Sleeping car attendant: **Michael Bird**
Albert: **Billy Cornelius**

When the Spirit Moves You
w Tony Williamson
d Ray Austin

There are some things a ghost detective can do better than his mortal counterparts. One is to act as an unseen bodyguard. But what happens when the client can not only see you - but wants to hear your side of the story?

Inspector Large: **Ivor Dean**
Miklos Corri: **Kieron Moore**
Calvin P. Bream: **Anton Rodgers**
Perrin: **Michael Gothard**
Wilks: **Peter J. Elliott**
Manny: **Reg Lye**
Cranley: **Anthony Marlowe**
Plain clothes Police Sergeant: **Richard Kerley**
Girl in luxury flat: **Penny Brahms**
Parkin: **Bill Reed**

The Trouble with Women
w Tony Williamson
d Cyril Frankel

When Jeff is hired to find out if a woman's husband is having an affair, he finds that having a ghost for a partner has its uses - especially if you're gambling for your life with the cards stacked against you.

Alan Corder: **Paul Maxwell**
Susan Lang: **Denise Buckley**
Paul Lang: **Edward Brayshaw**
Harry: **Robert Russell**
Brin: **Nik Zaran**
Mrs. Halloway: **Gwen Nelson**
Poker player: **Arnold Diamond**
Second player: **Neil Arden**
Inspector: **Frederick Treves**
First ghost: **Howard Goorney**
Second ghost: **Harry Hutchinson**
PC Russell: **Keith Grenville**

It's Supposed to Be Thicker Than Water
w Donald James
d Leslie Norman

Playing postman to deliver an envelope to an escaped convict strikes Jeff as a simple affair - until he discovers that the envelope contains an invitation to murder and he finds his own life on the line.

Joshua Crackan: **Felix Aylmer**
Fay Crackan: **Liz Fraser**
Rev. Henry Crackan: **Neil McCallum**
Mesmero: **Dick Bentley**
Hodder: **Meredith Edwards**
Johnny Crackan: **John Hallam**
Ramon: **Earl Green**
Sung Lee Crackan: **John A. Tinn**
Punter: **Michael Ripper**
Young stage director: **Graham Armitage**

The Man from Nowhere
w Donald James
d Robert Tronson

Why should a stranger enter Jean's flat and claim to be her husband? Everyone knows that Marty died - don't they? One man who wishes to get to the bottom of the strange event is the ghostly Hopkirk himself - but Jeff doesn't appear to be interested!

'Marty': **Ray Brooks**
Hyde Watson: **Michael Gwynn**
Mannering: **Patrick Newell**
Griggs: **Neil McCarthy**
Mullet: **James Bree**

Could You Recognise the Man Again?
w **Donald James**
d **Jeremy Summers**

When Jeff and Jean observe gangster George Roden leaving their car - and find a dead body in the back seat - it leads to Jean being held hostage to stop her giving evidence, and Marty enlisting unusual help to find her.

Inspector Large: **Ivor Dean**
Mrs. Roden: **Madge Ryan**
George Roden: **Stanley Meadows**
Mort Roden: **Dudley Sutton**
Mike Hales: **Norman Eshley**
Ralph Sorrel: **John Bryans**
Jennings: **Roland Curram**
The Judge: **A. J. Brown**
Prosecuting Counsel: **John Harvey**
Sgt. Hinds: **Richard Kerley**
Loftus: **Billy Milton**
Tina: **Tricia Chapman**
Ben Craddock: **Dudley Jones**
Tramp: **Walter Sparrow**
Shop assistant: **David Cargill**
Harry: **Michael Gover**
Uniformed Inspector: **John Arnatt**
Chalmers: **Bruce Beeby**

Vendetta for a Dead Man
w **Donald James**
d **Cyril Frankel**

Jansen, a vengeance-seeking escaped prisoner, decides that since Hopkirk, the man who put him away, is dead, his widow Jean must suffer - but he's reckoned without the ghostly guardian's devotion to his wife.

Jansen: **George Sewell**
Emil Cavallo-Smith: **Barrie Ingham**
Mrs Cavallo-Smith: **Ann Castle**
Sam Grimes: **Timothy West**
Fairground Concessionaire: **Ron Pember**
Police Sgt. bodyguard: **Richard Owens**
Police Inspector: **William Dysart**
Police Sgt. in car: **Harry Davies**
Police driver: **Colin Rix**
Blonde girl in car: **Sue Vaughan**

Money to Burn
w **Donald James**
d **Ray Austin**

Hot money proves a big temptation for Jeff Randall - but puts him in a hot spot. He finds himself accused of stealing money intended for incineration, and when there's smoke there's fire - this time in the shape of a sultry torch singer.

Inspector Large: **Ivor Dean**
Elizabeth Saxon: **Sue Lloyd**
Kevin O'Malley: **Roy Desmond**
Anne-Marie Benson: **Linda Cole**
Angela Kendon: **Olga Lowe**

Sgt. Hinds: **Richard Kerley**
Policeman: **Norman Beaton**
Chemist: **John Glyn-Jones**
Bank worker: **John Hughes**
Security man: **Tom Bowman**
Uniformed policeman: **Roger Avon**
Choreographer: **Don Vernon**

The Ghost Talks
w **Gerald Kelsey**
d **Cyril Frankel**

With Jeff confined to a hospital bed, Marty seizes the opportunity to increase his ill-temper by telling his partner about a spy drama he handled before they became partners.

Major Brenan: **Alan MacNaughtan**
Jackson: **John Collin**
Joe Hudson: **Jack MacGowran**
Parker: **James Culliford**
Chief Inspector Horner: **Thomas Heathcote**
Captain Rashid: **Marne Maitland**
Sir Basil Duggan: **Geoffrey King**
Long: **Peter Cellier**
First man in steamroom: **Hilary Wontner**
Second man in steamroom: **Jack Lambert**
Dr. Musgrove: **John Boxer**
Groves: **Martin Carrol**
Page Boy: **Ian Butler**

All Work and No Pay
w **Donald James**
d **Jeremy Summers**

Why are the Foster brothers trying to convince Jean Hopkirk that her late husband is trying to contact her? The subject of some strange psychic phenomena, Jean is distraught enough to believe them - until Marty lends a hand.

Henry Foster: **Alfred Burke**
George Foster: **Dudley Foster**
Laura: **Adrienne Corri**
Pawnbroker's clerk: **Noel Davis**
Man in Laundromat: **Michael Rathbone**

Somebody Just Walked Over My Grave
w **Donald James**
d **Cyril Frankel**

People popping in and out of Marty's grave! Men dressed in tricorn hats! What's it all about? Marty finds himself accusing his partner of seeing things and Jeff gets plastered - twice!

Mandrake: **George Murcell**
Dighton: **Bernard Kay**
Martha: **Patricia Haines**
Harry: **Nigel Terry**
Harper: **Geoffrey Hughes**
Dr. Cholmond: **Cyril Shaps**
Valerie: **Beverly Winn**
Commentator: **Andrew Sachs**
German commentator: **Michael Sheard**

Randall and Hopkirk [Deceased]:

Series created by: **Dennis Spooner**
Producer: **Monty Berman**
Music by: **Edwin Astley**
Production Supervisor: **Ronald Liles**
Executive Story Consultant: **Dennis Spooner**
Creative Consultant: **Cyril Frankel**
Production Manager: **Malcolm Christopher**
Casting Director: **Jack Owen**
Assistant Director: **Michael Meighan, Ken Baker**
Second Unit Director: **Jack Lowin**
Stunt Co-ordinator: **Frank Maher**
Music Editor: **Alan Willis, Deveril Goodman**
Make-up: **Elizabeth Romanoff**
Hairdressing: **Jeannette Freeman, Henry Montash**
Wardrobe Supervisor: **Laura Nightingale**

An ITC Production for the Incorporated Television
Co., Ltd, for ITC World Wide Distribution.
Made on location and at Associated British Elstree
Studios

26 colour 60-minute episodes
1969

Return of the Saint

The further adventures of Simon Templar, alias the Saint. A daredevil 20th-century swashbuckler who lived for excitement and danger. A pirate or a philanthropist as the occasion demanded. A freelance troubleshooter whose debonair outlook on life brought him into contact with the life he loved best - those triumphant moments when, having rescued the damsel in distress, or solved the affairs of the British Secret Service, he could stand back to proclaim that victory was his alone.

The adventures as before - well, not quite. The original recipe concocted by his creator Leslie Charteris had been juiced up in an attempt to garner worldwide sales and this series was no better [though certainly no worse] than its contemporaries.

'The Saint is back', proclaimed the media, 'The King of swashbucklers returns to television in a new series of adventures that will delight his fans.'

But it wasn't the 'King', just a lookalike pretender to his throne. The real Simon Templar had abdicated some 16 years earlier, leaving behind a legacy that the newcomer found difficult to replace. The King was dead - long live the King. The newcomer was an impostor - and his 'subjects' hardly raised a cheer!

[see The Saint]

Regular cast:
Simon Templar: **Ian Ogilvy**

The Judas Game
w **Morris Farhi**
d **Jeremy Summers**

Simon takes on a dangerous mission amid the Italian Alps. His task: to rescue a girl he once loved from a group of ruthless terrorists. But treachery dogs his every step and he soon find himself in trouble.

Dame Edith: **Mona Bruce**
Wilcox: **Maurice Roeves**
Selma: **Judy Geeson**
Buckingham: **Moray Watson**
Algernon: **Richard Wyler**
Vlora: **Olga Karlatos**
Xexo: **Venantino Venantini**
Shehu: **Luciano Bartoli**
Quirko: **Marino Mase**
Noli: **Carlos De Carvalho**
Non-Com: **Guido Mastrogiacomo**

Duel in Venice
w **Terence Feely**
d **Jeremy Summers**

A quiet interlude in Venice with Sally, the daughter of an old friend, erupts into more mayhem for Simon. The girl is kidnapped by a killer who uses her as a bait to lure Simon into a trap - with violent results.

Linda: **Cathryn Harrison**
Jed Blackett: **Maurice Colbourne**
Claudia: **Carole Andre**
Luigi: **Carlo Delle Piane**
Guido: **Enzo Fiermonte**

The Nightmare Man
w **John Kruse**
d **Peter Sasdy**

Simon must find out why an assassination has been arranged - and by whom? He winds up to his neck in danger, which could result in his own death - as Big Ben tolls a death knell for The Saint.

Gunther: **Joss Ackland**
Gayle: **Kathryn Leigh Scott**
Livia Moreno: **Moira Redmond**
Canfield: **Norman Eshley**
Carmela: **Sharon Maughan**
Di Vallesi: **John Bailey**
Dalby: **Stanley Lebor**
Dillon: **Roy Evans**
Concierge: **Olga Lowe**
Margarita Di Vallesi: **Juliette James**
Mila: **Ziena Merton**
Plump Policeman: **Georgio Bosso**
Young Policeman: **Raul Newney**
Desk Clerk: **Eve Karpf**
Victor: **Trevor Ward**

One Black September
w **John Goldsmith**
d **Leslie Norman**

The Saint finds himself teamed up with the beautiful Leila Sabin, an Israeli agent, when he is asked to track down a terrorist hiding somewhere in London. But where - and why is Simon being followed?

Captain Leila Sabin: **Prunella Gee**
Yasmina: **June Bolton**
Abdul Hakim: **Garrick Hagon**
Col. Leon Garvi: **Amos Mokadi**
Yakovitz: **Geoffrey Greenhill**
Garton: **Aubrey Morris**
Rahman: **Nadim Sawalha**
Caliban: **Shango Baku**
The Gorilla: **Ron Tarr**
Stern: **Reuben Elvy**

The Village that Sold its Soul
w **John Goldsmith**
d **Leslie Norman**

Simon's arrival at the isolated village of Santa Maria spells upheaval for the gang behind a series of violent outbreaks in the area. He is made far from welcome, but repays his hosts - explosively.

Sophia: **Katia Christine**
Prince Lorenzo: **Maurice Denham**
Father Vincenzo: **Tony Calvin**
Guzzi: **Loris Bazzocchi**
Signora Manelli: **Clelia Matania**
Boldini: **Giancarlo Prete**
Moreno: **Cyrus Elyas**
Signora Streso: **Alba Maiolini**
Mario: **Giovanni Bachino**
Dolores: **Laura De Marchi**

Assault Force
w **Moris Farhi**
d **Peter Sasdy**

Overhearing a young Eurasian girl pleading for her life, Simon intervenes - and soon finds himself involved in a dangerous web of political intrigue in the East. No stranger to trouble, he needs his wits this time around.

O'Hara: **Bryan Marshall**
Colonel Dibha: **Carolle Rousseau**
Randolph Smith: **Neil Stacy**
Chula: **Burt Kwouk**
Cornelius: **Trevor Thomas**

Wilks: **Eamonn Boyce**
Francois: **Timothy Morand**
Marek: **Jack McKenzie**
Surinit: **Eric Young**
Kuon: **Anthony Chinn**
Policeman: **Jason Good**
Plainclothes P.C.: **Clifford Earl**

Yesterday's Hero
w **John Kruse** [from a story by **Roger Parkes**]
d **Roy Ward Baker**

When a 'dead' man returns to pursue his trail of vengeance and seeks Simon's help, the Saint finds himself involved in a deadly escapade of treachery and blackmail with an unknown victim marked for death.

Roy Gates: **Ian Hendry**
Sandy: **Annette Andre**
Michael: **Matthew Ryan**
Cleaver: **Gerald Flood**
Diskett: **Tony Vogel**
Inspector Canfield: **Norman Eshley**
Brig. Danvers: **Tony Steedman**
Doland: **John Rolfe**
Security Man: **Charles Pemberton**
Cleaver's P.A.: **Maggie Wright**
Prefect: **Rupert Graves**
Headmaster: **Reginald Jessup**

The Poppy Chain
w **John Kruse**
d **Charles Crichton**

Simon finds himself infiltrating a drugs syndicate to teach its board members that it doesn't pay to rake in millions at the expense of lives - or try to get one jump ahead of the Saint!

General Platt: **Laurence Naismith**
Scorbesi: **Gregoire Anslan**
Sandy: **Jenny Hanley**
Dominic: **Jonathan Burn**
Robbie: **Kim Fortune**
The Gent: **Christopher Timothy**
Gent's Wife: **Zuleika Robson**
Inspector Sullivan: **Patrick Jordan**
Businessman: **Paul Gregory**
Doctor: **Anton Phillips**
Rickman: **Gary Waldhorn**
Falkner: **Mike Savage**

The Arrangement
w **Anthony Terpiloff**
d **Peter Medak**

Never one to raise overtures from a beautiful woman, Simon's meeting with two lovely girls develops into a nightmare situation. The women are arranging to murder, their husbands - and require Simon's assistance!

Lady Greer Stevens: **Carolyn Seymour**
Sheila Northcott: **Sarah Douglas**
Guy Northcott: **Michael Medwin**
Sir Trevor Stevens: **Donald Pickering**
Inspector Stone: **Ian McCulloch**
Nina: **Vikki Richards**
Otis: **Gregory Munroe**
Aileen: **Jane Hayden**
Dr. Evans: **Peter Burton**
Lou: **Reg Lye**
Bartender: **Brian Pettifer**
Hansen: **David Healy**
Police Officer: **Edmund Pegge**
Girl at airport: **Sandra Dickinson**
and **The Saints Punk Rock Band**

The Armageddon Alternative
w **Terence Feely**
d **Leslie Norman**

When a man threatens to blow up London if a beautiful girl is not guillotined in public, Simon finds himself chasing shadows in an attempt to run his quarry to earth before he can carry out his threat.

Fred: **George Cole**
Lynn Jackson: **Anouska Hempel**
Commander Denning: **Donald Houston**
Loader: **Frank Gatliff**
Parkinson: **Gordon Gostelow**
Army Captain: **Ian Collier**
Bomb Squad Officer: **Peter Quince**
Telex Operator: **Brian Haughton**
Police Officer: **Edward Lyon**
Hotel Clerk: **Ray Callaghan**

The Imprudent Professor
w **Terence Feely**
d **Kevin Connor**

When two pretty girls attempt to use Simon in their scheme to lure a learned professor into defecting to a foreign power, the Saint teaches them that those who play with fire should expect to get burned.

Samantha: **Catherine Schell**
Max Boothroyd: **Anthony Steel**
Emma: **Susan Penhaligon**
Professor Bartlett: **Bill Simpson**
Cartwright: **Peter Childs**
Pierre: **John Moreno**
Demmell: **Richard Parmentier**
Inspector Lebeau: **Godfrey James**
First Professor: **Gerard Camp**
Second Professor: **John Kidd**

Signal Stop
w **John Kruse**
d **Ray Austin**

The Saint takes a train ride into murder and intrigue when he meets a young girl who leads him into a very nasty affair. Simon soon finds himself under the scrutiny of two policemen who make him bemoan the retirement of Claude Eustace Teal.

Janie Lennox: **Ciaran Madden**
Inspector Grant: **Frederick Jaeger**
Sgt. Taylor: **Ian Cullen**
Plackett: **Brian Glover**
Sally: **Heather Wright**
Billy Bradshaw: **Royston Tickner**
Tad: **George Sweeney**
Malc: **Ralph Arliss**
Smiler: **Kevin Selway**
Pam Plackett: **Kim Hardy**
Linda: **Sabina Franklyn**
Train Guard: **Michael Segal**
Policeman: **Graham Ashley**
Shopkeeper: **Renu Setna**

The Roman Touch
w **John Goldsmith** [from a story by **William Fairchild**]
d **Jeremy Summers**

The beautiful city of Rome holds a danger for pop star Michelle. And when Simon tries to help her, it looks like the end for the Saint - with Michelle left to sing his requiem.

Bruno: **Larry Luckenbill**

Diamond: **Linda Thorson**
Michelle: **Kim Goody**
Petrucci: **Piero Gerlini**
Capo: **Daniele Vargas**
Abelardo: **Duccio Dugoni**
Marcello: **Massimo Sarchielli**
Mrs Marcello: **Alina De Simone**
Paolo: **Vito Domenighini**
Heavy: **Franco Beltramme**
First Reporter: **Giuliano Persica**
Second Reporter: **Piero Pugnalini**
Third Reporter: **Gustavo Nasti**
Nurse: **Andrea Smith**
Enrico: **Selan Karay**
Second Heavy: **Rajvir Deswal**

Tower Bridge is Falling Down
w **Leon Griffiths**
d **Roy Ward Baker**

When asked to help expose an embezzler and killer, The Saint believes that he has found the perfect ploy. He intends to sell off Tower Bridge to draw the villain into the open!

Ray Dennis: **John Woodvine**
Sammy: **Alfie Bass**
Jenny: **Fiona Curzon**
Buzz Wepner: **Paul Maxwell**
Inspector Ashton: **Stanley Meadows**
Mrs Steward: **Sally Lahee**
Charlie Steward: **Sam Kydd**
Henry: **Alan Browning**
Andrew: **Neil Hallett**
3 Card Dealer: **John Wade**
Shill: **Paddy Joyce**
American Tourist: **Thick Wilson**
Terry: **Jackie Pallo**
Rex: **Terry Duggan**
Sally: **Jack Piper**

The Debt Collectors
w **George Markstein**
d **Leslie Norman**

When Simon rescues a young girl from a runaway horse, he soon discovers that she is not all she seems to be. Or is she? And what part in the mystery does Christine, her sister, play? It's double trouble, whatever the outcome.

Geoffrey Connaught: **Anton Rodgers**
Jeri Hanson: **Mary Tamm**
Christine: **Diane Keen**
Charles Medley: **Geoffrey Keen**
Jimmy: **Bob Sherman**
Paul Hanson: **Esmond Knight**
Bradley: **Neil McCarthy**
Prison Governor: **Rosemary Dunham**
Maureen: **Lesley Diane**
Forbes: **Stephan Chase**
Wardress: **Marianne Stone**
Prison Guard: **Milton Cadman**
Bradley's Aide: **Chris Dillinger**
Girl in negligee: **Cheryl Cilham**

Collision Course [Part 1 of 2 'The Brave Goose']
w **John Kruse**
d **Cyril Frankel**

After her husband is killed in a power-boat race, Simon befriends the beautiful Annabel and decides to help her overcome the threats to her life. But who is behind the threats?

Annabel: **Gayle Hunnicutt**

Georges Duchamps: **Stratford Johns**
Inspector Lebec: **Derren Nesbitt**
Captain Finnigan: **Joe Lynch**
Bernadotti: **John Hallam**
Pancho: **Leon Lissek**
Oscar West: **Edward Brayshaw**
Beeky: **Michael Robbins**
Vic: **Prentis Hancock**
Franklyn: **Wensley Pithey**
Genevieve: **Michelle Newell**
Coroner: **Cyril Luckham**
Mrs Cloonan: **Peggy Thorpe-Bates**
Salesman: **David English**
French Tough: **Marc Zuber**

Collision Course [Part 2 of 2 'The Sixth Man']
w **John Kruse**
d **Cyril Frankel**

Surrounded by danger and intrigue, Simon and Annabel set out to unravel the mystery of buried gold. Who holds the secret to a bullion robbery? And who is behind the attempts on their lives?

Annabel: **Gayle Hunnicutt**
Duchamps: **Stratford Johns**
Lebec: **Derren Nesbitt**
Finnigan: **Joe Lynch**
Bernadotti: **John Hallam**
Pancho: **Leon Lissek**
Oscar West: **Edward Brayshaw**
Crewman: **Peter Brace**

Hot Run
w **Tony Williamson**
d **Peter Sasdy**

An avalanche of danger threatens to engulf Simon when he books into an Alpine resort for a holiday. Murder strikes shortly afterwards, and the Saint finds himself on a ski ride that could result in a man's death - his own!

Diana: **Rula Lenska**
Korvis: **John Nolan**
Harland: **Barry Andrews**
Erhart: **Struan Rodger**
Maria: **Lorraine De Salle**

The Murder Cartel
w **John Goldsmith** [from a story by **Moris Farhi & John Kruse**]
d **Tom Clegg**

An assassination attempt on a powerful - but despised - oil sheik propels Simon into doing a little undercover work for the CIA to expose a murder cartel who are killing for profit.

Laura: **Britt Ekland**
Vidal: **Helmut Berger**
Lomax: **Don Powell**
Valerio: **Gigi Reder**
Hendricks: **Roger Browne**
Brown: **Sergio Doria**
Kemal: **Marne Maitland**
Gunman No 1: **Raffaele De Paola**
Gunman No 2: **Mario Novelli**
Contessa Fardango: **Heidy Von Salvesberg**
Pietro: **Marco Stefanelli**
Carlo: **Franco Moruzzi**
American journalist: **Don Tesdahl**
Hotel Clerk: **Karin Skarreso**
Bartender: **Piero Palermini**
Mario: **Roberto Messina**

The Obono Affair
w **Michael Pertwee**
d **Peter Sasdy**

When the son of a visiting African president is kidnapped in London, who better to turn to than Simon Templar for help. But as the African soon discovers, the Saint has his own way of dealing with treachery.

Colonel Dyson: **Jack Hedley**
President Obono: **Thomas Baptiste**
Mora: **Muriel Odunton**
Joey: **Paul Medford**
Wright: **Derek Newark**
Rose: **Marjie Lawrence**
Assassin: **Willie Jonah**
Mombasa: **Oscar James**
Publican: **Jason Rose**
Inspector Thornton: **Jerome Willis**
Records Officer: **Emrys Leyshon**
Reiter: **John Barrett**
Jim Batley: **John Atkinson**
Fred Batley: **Robert Gillespie**

Vicious Circle
w **John Goldsmith** [from a story by **Michael Armstrong** and **John Kruse**]
d **Sam Wanamaker**

When former racing-driver Robert Lucci - husband of a leading Italian fashion designer - dies in a car crash, Simon finds himself seeking a killer and trying to find a girl on the run.

Renata: **Elsa Martinelli**
Anna: **Tessa Wyatt**
Dr Brogli: **Mel Ferrer**
Rotti: **Luciano Pigozzi**
Roberto: **Michael Forest**
Captain Gennaro: **Stelio Candelli**
Antonio: **Gianrico Tondinelli**
Cesare: **Renato De Carmine**
Padrone: **Dante Fioretti**
Fabio: **Silvio Laurenzi**
Franco: **Guido Mannari**
Benito: **Brizio Montinaro**

Dragonseed
w **John Kruse**
d **Leslie Norman**

When a rich man's son meets his death in a helicopter accident and Simon finds evidence to prove the boy was murdered, it spells trouble for the assassins as the Saint metes out his own kind of justice.

Carla: **Annamaria Macchi**
Domenico: **Sam Wanamaker**
Doctor: **Michael Graham**
Falco: **Shane Rimmer**
Gabriel: **Paolo Malco**
Lucia: **Barbara Pilavin**
Inga: **Greta Vayant**
Tino: **Antonio Cascio**
Captain George: **Bill Vanders**
Leo: **Andrea Occhipinti**
Steward: **Stefano Galantucci**
Night Club Manager: **Geoffrey Copplestone**
Gabriel's Driver: **Alessandro Romoli**
Peasant: **Fortuanto Arena**

Appointment in Florence
w **Philip Broadley**
d **Peter Sasdy**

When his close friend Christian is kidnapped and murdered by Italian terrorists, Simon vows to avenge his death. But his attempts to track down the killers are distracted by a beautiful girl.

Manfred: **Stuart Wilson**
Ingo: **James Aubrey**
Lea: **Carla Romanelli**
Paolo: **Rodolfo Bigotti**
Karl: **Rosalino Cellamare**
Helga: **Tamara Triffez**
Gaby: **Nicole Stoliaroff**
Sheffer: **Giacomo Rossi Stuart**
Christian: **Bryan Pinero**
Giselle: **Licia Dotti**

The Diplomat's Daughter
w **Michael Pertwee**
d **Charles Crichton**

A chance encounter with a beautiful girl leads Simon into the deadly world of drug smuggling and an encounter with a gang who are prepared to remove anyone who gets too close to their secret.

Marie de la Garde: **Lynn Dalby**
Pierre: **Murray Head**
Shriver: **Karl Held**
Michel: **Weston Gavin**
Louis: **Artro Morris**
Hotel Porter: **Jean Driant**
Desk Clerk: **Graeme Eton**
First Customs Officer: **Stacy Davies**
Second Customs Officer: **Stanley McGeagh**
Harbour Gendarme: **Jeremy Anthony**

✍

A feature, *The Saint and the Brave Goose*, was issued, being a compilation of the episodes *Collision Course*, parts 1 and 2.

Return of the Saint:

Based on the character created by **Leslie Charteris**
Producer: **Anthony Spinner**
Executive Producer: **Robert S. Baker**
Music by: **Johnny Scott**
Saint theme by: **Brian Dee** and **Irving Martin**
[Original Saint Theme by **Leslie Charteris**]
Production Supervisor: **Malcolm Christopher**
Casting Director: **Weston Drury Jnr.**
Assistant Director: **Gino Marotta**
Music Editor: **Brian Lintern**
Production Designer: **John Stoll**

Filmed on location and at EMI Studios Elstree
A Robert S. Baker Tribune Films,
Rai/ITC Co-Production for ITC World Wide Distribution
Filmed on location and at EMI Elstree Studios

24 colour 60-minute episodes
1978

The Saint

The Adventures of Simon Templar, aka the Saint, a modern-day Robin Hood who raised hell with his adversaries, rescued damsels in distress with a twinkle in his eye, and found himself involved in hair-raising adventures that took him all over the world.

Known as the Saint, because of his initials, S. T., Templar's zest for adventure lead him into many dangerous situations from which he always emerged triumphant - usually with a pretty girl at his side. A man with impeccable taste, a connoisseur of fine food and wine, and an appreciative eye for the best things in life, women found his handsome looks and suave charm irresistible.

Wherever he travelled, trouble and the Saint were seldom far apart. One adventure would find him helping a lady friend escape from the clutches of a cruel blackmail attempt; another thwarting an ingenious scheme to pull off the crime of the century - more often than not right under the nose of his hapless Scotland Yard adversary, the peppermint-chewing Chief Inspector Claud Eustace Teal [a man jokingly regarded by Templar as 'Scotland Yard's finest'].

The series contained more than its share of fisticuffs and for the first 71 adventures at least stuck closely to the stories of Templar's creator, Leslie Charteris, which were adapted for the series. Thereafter the plots got more extreme - some say downright foolish - but with world sales estimated to have passed the £370-million mark, the production company [not to mention Roger Moore, who owns the rights to the colour series] must be well satisfied with the end result.

See also *Return of the Saint*.

Regular cast:
Simon Templar: **Roger Moore**
Chief Inspector Teal: **Ivor Dean**
[**Campbell Singer, Wensley Pithey & Norman Pitt** appeared as Teal in three first-season stories]

✍

To avert any confusion re individual season entries, all episodes are listed as they appear in the ITC official holdings.

season one
39 monochrome 60-minute episodes
1962-64

The Talented Husband
w **Jack Sanders**
d **Michael Truman**

Was the death of playwright John Clarron's wife an accident or murder? Together with Adrienne, a glamorous insurance agent, Simon Templar delves into Clarron's background - and turns up a few surprises.

John Clarron: **Derek Farr**
Adrienne Halberd: **Shirley Eaton**
Madge Clarron: **Patricia Roc**
Mario: **George Roderick**
Dr. Sprague: **Donald Churchill**
Mr Smith: **Norman Mitchell**
Gilbert: **John Kelland**
Ticket Collector: **Howard Douglas**
Chemist: **Clemence Bettany**

The Latin Touch
w **Gerald Kelsey** and **Dick Sharples**
d **John Gilling**

Going to the rescue of an American girl who is being overcharged by a taxi-driver in Rome, Simon soon finds himself involved in an intriguing kidnapping case - and uncovers a few guilty secrets along the way.

Hudson Inverest: **Alexander Knox**
Maude Inverest: **Doris Nolan**
Tony Unciello: **Bill Nagy**
Marco: **Warren Mitchell** [intro]
Inspector Buono: **Peter Illing**
Signora Unciello: **Marie Burke**
Sue Inverest: **Suzan Farmer**
Benson: **Robert Easton**
Maria: **Carroll Simpson**
Ada Harmer: **Anita Sharp Bolster**
Eddie Harmer: **Charles Irwin**
Georgio: **Roy Patrick**
Vittorio: **David Calderisi**
Warder: **Tony Arpino**

The Careful Terrorist
w **Gerald Kelsey** and **Dick Sharples**
d **John Ainsworth**

When Simon's journalist friend Lester Boyd decides to run an expose of a crooked union boss, and is murdered before he can submit his story, the Saint decides to continue the crusade - but doing so places his life in danger.

Herman: **David Kossof**
Nat Grendel: **Peter Dyneley**
Hoppy: **Percy Herbert**
Inspector Fernack: **Allan Gifford** [intro]
Jenny Hallam: **Sally Bazeley**
Lester Boyd: **Gary Cockrell**
Clinton: **Robert Ayres**
Doctor Grant: **Nicholas Stuart**
Verna: **Dorinda Stevens**
Ricci: **George Sperdakos**
Telephone Repair Man: **Jared Allen**
Floor Manager: **Clay Johns**

The Covetous Headman
w **John Roddick**
d **Michael Truman**

The Saint tests the theory that wearing a Saint Christopher medallion protects one from harm. For Valerie North, a girl he meets during a flight to Paris, the opposite proves true, and Simon finds himself up to his neck in danger and intrigue.

Valerie North: **Barbara Shelley**
Inspector Quercy: **Eugene Deckers** [intro]
Georges Olivant: **George Pastell**
Antoine Louvois: **Esmond Knight**
Sergeant Ludoc: **Robert Cawdron**
Josie Claval: **Carol Gray**
Madame Duras: **Josephine Browne**
Kaplan: **Michael Spear**
Mario: **Andre Boulay**
Matron: **Natalie Benesch**
Air Hostess: **Barbara Roscoe**

The Loaded Tourist
w **Richard Harris**
d **Jeremy Summers**

Witnessing a murder leads to the Saint becoming involved with an emigre family - and joining in the hunt for a briefcase containing valuable papers which the family can ill-afford to lose.

Helen Ravenna: **Barbara Bates**
Fillipo Ravenna: **Edward Evans**

Oscar Kleinhaus: **Guy Deghy**
Alfredo Ravenna: **Joseph Cuby**
Carlo Visconti: **Norman Florence**
Galen: **Michael Ritterman**
Inspector Coudot: **John Dearth**
Jacques: **Andrew Sachs**
Butler: **Raymond Ray**
Garcia: **David Cargill**
Bellhop: **John Gray**

The Pearls of Peace
w **Richard Harris**
d **David Greene**

When Simon invests money in his friend's quest to find gems, it isn't long before both men find themselves facing a dangerous enemy. Simon's intervention proves costly - and his friend Brad discovers pearls of wisdom.

Consuelo: **Dina Paisner**
Joss Hendry: **Erica Rogers**
Brad Ryan: **Bob Kanter**
Harry Tiltman: **Robin Hughes**
Pedlar: **John Barrard**
Mike Harris: **Warren Stanhope**
Bartender: **Frank Olegario**
Delivery Boy: **Hugh Futcher**
Hotel Clerk: **Steven Scott**

The Arrow of God
w **Julian Bond**
d **John Paddy Carstairs**

Simon finds danger in the most unlikely surroundings - murder and mayhem between a number of hotel guests explode into his holiday break in Nassau.

Lucy Wexall: **Elspeth March**
Herbert Wexall: **Ronald Leigh Hunt**
Pauline Stone: **Honor Blackman**
John Herrick: **Tony Wright**
Floyd Vosper: **Anthony Dawson**
Janet Blaise: **Anne Sharp**
Arthur Gresson: **Gordon Tanner**
Major Fanshire: **John Arnatt**
Astron: **John Carson**
Dr. Rahn: **Alec Mango**
Police Sergeant: **Thomas Baptiste**
Hotel Maid: **Pearl Prescod**
Maria: **Hazel Futa**

The Element of Doubt
w **Norman Borisoff**
d **John Ainsworth**

Carlton Rood is a brilliant but corrupt attorney. He wins acquittals for his clients by any means open to him. Nothing, it seems, can halt his criminal activities - until a brush with the law sets the Saint on his heels.

Carlton Rood: **David Bauer**
Inspector Fernarck: **Alan Gifford**
Agnes Yarrow: **Margaret Vines**
Joe Sholto: **Bill Nagy**
Gilroy: **Ken Wayne**
Mary Hammond: **Anita West**
Willis Burnham: **Robert O'Neill**
Miss Donaldson: **Stella Bonheur**
Stan Johnson: **Graydon Gould**
Judge: **Basil Howes**
Dibs Brown: **Alistair Williamson**
Court Clerk: **John Bloomfield**
Nurse: **Sarah Brackett**
Jury Foreman: **Victor Chenet**

The Effete Angler
w **Norman Borisoff**
d **Anthony Bushell**

When Simon takes a fishing holiday in Miami and discovers a beautiful 'mermaid' casting her magic over a ship-owner, he finds himself swimming in dangerous waters - and netting a bigger catch than he expected.

Gloria Uckrose: **Shirley Eaton**
Clinton Uckrose: **George Pravda**
Patsy O'Kevin: **Patrick McAlinney**
Vincent Innutio: **Paul Stassino**
Superintendent Marsh: **Jack Gwillim**
Dan Morrow: **Roland Brand**
Des: **Kevin Scott**
Housekeeper: **Gladys Taylor**
Hotel bartender: **Ronald Wilson**

The Charitable Countess
w **Gerald Kelsey** and **Dick Sharples**
d **Jeremy Summers**

Simon meets a Countess who can't count very well: someone is using her to feather their own nests at her expense - with money meant for a charity. Their chance meeting paves the way for Simon to trim the gang's feathers and prove that charity begins at home.

Countess Rovagna: **Patricia Donahue**
Aldo Petri: **Nigel Davenport**
Marco De Cesari: **Warren Mitchell**
Father Bellini: **Anthony Newlands**
Franco: **Philip Needs**
Enrico Vespa: **Anthony Jacobs**
Princess De Ribes: **Marie Burke**
Signora Vespa: **Irene Prador**
Count Alzerno: **Victor Rietty**
Doctor: **Neville Becker**
Angelina: **Loretta Parry**
Butler: **Hugo de Vernier**

The Golden Journey
w **Lewis Davidson**
d **Robert S. Baker**

She is beautiful, warm-hearted and generous - but has been spoilt by doting parents. Her name is Belinda and a chance encounter provides the Saint with the opportunity to show the girl that there are other things in life besides wealth.

Belinda: **Erica Rogers**
Joan West: **Stella Bonheur**
Woodcutter: **Paul Whitsun-Jones**
Hotel Manager: **Roger Delgado**
Guardia Civile: **David Lawton**
Head Waiter: **Richard Montez**
Guitarist: **Ricardo Cortes**

The Romantic Matron
w **Larry Forrester**
d **John Paddy Carstairs**

Trouble is seldom far away from Simon Templar, but even the Saint is surprised when a beautiful girl bursts into his Buenos Aires hotel bedroom and beseeches him to help her. From that moment Simon's life hangs from a thread.

Beryl Carrington: **Ann Gillis**
Ramon Venino: **John Carson**
Bernabe: **Christopher Rhodes**
Police Inspector: **Patrick Troughton** [intro]
Hotel Manager: **Michael Ritterman**
Ernesto: **Joby Blanshard**

Commissionaire: **Victor Spinetti**
Landlady: **Madge Brindley**
Juanito: **Laurence Taylor**
Miguel: **Peter Diamond**
Chico: **Kaplan Kaye**
Manuel: **Peter Elliott**
Guard: **Georges Robin**
Driver: **Bill Cartwright**

The Man Who Was Lucky
w **John Gilling**
d **John Gilling**

With the help of two lovely girls, Simon deals with a protection gang who are threatening a bookmaker. But his involvement in the affair brings him to the attention of Inspector Claude Eustace Teal - a policeman with whom Simon will share many adventures.

Lucky Joe Luckner: **Eddie Byrne**
Cora: **Delphi Lawrence**
Inspector Teal: **Campbell Singer**
Jane: **Vera Day**
Marty O'Connor: **Harry Towb**
Eddy Toscelli: **Charles Houston**
Bailey: **Nicholas Selby**
Sergeant Stevens: **John Forbes Robertson**
Frank: **Jack Taylor**
Harry: **John Sullivan**
Cab Driver: **Dickie Owen**

The Invisible Millionaire
w **Kenneth Hayles**
d **Jeremy Summers**

When strange things start to happen after a millionaire and his assistant are reported killed in a car crash, Simon's suspicions lead him to unravel the unusual affair of a man who continues spending his money from the grave.

Rosemary Chase: **Katherine Blake**
Dr. Quintus: **Michael Goodliffe**
Jim Chase: **Nigel Stock**
Nora Prescott: **Eunice Gayson**
Ellen Chase: **Jane Asher**
Marvin Chase: **Basil Dignam**
Bertrand Tamblin: **Mark Eden**
Inspector Welland: **Charles Morgan**
Franklyn: **John Gabriel**
Thompson: **Ian Ainsley**
Charley Dodds: **Frank Atkinson**
Bartender: **Peter Lawrence**
Waiter: **Michael McKevitt**

The Gentle Ladies
w **John Graeme**
d **Jeremy Summers**

They are three gentle ladies - not so young, but not too old. What awful secret do they suspect will fall upon them when a blackmailer enters their lives? Simon Templar determines to find out.

Florence Warshed: **Avice Landon**
Ida Warshed: **Renee Houston**
Violet Warshed: **Barbara Mullen**
Alfred Powls: **Philip O'Flynn**
George Marsh: **Anthony Nicholls**
Charley Butterworth: **Timothy Bateson**
Kathleen Howard: **Christina Gregg**
Joe Tracey: **Frank Sieman**
Miss Wilson: **Gwenda Ewen**
Detective Sergeant: **Donald Tandy**
Waiter: **Barry Wilsher**

The Ever-loving Spouse
w **Norman Borisoff**
d **Ernest Morris**

Convention delegate Otis Q. Fennick is alone in his room when a near-naked girl bursts in ... followed by a photographer. Grounds for blackmail? Then why should the Saint suspect that murder is afoot?

Otis Q. Fennick: **Barry Jones**
Liane Fennick: **Jeanne Moody**
Norma Upton: **Jacqueline Ellis**
Brent Kingman: **Paul Carpenter**
Vern Balton: **David Bauer**
Alec Misner: **Alexis Kanner**
Detective Williams: **Robert Arden**
Miss Grimshaw: **Janet Brandes**
Desk Clerk: **Max Faulkner**
Bartender: **Hal Gallili**
Pete: **Stuart Nichol**
Stout Man: **John Bloomfield**
Bald Man: **Bartlett Mullins**

The Saint Sees it Through
w **Ian Kennedy Martin**
d **Robert S. Baker**

The Saint is asked to assist the police in the breaking of an international art-smuggling ring, when a valuable Raphael miniature, stolen in Moscow, is discovered in the New York locker of Lili, a friend of Simon's.

Lili: **Margit Saad**
Dr. Zellerman: **Joseph Furst**
Tante Ada: **Elspeth March**
Eberhard: **Guy Deghy**
John Hamilton: **Larry Cross**
Fritz Kapel: **Gordon Sterne**
Police Captain: **Carl Duering**
Otto: **Peter Perkins**
Policeman: **Graeme Bruce**
Hat-Check-Girl: **Caron Gardner**

The King of the Beggars
w **John Gilling**
d **John Gilling**

When several attempts are made on the life of a beautiful Italian actress, the Saint dons a beggar's disguise to get to the bottom of the villainy - and the gang behind the attacks are soon begging for mercy.

Dolores Marcello: **Maxine Audley**
Joe Catelli: **Oliver Reed**
Theresa Mantania: **Yvonne Romain**
Marco: **Warren Mitchell**
Stephen Elliot: **John McLaren**
Leghetti: **Charles Houston**
Maria Calvetti: **Jessie Robins**
Inspector Mateoli: **Bruno Barnabe**
Call Boy: **Ronald Corbett**
Italian Policeman: **Cesare Maranzana**
Italian Policeman: **Gino Coia**

The Benevolent Burglary
w **Larry Forrester**
d **Jeremy Summers**

Vascoe is an arrogant millionaire who is used to getting his own way. But when Simon bets him that his 'impregnable' Riviera home will be burgled within four days - and it appears that the Saint will win the stake of £5,000 - Vascoe employs tactics unbecoming to a gentleman.

Elliot Vascoe: **John Barrie**
Bill Fulton: **Gary Cockrell**
Delphine Chambers: **Rachel Gurney**
Meryl Vascoe: **Suzanne Neve**
Jules Brant: **Raymond Adamson**
Colonel Latignant: **Arnold Diamond** [intro]
Morgan Dean: **Allan McClelland**
Martin Grahame: **Barry Keegan**
Peter Davos: **Henry Vidon**
Deslauriers: **Neal Arden**
Henri: **Ian Parsons**
Jacques: **Richard Clarke**
Germaine: **Ivor Salter**
Radio Operator: **Andre Maranne**

The Fellow Traveller
w **Harry W. Junkin**
d **Peter Yates**

'Get Maria ...go to the Blue Goose' - words spoken to Simon by a dying man lead the Saint into putting his life on the line to expose a killer. The Blue Goose is owned by a beautiful Maria - and she wants Simon dead!

Magda Vamoff: **Dawn Addams**
Superintendent Kinglake: **Glyn Owen**
Nick Vashetti: **Neil McCallum**
Hans Blatt: **Michael Peake**
Mactavish: **Angus Lennie**
Mrs. Matson: **Jeanne Watts**
Joe: **Brian Oulton**
Gower: **Charles Simon**
Marsh: **Ray Austin**
Sergeant Lashbrook: **Fred Ferris**
Inspector in Grey Goose: **John Barrett**
Receptionist: **Janine Gray**
Guard: **Richard McNeff**

Marcia
w **Harry W. Junkin**
d **John Krish**

After her face is disfigured in an acid attack, international film starlet Marcia Landon commits suicide. Her death presents a convenient opportunity for Claire Avery to step into the dead star's shoes - but the Saint steps into trouble when Claire is threatened with the same fate.

Claire Avery: **Samantha Eggar**
Mike Sentinal: **Kenneth Mackintosh**
Sheila Sentinal: **Marion Mathie**
Johnny Desmond: **Johnny Briggs**
Irene Cromwell: **Jill Melford**
Inspector Carlton: **Phillip Stone**
Frank Landon: **Stranley Meadows**
Barry Aldon: **Tony Beckley**
Pearl: **Janet Davies**
Assistant Director: **Philip Anthony**
Nurse: **Virginia Clay**
Prop Man: **Peter Duguid**

The Bunco Artists
w **Lewis Davidson**
d **Peter Yates**

When two confidence tricksters divert the funds they received for the restoration of the village church into their own pockets, the Saint steps in and plays a confidence trick of his own - one which benefits the church twofold.

Sophie Yarmouth: **Mary Merral**
Richard Eade: **Peter Dyneley**
Jean Yarmouth: **Justine Lord**
Joyce Eade: **Louise King**

Charlie: **Victor Platt**
Vicar Stone: **John Glyn Jones**
Miss Emmar: **Marie Makino**
Mrs Rance: **Barbara Ogilvie**
Louis: **Andre Maranne**
Gendarme: **John Standing**
Stage Door Keeper: **Meadows White**

Judith
w **Leonard Grahame**
d **Robert Lynn**

A quiet drive in the country turns into a headlong chase to stop a cunningly conceived fraud attempt taking place. Simon is accused of trespassing, and the accusation leads to an exciting adventure in the Swiss Alps.

Judith: **Julie Christie**
Burt Northwade: **David Bauer**
Ellen Northwade: **Margo Johns**
Dr. Northwade: **John McLaren**
Inspector Lavin: **John Serret**
Sgt. Soustelle: **Ross Parker**
Tom Mackinnon: **Warren Stanhope**
Hal Sinfield: **Robert MacLeod**
Jim Wallace: **William Greene**
Garner: **Andre Boulay**
Desk Clerk: **Ronald Wilson**
French Waiter: **Georges Robin**

The Work of Art
w **Harry W. Junkin**
d **Peter Yates**

The Saint's springtime sojourn in Paris with the bewitching Juliette leads to drama when her brother, Andre, is suspected of murdering his partner to gain control of their fashion concern.

Juliette: **Yolande Turner**
Andre Grillot: **Alex Scott**
Major Quintana: **Martin Benson**
Jean Bourgrenet: **John Bailey**
Sgt. Luduc: **Robert Cawdron**
Insp. Quercy: **Manning Wilson**
Vladek Urivetsky: **Hamilton Dyce**
Mere Lafond: **Hazel Hughes**
Lt. Prevost: **Neville Becker**
Maria: **Miki Iveria**
Receptionist: **Anne Sharp**
Paul Fouchet: **Tom Naylor**
Annette Dosterd: **June Smith**

The Elusive Ellshaw
w **Harry W. Junkin** [from a story by **John Kruse**]
d **John Moxey**

A cashier's strange behaviour before her death leads Simon to suspect foul play. Before he's done, he will have thwarted an assassination attempt, unearthed the woman's 'dead' husband - and caused much annoyance to a gang of cut-throats.

Anne Ripwell: **Angela Browne**
Sir John Ripwell: **Richard Vernon**
Mrs Ellshaw: **Ellen McIntosh**
Ellshaw: **Philip Latham**
Martin Irelock: **Anthony Bate**
Hugo Meyer: **Walter Brown**
Kenneth Ripwell: **Philip Bond**
Teal: **Norman Pitt**
Gunsmith: **Arthur Hewlett**
Dr. Cranston: **James Ottaway**
Young Cop: **Nicholas Pennell**

Starring the Saint
w **Harry W. Junkin**
d **James Hill**

When Simon agrees to star as the Saint in a new film, it isn't long before someone rewrites the scenario with scenes of Simon's death. But why should anyone wish to kill their leading star? The answer leads Simon into danger beneath the floodlights.

Byron Ufferlitz: **Ronald Radd**
Teal: **Wensley Pithey**
Jack Groom: **Alfred Burke**
Peggy Warden: **Monica Stevenson**
Orland Flane: **Alexander Davion**
Vic Lazaroff: **Paul Whitsun-Jones**
Bob Kendricks: **Jerry Stovin**
David Brown: **Ivor Dean**
Sgt. Graham: **John Dunbar**
Cabbie: **Brian Weske**
April Quest: **Jackie Collins**
Barman: **John Gayford**
Medical Examiner: **John Martin**
P. C. Burns: **Bryan Marshall**

Sophia
w **Robert Stewart**
d **Roger Moore**

On holiday in a Greek village, Simon takes time out from his sightseeing to settle accounts with an Americanised crook who is threatening the peace of the inhabitants with his reign of bully-boy tactics.

Aristides: **Oliver Reed**
Sophia: **Imogen Hassall**
Niko: **Peter Kriss**
Stavros: **Tommy Duggan**
Professor Grant: **John Wentworth**
Joe Martin: **Hal Gallili**
Gorgo: **Wolfe Morris**
First Villager: **Andreas Malandrinos**
Second Villager: **Tony Arpino**
American Tourist: **Donna Pearson**
Photographer: **Raymond Ray**

Teresa
w **John Kruse**
d **Roy Baker**

When Simon becomes involved with a beautiful woman trying to solve the disappearance of her husband, he finds himself being chased by Mexican bandits - and discovers that life under the big top is not as it first appears.

Teresa: **Lana Morris**
Casemegas: **Eric Pohlmann**
Borota: **Marne Maitland**
El Rojo: **Lawrence Dane**
Senora Artigas: **Marie Burke**
Miguel Artigas: **Alexander Davion**
Carlos Segoia: **Richard Montez**
Sebastian: **Paul Whitsun-Jones**
Cafe Proprietor: **Alan Browning**
Padron: **Frank Olegario**
Police Lieutenant: **George Little**
Lucito: **Peter Exposite**

Iris
w **Bill Strutton**
d **John Gilling**

The Saint becomes involved in the schemes of a racketeer and his wife to frame a man for blackmail. The 'man'

marked down to be the hapless recipient of bad news is Simon himself - so he plays out enough rope to hang his adversaries.

Iris Lansing: **Barbara Murray**
Rick Lansing: **David Bauer**
Inspector Teal: **Ivor Dean** [intro]
Jack Hardy: **Cyril Luckham**
Stratford Keene: **Ferdy Mayne**
Mark Belden: **John Ronane**
Calder: **Anthony Wager**
Thatcher: **Barry Linehan**
Harry Blundell: **Meadows White**
Mary Hardy: **April Wilding**

The Rough Diamonds
w **Bill Strutton**
d **Peter Yates**

A consignment of industrial diamonds is hijacked on arrival in England. Two security guards are murdered - and someone is out to lay the blame at the Saint's door. Inspector Teal of Scotland Yard refuses to believe Simon's alibi - so the Saint sets out to throw a halo around the real culprits.

Alan Uttershaw: **Douglas Wilmer**
Inspector Teal: **Ivor Dean**
Milton Ourley: **George A. Cooper**
Tina Ourley: **Vanda Godsell**
Ricco: **Paul Stassino**
Barbara Sinclair: **Jemma Hyde**
George Stanton: **Michael Meacham**
Gabriel Linnet: **William Dexter**
Joe: **Ray Austin**
Pete Ferguson: **Geoffrey Palmer**
Johnny Maxwell: **Frank Jarvis**

The Saint Plays with Fire
w **John Kruse**
d **Robert S. Baker**

What connects the death of a journalist to a dark and isolated country house? Simon intends to find out, even if it means taking on the powerful force behind a new Nazi party - a man who has signed the Saint's death warrant.

Kane Luker: **Joseph Furst**
Lady Valerie: **Justine Lord**
Sidney Fairweather: **John Robinson**
Lady Sangore: **Margaretta Scott**
Sir Robert Sangore: **Geoffrey Denton**
Inspector Teal: **Ivor Dean**
Jackman: **Robert Brown**
Norton: **Raymond Adamson**
West: **John Hollis**
Austin: **Joe Robinson**
John Kennet: **Tony Beckley**
Ralph Windlay: **John Kelland**

The Well-Meaning Mayor
w **Robert Stewart**
d **Jeremy Summers**

Following up the death of a councillor, the Saint discovers corruption and treachery permeating through to the very heart of local government. One alone bears investigation - the Mayor - but who is pulling his strings?

Sam Purdell: **Leslie Sands**
Alice Purdell: **Mary Kenton**
Hackett: **Norman Bird**
Molly: **Mandy Miller**
Jack Bryant: **Noel Trevarthen**
Alderman Greer: **Cameron Hall**

Ironside: **Kenneth Henry**
Maxin: **David Morell**
Coroner: **Robert Sansom**
Dr. Yates: **John Gill**

The Wonderful War
w **John Graeme**
d **Robert S. Baker**

When greed, murder and intrigue follow the discovery of oil in the Middle East state of Sayeda, the Saint wages his own kind of war on behalf of the deposed ruler's son Karim, who suspects his father's advisers of plotting to assassinate him.

Mrs McAlister: **Renee Houston**
Mike Kelly: **Noel Purcell**
Harry Shannet: **Alfred Burke**
Abdul Aziz: **Alec Mango**
Major Hussein: **Patrick Westwood**
Ahmed: **David Graham**
Raschid: **John Bennet**
The Iman: **Ferdy Mayne**
Karim: **Louis Raynor**
John McAndrew: **Jack Lambert**
Lilla McAndrew: **Suzanna Leigh**

The Sporting Chance
w **John Kruse**
d **Jeremy Summers**

In Canada on a fishing holiday, the Saint uncovers a plot to bring a German scientist back to the East - against his best interests. So Simon goes fishing for the villains - and hooks a major prize by way of a result.

Netchideff: **Derren Nesbitt**
Professor Mueller: **Gerard Heinz**
Pavan: **Godfrey Quigley**
Marion Kent: **Carol Cleveland**
Cleaver: **Brandon Brady**
Beaver Johnson: **Harry Webster**
Jack Williams: **Bruce Boa**
Inspector Hackett: **Nicholas Stuart**
Mrs Whicker: **Nan Marriot-Watson**
Detective Gorman: **William Buck**
Dr. Beamish: **Evan Thomas**

The Noble Sportsman
w **John Graeme**
d **Peter Yates**

When her husband Lord Yearley starts to receive threats to his life, Lady Anne seeks Simon's help to find out why anyone should want to kill him. The Saint uncovers a web of intrigue which reaches back into her husband's past.

Lady Anne Yearley: **Sylvia Syms**
Lord Yearley: **Anthony Quayle**
Paula Farley: **Francis Matthews**
Bruno Walmar: **Paul Curran**
Rose Yearley: **Jane Asher**
Kelly: **Russell Walters**
Bates: **Martin Wyldeck**
Tom Crofton: **Howard Douglas**

Luella
w **John Kruse** and **Harry W. Junkin**
d **Roy Baker**

When Simon bumps into his old friend Bill Harvey, he finds himself painting the town red as Harvey sallies into one bar after another. But Simon tires of the game when he finds himself the victim of blackmail attempts.

Bill Harvey: **David Hedison**
Doris Harvey: **Suzanne Lloyd**
Luella: **Susan Lloyd**
Matt Joyson: **Aidan Turner**
Ted Kermein: **Michael Wynne**
Miss Hill: **Jean St Clair**
Head Porter: **John Woodnutt**
Waiter: **Julian Holloway**
Hotel Clerk: **Peter Fontaine**

The Lawless Lady
w **Harry W. Junkin**
d **Jeremy Summers**

To avenge a murder, Simon joins forces with the glamorous Countess Audrey Marova - one of the most astute crooks in London. Their combined efforts result in a team of modern-day pirates biting the dust - before Simon sets out to reform his companion.

Audrey: **Dawn Addams**
Hilloran: **Julian Glover**
Inspector Teal: **Ivor Dean**
Sanders: **Ronald Ibbs**
Jacques Boucher: **John G. Heller**
Dickie Tremaine: **David Sumner**
Photographer: **James Bellchamber**
Miss Williams: **Anthea Wyndham**
Lord Wentworth: **Kenneth Benda**
Lady Wentworth: **Dorothy Black**
George Ulrig: **Stuart Saunders**
May Ulrig: **Anne Sharp**
Sir Edras Levy: **Gerald Young**
Lady Levy: **Edith Saville**

The Good Medicine
w **Norman Borisoff**
d **Roy Baker**

When Simon meets the elegant and lovely Denise Dumont, the woman behind the Dumont beauty combine, he discovers the scent of something nasty hiding behind the facade of the woman's loving husband.

Denise: **Barbara Murray**
Phillipe: **Anthony Newlands**
Marie: **Jean Marsh**
David Stern: **Bill Nagy**
Alfredo: **John Bennet**
Madame Dumont: **Veronica Turleigh**
Jacques: **Bruce Montague**
Mathilde: **Alexandra Dane**

The High Fence
w **Harry W. Junkin**
d **James Hill**

A dinner date with glamorous actress Gabrielle leads the Saint to a murder investigation and a grim hunt for one of London's most notorious master-criminals- an old enemy of Simon's and one who swore to kill him should they ever meet again.

Inspector Pryor: **James Villiers**
Gabby: **Suzanne Lloyd**
Inspector Teal: **Ivor Dean**
Enderby: **Reginald Beckwith**
Bob Stryker: **Stanley Meadows**
Johnny: **Harry Towb**
Jim Fasson: **Dyson Lovell**
Mary: **Clare Kelly**
Quincy: **Peter Jeffrey**
Mrs Stewart: **Hazel Hughes**
Robbins: **Richard Poore**

season two
32 monochrome 60-minute episodes
1964-65

The Scorpion
w **Paul Erickson**
d **Roy Barker**

Hiding somewhere in the background of unexplained happenings, blackmail and murder in which Simon finds himself involved, there hides a mysterious mastermind known only as The Scorpion. Who is he? Unless Simon unmasks the villain, a young girl faces certain death.

Karen Bates: **Catherine Woodville**
Patsy Butler: **Nyree Dawn Porter**
Eddy: **Dudley Sutton**
Long Harry: **Philip Latham**
Inspector Teal: **Ivor Dean**
Birdie: **Leon Cortez**
Wilfred Garniman: **Geoffrey Bayldon**
Mark Deverest: **Ronald Leigh-Hunt**
Cynthia Deverest: **Eve Lister**

The Miracle Tea Party
w **Paddy Manning O'Brine**
d **Roger Moore**

When a pretty young nurse visits London and a packet of tea is slipped into her bag, and then a man who has been following her is murdered, Simon Templar finds himself involved in a tense adventure with danger at every turn.

Aunt Hattie: **Fabia Drake**
Geraldine McLeod: **Nanette Newman**
Dr. Sandberg: **Conrad Phillips**
Commander Richardson: **Basil Dignam**
Norton: **Charles Houston**
Inescue: **Viktor Viko**
Osbett: **Patrick Westwood**
Atkins: **Robert Brown**
Franklin: **Edward Jewesbury**
Wilson: **Neville Whiting**
Barlow: **Michael Standing**

The Saint Steps In
w **John Kruse**
d **John Gilling**

The Saint becomes involved in big business to break apart the highly explosive relationship between a tycoon's daughter and the daughter of a scientist who is out to seek revenge for her father's failure to win a large contract.

Hobart Quennel: **Geoffrey Keen**
Andrea Quennel: **Justine Lord**
Walter Devan: **Peter Vaughan**
Calvin Gray: **Moultrie Kelsall**
Madeline Gray: **Annette Andre**
Morgen: **Neil McCarthy**
Smith: **Michael Robbins**
Cy Imberline: **Edward Bishop**
Intelligent Undergraduate: **Nicholas Pennell**
Husky Undergraduate: **David Jackson**
Det. Insp. Malloy: **Robert Bruce**

The Death Penalty
w **Ian Stuart Black**
d **Jeremy Summers**

Holidaying in the South of France would be a breeze for anyone else, but when you're the Saint and you give a lift to a young girl, you can expect trouble to follow. It does, and

Templar finds himself sorting out a vice ring - and a witness to murder.

Abdul Osman: **Paul Stassino**
Galbraith Stride: **Brewster Mason**
Laura Stride: **Wanda Ventham**
Toby Haildon: **Scot Finch**
Colonel Latignant: **Arnold Diamond**
Clements: **Rory MacDermot**
Smith: **William Marlow**
Trape: **Alan Curtis**
Dali: **Arthur Gomez**
Suza: **Philo Hauser**

The Revolution Racket
w **Terry Nation** [from a story by **Harry W. Junkin**]
d **Pat Jackson**

Suspicious that an astute South American policeman is combining duty with personal gain, Simon dupes the man into showing his true colours by laying the seeds of doubt in the policeman's mind.

Doris Inkler: **Suzanne Lloyd**
Carlos Xavier: **Eric Pohlman**
Pablo Enriquez: **Peter Arne**
Sherm Inkler: **Edward Bishop**
Manuel Enriquez: **Michael Godfrey**
Vincente: **Hal Gallili**
Jose Jalisco: **Alec Mango**
Esteban: **Clive Cazes**
Immigration Officer: **Richard Montez**
Rainer: **Michael Lynch**
Francisco: **Reginald Jessup**
Juan: **Walter Randall**

Jeannine
w **Harry W. Junkin**
d **John Moxey**

When Simon visits Paris at the same time as Madame Chen, and their paths cross, the Saint is off and running into a new adventure to find a valuable pearl necklace which has been stolen from the girl.

Jeannine Roger: **Sylvia Syms**
Madam Chen: **Jacqui Chan**
Sergeant Leduc: **Robert Cawdron**
Inspector Quercy: **Manning Wilson**
Lo Yung: **Eric Young**
Jerome: **Martin Miller**
Kwan Li: **Peter Elliott**
Fouquet: **John Dearth**
Peyrac: **Peter Diamond**
Hotel Manager: **Michael Anthony**
Girl Receptionist: **Maggie Wright**

The Unkind Philanthropist
w **Marcus Demian**
d **Jeremy Summers**

A girl with a boy's name can lead to misunderstandings. The Saint takes advantage of this fact to repay a cruel and uncaring father for the selfish way he has been treating his step-children.

Elmer Quire: **Charles Farrell**
Dolores Gamma: **Pat Michon**
Juan Gamma: **David Graham**
Tristan Brown: **Sarah Brackett**
Victor Gamma: **Garry Fulsham**
Twinewright: **John Bloomfield**
Maria Gamma: **Dawn Davies**
Portagee: **Anthony Morton**

Alicron: **Larry Taylor**
Mrs Hendricks: **Joan Ingram**
Chic Woman: **Olive Lucius**

The Man Who Liked Toys
w **Basil Dawson**
d **John Gilling**

When he tries to investigate the shady dealings of a toy-loving business executive whom he suspects of bribery and corruption, Simon finds out that toy soldiers can sometimes win battles all on their own. Well, not quite, they sometimes require the help of the Saint.

Inspector Teal: **Ivor Dean**
Lewis Enstone: **John Baskcomb**
Marjorie Enstone: **Jeanne Moody**
John Hammel: **John Paul**
George Fowler: **Mauice Kaufmann**
Claire Wheeler: **Rosemary Reede**
Harry Duggan: **David Lodge**
Albert Costello: **Inigo Jackson**

Lida
w **Michael Cramoy**
d **Leslie Norman**

Wealthy Lida Verity falls victim to the smooth-talking nightclub blackmailer Maurice Kerr. Her sister, Joan, is alarmed at their relationship so she is delighted when her old friend Simon Templar arrives on the scene.

Joan Wingate: **Erica Rogers**
Lida Verity: **Jeanne Moody**
Bosun: **Barry Keegan**
Maurice Kerr: **Peter Bowles**
Esteban: **Marne Maitland**
Pebbles: **Aubrey Morris**
Inspector Maxwell: **Robert Raglan**
Mara: **Maggie Wright**
American Man: **Henry McCarthy**

The Hi-Jackers
w **Paul Erickson**
d **David Eady**

In Munich to visit an old friend, the Saint meets a beautiful Fraulein and finds himself plunged headlong into an audacious scheme to rob the American army of high-powered weapons.

Mathilde Baum: **Ingrid Schoeller**
Robert Pargo: **Robert Nichols**
Ed Jopley: **Neil McCallum**
Hans Lasser: **Walter Gotell**
Sergeant Henry Johns: **Kevin Scott**
Borieff: **Michael Collins**
Schultz: **Richard Shaw**
Major Smith: **Shane Rimmer**
P.F.C. Kirk: **Roy Stephens**

Sibao
w **Terry Nation**
d **Peter Yates**

When the Saint meets the beautiful Sibao in a Haitan bar, he suddenly finds himself involved in the shadowy world of native superstition and voodoo practice - with himself and the girl as the sacrificial lambs.

Theron Netlord: **John Carson**
Sibao: **Jeanne Roland**
Tony Kreiger: **Jerry Stovin**
Atherton Lee: **Nicholas Stuart**

Dr. Farrere: **Kevin Stoney**
Manon: **Christopher Carlos**
Tarno: **Tracey Connell**
Hamilton: **Bruce Boa**
Brinkley: **John McClaren**
Male Dancer: **Boscoe Holder**

The Imprudent Politician
w **Norman Hudis**
d **John Moxey**

When a politician allows himself to become involved with a scheming girl and betrays secrets to make a killing on the stock market, he is asking for trouble. When the trouble arrives in the shape of blackmail, the man turns to the Saint for help.

Christopher Waites: **Anthony Bate**
Janet Waites: **Jennifer Wright**
Denise Grant: **Justine Lord**
Colin Phillips: **Michael Gough**
Spencer Vallance: **Maxwell Shaw**
Tim Burton: **Jeremy Burnham**
Alex Morgan: **Mike Pratt**
Helen Phillips: **Jean Marsh**
Mister Anthony: **John Bryans**
Ken Shield: **Moray Watson**
Marine Mechanic: **Jimmy Gardner**

The Loving Brothers
w **John Graeme**
d **Leslie Norman**

Simon becomes involved with an old Australian prospector who believes he's struck it rich by discovering a silver mine. He needs finance to work the dig, but his two wealthy sons refuse to cough up - until Simon tries a little gentle persuasion.

Pop Kinsall: **Reg Lye**
Willie Kinsall: **Ray Barrett**
Wally Kinsall: **Ed Devereaux**
Linda Henderson: **Annette Andre**
Edna Kinsall: **Betty McDowell**
Charley O'Shea: **Dick Bentley**
Peter Grove: **Grant Taylor**
Joe Casey: **Noel Trevarthen**
Assayer: **John Tate**

The Damsel in Distress
w **Paul Erickson**
d **Peter Yates**

The owner of Templar's favourite restaurant is distraught... his daughter is pregnant, but has no husband. Her betrothed has absconded with a lot of money, so Simon plays matchmaker to restore the status quo.

Allessandro Naccaro: **Richard Wyler**
Barbara Astral: **Catherine Woodville**
Domenick Naccaro: **Paul Whitsun-Jones**
Guiseppe Rolfieri: **Harold Kasket**
Inspector Teal: **Ivor Dean**
Arturo: **Ray Austin**
Guido Naccaro: **John Bluthal**
Maria Naccaro: **Camilla Hasse**
Jennifer: **Gwynneth Tighe**

The Contract
w **Terry Nation**
d **Roger Moore**

Eight years after robbing an American airbase in England, the thief returns to his old haunts to recover the money he

secreted away. The Saint's evidence put him away - and he's out for revenge.

Dunstan: **Dick Haymes**
Farnberg: **Robert Hutton**
Eileen Ballinger: **Elizabeth Weaver**
Insp. Teal: **Ivor Dean**
Ardossi: **John Bennett**
Friste: **Michael Peake**
Chuck Powers: **Richard Easton**
Doctor Jerome: **Douglas Muir**
Mrs. Evans: **Mary Jones**

The Set-Up
w **Paddy Manning O'Brine**
d **Roy Baker**

When Simon finds his life threatened, a beautiful film starlet uses her acting talent to lead his unseen adversary into the open so that he can foil an ingenious plot to kill him - and lay the blame on someone else.

Oonagh O'Grady: **Penelope Horner**
Ted Orping: **John Stone**
Tex Goldman: **Henry Gilbert**
Chief. Inp. Teal: **Ivor Dean**
Jack Laurie: **Edward Underdown**
Nilder: **Redmond Phillips**
Clem Enright: **Norman Florence**
Corrigan: **Anthony Wager**
Mrs. Donaldson: **Faith Kent**

The Rhine Maiden
w **Brian Degas**
d **James Hill**

Quick action by the Saint saves the life of a pretty girl and plunges him into an intriguing mystery from which he barely escapes with his halo intact.

Charles Voyson: **Nigel Davenport**
Dr. Schreiber: **Victor Beaumont**
Julia Harrison: **Stephanie Randall**
Hans: **Anthony Booth**
Inspector Glessen: **George Pravda**
Helga: **Adlina Mandlova**
Otto: **Frederick Schiller**
Train Steward: **Ernst Walder**
English Man: **Ernest Hare**
English Woman: **Tutti Truman Taylor**
Barman: **Michael Wolf**

The Inescapable Word
w **Terry Nation**
d **Roy Baker**

While on a grouse-shooting holiday in the Scottish highlands, Simon finds himself confronted by some weird happenings surrounding the staff who work at a top-secret government research laboratory.

Marjorie North: **Ann Bell**
Jock Ingram: **James Maxwell**
Ivor North: **Maurice Hedley**
Professor Soren: **Robert Dean**
Professor Oakridge: **Robert McLeod**
Professor Walter Rand: **Ronald Ibbs**
Simms: **Donald Bisset**
Dr. Carey: **James Copeland**
Thompson: **Russell Waters**

The Golden Frog
w **Michael Cramoy**
d **John Moxey**

No one could be more gallant towards the fair sex than the Saint. But when an attractive girl uses Simon Templar to score a point with her rival, Simon decides to teach the girl a sharp lesson.

Alice Nestor: **Jacqueline Ellis**
Nestor: **Hugh McDermott**
Capt. Quintana: **Alan Tilvern**
General Cuevas: **Walter Brown**
Fergus Maclish: **Alex McCrindle**
Loro: **Inia Te Wiata**
Julio: **Alvaro Fontana**
Paco: **Barry Shawzin**
Vargos: **Alan Curtis**

The Sign of the Claw
w **Terry Nation**
d **Leslie Norman**

The Saint finds himself involved in an anti-terrorist campaign in Southeast Asia. He has been invited there by a girl, but upon arrival she is nowhere to be found. Concerned for her safety, Simon delves deeper - and finds himself held prisoner by terrorists.

Jean Morland : **Suzan Farmer**
Don Morland: **Peter Copley**
Max Valmon: **Godfrey Quigley**
Major Rowney: **Geoffrey Frederick**
Dr. Julias: **Leo Leyden**
Angkor: **Kenjin Takaki**
Tawau: **Burt Kwouk**
Gale: **John Rees**
Harlun: **Kristopher Kum**
Rawach: **Michael Chow**

The Frightened Inn-Keeper
w **Norman Hudis**
d **Roy Baker**

In response to an intriguing SOS from his friend Martin, the Saint travels to Cornwall. His arrival there appears to cause consternation to the local innkeeper, and Martin is nowhere to be found.

Martin Jeffroll: **Michael Gwynn**
Julia Jeffroll: **Susanne Neve**
Tom Kane: **Percy Herbert**
Portmore: **Howard Marion-Crowford**
Weems: **Norman Bird**
Yesterman: **John Gabriel**
Bellamy: **Edward Cast**

The Crime of the Century
w **Terry Nation**
d **John Gilling**

When the Saint impersonates a tough, greying American safebreaker to foil a crime, he is amused to find that he his working side by side with his old Scotland Yard adversary.

Bernhard Raxel: **Andre Morell**
Betty Tregarth: **Sarah Lawson**
Crantor: **William Lucas**
Inspector Teal: **Ivor Dean**
Gregory Marring: **Peter Jeffrey**
David Tregarth: **David Saire**
Philip Grey: **John Forbes-Robertson**
Gloria Mancini: **Carol Cleveland**
Joan Vendel: **Alexandra Bastedo**
Flavel: **Cyril Chamberlain**
Madeline: **Maggie Wright**

The Happy Suicide
w **Brian Degas**
d **Robert Tronson**

Ziggy Zaglan enjoys the standing ovation he receives nightly from the crowds gathered to watch his television chat show. But Simon finds that sinister mischief lurks behind Ziggy's smiling face.

Lois Norroy: **Jane Merrow**
Ziggy Zaglan: **John Bluthal**
Ralph Damian: **William Sylvester**
Ted Coblin: **Jerry Stovin**
Paul Zaglan: **William Dexter**
McCleery: **Donald Sutherland**
Capt. Williams: **Fred Sadoff**
Texas Mother: **Mavis Villiers**
Jack Gill: **Kevin Brennan**
Annie Ross: **Annie Ross**

The Crooked Ring
w **Harry W. Junkin**
d **Leslie Norman**

Simon becomes involved in bribery and corruption in the fight game when he is asked to help a young boxer, Steve Nelson, whose life has been threatened unless he follows orders and takes a 'dive' in his next contest.

'Doc' Spangler: **Walter Brown**
Steve Nelson: **Tony Wright**
Whitey Mullins: **Meredith Edwards**
Connie Grady: **Jean Aubrey**
The Angel: **Nosher Powell**
Dave Snyders: **John Tate**
Max: **Barry Linehan**
Torpedo Smith: **Irvin Allen**
Mrs. Barlow: **Doris Hare**
Radio Commentator: **Macdonald Hobley**

The Smart Detective
w **Michael Cramoy**
d **John Moxey**

When a private detective boasts that his security precautions at a jewel exhibition are foolproof, Simon becomes suspicious and decides to find out if the building is really as secure as it seems.

Peter Corrio: **Brian Worth**
Janice Dixon: **Anne Lawson**
Aunt Prudence: **Fabia Drake**
Inspector Teal: **Ivor Dean**
Nick Nigkoma: **Barry Shawzin**
Mr. Justin: **Martin Miller**
George: **Reg Lye**
Swann: **Larry Taylor**
Miller: **Dennis Blake**
Garage Mechanic: **Ron Welling**

The Chequered Flag
w **Norman Hudis**
d **Leslie Norman**

The Saint finds himself helping a friend to discover what lies behind a long spell of bad 'luck' that has dogged a former racing-driver. He comes to the grim decision that one of the man's competitors is playing the game by his own sordid rules.

Oscar Newley: **Eddie Byrne**
Mandy Ellington: **Justine Lord**
Beau Ellington: **Edward De Souza**
Catherine Marshall: **Pamela Conway**

Lee Leonard: **Tim Barrett**
Alec Hunter: **Neil McCarthy**
Bateman: **John Kidd**
Hunter's Landlady: **Dorothy Frere**
Bank Clerk: **Eliza Buckingham**

The Abductors
w **Brian Degas** [from a story by **Harry W. Junkin**]
d **Jeremy Summers**

An English girl wins a prize of a weekend in Paris but finds it very dull - until she bumps into The Saint. Within minutes, the couple find themselves pursued by a gang of crooks and Simon finds himself investigating a kidnap plot.

Jones: **Dudley Foster**
Brian Quell: **Robert Urquhart**
Madeline: **Annette Andre**
Olga: **Jennifer Jayne**
Sgt. Leduc: **Robert Cawdron**
Insp. Quercy: **John Serrett**
Alain: **Nicholas Courtney**
Professor Quell: **Ronald Ibbs**
Hotel Clerk: **Sandor Eles**
Peter: **David Garfield**
Mr. Mason: **Martin Wyldeck**

The Persistent Parasite
w **Norman Hudis**
d **Robert Tronson**

When the Saint is invited to join Waldo his millionaire friend on an island off the South of France, believing that he's in for a pleasant weekend sojourn, he accepts - but the weekend ends in tragedy.

Waldo: **Cec Linder**
Vera: **Jan Holden**
Wilma: **Ann Gillis**
Katerina: **Annette Carrell**
Nadine: **Sonia Fox**
Latignant: **Arnold Diamond**
Pierre: **Brian MacDermott**
George McGeorge: **Jeremy Longhurst**
Howard: **Donald Hewlett**
Monsieur Phillippe: **David Garth**
Latignant's Assistant: **Keith Smith**

The Spanish Cow
w **Paul Erickson** [from a story by **Michael Cramoy**]
d **John Gilling**

The Saint becomes involved with the lovely widow of an assassinated South American politician who believes that the men who killed her husband will not rest until she, too, is dead. Simon's dilemma: is the woman telling the truth?

Gilberto Arroyo: **Gary Raymond**
Consuela Flores: **Viviane Ventura**
Dona Luisa Arroyo: **Nancy Nevinson**
Col. Latignant: **Arnold Diamond**
Deigo Ramiriz: **Leonard Sachs**
Rene: **Michael Wynne**
Chico: **David Jackson**
Jean: **Nicholas Donnelly**
Sancho: **Terry Yorke**

The Saint Bids Diamonds
w **Norman Hudis**
d **Leslie Norman**

Alarmed that a friend is facing bankruptcy because his most valuable asset, a famous diamond, has been stolen, Simon

impersonates a diamond-cutter in an attempt to track down the jewel thieves.

Christine Graner: **Eunice Gayson**
Abdul Graner: **George Murcell**
Madame Calliope: **Jean St. Clair**
Joris Vanlinden: **Gerard Heinz**
Captain Garcia: **Peter Illing**
George Felson: **Edward Bishop**
Palerno: **Neville Becker**
Lauber: **Laurence Herder**
Teneriffe Policeman: **Richard Montee**

The Man Who Could Not Die
w **Terry Nation**
d **Roger Moore**

The Saint goes underground in an attempt to save a friend who has been tricked into going pot-holing with a dangerous man - a man who has already killed once, and looks set to do so again, unless Simon can stop him.

Miles Hallin: **Patrick Allen**
Moyna Stanford: **Jennie Linden**
Nigel Perry: **Robin Phillips**
Roddy Morton: **Richard Wyler**
Inspector Teal: **Ivor Dean**
Emrys Pugh: **Meredith Edwards**
Mrs. Pugh: **Mary Jones**

The Old Treasure Story
w **Ronald Duncan**
d **Roger Moore**

An old seafaring friend of Simon's leads him into a strange treasure hunt that takes them from Cornwall to the West Indies. Simon's suspicions that they are on a wild goose chase are confirmed when someone tries to kill them.

Duncan Rawl: **Jack Hedley**
Jack Forrest: **Robert Hutton**
April Mallory: **Erica Rogers**
Captain Bill Williams: **Reg Lye**
Jim Reston: **Frank Wolff**
Maria Cavallini: **Jill Curzon**
Big Tom: **Roy Patrick**
First Sailor: **Joby Blanshard**
Second Sailor: **Timmy Gardner**
Third Sailor: **George Lowdell**

season three
30 colour 60-minute episodes
1966-67

The Russian Prisoner
w **Harry W. Junkin**
d **John Moxey**

A beautiful girl and a Russian professor combine to make the Saint's holiday in Switzerland one of the most memorable of his career. Someone is out to return the scientist to his homeland - until the Saint intervenes.

Irma Jorovitch: **Penelope Horner**
Professor Karel Jorovitch: **Joseph Furst**
Insp. Oscar Kleinhaus: **Guy Deghy**
Milanov: **Yootha Joyce**
Kirill: **Godfrey Quigley**
Pyotr: **Anthony Booth**
Mikhail Zhukov: **Robert Crewdson**
Andre: **Sandor Eles**
Guard at Villa: **Raymond Adamson**
Aristov: **Alexis Chesnakov**
Clerk: **William Buck**

The House on Dragon's Rock
w **John Kruse**
d **Roger Moore**

What is the secret of the mysterious rambling old house in the Welsh mountains which is being used as a research laboratory? Holidaying in Wales, Simon tries to crack its secret - and comes face to face with a diabolical enemy.

✍ In some areas, this episode carried a warning: 'Unsuitable for children and people of a nervous disposition'. In others it was banned altogether - until repeat transmission.

Dr. Sardon: **Anthony Bate**
Carmen: **Annette Andre**
Dr. Davis: **Mervyn Johns**
Armstrong: **Alex Scott**
Dylan Williams: **Glyn Houston**
Shoni Morgan: **Richard Owens**
Owen Thomas: **Talfyn Thomas**
Mary: **Heather Seymour**
The Guard: **Anthony Blackshaw**
First Local: **David Garfield**
Second Local: **Dafyd Havard**
Third Local: **Peter Lawrence**
Fourth Local: **Reg Pritchard**

The Convenient Monster
w **Michael Cramoy**
d **Leslie Norman**

When the Saint encounters a monster mystery in Scotland - none other than the Loch Ness Monster itself - he must decide if 'Nessie' is behind a series of macabre killings, or is it the work of human hands?

Anne Clanraith: **Suzan Farmer**
Noel Bastion: **Laurence Payne**
Eleanor Bastion: **Caroline Blakiston**
Fergus Clanraith: **Moultrie Kelsall**
Willie: **Fulton Mackay**
Angus McGraw: **William Holmes**
Mrs. Mongrieff: **Anne Blake**
Inspector Mackenzie: **Ewan Roberts**
The Publican: **Alistair Hunter**
The Pathologist: **Brown Derby**
First Reporter: **Michael Graham**
Second Reporter: **Harry Littlewood**

The Helpful Pirate
w **Roy Russell**
d **Roy Baker**

Few people are able to resist the attraction of money for nothing, but when it is wrapped up in the guise of hidden treasure which is providing a profitable racket for confidence trickster Kolben, The Saint steps in to see fair play.

Eva: **Erika Remberg**
Kolben: **Paul Maxwell**
Nikita Roskin: **Vladek Sheybal**
Fran Roeding: **Anneke Wills**
Prof. Roeding: **Redmond Phillips**
Uhrmeister: **George Pravda**
Major Carter: **Jack Gwillim**
The Hotel Receptionist: **Michael Wolf**
Alexi: **Laurence Herder**
Erich Brauer: **Ray Austin**
The Pawnbroker: **Otto Diament**

The Angel's Eye
w **Paul Erickson**
d **Leslie Norman**

Why should a respected Dutch jeweller lie about a valuable stone which the Saint knows he has been given for cutting? When the man refuses to acknowledge receiving the diamond, Simon determines to find out why.

Mabel: **Jane Merrow**
Tom Upwater: **Liam Redmond**
Lord Cranmore: **Anthony Nicholls**
Jeremy: **Donald Pickering**
Malone: **T.P. McKenna**
Corbett: **Frederic Abbott**
Jonkheer: **Cyril Shaps**
Zuilen: **Terence Rigby**
Van Effen: **Martin Wyldeck**
Police Sgt.: **Arthur Gross**
Receptionist: **Katherine Schofield**
Hotel Clerk: **Steven Brook**
Waiter: **Jean Benedetti**

The Queen's Ransom
w **Leigh Vance**
d **Roy Baker**

The Saint moves into regal circles. He comes to the aid of Queen Adana, whose husband is the deposed ruler of a Middle Eastern country. But Simon's problems are compounded by the woman herself, when she insists on having her own way.

Queen Adana: **Dawn Addams**
King Fallouda: **George Pastell**
Hortense: **Nora Nicholson**
Michele: **Catherine Feller**
Georges: **Stanley Meadows**
Major Aboukir: **Gary Hope**
Saleb: **Patrick Westwood**
Farid: **Peter Madden**
Mahmoud: **Neville Becker**
Pilot: **John Woodvine**
Mustafa: **Larry Taylor**
Claude: **John Forbes Robertson**
Bank Manager: **Jean Serret**
First Gendarme: **Andre Charise**
Arab Servant: **Ernst Ulman**

The Reluctant Revolution
w **John Stanton**
d **Leslie Norman**

Simon stumbles into the activities of a girl he finds carrying a gun and determined to kill a man. He sets out to find out why - and ends up organising a revolution to overthrow a ruthless president.

Victor Lawrence: **Barry Morse**
Diane: **Jennie Linden**
Sanches: **Martin Benson**
President Alverez: **Peter Illing**
Hortel: **Gerard Heinz**
Delgado: **Michael Godfrey**
Vargas: **Peter Halliday**
Enrico: **John Garrie**
Pablo: **Louis Raynor**
Consuela: **Maria Roza**
Morales: **Norman Florence**
Sentry: **Clive Gazes**
Head Waiter: **Walter Randall**

Interlude in Venice
w **Paddy Manning O'Brine**
d **Leslie Norman**

Simon finds out that the sun doesn't always shine in Italy - and there is always a warm welcome when you're the Saint

and hot on the trail of a gang of racketeers, who intend to seek revenge.

Helen: **Lois Maxwell**
Foots Fortunati: **William Sylvester**
Cathy: **Quinn O'Hara**
Prince Ubaldo: **Paul Stassino**
Goldilocks: **Joyce Blair**
Don Battista: **Richard Warner**
John Allardyce: **Robert Ayres**
Inspector Gambetti: **Patrick Troughton**
O'Mallamo: **Derek Sydney**
Carlo: **Earl Green**
Tchi: **Hal Galili**
The Nun: **Tita Dane**

Locate and Destroy
w **John Stanton**
d **Leslie Norman**

In South America to visit a friend, Simon finds himself the unwilling prey of a gang of Israeli patriots who are searching for a former Nazi prisoner-of-war officer, who they believe to be alive and living in a local village.

Coleman: **John Barrie**
Maria: **Francesca Annis**
Ingrid: **Julia Arnall**
Karsh: **Victor Beaumont**
Nathan: **Maurice Kaufmann**
Jacob: **Alan Lake**
Bloom: **Harry Landis**
Salter: **Simon Lack**
Captain Rodrigues: **Roger Delgado**
Dr. Lopez: **Wolfe Morris**
Gonzales: **Andreas Malandrinos**
Merkin: **Harvey Hall**
Dr. Pineda: **Gordon Whiting**
Nurse: **Katerina Holden**
Peon: **Richard Montez**

The Man Who Liked Lions
w **Douglas Enefer**
d **Jeremy Summers**

When Simon's journalist friend is murdered while on the biggest story of his life, the Saint decides to put a stop to the antics of a modern-day Caesar - a man who refuses to accept that the glory of Rome is over.

Tiberio: **Peter Wyngarde**
Claudia Molinelli: **Suzanne Lloyd**
Franco De Cesarie: **Michael Wynne**
Inspector Galba: **Jeremy Young**
Vittorio Leale: **Michael Forrest**
Tony Allard: **Edward Bishop**
Berreeni: **Peter Elliott**
Serafino: **Mike Arrighi**
Guido: **Robert Russell**
Frascatto: **Steven Scott**
Princess Alexandra: **Phyllis Montefiore**

The Better Mousetrap
w **Leigh Vance**
d **Gordon Fleming**

Simon combines romance with acute observation when he decides to expose the woman behind a series of audacious jewel thefts in the South of France - but by becoming involved, he finds himself arrested and charged as the real thief.

Natalie Sheridan: **Alexandra Stewart**
Bertha Noversham: **Madge Ryan**

Alphonse: **Ronnie Barker**
Col. Latignant: **Arnold Diamond**
Milo Gambodi: **Lisa Daniely**
Bernie Kovar: **Patrick Whyte**
Tench: **Eddie Byrne**
Hugo: **Michael Coles**
Lady Haverstock: **Aimee Delamain**
Receptionist: **Marika Rivera**
Marie-Therese: **Pauline Collins**
Gendarme: **Allan Downer**
Fat Man: **Robert Bridges**
Banker: **Tom Macaulay**
Mirelle: **Vicky Hughes**

Little Girl Lost
w **Leigh Vance**
d **Roy Baker**

When Simon visits Ireland and meets with Mildred, a young girl who claims to be Hitler's daughter, he finds himself dancing a merry Irish jig to escape from the clutches of a ruthless gang of Irish patriots.

Mildred: **June Ritchie**
Brendan Cullin: **Noel Purcell**
Mullins: **Shay Gorman**
Brine: **Maurice Good**
Eugene Drew: **Edward Burnham**
Receptionist: **Colette Dunn**
Blaney: **Leo Leyden**
Mulloon: **Gerry Duggan**
Mrs. Mulloon: **Betty Cardno**
Patrick: **Peter Ellis**
Tessa: **Eve Belton**
Sgt. Finnegan: **Kevin Flood**

The Paper Chase
w **Michael Cramoy** [from a story by **Harry W. Junkin**]
d **Leslie Norman**

Persuaded to follow a defecting Civil Servant who has been tricked into smuggling secret papers into East Germany, Simon finds himself playing the part of a British agent to save the man's life.

Redman: **Ronald Hines**
Col. Probst : **Nial MacGinnis**
Hanya: **Penelope Horner**
Metz: **Gordon Gostelow**
Major Carter: **Jack Gwillim**
Kruger: **Carl Duering**
Dieter: **Michael Beint**
Ernst Schwerin: **Steve Plytas**
The Lieutenant: **Anthony Wager**
Receptionist: **Norma West**
Major: **John G. Heller**
Sergeant: **Hans De Vries**
London Policeman: **Paul Williamson**
Vopos: **Gordon Sterne**
Kraft: **Frank Maher**
Porter: **John Herrington**
Steward: **Carl Conway**

Flight Plan
w **Alfred Shaughnessy** [from a story by **Anthony Squire**]
d **Roy Baker**

When he spots a nun wearing high-heeled shoes whilst collecting for charity at a London railway station, Simon's interest is aroused and he is soon plunged into an exciting cross-London chase to thwart the schemes of a clever gang of criminals.

Mike: **William Gaunt**

Diana: **Fiona Lewis**
Nadya: **Imogen Hassell**
Landek: **Ferdy Mayne**
F/Lt. Wills: **Jeremy Burnham**
Kovicek: **Tommy Duggan**
Col. Zaglia: **Robert Crewdson**
Hassan: **Marne Maitland**
Ahmed: **Salmaan Peer**
Nursing Sister: **Mary Jones**
Policeman: **Donald Oliver**
Cpl. Buller: **Ray Lonnen**
Atar: **David Spenser**
Reeves: **Henry McGhee**
Dragisha: **John Cazabon**

The Fast Women
w **Leigh Vance**
d **Leslie Norman**

The Saint finds himself caught in the crossfire between two unscrupulous women who are rivals in love as well. Simon's intervention pleases neither woman - and he's soon in trouble again.

Cynthia Quillen: **Jan Holden**
Godfrey Quillen: **John Carson**
Errico Montesino: **Victor Maddern**
Teresa Montesino: **Kate O'Mara**
Tordoff: **John Hollis**
Paddy: **P. G. Stephens**
Thelma: **Valerie Bell**
Inspector Daws: **Donald Morley**
Porter: **Patrick Durkin**
Barmaid: **Vilma Ann Leslie**
The Night Watchman: **Stan Jay**
The Stage Door-Keeper: **Harry Brunning**
Glenda: **Mandy Mayer**

Escape Route
w **Michael Winder**
d **Roger Moore**

The Saint finds himself behind bars, staring at the delighted features of Claude Eustace Teal - but his sentence is part of a police plan to smash a major international escape organisation.

Colonel Roberts: **John Gregson**
Penny: **Wanda Ventham**
Insp. Teal: **Ivor Dean**
John Wood: **Donald Sutherland**
Ann: **Jean Marsh**
Harry: **Jeremy Burnham**
Jim: **Terry Yorke**
Dave: **Romo Gorrara**
Maggie: **Vicki Woolf**
Snooper: **Tony Doonan**
Hal: **Eric Mason**
Wilson: **Edwin Brown**
The Judge: **Walter Horsbrugh**
Nicky: **George Zenios**

The Persistent Patriots
w **Michael Pertwee**
d **Roy Baker**

Having rescued Liskard from death, Simon discovers that the man's enemies will stop at nothing to get their man. Liskard, it appears, is more vulnerable than most - he has political as well as personal enemies.

Jack Liskard: **Edward Woodward**
Mary Ford: **Jan Waters**
Anne Liskard: **Judy Parfitt**

Stewart: **Richard Leech**
Inspector Teal: **Ivor Dean**
Todd: **Tenniel Evans**
Jeff Peterson: **Mike Pratt**
Rogers: **Patrick O'Connell**
Benson: **Nosher Powell**
Lockhart: **Michael Graham**
The Manservant: **Hugh Morton**
The Old Boatman: **Joseph Greig**
The Young Boatman: **Gil Sutherland**
Dr. Eutcher: **Eric Longworth**

The Death Game
w **Harry W. Junkin** [from a story by **John Kruse**]
d **Leslie Norman**

A remarkable modern-day death cult has spread among students throughout the world. But when Simon finds himself marked down as the latest victim - and the threatened events become the real thing - he turns his attention to preventing further deaths.

Jenny Turner: **Angela Douglas**
Dr. Manders: **Alan MacNaughtan**
Vogler: **George Murcell**
Grey Wyler: **John Steiner**
Bill Bast: **Bernard Horsfall**
Inspector Teal: **Ivor Dean**
Gretl: **Katharine Schofield**
Joe Halston: **Stuart Cooper**
John Garton: **Rick Jones**
Duval: **Michael Anthony**
The French Girl: **Karen Ford**

The Art Collectors
w **Michael Pertwee**
d **Roy Baker**

Paris, and a damsel in distress. A combination which leads the Saint into meeting a girl who is selling her family's art treasures - before someone tries to steal them. Disbelieving her, Simon digs deeper to get at the truth.

Natasha: **Ann Bell**
Serge: **Peter Bowles**
Lucille: **Nadja Regin**
Marcel Legrand: **Geoffrey Bayldon**
Joseph: **James Maxwell**
Hans: **Philo Hauser**
Gunter: **Richard Shaw**
Mundt: **Garfield Morgan**
Bernard: **Bryan Kendrick**

To Kill a Saint
w **Michael Winder**
d **Robert Asher**

It's the most unusual assignment he's ever undertaken - Simon is hired to disguise himself as a gangster and kill...the Saint! Determined to find out who is behind the scheme, Simon arranges his own death.

Paul Verrier: **Peter Dyneley**
Annette: **Annette Andre**
Fellows: **Derek Bond**
Andre: **Francis Matthews**
Le Duc: **Robert Cawdron**
Quercy: **John Serret**
Justine: **Pamela Ann Davy**
Bolande: **Michael Bilton**
Pierre: **Robert Gillespie**
Braddock: **Victor Winding**
Maitre D: **Lawrence Davidson**
Jacqueline: **Maggie Wright**

Therese: **Valerie Leon**
Celeste: **Nita Lorraine**

The Counterfeit Countess
w **Philip Broadley**
d **Leslie Norman**

A plane crash sets the Saint on the trail of a counterfeiting gang, which takes him from London to Switzerland. While there he develops an interest in a wine of a very unusual vintage.

Nadine/Yvette: **Kate O'Mara**
Mireille: **Alexandra Bastedo**
Alzon: **Philip Madoc**
Carl: **Derek Newark**
C.I. Teal: **Ivor Dean**
Warburg: **Henry Soskin**
Miles: **David Kelsey**
Larry: **Ray Brown**
The Barman: **Gertan Klauber**
Maurice: **Cliff Dickens**
The Gendarme: **Terry Mountain**

Simon and Delilah
w **C. Scott Forbes**
d **Roy Baker**

A temperamental film star is kidnapped. Is it a publicity stunt or something more sinister? On a visit to Rome, the Saint finds himself involved with the petty bickerings of a film production team - one of whom is a killer.

Roberto Vittorini: **Ronald Radd**
Beth: **Lois Maxwell**
Serena: **Suzanne Lloyd**
David Bradley: **Guy Rolfe**
Tig Jordan: **Leon Greene**
Hal Ward: **David Healy**
Herbert Wheeler: **Patrick Holt**
Sergio: **John Collin**
Renzo: **Ray Charella**
Toni Amato: **Peter Birrel**
Inspector Crepi: **David Nettheim**
Electrician: **Gino Meldazzi**
Maria: **Vicki Hughes**

Island of Chance
w **John Stanton** [from a story by **Leigh Vance**]
d **Leslie Norman**

Murder is unpleasant at the best of times, but when the gaiety of a West Indian holiday turns into a macabre murder enquiry, Simon finds himself dancing to the rhythm of a calypso death march.

Marla Clayton: **Sue Lloyd**
Dr. Charles Krayford: **David Bauer**
Arlene Bland: **Patricia Donahue**
Jan Vanderfelt: **Alex Scott**
Vargas: **Milton Johns**
Grant: **Thomas Baptiste**
Inspector: **Christopher Carlos**
Pete: **Norman Jones**
Cody: **Richard Owens**
Rig: **Kenneth Gardnier**
Barman: **Danny Daniels**
Calypso Singer: **Tommy Eytle**
Maitre D' Hotel: **Charles Hyatt**

The Gadget Lovers
w **John Kruse**
d **Jim O'Connolly**

When he finds himself involved in a strange death campaign - the organised assassination of British intelligence agents - Simon dons the identity of a Russian Secret Police Chief to track the people responsible.

Smolenko: **Mary Peach**
Fenton: **Campbell Singer**
Igor: **Glynn Edwards**
Ivan: **Nicholas Donnelly**
Muller: **John Bennett**
Col. Wing: **Burt Kwouk**
Vogel: **Vernon Dobtcheff**
Anton: **Wolf Frees**
Blagot: **Maurice Browning**
Klaus: **Stephen Hubay**
Molliere: **Peter Burton**
The Waiter: **Stefan Griff**
Gretchen: **Trudi Neilsen**

A Double in Diamonds
w **Harry W. Junkin, Donald Ford** and **Derek Ford**
d **John Gilling**

Why should wealthy Lord Gillingham wish to purchase a copy of his fabulous family diamond necklace? Intrigued, the Saint attends a fashion show - and ends up preventing a robbery.

Lord Gillingham: **Cecil Parker**
Pierre: **Anton Rodgers**
Kate: **Yolande Turner**
Chief Inspector Teal: **Ivor Dean**
Mary: **Ilona Rodgers**
Nicholas: **Ferdy Mayne**
Mercier: **Howard Goorney**
Charlie Hallowes: **Jack Woolgar**
Valerie & Veronica: **The Graham Twins**
Garton: **John Clive**
Michelle: **Yvette Herries**
The Steward: **Tim Barrett**
Sgt. Knox: **Alan Haywood**
The Commentator: **Pauline Clifford**
The Pilot: **Brian Harrison**

The Power Artist
w **John Kruse**
d **Leslie Norman**

Finding himself dropped outside a Chelsea studio instead of his own apartment by a taxi-driver, who instructs him to go to the top floor, a mystified Simon climbs the staircase - and finds himself framed for murder.

Cassie: **Pauline Munro**
Vogler: **George Murcell**
C. I. Teal: **Ivor Dean**
Finlay-Thorp-Jones: **Tristam Jellinek**
Perry: **Peter Bourne**
Shard: **John Bown**
Clay: **John J. Carney**
Carter: **George Roubicek**
Sgt. Knox: **Alan Haywood**
The Clerk: **Anthony Dawes**
Jack: **Charles Rea**
The Taxi-Driver: **Tommy Godfrey**
The Policeman: **Michael Pemberton**
Dolly Girl: **Caron Gardner**
Dolly Girl: **Charlotte Selwyn**
Boy with Banjo: **John Bull**
Doorman: **Edward Higgins**

When Spring is Sprung
w **Michael Pertwee**
d **Jim O' Connolly**

The combination of the French Riviera and an attractive girl lands the Saint in the unexpected position of being asked to rescue her father, a Russian spy who is being held against his will.

Joanne Dell: **Toby Robins**
Marie Spring: **Ann Lynn**
Col. Hannerly: **Allan Cuthbertson**
C. I. Teal: **Ivor Dean**
Vulanin: **George Pastell**
John Spring: **Gary Watson**
Peter Quentin: **Harvey Ashby**
Watters: **Douglas Livingstone**
First Sleuth: **Bryan Mosley**
Prosecuting Counsel: **Eric Dodson**
First Russian Guard: **Lee Crawford**
Second Russian Guard: **Peter Brace**
Police Officer Witness: **Doel Luscombe**
The Judge: **Kenneth Edwards**
The Radio Expert: **Colin Rix**
The Cleaner: **Leslie Anderson**
The Doctor: **John Frawley**

The Gadic Collection
w **Philip Broadley**
d **Freddie Francis**

After finding a girl participating in a robbery in an Istanbul museum, the Saint soon finds the taste of Turkish delight a little hard to swallow. Someone is out to silence her - and Simon soon finds himself in the gunman's sights.

Turin: **Peter Wyngarde**
Diya: **Georgia Brown**
Sukan: **Michael Ripper**
Inspector Yolu: **Martin Benson**
Ahmed Bayer: **Andre Van Gyseghem**
Ayesha: **Nicole Shelby**
Geoffrey Bane: **Hedger Wallace**
Kemal: **Henry Soskin**
Omar: **Paul Darrow**
Zoltan: **Geoff Cheshire**
The Old Woman: **Ann Tirard**
The Old Man: **Andreas Malandrinos**
The Waiter: **Bakshi Prem**

Invitation to Danger
w **Terry Nation**
d **Roger Moore**

When a daring attempt is made to frame him, Simon finds himself surrounded by suspicion and intrigue - and smack in the middle of an international secrets-for-sale drama. But is the cool blonde really a British secret agent - or his true enemy?

Reb Denning: **Shirley Eaton**
Brett Sunley: **Robert Hutton**
Ramon Falconi: **Julian Glover**
Moreno: **Bryan Marshall**
Al Vitale: **Charles Houston**
Marty Bressett: **Warren Stanhope**
Peter Rendo: **Les Crawford**
Inez: **Ros Drinkwater**
Carson: **Dennis Chinnery**

The Best Laid Schemes
w **Joseph Morhain** and **A. Sandford Wolfe**
d **John Moxey**

Who is the victim of a drowning tragedy? The Saint meets with more than he bargained for when he sets out to prove that the 'dead' man is still alive. But why would anyone wish to convince his family that he's the victim of murder?

Arlene: **Sylvia Syms**
Dr. Ormsby: **Paul Daneman**
Diana: **Gabrielle Drake**
Inspector Mitchell: **Norman Bird**
John Everett: **Fulton Mackay**
Skinner: **John Tate**
Ballard: **Godfrey Quigley**
Captain Flemming: **Francis De Wolfe**
Mrs Haggerty: **Olive Milbourne**
Andrew: **Jonathan Elsom**
Joe Carney: **Fredric Abbott**
Coroner: **Geoffrey Lumsden**
Dr. Russell: **John Ringham**
Nurse: **Joanne Dainton**
Sailor: **Erik Mason**

season four
17 colour 60-minute episodes
1967-69

Legacy for the Saint
w **Michael Winder**
d **Roy Ward Baker**

Ed Brown is a retired gangster with a sense of humour - which includes getting his four greatest enemies at one another's throats. Simon helped to put him in jail the last time and intends to repeat the favour - providing Brown allows him to live.

Chief Insp. Teal: **Ivor Dean**
Charlie Lewis: **Alan MacNaughtan**
Tony: **T. P. McKenna**
Ed Brown: **Reginald Marsh**
Penny: **Stephanie Beacham**
Ashford: **Kenneth Farrington**
Pietro: **Edward Brayshaw**
Mark: **Bruce Boa**
Dickie: **Brian Coburn**
Cynthia Ffouldes: **Sheila Keith**
Williams: **Edward Kelsey**

The Desperate Diplomat
w **Terry Nation**
d **Ray Austin**

When diplomat Jason Douglas disappears with a million dollars of aid destined for an African country, Simon finds himself pleading his old friend's innocence to a less-than-interested Claude Eustace Teal.

C. Insp. Teal: **Ivor Dean**
Walter Faber: **Robert Hardy**
Sara Douglas: **Suzan Farmer**
Jason Douglas: **John Robinson**
Eddie Margoles: **David Cargill**
John Chatto: **Kenneth Gardnier**
Carla Lawrence: **Lorna Wilde**
Dunn: **Leslie Crawford**
Healey: **Terry Plummer**
Julie: **Maggie London**
Shop Assistant: **Charlotte Selwyn**
Telephone Operator: **Yutte Stensgaard**
Police Doctor: **Brian Harrison**

The Organisation Man
w **Donald James**
d **Leslie Norman**

When the Saint signs on as a mercenary and finds that things are none too healthy on the health farm where he's being trained, he decides to find out the real function of the establishment. Is it a school for murder?

Jonathan Roper: **Tony Britton**

Kate Barnaby: **Caroline Mortimer**
Leander: **Glynn Edwards**
Mr. Spode: **Norman Bird**
Cable: **John Collin**
Craddock: **Simon Lack**
Major Carter: **Mark Dignam**
Captain Yates: **Terence Edmond**
Mason: **Tony Caunter**
Highland Driver: **Douglas Ditta**

The Double Take
w **John Kruse**
d **Leslie Norman**

Which man is which? That's the problem facing Simon when a business tycoon claims he is being impersonated by a perfect double who intends to grind his business empire into obscurity.

Eugene Patroclos: **Gregoire Aslan**
Annabel II: **Kate O'Mara**
Annabel I: **Denise Buckley**
Bainter : **Blake Butler**
Pat Hurst: **Michael Robbins**
Girl in London Airport: **June Abbott**
Hotel Clerk: **Michael Mellinger**
First Man at Party: **Martin Wyldeck**
Second Man at Party: **Geoffrey Morris**
First Woman at Party: **Rose Alba**
Second Woman at Party: **Anne Godfrey**
Egan [Footman]: **Michael Pemberton**
Chuck Spendelton: **Iain Blair**

The Time to Die
w **Terry Nation**
d **Robert Tronson**

The Saint finds himself playing a deadly game of cat and mouse with a would-be killer. Simon's dilemma is twofold: why should anyone want to put a dent in his halo, and who is the man known only as 'The Avenger'?

Mary Ellen Brent: **Suzanne Lloyd**
Steven Lyall: **Maurice Good**
Dinni Haigh: **John Barcroft**
Charlie Mason: **Terence Rigby**
Martin Graves: **Freddie Jones**
Donna Sumrie: **Monica Grey**
Laura Carlton: **Linda Marlowe**

The Master Plan
w **Harry W. Junkin**
d **Leslie Norman**

When he discovers a plan to turn Britain and America into a dumping ground for some dangerous drugs, Simon sets out to crush the diabolical drugs-smuggling organisation at its source - a small island off the China coast.

Cord Thrandel: **John Turner**
Jean Lane: **Lyn Ashley**
Mr. Ching: **Burt Kwouk**
Fish: **Christopher Benjamin**
Max: **Robert Morris**
Tony Lane: **Paul Greenhalgh**
Dr. King: **James Locker**
Nurse: **Brenda Kempner**
Porter: **Leslie Anderson**
Van Driver: **Edwin Brown**
Girl Customer: **Prudence Drage**

The People Importers
w **Donald James**
d **Ray Austin**

The Saint investigates a racket in which illegal immigrants are being smuggled into Britain to serve as slave-labour in various Mafia-run establishments. His involvement leads him to personal tragedy - and the head of the enterprise.

Bonner: **Neil Hallett**
Laura: **Susan Travers**
Slater: **Gary Miller**
Jackson: **Ray Lonnen**
Suresh: **Salmaan Peer**
Malia: **Imogen Hassall**
Chaudri: **Nik Zaran**
Kumar: **Shivendra Sinha**
Hima dri: **Kevork Malikyan**
Mrs Reynold: **Joan Newell**
Harry: **Michael Robbins**
Sam: **Ron Pember**
Mr. Sen: **Julian Sherrier**
First Pakistani: **Jeremy Anthony**
Photographer: **Christopher Sandford**
First Policeman: **Robert Arnold**
Roberts: **John Downing**
Doctor: **Michael Da Costa**
Ministry of Health Official: **John Garvin**

The Scales of Justice
w **Robert Holmes**
d **Robert Asher**

When four directors of a large business combine die in mysterious circumstances, Simon finds himself investigating a fiendishly clever murder market - and a race against time to save the life of a fifth director.

Gilbert Kirby: **Andrew Keir**
Anne Kirby: **Jean Marsh**
Elliott Stratton: **Mark Burns**
Mrs. Stratton: **Gillian Lind**
Neal Lammerton: **John Barron**
Carl Howard: **Geoffrey Chater**
John Ramsey: **Ronald Leigh-Hunt**
Jim Cowdry: **Victor Maddern**
Sir John Mulliner: **John Boxer**
Dr. Downray: **Brian Badcoe**
Mac: **Leon Cortez**
The Blind Man: **John Crocker**
The Sheriff: **Edward Harvey**
Mr. Roach: **Clifford Parrish**
Mrs. Barnes: **Dorothea Phillips**

The Fiction Makers [part 1 of 2]
w **John Kruse**
[additional scenes and dialogue by **Harry W. Junkin**]
d **Roy Baker**

When he is mistaken for the author of several way-out thrillers, the world of fiction comes vividly to life for the Saint - as does the real 'Amos Klein', a beautiful young woman with a more-than-vivid imagination.

Amos Klein: **Sylvia Syms**
Galaxy Rose: **Justine Lord**
Warlock: **Kenneth J. Warren**
Frug: **Philip Lock**
Monk: **Tom Clegg**
Bishop: **Nicholas Smith**
Nero Jones: **Roy Hanlon**
Finlay Hugoson: **Peter Ashmore**
Carol Henley: **Caron Gardner**
Rip Savage: **Frank Maher**
Carson: **Graham Armitage**
Ma: **Lila Kaye**
Pa: **Joe Gibbons**
Gamekeper, Guard: **Shaun Curry**

Morgan: **Clifford Earl**
Duty Guard 1: **Vincent Harding**
Duty Guard 2: **Richard Franklin**
McCord: **Roy Boyd**
Photographer 2: **Ralph Ball**
Reporter: **Oswald Laurence**
Reporter: **David Rendell**
Reporter: **Richard Davies**
Reporter: **Ian Kingsley**

The Fiction Makers [part 2 of 2]
w **John Kruse**
[additional scenes and dialogue by **Harry W. Junkin**]
d **Roy Baker**

Simon finds himself abducted with a girl who has been using the nom-de-plume Amos Klein. But why? Before he discovers the answer to that question, Simon and the girl share several hair-raising adventures.

Amos Klein: **Sylvia Syms**
Galaxy Rose: **Justine Lord**
Warlock: **Kenneth J. Warren**
Frug: **Philip Lock**
Monk: **Tom Clegg**
Bishop: **Nicholas Smith**
Nero Jones: **Roy Hanlon**
Finlay Hugoson: **Peter Ashmore**
Carol Henley: **Caron Gardner**
Rip Savage: **Frank Maher**
Carson: **Graham Armitage**
Ma: **Lila Kaye**
Pa: **Joe Gibbons**
Gamekeeper, Guard: **Shaun Curry**
Morgan: **Clifford Earl**
Duty Guard 1: **Vincent Harding**
Duty Guard 2: **Richard Franklin**
McCord: **Roy Boyd**
Photographer 2: **Ralph Ball**
Reporter: **Oswald Laurence**
Reporter: **David Rendell**
Reporter: **Richard Davies**
Reporter: **Ian Kingsley**

The World Beater
w **Donald James**
d **Leslie Norman**

With a beautiful blonde by his side the Saint mops up the mysterious events surrounding a series of deaths among drivers at a car rally meeting - and finds himself steering around dangerous bends.

Kay Collingwood: **Patricia Haines**
Justine Pritchard: **John Ronane**
George Hapgood: **James Kerry**
Harold Laker: **George A. Cooper**
Mr Hapgood [Snr]: **Eddie Byrne**
Tom Stevens: **William Wilde**
Dilys: **Rosemary Donnelly**
Microphone Man: **Reg Whitehead**
Rally Official: **Anthony Sheppard**
Rally Official: **Clifford Earl**
Radio Man 1: **Bernard G. High**

Where the Money Is
w **Terry Nation**
d **Roger Moore**

When a film producer's daughter disappears and he suspects that she has been kidnapped, then an unusual ransom demand arrives in the form of scenes cut from a film, the man seeks Simon's help in obtaining his daughter's release.

Ben Kersh: **Kenneth J. Warren**
Jenny Kersh: **Judee Morton**
Jean Latour: **Sandor Eles**
German: **Derek Newark**
Arnie Garnett: **Warren Stanhope**
Frank Lomax: **John Savident**
Largo: **Tony Wright**
Lila Prentice: **Jane Bates**

The Ex-King of Diamonds
w **John Kruse**
d **Alvin Rakoff**

Simon finds himself mixed up with drama on the French Riviera when he meets an ex-king who cheats at cards, and a beautiful young girl with an infallible system for winning at the casino tables.

✍ This episode is seen as a try-out for *The Persuaders!*.

Rod Huston: **Stuart Damon**
Henri Flambeau: **Ronald Radd**
Janine Flambeau: **Isla Blair**
Boris: **Willoughby Goddard**
Col. Rakos: **Paul Stassino**
Gregorio: **Jeremy Young**
Franco: **Antony Stambolieh**
Lafitro: **Alan Rowe**
Ben: **Ray Chiarella**
Alba: **Karen Young**
Henriette: **Jacky Allouis**
Josette: **Carol Friday**
Young Man at Airport: **Derek Smee**
American Lady: **Araby Lockhart**
Attendant: **Hugh Morton**
Frogman: **Les White**
Boy Pupil I: **David Mayberry**
Boy Pupil II: **Darryl Read**
Girl Pupil: **Stephanie Marrian**

The Man Who Gambled with Life
w **Harry W. Junkin** [from a story by **Michael Cramoy**]
d **Freddie Francis**

The Saint has led a long and adventurous life. But now he's been chosen as the subject for an experiment which entails being frozen to death and later being brought back to life. Will he give the scientist the cold shoulder?

Keith Longman: **Clifford Evans**
Stella Longman: **Jayne Sofiano**
Vanessa Longman: **Veronica Carlson**
Carl: **Steven Berkoff**
Ronald: **Valentine Palmer**
Chick: **John D. Collins**
Morris: **Iain Blair**
Tom: **Barry Andrews**
Ian: **Hedger Wallace**
James: **James Vallon**
Dr. Williams: **Geoffrey Lumsden**
Dr. Grange: **Brian Tully**
Dennis: **David Kelsey**
Pete: **Barry Stanton**

Vendetta for the Saint [part 1 of 2]
w **John Kruse** and **Harry W. Junkin**
[adapted from the original story by **Leslie Charteris**]
d **Jim O'Connolly**

Suspecting that a man named Destamio is tied up with the Mafia, Simon attempts to prove it, but all he receives for his pains are threats to his life - which make him more determined than ever to reveal the truth.

Destamio: **Ian Hendry**
Gina: **Rosemary Dexter**
Lily: **Aimi MacDonald**
Marco Ponti: **George Pastell**
Donna Maria: **Marie Burke**
Euston: **Fulton Mackay**
Giorgio: **Peter Kristof**
Lo Zio: **Peter Madden**
Maresciallo: **Guy Deghy**
The Maid: **Eileen Way**
The Bank Manager: **Edward Evans**
The Bank Clerk: **Malya Nappi**
Hotel Reception Clerk: **Charles Houston**
Airline Clerk: **Salmaan Peer**
Maitre 'D': **Derek Sydney**
Barman: **Gabor Baraker**
Doorman: **Agath Angelos**

Vendetta for the Saint [part 2 of 2]
w **Harry W. Junkin** and **John Kruse**
[adapted from the original story by **Leslie Charteris**]
d **Jim O'Connolly**

Continuing his investigations into Destamio's background, Simon discovers that the present Mafia head is dying. Suspecting that Destamio is plotting to take his place, the Saint decides to face his enemy.

Destamio: **Ian Hendry**
Gina: **Rosemary Dexter**
Lily: **Aimi Macdonald**
Don Pasquale: **Finlay Currie**
Marco Ponti: **George Pastell**
Donna Maria: **Marie Burke**
Lo Zio: **Peter Madden**
The Major: **Alex Scott**
The Doctor : **Anthony Newlands**
The Maid: **Eileen Way**
Giorgio: **Peter Kristof**
Cirano: **Steve Plytas**
Renato: **Gertan Klauber**
Nino: **Richard Montez**
The Bus Driver: **Hal Galili**

Portrait of Brenda
w **Harry W. Junkin**
d **John Gilling**

Gurus, pop singers and disc jockeys combine to set the Saint spinning at 45rpm when he finds himself involved in a large-scale swindle involving a fake guru and a group of music-loving innocents.

Diane Huntley: **Anna Carteret**
Chief Inspector Teal: **Ivor Dean**
Josephine: **Ann de Vigier**
Johnny Fox: **Trevor Bannister**
Mrs White: **Petra Davies**
The Guru: **Marne Maitland**
Mrs Blondel: **Hazel Coppen**
Opera Singer: **Tina Ruta**
Ashok: **Larry Taylor**
Tony: **David Prowse**
Postman: **Harry Littlewood**

The Saint:

season one and two
Producers: **Robert S. Baker** and **Monty Berman**
Production Supervisor: **Johnny Goodman**
Script Supervision: **Harry W. Junkin**
Music by: **Edwin Astley**
[Original Saint Theme by **Leslie Charteris**]
Assistant Director: **Bruce Sharman, Ernie Lewis**
Casting Director: **David Booth**
Make-up: **Kenneth Mackay, Dick Bonner-Morris**
Hair: **Helen Penfold**
Wardrobe: **Joyce Stoneman**

Filmed at Associated British Elstree Studios and on location
A New World Production for ITC World Wide Distribution.

season one:
39 monochrome 60-minute episodes 1962-64
season two:
32 monochrome 60-minute episodes 1964-65

season three and four
Producer: **Robert S. Baker**
Production Supervisor: **Peter Manley**
Associate Producer: **Johnny Goodman** [season 4]
Script Supervision: **Harry W. Junkin**
Music by: **Edwin Astley**
[Original Saint Theme by **Leslie Charteris**]
Assistant Director: **Gordon Gilbert**
Music Editor: **Michael Clifford**
Casting Director: **Anthony Arnell**
Make-up: **George Blackler**
Hair: **Elsie Alder**
Wardrobe: **Johnny Briggs**

Filmed on location and at Associated British Elstree Studios
A Bamore Production for ITC World Wide Distribution

season three:
30 colour 60-minute episodes 1966-67
season four:
17 colour 60-minute episodes 1967-69

Sapphire and Steel

'All irregularities will be handled by the forces controlling each dimension. Transuranic heavy elements may not be used where there is life. Medium atomic weights are available: Gold! Lead! Copper! Jet! Diamond! Radium! Sapphire, Silver and Steel ... Sapphire and Steel have been assigned!'

Those words, spoken by a God-like voice, introduced us to one of the most unusual fantasy programmes ever to appear on television - the time-hopping adventures of Sapphire and Steel, two 'time detectives' who materialised out of nowhere to repair breaks in the fabric of time and do battle with the dark forces which had crept into our world through the broken time corridor. Exactly what they were doing, or where they came from was never made clear [although hints were made that they were elements, working for a superior race of elementals]. What we knew [or were told by Sapphire character in the first story] was that: 'Time is a corridor. It surrounds all things. You can't see it - only sometimes... and that's when it is dangerous. You cannot enter into time but, once in a while, Time itself can try to enter into the Present - break in, burst through, to take things ... take people. Sometimes, the present becomes weakened - like fabric. And when there is pressure upon the fabric, Time reaches in.'

That's where Sapphire and Steel came in. It was their job to restore the rip in time and restore the equilibrium - two time agents sent to discover what had crept through the time warp and use their special talents to destroy the alien entity and repair time itself.

Totally original in concept and execution. A pure delight.

✍ the entire series carried no individual story titles or episode identification numbers. For easy reference, each story has been clubbed together under one compact entry.

Regular cast:
Sapphire: **Joanna Lumley**
Steel: **David McCallum**

season one
14 colour 30-minute episodes
1979

Adventure One A 6-part story
d **Shaun O'Riordan**

Young Robert Jardine is doing his homework. His parents are reading nursery rhymes to his younger sister, Helen.
Suddenly, the clock stops ticking. Robert races upstairs to find his sister alone - their parents have vanished! Enter Sapphire and Steel to take on the challenge of the invader through time who has whisked away their parents. The battle begins and Sapphire finds herself trapped in an old painting where Roundhead soldiers are trying to kill her. Steel tries to save her by reducing his body temperature, but he fails and calls for the assistance of Lead.
Together they finally overcome their enemy, reunite the children with their parents and restore the rip in time.

Rob: **Steven O'Shea**
Helen: **Tamasin Bridge**
Mother: **Felicity Harrison**
Father: **John Golightly**
Countryman: **Ronald Goodale**
Policeman: **Charles Pemberton** [part 2]
Lead: **Val Pringle** [part 4]

Adventure Two An 8-part story
d **Shaun O'Riordan** and **David Foster**

Station-owner and psychic expert George Tully is convinced his railway station is haunted. He's right, but he has no idea by what. In fact it's a being that creates havoc with the balance of time and Sapphire and Steel are caught up in its struggle for vengeance. Together with Tully they begin their search and Steel attempts to identify their opponent - a ghostly figure, dressed in the uniform of a World War I soldier.
Steel's attempts to defeat the spectre almost result in Sapphire losing her life, but Tully finally makes contact with the dead man and unleashes a new and frightening force - a duplicate of Sapphire, which is every bit as malevolent as its creator. The tension mounts as Steel is forced to negotiate with the dead for the lives of his partners and himself.

Tully: **Gerald James**
Soldier [Pearce]: **Tom Kelly**
First Voice: **David Woodcock** [part 2]
Second Voice: **David Cann** [part 2]
Pilot: **David Cann** [part 3]
Submariner: **David Woodcock** [part 4]

season two
10 colour 30-minute episodes
1981

Adventure Three A 6-part story
d **Shaun O'Riordan**

A modern block of flats holds the secret of a strange mystery. It has an extra penthouse that no one can see. It's invisible and it is occupied by two time travellers from the future. Sapphire and Steel are aware of its occupants, but cannot hear or see them.
They are certain, however, that the strange couple have brought a strange creation with them - something that snatches Sapphire away when she tries to contact the strangers.
Joined by Silver, who tells Steel that unless they close the time source, the whole of Earth is in danger, they attempt to rescue Sapphire from the creature, but it releases Sapphire unharmed and escapes into time.

Rothwyn: **Catherine Hall**
Eldred: **David Gant**
Changeling: **Russell Wootton** [part 2]
Silver: **David Collings** [part 3]

Adventure Four A 4-part story
d **David Foster**

Discovering that something new has broken through the time corridor, Sapphire and Steel have their first encounter with the 'shape', a being which can slip in and out of any photograph and take refuge in its time zone - taking with it humans, who are then trapped forever in the photograph. If they allow the shape to continue its work, it will tear apart the slender fabric of time itself. So the two agents are forced to enter a photograph to fight their enemy in its own environment.

Liz: **Alyson Spiro**
Shapes: **Philip Bird, Bob Hornery**
Parasol Girl: **Natalie Hedges**
Ruth: **Shelagh Stephenson** [part 3]

season three
6 colour 30-minute episodes
1981

Adventure Five A 6-part story
d **Shaun O'Riordan**

When Lord Mullrine celebrates 50 years of business in a partnership to set up with his late friend Dr McDee, and

Sapphire and Steel attend as two of the party guests, Sapphire immediately senses that the place is subject to a time tear. But she is unable to pinpoint its source - until Mullrine's partner graces the party with an unexpected visit and his arrival is greeted with murder.

The entire surroundings revert to a 1930s setting and the 'death' of Dr McDee begins all over again.

Emma Mullrine: **Patience Collier**
Lord Mullrine: **David Kaye**
Felicity McDee: **Nan Munro**
Howard McDee: **Jeremy Child**
Felix Harborough: **Jeffry Wickham**
Annabelle Harborough: **Jennie Stoller**
Greville: **Peter Laird**
Anne Shaw: **Patricia Shakesby**
Radio Announcer: **Valentine Dyall**
George McDee: **Stephen Macdonald** [part 2]
Tony Purnell: **Christopher Bramwell** [part 2]
Debbie Farrington: **Veronica Blamey** [part 2]

season four
4 colour 30-minute episodes
1982

Adventure Six A 4-part story
d **David Foster**

Sapphire and Steel find themselves at a present-day service station where the only travellers are from the past - 1948. Hearing a man approach, they hide, but only a shadow arrives. Joined by Silver, they attempt to solve the strange mystery of the people from the past - only to discover that they themselves must play their part in the scenario in which they have been cast as the principal players. The die is cast, the executioners assembled and the time agents must face their destiny - to be imprisoned forever in a window in the sky and drift endlessly through space and time!

Silver: **David Collings**
Man: **Edward de Souza**
Woman: **Johanna Kirby**
Old Man: **John Boswall**
Johnny Jack: **Chris Fairbank** [part 3]

Sapphire and Steel [1979: Peter J. Hammond: Star Books: hard back W H Allen: novelisation of the first six episodes of the first season].

Sapphire and Steel:

Created and written by: **P. J. Hammond**
Producer: **Shaun O'Riordan**
Executive Producer: **David Reid**
Music by: **Cyril Ornadel**
Special Effects: **George Leuenberger** [season 2 & 3]
Designer: **Stanley Mills, Sue Chases** [*Adventure 5*]
Make-up: **Mary Southgate** [season 1 & 2] **Anita Harris** [season 3 & 4]
Wardrobe: **Dawn Evans** [*Adventure 1*] **Mary Gibson**

An ATV Network Production for ITC World-Wide Distribution

34 colour 30-minute episodes
1979 - 1982

The Scarlet Pimpernel

While heads were rolling in France under the terror of the guillotine, life at the Court of the Prince of Wales in England went on undisturbed by the violent events across the Channel. No-one seemed to care what happened in France, least of all the rich Sir Percy Blakeney.

Yet beneath the foppish exterior of this seeming dissipate there lay the mind and fame of the courageous and elusive Scarlet Pimpernel, the man the French revolutionary leaders would have paid millions to capture and kill. Declared friend of the innocent, the Pimpernel adopted the disguise of the freedom fighter whenever oppression and injustice reared its head. For no personal gain, Blakeney risked his life to protect the innocent from the cruel and sadistic Chauvelin - an enemy determined to see the Pimpernel's head gracing the guillotine's blade.

Baroness Orczy's classic hero brought to life in a short-lived, but enjoyable costumed drama. Viewers had the time of their lives trying to penetrate the astonishing variety of disguises adopted by actor Marius Goring, who would appear as a 60-year old duchess one minute, only to reappear moments later as a barrow boy or a wizened beggarwoman.

"They seek him here. They seek him there,
those Frenchies seek him everywhere....
Is he in heaven? Is he in Hell?
That cursed, elusive Pimpernel".

Regular cast:
Sir Percy/The Scarlet Pimpernel: **Marius Goring**
Chauvelin: **Stanley van Beers**
Lord Richard Hastings: **Anthony Newlands**
Sir Andrew Ffoulkes: **Patrick Troughton**
Prince of Wales: **Alexander Gauge**
Countess de la Valliere: **Lucie Mannheim**

The Hostage
w **Ralph Gilbert Bettinson**
d **Michael McCarthy**

The Baroness Suzanne de Fleury awaits the guillotine. Sir Percy sets out to rescue her. Extra cunning is called for - Chauvelin is holding the woman's son hostage. He, too, will feel the blade if the Pimpernel fails.

Suzanne de Fleury: **Yvonne Furneaux**
Chauvelin: **Stanley van Beers**
Lord Anthony Dewhurst: **Robert Shaw**
The Prince Regent: **Alexander Gauge**
The Countess: **Lucie Mannheim**

The Farmer's Boy
w **John Moore**
d **David Macdonald**

One of Sir Percy's agents is supplied with false information by Chauvelin, who hopes to lure the man he suspects of being the Pimpernel into the open. He achieves his aim - but who is the 'simple-minded' farmer's boy who arrives at court.

Lord Richard Hastings: **Anthony Newlands** [intro]
Chauvelin: **Stanley van Beers**
Jeanette: **Elvi Hale**
Andre: **Roger Delgado**
Elbeuf: **Michael Ripper**
The Tax Inspector: **Reginald Beckwith**
Madame Elbeuf: **Janet Burnell**
The First Agent: **Ivor Dean**
The Second Agent: **Monti de Lyle**
The Labourer: **Stuart Mitchell**

Gentlemen of the Road
w **Ralph Gilbert Bettinson**
d **David Macdonald**

Hearing that a beautiful woman is showing an unusual interest in the Prince Regent's affairs, convinced that she is up to mischief, Sir Percy decides that it's time for the Pimpernel to show his true colours.

Madame Melanie: **Maureen Connell**
Rachell: **Jean Aubrey**
Sir Andrew Ffoulkes: **Patrick Troughton** [intro]
The Prince Regent: **Alexander Gauge**
Lord Hastings: **Anthony Newlands**
Latour: **Conrad Phillips**
Bibot: **Cyril Shaps** [intro]
Soldier: **Michael Collins**
Thief: **Alfie Bass**
Robber: **Dennis Shaw**

The Winged Madonna
w **Joel Murcott** and **Ralph Gilbert Bettinson**
d **Wolf Rilla**

The Abbey of Nanterre has been plundered. It's monks lie dead - slain by Chauvelin and his troops. Sir Percy decides to set the Pimpernel's hand on his enemy's shoulders - and Chauvelin is forced into begging for heavenly intervention.

Madeleine: **Renee Goddard**
Chauvelin: **Stanley van Beers**
Lord Hastings: **Anthony Newlands**
Delong: **Nicholas Bruce**
Jean: **Jimmy Ray**
Valisse: **Robert Cawdron**
Major Domo: **Theo Gregory**

Antoine and Antoinette
w **Angus McPhail** and **Diana Morgan**
d **David Macdonald**

The wedding takes place and the couple take off for their honeymoon. But Chauvelin has other plans for the newly-weds. Flung into a rat-infested prison. Antoine and Antoinette pray for deliverance. It arrives in the shape of the Pimpernel.

Sir Andrew Ffoulkes: **Patrick Troughton**
Lord Hastings: **Anthony Newlands**
Chauvelin: **Stanley van Beers**
Antoine: **Eric Lindsay**
Antoinette: **Greta Watson**
Elise: **Gillian Towne**
Joubert: **Peter la Trobe**
Madame Cassis: **Nancy Nevinson**
Corporal: **David Tudor-Jones**

The Imaginary Invalides
w **Dennis Vance**
d **David Macdonald**

Hearing that the daughter of Rothstein, an old enemy, is being held for ransom by Chauvelin, Sir Percy sets out to ensure that the ransom is never paid - at least, not into Chauvelin's coffers...

Sir Andrew: **Patrick Troughton**
Lord Hastings: **Anthony Newlands**
Chauvelin: **Stanley van Beers**
Dr Dufay: **John Laurie**
Rothstein: **Milton Rosmer**
Rachelle Rothstein: **Jean Aubrey**
Lady Snatterthwaite: **Griselda Harvey**

Gaston de Long: **Vincent Edward**
The Landlord: **Ben Williams**
The Footman: **Donald Conlon**
The Duchess of Northumberland: **Jean Maude**

The Flower Woman
w **Marius Goring**
d **David Macdonald**

The Countess de la Valliere, Chauvelin's spy at the Regent's Court, has a change of heart and joins Sir Percy's crusade. Or does she? Can the Pimpernel really trust the woman with his secret?

Countess de la Valliere: **Lucie Mannheim**
Sir Andrew: **Patrick Troughton**
Lord Hastings: **Anthony Newlands**
Chauvelin: **Stanley van Beers**
The Prince of Wales: **Alexander Gauge**
Lady Arabella: **Joanna Duncan**
The Assassin: **Michael Hitchman**
The Sergeant: **Peter Halliday**
The Prison Sergeant: **Raymond Rollet**
The Boy: **Malcolm Knight**
The Messenger: **Michael Collins**

The Christmas Present
w **Ralph Gilbert Bettinson**
d **David Macdonald**

It's Christmas. So why has Sir Percy no time for festivities? Busy helping a group of children to escape Chauvelin's clutches, Sir Percy has other things on his mind - like a Christmas game ... and the prize is freedom.

Sir Andrew: **Patrick Troughton**
Lord Hastings: **Anthony Newlands**
The Prince: **Alexander Gauge**
Mrs Burton: **Sybil Arundale**
Chauvelin: **Stanley van Beers**
Jacques: **Arthur Young**
Antoinette: **Lesley Dudley**
Marie: **Ann Padwick**
Dr Maurois: **Mark Lawton**
Charles: **Richard Rogers**
Renee: **Nicola Braithwaite**
Berthe: **Amanda Coxell**
Chauvelin's agent: **Paul Williamson**
The Soldier: **Alan Gore-Lewis**

The Ambassador's Lady
w **Joel Murcott and Ralph Gilbert Bettinson**
d **David Macdonald**

Lord Richard Hasting's eye for a pretty girl puts both himself and Sir Percy in the foreground - and right under Chauvelin's nose. Can the Pimpernel discern Chauvelin's intentions and thwart his ruthless scheme to make light of Hasting's indiscretions?

Lord Hastings: **Anthony Newlands**
Sir Andrew: **Patrick Troughton**
Countess de la Valliere: **Lucie Mannheim**
Fleury: **William Franklyn** [intro]
Renee: **Simone Lovell**
Chauvelin: **Stanley van Beers**
Chicon: **Robert Cawdron**
The Landlord: **Alan Jeayes**
Lady Ponsonby: **Nicolette Bernard**
Major Domo: **Arthur Dibbs**

Sir Andrew's Fate
w **Ralph Gilbert Bettinson**
d **Wolf Rilla**

How can a wax effigy of the Pimpernel lead his enemy Chauvelin to the original? As Sir Percy finds to his cost, his reputation of being elusive will lead Sir Andrew to being captured and, badly wounded, lying low somewhere in Paris.

Chauvelin: **Stanley van Beers**
Sir Andrew: **Patrick Troughton**
Lord Hastings: **Anthony Newlands**
Balbina: **Colette Duclos**
Madame Tussaud: **Susan Richmond**
The First Agent: **Ivor Dean**

Thanksgiving Day
w **Michael Hogan, Angus McPhail and John Cousins**
d **David Macdonald**

An American, who desperately seeks the Pimpernel's help, challenges Sir Percy to a duel? The man's sister, a less than skilful American 'Pimpernel', is in in Chauvelin's hands. Can Sir Percy launch a remarkable rescue attempt?

Chauvelin: **Stanley van Beers**
Sir Andrew: **Patrick Troughton**
Frank Rawlinson: **Phil Brown**
The Prince: **Alexander Gauge**
John Adams: **William Abney**
Myra Rawlinson: **Ginger Hall**
Sir Reginald Compton: **Dennis Edwards**
The Marquis: **Arnold Diamond**
Lieutenant Gorschen: **Glen Farmer**
The Soldier: **Alex Scott**

The Sword of Justice
w **Ralph Gilbert Bettinson**
d **Dennis Vance**

Hearing that the Pimpernel is being impersonated in France by an Englishman who is robbing and murdering French aristocrats, Sir Percy sets out to clear his good name - and teach his enemy Chauvelin, the man behind the scheme, a lesson.

Chauvelin: **Stanley van Beers**
The Prince: **Alexander Gauge**
Countess de la Villiere: **Lucie Mannheim**
Sir Andrew: **Patrick Troughton**
Christine: **Theo Gregory**
Count Latour: **Christopher Steele**
Sir Thomas Landers: **Brian Wilde**
Georgette: **Clair Pollock**
Biggs: **Dennis Shaw**

The Elusive Chauvelin
w **Ralph Gilbert Bettinson**
d **Michael McCarthy**

It's his strangest mission yet. The Pimpernel must rescue the 'Pimpernel' - a young man set-up by Chauvelin to ensnare the real thing. The plan went awry and the imposter has been sentenced to death. So, naturally, Sir Percy mounts a rescue operation.

The Prince: **Alexander Gauge**
The Countess: **Lucie Mannheim**
Chauvelin: **Stanley van Beers**
'Sir Anthony Dewhurst': **Patrick Troughton**
Harding: **Gordon Whiting**
Louis: **Christopher Lee**
Hobson: **Richard Nennett**
Christine: **Theo Gregory**

Something Remembered
w **Joel Murcot and Ralph Gilbert Bettinson**
d **David Macdonald**

Answering an appeal from the Comtesse de la Fleury to bring her brother Jacques safely from France, the Pimpernel finds his rescue bid thwarted when Jacques says he intends to stay and lead the underground army against Chauvelin.

Sir Andrew: **Patrick Troughton**
Lord Hastings: **Anthony Newlands**
Chauvelin: **Stanley van Beers**
Melanie, Princess de Monsantes: **Maureen Connell**
Fleury: **William Franklyn**
The First Agent: **Robert Cawdron**
The Blind Man: **Esme Percy**
The Captain: **Philip Merant**
Lord Fenton: **Robert Bruce**

Lady in Distress
w **Ralph Gilbert Bettinson**
d **Dennis Vance**

The latest bait to catch the Pimpernel - Cecille, a lady in distress. Chauvelin's accomplice, Cecille is condemned to Madame Guillotine and allowed to 'escape' - straight into the arms of Sir Percy, the man alleged to be her brother's murderer!

Chauvelin: **Stanley van Beers**
The Prince: **Alexander Gauge**
The Countess: **Lucie Mannheim**
Cecille: **Ingeborg Wells**
Bibot: **Cyril Shaps**
Sir Andrew: **Patrick Troughton**
Durand: **Harold Young**
The Labourer: **Alfie Bass**
Baron de Rougement: **Walter Horsborough**

A Tale of Two Pigtails
w **Angus McPhail** and **Diana Morgan**
d **David Macdonald**

Determined to identify the Scarlet Pimpernel, Chauvelin travels to the Court of the Prince Regent. Sir Percy, quick to spot the motive for his visit, engineers the release of Princess Melanie from abduction by Chauvelin's men - a move guaranteed to inflame the Frenchman's hatred.

Sir Andrew: **Patrick Troughton**
Lord Hastings: **Anthony Newlands**
Chauvelin: **Stanley van Beers**
The Prince: **Alexander Gauge**
Princess Melanie: **Maureen Connell**
Alice: **Sybil Wise**
Joubert: **Peter la Trobe**
Sabot: **Eric Corrie**
The First Soldier: **Peter O'Toole**
Sir Reginald Compton: **Dennis Edwards**
Jellybrand: **Alan Jeayes**
Hempseed: **Clifford Buckton**

The Princess
w **Ralph Gilbert Bettinson**
d **David Macdonald**

Having rescued the Marquise de Manton from the revolutionaries, Sir Percy must now set his mind to freeing a gallant and faithful servant girl from Chauvelin's evil clutches. He does so by arranging his own arrest and sharing a cell with the girl he intends to save.

Sir Andrew: **Patrick Troughton**
Lord Hastings: **Anthony Newlands**
Chauvelin: **Stanley van Beers**
Ginette: **Susan Lyall Grant**
The Marquise de Manton: **Rachel Gurney**
The Prince: **Alexander Gauge**

The Sergeant: **Julian Somers**
Prison Guard: **Hugo de Vernier**
First Soldier: **Anthony Carlyon**
Second Soldier: **Michael Collins**
The Captain: **Phillip Morant**

Sir Percy's Wager
w **Joel Murcott** and **Ralph Gilbert Bettinson**
d **Dennis Vance**

By holding Lady Caroline Wells as hostage, Chauvelin makes his most ruthless bid yet to ensure the Pimpernel's capture and date with Madame Guillotine. But the foppish Sir Percy has other plans and is soon in Paris playing havoc with his enemy's plans - and fortune.

Lord Hastings: **Anthony Newlands**
Sir Andrew: **Patrick Troughton**
Countess de la Valliere: **Lucie Mannheim**
Bibot: **Cyril Shaps**
Lady Caroline: **Peggy Thorpe-Bates**
Chauvelin: **Stanley van Beers**
The Concierge: **Edmund Willard**
The Fisty Coachman: **Jimmy Thompson**
Francois: **Edgar Bruce**

The Scarlet Pimpernel:

Producers: **Dennis Vance, David Macdonald, Anthony Gilkison, Marius Goring**
Music by: **John Bath** [episodes 5 to 10 - 12 to 18]
Edwin Astley [episodes 2 to 4 - 11]
Production Manager: **Fraser Foulsham**
Production Associate: **Marius Goring**

A Rayant Pictures / Towers of London Production for the Incorporated Television Programme Co. Filmed at National Studios, Elstree

18 monochrome 30-minute episodes
1956

The Secret Service

Country priest, Father Unwin, and his slow-thinking yokel gardener, Matthew Harding, are hardly likely to be suspected of being one of the most efficient teams in British Intelligence. But Father Unwin, has a remarkable electronic device hidden in a book left in his care by a member of his parish - a device he can use in whatever way he sees fit for the good of mankind. The device has the remarkable property of being able to shrink a person or object to about one-third its original size.

When duty calls, Matthew drops his slow-thinking act and becomes his real self, an alert, athletic, intelligent counter-agent. Miniaturised until he is about two feet high, Matthew embarks with Father Unwin on their next case. But why would a vicar do such a thing? Answer: he isn't a vicar at all, but a highly-trained agent working for B.I.S.H.O.P [British Intelligence Secret Headquarters, Operation Priest], who kept in contact with other BISHOP operatives via a radio device in his hearing aid, and carried the miniature Matthew around in a specially designed briefcase!

At the time a new departure for the master of Supermarionation [Anderson elected to combine puppets with real-life actor Stanley Unwin], the series failed to attract good ratings and only 13 episodes were produced.

Regular cast:
Father Unwin: **Stanley Unwin**

Character voices:
Father Unwin: **Stanley Unwin**
Mrs Appleby: **Sylvia Anderson**
Matthew: **Keith Alexander**
The Bishop: **Jeremy Wilkin**
and
Gary Files
David Healy

A Case for the Bishop
w **Gerry Anderson** and **Sylvia Anderson**
d **Alan Perry**

The theft of the XK20 mini-computer threatens the exports of the Healy Automation Company. Discovering that the device is to be smuggled out of Britain by the Ambassador Dreisenburg in a diplomatic pouch, The Bishop contacts Father Unwin who places a miniaturised Matthew aboard the Ambassador's aircraft.

A Question of Miracles
w **Donald James**
d **Leo Eaton**

Why should new desalination plants explode after only 250 hours of operation? The Bishop asks Father Unwin to find out if sabotage is the answer - and to save another plant which is nearing the 250 zero deadline.

To Catch a Spy
w **Tony Barwick**
d **Brian Heard**

When top spy Grey is sprung from prison in a daring helicopter raid, Father Unwin sends Matthew to check out the home of Sir Humphrey Burton - the man suspected of being behind the breakout.

The Feathered Spies
w **Tony Barwick**
d **Peter Anderson**

Aerial photographs of a new fighter plane are being sold on the international espionage market. The Bishop asks Father Unwin to find out how the photographs were taken and the priest becomes a pigeon fancier - to avert bomb threat.

Last Train to Bufflers Halt
w **Tony Barwick**
d **Alan Perry**

After one attempt to hijack a gold shipment fails, Father Unwin is assigned to accompany the gold shipment during a train journey. It isn't long before he and the train crew are hijacked - leaving a miniaturised Matthew to rout the hijackers.

A Hole in One
w **Shane Rimmer**
d **Brian Heard**

When a satellite's orbit is tampered with by someone with inside information, Father Unwin is assigned to keep an eye on General Brompton, the only man who had access to the information. Unwin joins him on the golf course - and learns the secret of the 15th hole.

Recall to Service
w **Pat Dunlop**
d **Peter Anderson**

Father Unwin is asked to attend the NATO demonstration of the Army's latest tank which has suffered control failures to its on-board computer. It soon becomes clear that the tank is going to attack the lookout post - but fortunately Matthew is secreted inside it.

Errand of Mercy
w **Tony Barwick**
d **Leo Eaton**

Confined to bed by illness, Father Unwin falls asleep and dreams that he and Matthew are flying to Africa in Gabriel, his Model T-Ford to deliver urgent medical supplies. His dream continues unabated - and ends up with him fending off a rocket attack.

The Deadly Whisper
w **Donald James**
d **Leo Eaton**

While Father Unwin is away visiting friends, Matthew discovers that Professor Soames and his daughter are being held hostage by saboteurs who plan to use the scientist's sonic rifle to shoot down a new test aircraft.

The Cure
w **Pat Dunlop**
d **Leo Eaton**

Father Unwin follows notorious agent Sakov to the Klam Health Centre. His mission: to head off a sabotage attempt by Sakov on a car being used to test a new fuel. Matthew is hidden in the car, but Father Unwin, trapped by Sakov at the Klam Centre, cannot warn him of the impending attack.

School for Spies
w **Donald James**
d **Ken Turner**

When several priests are seen at a series of sabotage operations, Father Unwin unearths a group of mercenaries posing as clergy. Hearing they need a new explosives expert, he knocks out the man summoned and takes his place.

May-day, May-day
w Bob Kelson
d Alan Perry

Assigned to safeguard the welfare of an Arab King after several attempts have been made on his life, Father Unwin and Matthew usher the Arab aboard a plane to New York, content that all is well. It's not. The crew have been gassed - and the priest will have to land the plane himself.

More Haste - Less Speed
w Tony Barwick
d Ken Turner

Hoping that Mullins, a counterfeiter released from jail, will lead them to where he has hidden his printing plates, the Bishops asks Father Unwin to follow the man. All they find are a bunch of thieves - each determined to reach the plates before anyone else.

📖 Both, original stories:
The Secret Service: The Destroyer [1969: John Theydon: Armada Paperbacks (May Fair Books) Century 21 Merchandising Limited]; *The Secret Service: The V.I.P.* [1969: John Theydon: Armada Paperbacks (May Fair Books) Century 21 Merchandising Limited].

The Secret Service:

Series format by: **Gerry Anderson** and **Sylvia Anderson**
Characters created by: **Sylvia Anderson**
Producer: **David Lane**
Executive Producer: **Reg Hill**
Production Supervisor: **Des Saunders**
Music by: **Barry Gray**
Vocal title music by: **The Mike Sammes Singers**
Supervisor Visual Effects: **Derek Meddings**
Senior Visual Effects Director: **Jimmy Elliott**
Visual Effects Designer: **Mike Trim**
Story Editor: **Tony Barwick**
Supervising Editor: **Alan Killick**
Puppet Co-ordination: **Mary Turner**
Puppet Operation: **Christine Glanville, Rowena White**

Filmed in Supermarionation

A Century 21 Production for ITC World Wide Distribution

13 colour 30-minute episodes
1969

The Sentimental Agent

The series that gave us the opportunity to catch up on the further adventures of Carlos Varela, the devil-may-care import-export agent with a nose for trouble first seen in *Man of the World* [see entry under that name].

Now based in London, the impeccably dressed, cigar-smoking import-export agent who has a finger in every possible pie and uses his legitimate business as a cover for other activities, jets off to some exotic location for excitement, danger and romance. Vulnerable, he doesn't always come out on top, doesn't always win the girl, doesn't always avoid falling into deliberately-set traps. Varela turns danger into a light-hearted battle against adversity. Using wit, ingenuity and charm, he is content to rescue a fair maiden's honour [two of the more notable damsels in distress being the then comparatively unknown Diana Rigg and Sue Lloyd] and allow someone else to walk away with the girl.

Popular at the time, the series has long since disappeared from our screens - a victim of the 'monochrome' syndrome.

Regular cast:
Carlos Varela: **Carlos Thompson**
Bill Randle: **John Turner** [episodes 6, 10 - 13]
Miss Carter: **Clemence Bettany**

All that Jazz
w **Julian Bond**
d **Charles Frend**

When Varela undertakes responsibility for a jazz group making its debut in England, he soon finds himself with more problems than he bargained for and it isn't long before the band are serenading a group of spies to save the life of a musician.

Major Nelson: **Anthony Bushell**
Stirink: **Peter Arne**
Sarah: **Anneka Wills**
Tania: **Dora Reisser**
Bill: **Riggs O'Hara**
Art: **Jeremy Bulloch**
Mooney: **Hugh Futcher**
Leavis: **Stewart Guidotti**
Mr Wilson: **James Luck**
Piano Tuner: **Tony Quinn**
Insp. Shaunnesy: **David Blake Kelly**
Special Branch Man: **Brian Cant**
Delivery Boy: **Wilfred Downing**

The Beneficiary
w **Julian Bond**
d **John Paddy Carstairs**

Finding himself in trouble in Greece, Farrell, a wartime colleague of Varela's, sends his ex-comrade a prearranged distress signal: a campaign ribbon and a torn half of a document - the two items that spell 'danger'.

Anna: **Lubna Aziz**
Klaus: **Derek Francis**
Rattan: **Aubrey Morris**
Santos: **Michael Godfrey**
Bank Manager: **Robert Rietty**
Farell: **Bill Mitchell**
Hotel Clerk: **Artro Morris**
Bank Attendant: **David Graham**
Croupier: **Andre Charisse**
Fred: **Wilfred Grove**

Express Delivery
w **Lindsay Hardy**
d **Charles Frend**

When Varela promises to help a young Polish girl escape across the border, he finds himself involved in more than a simple escape attempt. It appears that the girl has witnessed a crime - and someone wants to silence her.

Katrina: **Ann Bell**
Major: **Patrick Magee**
Anders: **Gabriel Woolf**
Priest: **Donald Morley**
Captain: **Lawrence Davidson**
Police Sergeant: **Frederick Schiller**
Man in Trenchcoat: **Robin Chapman**
Official: **Philo Hauser**
Hotel Clerk: **Sandor Eles**
Policeman on Train: **Michael Goldie**
Sergeant: **John Stark**

Never Play Cards with Strangers
w **Julian Bond**
d **John Paddy Carstairs**

Hearing that some passengers have been fleeced of their savings while on a cruise booked through his agency, Varela decides to give the cardsharps a taste of their own medicine by settling the score personally.

Mamie: **Bessie Love**
Elmer: **Donald Stewart**
Lyons: **Hugh McDermott**
Jean: **Suzanna Leigh**
Phillips: **Peter Stephens**
Manager: **John Glyn-Jones**
Colonel Dewar: **Jack Melford**
Mrs Dewar: **Olive Milbourne**
Mr Johnson: **Bert Brownbill**
Mrs Johnson: **Eve Eden**

May the Saints Preserve Us
w **Patrick Campbell**
d **Charles Frend**

It's an unusual job - shipping an ancient Irish castle to America for a wealthy Texan heiress, but when there's money to be made Varela doesn't stop to think. Perhaps he should have done so - someone doesn't approve of the deal.

Shelah: **Carol Cleveland**
Sylvester O'Toole: **Brian Phelan**
Burke: **Patrick McAlinney**
Sgt Dooley: **Geoffrey Quigley**
Larry: **Donal Donnelly**
Mrs Maloney: **Peggy Marshall**
Hogan: **Liam Gaffney**
Northern Ireland Sgt: **Desmond Perry**
Labourer: **Desmond Perry**
Civic Guards: **Jerry Sullivan, David Burke**

Meet My Son, Henry
w **Lindsay Hardy**
d **John Paddy Carstairs**

Varela finds himself involved with the mysterious disappearance of top-secret flight plans from a Space Development Centre. At the request of a millionaire, he embarks on an intriguing escapade to recover the plans.

Bill Randall: **John Turner** [intro]
Henry Peabody Sr.: **John Phillips**
Henry Peabody Jr.: **Stephen Loegering**
Darrin: **Glyn Edwards**
Lewis: **Derren Nesbitt**
Arva: **Vladek Sheybal**
Bookshop Manager: **John Glyn-Jones**
Woman in Bookshop: **Nancy Seabrooke**
Taxi Driver: **Howard Douglas**

179

A Little Sweetness and Light
w **Tudor Gates**
d **Harold French**

Informed that his business representative has been killed in a motoring accident, Varela flies to the Greek island of Athos to investigate the man's death - and why his trade figures with the island have suddenly decreased.

Petrides: **Patrick Allen**
Melina: **Zena Marshall**
Ridou: **Patrick Newell**
Astolat: **Martin Miller**
Miss Mithras: **Eileen Way**
Isigonnis: **Charles Farrell**
Andrea: **Raymond Lay**
Waiter: **Louis Manzi**
Martis: **Andreas Markos**
Plessis: **Dimitris Andreas**

A Very Desirable Plot
w **Brian Clemens**
d **Harry Booth**

It must be a con trick. Someone is selling off worthless plots of land in the Bahamas to unsuspecting holidaymakers. Varela sends his representative along to report on the situation.

Colonel Wilde: **William Mervyn**
Lamont: **Paul Maxwell**
Francy: **Diana Rigg** [introducing]
Prentice: **David Healy**
Betty: **Dorothea Phillips**
Vincent: **Al Mulock**
Woman in Plane: **Jessie Robins**
Hotel Clerk: **Donald Sutherland**
Stewardess: **Jackie Wallis**

The Height of Fashion
w **Peter Lambda** and **Betty Lambda**
d **Charles Frend**

Varela moves in fashion circles and discovers that anything can be sold as the latest vogue - provided you sell your product with panache and style. Yes, anything - including horse blankets!

Victor Frey: **Dennis Price**
Pugh: **Warren Mitchell**
Jackie: **Sue Lloyd** [introducing]
Mr Fripp: **Anton Rodgers**
Dr Abu: **Marne Maitland**
Sally Clare: **Judy Parfitt**
Mr Giddy: **Noel Howlett**
Miss Smyth Wilberforce: **Judith Furse**
Anita: **Hazel Hughes**
Mac: **Fred Griffiths**
Ship's Officer: **Denys Graham**
Telephonist: **Rita Smythe**
Commissionaire: **George Street**
Princess: **Diana Lloyd**

Finishing School
w **Peter Lambda** and **Betty Lambda**
d **Harold Fine**

When a young girl goes missing from an exclusive ladies' finishing school, everyone suspects she has been kidnapped. Varela thinks otherwise and at the headmistress's request he sends Bill Randall to investigate.

Lady Graffham: **Helen Cherry**
Philippa: **Susan Clark**
Betsy Ann: **Annette Andre**

Chips: **Andrew Ray**
Caroline: **Sonia Fox**
Miss Woodfall: **Josphine Woodford**
Marlow: **Michael Forrest**
Doctor: **Ballard Berkeley**
Ling: **Robert Lee**

Not Quite Fully Covered
w **Leslie Harris** and **Roger East**
d **Charles Frend**

Assigned to transport a consignment of rare furniture which has been smuggled out of Gregoria to England, Bill Randall soon finds himself involved in the shadier side of the antiques business.

Yanni: **Keith Baxter**
Nikki: **Imogen Hassall**
Truman-Jones: **Reginald Beckwith**
Pettygrew: **Charles Lloyd Pack**
Saphodes: **Cyril Shaps**
Uncle Georgi: **Barry Shawzin**

The Scroll of Islam
w **Jack Davies**
d **John Paddy Carstairs**

Varela is intrigued when professor Fletcher approaches him and requests his help in obtaining photographs of a relic which could prove more important that the dead Sea Scrolls.

Shaw: **William Sylvester**
Fletcher: **Alan Gifford**
Shiekh: **Patrick Troughton**
Mahmoud: **Clifford Elkin**
Dancer: **Lisa Peake**
Hanif: **John Dimech**
Tailor: **Frank Thornton**
Pilot: **Terence Brook**
Commissionaire: **Joe Enrika**

Box of Tricks
w **Ian Stuart Black**
d **Harold French**

Why won't the Palabria people receive an £11 million gift to their country? Bill Randall is sent to investigate - and finds himself playing the role of an African witch-doctor to encourage them to do so.

Mateo: **Gary Raymond**
Rita: **Zena Marshall**
Miss Ryman: **Louise King**
General: **Richard Warner**
Count de Rici: **Ferdy Mayne**
Souza: **Walter Gotell**
Dali: **George Pastell**
Torta: **Robert Rietty**
Bilbo: **John Gabriel**
Piero: **Michael Golden**
Nalo: **Noel Trevarthen**
Marco: **Anthony Vicars**
Fellow Traveller: **Sheree Winton**

The Sentimental Agent:

Producer: **Harry Fine**
Music by: **Ivor Slaney**
Script Supervisor: **Ian Stuart Black**
An Associated Television Programmes Production for ITC World Wide Distribution
13 monochrome 60-minute episodes
1962

Shirley's World

The adventures of Shirley Logan, photo-journalist for World Illustrated magazine. Juggling with magazine deadlines - and datelines in many different countries - Shirley's wanderlust, insatiable curiosity and warm-hearted nature draws her into other people's problems. Tough. Easy. Comical. Tragic. She tackles her assignments with vitality and charm - much to the chagrin of her editor.

Regular cast:
Shirley Logan: **Shirley MacLaine**
Dennis Croft [her editor]: **John Gregson**

The Berkeley Club Caper
w **Frank Tarloff**
d **Ralph Levy**

Shirley arrives in London - and causes an uproar when she volunteers to lead a feminine march on a club with a long tradition: a club to which no woman has ever been admitted.

Sir Harold: **Charles Lloyd-Pack**
Commissionaire: **Erik Chitty**
Elderly Member: **Arthur Howard**
Lord Arthur: **Rayner Newmark**

To Dream the Improbable Dream
w **Philip Mishkin & Bob Reiner**
d **Ralph Levy**

Shirley's attempts to become a patron of the arts by sponsoring Quick, a scruffy pavement artist, lead to her crossing swords with his 'manager', the equally scruffy Beanie - who sees the good life beckoning.

Matthew Quick: **Ron Moody**
Beanie: **Nicky Henson**
Office Boy: **Kim Smith**

Thou Shall Not Be Found Out
w **Peter Miller**
d **Ray Austin**

Famous film star, Richard Burley, has matrimonial trouble. Enter Shirley, to succeed in interviewing the star where others have failed - and find herself walking where angel's fear to tread.

Richard Burley: **Nigel Davenport**
Mary Burley: **Lelia Goldini**
Henry: **Jeremy Lloyd**

A Girl Like You
w **Anthony Skene**
d **Ray Austin**

In Tokyo for a session with the Kabuki Theatre Company, an English couple on honeymoon and the pleasures of a Geisha house combine to bring an unexpected outcome for Shirley's photo assignment.

Ralph: **Rodney Bewes**
Marion: **Una Stubbs**
Okiyo: **Yoko Tani**

A Mother's Touch
w **Richard DeRoy**
d **Leslie Norman**

Millionaire Edmund Remberg conducts his business affairs with an iron fist. There's no disgrace in that - until he crosses Shirley's path and showers her dress with muddy water and has both his business and personal life reorganised.

Edmund Remberg: **James Booth**
Mina Remberg: **Dandy Nichols**

A Hell of an Engineer
w **Lew Schwarz**
d **Ray Austin**

On the way to shoot pictures of a Japanese temple in the resort of Nikko, Shirley gets waylaid by a cab-driver and ends up on a farm teaching him how to become an engineer!

Shunji: **Burt Kwouk**
Moriko: **Yasuko Nagazumi**

The Lovers
w **Peter Miller**
d **Ray Austin**

Why should a beautiful Japanese girl have a tear running down her cheek? Shirley determines to find the answer - and unravels an 'arranged' marriage for a couple who don't love each other.

Tamiko: **Akiko Wakabayashi**
Riko Miura: **Morko**
Shinzo Hotta: **Akira**

The Islanders
w **Lew Schwarz**
d **Charles Crichton**

When Shirley gets into her buccaneering spirit, it's yo-ho-ho and a bottle of rum - except the rum is illicit whisky brewed by Duncan Macdonald and his family on a quiet little Scottish island.

Duncan Macdonald: **Peter Dyneley**
Catriona Macdonald: **Sally Thomsett**
Angus McRuddy: **Roddy McMillan**

The Defective Defector
w **John Muir & Brian Degas**
d **Ray Austin**

Shirley encounters a romantic Russian in the back of a car - but dare she help a defector? When Shirley's around the simplest of assignments can have unexpected - and sinister overtones.

Igor Kuraganovitch: **Stuart Damon**
Agent: **Bill Nagy**

The Colonel
w **Peter Miller**
d **Charles Crichton**

A struggle to save the countryside from invasion by a new oil refinery sees Shirley involved in a battle for human rights with a 65-year old veteran ex-soldier - a lone voice against the ruination of the environment.

The Colonel: **Michael Shrubshawe**
Joe Burns: **Bill Owen**
Sir Matthew Hardcastle: **Derek Francis**

The Reunion
w **Peter Miller**
d **Frank Cvitanovich**

It looks as though Shirley has turned to crime when the Matchworth Diamonds are stolen. She was one of a dozen

visitors to the heavily guarded exhibition and seems to be the only person who could have carried out the theft.

Charlie: **Cyril Cusack**
Inspector Vaughan: **Joss Ackland**
Ron: **Tommy Godfrey**

Knightmare
w **Jeremy Burnham**
d **Peter Sasdy**

Shirley becomes queen for a day - but finds that merry-making can have knightmarish overtones, particularly when your knight in shining armour is eccentric - some might say insane!

Sir Everard: **John Neville**
Sir Nigel: **Brian Blessed**
Morgan: **James Villiers**

Always Leave Them Laughing
w **Jack Seddon & David Pursall**
d **Sidney Hayers**

Always leave them laughing. It's a rule by which the circus clowns survive. But when Shirley becomes a red-nosed clown and a movie star goes missing, someone ends up laughing on the other side of their face.

Addison Carshaw: **Jeremy Hawk**
Lillian: **Isa Miranda**
Mr Brown: **Skip Martin**

Follow That Rickshaw
w **Tom Brennand & Roy Bottomley**
d **Ralph Levy**

Shirley manages to put a fading pop star firmly back on his feet, helps to fulfil the lifetime dream of an ex-patriate London Jewish cabbie - and becomes a thorn in the side of her editor Dennis Croft.

Bernie Greenberg: **Joe Baker**
Ray King: **Murray Head**
Choa Chun: **Barbara Yu-Ling**

Evidence in Camera
w **T.E.B. Clarke**
d **Ralph Levy**

Shirley helps an Hong Kong fisherman to get money to repair his fishing boat. But not before she lands a scoop, mislays her camera and wins a jeraboam of champagne.

Min-Lau: **Kathy Hu**
Inspector Freeman: **Norman Bird**
Chi-Kwan: **Hao Lui-Wan**

The Rally
w **Peter Miller**
d **Peter Hunt**

The suggestion from her editor Dennis Croft, that a week's vacation will bring the spring back into her heels, is regarded with suspicion by Shirley. She was right to think so. An auto rally has more thrills than she bargained for!.

Mayhew: **Neil Hallett**
Sandra: **Aimi Macdonald**
Welsh Man: **John Glyn-Jones**

Figuratively Speaking
w **Patrick Alexander**
d **Ralph Levy**

Shirley goes dancing and picks up a nasty case of blackmail among the characters who haunt the docks of Hong Kong. A pretty Chinese hostess has a secret to hide - one that Shirley intends to solve with a little blackmail of her own.

Lilian: **Jacqui Chan**
Chen: **Patrick Newell**
Hank: **Robert Rothman**

Shirley's World:

Series created by: **Frank Tarloff** and **Melville Shavelson**
Producer: **Barry Delmaine, Ray Austin**
Executive Producer: **Sheldon Leonard**
    in association with **Ronald Rubin**
Music by: **Laurie Johnson**

An ITC Production for ITC World Wide Distribution
Filmed in Japan, Hong Kong, Spain and locations around the world.

17 colour 30-minute episodes
1971

Sir Francis Drake

The sea-faring adventures of Sir Francis Drake, sailor, explorer, adventurer and confidant of Queen Elizabeth I. The man who repelled the invading Spanish Armada and was appointed Admiral of the Queen's Navy.

Aboard the pride of the fleet, the *Golden Hind*, Drake led his adventurous Elizabethan crew into many exciting exploits and Drake's fame spread before him. A lone wolf, and expert swordsman, Drake took his orders directly from the Queen and defended her throne and the shores of England against the warring invaders.

High-spirited adventures that found favour with an audience seeking thrills.

Regular cast:
Sir Francis Drake: **Terence Morgan**
Queen Elizabeth I: **Jean Kent**
John Drake: **Michael Crawford**
Diego: **Milton Reid**
Mendoza: **Roger Delgado** [episodes 4 - 17]
Trevelyan: **Patrick McLoughlin** [episodes 4 -8]
Grenville: **Howard Lang** [episodes 10 -26]

The Garrison
w **Ian Stuart Black**
d **David Greene**

When he fails to deliver fresh supplies to an English garrison, Drake and his crew are accused of cowardice and treason and sent for trial. Only one man can prove their innocence - but he's been captured by the Spaniards.

Sir Miles: **Laurence Naismith**
Captain Williams: **Patrick Wymark**
Bosun: **Peter Diamond**
Master Gunner: **Bill Dancy**
Corporal: **Brian Cant**
Lacey: **Gordon Gardner**
Lady-in-Waiting: **Gabriella Licudi**
Captain-of-the-Guard: **Michael Bell**
Lord Loudon: **Reginald Jarman**
Bolton: **Desmond Newling**

The Prisoner
w **Ian Stuart Black**
d **Peter Maxwell**

Sir Francis Drake sails into the life of the haughty but beautiful Countess Inez, a Spanish aristocrat whose life he saves. In return she attempts to sink the *Golden Hind* with all hands!

Countess Inez: **Natasha Parry**
Roberto: **Warren Mitchell**
Don Antonio: **Clifford Elkin**
Consuelo: **Lynne Parry**
Pedro: **Peter Hampson**

Mary, Queen of Scots
w **Lindsay Galloway**
d **David Greene**

Drake foils a plot by Mendoza to dupe Queen Elizabeth into signing the death warrant of Mary, Queen of Scotland. But trouble awaits his return to England and Drake finds himself occupying a prison cell.

Mary: **Noelle Middleton**
Sir Amyas Paulet: **Alfred Burke**
Thomas Phillips: **Harvey Hall**
Munroe: **Ewan Roberts**
Walsingham: **Richard Warner**

Bess Pierpoint: **Grazina Frame**
Sergeant: **Reginald Jessup**
Sentry: **Howard Green**

The Governor's Revenge
w **John Baines**
d **Clive Donner**

Whilst buying provisions at a Spanish port, Drake finds that the Governor's brother died in a sea battle with the *Golden Hind*. To take his revenge, the Governor traps Drake's crew - and sentences them to death.

Hawkins: **Ronald Leigh-Hunt**
The Governor [Mendoza]: **Roger Delgado**
Donna Inez: **Marie Burke**
Isabel: **Maureen Moore**
Dona Clara: **Pauline Letts**
Tomas: **John Bennett**
Don Gonzalo: **Will Stampe**

Lost Colony of Virginia
w **Larry Forrester**
d **David Greene**

Hearing that a colony of English settlers in Virginia are badly in need of provisions, and face disaster unless they receive aid, Drake and his crew ignore the threat of Don Pedro's fleet to help them.

Jenny: **Olive McFarland**
Tom Brewster: **Barry Foster**
Governor Walters: **John Welsh**
Parson Maine: **Fred Johnson**
Mistress Seaton: **Ruth Lodge**
Crombie: **Robert Cawdron**
Daniel Peters: **Charles Lloyd-Pack**
Walsingham: **Richard Warner**
Lambert: **William Peacock**
Martin Armstrong: **Glyn Edwards**
Davey Preston: **Wensley Pithey**

Boy Jack
w **Cedric Wells and Ian Stuart Black**
d **Clive Donner**

Queen Elizabeth's godson John Harrington finds himself on a mission to Spain in the company of Sir Francis Drake. While there, he proves to the Captain that he has more courage and character than his colleague gave him credit for.

Boy Jack: **Michal Anderson**
The Ambassador: **Clive Morton**
Munro: **Ewan Roberts**
Ship's Cook: **Victor Maddern**
Spanish Captain: **John Moffatt**
Spanish Soldier: **Timothy Pearce**
Sophia: **Isobel Black**

Bold Enterprise
w **Jon Roddick**
d **Anthony Bushell and Harry Booth**

Financed by a wealthy merchant banker, Drake sails to the West Indies to raid one of Spain's treasure-filled gold vaults. No sooner has he set to sea, his ship comes under Spanish fire.

Bosanquet: **Richard Pearson**
Lord Westbrook: **Patrick Holt**
Munro: **Ewan Roberts**
Governor: **Michael Peake**
Eastwood: **Leon Peters**
Laura: **Joanne Dainton**

Doctor Dee
w **Doreen Montgomery**
d **Clive Donner**

Having seen success in the Queen's horoscope, Doctor Dee, Elizabeth's alchemist, advises Drake that the time is favourable to attack a Spanish fleet carrying fabulous wealth. He does so - and finds himself under heavy fire.

Doctor Dee: **Raymond Huntley**
Don Petro: **Alex Scott**
Rafe: **Michael Golden**
Captain-of-the-Guards: **Edward Cast**
Katharine: **Eve Lucette**

Mission to Paris
w **Lindsay Galloway** and **David Greene**
d **David Greene**

The Queen hands Drake the delicate task of visiting Paris to discover why a young French woman, who promised to visit her, has not done so - although Elizabeth has received notice of her arrival in England.

Catherine de Medici: **Pamela Brown**
Alencon: **Leon Peters**
Navarre: **Patrick Allen**
Walsingham: **Richard Warner**
Munro: **Ewan Roberts**
Caylus: **Michael Ripper**
De Luc: **Peter Diamond**
Rietti: **Desmond Newling**
Martier: **Ryan Jeffs**
Heloise: **Yvonne Buckingham**

Johnnie Factotum
w **John Keir Cross**
d **Peter Graham Scott**

On his way home after a successful mission against the Spanish, Drake hears word that a gang of cut-throats intend to deprive him of the booty he has stolen in battle. Forewarned is forenamed, and the thieves receive an unwelcome surprise.

The Dark Lady: **Katharine Blake**
Johnnie Factotum: **Philip Guard**
Lord Marmont: **Laurence Davidson**
Boy Actor: **Duncan Burns**
Chamberlain: **Barry Shawzin**
Janitor: **Lawrence Taylor**

The English Dragon
w **Ian Stuart Black**
d **Clive Donner**

When Queen Elizabeth's favourite ward of court falls deeply in love with a French Countess, it sets in operation a series of events which almost cost Drake his life - and culminates with the Spanish invasion almost succeeding.

Lord Oakeshot: **David McCallum**
The Countess: **Delphi Lawrence**
Don Pedro: **Alex Scott**
The Prefect: **Henry Vidon**
Lady-in-Waiting: **Eve Lucette**

The Irish Pirate
w **David Giltinan**
d **Peter Graham Scott**

Ordered by the Queen to capture the Lord O'Neill, a rebellious Irish earl, Drake finds himself totally unprepared for the events which follow: O'Neill has plans of his own - ones which don't include Sir Francis Drake.

Grace O'Malley: **Elspeth March**
The O'Neill: **Liam Gaffney**
Theobald Burke: **Peter Halliday**
Richard Burke: **John McCarthy**
Skipper Staunton: **Patrick McAlinney**
The Abbot: **Gordon Phillpott**
The Sergeant: **Wesley Murphy**

King of America
w **Ian Stuart Black**
d **David Greene**

When Drake's nephew, John, sets off with a crewman who states that he's off to the New World and will proclaim himself King of America, neither man has reckoned with the Spanish, the weather - or Drake's temper.

Thomas Stukeley: **Kieron Moore**
Flavel: **Andrew Keir**
Celia: **Susan Hampshire**
Spanish Admiral: **Charles Hill**
Spanish Captain: **Walter Randall**
Indian Chief: **Frederick Rawlings**

Beggars of the Sea
w **Ian Stuart Black**
d **Terry Bishop**

Despite the Queen's command that no ships should interfere with a special Spanish cargo, Dutch freedom-fighters, 'The Beggars of the Sea', ignore her words - and enable Drake to help himself to another victory.

Count Julio: **William Lucas**
Jan: **Michael Forrest**
Alva: **Gerard Heinz**
Captain Riccardo: **Robert Rietty**
Lieutenant: **George Little**
Banker: **David Graham**

Drake on Trial
w **Tudor Gates**
d **John Lemont**

Graveney, a ruthless pirate bearing a strong resemblance to Drake, decides to plunder English shipping and leave Drake to take the blame - but his lookalike knows no bounds when seeking revenge on his enemy.

Consellor: **Peter Stevens**
Governor: **Arnold Diamond**
Vanderhof: **Richard Shaw**
Sykes: **David Davies**
Mate: **Tom Bowman**
Lieutenant: **Stanley Morgan**
Hugh Graveney: **Terence Morgan**

The Bridge
w **Brian Clemens**
d **Terry Bishop**

When Drake sets out to rescue a Portuguese hero held by the Spanish, he finds his attempts to do so frustrated by the reluctance of the man to be saved. Why should this be? Drake is astonished when he finds the answer.

Maria: **Zena Marshall**
Gazio: **Patrick Troughton**
De Vazim: **Dennis Edwards**
Corsia: **Bill Nagy**

Tilsto: **Anthony Bate**
Spanish Officer: **John Ronane**
Prisoner: **Vicki Woolf**

The Flame Thrower
w **Doreen Montgomery**
d **Clive Donner** and **Harry Booth**

Sir Martin has invented a powerful weapon - one which Drake believes could win the war, but should only be used for peaceful purposes. Count Julio thinks otherwise - and sets out to steal the invention for the Spaniards.

Count Julio: **William Lucas**
Sir Martin Amyas: **Neil McCullum**
Lambert: **William Peacock**
Gomez: **Reginald Hearne**
Munro: **Ewan Roberts**
Alonzo: **Richard Huggett**
Lady Amyas: **Helen Christine**

The Fountain of Youth
w **Ian Stuart Black**
d **Terry Bishop**

Has the Queen been duped? Drake believes so as he sets out to find an Indian well in Florida. Legend has it that its waters possess magical qualities which prevent the ageing process. The Queen is determined to find it - but Drake has other ideas.

Sir Henry Rainsford: **Reginald Beckwith**
Little Dove: **Catherine Woodville**
Black Eagle: **Endre Muller**

Gentlemen of Spain
w **John Keir Cross**
d **John Lemont**

When Barbary pirates attack Wales and capture a kinsman of Queen Elizabeth's, she instructs Drake to rescue the prisoner and return him to court unharmed. But the captain makes alternative arrangements to save the prisoner.

Don Miguel: **Nigel Davenport**
Hassan Bey: **Paul Stassino**
Martin: **Glynn Edwards**
Sir Owen: **Jack Melford**
Uluch Ali: **Marne Maitland**
Zarque: **Guy Deghy**
Zaharra: **Kim Tracy**
Olwen: **Waverly Lee**
Stephens: **Norman Scace**
Lady-in-Waiting: **Helen Buckley**

The Reluctant Duchess
w **Gordon Wellesley** and **Paul Tabori**
d **Terry Bishop**

Whilst trying to persuade the ruler of a small European state, threatened by a Spanish invasion, to leave the country, Drake finds himself having to use all his guile to escape from his enemy.

The Duchess: **Mary Merrall**
Joos: **Ferdy Mayne**
Munro: **Ewan Roberts**
Duke of Alva: **Basil Dignam**
Count Toledo: **Andrew Faulds**
Lady Elena: **Susan Burnett**
Gretchen: **Nancy Egerton**
Spanish Officer: **Thomas Kempinski**
Major Domo: **John Dunbar**
Sergeant: **Kenneth Gilbert**

Escape
w **David Greene**
d **David Greene**

After escaping from his enemy by jumping overboard, Drake struggles ashore to find he's landed on Spanish territory. Dragged from the sea by two soldiers, he is taken before a sadistic Governor.

Governor: **Barry Morse**
Withers: **Charles Heslop**
Estaban: **Brian Bedford**
Gomez: **Barry Keegan**
The Colonel: **Martin Boddey**

The Doughty Plot
w **Margaret Irwin** and **David Greene**
d **David Greene**

It's a sea-going captain's nightmare. Drake must face the terrible ordeal of having to decide the fate of one of his crew who has been found guilty of mutiny. The law specifies hanging - but Drake believes his friend innocent.

Tom Doughty: **Anthony Bushell**
Vicary: **Frederick Jaeger**
Brewer: **Victor Maddern**
Martin: **Glynn Edwards**
Clements: **Bob Grant**
Cooper: **Marshall Jones**
Fletcher: **Rory McDermott**

The Gypsies
w **John Baines**
d **John Lemont**

When Drake and his crew rescue four people from an abandoned boat and take them aboard his ship, the dark clouds of defeat loom large on the horizon. The people are gypsies - and are being hunted by Don Pedro.

Sara: **Sara Branch**
Pastora: **Eileen Way**
Rafael: **Harry Lockhart**
Baltasar: **Christopher Carlos**
Will Martin: **Glynn Edwards**
Obadiah: **Larry Burns**
Don Pedro: **William Abney**

Court Intrigue
w **Hugh Ross Williamson**
d **Terry Bishop**

The Spanish hatch a cunning plot to keep Drake on English soil until a Spanish treasure ship deposits its cargo safely in Seville - but the scheme misfires and Drake and his crew attack the ship at sea.

Sir Christopher: **Bernard Archard**
Munro: **Ewan Roberts**
Spanish Ambassador: **John Arnatt**
Adam Forrester: **Robin Hughes**
Spanish Admiral: **Charles Carson**
Spanish Captain: **Edward Woodward**
Officer: **Colin Jeavons**
Servant: **Michael Mellinger**
Lady-in-Waiting: **Vicki Woolf**

Visit to Spain
w **Doreen Montgomery**
d **Terry Bishop**

Alarmed that Queen Elizabeth has promised the hand of Anne to an heir of the Spanish throne, Drake finds himself

risking his position with Elizabeth to save the girl from a loveless marriage.

King Phillip: **Zia Mohyeddin**
Anne: **Catherine Woodville**
Cordova: **John Arnatt**
Wenham: **Bryan Coleman**
Don Carlos: **Joseph Cuby**
Mariella: **Francesca Annis**
Major Domo: **Emrys Leyshon**
Duenna: **Nancy Beck**
Spanish Officer: **Carlos Douglas**
Spanish Soldier: **John Hatton**

The Slaves of Spain
w **Ian Stuart Black**
d **Anthony Bushell** and **Harry Booth**

Dropping anchor off the isle of Tobago, Drake finds the islanders have been enslaved by the Spaniards to help build a garrison which would overlook British shipping lanes and give the enemy the upper hand.

Yana: **Nanette Newman**
Agila: **Mark Eden**
Almighty Jones: **Michael Ripper**
Governor: **Derek Sydney**
His Wife: **Catherine Finn**
Garrett: **Marshall Johns**
Lieutenant: **Dallas Cavell**
Prisoner: **Colin Rix**

Sir Francis Drake:

Producer: **Anthony Bushell**
Executive Producer: **Leslie Harris**
Associate Producer: **Harry Fine**
Music by: **Ivor Slaney**
Script Editor: **Ian Stuart Black**
Production Manager: **John Comfort**
Assistant Director: **Gino Marotta**
Fights Arranger: **Peter Diamond**
Make-up: **Bill Lodge**

Filmed at Associated British Elstree Studios and at actual historical sites in Great Britain

An ITC Production in association with ABC Television
Filmed at Associated British Elstree Studios and at Actual Historic Sites in Great Britain

26 monochrome 30-minute episodes
1961

Space 1999

Gerry Anderson's third outing into the live-action field, a science-fiction opus distinguished by two formats.

The first format showed how Commander John Koenig arrived at Moonbase Alpha to supervise a deep-space-probe experiment, only to find himself and the Alphans marooned in space when a freak nuclear accident blasted the moon from its orbit and into a space-time warp light years away from Earth [thereby allowing the scriptwriters to dish up adventures which had Koenig and his people encountering alien life forms during their endless drift through space and, on several occasions, time].

Year Two [as the second season was known] found the Alphans stationed underground in a gigantic space complex that rivalled the sets of *Star Trek*, but the adventures remained the same - further encounters of the alien kind.

'...Moonbase Alpha...Massive Nuclear Explosion...Moon Torn Out Of Earth Orbit...Hurled Into Outer Space... RED ALERT!!'

Regular cast:
Cmdr John Koenig: **Martin Landau**
Dr Helena Russell: **Barbara Bain**
Prof. Victor Bergman [season one]: **Barry Morse**
Alan Carter: **Nick Tate**
Sandra Benes: **Zienia Merton**
Paul Morrow [season one]: **Prentis Hancock**
David Kano -[season one]: **Clifton Jones**
Tony Verdeschi [season two]: **Tony Anholt**
Maya [season two]: **Catherine Schell**
Dr Mathias: **Anton Phillips**
Yasko [season two]: **Yasuko Nagazumi**
First Operative [season two]: **Sarah Bullen**
Bill Fraser [season two]: **John Hug**
Dr Ben Vincent [season two]: **Jeffrey Kissoon**
Alibe [season two]: **Alibe Parsons**
Voice of Moonbase Computer: **Barbara Kelly**

season one
24 colour 60-minute episodes
1975

Breakaway
w **George Bellak**
d **Lee Katzin**

When John Koenig arrives at Moonbase Alpha to supervise a deep-space-probe project, and radiation plague hits the Moonbase crew, Koenig has no idea that within hours of his arrival a chain reaction will blast the Moon - and its occupants - into the far reaches of outer space.

John Koenig: **Martin Landau**
Helena Russell: **Barbara Bain**
Commissioner Simmonds: **Roy Dotrice**

Force of Life
w **John Byrne**
d **David Tomblin**

Technician Zoref becomes infused with an all-consuming need for heat. The people he touches freeze on contact and he is pulling life-giving energy from the Moonbase generators. Koenig must destroy him - before Alpha itself is destroyed.

Anton Zoref: **Ian McShane**
Eva Zoref: **Gay Hamilton**
Dominick: **John Hamill**

Collision Course
w **Anthony Terpiloff**
d **Ray Austin**

Should he allow the moon to collide with Astheria? That's the dilemma facing Koenig. He wants to use explosives to blast the moon out of the rogue planet's path, but Arra, Astheria's Queen, ask him to do nothing.

Arra: **Margaret Leighton**

War Games
w **Christopher Penfold**
d **Charles Crichton**

Attacked by a fleet of mysterious warships, with 129 dead and its life-support system smashed, Moonbase Alpha is no longer habitable. Joined by Dr Russell, Koenig pleads with the aliens for mercy but receives death in return.

Alien man: **Anthony Valentine**
Alien woman: **Isla Blair**

Death's Other Dominion
w **Anthony Terpiloff** and **Elizabeth Barrows**
d **Charles Crichton**

The Moonbase Alpha personnel discover Ultima Thule, a planet of ice. There are no signs of life but someone has left a message inviting Koenig and his people to share this 'paradise' with Earthmen who have lived for over 800 years!

Rowland: **Brian Blessed**
Jack Turner: **John Shrapnel**
Freda: **Mary Miller**

Voyager's Return
w **Johnny Byrne**
d **Bob Kellett**

Alpha catches up with a space-probe launched from Earth years before the Moon was shot into space. The ship is out of control and could kill millions of lives if left to roam the galaxy. Koenig wants to destroy it - Dr Russell has other ideas.

Dr Linden: **Jeremy Kemp**
Aarchon: **Alex Scott**
Haines: **Barry Stokes**

Alpha Child
w **Christopher Penfold**
d **Ray Austin**

The first birth on Alpha - a young male, who adopts the name Jarak and quickly develops from a five-year-old child into an adult - plunges Koenig into further danger. Aliens are after the new-born's secret - and threaten to annihilate Alpha to get it.

Jarak: **Julian Glover**
Cynthia: **Cyd Hayman**
Jackie: **Wayne Brooks**

Dragon's Domain
w **Christopher Penfold**
d **Charles Crichton**

Nobody believes Tony Cellini's story of a graveyard for spaceships, guarded by a terrible monster - until frightening events overtake Moonbase Alpha and Koenig and Dr Russell almost meet their deaths.

Cellini: **Gianni Garko**
Commissioner Dixon: **Douglas Wilmer**
Gina: **Barbara Kellerman**

Mission of the Darians
w **Johnny Byrne**
d **Ray Austin**

A spaceship which has been broadcasting its distress signal for over 800 years is discovered by Moonbase, who send a mission to help any survivors aboard. But a shock awaits them - the ship's occupants have been kept alive by cannibalism!

Kara: **Joan Collins**
High Priest: **Aubrey Morris**
Neman: **Denis Burgess**

Black Sun
w **David Weir**
d **Lee Katzin**

When Moonbase Alpha is under threat of being drawn into a 'black sun' and there appears to be little hope of averting the crisis, Koenig banks on Dr Bergman's force field for salvation.

Ryan: **Paul Jones**
Smithy: **Jon Laurimore**

Guardian of Piri
w **Christopher Penfold**
d **Charles Crichton**

Lured by false computer information, the Alphans land on Piri. To their joy, they find a seductive woman who can apparently satisfy their every whim - but Koenig alone sees through her magic and fights to free his people from her influence.

Guardian of Piri: **Catherine Schell**
Irving: **Michael Culver**

End of Eternity
w **Johnny Byrne**
d **Ray Austin**

Koenig finds himself risking his life to destroy an injured humanoid, which is doomed to spend eternity on a rock floating in space. Released by the Alphans, the creature is now hungry to inflict pain and destruction upon his saviours.

Balor: **Peter Bowles**
Baxter: **Jim Smilie**

Matter of Life and Death
w **Art Wallace** and **Johnny Byrne**
d **Charles Crichton**

When Dr Russell's husband mysteriously appears after years spent drifting in space, and warns the Alphans that his planet is composed of anti-matter, his warning arrives too late to save several of Koenig's team from being destroyed.

Lee Russell: **Richard Johnson**
Parks: **Stuart Damon**

Earthbound
w **Anthony Terpiloff**
d **Charles Crichton**

When an alien spaceship crash-lands on Alpha, Commissioner Simmonds, who was visiting Moonbase when it was blasted out of orbit, sees a chance to return to Earth - providing its captain, Zandor, allows him to do so.

Commissioner Simmonds: **Roy Dotrice**
Zandor: **Christopher Lee**

The Full Circle
w **Jesse Lasky Jr** and **Pat Silver**
d **Bob Kellett**

When two Alpha cruisers get caught in a time warp, the crews find they are hunting themselves in an age before they were born. Koenig nearly loses his life and, little realising that he is hunting his friends, Carter sets out to destroy the 'primitives'.

Spearman: **Oliver Cotton**

Another Time Another Place
w **Johnny Byrne**
d **David Tomblin**

Alpha finds itself and its occupants duplicated by a strange space phenomenon, and Koenig is surprised to see Earth again. But it is a duplicate earth, with an identical moon - and the Alphans meet themselves!

Regina: **Judy Geeson**

The Last Sunset
w **Christopher Penfold**
d **Charles Crichton**

The Alphans prepare for Operation Exodus. A new planet, Ariel-Alpha, has been discovered which closely resembles Earth and offers hope of a new life - but their dreams fade when they discover a new alien force.

The Infernal Machine
w **Anthony Terpiloff** and **Elizabeth Barrows**
d **David Tomblin**

Koenig and Dr Russell met the Companion, an old man who built a computerised spaceship and programmed his own personality into its computers. He is now the computer's slave - and he wants the earthlings to remain until they die!

Companion: **Leo McKern**

Ring Around the Moon
w **Edward Di Lorenzo**
d **Ray Austin**

Moonbase Alpha comes under threat from the Tritons, an alien race who plan to attack Earth. To gather information for their invasion, they begin killing off Koenig's people - and beam Dr Russell aboard their ship.

Ted Clifford: **Max Faulkner**

Missing Link
w **Edward Di Lorenzo**
d **Ray Austin**

A scientist from the planet Zenno takes Koenig prisoner to study him as a representative of ancient Earth. His daughter, Vana, falls in love with the Earthman - and Koenig finds himself bewitched by her charms.

Raan: **Peter Cushing**
Vana: **Joanna Dunham**

Space Brain
w **Christopher Penfold**
d **Charles Crichton**

Two Alphan astronauts are sent to investigate a strange organism in space. Their Eagle is destroyed and the alien being takes possession of crew-member Kelly's mind.

Meanwhile Koenig and his team are threatened with total extinction.

Kelly: **Shane Rimmer**
Melita: **Carla Romanelli**
Wayland: **Derek Anders**

The Troubled Spirit
w **Johnny Byrne**
d **Ray Austin**

When Koenig refuses to allow Mateo to continue with his experiments [he has been trying to communicate with plants], and the man dies, within hours a strange spirit materialises to avenge his death - which has yet to occur!

Mateo: **Giancarlo Prette**
Laura Adams: **Hilary Dwyer**
Dr Warren: **Anthony Nicholls**

The Testament of Arkadia
w **Johnny Byrne**
d **David Tomblin**

Koenig finds himself trying to save Moonbase Alpha from the power of Arkadia, a planet that once sustained life but is now barren. His attempts to do so are hampered by two Alphans - who wish to start a new civilisation on the planet.

Ferro: **Orso Maria Guerrini**
Anna: **Lisa Harrow**

The Last Enemy
w **Bob Kellett**
d **Bob Kellett**

Finding itself in the middle of an interplanetary war between two hostile planets, Koenig must try to negotiate a ceasefire so that Dione, a commander from one of the planets who has crash-landed on Alpha, can return home - but her enemies refuse to concede defeat.

Dione: **Caroline Mortimer**
Theia: **Maxine Audley**
Talos: **Kevin Stoney**

season two
24 colour 60-minute episodes
1975

The Metamorph
w **Johnny Byrne**
d **Charles Crichton**

When two of his crew are captured by Mentor, an evil alien from the planet Psychon, Koenig and Dr Russell lead a rescue mission to save them. They too become captives - but are helped to escape by Maya, Mentor's daughter.

Maya: **Catherine Schell** [intro]
Mentor: **Brian Blessed**
Annette: **Anouska Hempel**

The Exiles
w **Donald James**
d **Ray Austin**

Two innocent-looking young aliens, rescued by Koenig's team, wreak disaster and havoc on Moonbase when they take over Alpha and abduct Tony and Dr Russell - whom they transport to their home planet.

Cantar: **Peter Duncan**

Zova: **Stacy Dorning**
Mirella: **Margaret Inglis**

Journey to Where
w **Donald James**
d **Tom Clegg**

When Alpha receives a radio message from the USA [!], Koenig, Dr Russell and Alan Carter become involved in a strange journey through time and they end up back on Earth in the year 1339 - during the scourge of the Black Death.

Dr Logan: **Freddie Jones**
Carla : **Isla Blair**
MacDonald: **Roger Bizley**

One Moment of Humanity
w **Tony Barwick**
d **Charles Crichton**

Dr Russell and Tony Verdeschi are taken captive by Zamara, a beautiful female alien who wishes them to give her the secrets of emotion. She is the leader of a species of androids and she wants to make them human.

Zamara: **Billie Whitelaw**
Zarl: **Leigh Lawson**
Number Eight: **Geoffrey Bayldon**

Brian the Brain
w **Jack Ronder**
d **Kevin Connor**

An all-powerful robot, originally created on Earth, kidnaps Koenig and Dr Russell and takes them to a distant planet. Tony and Maya mount a rescue mission - not knowing that they're placing Koenig's life in danger.

Captain Michael: **Bernard Cribbins**

New Adam, New Eve
w **Terence Feely**
d **Charles Crichton**

Magus, a space being who believes himself to be 'God', offers the Alphans the opportunity to begin a new Garden of Eden - by matching Koenig and Maya as the new Adam and Eve.

Magus: **Guy Rolfe**

The Mark of Archanon
w **Lew Schwartz**
d **Charles Crichton**

Alan Carter and crewman Johnson find a man-made metal coffin. Dr Russell revives its two occupants, Pasc and his son, Etrec, with disastrous results. A deadly disease affects Pasc which threatens to infect the whole of Moonbase.

Pasc: **John Standing**
Etrec: **Michael Gallagher**

The Rules of Luton
w **Charles Woodgrove** [aka **Fred Freiberger**]
d **Val Guest**

When Koenig and Maya land their Eagle on a lush green planet, within minutes they find themselves transported to another planet where they are forced to fight three hideous aliens.

Alien 1: **David Jackson**

Alien 2: **Godfrey James**
Alien 3: **Roy Marsden**

All That Glisters
w **Keith Miles**
d **Ray Austin**

A planet possessed by living rocks, beings that can communicate, move and fire death-bringing rays. That's the situation that Tony Berdeschi and Dr Russell find themselves facing when they land on a planet to search for mineral specimens.

Reilly: **Patrick Mower**

Seed of Destruction
w **John Goldsmith**
d **Kevin Connor**

Jewel-like asteroids seem to be causing a power-loss on Alpha. Koenig and Alan Carter fly to a asteroid to investigate - and Koenig finds himself facing a duplicate of himself, which returns to Alpha in his place!

The Taybor
w **Thom Keyes**
d **Bob Brooks**

Taybor, a interstellar slave-trader, lands on Alpha bearing the 'gift' of a jump-drive device that could take Koenig's people back to Earth. There's just one catch - he wants Maya as payment!

Taybor: **Willoughby Goddard**

The A-B Chrysalis
w **Tony Barwick**
d **Val Guest**

A planet sending energy beams into space is causing serious damage to Alpha - which finds itself being drawn into a collision course with the planet. Koenig leads a team to investigate - and discovers a species of horrifying alien monsters.

A: **Ina Skriver**
B: **Sarah Douglas**

A Matter of Balance
w **Pip Baker** and **Jane Baker**
d **Charles Crichton**

Whilst exploring an apparently lifeless planet, the Alphans find an ancient temple, but its guardian allows only crew-woman Shermeen to enter. She meets Vindrus, the keeper of the temple - who has plans to enslave the Alphans.

Shermeen: **Lynne Frederick**
Vindrus: **Stuart Wilson**

Space Warp
w **Charles Woodgrove** [aka **Fred Freiberger**]
d **Peter Medak**

When Alpha slips through a space warp and is thrown 500 miles off its course - Tony Verdeschi and Alan Carter, returning from a mission in an Eagle, are left behind. Meanwhile, a strange fever begins to affect the Alphans.

The Beta Cloud
w **Charles Woodgrove** [aka **Fred Freiberger**]
d **Robert Lynn**

Koenig's people are attacked by a huge terrifying space creature which appears impervious to the Alphans' laser blasts. The creature seems unstoppable - unless Maya can transform herself into a deadly virus.

The Lambda Factor
w **Terence Dicks**
d **Charles Crichton**

With Koenig suffering from terrible nightmares and Alpha affected by a series of strange incidents. Dr Russell investigates a gas cloud which has turned Carolyn Powell into a superhuman being.

Carolyn Powell: **Deborah Fallander**
Mark Saunders: **Jess Conrad**

The Bringers of Wonder [part 1 of 2]
w **Terence Feely**
d **Tom Clegg**

When a spaceship from Earth lands on Moonbase Alpha and its pilot, Tony Verdeschi's brother Guido, steps out to greet the Alphans, it appears that the Alphans have finally won their battle to return home. Then why is Koenig ordering the newcomers to be destroyed?!

The Bringers of Wonder [part 2 of 2]
w **Terence Feely**
d **Tom Clegg**

Being treated by an experimental Brain Impulse Machine, Koenig appears to be the only Alphan who sees the strangers as aliens. Is he alone suffering from hallucinations - or will Maya learn the truth and rescue her comrades?

Guido: **Stuart Damon**
Dr Shaw: **Patrick Westwood**

The Seance Spectre
w **Donald James**
d **Peter Medak**

Sighting a giant planet on a direct collision course with Alpha, Koenig and Maya take off in Eagle One to examine the planet. Unknown to them, a group of dissident Alphans have sabotaged their spaceship - and Eagle One crashes.

Sanderson: **Ken Hutchison**
Eva: **Carolyn Seymour**

Dorzak
w **Christopher Penfold**
d **Val Guest**

When a spaceship carrying Sahala, a pretty young alien, requests permission to land on Alpha, it plunges Maya into a battle of wits with Dorzac, a dangerous criminal from her own planet.

Dorzac: **Lee Montague**
Sahala: **Jill Townsend**

Devil's Planet
w **Michael Winder**
d **Tom Clegg**

Koenig is captured and held prisoner by three alien catwomen, who carry electrical whips with which to overpower their enemies. He is told that the only way to win his freedom is through an ordeal called 'The Hunt'.

Catwoman: **Hildegard Neil**

The Dorcons
w Johnny Byrne
d Tom Clegg

A Dorcon battle-cruiser attacks Moonbase Alpha, and the Dorcon leader Varda demands that Koenig hands over Maya. Aware that they intend to use her as a guinea pig, Koenig refuses - and the Dorcons invade Alpha.

Varda: **Ann Firbank**
Archon: **Patrick Troughton**
Malik: **Gerry Sundquist**

The Immunity Syndrome
w Johnny Byrne
d Tom Clegg

Koenig leads a reconnaissance team to investigate an Earth-type planet. Landing on its surface the group separate. Moments later Koenig and Alan Carter find Tony Verdeschi nearly dead. They try to take him back to Alpha - but their Eagle crash-lands back on the planet's surface.

Zoran: **Nadine Sawalha**
Travis: **Karl Held**
Joe: **Ron Boyd**

Catacombs of the Moon
w Anthony Terpiloff
d Robert Lynn

Laying explosive charges in an underground cavern. Crewman Osgood begins to receive strange visions of doom. The Alpha sensors detect a strange heat surge, Osgood goes insane and Koenig is left to face the terrible force which has caused the mystery.

Osgood: **James Laurenson**
Michelle Osgood: **Pamela Stephenson**

📖 h/b = hardback: *Space 1999 - Breakaway* [1975: E.C. Tubb: Orbit Books (Futura Pub.): h/b Dobson Books: novelisation of *Breakaway, Matter of Life and Death, Ring Around the Moon & Black Sun*]; *Space 1999 - Moon Odyssey* [1975: John Rankine: Orbit Books (Futura Pub.): h/b Dobson Books: novelisation of *Alpha Child, The Last Sunset, Voyager's Return & Another Time, Another Place*]; *Space 1999: 3 - The Space Guardians* [1975: Brian Ball: Orbit Books (Futura Pub.): h/b Dobson Books: novelisation of *Missing Link, Force of Life & Guardian of Piri*]; *Space 1999: 4 - Collision Course* [1975: E.C. Tubb: Orbit Books (Futura Pub.): h/b Dobson Books: novelisation of *Collision Course, The Full Circle, End of Eternity & Death's Other Dominion*]; *Space 1999: 5 - Lunar Attack* [1975: John Rankine: Orbit Books (Futura Pub.): h/b Dobson Books: novelisation of *War Games, The Troubled Spirit, The Last Enemy & Space Brain*]; *Space 1999: 6 - Astral Quest* [1975: John Rankine: Orbit Books (Futura Pub.): h/b Dobson Books: novelisation of *The Infernal Machine, Mission of the Darians, Dragon's Domain & The Testament of Arcadia*]; *Space 1999: 7 - Alien Seed* [1976: E.C. Tubb: Orbit Books (Futura Pub.): h/b Arthur Baker Ltd.: original story based on the first season]; *Space 1999: 8 - Android Planet* [1976: John Rankine: Orbit Books (Futura Pub.): h/b Arthur Baker Ltd.: original story based on the first season]; *Space 1999: 9 - Rogue Planet* [1976/77: E.C. Tubb: 1977: Orbit Books (Futura Pub.): 1976: h/b Arthur Baker Ltd.: original story based on the first season]; *Space 1999: 10 - Phoenix of Megaron* [1976: John Rankine: Pocket Books (Simon and Schuster Inc.): USA only: original story based on first season]; *Space 1999 - Earthfall* [1977: E.C. Tubb: Orbit Books (Futura Pub.): alternative novelisation of *Breakaway* plus new material]; *Space 1999 - Planets of Peril* [1977: Michael Butterworth: Star Books (W.H. Allen/Wyndham): h/b Allan Wingate: novelisation, with photos, of *The Metamorph, The AB Chrysalis, The Rules of Luton & New Adam, New Eve*]; *Space 1999 - Mind Breaks of Space* [1977/78: Michael Butterworth and J. Jeff Jones: 1977: Star Books (W.H. Allen/Wyndham): 1978: h/b Allan Wingate: novelisation, with photos, of *Brian the Brain, The Mark of Archanon, Catacombs of the Moon & One Moment of Humanity*]; *Space 1999 - The Space-Jackers* [1977: Michael Butterworth: Star Books (W.H. Allen/Wyndham): novelisation, with photos, of *Seed of Destruction, A Matter of Balance, The Exiles & The Beta Cloud*]; *Space 1999 - The Psychomorph* [1977: Michael Butterworth: Star Books (W.H. Allen/Wyndham): novelisation, with photos, of *The Lambda Factor & The Bringers of Wonder*]; *Space 1999 - The Time Fighters* [1977: Michael Butterworth: Star Books (W.H. Allen/Wyndham): novelisation, with photos, of *Space Warp, Dorzak, Devil's Planet & The Seance Spectre*]; *Space 1999 - The Edge of the Infinite* [1977: Michael Butterworth: Warner Books USA only: novelisation, with photos, of *All That Glisters, Journey to Where, The Immunity Syndrome & The Dorcons*]; *The Making of Space 1999* [1976: Tim Heald: Ballantine Books: USA only].

Space 1999:

Created by **Gerry Anderson** and **Sylvia Anderson**
Produced by: **Sylvia Anderson** [season 1] & **Fred Freiberger** [2]
Executive Producer: **Gerry Anderson**
Associate Producer [2]: **F. Sherwin Green**
Production Executive: **Reg Hill**
Music: **Barry Gray** [1] & **Derek Wadsworth** [2]
Special Effects designed & directed by: **Brian Johnson**
Story Consultant [season 1]: **Christopher Penfold**
Script Editor: **Edward di Lorenzo, Johnny Byrne** [season 1]
Technical Director/Supervising Editor: **David Lane**
Production Designer: **Keith Wilson**
Production Manager: **Donald Toms, Ron Fry**
Director of Photography: **Frank Watts BSC**
Casting Director: **Michael Barnes**
Assistant Director: **Ken Baker**
Editor: **Alan Killick**
Sound Editor: **Peter Pennell**
Music Editor: **Alan Willis**
Continuity: **Gladys Goldsmith**
Make-up: **Ann Cotton**
Hair Designer: **Helene Bevan**
Wardrobe: **Eileen Sullivan**
Moon City Costumes designed by: **Rudi Gernreich**

An ITC/RAI co-production, produced by Group Three for worldwide distribution.
Filmed at Pinewood and Bray Studios

Season one: 24 colour 60-minute episodes 1975

Season two: 24 colour 60-minute episodes 1976

Stingray

*'Stand by for action! Anything can happen
in the next half hour!'*

Those words, spoken by Commander Shore [a character in the series], introduced us to Gerry Anderson's latest puppet creation, Captain Troy Tempest, Phones and the green-haired Marina, members of the World Aquanaut Security Patrol [WASP] - the crew of Stingray, a 'super-submarine equipped with an atomic engine, 16 Sting missiles and the ability to leap in and out of the sea 'salmon fashion'. A deadly killer-sub whose mission was to protect earthlings in the year 2000 from any sort of undersea dangers.

Troy Tempest [described in the original press release as the 'dynamic hero, a strikingly handsome, fearless, conscientious man'] captained the team. Assisting him was George Sheridan, nicknamed Phones, because he operated the ship's hydrophones [short-range sonar equipment].

The third [unofficial] member of the crew was Marina, the young daughter of Aphony, Emperor of the peaceful undersea kingdom of Pacifica, a huge shell city on the bed of the Pacific ocean.

In command of Marineville [an undersea city based somewhere off the North American coast, which served as WASP headquarters] was Commander Shore. Crippled during a mission [he relied on a hover chair for mobility], Shore had set up and run the WASP team for five years.

Other characters were: Shore's, daughter, Atlanta; Sub-Lieutenant Fisher; and the inevitable pet, Oink, Marina's seal cub.

Their enemies were: Titan, the tyrannical ruler of Titanica, who had vowed to destroy the WASPS; and the Aquaphibians, a monstrous ocean race who obeyed Titan and attacked Marineville in their mechanical fish [Terror Fish, which fired missiles from their gaping 'mouths'].

Notable for being the first Gerry Anderson series to be filmed in colour - but shown in monochrome until the 70s.

Character voices:
Troy Tempest: **Don Mason**
Commander Shore: **Ray Barrett**
Phones: **Robert Easton**
Atlanta: **Lois Maxwell**
Titan / SL Fisher: **Ray Barrett**
X20: **Robert Easton**
Marina: Non-speaking
[but voiced by **Sylvia Anderson** in *Raptures of the Deep*]

The Pilot aka Stingray
w **Gerry Anderson** and **Sylvia Anderson**
d **Alan Pattillo**

Investigating the destruction of a World Navy sub, Captain Troy Tempest and Phones come under attack from an enemy submarine in the form of a giant fish. They are taken prisoner and sent to the undersea kingdom of Titanica.

Plant of Doom
w **Alan Fennell**
d **David Elliott**

Enraged when Stingray escapes, Titan has Surface agent X20 deliver a deadly plant to Marina's father, who then gives it to his daughter - who is suspected of being a spy.

Sea of Oil
w **Dennis Spooner**
d **John Kelly**

When Atlanta is captured by an undersea race while Stingray is investigating the collapse of an oil rig, and her kidnappers plant a bomb aboard Stingray, the girl finds herself racing against time to contact Troy before the bomb explodes.

Hostages of the Deep
w **Alan Fennell**
d **Desmond Saunders**

When Admiral Carson and his wife are taken prisoner by Gadus, Stingray is sent to secure their release but Marina, attempting a rescue, is captured - leaving Troy and Phones to rescue her before she is killed by a giant swordfish.

Treasure Down Below
w **Dennis Spooner**
d **Alan Pattillo**

Following a treasure map obtained by Phones, the crew of Stingray meet two underwater pirates who are over 300 years old. Troy and Phones are captured and when they refuse to agree to the pirates' terms, an undersea battle breaks out.

The Big Gun
w **Alan Fennell**
d **David Elliott**

After destroying an underwater gunship, Stingray pursues a second ship into an undersea tunnel and discovers Solarstar, the refuge of the gunships - but the water pressure threatens to crush Stingray and Troy turns to Marina for help.

The Golden Sea
w **Dennis Spooner**
d **John Kelly**

Titan plans to trap Stingray during its regular visits to a group of scientists who are mining the sea bed for gold. His weapon is to be a giant killer swordfish - but Troy Tempest turns the tables once again.

The Ghost Ship
w **Alan Fennell**
d **Desmond Saunders**

When Commander Shore and Phones are taken prisoner by Idotee, who is based on a sunken Spanish galleon, Shore orders Troy to launch missiles against Idotee, but Tempest attempts a rescue bid - and sends the enemy into fits of laughter.

Countdown
w **Dennis Spooner**
d **Alan Pattillo**

Disguised as a professor who can make mute people speak, agent X20 convinces Troy and Phones to hand Marina over to him. He then ties her up and leaves her beside a time bomb - set to explode when Troy attempts a rescue bid.

Ghost of the Sea
w **Alan Fennell**
d **David Elliott**

During a flashback sequence, the viewer is told how Commander Shore was crippled during a sea battle with the enemy. He was saved by a mysterious stranger whom he never saw again - until Troy repays the Commander's debt by rescuing the stranger.

Emergency Marineville
w **Alan Fennell**
d **John Kelly**

Having tracked down the launching side of missiles aimed at Marineville, Troy and his crew are captured. Marina is tortured in an attempt to get her to betray the coded signal that would destroy Marineville's interceptor missiles.

Subterranean Sea
w Alan Fennell
d Desmond Saunders

Stingray's crew probe the ocean depths and discover a deep shaft that leads to a desert plateau, but before they can leave, a wall of water turns the desert into an underground sea. Will they be able to escape?

Loch Ness Monster
w Dennis Spooner
d Alan Pattillo

When Admiral Denver finds himself the prey of the Loch Ness monster, Troy and his crew investigate. But the creature attacks as they enter the Loch and Stingray launches a missile at the monster - only to discover that it is a fake, designed to attract tourists.

The Invaders
w Dennis Spooner
d David Elliott

When aliens set up a trap at a weather station and the Stingray crew are captured - then unknowingly give away vital Marineville secrets - Troy Tempest finds himself fighting a lone battle to stop an alien invasion.

Secret of the Giant Oyster
w Alan Fennell
d John Kelly

Two amateur divers trick Troy and his crew into helping them obtain a priceless pearl from a giant oyster. Marina is worried about a legend that says bad luck will befall anyone who steals the pearls - and Troy suddenly finds himself in danger.

Raptures of the Deep
w Alan Fennell
d Desmond Sanders

Racing to the rescue of two madcap treasure-hunters, Troy runs out of air and dreams that he is the ruler of an undersea castle with Atlanta and a talking Marina at his side. But the Aquaphibians attack and the castle falls to ruins - as he wakes up.

Stand by for Action
w Dennis Spooner
d Alan Pattillo

Marineville as the location for a film and everyone playing themselves - except Troy Tempest, who is replaced by a handsome actor to whom Atlanta and Marina are attracted. Is it another dream? And why does the film director resemble agent X20?

The Disappearing Ships
w Alan Fennell
d David Elliott

Searching for three freighter ships that were to be blown up, Troy and his crew discover a strange ship's graveyard inhabited by Nomads - who have no idea that the ships they live in are about to explode.

Man from the Navy
w Alan Fennell
d John Kelly

Troy becomes involved with a Naval Captain who has come to Marineville to demonstrate a new missile, little knowing that agent X20 had replaced the missile heads with real explosives. When the Captain is accused of treason, Troy must prove him innocent.

Marineville Traitor
w Alan Fennell
d Desmond Saunders

When a vital piece of equipment is stolen from Marineville and Commander Shore is accused of being a traitor, Troy finds himself having to arrest his friend and place him in the brig.

Tom Thumb Tempest
w Alan Fennell
d Alan Pattillo

Troy and the crew of Stingray find themselves shrunken to Tom Thumb size and trapped in a fishtank. They discover that Titan is hatching a plot to overthrow Marineville and Stingray cannot stop him - until Troy awakens from his dream.

Pink Ice
w Alan Fennell
d David Elliott

When it is reported that pink ice is falling all over the world, Stingray investigates, but becomes trapped in a block of frozen flesh-coloured water. Troy calls for the ice to be bombed - but will Stingray escape damage?

The Master Plan
w Alan Fennell
d John Kelly

It looks like the end for Troy Tempest. Poisoned by Titan, who wants Marina returned to him before he gives Troy the antidote, will Troy and Phones be able to overcome this latest threat?

Star of the East
w Alan Fennell
d Desmond Saunders

Blaming Marineville for the revolt in his country, El Hudat is ordered from the city. But he takes Marina with him against her will and Troy and Phones try to rescue her before the deposed leader can cause her harm.

An Echo of Danger
w Dennis Spooner
d Alan Pattillo

Disguised as a psychiatrist, X20 finds a way to discredit Phones, who fails to report a distress signal from Stingray. But one of Troy's crew finds a way to restore the status quo - and save Phone's honour.

Invisible Enemy
w Alan Fennell
d David Elliott

Returning to Marineville from a rescue mission with a man in a comatose state, Troy reports to Commander Shore.

Meanwhile the patient recovers and places everyone in the city in an hypnotic trance. Can Troy save the day before an attack is launched?

Deep Heat
w **Alan Fennell**
d **John Kelly**

Investigating the disappearance of a robot probe, Stingray finds itself drawn to the bottom of the ocean where two survivors from a doomed city attempt to steal the vehicle to use it in their escape attempt.

In Search of the Tajmanon
w **Dennis Spooner**
d **Desmond Saunders**

Assigned to help Professor Graham find the missing temple of Tajmanon, which was submerged when a dam was built in Africa, Troy and his crew encounter danger and intrigue at the bottom of the sea.

Titan goes Pop
w **Alan Fennell**
d **Alan Pattillo**

Believing that he has captured a VIP visiting Marineville, X20 takes his prisoner to Titan. But the man turns out to be Duke Dexter - a pop singer, whose 'weird music' lies heavy on Titan's ears.

Set Sail for Adventure
w **Dennis Spooner**
d **David Elliott**

When Commander Shore accepts a challenge that his agents cannot take the rigours of an old-time sailing vessel, Phones and Lt. Fisher find themselves all at sea when a storm overturns their boat.

Tune of Danger
w **Alan Fennell**
d **John Kelly**

When a jazz group visits Marineville everyone expects the evening to go with a bang - but not the kind that threatens to explode in their faces when X20 plants a bomb in a bass player's fiddle.

Rescue from the Skies
w **Dennis Spooner**
d **Desmond Saunders**

During his training to become an aquanaut, Lt. Fisher takes command of Stingray. His assignment involves target practice on a Terrorfish, but X20 has attached a limpet-bomb to Stingray's hull and Troy must attempt to remove it.

The Cool Caveman
w **Alan Fennell**
d **Alan Pattillo**

Troy's dream that he and Phones are pitted against a race of underwater cavemen who plunder the cargo of a vessel carrying radioactive fuel, gives him the idea of wearing a caveman's outfit at Marineville's fancy-dress ball.

A Nut for Marineville
w **Gerry Anderson** and **Sylvia Anderson**
d **David Elliott**

Professor Burgoyne, a man developing a new super-missile needed to destroy an indestructible craft heading towards Marineville, is presumed dead when his lab is destroyed by flames. Things look bleak for WASP headquarters.

Trapped in the Depths
w **Alan Fennell**
d **John Kelly**

When Atlanta is taken prisoner by Cordo, the ruler of a race of underwater people, Stingray is sent to rescue her. But Cordo lures Troy and Phones into a duplicate Stingray while his men steal the real one - and set off to destroy Marineville.

Eastern Eclipse
w **Alan Fennell**
d **Desmond Saunders**

El Hudat returns to wreak havoc on Marineville, by substituting his twin brother for himself and escaping from his cell. But Stingray is soon hot on his trail and Commander Shore has to make a double-sided decision.

A Christmas to Remember
w **Dennis Spooner**
d **Alan Pattillo**

In an attempt to brighten up the Christmas festivities for the orphaned son of an aquanaut, Troy asks the boy to join his Stingray crew and re-enact a famous battle. Unknown to either of them, Phones has been hypnotised to lead them into a trap.

The Lighthouse Dwellers
w **Alan Fennell**
d **David Elliott**

When disaster strikes a pilot approaching a new airfield and his ship crashes because a lighthouse beacon flashes on, then off again, confusing the pilot, it isn't long before Stingray is sent to investigate.

Aquanaut of the Year
w **Gerry Anderson** and **Sylvia Anderson**
d **Alan Pattillo**

Having received the 'Aquanaut of the Year' award, Troy finds himself the subject of 'This is Your Life'. His most exciting adventures are relived before his eyes - but it's the question from the host-master that worries him. Are you and Atlanta more than 'good friends'?

📖 both, original stories: *Stingray* [1965: John Theydon: Armada Paperbacks (May Fair Books): illustrated]; *Stingray and the Monster* [1966: John Theydon: Armada Paperbacks (May Fair Books): illustrated].

Stingray:

Producer: **Gerry Anderson**
Character visualisation: **Sylvia Anderson**
Associate Producer: **Reg Hill**
Special Effects: **Derek Meddings** and **Reg Hill**
Art Director: **Bob Bell**
Puppetry Supervision: **Christine Glanville**, **Mary Turner**
Music by: **Barry Gray**
Title Vocal by: **Gary Miller**

An A. P. Films Production in association with ATV for ITC Worldwide Distribution

39 colour 30-minute episodes
1964

Strange Report

The unusual cases solved by ex-police criminologist, Adam Strange, a man who investigated cases that had baffled the best minds of Scotland Yard. Crimes of such complexity that the powers that be only turned to him when they had exhausted all other avenues of detection open to them. Crimes of the 'impossible' variety, which the criminologist solved with monotonous regularity - that isn't to say that the programme itself was boring. Far from it. It was in fact one of the best of its genre and gave the viewer a seldom repeated opportunity to watch the multi-talented Anthony Quayle going through his paces, with tongue firmly in cheek.

Strange himself had developed his talent for solving crime while working at the Home Office, but was now retired and able to pursue his 'hobby' without the restrictions placed on him by his former job. One moment he'd be bringing his specialised talent to bear on a uniquely-executed crime, the next he'd be speeding through the London streets in his somewhat unusual transport - a black, unlicensed London taxi.

Never far away was Hamlyn Gynt, his young assistant, who shared a lab with Strange at his London home, and Evelyn McLean, who lived next door to the criminologist and sometimes helped him in his work.

Splendid stuff.

Regular cast:
Adam Strange: **Anthony Quayle**
Hamlyn Gynt: **Kas Garas**
Evelyn McLean: **Anneke Wills**
Semi regulars:
Chief Superintendent Cavanagh: **Gerald Sim**
Professor Marks: **Charles Lloyd Pack**

Report 0649: SKELETON:
'Let Sleeping Heroes Lie'
w **Brian Degas** and **Tudor Gates**
d **Peter Medak**

When the skeleton of a man found on a London bomb site is discovered to have been killed not by bombs but a bullet, Adam Strange is asked to roll back the years to trace what he was up to 30 years earlier!

Elleston: **Eric Portman**
James: **Hugh Burden**
Clinton: **Tom Adams**
Llewellyn: **Edward Cast**
Old Man: **Billy Russell**
Mrs Llwellyn: **Sylvia Kaye**
Professor Marks: **Charles Lloyd Pack** [intro]
Mrs. Tompkin: **Julie May**
Keymaker: **Erik Chitty**
Coroner: **Victor Platt**
Chief Inspector: **Allan McClelland**
Maid: **Patti Brooks**
Emma Llewellyn: **Julie Collins**
Attendant: **Raymond Graham**
Ticket Collector: **Leslie Sarony**

Report 2641: HOSTAGE:
'If You Won't Learn, Die!'
w **John Kruse**
d **Charles Crichton**

The Chinese Charge D'Affaire is kidnapped in London and held as hostage for the release of a man in Peking. When the Chinese threaten to retaliate, Strange is called in to ease the situation.

Blake: **Kenneth Haigh**
Sung-Lee: **Eric Young**

Mrs Deeds: **Peggy Thorpe-Bates**
Roger: **Peter Craze**
Chief Superintendent Cavanagh: **Gerald Sim** [intro]
Ho-Chai: **Robert Lee**
Doctor Ward: **Lockwood West**
Mr Watkins: **Geoffrey Colville**
Laboratory Assistant: **David Ashford**
Miss Blake: **Nan Braunton**

Report 0846: LONELYHEARTS:
'Who Killed Dan Cupid?'
w **Roger Parkes**
d **Peter Duffell**

What's so special about Leonard Grey that leads the police to arrest him for the murder of the boss of a Lonely Hearts Club? With the help of Ham and Evelyn, Adam Strange unearths what appears to be a case with political implications.

Tessa O'Neill: **Geraldinne Moffatt**
Leonard Grey: **Donald Douglas**
Jack White: **John Bennett**
Chief Superintendent Cavanagh: **Gerald Sim**
Barbara Coles: **Ruth Trouncer**
Carter: **Glyn Jones**
Professor Marks: **Charles Lloyd Pack**
Stevan Milner: **Donald Scott**
Baiteson: **Ewan Roberts**
Mark Harper: **Jonathan Holt**
Grantley: **Jeffrey Gardiner**
Jones: **Dennis Chinnery**
Helga Bauer: **Lyn Pinkney**

Report 8319: GRENADE:
'What Price Change?'
w **Bill Strutton**
d **Charles Crichton**

To air their views, two opposing factions at Radcliffe University are planning various activities to stop defence research taking place at the establishment. Because the campus is outside their jurisdiction, the police ask Adam Strange to look into the affair.

Arthur Pater: **Bernard Lee**
Superintendent Shaw: **Peter Jeffrey**
Ferdy Walker: **Anthony Corlan**
Voss: **Alex Scott**
Bob Tremayne: **Jeremy Bulloch**
Moira: **Susan Jameson**
Dean Jordan: **Basil Dignam**
Registrar: **Lionel Murton**
Liz: **Helen Cotterill**
Cliff Hunt: **John Nolan**
H. Birrell: **Alan Gerrard**
Bus Conductor: **John Hamilton**

Report 3906: COVER GIRL:
'Last Year's Model'
w **Terence Maples**
d **Peter Duffell**

When fear enters the fashion world, Adam finds himself involved in the affairs of a fashion designer whose latest creations have been stolen and who is now being threatened unless she pulls out of the parade.

Cricket: **Elaine Taylor**
Madeleine: **Lisa Daniely**
Bruce: **Richard Vanstone**
Mr Alsbury: **David Healy**
Shop Manager: **Ron Pember**
Mrs Olgilvie: **Doreen Mantle**

Hayes: **Albert Shepherd**
Sloan: **Christopher Malcolm**
Miss Gray: **Doris Nolan**
Lou Oliver: **John Rees**
Mimi: **Bobbie Oswald**
Bert: **Daniel Moynihan**
Security Guard: **Edwin Brown**
Model Girls: **Unity Grimwood, Pauline Long, Hilary Pritchard, Meg Walter**

Report 3424: EPIDEMIC:
'A Most Curious Crime'
w **Don Brinkley**
d **Daniel Petrie**

Adam finds himself facing a man who turns blood into gold - by smuggling illegal immigrants into the country and making vast profits from their misery. With Ham's help, he teaches the rogue a lesson.

Morrison: **Peter Vaughan**
Zeba: **Zienia Merton**
Ameen: **Saeed Jaffrey**
Mehdi: **Shivendra Sinha**
Jamal: **Roshan Seth**
Tork: **Graham Haberfield**
Professor Marks: **Charles Lloyd Pack**
Bus Boy: **Salmaan Peer**
Intern: **Raymond Armstrong**
Morgue Assistant: **John F. Landry**
Reggie: **Dallas Adams**
Ward Nurse: **Karol Keyes**
Waiter: **Tim Wylton**
Waitress: **Penny Service**

Report 2475: REVENGE:
'When a Man Hates'
w **Martin Hall**
d **Charles Crichton**

When an ex-convict vows to carry out his threat to kill those who put him inside - one of whom was Adam Strange - the criminologist finds himself involved in a race against time to discover the man's hiding place.

James Hanson: **Julian Glover**
Mary Hanson: **Rosemary Leach**
Inspector Jenner: **John Thaw**
Churchill: **James Cossins**
Mrs Rogers: **Gabrielle Hamilton**
Brinkley: **Alfred Bell**
Secretary: **Geraldine Sherman**
Michael: **Wade Barker**
Bill: **Richard Beaumont**
Antrobus: **Llewellyn Rees**
Office Boy: **Stephen Whittaker**

Report 1021: SHRAPNEL:
'The Wish in the Dream'
w **Jan Read**
d **Brian Smedley-Ashton**

A piece of shrapnel in a dead man's body reveals an unexpected twist in an eternal triangle that reaches out of the past. Called in to attend the autopsy, Adam Strange finds himself personally involved.

Carol Webber: **Sylvia Syms**
Paul Webber: **Gerald Flood**
George Halliday: **Leo Genn**
Inspector Purcell: **Bryan Marshall**
Joey Benjamin: **Barry Fantoni**
Professor Marks: **Charles Lloyd Pack**
Jeweller: **Ian Gray**

Coroner: **John Dunbar**
Valet Manager: **Reginald Barrett**
Messenger Boy: **Michael Holden**

Report 8944: HAND:
'A Matter of Witchcraft?'
w **Edward De Blasio**
d **Peter Duffell**

Adam and Ham find themselves immersed in the chilling world of witchcraft when a beautiful young secretary is murdered in brutal circumstances. Murder is one thing but as Adam finds out - the black-magic variety is difficult to solve.

Miss Dalton: **Renee Asherson**
Inspector Graves: **Keith Barron**
Joanna: **Cecillia Darby**
Mrs Brearley: **Helen Lindsay**
Miss Nightingale: **Rosalind Atkinson**
Brinkley: **Alfred Bell**
Professor Marks: **Charles Lloyd Pack**
Dean: **Carleton Hobbs**
Laboratory Assistant: **Richard Coe**
Police Sergeant: **Peter Welch**
Russian Lady: **Malya Woolf**
Birthday Girl: **Maxine Casson**

Report 1553: RACIST:
'A Most Dangerous Proposal'
w **Arthur Dales**
d **Peter Duffell**

Trouble and heartbreak is a foregone conclusion when the ideals of a father and daughter clash. He is the leader of an anti-black organisation, she is strong in her belief for racial equality. But no one expected the result to be murder, least of all Adam Strange.

Jill: **Jane Merrow**
Crowley: **Guy Doleman**
Sir George Davies: **Griffith Jones**
Drake: **Karl Held**
Brandt: **Clive Francis**
Margaret: **Cleo Sylvestre**
Rick: **Ram John Holder**
Barbara: **Sarah Marshall**
Canon Lewis: **Phillip Ross**
Inspector Matthews: **Frank Gatliff**
American Athlete: **Kenneth Gardnier**
Guard: **Michael Goldie**
Airport Attendant: **Graham Ashley**

Report 7931: SNIPER:
'When is Your Cousin Not?'
w **Nicholas Palmer**
d **Peter Medak**

Student demonstrations in a East European country, and murder, involve Adam Strange in a search for truth as well as a killer. Back in London, Ham comes up with a startling piece of evidence.

Marisha: **Lelia Goldoni**
Kulik: **Vladek Sheybal**
Olenka: **Kika Markham**
Savi: **Martin Shaw**
Colonel Vajda: **Alan MacNaughtan**
Pavel Gordy: **Sandor Eles**
Taran: **Michael Turner**
Security Man: **John Abineri**
T.V. Manager: **Michael Sheard**
Cafe Proprietor: **Rod Beacham**
Medical Student: **Scott Frederics**
Hotel Proprietress: **Joan Newell**

Young Man: **Oliver Cotton**
Soldiers: **John Challis, Alan Mason**

Report 4821: X-RAY:
'Who Weeps For the Doctor?'
w **Roger Parkes**
d **Charles Crichton**

Has anyone the right to help a man take his own life even though death is threatening to close in at any day? That's the dilemma facing Adam Strange when he finds himself in a human tragedy.

Miss Collingford: **Ann Firbank**
Doctor Hornsey: **John Laurie**
Peggy Gale: **Trisha Mortimer**
Caine: **Ewan Hooper**
Inspector Franklin: **Nicholas Selby**
House Surgeon: **Richard Carpenter**
Anders: **David Collings**
Professor Marks: **Charles Lloyd Pack**
Jennie: **Linda Renwick**
Miss Blake: **Annabelle Lee**
Clerk: **Isabel Metliss**

Report 2493: KIDNAP:
'Whose Pretty Girl Are You?'
w **Don Brinkley**
d **Daniel Petrie**

When a beauty queen is 'kidnapped', Adam must find out whether the event has been organised as a publicity stunt or is for real? If it's the latter, he has barely 24 hours to find the girl.

Toby: **Ian Ogilvy**
Otis Dean: **David Bauer**
Jennifer Dean: **Sally Geeson**
Perk: **Richard O'Sullivan**
George Lucas: **Peter Jones**
Louise: **Caroline Blakiston**
Inspector Lowe: **John Arnatt**
Reporter: **Neville Barber**

Report 4407: HEART:
'No Choice for the Donor'
w **Edward de Blasio**
d **Robert Asher**

The police are baffled. A famous heart surgeon has been kidnapped but no ransom note is delivered nor is anything heard from his abductors. Adam Strange is called in - and uncovers a most unusual reason for the man's disappearance.

Segarus: **Kenneth Griffith**
Mrs Sanders: **Barbara Murray**
Doctor Sanders: **Robert Hardy**
Inspector Collins: **Peter Cellier**
The Girl Friend: **Julie Samuel**
Inspector Lowe: **William Dysart**
Professor Marks: **Charles Lloyd Pack**
Doctor Comitas: **Gordon Faith**
Doctor Lambrus: **Michael Martin**
Tony Williams: **Mark Hawkins**
Landlady: **Hazel Hughes**
First Detective: **Kenneth Ives**
Man: **Frederic Abbot**

Report 4977: SWINDLE:
'Square Root of Evil'
w **Leigh Vance**
d **Brian Smedley-Aston**

When a Bank of England company responsible for printing genuine bank notes are duped into carrying out a massive order for a gang of swindlers. Adam Strange and his assistant Ham discover that greed lurks within.

Nils Paavo: **Derren Nesbitt**
Karen Rose: **Pauline Yates**
Klaus Frei: **Anton Diffring**
Dick Blaise: **Joe Baker**
David Covington: **John Carlisle**
Marla: **Louise Pajo**
Estelle: **Valerie Van Ost**
Inspector Peters: **Michael Forrest**
Otto: **Oliver MacGreevy**
Jago: **Patrick O'Connell**
Harbour Master: **Arthur Lovegrove**
Beth: **Ilona Rodgers**
Wiglow: **John Tate**
Penhollow: **Arthur Howard**

Report 5055: CULT:
'Murder Shrieks Out'
w **Morris Farhi**
d **Charles Crichton**

When a pop singer is electrocuted during a charity pop performance, Strange becomes involved in the twilight world of a charity-collecting religious sect. Suspecting that the death was no accident, he asks Ham to infiltrate the group.

Maggie: **Pamela Franklin**
Lars: **Ray McAnally**
Newcome: **John Ronane**
Pato: **George Mikell**
Inspector Morrell: **Tony Steedman**
Moran: **Edward Bishop**
Popescu: **Makki Marseilles**
Brand: **Christopher Mitchell**
Tanner: **Michael Rothwell**
Sergeant Harris: **Sebastian Breaks**
Foreman: **Godfrey James**

Strange Report [1970: John Burke: Hodder Paperbacks/Pan Books: novelisations of *Report 5055: Cult* and *Report 0649: Skeleton*].

Strange Report:

Producer: **Robert Buzz Berger**
Executive Producer: **Norman Felton**
Associate Producer: **Barry Delmaine**
Music by: **Roger Webb**
Story Editor: **Edward DeBlasio**
Associate Script Editor: **Jan Read**
Production Manager: **Ron Jackson**
Casting Director: **Mary Selway**
Assistant Director: **Malcolm Johnson**
Second Unit Director: **Brian Smedley-Aston**
Stunt Arranger: **Roy Vincente**
Music Editor: **John Taylor**
Make-up: **Sylvia Croft**
Hairdressing: **Freida Steiger**
Wardrobe: **Hilda Geerdts**
[Anneke Wills' clothes: **Harry Fox**]

An Arena Production for ITC World Wide Distribution.
Made on location and at Pinewood Studios

16 colour 60-minute episodes
1968

Supercar

Gerry Anderson's third outing into Supermarionation puppet land [or fourth, if one counts The Adventures of Twizzle] and his first encounter with the realms of science-fiction.

The 'star' of the series was Supercar, a vehicle which could travel on land, underwater, or through the skies. With eight rockets that retracted like wings, Supercar could travel anywhere, from cities to the dense jungles of Earth, to the limits of outer space - a wonder vehicle, the supercar of the future.

At its controls was Mike Mercury, Supercar's test pilot. Sharing his adventures were Professor Popkiss and his assistant Doctor Beaker, co-inventors of the wonder car, who spent much of their time fusing over their invention while trying to devise new components for it.

Rounding up the team were Jimmy Gibson, a ten-year-old boy who, together with his pet monkey Mitch, often joined Mike on his missions against the villain of the piece, Masterspy, a rogue who had set his mind on stealing the fabulous machine in order to use it for his own foul schemes. During most stories the villain shared the limelight with his worm-like assistant, Zarin.

Character voices:
Mike Mercury: **Graydon Gould**
Jimmy Gibson: **Sylvia Thamm**
Mitch: **David Graham**
Doctor Beaker: **David Graham**
Zarin: **David Graham**
Professor Popkiss [season one]: **George Murcell**
Professor Popkiss [season two]: **Cyril Shaps**
Masterspy [season one]: **George Murcell**
Masterspy [season two]: **Cyril Shaps**

season one
26 monochrome 30-minute episodes
1961

Rescue
w **Martin Woodhouse** and **Hugh Woodhouse**
d **David Elliott**

Mike Mercury uses Supercar's Clear-Vu device to rescue brothers Bill and Jimmy Gibson when their aeroplane crashes into the sea and their life raft becomes enveloped in thick dense fog.

Amazonian Adventure
w **Martin Woodhouse** and **Hugh Woodhouse**
d **Alan Pattillo**

Mitch the Monkey falls ill and Mike and his team take off to find a cure - a plant which grows only in a remote South American jungle. They find themselves captured by a tribe of head-hunters and Mike uses Supercar to conjure up a little 'white magic'.

Talisman of Sargon
w **Martin Woodhouse** and **Hugh Woodhouse**
d **David Elliott**

In disguise, masterspy tricks Dr Beaker into revealing the entrance of the Tomb of Sargon, which holds the Talisman of Sargon, a jewel reputed to have magic powers. Mike and Supercar must save the day.

False Alarm
w **Martin Woodhouse** and **Hugh Woodhouse**
d **Alan Pattillo**

Determined to steal Supercar, Masterspy and Zarin send out a phoney distress call. Mike sets out to rescue them but is overcome and drugged and the villains steal the vehicle - only to be given the ride of their lives when Mitch out-manoeuvres them.

What Goes Up
w **Martin Woodhouse** and **Hugh Woodhouse**
d **David Elliott**

Beaker and Popkiss are helping a USAF colonel to test-drive a new rocket fuel when things go wrong and the balloon carrying the fuel flies away. Mike must risk his own life to detonate the balloon at close range - a very risky mission.

Keep it Cool
w **Martin Woodhouse** and **Hugh Woodhouse**
d **Alan Pattillo**

Transporting a new experimental Supercar fuel across the desert, Bill Gibson and Beaker come under attack by Masterspy. Realising that the fuel will explode when it reaches above freezing point, Mike sets out to avert disaster.

Grounded
w **Martin Woodhouse** and **Hugh Woodhouse**
d **David Elliott**

Chasing after two villains who have stolen Beaker's printed circuits for Supercar, Mike crashes as a result of sabotage. However, the vehicle is still useful as a car so, for the very first time, Mike continues the journey by road.

Jungle Hazard
w **Martin Woodhouse** and **Hugh Woodhouse**
d **Alan Pattillo**

Little realising that Felicity, the girl from whom he's trying to take an estate in Malaya, is the cousin of Dr Beaker, Masterspy plans his next devious scheme. Enter Mike Mercury and Supercar to save the day - and Felicity's life.

High Tension
w **Martin Woodhouse** and **Hugh Woodhouse**
d **David Elliott**

Masterspy tries again to steal Supercar by kidnapping Dr Beaker. But Mike retaliates by using Supercar's remote control device to rescue his friend - and give Masterspy a very nasty shock.

A Little Art
w **Martin Woodhouse** and **Hugh Woodhouse**
d **Alan Pattillo**

Not realising that a painting he's purchased contains a visual clue to the location of a forger's counterfeit plates, Beaker is angry when the art-dealer steals back the artwork. But all is not lost - as Mike discovers.

Ice-Fall
w **Martin Woodhouse** and **Hugh Woodhouse**
d **Desmond Saunders**

On a trip to the mountains, Beaker finds himself in trouble when he sets out to find some ice-falls in a deep underground cavern. Encased in an ice avalanche, he shivers in anticipation as Mike attempts to release him via Supercar's engines.

Island Incident
w **Martin Woodhouse** and **Hugh Woodhouse**
d **David Elliott**

Asked to help the deposed leader of Pelota to regain power, Mike and his friends, finding themselves under fire, manage to negotiate an underwater escape route to expose the man's evil brother as a criminal.

The Tracking of Masterspy
w **Martin Woodhouse** and **Hugh Woodhouse**
d **David Elliott**

Posing as a reporter, Masterspy tricks Mike into giving him information about Supercar. He then steals the plans to the vehicle - or so he believes. In reality he has stolen a tracking device.

The Phantom Piper
w **Martin Woodhouse** and **Hugh Woodhouse**
d **Alan Pattillo**

Mike and his team travel to Scotland to help a woman solve the mystery of the Phantom Piper. They uncover a clever scheme to dupe the woman out of a fortune in buried treasure.

Deep Seven
w **Martin Woodhouse** and **Hugh Woodhouse**
d **Desmond Saunders**

To see how far it can dive underwater, Mike plunges Supercar into the ocean and descends to 400 feet. Suddenly the cockpit begins to leak and the engines stop working. Worse still, the vehicle becomes entangled in a mine cable and threatens to explode! Can Mike and his machine be saved?

Pirate Plunder
w **Martin Woodhouse** and **Hugh Woodhouse**
d **Alan Pattillo**

Black Morgan, a pirate, holds up ships and plunders their cargo. Mike sets out to stop him, but Morgan holds the aces - he has hostages and he will torpedo them if Mike interferes with his plans. Mike, however, has a trump card.

Flight of Fancy
w **Gerry Anderson** and **Sylvia Anderson**
d **Alan Pattillo**

Jimmy dreams that he and Mitch fly off in Supercar to rescue a Princess from the evil Hertz and Marzak. As a reward, Jimmy and Mitch are knighted by the King - then Jimmy wakes up.

Hostage
w **Martin Woodhouse** and **Hugh Woodhouse**
d **Desmond Saunders**

On holiday in Ireland, Dr Beaker finds himself in a kidnapping plot staged by two villains, who take a girl hostage and force Beaker to send for Mike and his Supercar - who spring a surprise on the villains with a baseball bat.

The Sunken Temple
w **Martin Woodhouse** and **Hugh Woodhouse**
d **David Elliott**

Whilst helping a Professor to escavate an underwater cavern, Mike and Dr Beaker find a safe containing stolen loot - but Professor Terman becomes trapped beneath a statue on the seabed and Mike finds himself using Supercar to save him.

Trapped in the Depths
w **Martin Woodhouse** and **Hugh Woodhouse**
d **Alan Pattillo**

Hearing that an American officer and an Australian scientist are trapped in a bathyscaph at the bottom of the sea and are under attack by giant fish, Mike dives into the ocean and uses Supercar's ultrasonic gun to rescue them.

Crash Landing
w **Gerry Anderson** and **Sylvia Anderson**
d **Desmond Saunders**

When Supercar and its team crash-lands in the jungle, it isn't long before Mitch discovers a new playmate - a female monkey - and Mike and his team find themselves lumbered with an extra passenger.

Dragon of Ho Meng
w **Martin Woodhouse** and **Hugh Woodhouse**
d **David Elliott**

Forced down by a terrible typhoon, Mike, Jimmy and Mitch come face to face with Ho Meng and his daughter Lotus Blossom, who look upon Supercar as a dragon. When the girl is kidnapped, Mike shows Ho Meng Supercar's full capabilities.

The Lost City
w **Gerry Anderson** and **Sylvia Anderson**
d **Alan Pattillo**

Professor Watson, a deranged scientist, plans to destroy Washington DC with a guided missile from his hideout beneath a lost city. Assigned to stop him, Mike and Dr Beaker are captured - but Supercar itself saves the day.

Magic Carpet
w **Martin Woodhouse** and **Hugh Woodhouse**
d **Desmond Saunders**

Sent to deliver some urgent medical supplies to Prince Hassan, Mike and his friends find themselves thrown into prison by Alif Bey, who wants the prince to die so that he can seize power. But Mitch escapes and enables the team to reach Supercar.

The White Line
w **Martin Woodhouse** and **Hugh Woodhouse**
d **Alan Pattillo**

The Supercar team are called in by Scotland Yard to help solve a series of bank and armoured car robberies carried out by two Chicago gangsters. Dr Beaker is sent out with the next armoured car delivery - and finds himself captured.

Supercar Take One
w **Gerry Anderson** and **Sylvia Anderson**
d **Desmond Saunders**

When Dr Beaker plays around with his new toy, a movie camera, and his exposed film gets mixed up with some film shot by spies, Mike and his team find themselves flying to New York to face the spies on their own ground.

---

season two
13 monochrome 30-minute episodes
1961

The Runaway Train
w **Gerry Anderson** and **Sylvia Anderson**
d **David Elliott**

Dr Beaker and Professor Popkiss find their journey aboard a new atomic train interrupted by the unwelcome entrance of

Masterspy and Zarin, who have sabotaged the train. When all seems lost, Mike enters the scene with Supercar.

Precious Cargo
w **Gerry Anderson** and **Sylvia Anderson**
d **Alan Pattillo**

Professor Popkiss, requiring a special wine for a dish he's preparing, visits wine-merchant Laval - an event which leads Mike and his friend into the problem of Zizi, a young girl.

Operation Superstork
w **Gerry Anderson** and **Sylvia Anderson**
d **Desmond Saunders**

When Mitch accidentally releases the guide rope of a new balloon being tested by Dr Beaker, sending Mike, Beaker and Jimmy off into danger, Mike finds himself parachuting to Earth to fetch Supercar to rescue them.

Hi-Jack
w **Gerry Anderson** and **Sylvia Anderson**
d **Bill Harris**

It appears that Masterspy and Zarin haven't learnt their lesson. This time they try to hijack an airliner, but Mike takes off in Supercar to teach them that they shouldn't build sky-high plans.

Calling Charlie Queen
w **Gerry Anderson** and **Sylvia Anderson**
d **Alan Pattillo**

When Professor Karloff plans to take over America by miniaturising its citizens and Mike and Dr Beaker find themselves cut down to size, with the help of Karloff's miniaturised assistant, they give the Professor a taste of his own medicine.

Space for Mitch
w **Gerry Anderson** and **Sylvia Anderson**
d **Desmond Saunders**

Mitch the Monkey finds himself in trouble again, this time as the unwilling pilot of a rocket that he fires off into orbit. Mike takes Supercar to rescue him and teaches the pet some monkey business of his own.

The Sky's the Limit
w **Gerry Anderson** and **Sylvia Anderson**
d **Bill Harris**

Their efforts to steal Supercar know no bounds: Masterspy and Zarin devise a new scheme - they attempt to buy the vehicle using phoney money. When this fails, they employ two villains to steal the machine, but all four are in for a surprise - Supercar has 'vanished'!

70-B-Low
w **Gerry Anderson** and **Sylvia Anderson**
d **Alan Pattillo**

Popkiss needs a blood transfusion. But his blood is a rare type and the nearest compatible donor, Professor Karlinsky, is trapped on the Artic wasteland. Mike and Supercar fly off to rescue him.

Atomic Witch Hunt
w **Gerry Anderson** and **Sylvia Anderson**
d **Desmond Saunders**

The Supercar team set out to discover who has planted atomic bombs all over the United States. They soon discover the culprit, a villainous Sheriff, but find themselves captured - leaving Mitch to save the day.

Jail Break
w **Gerry Anderson** and **Sylvia Anderson**
d **Bill Harris**

Using a helicopter, Red James attempts to free his friend Joe Anna from prison. Piloting the helicopter at gunpoint is Sam Weston, who is forced to take the two criminals to Black Rock - where Mike and Supercar are ordered to fly them to Mexico.

The Day Time Stood Still
w **Gerry Anderson** and **Sylvia Anderson**
d **Alan Pattillo**

Mike shares his birthday with his friends. Suddenly time itself is frozen: Mike's friends are motionless and a stranger from another planet presents Mike with a belt that will allow him to fly into the sky. What a present. But before Mike can use it, he wakes up. It was all a dream.

Transatlantic Cable
w **Gerry Anderson** and **Sylvia Anderson**
d **Desmond Saunders**

Masterspy is tapping into a transatlantic cable from his hideout under the sea. The Supercar team discover his hiding place and Mike uses the vehicle's latest device - a huge drill - to pour cold water on his enemy's scheme.

King Kool
w **Gerry Anderson** and **Sylvia Anderson**
d **Bill Harris**

When Mitch is tricked by King Kool, a famous TV gorilla jazz-drummer, and is locked in a cage, Mike and his friends find themselves up to their necks in monkey business of the most devious variety.

Supercar:

From an idea by: **Gerry Anderson** and **Reg Hill**
Producer: **Gerry Anderson**
Music by: **Barry Gray**
Dialogue Direction by: **Sylvia Thamm**
Special Effects: **Derek Meddings**
Puppets made and operated by:
Christine Glanville
Mary Turner
Roger Woodburn

Filmed by APF at A.P Films Studios, Slough

An A.P. Films Production in association with ATV Associated Television Ltd, for ITC World Wide Distribution.

39 monochrome 30-minute episodes
1961

Sword of Freedom

Set in sixteenth century Florence during the turbulent reign of the house of Medici, the series depicted the adventures of talented painter Marco del Monte. Artist and swordsman. Dashing and debonair. Courageous and romantic, del Monte's devotion and support of the Republican ideals brings him into conflict with would-be dictator, Duke de Medici, and his scheming supporter, Machiavelli.

Freedom-loving, del Monte uses his wits and brilliant swordsmanship to defend his fight for liberty. Helping him in his struggle were Angelica, a reformed pickpocket who has become his model, and Sandro, his friend and confidant.

Regular cast:
Marco del Monte: **Edmund Purdom**
Angelica [episodes 2 - 39]: **Adrienne Corri**
Sandro [episodes 1 - 27]: **Rowland Bartrop**
Duke de Medici: **Martin Benson**
Machiavelli [episodes 1 - 32]: **Kenneth Hyde**

Francesca
w **Lewis Hart**
d **Terry Bishop**

When the Duke de Medici promises the hand in marriage of his young sister, Francesca, to the Duke of Granada, help comes from an unexpected source - the artistic talents - both paintbrush and sword - of Marco del Monte, who paints a picture that de Medici is unlikely to forget.

Francesca: **Monica Stevenson** [intro]
Rodrigo: **Derek Sydney** [intro]
Umberto: **Bryan Coleman**
Spanish Ambassador: **Ferdy Mayne**
Attendant: **David Ritch**
First Bravo: **Peter Johnson**
Swiss Soldier: **Peter Wrubel**
First Guard: **Cecil Brock**
Second Guard: **John Brown**
Orator: **Richard Dunn**

The Sicilian
w **Samuel B. West**
d **Terry Bishop**

Pickpocket, Angelica, enters del Monte's life. Hoping to reform her, he takes her to supper at a bistro. There they meet Colonna, a Sicilian card sharp, who has already robbed del Monte's friend Sandro of his money. Perhaps Angelica can bring her talents to bear?

Colonna: **Peter Wyngarde**
Sebastiano: **Basil Dignam**
Tacco: **Charles Lamb**

Choice of Weapons
w **Samuel B. West**
d **Terry Bishop**

De Medici attempts to impose a tax on the Guild of Painters. Marco stops him. De Medici challenges him to a duel. Craven de Medici names De Foix, the finest swordsman in Europe, as his substitute. Angelica and Sandro beg Marco to leave Florence - but del Monte has a plan....

De Foix: **Charles Gray**
Muzio: **Geoffrey Bayldon**
Malchus: **Michael Peake**
Leonardo Da Vinci: **Edward Atienza** [intro]
Castellani: **John Moore**
Ugo: **John Dearth**

Caterina
w **Robert Westerby**
d **Bernard Knowles**

A realist, Marco has no objection to working for Baglione, the hated General of De Medici's Guard, because he knows he'll be well-paid. But when Sandro informs him that Baglione has sent to Venice for a painter to paint his daughter, Caterina's, portrait - an insult to Florentine painters, Marco determines to turn the tables.

Caterina: **Marianne Benet**
Baglione: **George Murcell**
Tortini: **William Lucas**
Maria: **Nora Gordon**
Paolo: **Neville Jason**
Majo Domo: **Howard Lang**

The Hero
w **Robert Westerby**
d **Bernard Knowles**

Marco is angry. He has heard that General Ferrucci, the hero of Florence, has accepted an amnesty from the Duke de Medici and is returning from exile. Ferrucci was the one man who could lead the republicans against the tyrant - now it appears that he has turned traitor....

Ferrucci: **John Robinson**
Rollo: **John Bailey**

Portrait in Emerald Green
w **Leighton Reynolds**
d **Bernard Knowles**

Master Butcher, Guilio Basti, opposes a tax imposed by De Medici, who orders his captain, Rodrigo, to dispose of Basti. Marco del Monte is painting a portrait of, Lucrezia, Basti's wife - it might be clever to make Basti jealous and stir up a quarrel between him and the artist .... a quarrel that would lead to a duel.

Lucrezia: **June Rodney**
Guilio Basti: **John Le Mesurier**
Rodrigo: **James Roughhead**
Consul: **Denis Edwards**

The Duke
w **Robert Westerby**
d **Terry Bishop**

De Medici, is a worried man. His taxes are causing unrest with the city's merchants - a situation that might lead to rebellion. An answer would be to police the city with Spanish mercenaries hired from the Duke of Ferrara, who will have no qualms about killing Florentines - including, perhaps, Marco del Monte.

Duke of Ferrara: **Richard Pasco**
Captain: **Robert Raikes**
Aldo: **Thomas Hare**
First Soldier: **Desmond Jordan**
Landlord: **Fred McNaughton**

The Eye of the Artist
w **William Templeton**
d **Terry Bishop**

A Courier carrying a message to a certain Senor Orsini, a promise of aid to Republican sympathisers, is ambushed by agents of De Medici. Their only clue to the identity of Orsini, is that his wife, Lisa, is having her portrait painted by Marco del Monte. De Medici's spy, Filippo, is ordered to get a description of the wanted man.

201

Lisa Orsini: **Norma Parnell**
Filippo: **John Carson**
Carlo Orsini: **Brian Nissen**
Julius: **Alex Scott**
Guilio: **Charles Houston**
Alfonso: **Paul Eddington**

The Tower
w **George Baxt**
d **Terence Fisher**

To impress the Duke and Duchess of Valencia, former enemies, De Medici has commissioned artists to contribute designs for a carnival - but does not intend to pay them. Machiavelli, sympathetic towards the artists, warns Marco del Monte of his trickery. So why is del Monte so amused?

Duke Di Luca: **Patrick Troughton**
Duchess: **Martita Hunt**
Captain: **Tony Thawnton**

Alessandro
w **George Baxt**
d **Peter Cotes**

Like most other painters Marco is penniless, and is relying on the St Luke's Day Exhibition of Art as a means of making money. When he meets local butcher, Alessandro, whose ambition is to become a great artist. Marco sees a way of helping the boy while helping himself - but Marlo, Alessandro's uncle does not approve.

Alessandro: **Michael Bryant**
Federici: **Manning Wilson**
Mario: **Colin Douglas**
President: **Carl Bernard**
De Bassi: **Elwyn Brook-Jones**
Lupo: **Patrick Crean**

The Ship
w **William Templeton**
d **Bernard Knowles**

Stephano, a Florentice merchant, has just returned from a visit to the east. In cahoots with the wealthy Duke of Urbino, De Medici plans to punish the Florentine Wool Guild who have refused to pay higher taxes. The common link - Marco del Monte, who has plans for all three personages.

Stephano: **Joseph O'Connor**
Duke of Urbino: **Andrew Cruikshank**
Duchess of Urbino: **Patricia Burke**
Pagolo: **Peter Asher**
Grifone: **Maxwell Shaw**
Physician: **Geoffrey Bayldon**

The Bracelet
w **Robert Westerby**
d **Terry Bishop**

Seeing Francesca, sister of De Medici, thrown from her horse, Marco goes to her aid, but is sent on his way by Paolo, the worthless nephew of Count Orlando, who is anxious to marry the girl. Later, Marco discovers that Francesca's bracelet has caught on the button of his cloak. On his way to return it, he is ambushed and the bracelet disappears.

Paolo: **Ronald Hines**
Francesca: **Monica Stevenson**
Carlo: **Ronald Leigh-Hunt**
Biotto: **Edward Harvey**
Rodrigo: **Derek Sydney**

The Slave
w **George Baxt**
d **Terry Bishop**

Disturbed when Sandro brings news of the arrival of a new batch of slaves from the east, Marco, striving for the abolition of slavery, visits Di Santi, the Slave Master, who is auctioning Natalia, a Turkish princess. Against the wishes of Angelica and Sandro, Marco decides to help her escape.

Safae: **Ziki Arnot**
Di Santi: **Thomas Heathcote**

The Bell
w **Michael Connor**
d **Terence Fisher**

Marco and Sandro are angry. Their elderly friend, Beppo, the bell-ringer, has been beaten by De Medici's guards for attempting to ring the liberty bell. It is customary for the bell to be rung once a year. If it does not, the bell is silenced forever. De Medici smells victory - Marco smells revenge.

Francesca: **Monica Stevenson**
Rodrigo: **Derek Sydney**
Beppo: **Wilfred Brambell**
Clerk: **Noel Davis**
Gonfalonier: **John Dearth**
Major Domo: **Philip James**

The Suspects
w **George Baxt**
d **Terry Bishop**

Six men meet in Marco's studio to discuss the distribution of pamphlets as a gesture of defiance of De Medici rule. Sent to collect the pamphlets from their hiding place in a warehouse, Sandro is disturbed by Medici and his guards. Hidden, what he hears sends terror to his heart.

Sebastiano: **Basil Dignam**
Bosti: **Leonard Sachs**
Porcelli: **Richard Wordsworth**
Varenza: **Charles Gray**
Rodrigo: **Derek Sydney**

Serenade in Red
w **Leighton Reynolds**
d **Terry Bishop**

De Medici's nephew, Tonio, is a promising young artist, studying under Marco del Monte. Tonio has fallen in love with and wants to marry, Laura Aro, daughter of a leading Republican, a match to which Medici and Laura's father would never agree - unless Marco can play matchmaker and paint a happy ending.

Rodrigo: **Derek Sydney**
Laura: **Jocelyn Britton**
Tonio: **Tony Wright**
Arno: **Alec Mango**
Guard: **Paul Hansard**

Marriage of Convenience
w **Robert Westerby**
d **Terry Bishop**

Girolamo and Zanobi, head two of the most powerful families in Italy. Their houses are to be united by the marriage between Girolamo's daughter, Ipolita, and Zanobi's son, Sigismondo. The two have never met - so how can Marco omit the one flaw in Ipolita's beauty, a long scar on her left cheek, from her wedding portrait?

Ipolita: **Concepta Fennell**
Sigismondo: **Maurice Kaufmann**
Zanobi: **Anthony Nicholls**
Battista: **Roger Cage**
Melozzo: **Edwin Richfield**
Girolamo: **Bruno Barnabe**

The Value of Paper
w **Michael Connor**
d **Terry Bishop**

Marco's friend, Umberto, has written a book "Treatise on Liberty" which could prove dangerous if word should reach De Medici. Umberto, a parchment maker, dislikes paper, so any chance that he will allow his daughter, Lisa, to marry Luigi, a printer and paper-maker seems out of the question - unless Marco can weave a magic spell.

Umberto: **John Longden**
Serlio: **Brian Haines**
Lisa: **Jennifer Jayne**
Luigi: **Patrick Doonan**
Magistrate: **Michael Peake**

The Pagan Venus
w **Robert Westerby**
d **Anthony Squire**

De Medici is anxious to buy cannons - weapons that will make him invincible. Realising that he will have to raise money to pay his armourers, the fact that the wealthy Duke of Milan is in Florence hasn't escaped his attention. Meanwhile, Marco and his friends set up a Guild of Vigilantes to ensure that justice prevails.

Grillo: **Leonard Sachs**
Agnolo: **Bill Fraser**
Cipriano: **John Carson**
Merula: **Alan Rowe**
Dealer: **Leonard Sharp**
Carlo: **Sheldon Allan**

Forgery in Red Chalk
w **Leighton Reynolds**
d **Terry Bishop**

Hearing that Leonardo de Vinci has invented an 'under the water machine' capable of remaining under the sea for long periods, De Medici wants to buy the plans - believed to be drawn in red chalk with construction details on the reverse side. Insisting that there are no plans, de Vinci arranges for his servant to slip the document into Marco del Monte's portfolio.

Rodrigo: **Derek Sydney**
Paolo: **Thomas Gallagher**
Leonardo de Vinci: **Andrew Keir**
Servant: **Russell Carr**

Vespucci
w **Michael Connor**
d **Anthony Squire**

Painting a portrait of explorer, Amerigo Vespucci, Marco learns that he is anxious for the Council of Florence to finance another voyage - one that will certainly open up trade links. Little Fawn, a young Indian girl Vespucci brought back to Florence provides Marco with a way to convince the council that the 'new world' really exists.

Vespucci: **John Gabriel**
Little Fawn: **Luciana Paoluzzi**
Bastiano: **Patrick Troughton**
Ginori: **Maxwell Shaw**
Gonfalonier: **Philip Ashley**

The School
w **William Templeton**
d **Terry Bishop**

Marco's friend, Tiberio, a printer and fellow Republican, has had his shop smashed by thugs in the pay of De Medici. Far worse, Tiberio's son, Crespino, tells him that the fathers of three of his school friends, also Republicans, have been attacked too. Someone is supplying information on Republican sympathisers to Medici. Marco determines to unmask the traitor.

Teofilo: **Patrick Troughton**
Tizio: **Kenneth Williams**
Brunetto: **Sean Barrett**
Angelo: **Bruce Sharman**
Crespino: **Colin Broadley**
Tiberio: **George Gee**

Chart of Gold
w **Leighton Reynolds**
d **Anthony Squire**

Master Cosimo, former commander of the Republican fleet, has returned to the city after an absence of ten years - during which time he was thought to be dead. Welcomed by his friend Marco, Cosimo is anxious to keep the news of his return a secret - but De Medici, Cosimo's bitter enemy has already set the dogs on him!

Rodrigo: **Derek Sydney**
Cosimo: **Richard Leech**
Viola: **Daphne Anderson**
Alberto: **Richard O'Sullivan**
Inspector: **John Dearth**
Serving Girl: **Lynette Mills**

The Ambassador
w **William Templeton**
d **Peter Maxwell**

Still plotting to consolidate his power, De Medici hopes to persuade the English government to grant him a considerable loan, supposedly for the benefit of the common people. Medici's sister, Francesca, brings the information to Marco - who sets out to show Medici in his true colours.

Ambassador: **Peter Hammond**
Francesca: **Monica Stevenson**
Cecci: **Patrick Troughton**
Vinci: **Bernard Brown**

The Lion and the Mouse
w **George Baxt**
d **Anthony Squire**

De Medici is playing the tax card again. This time he's increased the levy on alum, used by artists everywhere. Marco explains to Signora Valeska, that unless the tax is repealed the price of her portrait will have to be increased - and hell hath no fury....

Valeska: **Jean Kent**
Luigi: **Geoffrey Bayldon**
Rodrigo: **Derek Sydney**
Beatrice: **Anne Padwick**
Bella: **Geraldine Hagen**
Maria: **Charmian Eyre**

Angelica's Past
w **Michael Connor**
d **Coby Ruskin**

Virelli, a thief known as 'The Cord' because of his habit of using a cord as a weapon, returns to Florence. Angelica once

worked with Virelli, who insists that she returns to her former profession and help him to steal a valuable gold chain. If she refuses, Marco will be killed....

Virelli: **Roger Delgado**
Coppa: **Richard Wordsworth**
Marezza: **Barry Shawzin**
Merchant: **John Barron**

The Besieged Duchess
w **George Baxt**
d **Terry Bishop**

De Medici requires the Duchess of Crespi's derelict castle, necessary for conversion to a fortress in the defence of Florence, and doesn't care how he acquires it. When Marco arrives at the castle to sketch the landscape, the Duchess takes a liking to him and tells him her story - a tale which Marco ensures will have an happy ending.

Duchess Crespi: **Marita Hunt**
Rodrigo: **Derek Sydney**
Ugo: **Tom Clegg**

Cristina
w **Michael Connor**
d **Coby Ruskin**

Marco and Sandro rescue a young woman from two thugs. Before she runs off, Marco recognises her as Cristina, the girl he was to have married eight years earlier. That night, Arturo Bardi, Cristina's brother, and a loyal Republican, arrives at Marco's studio seeking help.

Cristina: **Julia Arnall**
Arturo Bardi: **George A. Cooper**
Duiseppe: **George Murcell**
Ronio: **Michael Cosmo**

The Strange Intruder
w **George Baxt**
d **Peter Maxwell**

De Medici plans to make an alliance with France by marrying Francesca to the Count Rene D' Albert. Unknown to him, the two are lovers already and intend to overthrow Medici and rule Florence together. Marco finds himself drawn into the intrigue when Machiavelli asks him to challenge the Count to a duel.

Francesca: **Monica Stevenson**
Count Rene D'Albert: **William Russell**

The Primavera
w **A. M. Caidden**
d **Peter Maxwell**

Commissioned by Medici to paint a portrait of his sister, Francesca, on the occasion of her birthday, Marco is astonished when his enemy shows him a priceless jewel, the 'Primavera', which tradition dictates Francesca must receive as a birthday gift - then produces an exact replica, which he substitutes for the original.

Francesca: **Monica Stevenson**
Rodrigo: **Derek Sydney**

A Game of Chance
w **George Baxt**
d **Coby Ruskin**

Giorgio, a Republican courier wounded by De Medici's men, manages to stagger to Marco's studio. The wounded man is taken to Orlando, the only Florentine physician who

dares treat Republican sympathisers. But Orlando has to leave Florence immediately, because of debts he owes to Medici. Marco decides to help - by making trick boxes for magicians!

Francesca: **Monica Stevenson**
Orlando: **Morton Lowry**
Rodrigo: **Derek Sydney**
Giorgio: **Peter Torquill**

The Marionettes
w **William Templeton**
d **Peter Maxwell**

Puppet masters, Poggio and Guidone, are giving a performance of their marionette show to the children of the Duke of Padua. During the performance, Galeotto, the Duke's minister, is stabbed to death and the puppet masters learn that an attempt will be made on the Duke's life the moment he returns home. Help arrives in the shape of Marco del Monte.

Duke of Padua: **Basil Dignam**
Poggio: **Charles Lamb**
Tristina: **June Asher**
Galeotto: **Carl Bernard**
Rodrigo: **Derek Sydney**
Guidone: **Paul Hansard**
Di Lucca: **Derry Nesbitt**

The Reluctant Duke
w **William Templeton**
d **Coby Ruskin**

Ludovico, the young Duke of Teano, is receiving threats to his life. His sister, Prospera, and Zampante, his chief minister, warn him of the danger of walking freely among his people. But Ludovico does not enjoy responsibility - his ambition is to be a clown. Another attempt on his life sees him fleeing the castle - and a fortuitous meeting with Marco.

Ludovico: **Murray Mayne**
Prospera: **Norma Parnell**
Zampante: **Bryan Coleman**
Clown: **Donald Morley**
Isabella: **Anne Padwick**

Vendetta
w **Michael Connor**
d **Peter Maxwell**

Goaded into a duel with Gambetta, a Corsican in the pay of De Vidici, Marco wins the encounter but spares the life of his adversary. But, as Marco turns away, Gambetta tries to stab him in the back. The villain falls on his own sword and dies. Furious by this turn of events, De Vidici sends a message to Lorenzo, Gambetta's brother, that his brother was murdered in cold blood.

Berto: **Nigel Davenport**
Niccolo: **Kevin Stoney**
Lorenzo: **Tim Seeley**
Rodrigo: **Derek Sydney**
Beppe: **Sheldon Allan**

Who is Felicia?
w **George Baxt**
d **Peter Maxwell**

Sebastiano and Marco are waiting the arrival of an agent carrying news vital to the Republican cause. The Duke of Arezzo is believed to be sympathetic to their intentions to mount a revolt against De Vidici's evil reign, but they must be sure. The revolt will begin in three days - at the cost to many lives.

Felicia: **Zena Walker**
Sebastiano: **Andrew Keir**
Dominick: **Walter Gotell**
Niccolo: **Kevin Stoney**

Violetta
w **Michael Connor**
d **Peter Maxwell**

Devoted to his niece, Violetta, the Count Origi accompanies her when she visits Marco's studio to have her portrait painted. Informing Marco that he wishes to see him later that evening., the Count returns home. Just before Marco's visit. the Count is stabbed to death by Antonio, his servant - who accuses Marco of the crime.

Violetta: **Jane Downs**
Count Origi: **Llewellyn Rees**
Antonio: **Alan Rowe**
Magistrate: **Michael Peake**
Captain: **Peter Torquill**

Adrianna
w **George Baxt**
d **Terry Bishop**

Francesca de Medici tells Marco that her brother has enlisted the services of the Lady Adrianna di Cervi to act as her governess. Convinced that her brother is determined to crush her spirit, she pleads with Marco to help.

Francesca: **Monica Stevenson**
Lady Adrianna: **Anne Padwick**
Rodrigo: **Derek Sydney**

The Assassin
w **Sidney Cole and Albert G. Ruben**
d ?

Attacked by three ruffians, Marco's life is saved when Otello, a stranger, comes to his rescue. Otello tells him that he is a professional assassin called to Florence by the Duke De Medici, to carry out a special mission - a task for which he will be well paid. Meanwhile, Medici tells his captain, Rodrigo, that he has arranged to have Marco del Monte assassinated...

Otello: **Bill Owen**
Rodrigo: **Derek Sydney**

The Woman in the Picture
sans info

Sword of Freedom:

Producer: **Sidney Cole**
Executive Producer: **Hannah Weinstein**

Filmed at Walton Studios
An Hannah Weinstein Production for Sapphire Films
for ITC World Wide Distribution

39 monochrome 30-minute episodes
1959

Thunderbirds

The rescue operations of International Rescue [IR], five fabulous life-saving machines operated by five fabulous heroes whose brief was to undertake rescue missions of every type, in any situation.

Based on a mountain-top fortress somewhere in the Pacific, the five Thunderbirds soared off to avert disaster and save the lives of people trapped in unusual predicaments with a blend of panache and determination that wouldn't have gone amiss in the control room of Captain Kirk's USS Enterprise.

Head of the operation was ex-astronaut Jeff Tracey and his five sons, each of whom had been named after the first five American astronauts in space.

There was Scott, pilot of Thunderbird I, a sleek craft capable of speeds in excess of 7,000 mph; Virgil, pilot of Thunderbird II, a freighter used for carrying the rescue equipment; Alan, who controlled Thunderbird III, a machine capable of flying into the outer reaches of space; Gordon, co-pilot of Thunderbird II, who also took over the controls of Thunderbird IV [a submersible, which was used in underwater rescue missions]; and John, the controller of Thunderbird V, the team's space satellite.

Rounding up the team were 'Brains' the scientist genius who invented the vehicles, and Lady Penelope, the organisation's upper-crust heroine, who was driven to her missions in her shocking-pink Rolls Royce [Reg. No: FAB 1] by her off-beat Cockney chauffeur and manservant Parker.

The villain of the piece was the Hood, a ruthless, dome-headed space-age villain who had taken a liking to the Thunderbirds and laid plans to steal them.

Without doubt, the best-loved of all the Gerry Anderson 'Supermarionation' series. Each adventure was a small-screen epic and the series [rightly] earned itself a niche in television history.

It also spawned two full-length feature films: *Thunderbirds Are Go* [1966] and *Thunderbirds Six* [1968].

Character voices:
Jeff Tracey: **Peter Dyneley**
Scott Tracey: **Shane Rimmer**
Virgil Tracey [season one]: **David Holliday**
Virgil Tracey [season two]: **Jeremy Wilkin**
Alan Tracey: **Matt Zimmerman**
Gordon Tracey: **David Graham**
John Tracey: **Ray Barrett**
Lady Penelope: **Sylvia Anderson**
Brains: **David Graham**
Parker: **David Graham**
The Hood: **Ray Barrett**
Tin Tin / Grandma: **Christine Finn**

season one
26 colour 60-minute episodes
1965

Trapped in the Sky [pilot story]
w **Gerry Anderson and Sylvia Anderson**
d **Alan Pattillo**

International Rescue set out on their first mission - to save the atomic airliner Fireflash from destruction. The Hood has planted a bomb in its landing gear and the superplane's passengers will be exposed to atomic radiation unless IR can avert disaster.

Pit of Peril
w **Alan Fennell**
d **Desmond Saunders**

Sidewinder, a US Army walking fortress, crashes into an underground pit of fire and US Army helicopters are unable to retrieve the vehicle, IR are called in to rescue the crew trapped in Sidewinder's control room.

The Perils of Penelope
w **Alan Pattillo**
d **Alan Pattillo and Desmond Saunders**

Assisting Sir Jeremy Hodge in his attempts to find the missing Professor Borender, a man who has discovered how to turn water into rocket fuel, Lady Penelope finds herself taken hostage by the evil Dr Godber.

Terror in New York City
w **Alan Fennell**
d **David Lane and David Elliott**

When TV reporter Ned Cook decides to take secret film of the Thunderbird's team during their rescue missions, Thunderbird II is accidentally shot down, and plans to move the Empire State building end in a state of collapse, IR are soon on the scene.

Edge of Impact
w **Donald Robertson**
d **Desmond Saunders**

Paid by General Bron to destroy the new British Red Arrow fighter-plane, the Hood is delighted when the plane crashes, but soon has cause for remorse when Red Arrow II hits a television relay tower, trapping two men.

Day of Disaster
w **Dennis Spooner**
d **David Elliott**

Lady Penelope and Brains, watching the Mars Probe rocket being taken to its launch site across the Arlington Bridge, find themselves involved in another IR rescue mission when the bridge collapses and the rocket becomes trapped in the river bed.

30 Minutes after Noon
w **Alan Fennell**
d **David Elliott**

Another tense mission for IR. This time they have to rescue Prescott, a man with a bomb locked securely to his wrist before he and Southern, a British agent, are destroyed in an office building.

Desperate Intruder
w **Donald Robertson**
d **David Lane**

Having joined the eccentric Professor Blakely on his mission to discover treasure in the underwater temple of Lake Anasta, Brains and Tin Tin are taken prisoner by The Hood - who buries Brains in the desert sand.

End of the Road
w **Dennis Spooner**
d **David Lane**

Determined to complete the building of a mountain road before the storm season breaks, Eddie Houseman finds himself trapped when his truck-load of explosives is blown onto a cliff-ledge. Gray, boss of the construction team, calls in IR.

The Uninvited
w **Alan Fennell**
d **Desmond Saunders**

Shot down over the Sahara desert by mysterious fighter planes, Scott lands Thunderbird I and meets two archaeologists who have found the lost tomb of Khamandides. Sometimes later, all three men are captured by Zombies - the creatures who shot down Thunderbird I.

Sun Probe
w Alan Fennell
d David Lane

Informed that three solarnauts from the Sun Probe project have accidentally left their orbit and are on course for the Sun, IR launch Thunderbirds II and III to attempt to fire Sun Probe's rockets by remote control.

Operation Crash Dive
w Martin Crump
d Desmond Saunders

Thunderbird IV is sent to rescue two crewmen trapped on board Fireflash, which has crashed into the sea. Meanwhile, suspecting sabotage, Scott tracks the next flight in Thunderbird II - and the saboteurs strike again.

Vault of Death
w Dennis Spooner
d David Elliott

A bank clerk finds himself trapped inside a new impregnable bank vault. The man will die of suffocation unless Lord Seton, the only man in England with a key to the vault, is located. Parker finds himself involved in a drama of his own making.

The Mighty Atom
w Dennis Spooner
d David Lane

The Hood plans to gain the secrets of a new atomic power station in the Sahara. To do so, he steals a robotic mouse - the Mighty Atom - and then sets fire to the plant so that IR will arrive to avert an atomic explosion.

City of Fire
w Alan Fennell
d David Elliott

When a car accident in one of its parking areas causes the Thompson Tower shopping complex to catch fire, Scott and Virgil use the Mole to burrow into the inferno to rescue some people trapped amid the flames.

The Imposters
w Dennis Spooner
d Desmond Saunders

Someone is impersonating IR, so Jeff shuts down operations. IR agent Jeremiah Tuttle gets a lead to the impostors, but Jeff is forced to resume operations when an American astronaut is lost in space and only Thunderbirds III can rescue him.

The Man from MI5
w Alan Fennell
d David Lane

Asked by Bob Bondson of MI5 to help him retrieve plans for a secret atomic weapon which was stolen, Lady Penelope agrees. Posing as model Gayle Williams, she is kidnapped - and left in a boathouse tied to a bomb!

Cry Wolf
w Dennis Spooner
d David Elliott

When two young Australian boys accidentally call out IR while playing a game of 'rescues' and the boys are then taken prisoner by The Hood, who plans to steal satellite photos from their father, their latest distress call convinces Jeff that it's just another hoax.

Danger at Ocean Deep
w Donald Robertson
d Desmond Saunders

When Ocean Pioneer I explodes after launching and Brains discovers that a cargo of liquid alsterene will explode when in contact with OD60, a chemical liquid dumped in the same region as that being used for Pioneer II's maiden voyage, IR find their services in great demand.

Move and You're Dead
w Alan Pattillo
d Alan Pattillo

After winning the Parola Sands motor race in Brain's new car, Alan falls foul of rival driver Victor Gomez, who traps Alan and Grandma on a bridge with an ultrasonic bomb that will detonate if they move. Enter IR to save the day.

The Duchess Assignment
w Martin Crump
d David Elliott

On holiday in France, Lady Penelope observes crooks swindling a Duchess out of her wealth at a casino, but is unable to stop their getaway. She contacts IR, and her friends retrieve the situation.

Brink of Disaster
w Alan Fennell
d David Lane

Approached by crooked businessman Grafton, who wants her to finance a Trans-American monorail, Lady Penelope alerts Jeff - and inadvertently places his life in danger when part of the monorail track collapses, leaving Jeff and Tin Tin in danger.

Attack of the Alligators!
w Alan Pattillo
d David Lane

When Dr Orchard develops Thuramine, a plant extract to enlarge animal and end famine, but his boatman Culp tries to steal some and flushes it into a creek, the IR team soon find themselves called out to avert the threat of giant alligators.

Martian Invasion
w Alan Fennell
d David Elliott

Posing as a film financier, The Hood traps two actors in a flooded cave while they are making a Martian invasion film. Using his hypnotic powers, he has Kyrano disable Thunderbird I's automatic camera detector so that he can film the rescue attempt.

The Cham - Cham
w Alan Pattillo
d Alan Pattillo

Every time that the Cass Carnaby Five do a live performance of their 'Dangerous Game' act, their fighter planes are destroyed. Disguised as Wanda L'Amour, Lady Penelope travels to Paradise Peak in Switzerland to investigate.

Security Hazard
w Alan Pattillo
d Desmond Saunders

Returning from a mission in England, Thunderbirds I and II find they have an unwanted guest on board - a young boy called Chip, who has stowed away in Pod I. While awaiting their next mission, the Tracey brothers tell Chip about some of their missions.

season two
6 colour 60-minute episodes
1966

Atlantic Inferno
w Alan Fennell
d Desmond Saunders

Having persuaded Jeff to take a holiday, Scott is in charge when a World Navy submarine test-missile ignites a gas pocket, which threatens a Seascape rig and the lives of its crew. Against his father's wishes, Scott mobilises IR.

Path of Destruction
w Donald Robertson
d David Elliott

When Crablogger One, an atomic tree-feller and pulp processor, goes on the rampage after its crew fall foul of food-poisoning, and the machine threatens to crush the San Martino dam atomic-reactor, IR receive an urgent distress call.

Alias Mr Hackenbacker
w Alan Pattillo
d Desmond Saunders

Brains, alias Hiram K. Hackenbacker, places a new secret safety-device on board the Skythrust aircraft, on which Lady Penelope is holding a fashion show with designer Francois Lemaire. Then Skythrust is hijacked by a gang seeking Lemaire's new fabric design.

Lord Parker's 'Oliday
w Tony Barwick
d Brian Burgess

Parker comes into his own. When a storm causes a solar-reflector dish to collapse and focus the sun's rays on the town below, 'Lord' Parker and Bruno distract the town's inhabitants by playing bingo.

Richochet
w Tony Barwick
d Brian Burgess

The Telesat 4 rocket from Sentinel Base goes rogue and IR have to designate a sector for its destruction - not knowing that the place they choose is occupied by DJ Rick O'Shea, a space pirate who runs an unlicensed TV station.

Give or Take a Million
w Alan Pattillo
d Desmond Saunders

Nicky, a child from Coralville children's hospital arrives at Tracey Island to spend Christmas with IR. The boy and the Traceys find themselves spending Christmas 2026 in a story of high adventure.

✍ Three features were issued, being a compilation of the episodes listed: *Thunderbirds To The Rescue* [*Trapped in the Sky & Operation Crash Dive*], *Thunderbirds in Outer Space* [*Sun Probe & Ricochet*] and *Countdown to Disaster* [*Terror in New York City & Atlantic Inferno*].

📖 All, original stories:
Thunderbirds [1966: John Theydon: Armada Paperbacks (May Fair Books): illustrated]; *Calling Thunderbirds* [1966: John Theydon: Armada Paperbacks (May Fair Books): illustrated]; *Thunderbirds - Ring of Fire* [1966: John Theydon: Armada Paperbacks (May Fair Books): illustrated]; *Thunderbirds - Lost World* [1966: John W. Jennison: World Distributors: hardback]; *Thunderbirds - Operation Asteroids* [1966: Angus P. Allan: World Distributors: hardback]; *Lady Penelope - A Gallery of Thieves* [1966: Kevin McGarry: World Distributors: hardback]; *Lady Penelope - Cool for Danger* [1966: Kevin McGarry: World Distributors: hardback]; *Lady Penelope - The Albanian Affair* [1967: John Theydon: Armada Paperbacks (May Fair Books)].

Thunderbirds:

Created by **Gerry Anderson** and **Sylvia Anderson**
Producer: **Gerry Anderson** [season one] **Reg Hill** [season two]
Associate Producer: **Reg Hill** [season one] **Jan Read** [two]
Executive Producer: **Gerry Anderson** [season two]
Music by: **Barry Gray**
Special Visual Effects: **Derek Meddings**
Art Director: **Bob Bell**
Director of Photography: **John Read**
Script Editor: **Alan Pattillo**

An AP Films Production for ATV for ITC World Wide distribution.
[AP Films not involved in season two].

32 colour 60-minute episodes
1965 - 1966

Timeslip

Spanning fifty years, from 1940 to 1990, but taking place in the present [?], this told how two young children, Simon Randall and Liz Skinner, break the time barrier and find themselves swept into a series of adventures in the past and in the future - experiences so fantastic that they actually met older versions of themselves!

Told in four episodic blocks, the programme lives long in the memory as being among the best SF outings of the Seventies... it most certainly cast a shade over the [unintentionally juvenile] past, present and future ramblings of the earlier [and infinitely higher budgeted] oater, *The Time Tunnel*.

Regular cast:
Simon Randall: **Spencer Banks**
Liz Skinner: **Cheryl Burfield**
Frank Skinner (Cheryl's dad): **Derek Benfield**
Jean Skinner (Cheryl's mum): **Iris Russell**
Commander Traynor: **Dennis Quilley**
Beth Skinner (Liz in the future): **Mary Preston**

The Wrong End of Time [Parts 1 - 6]
w **Bruce Stewart**
d **John Cooper**

The Midlands village of St Oswald hides a secret. Sited near to the nearby Naval base is a mysterious 'hole' in time. Invisible to the eye, the time bubble sucks young Simon Randall and Liz Skinner backwards through time into a vortex of adventure in 1940.

Frank Skinner (1940): **John Alken**
Gottfriend: **Sandor Eles**
Graz: **Paul Humpoletz**
Arthur Griffiths: **John Garrie** [1]
George Bradley: **Royston Tickner**
Ferris: **Peter Sproule**
Phipps: **John Abbott** [1]
Dr Fordyce: **Kenneth Watson** [1-2]
Alice Fortune: **Virginia Balfour** [1-2]
Sarah: **Sally Templer** [1-4]
German Sailor [Fritz]: **Hilary Minster**

✍

The first episode was introduced by television science correspondent, Peter Fairley.

The Time of the Ice Box [Parts 7 - 12]
w **Bruce Stewart**
d **Peter Jeffries**

Transported to 1990, Simon and Liz find themselves in the Ice Box, an Antarctic research establishment, where experiments are being carried out using the longevity drug HA57. There they encounter a human clone and Liz's father - preserved in a block of ice!

Devereaux: **John Barron** [intro]
Beth Skinner: **Mary Preston** [intro]
Dr Joynton: **Peggy Thorpe-Bates** [7-11]
Dr Bukov: **John Barcroft**
Larry: **Robert Oates**

✍

The first episode was introduced by television science correspondent, Peter Fairley.

The Year of the Burn-Up [Parts 13 - 20]
w **Bruce Stewart** [Episodes 13-19] **Victor Pemberton** [20]
d **Ron Francis** [Episodes 13-20] **Peter Jeffries** [14-19]

Still in the future, Simon and Liz meet a man known as 2957, a clone working on a project to change world climates. When the experiment goes wrong and threatens the world with extinction, the time-travellers must somehow avert the tragedy that will follow.

Beth: **Mary Preston**
2957: **David Graham**
Miss Stebbins: **Teresa Scoble**
Vera: **Merdel Jordine** [13-17]
Alpha 4: **Ian Fairbairn** [14-18]
Alpha 16: **Teresa Scoble** [14-18]
Alpha 17: **Lesley Scoble** [14-18]
Delta 22: **Patrick Durkin** [15-18]
Paul: **Brian Pettifer** [14-19]
Technician: **Stuart Henry** [16]

The Day of the Clone [Parts 21 - 26]
w **Victor Pemberton**
d **Dave Foster** [Episodes 21-24] **Ron Francis** [25 & 26]

Held prisoner at research station R1, by a duplicate of Commander Traynor, Liz is rescued by Simon and Dr Frazer. Escaping through the time bubble, they appear in 1965 and engage in a cat and mouse chase through time, pursued by Devereaux's clones!

Dr Frazer: **Ian Fairbairn**
Pitman: **John Swindells**
Stebbins: **Teresa Scoble**
Maria: **Mary Larkin**
Devereaux: **John Barron** [22-24]
De Saram: **Derek Sydney** [22-24]
Mr Randall: **John Cazabon** [24]
Desk attendant: **Bruce Beeby** [21-23]
Commissionaire: **Harry Davis** [21]
Driver: **Dennis Balcombe**
Newsvendor: **John Herrington** [22]
Ward Sister: **Hilary Liddell** [23]
Dr Ferguson: **Keith Grenville** [24]
George Pointer: **Richard Thorp** [24]

Timeslip:

Devised by: **Ruth Boswell**
Producer: **John Cooper**
Script Editor: **Ruth Boswell**
Scientific Adviser: **Geoffrey Hoyle**
Designers: **Gerry Roberts, Michael Eve**

An ATV Network Production

26 monochrome 30-minute episodes [in 4 episodic blocks]
1970-71

UFO

Puppet-master Gerry Anderson's first outing into the live-action field, a series that portrayed the activities of the Secret Headquarters, Alien Defence Organisation [SHADO], a group of scientists and military personnel who were brought together in the mid-eighties to defend Earth from the threat of invasion by aliens from another world. The series' opening episode introduced the viewer to SHADO's multi-faceted defence systems: Control, the operational HQ of SHADO command, a vast computer-orientated complex situated hundreds of feet below a bogus film studio; Moonbase, the organisation's moon defence arm from which Interceptor jets would zoom into outer space to repel the enemy UFOs whenever the Earth-orbiting Space Intruder Detector [SID] sighted alien spacecraft heading towards Earth: Skydiver, an atomic submarine from which Sky One, a jet fighter, could be launched into the stratosphere [or repel the invaders in an undersea environment]. The aliens themselves were green-skinned beings whose intention was to travel to Earth to capture humans and use their vital internal organs as spare parts to keep themselves alive.

A fast-paced, spectacular series complete with A1 special effects. The programme was given a raw deal by the ITV network, who obviously felt that the series' content was too provocative for 'family' viewing and hid it away in a late-night transmission spot. But you can't keep a good thing down and the series is now regarded as one of the best of its genre.

Regular cast:
CONTROL:
Commander Ed Straker: **Ed Bishop**
Colonel Alec Freeman: **George Sewell**
Colonel Paul Foster: **Michael Billington**
Colonel Virginia Lake: **Wanda Ventham**
Dr Jackson: **Vladek Sheybal**
MOONBASE:
Lt Gay Ellis: **Gabrielle Drake**
Joan Harrington: **Antonia Ellis**
Nina Barry: **Dolores Mantez**
SHADO PERSONNEL:
Captain Carlin: **Peter Gordeno**
Lt Mark Bradley: **Harry Baird**
General Henderson: **Grant Taylor**
Skydiver navigator: **Jeremy Wilkin**
Lew Waterman: **Gary Myers**
Lt. Ford: **Keith Alexander**
SHADO Operative: **Ayshea Brough**
Miss Ealand: **Norma Ronald**
Skydiver Engineer: **John Kelley**
Skydiver Operative: **Georgina Moon**

Identified
w **Gerry Anderson** and **Sylvia Anderson**, **Tony Barwick**
d **Gerry Anderson**

SHADO engages in its first battle with the enemy. Sky One cripples an alien ship which crash-lands in a lake. Staker's team capture its pilot, a strange blue-skinned humanoid - and the grim secret behind the aliens' plans are revealed.

Cabinet Minister: **Basil Dignam** [intro]
Kurt Mahler: **Peter Gillard**
Phil Wade: **Gary Files**
Ken Matthews: **Michael Mundell**
Dr Harris: **Matthew Roberton**
Nurse: **Annette Kerr**
Alien: **Gito Santana / Stanley Bray**

Exposed
w **Tony Barwick**
d **David Lane**

When an experimental plane being fight-tested by Paul Foster and his co-pilot is attacked and shot down by a UFO and the co-pilot loses his life, events lead Foster to a face to face confrontation with Ed Straker - and the start of a new career.

Janna: **Jean Marsh**
Kofax: **Robin Bailey**
Jim Wade [co-pilot]: **Matt Zimmerman**
Louis Graham: **Arthur Cox**
Dr Frazer: **Basil Moss**
Nurse: **Sue Gerrard**
Tsi: **Paula Li Schiu**

The Cat with Ten Lives
w **David Tomblin**
d **David Tomblin**

When Jim Regan, a SHADO interceptor pilot, is captured by the aliens, taken aboard a UFO, and put through a grim medical test, the events bring sinister drama for the pilot and his wife - and deadly trouble for Ed Straker.

Jim Regan: **Alexis Kanner**
Jean Regan: **Geraldine Moffatt**
Albert Thompson: **Colin Gordon**
Muriel Thompson: **Eleanor Summerfield**
Miss Holland: **Lois Maxwell** [intro]
Morgan: **Windsor Davies**
Capt Steve Minto [first astronaut]: **Steven Berkoff**
Second Astronaut: **Al Mancini**

Conflict
w **Ruric Powell**
d **Ken Turner**

Convinced that the aliens have hidden a satellite among the flying debris of space which is being used to knock out his re-entry craft, Straker requests to have the space junk cleared, but General Henderson opposes his plea - and Foster disobeys orders to prove his chief's theory.

Steve Maddox: **Drewe Henley**
Crewman [Lunar Module]: **David Courtland**
Navigator [Spaceship]: **Alan Tucker**
Pilot [Spaceship]: **Gerard Norman**
Steiner: **Michael Alexander**

A Question of Priorities
w **Tony Barwick**
d **David Lane**

When Straker's son is knocked down by a car and the plane carrying the drug that can save his life is threatened because of a communications breakdown, the SHADO commander finds himself having to choose between his duty to his son and his duty to protect Earth.

John Rutland: **Barnaby Shaw** [intro]
Mary Rutland: **Suzanne Neve** [intro]
Rutland: **Philip Madoc** [intro]
Alien: **Richard Aylen**
Doctor Segal: **Peter Halliday**
Mrs O'Connor: **Mary Merrall**
Doctor Green: **Russell Napier**
Nurse: **Andrea Allan**
SHADO Operative: **Penny Spencer**
Car Driver: **David Cargill**

E.S.P.
w **Alan Fennell**
d **Ken Turner**

When a UFO evades SHADO interceptors and crash-lands on Earth close to the house of a man named Croxley, and

Straker and Freeman find themselves facing death when Croxley is taken over by an alien - and given the power to read minds.

John Croxley: **John Stratton**
Stella Croxley: **Deborah Stanford**
Dr Ward: **Douglas Wilmer**
Dr Schroeder: **Maxwell Shaw**[intro]
Astronaut: **Harry Baird**
SHADO Security Man: **Stanley McGeagh**
Gateman: **Donald Tandy**

Kill Straker!
w **Donald James**
d **Alan Perry**

Straker takes a split-second decision when a lunar module captained by Paul Foster and Frank Craig is attacked by a UFO. The vehicle manages to land safely - but Craig immediately attempts to kill Straker.

Frank Craig: **David Summer**
Nurse: **Louise Pajo**
Astronaut: **Harry Baird**
Moonbase Guard: **Steve Cory**

Sub-Smash
w **Alan Fennell**
d **David Lane**

When a UFO sinks a freighter and Straker realises that the alien vessels can travel underwater, he and Nina Barry join Skydiver One in a search for the UFO. But Skydiver is hit during an attack - leaving Straker and his team trapped.

Lt Lewis: **Paul Maxwell**
Lt Chin: **Anthony Chinn**
Pilot: **Burnell Tucker**
SHADO Divers: **Alan Haywood, John Golightly**

Destruction
w **Dennis Spooner**
d **Ken Turner**

Faced with an information blackout, when a Navy ship shoots down a UFO but refuses to allow Straker and Colonel Lake to investigate the alien vessel - the matter, he is told, is secret - Straker is determined to seek the truth.

Sarah Bosanquet: **Stephanie Beacham**
Admiral Sheringham: **Edwin Richfield**
Ship's Captain: **Philip Madoc**
Second Officer Cooper: **Peter Blythe**
Rating: **Jimmy Winston**
Radar Technician: **Michael Ferrand**
Radar Officer: **Robert Lloyd**
Skydiver Captain: **David Warbeck**
Skydiver Navigator: **Jon Kelley**
Skydiver Engineer: **Barry Stokes**
Astronaut: **Steven Berkoff**

The Square Triangle
w **Alan Pattillo**
d **David Lane**

When Straker deliberately allows a UFO to land in England, in the hope of capturing the craft and its pilot, he has no idea that he will soon become involved in a murderous love triangle and the death of an alien.

Liz Newton: **Adrienne Corri**
Jack Newton: **Allan Cuthbertson**
Cass Fowler: **Patrick Mower**
Alien: **Anthony Chinn**

SHADO Mobile Operator: **Hugo Panczak**
Gamekeeper: **Godfrey James**
Astronaut: **Gary Myers**

Close up
w **Tony Barwick**
d **Alan Perry**

SHADO wait for the results of their latest experiment: a new electron telescope fitted to a tracking probe, which will allow them to photograph the alien's home planet and track a UFO to its origin in space.

Kelly: **Neil Hallett**
Dr Young: **James Beckett**
Rocket Launch Controller: **Frank Mann**
Interceptor Pilot: **Mark Hawkins**
Masters: **Jon Kelley**
Tracking Station Operative: **Alan Tucker**

The Psychobombs
w **Tony Barwick**
d **Jeremy Summers**

When three average people are taken over by the aliens and are given superhuman strength in order to seek out and destroy the SHADO organisation, Straker's team face danger and death.

Linda Simmons: **Deborah Grant**
Clem Mason: **Mike Pratt**
Daniel Clark: **David Collings**
Capt. Lauritzen: **Tom Adams**
The Executive: **Alex Davion**
Skydiver Navigator: **Christopher Timothy**
Police Motorcyclist: **Gavin Campbell**
Tracking station Officer: **Peter Blythe**
Tracking Station Guards: **Peter Davies, Derek Steen**
Skydiver Captain: **Robert Hawdon**
Security Men: **Nigel Gregory** and **Hans de Vries**
Skydiver engineers: **Peter Dolphin** and **Mark York**
Plain Clothes Officer: **Oscar James**
Room 22 Guard: **Aidan Murphy**

Survival
w **Tony Barwick**
d **Alan Perry**

The aliens land a UFO on the moon under the cover of a meteorite storm and an alien blasts his way through the leisure dome killing Bill Grant, Foster's close friend. Foster leads the mission to find the intruder - but finds himself marooned, far from Moonbase.

Tina Duval: **Suzan Farmer**
Bill Grant: **Robert Swann**
Alien: **Gito Santana**
Rescuers: **Ray Armstrong, David Weston**

Mindbender
w **Tony Barwick**
d **Ken Turner**

Why should two members of an interceptor crew suddenly go berserk and try to kill their colleagues, whom they believe to be their enemies? Straker must find the answer.

Howard Byrne: **Stuart Damon**
Beaver James: **Charles Tingwell**
Andy Conroy: **Al Mancini**
Film Director: **Stephen Case**
Cabinet Minister: **Basil Dignam**
John Rutland: **Barnaby Shaw**
Mary Rutland: **Suzanne Neve**

Rutland: **Philip Madoc**
Dale: **Craig Hunter**
Astronaut: **Steven Berkoff**
SHADO Operative: **James Marcus**
SHADO Guards: **John Lyons, Stanley McGeagh**
First Assistant Director: **Norton Clark**
Second Assistant Director: **Paul Greaves**
Mexican Bandits: **Larry Taylor, Richard Montez, Bill Morgan**

Flight Path
w **Ian Scott Stewart**
d **Ken Turner**

Forced into supplying secret data from SID - the Space Intruder Detector - because of his devotion to his wife who is being held hostage by the aliens, Moonbase operative Roper brings danger into Straker's life.

Paul Roper: **George Cole**
Carol Roper: **Sonia Fox**
Dawson: **Keith Grenville**
Dr Schroeder: **Maxwell Shaw**

The Man who Came Back
w **Terence Feely**
d **David Lane**

The return of Craig Collings, a spacecraft pilot who was presumed dead and has been missing for two months, spells trouble for Straker and a shock for his girlfriend, when his reappearance portends danger to the SHADO organisation.

Craig Collins: **Derren Nesbitt**
Col John Grey: **Gary Raymond**
Sir Esmond: **Ronald Culver**
Miss Holland: **Lois Maxwell**
Moonbase Operative: **Andrea Allan**
Chauffeur: **Mike Stevens**
Moonbase Doctor: **Robert Grange**
Housekeeper: **Navy Nevinson**
Porter: **Fred Real**
Hospital Doctor: **David Savile**
Nurse: **Rona Newton-John**

The Dalotek Affair
w **Ruric Powell**
d **Alan Perry**

The sudden failure of all radio and video equipment on Moonbase alarms Foster, who suspects that there is a fault in the geological scanner at the nearby research base run by the Dalotek company. He closes down the scanner - but the breakdown continues.

Jane Carson: **Tracy Reed**
Mark Tanner: **Clinton Greyn**
Phil Mitchell: **David Weston**
Blake: **Philip Latham**
Reed: **John Breslin**
Interceptor Pilot: **Gary Myers**
Lunar Module Pilot: **Alan Tucker**
Moonmobile Captain: **John Cobner**
Moonmobile Lieut: **Richard Poore**
Doctor: **Basil Moss**

Timelash
w **Terence Feely**
d **Cyril Frankel**

When Straker and Colonel Lake are attacked by a UFO, the SHADO commander finds himself fighting an unbeatable enemy. Time stands still and SHADO headquarters is locked in a time barrier - from which there is no escape.

Turner: **Patrick Allen**
Casting agent: **Ron Pember**
Actor: **Jean Vladon**
Actress: **Kirsten Lindhorn**
SHADO Maintenance Engineer: **Douglas Nottage**
Studio Guard: **John Lyons**
Studio Security Man: **John J. Carney**

Ordeal
w **Tony Barwick**
d **Ken Turner**

When Paul Foster gets drunk the night before entering a SHADO health-farm and falls asleep in the sauna, then wakes up to find aliens raiding the establishment and Straker ordering a UFO to be shot down, the SHADO member finds further troubles before his nightmare ends.

Joe Franklin: **David Healy**
Dr Harris: **Basil Moss**
Sylvia Graham: **Quinn O'Hara**
Astronaut: **Mark Hawkins**
Medic: **Joseph Morris**
Perry: **Peter Burton**

Court Martial
w **Tony Barwick**
d **Ron Appleton**

It's a clash between Straker's loyalty and Foster's courage. Paul Foster stands accused of being responsible for a security leak and is sentenced to death. Straker refuses to accept his guilt, and sets out to prove his innocence.

Webb: **Jack Hedley**
Carl Mason: **Neil McCallum**
Miss Grant: **Georgina Cookson**
Singleton: **Tutte Lemkow**
Diane: **Pippa Steel**
Miss Scott: **Louise Pajo**
Artist's Agent: **Noel Davis**
Ass Director: **Paul Greenhalgh**
Guard: **Michael Gover**
Masters: **John Kelley**

Reflections in the Water
w **David Tomblin**
d **David Tomblin**

It's a nightmare situation for the team of Straker and Freeman. To investigate reports of 'flying fish', the two men take Skydiver deep into the sea - and find themselves in a strange world in which they come face to face with their troubles.

Lt Anderson: **James Cosmo**
Skydiver Captain: **David Warbeck**
Skipper: **Conrad Phillips**
Film Producer: **Richard Caldicott**
Helmsman: **Gordon Sterne**
First Seaman: **Frederic Abbott**
Underwater Cameraman: **Mark Griffith**
Film Director: **Keith Bell**
Insurance Man: **Gerald Cross**
Skydiver Navigator: **Barry Stokes**
Astronaut: **Steven Berkoff**

Computer Affair
w **Tony Barwick**
d **David Lane**

The death of an astronaut has strange implications for Straker and his SHADO operatives when the Moonbase team are recalled to Earth to give evidence against a

computer which suggest that 'love' was responsible for the man's death.

Dr Murray: **Peter Burton**
Ken Matthews: **Michael Mundell**
Dr Schroeder: **Maxwell Shaw**
Lew Waterman: **Gary Myers**
Moonbase Operative: **Nigel Lambert**
SHADO Mobile 1 Personel: **Hein Viljoen, Dennis Plenty**
SHADO Mobile 3 Officer: **Hugh Armstrong**

Confetti Check A-O.K.
w **Tony Barwick**
d **David Lane**

The birth of a child to the wife of a SHADO operative causes Straker to think back to his own marriage. In the early seventies he was already involved in the creation of SHADO - and the work cost him the love of his wife.

Mary: **Suzanne Neve**
Mary's Father: **Michael Nightingale**
Doctor: **Tom Oliver**
Estate Agent: **Donald Palmer**
Lt Grey: **Julian Grant**
CIA Man: **Shane Rimmer**
Porter: **Frank Tregar**
Hotel Clerk: **Geoffrey Hinsliff**
Security Officer: **Michael Forrest**
English Delegate: **Jack May**
French Delegate: **Jeffrey Segal**
German Delegate: **Gordon Sterne**
US Delegate: **Alan Tilvern**
Nurse: **Penny Jackson**

The Sound of Silence
w **David Lane and Bob Bell**
d **David Lane**

When SHADO track a UFO heading towards Earth and it lands near the home of international showjumper Russel Stone, who then disappears. Paul Foster believes that the alien responsible has taken refuge in a nearby lake.

Russ Stone: **Michael Jayston**
Anne Stone: **Susan Jameson**
Alien: **Gito Santana**
Culley: **Nigel Gregory**
Stone: **Richard Vernon**
Doctor: **Basil Moss**
First Technician: **Tom Oliver**
GSP 4 Co-pilot: **Burnell Tucker**
GSP 4 Pilot: **Craig Hunter**
Second Technician: **Malcolm Reynolds**

The Responsibility Seat
w **Tony Barwick**
d **Alan Perry**

Left in charge of SHADO headquarters, Colonel Freeman takes command when three alien spacecraft are detected heading for the moon. Straker, meanwhile, is busy on a wild goose chase.

Jo Fraser: **Jane Merrow**
Russian Astronauts: **Janos Kurucz, Paul Tamarin**
Russian Base Commander: **Patrick Jordan**
Film Director: **Ralph Bell**
Stuntman: **Royston Rowe**
Astronaut: **Mark Hawkins**

The Long Sleep
w **David Tomblin**
d **Jeremy Summers**

When a young girl, Cathy, regains consciousness after being in a coma for 10 years, Straker becomes personally involved in the case. The girl had muttered something about a UFO before her long sleep - and Straker wishes to learn more.

Catherine Fraser: **Tessa Wyatt**
Tim: **Christian Roberts**
Bomb Disposal Expert: **Christopher Robbie**
Van Driver: **John Garrie**

✍ A feature, *Invasion U.F.O.*, was released, being a compilation of the episodes *Identified*, *The Computer Affair* & *Reflections in the Water*.

📖

U.F.O. [1970: Robert Miall aka John Burke: Pan Books: *U.F.O. #1 Flesh Hunters* in US Warner Books 1973: novelisations of *Exposed*, *Close Up* and *Court Martial*]; *U.F.O. #2* [1971: Robert Miall aka John Burke: Pan Books: *U.F.O. #2 Sporting Blood* in US Warner Books 1973: novelisations of *The Computer Affair*, *The Dalotek Affair* and *Survival*].

UFO:

Format: **Gerry Anderson** and **Sylvia Anderson** with **Reg Hill**
Produced by: **Gerry Anderson, Sylvia Anderson** and **Reg Hill**
Executive Producer: **Gerry Anderson**
Century 21 Fashions: **Sylvia Anderson**
Special Effects: **Derek Meddings**
Art Director: **Bob Bell**
Production Supervisor: **Norman Foster**
Assistant to Producer: **Des Saunders**
Lighting Cameraman: **Brendon Stafford**
Music: **Barry Gray**
Script Editor: **Tony Barwick**

Filmed at MGM Borehamwood and Pinewood Studios, England
A Century 21 Pictures Ltd. Production for ITC World Wide Distribution

26 colour 60-minute episodes
1969-70

Virgin of the Secret Service

The blood and thunder exploits of Captain Robert Virgin of the British Secret Service, a courageous soldier of fortune and Britain's last valiant hope of keeping 'the natives at bay' during the Northwest Indian Frontier campaign of the 1900s. A man of incredible bravery who would lay down his life to protect Britain's honour [and was frequently asked to do so by his superior, Colonel Shaw-Camberley], Virgin fought his way through his adventures with a stiff upper lip and considerable panache [not too mention a wicked smile on his face]. Using sword, knife or his fists [and highly proficient with all three], he blazed his way across the frontier protecting the honour of his regiment and saving the beautiful [though thoroughly emancipated] Edwardian lady spy, Mrs Virginia Cortez, from the dastardly overtures of their adversaries, the diabolically evil international agent, Karl Von Brauner and his equally evil [and deranged] aide, Klaus Striebeck, both of whom share an intense hatred for the upright and intrepid hero.

Played with tongue firmly in cheek, the series managed to spoof the likes of John Drake, James Bond [perhaps even, John Steed] without going over the top.

Regular cast:
Captain Robert Virgin [England's finest]: **Clinton Greyn**
Mrs Virginia Cortez [A British Agent]: **Veronica Strong**
Doublett [Virgin's batman/friend]: **John Cater**
Colonel Shaw-Camberley: **Noel Coleman**
Karl Von Brauner: **Alexander Dore**

Dark Deeds on the Northwest Frontier
w **Nicholas Palmer**
d **Paul Bernard**

Together with Doublett, Captain Virgin travels by balloon to the Northwest Frontier. His mission: to save India for the Empire - and outwit the diabolical plans of his old adversary, the thoroughly evil Karl Von Brauner.

Princess Katerina: **Patience Collier**
Theodor Green: **Cyril Luckham**
Polly Green: **Margo Andrew**
Colonel Richards: **Bernard Hepton**
Harry Crabb: **John Trigger**
Afghan: **Frank Seton**
First Hazarnao: **Ray Ford**
Second Hazarnao: **Peter Diamond**
Envoy: **David Grey**
Wazir: **Denis Shaw**
Hazarnao thief: **Arne Gordon**
Sergeant: **Ronald Mayer**
Guard: **Roy Stewart**

Russian Roundabout
w **Basil Dawson**
d **John Sichel**

During a mission to St Petersburg, Virgin finds a Prince who dreams of becoming Emperor of India. In a mission filled with intrigue and mystery, the agent puts paid to the man's dreams and once again foils Von Brauner's aspirations to greatness.

Prince Rouvaloff: **Michael Coles**
Countess Irene Kolinsky: **Gabrielle Drake**
Dmitri: **Geoffrey Russell**
Count Kolinsky: **Desmond Llewelyn**
Franz: **Peter Diamond**
Josep: **Bartlett Mullins**
Lieut. Anderson: **Malcolm Douglas**
Cmdr. Byng Howard: **Salvin Stewart**
Butler: **George Roumanov**

Grigori Rasputin: **Vernon Dobtcheff**
Raskolnikov: **Carl Paulsen**
President of Court: **Kevin Brennan**
Capt. Arapoff: **Jonathan Newth**
Sgt. Boyko: **Terence Rigby**

Entente Cordiale
w **Betty Lambda**
d **Paul Bernard**

When the entente cordiale is threatened by Von Brauner's attempts to have the Duke of Albany killed when he visits the opera, Virgin and Mrs Cortez, impersonating the Duke and his wife, find themselves held prisoner by a group of Chinese white slave traders.

Gerald: **Mark Hawkins**
Ching: **Keith Bonnard**
Cigarette: **Katherine Schofield**
Duke of Albany: **Frederick Peisley**
Major Trangmere: **Paul Williamson**
Marcel: **Laurence Davidson**
Cuthbert: **Roger Lloyd Pack**
Senor Curacha: **John Malcolm**
Prince Frederick: **Robert Crewsdon**
Duchess of Albany: **Noel Hood**
Chinese: **Tommy Yapp**
Helmut: **Juan Moreno**

The Great Ring of Akba
w **Ted Willis**
d **Paul Bernard**

Captain Virgin travels to Arabia alone, to meet a cruel usurper face to face - and finds himself held prisoner by Von Brauner and Klaus Striebeck, who put him through their 'ordeal by animal': a deep pit filled with venomous reptiles.

The Kalipha of Akba: **Erik Chitty**
Abu: **Mark Colleano**
Ozman Hassin: **John Collin**
Klaus Striebeck: **Peter Swanwick** [intro]
First Guard: **George Eugeniou**
Second Guard: **Archilles Georgiou**
Governor of Akba: **John Horsley**
Captain Watts: **Timothy Carlton**
Corporal: **Kevork Malikyan**
Fraulein Wellman: **Pearl Catlin**
Albert Smith: **Allen Sykes**
First Girl: **Veronica Page**
First Arab: **Sonny Caldinez**
Second Arab: **Peter Diamond**
Princess Selina: **Carmen Dene**
Miss Medlock: **Joan Geary**
Miss Fowler: **Etain O'Dell**
Schoolgirl: **Diane Cane**
Mohammed: **Gordon Whiting**
Belly Dancer: **Julie Mendez**
Third Guard: **Roy Stewart**
Hean Eunuch: **Harold Lang**
Sheik: **George Zenios**

The Amazons
w **Basil Dawson**
d **Robert D. Cardona**

Virgin, Doublett and Mrs Cortez arrive in Brazil and find themselves caught up in a plot to seize Inca gold. Lurking in the background are their enemies Brauner and Striebeck - who have a few nasty surprises in store for the trio.

Dermot O'Rourke: **John Welsh**
Manoel: **Sean Lynch**
Peterson: **Ken Haward**

Atahualpa: **Tom Kempinski**
Indian / Inca Guard: **Pete Diamond**
Sheila O'Rourke: **Elisabeth Murray**
Bridget O'Rourke: **Kate Ninchy**
Kitty O'Rourke: **Liz Davis**
Lady Pamela: **Pamela Miles**
Duchess of Didcott: **Elisabeth Digby-Smith**
Karakaan: **Frank Singuineau**

The Rajah and the Suffragette
w **Anthony Steven** and **Vincent Tilsley**
d **John Sichel**

When Virgin learns of a dastardly plot to entomb a British regiment in the valley of Sindra-Lal, he enters a Rajah's school of love to rescue a missing suffragette and save the honour of his regiment.

Hon. Maud la Moote: **Jennie Linden**
Rajah of Chundrapore: **Rodney Bewes**
Col. Devereaux: **Clive Morton**
Vizier: **Roger Delgado**
Vizier's servant: **Renu Setna**
Jam Singh: **Mohan Singh**
Lieut. Forbes Wintle: **Tom Browne**
Sgt. Polkinghorne: **Will Stampe**
Capt. Raffles Kirby: **John Challis**
Capt. Nigel Bratby: **Phillip Voss**
Roshan Cooch Benares: **Fay Sparks**
Guard Commander: **Allen Heider**

The Persuasion of a Million Drops
w **Ted Willis**
d **Robert D. Cardona**

A man who dreams of making the whole world a province of China by using a new and terrifying invention places Virgin's life at stake when he subjects our hero to the horrific Chinese torture of a thousand drips of water on the head.

Chu Chen Yu: **Norman Scace**
Professor Lemaire: **Michael Lees**
Klaus Striebeck: **Peter Swanwick**
Christa: **Pearl Catlin**
Gypsy Violinist: **John Lawrence**
Mrs Cherry White: **Marji Lawrence**
Capt. White: **Robin Ellis**
Major: **Ronald Mansell**
Ivan: **Nosher Powell**
Kontell: **David Nettheim**
Babette Lemaire: **Linda Marlowe**
Lily Jones: **Trisha Mortimer**
Concubines: **Talya Vashti, Marguerite Avril Gaynor**
Guards: **Peter Diamond, Gerry Wain**

Pride of Assassins
w **Anthony Steven**
d **Paul Bernard**

Virgin is assigned to hunt down the brilliant French marksman Bobo le Mec, who has been hired to assassinate the King of Croatia. To do so, Virgin infiltrates Le Mec's school for killers - but his cover is blown and he is taken prisoner.

Bobo le Mec: **Eugene Deckers**
Domino: **George Innes**
Gandolfio: **Tommy Godfrey**
Paola: **Julie Mendez**
Zafrini: **Austin Baptiste**
Zielgler: **Yuri Borienko**
Fleurette: **Felicity Gibson**
Grand Duke Pavlacek-Falkenberg: **Ralph Nossek**
Kaiser: **Michael Hall**
Ticket Collector: **Peter Boyes**

Across the Silver Pass of Gusri Song
w **Ted Willis**
d **Josephine Douglas**

Caught in a web of prophecy while searching for a missing comrade, Virgin finds himself imprisoned in a cage above a red-hot cauldron of fire. His only hope of escape is Doublett - but he, too, has been captured and subjected to torture.

Shang Si: **Georgina Hale**
Yuente: **Edward Brayshaw**
The Oracle: **Ewen Solon**
Priestess Shiao: **Marguerite**
Priestess Chaeo: **Yee Wah Young**
Mai Lung: **Thalia Kouri**
Chief Guard: **Peter Diamond**
Torturer: **Gerry Wain**
Private Watney: **David Rickard**
Corporal Reade: **Martin Pilcher**
Priest: **John Moore**

The Pyramid Plot
w **Basil Dawson**
d **Robert D. Cardona**

Who is behind the disappearance of seven British officers in Cairo? Virgin and his team are stumped - until the beautiful Lady Clea Merrion offers to help them. But can she be trusted - or do her true loyalties lie elsewhere?

Lady Clea Merrion: **Lisa Daniely**
Major Zaki: **Peter Birrel**
Lord Merrion: **William Kendall**
Sayid: **Paul Darrow**
Col. Blake Travers: **John Gill**
Ali: **Wilfred Grove**
Sheikh Abdul Amir: **Peter Madden**
Egyptian Sergeant: **Peter Maycock**
General Cookson: **Geoffrey Denton**
Dancers: **Julie Mendez, Katya Nadia, Birsen**
Drummer: **Austin Baptiste**

A Fate Worse Than Death
w **Stuart Douglas**
d **Henrich Hirsch**

When Von Brauner and Striebeck's latest scheme threatens the very heart of British rule in India, Captain Virgin and his friends expose their arch-enemies' diabolical plans with a clever scheme of their own.

Pell: **Oscar Quitak**
Stikow: **Sean Lynch**
Vlakon: **Michael Wynne**
Klaus Striebeck: **Peter Swanwick**
Constable: **Kenneth Edwards**
Prime Minister: **John Scott**
Geoffrey: **Geoffrey Colville**

The Professor Goes West
w **Nicholas Palmer**
d **Robert D. Cardona**

Attempting to engineer the release of an Englishman being held prisoner in deepest Texas, Captain Virgin comes face to face with Big Jack, the fastest gun in the West - and is ordered to prepare for a gunfight at dawn.

Big Jack: **David Bauer**
Jesse: **Al Mancini**
Professor Whitestone: **Carleton Hobbs**
Henry: **Jerry Stovin**
Sir Robert Fenton: **Jack Lambert**
Jake Reilly: **Glenn Beck**

Sunshine: **Carolyn Jones**
Sheriff: **John Brandon**
Man in Saloon: **Peter Diamond**
Judd: **Ray Ford**
Ed: **Gerry Wain**

Wings Over Glencraig
w **John Roberts**
d **Robert D. Cardonna**

In a desperate bid to save the world from a new and terrifying invention, Captain Virgin and his friends travel to Scotland to take on the greatest assignment they have yet faced - the threat of Lord Glencraig.

Laird of Glencraig: **John Grieve**
Prince Luigi: **Ian White**
Isla: **Lorna Heilbron**
Wullie: **Douglas Cummings**
Tosh: **Freddie Earle**
Taro: **Milton Reid**
Kemel: **Alex Donahue**
Tom: **John Kane**
Maclean: **Angus Lennie**

Virgin of the Secret Service:

Series devised by: **Ted Willis**
Producer: **Josephine Douglas**
Theme music composed and played by: **Larry Adler**
Edited by: **Nicholas Palmer**
Fights arranged by: **Peter Diamond**

An ATV Production. An ITC Presentation.

13 monochrome videotaped 60-minute episodes
1968

White Hunter

By far and away the best of the heroics-in-the-jungle oaters produced in the late fifties, this lively series of African Adventures [based on the real life exploits of John A. Hunter, 'the surest and fastest shot in Africa'] took little time to establish itself as a viewer's favourite - mainly due to some exciting scripts and the sincere approach of its subject material.

Regular cast:
John Hunter: **Rhodes Reason**
Atimbu [Hunter's Bearer]: **Harry Baird**

The General
w Frank L. Moss
d Ernest Morris

General Chip Walker is privy to State Department secrets. Therefore, the Pentagon is disturbed when he plans a hunting safari with his friend, John Hunter. Every precaution is taken - but enemy intelligence are aware of Walker's plans.

General Walker: **Robert Henderson**
Winfield: **Sheldon Lawrence**
Dubois: **Ferdy Mayne**
Ruysman: **Andre Mikhelson**
Ezra McGivney: **Peter Swanwick**

Voodoo Wedding
w Lee Loeb
d Ernest Morris

Asked to lead Sally Reynolds and her fiancee Fred on Safari. Hunter is happy to oblige, he likes the young couple. But the accidental violation of a sacred burial ground incurs the wrath of a Witch Doctor and Sally is struck down by a voodoo curse.

Fred Langton: **Edward Judd**
Bob Gordon: **Robert Shaw**
Sally: **Gene Anderson**
Napi: **Harry Quashie**
Commissioner: **Hugh Moxey**
Dr. Waring: **Jack Lambert**
Witch Doctor: **Sammy Wilde**
Clerk in Licence Office: **Eric Francis**
Policeman: **Fred Foddard**
Nurse: **Susan Travers**
Native Woman: **Mrs How**

A Moment of Truth
w Lee Loeb
d Peter Maxwell

Pete McAfee, one the best white hunters in Africa, has trained his son, Denny, to follow in his footsteps - a situation John Hunter takes an interest in when Denny is injured and forced into retirement.

Denny: **Tim Turner**
Barbara: **Jennifer Jayne**
Mrs McAfee: **Moira Lynd**
Pete McAfee: **John Rae**
Carol: **Jill Melford**
Pilot: **Anthony Bate**
Andy Stevenson: **Gerald Case**
Harry: **Michael Anthony**

Run to Earth
w Robert Yale Libbott
d Maurice Elvey

Released from prison, Manderley, makes no secret of the fact that he intends to kill John Hunter, the man who helped to put him away. Driven by an insane compulsion for revenge he opens his deadly campaign.

Manderley: **Andre Morell**
Gemma: **Sandra Dorne**
Tim Wallington: **Harry Fowler**
Prof. Rosehill: **Arnold Ridley**
Mrs Rosehill: **Madeline Thomas**
Alice Sutton: **Frances Guthrie**
Colonel Sutton: **Peter Bathurst**
Purley: **Hugh Moxey**
Banstead: **Jack Lambert**
Ral Guparji: **Michael Mellinger**

Decision
w Herb Purdom
d Maclean Rogers

Young city hoodlum, Vic Rader, is running from trouble when he's befriended by John Hunter. At Hunter's suggestion, his friend, Jamie, helps Vic to learn to use a rifle. When Jamie is found dead, all evidence points to Rader. But did he kill his mentor?

Paul Haggis: **John Stuart**
Vic Rader: **Charles Houston**
Jamie: **John Fabian**
Chato: **Dan Jackson**
Kagaya: **Andre Dakar**

One Fatal Weakness
w Lee Erwin
d Max Varnel

It's a safari with a difference. Hunter is asked to join Doak, a counter-intelligence agent in a hunt for a mysterious individual named Mr Sims - the head of an ivory smuggling ring and racketeer on an international scale.

Maria Varga: **Andrienne Corri**
Mr Doak: **Mervyn Johns**
Drunk: **Jack Taylor**

Sickness of Kilimanjaro
w Herb Purdom
d Joseph Sterling

Asked to locate the breeding-ground of man-eating lions, Hunter finds his task made that much more dangerous by the presence of a alcoholic hunter and his wife - he determined to make a name for himself, she determined to see him dead!

Superintendent: **Lloyd Lamble**
Kotitcu: **Andre Dakar**
Remaining cast unknown

Marked Man
w Lee Loeb
d Darcy Conyers

A man named Atherton dispatches a paid killer to Africa. He is to kill game reserve warden, Porter, presently on safari with John Hunter. The killer's reign of terror begins when they reach a game reserve lodge.

Steve Porter: **Jack Hedley**
Helen Porter: **Kay Callard**
Richardson: **Gordon Sterne**
Martin: **Carl Jaffe**
Smedley: **Alexander Archdale**
Atherton: **Desmond Roberts**
Peterson: **Nigel Fitzgerald**

Williams: **Sydney King**
Insp. Dunlap: **Frank Hawkins**

The Treasure of Tippu Tib
w **Lee Loeb**
d **Ernest Morris**

Baker and Anderson have been hunting with John Hunter for several years. Now they have made a bet to see who will be the first one to capture the giant Kudu. Their foolishness will place Hunter into an orgy of terror.

Steve Anderson: **John Loder**
Harvey Baker: **Leslie Perrins**
Harajo Sam: **Peter Sinclair**

No Survivors
w **Lee Erwin**
d **Joseph Sterling**

A plane has crash landed in the jungle. John Hunter leads the search party. Then Mr Doak, his friend from the C.I.D. in London, asks him to track down the people responsible - a collection of spies, saboteurs and murderers.

Mr Doak: **Mervyn Johns**
Capt. Hagen: **Hugh Moxey**
Major Royce: **Garard Green**
Volpo: **Maurice Duran**
Kramer: **Walter Gotell**
Zacharias: **Richard Goldring**
Kemp: **William Thorburn**
Gruber: **Steve Plytas**
Travers: **Laurence Brooks**

Deadfall
w **Lee Loeb**
d **Peter Maxwell**

Hunter's friend, Harvey Benson, springs a surprise. They're going hunting - house hunting! Benson has his eyes set on Table Top, one of the finest properties in the area. But murder and corruption join the house-safari.

Louise: **Patricia Dainton**
Harvey Benson: **Ronan O'Casey**
Westcott: **Conrad Phillips**
Bailey: **John Rae**

The Stepfathers
w **Donn Mullally**
d **Ernest Morris**

Hunter joins former ivory poacher, Mjumbino Barr, to curb an invasion of rhinos from across the North-western frontier. Crossing the border, they encounter Lord Trevor, an amateur lion-hunter - a meeting which spells trouble.

Mjumbino Barr: **Francis de Wolff**
Trevor: **Vincent Ball**
2nd Bearer: **Danny Daniels**
Spanish Officer: **Peter Allenby**
2nd Spanish Officer: **Marcel de Villiers**

The Fugitive
w **Lee Erwin**
d **Peter Maxwell**

Leeds and Parker, the wardens of a remote game reserve, have been virtually out of touch with civilisation except for radio - a loneliness that has bred hatred. Before Hunter arrives, the men engage in a fight and Leeds is killed.

Parker: **Charles Houston**

Leeds: **Tim Turner**
Komo: **Earl Cameron** [intro]
Anne: **Moira Lynd**

Operation Transfer
w **Frank L. Moss**
d **Darcy Conyers**

Albert Grunig, the Assistant Commissioner of a Valley-farm district, feels that Hunter, a civilian, is an interfering busybody. The two men clash when Grunig attempts to rule the Valley with a show of force.

Grunig: **Clifford Evans**
Robert Storm: **John Stone**
Henry Zender: **Tony Sheppard**
Peter Reyes: **Carl Conway**
Arthur Korvin: **Michael Kelly**
Edward Storm: **Henry Longhurst**
Martinson: **Colin Tapley**

Inside Story
w **Ellis Marcus**
d **Joseph Sterling**

Hunter is hired to guide American news photographer, Sherman Wick, and his researcher, Martha Locklin, to the village of Cambridge-educated tribal chief, Arusha. Things start to go wrong from the onset.

Martha: **Barbara Shelley**
Wick: **Phil Brown**
Arusha: **Cy Grant**
Sayville: **Neal Arden**
Kenduyu: **Jimmy Ramsay**

The No-Account
w **Lee Loeb**
d **Ernest Morris**

Hunter and missionary nurse, Barbara Sinclair, are asked to transport hospital drugs and equipment to Koona. Against Hunter's advice, Barbara engages a driver named Mason, a man with a record who intends to hi-jack the shipment.

Slater: **Ronald Leigh Hunt**
Mason: **Clifford Evans**
Barbara: **Mary Laura Wood**
A.D.C.: **Hugh Moxey**
Burrows: **Howard Lang**

Rogue Man
w **Herb Purdom**
d **Peter Maxwell**

Kells is a multiple killer who lives in the jungle like an animal. Too clever to be captured by the ordinary police, Kells is convinced that he will never be taken alive. John Hunter is hired to track him down.

Joe Kells: **Edwin Richfield**
Ruth Osterman: **Gwen Watford**
Davidson: **John Longden**
Amos Briggs: **Charles Farrell**
Sievers: **Peter Carver**
James Purley: **Hugh Moxey**

The Prisoner
w **Lee Loeb**
d **Ernest Morris**

Hunter is hired by Police Inspector Sommers, who hopes to capture Terry Flynn, a white hunter suspected of murder.

They catch Flynn easily, but returning him to face justice proves to be harder than they imagined.

Diane Kendrick: **Katherine Boyle**
Terry Flynn: **David Oxley**
Harijo Sam [Fergus]: **Peter Sinclair**
Nora Maxwell: **Paula Byrne**
Insp. Sommers: **Neil Hallett**
Messenger: **Bertie Green**

Big Bwana Brady
w **Lee Erwin**
d **Joseph Sterling**

Hunter finds himself trapped into the job of collaborating with an American politico to develop his prospects as a candidate for Governor of an un-named state.

Brady: **John Crawford**
Patricia: **Faith Brook**
J. W. Evans: **Robert Ayres**

Squire of the Serengeti
w **Donn Mullally**
d **Ernest Morris**

On Safari in the Northwest district with his friends, Lord Ashmore and Peter Carr, Hunter decides to return to camp when Lord Ashmore fails to capture the record elephant - a mistake. The party is being stalked by a man-eating lion.

Lenore Mason: **Rona Anderson**
Denis Ashmore: **John Witty**
Peter Carr: **Denis Shaw**
M'Kimba: **Phillip Rose**
Chief: **Samuel Mansaray**

Day of Reckoning
w **Donn Mullally**
d **Darcy Conyers**

During the course of a hunt, Hunter's bearer, Komo, is struck by a mamba. The boy dies and Hunter promises to take his money and personal effects to his family. Arriving at Kamo's village, he finds himself the victim of a curse.

Tracey Allen: **Jill Adams**
Peter Renard: **Barry Keegan**
Karl Dekker: **Ivor Salter**
Chief: **Orlando Martins**
Komo: **Earl Cameron**

Forest of the Night
w **Robert Yale Libott**
d **Bernard Lewis**

The discovery that Peter McLeod, his safari outfitter, has engaged him to escort Karen Lindeman, Hunter's one-time lover, into French Equatorial Africa, Hunter tries to duck the assignment.

Karen Lindeman: **Marianne Brauns**
Carl Lindeman: **Wolf Frees**
Peter McLeod: **John Rae**
Matron: **Enid Lorrimer**
Anatole: **Ken McGregor**

Sister My Spouse
w **Donn Mullally**
d **Ernest Morris**

Hunter and his gunbearer are mystified when they find a village that has recently and unaccountably been evacuated.

Only a helpless old crone remains, left to be devoured by wild animals.

Mother Superior: **Barbara Mullen**
Kamoba: **Thomas Baptiste**
Dr. Larau: **Arthur Lawrence**
Lida: **Zoremah**
Sister Agatha: **Joan Hooley**

The Trophy
w **Lee Erwin**
d **Ernest Morris**

A plane delivers two clients - and a lot of trouble - to Hunter. Bill and Laura West commission him to take them and their motion picture cameras on safari. Trouble is, a man named Kern will stoop to any lengths to get himself into the big game record book.

Bartley Kern: **Frank Leighton**
Laura West: **Jill Melford**
Bill West: **Charles Stapley**
Doug Gordon: **Robert Cawdron**

Web of Death
w **Ken Taylor**
d **Darcy Conyers**

Doctor Elvin has engaged Hunter to lead him on a mysterious safari. Only Elvin's assistant, Palmer, knows their destination - a disused copper mine in Tanganyika - rumoured to contain rich deposits of uranium.

Maria Conti: **Jeanette Sterke**
Dr. Elvin: **Peter Illing**
Jack Palmer: **Peter Reynolds**

Pegasus
w **Lee Loeb and Donn Mullally**
d **Ernest Morris**

When the man-made moon, Pegasus, comes to earth somewhere in the Kenyan jungle, Hunter is hired to guide an expedition led by scientist, Dr. Sheldon, who developed the satellite.

Marge Wilson: **Patricia Roc**
Dr. Sheldon: **Arthur Lawrence**
Harrison: **Trevor Reid**
First Security Officer: **John Baker**
Second Security Officer: **Harry Fine**
Second Bearer: **Danny Daniels**

The Jackals
w **Ellis Marcus**
d **Darcy Conyers**

Hoodlum, Tom Frazier, crashes out of prison and takes his cellmate, Lloyd Elsom, with him - at gunpoint. Escaping to the jungle, they meet Hunter, knock him to the ground and leave him for dead.

Stacey Clarke: **Leslie Dwyer**
Hannah Elsom: **Sarah Lawson**
Lloyd Elsom: **Richard Neilson**
Tom Frazier: **Victor Brooks**
Wembley: **Patrick Jordan**
Jerry Douglas: **Brian Nissen**
McCreery: **Gordon Harrison**

The Plague
w **Donn Mullally**
d **Ernest Morris**

The plague strikes Hunter's camp. Hunter sends his number one boy for medical aid, and then explains the situation to his clients Claude and Irene Holmby - but Claude is already in the early stages of the disease.

Claude Holmby: **William Lucas**
Irene Holmby: **Jennifer Jayne**
Dr. Redfern: **Robert Perceval**
Michael Bridges: **Stanley Van Beers**

The Lonely Place
w **Donn Mullally** and **Alan Cillou**
d **Ernest Morris**

Hunter and a client are fired upon from a fort set to protect a water hole. Investigating, Hunter discovers that the Semali tribe are about to mount an attack on the fort, which will lead to a native uprising.

Rankin: **Andre Morell**
Margaret Rankin: **Barbara Brown**
Richard Hyde: **Richard Peel**

Killer Leopard
w **Stanley Miller**
d **Joseph Sterling**

Atimbu, reports that leopards have been seen in the Oshowe country and Hunter is commissioned to obtain a live female leopard by a visiting scientist. But the local Witchdoctor proves to be far from friendly to the intruders.

Gomez: **Roger Delgado**
Mortimer: **Leonard Sachs**
M'Kame: **Zorenia Osborne**
Witch Doctor: **Chief Odengo**

Valley of the Dead
w **Norman Williams**
d **Ernest Morris**

The Maharaja of Kipung has money to burn. To impress his daughter, Laila, he mounts a lion hunt, led by the best white hunter in Africa, John Hunter - who soon finds himself the pawn in a dangerous game.

Maharaja: **Alec Mango**
Howard: **Lawrence Taylor**
Laila: **Edwina Carroll**
Gunsmith: **Billy Milton**
Atimbu: **Harry Baird**
Pilot: **Donavan Winter**
Chief Air Controller: **Frank Hawkins**
Air Controller: **Max Faulkner**

The Long Knife
w **Ian Stuart Black**
d **Ernest Morris**

Williams, owner of the "Williams and Crawford Collecting Station" has been attacked and is considering giving up his dangerous occupation. Hunter determines to coax his friend into changing his mind.

Sandy Williams: **Patrick Holt**
Anna Williams: **Barbara Shelley**
Dr. Mackenzie: **Jack Lambert**
Native Chef: **Andre Dakar**

Dead Man's Tale
w **Leonard Fincham**
d **Ernest Morris**

Narcotics are turning up in Mobassa and Inspector Burke of the Kenya Police cannot find the method employed. The policeman asks his friend John Hunter to join the investigation.

Kay Gibson: **Betty McDowell**
James Wilson: **Arnold Diamond**
Piet Ritter: **Martin Benson**
Insp. Burke: **Lloyd Lamble**

The Hungry Hell
w **Donn Mullally**
d **Joseph Sterling**

On safari with his client Mark Caldwell, Hunter receives a message that settlers, Alan and Thelma Thomas are in trouble. Alan has been savaged by a troop of baboons and his wife has run out of medical supplies.

Mark Caldwell: **Christopher Lee**
Thelma Thomas: **Eunice Gayson**
Alan Thomas: **Brian Worth**

Girl Hunt
w **Leonard Fincham**
d **Darcy Conyers**

Lee Holt, a rich and spoilt young heiress, wants to employ Hunter as her guide - an offer he refuses: killing wild animals for thrills doesn't appeal to him. Determined to have her own way, the girl employs two 'hunters' - who are in fact crooks.

Lee Holt: **Beth Rogan**
Paul Klinger: **Robert Cawdron**
Brad Holt: **John Longden**
Tallon: **Neal Arden**
Chauvet: **Peter Burton**
Game Warden: **Ted Archer**
Hotel Clerk: **Geoffrey Adams**

Gun Duel
w **Tony O'Grady** [aka **Brian Clemens**]
d **Ernest Morris**

Hunter is hired to escort Max Early on safari. A hunter of formidable reputation. Early has an almost pathological desire to prove himself "Top Man." To achieve this, he challenges Hunter to shoot against him - with Hunter as his prey!

Max Early: **Francis de Wolff**

Out of the Wind
w **Ken Taylor**
d **Joseph Sterling**

Hunter is employed to remove obstinate rhinos, which are trampling fields on a site where Assistant Agricultural Officer Dick Goodwyn has started a scheme to resettle Mau Mau prisoners.

Dr. Anne Clements: **Patricia Dainton**
Dick Goodwyn: **Ronan O'Casey**
Harrison: **Trevor Reid**
Kilmani: **Frank Singuineau**
Wireless Op: **Max Faulkner**
Secretary: **Leila Williams**

Second Dealer
w **Gilbert Winfield**
d **Ernest Morris**

Old timer George Stacey is swindled by two card-sharps, Harris and Farley. Determined to secure justice for his friend, Hunter and Police Superintendent Bradlow evolve a plan to teach the swindlers a lesson.

Farley: **Maurice Kaufmann**
Harris: **John McLaren**
George Stacey: **Thomas Gallagher**
Supt. Bradlow: **Tom Chatto**

Let My People Go
w **Gordon Wellesley** and **Charlotte Hastings**
d **Darcy Conyers**

Dr. Hudia combines the job of medical officer with that of chief of his tribe. When Kuyo, the Lion Man begins to terrorise his district, he calls on John Hunter for help.

Dr. Hudia: **Frank Singuineau**
Kuyo: **Danny Daniels**
Dr. Julian: **Jack Lambert**
Asst. Superintendent: **Lloyd Lamble**
Kruma: **Orlando Martins**
Hospital Assistant: **Edna McKenzie**

White Hunter:

Producer: **Norman Williams**
Executive Producer: **Sydney Box**
Music: **Philip Green**
Script Consultant: **Donn Mullally**
African Location Director: **Bernard Lewis**
Production Supervisor: **T. S. Lyndon-Hayes**

A Bernard L. Schubert Production, for ITP, for ITC World Wide Distribution
Filmed on location in Africa and at Twickenham Studios

39 monochrome 30-minute episodes
1958

William Tell

In the fourteenth century, the small town of Altdort in Switzerland was conquered by the Austrians, who ruled the community with a rod of iron wielded by the dreaded Landburgher Gessler, an obese and thoroughly evil tyrant who imposed heavy tax on his Swiss subjects and had his soldiers slay anyone who refused to pay. Only one man, a resident of the nearby village of Berglan, dared to oppose the Austrian governor - William Tell. With courage and cunning, Tell and his small band of followers fought for freedom and justice. Like England's Robin Hood, Tell robbed the rich to feed the poor, and his name became a symbol of hope for the downtrodden Swiss villagers. The first episode adapted the original story by Johann von Schiller: Tell, captured by Gessler's troops, was forced to display his renowned marksmanship with the crossbow by shooting an apple off his own son's head. With unfailing accuracy he did so but, as a precaution against Gessler's treachery, the archer secreted a second arrow upon his person with which he would have killed the Austrian governor if his marksmanship had failed him. Discovering this ruse, Gessler issued orders for Tell's arrest and the bowman was forced to retreat to a mountain hideaway where, outlawed to a cave with his wife, Hedda, and their son, Walter, he gathered around him a small group of followers who banded together in their attempt to free Swiss people from Austrian oppression.

"Come away, come away with William Tell,
Come away, to the land he loved so well.
What a day, what a day when the apple fell,
for Tell and Switzerland.
Come away with Tell to the mountain side,
look down to the pass where the tyrants ride.
Fit a bolt to your bow and down they go
for Tell and Switzerland.
Hurry on, hurry on to the dungeon cell,
hurry on, hurry on where the losers dwell.
But he'll escape from the jaws of Hell
for Tell and Switzerland."

Regular cast:
William Tell: **Conrad Phillips**
Hedda: **Jennifer Jayne**
Walter: **Richard Rogers**
Gessler: **Willoughby Goddard**
Fertog [The Bear]: **Nigel Greene**

The Emperor's Hat
w **Rene Wilde** and **Leslie Arliss** [from an original story by Rene Wilde]
d **Ralph Smart**

Overrun by Austrians, and ruled by the evil tyrant, Landburgher Gessler, Switzerland soon forms a resistance movement. One such band is led by William Tell.

Hedda Tell: **Jennifer Jayne**
Walter Tell: **Richard Rogers**
Gessler: **Willoughby Goddard**
Frederick: **Norman Mitchell**
Furst: **Ernest Milton**
Sentry: **Derry Nesbitt**

The Hostages
w **Doreen Montgomery** [from an original story by **Ralph Smart**]
d **Peter Maxwell**

Annoyed by Tell's activities, Gessler issues orders to have the archer arrested - but Tell has disappeared. Not to be outdone, Gessler seizes six villagers as hostage: each of them will die - unless Tell returns within 12 hours.

Hedda Tell: **Jennifer Jayne**
Walter Tell: **Richard Rogers**
Gessler: **Willoughby Goddard**
Captain Hofmanstahl: **Peter Hammond** [intro]
Fritz: **Roy Purcell** [intro]
Franz: **James Booth**
Gretel: **Celia Hewitt**

Secret Death
w **Doreen Montgomery** [from an original story by **Ralph Smart**]
d **Peter Maxwell**

When his wife is captured by Gessler's troops and sentenced to death, Tell offers himself in exchange - a dangerous move? Not when you have the loyalty of several trustworthy supporters.

Hedda Tell: **Jennifer Jayne**
Gessler: **Willoughby Goddard**
Captain Hofmanstahl: **Peter Hammond**
Judge Furst: **Jack Lambert** [intro]
First guard: **Peter Welch**
Schmidt: **Howard Lang**
and
Schaffner: **Sydney James**

The Gauntlet of St. Gerhardt
w **Doreen Montgomery** [from an original story by **Ralph Smart**]
d **Peter Maxwell**

A religious relic, the Gauntlet of St Gerhardt, appears to inspire the Swiss to feats of valour. Gessler makes plans to steal it by having the Abbot who guards it killed. Tell, however, has other plans.

Hedda Tell: **Jennifer Jayne**
Walter Tell: **Richard Rogers**
Gessler: **Willoughby Goddard**
Captain Werner: **Derry Nesbitt**
Major Augustin: **Howard Pays**
Trooper Strauss: **Edward Judd**
and
Father Abbot: **Ian Wallace** [intro]

The Prisoner
w **John Kruse**
d **Peter Maxwell**

On his way to deliver a message to William Tell, a resistance man is captured and taken to a secluded fortress. It appears Tell will never learn his secret - but the resistance leader has other plans.

Hedda Tell: **Jennifer Jayne**
Bullinger: **Bruce Seton** [intro]
Petitpierre: **Jerry Verno**
Max: **Michael Caine**
Karl: **John Howard Davies**
Erlanger: **Keith Pyott**
Tasker: **Richard Shaw**

Voice in the Night
w **Ralph Smart**
d **Terry Bishop**

After a disagreement with Gessler, Judge Furst is thrown into a dungeon. His clerk - a secret Austrian collaborator - is appointed Judge in his place, but Tell plans to expose him.

Hedda Tell: **Jennifer Jayne**
Walter Tell: **Richard Rogers**
Gessler: **Willoughby Goddard**

Frederick: **Derry Nesbitt**
Judge Furst: **Jack Lambert**
Jules Gunther: **Ronald Leigh-Hunt**
and
Schwartz: **Michael Ripper**

The Assassins
w **Ralph Smart** [from an original story by **Rene Wilde**]
d **Terry Bishop**

Two Swiss collaborators, arrested by Gessler for murdering Prince Karl, are given a chance to save their necks from the hangman's noose. They must discover Tell's hiding place and kill him!

Hedda Tell: **Jennifer Jayne**
Walter Tell: **Richard Rogers**
Gessler: **Willoughby Goddard**
Maddeaux: **Edwin Richfield**
Bolf: **Alfred Burke**
Captain Frederick: **Willoughby Gray**
Fritz: **Roy Purcell**

The Baroness
w **John Kruse** [from an original story by **Ralph Smart**]
d **Peter Maxwell**

When her husband is invited to visit the castle of a beautiful baroness who says she is being blackmailed, Hedda, suspecting the woman of working for Gessler, follows Tell and uncovers a devious plot.

Hedda Tell: **Jennifer Jayne**
Gessler: **Willoughby Goddard**
Baroness Ulbricht: **Delphi Lawrence**
Colonel Bullinger: **Bruce Seton**
Maria: **Norma Parnell**
Hilde: **Olive McFarland**
Johann: **Arthur Skinner**

The Elixir
w **Lindsay Galloway** [from an original story by **Ralph Smart**]
d **Terry Bishop**

A local monastery, run by Italian monks, is making a delicious brew, then donating the proceeds to founding a school for Swiss children. Never one to pass an opportunity to swell his coffers, Gessler arrests the holy men.

Hedda Tell: **Jennifer Jayne**
Walter Tell: **Richard Rogers**
Gessler: **Willoughby Goddard**
Ferdinand: **Jack Watling**
Brother Jules: **John McCarthy**
Gatekeeper: **Hamlyn Benson**
and
Father Abbot: **Ian Wallace**

The Suspect
w **Doreen Montgomery** [from an original story by **Larry Forester**]
d **Quentin Lawrence**

Tell must prove a young girl innocent of the charge of giving information to the Austrians about secret arms shipments to the resistance workers. If he doesn't, the girl will be hanged by the townspeople.

Waldmann: **Thomas G. Duggan**
Emil: **John McCarthy**
Gaston: **Harold Scott**
Cruner: **Peter Bennett**
Austrian Officer: **Edward Judd**

Josephine: **Sheila Raynor**
Dagma: **Marianne Benet**

The Cuckoo
w **Ralph Smart**
d **Peter Maxwell**

Early every morning, Gessler is awakened by a cuckoo. At his wits' end, his problem is compounded further when he receives a message from the Emperor demanding taxes Gessler hasn't yet collected!

Hedda Tell: **Jennifer Jayne**
Walter Tell: **Richard Rogers**
Gessler: **Willoughby Goddard**
Hofmanstahl: **Peter Hammond**
Ferdinand: **Jack Watling**
Sergeant: **David Davenport**
Conrad: **George Benson**

The Bear
w **Doreen Montgomery** [from an original story by **Michael Connor**]
d **Ernest Morris**

When his son joins Tell's group, and refuses to return home, the Bear, a robber, swears to seek revenge on Tell and his followers. As events turn out, the two men form a uneasy but beneficial alliance.

Gessler: **Willoughby Goddard**
Hofmanstahl: **Peter Hammond**
Fertog: **Nigel Green**
Bruno: **John Howard Davies**
Hans: **Graham Stewart**
Burgomaster: **Meadows White**

The Magic Powder
w **Martin Worth** [from an original story by **Ralph Smart**]
d **Peter Maxwell**

Doctor Klein, a scientist working for Gessler, invents an explosive powder for use in road-making. When his employer decides to use the invention for warfare, Klein seeks refuge with William Tell - who has greater need of such a discovery.

Hedda Tell: **Jennifer Jayne**
Gessler: **Willoughby Goddard**
Hofmanstahl: **Peter Hammond**
Doctor Kleine: **Henry Oscar**
Ludwig: **Gerald Cross**
Soldier: **Anthony Parker**

The Golden Wheel
w **Michael Connor**
d **Peter Maxwell**

Having discovered where the resistance hides its funds, Gessler makes plans to stop further money reaching them. As always, he has reckoned without William Tell's interference - and the Landburgher's coffers suffer as a result.

Gessler: **Willougyby Goddard**
Wolfgang: **Derek Godfrey**
Hanzler: **Patrick Troughton**
Fritz: **Charles Ross**
Headman of Dosten: **Richard Warner**

The Bride
w **Doreen Montgomery** [from an original story by **John Kruse**]
d **Quentin Lawrence**

Maddelenna is being forcibly taken to Altdorf Castle as a bride for Gessler. Tell sees this as an opportunity to teach their enemy a lesson, but his wife Hedda is not so sure.

Gessler: **Willoughby Goddard**
Maddelena: **Nadja Regen**
Anton: **Glyn Owen**
The Bear: **Nigel Green**
Marthe: **Mary Webster**
Captain Huber: **Richard Bebb**
Colonel: **Lloyd Lamble**

The Boy Slaves
w **John Kruse**
d **Terry Bishop**

Can Tell trust the word of his enemy? He must, if he is to obtain the release of several young boys whom Gessler is holding as slaves in a labour camp. Alone and unarmed he may be - but Tell has an ace up his sleeve.

Walter Tell: **Richard Rogers**
Gessler: **Willoughby Goddard**
Carl: **Frazer Hines**
Aunt Maria: **Marjorie Rhodes**
Count Heinemann: **Bryan Coleman**
Schulemburg: **Derry Nesbitt**

The Young Widow
w **Paul Christie**
d **Peter Maxwell**

Having escaped from Gessler's troops, Tell and his wife are given refuge by the beautiful Countess Von Marheim. Recognising her guests, Paul, her servant, threatens to inform Gessler of their whereabouts - unless the Countess agrees to marry him.

Hedda Tell: **Jennifer Jayne**
Gessler: **Willoughby Goddard**
Hofmanstahl: **Peter Hammond**
Paul: **Charles Houston**
Kurt: **Julian Somers**
Tina: **Norma Parnell**
Countess Von Markheim: **Melissa Stribling**

Landslide
w **John Kruse**
d **Terry Bishop**

Tell comes face to face with his exact double - an Austrian imported by Gessler to impersonate the resistance leader and rob Swiss peasants. But which of the look-alikes is which? Gessler's attempts to find out cost him dearly.

Hedda Tell: **Jennifer Jayne**
Gessler: **Willoughby Goddard**
Aunt Maria: **Marjorie Rhodes**
Herr Specker: **Charles Lloyd Pack**
Weber: **Charles Houston**
Josef: **Wilfred Brambell**
Tax Collector: **Frank Thornton**

The Trap
w **Doreen Montgomery** [from an original story by **Max Savage**]
d **Quentin Lawrence**

By using a traitor planted in Tell's camp, Gessler plans to smash the resistance movement in one swoop. But even the best-laid schemes are prone to failure - as the Landburgher soon discovers.

Hedda Tell: **Jennifer Jayne**

The Bear: **Nigel Green**
Max: **Richard Burrell**
Rudi: **Peter Torquill**
Ingrid: **Colette Wilde**
Officer: **Walter Gotell**
and
Peter: **Robert Shaw**

The Shrew
w **Max Savage**
d **Peter Maxwell**

Hedda, lured away by a message that her sister is ill, finds herself an unwilling pawn in Gessler's latest plot to squash the resistance. Confident that this time Tell will be taken, the Austrian is in for a surprise.

Hedda Tell: **Jennifer Jayne**
Gessler: **Willoughby Goddard**
Honest Karl: **Roy Godfrey**
Gretel: **Joanna Dunham**
Hans: **Keith Pyott**
Colonel Wentzel: **John Salew**
and
Gertrude: **Harriette Johns**

Manhunt
w **Doreen Montgomery** [from an original story by **Ralph Smart**]
d **Peter Maxwell**

Trapped on an island owned by Prince Erik, a man who enjoys hunting human prey, Tell's career appears to be at an end - but help arrives from a most unexpected quarter, and the resistance leader finds a new ally.

Heinrich: **Kevin Stoney**
Peter: **Scott Finch**
Prince Erik: **Christopher Lee**
Count Hegel: **Leslie Perrins**
Vogel: **Cyril Chamberline**

The Killer
w **Lindsay Galloway**
d **Peter Maxwell**

Accused of murdering a partisan helper and stealing his gold, Tell must find a way to prove his innocence - and that's not so easy when you suspect one of your accusers of being the real killer.

Gessler: **Willoughby Goddard**
Burgomaster: **Derek Godfrey**
Frau Anna: **Monica Grey**
Strauss: **Kevin Stoney**
Frau Strauss: **Sally Travers**
Merchant: **Richard Vernon**
Klaus: **Alex Scott**

The Surgeon
w **Doreen Montgomery**
d **Peter Maxwell**

Seriously wounded, Tell is taken to the home of a Swiss surgeon. To throw Gessler off their trail, Tell's followers pretend their leader is stricken with the plague. Will their ruse work? Tell's life depends on the outcome.

Hedda Tell: **Jennifer Jayne**
Gessler: **Willoughby Goddard**
The Bear: **Nigel Green**
Kramer: **Derek Aylward**
Von Eckenburg: **David Blake Kelly**
Heinburgher: **Frank Thornton**
Apothecary: **Stanley Van Beers**

The Ensign
w **Max Savage** and **Leslie Arliss**
d **Quentin Lawrence**

When faced with conflict between duty and conscience, Fritz, a young Austrian soldier, unexpectedly turns not to Gessler, but to William Tell for help - a move which places the resistance leader's life in great peril.

Gessler: **Willoughby Goddard**
The Bear: **Nigel Green**
Fritz: **John Carson**
Hoffman: **Edward Evans**
Grand Duke: **Andre Van Gyseghem**
Hugo: **Julian Somers**
Trooper Strauss: **John Maxim**

The Unwelcome Stranger
w **Paul Christie**
d **Peter Maxwell**

Investigating why people from the swordmaking village of Linzon have stopped sending arms to his headquarters. Tell's visit to the community is treated with an air of suspicion. What's more, the villagers are anxious to get rid of him. Why?

Karl: **David De Keyser**
Dina: **Susan Travers**
Hofer: **Peter Swanwick**
Martin: **Derren Nesbitt**
Heinz: **John McCarthy**
Andreas: **Norman Macowan**
Capt. Markheim: **John Maxim**

The Avenger
w **Lindsay Galloway**
d **Anthony Squire**

When Tell investigates why two envoys disappeared while on their way to him to discuss a treaty of friendship, he uncovers a far greater mystery - one that threatens to engulf his family and will ultimately test the loyalty of his followers.

Number One: **Willoughby Gray**
Quirini : **Ralph Michael**
Louis: **Derek Waring**
Anna: **Diana Lambert**
Aldo: **Raymond Young**
Hilaire: **Peter Reynolds**
Duke of Burgundy: **John Le Mesurier**

The Bandit
w **Doreen Montgomery** [from an original story by **Ralph Smart**]
d **Anthony Squire**

When one of his men fails to return from a mission to Rinaldo, a rival resistance leader, Tell suspects treachery. Unknown to him, a bandit is in the area, under orders from Gessler, seeking to cast doubt on Tell's activities.

Rinaldo: **Brian Rawlinson**
Carl: **Maurice Kaufman**
Marco: **Kenneth Cope**
Fritz: **William Abney**
Eva: **Simone Lovell**
Hans: **Robert Raglan**
Landlord: **Michael Peake**

Gessler's Daughter
w **Lindsay Galloway**
d **Ernest Morris**

With his daughter Anna kidnapped and held for ransom, Gessler knows of only one man who can help him obtain her release - his arch enemy, William Tell. But can he swallow his pride long enough to meet Tell on neutral ground?

Hedda Tell: **Jennifer Jayne**
Gessler: **Willoughby Goddard**
Anna: **Perlita Neilson**
Jakob Muller: **Michael Golden**
Frau Muller: **Catherine Finn**
Nurse: **Patsy Smart**
Vogler: **Howard Pays**

The Raid
w **Leslie Arliss** and **Rene Wilde**
d **Leslie Arliss**

Disguised as Austrian soldiers, Tell and Hans enter the fortress at Schwartzburg. Their mission is to seize arms needed by the resistance - but disaster strikes when Tell is recognised by a guard.

Walter Tell: **Richard Rogers**
Gessler: **Willoughby Goddard**
Hans: **Michael Brennan**
Fritz: **Tony Thawnton**
Officer of the Guard: **Terence Cooper**
Sergeant: **Peter Bennett**

The General's Daughter
w **Ian Stuart Black**
d **Peter Maxwell**

While collecting provisions from a Swiss patriot, the Bear is captured and flung into Gessler's dungeons. Tell must devise an ingenious method of engineering his friend's release.

Gessler: **Willoughby Goddard**
The Bear: **Nigel Green**
General: **Bruce Seton**
Maria: **Ann Hughes**
Stefan: **Scot Finch**
Sgt. Wiener: **Michael Caine**
Cpl. Muller: **Peter Torquill**

Castle of Fear
w **Roger Marshall** [from an original story by **Max Savage**]
d **Peter Maxwell**

Visiting Werner Castle to track down the murderer of a resistance leader, Tell finds himslef involved in a deadly game of fear and intrigue - with his own life offered to the victor.

Gustaf: **Ferdy Mayne**
Eric: **Edwin Richfield**
Hans: **Keith Rawlings**
Anton: **Alan Rowe**
Klein: **Erik Chitty**
Eva: **Caroline Denzil**
Klaus: **William Peacock**

The Black Brothers
w **Arnold Abbot**
d **Quentin Lawrence**

Stealing arms intended for the Swiss resistance movement is crime enough, but when three Italian rogues compound their crime by attempting to sell the weapons to William Tell, they have cause for concern indeed.

Hedda Tell: **Jennifer Jayne**
Granny Rossi: **Eileen Way**
Luigi: **Roger Delgado**

Pietro: **Paul Stassino**
Guiseppe: **Harry Lockhart**
Carlo: **Warren Mitchell**
Anna: **Gillian Vaughan**

The Lost Letter
w **Michael Connor**
d **Terry Bishop**

So anxious is he to read a letter from Judge Furst informing William Tell of the location of a large arms shipment, Gessler fails to realise that the missive is in the sole of his own boot. When finding it, the hapless Austrian really puts his foot into it!

Gessler: **Willoughby Goddard**
Frederick: **Derry Nesbitt**
Franz: **Alex Scott**
Judge Furst: **Jack Lambert**
Muller: **John Dearth**
Vera: **Olive McFarland**
and
Cobbler: **Max Bacon**

Secret Weapon
w **Doreen Montgomery** [story by **Arnold Abbott**]
d **Ernest Morris**

The resistance leader and The Bear set out to investigate reports that Gessler is erecting new fortifications along the Swiss coastline. Should the rumour be confirmed, it will effectively cut off the resistance group's escape route.

Gessler: **Willoughby Goddard**
The Bear: **Nigel Green**
Jacques Brun: **John Horsley**
Captain of Fort: **Jack Watling**
Hans: **Derrich Sherwin**
Heinrich: **Harvey Hall**
Gunmaster: **Willoughby Gray**

The Master Spy
w **Doreen Montgomery**
d **Ernest Morris**

Armed with a new 'secret weapon' - Mara, a beautiful, but highly dangerous spy known only as the Shadow - Gessler lures Tell and his followers into a trap. Could this spell the end of Tell's fight for freedom?

Gessler: **Willoughby Goddard**
The Bear: **Nigel Green**
Anton: **Glyn Owen**
Hofmanstahl: **Jack Watling**
Heinz: **Harvey Hall**
Rosa: **Maureen Beck**
and
Mara: **Adrienne Corri**

The Traitor
w **Roger Marshall** and **Leslie Arliss**
d **Peter Maxwell**

Certain that no one knows their whereabouts, Tell and his wife visit a friendly resistance leader's camp. During their journey home, they are attacked by a gang of rogues.

Kramer: **William Lucas**
Bullinger: **Bruce Seton**
Major: **Charles Ross**
Sergeant: **Derren Nesbitt**
Sentry: **Richard Clarke**
Rothman: **Neil Hallett**

The Spider
w **Roger Marshall** [original story by **Ralph Smart**]
d **Ernest Morris**

Hearing that a ruthless Austrian commander, nicknamed The Spider, has captured two of his men and threatens to torture them unless they divulge the location of Tell's camp, the resistance leader infiltrates The Spider's ranks.

Klaus: **John Horsley**
Johan: **Howard Pays**
Captain: **Robert Cawdron**
Von Brenen: **Trevor Reid**
Gerda: **Sheelah Wilcock**
First Child: **Deborah Watling**
Guest star
Donald Pleasance as The Spider

The Mountain People
w **Doreen Montgomery** [story by **John Kruse**]
d **Quentin Lawrence**

A beautiful young girl, rescued by Tell from a troop of Austrian soldiers, leads him into a situation from which the resistance leader barely escapes with his life - and reputation - intact.

Eve: **Maureen Davis**
Margit: **Catherine Finn**
Sgt. Johann: **Lee Montague**
Capt. Kraus: **Terence Cooper**
Josef: **James Booth**
Father: **Fred Johnson**
Major Richter: **John Dearth**

Undercover
w **Lindsay Galloway**
d **Ernest Morris**

Hearing that a close friend, an agent to the Emperor, has died, Tell enters enemy territory disguised as a trader. He intends to rescue Magda, the Emperor's daughter - but things go disastrously wrong.

Johann: **Peter Welch**
Magda: **Jill Browne**
Michaelis: **Ian Colin**
Reinhardt: **John Longden**
Sebastian: **David Peel**
Chancellor: **Stanley Van Beers**
Emperor: **Derek Bond**

William Tell:

Producer: **Leslie Arliss**
Executive Producer: **Ralph Smart**
Production Supervisor: **Aida Young**
Assistant Director: **David Tomblin**
Casting Director: **Harry Fine**
The William Tell song lyric by: **Harold Purcell**
The William Tell song sung by: **David Whitfield**
Music Director: **Sydney John Kay**

An Incorporated Television Programmes Co. Ltd. Production
Filmed at the National Studios, Elstree

39 monochrome 30-minute episodes
1957

The Zoo Gang

The exploits of four World War II French Resistance fighters who found themselves reunited 30 years later to fight crime and intrigue in Europe. Four service veterans who re-formed to use their resources, guile and experience to become modern-day Robin Hoods who stole from criminals and distributed the spoils of their 'crimes' to the needy.

Organiser of the team was Captain Tommy Devon, codename the Elephant, who ran a small jewellery business on the French Riviera. Lending his electronics expertise to the gang's cause was former American secret agent Stephen Halliday, codename the Fox, now a New York business executive. Madame Manouche Roget, codename the Leopard [and widow of Claude Roger, 'The Wolf', who was a member of the Resistance until his death at the hands of the Gestapo, and whose death the gang had sworn to avenge] ran a bar in Nice. An expert with explosives, her safe-cracking talents were put to good use by Tommy and Co. Rounding up the quarter was ex-Canadian Air Force Lieutenant Alec Marlowe, codename the Tiger, whose wizardry with mechanics kept the show on the road.

Appearing in all six stories was French policeman Lt. George Roget, Mamouche's son. Despite suspecting that his mother and her friends were up to 'something' [he recognised old 'Zoo Gang' tricks as those spoken about by his mother], he ignored their activities and allowed them to pull off jobs without reporting his suspicions to his superior.

Star-studded though it was, the series failed to live up to expectations. The enterprise folded after six stories.

Regular cast:
Tommy Devon: **John Mills**
Stephen Halliday: **Brian Keith**
Manouche Roget: **Lilli Palmer**
Alec Marlowe: **Barry Morse**
Lt George Roget: **Michael Petrovitch**
Jill Burton [Tommy's niece]: **Seretta Wilson**

Revenge: Post-dated
w **Reginald Rose**
d **Sidney Hayers**

The Gestapo had dubbed them 'The Zoo Gang' because of their French Resistance-adopted animal names. They had been betrayed to the Nazis and found themselves imprisoned and tortured. Thirty years later Tommy Devon recognises the man entering his shop as Maurice Boucher, the Nazi who had him arrested and tortured. Tommy contacts his Resistance comrades and they plan their revenge. The Zoo Gang are back in business.

Boucher: **Walter Gotell**
Calvin Smith: **Henry McCarthy**
Harry Crane: **Gordon Tanner**
Henry Davis: **Robert Henderson**
Mrs Darbot: **Betty Lynne**
Chauffeur: **Freddy Clarke**
Jill Burton: **Seretta Wilson** [intro]

Mindless Murder
w **Howard Dimsdale**
d **Johnny Hough**

Three apparently motiveless murders on the French Riviera lead the Zoo Gang to uncover an exortion racket. But in order to expose the ringleaders and protect the lives of two famous film stars, Manouche must set herself up as the killers' next target.

Lynn Martin: **Ingrid Pitt**
Anthony Martin: **Clinton Greyn**
Jean: **Alex Scott**
Claude: **Louis Negin**

Paul: **Aharon Ipale**
Michel: **Ray Boyd**
Herbault: **Morris Perry**
Jill Burton: **Seretta Wilson**

African Misfire
w **Peter Yeldham**
d **Sidney Hayers**

When a deposed African president's art collection is stolen on its way to an auction in France, the Zoo Gang make plans to recover it. Their interest is a matter of principle: the proceeds of the sale were earmarked for African famine relief - or so they're led to believe.

Jacques Picard: **Kieron Moore**
General Naganda: **Nathan Dambuza**
Jombote: **Earl Cameron**
Ferrand: **Leonard Trolley**
Major: **Edward Cast**
Jill Burton: **Seretta Wilson**

The Counterfeit Trap
w **John Kruse**
d **Johnny Hough**

It's a daring plan: to steal forged money to pay for smuggled gold. That's their intention, but playing two ends against the middle is a game fraught with danger - as Alec Marlowe discovers to his cost.

Judge Gautier: **Peter Cushing**
Brigitte Gautier: **Jacqueline Pearce**
Paul Sabot: **Philip Madoc**
Raoul: **Stephan Chase**
Carlo: **Mark Colleano**
Nico: **Chris Dillinger**
Pierre: **Leon Lissek**
Challon: **Anthony Stamboulich**
Jill Burton: **Seretta Wilson**

The Lion Hunt
w **Sean Graham**
d **Sidney Hayers**

The arrest by the French of El Leon, a Latin American revolutionary viewed as a hero by most of the world, proves to be an embarrassment to the French Government. The media are demanding his release, but to accede to their wishes could spark off an international incident. Solution: call in the Zoo Gang - but is it that simple?

Dupont: **Leo Genn**
Pedro: **Roger Delgado**
De Broux: **Ferdy Mayne**
Colonel Martin: **Ed Devereaux**
Mercier: **Bill Kenwright**
Reporter: **Neville Jason**
Pierre: **Vic Armstrong**
Guard: **Richard Woodworth**
Jill Burton: **Seretta Wilson**

The Twisted Cross
w **William Fairchild**
d **Johnny Hough**

Informed that Schroeder, a Nazi officer, has received - and concealed - a Nazi fortune in gold, the Zoo Gang set out to recoup the treasure and use the proceeds from its sale to help those more needy than themselves.

Hercule: **Michael da Costa**
Schroeder: **Bernard Kay**
Helene Schroeder: **Ann Lynn**

Andre: **Tim Hardy**
Inspector: **Olaf Pooley**
Phillipe: **Alf Joint**
Customs Man: **Kenneth Gilbert**
Jules: **Vic Armstrong**

The Zoo Gang [1971: Paul Galico: Pan Books: reprint of Galico's original story with TV cast cover].

The Zoo Gang:

Based on the book by **Paul Gallico**
Developed for television by **Reginald Rose**
Producer: **Herbert Hirschman**
Associated Producer: **John Pellatt**
'The Zoo Gang' theme by **Paul** and **Linda McCartney**
Music composed and conducted by - **Ken Thorne**
Music Editor: **Norman Cole**
Script Consultant: **Howard Dimsdale**
Production Manager: **Geoffrey Helman**
Assistant Director: **Bert Blatt**
Casting Director: **Weston Drury Jnr**
Make-up: **Philip Leakey**
Hairdresser: **Barbara Ritchie**
Wardrobe Supervisor: **Jackie Cummins**

An ITC Production for World Wide Distribution
Made on location in France and at Pinewood Studios
[Nice sequences filmed with the kind co-operation of Le Ville de Nice]

6 colour 60-minute episodes
1974

Other Shows

Other shows co-produced [or distributed by] ITC

Cannonball

39 monochrome 30-minute episodes
1958

The adventures of truckers Mike "Cannonball" Malone and his mate, Jerry Austin, who drive their International Transport Trucking Company lorry into unexpected danger and adventure as they speed their way across Canada and into the United States. Working on the theory that sinister forces are at work to prevent them from delivering their goods, the duo needs brawn to cope with the fraught situations they encounter and brains to forestall their adversaries. Mike has more than enough for both of them.

Mike "Cannonball" Malone: **Paul Birch**
Jerry Austin: **William Campbell**

Episode Titles:
The Runaway Truck
Pills
Willy
Sights on Safety *
The Iron Lung
The Big Ambulance
Hostage
Small Cargo
Green-Eyed Monster
Moose Hunt
Shock
Nitro Haul
Girl at Joe's Place
The Attack
Sauce for the Goose
Mark Time
The Dog
Butch
Fallout
The Necklace
Under Cover
Nanette
Big Buck
The Little Old Man
Marooned
Lil's Place
Vendetta
The Girl Reporter
The Has Been
Flying Dutchman
Rodeo
Trip to Buffalo
Wild Party
Ginny
The Racket
Driving School
Eye Witness
Snake Eyes
Tunnel Eyes

✍ Episode denoted * co-starred **Shane Rimmer**

The Forest Rangers

104 colour 30-minute episodes
1964 - 65

A series for the young viewer, combining the age-old appeal of trapping, trekking and forest life in the Canadian Woods.

Primarily about the Junior Rangers, four boys and two girls, attached to the Forest Rangers, the men responsible for the conservation of wild life, forest fire control and game regulating, there were plenty of dramatic incidents to keep the mums and dads glued to the set.

The Rangers:
Ranger Keeley: **Graydon Gould**
Joe Two-Rivers: **Mickael Zenon**
Sergeant Scott: **Gordon Pisdent**
Chub: **Ralph Endersby**

The Junior Rangers:
Peter: **Rex Hagen**
Steve: **Don Mason**
Mike: **Peter Tully**
Ted: **George Allen**
Kathy: **Susan Conway**
Denise: **Barbara Pierce**

Fury

116 monochrome 30-minute episodes
1955 - 56

The story of Joey Newton, a tough little waif from the city who is given the chance of a new life on a ranch where wild horses are caught and broken. His best friend is Fury, a magnificent stallion, leader of a herd of wild horses, presented to the boy by ranch-owner, Jim Newton, the man who brought him to his Broken Wheel Ranch and [eventually] adopts Joey.
As time passes, Fury comes to recognise no-one but Joey as his master - their adventures together providing the background to Joey's story.

Jim Newton: **Peter Graves**
Joey Newton: **Bobby Diamond**
Fury: **Gypsy**
Pete [a hired hand]: **William Fawcett**
Helen [Joey's schoolteacher]: **Ann Robinson**
Pee-Wee [his friend]: **Jimmy Baird**
Harriet [Jim's sister]: **Nan Leslie**
The Sheriff: **James Sealy**
The Deputy Sheriff: **Guy Teague**

Hawkeye and the Last of the Mohicans

39 monochrome 30-minute episodes
1957

The adventure of frontier scout Hawkeye 'the Long Rifle' and his blood brother. Chingachgook, the last of the Mohican race, who wage a never-ending battle against ruthless men who, for their own tawdry gain, stir up trouble between the "Redskins" and "Palefaces" in the New York State territories occupied by the Huron Indians - sworn enemies of the Mohican brave.

Hawkeye: **Jon Hart**
Chingachgook: **Lon Chaney Jr**

Episode Titles:
Hawkeye's Homecoming
The Way-Station *
The Delaware Hoax
The Contest
The Search
The Scapegoat *
The Snake Tattoo
The Medicine Man

The Stubborn Pioneer
The Washington Story
Circle of Hate
Powder Keg
False Witness
False Faces
The Threat
The Promised Valley
The Brute
The Servant
The Colonel and His Lady
The Ethan Allen Story
The Huron Tomahawk
The Coward
The Witch
The Soldier
Winter Passage
The Girl
The Prisoner **
The Franklin Story
The Wild One
The Reckoning
The Indian Doll
The Tolliver Gang
The Traunt
The Long Rifles
The Printer
The Royal Grant
La Salle's Treasure
The Morristown Story
Revenge

✍ Episode denoted * co-starred **James Doohan**
✍ Episode denoted ** co-starred **Shane Rimmer**

Mystery is My Business
32 monochrome 30-minute episodes
1955

His business - mystery. His name - Ellery Queen. Clever deduction combined with riveting danger see the master detective and his father, police officer Richard Queen, surviving threats from racketeers, blackmailers and undesirables from the criminal underworld.

Ellery Queen: **Hugh Marlow**
Inspector Richard Queen: **Florenz Ames**
Nikki [Ellery's secretary]: **Charlotte Keane**

The New Adventures of Charlie Chan
39 monochrome 30-minute episodes
1957

The adventures of Earl Derr Bigger's astute and inscrutable Chinese detective who, touring Europe with his "Number One Son", Barry, is asked to bring his shrewd Oriental mind to bear on a series of unexpected and baffling mysteries.
No matter what the port of call, Chan finds danger in the shadows and villains around every corner. Despite the bumbling antics of Barry, he uncovers clues in crimes of jealousy, greed and revenge. As adept at disguise as he is at intrigue, the ingenious investigator is as sly and as shady as the characters he encounters. Step by step, he outmanoeuvres crooks and solves cases armed with keen insight and wit... always with one more trick up his sleeve, the wisdom to surmount the dangers that surround him.
Hidden beneath masses of make-up, actor J. Carrol Naish had little to do beyond spouting the sayings of Confucius -

which apparently proved helpful to him when deliberating over some newly-found clue.

Regular cast:
Charlie Chan: **J. Carrol Naish**
Barry: **James Hong**
Inspector Duff: **Rupert Davies**
Inspector Marlowe: **Hugh Williams**

Episode Titles:
Charlie's Highland Fling
Backfire
Death of a Don
The Patient in Room 21
Final Curtain
The Counterfeiters
No Holiday For Murder
Exhibit in Wax
The Raiput Ruby
Hamlet in Flames
The Sweater
Voodoo Death
Circle of Fear
Patron of the Arts
The Ex-Patriot
The Hands of Hora Bass
The Airport Murder Case
Dateline Executioner
The Chippendale Racket
The Invalid
Something Old, Something New
The Man in the Wall
Man With 100 Faces
A Bowl by Cellini
Kidnap
Three Men On a Raft
Point of No Return
No Future For Frederick
The Nobel Art of Murder
Safe Deposit
Three Into One
Rhyme Or Treason
Without Fear
Death at High Tide
The Great Salvos
Blind Man's Bluff
The Lost Face
The Secret of the Sea
Your Money Or Your Wife

Produced by: **Rudolph Flothow**
Executive Producer: **Leon Fromkess**
Associate Producer: **Herman Blaser**
Story Editor: **Jerry Sackheim**
Production Manager: **Aida Young**
Assistant Director: **David Tomblin**
Make-up: **Colin Garde**
Directors:
Don Chaffey, Alvin Rakoff, Leslie Arliss, Charlie Haas, Charles Bennett, Les Goodwins, Jack Gage
Writers:
Richard Grey, John Butler, Terence Maples, Frederick Schiller, Gene Wang, Doris Gilbert, Lee Erwin, Sam Neuman.

A Television Programs of America Presentation, in association with the Incorporated Television Programme Company Limited.
Made on location in England

New York Confidential
39 monochrome 30-minute episodes
1958

Dateline: New York, a city teeming with gripping stories for a newspaperman. The investigations of city desk reporter, Lee Cochran, a man who's on the inside track of events that make front-page news. A man who gets his stories, whatever the danger they may lead him into, Cochran never lets go until he has learned the truth behind the story.

Ramar of the Jungle

52 monochrome 30-minute episodes
1952

Adventures set in the Nairobi jungle [later India] the series depicted the bond of friendship between Dr Tom Reynolds and the natives, who see him as their protector. Affectionately known as Ramar [White Witch Doctor], the doctor engages in scientific work in the wildest areas of the jungle, curing illness and defending his friends from the unscrupulous white men and tribal witch doctors.

Ramar: **Jon Hall**
Ogden [his assistant]: **Ray Montgomery**
Zahir [a native]: **Victor Millan**

Seaway

28 monochrome 60-minute episodes,
plus 2 colour 60-minute episodes.
1969

The investigations of Nick King, agent for an organisation responsible for security in the constant flow of teeming, vibrant life along the great Saint Lawrence Seaway in Canada.

Nick King: **Stephen Young**
Admiral Fox: **Austin Willis**

✍ Two 90-minute features were compiled from the colour episodes, plus two monochrome stories: *Affair With a Killer* and *Don't Forget to Wipe the blood Off* respectively.

Whiplash

18 monochrome 30-minute episodes
1960

The exciting era of the gold-rush in Australia in the 1950's, when the Cobb and Co. stageline opened up thousands of miles of the hinterland during a time when the country was emerging from its days of penal colony history.
Determined to forge lines of communication into the very heart of the 'new' country. Christopher Cobb, a man with steady-nerves, but dangerous when pushed, forges his way through the searing heat, choking dust and hundreds of miles of waterless country meeting violence, greed and murder along the way. Mixing with gamblers and fortune-hunters, he establishes his export-import business and freight line despite the bushrangers who would see him robbed - or dead.

Regulars:
Chris Cobb: **Peter Graves**
Dan Ledward: **Anthony Wickert**

Episode Titles:
Convict Town
Episode in Bathurst *
Sarong *
The Actress *
Rider on the Hill
Love Story in Gold

The Other Side of the Swan
Barbed Wire
Dutchman's Reef
The Bone that Whispered
The Secret of the Screaming Hills
Act of Courage *
The Twisted Road
Day of the Hunter
The Solid Gold Brigade
Stage for Two
Canoomba Incident
The Rushing Sands

✍ Episodes denoted * written by **Gene Roddenberry**.

Producer: **M. Bernard Fox, Maury Geraghty**
Associate Producer: **John Meredyth-Lucas**

An Artransa Production
Filmed on location in Australia

****

The People

Abbott Arnold
Wrote the **William Tell** episode *The Black Brothers* and the story for *Secret Weapon* [teleplayed by Doreen Montgomery].

Abbott Fredric
Also listed as Frederic and Frederick
Played Lovegrove in **The Baron** episode *Diplomatic Immunity*. Guested as White in **The Champions** episode *The Bodysnatchers*.
Appeared as the 'dead' man in the second season **Danger Man** [aka **Secret Agent**] episode *The Outcast* and the first counter agent in *The Black Book*. In the third season's *I'm Afraid you Have the Wrong Number* appeared as Stoian and as Callaghan in *The Man on the Beach*.
Played Johnson in the **Department S** episode *The Trojan Tanker*.
Played Smithy in the **G.S.5** episode *An Eye for An Eye*.
Played the porter in the **Man in a Suitcase** episode *Property of a Gentleman*.
Appeared as Potter in **The Prisoner** episode *Do Not Forsake Me Oh My Darling*.
Played Corbett in the third season **The Saint** episode *The Angel's Eye* and Joe Carney in *The Best Laid Schemes*.
Played the man in the **Strange Report** episode *Report 4407: HEART: 'No Choice for the Donor'*.
Played the first seaman in the **UFO** episode *Reflections in the Water*.

Abbott John
Played Phipps in the **Timeslip** story *The Wrong End of Time* [episode 1].

Abbott June
Played Estelle in the **Department S** episode *The Treasure of the Costa del Sol*.
Played the girl in London Airport in the fourth season **The Saint** episode *The Double Take*.

Abbott Len
Sound recordist on **The Champions**, **Department S** and **The Saint**.

Abbott Mary
Played the air hostess in the season two **Ghost Squad** episode *Lost in Transit*.

ABC Television
In association with ITC, produced **Sir Francis Drake**.

Abineri John
Played Spinoza in **The Baron** episode *Enemy of the State* and Cerdan in *The Edge of Fear*.
Played the security man in the **Strange Report** episode *Report 7931: SNIPER: 'When is Your Cousin Not?'*.

Abney William
Played the co-pilot in **The Adventurer** episode *Somebody Doesn't Like Me*.
Played Mayer in the **Jason King** episode *That Isn't Me, It's Somebody Else*.
Played John Adams in **The Scarlet Pimpernel** episode *Thanksgiving Day*.
Played Don Pedro in the **Sir Francis Drake** episode *The Gypsies* and Fritz in the **William Tell** episode *The Bandit*.

Acheson John
Played the aircraft Captain in the **Department S** episode *The Bones of Byrom Blain*.
Played Triver in **The Persuaders!** episode *Overture*.

Ackland Joss
Played Felix Meadows in **The Persuaders!** episode *Read and Destroy*.

Played Arthur Gordon in the second season **The Protectors** episode *Trial*.
Played Gunther in the **Return of the Saint** episode *The Nightmare Man*.
Played Inspector Vaughan in the **Shirley's World** episode *The Reunion*.

Ackland Noreen, G.B.E.E.
Editor on **The Prisoner** episode *Living in Harmony* and, with Eric Boyd-Perkins, on *Fall Out*.

Adam Joshua
Pseudonym of/see Lewis **Greifer**.

Adam Ronald
Played Gen. Le Claire in **The Count of Monte Cristo** episode *A Matter of Justice*.
Played Mr Baker in the **Gideon's Way** episode *The Lady Killer*.

Adams Craig
Played Andy Winters in **The Four Just Men** episode *The Discovery*.

Adams Dallas
Played Reggie in the **Strange Report** episode *Report 3424: EPIDEMIC: 'A Most Curious Crime'*.

Adams Dixon
Played Chauffeur in the season two **Ghost Squad** episode *The Menacing Mazurka*.

Adams Geoffrey
Played the hotel clerk in the **White Hunter** episode *Girl Hunt*.

Adams Jill
Appeared as Tracey Allen in the **White Hunter** episode *Day of Reckoning*.

Adams Kenneth
Played Sustri in the second series **Danger Man** [aka **Secret Agent**] episode *Fair Exchange* and the interrogator in *The Colonel's Daughter*.

Adams Ronald
Played Sir Robert Copthorne in the **Gideon's Way** episode *Morna*.

Adams Tom
Played Simon in the first series **Ghost Squad** episode *High Wire*.
Played Piers Emerson in **The Persuaders!** episode *Greensleeves*.
Played Clinton in the **Strange Report** episode *Report 0649: SKELETON: 'Let Sleeping Heroes Lie'*.
Played Capt. Lauritzen in the **UFO** episode *The Psychobombs*.

Adamson Raymond
Played Inspector Bob Weston in **The Baron** episode *There's Someone Close Behind You*.
Played Inspector Lothar in the first series **Ghost Squad** episode *Still Waters*.
Played Jack Lacey in the **Randall and Hopkirk [Deceased]** aka **My Partner the Ghost** episode *Murder Ain't what it Used to Be!*.
Played Gorton in the second series **Danger Man** [aka **Secret Agent**] episode *Fair Exchange & Don't Nail Him Yet*.
Played Norton in the first season **The Saint** episode *The Saint Plays with Fire* and Jules Brant in *The Benevolent Burglary*.
Played the guard at Villa in the third season's *The Russian Prisoner*.

Addams Dawn
Played Lady Anne Benson in **The Adventurer** episode *The Case of the Poisoned Pawn.*
Played Gerdi in the second series **Danger Man** [aka **Secret Agent**] episode *Fish on the Hook* and Martine in *The Battle of the Cameras.*
Played Diane Lynne in the **Department S** episode *Handicap Dead.*
Played Magda Vamoff in the first season **The Saint** episode *The Fellow Traveller* and Audrey in *The Lawless Lady.* Played Queen Adana in the third season's *The Queen's Ransom.*

Adem Yashar
Played the driver in the second series **Danger Man** [aka **Secret Agent**] episode *Judgement Day.*

Adler Larry
Composed and played the theme music for the series **Virgin of the Secret Service.**

Adolphe Hylette
Played Estelle in the **Jason King** episode *A Kiss for a Beautiful Killer.*

Adorni Guido
Played Jose in the second series **Danger Man** [aka **Secret Agent**] episode *A Date with Doris* & in the third season's *Two Birds with One Bullet.*
Played the barman in the **Man in a Suitcase** episode *Find the Lady.*

Adrian Max
Played The Chosen One in **The Baron** episode *The High Terrace.*

Ahlefeldt Karl
Played Beck in the season two **The Protectors** episode *Bagman.*

Ahrens Monique
Played Maria in the first season **Danger Man** episode *The Key.*

Aida Foster School
Some of its pupils appeared in the **O.S.S.** episode *Operation Powder Puff.*

Ainley Anthony
Played Josef Kerston in **The Adventurer** episode *The Bradley Way* and the supervisor in the **Department S** episode *A Ticket to Nowhere.*

Ainsley Ian
Played the neighbour in **The Count of Monte Cristo** episode *Burgundy* and Thompson in the first season **The Saint** episode *The Invisible Millionaire.*

Ainsworth John
Directed the first season **The Saint** episodes *The Careful Terrorist* & *The Element of Doubt.*

Aizlewood Philip
Post-production Supervisor on **The Champions** & **Jason King.**
Post-production on **Department S, Randall and Hopkirk** [**Deceased**] aka **My Partner the Ghost** and **The Saint.**

Ajibade Yemi
Played the barman in the second series **Danger Man** [aka **Secret Agent**] episode *Loyalty Always Pays.*

Akira
Played Shinzo Hotta in the **Shirley's World** episode *The Lovers.*

Alan Pamela
Played Constance in the season three **The Adventures of Robin Hood** episode *The Double.*

Alba Rose
Played Madame La Gata in **The Persuaders!** episode *Angie. . . Angie.*
Played the first woman at Party in the fourth season **The Saint** episode *The Double Take.*

Alberge Betty
Played Mrs Gow in the **Father Brown** episode *The Head of Caesar.*

Alder Elsie
Hairdresser on **The Adventures of Sir Lancelot** episodes *The Pirates, The Black Castle, The Lesser Breed, The Magic Book* and *Knight Errand.*
Hairdresser on **The Saint.**

Alderson John
Played Kyle Sandor in **The Persuaders!** episode *Angie... Angie.*

Aldridge James
Co-wrote, with Ralph Smart, the first series **The Adventures of Robin Hood** episode *The Sheriff's Boots* and wrote the third series episode *An Apple for the Archer.*

Aldridge Michael
Played Mazzini in **The Count of Monte Cristo** episode *The Mazzini Affair.*

Alexander Geoffrey
Played the police sergeant in the **G.S.5** episode *It Won't be a Stylish Marriage.*

Alexander Keith
Voiced Sam Loover in the **Joe 90** series, Matthew in **The Secret Service** and featured in **UFO** as, regular, Lt. Ford.

Alexander Michael
Played Croupier in **The Count of Monte Cristo** episode *Monaco* and Steiner in the **UFO** episode *Conflict.*

Alexander Patrick
Wrote the **Shirley's World** episode *Figuratively Speaking.*

Alexander Terence
Played Nigel Brockhurst in **The Baron** episode *Portrait of Louisa.*
Guested as Douglas Trennick in **The Champions** episode *The Night People.*
Played Elliott Chapman in the season two **Ghost Squad** episode *Escape Route.*
Played Gerald Farson in the **Man in a Suitcase** episode *Property of a Gentleman.*
Played Crane in **The Persuaders!** episode *Powerswitch.*

Alexis Brian
Played Will in the third series **The Adventures of Robin Hood** episode *Marian's Prize* and Edgar in the fourth's *The Lady Killer.*

Alexis Charles
Master-at-Arms [staff] throughout **The Adventures of Sir Lancelot** [not credited for *The Knight with the Red Plume, The Ferocious Fathers* and *The Queen's Knight*].

Alkazzi Raul
Played Kemal in the second series **Danger Man** [aka **Secret Agent**] episode *Yesterday's Enemies.*

Played Tom in the season two **Ghost Squad** episode *Sabotage.*

Alken John
Played Frank Skinner - 1940 - in the **Timeslip** story *The Wrong End of Time* [series parts 1 - 6].

Allan Andrea
Played Pru Gideon in the **Gideon's Way** episode *The Rhyme and the Reason.*
Played the tall girl in the **Jason King** episode *To Russia With ....Panache* .
Played the nurse in the **UFO** episode *A Question of Priorities.* and a Moonbase operative in *The Man who Came Back.*

Allan Julie
Played Suzan in the first season **Danger Man** episode *The Actor.*
Played Suzie in the first series **Ghost Squad** episode *Hong Kong Story* and Yvette in season two's *Mr Five Per Cent.*

Allan Ronald
Played Walter in the season three **The Adventures of Robin Hood** episode *The Bride of Robin Hood.*

Allan Sheldon
Played Beppe in the **Sword of Freedom** episode *Vendetta* and Carlo in *The Pagan Venus.*

Allbritton Louise
Played Zena Fleming in the **H. G. Wells' Invisible Man** episode *The Gun Runners.*

Allder Nick
Special Effects Director on **Space 1999**.

Allen Anthony
Played John Banks in the **Father Brown** episode *The Man with Two Beards.*

Allen George
Starred as, Junior Ranger, Ted in **The Forest Rangers** series.

Allen Irvin
Played Torpedo Smith in the second season **The Saint** episode *The Crooked Ring.*

Allen Jack
Played Sir Perry in the fourth series of **The Adventures of Robin Hood** episode *The Champion.*
Played the colonel in the third season **Danger Man** [aka **Secret Agent**] episode *To our Best Friend.*
Played the Doctor in **The Prisoner** episode *Arrival.*

Allen James
Second Unit Cameraman on **The Champions**.

Allen Jared
Played the telephone repair man in the first season **The Saint** episode *The Careful Terrorist.*

Allen Lesley
Played the girl in the taxi in the second series **Danger Man** [aka **Secret Agent**] episode *Are You Going to be More Permanent?*

Allen Patrick
Played Max Holder in **The Baron** episode *Something for a Rainy Day.*
Guested as Westerman in **The Champions** episode *Full Circle.*
Played Spender 'Todd' in the **Gideon's Way** episode *A Perfect Crime.*

Played Marcus Spencer in the **Man in a Suitcase** episode *The Whisper.*
Played Mallory in the first series **The Protectors** episode *A Matter of Life and Death.*
Played Miles Hallin in the second season **The Saint** episode *The Man who Could not Die.*
Played Petrides in **The Sentimental Agent** episode *A Little Sweetness and Light.*
Played Navarre in the **Sir Francis Drake** episode *Mission to Paris.*
Played Turner in the **UFO** episode *Timelash.*

Allen Ronald
Played Walter Bernard in the debut season **Danger Man** episode *Colonel Rodriguez* and Ted Baker in *The Honeymooners.*
Played Ted in **The Four Just Men** episode *The Bystanders.*

Allen Sheila
Played Diana in the second series **Danger Man** [aka **Secret Agent**] episode *Don't Nail Him Yet.*
Played Ilse in **The Four Just Men** episode *The Man Who Wasn't There* and Marie Clement in *The Godfather.*
Played Mary Calloway in the **Gideon's Way** episode *The Alibi Man.*
Guested as Number 14 in **The Prisoner** episode *A. B. and C.*

Allenby Peter
Played the police captain in the **G.S.5** episode *Scorpion Rock.*
Appeared as the Spanish officer in the **White Hunter** episode *The Stepfathers.*

Allison Dorothy
Played Matilda in the first series **The Adventures of Robin Hood** episode *The Ordeal* and, in season two, played Constance in *Ambush* & Duchess Constance in *The Bandit of Brittany.*

Allister David
Played the customs official in the second series **The Protectors** episode *Border Line.*

Allouis Jacky
Played Henriette in the fourth season **The Saint** episode *The Ex-King of Diamonds.*

Altman W. H.
Wrote the story for the **H. G. Wells' Invisible Man** episode *Flight into Darkness* [teleplayed by Ian Stuart Black].

Ames Florenz
Starred as Inspector Richard Queen, Ellery Queen's father, in the series **Mystery is My Business**.

Anders Derek
Played Manning in the second season **The Protectors** episode *Sugar and Spice.*
Played Wayland in the first season **Space 1999** episode *Space Brain.*

Andersen Jurgen
Played Hal in the **Jason King** episode *The Constance Missal.*

Anderson Bob
Played the first thug in the third season **Danger Man** [aka **Secret Agent**] episode *I can only Offer you Sherry.*
Played 'Assassin' in the first series **The Protectors** episode *The Big Hit.*

Anderson Brian
Played the garage manager in the second series **Danger Man** [aka **Secret Agent**] episode *Whatever Happened to George Foster?.*

Anderson Daphne
Starred as Kate Gideon in **Gideon's Way**.
Played Viola in the **Sword of Freedom** episode *Chart of Gold*.

Anderson Gene
Played Sally in the **White Hunter** episode *Voodoo Wedding*.

Anderson Gerry
Created, with Sylvia Anderson, **Captain Scarlet and the Mysterons**. Also executive produced and, with Sylvia Anderson, co-wrote its pilot: *The Mysterons*.
On **Fireball XL5**: Created [with Sylvia], produced, script supervisor [with Sylvia], voiced, co-pilot, Robert the Robot, wrote [with Sylvia] *Planet 46*, wrote *Space Monster* and directed *Planet 46*.
Created the format [with Sylvia] for the **Joe 90** series and co-wrote the episodes *The Most Special Agent* [with Sylvia], *Operation McClaine* [with David Lane], *The Professional* [with Sylvia] & *The Birthday* [format, with Sylvia: written by Tony Barwick].
Producer [with Reg Hill] on **The Protectors** series.
Created the series format [with Sylvia] for **The Secret Service** series and co-wrote the episode *A Case for the Bishop* [with Sylvia Anderson].
Created **Space 1999** [with Sylvia] and executive produced the first series.
Producer on the series **Stingray** and co-wrote, with Sylvia, *The Pilot* [aka *Stingray*], *A Nut for Marineville* and *Aquanaut of theYear*.
Created [original idea with Reg Hill] the **Supercar** series. Also produced and co-wrote [with Sylvia] the first season **Supercar** episodes *Flight of Fancy, Crash Landing, The Lost City & Supercar Take One* and the second season's *The Runaway Train, Precious Cargo, Operation Superstork, Hi-Jack, Calling Charlie Queen, Space for Mitch, The Sky's the Limit, 70-B-Low, Atomic Witch Hunt, Jail Break, The Day Time Stood Still, Transatlantic Cable & King Kool*.
Created **Thunderbirds** [with Sylvia], produced season one, executive producer on season two and co-wrote the pilot *Trapped in the Sky* [with Sylvia].
Created the format and produced the series **UFO** [with Sylvia & Reg Hill]. Also served as executive producer, directed *Identified* and co-wrote *Identified* [with Sylvia & Tony Barwick].

Anderson Jean
Played Tante Marie in the first series **Ghost Squad** episode *The Broken Doll*.
Played the Nun in the **Interpol Calling** episode *The Man's Clown*.

Anderson Jim
Played the demolition officer in **The Four Just Men** episode *Dead Man's Switch*.

Anderson Keith
Played Adam in the season three **The Adventures of Robin Hood** episode *My Brother's Keeper*, the second sentry in the third season's *The Genius* and the second soldier in season four's *The Loaf*.
Played the boy in the season two **Ghost Squad** episode *A First Class Way to Die*.
Played Det. Insp. Elmhurst in the **Gideon's Way** episode *The Alibi Man*.

Anderson Leslie
Played the cleaner in the third season **The Saint** episode *When Spring is Sprung* and the porter in the fourth season's *The Master Plan*.

Anderson Lindsay
Directed the first series of **The Adventures of Robin Hood** episode *Secret Mission* and the second's *The Impostor, Isabella, The Haunted Mill & Ambush*.

Anderson Margaret
Appeared as Lady Helen in **The Adventures of Sir Lancelot** episode *Knight Errant*.

Anderson Michael
Played Lt. Lenz in **The Count of Monte Cristo** episode *A Matter of Justice*.
Played the title role in the **Sir Francis Drake** episode *Boy Jack*.

Anderson Peggy
Continuity on **The Adventures of Sir Lancelot** episode *Lancelot's Banishment*.

Anderson Peter
Directed the **Joe 90** episodes *Most Special Astronaut, Project 90, Relative Danger, Three's a Crowd, Child of the Sun God, Attack of the Tiger, Viva Cordova* and *Test Flight*.
Directed **The Secret Service** episodes *The Feathered Spies* and *Recall to Service*.

Anderson Rona
Guested as Lena in the **Interpol Calling** episode *Eight Days Inclusive*.
Appeared as Lenore Mason in the **White Hunter** episode *Squire of the Serengeti*.

Anderson Sylvia
Created, with Gerry Anderson, **Captain Scarlet and the Mysterons**. Also provided the voice for Melody Angel and, with Gerry, co-wrote its pilot: *The Mysterons*.
On **Fireball XL5**: Created [with Gerry], script supervisor [with Gerry], voiced Venus and wrote [with Gerry] *Planet 46*.
Created the format [with Gerry] for the **Joe 90** series, created the characters, voiced Ada Harris and co-wrote the episodes *The Most Special Agent* [with Gerry], *The Professional* [with Gerry] & *The Birthday* [format, with Gerry: written by Tony Barwick].
Wrote the first season **The Protectors** episode *.....With a Little Help from my Friends*.
Created the series format [with Gerry] for **The Secret Service** series, created the characters, voiced Mrs Appleby and co-wrote *A Case for the Bishop* [with Gerry].
Created **Space 1999** [with Gerry] and produced the first series.
Character visualisation on the **Stingray** series, voiced, the usually silent, Marina in *Raptures of the Deep* and co-wrote, with Gerry, *The Pilot* [aka *Stingray*], *A Nut for Marineville* and *Aquanaut of theYear*.
Co-wrote [with Gerry] the first season **Supercar** episodes *Flight of Fancy, Crash Landing, The Lost City & Supercar Take One* and the second season's *The Runaway Train, Precious Cargo, Operation Superstork, Hi-Jack, Calling Charlie Queen, Space for Mitch, The Sky's the Limit, 70-B-Low, Atomic Witch Hunt, Jail Break, The Day Time Stood Still, Transatlantic Cable & King Kool*.
Created **Thunderbirds** [with Gerry], character visualisation, voiced Lady Penelope and co-wrote the pilot *Trapped in the Sky* [with Gerry].
Created the format and produced the series **UFO** [with Gerry & Reg Hill]. Also designed the Century 21 Fashions and co-wrote *Identified* [with Gerry & Tony Barwick].

Andre Annette
Played Samantha Ballard in **The Baron** episode *Roundabout*.
Played Sue Young in the **Gideon's Way** episode *The Nightlifers*.
Starred as, series regular, Jean Hopkirk in the series **Randall and Hopkirk [Deceased]** aka **My Partner the Ghost**.
Played Pekoe in **The Persuaders!** episode *Powerswitch*.
Guest starred as the watchmaker's daughter in **The Prisoner** episode *It's Your Funeral*.
Played Sandy in the **Return of the Saint** episode *Yesterday's Hero*.

Played Madeline Gray in the second season **The Saint** episode *The Saint Steps In*, Linda Henderson in *The Loving Brothers* and Madeline in *The Abductors*. In the third season, played Carmen in *The House on Dragon's Rock* & Annette in *To Kill a Saint*.
Played Betsy Ann in **The Sentimental Agent** episode *Finishing School*.

Andre Carole
Played Claudia in the **Return of the Saint** episode *Duel in Venice*.

Andreas Dimitris
Played Plessis in **The Sentimental Agent** episode *A Little Sweetness and Light*.

Andrew Margo
Appeared as the shop kiosk girl in **The Prisoner** episode *Hammer Into Anvil*.
Played Polly Green in the **Virgin of the Secret Service** episode *Dark Deeds on the Northwest Frontier*.

Andrews Barry
Played Gadden in the **Department S** episode *Spencer Bodily is 60 Years Old*.
Played Harland in the **Return of the Saint** episode *Hot Run*.
Played Tom in the fourth season **The Saint** episode *The Man Who Gambled with Life*.

Andrews Donna
Played Little Girl in **The Count of Monte Cristo** episode *Burgundy*.

Angelos Agath
Played the second seaman in the **Man in a Suitcase** episode *Variation on a Million Bucks* [part 2: also combined with part 1 to form a movie: *To Chase a Million*].
Played the doorman in the fourth season **The Saint** episode *Vendetta for the Saint* [part 1].

Anholt Tony
Played Armand in the **Jason King** episode *A Thin Band of Air*.
Starred in the series **The Protectors** as Paul Buchet.
Starred as, second season regular, Tony Verdeschi in **Space 1999**.

Annis Francesca
Played Judy in the second series **Danger Man** [aka **Secret Agent**] episode *No Marks for Servility* and Sheila in *That's Two of Us Sorry*.
Played Maria in the third season **The Saint** episode *Locate and Destroy*.
Played Mariella in the **Sir Francis Drake** episode *Visit to Spain*.

Ansah Tommy
Played Tchumbu in the **Man in a Suitcase** episode *The Whisper*.

Anslan Gregoire
Played Scorbesi in the **Return of the Saint** episode *The Poppy Chain*.

Anthony Brian
Played Philip Hawker in the **Father Brown** episode *The Head of Caesar*.

Anthony Jeremy
Played the harbour gendarme in the **Return of the Saint** episode *The Diplomat's Daughter*.
Played the first Pakistani in the fourth season **The Saint** episode *The People Importers*.

Anthony Michael
Played Barjou in the third season **Danger Man** [aka **Secret Agent**] episode *Dangerous Secret*.
Played Count De Ville in the **Jason King** episode *A Deadly Line in Digits*.
Played the hotel desk clerk in **The Persuaders!** episode *The Old, the New and the Deadly*.
Played the hotel manager in the second season **The Saint** episode *Jeannine* and Duval in the third season's *The Death Game*.
Appeared as Harry in the **White Hunter** episode *A Moment of Truth*.

Anthony Philip
Played the assistant director in the first season **The Saint** episode *Marcia*.

Antrim Paul
Played the policeman in the second season **The Protectors** episode *Blockbuster*.

Antrobus Yvonne
Played Katis Bergen in the second season **The Protectors** episode *Baubles, Bangles and Beads*.

Anvil Films Limited
Sound re-recording on **Joe 90** & **The Secret Service**.

AP Films
Produced, in association with ATV, for ITC World Wide Distribution: Gerry Anderson's **Fireball XL5**, **Stingray**, **Supercar** & **Thunderbirds** [not season two].

Appleby Basil
Associate Producer on **The Four Just Men**.

Appleton Ron
Directed the **UFO** episode *Court Martial*.

Apps Edwin
Played Mumford in the second series **Danger Man** [aka **Secret Agent**] episodes *Fair Exchange* & *Don't Nail Him Yet*.

Archard Bernard
Played Doctor Bryant in the first season **Danger Man** episode *The Leak* and Nubar in the third season [now aka **Secret Agent**] episode *I can only Offer you Sherry*.
Played Sheikh Ibrahim Ben Said in the first series **Man of the World** episode *The Nature of Justice*.
Played Sir Christopher in the **Sir Francis Drake** episode *Court Intrigue*.

Archdale Alexander
Played Fordyce in the first season **Danger Man** episode *The Lonely Chair*.
Appeared as Smedley in the **White Hunter** episode *Marked Man*.

Archer Barbara
Played Pamela in the season three **The Adventures of Robin Hood** episode *The Profiteer*.

Archer Ted
Appeared as the Game Warden in the **White Hunter** episode *Girl Hunt*.

Arden Blanche
Hairdresser on the **Man in a Suitcase** series.

Arden Neal
Played the commentator in the **Department S** episode *Handicap Dead* and the doctor in *Last Train to Redbridge*.

Played Florian in the first series **Ghost Squad** episode *Ticket for Blackmail*.

Guested as Commandant in the **Interpol Calling** episode *Desert Hi-Jack*.

Played the German Minister in the **O.S.S.** episode *Operation Eel*.

Played Inspector Flavel in **The Persuaders!** episode *Overture*.

Played the second poker player in the **Randall and Hopkirk [Deceased]** aka **My Partner the Ghost** episode *The Trouble with Women*.

Played Deslauriers in the first season **The Saint** episode *The Benevolent Burglary*.

Appeared as Sayville in the **White Hunter** episode *Inside Story* and as Tallon in *Girl Hunt*.

Arden Robert

Guested as Marston in the **Interpol Calling** episode *You Can't Die Twice*.

Played Carter in the second season **Man of the World** episode *The Prince*.

Played Joe Sammis in the **O.S.S.** episode *Operation Barbecue*.

Played Detective Williams in the first season **The Saint** episode *The Ever-loving Spouse*.

Arena

Produced **Strange Report** for ITC World Wide Distribution.

Arena Fortuanto

Played the peasant in the **Return of the Saint** episode *Dragonseed*.

Argent Douglas

In **The Adventures of Sir Lancelot**: played Hugh in *The Outcast*, Prince Boudwin in *Winged Victory*, the foppish man in *Sir Bliant*, Sir Hugh in *The Magic Sword*, Mador in *Shepherd's War*, the old man in *The Pirates*, Sir Trebizond in *The Black Castle*, Sir Paddagore in *The Magic Book* and the first knight in *Knight Errant*.

Ari Ben

Played David in the second series **Danger Man** [aka **Secret Agent**] episode *Judgement Day*. Played the first watcher in the third season's *I can only Offer you Sherry* and the agent in *The Paper Chase*.

Arliss Leslie

Directed **The Buccaneers** [aka **Dan Tempest**] episodes *Dan Tempest's War with Spain*, *Whale Gold*, *Gunpowder Plot*, *Articles of War*, *Conquest of New Providence* [with Robert Day], *Hurricane*, *Dangerous Cargo*, *Gentleman Jack and the Lady* and *Marooned*.

Wrote the **H. G. Wells' Invisible Man** episodes *Behind the Mask* [co-teleplayed with Stanley Mann: from a story by Stanley Mann], *Play to Kill* [teleplayed from a story by Robert Westerby], *Picnic with Death* [co-teleplayed with Leonard Fincham: from a story by Leonard Fincham] and *Man in Disguise* [story: teleplayed by Brenda Blackmore].

Served as a Director on **The New Adventures of Charlie Chan**.

On the series **William Tell**: teleplayed *The Emperor's Hat* [with Rene Wilde: original story by Rene Wilde], teleplayed *The Raid* [with Leslie Arliss: original story by Rene Wilde], wrote *The Ensign* [with Max Savage], and wrote *The Traitor* [with Roger Marshall]; directed *The Raid* and produced *The Prisoner*, *Gessler's Daughter*, *Manhunt*, *The Bandit*, *Undercover*, *The Bear*, *The Suspect*, *Golden Wheel*, *The Bride*, *The Avenger*, *The Young Widow*, *The Shrew*, *The Trap*, *The Killer*, *The Mountain People*, *The Surgeon*, *The Ensign*, *The Unwelcome Stranger*, *The Black Brothers*, *The General's Daughter*, *Secret Weapon*, *Castle of Fear*, *The Spider* & *The Master Spy*.

Arliss Ralph

Played Malc in the **Return of the Saint** episode *Signal Stop*.

Armitage Graham

Played the young stage director in the **Randall and Hopkirk [Deceased]** aka **My Partner the Ghost** episode *It's Supposed to be Thicker than Water*.

Played Carson in the fourth season **The Saint** two parter *The Fiction Makers*.

Armstrong Alun

Played Joe in the **Father Brown** episode *The Hammer of God*.

Armstrong Bridget

Played Yvette in **The Adventurer** episode *Going, Going....*

Played the young nurse in the **Jason King** episode *If it's Got to Go - It's Got to Go*.

Played Louise in the **Man in a Suitcase** episode *Jigsaw Man*.

Armstrong Hugh

Played the SHADO Mobile 3 officer in the **UFO** episode *Computer Affair*.

Armstrong Michael

Co-wrote the story, with John Kruse, for the **Return of the Saint** episode *Vicious Circle* [teleplayed by John Goldsmith].

Armstrong Paul

Played the policeman in the cafe in the second series **Danger Man** [aka **Secret Agent**] episode *The Affair at Castelevara* and the Spanish bus official in *The Outcast*.

Armstrong Ray

Played a rescuer in the **UFO** episode *Survival*.

Armstrong Raymond

Played the farmer in the **Department S** episode *The Pied Piper of Hambledown*.

Played the intern in the **Strange Report** episode *Report 3424: EPIDEMIC: 'A Most Curious Crime'*.

Armstrong Vic

Played Pierre in **The Zoo Gang** episode *The Lion Hunt* and Jules in *The Twisted Cross*.

Arnall Julia

Played Natalie Smith in the first season **Danger Man** episode *Dead Man Walks* and Josetta in *Josetta*.

Played Julie in the first series **Ghost Squad** episode *The Broken Doll*.

Played Ingrid in the third season **The Saint** episode *Locate and Destroy*.

Played Cristina in the **Sword of Freedom** episode *Cristina*.

Arnatt John

Played Sir Roger in the season three **The Adventures of Robin Hood** episode *The Challenge of the Black Knight* before becoming, series regular, Ralph the Deputy Sheriff [from season 4]: *The Devil You Don't Know*, *Goodbye, Little John*, *Hostage for a Hangman*, *Hue and Cry*, *The Oath*, *The Charm Pedlar*, *The Debt*, *Bride for an Outlaw*, *A Bushel of Apples*, *Double Trouble*, *The Champion*, *Trapped*, *The Edge and the Point* & *The Truce*.

Played Lord Peversham in the **H. G. Wells' Invisible Man** episode *The Big Plot*.

Played the uniformed Inspector in the **Randall and Hopkirk [Deceased]** aka **My Partner the Ghost** episode *Could You Recognise the Man Again?*.

Played Major Fanshire in the first season **The Saint** episode *The Arrow of God*.

Played the Spanish Ambassador in the **Sir Francis Drake** episode *Court Intrigue* and Cordova in *Visit to Spain*.

Played Inspector Lowe in the **Strange Report** episode *Report 2493: KIDNAP: 'Whose Pretty Girl Are You?'*.

Arne Peter

Played Marco Navini in **The Baron** episode *The Long, Long Day*.

Guested as Margoli in **The Champions** episode *Operation Deep-freeze*.

Played Major Hassler in the debut season **Danger Man** episode *Find and Destroy*. In series two [now aka **Secret Agent**] played Richardson in *Colony Three*, Chi Ling in *A Very Dangerous Game* and General G'Niore in *The Mercenaries*.

Played Slovik in the **Department S** episode *The Double Death of Charlie Crippen* and Segres in *The Soup of the Day*.

Played Rudnik in the **Man in a Suitcase** episode *The Boston Square*.

Played Chang in the first series **Man of the World** episode *The Frontier*.

Played Giocovetti in the first series **The Protectors** episode *The Numbers Game*.

Played Pablo Enriquez in the second season **The Saint** episode *The Revolution Racket*.

Played Stirink in **The Sentimental Agent** episode *All that Jazz*.

Arnell Anthony

Casting Director on **The Baron** & **The Saint**.

Arnold Grace

Played the female singer in the **Man in a Suitcase** episode *The Sitting Pigeon*.

Appeared as the maid, Martha, in **The Prisoner** episode *Many Happy Returns* and as Number 36 in *It's Your Funeral*.

Arnold Robert

Played the first policeman in the fourth season **The Saint** episode *The People Importers*.

Arnold Sydney

Played the Vice President in the **G.S.5** episode *Death of a Cop*.

Arnot Ziki

Played Safae in the **Sword of Freedom** episode *The Slave*.

Arpino Tony

Played the warder in the first season **The Saint** episode *The Latin Touch* and the second villager in *Sophia*.

Arrighi Mike

Played Serafino in the third season **The Saint** episode *The Man Who Liked Lions*.

Arrighi Nike

Guested as Corinne in **The Champions** episode *Reply Box No: 666*.

Played Angela in the **Man in a Suitcase** episode *Why they Killed Nolan* and Ivanna in episode *Jigsaw Man*.

Appeared as the gypsy girl in **The Prisoner** episode *Many Happy Returns*.

Arthy Judith

Played Jill Prentice in **The Baron** episode *The Maze*.

Played the model girl in the **Man in a Suitcase** episode *The Bridge*.

Played Monique in the first series **The Protectors** episode *Your Witness*.

Starred as Jennifer in the **Randall and Hopkirk [Deceased]** aka **My Partner the Ghost** episodes *A Disturbing Case* & *The House on Haunted Hill*.

Artransa

Produced the **Whiplash** series.

Arundale Sybil

Played Mrs Burton in **The Scarlet Pimpernel** episode *The Christmas Present*.

Ashby Harvey

Played Mora in the second series **Danger Man** [aka **Secret Agent**] episode *A Man to be Trusted*.

Played Peter Quentin in the third season **The Saint** episode *When Spring is Sprung*.

Asher Jane

Played Sarah Cookson in **The Adventurer** episode *To the Lowest Bidder*.

Played Alice in the first series **The Adventures of Robin Hood** episode *Children of the Greenwood*, Susan in the third season's *The Christmas Goose* and the first small girl in *The Minstrel*, also in series three.

Played the girl in **The Buccaneers** [aka **Dan Tempest**] episode *Mistress Higgins' Treasure* and Jenny in *Flip and Jenny*.

Played Yvonne in **The Four Just Men** episode *The Man in the Road*.

Played Ellen Chase in the first season **The Saint** episode *The Invisible Millionaire* and Rose Yearley in *The Noble Sportsman*.

Asher June

Played Tristina in the **Sword of Freedom** episode *The Marionettes*.

Asher Peter

Played Young Prince Arthur in **The Adventures of Robin Hood** [Richard O'Sullivan & Jonathan Bailey also had a stab at the role]: Played Arthur in the first season's *The Youngest Outlaw* and the second season's *Ambush* & *The Bandit of Brittany*. Also appeared in the first series episode *Children of the Greenwood* as Oswald.

Played Pagolo in the **Sword of Freedom** episode *The Ship*.

Asher Robert

Directed **The Baron** episodes *Time to Kill*, *The High Terrace*, *The Seven Eyes of Night* & *Countdown*.

Directed **The Champions** episodes *The Mission*, *The Silent Enemy*, *The Night People* and *The Gun-Runners*.

Directed **The Prisoner** episode *It's Your Funeral*.

Directed the third series **The Saint** episode *To Kill a Saint* and the fourth's *The Scales of Justice*.

Directed the **Strange Report** episode *Report 4407: HEART: 'No Choice for the Donor'*.

Asherson Renee

Played Miss Dalton in the **Strange Report** episode *Report 8944: HAND: 'A Matter of Witchcraft?'*.

Ashford David

Played the laboratory assistant in the **Strange Report** episode *Report 2641: HOSTAGE: 'If You Won't Learn, Die!*.

Ashley Elizabeth

Played Lady Fielding in the second series **Danger Man** [aka **Secret Agent**] episode *No Marks for Servility*.

Ashley Graham

Played the Police Inspector in the second season **The Protectors** episode *Trial*.

Played the policeman in the **Return of the Saint** episode *Signal Stop*.

Played the Airport attendant in the **Strange Report** episode *Report 1553: RACIST: 'A Most Dangerous Proposal'*.

Ashley Grantham

Played the police sergeant in the third season **Danger Man** [aka **Secret Agent**] episode *I'm Afraid you Have the Wrong Number*.

Ashley Keith

Played the manservant in **The Adventurer** episode *Miss Me Once, Miss Me Twice and Miss Me Once Again*.

Ashley Lyn
Played Ann in the first season **Danger Man** episode *Sabotage*.
Played Zoe Ballard in the **Jason King** episode *Buried in the Cold, Cold Ground*.
Played Jean Lane in the fourth season **The Saint** episode *The Master Plan*.

Ashley Philip
Played Count of Severne in the second series of **The Adventures of Robin Hood** episode *Ransom*.
Played the Spanish Officer in **The Buccaneers** [aka **Dan Tempest**] episode *The Surgeon of Sangre Rojo*.
Played Gonfalonier in the **Sword of Freedom** episode *Vespucci*.

Ashmore Peter
Played Finlay Hugoson in the fourth season **The Saint** two parter *The Fiction Makers*.

Ashton Brad
Wrote the **G.S.5** episode *It Won't be a Stylish Marriage*.

Ashwin Michael
Played Edward in the season three **The Adventures of Robin Hood** episode *The Rivals*.

Askew Maurice
Sound Recording on **Fireball XL5** & **Thunderbirds**.

Aslan Gregoire
Played Eugene Patroclos in the fourth season **The Saint** episode *The Double Take*.

Asprey Laurie
Guested as Jackson in **The Champions** episode *Twelve Hours*.
Played the photographer in the **Department S** episode *The Shift that Never was*.
Played William in the **Man in a Suitcase** episode *Dead Man's Shoes*.

Assar Shusha
Played Gina in the **G.S.5** episode *Pay Up or Else*.

Assinder Peter
Played the happy thief in **The Adventures of Sir Lancelot** episode *Thieves*.

Associated British Elstree Studios
Film studio used for the filming of: **The Baron, The Champions, The Count of Monte Cristo** [also shot in Hollywood], **Department S, Gideon's Way, Randall and Hopkirk [Deceased]** aka **My Partner the Ghost, The Saint** and **Sir Francis Drake**.

Associated TeleVision
The Four Just Men was a 'Hannah Fisher Production for Sapphire Films Ltd., for Associated TeleVision: an ITC Presentation'.

Associated Television [Overseas]
Produced the series **Joe 90**.

Associated Television Programmes
Produced **The Sentimental Agent** series for ITC World Wide Distribution.

Astley Edwin
Music on the first two seasons of **The Adventures of Robin Hood** [Albert Elms also worked on the first two].
Composed music for **The Adventures of Sir Lancelot** episodes *The Knight with the Red Plume, The Queen's Knight, The Magic Sword* and *The Lesser Breed*.
Music on **The Baron**.
Music on **The Buccaneers** [aka **Dan Tempest**] episodes *Blackbeard, The Raiders, Captain Dan Tempest, Dan Tempest's War with Spain, The Wasp, Whale Gold, Ghost Ship, Dead Man's Rock, Dangerous Cargo, Hand of the Hawk, Gentleman Jack and the Lady, Before the Mast, Dan Tempest and The Amazons, The Ladies, The Surgeon of Sangre Rojo* and *The Return of Calico Jack*.
Musical Director on **The Champions, Department S** & **Randall and Hopkirk [Deceased]** aka **My Partner the Ghost**.
Music throughout the four seasons of **Danger Man** [aka **Secret Agent**].
Music on **Gideon's Way**.
Music throughout **The Saint** series [original *Saint* Theme by Leslie Charteris].

Aston Anne
Played the nurse in the **Jason King** episode *Wanna Buy a Television Series* aka *A Face I Used to Know*.

Aston Peter
Models on **Joe 90** & **The Secret Service**.

Atienza Edward
Played Leonardo Da Vinci in the **Sword of Freedom** episode *Choice of Weapons*.

Atkinson Frank
Played Charley Dodds in the first season **The Saint** episode *The Invisible Millionaire*.

Atkinson John
Played Mr Aubrey Traill in the **Father Brown** episode *The Oracle of the Dog*.
Played Reg Cross in the second season **Ghost Squad** episode *The Thirteenth Girl*.
Played Jim Batley in the **Return of the Saint** episode *The Obono Affair*.

Atkinson Michael
Played Bowles Jr in **The Four Just Men** episode *National Treasure*.

Atkinson Reginald
Played the Doctor in **The Count of Monte Cristo** episode *Lichtenburg*.

Atkinson Rosalind
Played Miss Nightingale in the **Strange Report** episode *Report 8944: HAND: 'A Matter of Witchcraft?'*.

Atkinson Sarah
Played Anne Wilcox in the **Jason King** episode *Chapter One: The Company I Keep*.

Atkyns Norman
Played the shopkeeper in **The Adventurer** episode *Action!*.
Played the stage door keeper in the second season **The Protectors** episode *Dragon Chase*.

Attard Josef
Played the dealer in **The Four Just Men** episode *The Man With the Golden Touch*.
Played the hotel manager in the **H. G. Wells' Invisible Man** episode *The Gun Runners*.

ATV
Associated Television Corporation.
UK broadcasting company. Screened ITC's output in its Midland's franchise: see also **ITC**.
Produced **Man of the World** & **Sapphire and Steel** for ITC World Wide Distribution.

For ITC World Wide Distribution [and in association with A.P. Films], produced **Fireball XL5, Stingray, Supercar & Thunderbirds** [with AP Films on series one only].
Produced the first series of **Ghost Squad** for ITC World Wide Distribution. Season two was a Rank Organisation Television Film in association with Associated Television Ltd. for ITC World Wide Distribution] as was **G.S.5**.
The series **Interpol Calling** was 'An ATV Presentation' [produced by Rank/Wrather].

ATV Network Productions
Produced the **Father Brown** series for ITC World Wide Distribution.

Aubrey James
Played Ingo in the **Return of the Saint** episode *Appointment in Florence*.

Aubrey Jean
Played Connie Grady in the second season **The Saint** episode *The Crooked Ring*.
Played Rachell Rothstein in **The Scarlet Pimpernel** episodes *Gentlemen of the Road* & *The Imaginary Invalides*.

Audley Maxine
Appeared as Eunice in **The Adventures of Sir Lancelot** episode *The Witch's Brew*.
Played Maria in the debut season **Danger Man** episode *The Lovers* and Martine in *Colonel Rodriguez*. In series four [now aka **Secret Agent**] played Pauline in *Shinda Shima* [*Shinda Shima* was also merged with the only other surviving fourth season episode, *Koroshi*, to form a TVM entitled *Koroshi*].
Played Dolores Marcello in the first season **The Saint** episode *The King of the Beggars*.
Played Theia in the first season **Space 1999** episode *The Last Enemy*.

Aukin Liane
Played the receptionist in the first series **Man of the World** episode *The Sentimental Agent*.

Aulds Donald
Played the Flight Sgt. in the **O.S.S.** episode *Operation Newsboy*.

Aurelius Neville
Played Benny in the **Jason King** episode *Flamingos only Fly on Tuesdays*.

Austin Ray
Directed the **Department S** episodes *The Trojan Tanker, Black Out, Dead Men Die Twice* & *Death on Reflection*.
Appeared in several roles in season two of **Ghost Squad**: Joe Dunning in *Polsky*, Andret in *The Menacing Mazurka* and Ali in *Sabotage*. Played, series regular, Billy Clay in the subsequent **G.S.5**: *Party for Murder, Dead Men Don't Drive, Pay Up or Else, Rich Ruby Wine, Hideout*. Also served as Fight Arranger.
Directed the **Randall and Hopkirk [Deceased]** aka **My Partner the Ghost** episodes *A Disturbing Case, Who Ever Heard of a Ghost Dying?, The House on Haunted Hill, You Can Always find a Fall Guy, When the Spirit Moves You* & *Money to Burn* and wrote *That's How Murder Snowballs*.
Directed the **Return of the Saint** episode *Signal Stop*.
Played Joe in the first season **The Saint** episode *The Rough Diamonds*, Marsh in *The Fellow Traveller*, Arturo in the second season episode *The Damsel in Distress* and Erich Brauer in the third season's *The Helpful Pirate*. Directed the fourth season **The Saint** episodes *The Desperate Diplomat* & *The People Importers*.
Producer on the series **Shirley's World** and directed the episodes *Thou Shall Not Be Found Out, A Girl Like You, A Hell of an Engineer, The Lovers* & *The Defective Defector*.

Directed the first series **Space 1999** episodes *Collision Course, Alpha Child, Mission of the Darians, End of Eternity, Ring Around the Moon, Missing Link* & *The Troubled Spirit* and the second season's *The Exiles* & *All That Glisters*.

Avon Roger
Played Chateau Guide in the second series **Danger Man** [aka **Secret Agent**] episode *Have a Glass of Wine*.
Played the first maintenance man in the **Department S** episode *One of our Aircraft is Empty* and Hooper in *Last Train to Redbridge*.
Played the second security man in the season two **Ghost Squad** episode *The Grand Duchess*.
Played the uniformed policeman in the **Randall and Hopkirk [Deceased]** aka **My Partner the Ghost** episode *Money to Burn*.

Aylen Richard
Played the firearms expert in the **Father Brown** episode *The Mirror of the Magistrate* and the Alien in the **UFO** episode *A Question of Priorities*.

Aylmer Felix
Played the old man in **The Champions** episode *The Beginning* [this episode was combined with *The Interrogation* to form a 'feature' entitled *Legend of The Champions*].
Played Dr Wilstein in the **Jason King** episode *If it's Got to Go - It's Got to Go*.
Played Joshua Crackan in the **Randall and Hopkirk [Deceased]** aka **My Partner the Ghost** episode *It's Supposed to be Thicker than Water*.

Aylward Derek
Played King Marhaus in **The Adventures of Sir Lancelot** episodes *Lancelot's Banishment* and *The Bridge*.
Played the New Supervisor in **The Prisoner** episode *Hammer Into Anvil*.
Played Kramer in the **William Tell** episode *The Surgeon*.

Aymes Julian
Directed the first season **Danger Man** episode *Colonel Rodriguez*.

Ayres Robert
Played Hamilton in the first season **Danger Man** episode *The Nurse*.
Played the District Attorney in **The Four Just Men** episode *The Judge* and the Chairman in *The Prime Minister*.
Played the US Capt in the **O.S.S.** episode *Operation Eel*.
Played Clinton in the first season **The Saint** episode *The Careful Terrorist* and John Allardyce in the third season's *Interlude in Venice*.
Appeared as J. W. Evans in the **White Hunter** episode *Big Bwana Brady*.

Ayres Rosalind
Played Christabel Carstairs in the **Father Brown** episode *The Head of Caesar*.

Aziz Lubna
Played Anna in **The Sentimental Agent** episode *The Beneficiary*.

****

Baba Ali
Played a steward in the **Father Brown** episode *The Curse of the Golden Cross.*

Bachino Giovanni
Played Mario in the **Return of the Saint** episode *The Village that Sold its Soul.*

Backus Jim
Featured in the **Espionage** episode *A Tiny Drop of Poison.*

Bacon Max
Played Sam in the season two **Ghost Squad** episode *Hot Money.*
Played Bookie Thompson in the **Gideon's Way** episode *The Big Fix.*
Played Cobbler in the **William Tell** episode *The Lost Letter.*

Badcoe Brian
Played Travers in the **Department S** episode *The Man from X.*
Played Dr. Downray in the fourth season **The Saint** episode *The Scales of Justice.*

Baddeley Angela
Played Mrs Clark in the **Gideon's Way** episode *Big Fish, Little Fish.*

Baddeley Hermione
Played Mrs Grahame in the first season **Danger Man** episode *Under the Lake.*

Bailey Faith
Guested in the first season **The Adventures of Robin Hood** episode *Friar Tuck* as Mildred.

Bailey Gillian
Played Lizzy in **The Adventurer** episode *To the Lowest Bidder.*

Bailey John
Played John in **The Adventures of Sir Lancelot** episode *Double Identity.*
Guested as Umberto in **The Champions** episode *A Case of Lemmings.*
Played Kruger in the **Department S** episode *Handicap Dead.*
Played Rivera in the second season **Man of the World** episode *The Bullfighter.*
Played Di Vallesi in the **Return of the Saint** episode *The Nightmare Man.*
Played Jean Bourgrenet in the first season **The Saint** episode *The Work of Art.*
Played Rollo in the **Sword of Freedom** episode *The Hero.*

Bailey Jonathan
Played Young Prince Arthur in **The Adventures of Robin Hood** Played Prince Arthur in the season four **The Adventures of Robin Hood** episode *Race Against Time* [Peter Asher & Richard O'Sullivan also had a go at the role].

Bailey Robin
Appeared as Sir Bertram in the first season **The Adventures of Robin Hood** episode *The Knight Who Came To Dinner* and as Edmund Woodstock in the third season's *One Man's Meat.*
Played Rudyard in the **Man in a Suitcase** episode *The Sitting Pigeon.*
Played Kofax in the **UFO** episode *Exposed.*

Bain Barbara
Starred as Dr Helena Russell throughout the series **Space 1999**.

Baines John
Wrote **The Four Just Men** episode *The Deserter.*

Wrote the **Sir Francis Drake** episodes *The Governor's Revenge* & *The Gypsies.*

Baird Anthony
Played the Lieutenant in the second series of **The Adventures of Robin Hood** episode *The Goldmaker.*
Played Corteau in **The Count of Monte Cristo** episode *The Art of Terror* and Dardelle in *The Devil's Emissary.*
Played the British agent in the second series **Danger Man** [aka **Secret Agent**] episode *It's Up to the Lady.*
Played Mr Barnes in the **Gideon's Way** episode *A Perfect Crime.*
Played Hamilton in the **Randall and Hopkirk [Deceased]** aka **My Partner the Ghost** episode *A Sentimental Journey.*

Baird Harry
Played Carlos in the second series **Danger Man** [aka **Secret Agent**] episode *A Man to be Trusted*, the first removal man in *Loyalty Always Pays* and the cellar man in the third season's *The Man on the Beach.*
Played an astronaut [Lieutenant Mark Bradley] in the **UFO** episodes *E.S.P.* and *Kill Straker!.*
Starred as Atimbu [Hunter's Bearer] in the **White Hunter** series.

Baird Jimmy
Starred as Pee-Wee in the **Fury** series.

Baisley George
Played Adam in the third season **Danger Man** [aka **Secret Agent**] episode *Someone is Liable to Get Hurt.*

Baker Dell
Played Rhys Brown in **The Baron** episode *The High Terrace.*

Baker Derek
Played Leon in the third season **Danger Man** [aka **Secret Agent**] episode *Dangerous Secret.*

Baker George
Played Frank Ashton in **The Baron** episode *So Dark the Night.*
Played Bailey in the **Gideon's Way** episode *The Great Plane Robbery.*
Played Britten in **The Persuaders!** episode *Chain of Events.*
Played the New Number Two in **The Prisoner** episode *Arrival.*
Played Dixon in the first series **The Protectors** episode *Your Witness.*

Baker Jane
Co-wrote the second series **Space 1999** episode *A Matter of Balance* [with Pip Baker].

Baker Joe
Played Bernie Greenberg in the **Shirley's World** episode *Follow that Rickshaw.*
Played Dick Blaise in the **Strange Report** episode *Report 4977: SWINDLE: 'Square Root of Evil'.*

Baker John
Played Quentin in the season three **The Adventures of Robin Hood** episodes *The Christmas Goose* & *The Bride of Robin Hood.*
Played the first security officer in the **White Hunter** episode *Pegasus.*

Baker Ken
Assistant Director on **The Adventurer, The Baron, The Champions, Department S, Jason King, Randall and Hopkirk [Deceased]** aka **My Partner the Ghost** and **Space 1999**.

Baker Ken
Played the Croat in the first series **Man of the World** episode *Specialist for the Kill.*

Baker Mark
Played the first man in **The Four Just Men** episode *Panic Button*, the reporter in *The Judge* and Minelli in *Riot*.

Baker Pip
Wrote the second series **Space 1999** episode *A Matter of Balance* [with Jane Baker].

Baker Robert S.
Producer [with Monty Berman] on **Gideon's Way**.
Devised and produced **The Persuaders!** series.
Executive Producer on **Return of The Saint** [credited as: 'A Robert S. Baker Tribune Films, a RAI/ITC Co-Production for ITC World Wide Distribution'].
Producer thoughout **The Saint** series [with Monty Berman on the first two seasons]. Also directed the first season episodes *The Golden Journey, The Saint Sees it Through, The Saint Plays with Fire & The Wonderful War*.

Baker Roy
Sound Editor on **Jason King** .

Baker Roy
Directed **The Baron** episodes *There's Someone Close Behind You, Night of the Hunter, The Long, Long Day & The Man Outside*.
Directed the **Gideon's Way** episodes *The Firebug, The White Rat & Subway to Revenge*.
Directed the **The Saint** episodes *Teresa, Luella & The Good Medicine* [season 1]; *The Scorpion, The Set-Up, The Inescapable Word & The Frightened Inn-Keeper* [2]; *The Helpful Pirate, The Queen's Ransom, Little Girl Lost, Flight Plan, The Persistent Patriots, The Art Collectors & Simon and Delilah* [3] and the fourth series two parter *The Fiction Makers*.

Baker Roy Ward
Directed **The Champions** episodes *Nutcracker* and *Autokill*.
Directed the **Department S** episode *The Pied Piper of Hambledown*.
Directed the **Jason King** episode *Wanna Buy a Television Series* [aka *A Face I Used to Know*].
Directed **The Persuaders!** episodes *The Gold Napoleon, Someone Like Me, Read and Destroy & The Ozerov Inheritance*.
Directed the first season **The Protectors** episode *The Big Hit*.
Directed the **Randall and Hopkirk [Deceased]** aka **My Partner the Ghost** episodes *But what a Sweet Little Room & Who Killed Cock Robin*.
Directed the **Return of the Saint** episodes *Yesterday's Hero & Tower Bridge is Falling Down*.
Directed the fourth season **The Saint** episode *Legacy for the Saint*.

Bakshi Prem
Played the Captain in the second series **Danger Man** [aka **Secret Agent**] episode *Fish on the Hook*.

Baku Shango
Played Caliban in the **Return of the Saint** episode *One Black September*.

Balbina
Played Margie in the **Interpol Calling** episode *The Long Weekend* and the Sister in **The Persuaders!** episode *The Gold Napoleon*.

Balcombe Dennis
Played Driver in the **Timeslip** story *The Day of the Clone* [series parts 21 - 26].

Balcon Jill
Played Maria Karoleon in the first series **The Protectors** episode *Brother Hood*.

Balfour Michael
Played Gaston in the second series **Danger Man** [aka **Secret Agent**] episode *Have a Glass of Wine*.
Played Eccles in the **Department S** episode *The Trojan Tanker*.
Guested as Russ in the **Interpol Calling** episode *Trial at Cranby's Creek* and as Insp. Hill in *A Foreign Body*.
Played Donkey Cart Driver in **The Persuaders!** episode *The Man in the Middle*.
Played Will in **The Prisoner** episode *Living in Harmony*.

Balfour Virginia
Played Alice Fortune in the **Timeslip** story *The Wrong End of Time* [episodes 1 & 2].

Ball Ralph
Played Photographer 2 in the fourth season **The Saint** two parter *The Fiction Makers*.

Ball Sally
Continuity on **Jason King** and **Randall and Hopkirk [Deceased]** aka **My Partner the Ghost**.

Ball Vincent
Played Father Huggins in the season two **Ghost Squad** episode *The Big Time*.
Played Dalby in the **Man in a Suitcase** episode *The Boston Square*.
Played Trevor in the **White Hunter** episode *The Stepfathers*.

Ballard Edward
Played the sailor in the **O.S.S.** episode *Operation Orange Blossom*.

Balogh Elizabeth
Played the Hungarian peasant woman in the second series **The Protectors** episode *Border Line*.

Balsam Martin
Featured as a special guest star in the **Espionage** episode *Final Decision*.

Bamore
Produced the third and fourth seasons of The Saint for ITC World Wide Distribution [New World produced the first two].

Banes Lionel B.S.C.
Director of Photography on **Man in a Suitcase**.

Banks Spencer
Starred as Simon Randall in the **Timeslip** series.

Bannen Ian
Guested as Sir Walter in the debut season of **The Adventures of Robin Hood** episode *The May Queen*.
Played Felipe in **The Count of Monte Cristo** episode *Majorca*.

Bannister Trevor
Played PC John Moss in the **Gideon's Way** episode *The Reluctant Witness*.
Played Johnny Fox in the fourth season **The Saint** episode *Portrait of Brenda*.

Baptiste Austin
Played Zafrini in the **Virgin of the Secret Service** episode *Pride of Assassins* and the drummer in *The Pyramid Plot*.

Baptiste Thomas
Played Odzala in the second series **Danger Man** [aka **Secret Agent**] episode *Such Men are Dangerous*.

Played President Obono in the **Return of the Saint** episode *The Obono Affair*.

Played the police sergeant in the first season **The Saint** episode *The Arrow of God* and Grant in the third season's *Island of Chance*.

Played Kamoba in the **White Hunter** episode *Sister My Spouse*.

Baraker Gabor
Played the Innkeeper in **The Champions** episode *The Search*.

Played Abramov in the first series **Man of the World** episode *Specialist for the Kill*.

Played the barman in the fourth season **The Saint** episode *Vendetta for the Saint* [part 1].

Barber Neville
Played the plainclothes Inspector in the **Jason King** episode *Toki*; the attendant in the second season **The Protectors** episode *Shadbolt* and the reporter in the **Strange Report** episode *Report 2493: KIDNAP: 'Whose Pretty Girl Are You?'*.

Barbour Heather
Played the secretary in the **Jason King** episode *The Stones of Venice*.

Barbour Joyce
Played Landy Kempson in the first series **Man of the World** episode *Portrait of a Girl*.

Barclay Mary
Played Mrs Garnes in **The Four Just Men** episode *Dead Man's Switch*.

Barcroft John
Played the bank cashier in **The Baron** episode *The Legions of Ammak*.

Played Vernon in the third season **Danger Man** [aka **Secret Agent**] episode *The Hunting Party*.

Played Dinni Haigh in the fourth season **The Saint** episode *The Time to Die*.

Played Dr Bukov in the **Timeslip** story *The Time of the Ice Box* [series parts 7 - 12].

Baring Victor
Played the airport official in the first season **Danger Man** episode *An Affair of State*.

Played the hotel clerk in **The Four Just Men** episode *Rogue's Harvest*.

Played the barman in the **G.S.5** episode *Scorpion Rock*.

Played Escatore in the **Jason King** episode *That isn't Me, It's Somebody Else*.

Played the policeman in the first series **Man of the World** episode *Blaze of Glory*.

Played Guido in the **O.S.S.** episode *Operation Payday*.

Barker Eric
Played Mr Lovegrove in the second series **Danger Man** [aka **Secret Agent**] episode *The Ubiquitous Mr Lovegrove*.

Played Robert Gresham in the **Gideon's Way** episode *How to Retire without Really Working*.

Barker Ronnie
Played Alphonse in the third season **The Saint** episode *The Better Mousetrap*.

Barker Wade
Played Michael in the **Strange Report** episode *Report 2475: REVENGE: 'When a Man Hates'*.

Barnabe Bruno
Played Gomez in **The Buccaneers** [aka **Dan Tempest**] episode *Prize of Andalusia*.

Played Buller in the **Father Brown** episode *The Mirror of the Magistrate*.

Played Terranti in **The Four Just Men** episode *The Man With the Golden Touch* and Mark in *The Godfather*.

Played the First Secretary in the **H. G. Wells' Invisible Man** episode *The Decoy*.

Guested as Dekker in the **Interpol Calling** episode *No Flowers for Onno*.

Played the Maitre D in **The Persuaders!** episode *Overture*.

Played Inspector Mateoli in the first season **The Saint** episode *The King of the Beggars*.

Played Girolamo in the **Sword of Freedom** episode *Marriage of Convenience*.

Barnes Frank
Played Capt. Joubert in **The Count of Monte Cristo** episode *Point Counter Point*.

Barnes Michael
Casting on **The Protectors** and **Space 1999**.

Barnes Simon
Played the man with cards in the **Randall and Hopkirk [Deceased]** aka **My Partner the Ghost** episode *That's How Murder Snowballs*.

Barnham Daron
Appeared as the boy in the first series **The Protectors** episode *.....With a Little Help from my Friends*.

Barnikel Philip
Editor on **Department S**.

Barnsley Bernard
Played Berger in the **G.S.5** episode *Pay Up or Else*.

Baron Tony
Played Fausto in the second series **Danger Man** [aka **Secret Agent**] episode *You're Not in Any Trouble, Are You?*

Barr Patrick
Guested in **The Adventures of Robin Hood** first season episodes *Richard the Lionheart* and *Secret Mission* as Peregrinus.

Played Crawley in the **Department S** episode *The Bones of Byrom Blain*.

Played Mark Richmond in **The Four Just Men** episode *The Man in the Road*.

Played Yateman in the **Randall and Hopkirk [Deceased]** aka **My Partner the Ghost** episode *You Can Always find a Fall Guy*.

Barrard John
Played Concierge in **The Count of Monte Cristo** episode *Majorca*.

Played Milo in the **G.S.5** episode *Pay Up or Else*.

Played Gem Setter in the first series **The Protectors** episode *Triple Cross*.

Played Pedlar in the first season **The Saint** episode *The Pearls of Peace*.

Barrat Reginald
Played Barbier in the third season **Danger Man** [aka **Secret Agent**] episode *Dangerous Secret* and the porter in the **Department S** episode *Last Train to Redbridge*.

Barrett Claudia
Played Odette in **The Count of Monte Cristo** episode *The Duel*.

Barrett Jane
Played Jenny in the **H. G. Wells' Invisible Man** episode *Point of Destruction*.

Barrett John
Played the ministry clerk in **The Baron** episode *Masquerade* [Part 1 of a 2 parter: also exists, edited together with part 2, *The Killing*, to form a feature *Man In a Looking Glass*].
Played Melchek in the second series **Ghost Squad** episode *Interrupted Requiem*.
Played Reiter in the **Return of the Saint** episode *The Obono Affair*.
Played the Inspector in the Grey Goose in the first season **The Saint** episode *The Fellow Traveller*.

Barrett Ray
Played Mr Hicks in the season two **Ghost Squad** episode *Polsky* and starred as Peter Clarke in the series **G.S.5**.
Played Robert Carne in the **Gideon's Way** episode *The Lady Killer*.
Played Charlie West in the first series **Man of the World** episode *The Highland Story*.
Played Willie Kinsall in the second season **The Saint** episode *The Loving Brothers*.
Provided the voices for Commander Shore and Titan / SL Fisher on the series **Stingray**.
Voiced John Tracey and The Hood in **Thunderbirds**.

Barrett Reginald
Played the valet manager in the **Strange Report** episode *Report 1021: SHRAPNEL: 'The Wish in the Dream'*.

Barrett Sean
Played Brunetto in the **Sword of Freedom** episode *The School*.

Barrett Tim
Played John Radcliffe in **The Persuaders!** episode *Someone Waiting*.
Played Lee Leonard in the second season **The Saint** episode *The Chequered Flag* and the steward in the third season's *A Double in Diamonds*.

Barrie Amanda
Played Rosemary in the fourth season **Danger Man** [aka Secret Agent] episode *Koroshi* [also merged with the only other surviving fourth season colour episode, *Shinda Shima*, to form a TVM entitled *Koroshi*].

Barrie Frank
Played Werner in **The Adventurer** episode *I'll Get There Sometime*.

Barrie John
Played Vladimir Horvic in **The Adventurer** episode *Miss Me Once, Miss Me Twice and Miss Me Once Again*.
Played the Yeoman in the season three **The Adventures of Robin Hood** episode *The Ghost that Failed*.
Played Will Rikker in the **Gideon's Way** episode *The Wall*.
Played Harry Thyssen in the **Man in a Suitcase** episode *Man from the Dead*.
Played Elliot Vascoe in the first season **The Saint** episode *The Benevolent Burglary* and Coleman in the third season's *Locate and Destroy*.

Barrington Michael
Appeared as Emile in the second series of **The Adventures of Robin Hood** episode *Flight from France*.
Guested as the manager in **The Champions** episode *Nutcracker*.
Played Heppel in the **Department S** episode *Death on Reflection*.

Barron John
Played Byrom Blain in the **Department S** episode *The Bones of Byrom Blain*.
Played Lazenger in the season two **Ghost Squad** episode *The Grand Duchess*.

Played the insurance executive in the second season **The Protectors** episode *Baubles, Bangles and Beads*.
Played Neal Lammerton in the fourth season **The Saint** episode *The Scales of Justice*.
Played Merchant in the **Sword of Freedom** episode *Angelica's Past*.
Played Devereaux in the **Timeslip** story *The Time of the Ice Box* [series parts 7 - 12] and *The Day of the Clone* [series episodes 22-24].

Barron Keith
Played Jarvis in the **Randall and Hopkirk [Deceased]** aka **My Partner the Ghost** episode *When Did you Start to Stop Seeing Things?*.
Played Inspector Graves in the **Strange Report** episode *Report 8944: HAND: 'A Matter of Witchcraft?'*.

Barron Ray
Played the boy in the Bar in the second series **Danger Man** [aka **Secret Agent**] episode *You're Not in Any Trouble, Are You?*

Barrows Elizabeth
Co-wrote, with Anthony Terpiloff, the first series **Space 1999** episodes *Death's Other Dominion* & *The Infernal Machine*.

Barry Gene
Starred as Gene Bradley in the series **The Adventurer**.

Barry Hilda
Played Mrs Critchley in the **Gideon's Way** episode *The Firebug*.
Appeared as Number 38 in **The Prisoner** episode *The Chimes of Big Ben*.

Barry John
Wrote the title theme for **The Adventurer** & **The Persuaders!**.

Barry Rudolf
Played the attendant in the second season **The Protectors** episode *Wam* [part one].

Bartman Frederick
Played Lucien Holz in **The Baron** episode *A Memory of Evil*.
Played Philippe Granville in the second series **Danger Man** [aka **Secret Agent**] episode *English Lady Takes Lodgers* and Genicot in *The Battle of the Cameras*.
Played Henry Waldo in the **Gideon's Way** episode *Gang War*.

Bartoli Luciano
Played Shehu in the **Return of the Saint** episode *The Judas Game*.

Bartrop Roland
Played Father Justin in the season two **The Adventures of Robin Hood** episode *The Little People*.

Bartrop Rowland
Played Hogarth in the season three **The Adventures of Robin Hood** episode *The Angry Village*.
Played Brock in the **Interpol Calling** episode *Trial at Cranby's Creek* and Grimond in *Diamond S.O.S.*, *The Thousand Mile Alibi* & *Dead On Arrival*.
Starred as, series regular [episodes 1 - 27], Sandro in the series **Sword of Freedom**.

Barwick Tony
Script Editor on **Captain Scarlet and the Mysterons** and wrote the episodes *Winged Assassin*, *Big Ben Strikes Again*, *Manhunt*, *Spectrum Strikes Back*, *Special Assignment*, *The Heart of New York*, *Lunarville 7*, *The Traitor*, *Crater 101*, *Shadow of Fear*, *Dangerous Rendezvous*, *Treble Cross*, *Flight*

104, Noose of Ice, Inferno [with Shane Rimmer], *Flight to Atlantica, Attack on Cloudbase & The Inquisition.*

Script Editor on the **Joe 90** series and wrote the episodes *Most Special Astronaut, Project 90, Hi-jacked, Colonel McClaine, International Concerto, Splashdown, The Unorthodox Shepherd, Business Holiday, Arctic Adventure, Double Agent, Three's a Crowd, The Race, Talkdown, See You Down There, Attack of the Tiger, The Birthday* [format by Gerry and Sylvia Anderson] and *Viva Cordova.*

Wrote **The Persuaders!** episodes *Element of Risk & Nuisance Value* [co-wrote with David Rolfe].

Script Editor on **The Protectors** series and wrote the first season episodes *It Could be Practically Anywhere on the Island, The First Circle, King Con & For the Rest of your Natural ...* and the second's *Petard, The Last Frontier, Wam* [two parter], *Implicado, The Bridge, Shadbolt & Wheels.*

Script Editor on **The Secret Service** and wrote the episodes *To Catch a Spy, The Feathered Spies, Last Train to Bufflers Halt, Errand of Mercy* and *More Haste - Less Speed.*

Wrote the second season **Space 1999** episodes *One Moment of Humanity & The A B Chrysalis.*

Wrote the second season **Thunderbirds** episodes *Lord Parker's 'Oliday & Richochet.*

Script Editor on the series **UFO** and wrote the episodes *Exposed, Identified* [with Gerry Anderson & Sylvia Anderson], *A Question of Priorities, Close up, The Psychobombs, Survival, Mindbender, Ordeal, Court Martial, Computer Affair, Confetti Check A-O.K. & The Responsibility Seat.*

Basillsco Carlos

Played the Flamenco singer in the second season **Man of the World** episode *The Bullfighter.*

Baskcomb John

Played Lewis Enstone in the second season **The Saint** episode *The Man who Liked Toys.*

Bass Alfie

Played Edgar in the first series **The Adventures of Robin Hood** episodes *The Coming of Robin Hood, The Moneylender & The Ordeal* and Lepidus in the second season's *The Goldmaker & The Goldmaker's Return.*

Played Barney Brandygore in **The Adventures of Sir Lancelot** episode *The Theft of Excalibur.*

Played Sawney in **The Buccaneers** [aka **Dan Tempest**] episode *Blackbeard.*

Played Max Fischer in the **Gideon's Way** episode *State Visit.*

Played Sammy in the **Return of the Saint** episode *Tower Bridge is Falling Down.*

Played the thief in **The Scarlet Pimpernel** episode *Gentlemen of the Road* and the labourer in *The Lady in Distress.*

Bastedo Alexandra

Played Lola Wells in **The Adventurer** episode *Action!.*

Starred in **The Champions** as Sharron Macready.

Played Nicole in the **Department S** episode *The Man who got a New Face.*

Played Alexandra in the **Jason King** episode *Variations on a Theme.*

Played Carol Latimer in the **Randall and Hopkirk [Deceased] aka My Partner the Ghost** episode *Who Ever Heard of a Ghost Dying?.*

Played Joan Vendel in the second season **The Saint** episode *The Crime of the Century* and Mireille in the third season's *The Counterfeit Countess.*

Bate Anthony

Played Dr Pederson in **The Champions** episode *The Mission.*

Played Dr Kirk in the **Gideon's Way** episode *Boy with a Gun.*

Played Martin Irelock in the first season **The Saint** episode *The Elusive Ellshaw*, Christopher Waites in the second season's *The Imprudent Politician* and Sardon in the third season's *The House on Dragon's Rock.*

Played Tilsto in the **Sir Francis Drake** episode *The Bridge.* Appeared as the pilot in the **White Hunter** episode *A Moment of Truth.*

Bateman Tony

Played the barman in the first series **The Protectors** episode *The Big Hit.*

Bates Alan

Played Giorgio in **The Four Just Men** episode *Treviso Dam.*

Bates Barbara

Played Helen Ravenna in the first season **The Saint** episode *The Loaded Tourist.*

Bates Eileen

Hairdresser on the first season of **The Adventures of Robin Hood**.

Bates Jane

Played Lila Prentice in the fourth season **The Saint** episode *Where the Money Is.*

Bates Michael

Played Corporal Bates in **The Four Just Men** episode *The Deserter.*

Played Edward in the **Jason King** episode *As Easy as A B C.*

Played Delucroix in the **Man in a Suitcase** episode *Blind Spot.*

Bates Ralph

Played Alan Keeble in the **Jason King** episode *Variations on a Theme.*

Played Michel in **The Persuaders!** episode *Nuisance Value.*

Played David Lee in the second season **The Protectors** episode *Petard.*

Bateson Timothy

Played Parker in the **Gideon's Way** episode *The Lady Killer.*

Played Pfeiffer in the **Man in a Suitcase** episode *Man from the Dead.*

Played Charley Butterworth in the first season **The Saint** episode *The Gentle Ladies.*

Bath John

Music on **The Scarlet Pimpernel** [episodes 5 to 10 & 12 to 18: Edwin Astley did 2 to 4 & 11].

Bathurst Peter

Appeared as Colonel Sutton in the **White Hunter** episode *Run to Earth.*

Bauer David

Played Bruno Orsini in **The Baron** episode *The Man Outside.*

Provided the narration for **The Champions** series and guested as Doctor Glind in the episode *The Experiment.*

Played Harlan in the **Department S** episode *Dead Men Die Twice.*

Played Elliott Henderson in the **Gideon's Way** episode *The Millionaire's Daughter.*

Played Harry Carmel in the **Jason King** episode *Wanna Buy a Television Series* aka *A Face I Used to Know.*

Played the judge in **The Prisoner** episode *Living in Harmony.*

Played Carl Huron in the first series **The Protectors** episode *Disappearing Trick.*

Played Dr. Conrad in the **Randall and Hopkirk [Deceased] aka My Partner the Ghost** episode *A Disturbing Case.*

Played Vern Balton in the first season **The Saint** episode *The Ever-loving Spouse*, Carlton Rood in *The Element of Doubt*, Burt Northwade in *Judith* and Rick Lansing in *Iris.* Returned in the third series to play Doctor Charles Krayford in *Island of Chance.*

Played Otis Dean in the **Strange Report** episode *Report 2493: KIDNAP: 'Whose Pretty Girl Are You?'.*

Played Big Jack in the **Virgin of the Secret Service** episode *The Professor Goes West*.

Baulch Alan
Played Peter Wray in the **Gideon's Way** episode *Big Fish, Little Fish*.
Played Steve in the **Man in a Suitcase** episode *All that Glitters*.

Baxt George
Wrote the **Sword of Freedom** episodes *The Tower, Alessandro, The Slave, The Suspects, The Lion and the Mouse, The Strange Intruder, The Besieged Duchess, A Game of Chance, Who is Felicia?* and *Adrianna*.

Baxter Clive
Played the security officer in **The Four Just Men** episode *The Deserter* and the newspaperman in *The Prime Minister*.
Played the sentry in the **H. G. Wells' Invisible Man** episode *The Prize*.

Baxter David
Played Bob in the **Man in a Suitcase** episode *Variation on a Million Bucks* [first part: the instalment was also combined with part two to form a movie entitled *To Chase a Million*].

Baxter Keith
Played Geoffrey Miles in the **Gideon's Way** episode *The 'V' Men*.
Played Yanni in **The Sentimental Agent** episode *Not Quite Fully Covered*.

Baxter Stanley
Featured in the **Espionage** episode *The Frantic Rebel*.

Bay J. M.
Played Anderson in **The Persuaders!** episode *Element of Risk*.

Bay John
Played the second pilot in the **O.S.S.** episode *Operation Blackbird*.

Bayldon Geoffrey
Played Cal in the season three **The Adventures of Robin Hood** episode *The Angry Village* and Count de Severne in *The Genius*.
Played Dickinson in the second series **Danger Man** [aka Secret Agent] episode *A Very Dangerous Game*.
Played Ernst Hartmann in the **G.S.5** episode *Rich Ruby Wine*.
Played the Abwehr Lieutenant in the **O.S.S.** episode *Operation Dagger*.
Played Wilfred Garniman in the second season **The Saint** episode *The Scorpion* and Marcel Legrand in the third season's *The Art Collectors*.
Played Number Eight in the second season **Space 1999** episode *One Moment of Humanity*.
Made three appearances in **Sword of Freedom**: played the physician in *The Ship*, Luigi in *The Lion and the Mouse* and Muzio in *Choice of Weapons*.

Bayona Tanya
Played the girl with the pram in the first series **The Protectors** episode *It was All Over in Leipzig*.

Bazely Sally
Played Joan Baker in the first season **Danger Man** episode *The Honeymooners*.
Played Mrs Hunter in the first series **The Protectors** episode *The First Circle*.
Played Jenny Hallam in the first season **The Saint** episode *The Careful Terrorist*.

Bazzocchi Loris
Played Guzzi in the **Return of the Saint** episode *The Village that Sold its Soul*.

Beacham Rod
Played the cafe proprietor in the **Strange Report** episode *Report 7931: SNIPER: 'When is Your Cousin Not?'*.

Beacham Stephanie
Played Countess Maria in **The Adventurer** episode *Icons Are Forever*.
Played Simpson in the **Jason King** episode *Chapter One: The Company I Keep*.
Played Christie in the first series **The Protectors** episode *Your Witness*.
Played Penny in the fourth season **The Saint** episode *Legacy for the Saint*.
Played Sarah Bosanquet in the **UFO** episode *Destruction*.

Beale Basil
Played the Man-at-Arms in the second series of **The Adventures of Robin Hood** episode *The Secret Pool*.

Beale David
Played Sr Summers in **The Baron** episode *The Edge of Fear*.
Played Colin Whetlor in the **Department S** episode *Black Out*.

Beale Richard
Played Captain Vanner in the **Gideon's Way** episode *The White Rat*.

Beard Stanley
Played Yates in the **Department S** episode *The Pied Piper of Hambledown*.

Beaton John
Music Editor on **Gideon's Way**.

Beaton Norman
Played the chauffeur in the second season **The Protectors** episode *Route 27*.
Played the policeman in the **Randall and Hopkirk [Deceased]** aka **My Partner the Ghost** episode *Money to Burn*.

Beauman Frederick
Played the hotel proprietor in the **Man in a Suitcase** episode *Night Flight to Andora*.

Beaumont Diana
Played Lady Beth in the second series of **The Adventures of Robin Hood** episode *The Black Patch*.

Beaumont Richard
Played Bill in the **Strange Report** episode *Report 2475: REVENGE: 'When a Man Hates'*.

Beaumont Victor
Played Heuer in **The Baron** episode *Roundabout*.
Played Wim Harmsen in the first series **Ghost Squad** episode *Still Waters*.
Guested as Esler in the **Interpol Calling** episode *No Flowers for Onno*.
Played Doctor Schreiber in the second season **The Saint** episode *The Rhine Maiden* and Karsh in the third season's *Locate and Destroy*.

Bebb Richard
Played Dodge in **The Count of Monte Cristo** episode *The Portuguese Affair*.
Played Major Casado in the second series **Danger Man** [aka Secret Agent] episode *A Date with Doris*.

Played Gold in the first series **Ghost Squad** episode *The Broken Doll*.
Played Matelon in the **O.S.S.** episode *Operation Post Office*.
Played Captain Huber in the **William Tell** episode *The Bride*.

Beck Glenn
Played the Intern in the first season **Danger Man** episode *The Contessa* and Motril in *Josetta*.
Played Martin in the first series **Man of the World** episode *The Nature of Justice*.
Played Jake Reilly in the **Virgin of the Secret Service** episode *The Professor Goes West*.

Beck Maureen
Played Mary Sin Chui in the **G.S.5** episode *Seven Sisters of Wong*.
Played Rosa in the **William Tell** episode *The Master Spy*.

Beck Nancy
Played Duenna in the **Sir Francis Drake** episode *Visit to Spain*.

Beck Roy
Background [actor] on **The Prisoner**.

Becker Neville
Played Danny in the first season **Danger Man** episode *Colonel Rodriguez*, Messadi in the second series [now aka **Secret Agent**] episode *Sting in the Tail* and the airport official in *Judgement Day*.
Played Paco in the **Man in a Suitcase** episode *The Man who Stood Still*.
Played the Consulate official in the first series **Man of the World** episode *The Sentimental Agent*.
Played Lieutenant Prevost in the first season **The Saint** episode *The Work of Art*, the doctor in *The Charitable Countess*, Palermo in the second season's *The Saint Bids Diamonds* and Mahmoud in the third's *The Queen's Ransom*.

Becket Albert
Production Manager on **The Buccaneers** [aka **Dan Tempest**] episodes *Articles of War, Ghost Ship, Conquest of New Providence, Mother Doughty's Crew, Blood Will Tell, Hurricane, Dead Man's Rock, Dangerous Cargo, Hand of the Hawk, Gentleman Jack and the Lady, Mr. Beamish and the Hangman's Noose, Marooned, Dan Tempest and The Amazons, The Return of Calico Jack, Conquistador* and *Aztec Treasure*.

Beckett James
Played Previn in **The Persuaders!** episode *Chain of Events*.
Played Doctor Young in the **UFO** episode *Close up*.

Beckh Nancy
Played the housekeeper in the first season **Danger Man** episode *The Brothers*.

Beckley Tony
Played Giorgio in the **Jason King** episode *Toki*.
Played John Kennet in the first season **The Saint** episode *The Saint Plays with Fire* and Barry Aldon in *Marcia*.

Beckwith Reginald
Played Sir Louis in the third series **The Adventures of Robin Hood** episode *Elixir of Youth*.
Played Enderby in the first season **The Saint** episode *The High Fence*.
Played the tax inspector in **The Scarlet Pimpernel** episode *The Farmer's Boy*.
Played Truman-Jones in **The Sentimental Agent** episode *Not Quite Fully Covered*.
Played Sir Henry Rainsford in the **Sir Francis Drake** episode *The Fountain of Youth*.

Bedard Virginia
Played the woman in **The Four Just Men** episode *The Judge*.

Bedenes Pierre
Played the hotel porter in the second season **The Protectors** episode *Decoy*.

Bedford Brian
Played Estaban in the **Sir Francis Drake** episode *Escape*.

Bedford Patrick
Played the guard in the second series of **The Adventures of Robin Hood** episode *The Bandit of Brittany*.
Played John Cavendish in **The Baron** episode *Farewell to Yesterday*.
Played Casey in the **Gideon's Way** episode *A Perfect Crime*.

Beeby Bruce
Guested as the pilot in **The Champions** episode *Project Zero*.
Played Bob Royston in the first series **Ghost Squad** episode *Million Dollar Ransom*.
Played Chalmers in the **Randall and Hopkirk [Deceased]** aka **My Partner the Ghost** episode *Could You Recognise the Man Again?*.
Played the desk attendant in the **Timeslip** story *The Day of the Clone* [series episodes 21-23].

Beeson Paul, BSC
Director of Photography on **The Saint**.

Behr Arthur
Wrote the debut season of **The Adventures of Robin Hood** episodes *Trial by Battle* and *The Thorkill Ghost*.

Beint Michael
Played the ticket inspector in the season two **Ghost Squad** episode *Sentences of Death*.
Played Divisional Inspector Marsh in the **Gideon's Way** episode *How to Retire without Really Working*.
Played the senior official in the **Randall and Hopkirk [Deceased]** aka **My Partner the Ghost** episode *Just for the Record*.
Played Dieter in the third season **The Saint** episode *The Paper Chase*.

Bejerano Enrique
Played the guitarist in the second season **Man of the World** episode *The Bullfighter*.

Bell Alfred
Played Brinkley in the **Strange Report** episodes *Report 2475: REVENGE: 'When a Man Hates'* & *Report 8944: HAND: 'A Matter of Witchcraft?'*.

Bell Ann
Played Nikki Holtz in **The Baron** episode *A Memory of Evil*.
Played Leslie Vincent in the third season **Danger Man** [aka **Secret Agent**] episode *To our Best Friend*.
Played May Heywood in the **Department S** episode *The Duplicated Man*.
Played Netta Penn in the **Gideon's Way** episode *The Wall*.
Played Marjorie North in the second season **The Saint** episode *The Inescapable Word* and Natasha in the third season's *The Art Collectors*.
Played Katrina in **The Sentimental Agent** episode *Express Delivery*.

Bell Arnold
Played Villon in **The Count of Monte Cristo** episode *The Carbonari*.
Guested as Antigas in the **Interpol Calling** episode *Checkmate*.

Bell Bob
Art Director on **Fireball XL5**, **The Protectors**, **Stingray**, **Thunderbirds** and **UFO** [also co-wrote the episode *The Sound of Silence* - with David Lane].

Bell Keith
Played Bill in the second series **Danger Man** [aka **Secret Agent**] episode *Don't Nail Him Yet*.
Played Sammy in the **Gideon's Way** episode *Gang War*.
Played Sergeant Peters in the first series **The Protectors** episode *Thinkback*.
Played the film director in the **UFO** episode *Reflections in the Water*.

Bell Michael
Played the Captain-of-the-Guard in the **Sir Francis Drake** episode *The Garrison*.

Bell Ralph
Played the Film Director in the **UFO** episode *The Responsibility Seat*.

Bell Tom
Played the title role in the second season **The Protectors** episode *Shadbolt*.

Bell Valerie
Played Thelma in the third season **The Saint** episode *The Fast Women*.

Bellak George
Wrote the first series **Space 1999** episode *Breakaway*.

Bellchamber James
Played Mark in the **Randall and Hopkirk [Deceased]** aka **My Partner the Ghost** episode *That's How Murder Snowballs*.
Played the photographer in the first season **The Saint** episode *The Lawless Lady*.

Bellman Geoffrey
Co-wrote the season two **Ghost Squad** episode *Sentences of Death* [with John Whitney].

Belton Eve
Played Tessa in the third season **The Saint** episode *Little Girl Lost*.

Beltramme Franco
Played the heavy in the **Return of the Saint** episode *The Roman Touch*.

Benda Kenneth
Played the supervisor in **The Prisoner** episode *Free for All*.
Played Lord Wentworth in the first season **The Saint** episode *The Lawless Lady*.

Benedetti Jean
Played the waiter in the third season **The Saint** episode *The Angel's Eye*.

Benesch Natalie
Played Matron in the first season **The Saint** episode *The Covetous Headman*.

Benet Marianne
Played Renata in the **Jason King** episode *Chapter One: The Company I Keep*.
Played the title role in the **Sword of Freedom** episode *Caterina*.
Played Dagma in the **William Tell** episode *The Suspect*.

Benfield Derek
Played the scientist in **The Baron** episode *The Persuaders*.
Starred as, series regular, Frank Skinner [Cheryl's dad] in the **Timeslip** series.

Benham Joan
Played Lady Galloway in the **Father Brown** episode *The Secret Garden*.

Benjamin Christopher
Played Verel in **The Baron** episode *The Seven Eyes of Night*.
Played Potter in the fourth season **Danger Man** [aka **Secret Agent**] episode *Koroshi* [*Koroshi* was also merged with the only other surviving fourth season colour episode, *Shinda Shima*, to form a TVM entitled *Koroshi*].
Played Jukes in the **Father Brown** episode *The Quick One*.
Played the police Inspector in the **Jason King** episode *A Red, Red Rose Forever*.
Played the Labour Exchange Manager in **The Prisoner** episode *Arrival*, Number Two's assistant in *The Chimes of Big Ben* and added weight to the theory that *The Prisoner* was a sequel to *Danger Man* by playing Potter in *The Girl who was Death*.
Played the Banker in the first series **The Protectors** episode *The Quick Brown Fox*.
Played Fish in the fourth season **The Saint** episode *The Master Plan*.

Benke Timothy
Played Tim in the first season **Danger Man** episode *The Conspirators*.

Bennett Charles
Director of episodes of **The Count of Monte Cristo** and **The New Adventures of Charlie Chan**.

Bennett Compton
Directed the fourth series of **The Adventures of Robin Hood** episodes *Hue and Cry* & *The Oath*.
Directed **The Four Just Men** episode *The Deadly Capsule*.

Bennett Frances
Played Anne Fenwick in the **Randall and Hopkirk [Deceased]** aka **My Partner the Ghost** episode *But what a Sweet Little Room*.

Bennett Frederick
Played the security man in the first series **The Protectors** episode *The First Circle*.

Bennett Jill
Featured in the **Espionage** episode *The Frantic Rebel*.

Bennett John
Played Salan in **The Baron** episode *Red Horse, Red Rider*.
Played the Minister in the second series **Danger Man** [aka **Secret Agent**] episode *The Colonel's Daughter*.
Played Tomas in the **Sir Francis Drake** episode *The Governor's Revenge*.
In **The Saint**: played Raschid in *The Wonderful War* [series 1], Alfredo in *The Good Medicine* [1], Ardossi in *The Contract* [2] and Muller in the third season's *The Gadget Lovers*
Played Jack White in the **Strange Report** episode *Report 0846: LONELYHEARTS: 'Who Killed Dan Cupid?'*.

Bennett Norman
Played the croupier in the **G.S.5** episode *It Won't be a Stylish Marriage*.

Bennett Peter
Appeared in a number of roles in the second series of **The Adventures of Robin Hood**: the Guard Commander in *A Village Wooing*, the Librarian in *The Scientist*, the Lawyer in *A Year

and a Day, the Steward in *Blackmail*, Mercer in *The Gold-maker*, Edwin in *Ransom*, the Tavern Keeper in *Isabella*, the Woodman in *The Hero*, Edward in *The Haunted Mill*, Eldred in *The Black Patch*, Eldred in *The Trap* and Edwin in *Ambush*.
Played Leonides in **The Adventures of Sir Lancelot** episodes *The Knight with the Red Plume* and *The Queen's Knight*.
Played Costellaux in **The Buccaneers [aka Dan Tempest]** episode *Blackbeard*, Sikes in *The Raiders* and Murchison in *Captain Dan Tempest*.
Played the doctor in the **Man in a Suitcase** episode *All that Glitters*.
Played Cruner in the **William Tell** episode *The Suspect* and the sergeant in *The Raid*.

Benning Ingrid
Played Annalisa in the second season **Ghost Squad** episode *The Thirteenth Girl*.

Bennison Bill
Art Director on **The Adventures of Sir Lancelot** episodes *Double Identity, The Bridge, The Witch's Brew, The Mortaise Fair, Maid of Somerset, Sir Crustabread, The Ugly Duckling, The Prince of Limerick, The Lady Lilith, Knight's Choice, The Missing Princess & The Thieves*.
Art Director on **The Buccaneers [aka Dan Tempest]** episodes *To the Rescue, Indian Fighters, Mistress Higgins' Treasure, The Decoy, Pirate Honour, Instrument of War* and *Printer's Devil*.

Benson Court
Played Finch in the first season **Danger Man** episode *View from the Villa*.

Benson George
Played Sir Cedric in the second series **The Adventures of Robin Hood** episode *The Secret Pool*.
Appeared as the police chief in the second season **Danger Man [aka Secret Agent]** episode *Have a Glass of Wine*.
Played the gym instructor in the **Jason King** episode *If it's Got to Go - It's Got to Go*.
Played the Labour Exchange Manager in **The Prisoner** episode *Free For All*.
Played Conrad in the **William Tell** episode *The Cuckoo*.

Benson Hamlyn
Played the gatekeeper in the **William Tell** episode *The Elixir*.

Benson Martin
Played Nicky Asteri in **The Adventurer** episode *The Case of the Poisoned Pawn*.
Appeared as Hassim in **The Adventures of Sir Lancelot** episode *The Mortaise Fair*.
Guested as Garcian in **The Champions** episode *Full Circle*.
Played Fawzi in the debut season **Danger Man** episode *Position of Trust*. In series two [now aka **Secret Agent**] played General Ventura in *The Affair at Castelevara*.
Played Captain Renald in **The Four Just Men** episode *The Boy Without a Country*.
Played Zervas in the season two **Ghost Squad** episode *Death of a Sportsman*.
Played Omar in the **H. G. Wells' Invisible Man** episode *Crisis in the Desert*.
Guested as Ahmed in the **Interpol Calling** episode *Mr George*.
Played Tullio in the **O.S.S.** episode *Operation Payday*.
Played the President in the first series **The Protectors** episode *.....With a Little Help from my Friends*.
Played Piet Ritter in the **White Hunter** episode *Dead Man's Tale*.
Played Major Quintana in the first season **The Saint** episode *The Work of Art*, Sanches in the third season's *The Reluctant Revolution* and Inspector Yolu in *The Gadic Collection*.
Starred as, series regular, Duke de Medici in the series **Sword of Freedom**.

Bentley Arthur
Played the doctor in the **O.S.S.** episode *Operation Fracture*.

Bentley Dick
Played Mesmero in the **Randall and Hopkirk [Deceased]** aka **My Partner the Ghost** episode *It's Supposed to be Thicker than Water*.
Played Charley O'Shea in the second season **The Saint** episode *The Loving Brothers*.

Bentley John
Played Dave Carson in the **Interpol Calling** episode *Pipeline*.

Berens Harold
Played the hotel landlord in the second series **Danger Man [aka Secret Agent]** episode *Judgement Day*.
Played Bunny in the **H. G. Wells' Invisible Man** episode *The Mink Coat*.
Appeared as the reporter in **The Prisoner** episode *Free For All* and as the boxing M.C. in *The Girl Who Was Death*.
Played Tony Lang in the **Randall and Hopkirk [Deceased]** aka **My Partner the Ghost** episode *That's How Murder Snowballs*.

Beret Dawn
Played the lady croupier in the **Department S** episode *Handicap Dead*.

Berger Helmut
Played Vidal in the **Return of the Saint** episode *The Murder Cartel*.

Berger Robert Buzz
Producer on the **Strange Report** series.

Bergmann Erika
Played the girlfriend in the second season **The Protectors** episode *Decoy*.

Bergmayer Lisa
Played an auction client in the **Father Brown** episode *The Arrow of Heaven*.

Berkley Ballard
Guested as Count de Waldern in the first season **The Adventures of Robin Hood** episode *Queen Eleanor* and as Tybalt in the third season's *Roman Gold*.
Played Sir Urgan in **The Adventures of Sir Lancelot** episode *The Ferocious Fathers*.
Played Rafton in **The Buccaneers [aka Dan Tempest]** episode *Dan Tempest Holds an Auction*.
Played Lieber in the season two **Ghost Squad** episode *The Retirement of Gentle Dove*.
Played Manton in the **H. G. Wells' Invisible Man** episode *Play to Kill*.
Played the doctor in **The Sentimental Agent** episode *Finishing School*.

Berkoff Steven
Guested as Carlos in **The Champions** episode *The Iron Man*.
Played Nelson Rador in the **G.S.5** episode *A Cast of Thousands*.
Played Carl in the fourth season **The Saint** episode *The Man Who Gambled with Life*.
Played Captain Steve Minto [the first astronaut] in the **UFO** episode *The Cat with Ten Lives* and appeared as an astronaut in *Destruction, Mindbender & Reflections in the Water*.

Berlin Arthur
Wrote the season two **Man of the World** episode *The Prince*.

Berlinka Jose
Played several roles in the second series of **Danger Man** [aka **Secret Agent**]: the cafe owner in *Sting in the Tail*, the servant in *A Room in the Basement* and the barman in *The Battle of the Cameras*.
Played the desk clerk in the **Man in a Suitcase** episode *The Boston Square*.

Berman Monty
Created the series **The Adventurer** [with Dennis Spooner] and served as Producer.
Producer on **The Baron**.
Created **The Champions** [with Dennis Spooner] and produced.
Created the series **Department S** [with Dennis Spooner] and was the producer.
Producer [with Robert S. Baker] on **Gideon's Way**.
Created the series **Jason King** [with Dennis Spooner] and was the producer.
Producer on the series **Randall and Hopkirk [Deceased]** aka **My Partner the Ghost**.
Producer on the first two seasons of **The Saint** [with Robert S. Baker].

Bernaducci Don
Construction Superintendent on **The Count of Monte Cristo**.

Bernal Robert
Played Count Percy in the season three **The Adventures of Robin Hood** episode *An Apple for the Archer*.
Played Miguel in the first season **Danger Man** episode *Josetta*.

Bernard Carl
Played several roles in **The Adventures of Robin Hood**: the Archbishop in *The Inquisitor*, Lord Duquesne in *My Brother's Keeper*, Dick Banks in *The Rivals*, the Archbishop in *Farewell to Tuck*, the Archbishop in *The Oath* and the pedlar in *The Pharaoh Stones*.
Played Hesse in **The Count of Monte Cristo** episode *Mecklenburg* and Latoure in *The Barefoot Empress*.
Played Leonido in the first season **Danger Man** episode *The Lovers*.
Played Major Stone in the season two **Ghost Squad** episode *The Retirement of Gentle Dove*.
Played Karl Braun in the **Man in a Suitcase** episode *Somebody Loses, Somebody ...Wins?*.
Played Galeotto in the **Sword of Freedom** episode *The Marionettes* and the President in *Alessandro*.

Bernard Dennis
Played the Commandante in the **Department S** episode *Les Fleurs du Mal*.
Played Monsieur Roget in the season two **Ghost Squad** episode *The Magic Bullet*.

Bernard Nicolette
Played Lady Ponsonby in **The Scarlet Pimpernel** episode *The Ambassador's Lady*.

Bernard Paul
Directed the **Virgin of the Secret Service** episodes *Dark Deeds on the Northwest Frontier*, *Entente Cordiale*, *The Great Ring of Akba* & *Pride of Assassins*.

Bernelle Agnes
Appeared in the first season **The Adventures of Robin Hood** episode *Dead or Alive* as the Countess.

Bertroya Paul
Played Silvio in the **Man in a Suitcase** episode *Jigsaw Man*.
Played Jean-Claude in the **Randall and Hopkirk [Deceased]** aka **My Partner the Ghost** episode *For the Girl who has Everything*.

Besserman Ann
Continuity on **The Prisoner** episode *Do Not Forsake Me Oh My Darling*.

Best Gloria
Played the stewardess in the **G.S.5** episode *Dr. Ayre*.

Best Norman
Wrote the second series of **The Adventures of Robin Hood** episode *The Impostor*.

Beswick Martine
Played one of the girls in the second series **Danger Man** [aka **Secret Agent**] episode *Such Men are Dangerous*.

Bettany Clemence
Played the chemist in the first season **The Saint** episode *The Talented Husband*.
Played Monique in the first series **Man of the World** episode *A Family Affair*.
Starred as, regular, Miss Carter in **The Sentimental Agent**.

Bettinson Ralph Gilbert
Wrote **The Scarlet Pimpernel** episodes *The Hostage*, *Gentlemen of the Road*, *The Winged Madonna* [with Joel Murcott], *The Christmas Present*, *The Ambassador's Lady* [with Murcott], *Sir Andrew's Fate*, *The Sword of Justice*, *The Elusive Chauvelin*, *Something Remembered* [with Murcott], *The Lady in Distress*, *The Princess* and *Sir Percy's Wager* [with Murcott].

Bevan Helene
Hairdresser on the series **Man of the World** and Hair Designer on **Space 1999**.

Bevan Julie
Played the second model in the **Man in a Suitcase** episode *The Sitting Pigeon*.

Bewes Rodney
Played Tim Gormond in the **Man in a Suitcase** episode *The Bridge*.
Played Ralph in the **Shirley's World** episode *A Girl Like You*.
Played Rajah of Chundrapore in the **Virgin of the Secret Service** episode *The Rajah and the Suffragette*.

Bigotti Rodolfo
Played Paolo in the **Return of the Saint** episode *Appointment in Florence*.

Billington Michael
Played the second woodland man in **The Prisoner** episode *A Change of Mind*.
Starred in the series **UFO** as, regular, Colonel Paul Foster.

Bilton Michael
Guested as Dan in **The Champions** episode *The Night People*.
Played the M.C./announcer/councillor in **The Prisoner** episode *It's Your Funeral*.
Played Bolande in the third season **The Saint** episode *To Kill a Saint*.

Bindon John
Played Greer in the **Department S** episode *Who Plays the Dummy?*.

Binney Neil
Camera Operator on **Space 1999**.

Birch Derek
Played De Sarigny in the fourth series **The Adventures of Robin Hood** episode *The Lady Killer*.

Birch Paul
Starred as Mike 'Cannonball' Malone in the series **Cannonball**.

Bird Michael
Appeared as the conductor in the debut season **Danger Man** episode *The Gallows Tree*. On series two [now aka **Secret Agent**] wrote the original story for *Judgement Day* [teleplayed by Donald Johnson].
Played the sleeping car attendant in the **Randall and Hopkirk [Deceased] aka My Partner the Ghost** episode *A Sentimental Journey*.

Bird Norman
Played Brooks in **The Adventurer** episode *Going, Going....*
Played Inspector Macaulay in **The Baron** episode *Roundabout*.
Played Drayton in the **Department S** episode *The Ghost of Mary Burnham*.
Played the gunsmith in the first series **Ghost Squad** episode *Assassin*.
Played Supt. Fred Lee in the **Gideon's Way** episode *To Catch a Tiger*.
Played Detective Inspector Fields in the **Jason King** episode *It's Too Bad about Auntie*.
Played Elliot in the **Randall and Hopkirk [Deceased] aka My Partner the Ghost** episode *But what a Sweet Little Room*.
Played Hackett in the first season **The Saint** episode *The Well-Meaning Mayor*, Weems in the second season episode *The Frightened Inn-Keeper*, Inspector Mitchell in the third season's *The Best Laid Schemes* and Mr. Spode in the fourth season's *The Organisation Man*.
Played Inspector Freeman in the **Shirley's World** episode *Evidence in Camera*.

Bird Penny
Played Eccles' girlfriend in the **Department S** episode *The Trojan Tanker*.

Bird Philip
Played Shapes in *Adventure Four* of **Sapphire and Steel**.

Birrel Peter
Played the Assistant Director in **The Adventurer** episode *The Solid Gold Hearse*.
Played Rossiter in the **Man in a Suitcase** episode *The Bridge*.
Played Toni Amato in the third season **The Saint** episode *Simon and Delilah*.
Played Major Zaki in the **Virgin of the Secret Service** episode *The Pyramid Plot*.

Birsen
Played a dancer in the **Virgin of the Secret Service** episode *The Pyramid Plot*.

Birt Dan
Directed the first season **The Adventures of Robin Hood** episodes *Dead or Alive*, *Queen Eleanor* and *The Ordeal*.

Birtles Steve
Gaffer on **The Saint**.

Bishop Charles
Art Director on **The Champions, The Persuaders!** & **Randall and Hopkirk [Deceased] aka My Partner the Ghost**.

Bishop Ed
aka Edward Bishop
Played Wayne in **The Adventurer** episode *Miss Me Once, Miss Me Twice and Miss Me Once Again*.
Provided the voice for Captain Blue in **Captain Scarlet and the Mysterons**.
Played the American agent in the **Man in a Suitcase** episode *The Boston Square*.

Played Hunter in the first series **The Protectors** episode *The First Circle*.
Played Cy Imberline in the second season **The Saint** episode *The Saint Steps In*, Sherm Inkler in *The Revolution Racket* & George Felson in *The Saint Bids Diamonds*. Played Tony Allard in the third season episode *The Man Who Liked Lions*.
Played Moran in the **Strange Report** episode *Report 5055: CULT: 'Murder Shrieks Out'*.
Starred throughout the series **UFO** as Commander Ed Straker.

Bishop Sue
Played an art student in the **Father Brown** episode *The Head of Caesar*.

Bishop Terry
Director on the second, third and fourth seasons of **The Adventures of Robin Hood**: *The Scientist, The Goldmaker, Outlaw Money, The Black Patch, The Trap, The Shell Game, The Final Tax, The Bandit of Brittany, The Goldmaker's Return, Flight from France, Fair Play, The York Treasure, Food for Thought, Highland Fling & The Mystery of Ireland's Eye* [series 2], *A Tuck in Time, The Charter, Change of Heart, An Apple for the Archer, The Angry Village, The Profiteer, Elixir of Youth, Lincoln Green, Little Mother & Farewell to Tuck* [3] and *Sybella, The Lady Killer, Tuck's Love Day, Six Strings to his bow, The Bagpiper, The Parting Guest, Race Against Time, A Bushel of Apples, Double Trouble & Trapped* [4].
Directed **The Adventures of Sir Lancelot** episodes *Caledon, The Witch's Brew, The Lesser Breed* and *The Magic Book*.
Directed **The Buccaneers** [aka **Dan Tempest**] episodes *The Wasp* and *Slave Ship*.
Directed the first season **Danger Man** episodes *View from the Villa, The Prisoner, The Traitor* & *The Contessa*.
Directed the **Sir Francis Drake** episodes *Beggars of the Sea, The Fountain of Youth, The Bridge, The Reluctant Duchess, Court Intrigue* & *Visit to Spain*.
Directed the **Sword of Freedom** episodes *Francesca, The Sicilian, Choice of Weapons, The Duke, The Eye of the Artist, The Bracelet, The Slave, The Suspects, Serenade in Red, Marriage of Convenience, The Value of Paper, Forgery in Red Chalk, The School, The Besieged Duchess* & *Adrianna*.
Directed the **William Tell** episodes *The Assassins, Landslide, The Boy Slaves, Voice in the Night, The Lost Letter* and *The Elixir*.

Bisset Donald
Played the tax collector in the fourth series **The Adventures of Robin Hood** episode *The Pharaoh Stones*.
Played Simms in the second season **The Saint** episode *The Inescapable Word*.

Bizley Roger
Played Jack in the season three **The Adventures of Robin Hood** episode *To Be a Student*.
Played MacDonald in the second season **Space 1999** episode *Journey to Where*.

Black Derek
Camera Operator on **The Secret Service**.

Black Dorothy
Played Lady Wentworth in the first season **The Saint** episode *The Lawless Lady*.

Black Ian Stuart
Wrote **The Champions** episode *Desert Journey*.
Associate Producer on the first series of **Danger Man** [episodes 1-12] and wrote the episodes: *Time to Kill* [with Brian Clemens: teleplayed from a story by Clemens], *The Girl in Pink Pyjamas* [with Ralph Smart: teleplayed from a story by Brian Clemens], *Deadline* [original story: teleplayed by Jo Eisinger], *The Journey Ends Halfway* & *Sabotage* [with Michael Pertwee].

Wrote the **H. G. Wells' Invisible Man** episodes *The Mink Coat* [teleplayed from a story by Leonore Coffee], *The Gun Runners*, *Odds Against Death* [teleplayed from a story idea by Stanley Mann], *Jailbreak*, *Point of Destruction*, *The Vanishing Evidence*, *The Prize*, *The White Rabbit*, *Flight into Darkness* [teleplayed from a story by W. H. Altman], *Man in Power*, *Shadow Bomb* [co-teleplayed with Tony O'Grady - aka Brian Clemens: from a story by Tony O'Grady], *The Big Plot* [teleplayed from a story by Tony O'Grady and Ralph Smart] and *Shadow on the Screen* [teleplayed from a story by Ralph Smart and Philip Levene].
Script Editor on the series **Man of the World** and wrote the first season episodes *The Mindreader* & *Shadow of the Wall*.
Wrote the second season **The Saint** episode *The Death Penalty*.
Script Supervisor on **The Sentimental Agent** series and wrote the episode *Box of Tricks*.
Script Editor on the series **Sir Francis Drake** and wrote the episodes *The Garrison*, *The Prisoner*, *Boy Jack* [with Cedric Wells], *The English Dragon*, *King of America*, *Beggars of the Sea*, *The Fountain of Youth* & *The Slaves of Spain*.
Wrote the **White Hunter** episode *The Long Knife*.
Wrote the story and screenplay for the **William Tell** episode *The General's Daughter*.

Black Isobel
Played Maruja in the third season **Danger Man** [aka **Secret Agent**] episode *The Man with the Foot*.
Played Maria in the **Department S** episode *The Soup of the Day*.
Played Colette in the **H. G. Wells' Invisible Man** episode *The White Rabbit*.
Played Acquilina in the second series **Man of the World** episode *Jungle Mission*.
Played Sophia in the **Sir Francis Drake** episode *Boy Jack*.

Black Walter
Wrote **The Persuaders!** episode *The Morning After*.

Blackburn Jane
Played Ruth Parke in **The Baron** episode *Red Horse, Red Rider*.

Blackler George
Make-up on **Jason King** and Make-up Supervisor on **The Saint**.

Blackler Gordon
Make-up on **The Saint**.

Blackman Honor
Played Joan Bernard in the first season **Danger Man** episode *Colonel Rodriguez*.
Starred as, series regular, Nicole in the series **The Four Just Men** appearing in the episodes: *The Prime Minister*, *The Deadly Capsule*, *Marie*, *The Man in the Road*, *The Miracle of St. Philippe*, *The Princess*, *The Grandmother*, *The Godfather* & *The Moment of Truth*.
Played Laura in the first series **Ghost Squad** episode *Princess* [this episode was shot for the first series, but due to an actors' strike, was originally shown in season two].
Played Katherine in the **H. G. Wells' Invisible Man** episode *Blind Justice*.
Played Pauline Stone in the first season **The Saint** episode *The Arrow of God*.

Blackman Ron
Played the NCO in the second series **Danger Man** [aka **Secret Agent**] episode *The Galloping Major*.

Blackmore Brenda
Wrote the **H. G. Wells' Invisible Man** episodes *The Decoy* and *Man in Disguise* [teleplayed from a story by Leslie Arliss].

Blackshaw Anthony
Played the security guard in **The Baron** episode *The Killing* [Part 2 of a 2 parter: also exists, edited together with part 1, *Masquerade*, to form a feature *Man In a Looking Glass*].
Played the guard in the third season **The Saint** episode *The House on Dragon's Rock*.

Blackwell Charles
Arranged the title music on **Fireball XL5**.

Blackwell Patrick
Played Tom Didcot in the season two **Ghost Squad** episode *The Golden Silence*.

Blagden David
Played Grant in **The Adventurer** episode *The Case of the Poisoned Pawn*.

Blair Iain
Played Chuck Spendelton in the fourth season **The Saint** episode *The Double Take* and Morris in *The Man Who Gambled with Life*.

Blair Isla
Played Elaine in the **Department S** episode *The Treasure of the Costa del Sol*.
Played Anne Winters in the **Jason King** episode *A Red, Red Rose Forever*.
Played Janine Flambeau in the fourth season **The Saint** episode *The Ex-King of Diamonds*.
Played the alien woman in the season one **Space 1999** episode *War Games* and Carla in season two's *Journey to Where*.

Blair Joyce
Played Millicent in the debut season **The Adventures of Robin Hood** episode *The Alchemist*.
Played Tamara Luchovak in the first series **Ghost Squad** episode *The Green Shoes* [shot for the first series, but due to an actors' strike, was originally shown as a season two episode].
Played Goldilocks in the third season **The Saint** episode *Interlude in Venice*.

Blair Lionel
Played Quinn Travis in **The Persuaders!** episode *Powerswitch*.

Blake Anne
Played Mrs. Wainwright in **The Buccaneers** [aka **Dan Tempest**] episode *The Return of Calico Jack*.
Played Censor in the third season **Danger Man** [aka **Secret Agent**] episode *Two Birds with One Bullet*.
Played Professor Bryant in the **Department S** episode *The Man in the Elegant Room*.
Played Dr Arne in the season two **Ghost Squad** episode *The Man With the Delicate Hands*.
Played Mrs. Mongrieff in the third season **The Saint** episode *The Convenient Monster*.

Blake Dennis
Played Miller in the second season **The Saint** episode *The Smart Detective*.

Blake Katherine
Played Madame Nicharos in **The Baron** episode *Night of the Hunter*.
Played Rosemary Chase in the first season **The Saint** episode *The Invisible Millionaire*.
Played the dark lady in the **Sir Francis Drake** episode *Johnnie Factotum*.

Blakely Colin
Played The Interrogator in **The Champions** episode *The Interrogation* [this episode was combined with *The Beginning* to form a 'feature' entitled *Legend of The Champions*].

Played John in the **Man in a Suitcase** episode *Brainwash* and Father Loyola in *The Whisper*.

Blakemore Michael
Played Cedric in **The Adventures of Sir Lancelot** episode *The Black Castle*.

Blakiston Caroline
Played Felicia Talbot in **The Baron** episode *So Dark the Night*. Guested as Marianne Grant in **The Champions** episode *The Experiment*.
Played Kate Mortimer in the **Department S** episode *The Shift that Never was*.
Played Karen Howarth in the **Randall and Hopkirk [Deceased] aka My Partner the Ghost** episode *Never Trust a Ghost*.
Played Eleanor Bastion in the third season **The Saint** episode *The Convenient Monster*.
Played Louise in the **Strange Report** episode *Report 2493: KIDNAP: 'Whose Pretty Girl Are You?'*.

Blamey Veronica
Played Debbie Farrington in *Adventure Five* of **Sapphire and Steel** [part 2].

Blanshard Joby
Played Bill White in the **Gideon's Way** episode *The Firebug*.
Played the police inspector in the **Randall and Hopkirk [Deceased] aka My Partner the Ghost** episode *But what a Sweet Little Room*.
Played Ernesto in the first season **The Saint** episode *The Romantic Matron* and the first sailor in the second season's *The Old Treasure Story*.

Blaser Herman
Associate Producer on **The New Adventures of Charlie Chan**.

Blatt Bert
Assistant Director on the series **The Zoo Gang**.

Bleifer John
Played Dubois in **The Count of Monte Cristo** episode *The Pen and the Sword*.

Blessed Brian
Played Lawsey in the **Randall and Hopkirk [Deceased] aka My Partner the Ghost** episode *The Ghost who Saved the Bank at Monte Carlo*.
Played Sir Nigel in the **Shirley's World** episode *Knightmare*.
Played Rowland in the first season **Space 1999** episode *Death's Other Dominion* and Mentor in the second season's *The Metamorph*.

Blezard John
Art Director on **The Adventures of Robin Hood** [season three & four].

Blick Newton
Played the father in **The Four Just Men** episode *The Deadly Capsule*.

Bligh Jack
Played Charlie Hewitt in the series two **Danger Man** [aka **Secret Agent**] episode *Whatever Happened to George Foster?* and French in the **Man in a Suitcase** episode *The Girl who Never was*.

Bloom Judi
Played Maria Russi in the second series **The Protectors** episode *Lena*.

Bloomfield John
Played the Court Clerk in the first season **The Saint** episode *The Element of Doubt* and the stout man in *The Ever-loving Spouse*. In season two, played Twinewright in *The Unkind Philanthropist*.

Blueth Ellen
Played Inga in the **O.S.S.** episode *Operation Sardine*.

Blundall John
Sculptor on **Fireball XL5 & Thunderbirds**.

Blundell Geoff
Played the boy in the **Father Brown** episode *The Quick One*.

Bluthal John
Played Guiseppe Borzo in **The Baron** episode *The Long, Long Day*.
Voiced Commander Zero in Gerry Anderson's **Fireball XL5**.
Played Berger in the **Man in a Suitcase** episode *Jigsaw Man*.
Played Ziggy Zaglan in the season two **The Saint** episode *The Happy Suicide* & Guido Naccaro in *The Damsel in Distress*.

Blythe Dorothy
Played Ethelreda in the debut season **The Adventures of Robin Hood** episode *The Alchemist*.

Blythe Peter
Played Cooper, the second officer in the **UFO** episode *Destruction* and the tracking station officer in *The Psychobombs*.

Boa Bruce
Guested as American Colonel in **The Champions** episode *Autokill*.
Played the cop in **The Four Just Men** episode *The Judge* and Connolly in *The Night of the Precious Stones*.
Played Inspector Bergson in the **Man in a Suitcase** episode *The Revolutionaries*.
Played Jack Williams in the first season **The Saint** episode *The Sporting Chance*, Hamilton in the second season's *Sibao* and Mark in the fourth's *Legacy for the Saint*.

Bobrinskey Alexis
Played Petrov in **The Count of Monte Cristo** episode *The Luxembourg Affair*.

Boddey Martin
Guested as Gregson in **The Champions** episode *Operation Deep-freeze*.
Played the masseur in the first season **Danger Man** episode *The Journey Ends Halfway*.
Played Harry Finch in the **Department S** episode *The Man in the Elegant Room*.
Played Chief Officer Carmichael in the **Gideon's Way** episode *The Firebug*.
Played the Colonel in the **Sir Francis Drake** episode *Escape*.

Boetticher Bud
Director on **The Count of Monte Cristo**.

Bogany R. W.
Wrote the third series **The Adventures of Robin Hood** episode *Quickness of the Hand*.

Bohun Carl
Played the motor cyclist in the **Jason King** episode *A Red, Red Rose Forever*.
Played Dieter Schultz in **The Persuaders!** episode *Read and Destroy*.
Played Revell in the second season **The Protectors** episode *Route 27*.

Bolam James
Played Max in the first series **The Protectors** episode *See No Evil*.

Bolsover Philip
Wrote the third series **The Adventures of Robin Hood** episodes *The Fire, Woman's War & Little Mother* and the fourth season's *The Loaf*.

Bolton Jim
Played Abdullah in **The Baron** episode *The Legions of Ammak*.

Bolton June
Played Yasmina in the **Return of the Saint** episode *One Black September*.

Bonanova Fortunio
Starred as Mario in **The Count of Monte Cristo** episodes *The Affair of the Three Napoleons, The Pen and the Sword* and *The De Berry Affair*.

Bond Derek
Played John Norton in the **H. G. Wells' Invisible Man** episode *Picnic with Death*.
Played Fellows in the third season **The Saint** episode *To Kill a Saint*.
Played Emperor in the **William Tell** episode *Undercover*.

Bond Julian
Wrote the **Espionage** episode *Once a Spy*.
Wrote the season two **Ghost Squad** episodes *The Grand Duchess & The Heir Apparent*.
Wrote the season two **Man of the World** episode *The Enemy*.
Wrote the first season **The Saint** episode *The Arrow of God*.
Wrote **The Sentimental Agent** episodes *All that Jazz, The Beneficiary & Never Play Cards with Strangers*.

Bond Philip
Played the officer in **The Champions** episode *The Experiment*.
Played Jaevert in the **Jason King** episode *Flamingos only Fly on Tuesdays*.
Played Luis in the **Man in a Suitcase** episode *The Man who Stood Still* and Philip Oliver in *Web with Four Spiders*.
Played Kenneth Ripwell in the first season **The Saint** episode *The Elusive Ellshaw*.

Bond Richard
Played the radio operator in **The Champions** episode *The Dark Island*.

Bond Sidonie
Played the nurse in **The Baron** episode *Samurai West*.

Bonheur Stella
Played Joan West in the first season **The Saint** episode *The Golden Journey* and Miss Donaldson in *The Element of Doubt*.

Bonnard Keith
Played Ching in the **Virgin of the Secret Service** episode *Entente Cordiale*.

Bonner Tony
Played Jon in **The Persuaders!** episode *The Morning After*.

Bonner-Moris Dick
Make-up Supervisor on **Gideon's Way** and Make-up on **The Saint**.

Bonney John
Played Stashig in the first season **Danger Man** episode *The Trap*.

Played Lt. Keith Blanford in the season two **Ghost Squad** episode *The Last Jump*.

Boo Luis Bar
Played the taxi driver in the second season **The Protectors** episode *Quin*.

Booth Anthony
Played Hans in the second season **The Saint** episode *The Rhine Maiden* and Pyotr in the third season's *The Russian Prisoner*.

Booth Beryl
Continuity on *The Prisoner*.

Booth Buddy
Assistant Director on **The Adventures of Sir Lancelot** episodes *Double Identity, The Witch's Brew, Ruby of Radnor, The Mortaise Fair, Sir Crustabread, The Lady Lilith & The Thieves*.

Booth David
Casting Director on **Gideon's Way** and **The Saint**.

Booth Harry
Location Director on the series **Man of the World** and directed *Blaze of Glory, The Nature of Justice & Shadow of the Wall* [series 1] and *Jungle Mission & The Bullfighter* [2].
Directed the first season **The Protectors** episode *Chase*.
Directed **The Sentimental Agent** episode *A Very Desirable Plot*.
Supervising Film Editor on the series **Sir Francis Drake** and also co-directed the episodes *Bold Enterprise* [with Anthony Bushell], *The Flame Thrower* [with Clive Donner] & *The Slaves of Spain* [with Anthony Bushell].

Booth James
Played Ali in the **H. G. Wells' Invisible Man** episode *The Gun Runners*.
Played Edmund Remberg in the **Shirley's World** episode *A Mother's Touch*.
Played Franz in the **William Tell** episode *The Hostages* and Josef in *The Mountain People*.

Booth Jolyon
Played Swann in **The Baron** episode *Diplomatic Immunity*.
Played the radio man in the **Gideon's Way** episode *The Reluctant Witness*.

Borienko Yuri
Played Filipo in the **Department S** episode *A Fish out of Water*.
Played Maurice in the **Jason King** episode *Toki*.
Played Nikolai in **The Persuaders!** episode *The Ozerov Inheritance*.
Played Khukov in the second season **The Protectors** episode *The Last Frontier*.
Played Zielgler in the **Virgin of the Secret Service** episode *Pride of Assassins*.

Borin Alexander
Played the vendor in the series two **The Protectors** episode *Lena*.

Borisenko Don
Played Walter Farrow in **The Baron** episode *The Maze*.
Played Alan Blake in the **Gideon's Way** episode *The Millionaire's Daughter*.

Borisoff Norman
Wrote the story for the **Espionage** episode *To the Very End* [and co-teleplayed with David Greene] and for *Castles In Spain* [teleplayed by Raymond Bowers].

Co-wrote the first season **Man of the World** episode *A Family Affair* [with Robert Thompson].
Wrote the first season **The Saint** episodes *The Element of Doubt, The Effete Angler, The Ever-loving Spouse & The Good Medicine.*

Borneman Ernest
Wrote the second season **The Adventures of Robin Hood** episode *The Final Tax* [with Ralph Smart] and directed the third's *At the Sign of the Blue Boar.*

Boscoe Holder Dancers, The
Appeared in the second series **Danger Man** [aka **Secret Agent**] episode *A Man to be Trusted.*

Bosso Georgio
Played a policeman in the **Return of the Saint** episode *The Nightmare Man.*

Boswall John
Played the old man in *Adventure Six* of **Sapphire and Steel**.

Boswell Ruth
Devised the series **Timeslip** and served as its Script Editor.

Bott John
Played Dyson in the **Randall and Hopkirk [Deceased]** aka **My Partner the Ghost** episode *The Smile Behind the Veil.*

Bottomley Roy
Wrote the **Shirley's World** episode *Follow That Rickshaw* [with Tom Brennand].

Bough David
Played Michael in **The Adventures of Sir Lancelot** episode *The Theft of Excalibur.*

Boulay Andre
Played Mario in the first season **The Saint** episode *The Covetous Headman* and Garner in *Judith.*

Bourman Einar
Wardrobe on **The Count of Monte Cristo**.

Bourne Peter
Played Peter in **The Baron** episode *Night of the Hunter*, the projection operator in **The Prisoner** episode *The General* and Perry in the third season **The Saint** episode *The Power Artist.*

Bowen Dave
Sound Recordist on **The Champions, Department S, Jason King, Space 1999 & The Zoo Gang**.

Bower Dallas
Producer on **The Adventures of Sir Lancelot**: *The Outcast, Winged Victory, Sir Bliant, The Magic Sword, Lancelot's Banishment, Roman Wall, Caledon, Shepherd's War, The Pirates, The Black Castle, The Magic Book, Knight Errand & The Theft of Excalibur.*

Bowers Raymond
Script Supervisor on season four of **The Adventures of Robin Hood** and wrote the episodes *Goodbye, Little John & The Edge and the Point.*

Bowers Richard
Wrote the season four **The Adventures of Robin Hood** episode *Six Strings to his bow.*
Wrote the second season **Danger Man** [aka **Secret Agent**] episode *A Man to be Trusted* and the third's *The Man with the Foot.*

Teleplayed the **Espionage** episodes *Festival of Pawns* [from a story by Robert Dozier] and *Castles In Spain* [from a story by Norman Borisoff].
Wrote the **Man in a Suitcase** episode *The Man who Stood Still.*

Bowler Clive Colin
Played Danny Terrill in the **Department S** episode *The Man in the Elegant Room.*
Played Duke in the **Gideon's Way** episode *Gang War* and Rod Jenkins in *The Rhyme and the Reason.*

Bowler Norman
Played Michael Usher in the **Gideon's Way** episode *Morna.*

Bowles Peter
Played Menendez in **The Baron** episode *Time to Kill* and Jim Gaynor in *You Can't Win Them All.*
Played Gamal in the second series **Danger Man** [aka **Secret Agent**] episode *Fish on the Hook.*
Played Borowitsch in the **Department S** episode *Six Days.*
Played Mitchell in **The Persuaders!** episode *Element of Risk.*
Guest starred as "A" in **The Prisoner** episode *A. B. and C.*
Played Kofax in the first series **The Protectors** episode *Triple Cross.*
Played Maurice Kerr in the second season **The Saint** episode *Lida* and Serge in the third season's *The Art Collectors.*
Played Balor in the first season **Space 1999** episode *End of Eternity.*

Bowman Dulcie
Guested as Lady Donnington in the debut season of **The Adventures of Robin Hood** episode *The May Queen.*

Bowman Tom
Played Jocko in the season two **Ghost Squad** episode *The Desperate Diplomat* and Jack Berg in *Polsky.*
Played the prison officer in the **Man in a Suitcase** episode *The Sitting Pigeon.*
Played the Kapitan in the **O.S.S.** episode *Operation Meatball.*
Played the security man in the **Randall and Hopkirk [Deceased]** aka **My Partner the Ghost** episode *Money to Burn.*
Played the Mate in the **Sir Francis Drake** episode *Drake on Trial.*

Bown John
Played Tredgett in **The Baron** episode *You Can't Win Them All.*
Played Shard in the third season **The Saint** episode *The Power Artist.*

Box Sydney
Executive Producer [with Bernard L. Schubert] on the **White Hunter** series.

Boxer John
Played Dr. Musgrove in the **Randall and Hopkirk [Deceased]** aka **My Partner the Ghost** episode *The Ghost Talks.*
Played Sir John Mulliner in the fourth season **The Saint** episode *The Scales of Justice.*

Boxill Patrick
Played Vaughan in the season two **Ghost Squad** episode *The Man With the Delicate Hands.*

Boyce Eamonn
Played Wilks in the **Return of the Saint** episode *Assault Force.*

Boyd Ray
Played Michel in **The Zoo Gang** episode *Mindless Murder.*

Boyd Ron
Played Joe in the second season **Space 1999** episode *The Immunity Syndrome.*

Boyd Roy
Played McCord in the fourth season **The Saint** two parter *The Fiction Makers.*

Boyd-Perkins Eric
Editor on **The Prisoner** episodes *Do Not Forsake Me Oh My Darling, The Girl who was Death* and, with Noreen Ackland, on *Fall Out.*

Boyer Carole
Played Masie in the **G.S.5** episode *Seven Sisters of Wong.*

Boyers Jim
Lighting on **Sapphire and Steel**.

Boyes Peter
Played the ticket collector in the **Virgin of the Secret Service** episode *Pride of Assassins.*

Boyle Katherine
Played Diane Kendrick in the **White Hunter** episode *The Prisoner.*

Boyle Marc
Played Miguel in **The Adventurer** episode *Icons Are Forever.*

Brace Peter
Played Hamilton in **The Baron** episode *Countdown.*
Played Alex in the third season **Danger Man** [aka **Secret Agent**] episode *Dangerous Secret.*
Played Crick in the **Man in a Suitcase** episode *Essay in Evil.*
Appeared as the first guardian in **The Prisoner** episode *Arrival* and as the first mechanic in *Free for All.*
Played the crewman in the **Return of the Saint** episode *Collision Course* [Part 2: 'The Sixth Man': also exists, combined with part 1, as a movie: *The Saint and the Brave Goose*].
Played the second Russian guard in the third season **The Saint** episode *When Spring is Sprung.*

Brackett Sarah
Played the secretary in the second series **Danger Man** [aka **Secret Agent**] episode *It's Up to the Lady* and Annette in *Have a Glass of Wine.*
Played the nurse in the first season **The Saint** episode *The Element of Doubt* and Tristan Brown in *The Unkind Philanthropist.*

Bracknell David
Assistant Director on **The Protectors**.

Bradbury Jeanette
Played Katy in **The Four Just Men** episode *The Bystanders.*

Bradford Andrew
Played Max in **The Adventurer** episode *I'll Get There Sometime.*
Played the motor cyclist in the second season **The Protectors** episode *Baubles, Bangles and Beads.*

Bradford Richard
The star of the **Man in a Suitcase** series playing McGill. The series was, initially, produced under the title McGill.

Bradley Donald
Played Jaques, the Jester, in the first series of **The Adventures of Robin Hood** episode *The Prisoner.*

Bradley Leslie
Played Minister of Justice Bonjean in **The Count of Monte Cristo** episode *The Pen and the Sword.*

Brady Brandon
Played Tronson in the **Department S** episode *A Cellar full of Silence.*
Played the security guard in the second season **Man of the World** episode *In the Picture.*
Played Cleaver in the first season **The Saint** episode *The Sporting Chance.*

Brady Nicholas
Played Will in the second series of **The Adventures of Robin Hood** episode *Isabella.*

Brahms Penny
Played the girl in luxury flat in the **Randall and Hopkirk [Deceased]** aka **My Partner the Ghost** episode *When the Spirit Moves You.*

Braithwaite Nicola
Played Renee in **The Scarlet Pimpernel** episode *The Christmas Present.*

Bramall John
Sound Recordist on **The Prisoner**.

Brambell Wilfred
Appeared as Ned in the second series of **The Adventures of Robin Hood** episode *The Final Tax* and as the fisherman in *The York Treasure.*
Appeared as the fisherman in **The Adventures of Sir Lancelot** episode *The Lesser Breed.*
Played the old man in **The Buccaneers** [aka **Dan Tempest**] episode *The Spy Aboard.*
Played Beppo in the **Sword of Freedom** episode *The Bell.*
Played Josef in the **William Tell** episode *Landslide.*

Bramwell Christopher
Played Tony Purnell in *Adventure Five* of **Sapphire and Steel** [part 2].

Branch Sara
Played Miss Montgomery in the second series **Danger Man** [aka **Secret Agent**] episode *That's Two of Us Sorry.*
Played Sara in the **Sir Francis Drake** episode *The Gypsies.*

Brand Erika
Played Mara in the **G.S.5** episode *The Goldfish Bowl.*

Brand Roland
Played Coleman in **The Baron** two parter *Storm Warning* [*Storm Warning* - part 1 and *The Island* - part 2: also exists as a feature called *Mystery Island*].
Played Grunther in the series one **Ghost Squad** episode *Assassin.*
Played the military policeman in the **O.S.S.** episode *Operation Blackbird.*
Played Dan Morrow in the first season **The Saint** episode *The Effete Angler.*

Brand Ronald
Played the petty officer in the **O.S.S.** episode *Operation Orange Blossom.*

Brandel Marc
Wrote the first season **Danger Man** episodes *The Girl who Liked GIs* [with Ralph Smart], *The Gallows Tree* [with Ralph Smart] & *The Actor* and the second season's - now aka **Secret Agent** - *Fair Exchange* [with Wilfred Greatorex].

Wrote **The Four Just Men** episodes *The Judge, The Survivor, The Discovery, The Grandmother* and *The Boy without a Country.*
Wrote the season two **Man of the World** episode *The Bull-fighter.*

Brander Arthur
Played the club manager in the **O.S.S.** episode *Operation Eel.*

Brandes Janet
Played Miss Grimshaw in the first season **The Saint** episode *The Ever-loving Spouse.*

Brandon Bill
Played a guard in the **Man in a Suitcase** episode *Brainwash.*

Brandon John
Played Philip Kane in the **Man in a Suitcase** episode *Dead Man's Shoes* and the sheriff in the **Virgin of the Secret Service** episode *The Professor Goes West.*

Brauns Marianne
Appeared as Karen Lindeman in the **White Hunter** episode *Forest of the Night.*

Braunton Nan
Played Miss Blake in the **Strange Report** episode *Report 2641: HOSTAGE: 'If You Won't Learn, Die!.*

Bray Studios
Where **Space 1999** was filmed [also shot at Pinewood Studios].

Bray Stanley
Played the alien in the **UFO** episode *Identified.*

Brayham Peter
Appeared as the sergeant's man in the second season **Danger Man** [aka **Secret Agent**] episode *A Date with Doris* and as Stefan in the third season's *Dangerous Secret.*
Stuntman on **The Prisoner**: played the thug in *A. B. and C.* and a cowboy in *Living in Harmony.*
Stuntman on **Space 1999**.

Brayshaw Edward
Played Shamir in **The Baron** episode *Red Horse, Red Rider* and Carlos Lamas in *Time to Kill.*
Guested as Del Marco in **The Champions** episode *A Case of Lemmings.*
Played Vernon Brooks in the second series **Danger Man** [aka **Secret Agent**] episode *Parallel Lines Sometimes Meet.*
Played Vic Kent in the **Department S** episode *A Cellar full of Silence.*
Played Paul Lang in the **Randall and Hopkirk [Deceased]** aka **My Partner the Ghost** episode *The Trouble with Women.*
Played Oscar West in the **Return of the Saint** two parter *Collision Course* [Part 1: *The Brave Goose* & part 2: *The Sixth Man*: also exists as a movie entitled *The Saint and the Brave Goose*].
Played Pietro in the fourth season **The Saint** episode *Legacy for the Saint.*
Played Yuente in the **Virgin of the Secret Service** episode *Across the Silver Pass of Gusri Song.*

Breaks Sebastian
Played Haswell in **The Champions** episode *The Gilded Cage.*
Played Hazell in the **Jason King** episodes *Variations on a Theme* & *A Royal Flush.*
Played Sergeant Harris in the **Strange Report** episode *Report 5055: CULT: 'Murder Shrieks Out'.*

Breck Kathleen
Played Zelda in the second series **Danger Man** [aka **Secret Agent**] episode *Have a Glass of Wine.*

Played Number 42 in **The Prisoner** episode *A Change of Mind.*

Bree James
Played Bill Wilto in **The Persuaders!** episode *Chain of Events.*
Played Villiers in **The Prisoner** episode *Do Not Forsake Me Oh My Darling.*
Played Mullet in the **Randall and Hopkirk [Deceased]** aka **My Partner the Ghost** episode *The Man from Nowhere.*

Breem Reg
Draughtsman on **The Prisoner**.

Brennan Kevin
Played Jack Gill in the second season **The Saint** episode *The Happy Suicide.*
Played the President of the Court in the **Virgin of the Secret Service** episode *Russian Roundabout.*

Brennan Michael
Played Brenner in the **H. G. Wells' Invisible Man** episode *Jailbreak.*
Guested as Victor Perrot in the **Interpol Calling** episode *Last Man Lucky.*
Played Killer Karminski in **The Prisoner** episode *The Girl who was Death.*
Played Hans in the **William Tell** episode *The Raid.*

Brennan Sheila
Played Penelope Spencer in the **Man in a Suitcase** episode *The Whisper.*
Played Gabrielle in the **O.S.S.** episode *Operation Powder Puff.*

Brennand Tom
Wrote the **Shirley's World** episode *Follow That Rickshaw* [with Roy Bottomley].

Brent John Boyd
Played the police officer in the season two **Ghost Squad** episode *Sentences of Death.*
Played Larry Woods in the **G.S.5** episode *Hideout.*

Brent Simon
Played the watcher in the third season **Danger Man** [aka **Secret Agent**] episode *To our Best Friend* and Peter in *The Man who wouldn't Talk.*
Played Bert in the **Man in a Suitcase** episode *Variation on a Million Bucks* [two parter: also a movie: *To Chase a Million*].

Breslin John
Played Keith Turnbull in the second series **Danger Man** [aka **Secret Agent**] episode *A Room in the Basement.*
Played Reed in the **UFO** episode *The Dalotek Affair.*

Bresslaw Bernard
Played Sir Dunstan's Captain in the second series of **The Adventures of Robin Hood** episode *The Black Patch.*
Played Leo Perrins in the second series **Danger Man** [aka **Secret Agent**] episode *The Outcast.*

Brett Anna
Played Suzanne in the **Jason King** episode *If it's Got to Go - It's Got to Go.*
Played the bank secretary in **The Persuaders!** episode *Angie.. . Angie.*

Brett Jeremy
Played Jeff Walker in **The Baron** episode *The Seven Eyes of Night.*
Guested as The Bey in **The Champions** episode *Desert Journey.*

Played Kahan in the first series **The Protectors** episode .....*With a Little Help from my Friends.*

Brett Peter
Played the air steward in **The Baron** episode *Farewell to Yesterday.*
Played the secretary to Seretse in the **Department S** episode *The Man in the Elegant Room.*

Brice Bridget
Played Susan Blain in the **Department S** episode *A Ticket to Nowhere.*

Bridge Joan
Colour Consultant on **The Adventures of Sir Lancelot** episodes *The Mortaise Fair, The Missing Princess* and *The Thieves.*

Bridge Tamasin
Played Helen in *Adventure One* of **Sapphire and Steel.**

Bridgeman Kenneth 'Ken'
Set Dresser on **The Prisoner.**

Bridges Robert
Played Clifford Thornton in **The Baron** episode *The High Terrace.*
Played the fat man in the third season **The Saint** episode *The Better Mousetrap.*

Briggs Johnny
Wardrobe Supervisor on **The Persuaders!** and Wardrobe on **The Saint.**

Briggs Johnny
Played Charlie in **The Persuaders!** episode *Someone Like Me.*
Played Johnny Desmond in the first season **The Saint** episode *Marcia.*

Brill Don
Dialogue Editor on **Joe 90.**

Brill Michael
Played David Guy in the first series **The Adventures of Robin Hood** episode *The Brothers.*

Brimmel Max
Played Secchi in **The Count of Monte Cristo** episode *Sicily* and Dubois in *The Island.*
Played Inspector Nardi in **The Four Just Men** episode *The Crying Jester.*

Brimmel May
Played Brentano in **The Count of Monte Cristo** episode *Flight to Calais.*

Brindley Madge
Guested as the French woman in **The Champions** episode *A Case of Lemmings.*
Played the landlady in the first season **The Saint** episode *The Romantic Matron.*

Brinkley Don
Wrote the **Strange Report** episodes *Report 3424: EPIDEMIC: 'A Most Curious Crime'* and *Report 2493: KIDNAP: 'Whose Pretty Girl Are You?'.*

Bristow Jacky
Played an art student in the **Father Brown** episode *The Head of Caesar.*

Britt Leo
Played Cabane in **The Four Just Men** episode *Village of Shame.*

Britton Jocelyn
Played Laura in the **Sword of Freedom** episode *Serenade in Red.*

Britton Tony
Played Jonathan Roper in the fourth season **The Saint** episode *The Organisation Man.*

Broadley Colin
Played Owen in the second series of **The Adventures of Robin Hood** episode *Fair Play* and Brian in *The Little People.* Played Willie Steele in season three's *The Rivals.*
Played Crespino in the **Sword of Freedom** episode *The School.*

Broadley Philip
Wrote **The Adventurer** episodes *Love Always, Magda, Nearly the End of the Picture, Target!* & *The Case of the Poisoned Pawn.*
Wrote **The Champions** episodes *Reply Box No: 666, The Iron Man, The Gilded Cage, A Case of Lemmings* and *Nutcracker.*
Wrote the second season **Danger Man** [aka **Secret Agent**] episodes *The Battle of the Cameras, Don't Nail Him Yet, A Date with Doris, It's Up to the Lady* [teleplayed from a story by John Roddick], *The Mirror's New, You're Not in Any Trouble, Are You?, The Black Book, Sting in the Tail* & *Are You Going to Be More Permanent?* and the third's *The Man on the Beach, Someone is Liable to get Hurt* [with Ralph Smart], *The Hunting Party* & *The Paper Chase* [with Smart].
Wrote the **Department S** episodes *The Trojan Tanker, Handicap Dead, Black Out, The Treasure of the Costa del Sol, The Man who got a New Face, Les Fleurs du Mal, Dead Men Die Twice, The Mysterious Man in the Flying Machine, Death on Reflection* & *A Fish out of Water.*
Wrote the **Jason King** episodes *Buried in the Cold, Cold Ground, Variations on a Theme, All that Glisters* [2 parter], *Toki, Nadine, A Royal Flush* & *Zenia.* Also, directed *A Royal Flush, Zenia* & *That isn't Me, It's Somebody Else.*
Wrote the **Man in a Suitcase** episodes *Day of Execution, Sweet Sue* & *Find the Lady.*
Wrote the **Return of the Saint** episode *Appointment in Florence.*
Wrote the third series **The Saint** episodes *The Counterfeit Countess* & *The Gadic Collection.*

Brocco Peter
Played Dubois in **The Count of Monte Cristo** episode *The De Berry Affair.*

Brock Cecil
Played the head waiter in the first season **Danger Man** episode *Josetta.*
Played Sean in **The Four Just Men** episode *The Heritage* and the Impresario in *The Moment of Truth.*
Played the first guard in the **Sword of Freedom** episode *Francesca.*

Broderick Susan
Played the typist in the **Department S** episode *The Pied Piper of Hambledown*; the receptionist in the **Jason King** episode *Uneasy Lies the Head* and Carol in the **Randall and Hopkirk** [Deceased] aka **My Partner the Ghost** episode *Who Killed Cock Robin.*

Brodny Oscar
Wrote the first season **Danger Man** episode *An Affair of State.*

Brody Estelle
Played Mrs Chase in **The Four Just Men** episode *The Judge.*

Bromiley Dorothy
Appeared as Rowena in the second series of **The Adventures of Robin Hood** episode *Hubert*.

Bromilow Peter
Played Walsham in the **Department S** episode *Six Days*.

Brook Faith
Played Carol Norton in the **H. G. Wells' Invisible Man** episode *Picnic with Death*.
Played Eleanor in the **Man in a Suitcase** episode *Three Blinks of the Eyes*.
Appeared as Patricia in the **White Hunter** episode *Big Bwana Brady*.

Brook Lyndon
Played Colin Ashby in the third season **Danger Man** [aka **Secret Agent**] episode *Dangerous Secret*.
Played James in the **O.S.S.** episode *Operation Foulball*.

Brook Olga
Continuity on **The Adventures of Sir Lancelot** episode *Winged Victory*.

Brook Steven
Played the hotel clerk in the third season **The Saint** episode *The Angel's Eye*.

Brook Terence
Played the pilot in **The Sentimental Agent** episode *The Scroll of Islam*.

Brooke Michael
Played Niki in **The Count of Monte Cristo** episode *Athens*.

Brookes Harry
Played the young man in the bar in the second series **Danger Man** [aka **Secret Agent**] episode *A Very Dangerous Game*.

Brookes Olwen
Played Miss Reeves in the season two **Ghost Squad** episode *The Retirement of Gentle Dove*.

Brookes Victor
Played Jules in the second series **Danger Man** [aka **Secret Agent**] episode *Have a Glass of Wine*.

Brook-Jones Elwyn
Played De Bassi in the **Sword of Freedom** episode *Alessandro*.

Brooking John
Played Mather in the third season **Danger Man** [aka **Secret Agent**] episode *Dangerous Secret*.

Brooking Timothy
Appeared in the first season **The Adventures of Robin Hood** episode *The Inquisitor* as the scullery boy.

Brooks Bob
Directed the second series **Space 1999** episode *The Taybor*.

Brooks Harry
Played Jackie in the **Man in a Suitcase** episode *Dead Man's Shoes*.

Brooks Harry Jnr.
Played Gerard Reder in the **Jason King** episode *Nadine*.

Brooks Laurence
Played Travers in the **White Hunter** episode *No Survivors*.

Brooks Patti
Played the maid in the **Strange Report** episode *Report 0649: SKELETON: 'Let Sleeping Heroes Lie'*.

Brooks Ray
Played Lucas in the second series **Danger Man** [aka **Secret Agent**] episode *Loyalty Always Pays*.
Played Frank Romano in the **Gideon's Way** episode *Gang War*.
Played 'Marty' in the **Randall and Hopkirk [Deceased]** aka **My Partner the Ghost** episode *The Man from Nowhere*.

Brooks Victor
Guested as Collins in **The Champions** episode *Full Circle*.
Played the policeman in the **Department S** episode *Last Train to Redbridge*.
Played the sergeant in **The Four Just Men** episode *The Boy Without a Country*.
Played Supt. Ridgeway in the **Gideon's Way** episode *The Wall*.
Played Logan in the **Man in a Suitcase** episode *Property of a Gentleman*.
Played Tom Frazier in the **White Hunter** episode *The Jackals*.

Brooks Wayne
Played Jackie in the first season **Space 1999** episode *Alpha Child*.

Brough Arthur
Played Jenkins in the **Jason King** episode *The Constance Missal*.
Played Moorehead in **The Persuaders!** episode *Greensleeves*.
Played Snowy in the **Randall and Hopkirk [Deceased]** aka **My Partner the Ghost** episode *That's How Murder Snowballs*.

Brough Ayesha
Played Mireille in the **Jason King** episode *As Easy as A B C*.
Featured regularly in the series **UFO** as a SHADO operative.

Broughton Anthony
Played Tom in the **G.S.5** episode *Rich Ruby Wine*.

Brown A. J.
Appeared in the first season **The Adventures of Robin Hood** episode *Husband for Marian* as Uncle George & *The Brothers* as The Abbott and as Sir Edward in the second series episode *The Mystery of Ireland's Eye*.
Played Augustus Aylmer in the **Father Brown** episode *The Dagger With Wings*.
Played the Judge in the **Randall and Hopkirk [Deceased]** aka **My Partner the Ghost** episode *Could You Recognise the Man Again?*.

Brown Barbara
Appeared as Margaret Rankin in the **White Hunter** episode *The Lonely Place*.

Brown Bernard
Played Chris in **The Buccaneers** [aka **Dan Tempest**] episode *Dan Tempest Holds an Auction*.
Played Ralph Mason in the **Gideon's Way** episode *The Wall*.
Played Vinci in the **Sword of Freedom** episode *The Ambassador*.

Brown Edwin
Played the farmer in **The Adventurer** episode *Skeleton in the Cupboard*.
Played a warder in **The Baron** episode *You Can't Win Them All*.
Played Barrow in the season two **Ghost Squad** episode *The Big Time*.
Played Grinley in the **G.S.5** episode *Dead Men Don't Drive*.

Played Wilson in the third season **The Saint** episode *Escape Route* and the van driver in the fourth's *The Master Plan.*
Played the security guard in the **Strange Report** episode *Report 3906: COVER GIRLS: 'Last Year's Model'.*

Brown Georgia
Made two appearances in **The Protectors**: as Maria Ghardala in *One and One Makes One* [series one] and as Ilona Tabori in the second series episode *Border Line.*

Brown John
Guested as Walcott in **The Champions** episode *Nutcracker.*
Played Enrico in **The Four Just Men** episode *Treviso Dam.*
Played the second guard in the **Sword of Freedom** episode *Francesca.*

Brown John
Sculptor on **Thunderbirds**.

Brown Pamela
Featured as a special guest star in the **Espionage** episode *Never Turn Your Back On a Friend.*
Played Catherine de Medici in the **Sir Francis Drake** episode *Mission to Paris.*

Brown Phil
Played Albert Peterson in **The Four Just Men** episode *The Bystanders.*
Guested as Brownley in the **Interpol Calling** episode *The Money Game.*
Played Markos in the first series **The Protectors** episode *It was All Over in Leipzig.*
Played Frank Rawlinson in the **The Scarlet Pimpernel** episode *Thanksgiving Day.*
Appeared as Wick in the **White Hunter** episode *Inside Story.*

Brown Phil
Directed the season two **Ghost Squad** episodes *Lost In Transit, Mr Five Per Cent* & *P.G. 7.*

Brown Ray
Played Larry in the third season **The Saint** episode *The Counterfeit Countess.*

Brown Robert
Played Valpezzo in **The Count of Monte Cristo** episode *The Island* and Baron Buray in *The Barefoot Empress.*
Played Kauffman in the **G.S.5** episode *Death of a Cop.*
Played Bill Campbell in the **Gideon's Way** episode *The Big Fix.*
Played Prof. Howard in the **H. G. Wells' Invisible Man** episode *The Rocket.*
Guested as Attendant in the **Interpol Calling** episode *Dead On Arrival.*
Played Governor in the first series **The Protectors** episode *Brother Hood.*
Played Jackman in the first season **The Saint** episode *The Saint Plays with Fire* and Atkins in the second season's *The Miracle Tea Party.*

Brown Ron
Programme Administrator on **Sapphire and Steel**.

Brown Walter
Played Forbes in the first series **Ghost Squad** episode *Catspaw* [this episode was shot for the first series, but due to an actors' strike, was originally shown as a season two episode].
Played John Borgman in the **Gideon's Way** episode *To Catch a Tiger.*
Played Hugo Meyer in the first season **The Saint** episode *The Elusive Ellshaw.* Played 'Doc' Spangler in the second season's *The Crooked Ring* and General Cuevas in *The Golden Frog.*

Brown William Lyon
Played the gaunt man in **The Baron** episode *Epitath for a Hero.*
Played the second doctor in **The Prisoner** episode *Dance of the Dead.*

Brownbill Bert
Played Mr Johnson in **The Sentimental Agent** episode *Never Play Cards with Strangers.*

Browne Alexander
Played the operator in the season two **Ghost Squad** episode *Death of a Sportsman.*

Browne Angela
Played The Girl in the first season **Danger Man** episode *The Girl in Pink Pyjamas.*
Starred as Helen Winters in the series **G.S.5** [first appeared as Helen Winters in the first series **Ghost Squad** episode *Million Dollar Ransom*].
Played Rachel Thyssen in the **Man in a Suitcase** episode *Man from the Dead.*
Played Number 86 in **The Prisoner** episode *A Change of Mind.*
Played Anne Ripwell in the first season **The Saint** episode *The Elusive Ellshaw.*

Browne Jill
Played Magda in the **William Tell** episode *Undercover.*

Browne Josephine
Played Madame Duras in the first season **The Saint** episode *The Covetous Headman.*

Browne Roger
Played Hendricks in the **Return of the Saint** episode *The Murder Cartel.*

Browne Tom
Played Malherb in **The Count of Monte Cristo** episode *The Black Death.*
Played Lieut. Forbes Wintle in the **Virgin of the Secret Service** episode *The Rajah and the Suffragette.*

Browning Alan
Played Lewis in the **G.S.5** episode *Pay Up or Else.*
Played Wilson in the **Gideon's Way** episode *Subway to Revenge.*
Played Henry in the **Return of the Saint** episode *Tower Bridge is Falling Down.*
Played the cafe proprietor in the first season **The Saint** episode *Teresa.*

Browning Maurice
Played Zavar in **The Adventurer** episode *Poor Little Rich Girl.*
Guested as Wittering in **The Champions** episode *Project Zero.*
Played Blagot in the third season **The Saint** episode *The Gadget Lovers.*

Browning Michael
Played a steward in the season two **Ghost Squad** episode *A First Class Way to Die.*

Bruce Edgar
Played Francois in **The Scarlet Pimpernel** episode *Sir Percy's Wager.*

Bruce Edgar K.
Played Jack Harris in the season two **Ghost Squad** episode *The Desperate Diplomat.*

Bruce Graeme
Played the policeman in the first season **The Saint** episode *The Saint Sees it Through.*

Bruce Mona
Played Dame Edith in the **Return of the Saint** episode *The Judas Game.*

Bruce Nicholas
Played Delong in **The Scarlet Pimpernel** episode *The Winged Madonna.*

Bruce Robert
Played Det. Insp. Malloy in the second season **The Saint** episode *The Saint Steps In* and Lord Fenton in **The Scarlet Pimpernel** episode *Something Remembered.*

Brune Gabrielle
Played Mrs. Howe in the **Randall and Hopkirk [Deceased]** aka **My Partner the Ghost** episode *Who Killed Cock Robin.*

Brunius Jacques
Played the Mayor in **The Four Just Men** episode *The Miracle of St. Philippe.*

Brunnel Juanita
Played one of the Flamenco dancers in the second season **Man of the World** episode *The Bullfighter.*

Brunning Harry
Played the stage door-keeper in the third season **The Saint** episode *The Fast Women.*

Bryans John
Played Arko in **The Baron** episode *Red Horse, Red Rider* and the barman in *The Long, Long Day.*
Played Crolic in **The Champions** episode *The Ghost Plane.*
Played the plainclothes man in the second series **Danger Man** [aka **Secret Agent**] episode *It's Up to the Lady.*
Played Ralph Sorrel in the **Randall and Hopkirk [Deceased]** aka **My Partner the Ghost** episode *Could You Recognise the Man Again?.*
Played Mister Anthony in the second season **The Saint** episode *The Imprudent Politician.*

Bryant Gerry
Directed the season three **The Adventures of Robin Hood** episodes *The Crusaders* & *The Double.*

Bryant Michael
Played Alessandro in the **Sword of Freedom** episode *Alessandro.*

Buck David
Played Martin in **The Adventurer** episode *Nearly the End of the Picture.*
Featured in the **Espionage** episode *To the Very End.*
Played John Strake in the **Father Brown** episode *The Dagger With Wings.*
Played Oliver in the **Jason King** episode *Toki.*
Played Azon in the first series **The Protectors** episode *Vocal.*

Buck Harold
Production Supervisor on **The Adventures of Robin Hood** [season two to four] and on **The Four Just Men.**
Production Manager on **The Adventures of Sir Lancelot** episodes *The Knight with the Red Plume, The Ferocious Fathers* and *The Queen's Knight* and on the **The Buccaneers** [aka **Dan Tempest**] episode *Blackbeard.*

Buck Jules
Producer on the series **O.S.S.**

Buck William
Played Lt. Lang in **The Baron** episode *The Island* [part 2 of a two-parter: also exists, edited together with part 1 - *Storm Warning*, as a feature entitled *Mystery Island*].
Played Detective Gorman in the first season **The Saint** episode *The Sporting Chance* and the clerk in the third season's *The Russian Prisoner.*

Buckeye Enterprises
Produced, with ITC, the series **O.S.S.** [a Robert Siodmak production in association with LSQ].

Buckingham Eliza
Played the bank clerk in the second season **The Saint** episode *The Chequered Flag.*

Buckingham Yvonne
Played Heloise in the **Sir Francis Drake** episode *Mission to Paris.*

Buckley Denise
Played Libby Spear in the **Department S** episode *A Cellar full of Silence.*
Played the manageress in the **Man in a Suitcase** episode *Why they Killed Nolan.*
Appeared as the maid in **The Prisoner** episode *Dance of the Dead.*
Played Susan Lang in the **Randall and Hopkirk [Deceased]** aka **My Partner the Ghost** episode *The Trouble with Women.*
Played Annabel I in the fourth season **The Saint** episode *The Double Take.*

Buckley Helen
Played the Lady-in-Waiting in the **Sir Francis Drake** episode *Gentlemen of Spain.*

Buckley Keith
Played Kurt in the first series **The Protectors** episode *Chase.*
Played Lattimer in the **Randall and Hopkirk [Deceased]** aka **My Partner the Ghost** episode *The House on Haunted Hill.*

Buckton Clifford
Played a farmer in the **O.S.S.** episode *Operation Firefly.*
Played Hempseed in **The Scarlet Pimpernel** episode *A Tale of Two Pigtails.*

Bull John
Played the boy with banjo in the third season **The Saint** episode *The Power Artist.*

Bullen Sarah
Series regular, appearing as an operative, in the second series of **Space 1999.**

Bulloch Jeremy
Played Art in **The Sentimental Agent** episode *All that Jazz.*
Played Bob Tremayne in the **Strange Report** episode *Report 8319: GRENADE: 'What Price Change?'.*

Bunnage Avis
Played Bessie Cowan in the **Gideon's Way** episode *Big Fish, Little Fish.*

Burden Celestine
Played the girl in the cafe in the **Jason King** episode *All that Glisters* [part 2].

Burden Hugh
Played the tailor in the season two **The Adventures of Robin Hood** episode *The Frightened Tailor.*
Played Rockworth in the season two **Ghost Squad** episode *Escape Route.*

Played Dr Maza in the **Man in a Suitcase** episode *The Revolutionaries*.
Played James in the **Strange Report** episode *Report 0649: SKELETON: 'Let Sleeping Heroes Lie'*.

Burfield Cheryl
Starred as Liz Skinner in the **Timeslip** series.

Burge Stuart
Directed the third season **Danger Man** [aka **Secret Agent**] episode *Dangerous Secret*.

Burgess Brian
Directed the **Captain Scarlet and the Mysterons** episodes *Big Ben Strikes Again, Avalanche, Renegade Rocket, Dangerous Rendezvous* and *The Launching*.
Directed the second season **Thunderbirds** episodes *Lord Parker's 'Oliday & Ricochet*.

Burgess Dennis
Starred as, series regular, Flambeau in **Father Brown**: *The Mirror of the Magistrate, The Quick One, The Actor and the Alibi, The Eye of Apollo & The Head of Caesar*.
Played Neman in the first season **Space 1999** episode *Mission of the Darians*.

Burgess-Wall Harry
Played Tala in the **Jason King** episode *Zenia*.

Burice Rodney
Played the first airman in the first season **Danger Man** episode *The Brothers*.

Burke Alfred
Played Sir Simon in the second series of **The Adventures of Robin Hood** episode *The Trap* and Will Sharpe in the third season's *The Lottery*.
Played the Mate in **The Buccaneers** [aka **Dan Tempest**] episode *Ghost Ship* and Marsh in *Instrument of War*.
Played Craven in the first season **Danger Man** episode *The Conspirators*.
Played Kane in the first series **Ghost Squad** episode *Bullet With My Name on it*.
Guested as Bekker in the **Interpol Calling** episode *The Angola Brights*.
Played High Lama in the first series **Man of the World** episode *The Frontier*.
Played Henry Foster in the **Randall and Hopkirk [Deceased]** aka **My Partner the Ghost** episode *All Work and No Pay*.
Played Jack Groom in the first season **The Saint** episode *Starring the Saint* and Harry Shannet in *The Wonderful War*.
Played Sir Amyas Paulet in the **Sir Francis Drake** episode *Mary, Queen of Scots*.
Played Bolf in the **William Tell** episode *The Assassins*.

Burke David
Played Whetlor in **The Baron** episode *You Can't Win Them All*.
Played Roger Carson in **The Champions** episode *The Fanatics*.
Played the civic guard in **The Sentimental Agent** episode *May the Saints Preserve Us*.

Burke Honora
Played the night club singer in the second season **Man of the World** episode *Double Exposure*.

Burke Marie
Appeared in the first season **The Adventures of Robin Hood** episode *Maid Marian* as Nanny, as Granny in *Checkmate* and as the nurse in *The Traitor*. Played Nanny in the second series episode *The Dream*.

Played the housekeeper in the first season **Danger Man** episode *View from the Villa* and Carla in *The Trap*.
In the first season of **The Saint**: played Signora Unciello in *The Latin Touch*, Princess De Ribes in *The Charitable Countess* & Senora Artigas in *Teresa*. Played Donna Maria in the fourth season two parter *Vendetta for the Saint*.
Played Donna Inez in the **Sir Francis Drake** episode *The Governor's Revenge*.

Burke Patricia
Appeared as Lady Leonia in **The Adventures of Robin Hood**: season one: *The Challenge* [credited as Leonia], [credited as Lady Torrence] *The Youngest Outlaw, The Betrothal & The Byzantine Treasure*; two: *Blackmail & The Final Tax* [credited as Donia] and three: *Castle in the Air*.
Played Ann in **The Four Just Men** episode *The Survivor*.
Played Mrs Gully in the **Gideon's Way** episode *The Reluctant Witness*.
Played Mrs Willis in the **H. G. Wells' Invisible Man** episode *Death Cell*.
Played Duchess of Urbino in the **Sword of Freedom** episode *The Ship*.

Burleigh Andrew
Played the Bell Boy in the second season **The Protectors** episode *Route 27*.

Burn Jonathan
Guested as Jean in **The Champions** episode *The Experiment*.
Played Dominic in the **Return of the Saint** episode *The Poppy Chain*.

Burnell Janet
Played Madame Elbeuf in **The Scarlet Pimpernel** episode *The Farmer's Boy*.

Burnett Susan
Played Lady Elena in the **Sir Francis Drake** episode *The Reluctant Duchess*.

Burnham Edward
Played Insp. Bates in the **G.S.5** episode *Hideout*.
Played Eugene Drew in the third season **The Saint** episode *Little Girl Lost*.

Burnham Jeremy
Wrote the **Shirley's World** episode *Knightmare*.

Burnham Jeremy
Played Phillip Tremayne in **The Baron** episode *The Man Outside*.
Played Ellis in the second series **Danger Man** [aka **Secret Agent**] episode *You're Not in Any Trouble, Are You?*
Played Harold in the **Gideon's Way** episode *The Great Plane Robbery*.
Played Scott Maskell in **The Persuaders!** episode *Someone Like Me*.
Played Walter Previss in the **Randall and Hopkirk [Deceased]** aka **My Partner the Ghost** episode *The House on Haunted Hill*.
Played Tim Burton in the second season **The Saint** episode *The Imprudent Politician*, Flight Lieutenant Wills in the third season's *Flight Plan* and Harry in *Escape Route*.

Burns Duncan
Played the boy actor in the **Sir Francis Drake** episode *Johnnie Factotum*.

Burns Hamish Hamilton
aka H.H. Burns
Wrote **The Adventures of Sir Lancelot** episodes *Ruby of Radnor* [with Peggy Philips], *Thieves & The Theft of Excalibur*

Burns Larry
Played Franz in the **Interpol Calling** episode *The Thirteen Innocents*.
Played Obadiah in the **Sir Francis Drake** episode *The Gypsies*.

Burns Mark
Played Peter Langley in **The Baron** episode *Portrait of Louisa*.
Played Number 2's assistant in **The Prisoner** episode *It's Your Funeral*.
Played Elliott Stratton in the fourth season **The Saint** episode *The Scales of Justice*.

Burrell Richard
Played the deck officer in the season two **Ghost Squad** episode *A First Class Way to Die*.
Played Det. Sgt Doug Brown in the **Gideon's Way** episode *The Prowler*.
Played Smith in **The Persuaders!** episode *The Man in the Middle*.
Played Max in the **William Tell** episode *The Trap*.

Burrill Ena
Played Mother Doughty in **The Buccaneers** [aka **Dan Tempest**] episode *Mother Doughty's Crew*.

Burt Oliver
Played Abbe in **The Count of Monte Cristo** episode *The Devil's Emissary*.
Played Meisener in the first season **Danger Man** episode *Sabotage*.
Guested as Von Stegger in the **Interpol Calling** episode *The Sleeping Giant*.

Burton Donald
Played Gorman in **The Adventurer** episode *Return to Sender*.
Played Oran in the **Jason King** episode *Zenia*.
Played the doctor in the first series **The Protectors** episode *Thinkback*.

Burton John Nelson
Directed the second series **Ghost Squad** episodes *Interrupted Requiem, The Golden Silence* & *Hot Money*.

Burton Peter
Played Anderson in the **Man in a Suitcase** episode *The Sitting Pigeon*.
Played Spahi Major in the **O.S.S.** episode *Operation Eel*.
Played Doctor Evans in the **Return of the Saint** episode *The Arrangement*.
Played Molliere in the third season **The Saint** episode *The Gadget Lovers*.
Played Doctor Murray in the **UFO** episode *Computer Affair* and Perry in *Ordeal*.
Appeared as Chauvet in the **White Hunter** episode *Girl Hunt*.

Burville Sandra
Appeared as one of the dancers in the **Man in a Suitcase** episode *Three Blinks of the Eyes*.

Busby Joanna
Continuity on **The Adventures of Robin Hood**.

Busby Tom
Played Lefty in the season two **Ghost Squad** episode *Lost In Transit*.
Played Eilers in the **O.S.S.** episode *Operation Jingle Bells*.

Bushell Anthony
Directed the debut season **Danger Man** episodes *The Relaxed Informer* & *The Leak*.
Directed **The Four Just Men** episodes *Panic Button, Crack-Up* & *Riot* and played Cyril Bacon in *The Battle of the Bridge*.

Directed the first season **Man of the World** episodes *The Frontier* & *A Family Affair*.
Directed the first season **The Saint** episode *The Effete Angler*.
Producer on the series **Sir Francis Drake** and co-directed the episodes *Bold Enterprise* [with Harry Booth] & *The Slaves of Spain* [with Harry Booth].

Bushell Anthony
Played Lotsbeyer in the debut season **Danger Man** episode *The Girl who Liked GIs*.
Played General Martin in the **H. G. Wells' Invisible Man** episode *Shadow Bomb*.
Appeared as Major Nelson in **The Sentimental Agent** episode *All that Jazz*.
Played Tom Doughty in the **Sir Francis Drake** episode *The Doughty Plot*.

Bushelman John
Sound Editor on **The Count of Monte Cristo**.

Butler Blake
Played Bainter in the fourth season **The Saint** episode *The Double Take*.

Butler David
Wrote the second season **The Protectors** episode *Sugar and Spice*.

Butler Ian
Played the page boy in the **Randall and Hopkirk** [Deceased] aka **My Partner the Ghost** episode *The Ghost Talks*.

Butler John
Writer on **The New Adventures of Charlie Chan**.

Butler Robert
Directed the **Espionage** episode *Do You Remember Leo Winters?*.

Butterfield Max
Played Herd in the first series **Ghost Squad** episode *Still Waters*.

Butterworth Peter
Played 'Umbrella' in the second series **Danger Man** [aka **Secret Agent**] episode *The Ubiquitous Mr Lovegrove*.

Byers Isabelle
Continuity on **The Champions**.

Byrne Eddie
Played Rolf in the season two **The Adventures of Robin Hood** episode *The Mystery of Ireland's Eye* and Lord Humphrey in the third's *Change of Heart*.
Played Murphy in **The Baron** episode *The Long, Long Day*.
Played Benedetto in **The Count of Monte Cristo** episode *Sicily*.
Played Bellman in the **Department S** episode *The Shift that Never was*.
Played Santolla in **The Four Just Men** episode *The Last Days of Nick Pompey*.
Played Lucky Joe Luckner in the first season **The Saint** episode *The Man who was Lucky*, Oscar Newley in the second season's *The Chequered Flag*, Tench in the third's *The Better Mousetrap* and Mr Hapgood [Senior] in the fourth's *The World Beater*.

Byrne Johnny
First series Script Editor on **Space 1999**. Wrote the first series episodes *Force of Life, Voyager's Return, Mission of the Darians, End of Eternity, Matter of Life and Death* [with Art Wallace], *Another Time Another Place, The Troubled Spirit* &

The Testament of Arkadia and the second season's *The Meta-morph, The Dorcans & The Immunity Syndrome.*

Byrne Paula
Appeared as Ethel in the debut season of **The Adventures of Robin Hood** episode *Errand of Mercy* and as Edward's wife in *The Wanderer*.
Guested as Blanche in the **Interpol Calling** episode *Game for Three Hands* and as Mamie in *Dressed To Kill*.
Played Mrs Nolan in the **Man in a Suitcase** episode *Why they Killed Nolan*.
Played Suzanne in the **O.S.S.** episode *Operation Yodel*.
Appeared as Nora Maxwell in the **White Hunter** episode *The Prisoner*.

Byrne Shamus
Third Assistant Director on **The Prisoner**.

Byron Kathleen
Played Deirdre in the first season **Danger Man** episode *Name, Date and Place*.

****

Caddick Edward
Played Alain in the **Department S** episode *Dead Men Die Twice*.
Played the patient in the **Randall and Hopkirk [Deceased]** aka **My Partner the Ghost** episode *You Can Always find a Fall Guy*.

Cadell Jean
Played Marquesa in **The Buccaneers** [aka **Dan Tempest**] episode *Prize of Andalusia*.

Cadman Milton
Played the prison guard in the **Return of the Saint** episode *The Debt Collectors*.

Caffrey Sean
Played Borislav in **The Adventurer** episode *The Bradley Way*.

Cage Roger
Played Battista in the **Sword of Freedom** episode *Marriage of Convenience*.

Caidden A. M.
Wrote the **Sword of Freedom** episode *The Primavera*.

Caine Michael
Played Max in the **William Tell** episode *The Prisoner* and Sergeant Wiener in *The General's Daughter*.

Cairney John
Played Jack Taylor in the second series **Danger Man** [aka **Secret Agent**] episode *Such Men are Dangerous*.
Played Moker in the first series **Ghost Squad** episode *High Wire*.
Played Captain Robbie McGregor in the **Gideon's Way** episode *The Thin Red Line*.
Guested as Lt. Gupta in the **Interpol Calling** episode *Ascent to Murder*.
Played Peters in the **Man in a Suitcase** episode *Essay in Evil*.
Played Jenkins Brothers in **The Persuaders!** episode *Someone Waiting*.

Calderisi David
Played the hotel clerk in **The Baron** episode *Time to Kill*.
Played the garage mechanic in the first series **The Protectors** episode *Disappearing Trick*.
Played Vittorio in the first season **The Saint** episode *The Latin Touch*.

Caldicot Richard
Played Sir Ralph in the third series of **The Adventures of Robin Hood** episode *Quickness of the Hand* and Lord Repton in the final season's *The Truce*.
Played the Abbot in **The Count of Monte Cristo** episode *A Toy for the Infanta*.
Played Commander Marsden in the second series **Danger Man** [aka **Secret Agent**] episode *The Outcast* and Sir Joseph Manton in *Whatever Happened to George Foster?*.
Played Robin Skelton/Peter Sinclair in the **Department S** episode *Black Out*.
Played Sir Thomas Glanville in the season two **Ghost Squad** episodes *The Desperate Diplomat* and *Gertrude*.
Appeared as the Commander in **The Prisoner** episode *Many Happy Returns*.
Played the doctor in the **Randall and Hopkirk [Deceased]** aka **My Partner the Ghost** episode *Who Ever Heard of a Ghost Dying?*.
Played the film Producer in the **UFO** episode *Reflections in the Water*.

Caldinez Sonny
Played the first Arab in the **Virgin of the Secret Service** episode *The Great Ring of Akba*.

Callaghan Ray
Played the hotel clerk in the **Return of the Saint** episode *The Armageddon Alternative*.

Callander Peter
Wrote the lyrics for **The Protectors** theme *Avenues and Alleyways* [music composed by Mitch Murray].

Callard Kay
Played Jean Lawson in **The Four Just Men** episode *The Judge* and Helen Porter in the **White Hunter** episode *Marked Man*.

Calvin Tony
Played Father Vincenzo in the **Return of the Saint** episode *The Village that Sold its Soul*.

Cameron David
Played Garth in the second series of **The Adventures of Robin Hood** episode *The Dowry*.
Played Sir Abelard in the season three **The Adventures of Robin Hood** episode *My Brother's Keeper*.
Played David in the **Interpol Calling** episode *The Sleeping Giant*.

Cameron Earl
Played Professor Moma in the first season **Danger Man** episode *Deadline*, Kassawan in the second season's *The Galloping Major* [now aka **Secret Agent**], Darcy in *Parallel Lines Sometimes Meet* and the Prime Minister in *Loyalty Always Pays*. In series three played Chand in *Someone is Liable to get Hurt*.
Played the Supervisor in **The Prisoner** episode *The Schizoid Man*.
Played Komo in the **White Hunter** episodes *The Fugitive* & *Day of Reckoning*.
Played Jombote in **The Zoo Gang** episode *African Misfire*.

Cameron Gay
Played Sheila McLellan in **The Buccaneers** [aka **Dan Tempest**] episode *Instrument of War*.
Played Number 36 in **The Prisoner** episode *The Schizoid Man*.

Cameron John
Composed and Directed the music on **The Protectors**.

Camiller George
Played the cafe waiter in the **Jason King** episode *Toki*.

Camp Gerard
Played the first professor in the **Return of the Saint** episode *The Imprudent Professor*.

Campanella Joe
Featured in the **Espionage** episode *We, the Hunted*.

Campbell Gavin
Played Spencer Bodily in the **Department S** episode *Spencer Bodily is 60 Years Old*.
Played the police motorcyclist in the **UFO** episode *The Psychobombs*.

Campbell Patrick
Wrote the first series **Ghost Squad** episode *The Broken Doll*.
Wrote **The Sentimental Agent** episode *May the Saints Preserve Us*.

Campbell William
Starred as Jerry Austin in the series **Cannonball**.

Campion Gerald
Played Eldon in the **Department S** episode *The Bones of Byrom Blain*.

Campos Ricardo
Played the boy in the **Department S** episode *Les Fleurs du Mal.*

Camps Professor Francis E.
Forensic Adviser on **Strange Report**.

Candelli Stelio
Played Captain Gennaro in the **Return of the Saint** episode *Vicious Circle.*

Cane Diane
Played the schoolgirl in the **Virgin of the Secret Service** episode *The Great Ring of Akba.*

Cann David
Was the second voice in part 2 of *Adventure Two* of **Sapphire and Steel** and played the pilot in part 3.

Canning Victor
Wrote the **Man in a Suitcase** episode *Blind Spot.*

Cannon John
Played the policeman in the **Father Brown** episode *Three Tools of Death.*

Cannon Roy
Props on **The Prisoner** [also appeared as a corpse in the episode *Dance of the Dead*].

Cant Brian
Played the Special Branch man in **The Sentimental Agent** episode *All that Jazz.*
Played the corporal in the **Sir Francis Drake** episode *The Garrison.*

Cantor Terry
Played Joe in the second season **The Protectors** episode *A Pocketful of Posies.*

Cardew Jane
Played Isabella in the **Jason King** episode *The Constance Missal.*

Cardew Valerie
Played Sally in the first series of **The Adventures of Robin Hood** episode *The Prisoner.*

Cardno Betty
Played Mrs. Mulloon in the third season **The Saint** episode *Little Girl Lost.*

Cardona Robert D.
Directed the **Virgin of the Secret Service** episodes *The Amazons, The Persuasion of a Million Drops, The Pyramid Plot, The Professor Goes West & Wings Over Glencraig.*

Carera Leo
Played Rahman in the season two **Ghost Squad** episode *Death of a Sportsman.*
Played Ananga in the second season **Man of the World** episode *Jungle Mission.*

Carey Joyce
Played Lady Ammanford in the second series **Danger Man** [aka **Secret Agent**] episode *Whatever Happened to George Foster?.*
Played Mrs Coles in the **Gideon's Way** episode *The Nightlifers.*
Played Mrs. Maddox in the **Randall and Hopkirk [Deceased]** aka **My Partner the Ghost** episode *Murder ain't what it Used to Be!.*

Cargill David
Played Narouz in **The Adventurer** episode *Love Always, Magda.*
Played Richards in **The Baron** episode *The Edge of Fear.*
Appeared as the van driver in the second season **Danger Man** [aka **Secret Agent**] episode *A Date with Doris* and as Harry Hutchinson in *Such Men are Dangerous.*
Played the tout in the **Man in a Suitcase** episode *Web with Four Spiders* and Yuseef in *The Revolutionaries.*
Played Patterson in **The Persuaders!** episode *Nuisance Value.*
Played the shop assistant in the **Randall and Hopkirk [Deceased]** aka **My Partner the Ghost** episode *Could You Recognise the Man Again?.*
Played Garcia in the first season **The Saint** episode *The Loaded Tourist* and Eddie Margoles in the fourth season's *The Desperate Diplomat.*
Played the car driver in the **UFO** episode *A Question of Priorities.*

Cargill Patrick
Featured in the **Espionage** episode *The Dragon Slayer.*
Played the Commandante in the **Man in a Suitcase** episode *Find the Lady.*
Guest starred as Thorpe in **The Prisoner** episode *Many Happy Returns* and as *'The new No. 2'* in *Hammer into Anvil.*

Carhartt James
Co-wrote, with Nicolas Winter, **The Adventures of Robin Hood** episodes *The Mystery of Ireland's Eye & The Little People* [season 2] and *A Tuck in Time* [3].

Caridia Michael
Played Edwin in **The Buccaneers** [aka **Dan Tempest**] episode *Pirate Honour.*

Carlin John
Played Tim Casey in the season two **Ghost Squad** episode *Quarantine at Kavar.*

Carlisle John
Played David Covington in the **Strange Report** episode *Report 4977: SWINDLE: 'Square Root of Evil'.*

Carlos Christopher
Played Ajali in the first season **Danger Man** episode *Deadline.*
In season two [now aka **Secret Agent**]: played Papa Camille in *A Man to be Trusted*, Victor N'Dias in *Parallel Lines Sometimes Meet* and the PM's Secretary in *The Mercenaries.*
Played the Doctor in **The Champions** episode *Shadow of the Panther.*
Played Captain Hann in the season two **Ghost Squad** episode *East of Mandalay.*
Played Manon in the second season **The Saint** episode *Sibao* and the Inspector in the third season's *Island of Chance.*
Played Baltasar in the **Sir Francis Drake** episode *The Gypsies.*

Carlson Veronica
Played Gina in the **Department S** episode *The Double Death of Charlie Crippen.*
Played Suzanne in the **Randall and Hopkirk [Deceased]** aka **My Partner the Ghost** episode *The Ghost who Saved the Bank at Monte Carlo.*
Played Vanessa Longman in the fourth season **The Saint** episode *The Man Who Gambled with Life.*

Carlton Pam
Continuity on **The Buccaneers** [aka **Dan Tempest**] episodes *The Raiders, Captain Dan Tempest, Dan Tempest's War with Spain, The Wasp, Whale Gold, Slave Ship, Gunpowder Plot, Articles of War, Ghost Ship, Conquest of New Providence, Mother Doughty's Crew, Blood Will Tell, Hurricane, Dead Man's Rock, Dangerous Cargo, Hand of the Hawk, Gentleman Jack and the Lady, Mr. Beamish and the Hangman's*

Noose, Marooned, Dan Tempest and The Amazons, The Ladies, The Return of Calico Jack, Conquistador, Aztec Treasure, Flip and Jenny, To the Rescue, Indian Fighters, Mistress Higgins' Treasure, The Spy Aboard, The Decoy, Pirate Honour, Instrument of War and *Printer's Devil.*

Carlton Timothy
Played Captain Watts in the **Virgin of the Secret Service** episode *The Great Ring of Akba.*

Carlvon Anthony
Played the first soldier in **The Scarlet Pimpernel** episode *The Princess.*

Carne Judy
Played Juanita in the first season **Danger Man** episode *Hired Assassin.*

Carney John J.
Played Clay in the third season **The Saint** episode *The Power Artist* and the security man in the **UFO** episode *Timelash.*

Caro Norman
Played General Schlessen in **The Adventurer** episode *The Bradley Way.*

Carr Russell
Played the servant in the **Sword of Freedom** episode *Forgery in Red Chalk.*

Carrell Annette
Played Eleanor Saumarez in **The Baron** episode *Long Ago and Far Away.*
Played "B" in **The Prisoner** episode *A. B. and C..*
Played Katerina in the second season **The Saint** episode *The Persistent Parasite.*

Carriello Frank
Played Vittorio in **The Count of Monte Cristo** episode *Point Counter Point.*

Carrigan Anarose
Appeared in **The Adventures of Sir Lancelot** episode *Thieves.*

Carrol Martin
Played Groves in the **Randall and Hopkirk [Deceased]** aka **My Partner the Ghost** episode *The Ghost Talks.*

Carroll Anne
Played the maid in the season two **Ghost Squad** episode *The Desperate Diplomat.*

Caroll Annette
Played Gilchrist in the **Man in a Suitcase** episode *The Girl who Never was.*

Carroll Edwina
Played the nurse in the **Department S** episode *The Double Death of Charlie Crippen.*
Played Laila in the **White Hunter** episode *Valley of the Dead.*

Carroll Martin
Played the second businessman in **The Adventurer** episode *Make it a Million.*

Carroll Sidney
Co-wrote the **Espionage** episode *The Incurable One* [with Halstead Welles].

Carpenter Paul
Played Ray Pearson in **The Four Just Men** episode *Panic Button.*

Played Brent Kingman in the first season **The Saint** episode *The Ever-loving Spouse.*

Carpenter Richard
Played Ronald Bell in **The Baron** episode *Enemy of the State.*
Played Michael Penn in the **Gideon's Way** episode *The Wall.*
Played the house surgeon in the **Strange Report** episode *Report 4821: X-RAY: 'Who Weeps For the Doctor?'.*

Carruthers Benito
Played Perango in **The Champions** episode *The Dark Island.*

Carson Charles
Played Maurine Ronda in **The Count of Monte Cristo** episode *A Matter of Justice.*
Played the Ambassador in the first season **Danger Man** episode *The Key* and George in the second season's [now aka **Secret Agent**] *A Very Dangerous Game.*
Played the Professor in the **Gideon's Way** episode *The Millionaire's Daughter.*
Played the Spanish Admiral in the **Sir Francis Drake** episode *Court Intrigue.*

Carson Clive
Played Marco in the **O.S.S.** episode *Operation Payday.*

Carson John
Played Sir Nigel Fitzhulme in the fourth series **The Adventures of Robin Hood** episode *A Touch of Fever* and Sir Geoffrey in *The Reluctant Rebel.*
Played Revell in **The Baron** two parter *Masquerade* [*Masquerade* - part 1 and *The Killing* - part 2: edited together, also exists as a feature entitled *Man In a Looking Glass*].
Played Symond in **The Champions** episode *The Gilded Cage.*
Played Arny Long in the first series **Ghost Squad** episode *Still Waters* and Franz Hartmann in the second season's *The Thirteenth Girl.*
Played John Gilsen in the **Man in a Suitcase** episode *Dead Man's Shoes.*
Played Said in the first series **Man of the World** episode *Death of a Conference.*
Played Ramon Venino in the first season **The Saint** episode *The Romantic Matron*, Astron in *The Arrow of God*; Theron Netlord in the second season's *Sibao* and Godfrey Quillen in the third's *The Fast Women.*
Played Filippo in the **Sword of Freedom** episode *The Eye of the Artist* and Cipriano in *The Pagan Venus.*
Played Fritz in the **William Tell** episode *The Ensign.*

Carstairs John Paddy
Directed the first season **The Saint** episodes *The Arrow of God* & *The Romantic Matron.*
Directed **The Sentimental Agent** episodes *The Beneficiary, Never Play Cards with Strangers, Meet my Son, Henry* & *The Scroll of Islam.*

Carter Dave
Played Kazakov in the **Jason King** episode *Zenia.*
Played the electrician in the **Randall and Hopkirk [Deceased]** aka **My Partner the Ghost** episode *My Late Lamented Friend and Partner.*

Carter Patrick
Played the air captain in the second series **Ghost Squad** episode *Interrupted Requiem* and Ali in *Quarantine at Kavar.*

Carter Peter
Location Manager on **The Protectors**.

Carter Wilfred
Played the Berlin policeman in the season two **Ghost Squad** episode *Lost in Transit.*

Carteret Anna
Played Diane Huntley in the fourth season **The Saint** episode *Portrait of Brenda*.

Cartland Bob
Played Peter Maller in **The Adventurer** episode *Action!*.

Cartwright Bill
Played the driver in the first season **The Saint** episode *The Romantic Matron*.

Caruso Anthony
Played Thiers in **The Count of Monte Cristo** episode *The De Berry Affair*.

Carver Peter
Appeared as Sievers in the **White Hunter** episode *Rogue Man*.

Cascio Antonio
Played Tino in the **Return of the Saint** episode *Dragonseed*.

Case Gerald
Appeared as Andy Stevenson in the **White Hunter** episode *A Moment of Truth*.

Case Stephen
Played the film director in the **UFO** episode *Mindbender*.

Cash John
Played an art student in the **Father Brown** episode *The Head of Caesar*.

Cash Murray
Played the American in the second series **Danger Man** [aka **Secret Agent**] episode *Are You Going to Be More Permanent?* Played the pilot in the **O.S.S.** episode *Operation Fracture*.

Cashman Michael
Played Syd Benson in the **Gideon's Way** episode *The Tin God*.

Cashmere Centre, The
Provided the Cashemeres for **Jason King**.

Caspi Michael
Played the page in the first series **Man of the World** episode *The Sentimental Agent*.

Cassie Alan
Assistant Art Director on **The Zoo Gang**.

Casson Maxine
Played the birthday girl in the **Strange Report** episode *Report 8944: HAND: 'A Matter of Witchcraft?'*.

Cast Edward
Played Rossi in the first season **Danger Man** episode *The Contessa*. Played Bennett in the second series [now aka **Secret Agent**] episode *Don't Nail Him Yet* and Luke in *A Room in the Basement*.
Played Hallam in the **Department S** episode *The Duplicated Man*.
Played Peter in the first series **Ghost Squad** episode *Eyes of the Bat* and the stage manager in *The Green Shoes* [this episode was shot for the first series, but due to an actors' strike, was originally shown in season two].
Played Pec in the second season **Man of the World** episode *In the Picture*.
Played Bellamy in the second season **The Saint** episode *The Frightened Inn-Keeper*.
Played the Captain-of-the-Guards in the **Sir Francis Drake** episode *Doctor Dee*.

Played Llewellyn in the **Strange Report** episode *Report 0649: SKELETON: 'Let Sleeping Heroes Lie'*.
Played Major in **The Zoo Gang** episode *African Misfire*.

Castle Ann
Played Mrs Cavallo-Smith in the **Randall and Hopkirk [Deceased]** aka **My Partner the Ghost** episode *Vendetta for a Dead Man*.

Castle Don
Co-wrote the story for **The Four Just Men** episode *The Battle of the Bridge* [with Miriam Geiger: teleplayed by Gene Coon].

Castle John
Played Number 12 in **The Prisoner** episode *The General*.

Cater John
Played Ronnie Osborne in **The Baron** episode *You Can't Win Them All*.
Played the male receptionist in the second series **Danger Man** [aka **Secret Agent**] episode *A Room in the Basement*.
Played Charles Barjou in the **Department S** episode *Dead Men Die Twice*.
Starred as Doublett [Virgin's batman/friend] in **Virgin of the Secret Service**.

Catlin Pearl
Played Fraulein Wellman in the **Virgin of the Secret Service** episode *The Great Ring of Akba* and Christa in *The Persuasion of a Million Drops*.

Caunter Tony
Played Darby in **The Baron** episode *You Can't Win Them All*.
Played Brandon in **The Champions** episode *The Gilded Cage*.
Played the male nurse in the **Department S** episode *The Man in the Elegant Room*.
Played Mason in the fourth season **The Saint** episode *The Organisation Man*.

Cavallaro Gaylord
Guested as Baker in the **Interpol Calling** episode *Checkmate*.
Played Frenchy in the **O.S.S.** episode *Operation Meatball* and Sammartino in *Operation Blackbird*.

Cavanaugh Paul
Played Morrell in **The Count of Monte Cristo** episode *The Affair of the Three Napoleons*.

Cavell Dallas
Played the Ship's Captain in **The Champions** episode *Operation Deep-freeze*.
Played Gholam in the season two **Ghost Squad** episode *Quarantine at Kavar*.
Played the Lieutenant in the **Sir Francis Drake** episode *The Slaves of Spain*.

Cawdron Robert
Starred as, series regular, Rico in **The Count of Monte Cristo** [episodes 8 - 39].
Played President Varnold in the first season **Danger Man** episode *The Girl in Pink Pyjamas*.
Played the Police Inspector in the **Department S** episode *The Soup of the Day*.
Played the farmer in **The Four Just Men** episode *Village of Shame*.
Played Ryan in the **H. G. Wells' Invisible Man** episode *Strange Partners*.
Guested as Debre in the **Interpol Calling** episode *The Two-Headed Monster*.
Played Leyland in **The Persuaders!** episode *Greensleeves*.
Played Sergeant Luduc in the **The Saint**: *The Covetous Headman & The Work of Art* [season 1] and *The Abductors & Jeannine* [2]. Played Le Duc in the third season's *To Kill a Saint*.

Played Valisse in **The Scarlet Pimpernel** episode *The Winged Madonna*, Chicon in *The Ambassador's Lady* and the first agent in *Something Remembered*.
Played Crombie in the **Sir Francis Drake** episode *Lost Colony of Virginia*.
Appeared as Doug Gordon in the **White Hunter** episode *The Trophy* and as Paul Klinger in *Girl Hunt*.
Played the Captain in the **William Tell** episode *The Spider*.

Cazabon John
Played Father Telford in **The Adventures of Sir Lancelot** episode *The Magic Book*.
Played Granger in **The Baron** episode *A Memory of Evil*.
Played Strotti in the second season **Danger Man** [aka **Secret Agent**] episode *No Marks for Servility*, the man in black in *The Ubiquitous Mr Lovegrove* and Ernesto in *You're Not in Any Trouble, Are You?* Played Aurel in the third season's *I'm Afraid you Have the Wrong Number*.
Played the chemist in the **Department S** episode *A Fish out of Water*.
Played Marco in the **Jason King** episode *The Stones of Venice*.
Played the nun in the **O.S.S.** episode *Operation Powder Puff*.
Played the man in the cave in **The Prisoner** episode *Free for All* and appeared as the Umbrella Man in *Once Upon a Time*.
Played Heller in the first series **The Protectors** episode *Brother Hood*.
Played the doctor in the **Randall and Hopkirk [Deceased]** aka **My Partner the Ghost** episode *That's How Murder Snowballs*.
Played Dragisha in the third season **The Saint** episode *Flight Plan*.
Played Mr Randall in the **Timeslip** story *The Day of the Clone* [series episode 24].

Cazes Clive
Played Mikos in **The Baron** episode *Night of the Hunter* and the police Captain in *Farewell to Yesterday*.
Appeared as the prison guard in the second season **Danger Man** [aka **Secret Agent**] episode *The Affair at Castelevara* & as the taxi driver in *English Lady Takes Lodgers*. Played a guard in the third season's *Two Birds with One Bullet*.
Played Kyriacon in the **Jason King** episode *Nadine*.
Played Giuseppe in the **Man in a Suitcase** episode *Find the Lady*.
Played Matra in **The Persuaders!** episode *Nuisance Value*.
Played Claude in the **Randall and Hopkirk [Deceased]** aka **My Partner the Ghost** episode *The Ghost who Saved the Bank at Monte Carlo*.
Played Esteban in the second season **The Saint** episode *The Revolution Racket*.

Cellamare Rosalino
Played Karl in the **Return of the Saint** episode *Appointment in Florence*.

Cellier Peter
Played the auctioneer in the first series **The Protectors** episode *King Con* and Jones in the second season's *The Last Frontier*.
Played Long in the **Randall and Hopkirk [Deceased]** aka **My Partner the Ghost** episode *The Ghost Talks*.
Played Inspector Collins in the **Strange Report** episode *Report 4407: HEART: 'No Choice for the Donor'*.

Central Casting [UK] Limited
Provided extras for **The Prisoner** whilst shooting at MGM.

Century 21
Produced **Joe 90** and **The Secret Service** series for ITC World Wide Distribution.

Century 21 Film Props
Provided BIG RAT for **Joe 90** and instrumentation for **UFO**.

Century 21 Pictures Limited
Produced **UFO** for ITC World Wide Distribution.

Century 21 Studios, Pinewood
Where **UFO** was filmed.

Cey Jacques
Played Frenchman in **The Champions** episode *A Case of Lemmings*.
Played the taxi driver in the **Department S** episode *Dead Men Die Twice*.
Played Claude in the **O.S.S.** episode *Operation Death Trap*.

Chadbon Tom
Played Vent in the first series **The Protectors** episode *Chase*.

Chaffey Don
Directed the second series **The Adventures of Robin Hood** episodes *The Secret Pool*, *The Borrowed Baby* & *The Little People* and the third's *The Salt King*, *My Brother's Keeper*, *The Christmas Goose* & *One Man's Meat*.
Directed **The Baron** episodes *A Memory of Evil* & *You Can't Win Them All*.
Directed the second season **Danger Man** [aka **Secret Agent**] episodes *Colony three*, *The Battle of the Cameras*, *No Marks for Servility*, *Such Men are Dangerous*, *Whatever Happened to George Foster?*, *A Room in the Basement*, *The Ubiquitous Mr Lovegrove*, *Parallel Lines Sometimes Meet*, *You're Not in Any Trouble, Are You?*, *A Very Dangerous Game*, *The Mercenaries*, *Judgement Day* & *Are You Going to Be More Permanent?* and the third's *Not So Jolly Roger*.
Directed the **Man in a Suitcase** episode *The Boston Square*.
Directed episodes of **The New Adventures of Charlie Chan**.
Directed **The Prisoner** episodes *Arrival*, *The Chimes of Big Ben*, *Dance of the Dead* and *Checkmate*.
Directed the first season **The Protectors** episodes *Brother Hood*, *It was All Over in Leipzig*, *The Quick Brown Fox*, *Balance of Terror*, *The Numbers Game*, *The Bodyguards*, *A Matter of Life and Death*, *One and One Makes One* & *The First Circle*.

Chagrin Francis
Music on **The Four Just Men**.

Chagrin Nicholas
Played the Ministry Clerk in **The Champions** episode *The Gun-Runners*.
Played Petrangeli in the **Department S** episode *The Double Death of Charlie Crippen*.
Played Andre in the **Randall and Hopkirk [Deceased]** aka **My Partner the Ghost** episode *The Ghost who Saved the Bank at Monte Carlo*.

Challis John
Played the soldier in the **Strange Report** episode *Report 7931: SNIPER: 'When is Your Cousin Not?'*.
Played Captain Raffles Kirby in the **Virgin of the Secret Service** episode *The Rajah and the Suffragette*.

Chamberlain Cyril
Played the wardrobe master in the second series **Danger Man** [aka **Secret Agent**] episode *A Very Dangerous Game*.
Played the courier in the **O.S.S.** episode *Operation Lovebird* and the Field Comm. in *Operation Yo Yo*.
Played Flavel in the second season **The Saint** episode *The Crime of the Century*.
Played Vogel in the **William Tell** episode *Manhunt*.

Chambers + Partners
Titles on **Department S**, **Jason King** & **Randall and Hopkirk [Deceased]** aka **My Partner the Ghost**.

Chambers Philip
Writer on **Interpol Calling**: co-teleplayed *Dead On Arrival* [with Max Marquis: story by Leonard Fincham] and wrote the story for *The Heiress* [teleplayed by Fincham & Marquis].

Chan Donald
Played the manservant in the second series **Danger Man** [aka **Secret Agent**] episode *A Very Dangerous Game*.

Chan Jacqui
Played Sara Van Neikerk in the season two **Ghost Squad** episode *East of Mandalay*.
Played Madam Chen in the second season **The Saint** episode *Jeannine*.
Played Lilian in the **Shirley's World** episode *Figuratively Speaking*.

Chance Naomi
Played Helen in **The Four Just Men** episode *The Judge*.
Played Liz Esposito in the season two **Ghost Squad** episode *Mr Five Per Cent* and Anna in *The Desperate Diplomat*.
Played Sheila in the **O.S.S.** episode *Operation Foulball*.

Chancer Norman
Played Max Rinston in the **Department S** episode *The Man from X*.

Chandler David
Wrote the **Gideon's Way** episodes *The Firebug, Gang War & The Wall*.

Chandos John
Played Reiker in **The Count of Monte Cristo** episode *The Mazzini Affair*.
Guested as Landau in the **Interpol Calling** episode *A Foreign Body*.
Played the club manager in the **Man in a Suitcase** episode *Burden of Proof*.

Chaney Lon Jnr.
Starred as Chingachgook, the last of the Mohican race, in **Hawkeye and the Last of the Mohicans**.

Chantler David
Wrote the **Gideon's Way** episodes *The Housekeeper & The Lady Killer*.
Wrote the **Interpol Calling** episodes: *The Long Weekend, The Thirteen Innocents, The Two-Headed Monster, Mr George, The Collector* - with Wilton Schiller and *Dressed To Kill* - with Robert Stewart.

Chapman Ann
Appeared as one of the dancers in the **Man in a Suitcase** episode *Three Blinks of the Eyes*.

Chapman Edward
Played Sir Ralph in the second series **Danger Man** [aka **Secret Agent**] episode *Don't Nail Him Yet*.

Chapman Robin
Played the man in the trenchcoat in **The Sentimental Agent** episode *Express Delivery*.

Chapman Tricia
Played Tina in the **Randall and Hopkirk [Deceased]** aka **My Partner the Ghost** episode *Could You Recognise the Man Again?*.

Chappell Connery
Producer on the first series of **Ghost Squad** and wrote the episodes *Hong Kong Story* [with Anthony Marriott] & *Death from a Distance* [with Lindsay Galloway].

Producer on the series **Interpol Calling**. Also, co-wrote *In the Swim* [with Robert Stewart] and co-teleplayed *The Three Keys* [with Robert Stewart: from a story by Paul Erickson].

Chappell Norman
Played the janitor in **The Adventurer** episode *Has Anyone Here Seen Kelly?*.
Played Johnny Pitt in the **G.S.5** episode *Hideout*.

Charella Ray
Played Renzo in the third season **The Saint** episode *Simon and Delilah*.

Charise Andre
Played Louis Brion in **The Buccaneers** [aka **Dan Tempest**] episode *To the Rescue*.
Played the groupier in the first season **Danger Man** episode *An Affair of State*.
Played the waiter in the **Department S** episode *One of our Aircraft is Empty* and the train steward in *The Bones of Byrom Blain*.
Played Cure in **The Four Just Men** episode *The Deadly Capsule* and the fisherman in *Village of Shame*.
Played Brun Played Hugo in the **H. G. Wells' Invisible Man** episode *The White Rabbit*.
Played the French Delegate in the **Jason King** episode *Uneasy Lies the Head*.
Played the first gendarme in the third season **The Saint** episode *The Queen's Ransom*.
Played the Croupier in **The Sentimental Agent** episode *The Beneficiary*.

Charles Oscar
Played a steward in the **Father Brown** episode *The Curse of the Golden Cross*.

Charlesworth David
Played the sergeant in the second series **Danger Man** [aka **Secret Agent**] episode *A Date with Doris*.

Charlesworth John
Appeared as Robert in **The Adventures of Sir Lancelot** episode *The Theft of Excalibur*.

Charteris Leslie
Creator of the Simon Templar character.
Credited for the original character creation and credited for the original Saint theme on the **Return of the Saint** series.
The Saint series was based, initially at least, on his *Saint* short stories. Scored the original Saint theme.

Chase James
Played the cowboy in the **Gideon's Way** episode *Gang War*.

Chase Stephan
Played Christian in the second season **The Protectors** episode *Bagman*.
Played Forbes in the **Return of the Saint** episode *The Debt Collectors*.
Played Raoul in **The Zoo Gang** episode *The Counterfeit Trap*.

Chasen Heather
Played Lorain Zameda in the first season **Danger Man** episode *The Deputy Coyannis Story* and Helen Hamilton in *The Nurse*.

Chases Sue
Designer on *Adventure 5* of **Sapphire and Steel**.

Chater Geoffrey
Played William Blount in the third series **The Adventures of Robin Hood** episode *At the Sign of the Blue Boar* and David in *Lincoln Green*.

Guested as Forster in **The Champions** episode *Project Zero*.
Played Peck in the **Department S** episode *Six Days*.
Played Leonard Smyth in the **Father Brown** episode *The Curse of the Golden Cross*.
Played Mr Jason in the season two **Ghost Squad** episode *The Big Time*.
Played Mr Horner in the **Jason King** episode *It's Too Bad about Auntie*.
Played Carl Howard in the fourth season **The Saint** episode *The Scales of Justice*.

Chatto Tom
Played Preston in the season two **Ghost Squad** episode *Sentences of Death*.
Played the doctor in the **Randall and Hopkirk [Deceased]** aka **My Partner the Ghost** episode *My Late Lamented Friend and Partner*.
Appeared as Supt. Bradlow in the **White Hunter** episode *Second Dealer*.

Chaudhuri Rajah
Played Canteyo in **The Buccaneers** [aka Dan Tempest] episode *Dead Man's Rock*.

Chaza Kubi
Played Jill in the first series **The Protectors** episode *A Kind of Wild Justice*.

Chegwidden Ann
Editor on the second season of **Danger Man** [aka **Secret Agent**].

Chenery Ronald
Played Edwards in **The Adventurer** episode *Has Anyone Here Seen Kelly?*.
Played Kyriascu in the **Jason King** episode *Wanna Buy a Television Series* aka *A Face I Used to Know*.

Chenet Victor
Played the Jury Foreman in the first season **The Saint** episode *The Element of Doubt*.

Cheng Cecil
Played the watcher in the second series **Danger Man** [aka **Secret Agent**] episode *A Very Dangerous Game*.
Played the waiter in the **Department S** episode *The Soup of the Day*.
Played Teller in the **Jason King** episode *Every Picture Tells a Story*.

Cherrell Gwen
Played Anne Gordon in the second season **The Protectors** episode *Trial*.

Cherry Helen
Played Avice in the second series of **The Adventures of Robin Hood** episode *Isabella*.
Played Mrs Pearson in the second series **Danger Man** [aka **Secret Agent**] episode *The Professionals*.
Played Barbara Crane in the **H. G. Wells' Invisible Man** episode *Play to Kill*.
Played Lady Graffham in **The Sentimental Agent** episode *Finishing School*.

Cheshire Geoff
Played Zoltan in the third season **The Saint** episode *The Gadic Collection*.

Chesnakov Alexis
Played Professor Brodny in the season two **Ghost Squad** episode *The Magic Bullet*.
Played Aristov in the third season **The Saint** episode *The Russian Prisoner*.

Chesterton G. K.
His *Father Brown* stories were adapted by Hugh Leonard for the **Father Brown** series.

Chevreau Cecile
Played Martha Frenke in **The Four Just Men** episode *The Godfather*.

Cheyney Nora
Played Lydia in **The Adventures of Sir Lancelot** episode *The Magic Sword*.

Chiarella Ray
Played the hotel clerk in **The Adventurer** episode *Miss Me Once, Miss Me Twice and Miss Me Once Again*.
Played Fausto in the **Jason King** episode *The Stones of Venice*.
Played Ben in the fourth season **The Saint** episode *The Ex-King of Diamonds*.

Chilcott Barbara
Played Mai in the first season **Danger Man** episode *Deadline*.
Played Maria in the **H. G. Wells' Invisible Man** episode *Behind the Mask*.

Child Christine
Played the air stewardess in **The Baron** episode *Farewell to Yesterday*.
Played the model in the second series **Danger Man** [aka **Secret Agent**] episode *Sting in the Tail*.

Child Jeremy
Played Carlton in **The Persuaders!** episode *Chain of Events*.
Played Howard McDee in *Adventure Five* of **Sapphire and Steel**.

Childs Peter
Played Cartwright in the **Return of the Saint** episode *The Imprudent Professor*.

Chin Dennis
Played policeman number one in **The Baron** episode *Storm Warning* [part 1 of a two-parter: also exists, edited together with part 2 - *The Island*, as a feature entitled *Mystery Island*].

Chin Tai
Played Souen in the second season **Man of the World** episode *The Enemy*.

Chinn Anthony
Played Mitchu in the first season **Danger Man** episode *The Honeymooners* and Chang in *The Journey Ends Halfway*. In the second series [now aka **Secret Agent**], played the questioner in *A Very Dangerous Game*.
Starred in the series **The Protectors** as Chino [season one].
Played Kuon in the **Return of the Saint** episode *Assault Force*.
Played Lieutenant Chin in the **UFO** episode *Sub-smash* and the alien in *The Square Triangle*.

Chinn Donald
Played the foreman miner in the season two **Ghost Squad** episode *East of Mandalay*.
Played the Chinese Doctor in the first series **Man of the World** episode *The Frontier*.

Chinnery Dennis
Played Bridges in **The Champions** episode *The Ghost Plane*.
Played Gunther in **The Prisoner** episode *Many Happy Returns*.
Played Carson in the third season **The Saint** episode *Invitation to Danger*.
Played Jones in the **Strange Report** episode *Report 0846: LONELYHEARTS: 'Who Killed Dan Cupid?'*

Chitty Eric
also spelled as Erik.
Played the butler in the second series **Danger Man** [aka **Secret Agent**] episode *Such Men are Dangerous*.
Played Hans Delarge in the season two **Ghost Squad** episode *The Man with the Delicate Hands*.
Played the Commissionaire in the **Shirley's World** episode *The Berkeley Club Caper*.
Played the keymaker in the **Strange Report** episode *Report 0649: SKELETON: 'Let Sleeping Heroes Lie'*.
Played The Kalipha of Akba in the **Virgin of the Secret Service** episode *The Great Ring of Akba*.
Played Klein in the **William Tell** episode *Castle of Fear*.

Chong Mona
Played the hostess in the second series **Danger Man** [aka **Secret Agent**] episode *A Very Dangerous Game* and the first girl islander in the fourth season's *Shinda Shima* [*Shinda Shima* was also merged with the only other surviving fourth season colour episode, *Koroshi*, to form a TVM entitled *Koroshi*].
Played Pearl Yenn in the **Jason King** episode *Every Picture Tells a Story*.

Chono Geoff
Played the Chinese assistant in the **Jason King** episode *Wanna Buy a Television Series* aka *A Face I Used to Know*.

Chow Michael
Played Chee in **The Baron** episode *Storm Warning* [part 1 of a two-parter: also exists, edited together with part 2 - *The Island*, as a feature entitled *Mystery Island*].
Played the second member of the Social Group in **The Prisoner** episode *A Change of Mind*.
Played Rawach in the second season **The Saint** episode *The Sign of the Claw*.

Chowdhary Sam
Played Karibz in the first season **Danger Man** episode *The Actor*.

Christian Hildy
Played Bianca in **The Count of Monte Cristo** episode *Naples*.

Christian Roger
Set Dresser on **Jason King** .

Christie Gordon
Played an auction client in the **Father Brown** episode *The Arrow of Heaven*.

Christie Julie
Played the title role in the first season **The Saint** episode *Judith*.

Christie Madeleine
Played Mrs Moss in the **Gideon's Way** episode *The Reluctant Witness*.

Christie Tony
Sang **The Protectors** theme *'Avenues and Alleyways'*.

Christine Helen
Played Lady Amyas in the **Sir Francis Drake** episode *The Flame Thrower*.

Christine Katia
Played Sophia in the **Return of the Saint** episode *The Village that Sold its Soul*.

Christopher Malcolm
Production Manager on **The Champions** and **The Persuaders!**, **The Protectors** & **Randall and Hopkirk [Deceased]** aka **My Partner the Ghost**.

Production Supervisor on the **Return of the Saint** series.

Chuntz Alan
Played the second watcher in the third season **Danger Man** [aka **Secret Agent**] episode *I can only Offer you Sherry*.

Church Tony
Played Professor Kenig in the **H. G. Wells' Invisible Man** episode *The Prize*.

Churchill Donald
Played Joe Kenton in the first series **Ghost Squad** episode *Eyes of the Bat*.
Played James Lane in the **Gideon's Way** episode *Subway to Revenge*.
Played Dr. Sprague in the first season **The Saint** episode *The Talented Husband*.

Cilento Diane
Featured as a special guest star in the **Espionage** episode *Festival of Pawns*.
Played Kate in **The Persuaders!** episode *A Death in the Family*.

Cilham Cheryl
Played the girl in a negligee in the **Return of the Saint** episode *The Debt Collectors*.

Cillou Alan
Wrote the **White Hunter** episode *The Lonely Place* [with Donn Mullally].

Cinesound
Sound Effects on **Department S, Randall and Hopkirk [Deceased]** aka **My Partner the Ghost** & **Strange Report**.
Post Production Sound on **Jason King**.

Clapton Patricia
Played Sally in the season two **Ghost Squad** episode *The Missing People*.

Clare Karen
Played Dr Zoren's nurse in the second series **Danger Man** [aka **Secret Agent**] episode *Fish on the Hook*.

Claridge Norman
Played Sir David Andrews in the season two **Ghost Squad** episode *The Magic Bullet*.

Clark Ernest
Played Sir Charles Anderson in the **H. G. Wells' Invisible Man** episodes *Secret Experiment*, *Picnic with Death* & *Shadow on the Screen* and Colonel Ward in *The Vanishing Evidence*.
Played Mac Andrew in the **Interpol Calling** episode *Private View*.

Clark Ian
Played the doctor in the season two **Ghost Squad** episode *The Missing People* and Fulroy in the **G.S.5** episode *It Won't be a Stylish Marriage*.

Clark Norton
Played the first assistant director in the **UFO** episode *Mindbender*.

Clark Susan
Played Philippa in **The Sentimental Agent** episode *Finishing School*.

Clarke Basil
Played the porter in the **Man in a Suitcase** episode *Which Way did he Go, McGill?*.

Played the coroner in the **Randall and Hopkirk [Deceased]** aka **My Partner the Ghost** episode *For the Girl who has Everything*.

Clarke Bob
Played Ferrar in **The Count of Monte Cristo** episode *Affair of Honour*.

Clarke Freddy
Played the chauffeur in **The Zoo Gang** episode *Revenge: Post-dated*.

Clarke Jean
Played Simone in the first series **Ghost Squad** episode *Eyes of the Bat*.

Clarke Martin
Sound Editor on **Strange Report**.

Clarke Richard
Played Fedor in the first season **Danger Man** episode *Find and Destroy* and Ricki in *Vacation*.
Played Robert in **The Four Just Men** episode *The Man in the Road* and Krager in *Crack-Up*.
Played Capt. Bera in the **H. G. Wells' Invisible Man** episode *The Prize*.
Played Jacques in the first season **The Saint** episode *The Benevolent Burglary*.
Played the sentry in the **William Tell** episode *The Traitor*.

Clarke T.E.B.
Wrote the **Shirley's World** episode *Evidence in Camera*.

Clarke T.E.V.
Wrote **The Four Just Men** episode *Rogue's Harvest*.

Clay Paul
Music on **The Adventurer** [theme was by John Barry] and Music Co-ordinator on **Jason King**.

Clay Virginia
Played the nurse in the first season **The Saint** episode *Marcia*.

Cleal Len
Film Editor on **Joe 90**.

Clegg Tom
Directed the **Return of the Saint** episode *The Murder Cartell*.
Directed the second season **Space 1999** episodes *Journey to Where*, *The Bringers of Wonder* [2 parter], *Devil's Planet*, *The Dorcans* & *The Immunity Syndrome*.

Clegg Tom
Played Hugo in **The Four Just Men** episode *The Godfather*.
Played the Monk in the fourth season **The Saint** two parter *The Fiction Makers*.
Played Ugo in the **Sword of Freedom** episode *The Besieged Duchess*.

Clemens Brian
Wrote **The Adventurer** episode *Action!*.
Using the pen name Tony O'Grady, wrote **The Baron** episodes *The Maze* & *The Long, Long Day*.
Wrote **The Champions** episodes *Happening* and *Autokill*.
Wrote the debut series **Danger Man** episodes *View from the Villa* [with Ralph Smart], *Time to Kill* [teleplayed with Ian Stuart Black: from a story by Brian Clemens], *The Girl in Pink Pyjamas* [original story: teleplayed by Ian Stuart Black & Ralph Smart], *The Sisters* [original story: teleplayed by Jo Eisinger], *The Island* [with Ralph Smart], *Bury the Dead* [original story: teleplayed by Smart], *The Leak* [with Smart], *The Nurse* [with Smart] & *Dead Man Walks* [with Smart].

Using the pen name Tony O'Grady, wrote the first series **Ghost Squad** episode *Bullet With My Name on it*.
Script Editor on **G.S.5** and wrote the episodes *Dr. Ayre* & *Seven Sisters of Wong*.
Using the pen name Tony O'Grady, wrote for the series **H. G. Wells' Invisible Man**: *Shadow Bomb* [co-teleplayed with Ian Stuart Black: from Clemens' story] and *The Big Plot* [co-wrote the story with Ralph Smart: teleplayed by Ian Stuart Black].
Co-wrote the **Interpol Calling** episode *Diamond S.O.S.* [used the pen name Tony O'Grady: with Leonard Fincham]
Wrote the second season **Man of the World** episode *In the Picture*.
Wrote **The Persuaders!** episodes *Overture*, *The Old, the New and the Deadly* & *That's Me Over There*.
Wrote the first season **The Protectors** episodes *Disappearing Trick*, *Thinkback*, *Vocal* & *Chase* and the second's *Goodbye George* & *Decoy*.
Wrote **The Sentimental Agent** episode *A Very Desirable Plot*.
Wrote the **Sir Francis Drake** episode *The Bridge*.
Wrote the **White Hunter** episode *Gun Duel* [using the pen name Tony O'Grady].

Clements Ted
Art Director on **The Buccaneers** [aka **Dan Tempest**]: *The Raiders*, *Captain Dan Tempest*, *Dan Tempest's War with Spain*, *The Wasp*, *Whale Gold*, *Gunpowder Plot*, *Articles of War*, *Ghost Ship*, *Conquest of New Providence*, *Mother Doughty's Crew*, *Blood Will Tell*, *Hurricane*, *Dead Man's Rock*, *Dangerous Cargo*, *Hand of the Hawk*, *Gentleman Jack and the Lady*, *Mr. Beamish and the Hangman's Noose*, *Marooned*, *Dan Tempest and The Amazons*, *The Ladies*, *The Surgeon of Sangre Rojo*, *The Return of Calico Jack*, *Conquistador*, *Aztec Treasure*, *Prize of Andalusia*, *Cutlass Wedding*, *Dan Tempest Holds an Auction*, *Flip and Jenny* & *The Spy Aboard*.

Cleveland Carol
Played Miss Dinsdale in the **Man in a Suitcase** episode *The Sitting Pigeon*.
Played the girl at the airport in **The Persuaders!** episode *Element of Risk*.
Played Laura Slade in the **Randall and Hopkirk [Deceased]** aka **My Partner the Ghost** episode *For the Girl who has Everything*.
Played Marion Kent in the first season **The Saint** episode *The Sporting Chance* and Gloria Mancini in the second season's *The Crime of the Century*.
Played Shelah in **The Sentimental Agent** episode *May the Saints Preserve Us*.

Clifford Jefferson
Played Dickon in the season two **The Adventures of Robin Hood** episode *The Mystery of Ireland's Eye*.
Appeared as the Retainer in the second series of **The Adventures of Robin Hood** episode *The Final Tax*.

Clifford Michael
Music Editor on **The Saint**.

Clifford Peggy Ann
Played Madame Susa in **The Four Just Men** episode *Marie*.

Clifford Pauline
Played the commentator in the third season **The Saint** episode *A Double in Diamonds*.

Clinton Dennis
Played British Delegate in the second season **The Protectors** episode *The Last Frontier*.

Clive John
Played the clerk in the **Man in a Suitcase** episode *Sweet Sue*.

Played Garton in the third season **The Saint** episode *A Double in Diamonds*.

Clulow Jennifer
Played Ann in **The Baron** episode *The Persuaders*.
Played Julie in the **Department S** episode *Handicap Dead*.

Clunes Alec
Played Woodes Rogers in **The Buccaneers** [aka **Dan Tempest**] episodes *The Raiders* and *Captain Dan Tempest*.

Coats Athol
Played Ivan in the **Father Brown** episode *The Secret Garden*.

Cobner John
Played the Moonmobile captain in the **UFO** episode *The Dalotek Affair*.

Coburn Brian
Played Dickie in the fourth season **The Saint** episode *Legacy for the Saint*.

Coccoran Michael
Played Pierre in the second series **Danger Man** [aka **Secret Agent**] episode *Have a Glass of Wine*.

Cockrell Gary
Played Al Jason in the first season **Danger Man** episode *The Actor*.
Played Frank in **The Persuaders!** episode *The Old, the New and the Deadly*.
Played Bill Fulton in the season one **The Saint** episode *The Benevolent Burglary* and Lester Boyd in *The Careful Terrorist*.

Coda Frank
Played the barman in the second series **Danger Man** [aka **Secret Agent**] episode *You're Not in Any Trouble, Are You?*

Coe Richard
Played Charlie in the **Man in a Suitcase** episode *Burden of Proof*.
Played the laboratory assistant in the **Strange Report** episode *Report 8944: HAND: 'A Matter of Witchcraft?'*.

Coffee Leonore
Wrote the story for the **H. G. Wells' Invisible Man** episode *The Mink Coat* [teleplay by Ian Stuart Black].

Cogan Dave
Sound on **The Buccaneers** aka **Dan Tempest**.

Cohen Larry
Wrote the **Espionage** episode *Medal For a Turned Coat*.

Cohen Vivienne
Played Marie in the **Department S** episode *Death on Reflection*.

Coia Gino
Played Italian policeman in the first season **The Saint** episode *The King of the Beggars*.

Coke Peter
Played Torwald in **The Adventures of Sir Lancelot** episode *The Black Castle*.

Colbourne Maurice
Played Sir Ian Rand-Fuller in the season two **Ghost Squad** episode *Sabotage*.
Played Jed Blackett in the **Return of the Saint** episode *Duel in Venice*.

Cole David
Played Anselmo in **The Four Just Men** episode *The Crying Jester*.
Played Charles in the **Man in a Suitcase** episode *Sweet Sue*.

Cole George
Played Bishop in the **Gideon's Way** episode *The Firebug*.
Played Fred in the **Return of the Saint** episode *The Armageddon Alternative*.
Played Paul Roper in the **UFO** episode *Flight Path*.

Cole Linda
Played Anne-Marie Benson in the **Randall and Hopkirk [Deceased]** aka **My Partner the Ghost** episode *Money to Burn*.

Cole Norman
Assistant Editor on **The Prisoner** and Music Editor on **The Zoo Gang**.

Cole Norman A.
Film Editor on **The Secret Service**.

Cole Paul
Played the bellboy in **The Four Just Men** episode *The Man With the Golden Touch*.

Cole Sidney
Producer on the four seasons of **The Adventures of Robin Hood** [Associate Producer on the first season].
Producer on **The Adventures of Sir Lancelot**: *The Knight with the Red Plume*, *The Ferocious Fathers* and *The Queen's Knight*.
Produced **The Buccaneers** [aka **Dan Tempest**] episodes *Blackbeard*, *The Raiders*, *Captain Dan Tempest*, *Conquest of New Providence*, *Hurricane*, *The Return of Calico Jack*, *Conquistador*, *Aztec Treasure*, *Prize of Andalusia*, *Cutlass Wedding*, *Dan Tempest Holds an Auction*, *Flip and Jenny*, *To the Rescue*, *Indian Fighters*, *Mistress Higgins' Treasure*, *The Spy Aboard*, *The Decoy*, *Pirate Honour*, *Instrument of War* and *Printer's Devil*.
Producer on the second, third & fourth seasons of **Danger Man** [aka **Secret Agent**] - episodes 9 - 32 only of series two.
Producer on the pilot - *The Battle of the Bridge* - and the Hawkins / de Sica episodes of **The Four Just Men** [Jud Kinberg was Producer on the Dailey / Conte episodes. The series was filmed in four separate blocks with the four stars actually appearing together in the pilot only. Dan Dailey & Richard Conte were each allocated ten episodes and Jack Hawkins & Vittorio de Sica each appeared in nine]: *Village of Shame*, *The Deserter*, *Their Man in London*, *National Treasure*, *The Survivor*, *Money to Burn*, *The Man Who Wasn't There*, *The Heritage* & *The Boy Without a Country* and *The Crying Jester*, *The Night of the Precious Stones*, *Mava*, *The Man With the Golden Touch*, *The Rietti Group*, *The Slaver*, *The Man in the Royal Suite*, *Rogue's Harvest* & *Treviso Dam*.
Producer on the **Man in a Suitcase** series.
Producer on the series **Sword of Freedom** and wrote the episode *The Assassin* [with Albert G. Ruben].

Colebrook Merrill
Played the third woman in **The Buccaneers** [aka **Dan Tempest**] episode *Dan Tempest and The Amazons*.
Played the first model in the **Man in a Suitcase** episode *The Sitting Pigeon*.

Coleby Robert
Played Anton in the second season **The Protectors** episode *Wheels*.

Coleman Bryan
Appeared in the second series of **The Adventures of Robin Hood** as Sir Peter in *The Goldmaker's Return* and the fat Duke

in *Flight from France*. In season three he played Baron Barclay in *The Healing Hand* & Beaumont in *The Crusaders*.
Played Professor Hanbury in the first season **Danger Man** episode *Dead Man Walks*.
Played Wenham in the **Sir Francis Drake** episode *Visit to Spain*.
Played Umberto in the **Sword of Freedom** episode *Francesca* and Zampante in *The Reluctant Duke*.
Played Count Heinemann in the **William Tell** episode *The Boy Slaves*.

Coleman Elizabeth
Wardrobe on **Thunderbirds**.

Coleman Noel
Played Baron Mark in the season two **The Adventures of Robin Hood** episode *The Little People*.
Played Sir Joplin James in **The Buccaneers** [aka **Dan Tempest**] episode *Printer's Devil*.
Played Phillips in the **H. G. Wells' Invisible Man** episode *The Locked Room*.
Played Stavros in the first series **Man of the World** episode *Masquerade in Spain*.
Starred as, series regular, Colonel Shaw-Camberley in **Virgin of the Secret Service**.

Coleman Richard
Starred as Alan-a-Dale in the fourth series of **The Adventures of Robin Hood** episodes *Six Strings to his Bow*, *The Devil You Don't Know* and *Hostage for a Hangman*.

Coleridge Sylvia
Played Mrs Bishop in the **Jason King** episode *It's Too Bad about Auntie*.

Coles Michael
Played Vince Florio in **The Baron** episode *The Man Outside*.
Played Rupert Fallon in the **Department S** episode *The Soup of the Day*.
Played Sandven in the second season **The Protectors** episode *Route 27*.
Played Larry Wentworth in the **Randall and Hopkirk [Deceased] aka My Partner the Ghost** episode *For the Girl who has Everything*.
Played Hugo in the third season **The Saint** episode *The Better Mousetrap*.
Played Prince Rouvaloff in the **Virgin of the Secret Service** episode *Russian Roundabout*.

Colin Ian
Played Michaelis in the **William Tell** episode *Undercover*.

Coll Christopher
Played the second yobbo in the **Man in a Suitcase** episode *The Bridge*.
Played the London Agent in **The Persuaders!** episode *Anyone Can Play*.

Colleano Mark
Played Abu in the **Virgin of the Secret Service** episode *The Great Ring of Akba*.
Played Carlo in **The Zoo Gang** episode *The Counterfeit Trap*.

Colley Kenneth
Played Dinny Brand in **The Baron** episode *The Legions of Ammak*.
Played the bank teller in the season two **Ghost Squad** episode *Hot Money*.
Played Devlin in the second season **The Protectors** episode *Dragon Chase*.

Collier Gerry Massy
Camera Operator on **Man in a Suitcase**.

Collier Ian
Played the army captain in the **Return of the Saint** episode *The Armageddon Alternative*.

Collier John
Co-wrote **The Four Just Men** episode *The Man in the Royal Suite* [with Samuel B. West: from an idea by Alec Coppel].

Collier Patience
Played Mrs Zaleski in the **Jason King** episode *A Thin Band of Air*.
Played Emma Mullrine in *Adventure Five* of **Sapphire and Steel**.
Played Princess Katerina in the **Virgin of the Secret Service** episode *Dark Deeds on the Northwest Frontier*.

Collin Ian
Played the pub landlord in the second series **Danger Man** [aka **Secret Agent**] episode *Don't Nail Him Yet*.

Collin Ivor
Played the first Man-at-Arms in the season four **The Adventures of Robin Hood** episode *A Bushel of Apples*.
Master-of-Horse [staff] on **The Adventures of Sir Lancelot** episode *Caledon*.

Collin John
Played John Campbell in **The Adventurer** episode *Action!*.
Played Bishop in **The Baron** episode *And Suddenly You're Dead* and Inspector Summers in *The High Terrace*.
Played Ciro in the **Man in a Suitcase** episode *Jigsaw Man*.
Played Jackson in the **Randall and Hopkirk [Deceased] aka My Partner the Ghost** episode *The Ghost Talks*.
Played Slade in the first series **The Protectors** episode *The First Circle*.
Played Sergio in the third season **The Saint** episode *Simon and Delilah* and Cable in the fourth season's *The Organisation Man*.
Played Ozman Hassin in the **Virgin of the Secret Service** episode *The Great Ring of Akba*.

Collings David
Played Stephen Miller in the second series **Danger Man** [aka **Secret Agent**] episode *Sting in the Tail*.
Played Silver in *Adventure Three* and *Six* [part 3] of **Sapphire and Steel**
Appeared as Anders in the **Strange Report** episode *Report 4821: X-RAY: 'Who Weeps For the Doctor?'*.
Played Daniel Clark in the **UFO** episode *The Psychobombs*.

Collins David
Played Alan Campbell-Gore in the **Gideon's Way** episode *The Prowler*.

Collins Jackie
Played Lucia in the first season **Danger Man** episode *The Contessa* and April Quest in the first season **The Saint** episode *Starring the Saint*.

Collins Joan
Played Sidonie in **The Persuaders!** episode *Five Miles to Midnight*.
Played Kara in the first season **Space 1999** episode *Mission of the Darians*.

Collins John D.
Played Chick in the fourth season **The Saint** episode *The Man Who Gambled with Life*.

Collins Julie
Played Emma Llewellyn in the **Strange Report** episode *Report 0649: SKELETON: 'Let Sleeping Heroes Lie'*.

Collins Louise
Played Sally Raymond in the first season **Danger Man** episode *Time to Kill* and Liz in *The Trap*.
Played Inga in **The Four Just Men** episode *Justice for Gino*.

Collins Michael
Played the Man-at-Arms in the second series of **The Adventures of Robin Hood** episode *The Trap*.
Played the police sergeant in the second series **Danger Man** [aka **Secret Agent**] episode *Whatever Happened to George Foster?*.
Played Det. Supt. Brown in the **Gideon's Way** episode *The Alibi Man*.
Played Borieff in the second season **The Saint** episode *The Hi-Jackers*.
Played the soldier in **The Scarlet Pimpernel** episode *Gentlemen of the Road*, the messenger in *The Flower Woman* and the second soldier in *The Princess*.

Collins Neil R.
Wrote the second series of **The Adventures of Robin Hood** episodes *A Village Wooing, The Scientist, A Year and a Day, Isabella & The Dowry* and the third's *My Brother's Keeper & Lincoln Green*.
Wrote **The Buccaneers** [aka **Dan Tempest**] episodes *Flip and Jenny, Indian Fighters* and *The Spy Aboard*.

Collins Pauline
Played Marie-Therese in the third season **The Saint** episode *The Better Mousetrap*.

Colston Ann
Played one of the girls in the second series **Danger Man** [aka **Secret Agent**] episode *Such Men are Dangerous*.

Colville Geoffrey
Played Mr. Watkins in the **Strange Report** episode *Report 2641: HOSTAGE: 'If You Won't Learn, Die!*.
Played Geoffrey in the **Virgin of the Secret Service** episode *A Fate Worse Than Death*.

Comfort John
Production Manager on the series **Sir Francis Drake**.

Conlon Donald
Played the footman in **The Scarlet Pimpernel** episode *The Imaginary Invalides*.

Connell Maureen
Played Eugenie in **The Count of Monte Cristo** episode *Majorca* and Carla in *The Mazzini Affair*.
Played Jo Dutton in the second series **Danger Man** [aka **Secret Agent**] episode *Yesterday's Enemies*.
Featured in the **Espionage** episode *Snow on Mount Kama*.
Played Janis in **The Four Just Men** episode *The Protector*.
Played Melanie, Princess de Monsantes, in **The Scarlet Pimpernel** episodes *Something Remembered, A Tale of Two Pigtails & Gentlemen of the Road*.

Connell Patrick
Played Smith in the **Man in a Suitcase** episode *No Friend of Mine*.

Connell Paul
Appeared in the first season of **The Adventures of Robin Hood** in a variety of roles: as the Manservant in *Husband for Marian*, as Lt. Howard in *The Miser*, as Mercer in *The Byzantine Treasure* and as the Innkeeper in *Secret Mission*.

Connell Thelma
Associate Producer on the seasons one to three of **The Adventures of Robin Hood** [also served as Supervising Editor].

Supervising Editor on **The Adventures of Sir Lancelot** episodes *The Knight with the Red Plume, The Ferocious Fathers, The Queen's Knight, The Outcast, Winged Victory, Sir Bliant, The Magic Sword, Lancelot's Banishment, Caledon, Roman Wall, Shepherd's War, The Pirates, The Black Castle, The Witch's Brew, Ruby of Radnor, The Lesser Breed, The Magic Book, Knight Errant, The Theft of Excalibur* and *Sir Crustabread*.
Supervising Editor on **The Buccaneers** [aka **Dan Tempest**] episode *Blackbeard*.

Connell Tracy
Played the manservant in the second series **Danger Man** [aka **Secret Agent**] episode *A Man to be Trusted*.
Played Tarno in the second season **The Saint** episode *Sibao*.

Connor Edrich
Played Thompson in the first season **Danger Man** episode *Deadline* and Doctor Manudu in the second season's *The Galloping Major*.
Played Captain Abdul in **The Four Just Men** episode *The Slaver*.
Played Doctor Gwabe in the **Man in a Suitcase** episode *Brainwash*.

Connor Kenneth
Played Milotti in **The Four Just Men** episode *The Man in the Royal Suite*.

Connor Kevin
Directed the **Return of the Saint** episode *The Imprudent Professor*.
Directed the first series **Space 1999** episode *Seed of Destruction* and the second season's *Brian the Brain*.

Connor Michael
Writer on **The Adventures of Robin Hood**: *The Carlotta* [with Basil Dawson], *The Black Five, & Frightened Tailor* [series 2]; *Pepper & Knight Errant* [3] and *Sybella* [4].
Wrote the story for **The Four Just Men** episode *Justice for Gino* [teleplayed by Lindsay Galloway].
Wrote the **H. G. Wells' Invisible Man** episodes *Secret Experiment* [with Michael Cramoy] and *Death Cell*.
Co-wrote the **Interpol Calling** episode *Cargo of Death* [with Leonard Fincham].
Wrote the **Sword of Freedom** episodes *The Bell, The Value of Paper, Vespucci, Angelica's Past, Cristina, Vendetta & Violetta*.
Wrote the **William Tell** episodes *The Lost Letter, Golden Wheel* and *The Bear* [original story: teleplayed by Doreen Montgomery].

Connor Patrick
Played Sergeant in **The Buccaneers** [aka **Dan Tempest**] episode *Pirate Honour*.
Played the receptionist in the second series **Danger Man** [aka **Secret Agent**] episode *The Ubiquitous Mr Lovegrove* and the gateman in *Such Men are Dangerous*.
Played the train guard in **The Persuaders!** episode *Anyone Can Play*.
Played Harry in the **Randall and Hopkirk [Deceased]** aka **My Partner the Ghost** episode *Murder ain't what it Used to Be!*.

Conrad Jan
Played Landlord in the second series **Danger Man** [aka **Secret Agent**] episode *The Professionals*.

Conrad Jess
Played Carl Willett in **The Four Just Men** episode *Panic Button*.
Played Mark Saunders in the second season **Space 1999** episode *The Lambda Factor*.

Conrad Les
Played the police constable in the **Father Brown** episode *The Head of Caesar* and the technician/policeman in *Three Tools of Death*.

Conte Richard
Starred as Jeff Ryder in the series **The Four Just Men** [The series was filmed in four separate blocks with the four stars actually appearing together in *The Battle of the Bridge* only. Dan Dailey & Conte were each allocated ten episodes and Jack Hawkins & Vittorio de Sica each appeared in nine]: *The Judge, Dead Man's Switch, Panic Button, The Discovery, Crack-Up, The Protector, The Bystanders, Riot, The Last Days of Nick Pompey & Justice for Gino*.

Conway Carl
Played Kurt in the **O.S.S.** episode *Operation Sardine*.
Played the steward in the third season **The Saint** episode *The Paper Chase*.
Appeared as Peter Reyes in the **White Hunter** episode *Operation Transfer*.

Conway Pamela
Played Ella Gante in the season two **Ghost Squad** episode *A First Class Way to Die*.
Played Phyllis in the **Gideon's Way** episode *The Great Plane Robbery*.
Played Catherine Marshall in the second season **The Saint** episode *The Chequered Flag*.

Conway Richard
Wrote the **Captain Scarlet and the Mysterons** episode *Operation Time* [with Stephen Mattick].

Conway Susan
Starred as, Junior Ranger, Kathy in the series **The Forest Rangers**.

Conyers Darcy
Directed the **White Hunter** episodes *Marked Man, Operation Transfer, Day of Reckoning, Web of Death, The Jackals, Girl Hunt* and *Let My People Go*.

Cook Fielder
Directed the **Espionage** episode *A Camel to Ride*.

Cook Vera
Played Paula's mother in the second series **Danger Man** [aka **Secret Agent**] episode *It's Up to the Lady*.

Cooklin Shirley
Played the title role in **The Adventures of Sir Lancelot** episode *The Lady Lilith*.

Cooksey Tim
Puppet Sculptor on **Joe 90 & The Secret Service**.

Cookson Barrie
Played Carl in **The Adventurer** episode *Has Anyone Here Seen Kelly?*.

Cookson Georgina
Played Miss Bishop in the first season **Danger Man** episode *The Trap*.
Appeared as the blonde lady in **The Prisoner** episode *A. B. and C.* and as Mrs Butterworth in *Many Happy Returns*.
Played Miss Grant in the **UFO** episode *Court Martial*.

Coon Gene
Teleplayed **The Four Just Men** episode *The Battle of the Bridge* [from a story by Miriam Geiger & Don Castle].

Cooper Bernie
Co-wrote, with Frances Megahy, the **Man in a Suitcase** episodes *Brainwash* and *Which Way did He Go, McGill?*.

Cooper Bryan
Wrote the **Captain Scarlet and the Mysterons** episode *Fire at Rig 15*.

Cooper Dene
Played the photographer in **The Prisoner** episode *Free for All*.

Cooper George A.
Played Dr. Quince in the season three **The Adventures of Robin Hood** episode *Roman Gold*.
Played Blatta in the first season **Danger Man** episode *The Traitor*.
Featured in the **Espionage** episode *Do You Remember Leo Winters?*.
Played Heppie in the **G.S.5** episode *It Won't be a Stylish Marriage*.
Played Mandel in the **Man in a Suitcase** episode *Sweet Sue*.
Played Webster in the **Randall and Hopkirk [Deceased]** aka **My Partner the Ghost** episode *The House on Haunted Hill*.
Played Milton Ourley in the first season **The Saint** episode *The Rough Diamonds* and Harold Laker in the fourth season's *The World Beater*.
Played Arturo Bardi in the **Sword of Freedom** episode *Cristina*.

Cooper Gladys
Played Grand Duchess Ozerov in **The Persuaders!** episode *The Ozerov Inheritance*.

Cooper Jack 'Jackie'
Appeared as the second corridor guard in **The Prisoner** episode *The General*, arranged the fight for *Do Not Forsake Me Oh My Darling* and played the first guardian in *Hammer Into Anvil*.
➔ Drove the Lotus 7 for the opening sequence of **The Prisoner**

Cooper John
Producer on the series **Timeslip** and directed the story *The Wrong End of Time* [series parts 1 - 6].

Cooper Maxine
Played Susan in **The Count of Monte Cristo** episode *Affair of Honour*.

Cooper Stuart
Played Joe Halston in the third season **The Saint** episode *The Death Game*.

Cooper Terence
Played Costellaux in **The Buccaneers** [aka **Dan Tempest**] episodes *Dan Tempest's War with Spain, Conquest of New Providence, Blood Will Tell, Hand of the Hawk, Gentleman Jack and the Lady, Dan Tempest and The Amazons & The Return of Calico Jack*, Grimes in *Whale Gold*, the Spanish jailer in *Dead Man's Rock*, Sergeant in *Mr. Beamish and the Hangman's Noose*, Macarty in *Marooned* and Blackbeard in *The Wasp & The Ladies*.
Played the singer in the first season **Danger Man** episode *The Contessa*.
Played John in **The Four Just Men** episode *The Last Days of Nick Pompey*.
Played Hanstra in the **H. G. Wells' Invisible Man** episode *The Big Plot*.
Played the Officer of the Guard in the **William Tell** episode *The Raid* and Captain Kraus in *The Mountain People*.

Cope Kenneth
Appeared in season three of **The Adventures of Robin Hood**: as Timothy Cox in *An Apple for the Archer*, Diccon in *The Mark* and Alwyn in *Elixir of Youth*.

Starred as Marty Hopkirk throughout the series **Randall and Hopkirk [Deceased]** aka **My Partner the Ghost**.
Played Marco in the **William Tell** episode *The Bandit*.

Copeland James
Played Dr. Carey in the second season **The Saint** episode *The Inescapable Word*.

Copeley Peter
Guested as Antrobus in **The Champions** episode *Project Zero*.
Played Brett in the second series **Danger Man** [aka **Secret Agent**] episode *Yesterday's Enemies*.
Played the auctioneer in the **Department S** episode *Death on Reflection*.
Played Rev. John Walters in the **Father Brown** episode *The Curse of the Golden Cross*.
Played Don Morland in the second season **The Saint** episode *The Sign of the Claw*.

Coppel Alec
Wrote the original stories for **The Four Just Men** episodes *The Prime Minister* [teleplayed by Oliver Skene] & *The Beatniques* [teleplayed by Wilton Schiller] and the original idea for *The Man in the Royal Suite* [written by Samuel B. West & John Collier].

Coppen Hazel
Played Mrs Blondel in the fourth season **The Saint** episode *Portrait of Brenda*.

Copplestone Geoffrey
Played the night club manager in the **Return of the Saint** episode *Dragonseed*.

Corbett Harry H.
Appeared in **The Adventures of Robin Hood**: as Sir Bascom in *The Charter*, as Jason in *The Angry Village* & as Nicodemus in *The Genius* [series 3] and as Sir Watkyn in *A Bushel of Apples* [4].

Corbett Ronald 'Ronnie'
Played the call boy in the first season **The Saint** episode *The King of the Beggars*.

Cordeau Evelyn
Played the first sister in **The Adventures of Sir Lancelot** episode *Sir Bliant*.

Corden Henry
Starred as Carlo in **The Count of Monte Cristo** episodes: *Affair of Honour*, *First Train to Paris* and *The Sardinia Affair*.

Corder Alan
Sound Editor on **The Champions**.

Corlan Anthony
Played Euzio in the **Jason King** episode *A Royal Flush*.
Played Ferdy Walker in the **Strange Report** episode *Report 8319: GRENADE: 'What Price Change?'*.

Corlett Bill
Played the garage attendant in the second series **Danger Man** [aka **Secret Agent**] episode *Whatever Happened to George Foster?*.

Cormack George
Played the man in the museum in the second series **Danger Man** episode *Are You Going to Be More Permanent?*

Cornelius Billy
Played Albert in the **Randall and Hopkirk [Deceased]** aka **My Partner the Ghost** episode *A Sentimental Journey*.

Corri Adrienne
Played Nita in **The Adventurer** episode *The Good Book*.
Played Mistress Higgins in **The Buccaneers** [aka **Dan Tempest**] episode *Mistress Higgins' Treasure*.
Guested as Mrs Trennick in **The Champions** episode *The Night People*.
Played Gabrielle in **The Count of Monte Cristo** episode *Monaco* and Simone in *Flight to Calais*.
Played Pauline in the second series **Danger Man** [aka **Secret Agent**] episode *Whatever Happened to George Foster?* and Elaine in *The Ubiquitous Mr Lovegrove*.
Played Monique in the **Department S** episode *The Man who got a New Face*.
Played Yolanda in the **H. G. Wells' Invisible Man** episode *Crisis in the Desert*.
Played Laura in the **Randall and Hopkirk [Deceased]** aka **My Partner the Ghost** episode *All Work and No Pay*.
Starred as, series regular [episodes 2 - 39], Angelica in the series **Sword of Freedom**.
Played Liz Newton in the **UFO** episode *The Square Triangle*.
Appeared as Maria Varga in the **White Hunter** episode *One Fatal Weakness*.
Played Mara in the **William Tell** episode *The Master Spy*.

Corrie Eric
Appeared in **The Adventures of Sir Lancelot**: as a peasant in *Double Identity*, a Priest in *The Bridge*, a jailer in *The Witch's Brew*, as Robert in *Ruby of Radnor*, as an overseer in *The Lesser Breed*, as Osbert in *The Mortaise Fair*, as the Saracen in *Maid of Somerset*, as Seneschal in *The Lady Lilith* and as a herald in *Knight's Choice*.
Played Sabot in **The Scarlet Pimpernel** episode *A Tale of Two Pigtails*.

Cortes Ricardo
Appeared as the guitarist in the first season **The Saint** episode *The Golden Journey*.

Cortez Leon
Played Birdie in the second season **The Saint** episode *The Scorpion* and Mac in the fourth season's *The Scales of Justice*.

Corvin Maria
Played Mlle Danois in the first series **Man of the World** episode *A Family Affair*.

Cory Steve
Played the moonbase guard in the **UFO** episode *Kill Straker!*.

Cosmo James
Played Inspector Williams in **The Persuaders!** episode *Element of Risk*.
Played Lieutenant Anderson in the **UFO** episode *Reflections in the Water*.

Cosmo Michael
Played Ronio in the **Sword of Freedom** episode *Cristina*.

Cossins James
Played Churchill in the **Strange Report** episode *Report 2475: REVENGE: 'When a Man Hates'*.

Costa Alf
Played the chauffeur in the second season **The Protectors** episode *The Insider*.

Cotes Peter
Directed the **Sword of Freedom** episode *Alessandro*.

Cotterill Helen
Played Liz in the **Strange Report** episode *Report 8319: GRENADE: 'What Price Change?'*.

Cotton Ann
Make-up on **Space 1999**.

Cotton Oliver
Played Spearman in the first season **Space 1999** episode *The Full Circle*.
Played the young man in the **Strange Report** episode *Report 7931: SNIPER: 'When is Your Cousin Not?'*.

Couch Lionel
Art Director on the second & third season of **Danger Man** [aka **Secret Agent**].

Coulouris George
Played the Police Commissioner in the debut season **Danger Man** episode *The Brothers*. In series four [now aka **Secret Agent**] played the Controller in *Shinda Shima* [*Shinda Shima* was also merged with the only other surviving fourth season colour episode, *Koroshi*, to form a TVM entitled *Koroshi*].
Played Kowska in the first series **Ghost Squad** episode *Assassin*.
Played Gomez in the first series **Man of the World** episode *Masquerade in Spain*.
Guest starred as the man with the stick in **The Prisoner** episode *Checkmate*.

Counsell Elizabeth
Played Veronica Kendal in the **Gideon's Way** episode *The Alibi Man*.
Played Anna Brenskaja in the **Jason King** episode *To Russia With ....Panache* .

Couper Barbara
Played Jean Anderson in the **Gideon's Way** episode *The Housekeeper*.

Court Hazel
Played Anne "Gentleman Jack" Bon in **The Buccaneers** [aka **Dan Tempest**] episode *Gentleman Jack and the Lady*.
Played Noelle Laurence in the debut season **Danger Man** episode *The Lonely Chair* and Francesca in *The Contessa*.
Played Jackie in the first series **Ghost Squad** episode *Death from a Distance*.
Played Penny Page in the **H. G. Wells' Invisible Man** episode *The Mink Coat*.
Played Carol in the **Interpol Calling** episode *Dressed to Kill*.

Courtenay Margaret
Played Flight Officer Sarah Glindon in the season two **Ghost Squad** episode *The Last Jump*.

Courtland David
Played the lunar module crewman in the **UFO** episode *Conflict*.

Courtneidge Cecily
Played Mrs Rosewall in the second season **Man of the World** episode *Double Exposure*.

Courtney Nicholas
Guested as Doctor Farley in **The Champions** episode *The Experiment*.
Played Dr Stayman in the **Jason King** episode *Wanna Buy a Television Series* aka *A Face I Used to Know*.
Played Max in the **Randall and Hopkirk [Deceased]** aka **My Partner the Ghost** episode *The Ghost who Saved the Bank at Monte Carlo*.
Played Alain in the second season **The Saint** episode *The Abductors*.

Courtney Stella
Played Nadia in the second series **Danger Man** [aka **Secret Agent**] episode *The Professionals*.

Cousins John
Wrote the first series of **The Adventures of Robin Hood** episode *Children of the Greenwood*.
Wrote **The Buccaneers** [aka **Dan Tempest**] episode *Slave Ship*.
Wrote **The Scarlet Pimpernel** episode *Thanksgiving Day* [with Michael Hogan and Angus McPhail].

Cowan James
Dialogue Synchronisation on **Joe 90** & **The Secret Service**.

Cowan Kenneth
Played Detective Constable in the **Man in a Suitcase** episode *Which Way did he Go, McGill?*.

Cox Arthur
Played Green in the **Department S** episode *Spencer Bodily is 60 Years Old*.
Played Louis Graham in the **UFO** episode *Exposed*.

Cox Brian
Appeared in **The Prisoner**.

Cox Clifford
Played the first security man in the season two **Ghost Squad** episode *The Grand Duchess*.
Played the attendant in the **Randall and Hopkirk [Deceased]** aka **My Partner the Ghost** episode *Just for the Record*.

Coxell Amanda
Appeared as the child in the second series of **The Adventures of Robin Hood** episode *A Year and a Day*.
Played Berthe in **The Scarlet Pimpernel** episode *The Christmas Present*.

Crabtree Arthur
Directed **The Adventures of Robin Hood** first season episode *The Vandals* and the second season's *The Friar's Pilgrimage*.
Directed **The Adventures of Sir Lancelot** episodes *Winged Victory*, *The Magic Sword* and *Roman Wall*.

Craig Bill
Wrote the first series **Ghost Squad** episode *Catspaw* [this episode was shot for the first series, but due to an actors' strike, was originally shown as a season two episode] and the second season's *Interrupted Requiem* & *East of Mandalay*.

Craig Ivan
Played Captain Steele in **The Buccaneers** [aka **Dan Tempest**] episode *Dangerous Cargo*.
Played the Ambassador in the **H. G. Wells' Invisible Man** episode *Man in Power*.

Craig Valerie
Played Madame Hubert in **The Four Just Men** episode *Panic Button*.

Craig Wendy
Played Jean in the debut season **Danger Man** episode *The Gallows Tree*. In series three [now aka **Secret Agent**] played Jean Smith in *I can only Offer you Sherry*.

Cramoy Michael
Wrote **The Baron** episode *The Legions of Ammak*.
Wrote the **H. G. Wells' Invisible Man** episodes *Secret Experiment* [with Michael Connor] and *Strange Partners*.
Wrote **The Prisoner** episode *It's Your Funeral*.
Wrote the **The Saint** episodes *Lida*, *The Golden Frog*, *The Spanish Cow* [story: teleplayed by Paul Erickson] & *The Smart Detective* [season 2]; *The Paper Chase* [teleplayed from a story by Harry W. Junkin] & *The Convenient Monster* [3] and *The Man Who Gambled with Life*, [story: teleplayed by Junkin] [4].

Crampton Gerry
Appeared as the Guardian in **The Prisoner** episode *The Schizoid Man* and as the Kosho opponent in *It's Your Funeral*.
Played Barnes in the second season **The Protectors** episode *Sugar and Spice*.

Crane John
Vision Control on **Sapphire and Steel**.

Cravat Nick
Starred as, regular, Jacopo in **The Count of Monte Cristo**.

Craven Timothy
Played Mavitch in the **Jason King** episode *To Russia With ....Panache* .

Crawford Andrew
Appeared as Hugh in the second series of **The Adventures of Robin Hood** episode *The Scientist*.
Played Sir Gawaine in **The Adventures of Sir Lancelot** episode *The Knight with the Red Plume* and Sir Gawaine in *The Queen's Knight*.
Played Captain Hornigold in **The Buccaneers** [aka **Dan Tempest**] episodes *Blackbeard*, *The Raiders* and *Captain Dan Tempest*.
Played Mackenzie in the first season **Danger Man** episode *The Gallows Tree*.

Crawford Howard Marion
Played Archer in the second season **Danger Man** [aka **Secret Agent**] episode *Yesterday's Enemies*, Gregori in *No Marks for Servility* and Commander Collinson in *English Lady Takes Lodgers*.
Guested as Reg Couts in the **Interpol Calling** episode *The Chinese Mask* and as Peters in *Ascent to Murder*.
Played Colonel Davies in the **Man in a Suitcase** episode *Brainwash*.

Crawford John
Played Dr. Keller in the first season **Danger Man** episode *The Girl in Pink Pyjamas*.
Played Pavelich in the first series **Ghost Squad** episode *Death from a Distance*.
Played Kustrinski in the **Interpol Calling** episode *The Sleeping Giant*, Keflik in *The Man's Clown* and Ben Stack in *A Foreign Body*.
Played Crawford in the **O.S.S.** episode *Operation Yo Yo*.
Appeared as Brady in the **White Hunter** episode *Big Bwana Brady*.

Crawford John Ernest
Played Gerard in **The Count of Monte Cristo** episode *Andorra*.

Crawford Lee
Played the first Russian guard in the third season **The Saint** episode *When Spring is Sprung*.

Crawford Leslie 'Les'
Played Jan in **The Adventurer** episode *Target!*.
Played Ravel in **The Persuaders!** episode *Powerswitch*.
Appeared as the second gunman in **The Prisoner** episode *Living in Harmony*.
Played Peter Rendo in the third season **The Saint** episode *Invitation to Danger* and Dunn in the fourth season's *The Desperate Diplomat*.

Crawford Michael
Starred in the series **Sir Francis Drake** as John Drake.

Craze Michael
Played Vince Kelly in the **Gideon's Way** episode *Boy with a Gun*.

Craze Peter
Played Roger in the **Strange Report** episode *Report 2641: HOSTAGE: 'If You Won't Learn, Die!*.

Crean Patrick
Played Lupo in the **Sword of Freedom** episode *Alessandro*.

Creasey John
Created [writing as Anthony Morton] the character which inspired **The Baron**.
Gideon's Way was based on his character creation.

Cresswell Colin
Played the barman in the season two **Ghost Squad** episode *The Menacing Mazurka*.

Crewdson Robert
Played the harpist in **The Adventures of Sir Lancelot** episode *Lancelot's Banishment*.
Played Laslo Polk in **The Baron** episode *Diplomatic Immunity*.
Played Gallezan in **The Champions** episode *The Iron Man*.
Played Luis in the **Man in a Suitcase** episode *Night Flight to Andora*.
Played Mikhail Zhukov in the third season **The Saint** episode *The Russian Prisoner* and Colonel Zaglia in *Flight Plan*.
Played Prince Frederick in the **Virgin of the Secret Service** episode *Entente Cordiale*.

Cribbins Bernard
Played Sid in the **Interpol Calling** episode *Slow Boat to Amsterdam*.
Played Captain Michael in the second season **Space 1999** episode *Brian the Brain*.

Crichton Charles
Directed the second season **Danger Man** [aka **Secret Agent**] episodes *Yesterday's Enemies* & *Fair Exchange*.
Directed the **Man in a Suitcase** episodes *Brainwash*, *Day of Execution*, *The Whisper*, *Why they Killed Nolan*, *No Friend of Mine* & *Three Blinks of the Eyes*.
Directed the first season **Man of the World** episode *The Runaways* and the second season's *The Bandit* & *The Prince*.
Directed the second season **The Protectors** episodes *The Last Frontier*, *Dragon Chase*, *Border Line*, *Sugar and Spice* & *Trial*.
Directed the **Return of the Saint** episodes *The Poppy Chain* & *The Diplomat's Daughter*.
Directed the **Shirley's World** episode *The Islanders* & *The Colonel*.
Directed the first series **Space 1999** episodes *War Games*, *Death's Other Dominion*, *Dragon's Domain*, *Guardian of Piri*, *Matter of Life and Death*, *Earthbound*, *The Last Sunset*, *Space Brain* and the second season's *The Metamorph*, *One Moment of Humanity*, *New Adam, New Eve*, *The Mark of Archanon*, *A Matter of Balance* & *The Lambda Factor*.
Directed the **Strange Report** episodes *Report 2641: HOSTAGE: 'If You Won't Learn, Die!*, *Report 8319: GRENADE: 'What Price Change?'*, *Report 2475: REVENGE: 'When a Man Hates'*, *Report 4821: X-RAY: 'Who Weeps For the Doctor?'* and *Report 5055: CULT: 'Murder Shrieks Out'*.

Criddle Tom
Played Fulton in the **Man in a Suitcase** episode *Which Way did he Go, McGill?*.

Crieg Isobel
Played the Maid in Waiting in the second series of **The Adventures of Robin Hood** episode *Isabella* and Agatha in *Fair Play*.

Crimmins Halstan
Played Bardo in **The Count of Monte Cristo** episode *Naples*.

Cripps Arthur
Property Master on **Thunderbirds**.

Crisp Tracey
Played Dandy Garrison in the **Randall and Hopkirk [Deceased]** episode *A Sentimental Journey*.

Cristie Paul
Wrote the **William Tell** episodes *The Young Widow* and *The Unwelcome Stranger*.

Crocker John
Played Reynolds in **The Baron** episode *The High Terrace*.
Played the blind man in the fourth season **The Saint** episode *The Scales of Justice*.

Croft Colin
Played Fitzrobert in the second series of **The Adventures of Robin Hood** episode *The Black Patch*.
Played Bill in the **H. G. Wells' Invisible Man** episode *The Rocket*.
Played Pat Adams in the **Interpol Calling** episode *Air Switch*.

Croft John
Played the reporter in the second season **The Protectors** episode *A Pocketful of Posies*.

Croft Jon
Played Morgan in the **Jason King** episode *If it's Got to Go - It's Got to Go*.

Croft Sylvia
Make-up on **Man in a Suitcase & Strange Report**.

Crole-Rees Trevor
Make-up on the first series of **Ghost Squad**.

Cronin John
Played the second Nazi in the **O.S.S.** episode *Operation Jingle Bells*.

Crooks Christopher
Played the first guard in the **Father Brown** episode *The Arrow of Heaven*.

Cross Cyril
Played Poltyev in the third season **Danger Man [aka Secret Agent]** episode *To our Best Friend*.
Played the second American in the season two **Ghost Squad** episode *Mr Five Per Cent*.

Cross Eric
Visual Effects Unit lighting cameraman on **The Secret Service**.

Cross Gerald
Appeared in the first season **The Adventures of Robin Hood** episode *Queen Eleanor* as Bruno.
Played Trullus in **The Adventures of Sir Lancelot** episode *Roman Wall*.
Played Mr Minto in the season two **Ghost Squad** episode *Polsky*.
Played the insurance man in the **UFO** episode *Reflections in the Water*.
Played Ludwig in the **William Tell** episode *The Magic Powder*.

Cross Hugh
Played Jim Stark in the season four **The Adventures of Robin Hood** episode *The Reluctant Rebel*.

Cross John Keir
Wrote the **Sir Francis Drake** episodes *Johnnie Factotum & Gentlemen of Spain*.

Cross Larry
Played the Warden in **The Four Just Men** episode *Riot* and Meadows in *The Protector*.
Played General Denmayer in the **Man in a Suitcase** episode *All that Glitters*.
Played Burton in the second season **Man of the World** episode *The Prince*.
Played John Hamilton in the first season **The Saint** episode *The Saint Sees it Through*.

Cross Mel
Puppet Operator on **Joe 90**.

Crossthwaite Julie
Played the air hostess in the **Jason King** episode *That isn't Me, It's Somebody Else*.
Played Mandy in **The Persuaders!** episode *Take Seven*.
Played Mallory's girl in the first series **The Protectors** episode *A Matter of Life and Death*.

Croucher Brian
Played Daniel Devine in the **Father Brown** episode *The Man with Two Beards*.

Croucher Roger
Played Terry in the **Randall and Hopkirk [Deceased]** aka **My Partner the Ghost** episode *The Ghost who Saved the Bank at Monte Carlo*.

Crowden Graham
Appeared as Friar Dennis in the second series of **The Adventures of Robin Hood** episode *Hubert*.
Played Braithwaite in the second series **Danger Man [aka Secret Agent]** episode *That's Two of Us Sorry*.
Played Colonel Bohun in the **Father Brown** episode *The Hammer of God*.

Crowest John
Played the Navy Lieutenant in the **O.S.S.** episode *Operation Powder Puff*.

Cruikshank Andrew
Played Duke of Urbino in the **Sword of Freedom** episode *The Ship*.

Cruikshank Rufus
Starred as Little John in **The Adventures of Robin Hood** [took over the role for ten first series episodes to cover for the injured Archie Duncan]: *Husband for Marian, The Highlander, The Youngest Outlaw, The Betrothal, The Alchemist, The Jongleur, The Intruders, The Sheriff's Boots, Errand of Mercy & The Vandals*.
Guested as Sgt. Logie in the **Interpol Calling** episode *The Sleeping Giant*.

Crump Martin
Wrote the first season **Thunderbirds** episodes *Operation Crash Dive & The Duchess Assignment*.

Crutchley Rosalie
Played the Queen in **The Prisoner** episode *Checkmate*.

Cuby Joseph
Played Hassan in the first season **Danger Man** episode *The Blue Veil* and Sadi in *The Leak*.
Played Guido [as a boy] in **The Four Just Men** episode *The Battle of the Bridge* and Vito in *The Boy Without a Country*.
Played Luiz in the second season **Man of the World** episode *The Bullfighter*.
Appeared as the first member of the Social Group in **The Prisoner** episode *A Change of Mind*.
Played Alfredo Ravenna in the first season **The Saint** episode *The Loaded Tourist*.

Played Don Carlos in the **Sir Francis Drake** episode *Visit to Spain*.

Cuka Frances
Guested as Anna Maria Martes in **The Champions** episode *Get Me Out of Here!*.

Cullen Ian
Played the Special Branch man in the **Department S** episode *The Bones of Byrom Blain*.
Played Sgt. Taylor in the **Return of the Saint** episode *Signal Stop*.

Culliford James
Played Eric Little in the **Gideon's Way** episode *The Alibi Man*.
Played Ginter in the first series **The Protectors** episode *Thinkback*.
Played Parker in the **Randall and Hopkirk [Deceased]** aka **My Partner the Ghost** episode *The Ghost Talks*.

Cullum Charles
Played Lord Eastleigh in **The Four Just Men** episode *National Treasure*.

Cullum-Jones Desmond
Played Jordon in the second series **Danger Man** [aka **Secret Agent**] episode *Are You Going to Be More Permanent?*
Played the police constable in the **Father Brown** episode *The Dagger With Wings*.

Culver Michael
Played Danny in the **Man in a Suitcase** episode *The Bridge*.
Played Kurt in **The Persuaders!** episode *Nuisance Value*.
Played Irving in the first season **Space 1999** episode *Guardian of Piri*.

Culver Roland
Featured in the **Espionage** episode *Castles In Spain*.

Culver Ronald
Played Sir Arthur Vane in the **Gideon's Way** episode *The 'V' Men*.
Played Duke of Caith in **The Persuaders!** episode *A Death in the Family*.
Played Sir Esmond in the **UFO** episode *The Man who Came Back*.

Cummin Dave
Wrote the **G.S.5** episode *Pay Up or Else*.

Cummings Bill
Guested as Aston in **The Champions** episode *Happening*.
Played the henchman in **The Prisoner** episode *A. B. and C.* and the second horseman in *Living in Harmony*.

Cummings Douglas
Played Wullie in the **Virgin of the Secret Service** episode *Wings Over Glencraig*.

Cummings Susan
Played Duchess De Barry in **The Count of Monte Cristo** episode *The De Berry Affair*.

Cummins Jackie
Wardrobe Supervisor on the series **The Zoo Gang**.

Cunningham Chris
Played Vladimir in the **Jason King** episode *A Royal Flush*.

Cunningham Dan
Played Sir Bernard in **The Adventures of Sir Lancelot** episode *The Magic Sword*.

Cunningham Jack
Played the landlord in **The Count of Monte Cristo** episode *Lichtenburg*.
Played the driver in the first season **Danger Man** episode *Under the Lake*.

Cunningham Linda
Played the second fan in the **Jason King** episode *That isn't Me, It's Somebody Else*.

Curacao Harcourt
Played the officer in the first season **Danger Man** episode *Deadline*.
Played the third removal man in the second series **Danger Man** [aka **Secret Agent**] episode *Loyalty Always Pays*.

Curnow Graham
Played P.C. Awkwright in the **Gideon's Way** episode *The Lady Killer*.

Curram Roland
Played Jennings in the **Randall and Hopkirk [Deceased]** aka **My Partner the Ghost** episode *Could You Recognise the Man Again?*.

Curran Paul
Played Gomez in the third season **Danger Man** [aka **Secret Agent**] episode *The Man with the Foot* and Dr Shargis in *Two Birds with One Bullet*.
Played Sir Humphrey Gwynne in the **Father Brown** episode *The Mirror of the Magistrate*.
Played Kasankas in the second series **The Protectors** episode *Zeke's Blues*.
Played Bruno Walmar in the first season **The Saint** episode *The Noble Sportsman*.

Curran Peter
Co-wrote, with David Williams, the **Captain Scarlet and the Mysterons** episodes *White as Snow*, *Point 783*, *Seek and Destroy* and *The Launching*.

Currie Finlay
Played Palmerstone in **The Count of Monte Cristo** episode *The Talleyrand Affair*.
Played "Jock" in the **Danger Man** episode *The Gallows Tree* and, in the second series [now aka **Secret Agent**], played the landlord in *That's Two of Us Sorry*.
Played General Sir Hector McGregor in the **Gideon's Way** episode *The Thin Red Line*.
Played Donald in the first series **Man of the World** episode *The Highland Story*.
Guest starred as the General in **The Prisoner** episode *The Chimes of Big Ben*.
Played Don Pasquale in the fourth season **The Saint** episode *Vendetta for the Saint* [part 2].

Curry Shaun
Played the gamekeeper, guard in the fourth season **The Saint** two parter *The Fiction Makers*.

Curtis Alan
Played the commissionaire in the **Jason King** episode *An Author in Search of Two Characters*.
Played Trape in the second season **The Saint** episode *The Death Penalty* and Vargos in *The Golden Frog*.

Curtis Martin
Director of Photography on **The Buccaneers** [aka **Dan Tempest**] episodes *The Raiders*, *Captain Dan Tempest*, *Dan Tempest's War with Spain*, *The Wasp*, *Whale Gold*, *Slave Ship*, *Gunpowder Plot*, *Articles of War*, *Mr. Beamish and the Hangman's Noose*, *Marooned*, *Before the Mast*, *Dan Tempest and The Amazons*, *The Ladies & The Surgeon of Sangre Rojo*.

Curtis Tony
Starred as Danny Wilde throughout **The Persuaders!** series.

Curzon Fiona
Played Jenny in the **Return of the Saint** episode *Tower Bridge is Falling Down.*

Curzon Jill
Played the stewardess in **The Champions** episode *Project Zero.*
Played Maria Cavallini in the second season **The Saint** episode *The Old Treasure Story.*

Cusack Cyril
Played Charlie in the **Shirley's World** episode *The Reunion.*

Cusack Sinead
Played Jenny Lindley in **The Persuaders!** episode *Take Seven.*
Played Anne Ferris in the second season **The Protectors** episode *Burning Bush.*

Cushing Peter
Played Raan in the first season **Space 1999** episode *Missing Link.*
Played Judge Gautier in **The Zoo Gang** episode *The Counterfeit Trap.*

Cuthbertson Allan
Played Malbete in the second series of **The Adventures of Robin Hood** episode *The York Treasure.*
Played Cranmore in **The Champions** episode *The Experiment.*
Played Metz in **The Count of Monte Cristo** episode *Lichtenburg.*
Played Mr Wilson in the first season **Danger Man** episode *The Island.*
Featured in the **Espionage** episode *Covenant With Death.*
Played Cowen in **The Four Just Men** episode *The Survivor.*
Played Chief Superintendent Bill Parsons in the **Gideon's Way** episode *The 'V' Men* and Major Donald Ross in *The Thin Red Line.*
Played Rutledge in the **Jason King** episode *Every Picture Tells a Story.*
Played Turner in the **Man in a Suitcase** episode *No Friend of Mine.*
Played Colonel Wright in **The Persuaders!** episode *That's Me Over There.*
Played Colonel Hannerly in the third season **The Saint** episode *When Spring is Sprung.*
Played Jack Newton in the **UFO** episode *The Square Triangle.*

Cuthbertson Iain
Played Kendall in the **Department S** episode *Spencer Bodily is 60 Years Old.*
Played Wyatt in the second season **The Protectors** episode *Petard.*

Cutlack Ted
Camera Operator [Visual Effects Main Unit] on **Joe 90**.

Cvitanovich Frank
Directed the **Shirley's World** episode *The Reunion.*

Cyrus Tony
Guested as Major Tuat in **The Champions** episode *Desert Journey.*

****

Da Costa Michael
Played the cafe owner in the first series **The Protectors** episode *Disappearing Trick*, Emil in *King Con* and the hotel manager in *It Could be Practically Anywhere on the Island*.
Played the doctor in the fourth season **The Saint** episode *The People Importers*.
Played Hercule in **The Zoo Gang** episode *The Twisted Cross*.

Dailey Dan
Starred as Tim Collier in the series **The Four Just Men** [the series was filmed in four separate blocks with the four stars actually appearing together in *The Battle of the Bridge* only. Dailey & Richard Conte were each allocated ten episodes and Jack Hawkins & Vittorio de Sica, nine]: *The Prime Minister, The Beatniques, The Deadly Capsule, Marie, The Man in the Road, The Miracle of St. Philippe, The Princess, The Grandmother, The Godfather & The Moment of Truth*.

Daine Lois
Played Valerie in the **Man in a Suitcase** episode *The Sitting Pigeon*.

Dainton Joanne
Played the nurse in the **O.S.S.** episode *Operation Blackbird*.
Played Miss Lindsay in **The Persuaders!** episode *Someone Like Me*.
Played the nurse in the third season **The Saint** episode *The Best Laid Schemes*.
Played Laura in the **Sir Francis Drake** episode *Bold Enterprise*.

Dainton Patricia
Appeared as Louise in the **White Hunter** episode *Deadfall* and as Dr. Anne Clements in *Out of the Wind*.

Dakar Andre
Played Sir Aaron Nelson in the first season **Danger Man** episode *Deadline*.
Appeared as Kagaya in the **White Hunter** episode *Decision*, Kotitcu in *Sickness of Kilimanjaro* and as the Native Chief in *The Long Knife*.

Dalby Amy
Played Mrs Kerman in the **G.S.5** episode *Dead Men Don't Drive*.

Dalby Lynn
Played Marie de la Garde in the **Return of the Saint** episode *The Diplomat's Daughter*.

Dale Ellis
Played Finlay in the **Department S** episode *The Soup of the Day* and the priest in *The Ghost of Mary Burnham*.

Dale John
Played Will in **The Adventures of Sir Lancelot** episode *The Outcast*.

Dales Arthur
Writer on **The Adventures of Robin Hood**: The *Youthful Menace & Farewell to Tuck* [series 3] and *Hostage for a Hangman, The Oath & Race Against Time* [4].
Wrote the **Strange Report** episode *Report 1553: RACIST: 'A Most Dangerous Proposal'*.

Dambuza Nathan
Played General Naganda in **The Zoo Gang** episode *African Misfire*.

Damon Mark
Played Nick Archer in the second season **The Protectors** episode *Decoy*.

Damon Stuart
Played Vince in **The Adventurer** episodes *The Good Book & Poor Little Rich Girl*.
Starred throughout **The Champions** as Craig Sterling.
Played Williams in the **Man in a Suitcase** episode *Man from the Dead*.
Played Rod Huston in the fourth season **The Saint** episode *The Ex-King of Diamonds*.
Played Igor Kuraganovitch in the **Shirley's World** episode *The Defective Defector*.
Played Parks in the first season **Space 1999** episode *Matter of Life and Death* and Guido in the second season two parter *The Bringers of Wonder*.
Played Howard Byrne in the **UFO** episode *Mindbender*.

Dan Dafna
Played the air hostess in **The Baron** episode *The Edge of Fear*.

Dance Charles
Played Commandant Neil O'Brien in the **Father Brown** episode *The Secret Garden*.

Dancy Bill
Played the master gunner in the **Sir Francis Drake** episode *The Garrison*.

Dancy Brad
Played Corto in the first season **Danger Man** episode *Find and Destroy*.

Dane Alexandra
Played Mathilde in the first season **The Saint** episode *The Good Medicine*.

Dane Lawrence
Played El Rojo in the first season **The Saint** episode *Teresa*.

Dane Tita
Played the Nun in the third season **The Saint** episode *Interlude in Venice*.

Daneman Paul
Played Stopford in **The Adventurer** episode *Mr Calloway is a Very Cautious Man*.
Played Sir Guy in the second series of The **Adventures of Robin Hood** episode *Ransom*.
Played Dr. Bakalter in the first season **Danger Man** episode *The Journey Ends Halfway*.
Played Dante in **The Four Just Men** episode *The Miracle of St. Philippe*.
Played Rocher Played Hugo in the **H. G. Wells' Invisible Man** episode *The White Rabbit*.
Played Dr. Ormsby in the third season **The Saint** episode *The Best Laid Schemes*.

Daniel Jennifer
Played Anya Krovchuk in the season two **Ghost Squad** episode *A First Class Way to Die* and Majorie Bellman in the **Gideon's Way** episode *The Alibi Man*.

Daniels Danny
Played the adjutant in the second series **Danger Man** [aka **Secret Agent**] episode *The Galloping Major*.
Played the ringleader in the **Man in a Suitcase** episode *No Friend of Mine*.
Played the barman in the third season **The Saint** episode *Island of Chance*.
Appeared in **White Hunter** as Kuyo in *Let My People Go* and as the second bearer in *The Stepfathers & Pegasus*.

Daniely Lisa
Played Lisa Declair in **The Baron** episode *Roundabout*.

Played Linda Janson in the third season **Danger Man** [aka **Secret Agent**] episode *Not So Jolly Roger*.
Starred as, series regular, Diane 'Dee' Brady in the series **H. G. Wells' Invisible Man**: *Secret Experiment, The Locked Room, Play to Kill, The Mink Coat, Picnic with Death, Blind Justice, Strange Partners, Odds Against Death, Jailbreak, Bank Raid, Death Cell, Point of Destruction & The Prize*.
Guested as Helene in the **Interpol Calling** episodes *Diamond S.O.S.* and *The Man's Clown*.
Played Marquesa Visconti in the second season **The Protectors** episode *Fighting Fund*.
Played Milo Gambodi in the third season **The Saint** episode *The Better Mousetrap*.
Played Madeleine in the **Strange Report** episode *Report 3906: COVER GIRLS: 'Last year's Model'*.
Played Lady Clea Merrion in the **Virgin of the Secret Service** episode *The Pyramid Plot*.

Danquah Paul
Played James Owen in the second series **Danger Man** [aka **Secret Agent**] episode *Parallel Lines Sometimes Meet*, the cleaner in *The Mercenaries* and the barman in the third season's *The Man on the Beach*.

Darbon Leslie
Wrote the **Department S** episodes *The Perfect Operation, The Double Death of Charlie Crippen & The Soup of the Day*.

Darby Cecillia
Played Joanna in the **Strange Report** episode *Report 8944: HAND: 'A Matter of Witchcraft?'*.

Dare Richard
Played Jan Kupra in the second series **Ghost Squad** episode *Interrupted Requiem*.

Darke Dorothy
Appeared as the landlady in **The Four Just Men** episode *The Survivor*.

Darrow Paul
Played Omar in the third season **The Saint** episode *The Gadic Collection*.
Played Sayid in the **Virgin of the Secret Service** episode *The Pyramid Plot*.

Dasey Neville
Wrote the **Interpol Calling** episode *Last Man Lucky*.

Davenport Claire
Played Anna Lobovitch in **The Baron** episode *Diplomatic Immunity*.

Davenport David
Played the Man-at-Arms in the season three **The Adventures of Robin Hood** episode *Roman Gold*.
Played the detective in the season two **Ghost Squad** episode *Hot Money* and Ft. Lt. Ward in *The Last Jump*.
Played Sergeant in the **William Tell** episode *The Cuckoo*.

Davenport Mel
Wrote the **Espionage** episode *Never Turn Your Back On a Friend*.

Davenport Nigel
Played Barty in the second series of **The Adventures of Robin Hood** episode *The Path of True Love* [aka *Locksley Hall*[, Lord Lawrence in *Too Many Earls*, the sentry in *The Frightened Tailor*, the captain in *The Mystery of Ireland's Eye*, Sir James in *The Little People* & Claud in *The Road in the Air*.
Played Sir Peter in the fourth season's *Bride for an Outlaw*.
Played Stranger in **The Count of Monte Cristo** episode *Naples*.

Featured in the **Espionage** episode *Snow on Mount Kama*.
Played Grabowsky in the second season **Man of the World** episode *Double Exposure*.
Played Aldo Petri in the first season **The Saint** episode *The Charitable Countess* and Charles Voyson in the second season's *The Rhine Maiden*.
Played Richard Burley in the **Shirley's World** episode *Thou Shall Not Be Found Out*.
Played Don Miguel in the **Sir Francis Drake** episode *Gentlemen of Spain*.
Played Berto in the **Sword of Freedom** episode *Vendetta*.

Davey Anne
Played Suzette in the first series of **The Adventures of Robin Hood** episode *Table's Turned*.

David Hugh
Played Benjy in **The Buccaneers** [aka **Dan Tempest**] episodes *Blackbeard, The Raiders* and *Captain Dan Tempest*.

David Michael
Played Dischev in the **Jason King** episode *Variations on a Theme* and Jean Pierre in the **O.S.S.** episode *Operation Death Trap*.

Davidson Lawrence
Played Gautier in the first season **Danger Man** episode *Vacation* and Finch in *The Leak*.
Played the Maitre D in the third season **The Saint** episode *To Kill a Saint*.
Played the Captain in **The Sentimental Agent** episode *Express Delivery*.
Played Lord Marmont in the **Sir Francis Drake** episode *Johnnie Factotum*.
Played Marcel in the **Virgin of the Secret Service** episode *Entente Cordiale*.

Davidson Lew
Wrote the first season **The Protectors** episode *Triple Cross*.

Davidson Lewis
Co-wrote, with Ralph Smart the first season **Danger Man** episode *The Honeymooners*.
Wrote the first series **Ghost Squad** episode *High Wire*.
Wrote the **Interpol Calling** episodes *The Money Game* and *The Chinese Mask*.
Wrote the first season **The Saint** episodes *The Golden Journey & The Bunco Artists*.

Davies Bernard
Played the German taxi driver in the second series **Danger Man** [aka **Secret Agent**] episode *Fair Exchange*.

Davies David
Played Baron Onslow in the fourth series **The Adventures of Robin Hood** episode *Sybella* and Sir Hartley in *Race Against Time*.
Played Sergeant Syd Taylor in the **Gideon's Way** episode *The White Rat*.
Played Col. Briggs in the **Interpol Calling** episode *Slave Ship*.
Played Sykes in the **Sir Francis Drake** episode *Drake on Trial*.

Davies Desmond
Played the photographer in the season two **Ghost Squad** episode *The Menacing Mazurka*.

Davies Dawn
Played Maria Gamma in the second season **The Saint** episode *The Unkind Philanthropist*.

Davies Griffith
Played Black in the **Department S** episode *A Ticket to Nowhere*.

Played Jimmy in the **Gideon's Way** episode *The Big Fix*.

Davies Harry
Played the police sgt. in the car in the **Randall and Hopkirk [Deceased] aka My Partner the Ghost** episode *Vendetta for a Dead Man*.

Davies Howard
Played Karl John in the **William Tell** episode *The Prisoner* and Bruno John in *The Bear*.

Davies Howell
Played the farmer in **The Count of Monte Cristo** episode *Lichtenburg*.

Davies Jack
Wrote the first season **Man of the World** episode *The Sentimental Agent* and the second season's *Double Exposure*. Wrote **The Sentimental Agent** episode *The Scroll of Islam*.

Davies Janet
Played Pearl in the first season **The Saint** episode *Marcia*.

Davies Peter
Played a tracking station guard in the **UFO** episode *The Psychobombs*.

Davies Petra
Played Christine in **The Buccaneers [aka Dan Tempest]** episode *The Ladies*.
Played Suzanne in the first series **Ghost Squad** episode *Ticket for Blackmail*.
Played Mrs White in the fourth season **The Saint** episode *Portrait of Brenda*.

Davies Richard
Played the postman in the **Gideon's Way** episode *The Housekeeper* and the taxi driver in *A Perfect Crime*.
Played a reporter in the fourth season **The Saint** two parter *The Fiction Makers*.

Davies Rita
Played the W.P.C. in the second season **Ghost Squad** episode *The Thirteenth Girl*.

Davies Robert
Played a guard/auction client in the **Father Brown** episode *The Arrow of Heaven*.

Davies Rowland
Played Dr. Bernard Simon in the **Father Brown** episode *The Secret Garden*.

Davies Rupert
Played Simon Dexter in the season three **The Adventures of Robin Hood** episode *The Ghost that Failed*.
Guested as Voss in **The Champions** episode *Project Zero*.
Played Colonel Graves in the first season **Danger Man** episode *The Actor*.
Played Colonel Druce in the **Father Brown** episode *The Oracle of the Dog*.
Played Dushkin in the **H. G. Wells' Invisible Man** episode *The Locked Room*.
Guested as Coetzee in the **Interpol Calling** episode *The Angola Brights*.
Voiced Professor McClaine on the **Joe 90** series.
Played Gomez in the **Man in a Suitcase** episode *The Man who Stood Still*.
Starred as, series regular, Inspector Duff in **The New Adventures of Charlie Chan**.
Played Dupont in the **O.S.S.** episode *Operation Eel*.

Davies Stacy
Played the first customs officer in the **Return of the Saint** episode *The Diplomat's Daughter*.

Davies Tessa
Set Dresser on **The Zoo Gang**.

Davies Tina
Production secretary on **Danger Man & The Prisoner**.

Davies Windsor
Played Morgan in the **UFO** episode *The Cat with Ten Lives*.

Davion Alex
Played the executive in the **UFO** episode *The Psychobombs*.

Davion Alexander
Starred as Detective Chief Inspector David Keen in **Gideon's Way**.
Played Padrone in the second season **Man of the World** episode *Jungle Mission*.
Played Orland Flane in the first season **The Saint** episode *Starring the Saint* & Miguel Artigas in *Teresa*.

Davis Allan
Directed the **O.S.S.** episodes *Operation Jingle Bells, Operation Sardine* & *Operation Barbecue*.

Davis Desmond
Camera operator on **The Adventures of Sir Lancelot** episode *Lancelot's Banishment* and directed *The Missing Princess*.

Davis Fred
Played a commercial traveller in the **Father Brown** episode *The Quick One*.

Davis Harry
Played the Commissionaire in the **Timeslip** story *The Day of the Clone* [series episode 21].

Davis Liz
Played Kitty O'Rourke in the **Virgin of the Secret Service** episode *The Amazons*.

Davis Maureen
Played Alice in the second series of **The Adventures of Robin Hood** episode *The Friar's Pilgrimage*, Agnes in the season three episode *To Be a Student* and Alice Dale in season four's *The Debt*.
Appeared as a handmaiden in **The Adventures of Sir Lancelot** episode *Knight Errant*.
Played Emily in **The Buccaneers [aka Dan Tempest]** episode *Cutlass Wedding*.
Played Barjou's secretary in the third season **Danger Man [aka Secret Agent]** episode *Dangerous Secret*.
Played Lucie in **The Four Just Men** episode *The Miracle of St. Philippe*.
Played Eve in the **William Tell** episode *The Mountain People*.

Davis Noel
Played the Sheriff's doctor in the third series **The Adventures of Robin Hood** episode *The Doctor*.
Played the traveller in **The Adventures of Sir Lancelot** episode *The Bridge* and the bartender in *Thieves*.
Played Jenks in **The Buccaneers [aka Dan Tempest]** episode *To the Rescue*.
Played the pawnbroker's clerk in the **Randall and Hopkirk [Deceased] aka My Partner the Ghost** episode *All Work and No Pay*.
Played the clerk in the **Sword of Freedom** episode *The Bell*.
Played the artist's agent in the **UFO** episode *Court Martial*.

Davis Stringer
Played Admiral Bingham in **The Buccaneers** [aka **Dan Tempest**] episode *Mr. Beamish and the Hangman's Noose*.

Davis-Goff Annabel
Continuity on **The Champions**.

Davy Pamela Ann
Played Melissa in the **Department S** episode *The Soup of the Day*.
Played Josie in the season two **Ghost Squad** episode *The Missing People*.
Played Justine in the third season **The Saint** episode *To Kill a Saint*.

Dawes Anthony
Played Lawson in **The Adventurer** episode *Make it a Million* and a clerk in the season three **The Saint** episode *The Power Artist*.

Dawes Kathryn
Script Supervision on **The Buccaneers** [aka **Dan Tempest**] episodes *The Raiders, Captain Dan Tempest, Dan Tempest's War with Spain, The Wasp, Whale Gold, Slave Ship, Gunpowder Plot, Articles of War, Ghost Ship, Conquest of New Providence, Mother Doughty's Crew, Blood Will Tell, Hurricane, Dead Man's Rock, Dangerous Cargo, Hand of the Hawk, Gentleman Jack and the Lady, Mr. Beamish and the Hangman's Noose, Marooned, Before the Mast, Dan Tempest and The Amazons, The Ladies, The Surgeon of Sangre Rojo, The Return of Calico Jack, Conquistador* and *Aztec Treasure*.

Dawkins Paul
Played Dr Poulton in **The Baron** episode *The Edge of Fear* and Davidson in the season two **The Protectors** episode *Bagman*.

Dawson Anthony
Appeared as Lucas in the second series of **The Adventures of Robin Hood** episode *Blackmail*.
Played Captain Flash in **The Buccaneers** [aka **Dan Tempest**] episode *Hand of the Hawk*.
Played the security officer in the first season **Danger Man** episode *The Sisters* and Martin in *The Leak*. In the second series [now aka **Secret Agent**], played Lucus in *Don't Nail Him Yet* and Simpson in *A Very Dangerous Game*.
Played Clouston in the **Interpol Calling** episode *Ascent to Murder*.
Played Floyd Vosper in the first season **The Saint** episode *The Arrow of God*.

Dawson Basil
Wrote the second series of **The Adventures of Robin Hood** episodes *The Path of True Love* aka *Locksley Hall* with [Alan Moreland], *The Infidel* [with John Dyson] &*Carlotta* [with Michael Connor]. Wrote the third season's *Change of Heart, The Double* & *Roman Gold*.
Wrote **The Buccaneers** [aka **Dan Tempest**] episodes *The Return of Calico Jack* [with Zachary Weiss], *Conquistador* [with Terence Moore] and *Prize of Andalusia* [with Weiss].
Wrote the season two **Ghost Squad** episodes *Lost In Transit, Quarantine at Kavar, Death of a Sportsman* & *P.G. 7*.
Wrote the second season **The Saint** episode *The Man who Liked Toys*.
Wrote the **Virgin of the Secret Service** episodes *Russian Roundabout, The Amazons* & *The Pyramid Plot*.

Dawson Gladys
Played the cleaning woman in the **G.S.5** episode *Death of a Cop*.

Day Robert
Director on **The Adventures of Robin Hood**: *Too Many Earls* & *The Road in the Air* [series 2]; *Pepper, Brother Battle, The*

Mark, To Be a Student, Too Many Robins, The Fire, The Rivals, Quickness of the Hand & *The Youthful Menace* [3] and *Goodbye, Little John* [4].
Directed **The Buccaneers** [aka **Dan Tempest**] episodes *Ghost Ship, Conquest of New Providence* [with Leslie Arliss], *Blood Will Tell, Dead Man's Rock, Hand of the Hawk, Conquistador, Cutlass Wedding* and *The Spy Aboard*.
Directed the second season **Danger Man** [aka **Secret Agent**] episode *Fish on the Hook*.
Directed the **O.S.S.** episode *Operation Chopping Block*.

Day Vera
Played Jane in the first season **The Saint** episode *The Man who was Lucky*.

Dayvis Denny
Played Doris in the **H. G. Wells' Invisible Man** episode *Jailbreak*.

de Banzie Brenda
Played Lady Pomfret in the second series of The **Adventures of Robin Hood** episode *The Impostor*.
Played Duchess Della Riviero in **The Four Just Men** episode *The Night of the Precious Stones*.

De Blasio Edward
Story Editor on the **Strange Report** series and wrote the episodes *Report 8944: HAND: 'A Matter of Witchcraft?'* & *Report 4407: HEART: 'No Choice for the Donor'*.

De Bray Harry
Played the van driver in the second season **Man of the World** episode *In the Picture*.

De Bray Henry
Played the chief chemist in the second series **Danger Man** [aka **Secret Agent**] episode *The Battle of the Cameras*.
Played the butler in **The Four Just Men** episode *The Battle of the Bridge*.

De Carmine Renato
Played Cesare in the **Return of the Saint** episode *Vicious Circle*.

De Carvalho Carlos
Played Noli in the **Return of the Saint** episode *The Judas Game*.

de Crespo Helena
Played Esther in the second series of **The Adventures of Robin Hood** episode *The York Treasure*.

de Goguel Constantin
Played Volodin in the **Department S** episode *The Duplicated Man*.

De Keyser David
Played Karl in the **William Tell** episode *The Unwelcome Stranger*.

de la Motte Andrew
Guested as Francoise in the first series of **The Adventures of Robin Hood** episode *Table's Turned*.

De La Motte Mischa
Played Bolton in **The Adventurer** episode *Going, Going....*
Played Dr Bianco in the second season **The Protectors** episode *Fighting Fund*.

De La Torre Raf
Played Durracq in **The Count of Monte Cristo** episode *Naples*.

Played Ali in the season two **Ghost Squad** episode *Gertrude*.

De Lyle Monti
Played the Town Dignitary in **The Prisoner** episode *Living in Harmony*.
Played the second agent in **The Scarlet Pimpernel** episode *The Farmer's Boy*.

De Marchi Laura
Played Dolores in the **Return of the Saint** episode *The Village that Sold its Soul*.

De Marney Derek
Played Colonel Coote in the second series **Danger Man** [aka **Secret Agent**] episode *The Mercenaries*.
Played Clive Errington in the season two **Ghost Squad** episode *The Desperate Diplomat*.

De Paola Raffaele
Played a gunman in the **Return of the Saint** episode *The Murder Cartel*.

de Rouen Reed
Played Andre Soult in **The Count of Monte Cristo** episode *The Texas Affair* and Von Hanstein in *Athens*.
Played Nick Pompey in **The Four Just Men** episode *The Last Days of Nick Pompey*.
Wrote the season two **Ghost Squad** episode *Sabotage*.
Played Bassett in the **G.S.5** episode *Seven Sisters of Wong*.
Played Max Played Hugo in the **H. G. Wells' Invisible Man** episode *The White Rabbit*.
Played Simms in the **Interpol Calling** episode *Act of Piracy*.
Played Buck in the **Man in a Suitcase** episode *Night Flight to Andora*. Wrote the episodes *Jigsaw Man* [with Stanley R. Greenberg] and *Night Flight to Andora* [with Jan Read].
Played Hartley in the **O.S.S.** episode *Operation Post Office*.

De Salle Lorraine
Played Maria in the **Return of the Saint** episode *Hot Run*.

de Sica Vittorio
Starred as Ricco Poccari in the series **The Four Just Men** [The series was filmed in four separate blocks with the four stars actually appearing together in *The Battle of the Bridge* only. Dan Dailey & Richard Conte were each allocated ten episodes and Jack Hawkins & de Sica each appeared in nine]: *The Crying Jester, The Night of the Precious Stones, Mava, The Man With the Golden Touch, The Rietti Group, The Slaver, The Man in the Royal Suite, Rogue's Harvest* & *Treviso Dam*.

De Simone Alina
Played Mrs Marcello in the **Return of the Saint** episode *The Roman Touch*.

de Souza Edward
Played Paul Dupont in the **Department S** episode *The Double Death of Charlie Crippen*.
Appeared in *Adventure Six* of **Sapphire and Steel**.
Played Beau Ellington in the second season **The Saint** episode *The Chequered Flag*.

de Temple Charles
Played Wilson in **The Four Just Men** episode *The Protector*.

De Vernier Hugo
Appeared as the servant in the second season **Danger Man** [aka **Secret Agent**] episode *Fair Exchange* and the night manager in *The Battle of the Cameras*.
Played the hospital porter in **The Persuaders!** episode *The Gold Napoleon*.
Played the croupier in the first series **The Protectors** episode *Your Witness*.

Appeared as the butler in the first season **The Saint** episode *The Charitable Countess*.
Played the prison guard in **The Scarlet Pimpernel** episode *The Princess*.

de Vigier Anne
Played Nurse Crane in **The Persuaders!** episode *Someone Like Me*.
Played Julia Fenwick in the **Randall and Hopkirk [Deceased]** aka **My Partner the Ghost** episode *But what a Sweet Little Room*.
Played Josephine in the fourth season **The Saint** episode *Portrait of Brenda*.

de Villiers Marcel
Appeared as the second Spanish officer in the **White Hunter** episode *The Stepfathers*.

De Vries Hans
Played the barman in the **Man in a Suitcase** episode *Three Blinks of the Eyes*.
Played Hibert in the **Randall and Hopkirk [Deceased]** aka **My Partner the Ghost** episode *The Ghost who Saved the Bank at Monte Carlo*.
Played the sergeant in the third season **The Saint** episode *The Paper Chase*.
Played a security man in the **UFO** episode *The Psychobombs*.

de Woolf Francis
Played Brother Wootan in the season three **The Adventures of Robin Hood** episode *Brother Battle*.
Played Mr Alexander in the second series **Danger Man** [aka **Secret Agent**] episode *The Ubiquitous Mr Lovegrove*.
Played Capt. Gallard in the **Interpol Calling** episode *The Long Weekend* and Blink in *Slow Boat to Amsterdam*.
Played Captain Flemming in the third season **The Saint** episode *The Best Laid Schemes*.
Appeared as Mjumbino Barr in the **White Hunter** episode *The Stepfathers* and as Max Early in *Gun Duel*.

Dean Bill
Played the British soldier in the **Man in a Suitcase** episode *The Girl who Never was*.

Dean Ivor
Played Chief Inspector Hughes in the **Jason King** episode *An Author in Search of Two Characters*.
Played Mr Beebe in **The Persuaders!** episode *A Death in the Family*.
Played Inspector Large in the **Randall and Hopkirk [Deceased]** aka **My Partner the Ghost** episodes *Who Ever Heard of a Ghost Dying?, When Did you Start to Stop Seeing Things?, When the Spirit Moves You, Could You Recognise the Man Again?* & *Money to Burn*.
Debuted in **The Saint** in the first season episode *Starring the Saint* as David Brown before going on to star as, regular, Inspector/Chief Inspector Teal: in the first season's *Iris, The Rough Diamonds, The Saint Plays with Fire, The Lawless Lady* &*The High Fence*; the second season's *The Scorpion, The Man who Liked Toys, The Crime of the Century, The Damsel in Distress, The Contract, The Smart Detective, The Man who could not Die* and *The Set-Up*; the third's *Escape Route, The Persistent Patriot, The Death Game, The Counterfeit Countess, A Double in Diamonds, The Power Artist* & *When Spring is Sprung* and the fourth's *Legacy for the Saint, The Desperate Diplomat* & *Portrait of Brenda*.[Campbell Singer, Wensley Pithey & Norman Pitt also appeared as Teal].
Played an agent in **The Scarlet Pimpernel** episodes *The Farmer's Boy* and *Sir Andrew's Fate*.

Dean Robert
Played David Elliot in the second series **Danger Man** [aka **Secret Agent**] episode *Parallel Lines Sometimes Meet*.

Played Professor Soren in the second season **The Saint** episode *The Inescapable Word*.

Deane Sally
Played the first maiden in **The Adventures of Sir Lancelot** episode *The Outcast*.

Dearberg Bob
Music Editor on **The Prisoner** episodes *Arrival*, *The Chimes of Big Ben* and *Checkmate*.

Dearden Basil
Directed **The Four Just Men** episodes *The Battle of the Bridge, Village of Shame, The Deserter, Their Man in London, National Treasure, The Man With the Golden Touch, The Survivor, Money To Burn, The Man Who Wasn't There, Rogue's Harvest, The Heritage, The Boy Without a Country & Treviso Dam*.
Directed **The Persuaders!** episodes *Overture, Powerswitch & To the Death, Baby*.

Dearman Glyn
Played Leather Jacket in the season two **Ghost Squad** episode *The Missing People*.

Dearth John
Played a variety of roles in the second series of **The Adventures of Robin Hood**: Sir Blaise in *The Betrothal*, the Physician in *The Jongleur*, the second Pilgrim in *The Intruders*, Master Higgs in *The Sheriff's Boots*, the Informer in *Errand of Mercy*, Baron Hubert in *The Vandals*, De Belvoir in *Richard the Lionheart*, Will in *Ladies of Sherwood*, Captain Lash in *Will Scarlet*, Arthur in *The Miser*, Cook in *Children of the Greenwood*, De Clifford in *The May Queen*, the second healer in *The Wanderer*, Goldsmith in *The Byzantine Treasure*, Hubert in *Table's Turned*, Faversham in *The Traitor*, Bodo in *The Thorkill Ghost* & the feeble beggar in *The Wager*. Returned as Sorel in season two's *The Hero* and as the Lieutenant in the third season's *Quickness of the Hand*.
Played King Pell in **The Adventures of Sir Lancelot** episode *The Queen's Knight* and Piggott in *Thieves*.
Played Bellows in **The Buccaneers** [aka **Dan Tempest**] episode *Blood Will Tell*.
Played the waiter in **The Four Just Men** episode *The Grandmother*.
Played Detective Superintendent Warr in the **Gideon's Way** episode *The Housekeeper*.
Played the French soldier in the **O.S.S.** episode *Operation Eel*.
Played Inspector Coudot in the first season **The Saint** episode *The Loaded Tourist* and Fouquet in the second season's *Jeannine*.
Played Ugo in the **Sword of Freedom** episode *Choice of Weapons*, Gonfalonier in *The Bell* and the inspector in *Chart of Gold*.
Played Muller in the **William Tell** episode *The Lost Letter* and Major Richter in *The Mountain People*.

Deason Splinters
Continuity on **The Adventures of Sir Lancelot** episode *The Ugly Duckling*.

Deckers Eugene
Played Corbett in the first series **Man of the World** episode *A Family Affair*.
Played Inspector Quercy in the first season **The Saint** episode *The Covetous Headman*.
Played Bobo le Mec in the **Virgin of the Secret Service** episode *Pride of Assassins*.

Dee Brian
Composed, with Irving Martin, the theme for **Return of The Saint** [original *Saint* theme by Leslie Charteris].

Deeley Michael
Dubbing Editor on **The Adventures of Robin Hood** and on **The Adventures of Sir Lancelot** episodes *The Knight with the Red Plume, The Ferocious Fathers, The Queen's Knight, The Outcast, Winged Victory, Sir Bliant, The Magic Sword, Lancelot's Banishment, Roman Wall, Caledon, Shepherd's War, The Pirates, The Black Castle, The Magic Book, Knight Errand & The Theft of Excalibur*.

Deeming Marianne
Played Frau Dorfer in the first series **Man of the World** episode *Specialist for the Kill*.

Degas Brian
Wrote **The Baron** episode *Samurai West*.
Wrote the second season **The Saint** episodes *The Rhine Maiden, The Happy Suicide & The Abductors* [teleplayed from a story by Harry W. Junkin].
Co-wrote the **Shirley's World** episode *The Defective Defector* [with John Muir].
Co-wrote [with Tudor Gates] the **Strange Report** episode *Report 0649: SKELETON: 'Let Sleeping Heroes Lie'*.

Deghy Guy
Played Willet Mosselman in **The Adventurer** episode *Target!*.
Guested as Schroeder in **The Champions** episode *The Gun-Runners*.
Played Kirov in the **Department S** episode *The Duplicated Man*.
Appeared as the guard on the train in the debut season **Danger Man** episode *The Traitor* and Vogel in *Name, Date and Place*. In series two [now aka **Secret Agent**] played Garriga in *Judgement Day* and Leontine in the third season's *I'm Afraid You Have the Wrong Number*.
Played Poppa in the first series **Ghost Squad** episode *Bullet With My Name on it* and Rosendo in *Catspaw* [*Catspaw* was shot for the first series, but due to an actors' strike, was originally shown as a season two episode]. Played Anton Dukavic in the season two episode *Mr Five Per Cent*.
Played the owner of Krootnings in the **Gideon's Way** episode *The Thin Red Line*.
Guested as Ritter in the **Interpol Calling** episode *The Thirteen Innocents*.
Played Inspector Gruman in the **Jason King** episode *If it's Got to Go - It's Got to Go*.
Played Simon in the **O.S.S.** episode *Operation Death Trap*.
Played Oscar Kleinhaus in the first season **The Saint** episode *The Loaded Tourist* & Inspector Oscar Kleinhaus in the third season's *The Russian Prisoner*. Played Eberhard in the first season's *The Saint Sees it Through* & Maresciallo in the fourth's *Vendetta for the Saint* [part 1].
Played Zarque in the **Sir Francis Drake** episode *Gentlemen of Spain*.

Delamain Aimee
Played Lady Haverstock in the third season **The Saint** episode *The Better Mousetrap*.

Delavanti Cyril
Played Abbe Faria in **The Count of Monte Cristo** episode *Return to the Chateau d'If*.

Delgado Roger
Played the Ambassador in the season three **The Adventures of Robin Hood** episode *The Minstrel*.
Played Estaban in **The Buccaneers** [aka **Dan Tempest**] episode *Conquest of New Providence*, Captain Mendoza in *Dangerous Cargo* and Estaban in *Conquistador*.
Guested as Yussef in **The Champions** episode *Desert Journey*.
Played Von Golling in the first season **Danger Man** episode *Under the Lake*.
Featured in the **Espionage** episode *A Camel to Ride*.

Played Inspector Russo in **The Four Just Men** episodes *The Slaver & Rogue's Harvest.*

Played Holgar in the first series **Ghost Squad** episode *Death from a Distance.* In season two, played Major Sayid in *Quarantine at Kavar* and Ben Ali in *The Heir Apparent.* In **G.S.5**, played De Souza in *Death of a Cop.*

Played Capitano Garrozo in the **Jason King** episode *The Stones of Venice.*

Played Ambassador in the **Man in a Suitcase** episode *Burden of Proof.*

Played Luigi in the **O.S.S.** episode *Operation Big House.*

Played Estoban in **The Persuaders!** episode *To the Death, Baby.*

Played Tapiro in the **Randall and Hopkirk [Deceased]** episode *The Ghost who Saved the Bank at Monte Carlo.*

Appeared as the hotel manager in the first season **The Saint** episode *The Golden Journey* and as Captain Rodrigues in the third season's *Locate and Destroy.*

Played Andre in **The Scarlet Pimpernel** episode *The Farmer's Boy.*

Starred as series regular Mendoza in **Sir Francis Drake** [episodes 4 - 17].

Played Virelli in the **Sword of Freedom** episode *Angelica's Past.*

Played Vizier in the **Virgin of the Secret Service** episode *The Rajah and the Suffragette.*

Played Gomez in the **White Hunter** episode *Killer Leopard.*

Played Luigi in the **William Tell** episode *The Black Brothers.*

Played Pedro in **The Zoo Gang** episode *The Lion Hunt.*

Delle Piane Carlo
Played Luigi in the **Return of the Saint** episode *Duel in Venice.*

Delmaine Barry
Production Supervisor on the second series of **Danger Man** [aka **Secret Agent**], Associate Producer on the second season episodes eight & 27 - 32, and throughout series three & four.
Production Supervisor on **Man of the World**.
Associate Producer on **The Adventurer**, **Man in a Suitcase** & **Strange Report** series.
Producer on **Shirley's World**.

Demian Marcus
Wrote the second season **The Saint** episode *The Unkind Philanthropist.*

Dench Judi
Played Anna in **The Four Just Men** episode *Treviso Dam.*

Dene Carmen
Played Princess Selina in the **Virgin of the Secret Service** episode *The Great Ring of Akba.*

Denham Maurice
Played Volos in the third season **Danger Man** episode *Someone is Liable to get Hurt* and Prince Lorenzo in the **Return of the Saint** episode *The Village that Sold its Soul.*

Denise Gita
Played Natalie in the third season **Danger Man** [aka **Secret Agent**] episode *To our Best Friend.*

Dennis Winifred
Played Mrs Bigley in the **G.S.5** episode *The Goldfish Bowl.*

Denny Susan
Played Cynthia in the **Department S** episode *Death on Reflection.*

Dent Brian
Played the police Inspector in the season two **Ghost Squad** episode *The Man With the Delicate Hands.*

Dentith Edward
Played the Commissionaire in **The Adventurer** episode *Somebody Doesn't Like Me.*
Played Det. Insp. Dillon in the **Gideon's Way** episode *The Firebug.*

Denton Geoffrey
Played the Assistantt Commissioner in the **G.S.5** episode *Death of a Cop.*
Played the Chairman in the **Jason King** episode *Uneasy Lies the Head.*
Played Sir Robert Sangore in the first season **The Saint** episode *The Saint Plays with Fire.*
Played General Cookson in the **Virgin of the Secret Service** episode *The Pyramid Plot.*

Denville Roma
Appeared as Lady Eleanor in **The Adventures of Sir Lancelot** episode *Sir Crustabread.*

Denzil Caroline
Played Isobel in **The Adventures of Sir Lancelot** episode *The Queen's Knight.*
Played Eva in the **William Tell** episode *Castle of Fear.*

Depita Mario
Played the pursuer in **The Protectors** episode *Lena.*

Derby Brown
Appeared as John in **The Adventures of Sir Lancelot** episode *Maid of Somerset.*
Played Carl Grant in **The Baron** episode *So Dark the Night.*
Played Inspector Angus in the **Interpol Calling** episode *The Chinese Mask.*
Played the pathologist in the third season **The Saint** episode *The Convenient Monster.*

Derosa Franco
Played an hotel clerk in **The Adventurer** episode *Return to Sender* and in the **Jason King** episode *Chapter One: The Company I Keep.*

DeRoy Richard
Wrote the **Shirley's World** episode *A Mother's Touch.*

Desmond Robert
Appeared in the first season **The Adventures of Robin Hood** episode *A Guest for the Gallows* as Will Stutely.

Desmond Roy
Played Kevin O'Malley in the **Randall and Hopkirk [Deceased]** aka **My Partner the Ghost** episode *Money to Burn.*

Deswal Rajvir
Played second heavy in the **Return of the Saint** episode *The Roman Touch.*

Devereaux Ed
Played Ryker in **The Persuaders!** episode *Anyone Can Play.*
Played Wally Kinsall in the second season **The Saint** episode *The Loving Brothers.*
Played Colonel Martin in **The Zoo Gang** episode *The Lion Hunt.*

Devereaux William Thorpe
Played Mottier in the **Interpol Calling** episode *The Absent Assassin.*
Played Van Groot in the **O.S.S.** episode *Operation Tulip.*

Devis Jimmy
Camera Operator on **The Persuaders!**

Devlin J. G.

Guested as Frank Nicholls in **The Champions** episode *The Bodysnatchers*.
Eddy in the **Man in a Suitcase** episode *Which Way did he Go, McGill?*.

Dexter Rosemary

Played Gina in the fourth season **The Saint** two parter *Vendetta for the Saint*.

Dexter William

Played Meyer in the third season **Danger Man** [aka **Secret Agent**] episode *Say it with Flowers*.
Appeared as Nickolai in the second season **The Protectors** episode *Dragon Chase*.
Played Gabriel Linnet in the first season **The Saint** episode *The Rough Diamonds* and Paul Zaglan in the second season's *The Happy Suicide*.
Played Inspector Banard in the **Man in a Suitcase** episode *Blind Spot*.

Di Lorenzo Edward

Script editor on the **Space 1999** series and wrote the first season episodes *Ring Around the Moon & Missing Link*.

Diament Otto

Played the pawnbroker in the third season **The Saint** episode *The Helpful Pirate*.

Diamond Arnold

Played Eisen in **The Adventurer** episode *Going, Going....*
Played Insp. Lamille in **The Baron** episode *The Seven Eyes of Night* and the train steward in *Farewell to Yesterday*.
Played Lasalle in the second series **Danger Man** [aka **Secret Agent**] episode *The Galloping Major*.
Played Kolliatis in the **Department S** episode *The Man who got a New Face*.
Played Nicholas Mayer in the second season **Ghost Squad** episode *Lost In Transit* and Roger Belcher in *The Heir Apparent*. In **G.S.5**, played Costa in *Death of a Cop*.
Played Professor Blaire Played Hugo in the **H. G. Wells' Invisible Man** episode *The White Rabbit*.
Guested as Inspector Krantz in the **Interpol Calling** episode *You Can't Die Twice* and as Lambert in *The Three Keys*.
Played Brig. Bosville in the **O.S.S.** episode *Operation Powder Puff*.
Played Brusati in **The Persuaders!** episode *Five Miles to Midnight*.
Played the policeman in the second season **The Protectors** episode *Goodbye George*.
Played the poker player in the **Randall and Hopkirk [Deceased]** aka **My Partner the Ghost** episode *The Trouble with Women*.
Played Colonel Latignant in **The Saint**: *The Benevolent Burglary* [season 1], *The Death Penalty*, *The Persistent Parasite* & *The Spanish Cow* [2] and *The Better Mousetrap* [3].
Played The Marquis in **The Scarlet Pimpernel** episode *Thanksgiving Day*.
Played the Governor in the **Sir Francis Drake** episode *Drake on Trial*.
Appeared as James Wilson in the **White Hunter** episode *Dead Man's Tale*.

Diamond Bobby

Starred as Joey Newton in the **Fury** series.

Diamond Margaret

Guested as Zita McGrath in the **Interpol Calling** episode *The Thousand Mile Alibi*.

Diamond Marian

Played the telephone operator in the first season **Danger Man** episode *The Girl in Pink Pyjamas*.

Diamond Peter

Appeared in several roles in season two of **Ghost Squad**: the native guard in *East of Mandalay*, Beni in *Death of a Sportsman* and Pinto in *The Thirteenth Girl*.
Played Miguel in the first season **The Saint** episode *The Romantic Matron* and Peyrac in the second season's *Jeannine*.
Fight Arranger on the series **Sir Francis Drake** and appeared in *The Garrison* as the Bosun and *Mission to Paris* as De Luc.
Fight Arranger on **Virgin of the Secret Service** and appeared in a number of roles: the second Hazarnao in *Dark Deeds on the Northwest Frontier*, Franz in *Russian Roundabout*, the second Arab in *The Great Ring of Akba*, the Indian / Inca guard in *The Amazons*, a guard in *The Persuasion of a Million Drops*, the chief guard in *Across the Silver Pass of Gusri Song* and the man in the saloon in *The Professor Goes West*.

Diane Lesley

Played Maureen in the **Return of the Saint** episode *The Debt Collectors*.

Dibbs Arthur

Played Major Domo in **The Scarlet Pimpernel** episode *The Ambassador's Lady*.

Dickens Cliff

Played Maurice in the third season **The Saint** episode *The Counterfeit Countess*.

Dickinson Sandra

Played the girl at the airport in the **Return of the Saint** episode *The Arrangement*.

Dickon Dolores

Played the nurse in the second season **Man of the World** episode *The Enemy*.

Dicks Terence

Wrote the second series **Space 1999** episode *The Lambda Factor*.

Dickson Bettina

Played Miss Beck in the **H. G. Wells' Invisible Man** episode *Death Cell*.

Dickson Paul

Directed **The Adventurer** episodes *Thrust and Counter Thrust & Counterstrike*.
Directed **The Champions** episodes *Operation Deep-freeze, Twelve Hours, A Case of Lemmings, The Bodysnatchers* and *Desert Journey*.
Directed the **Department S** episodes *One of our Aircraft is Empty, The Duplicated Man & The Bones of Byrom Blain*.
Directed the **Jason King** episode *To Russia With ....Panache*.
Directed the **Randall and Hopkirk [Deceased]** aka **My Partner the Ghost** episode *That's How Murder Snowballs*.

Dietrich Monika

Played Fausta in the **Department S** episode *The Trojan Tanker*.
Played Miranda in the **Jason King** episode *A Deadly Line in Digits*.

Diffring Anton

Played Jadwiga Szoblik in **The Baron** episode *Enemy of the State*.
Played Ronter in the first series **Ghost Squad** episode *Death from a Distance*.
Played Gunzi in the **H. G. Wells' Invisible Man** episode *The Prize*.
Played Schneider in the **O.S.S.** episode *Operation Eel*.
Played Klaus Frei in the **Strange Report** episode *Report 4977: SWINDLE: 'Square Root of Evil'*.

Digby-Smith Elisabeth
Played the Duchess of Didcott in the **Virgin of the Secret Service** episode *The Amazons*.

Dignam Basil
Played John Ballard in **The Adventurer** episode *Skeleton in the Cupboard*.
Played the rich merchant in the third series **The Adventures of Robin Hood** episode *The Rivals* and, in series four, Sir Geoffrey in *Tuck's Love Day*.
Guested as Sir Frederic in **The Champions** episode *The Invisible Man*.
Played the man in the taxi in the third season **Danger Man** [aka **Secret Agent**] episode *Say it with Flowers*.
Played Howard Finch in the **Department S** episode *One of our Aircraft is Empty*, Smith in *The Perfect Operation* and Henry Smith in *The Duplicated Man*.
Played the Judge Advocate in **The Four Just Men** episode *The Deserter*.
Played Henry Dickenson in the season two **Ghost Squad** episode *The Man With the Delicate Hands*.
Played Commissioner Scott-Marle in the **Gideon's Way** episodes *State Visit*, *The 'V' Men*, *The Thin Red Line*, *A Perfect Crime* & *Morna*.
Played the Minister in the **H. G. Wells' Invisible Man** episode *The Big Plot*.
Guested as Insp. Hopkins in the **Interpol Calling** episode *The Three Keys*.
Played Viney in the **Jason King** episode *Variations on a Theme*.
Played Todd in the **Man in a Suitcase** episode *The Girl who Never was* and Sir Edric Coulsdon in *The Boston Square*.
Played Bosville in the **O.S.S.** episode *Operation Barbecue*.
Played the Prime Minister in **The Persuaders!** episode *The Time and the Place*.
Played the Supervisor, Number 56, in **The Prisoner** episode *Checkmate*.
Played Engleton in the second season **The Protectors** episode *Petard*.
Played Hepple in the **Randall and Hopkirk [Deceased]** aka **My Partner the Ghost** episode *When Did you Start to Stop Seeing Things?*.
Played Marvin Chase in the first season **The Saint** episode *The Invisible Millionaire* and Commander Richardson in the second season episode *The Miracle Tea Party*.
Played the Duke of Alva in the **Sir Francis Drake** episode *The Reluctant Duchess*.
Played Dean Jordan in the **Strange Report** episode *Report 8319: GRENADE: 'What Price Change?'*.
Played the Duke of Padua in the **Sword of Freedom** episode *The Marionettes* and Sebastiano in *The Suspects* & *The Sicilian*.
Played the Cabinet Minister in the **UFO** episodes *Identified* & *Mindbender*.

Dignam Mark
Played Coburn in **The Baron** episode *You Can't Win Them All*.
Played the British Ambassador in the second series **Danger Man** [aka **Secret Agent**] episode *A Room in the Basement*.
Played Falworth in **The Four Just Men** episode *Their Man in London*.
Played Dolguib in the first series **Man of the World** episode *Death of a Conference*.
Played Major Carter in the fourth season **The Saint** episode *The Organisation Man*.

Dignam Rebecca
Played Pia in the first season **Danger Man** episode *Find and Destroy*.

Dillinger Chris
Played Bradley's aide in the **Return of the Saint** episode *The Debt Collectors*.

Played Nico in **The Zoo Gang** episode *The Counterfeit Trap*.

Dillman Bradford
Featured in the **Espionage** episode *Covenant With Death*.

Dillon Micky
Played Marty Evans in the **G.S.5** episode *Pay Up or Else*.

Dilworth Carol
Played the girl in the **Randall and Hopkirk [Deceased]** episode *For the Girl who has Everything*.

Dimech John
Played Hanif in **The Sentimental Agent** episode *The Scroll of Islam*.

Dimitri Ann
Played the receptionist in the **H. G. Wells' Invisible Man** episode *The Gun Runners*.

Dimsdale Howard
Script Consultant on **The Zoo Gang** and wrote the episode *Mindless Murder*.

Ditta Douglas
Played the highland driver in the fourth season **The Saint** episode *The Organisation Man*.

Dobtcheff Vernon
Played the Manager in **The Champions** episode *The Gilded Cage*.
Played Simon Vesty in the **Father Brown** episode *The Dagger With Wings*.
Played Joe Flynn in the first series **The Protectors** episode *It Could be Practically Anywhere on the Island*.
Played Vogel in the third season **The Saint** episode *The Gadget Lovers*.
Played Grigori Rasputin in the **Virgin of the Secret Service** episode *Russian Roundabout*.

Dodson Eric
Played the auctioneer in the **Father Brown** episode *The Arrow of Heaven*.
Played Doyle in the second season **The Protectors** episode *Blockbuster*.
Played the vicar in the **Randall and Hopkirk [Deceased]** aka **My Partner the Ghost** episode *For the Girl who has Everything*.
Played the prosecuting counsel in the third season **The Saint** episode *When Spring is Sprung*.

Doig Lee
Editor on the second & third season of **Danger Man** [aka **Secret Agent**]. Edited the fourth series episode *Koroshi* which, was also joined with the other season four episode *Shinda Shima*, to form a feature entitled *Koroshi*.
Editor on **Jason King** & **The Zoo Gang**.
Editor on **The Prisoner** episodes *Arrival*, *Checkmate*, *Hammer into Anvil*, *A Change of Mind* and *Once Upon a Time*.

Dolan Leo
Played the barman in the second series **The Protectors** episode *Lena*.

Doleman Guy
Played the first Number Two in **The Prisoner** episode *Arrival*.
Played Crowley in the **Strange Report** episode *Report 1553: RACIST: 'A Most Dangerous Proposal'*.

Dolenz George
Starred as The Count of Monte Cristo [Edmund Dantes] in **The Count of Monte Cristo**.

Dolphin Peter
Played the co-pilot in the first season **Danger Man** episode *Sabotage*.
Played a Skydiver engineer in the **UFO** episode *The Psychobombs*.

Domanske Marlene
Appeared as one of the dancers in the **Man in a Suitcase** episode *Three Blinks of the Eyes*.

Domenighini Vito
Played Paolo in the **Return of the Saint** episode *The Roman Touch*.

Domergue Faith
Played Renee Morrell in **The Count of Monte Cristo** episode *The Affair of the Three Napoleons*.

Donaghy Philip
Played Nicolas in the **Jason King** episode *Zenia*.

Donahue Alex
Played Kemel in the **Virgin of the Secret Service** episode *Wings Over Glencraig*.

Donahue Patricia
Played Lorna Corlander in the second series **Danger Man** [aka **Secret Agent**] episode *A Man to be Trusted* and Caroline Winter in *The Mercenaries*.
Played Ingrid Von Elzdorf in the **Department S** episode *Spencer Bodily is 60 Years Old*.
Played Kim in the first series **Man of the World** episode *Blaze of Glory*.
Played Countess Rovagna in the first season **The Saint** episode *The Charitable Countess* and Arlene Bland in the third season's *Island of Chance*.

Donlevy Jim
Wardrobe on **The Buccaneers** [aka **Dan Tempest**] episodes *The Raiders, Captain Dan Tempest, Dan Tempest's War with Spain, The Wasp, Whale Gold, Gunpowder Plot, Articles of War, Ghost Ship, Conquest of New Providence, Mother Doughty's Crew, Blood Will Tell, Hurricane, Dead Man's Rock, Dangerous Cargo, Hand of the Hawk, Gentleman Jack and the Lady, Mr. Beamish and the Hangman's Noose, Marooned, Before the Mast, Dan Tempest and The Amazons, The Ladies, The Surgeon of Sangre Rojo, The Return of Calico Jack, Conquistador, Aztec Treasure, Prize of Andalusia, Cutlass Wedding, Dan Tempest Holds an Auction, Flip and Jenny, To the Rescue, Indian Fighters, Mistress Higgins' Treasure, The Spy Aboard, The Decoy, Pirate Honour, Instrument of War* and *Printer's Devil*.

Donna Christine
Played the secretary in **The Adventurer** episode *The Case of the Poisoned Pawn*.

Donne Ann
Casting Director on **The Adventurer** and Casting on **Jason King**.

Donnelly Donal
Played Stacey in the **Department S** episode *Les Fleurs du Mal*.
Played Larry in **The Sentimental Agent** episode *May the Saints Preserve Us*.

Donnelly James
Guested as Pickering in **The Champions** episode *Full Circle*.
Played Gerald in the **Department S** episode *The Duplicated Man*.
Played Frank Calder in the **Jason King** episode *Wanna Buy a Television Series* aka *A Face I Used to Know*.

Played the detective in the **Randall and Hopkirk [Deceased]** episode *My Late Lamented Friend and Partner*.

Donnelly Nicholas
Played Jean in the second season **The Saint** episode *The Spanish Cow* and Ivan in the third season's *The Gadget Lovers*.

Donnelly Rosemary
Played the receptionist in the **Department S** episode *The Man from X*.
Played Diana in the **Randall and Hopkirk [Deceased]** aka **My Partner the Ghost** episode *When Did you Start to Stop Seeing Things?*.
Played Dilys in the fourth season **The Saint** episode *The World Beater*.

Donner Clive
Directed the first season **Danger Man** episodes *The Journey Ends Halfway & Bury the Dead*.
Directed the **Sir Francis Drake** episodes *The Governor's Revenge, Boy Jack, Doctor Dee, The Flame Thrower* [with Harry Booth] & *The English Dragon*.

Donovan Sue
Played Pia Vallachio in **The Baron** episode *The Long, Long Day*.

Donovan Terence
Played Brent in the **Man in a Suitcase** episode *Sweet Sue*.
Played the sailor in **The Prisoner** episode *Checkmate*.

Doohan James
Co-starred in the **Hawkeye and the Last of the Mohicans** episodes *The Way-Station & The Scapegoat*.

Doonan Anthony
Played Johnny in the **Man in a Suitcase** episode *Web with Four Spiders* and Grant in **The Persuaders!** episode *Element of Risk*.

Doonan Patrick
Played Luigi in the **Sword of Freedom** episode *The Value of Paper*.

Doonan Tony
Played Eckler in the **O.S.S.** episode *Operation Chopping Block* and Snooper in the season three **The Saint** episode *Escape Route*.

Doone Holly
Appeared as the waitress in **The Prisoner** episode *Free for All*.

Dore Alexander
Played the porter in the **H. G. Wells' Invisible Man** episode *The Locked Room*.
Starred as, series regular, Karl Von Brauner in **Virgin of the Secret Service**.

Dore Jane
Played the dancer in the **O.S.S.** episode *Operation Eel*.

Doria Sergio
Played Brown in the **Return of the Saint** episode *The Murder Cartel*.

Dorken Rosemary
Played Helen Lambert in the season two **Ghost Squad** episode *The Man With the Delicate Hands*.

Dorne Sandra
Played Helen Mills in the **Interpol Calling** episode *Last Man Lucky*.

Played Ilse in the **O.S.S.** episode *Operation Tulip* and Gizi in *Operation Post Office*.
Played Gemma in the **White Hunter** episode *Run to Earth*.

Dorner Albert A.
Wrote the season two **The Adventures of Robin Hood** episode *The Road in the Air* [with Carol Warner Gluck].

Dorning Stacy
Played Zova in the second season **Space 1999** episode *The Exiles*.

Dotrice Michele
Played Felicity in the **Jason King** episode *Buried in the Cold, Cold Ground*.

Dotrice Roy
Played Commissioner Simmonds in the first season **Space 1999** episodes *Breakaway* & *Earthbound*.

Dotti Licia
Played Giselle in the **Return of the Saint** episode *Appointment in Florence*.

Douglas Angela
Played Vanessa in **The Adventurer** episode *The Not-So-Merry Widow*.
Featured in the **Espionage** episode *The Gentle Spies*.
Played Petra Merton in the **Father Brown** episode *The Arrow of Heaven*.
Played the title role in the **Gideon's Way** episode *Morna* and Cathy Miller in *The 'V' Men*.
Played Dana in the **Jason King** episode *Zenia*.
Played Linda in the second season **The Protectors** episode *Petard*.
Played Jenny Turner in the third season **The Saint** episode *The Death Game*.

Douglas Carlos
Played the reception clerk in the second series **Danger Man** [aka **Secret Agent**] episode *A Date with Doris*.
Played Nicoyram in the **Jason King** episode *Zenia*.
Played the receptionist in the **Man in a Suitcase** episode *Find the Lady*.
Played the Spanish officer in the **Sir Francis Drake** episode *Visit to Spain*.

Douglas Colin
Played De Groot in **The Buccaneers** [aka **Dan Tempest**] episode *Ghost Ship* and Purdy in *Flip and Jenny*.
Played Capt. Bodine in **The Count of Monte Cristo** episode *A Matter of Justice*.
Played Mego in the first season **Danger Man** episode *View from the Villa* and the stranger in the second series [now aka **Secret Agent**] episode *Whatever Happened to George Foster?*.
Played Barron in the season two **Ghost Squad** episode *The Grand Duchess*.
Played the doctor in the **G.S.5** episode *Dead Men Don't Drive*.
Played Sewell in the **H. G. Wells' Invisible Man** episode *Flight into Darkness*.
Played Mario in the **Sword of Freedom** episode *Alessandro*.

Douglas Donald
Played Douglas Macrae in **The Baron** episode *The Man Outside*.
Played Leonard Grey in the **Strange Report** episode *Report 0846: LONELYHEARTS: 'Who Killed Dan Cupid?'*.

Douglas Howard
Played Harry in the **Gideon's Way** episode *The Lady Killer*.

Played the ticket collector in the first season **The Saint** episode *The Talented Husband* and Tom Crofton in *The Noble Sportsman*.
Played the taxi driver in **The Sentimental Agent** episode *Meet my Son, Henry*.

Douglas Josephine
Producer on the series **Virgin of the Secret Service** and directed the episode *Across the Silver Pass of Gusri Song*.

Douglas Malcoln
Played Lieut. Anderson in the **Virgin of the Secret Service** episode *Russian Roundabout*.

Douglas Sally
Played the girl in the second series **Danger Man** [aka **Secret Agent**] episode *It's Up to the Lady*.
Played the cigarette girl in the second season **Man of the World** episode *Double Exposure*.

Douglas Sarah
Played Sheila Northcott in the **Return of the Saint** episode *The Arrangement*.
Played B in the second season **Space 1999** episode *The A B Chrysalis*.

Douglas Stuart
Wrote the **Virgin of the Secret Service** episode *A Fate Worse Than Death*.

Dowie Freda
Played Opal Banks in the **Father Brown** episode *The Man with Two Beards*.

Downer Allan
Played the police Inspector in **The Adventurer** episode *Target!*.
Played the gendarme in the third season **The Saint** episode *The Better Mousetrap*.

Downer David
Played Hinch in the **Randall and Hopkirk [Deceased]** aka **My Partner the Ghost** episode *When Did you Start to Stop Seeing Things?*.

Downie Andrew
Played Tom O'Gaunt in the second series of **The Adventures of Robin Hood** episode *The Trap* and Tam in season four's *The Bagpiper*.
Played the porter in the first season **Danger Man** episode *Under the Lake*.
Played Alastair in the first series **Man of the World** episode *The Highland Story*.

Downing John
Played Roberts in the fourth season **The Saint** episode *The People Importers*.

Downing Michael S.E.
Special Effects Electronics on **Space 1999**.

Downing Wilfrid
Appeared as Jeremy in the third series of **The Adventures of Robin Hood** episode *A Tuck in Time*.
Played The Boy [Dickon] in **The Buccaneers** [aka **Dan Tempest**] episode *The Wasp*, and Dickon in *Whale Gold, Gunpowder Plot, Ghost Ship, Blood Will Tell, Dead Man's Rock, Dangerous Cargo, Hand of the Hawk, Gentleman Jack and the Lady, Mr. Beamish and the Hangman's Noose, Marooned, Before the Mast, Dan Tempest and The Amazons, The Surgeon of Sangre Rojo, Flip and Jenny* and *Pirate Honour*.

Played the delivery boy in **The Sentimental Agent** episode *All that Jazz*.

Downs Jane
Played Violetta in the **Sword of Freedom** episode *Violetta*.

Dozier Robert
Wrote the original story for the **Espionage** episode *Festival of Pawns* [teleplayed by Raymond Bowers].

Drage Prudence
Played the girl customer in the fourth season **The Saint** episode *The Master Plan*.

Drake Fabia
Played Lady Pulman in the **Father Brown** episode *The Man with Two Beards*.
Played the receptionist in the **Man in a Suitcase** episode *Man from the Dead*.
Played the welfare worker in **The Prisoner** episode *Arrival*.
Played Aunt Prudence in the season two **The Saint** episode *The Smart Detective* and Aunt Hattie in *The Miracle Tea Party*.

Drake Frank
Special Effects Camera Operator on **Space 1999**.

Drake Gabrielle
Played Marian in **The Adventurer** episode *The Good Book*.
Guested as Sara in **The Champions** episode *Full Circle*.
Played Diana in the third season **The Saint** episode *The Best Laid Schemes*.
Starred in the series **UFO** as, regular, Lt Gay Ellis.
Played Countess Irene Kolinsky in the **Virgin of the Secret Service** episode *Russian Roundabout*.

Drake James
Played Bill in the **Department S** episode *Handicap Dead*.

Drake John
Guested in the first series of **The Adventures of Robin Hood**: *The Moneylender* - as Howard, *Friar Tuck* - as Harold, *Maid Marian* - as Ned, *The Challenge* - as Simon, *Queen Eleanor* - as Sir Giles and *The Ordeal* - as Alvin.
Played the cricket bowler in **The Prisoner** episode *The Girl who was Death*.

Driant Jean
Played Douane in **The Persuaders!** episode *The Gold Napoleon* and the hotel porter in the **Return of the Saint** episode *The Diplomat's Daughter*.

Drinkwater Ros
Played Inez in the third season **The Saint** episode *Invitation to Danger*.

Driscoll Paricia
Starred as, series regular, Lady Marian Fitzwalter aka Maid Marian in **The Adventures of Robin Hood** [Bernadette O'Farrell also starred in the role]: *The Salt King, A Tuck in Time, Pepper, The Charter, My Brother's Keeper, The Bride of Robin Hood, Knight Errant, Too Many Robins, Castle in the Air, The Ghost that Failed, The Minstrel, Elixir of Youth, The Youthful Menace, The Lottery, Lincoln Green, Woman's War, Little Mother & Marian's Prize* [series three] and *Sybella, The Lady Killer, A Touch of Fever, The Flying Sorcerer, Six Strings to his bow, The Devil You Don't Know, Hostage for a Hangman, Hue and Cry, The Charm Pedlar, The Bagpiper, The Parting Guest, The Debt, A Bushel of Apples, The Pharaoh Stones, Double Trouble, The Champion, Trapped, The Edge and the Point & The Truce* [season four].
Played Lady Lindsay in the first season **Danger Man** episode *The Conspirators* and Mrs Archer in the second series [now aka **Secret Agent**] episode *Yesterday's Enemies*.

Drummond Vivienne
Played Mrs Fellows in **The Four Just Men** episode *The Discovery*.

Drury Weston Jnr.
Casting Director on **Return of The Saint** & **The Zoo Gang**.

Duclos Colette
Played Balbina in **The Scarlet Pimpernel** episode *Sir Andrew's Fate*.

Dudley Lesley
Played Ilse in the **O.S.S.** episode *Operation Meatball*.
Played Antoniette in **The Scarlet Pimpernel** episode *The Christmas Present*.

Dudley Paul
Wrote all of the **O.S.S.** episodes [with Manning O'Brine on *Operation Big House* and with Robert Spafford on *Operation Death Trap*].

Duering Carl
Played Colonel Kazan in **The Adventurer** episode *Double Exposure*.
Played Count Marrais in the **G.S.5** episode *It Won't be a Stylish Marriage*.
Guested as Dr. Berger in the **Interpol Calling** episode *Payment in Advance* and as D'Ambrosio in *A Foreign Body*.
Played Lanik in the **Jason King** episode *A Page Before Dying*.
Played MfS Colonel in the **Man in a Suitcase** episode *Somebody Loses, Somebody ...Wins?*.
Played the German officer in the **O.S.S.** episode *Operation Flint Axe*.
Played the police captain in the first season **The Saint** episode *The Saint Sees it Through* and Kruger in the third season's *The Paper Chase*.

Duffell Bee
Played the secretary in **The Four Just Men** episode *Money To Burn*.
Played the Psychiatrist in **The Prisoner** episode *Dance of the Dead* and the second Psychiatrist in *Checkmate*.

Duffell Peter
Directed the **Man in a Suitcase** episodes *Dead Man's Shoes, The Man who Stood Still, Burden of Proof, Property of a Gentleman, The Revolutionaries & Castle in the Clouds* and teleplayed, with Jan Read, *The Revolutionaries* [from a story by Kevin B. Laffan].
Directed the **Strange Report** episodes *Report 0846: LONELYHEARTS: 'Who Killed Dan Cupid?', Report 3906: COVER GIRLS: 'Last year's Model', Report 8944: HAND: 'A Matter of Witchcraft?' & Report 1553: RACIST: 'A Most Dangerous Proposal'*.

Dugay Yvette
Played Marie in **The Count of Monte Cristo** episode *Affair of Honour*.

Duggan Gerry
Played Sidney Grafton in the **G.S.5** episode *Dr. Ayre*.
Played Mulloon in the third season **The Saint** episode *Little Girl Lost*.

Duggan Terry
Played Jackson in the **Randall and Hopkirk [Deceased]** aka **My Partner the Ghost** episode *The House on Haunted Hill*.
Played Rex in the **Return of the Saint** episode *Tower Bridge is Falling Down*.

Duggan Thomas
Guested as Cranby in the **Interpol Calling** episode *Trial at Cranby's Creek*.

Played Cesare in the **O.S.S.** episode *Operation Payday*.

Duggan Thomas G.
Played Martin in **The Buccaneers** [aka **Dan Tempest**] episode *Aztec Treasure*.
Played Waldmann in the **William Tell** episode *The Suspect*.

Duggan Thomas R.
Appeared as Baron Wicklaw in **The Adventures of Sir Lancelot** episode *The Prince of Limerick*.

Duggan Tommy
Played Stavros in the first season **The Saint** episode *Sophia* and Kovicek in the third season's *Flight Plan*.

Dugoni Duccio
Played Abelardo in the **Return of the Saint** episode *The Roman Touch*.

Duguid Peter
Played the prop man in the first season **The Saint** episode *Marcia*.

Dumas Alexandre
His novel *The Count of Monte Cristo* was adapted to provide the basic storyline for the series **The Count of Monte Cristo**.

Dunbar John
Played the police Inspector in **The Adventurer** episode *Action!*.
Played the House of Lords Messenger in the third season **Danger Man** [aka **Secret Agent**] episode *The Hunting Party*.
Played the barman in the second season **Ghost Squad** episode *P.G. 7*.
Played Sgt. Graham in the first season **The Saint** episode *Starring the Saint*.
Played Major Domo in the **Sir Francis Drake** episode *The Reluctant Duchess*.
Played the Coroner in the **Strange Report** episode *Report 1021: SHRAPNEL: 'The Wish in the Dream'*.

Duncan Archie
Starred as, series regular, Little John in **The Adventures of Robin Hood** [Rufus Cruikshank took over the role for ten episodes to cover him after he broke his leg on set]: *Dead or Alive, A Guest for the Gallows, The Inquisitor, The Knight Who Came To Dinner, The Challenge, Queen Eleanor, Checkmate, The Ordeal, Richard the Lionheart, Will Scarlet, The Deserted Castle, The Miser, Trial by Battle, Children of the Greenwood, The May Queen, The Byzantine Treasure, Secret Mission, Table's Turned & The Traitor* [series 1]; *A Village Wooing, The Scientist, Blackmail, A Year and a Day, The Impostor, Ransom, Isabella, The Hero, The Haunted Mill, Outlaw Money, The Black Patch, The Friar's Pilgrimage, The Trap, Hubert , The Dream, The Blackbird, The Shell Game, The Final Tax, Ambush, The Goldmaker's Return, Fair Play, The Dowry, The York Treasure, The Borrowed Baby, Food for Thought, Too Many Earls, The Little People, The Frightened Tailor, The Black Five, The Road in the Air & Carlotta* [2]; *The Salt King, A Tuck in Time, Pepper, Change of Heart, Brother Battle, My Brother's Keeper, An Apple for the Archer, The Angry Village, The Mark, The Bride of Robin Hood, To Be a Student, The Christmas Goose, The Challenge of the Black Knight, The Rivals, The Profiteer, Knight Errant, The Healing Hand, Too Many Robins, The Crusaders, Castle in the Air, The Double, Roman Gold, The Ghost that Failed, The Minstrel, The Doctor, The Fire, At the Sign of the Blue Boar, Quickness of the Hand, Elixir of Youth, The Genius, The Youthful Menace, The Lottery, Lincoln Green, Woman's War, Little Mother, Marian's Prize & Farewell to Tuck* [3] and *Goodbye, Little John, Hostage for a Hangman, Hue and Cry, The Reluctant Rebel, The Oath, The Charm Pedlar, The Bagpiper, The Parting Guest, The Debt, Race Against Time, A*

Bushel of Apples, The Pharaoh Stones, Double Trouble, The Champion, Trapped, The Edge and the Point & The Truce [4].
Played Henry Cameron in the season two **Ghost Squad** episode *Gertrude*.

Duncan Joanna
Played Lady Arabella in **The Scarlet Pimpernel** episode *The Flower Woman*.

Duncan Peter
Played Cantar in the season two **Space 1999** episode *The Exiles*.

Duncan Ronald
Wrote the second season **The Saint** episode *The Old Treasure Story*.

Dunham Christopher
Played Kramer in the first series **The Protectors** episode *One and One Makes One*.

Dunham Joanna
Played Gerda Hoffman in **The Adventurer** episode *The Bradley Way*.
Played Nawi in the first season **Danger Man** episode *Dead Man Walks*.
Played Madeleine de Seiberd in **The Four Just Men** episode *The Grandmother*.
Played Pat Stephens in the **H. G. Wells' Invisible Man** episode *Flight into Darkness*.
Played Martine in the **Jason King** two parter *All that Glisters*.
Played Vana in the first season **Space 1999** episode *Missing Link*.
Played Gretel in the **William Tell** episode *The Shrew*.

Dunham Rosemarie
Played the Duchess of Mont.St. Michel in the **Father Brown** episode *The Secret Garden*.

Dunham Rosemary
Played the first tart in **The Four Just Men** episode *The Boy Without a Country*.
Played Sophie Murdoch in the **Gideon's Way** episode *The Prowler*.
Played the prison governor in the **Return of the Saint** episode *The Debt Collectors*.

Dunlop Pat
Wrote the **Joe 90** episode *Mission X-41* and **The Secret Service** episodes *Recall to Service & The Cure*.

Dunlop Peter
Production Buyer on **Jason King & Randall and Hopkirk** [Deceased] aka **My Partner the Ghost**.

Dunn Colette
Played the receptionist in the third season **The Saint** episode *Little Girl Lost*.

Dunn Richard
Played the orator in the **Sword of Freedom** episode *Francesca*.

Dunne Joe
Appeared as the first tower guard in **The Prisoner** episode *Checkmate*.

Dunrich Brenda
Played the secretary in the second series **Danger Man** [aka **Secret Agent**] episode *The Professionals*.

Durant Maurice

Played John Mallory in the season two **Ghost Squad** episode *Sabotage*.

Played the sergeant in the **H. G. Wells' Invisible Man** episode *The Rocket*.

Appeared as Volpo in the **White Hunter** episode *No Survivors*.

Durden Richard
Played the head waiter in the **Department S** episode *The Bones of Byrom Blain*.

Durkin Patrick
Played Gill in **The Baron** episode *Diplomatic Immunity* and Marsh in *The Maze*.

Played Albert in the **Department S** episode *The Soup of the Day*.

Played Lefty in the **Gideon's Way** episode *Gang War*.

Played the porter in the third season **The Saint** episode *The Fast Women*.

Played Delta 22 in the **Timeslip** story *The Year of the Burn-Up* [series episodes 15-18].

Durra
Played the Arab girl in the second series **Danger Man** [aka **Secret Agent**] episode *Fish on the Hook*.

Dutton Anthony
Played Frank in the **Department S** episode *The Shift that Never was*.

Played Chief Insp. Gilder in the **Father Brown** episode *Three Tools of Death*.

Duval Denis
Played the engineer in the **Jason King** episode *Uneasy Lies the Head*.

Dwyer Hilary
Played Number 73 in **The Prisoner** episode *Hammer Into Anvil*.

Played Laura Adams in the first season **Space 1999** episode *The Troubled Spirit*.

Dwyer Leslie
Appeared as Stacey Clarke in the **White Hunter** episode *The Jackals*.

Dyall Valentine
Played the radio announcer in *Adventure Five* of **Sapphire and Steel**.

Dyce Hamilton
Played Justo Vitale in **The Baron** episode *Time to Kill*.

Played Chief Inspector Poron in the **Jason King** episode *As Easy as A B C*.

Played Vladek Urivetsky in the first season **The Saint** episode *The Work of Art*.

Dyer Hal
Played Miss Chanter in **The Baron** episode *Samurai West*.

Dyneley Peter
Played Julius K. Brayne in the **Father Brown** episode *The Secret Garden*.

Played the Police Chief in **The Four Just Men** episode *The Judge* and Dougan in *Riot*.

Played Phil Slade in the first series **Ghost Squad** episode *Million Dollar Ransom* and Larry Arnell in season two's *A First Class Way to Die*.

Guested as Leroy in the **Interpol Calling** episode *Game for Three Hands*.

Played Tony Gardner in the first series **Man of the World** episode *Blaze of Glory*.

Played Nat Grendel in the first season **The Saint** episode *The Careful Terrorist*, Richard Eade in *The Bunco Artists* and Paul Verrier in the third season's *To Kill a Saint*.

Played Duncan Macdonald in the **Shirley's World** episode *The Islanders*.

Voiced Jeff Tracey in **The Thunderbirds** series.

Dyrenforth James
Played Dr. Chase in **The Four Just Men** episode *The Judge* and Frank Appleby in *The Man in the Road*.

Played the US doctor in the **O.S.S.** episode *Operation Fracture*.

Dysart William
Played Grant in the **Father Brown** episode *The Quick One*.

Played the police Inspector in the **Randall and Hopkirk [Deceased]** aka **My Partner the Ghost** episode *Vendetta for a Dead Man*.

Played Inspector Lowe in the **Strange Report** episode *Report 4407: HEART: 'No Choice for the Donor'*.

Dyson John
Writer on **The Adventures of Robin Hood**: *Husband for Marian, The Youngest Outlaw, The Jongleur, Errand of Mercy & Will Scarlet* [series 1]; *Ransom, The Hero, Outlaw Money, The Black Patch & The Secret Pool* [2] and *The Infidel* [with Basil Dawson], *The Charter & Too Many Robins* [3].

Dyson Noel
Played Mrs Lane in the **Gideon's Way** episode *Subway to Revenge*.

****

Eady David
Directed the second season **The Saint** episode *The Hi-Jackers*.

Eagleton Ron
Played the assassin in the second season **The Protectors** episode *Implicado*.

Earl Clifford
Played the Det. Sgt. in **The Baron** episode *Samurai West*.
Played Porter in the first season **Danger Man** episode *The Lonely Chair*.
Played Dave in the **Department S** episode *The Man who got a New Face*.
Played Sgt. Bailey in the **Gideon's Way** episode *Fall High, Fall Hard*.
Played the police doctor in the **Jason King** episode *It's Too Bad about Auntie*.
Played the policeman in the **Man in a Suitcase** episode *Man from the Dead*.
Played the first detective in the **Randall and Hopkirk [Deceased]** aka **My Partner the Ghost** episode *You Can Always find a Fall Guy*.
Played the plainclothed policeman in the **Return of the Saint** episode *Assault Force*.
Played Morgan in the fourth season **The Saint** two parter *The Fiction Makers* and the rally official in *The World Beater*.

Earle Freddie
Played Tommy Farrell in the **G.S.5** episode *Dr. Ayre*.
Played Tosh in the **Virgin of the Secret Service** episode *Wings Over Glencraig*.

Early Charles
Wrote the second series of **The Adventures of Robin Hood** episode *The Trap*.

East Roger
Co-wrote **The Sentimental Agent** episode *Not Quite Fully Covered Not* [with Leslie Harris].

Easton Richard
Played Dave Sherman in the **G.S.5** episode *A Cast of Thousands*.
Played Savage in the first series **The Protectors** episode *The Numbers Game*.
Played Chuck Powers in the second season **The Saint** episode *The Contract*.

Easton Robert
Played Benson in the first season **The Saint** episode *The Latin Touch*.
Provided the voices for Phones and X20 on the series **Stingray**.

Eaton Leo
Directed the **Captain Scarlet and the Mysterons** episodes *Place of Angels* [and wrote], *Expo 2068* & *Flight to Atlantica*.
Directed the **Joe 90** episodes *The Fortress*, *King for a Day*, *Splashdown*, *Breakout*, *See You Down There*, *Trial at Sea*, and *The Birthday*.
Directed **The Secret Service** episodes *A Question of Miracles*, *Errand of Mercy*, *The Deadly Whisper* and *The Cure*.

Eaton Shirley
Played Lee in the first series **Man of the World** episode *The Sentimental Agent*.
Played Adrienne Halberd in the first season **The Saint** episode *The Talented Husband*, Gloria Uckrose in *The Effete Angler* and Reb Denning in the third season's *Invitation to Danger*.

Eaton Wallace
Played Detective Inspector Samuels in the **Man in a Suitcase** episode *The Whisper*.

Eccles Donald
Played Andre Gustave in **The Adventurer** episode *Full Fathom Five*.
Played Perston in the first series **The Protectors** episode *Chase*.

Eccles Jane
Played the old woman in **The Buccaneers** [aka **Dan Tempest**] episode *The Surgeon of Sangre Rojo*.

Eddington Paul
Played Charlesworth in **The Adventurer** episode *Make it a Million*.
Starred as, fourth series regular, Will Scarlett in **The Adventures of Robin Hood** [Will Scarlet appeared twice before he assumed the role, played by Ronald Howard]: *The Lady Killer*, *A Touch of Fever*, *Tuck's Love Day*, *The Loaf*, *Six Strings to his Bow*, *The Devil You Don't Know*, *Goodbye, Little John*, *Hostage for a Hangman*, *Hue and Cry*, *The Reluctant Rebel*, *The Oath*, *The Charm Pedlar*, *The Bagpiper*, *The Parting Guest*, *The Debt*, *Bride for an Outlaw*, *Race Against Time*, *A Bushel of Apples*, *The Pharaoh Stones*, *Double Trouble*, *The Champion*, *The Edge and the Point* and *The Truce*. Originally joined the show in season two playing a variety of parts: the second villager in *The Hero*, Count William in *Outlaw Money*, Count Duprez in *The Friar's Pilgrimage*, Sir Walter in *Hubert*, the look-out in *The Dream*, the Man-at-Arms in *The Blackbird*, Sad Simon in *The Shell Game*, Sir Charles in *The Final Tax*, Leborgne in *The Bandit of Brittany*, Sir Paul in *The Goldmaker's Return*, Duc de Guise in *Flight from France*, Tom in *Fair Play*, Henry in *The Secret Pool*, Sir Harold in *The Dowry*, Aaron in *The York Treasure*, the Man-at-Arms in *The Borrowed Baby*, Baron Mornay in *Highland Fling* & Connor in *The Little People*. Also appeared in a number of roles in season three: Wilfrid in *The Salt King*, Sir Reginald in *A Tuck in Time*, Sir Eustace in *The Charter*, Colin in *Change of Heart*, Howard in *Brother Battle*, Satan in *My Brother's Keeper*, Pierre of Bordeaux in *An Apple for the Archer*, the Captain in *The Angry Village*, Rolfe in *To Be a Student*, the Bailiff in *The Christmas Goose*, Tom in *The Challenge of the Black Knight*, the Seneschal in *The Rivals*, Rypon in *The Profiteer*, the Captain in *Knight Errant*, the Captain in *The Healing Hand*, Patrick in *One Man's Meat*, Sir Hugh in *The Crusaders*, Howard in *The Doctor*, the Lieutenant in *The Fire*, Walter in *Marian's Prize* & the Lieutenant in *Farewell to Tuck*.
Played La Forte in **The Buccaneers** [aka **Dan Tempest**] episode *Cutlass Wedding*.
Guested as Klein in **The Champions** episode *Autokill*.
Played Captain Schulman in the third season **Danger Man** [aka **Secret Agent**] episode *I'm Afraid you Have the Wrong Number*.
Played Rustie in **The Four Just Men** episode *Crack-Up*.
Guested as Mike McGrath in the **Interpol Calling** episode *The Thousand Mile Alibi*.
Guest starred in **The Prisoner** episode *Arrival* as Cobb.
Played Alfonso in the **Sword of Freedom** episode *The Eye of the Artist*.

Eddon Eddie
Played the third horseman in **The Prisoner** episode *Living in Harmony*.

Eden Eve
Played Mrs Johnson in **The Sentimental Agent** episode *Never Play Cards with Strangers*.

Eden Mark
Featured in the **Espionage** episode *Never Turn Your Back On a Friend*.
Played Jackson in the **Man in a Suitcase** episode *The Sitting Pigeon*.
Played Number 100 in **The Prisoner** episode *It's Your Funeral*.

Played Bertrand Tamblin in the first season **The Saint** episode *The Invisible Millionaire*.
Played Agila in the **Sir Francis Drake** episode *The Slaves of Spain*.

Edis Janey
Played the girl revolutionary in the **Jason King** episode *Zenia*.

Edmond Terence
Played Cliff Turner in **The Persuaders!** episode *That's Me Over There*.
Played Captain Yates in the fourth season **The Saint** episode *The Organisation Man*.

Edmonds Larry
Production accountant on **The Prisoner**.

Edward Vincent
Played Gaston de Long in **The Scarlet Pimpernel** episode *The Imaginary Invalides*.

Edwards Alan
Played a range of roles in the second series of **The Adventures of Robin Hood**: Pembroke in *Isabella*, The Reeve in *The Final Tax*, Howard in *The Goldmaker's Return*, Sir Robert Gascon in *Flight from France*, Quentin in *Fair Play* and Howard in *The Secret Pool*.
Appeared as Sir Gringamore in **The Adventures of Sir Lancelot** episode *Sir Crustabread*.

Edwards Bill
Played Sergeant Poole in the first season **Danger Man** episode *The Girl who Liked Gis* and Dave in the season two[now aka **Secret Agent**] episode *You're Not in Any Trouble, Are You?*
Played the Sergeant in the second season **Man of the World** episode *The Prince*.
Played the U.S. Sergeant in the **O.S.S.** episode *Operation Yo Yo* and the navigator in *Operation Blackbird*.

Edwards David
Played the lieutenant in the first season **The Adventures of Robin Hood** episode *Maid Marian* and the ploughman in *The Inquisitor*.

Edwards Dennis
Appeared as the Bailiff in the second series of **The Adventures of Robin Hood** episode *The Final Tax* and as the Sheriff's Seneschal in *The Black Five*.
Played the second guard in **The Buccaneers** [aka **Dan Tempest**] episode *Instrument of War* and the officer in *Printer's Devil*.
Played the journalist in **The Four Just Men** episode *The Beatniques*.
Played the doctor in the **Father Brown** episode *The Mirror of the Magistrate*.
Played the doctor in the season two **Ghost Squad** episode *The Big Time*.
Played the bank manager in the **G.S.5** episode *Dr. Ayre*.
Played Sir Reginald Compton in **The Scarlet Pimpernel** episodes *Thanksgiving Day* & *A Tale of Two Pigtails*.
Played De Vazim in the **Sir Francis Drake** episode *The Bridge*.
Played Consul in the **Sword of Freedom** episode *Portrait in Emerald Green*.

Edwards Dorothy
Played Mrs Hart in the **Man in a Suitcase** episode *All that Glitters*.

Edwards Glyn
Played Det. Insp. Walsh in **The Baron** episode *The Maze*.
Played Boris in **The Persuaders!** episode *The Long Goodbye*.

Played Igor in the third season **The Saint** episode *The Gadget Lovers* and Leander in the fourth season's *The Organisation Man*.
Played Darrin in **The Sentimental Agent** episode *Meet my Son, Henry*.
Played Martin Armstrong in the **Sir Francis Drake** episode *Lost Colony of Virginia* and Will Martin in *Gentlemen of Spain*, *The Gypsies* & *The Doughty Plot*.

Edwards Kenneth
Appeared in the first season **The Adventures of Robin Hood** episode *The Moneylender* as Hawkins and as a villager in *The Sheriff's Boots*.
Played Bowles Sr in **The Four Just Men** episode *National Treasure*.
Played the Coroner in the **Gideon's Way** episode *The Lady Killer*.
Played Smithers in the **G.S.5** episode *The Goldfish Bowl*.
Played the judge in the third season **The Saint** episode *When Spring is Sprung*.
Played the constable in the **Virgin of the Secret Service** episode *A Fate Worse Than Death*.

Edwards Meredith
Played Sam Ludlow in the second series **The Adventures of Robin Hood** episode *Food for Thought*.
Played Inspector Powell in **The Baron** episode *Portrait of Louisa*.
Played Paul Samuels in the **Gideon's Way** episode *To Catch a Tiger*.
Guested as Doctor Gorman in the **Interpol Calling** episode *Slave Ship*.
Played Hodder in the **Randall and Hopkirk [Deceased]** aka **My Partner the Ghost** episode *It's Supposed to be Thicker than Water*.
Played Emrys Pugh in the season two **The Saint** episode *The Man who could not Die* and Whitey Mullins in *The Crooked Ring*.

Eedy Christopher
Played the bell boy in the **Randall and Hopkirk [Deceased]** aka **My Partner the Ghost** episode *The Ghost who Saved the Bank at Monte Carlo*.

Egerton Nancy
Played Gretchen in the **Sir Francis Drake** episode *The Reluctant Duchess*.

Eggar Samantha
Played Mina in the season two **Ghost Squad** episode *Hot Money*.
Played Claire Avery in the first season **The Saint** episode *Marcia*.

Eisinger Jo
Wrote the series one **Danger Man** episodes *The Lovers* [with Doreen Montgomery], *Position of Trust* [teleplayed from a story by Ralph Smart], *The Sisters* [teleplayed from a story by Brian Clemens], *Deadline* [teleplayed from a story by Ian Stuart Black], *Find and Return* & *The Deputy Coyannis Story*.

Ekland Britt
Played Laura in the **Return of the Saint** episode *The Murder Cartel*.

Elboz Jerry
Played the second guard in the season two **Ghost Squad** episode *Gertrude*.

Elderedge John
Played Gerald in **The Count of Monte Cristo** episode *First Train to Paris*.

Eles Sandor
Played Gerard Laroche in **The Adventurer** episode *Has Anyone Here Seen Kelly?*.

Played Peter Savel in **The Baron** episode *Roundabout* and Alifa in *Red Horse, Red Rider*.

Played Canesi in the third season **Danger Man** [aka **Secret Agent**] episode *The Paper Chase*.

Played Dominic in the **Department S** episode *The Soup of the Day*.

Played Shimoon in the **Jason King** episode *Uneasy Lies the Head*.

In **The Saint**: appeared as the hotel clerk in *The Abductors* [series 2], as Andre in *The Russian Prisoner* [3] and as Jean Latour in *Where the Money Is* [4].

Played the hotel clerk in **The Sentimental Agent** episode *Express Delivery*.

Played Pavel Gordy in the **Strange Report** episode *Report 7931: SNIPER: 'When is Your Cousin Not?'*.

Played Gottfriend in the **Timeslip** story *The Wrong End of Time* [series parts 1 - 6].

Elgar Avril
Played Mrs Tennison in the **Gideon's Way** episode *The Firebug*.

Eliscu William
Executive Producer on the series **O.S.S.**

Elkin Clifford
Played Mahmoud in **The Sentimental Agent** episode *The Scroll of Islam*.

Played Don Antonio in the **Sir Francis Drake** episode *The Prisoner*.

Elliott David
Production Supervisor on **Fireball XL5** and directed the episodes *Planet of Platonia, Wings of Danger, The Triads, Flight to Danger, The Forbidden Planet, The Robot Freighter Mystery, The Day the Earth Froze & A Day in the Life of a Space General*.

Directed the **Stingray** episodes *Plant of Doom, The Big Gun, Ghost of the Sea, The Invaders, The Disappearing Ships, Pink Ice, Invisible Enemy, Set Sail for Adventure, A Nut for Marineville* and *The Lighthouse Dwellers*.

Directed the first season **Supercar** episodes *Rescue, Talisman of Sargon, What Goes Up, Grounded, High Tension, Island Incident, The Tracking of Masterspy, The Sunken Temple & Dragon of Ho Meng* and *The Runaway Train* [season two].

Directed the first season **Thunderbirds** episodes *Terror in New York City* [with David Lane], *Day of Disaster, 30 Minutes after Noon, Vault of Death, City of Fire, Cry Wolf, The Duchess Assignment & Martian Invasion* and the second season's *Path of Destruction*.

Elliott Denholm
Played Basil Jordan in the third season **Danger Man** [aka **Secret Agent**] episode *The Hunting Party* and Roland in **The Persuaders!** episode *A Death in the Family*.

Elliott Jimmy
Senior Visual Effects Director on **Joe 90** & **The Secret Service** and Camera Operator on **Thunderbirds**.

Elliott Peter
Sound editor on **The Prisoner** episode *A. B. and C.*

Elliott Peter
Played the sergeant in the second series **Danger Man** [aka **Secret Agent**] episode *A Room in the Basement*.

Played Truloff in the season two **Ghost Squad** episode *The Grand Duchess*.

Played the croupier in the **H. G. Wells' Invisible Man** episode *Odds Against Death*.

Played Manuel in the first season **The Saint** episode *The Romantic Matron*, Kwan Li in the second season's *Jeannine* and Berreeni in the third's *The Man Who Liked Lions*.

Elliott Peter J.
Guested as Paul in **The Champions** episode *The Experiment*.

Played Thorn in the **Department S** episode *The Treasure of the Costa del Sol*.

Played Wilks in the **Randall and Hopkirk [Deceased]** aka **My Partner the Ghost** episode *When the Spirit Moves You*.

Ellis Antonia
Starred in the series **UFO** as, regular, Joan Harrington.

Ellis Ian
Played Kip in the first season **Danger Man** episode *The Conspirators*.

Ellis Jacqueline
Played Veronica in the first season **Danger Man** episode *Vacation*.

Played Ilse Virany in the season two **Ghost Squad** episode *The Menacing Mazurka*.

Played Martha in the **Man in a Suitcase** episode *Web with Four Spiders*.

Played Jane in the first series **Man of the World** episode *The Nature of Justice*.

Played Norma Upton in the first season **The Saint** episode *The Ever-loving Spouse* and Alice Nestor in the second season's *The Golden Frog*.

Ellis James
Played the thin man in the season three **The Adventures of Robin Hood** episode *The Healing Hand*.

Ellis June
Played Number 48 in **The Prisoner** episode *A Change of Mind*.

Ellis Peter
Played Patrick in the third season **The Saint** episode *Little Girl Lost*.

Ellis Robin
Played Capt. White in the **Virgin of the Secret Service** episode *The Persuasion of a Million Drops*.

Ellison Catherine
Played the first woman in **The Adventures of Sir Lancelot** episode *The Missing Princess*.

Ellison Michael
Played fhe boy in the season three **The Adventures of Robin Hood** episode *The Charter*.

Elms Albert
Music on the four seasons of **The Adventures of Robin Hood** [Edwin Astley also worked on the first two].

Music on **The Adventures of Sir Lancelot** episodes *The Ferocious Fathers, The Outcast, Winged Victory, Sir Bliant, Lancelot's Banishment, Roman Wall, Caledon, Shepherd's War, The Pirates, The Black Castle, Double Identity, The Bridge, The Witch's Brew, Ruby of Radnor, The Magic Book, Knight Errand, The Theft of Excalibur, The Mortaise Fair, Maid of Somerset, Sir Crustabread, The Ugly Duckling, The Prince of Limerick, The Lady Lilith, Knight's Choice, The Missing Princess* and *The Thieves*.

Music for **The Buccaneers** [aka **Dan Tempest**] episodes *Gunpowder Plot, Articles of War, Conquest of New Providence, Mother Doughty's Crew, Blood Will Tell, Hurricane, Mr. Beamish and the Hangman's Noose, Marooned, Conquistador, Aztec Treasure, Prize of Andalusia, Cutlass Wedding, Dan Tempest Holds an Auction, Flip and Jenny, To the Res-*

cue, *Indian Fighters, Mistress Higgins' Treasure, The Spy Aboard, The Decoy, Pirate Honour, Instrument of War* and *Printer's Devil*.

Composed music for **The Champions** episodes *The Invisible Man* and *The Search*.

Musical Director on on the **Man in a Suitcase** series [title theme by Ron Grainer].

Music Director on **The Prisoner**: *The Schizoid Man, Many Happy Returns, Dance of the Dead, Hammer Into Anvil, It's Your Funeral, A Change of Mind, Do Not Forsake Me Oh My Darling, Living in Harmony, The Girl who was Death* and *Fall Out*. Composer of incidental music for *A. B. and C., Free for All, The General* and *Once Upon A Time*.

Elms Vic
Music associate on **Space 1999**.

Eloor Jean
Played Mrs. Miles in **The Buccaneers** [aka **Dan Tempest**] episode *Printer's Devil*.

Elsom Jonathan
Played the lieutenant in **The Baron** episode *Long Ago and Far Away*.

Played Andrew in the third season **The Saint** episode *The Best Laid Schemes*.

Elton Eileen
Played Molly in **The Buccaneers** [aka **Dan Tempest**] episode *Cutlass Wedding*.

Elvey Maurice
Directed the **White Hunter** episode *Run to Earth*.

Elvy Reuben
Played the second prison guard in the third season **Danger Man** [aka **Secret Agent**] episode *Two Birds with One Bullet*.

Played Stern in the **Return of the Saint** episode *One Black September*.

Elweg Mark
Played Corbett in the **Department S** episode *A Small War of Nerves*.

Elwes Mark
Played the cashier in the **Man in a Suitcase** episode *Why they Killed Nolan*.

Elyas Cyrus
Played Moreno in the **Return of the Saint** episode *The Village that Sold its Soul*.

EMI/MGM Elstree Studios
Studio used for the filming of **The Adventurer, Jason King, The Protectors** and **Return of the Saint**.

Emma Gay
Played The Infanta in **The Count of Monte Cristo** episode *A Toy for the Infanta*.

Emmanuel Heather
Played the girl in the second series **Danger Man** [aka **Secret Agent**] episode *The Galloping Major* and the lab assistant in *The Mercenaries*.

Endersby Ralph
Starred as Chub in the series **The Forest Rangers**.

Enefer Douglas
Wrote the third season **The Saint** episode *The Man Who Liked Lions*.

Enger Eva
Played the young lady in the **Randall and Hopkirk [Deceased]** aka **My Partner the Ghost** episode *The Ghost who Saved the Bank at Monte Carlo*.

England Betty
Played the hotel receptionist in the **G.S.5** episode *Dr. Ayre*.

English David
Played the salesman in the **Return of the Saint** episode *Collision Course* [Part 1: *'The Brave Goose'*: also exists, combined with the second installment as a movie entitled *The Saint and the Brave Goose*].

English Patricia
Played Madame Devereaux in **The Baron** episode *The Seven Eyes of Night*.

Guested as Suzanne Taylor in **The Champions** episode *The Search*.

Played Mrs Taylor in the **Department S** episode *Last Train to Redbridge*.

Played Jean Cox in the **Gideon's Way** episode *State Visit*.

Played Leila in the **Jason King** episode *Zenia*.

Enrika Joe
Played the commissionaire in **The Sentimental Agent** episode *The Scroll of Islam*.

Erickson Paul
Wrote the story for the **Interpol Calling** episode *The Three Keys* [teleplayed by Connery Chappell and Robert Stewart].

Wrote **The Saint** episodes *The Scorpion, The Hi-Jackers, The Spanish Cow* [teleplayed from a story by Michael Cramoy] & *The Damsel in Distress* [season 2] and *The Angel's Eye* [3].

Erith J. Leslie
Played Viccenti in the first season **Danger Man** episode *Hired Assassin*.

Ernst Frank
Assistant Director on the first series of **Ghost Squad**.

Assistant director on **The Persuaders!** series.

Erwin Lee
Writer on **The New Adventures of Charlie Chan**.

Wrote the **White Hunter** episodes *One Fatal Weakness, No Survivors, The Fugitive, Big Bwana Brady* and *The Trophy*.

Eshley Norman
Played Red in the **Department S** episode *Handicap Dead*.

Played Mike Hales in the **Randall and Hopkirk [Deceased]** episode *Could You Recognise the Man Again?*.

Played Inspector Canfield in the **Return of the Saint** episodes *The Nightmare Man* & *Yesterday's Hero*.

Esmond Jill
Guested as Queen Eleanor in the debut season **The Adventures of Robin Hood** episodes *Queen Eleanor* and *The Deserted Castle*.

Essame Richard
Played the boy in the **Department S** episode *A Fish out of Water*.

Eton Graeme
Played desk clerk in the **Return of the Saint** episode *The Diplomat's Daughter*.

Ettlinger Norman
Played Lynsky in **The Adventurer** episode *Going, Going....*

Played Sir Charles Standish in the second season **The Protectors** episode *Sugar and Spice*.

Eu Kathleen
Played Ming Finnigin in the **Jason King** episode *Every Picture Tells a Story*.

Eugeniou George
Played the barman in the first series **Danger Man** episode *Bury the Dead* and the immigration officer in the second season's *Yesterday's Enemies*.
Played Hassan in the season two **Ghost Squad** episode *Quarantine at Kavar* and Dr. Diaz in *The Magic Bullet*.
Played Stefano in the first series **Man of the World** episode *The Sentimental Agent* and Luis in the second season's *Jungle Mission*.
Played the first guard in the **Virgin of the Secret Service** episode *The Great Ring of Akba*.

Evans Barbara
Played Nadia in the first series **Ghost Squad** episode *Princess* [this episode was shot for the first series, but due to an actors' strike, was originally shown as a season two episode].

Evans Clifford
Played Denzo in the first series **Man of the World** episode *Masquerade in Spain*.
Played Baron Drovotkin in **The Adventurer** episode *Thrust and Counter Thrust*.
Played Franz/Colonel Reitz in **The Champions** episode *The Survivors*.
Featured in the **Espionage** episode *To the Very End*.
Played Cordober in the **Jason King** episode *A Kiss for a Beautiful Killer* and Arthur Tsumg in *Every Picture Tells a Story*.
Played No.2 in **The Prisoner** episode *Do Not Forsake Me Oh My Darling*.
Played Sir Oliver Norenton in the **Randall and Hopkirk [Deceased]** aka **My Partner the Ghost** episode *When Did you Start to Stop Seeing Things?*.
Played Keith Longman in the fourth season **The Saint** episode *The Man Who Gambled with Life*.
Appeared as Grunig in the **White Hunter** episode *Operation Transfer* and as Mason in *The No-Account*.

Evans Dawn
Wardrobe on *Adventure 1* of **Sapphire and Steel**.

Evans Edward
Played Inspector Cole in the **Father Brown** episode *The Oracle of the Dog*.
Played the barber in **The Four Just Men** episode *The Man in the Royal Suite* and the priest in *Justice For Gino*.
Played Fred Norton in the **Gideon's Way** episode *The Rhyme and the Reason*.
Played Frederick in the **Man in a Suitcase** episode *Web with Four Spiders*.
Played Fillipo Ravenna in the first season **The Saint** episode *The Loaded Tourist* and the bank manager in the fourth season's *Vendetta for the Saint* [part 1].
Played Hoffman in the **William Tell** episode *The Ensign*.

Evans Eynon
Played Deacon in **The Buccaneers** [aka **Dan Tempest**] episode *Slave Ship* and played the schoolmaster in the second series **Danger Man** [aka **Secret Agent**] episode *Whatever Happened to George Foster?*.

Evans Jim
Make-up on the **Man in a Suitcase** series.

Evans Murray
Played Van Ruys in the **Man in a Suitcase** episode *Dead Man's Shoes*.

Evans Nicholas
Played the reporter in **The Adventurer** episode *The Not-So-Merry Widow* and Arnold Aylmer in the **Father Brown** episode *The Dagger With Wings*.

Evans Roy
Played Dillon in the **Return of the Saint** episode *The Nightmare Man*.

Evans Rupert
Master-at-Arms [crew] on **The Buccaneers** [aka **Dan Tempest**] episodes: *Ghost Ship* [and played Martin], *Conquest of New Providence*, *Mother Doughty's Crew*, *Blood Will Tell*, *Hurricane*, *Dead Man's Rock*, *Dangerous Cargo* [and played the Merchant Mate], *Gentleman Jack and the Lady* [and played the Spanish gunner], *The Return of Calico Jack*, *Conquistador*, *Aztec Treasure*, *Prize of Andalusia*, *Cutlass Wedding*, *Dan Tempest Holds an Auction*, *Flip and Jenny*, *To the Rescue*, *Indian Fighters*, *Mistress Higgins' Treasure*, *The Decoy*, *Pirate Honour*, *Instrument of War* and *Printer's Devil*. Also appeared as the sailor in *Articles of War*, the look-out in *Dan Tempest and The Amazons*, a Marine in *Mr. Beamish and the Hangman's Noose*, a sentry in *Marooned*, a man shaving in *The Ladies* and Jack in *The Surgeon of Sangre Rojo*.

Evans Tenniel
Played James Howe in the **Randall and Hopkirk [Deceased]** aka **My Partner the Ghost** episode *Who Killed Cock Robin*.
Played Todd in the third season **The Saint** episode *The Persistent Patriots*.

Evans Winifred
Played Mrs. Harvey in the **Department S** episode *The Duplicated Man*.

Eve Michael
Designer on **Father Brown** and **Timeslip**.

Everhart Rex
Played Packard in the **Man in a Suitcase** episode *The Boston Square*.

Everyman Films Limited
Patrick McGoohan's production company, named after the 15th Century book *Every Man*, set up by McGoohan and David Tomblin in 1960. Was wound up by the Inland Revenue in 1975.
Produced **The Prisoner**.

Eves Grenville
Played the Superintendent in the season two **Ghost Squad** episode *The Man With the Delicate Hands*.

Ewen Gwenda
Played Miss Wilson in the first season **The Saint** episode *The Gentle Ladies*.

Exposite Peter
Played Lucito in the first season **The Saint** episode *Teresa*.

Eyre Charmian
Played Maria in the **Sword of Freedom** episode *The Lion and the Mouse*.

Eytle Tommy
Played the Calypso singer in the third season **The Saint** episodes *Island of Chance* and in the third season **Danger Man** [aka **Secret Agent**] episode *The Man on the Beach*.

****

Fabian John
Played Ferdinand in **The Count of Monte Cristo** episode *Mecklenburg*.
Played Jamie in the **White Hunter** episode *Decision*.

Fabiani Joel
Starred throughout **Department S** as Stewart Sullivan.

Fagan Don
Instrumentation on UFO.

Fairbairn Ian
Played Alpha 4 in the **Timeslip** story *The Year of the Burn-Up* [series episodes 14-18] and Dr Frazer in *The Day of the Clone* [series episodes 21 - 26].

Fairbank Chris
Played Johnny Jack in *Adventure Six* of **Sapphire and Steel** [part 3].

Fairchild William
Wrote **The Four Just Men** episodes *The Crying Jester, Mava, The Godfather* [story with Wilton Schiller: teleplayed by Schiller] and *The Rietti Group*. Directed *The Crying Jester, The Night of the Precious Stones, Mava, The Rietti Group & The Man in the Royal Suite*.
Wrote the story for the **Return of the Saint** episode *The Roman Touch* [teleplayed by John Goldsmith].
Wrote **The Zoo Gang** episode *The Twisted Cross*.

Fairfax Diana
Played Lady Margaret in **The Adventures of Sir Lancelot** episode *Double Identity*.
Played Suzanne in **The Count of Monte Cristo** episode *The Experiment*.

Fairlie Jean
Wardrobe Supervisor on UFO.

Fairley Peter
Introduced the first episodes of the **Timeslip** stories *The Wrong End of Time & The Time of the Ice Box*.

Faith Gordon
Played Doctor Comitas in the **Strange Report** episode *Report 4407: HEART: 'No Choice for the Donor'*.

Falana Jimmy
Played the attendant in the second series **Danger Man** [aka **Secret Agent**] episode *The Galloping Major*.

Falconer Alan
Wrote the **Gideon's Way** episodes *The 'V' Men, Big Fish, Little Fish, The Great Plane Robbery, A Perfect Crime & Morna*.

Fallander Deborah
Played Carolyn Powell in the second season **Space 1999** episode *The Lambda Factor*.

Fallon Terence
Played the driver in the first series **Man of the World** episode *Shadow of the Wall*.

Fanning Rio
Played Mike Kelly in **The Adventurer** episode *Has Anyone Here Seen Kelly?*.
Played the lighthouse keeper in **The Champions** episode *The Silent Enemy* and as the telegraphist in *Twelve Hours*.
Played Smith in the season two **Ghost Squad** episode *The Missing People*.

Fantoni Barry
Played Joey Benjamin in the **Strange Report** episode *Report 1021: SHRAPNEL: 'The Wish in the Dream'*.

Fares Gamel
Played Captain Omar in the **Interpol Calling** episode *Dead On Arrival*.

Farhi Moris
Wrote the **Man in a Suitcase** episode *The Whisper*.
Wrote the unused **The Prisoner** episode script *The Outsider*.
Wrote the **Return of the Saint** episodes *The Judas Game, Assault Force & The Murder Cartel* [story with John Kruse: teleplayed by John Goldsmith].
Wrote the **Strange Report** episode *Report 5055: CULT: 'Murder Shrieks Out'*.

Farley Frederick
Played Solomin in the third season **Danger Man** [aka **Secret Agent**] episode *To our Best Friend*.
Played the doctor in the season two **Ghost Squad** episode *Hot Money*.

Farmer Glen
Played Lieutenant Gorschen in **The Scarlet Pimpernel** episode *Thanksgiving Day*.

Farmer Suzan
Played Helen in the second series **Danger Man** [aka **Secret Agent**] episode *No Marks for Servility*.
Played Ada Lee in the **Gideon's Way** episode *Big Fish, Little Fish*.
Played Judy in the **Man in a Suitcase** episode *Brainwash*.
Played Ann Summers in **The Persuaders!** episode *That's Me Over There*.
Played Sue Inverest in the first season **The Saint** episode *The Latin Touch*, Jean Morland in the second season's *The Sign of the Claw*, Anne Clanraith in the third's *The Convenient Monster* and Sara Douglas in the fourth's *The Desperate Diplomat*.
Played Tina Duval in the **UFO** episode *Survival*.

Farnon Robert
Composed & directed music on **The Champions**.

Farquhar Malcolm
Played the film director in **The Baron** episode *Countdown*.

Farr Derek
Played John Clarron in the first season **The Saint** episode *The Talented Husband*.

Farrell Charles
Played the Warden in the second series of **The Adventures of Robin Hood** episode *The Bandit of Brittany*.
Played Cadeaux in **The Count of Monte Cristo** episode *Burgundy*.
Played Anders in the first season **Danger Man** episode *The Sanctuary* and Krug in *The Girl who Liked GIs*.
Played the foreman in the season two **Ghost Squad** episode *The Golden Silence*.
Played Taylor in the **H. G. Wells' Invisible Man** episode *Jailbreak*.
Played Elmer Quire in the second season **The Saint** episode *The Unkind Philanthropist*.
Played Isigonnis in **The Sentimental Agent** episode *A Little Sweetness and Light*.
Appeared as Amos Briggs in the **White Hunter** episode *Rogue Man*.

Farrell Paul
Played Rooney in the season two **Ghost Squad** episode *The Big Time*.

Farrington Kenneth
Played Ashford in the fourth season **The Saint** episode *Legacy for the Saint*.

Fashion Group of London
Members of the Group created clothes for **Danger Man** and **Man of the World**.

Fass George
Wrote the season three **The Adventures of Robin Hood** episode *One Man's Meat* [with Gertrude Fass].

Fass Gertrude
Co-wrote, with George Fass, the third series **The Adventures of Robin Hood** episode *One Man's Meat*.

Faulds Andrew
Played Davy in the season two **The Adventures of Robin Hood** episode *Highland Fling*.
Played Saveau in **The Count of Monte Cristo** episode *The Art of Terror* and Freidrich in *The Mazzini Affair*.
Played Gen. Khan in the first season **Danger Man** episode *The Nurse* and Mullins in the third season's *Not So Jolly Roger*.
Played Count Toledo in the **Sir Francis Drake** episode *The Reluctant Duchess*.

Faulkner Max
Appeared in **The Adventures of Robin Hood**: as the old Martin in *The Path of True Love* [aka *Locksley Hall*] & the Sheriff's Lieutenant in *Carlotta* [series 2]; the first Lord in *The Salt King*, a guard in *The Charter*, a Lieutenant in *The Double* & the clerk in *Lincoln Green* [3] and the clerk in *Race Against Time* [4].
Played the peasant in **The Adventures of Sir Lancelot** episode *The Bridge*.
Played a guard in **The Buccaneers** [aka **Dan Tempest**] episode *Dan Tempest Holds an Auction* and the servant in *Indian Fighters*.
Played Bob in **The Four Just Men** episode *The Beatniques* and a guard in *Riot*.
Played the house servant in the second season **Man of the World** episode *In the Picture*.
Played the crewman in the **O.S.S.** episode *Operation Yodel* and the Nazi officer in *Operation Chopping Block*.
Appeared as the first horseman in **The Prisoner** episode *Living in Harmony* and as the Scots Napoleon/Marshall in *The Girl who was Death*.
Played Jarman in the second season **The Protectors** episode *The Tiger and the Goat*.
Played a nurse in the **Randall and Hopkirk [Deceased]** aka **My Partner the Ghost** episode *A Disturbing Case*.
Played the desk clerk in the first season **The Saint** episode *The Ever-loving Spouse*.
Played Ted Clifford in the first season **Space 1999** episode *Ring Around the Moon*.
Appeared as the wireless operator in the **White Hunter** episode *Out of the Wind*.
Played the Air Controller in the **White Hunter** episode *Valley of the Dead*.

Faulkner Trader
Played Guy de Seiberd in **The Four Just Men** episode *The Grandmother*.

Faure Michel
Played Durand in the **Department S** episode *The Mysterious Man in the Flying Machine*.

Fawcett William
Starred as Pete in the **Fury** series.

Feely Terence
Wrote **The Persuaders!** episode *Greensleeves*.
Wrote **The Prisoner** episode *The Schizoid Man* and *The Girl who was Death* [from an idea by David Tomblin].
Wrote the first season **The Protectors** episode *2,000ft to Die*.
Wrote the **Return of the Saint** episodes *Duel in Venice*, *The Armageddon Alternative* & *The Imprudent Professor*.
Wrote the second series **Space 1999** episodes *New Adam, New Eve* & *The Bringers of Wonder* [2 parter].
Wrote the **UFO** episodes *The Man who Came Back* & *Timelash*.

Feller Catherine
Played Gina in the first series **Ghost Squad** episode *Bullet With My Name on it* and Michele in the third season **The Saint** episode *The Queen's Ransom*.

Felton Felix
Played Demaris in the **G.S.5** episode *Pay Up or Else*.
Played Aylmer in the **H. G. Wells' Invisible Man** episode *Man in Disguise*.

Felton Norman
Executive Producer on the **Strange Report** series.

Fennell Alan
Wrote the **Fireball XL5** episodes *Hypnotic Sphere*, *Planet of Platonia*, *The Doomed Planet*, *XL5 to H₂O*, *Spies in Space*, *Convict in Space*, *Wings of Danger*, *The Triads*, *Flight to Danger*, *The Granatoid Tanks*, *The Robot Freighter Mystery*, *The Day the Earth Froze*, *Ghosts of Space*, *A Day in the Life of a Space General*, *Trial by Robot* and *The Fire Fighters*.
Wrote the **Stingray** episodes *Plant of Doom*, *Hostages of the Deep*, *The Big Gun*, *The Ghost Ship*, *Ghost of the Sea*, *Emergency Marineville*, *Subterranean Sea*, *Secret of the Giant Oyster*, *Raptures of the Deep*, *The Disappearing Ships*, *Man from the Navy*, *Marineville Traitor*, *Tom Thumb Tempest*, *Pink Ice*, *The Master Plan*, *Star of the East*, *Invisible Enemy*, *Deep Heat*, *Titan goes Pop*, *Tune of Danger*, *The Cool Caveman*, *Trapped in the Depths*, *Eastern Eclipse* and *The Lighthouse Dwellers*.
Wrote the first season **Thunderbirds** episodes *Pit of Peril*, *Terror in New York City*, *30 Minutes after Noon*, *The Uninvited*, *Sun Probe*, *City of Fire*, *The Man from MI5*, *Brink of Disaster* & *Martian Invasion* and *Atlantic Inferno* [season two]
Wrote the **UFO** episodes *E.S.P.* & *Sub-smash*.

Fennell Barry
Appeared as Simon in the second series of **The Adventures of Robin Hood** episode *The Final Tax*.
Appeared as Richard in **The Adventures of Sir Lancelot** episode *Maid of Somerset*.
Played the boy in **The Buccaneers** [aka **Dan Tempest**] episode *Mistress Higgins' Treasure*.

Fennell Concepta
Played Brigid in the season two **The Adventures of Robin Hood** episode *The Mystery of Ireland's Eye*.
Played Cathy O'Shaughnessy in **The Four Just Men** episode *The Heritage*.
Played Ipolita in the **Sword of Freedom** episode *Marriage of Convenience*.

Fennell Eithne
Hairdresser on **The Adventurer**.

Fennessy Jill
Assistant accountant on **The Prisoner**.

Ferdorqui Productions
Production company on **The Protectors** series.

Ference Ilona
Played Mrs Drewitt in **The Buccaneers** [aka **Dan Tempest**] episode *Pirate Honour*.

Played Anna in the season two **Ghost Squad** episode *The Retirement of Gentle Dove.*

Ferguson Perry
Art Director on **The Count of Monte Cristo**.

Ferman James
Directed the season two **Ghost Squad** episodes *Death of a Sportsman* & *The Magic Bullet.*

Ferrand Michael
Played the radar technician in the **UFO** episode *Destruction.*

Ferraz Catharina
Played Romano in **The Four Just Men** episode *The Bystanders.*

Ferrer Mel
Played Doctor Brogli in the **Return of the Saint** episode *Vicious Circle.*

Ferris Fred
Played Sergeant Lashbrook in the first season **The Saint** episode *The Fellow Traveller.*

Ferris Paul
Starred as, series regular, David Marlowe in **The Baron**: *Diplomatic Immunity, Red Horse, Red Rider, The Persuaders, Epitath for a Hero, The Legions of Ammak, Samurai West, Portrait of Louisa* & *Farewell to Yesterday.*

Fiander Lewis
Played Lanz in the **Jason King** episode *Buried in the Cold, Cold Ground.*

Field Margot
Played Miss Howe in the **Jason King** episode *It's Too Bad about Auntie.*

Fielding Fenella
Played the hostess in the first season **Danger Man** episode *An Affair of State.*
Played the Contessa in **The Four Just Men** episode *Treviso Dam.*
Provided the Village Tanoy voice in **The Prisoner** episode *Arrival.*

Fiermonte Enzo
Played Guido in the **Return of the Saint** episode *Duel in Venice.*

Files Gary
Provided the voice for Captain Magenta on **Captain Scarlet and the Mysterons**.
Provided voices for **The Secret Service**.
Played Phil Wade in the **UFO** episode *Identified.*

Finch Scott
Played Vesper in the first series **Man of the World** episode *Shadow of the Wall.*
Played Toby Haildon in the second season **The Saint** episode *The Death Penalty* and Stefan in the **William Tell** episode *The General's Daughter* & Peter in *Manhunt.*

Fincham Leonard
Wrote the **H. G. Wells' Invisible Man** episode *Picnic with Death* [co-teleplayed with Leslie Arliss: from his story].
Writer on **Interpol Calling**: wrote the story for *You Can't Die Twice* [teleplayed by Barbara Hammer], wrote the story for *The Thousand Mile Alibi* [teleplayed by John Kruse], wrote *Air Switch* [with Gil Winfield], wrote *Diamond S.O.S.* [with Tony O'Grady aka Brian Clemens], wrote the story for *Dead On Arrival* [teleplayed by Max Marquis and Philip Chambers], wrote *The Girl with Grey Hair* [with Michael Hankinson and Robert Stewart], teleplayed *The Heiress* [with Max Marquis: from a story by Philip Chambers] and wrote *Cargo of Death* [with Michael Connor].
Wrote the **White Hunter** episodes *Dead Man's Tale* and *Girl Hunt.*

Fine Harold 'Harry'
Casting Director on the first series of **Danger Man** and on **William Tell**.
Produced the series **Man of the World**.
Producer on **The Sentimental Agent** series and directed the episode *Finishing School.*
Associate Producer on **Sir Francis Drake**.

Fine Harry
Played the second security officer in the **White Hunter** episode *Pegasus.*

Finn Catherine
Played Martha in the season three **The Adventures of Robin Hood** episode *The Profiteer* and Catherine in *Farewell to Tuck.*
Played the Governor 's wife in the **Sir Francis Drake** episode *The Slaves of Spain.*
Played Frau Muller in the **William Tell** episode *Gessler's Daughter* and Margit in *The Mountain People.*

Finn Christine
Played Majorie Bennett in the **Gideon's Way** episode *The 'V' Men.*
Voiced Tin Tin / Grandma in **The Thunderbirds** series.

Fioretti Dante
Played Padrone in the **Return of the Saint** episode *Vicious Circle.*

Firbank Ann
Played Mary Quartermaine in the season three **The Adventures of Robin Hood** episode *An Apple for the Archer.*
Played Bobby in the first season **Danger Man** episode *The Island.*
Played Varda in the second season **Space 1999** episode *The Dorcans.*
Played Miss Collingford in the **Strange Report** episode *Report 4821: X-RAY: 'Who Weeps For the Doctor?'.*

Firth Anne
Played Stella in the season three **The Adventures of Robin Hood** episode *The Christmas Goose* and the mother in the fourth season's *The Loaf.*

Firth David
Played the photographer in the **Jason King** episode *It's Too Bad about Auntie.*

Firth Peter
Played Stephen Douglas in the second season **The Protectors** episode *Implicado.*

Fisher Doug
Played Merrick in **The Adventurer** episode *Make it a Million.*
Played Tom Watt in the second season **The Protectors** episode *The Tiger and the Goat.*

Fisher George
Played Kramer in **The Persuaders!** episode *Element of Risk.*

Fisher Hannah
aka/see Hannah **Weinstein**
Season four of **The Adventures of Robin Hood** was credited as 'A Hannah Fisher Production for Sapphire Films, for the Incorporated Television Programme Co.': Season one & two

was as 'A Sapphire Films Production for the Incorporated Television Programme Co.' - Hannah Weinstein, Executive Producer, and season three as 'A Weinstein Production for Sapphire Films, for the Incorporated Television Programme Co.'

The Four Just Men was 'A Hannah Fisher Production for Sapphire Films Ltd., for Associated TeleVision: an ITC Presentation'.

Fisher Terence
Directed the debut season of **The Adventures of Robin Hood** episodes *Trial by Battle, The Byzantine Treasure, The Traitor & The Thorkill Ghost* and the second season's *Ransom, The Hero, Hubert, The Dream, The Blackbird, The Path of True Love* [aka *Locksley Hall*] & *The Infidel*.
Directed the **Sword of Freedom** episodes *The Tower* and *The Bell*.

Fitz Paddy
Pseudonym of/see Patrick **McGoohan**. Wrote **The Prisoner** episode *Free for All*.

Fitzgerald Nigel
Played Peterson in the **White Hunter** episode *Marked Man*.

Fitzgerald Walter
Played Professor Owens in the **H. G. Wells' Invisible Man** episode *Odds Against Death*.

Fitzgibbon Maggie
Played Peta in the first season **Danger Man** episode *Sabotage*.

Fitzroy Katie
Played the girl in the **Man in a Suitcase** episode *Web with Four Spiders*.

Flanagan John
Played Patrick Royce in the **Father Brown** episode *Three Tools of Death*.

Flannery Seamus
Art Director on the second season of **Danger Man** [aka **Secret Agent**].

Fleetwood Susan
Played Miss Bronson in the **Department S** episode *The Ghost of Mary Burnham*.

Fleming Ian
Played Louis Martell in **The Count of Monte Cristo** episode *The Devil's Emissary*.
Played Sir Charles Thorne in the season two **Ghost Squad** episode *East of Mandalay*.
Played the man at the cafe and the first Top Hat in **The Prisoner** episode *The General*.

Flemyng Gordon
Directed **The Baron** episodes *Storm Warning* [two parter: *Storm Warning* - part 1 and *The Island* - part 2: also exists as a feature entitled *Mystery Island*].
Directed the third season **The Saint** episode *The Better Mousetrap*.

Flemyng Robert
Played Logan in the first season **Danger Man** episode *The Key*.
Played O'Connor in the first series **Man of the World** episode *The Nature of Justice*.
Played Sir George in **The Persuaders!** episode *The Time and the Place*.

Fletcher Gerry
Make up Supervisor on **The Champions & Department S** and Make-up on **The Persuaders!**

Fletcher Hugh
Played Jean in the **Jason King** episode *That isn't Me, It's Somebody Else*.

Fletcher Wilfred
Played the tramp in **The Four Just Men** episode *The Boy Without a Country*.

Flintoff Ian
Played Nikita in the second series **Danger Man** [aka **Secret Agent**] episode *That's Two of Us Sorry*.

Flood Gerald
Played Sir Dennis Salt in the **Man in a Suitcase** episode *Castle in the Clouds*.
Played Duchamp in the first series **Man of the World** episode *Death of a Conference*.
Played Dr. Lambert in the **Randall and Hopkirk [Deceased]** aka **My Partner the Ghost** episode *A Disturbing Case*.
Played Cleaver in the **Return of the Saint** episode *Yesterday's Hero*.
Played Paul Webber in the **Strange Report** episode *Report 1021: SHRAPNEL: 'The Wish in the Dream'*.

Flood Kevin
Played Sergeant Finnegan in the third season **The Saint** episode *Little Girl Lost*.

Florence Norman
Guested as Cabello in **The Champions** episode *The Iron Man* and as the Police Captain in *Get Me Out of Here!*.
Played the attendant in the first season **Danger Man** episode *Under the Lake*.
Played Ricky Cirrano in the first series **Man of the World** episode *Blaze of Glory*.
Played Carlo Visconti in the first season **The Saint** episode *The Loaded Tourist*, Clem Enright in the second season's *The Set-Up* and Morales in the third's *The Reluctant Revolution*.

Florenz Nyall
Played Edouardo in the **Danger Man** episode *Hired Assassin*.

Flothow Rudolph
Production Supervisor on **The Count of Monte Cristo**.
Producer on **The New Adventures of Charlie Chan**.

Foddard Fred
Played the policeman in the **White Hunter** episode *Voodoo Wedding*.

Foley John
Camera Operator [Special Effects Second Unit] on **Thunderbirds**.

Fontaine Peter
Played the secretary in **The Count of Monte Cristo** episode *Mecklenburg*.
Played the bartender in the first series **The Protectors** episode *It Could be Practically Anywhere on the Island*.
Played the hotel clerk in the first season **The Saint** episode *Luella*.

Fontana Alvaro
Played the customs officer in the second series **Danger Man** [aka **Secret Agent**] episode *A Man to be Trusted* and the police officer in *A Date with Doris*.
Played Julio in the second season **The Saint** episode *The Golden Frog*.

Foot Geoffrey, G.B.F.E.
Editor on **The Prisoner** episodes *A. B. and C., Free for All, The Schizoid Man* and *Many Happy Returns*.

Forbes C. Scott
Wrote the third series **The Saint** episode *Simon and Delilah*.

Forbes David
Played the police constable in the **Randall and Hopkirk [Deceased] aka My Partner the Ghost** episode *The Smile Behind the Veil*.

Forbes-Robertson John
Played Stretfield in the **Jason King** episode *A Deadly Line in Digits*.
Played Philip Grey in the second season **The Saint** episode *The Crime of the Century*.

Forbes-Robertson Peter
Played Yeldham in **The Baron** episode *There's Someone Close Behind You*.
Played Tanfield in the **Jason King** episode *A Deadly Line in Digits*.
Played Inspector Langford in **The Persuaders!** episode *Anyone Can Play*.
Played Sergeant Stevens in the first season **The Saint** episode *The Man who was Lucky* and Claude in the third season's *The Queen's Ransome*.

Ford Derek
Wrote the third season **The Saint** episode *A Double in Diamonds* [with Harry W. Junkin & Donald Ford].

Ford Donald
Wrote the third season **The Saint** episode *A Double in Diamonds* [with Harry W. Junkin & Derek Ford].

Ford Karen
Played the French girl in the third season **The Saint** episode *The Death Game*.

Ford Michael
Assistant Art Director on **The Protectors**.

Ford Ray
Played the first Hazarnao in the **Virgin of the Secret Service** episode *Dark Deeds on the Northwest Frontier* and Judd in *The Professor Goes West*.

Ford Robin
Played the messenger in the **Jason King** episode *A Deadly Line in Digits*.

Ford-Davies Oliver
Played Corliss in the **Father Brown** episode *The Eye of Apollo*.
Played Hansen in **The Protectors** episode *Bagman*.

Fordyce Ian
Producer on the **Father Brown** series and directed the episode *The Quick One*.

Forgeham John
Played Simeon Barnes in the **Father Brown** episode *The Hammer of God*.

Forgione Carl
Played the waiter in **The Protectors** episode *Implicado*.

Forrest Helen
Played Joan in the first series of **The Adventures of Robin Hood** episodes *Table's Turned* & *The Traitor*. Returned to the series, as Helen, in the second season's *The Trap*.

Forrest John
Played Edgar in the fourth series **The Adventures of Robin Hood** episode *The Pharaoh Stones*.

Forrest Michael
Played Dino in **The Adventurer** episode *Has Anyone Here Seen Kelly?*.
Played Gautler in **The Baron** episode *Long Ago and Far Away*.
Played Abelardo in the third season **Danger Man [aka Secret Agent]** episode *The Man with the Foot*.
Played the manager of the nightclub in the season two **Ghost Squad** episode *The Heir Apparent*.
Played Verrier in the **Randall and Hopkirk [Deceased] aka My Partner the Ghost** episode *The Ghost who Saved the Bank at Monte Carlo*.
Played Roberto in the **Return of the Saint** episode *Vicious Circle*.
Played Vittorio Leale in the third season **The Saint** episode *The Man Who Liked Lions*.
Played Marlow in **The Sentimental Agent** episode *Finishing School*.
Played Jan in the **Sir Francis Drake** episode *Beggars of the Sea*.
Played Inspector Peters in the **Strange Report** episode *Report 4977: SWINDLE: 'Square Root of Evil'*.
Played the security officer in the **UFO** episode *Confetti Check A-O.K.*.

Forrest Steve
Starred as John Mannering, aka The Baron, in the series **The Baron**.

Forrester Larry
Wrote the **G.S.5** episode *A Cast of Thousands*.
Wrote the **Interpol Calling** episodes *The Angola Brights*, *The Sleeping Giant*, *Payment in Advance*, *Trial at Cranby's Creek*, *Pipeline*, *Ascent to Murder* & *The Absent Assassin*.
Wrote the first season **The Saint** episodes *The Romantic Matron* & *The Benevolent Burglary*.
Wrote the **Sir Francis Drake** episode *Lost Colony of Virginia*.
Wrote the original story for the **William Tell** episode *The Suspect* [teleplayed by Doreen Montgomery].

Forsyth Frank
Played Norman Fowler in the **Department S** episode *A Cellar full of Silence* and Sawyer in *Last Train to Redbridge*.
Played the lorry driver in the **Man in a Suitcase** episode *Essay in Evil*, the commissionaire in *Web with Four Spiders* and the steward in *Which Way did he Go, McGill?*.

Fortell Bert
Played the manager in the second season **The Protectors** episode *Wam* [part one].

Fortune Kim
Played Robbie in the **Return of the Saint** episode *The Poppy Chain*.

Foss Roger
Played Mick in the **Gideon's Way** episode *Boy with a Gun*.

Foster Barry
Featured in the **Espionage** episode *The Gentle Spies*.
Played Tom Brewster in the **Sir Francis Drake** episode *Lost Colony of Virginia*.

Foster David 'Dave'
Directed *Adventure Two* of **Sapphire and Steel** [with Shaun O'Riordan], *Adventure Four* and *Six*.
Directed episodes 21-24 of the **Timeslip** story *The Day of the Clone* [Ron Francis directed 25 & 26].

Foster Dudley
Played Giorgio in the first season **Danger Man** episode *The Contessa*.

Played Luigi in **The Four Just Men** episode *The Crying Jester*.

Played Vic Diamond in the first series **Ghost Squad** episode *Eyes of the Bat*.

Played Ackroyd in the **Jason King** episode *An Author in Search of Two Characters*.

Played Heather in **The Persuaders!** episode *Anyone Can Play*.

Played George Foster in the **Randall and Hopkirk [Deceased]** aka **My Partner the Ghost** episode *All Work and No Pay*.

Played Jones in the second season **The Saint** episode *The Abductors*.

Foster James
Wrote the second season **Danger Man [aka Secret Agent]** episode *The Affair at Castelevara*.

Foster Marianne
Co-wrote **The Four Just Men** episode *Panic Button* [with Samuel B. West].

Foster Maxwell
Played Sir Kenneth Ingram in the season two **Ghost Squad** episode *The Retirement of Gentle Dove*.

Foster Norma
Played Angela in the **Man in a Suitcase** episode *Find the Lady*.

Foster Norman
Production Manager on **The Protectors** and Production Supervisor on **UFO**.

Foster Norman
Featured in the **Espionage** episode *A Free Agent*.

Foulger Sally
Played a passenger in the **Father Brown** episode *The Curse of the Golden Cross*.

Foulkes Thomas
Played Otto Weiner in the **O.S.S.** episode *Operation Tulip*.

Foulsham Fraser
Production Manager on **The Scarlet Pimpernel**.

Fowlds Derek
Played Tim Coles in the **Gideon's Way** episode *The Nightlifers*.

Fowler Bruce Jnr.
Assistant Director on **The Count of Monte Cristo**.

Fowler Harry
Played Ralph Maricut in the **Gideon's Way** episode *The Housekeeper*.

Appeared as Tim Wallington in the **White Hunter** episode *Run to Earth*.

Fox Edward
Played Ezard in the **Man in a Suitcase** episode *Castle in the Clouds*.

Fox Franklyn
Played Mike in the **O.S.S.** episode *Operation Yo Yo*, Karl Wagner in *Operation Blackbird* and Patsy in *Operation Meatball*.

Fox Harry
Designed the clothes for Anneke Wills on **Strange Report**.

Fox Hilda
Hairdresser on **Department S** and Hairdressing Supervisor on **Gideon's Way**.

Fox James
Featured in the **Espionage** episode *To the Very End*.

Fox M. Bernard
Producer on the **Whiplash** series.

Fox Marcia
Played the female clerk in the **Jason King** episode *Flamingos only Fly on Tuesdays*.

Fox Sonia
Played the airport clerk in the second series **Danger Man [aka Secret Agent]** episode *Whatever Happened to George Foster?* and Maite in *The Affair at Castelevara*.

Played Chantal in the **Man in a Suitcase** episode *The Revolutionaries*.

Played Nadine in the second season **The Saint** episode *The Persistent Parasite*.

Played Caroline in **The Sentimental Agent** episode *Finishing School*.

Played Carol Roper in the **UFO** episode *Flight Path*.

Fox-Roberts Ronnie
Second Unit camera operator on **The Prisoner**.

Frame Grazina
Played Gloria Marsh in the **Randall and Hopkirk [Deceased]** aka **My Partner the Ghost** episode *That's How Murder Snowballs*.

Played Bess Pierpoint in the **Sir Francis Drake** episode *Mary, Queen of Scots*.

France Dawson
Played Piggott in **The Buccaneers [aka Dan Tempest]** episode *Blood Will Tell*.

France Gilbert
Played the croupier in the second series **Danger Man [aka Secret Agent]** episode *The Battle of the Cameras*.

France Marie
Played Cleo in the first series **Man of the World** episode *Masquerade in Spain*.

Francis Clive
Played Brandt in the **Strange Report** episode *Report 1553: RACIST: 'A Most Dangerous Proposal'*.

Francis Dean
Played the barman in the second series **Danger Man [aka Secret Agent]** episode *The Colonel's Daughter*.

Francis Derek
Played Fenton in the third season **Danger Man [aka Secret Agent]** episode *Dangerous Secret*.

Played Peter Brenner in the season two **Ghost Squad** episode *The Man With the Delicate Hands*.

Played Umberto Bellini in the **Jason King** episode *Wanna Buy a Television Series* aka *A Face I Used to Know*.

Played Doctor James Vance in the **Man in a Suitcase** episode *Property of a Gentleman*.

Played Klaus in **The Sentimental Agent** episode *The Beneficiary*.

Played Sir Matthew Hardcastle in the **Shirley's World** episode *The Colonel*.

Francis Eric
Played the clerk in the Licence Office in the **White Hunter** episode *Voodoo Wedding*.

Francis Freddie
Directed **The Champions** episode *Shadow of the Panther*.

Directed the **Man in a Suitcase** episodes *Essay in Evil, Which Way did he Go, McGill?, Who's Mad Now? & Night Flight to Andora*.

Directed the third season **The Saint** episode *The Gadic Collection* and the fourth's *The Man Who Gambled with Life*.

Francis Ron
Directed episodes 13-20 of the **Timeslip** story *The Year of the Burn-Up* [Peter Jefferies directed 14-19] and episodes 25 & 26 of *The Day of the Clone* [Dave Foster directed 21-24].

Francis Sandra
Played Maria in the **O.S.S.** episode *Operation Payday*.

Frank Astrid
Played Astrid in **The Adventurer** episode *Target!*.

Frankel Cyril
Creative Consultant on **The Adventurer** and directed the episodes *The Good Book, Poor Little Rich Girl, Return to Sender, Double Exposure, Miss Me Once, Miss Me Twice and Miss Me Once Again, Love Always, Magda, Nearly the End of the Picture, Skeleton in the Cupboard, Target!, The Not-So-Merry Widow, The Case of the Poisoned Pawn, Icons Are Forever & Somebody Doesn't Like Me*.

Directed **The Baron** episodes *Something for a Rainy Day, And Suddenly You're Dead* and *Masquerade* [two parter: *Masquerade* - part 1 and *The Killing* - part 2: edited together, also exists as a feature entitled *Man In a Looking Glass*].

Directed **The Champions** episodes *The Beginning, The Invisible Man, Reply Box No: 666, The Experiment, Happening, The Survivors, The Dark Island, The Gilded Cage, The Interrogation* and *Get Me Out of Here!*. [*The Beginning* & *The Interrogation* were also combined to form a 'feature' entitled *Legend of The Champions*].

Creative Consultant on the **Department S** series and directed *Six Days, The Man in the Elegant Room, The Man who got a New Face, Les Fleurs du Mal, A Ticket to Nowhere, The Perfect Operation, The Mysterious Man in the Flying Machine, The Ghost of Mary Burnham & A Fish out of Water*.

Directed the **Gideon's Way** episodes *The 'V' Men, Big Fish, Little Fish, The Alibi Man, The Thin Red Line, The Millionaire's Daughter & Morna*.

Creative Consultant on the **Jason King** series and directed the episodes *Variations on a Theme, A Red, Red Rose Forever, All that Glisters* [2 parter], *Uneasy Lies the Head, Nadine, A Kiss for a Beautiful Killer, If it's Got to Go - It's Got to Go, A Thin Band of Air, Every Picture Tells a Story, Chapter One: the Company I Keep & An Author in Search of Two Characters*.

Directed the first season **The Protectors** episodes *Thinkback & Vocal* and the second's *Petard & A Pocketful of Posies*.

Creative Consultant on **Randall and Hopkirk [Deceased]** aka **My Partner the Ghost** and directed the episodes *My Late Lamented Friend and Partner, For the Girl who has Everything, The Trouble with Women, Vendetta for a Dead Man, The Ghost Talks & Somebody just Walked over my Grave*.

Directed the **Return of the Saint** episodes *Collision Course* [2 parter: part 1:*The Brave Goose* and part 2: *The Sixth Man*: also exists as a feature entitled *The Saint and the Brave Goose*].

Directed the **UFO** episode *Timelash*.

Franklin Gretchen
Played Miss Wallace in the third season **Danger Man** [aka **Secret Agent**] episode *Say it with Flowers*.

Played Martha Bray in the **Gideon's Way** episode *The Reluctant Witness*.

Nelly Baxter in the second season **The Protectors** episode *A Pocketful of Posies*.

Franklin Pamela
Played Maggie in the **Strange Report** episode *Report 5055: CULT: 'Murder Shrieks Out'*.

Franklin Richard
Played duty guard 2 in the fourth season **The Saint** two parter *The Fiction Makers*.

Franklyn Leo
Played Innkeeper in **The Count of Monte Cristo** episode *Point Counter Point*.

Franklyn Sabina
Played Linda in the **Return of the Saint** episode *Signal Stop*.

Franklyn William
Appeared as Baron Mortaise in **The Adventures of Sir Lancelot** episode *The Mortaise Fair*.

Played Kent Jordan in **The Baron** episode *The Edge of Fear*.

Played Hartington in **The Champions** episode *The Gun-Runners*.

Played Phillipe in **The Count of Monte Cristo** episode *Burgundy* and Dubroc in *The Carbonari*.

Played Nevil in the **Interpol Calling** episode *Slow Boat to Amsterdam*.

Played Fleury in **The Scarlet Pimpernel** episodes *The Ambassador's Lady & Something Remembered*.

Franklyn-Robbins John
Played Dr Richard Thornton in **The Baron** episode *So Dark the Night*.

Guested as Warre in **The Champions** episode *Nutcracker*.

Franks David
Played Tony Romano in **The Four Just Men** episode *The Bystanders*.

Fraser Bill
Played Pietro in the **O.S.S.** episode *Operation Blue Eyes*.

Played Agnolo in the **Sword of Freedom** episode *The Pagan Venus*.

Fraser John
Played Rawson in the second series **Danger Man** [aka **Secret Agent**] episode *Don't Nail Him Yet*.

Played Hellingworth in the **Randall and Hopkirk [Deceased]** aka **My Partner the Ghost** episode *Who Ever Heard of a Ghost Dying?*.

Fraser Liz
Played Claire in the **Jason King** episode *An Author in Search of Two Characters*.

Played Fay Crackan in the **Randall and Hopkirk [Deceased]** aka **My Partner the Ghost** episode *It's Supposed to be Thicker than Water*.

Fraser Peter
Played Jeans in the season two **Ghost Squad** episode *The Missing People*.

Fraser Ronald
Played Guiseppe in the first season **Danger Man** episode *The Brothers*.

Played Sharp in the **H. G. Wells' Invisible Man** episode *Jailbreak*.

Played the Nazi guard in the **O.S.S.** episode *Operation Death Trap*.

Fraser Shelagh
Played Lady Copthorne in the **Gideon's Way** episode *Morna*.

Frawley John
Played the detective in the season two **Ghost Squad** episode *Escape Route*.

Played the flowerman in **The Prisoner** episode *Dance of the Dead*.

Played the doctor in the third season **The Saint** episode *When Spring is Sprung*.

Frederick Geoffrey
Played Major Rowney in the second season **The Saint** episode *The Sign of the Claw*.

Frederick Lynne
Played Shermeen in the second season **Space 1999** episode *A Matter of Balance*.

Frederics Scott
Played the medical student in the **Strange Report** episode *Report 7931: SNIPER: 'When is Your Cousin Not?'*.

Freeman Jeannette
Hairdresser on **Randall and Hopkirk [Deceased]** aka **My Partner the Ghost**.

Freeman Paul
Played the male revolutionary in the **Jason King** episode *Zenia*. Played the mechanic in the first series **The Protectors** episode *A Kind of Wild Justice*.

Frees Wolf
Guested as Neinmann in **The Champions** episode *The Final Countdown*.
Played General de Santos in **The Four Just Men** episode *Money To Burn*.
Played the Kommandant in the **O.S.S.** episode *Operation Chopping Block*.
Played Anton in the third season **The Saint** episode *The Gadget Lovers*.
Appeared as Carl Lindeman in the **White Hunter** episode *Forest of the Night*.

Freiberger Fred
Produced the second series of **Space 1999** and, using the pseudonym of Charles Woodgrove, wrote *The Rules of Luton, Space Warp* & *The Beta Cloud*.

French Gillian
Played Jennifer Lewis in the **Gideon's Way** episode *The Prowler*.

French Harold
Directed **The Sentimental Agent** episodes *A Little Sweetness and Light* & *Box of Tricks*.

French Hermene
Played Lorraine in **The Adventures of Sir Lancelot** episode *The Black Castle*.

French Leslie
Guested as Pimm in the **Interpol Calling** episode *Private View*.
Played Deshfield in the **Jason King** two parter *All that Glisters*.
Played Blyvus in the first series **Man of the World** episode *The Mindreader*.

French Valerie
Guest starred as Kathy in **The Prisoner** episode *Living in Harmony*.

Frend Charles
Directed the first season **Danger Man** episodes *The Blue Veil, The Sanctuary, The Lonely Chair, Name, Date and Place, The Honeymooners, The Brothers, Hired Assassin, Find and Destroy* & *Dead Man Walks*.
Directed the **Interpol Calling** episodes *The Long Weekend, Diamond S.O.S., The Man's Clown, The Girl with Grey Hair* and *Mr George*.

Directed the **Man in a Suitcase** episode *Jigsaw Man*.
Directed the first season **Man of the World** episodes *The Sentimental Agent, The Highland Story* & *Portrait of a Girl*.
Directed **The Sentimental Agent** episodes *All that Jazz, Express Delivery, May the Saints Preserve Us, The Height of Fashion* & *Not Quite Fully Covered*.

Frere Dorothy
Played Hunter's Landlady in the second season **The Saint** episode *The Chequered Flag*.

Friday Carol
Played Josette in the fourth season **The Saint** episode *The Ex-King of Diamonds*.

Friend Philip
Played Arthur Hold in the **H. G. Wells' Invisible Man** episode *Blind Justice*.

Frift Ray
Production Manager on **Department S** and Location Manager on **UFO**.

Fromkess Leon
Executive Producer on **The Count of Monte Cristo** and **The New Adventures of Charlie Chan**.

Fry Ron
Production Manager on **Space 1999**.

Fulford Josie
Continuity on **The Prisoner** episodes *Many Happy Returns* and *Hammer into Anvil*.

Fulsham Garry
Played Victor Gamma in the second season **The Saint** episode *The Unkind Philanthropist*.

Fung Jimmy
Played the receptionist in the first season **Danger Man** episode *The Honeymooners* and the taxi-driver in *Sabotage*.

Furia John Jnr.
Wrote the **Espionage** episodes *A Camel to Ride* & *The Liberators*.

Furlong Lynne
Appeared as Princess Kathleen in **The Adventures of Sir Lancelot** episode *The Prince of Limerick*.
Played Florrie in the **Father Brown** episode *The Mirror of the Magistrate*.

Furneaux Yvonne
Played Selina Travis in **The Baron** two parter *Masquerade* [*Masquerade* - part 1 and *The Killing* - part 2: edited together, also exists as a feature entitled *Man In a Looking Glass*].
Played Lisa Lee in the second series **Danger Man** [aka **Secret Agent**] episode *A Very Dangerous Game*.
Played Suzanne de Fleury in **The Scarlet Pimpernel** episode *The Hostage*.

Furse Judith
Played Miss Smyth Wilberforce in **The Sentimental Agent** episode *The Height of Fashion*.

Furst Joseph
Played Colonel Bucholz in **The Baron** episode *Enemy of the State*.
Played Chislenka in **The Champions** episode *The Beginning* [this episode was combined with *The Interrogation* to form a 'feature' entitled *Legend of The Champions*]. Also played Dr Mueller in *The Search*.

Featured in the **Espionage** episode *Medal For a Turned Coat.*

Played Koster in the first series **Ghost Squad** episode *Assassin.*

Played Wilhelm in the first series **Man of the World** episode *Shadow of the Wall.*

Played Yelker in **The Persuaders!** episode *The Ozerov Inheritance.*

Played Dr. Zellerman in the first season **The Saint** episode *The Saint Sees it Through*, Kane Luker *The Saint Plays with Fire* and Professor Karel Jorovitch in the third season's *The Russian Prisoner.*

Fusek Vera

Played Simone Laforque in **The Adventurer** episode *Love Always, Magda.*

Played Coralie Marlow in **The Four Just Men** episode *Rogue's Harvest.*

Futa Hazel

Played Maria in the first season **The Saint** episode *The Arrow of God.*

Futcher Hugh

Played the delivery boy in the first season **The Saint** episode *The Pearls of Peace.*

Played Mooney in **The Sentimental Agent** episode *All that Jazz.*

****

Gabriel John

Played Bolbec in the season three **The Adventures of Robin Hood** episode *The Double*.

Played Castle in **The Baron** episode *The Killing* [Part 2 of a 2 parter: also exists, edited together with part 1, *Masquerade*, to form a feature *Man In a Looking Glass*].

Played Pierre Deschamps in the second series **Danger Man** [aka **Secret Agent**] episode *The Mercenaries* and Rutledge in the third season's *To our Best Friend*.

Appeared as the Air Traffic Controller in the **Department S** episode *Six Days* and played George Grant in *One of our Aircraft is Empty*.

Played Cure in **The Four Just Men** episode *Village of Shame*, Legari in *The Discovery* and Leclerc in *The Miracle of St. Philippe*.

Played Cuthbertson in the **Gideon's Way** episode *To Catch a Tiger*.

Played Inspector Lamotte in the **Man in a Suitcase** episode *Three Blinks of the Eyes*.

Played the hotel clerk in the **O.S.S.** episode *Operation Orange Blossom* and Schuster in *Operation Chopping Block*.

Played Franklyn in the first season **The Saint** episode *The Invisible Millionaire* and Yesterman in the second season's *The Frightened Inn-Keeper*.

Played Bilbo in **The Sentimental Agent** episode *Box of Tricks*.

Played Vespucci in the **Sword of Freedom** episode *Vespucci*.

Gael Anna

Played Ingrid and Teresa Bonival in the **Jason King** episode *The Stones of Venice*.

Played Suzy in **The Persuaders!** episode *The Old, the New and the Deadly*.

Gaffney Liam

Played Captain Achard in the first season **Danger Man** episode *The Deputy Coyannis Story*.

Played Hogan in **The Sentimental Agent** episode *May the Saints Preserve Us*.

Played O'Neill in the **Sir Francis Drake** episode *The Irish Pirate*.

Gage Jack

Director on **The New Adventures of Charlie Chan**.

Gage Roger

Played Juan in **The Buccaneers** [aka **Dan Tempest**] episode *Conquistador*.

Gail Philippa

Played Patricia Baldwin in the **Man in a Suitcase** episode *No Friend of Mine*.

Gainsborough Louis

Played Elena in **The Count of Monte Cristo** episode *Athens*.

Galantucci Stefano

Played the steward in the **Return of the Saint** episode *Dragonseed*.

Gale John

Appeared in a variety of roles in **The Adventures of Sir Lancelot**: the torture master in *Winged Victory*, the first knight in *The Magic Sword*, the second guard in *Lancelot's Banishment*, Amadeus in *Roman Wall*, the farmer's son in *Caledon*, Sir Christopher in *Shepherd's War & Knight Errant*, the Captain in *The Pirates* and the peasant in *The Black Castle*.

Gale Pamela

Played Maisie in the season two **Ghost Squad** episode *Polsky*.

Gale Richard

Played Ember in the **Interpol Calling** episode *Act of Piracy*.

Galih Gail

Played the stewardess in **The Adventurer** episode *Make it a Million*.

Galili Hal

Played Masiol in the **Department S** episode *The Mysterious Man in the Flying Machine*.

Played the first oilman in the **Jason King** episode *That isn't Me, It's Somebody Else*.

Played the bartender in the first season **The Saint** episode *The Ever-loving Spouse*, Joe Martin in *Sophia*, Vincente in the second season's *The Revolution* Racket, Tchi in the third's *Interlude in Venice* and the bus driver in the fourth's *Vendetta for the Saint* [part 2].

Gallagher Michael

Played Etrec in the second season **Space 1999** episode *The Mark of Archanon*.

Gallagher Sheila

Played Sue Pearson in **The Four Just Men** episode *Panic Button*.

Gallagher Thomas

Played Herr Mielke in the second series of **The Adventures of Robin Hood** episode *Fair Play*.

Played the German farmer in the second series **Danger Man** [aka **Secret Agent**] episode *Fair Exchange*.

Played Willi in the season two **Ghost Squad** episode *Mr Five Per Cent*.

Played Bull Hoolahan in the **O.S.S.** episode *Operation Barbecue*.

Played Paolo in the **Sword of Freedom** episode *Forgery in Red Chalk*.

Appeared as George Stacey in the **White Hunter** episode *Second Dealer*.

Gallico Paul

The series **The Zoo Gang** was based on his original book [In 1971, Pan Books reprinted his book with the cast on its cover].

Gallico Robert

Played Mac in **The Four Just Men** episode *Dead Man's Switch* and Ed Forrest in *The Bystanders*.

Played Captain Rubens in the **H. G. Wells' Invisible Man** episode *The Decoy*.

Guested as Hunter in the **Interpol Calling** episode *White Blackmail*.

Starred as, series regular, Sergeant O'Brien the series **O.S.S.**.

Played Manny Howard in **The Persuaders!** episode *Five Miles to Midnight*.

Gallier Alex

Played the bridge player in the **Department S** episode *A Fish out of Water*.

Galloway Jack

Played the student, Jasper in the second season **The Protectors** episode *Dragon Chase*.

Galloway Lindsay

Wrote **The Four Just Men** episodes *Village of Shame*, *The Slaver*, *The Man Who Wasn't There*, *Justice For Gino* [teleplayed from a story by Michael Connor] and *Treviso Dam*.

Wrote the first series **Ghost Squad** episodes *Death from a Distance* [with Connery Chappell] and *Ticket for Blackmail*.

Teleplayed the **H. G. Wells' Invisible Man** episode *The Locked Room* [from a story by Ralph Smart].

Wrote the **Interpol Calling** episode *Slow Boat to Amsterdam*.

Wrote the first season **Man of the World** episodes *The Frontier*, *The Highland Story* & *Portrait of a Girl* and the second season's *Jungle Mission*.

Wrote the **Sir Francis Drake** episodes *Mission to Paris* [with David Greene] & *Mary, Queen of Scots*.
Wrote the **William Tell** episodes *The Elixir* [teleplayed from an original story by Ralph Smart], *Gessler's Daughter*, *Undercover*, *The Avenger* and *The Killer*.

Galvani Dino
Played Francisco in **The Buccaneers** [aka **Dan Tempest**] episode *The Surgeon of Sangre Rojo*.

Gammel Robin
Played the Flt. Sgt. in the **O.S.S.** episode *Operation Jingle Bells* and the second seaman in *Operation Barbecue*.

Gannon Chris
Played the salesman in the **Randall and Hopkirk [Deceased]** aka **My Partner the Ghost** episode *But what a Sweet Little Room*.

Gant David
Played Eldred in *Adventure Three* of **Sapphire and Steel**.

Garas Kas
Starred as Hamlyn Gynt in the **Strange Report** series.

Garcia Al
Played the Inspector in **The Adventurer** episode *Deadlock*.
Played Tony Mussoni in the **Jason King** episode *Nadine*.

Garde Colin
Make-up on **The Adventurer, Man of the World** & **The New Adventures of Charlie Chan**.

Gardiner Jeffrey
Played Grantley in the **Strange Report** episode *Report 0846: LONELYHEARTS: 'Who Killed Dan Cupid?'*.

Gardiner John
Played the bank clerk in the first season **Danger Man** episode *Name, Date and Place*.

Gardiner Kenneth
Guested as the waiter in **The Champions** episode *Shadow of the Panther*.

Gardner Brenda
Wardrobe on the first season of **The Adventures of Robin Hood**.
Wardrobe on **The Buccaneers** [aka **Dan Tempest**] episode *Blackbeard*.
Wardrobe Supervisor on **The Adventures of Sir Lancelot** and **The Four Just Men**.

Gardner Carol
Played Lieutenant Barrington in the second series **Danger Man** [aka **Secret Agent**] episode *The Outcast*.
Played Billie in the **Department S** episode *Black Out*.
Played Muriel in the **Gideon's Way** episode *The Prowler* and Daisy in *Boy with a Gun*.
Played the hat-check-girl in the first season **The Saint** episode *The Saint Sees it Through*, the dolly girl in the third season's *The Power Artist* and Carol Henley in the fourth season's two parter *The Fiction Makers*.

Gardner Gordon
Played Lacey in the **Sir Francis Drake** episode *The Garrison*.

Gardner Jimmy
Played the caretaker in the **Man in a Suitcase** episode *Day of Execution*.
Played the marine mechanic in the second season **The Saint** episode *The Imprudent Politician*.

Gardner Timmy
Played the second sailor in the second season **The Saint** episode *The Old Treasure Story*.

Gardnier Kenneth
Played Rig in the third season **The Saint** episode *Island of Chance* and John Chatto in the fourth season's *The Desperate Diplomat*.
Played the American athlete in the **Strange Report** episode *Report 1553: RACIST: 'A Most Dangerous Proposal'*.

Garfath Alex
Chief Make-up Artist on **UFO**.

Garfield David
Played Nicholas in **The Baron** episode *Night of the Hunter*.
Played Baxter in the **Man in a Suitcase** episode *The Sitting Pigeon* and Bateson in *The Girl who Never was*.
Played the hospital attendant in **The Prisoner** episode *Arrival*.
Played Peter in the second season **The Saint** episode *The Abductors* and the first local in the third season's *The House on Dragon's Rock*.

Garko Gianni
Played Cellini in the first season **Space 1999** episode *Dragon's Domain*.

Garland Beverly
Played Jo Harris in the first season **Danger Man** episode *Bury the Dead*.

Garrie John
Played Ben Cross in **The Baron** episode *So Dark the Night*.
Played the old Japanese man in the fourth season **Danger Man** [aka **Secret Agent**] episode *Koroshi* [*Koroshi* was also merged with the only other surviving fourth season colour episode, *Shinda Shima*, to form a TVM entitled *Koroshi*].
Played Mori in the **Man in a Suitcase** episode *Find the Lady*.
Played Enrico in the third season **The Saint** episode *The Reluctant Revolution*.
Played Arthur Griffiths in the **Timeslip** story *The Wrong End of Time*.
Played the van driver in the **UFO** episode *The Long Sleep*.

Garside John
Played Baron Lhota in **The Count of Monte Cristo** episode *Albania*.

Garstin Peter
Played the Spanish prisoner in **The Buccaneers** [aka **Dan Tempest**] episode *Dead Man's Rock*,
Played Dupre in **The Count of Monte Cristo** episode *The Devil's Emissary*.

Garth David
Played Vincente Carreras in **The Baron** episode *Time to Kill*.
Played Blakestone in the season two **Ghost Squad** episode *The Golden Silence*.
Played Duval in the **G.S.5** episode *It Won't be a Stylish Marriage*.
Played Monsieur Phillippe in the second season **The Saint** episode *The Persistent Parasite*.

Garvin John
Played Tully in the **Randall and Hopkirk [Deceased]** episode *When Did you Start to Stop Seeing Things?*.
Played the Ministry of Health official in the fourth season **The Saint** episode *The People Importers*.

Gastoni Lisa
Played Clare in the first season **Danger Man** episode *The Blue Veil* and Lita Rossi in *The Brothers*.

Starred as, series regular, Guilia in the series **The Four Just Men**: *The Night of the Precious Stones*, *Mava*, *The Rietti Group*, *The Slaver*, *The Man in the Royal Suite* & *Treviso Dam*.
Played Blue Eyes in the **O.S.S.** episode *Operation Blue Eyes*.

Gates Larry
Featured in the **Espionage** episode *The Whistling Shrimp*.

Gates Tudor
Wrote the season two **Ghost Squad** episode *Polsky*.
Wrote the **G.S.5** episodes *Dead Men Don't Drive* & *The Goldfish Bowl*.
Wrote the first season **Man of the World** episodes *Death of a Conference* [with Robert E. Thompson] and *The Nature of Justice*.
Wrote **The Sentimental Agent** episode *A Little Sweetness and Light*.
Wrote the **Sir Francis Drake** episode *Drake on Trial*.
Co-wrote [with Brian Degas] the **Strange Report** episode *Report 0649: SKELETON: 'Let Sleeping Heroes Lie'*.

Gatliff Frank
Played Georges Sforza in **The Baron** episode *Diplomatic Immunity*.
Played Doctor Radev in the third season **Danger Man** [aka **Secret Agent**] episode *The Man who wouldn't Talk*.
Played the police inspector in the **Department S** episode *The Man in the Elegant Room*.
Played Geoffrey Haydon in the season two **Ghost Squad** episode *P.G. 7*.
Played the managing director in the **Man in a Suitcase** episode *Which Way did He Go, McGill?* and the auctioneer in *Property of a Gentleman*.
Played Anderson in **The Persuaders!** episode *The Morning After*.
Played Loader in the **Return of the Saint** episode *The Armageddon Alternative*.
Played Inspector Matthews in the **Strange Report** episode *Report 1553: RACIST: 'A Most Dangerous Proposal'*.

Gatrell John
Appeared in season three of **The Adventures of Robin Hood**: as Uncle Robert in *An Apple for the Archer* and as the peasant in *The Youthful Menace*.
Played Coleman in **The Baron** episode *The Edge of Fear*.
Played Phelps in **The Buccaneers** [aka **Dan Tempest**] episode *Conquest of New Providence*, the captain in *Mother Doughty's Crew*, the tavern keeper in *Dangerous Cargo*, William in *Gentleman Jack and the Lady*, and the Merchant officer in *Prize of Andalusia*.
Played Buchanan in the **Interpol Calling** episode *Cargo of Death*.
Played Butler in the first series **The Protectors** episode *.....With a Little Help from my Friends*.

Gauge Alexander
Starred as, series regular, Friar Tuck in **The Adventures of Robin Hood** appearing in: *Friar Tuck*, *A Guest for the Gallows*, *The Inquisitor*, *The Knight Who Came To Dinner*, *The Challenge*, *Queen Eleanor*, *Checkmate*, *The Ordeal*, *Husband for Marian*, *The Highlander*, *The Youngest Outlaw*, *The Betrothal*, *The Alchemist*, *The Jongleur*, *The Brothers*, *The Sheriff's Boots*, *The Vandals*, *Richard the Lionheart*, *Will Scarlet*, *The Deserted Castle*, *The Miser*, *Trial by Battle*, *Children of the Greenwood*, *The May Queen*, *The Wanderer*, *The Byzantine Treasure*, *Secret Mission*, *The Traitor* & *The Wager* [series 1]; *A Village Wooing*, *The Scientist*, *Blackmail*, *A Year and a Day*, *The Impostor*, *Ransom*, *The Haunted Mill*, *Outlaw Money*, *The Black Patch*, *The Friar's Pilgrimage*, *Hubert*, *The Blackbird*, *The Shell Game*, *The Final Tax*, *Ambush*, *The Bandit of Brittany*, *Flight from France*, *The Borrowed Baby*, *Highland Fling*, *The Mystery of Ireland's Eye* &

The Little People [2]; *The Salt King*, *A Tuck in Time*, *The Charter*, *Change of Heart*, *Brother Battle*, *My Brother's Keeper*, *The Mark*, *The Bride of Robin Hood*, *To Be a Student*, *The Christmas Goose*, *The Rivals*, *The Profiteer*, *One Man's Meat*, *The Crusaders*, *The Double*, *Roman Gold*, *The Ghost that Failed*, *The Minstrel*, *The Doctor*, *The Fire*, *Quickness of the Hand*, *Elixir of Youth*, *The Genius*, *The Lottery*, *Little Mother*, *Marian's Prize* & *Farewell to Tuck* [3] and *Tuck's Love Day*, *The Loaf*, *Goodbye, Little John*, *The Oath*, *The Charm Pedlar*, *The Debt*, *Bride for an Outlaw*, *A Bushel of Apples*, *Double Trouble*, *The Champion*, *Trapped*, *The Edge and the Point* & *The Truce* [4]. Also appeared as Edgar in season three's *A Tuck in Time* and the fourth season's *Double Trouble*.
Played Monevido in **The Count of Monte Cristo** episode *Sicily*.
Starred as, series regular, The Prince of Wales/The Prince Regent in **The Scarlet Pimpernel**: *The Hostage*, *Gentlemen of the Road*, *The Flower Woman*, *The Christmas Present*, *Thanksgiving Day*, *The Sword of Justice*, *The Elusive Chauvelin*, *The Lady in Distress*, *A Tale of Two Pigtails* & *The Princess*.

Gaunt William
Starred in **The Champions** as Richard Barrett.
Played Voyce in the season two **Ghost Squad** episode *The Grand Duchess*.
Played Mike in the third season **The Saint** episode *Flight Plan*.

Gavin Weston
Played Novack in the **Department S** episode *The Ghost of Mary Burnham*.
Played Michel in the **Return of the Saint** episode *The Diplomat's Daughter*.

Gay John
Wrote the **Espionage** episode *The Light of the Friendly Star*.

Gayford John
Played the barman in the first season **The Saint** episode *Starring the Saint*.

Gaylor Anna
Played Vicki in the first season **Danger Man** episode *The Girl who Liked GIs*.

Gaynor Marguerite Avril
Played one of the Concubines in the **Virgin of the Secret Service** episode *The Persuasion of a Million Drops*.

Gayson Eunice
Played Countess Marie in **The Adventurer** episode *Thrust and Counter Thrust*.
Played Louise Bancroft in the second series **Danger Man** [aka **Secret Agent**] episode *A Man to be Trusted*.
Played Nora Prescott in the first season **The Saint** episode *The Invisible Millionaire* and Christine Graner in the second season's *The Saint Bids Diamonds*.
Played Thelma Thomas in the **White Hunter** episode *The Hungry Hell*.

Gazes Clive
Played the sentry in the third season **The Saint** episode *The Reluctant Revolution*.

Geary Joan
Played Miss Medlock in the **Virgin of the Secret Service** episode *The Great Ring of Akba*.

Gedge Lewis
Played Mainwaring in **The Buccaneers** [aka **Dan Tempest**] episode *Mr. Beamish and the Hangman's Noose*.

Gee George
Played Tiberio in the **Sword of Freedom** episode *The School*.

Gee Prunella
Played Captain Leila Sabin in the **Return of the Saint** episode *One Black September*.

Geerdts Hilda
Wardrobe on **Man in a Suitcase** and **Strange Report**.

Geeson Judy
Played Suzy Dolman in **The Adventurer** episode *Poor Little Rich Girl*.
Played Helen Cazalet in the second series **Danger Man** [aka **Secret Agent**] episode *The Outcast*.
Played Sue in the **Man in a Suitcase** episode *Sweet Sue*.
Played Selma in the **Return of the Saint** episode *The Judas Game*.
Played Regina in the first season **Space 1999** episode *Another Time Another Place*.

Geeson Sally
Played the girl at the cleaners in the **Man in a Suitcase** episode *Day of Execution* and Jennifer Dean in the **Strange Report** episode *Report 2493: KIDNAP: 'Whose Pretty Girl Are You?'*.

Geiger Miriam
Co-wrote the story for **The Four Just Men** episode *The Battle of the Bridge* [with Don Castle: teleplayed by Gene Coon].

Gelman Milton S.
Co-Story Consultant on **The Persuaders!** and wrote *Angie. . . Angie*.

Genn Leo
Played Sir Hugo Chalmers in **The Persuaders!** episode *The Long Goodbye*.
Played George Halliday in the **Strange Report** episode *Report 1021: SHRAPNEL: 'The Wish in the Dream'*.
Played Dupont in **The Zoo Gang** episode *The Lion Hunt*.

George Susan
Played Michelle Devigne in **The Persuaders!** episode *The Gold Napoleon*.

Georgiou Archilles
Played the second guard in the **Virgin of the Secret Service** episode *The Great Ring of Akba*.

Geraghty Maury
Producer on **Whiplash**.

Gerard Tom
Played the student in **The Four Just Men** episode *Panic Button*.

Gerlini Piero
Played Petrucci in the **Return of the Saint** episode *The Roman Touch*.

Gernreich Rudi
Designed the Moon City costumes for **Space 1999**.

Gerrard Alan
Played the grocer in the **Father Brown** episode *The Man with Two Beards*.
Played H. Birrell in the **Strange Report** episode *Report 8319: GRENADE: 'What Price Change?'*.

Gerrard Sue
Played Jane in **The Adventurer** episodes *Love Always, Magda* and *Has Anyone Here Seen Kelly?*.

Played Veronica in the **Department S** episode *The Mysterious Man in the Flying Machine*.
Played Susan Kirstner in the **Randall and Hopkirk [Deceased]** aka **My Partner the Ghost** episode *Murder ain't what it Used to Be!*.
Played a nurse in the UFO episode *Exposed*.

Gibbons Joe
Played the steward in the season two **Ghost Squad** episode *Escape Route*.
Played Pa in the fourth season **The Saint** two parter *The Fiction Makers*.

Gibbs Gerald B.S.C
Director of Photography on **Strange Report**.

Gibbs Ken
Played Rabat in **The Count of Monte Cristo** episode *Return to the Chateau d'If*.

Gibson Felicity
Played Fleurette in the **Virgin of the Secret Service** episode *Pride of Assassins*.

Gibson Mary
Wardrobe on **Sapphire and Steel** [not *Adventure 1*].

Gifford Alan
Played the Admiral in **The Champions** episode *The Dark Island*.
Played Whitmore in the first season **Danger Man** episode *The Trap*, Mr Hartley in *An Affair of State* and Van Horn in the second series [now aka **Secret Agent**] episode *The Affair at Castelevara*.
Featured in the **Espionage** episode *Final Decision*.
Played Gino in **The Four Just Men** episode *Justice For Gino*.
Guested as Bonnier in the **Interpol Calling** episode *Game for Three Hands*.
Played Henry Burton in the first series **Man of the World** episode *A Family Affair*.
Played Fletcher in **The Sentimental Agent** episode *The Scroll of Islam*.
Played Paul Kirstner in the **Randall and Hopkirk [Deceased]** episode *Murder ain't what it Used to Be!*.
Played Inspector Fernack in the first season **The Saint** episodes *The Careful Terrorist* and *The Element of Doubt*.

Gilbert Doris
Writer on **The New Adventures of Charlie Chan**.

Gilbert Gordon
Assistant Director on **The Saint**.

Gilbert Henry
Guested as Drobnic in **The Champions** episode *Twelve Hours*.
Played Seghir in the third season **Danger Man** [aka **Secret Agent**] episode *I can only Offer you Sherry*.
Played Tex Goldman in the second season **The Saint** episode *The Set-Up*.

Gilbert Henry G.
Played Schulz in the **Jason King** episode *A Page Before Dying*.

Gilbert Kay
Wardrobe Supervisor on **Man in a Suitcase**.

Gilbert Kenneth
Played the detective in the first series **The Protectors** episode *For the Rest of your Natural ....*
Played the Sergeant in the **Sir Francis Drake** episode *The Reluctant Duchess*.

Played the Customs man in **The Zoo Gang** episode *The Twisted Cross.*

Gilkison Anthony
Producer on **The Scarlet Pimpernel.**

Gill James
Played the Arab in the season two **Ghost Squad** episode *The Heir Apparent* and the Arab son in *Gertrude.*

Gill John
Played Brooks in **The Baron** episode *The Killing* [Part 2 of a 2 parter: also exists, edited together with part 1, *Masquerade*, to form a feature *Man In a Looking Glass*].
Played Dr. Yates in the first season **The Saint** episode *The Well-Meaning Mayor.*
Played Col. Blake Travers in the **Virgin of the Secret Service** episode *The Pyramid Plot.*

Gill Peter
Played Fletcher in the second series **Danger Man** [aka **Secret Agent**] episode *The Ubiquitous Mr Lovegrove.*

Gill Tom
Played Captain Brandt in the first season **Danger Man** episode *The Relaxed Informer*. In the second series [now aka **Secret Agent**], played Edwin Bowden in *Such Men are Dangerous.*
Played the Vet in the **Gideon's Way** episode *The Big Fix* and the hotel manager in *How to Retire without Really Working.*
Played the General in the **H. G. Wells' Invisible Man** episode *The Prize.*

Gillam Harry
Camera Operator on **The Champions & Strange Report.**

Gillard Peter
Played Kurt Mahler in the **UFO** episode *Identified.*

Gilles Jacques
Co-wrote, with Ralph Smart, the third season **Danger Man** [aka **Secret Agent**] episode *Say it with Flowers.*

Gillespie Robert
Played the customs officer in **The Adventurer** episode *Mr Calloway is a Very Cautious Man.*
Played Fred Batley in the **Return of the Saint** episode *The Obono Affair.*
Played Pierre in the third season **The Saint** episode *To Kill a Saint.*

Gilliat Leslie
MGM producer on **The Prisoner**: involved in pre-production.

Gilling John
Directed **The Champions** episodes *The Ghost Plane, The Fanatics, Full Circle* and *The Final Countdown.*
Directed the **Department S** episodes *A Cellar full of Silence, Handicap Dead, Who Plays the Dummy?, The Treasure of the Costa del Sol, The Shift that Never was, The Double Death of Charlie Crippen & Last Train to Redbridge.*
Directed the **Gideon's Way** episodes *The Tin God & The Rhyme and the Reason.*
Directed **The Saint** episodes *The Latin Touch, The Man who was Lucky, The King of the Beggars & Iris* [season 1]; *The Saint Steps In, The Man who Liked Toys, The Crime of the Century & The Spanish Cow* [2]; *A Double in Diamonds* [3] and *Portrait of Brenda* [4]. Also wrote the first series episodes *The Man who was Lucky & The King of the Beggars.*

Gillis Ann
Played Susan Forrester in the second season **Man of the World** episode *The Prince.*

Played Beryl Carrington in the first season **The Saint** episode *The Romantic Matron* and Wilma in the second season's *The Persistent Parasite.*

Gillis Jackson
Wrote **The Four Just Men** episode *The Last Days of Nick Pompey.*

Gilmar Brian
Played the first agent in the second series **Danger Man** [aka **Secret Agent**] episode *Are You Going to Be More Permanent?*

Gilmore Peter
Played Mather in **The Persuaders!** episode *That's Me Over There.*

Gilpin Antonia
Played Maria in the first season **Danger Man** episode *The Sisters.*

Giltinan David
Wrote the **Sir Francis Drake** episode *The Irish Pirate.*

Giovannini Rita
Played Irene Maroni in the **Father Brown** episode *The Actor and the Alibi.*

Gish Sheila
Played Laura in **The Adventurer** episode *To the Lowest Bidder.*

Gladstone Zeph
Played Scott in **The Baron** episode *The Persuaders* and Daniella in *Night of the Hunter.*

Gladwin Joe
Played Finny in the **Gideon's Way** episode *Boy with a Gun.*
Played the Yorkshire Napoleon/Marshall in **The Prisoner** episode *The Girl who was Death.*

Glanville Christine
Puppetry Supervisor on **Stingray** and **Fireball XL5.**
Puppet Operator on **The Secret Service.**
Made and operated puppets on the **Supercar** series.

Glen Glenn Sound Co.
Sound facilities for **The Count of Monte Cristo.**

Glen John
Editor on the second & third season of **Danger Man** [aka **Secret Agent**]. Edited the fourth series episode *Shinda Shima* which, edited together with the other season four episode *Koroshi*, also exists as a feature entitled *Koroshi.*
Editor and Second Unit Director on the **Man in a Suitcase** series and directed the episode *Somebody Loses, Somebody ...Wins?.*

Glover Brian
Played Allen in the second season **The Protectors** episode *Quin.*
Played Plackett in the **Return of the Saint** episode *Signal Stop.*

Glover David
Played the Doctor in the first series **The Protectors** episode *It Could be Practically Anywhere on the Island.*

Glover Julian
Guested as Anderson in **The Champions** episode *The Fanatics.*
Played John in the **Jason King** episode *Variations on a Theme.*
Played Hilloran in the first season **The Saint** episode *The Lawless Lady* and Ramon Falconi in the third season's *Invitation to Danger.*

Played Jarak in the first season **Space 1999** episode *Alpha Child*.

Played James Hanson in the **Strange Report** episode *Report 2475: REVENGE: 'When a Man Hates'*.

Glover Michael
Played Davies in the second season **The Protectors** episode *Wam* [part one].

Gluck Carol Warner
Wrote the season two **The Adventures of Robin Hood** episode *The Road in the Air* [with Albert A Dorner].

Glyn-Jones John
Played Hamish in the first season **Danger Man** episode *The Gallows Tree*.

Played Percy Knox in the **Gideon's Way** episode *The Big Fix*.

Played Dr. Rogers in **The Persuaders!** episode *Chain of Events*.

Played the Welsh man in the **Shirley's World** episode *The Rally*.

Played the chemist in the **Randall and Hopkirk [Deceased] aka My Partner the Ghost** episode *Money to Burn*.

Played the manager in **The Sentimental Agent** episode *Never Play Cards with Strangers* & the bookshop manager in *Meet my Son, Henry*.

Goddard Fred
Played the sergeant in the second series of **The Adventures of Robin Hood** episode *The Blackbird* & Tom in *The Final Tax*. Appeared as a guard in season three's *Brother Battle*.

Appeared as Horg in **The Adventures of Sir Lancelot** episode *The Lesser Breed*.

Goddard Ian
Production Manager on **The Adventurer**.

Goddard Rene
Played the nurse in the **O.S.S.** episode *Operation Fracture*.

Played Madeleine in **The Scarlet Pimpernel** episode *The Winged Madonna*.

Goddard Willoughby
Played Colbert in **The Baron** episode *The Edge of Fear*.

Played Pym in **The Buccaneers** [aka **Dan Tempest**] episode *Blood Will Tell* and Phineas Bunch in *Marooned*.

Played McFadden in the first season **Danger Man** episode *The Journey Ends Halfway*.

Played Slim Salmon in the season two **Ghost Squad** episode *The Missing People*.

Played Crowther in the **H. G. Wells' Invisible Man** episode *Bank Raid*.

Played Boris in the fourth season **The Saint** episode *The Ex-King of Diamonds*.

Played Taybor in the second season **Space 1999** episode *The Taybor*.

Regular in **William Tell** as Gessler: *The Emperor's Hat, The Raid, The Assassins, The Hostages, Landslide, The Boy Slaves, The Baroness, Secret Death, Voice in the Night, The Lost Letter, The Gauntlet of St. Gerhardt, The Cuckoo, The Elixir, The Magic Powder, Gessler's Daughter, The Bear, Golden Wheel, The Bride, The Young Widow, The Shrew, The Killer, The Surgeon, The Ensign, The General's Daughter, Secret Weapon* and *The Master Spy*.

Godfrey Anne
Played the second woman at the party in the fourth season **The Saint** episode *The Double Take*.

Godfrey Derek
Played the General in **The Baron** episode *Night of the Hunter*.

Played the casino manager in the first season **Danger Man** episode *Position of Trust*.

Played Walker in the **H. G. Wells' Invisible Man** episode *The Mink Coat*.

Played David Barsella in the second season **The Protectors** episode *The Tiger and the Goat*.

Played Wolfgang in the **William Tell** episode *Golden Wheel* and the Burgomaster in *The Killer*.

Godfrey Michael
Played Captain Arilla in **The Adventurer** episode *Target!*.

Played Colonel Ahmed Bey in **The Baron** episode *The Legions of Ammak*.

Guested as Mendoza in **The Champions** episode *Operation Deep-freeze*.

Played Abdul in the second series **Danger Man** [aka **Secret Agent**] episode *Fish on the Hook* and Gandon in the third season's *The Hunting Party*.

Played Stanic in the **Department S** episode *The Double Death of Charlie Crippen*.

Played Dupont in **The Persuaders!** episode *Overture*.

Played Santos in **The Sentimental Agent** episode *The Beneficiary*.

Played Manuel Enriquez in the second season **The Saint** episode *The Revolution Racket* and Delgado in the third season's *The Reluctant Revolution*.

Godfrey Roy
Played Honest Karl in the **William Tell** episode *The Shrew*.

Godfrey Tommy
Played the taxi driver in the **Department S** episode *Last Train to Redbridge*.

Played Falpiaz in the **Jason King** episode *That isn't Me, It's Somebody Else*.

Played Benny Ryan in **The Persuaders!** episode *Greensleeves*.

Played the taxi-driver in the third season **The Saint** episode *The Power Artist*.

Played Ron in the **Shirley's World** episode *The Reunion*.

Played Gandolfio in the **Virgin of the Secret Service** episode *Pride of Assassins*.

Goding Jim
Camera Operator on **The Buccaneers** [aka **Dan Tempest**] episodes *The Raiders, Captain Dan Tempest, Dan Tempest's War with Spain, The Wasp, Whale Gold, Slave Ship, Gunpowder Plot, Articles of War, Ghost Ship, Conquest of New Providence, Hurricane, Dead Man's Rock, Dangerous Cargo, Hand of the Hawk, Gentleman Jack and the Lady, Mr. Beamish and the Hangman's Noose, Marooned, Before the Mast, Dan Tempest and The Amazons, The Ladies, The Surgeon of Sangre Rojo, The Return of Calico Jack, Conquistador, Aztec Treasure, Prize of Andalusia, Cutlass Wedding, Dan Tempest Holds an Auction, Flip and Jenny, To the Rescue, Indian Fighters, Mistress Higgins' Treasure, The Spy Aboard, The Decoy, Pirate Honour, Instrument of War* & *Printer's Devil*.

Godsell Vanda
Played Charlotte Borgman in the **Gideon's Way** episode *To Catch a Tiger*.

Played Tina Ourley in the first season **The Saint** episode *The Rough Diamonds*.

Goghan Dave
Sound on **The Buccaneers** [aka **Dan Tempest**] episodes *The Raiders, Captain Dan Tempest, Dan Tempest's War with Spain, The Wasp, Whale Gold, Slave Ship, Gunpowder Plot, Articles of War, Ghost Ship, Conquest of New Providence, Mother Doughty's Crew, Blood Will Tell, Hurricane, Dead Man's Rock, Dangerous Cargo, Hand of the Hawk, Gentleman Jack and the Lady, Mr. Beamish and the Hangman's Noose, Marooned, Before the Mast, Dan Tempest and The Amazons, The Ladies, The Surgeon of Sangre Rojo, The Return of Calico Jack, Conquistador, Aztec Treasure, Prize of Andalusia, Cutlass Wedding, Dan Tempest Holds an Auction,*

Flip and Jenny, To the Rescue, Indian Fighters, Mistress Higgins' Treasure, The Spy Aboard, The Decoy, Pirate Honour, Instrument of War and *Printer's Devil*.

Goguel Constantinde
Played the jeweller in the **Man in a Suitcase** episode *Blind Spot*.

Goh Pat
Played the orderly in the second season **Man of the World** episode *The Enemy*.

Goldblatt Harold
Played Olmira in **The Baron** episode *Red Horse, Red Rider*.
Played Ramon Torres in the second series **Danger Man** [aka **Secret Agent**] episode *The Affair at Castelevara*.
Played Mayer in the **G.S.5** episode *Rich Ruby Wine*.
Played Devigne in **The Persuaders!** episode *The Gold Napoleon*.

Golden Michael
Played Captain Barker in **The Buccaneers** [aka **Dan Tempest**] episode *To the Rescue*.
Played Larry Montague in the **G.S.5** episode *Death of a Cop*.
Played Rafe in the **Sir Francis Drake** episode *Doctor Dee*.
Played Jakob Muller in the **William Tell** episode *Gessler's Daughter*.

Goldie Michael
Played Gimbal in the **Randall and Hopkirk [Deceased]** aka **My Partner the Ghost** episode *Who Killed Cock Robin*.
Played the policeman on the train in **The Sentimental Agent** episode *Express Delivery* and Piero in *Box of Tricks*.
Played the guard in the **Strange Report** episode *Report 1553: RACIST: 'A Most Dangerous Proposal'*.

Golding Richard
Played the Aran vendor in the **O.S.S.** episode *Operation Eel*.

Golding Sarah
Played Hazel in the **Father Brown** episode *The Dagger With Wings*.

Goldman Bernard
Played the jailer in the second series of **The Adventures of Robin Hood** episode *The Blackbird*.

Goldoni Lelia
Played Lisa in the second series **Danger Man** [aka **Secret Agent**] episode *Fair Exchange* and Pilar Lin in the third season's *Two Birds with One Bullet*.
Featured in the **Espionage** episode *The Liberators*.
Played Mary Burley in the **Shirley's World** episode *Thou Shall Not Be Found Out*.
Played Marisha in the **Strange Report** episode *Report 7931: SNIPER: 'When is Your Cousin Not?'*.

Goldring Richard
Played Zacharias in the **White Hunter** episode *No Survivors*.

Goldsmith Gladys
Continuity on **Space 1999**.

Goldsmith John
Wrote the first season **The Protectors** episodes *Brother Hood* & *Balance of Terror*.
Wrote the **Return of the Saint** episodes *One Black September, The Village that Sold its Soul, The Roman Touch* [teleplayed from a story by William Fairchild], *The Murder Cartel* [teleplayed from a story by Moris Farhi & John Kruse] and *Vicious Circle* [teleplayed from a story by Michael Armstrong and John Kruse].
Wrote the first series **Space 1999** episode *Seed of Destruction*.

Golightly John
Played Father in *Adventure One* of **Sapphire and Steel**.
Played the SHADO diver in the **UFO** episode *Sub-smash*.

Gomez Arthur
Played a variety of roles in **The Four Just Men**: the stout man in *The Prime Minister*, a gendarme in *Village of Shame*, the clerk in *The Deserter*, a gendarme in *The Beatniques*, the taxi driver in *National Treasure*, Stoyen Matchek in *The Survivor*, Rodrigo in *The Rietti Group*, the train conductor in *The Princess*, the manservant in *The Grandmother*, Kalmar in *The Godfather* and the bartender in *The Moment of Truth*.
Played President Domecq in the **H. G. Wells' Invisible Man** episode *Behind the Mask*.
Played Costa in the **Interpol Calling** episode *The Angola Brights*.
Played Dali in the second season **The Saint** episode *The Death Penalty*.

Good Christopher
Played Gerald Lloyd in the **Father Brown** episode *The Eye of Apollo*.

Good Jason
Played the policeman in the **Return of the Saint** episode *Assault Force*.

Good Maurice
Played Harris in the **Man in a Suitcase** episode *Essay in Evil*.
Played Brine in the third season **The Saint** episode *Little Girl Lost* and Steven Lyall in the fourth season's *The Time to Die*.

Goodale Ronald
Played the guard/porter in the **Father Brown** episode *The Arrow of Heaven*.
Played the countryman in *Adventure One* of **Sapphire and Steel**.

Goodliffe Michael
Played Ribas in the first series **Ghost Squad** episode *Catspaw* [this episode was shot for the first series, but due to an actors' strike, was originally shown as a season two episode].
Played Crompton in the **H. G. Wells' Invisible Man** episode *Secret Experiment*.
Played the President in the **Jason King** episode *Zenia*.
Guested as Wolf Barstrom in the **Interpol Calling** episode *Private View*.
Played Michael Hornsby in the **Man in a Suitcase** episode *All that Glitters*.
Played Galworth in the first series **Man of the World** episode *Portrait of a Girl*.
Played De Santos in the second season **The Protectors** episode *The Bridge*.
Played Arthur de Crecy in the **Randall and Hopkirk [Deceased]** aka **My Partner the Ghost** episode *But what a Sweet Little Room*.
Played Dr. Quintus in the first season **The Saint** episode *The Invisible Millionaire*.

Goodman Deveril
Music Editor on **The Baron, The Champions, Department S, The Persuaders!** & **Randall and Hopkirk [Deceased]** aka **My Partner the Ghost** and **The Saint**.

Goodman Johnny
Production Supervisor on **The Baron**.
Associate Producer on **The Champions** [not *Reply Box. No. 666, Happening, The Survivors, Shadow of the Panther, Desert Journey, Nutcracker, The Final Countdown* and *Autokill*].
In charge of production on **The Persuaders!**
Production Supervisor on the first two seasons of **The Saint** series and Associate Producer on season four.

Goodman Keith
Played the passport officer in the first season **Danger Man** episode *The Prisoner*.

Goodman Michael
Played Ron Short in the **Gideon's Way** episode *The Big Fix*.

Goodman Tim
Played Webster in **The Persuaders!** episode *Anyone Can Play*.

Goodwin Harold
Played Saunders in the third series **The Adventures of Robin Hood** episode *At the Sign of the Blue Boar* and Jack in *Farewell to Tuck*.
Played the peasant in **The Adventures of Sir Lancelot** episode *Ruby of Radnor*.
Played Corporal Jeavons in **The Four Just Men** episode *The Deserter*.
Played Driver Evans in the **H. G. Wells' Invisible Man** episode *The Rocket*.
Played Foley in the **Man in a Suitcase** episode *The Girl who Never was* and the taxi driver in *Why they Killed Nolan*.

Goodwins Les
Director on **The New Adventures of Charlie Chan**.

Goody Kim
Played Michelle in the **Return of the Saint** episode *The Roman Touch*.

Goorney Howard
Played the hotel clerk in **The Adventurer** episode *Deadlock*.
Played Joseph Laclos in the second series **Danger Man** [aka **Secret Agent**] episode *Are You Going to Be More Permanent?*
Played Professor Leros in the **Man in a Suitcase** episode *The Boston Square*.
Played the first ghost in the **Randall and Hopkirk [Deceased]** aka **My Partner the Ghost** episode *The Trouble with Women*.
Played Mercier in the third season **The Saint** episode *A Double in Diamonds*.

Gordeno Peter
Featured in the series **UFO** as, regular, Captain Carlin.

Gordon Arne
Played the Hazarnao thief in the **Virgin of the Secret Service** episode *Dark Deeds on the Northwest Frontier*.

Gordon Clair
Played Sandra in the first season **Danger Man** episode *Josetta*.
Played Gloria in the third season **Danger Man** [aka **Secret Agent**] episode *The Paper Chase*.

Gordon Colin
Starred as, series regular, John Templeton-Green in **The Baron**: *Diplomatic Immunity, The Persuaders, Epitath for a Hero, Enemy of the State, A Memory of Evil & Farewell to Yesterday*.
Played Doctor Stickney in the **Department S** episode *A Small War of Nerves*.
Played the Colonel in the **H. G. Wells' Invisible Man** episode *Play to Kill*.
Played Langford in the first series **Man of the World** episode *Portrait of a Girl*.
Guest starred as *'The New No. 2'* in **The Prisoner** episodes *A. B. and C.* and *The General*.
Played Albert Thompson in the **UFO** episode *The Cat with Ten Lives*.

Gordon Dorothy
Played Kate in the second series of **The Adventures of Robin Hood** episode *The Borrowed Baby*.

Gordon Hannah
Guested as Anna in **The Champions** episode *The Final Countdown*.
Played Laura in the first series **The Protectors** episode *.....With a Little Help from my Friends*.
Played Lucy in **The Persuaders!** episode *A Home of One's Own*.

Gordon Norah
Played Nurse in the first series of **The Adventures of Robin Hood** episode *Table's Turned*.
Played Mrs Harrow in the **Gideon's Way** episode *The Lady Killer*.
Played Maria in the **Sword of Freedom** episode *Caterina*.

Gore-Lewis Alan
Played the soldier in **The Scarlet Pimpernel** episode *The Christmas Present*.

Goring Marius
Played Henry Thibaud in the **Man in a Suitcase** episode *Blind Spot*.
Starred as Sir Percy Blakeney [The Scarlet Pimpernel] in **The Scarlet Pimpernel**. Also served as Producer, Production Associate and wrote the episode *The Flower Woman*.

Gorman Shay
Played Brannigan in the first season **Danger Man** episode *The Sanctuary*.
Played O'Rorke in **The Four Just Men** episode *The Heritage*.
Played Mullins in the third season **The Saint** episode *Little Girl Lost*.

Gorrara Romo
Appeared as the second tower guard in **The Prisoner** episode *Checkmate*.
Played Ray in the **Randall and Hopkirk [Deceased]** aka **My Partner the Ghost** episode *Who Ever Heard of a Ghost Dying?*.
Played Dave in the third season **The Saint** episode *Escape Route*.

Gorsen Norah
Played Helen in **The Adventures of Sir Lancelot** episode *The Ferocious Fathers*.

Gosling John
An ex-detective, wrote the book 'Ghost Squad'.

Goss Helen
Played Lady M. Ingram in the season two **Ghost Squad** episode *The Retirement of Gentle Dove*.

Gostelow Gordon
Played Thompson in the **Gideon's Way** episode *Fall High, Fall Hard*.
Played Chester Farson/Gray in the **Man in a Suitcase** episode *Property of a Gentleman*.
Played Parkinson in the **Return of the Saint** episode *The Armageddon Alternative*.
Played Metz in the third season **The Saint** episode *The Paper Chase*.

Gotell Walter
Played Capt. Brandt in **The Baron** episode *Night of the Hunter*.
Guested as Jost in **The Champions** episode *Operation Deepfreeze*.
Played Le Drue in **The Count of Monte Cristo** episode *Burgundy* and Florian in *Bordeaux*.
Played Colonel Perar in the debut season **Danger Man** episode *The Leak* and the receptionist in *Under the Lake*.

Played Lloyd in the **H. G. Wells' Invisible Man** episode *Shadow Bomb*.

Guested as Zeist in the **Interpol Calling** episode *The Money Game* and as Fischer in *Payment in Advance*.

Played the Kommandant in the **O.S.S.** episode *Operation Tulip*.

Played Hans Lasser in the second season **The Saint** episode *The Hi-Jackers*.

Played Souza in **The Sentimental Agent** episode *Box of Tricks*.

Played Dominick in the **Sword of Freedom** episode *Who is Felicia?*.

Appeared as Kramer in the **White Hunter** episode *No Survivors*.

Played the officer in the **William Tell** episode *The Trap*.

Played Boucher in **The Zoo Gang** episode *Revenge: Postdated*.

Gothard Michael
Played Weber in the **Department S** episode *Les Fleurs du Mal*.
Played Perrin in the **Randall and Hopkirk [Deceased]** aka **My Partner the Ghost** episode *When the Spirit Moves You*.

Gough Michael
Played Boland in the fourth series **The Adventures of Robin Hood** episode *The Edge and the Point*.
Guested as Joss in **The Champions** episode *Happening*.
Played Shkoder in the first series **The Protectors** episode *One and One Makes One*.
Played Colin Phillips in the second season **The Saint** episode *The Imprudent Politician*.

Gough Roy
Stills photographer on **Danger Man** & **The Prisoner**.

Gough Simon
Played the crew member in the **Jason King** episode *A Royal Flush*.

Gould Graydon
Played Sergeant Peter Ross in the first season **Danger Man** episode *The Girl who Liked GIs*.
Starred as Ranger Keeley in the series **The Forest Rangers**.
Played Stan Johnson in the first season **The Saint** episode *The Element of Doubt*.
Voiced Mike Mercury in the **Supercar** series.

Gover Michael
Played Harry in the **Randall and Hopkirk [Deceased]** aka **My Partner the Ghost** episode *Could You Recognise the Man Again?*.
Played the guard in the **UFO** episode *Court Martial*.

Grace Martin
Played a gang member in the second season **The Protectors** episode *Baubles, Bangles and Beads*.

Grade Lew, Lord
Lew entered the world of TV production in 1954 forming ITC and in 1955, broadcasting, by joining the board of ATV.
Was MD of ATV until 1973 and then Chairman till 1977.
➔ Made Chairman for life when ITC was bought by Polygram.
'All of my shows are great.
Some of them are bad, but they're all great.'

Graeme John
Wrote **The Saint** episodes *The Gentle Ladies, The Wonderful War* & *The Noble Sportsman* [series 1] and *The Loving Brothers* [2].

Graham Twins, The
Played Valerie & Veronica in the third season **The Saint** episode *A Double in Diamonds*.

Graham Arthur
Director of Photography on **William Tell**.

Graham Cathy
Played Moira in the **Department S** episode *Death on Reflection*.

Graham David
Played the detective in the second series **Danger Man [aka Secret Agent]** episode *The Affair at Castelevara*.
Voiced Professor 'Matt' Matic, Fireball's science officer and navigator in Gerry Anderson's **Fireball XL5**. Also voiced Lieutenant 90 and Zoonie - Venus's pet Lazoon .
Played Pantin in **The Four Just Men** episode *The Beatniques*.
Played Hafiz in the first series **Man of the World** episode *Death of a Conference*.
Played the pilot in the **O.S.S.** episode *Operation Yo Yo*.
Played Ahmed in the first season **The Saint** episode *The Wonderful War* and Juan Gamma in the second season's *The Unkind Philanthropist*.
Played the bank attendant in **The Sentimental Agent** episode *The Beneficiary*.
Played the banker in the **Sir Francis Drake** episode *Beggars of the Sea*.
Voiced Mitch, Zarin and Doctor Beaker in the **Supercar** series.
Voiced Brains, Parker and Gordon Tracey in **The Thunderbirds** series.
Played 2957 in the **Timeslip** story *The Year of the Burn-Up* [series parts 13-20].

Graham Denys
Played the ship's officer in **The Sentimental Agent** episode *The Height of Fashion*.

Graham Michael
Played Jacquet in **The Champions** episode *A Case of Lemmings*.
Appeared as the anaesthetist in the **Randall and Hopkirk [Deceased]** aka **My Partner the Ghost** episode *You Can Always find a Fall Guy*.
Played Doctor in the **Return of the Saint** episode *Dragonseed*.
Played Lockhart in the third season **The Saint** episode *The Persistent Patriots* and the first reporter in *The Convenient Monster*.

Graham Raymond
Played the attendant in the **Strange Report** episode *Report 0649: SKELETON: 'Let Sleeping Heroes Lie'*.

Graham Sean
Wrote **The Zoo Gang** episode *The Lion Hunt*.

Graham Vicki
Played Joanna in the **Department S** episode *Death on Reflection*.

Grahame Leonard
Wrote the first season **The Saint** episode *Judith*.

Grainer Ron
Wrote the theme for **Man in a Suitcase** & **The Prisoner**.

Grainger Dawn
Played Gregoire in the **Jason King** episode *A Thin Band of Air*.

Graley Barbara
Played Martine in the third season **Danger Man [aka Secret Agent]** episode *The Hunting Party*.

Grange Robert
Played the Moonbase doctor in the **UFO** episode *The Man who Came Back*.

Grant Angie
Played Monica in the first series **The Protectors** episode *The Quick Brown Fox*.

Grant Bob
Played Clements in the **Sir Francis Drake** episode *The Doughty Plot*.

Grant Cy
Provided the voice for Lieutenant Green on **Captain Scarlet and the Mysterons**.
Played Richard Congoto in **The Persuaders!** episode *Greensleeves*.
Appeared as Arusha in the **White Hunter** episode *Inside Story*.

Grant Deborah
Played Linda Simmons in the **UFO** episode *The Psychobombs*.

Grant Joyce
Played Margaret Gresham in the **Gideon's Way** episode *How to Retire without Really Working*.

Grant Julian
Played Lt. Grey in the **UFO** episode *Confetti Check A-O.K.*

Grant Pat
Hairdresser on **The Champions**.

Grant Richard
Played a guard in **The Count of Monte Cristo** episode *The Experiment*.

Grant Susan Lyall
Played Ginette in **The Scarlet Pimpernel** episode *The Princess*.

Grassom Lilian
Played Rita in the **G.S.5** episode *Hideout*.

Graves Peter
Played Reggie in the **Department S** episode *A Small War of Nerves*.
Played Sir Leopold Pulman in the **Father Brown** episode *The Man with Two Beards*.

Graves Peter
Starred as Jim Newton in the **Fury** series.
Starred as Chris Cobb in the **Whiplash** series.

Graves Rupert
Played the prefect in the **Return of the Saint** episode *Yesterday's Hero*.

Gray Barry
Music composer on: **Captain Scarlet and the Mysterons**, **Fireball XL5** [and arranged & conducted], **Joe 90** [and directed music], **The Secret Service**, **Space 1999** [first series: Derek Wadsworth did season two], **Stingray**, **Supercar**, **Thunderbirds** and **UFO**.

Gray Carol
Played Josie Claval in the first season **The Saint** episode *The Covetous Headman*.

Gray Chantal
Played an auction client in the **Father Brown** episode *The Arrow of Heaven*.

Gray Charles
Played Sir Blaise in the season three **The Adventures of Robin Hood** episode *The Mark*.

Played Alex in the first season **Danger Man** episode *The Key* and Zameda in *The Deputy Coyannis Story*.
Played Paul Lederer in **The Four Just Men** episode *The Man in the Road*, Doninguez in *Money To Burn* and Sadik Bey in *The Slaver*.
Played Peter Thal in the **H. G. Wells' Invisible Man** episode *The Vanishing Evidence*.
Played De Foix in the **Sword of Freedom** episode *Choice of Weapons* and Varenza in *The Suspects*.

Gray Donald
Provided the voice of Colonel White for **Captain Scarlet and the Mysterons** and was the Voice of Mysterons.

Gray Ian
Played the jeweller in the **Strange Report** episode *Report 1021: SHRAPNEL: 'The Wish in the Dream'*.

Gray Janine
Played the receptionist in the first season **The Saint** episode *The Fellow Traveller* and the nurse in the first season **Danger Man** episode *The Girl in Pink Pyjamas*.

Gray John
Played the bellhop in the first season **The Saint** episode *The Loaded Tourist*.

Gray Linda
Appeared as Marta in **The Adventures of Sir Lancelot** episode *The Missing Princess*.

Gray Nadia
Played Nadia, Number 8, in **The Prisoner** episode *The Chimes of Big Ben*.

Gray Peter
Played Sevier in **The Count of Monte Cristo** episode *The De Berry Affair*.

Gray Willoughby
Played a number of roles in **The Adventures of Robin Hood**: Gilbert in *The Coming of Robin Hood*, Nailer in *The Moneylender*, Much in *Maid Marian*, the Inquisitor in *The Inquisitor*, Aubrey in *The Knight Who Came To Dinner*, Major Domo in *Checkmate*, Humphrey in *The Ordeal*, Otto in *The Highlander*, Otto in *The Youngest Outlaw*, Count de Waldern in *The Jongleur*, Stationarius in *The Brothers*, Hildebrand in *The Intruders*, Master Giles in *Errand of Mercy*, Hubert in *Richard the Lionheart*, Arthur of Tetsbury in *Ladies of Sherwood*, the Sergeant in *Will Scarlet*, Hodge in *The Miser*, Earl of Drune in *Trial by Battle*, the Sergeant in *Children of the Greenwood*, the first healer in *The Wanderer*, Nicholas in *The Byzantine Treasure*, the High Constable in *The Traitor*, the tall monk in *The Wager* & Blondel in *The Prisoner* [series 1] and Sir Godfrey in *A Village Wooing*, Roger of Danby in *The Scientist*, Bafe in *Blackmail*, Tinker in *A Year and a Day* & a forester in *The Goldmaker* [2].
Appeared in several parts in **The Buccaneers** [aka **Dan Tempest**]: played Harris in *Slave Ship*, the Bosun in *Before the Mast* and the first man shaving in *The Ladies*. Was also a regular as Pop appearing in *The Wasp*, *Whale Gold*, *Articles of War*, *Marooned*, *The Surgeon of Sangre Rojo*, *The Return of Calico Jack*, *Conquistador*, *Prize of Andalusia*, *To the Rescue*, *Pirate Honour* and *Printer's Devil*.
Played Captain Frederick in the **William Tell** episode *The Assassins*, Number One in *The Avenger* and the Gunmaster in *Secret Weapon*.

Graysmark John
Associate Art Director on **The Champions**.

Greatorex Wilfred

Script Editor on season two & three of **Danger Man** [aka Secret Agent]. Also, wrote the second series episodes *The Professionals* [with Louis Marks] & *Fair Exchange* [with Marc Brandel].
Wrote the **Man in a Suitcase** episodes *The Boston Square* & *Property of a Gentleman*.

Greaves Paul
Played the aide in **The Adventurer** episode *Miss Me Once, Miss Me Twice and Miss Me Once Again*.
Played the second assistant director in the **UFO** episode *Mindbender*.

Green Anthony
Played the peasant boy in the third series **The Adventures of Robin Hood** episode *Little Mother*.

Green Bertie
Appeared as the messenger in the **White Hunter** episode *The Prisoner*.

Green Danny
Played Noah in **The Buccaneers** [aka **Dan Tempest**] episode *The Spy Aboard*.
Played Lord Surrey in the **Randall and Hopkirk [Deceased]** aka My **Partner the Ghost** episode *Just for the Record*.

Green Earl
Played the car salesman in the **Department S** episode *The Double Death of Charlie Crippen*.
Played the hotel receptionist in the second season **Man of the World** episode *In the Picture*.
Played Ramon in the **Randall and Hopkirk [Deceased]** aka My **Partner the Ghost** episode *It's Supposed to be Thicker than Water*.
Played Carlo in the third season **The Saint** episode *Interlude in Venice*.

Green F. Sherwin
Executive Producer on the series **Interpol Calling**.
Associate Producer on the second series of **Space 1999**.

Green Garard
Played Kubitz in the first series **Ghost Squad** episode *Assassin*.
Appeared as Major Royce in the **White Hunter** episode *No Survivors*.

Green Janet
Wrote the story for **The Four Just Men** episode *National Treasure* [teleplayed by Owen Holder].

Green Nigel
Played Prival in the second series of **The Adventures of Robin Hood** episode *The Impostor*.
In **The Adventures of Sir Lancelot**: played King Mark in *Winged Victory*, Bart in *Sir Bliant*, the second peasant in *The Magic Sword*, Sir Grint in *Lancelot's Banishment*, Probus in *Roman Wall*, the farmer in *Caledon*, the jailer in *Knight Errant* and the second thief in *The Theft of Excalibur*.
Played Wetzel in the **Danger Man** episode *The Girl who Liked Gis* and Magnus Sutherland in the second series [now aka Secret Agent] episode *That's Two of Us Sorry*.
Played Cresswell in the season two **Ghost Squad** episode *The Missing People*.
Played Charles in the **Jason King** episode *As Easy as A B C*.
Played Cavendish in **The Persuaders!** episode *Read and Destroy*.
Played Krassinkov in the first series **The Protectors** episode *Balance of Terror*.
Regular in **William Tell** as 'The Bear', debuting as Fertog in *The Bear* and going on to appear in *The Bride, The Trap, The Surgeon, The Ensign, The General's Daughter, Secret Weapon* & *The Master Spy*.

Green Philip
Music on the first and second series of **Ghost Squad** and on **G.S.5** [also whistled the theme].
Music on **White Hunter**.

Green Seymour
Played Constable Herridge in **The Buccaneers** [aka **Dan Tempest**] episode *Flip and Jenny*.

Greenberg Stanley R.
Devised the **Man in a Suitcase** series [Created by Richard Harris and Dennis Spooner], served as executive story consultant and wrote the episodes *Man from the Dead, Variation on a Million Bucks* [2 parter: also exists a movie: *To Chase a Million*], *Jigsaw Man* [with Reed de Rouen] & *All that Glitters*.

Greene Bill
Construction Manager on **The Champions, Department S & Randall and Hopkirk [Deceased]** aka My **Partner the Ghost** and **The Saint**.

Greene David
Directed the **Espionage** episodes *He Rises On Sunday, and We On Monday, The Gentle Spies, To the Very End* [and co-teleplayed with Norman Borisoff: from an original story by Norman Borisoff], *Medal For a Turned Coat* and *Once a Spy*.
Directed the first season **Man of the World** episodes *Death of a Conference, Masquerade in Spain* & *The Mindreader*.
Directed **The Persuaders!** episode *Greensleeves*.
Directed the first season **The Saint** episode *The Pearls of Peace*.
Directed the **Sir Francis Drake** episodes *The Garrison, Mary, Queen of Scots, Lost Colony of Virginia, Mission to Paris, King of America, Escape* & *The Doughty Plot* and wrote *Mission to Paris* [with Lindsay Galloway], *The Doughty Plot* [with Margaret Irwin] & *Escape*.

Greene Howard
Played the servant in the first season **Danger Man** episode *Name, Date and Place*.
Played the first Man-at-Arms in the second series of **The Adventures of Robin Hood** episode *The Hero*.
Played the sentry in the **Sir Francis Drake** episode *Mary, Queen of Scots*.

Greene Leon
Played Abel Gaunt in **The Persuaders!** episode *A Home of One's Own*.
Played Tig Jordan in the third season **The Saint** episode *Simon and Delilah*.

Greene Richard
Starred as Robin Hood in **The Adventures of Robin Hood**. [note: did not appear in season two's *The Goldmaker's Return* but made up by also playing Luke Tanner in the third season's *The Double*]. Was production associate on the fourth series.

Greene William
Appeared as Sir Hubert in the second series of **The Adventures of Robin Hood** episode *Hubert*.
Played Frank O'Hara in the first series **Ghost Squad** episode *Bullet With My Name on it*.
Played Jim Wallace in **The Saint** episode *Judith*.

Greenhalgh Paul
Played the waiter in the **Jason King** episode *A Royal Flush*.
Played Tony Lane in the fourth season **The Saint** episode *The Master Plan*.
Played the assistant director in the **UFO** episode *Court Martial*.

Greenhill Geoffrey
Played Yakovitz in the **Return of the Saint** episode *One Black September*.

Greenway Lee
Make-up on **The Count of Monte Cristo**.

Greenwood Joan
Played Nandina in the third season **Danger Man** [aka **Secret Agent**] episode *The Paper Chase*.

Greenwood Rosamund
Played Miss Ammerley in the **Father Brown** episode *The Eye of Apollo*.

Greer Luanshya
Played Diana in the **Man in a Suitcase** episode *Who's Mad Now?* and Anne Weeks in *Night Flight to Andora*.

Gregg Beverly
Played Madame Lenz in **The Count of Monte Cristo** episode *A Matter of Justice*.

Gregg Christina
Played Maria in the **Interpol Calling** episode *The Collector*.
Played Melissa in the first series **Man of the World** episode *Masquerade in Spain*.
Played Kathleen Howard in the first season **The Saint** episode *The Gentle Ladies*.

Gregg Hubert
Starred as Prince John in **The Adventures of Robin Hood** [the role was also played by Donald Pleasence & Brian Haines].

Gregg Stacey
Played Kim in the **Jason King** episode *Nadine*.

Gregory David
Played Cal in the **Department S** episode *The Treasure of the Costa del Sol*.
Played the yob in the **Gideon's Way** episode *The White Rat* and Syd Carter in *The Reluctant Witness*.

Gregory Hermione
Played Rosa in the **Danger Man** episode *The Lovers*.

Gregory Nigel
Played Culley in the **UFO** episode *The Sound of Silence* and a security man in *The Psychobombs*.

Gregory Paul
Played the businessman in the **Return of the Saint** episode *The Poppy Chain*.

Gregory Theo
Played Major Domo in **The Scarlet Pimpernel** episode *The Winged Madonna* and Christine in the episodes *The Sword of Justice* & *The Elusive Chauvelin*.

Gregson John
Featured in the **Espionage** episode *The Weakling*.
Starred as Commander George Gideon in the series **Gideon's Way**.
Played Harry Faversham in the **Man in a Suitcase** episode *Burden of Proof*.
Played Colonel Roberts in the third season **The Saint** episode *Escape Route*.
Starred as Dennis Croft [Shirley's Editor] in the series **Shirley's World**.

Greif Stephen
Played Krilov in **The Persuaders!** episode *The Man in the Middle*.
Played the policeman at the cafe in the second season **The Protectors** episode *Implicado*.

Greifer Lewis
Using the pen name Joshua Adam, wrote the season two **Ghost Squad** episodes *The Desperate Diplomat & The Thirteenth Girl* and the **G.S.5** episode *Rich Ruby Wine*.
As Joshua Adam, wrote **The Prisoner** episode *The General*.

Greig Joseph
Played Fergus in **The Baron** episode *The Man Outside*.
Played the old boatman in the third season **The Saint** episode *The Persistent Patriots*.

Grellis Brian
Played Detective Sergeant Watkins in the **Jason King** episode *An Author in Search of Two Characters*.

Grenville Keith
Played PC Russell in the **Randall and Hopkirk [Deceased]** aka **My Partner the Ghost** episode *The Trouble with Women*.
Played Dr Ferguson in the **Timeslip** story *The Day of the Clone* [series episode 24].
Played Dawson in the **UFO** episode *Flight Path*.

Gres Marie-Lise
Played the first model in the **Man in a Suitcase** episode *Variation on a Million Bucks*.

Grey Monica
Played Donna Sumrie in the fourth season **The Saint** episode *The Time to Die*.
Played Frau Anna in the **William Tell** episode *The Killer*.

Grey David
Played Envoy in the **Virgin of the Secret Service** episode *Dark Deeds on the Northwest Frontier*.

Grey Richard
Writer on **The New Adventures of Charlie Chan**.

Grey Timothy
Played Bond in **The Four Just Men** episode *The Discovery*.
Played the junior officer in the **O.S.S.** episode *Operation Yo Yo*.

Greyn Clinton
Played Lovegrove in **The Champions** episode *The Gilded Cage*.
Played Gerard in the **Department S** episode *The Mysterious Man in the Flying Machine*.
Played John Mallen in the **Jason King** two parter *All that Glisters*.
Played David Cameron in the second season **The Protectors** episode *Petard*.
Played Mark Tanner in the **UFO** episode *The Dalotek Affair*.
Starred as Captain Robert Virgin [England's finest] in **Virgin of the Secret Service**.
Played Anthony Martin in **The Zoo Gang** episode *Mindless Murder*.

Grieve John
Played Laird of Glencraig in the **Virgin of the Secret Service** episode *Wings Over Glencraig*.

Griff Stefan
Played the Waiter in the third season **The Saint** episode *The Gadget Lovers*.

Griffin Alison
Played the secretary in the second season **The Protectors** episode *The Insider*.

Griffith Kenneth
Played Richards in the fourth season **Danger Man** [aka **Secret Agent**] episode *Shinda Shima* [*Shinda Shima* was also merged

with the only other surviving fourth season colour episode, *Koroshi*, to form a TVM entitled *Koroshi*].

Guested as Schnipps in **The Prisoner** episode *The Girl who was Death* and as the President in *Fall Out*.

Played Segarus in the **Strange Report** episode *Report 4407: HEART: 'No Choice for the Donor'*.

Griffith Mark
Played the underwater cameraman in the UFO episode *Reflections in the Water*.

Griffiths Arthur
Played the newspaper seller in the **Man in a Suitcase** episode *Castle in the Clouds*.

Griffiths Bill
Hairdresser on the first season of **The Adventures of Robin Hood**.

Griffiths Fred
Played Mac in **The Sentimental Agent** episode *The Height of Fashion*.

Griffiths Jane
Played Ivy in **The Buccaneers** [aka **Dan Tempest**] episode *The Raiders*, Paula Meadows in *Dan Tempest Holds an Auction* and Paula in *To the Rescue & Indian Fighters*.

Played Anna in **The Count of Monte Cristo** episode *The Barefoot Empress*.

Griffiths Leon
Wrote the third series **The Adventures of Robin Hood** episodes *The Challenge of the Black Knight*, *The Healing Hand & The Ghost that Failed* and the fourth's *A Touch of Fever*, *The Reluctant Rebel*, *The Debt*, *The Champion* and *The Truce*.

Writer on **The Four Just Men**: *Their Man in London*, *The Protector* [co-teleplayed with Alan Moreland: from a story by Alan Moreland & Samuel B. West] and *Riot* [teleplayed from a story by Louis Marks].

Wrote the season two **Ghost Squad** episode *The Big Time*.

Wrote the **Return of the Saint** episode *Tower Bridge is Falling Down*.

Griffiths Lucy
Played the third Judge in **The Prisoner** episode *The Chimes of Big Ben* and appeared as the Lady in the corridor in *Dance of the Dead*.

Griffiths Michael
Played Superintendent Collins in the **Department S** episode *The Bones of Byrom Blain*.

Played Inspector Nelson in the **Randall and Hopkirk [Deceased]** aka **My Partner the Ghost** episodes *A Disturbing Case & That's How Murder Snowballs*.

Grimwood Unity
Played one of the models in the **Strange Report** episode *Report 3906: COVER GIRLS: 'Last year's Model'*.

Grist Paul
Played the pilot in **The Champions** episode *The Ghost Plane*.

Grizzard George
Featured in the **Espionage** episode *Festival of Pawns*.

Groome Stanley
Played Marat in **The Count of Monte Cristo** episode *The Art of Terror*.

Gross Arthur
Played the passport man in **The Four Just Men** episode *The Last Days of Nick Pompey*.

Played the control room operator in **The Prisoner** episode *Hammer into Anvil*.

Played the police sergeant in the third season **The Saint** episode *The Angel's Eye*.

Group Three
Produced **The Protectors** for ITC World Wide Distribution and **Space 1999** [an ITC/RAI co-production for worldwide distribution].

Grout James
Played Petroc in **The Adventures of Sir Lancelot** episode *Shepherd's War*.

Played the film Director in the **Jason King** episode *An Author in Search of Two Characters*.

Played Franklin in the **Man in a Suitcase** episode *The Sitting Pigeon*.

Grove Wilfred
Played the French postman in the third season **Danger Man** [aka **Secret Agent**] episode *The Hunting Party*.

Played Ramon in the first series **Man of the World** episode *The Sentimental Agent*.

Played Fred in **The Sentimental Agent** episode *The Beneficiary*.

Played Ali in the **Virgin of the Secret Service** episode *The Pyramid Plot*.

Gryff Stefan
Played Beaumont in the **Father Brown** episode *The Secret Garden*.

Guard Phillip
Played Sir Claude in the debut season of **The Adventures of Robin Hood** episode *The Betrothal*.

Played Lt. Nigel Brookes in the season two **Ghost Squad** episode *Sabotage*.

Played the title role in the **Sir Francis Drake** episode *Johnnie Factotum*.

Gudrun Ann
Played Mistress Rawlins in the first series of **The Adventures of Robin Hood** episode *The Wager*.

Guerin Charles
Wardrobe on **The Buccaneers** [aka **Dan Tempest**] episode *Slave Ship*.

Wardrobe supervisor on **The Saint**.

Guerrini Orso Maria
Played Ferro in the first season **Space 1999** episode *The Testament of Arkadia*.

Guest Michael
Played an ambulanceman in **The Champions** episode *To Trap a Rat*.

Played Rogers in the **Department S** episode *The Soup of the Day*.

Guest Val
Directed **The Adventurer** episodes *The Bradley Way*, *Has Anyone Here Seen Kelly?*, *Deadlock*, *I'll Get There Sometime*, *The Solid Gold Hearse*, *To the Lowest Bidder*, *Full Fathom Five & Going, Going....*

Directed **The Persuaders!** episodes *Five Miles to Midnight & Angie... Angie* and wrote *The Gold Napoleon*.

Directed the second season **Space 1999** episodes *The Rules of Luton*, *The A B Chrysalis & Dorzak*.

Guidotti Stewart
Played Rene in the **O.S.S.** episode *Operation Jingle Bells*.

Played Leavis in **The Sentimental Agent** episode *All that Jazz*.

Gunning Fred
Construction Manager on **UFO**.

Gur Aliza
Played Maria in the season two **Ghost Squad** episode *Sabotage*.

Gurney Rachel
Played Margaret Mandeville in the **Father Brown** episode *The Actor and the Alibi*.
Played Delphine Chambers in the first season **The Saint** episode *The Benevolent Burglary*.
Played The Marquise de Manton in **The Scarlet Pimpernel** episode *The Princess*.

Gurney Sharon
Played Valerie Green in **The Adventurer** episode *Return to Sender*.
Played Nerine in the **Jason King** episode *Zenia*.

Guthrie Frances
Appeared as Alice Sutton in the **White Hunter** episode *Run to Earth*.

Gwillim Jack
Guested as Carrington in **The Champions** episode *Full Circle*.
Played the General in the second series **Danger Man** [aka **Secret Agent**] episode *Such Men are Dangerous*, General Carteret in *The Black Book* and General White in *The Mercenaries*.
Played Commander Ripple in the **Gideon's Way** episode *State Visit*.
Played Superintendent Marsh in the first season **The Saint** episode *The Effete Angler*. Played Major Carter in the third season episodes *The Paper Chase* & *The Helpful Pirate*.

Gwynn Michael
Played Sir Richard in **The Adventurer** episode *Full Fathom Five*.
Played Mark Seldon in **The Baron** episode *Something for a Rainy Day*.
Played the Military Attache in the second series **Danger Man** [aka **Secret Agent**] episode *A Room in the Basement*.
Played Drieker in the **Department S** episode *A Ticket to Nowhere*.
Featured in the **Espionage** episode *The Incurable One*.
Played Sebastian Boone in the season two **Ghost Squad** episode *P.G. 7*.
Played Vaturia in the **Jason King** two parter *All that Glisters*.
Played Hyde Watson in the **Randall and Hopkirk [Deceased]** aka **My Partner the Ghost** episode *The Man from Nowhere*.
Played Martin Jeffroll in the second season **The Saint** episode *The Frightened Inn-Keeper*.

Gynt Greta
Played Lady Matilda in the second series of **The Adventures of Robin Hood** episode *The Friar's Pilgrimage*.
Played Sonia Vasa in the **H. G. Wells' Invisible Man** episode *Shadow on the Screen*.

Gypsy
Starred as Fury in the **Fury** series.

****

Haas Charlie
Director on **The New Adventures of Charlie Chan**.

Haberfield Graham
Played Tork in the **Strange Report** episode *Report 3424: EPIDEMIC: 'A Most Curious Crime'*.

Haby Nina
Played Arlette in the **Man in a Suitcase** episode *Blind Spot*.

Hackney Alan
Wrote the season four **The Adventures of Robin Hood** episodes *Tuck's Love Day, Hue and Cry* & *The Charm Pedlar*.

Hagan Geraldine
Played Jenny in the season four **The Adventures of Robin Hood** episode *Hue and Cry* and Maud in *The Lady Killer*.
Played Bella in the **Sword of Freedom** episode *The Lion and the Mouse*.

Hagen Rex
Starred as, Junior Ranger, Peter in **The Forest Rangers**.

Hagar Peter
Played the officer in the **G.S.5** episode *The Goldfish Bowl*.
Played the German police officer in the **Jason King** episode *As Easy as A B C*.
Played Fedora in the **Man in a Suitcase** episode *Somebody Loses, Somebody ...Wins?*.

Haggerty Fred
Played the agent in the **Man in a Suitcase** episode *Man from the Dead*.
Played the second guardian in **The Prisoner** episode *Hammer into Anvil*.

Hagon Garrick
Starred as Gavin Jones in the series **The Adventurer**: *Return to Sender, Double Exposure, Thrust and Counter Thrust, Counterstrike, I'll Get There Sometime, The Solid Gold Hearse, Full Fathom Five, Going, Going...., Make it a Million* & *Somebody Doesn't Like Me*.
Played Abdul Hakim in the **Return of the Saint** episode *One Black September*.

Haigh Kenneth
Played Juan in the first season **Danger Man** episode *Josetta*.
Played Blake in the **Strange Report** episode *Report 2641: HOSTAGE: 'If You Won't Learn, Die!*.

Haine Geoffrey
Assistant Director on **The Adventures of Sir Lancelot** episode *The Prince of Limerick*.
Production Supervisor on **The Champions** episodes *Reply Box No. 666, The Survivors, Shadow of the Panther, Nutcracker, The Final Countdown* and *Autokill*.

Haines Brian
Played Prince John in the season three **The Adventures of Robin Hood** episode *The Minstrel* [the role was also played by Donald Pleasence & Hubert Gregg].
Played Burton in the season two **Ghost Squad** episode *East of Mandalay*.
Played Withers in the **G.S.5** episode *Party for Murder*.
Played Kellerman in the **O.S.S.** episode *Operation Fracture*.
Played Serlio in the **Sword of Freedom** episode *The Value of Paper*.

Haines Patricia
Played Helga Sorenson in **The Baron** episode *Epitath for a Hero*.
Guested as Sophia in **The Champions** episode *The Mission*.

Played Nora Cazalet in the second series **Danger Man** [aka **Secret Agent**] episode *The Outcast* and Lady Blanchard *The Black Book*.
Played Veronica Bray in the **Department S** episode *The Trojan Tanker*.
Played Caroline Deeds in the season two **Ghost Squad** episode *Death of a Sportsman*.
Played Mrs Andersen in the second season **The Protectors** episode *Bagman*.
Played Martha in the **Randall and Hopkirk [Deceased]** aka **My Partner the Ghost** episode *Somebody just Walked over my Grave*.
Played Kay Collingwood in the fourth season **The Saint** episode *The World Beater*.

Hale Elvi
Played Sazi Keller in the season two **Ghost Squad** episode *Quarantine at Kavar*.
Played Jeanette in **The Scarlet Pimpernel** episode *The Farmer's Boy*.

Hale Georgina
Played the girl in the second season **The Protectors** episode *Shadbolt*.
Played Shang Si in the **Virgin of the Secret Service** episode *Across the Silver Pass of Gusri Song*.

Hale Nancy
Played Marguerite in **The Count of Monte Cristo** episode *Return to the Chateau d'If*.

Hall Adrian
Played the bell boy in the **Jason King** episode *Variations on a Theme*.

Hall Cameron
Played the caterer in the season two **Ghost Squad** episode *The Grand Duchess*.
Played Alderman Greer in the first season **The Saint** episode *The Well-Meaning Mayor*.

Hall Catherine
Played Rothwyn in *Adventure Three* of **Sapphire and Steel**.

Hall Elvi
Played Jeanine in **The Count of Monte Cristo** episode *The Art of Terror*.

Hall Frederick
Played the landlord in the **Father Brown** episode *The Hammer of God*.

Hall Ginger
Played Myra Rawlinson in **The Scarlet Pimpernel** episode *Thanksgiving Day*.

Hall Harvey
Played the frontier guard in the first season **Danger Man** episode *Time to Kill*, Franz in *The Girl in Pink Pyjamas* and Maxwell in the second series [now aka **Secret Agent**] episode *Fish on the Hook*.
Played Rogers in the **Department S** episode *Last Train to Redbridge*.
Played Bates in the **Man in a Suitcase** episode *No Friend of Mine*.
Played Smedley in the first series **Man of the World** episode *The Runaways*.
Played Ivanov in **The Persuaders!** episode *Read and Destroy*.
Played Reiwald in the first series **The Protectors** episode *2,000ft to Die*.
Played Merkin in the third season **The Saint** episode *Locate and Destroy*.

Played Thomas Phillips in the **Sir Francis Drake** episode *Mary, Queen of Scots*.
Played Heinz in the **William Tell** episode *The Master Spy* and Heinrich in *Secret Weapon*.

Hall Jacqueline
Played the girl in the third season **Danger Man** [aka **Secret Agent**] episode *Dangerous Secret*.

Hall John
Played Sid Kautsky in the **Gideon's Way** episode *The Great Plane Robbery*.

Hall Jon
Starred as Ramar [Dr Tom Reynolds] in the series **Ramar of the Jungle**.

Hall Martin
Wrote the **Strange Report** episode *Report 2475: REVENGE: 'When a Man Hates'*.

Hall Michael
Played Ralph Randall in the **Father Brown** episode *The Actor and the Alibi*.
Played Kaiser in the **Virgin of the Secret Service** episode *Pride of Assassins*.

Hall Wendy
Played Lucinda Masters in the **Man in a Suitcase** episode *Essay in Evil* and the receptionist in *Somebody Loses, Somebody ...Wins?*.

Hallam John
Played Doug Martin in the **Department S** episode *The Man in the Elegant Room*.
Played John Hewlett in the **Jason King** episode *A Thin Band of Air*.
Played Johnny Crackan in the **Randall and Hopkirk [Deceased]** aka **My Partner the Ghost** episode *It's Supposed to be Thicker than Water*.
Played Bernadotti in the **Return of the Saint** two parter *Collision Course* [Part 1: *The Brave Goose* & part 2: *The Sixth Man*: also exists as a movie entitled *The Saint and the Brave Goose*].

Hallett Neil
Played the forester in the third series **The Adventures of Robin Hood** episode *The Fire*, Michael in *Woman's War* and the commander in the fourth season's *The Loaf*.
Played Sam Bassett in **The Buccaneers** [aka **Dan Tempest**] episodes *Dan Tempest's War with Spain, The Wasp, Gunpowder Plot, Articles of War, Conquest of New Providence, Blood Will Tell, Hurricane, Dead Man's Rock, Gentleman Jack and the Lady, Mr. Beamish and the Hangman's Noose, Marooned, Dan Tempest and The Amazons, The Ladies, The Surgeon of Sangre Rojo, The Return of Calico Jack, Conquistador* and *Cutlass Wedding*. Played Hornigold in *Slave Ship*, the pirate in *Dangerous Cargo* and the barman in *Before the Mast*.
Played Doctor Lang in the **Department S** episode *Black Out*.
Played the Sergeant in **The Four Just Men** episode *The Deserter*.
Played Snaith in the first series **Ghost Squad** episode *The Green Shoes* [this episode was shot for the first series, but due to an actors' strike, was originally shown as a season two episode]. Return to the series, and the subsequent **G.S.5**, as regular Tony Miller.
Played Falkenburg in the **O.S.S.** episode *Operation Newsboy*.
Played Prentice in **The Persuaders!** episode *That's Me Over There*.
Played Doctor Dove in the second season **The Protectors** episode *Implicado*.
Played Andrew in the **Return of the Saint** episode *Tower Bridge is Falling Down*.

Played Bonner in the fourth season **The Saint** episode *The People Importers*.
Played Mayhew in the **Shirley's World** episode *The Rally*.
Played Kelly in the **UFO** episode *Close up*.
Appeared as Insp. Sommers in the **White Hunter** episode *The Prisoner*.
Played Rothman in the **William Tell** episode *The Traitor*.

Halliday Peter
Played Alfred in the season three **The Adventures of Robin Hood** episode *The Bride of Robin Hood*.
Played Secretary in **The Count of Monte Cristo** episode *The Grecian Gift* [aka *The Brothers*].
Played James in the second series **Danger Man** [aka **Secret Agent**] episode *Judgement Day*.
Played Ettore Scaccia in the season two **Ghost Squad** episode *A First Class Way to Die*.
Played James Baldwin in the **Man in a Suitcase** episode *No Friend of Mine*.
Played Vargas in the third season **The Saint** episode *The Reluctant Revolution*.
Played the Sergeant in **The Scarlet Pimpernel** episode *The Flower Woman*.
Played Theobald Burke in the **Sir Francis Drake** episode *The Irish Pirate*.
Played Dr. Segal in the **UFO** episode *A Question of Priorities*.

Halliwell Ken
Played the police constable in the **Father Brown** episode *The Eye of Apollo*.

Hallows Ted
Supervising Electrician on **The Champions, Department S** & **Jason King**.

Hamblin John
Played the first woodland man in **The Prisoner** episode *A Change of Mind*.

Hamill John
Played Chuck in the **Jason King** episode *Nadine*.
Played Dominick in the first season **Space 1999** episode *Force of Life*.

Hamilton Aileen
Wrote the second series **The Adventures of Robin Hood** episode *The Borrowed Baby*.

Hamilton Gabrielle
Played Mrs Rogers in the **Strange Report** episode *Report 2475: REVENGE: 'When a Man Hates'*.

Hamilton Gary
Played the student, Mike in the second season **The Protectors** episode *Dragon Chase*.

Hamilton Gay
Played Lucia in the **Man in a Suitcase** episode *Variation on a Million Bucks* [part 2: also combined with the first installment to form a movie: *To Chase a Million*] and Magda in *Castle in the Clouds*.
Played Eva Zoref in the first season **Space 1999** episode *Force of Life*.

Hamilton Hal
Played the police Sergeant in the **Man in a Suitcase** episode *The Revolutionaries*.

Hamilton John
Played Vicomte de Combray in **The Count of Monte Cristo** episode *The Duel*.
Played the bus conductor in the **Strange Report** episode *Report 8319: GRENADE: 'What Price Change?'*.

Hamilton Lee
Played Father Martin in **The Four Just Men** episode *Dead Man's Switch* and the customs man in *The Last Days of Nick Pompey*.

Hammer Barbara
Wrote the story for **The Four Just Men** episode *The Miracle of St. Philippe* [teleplayed by Jan Read and Louis Marks].
Wrote the **Interpol Calling** episode *You Can't Die Twice* [from a story by Leonard Fincham].

Hammond P. J.
Created and wrote the **Sapphire and Steel** series.
Wrote the book *Sapphire and Steel* [1979: novelisation of the first six episodes of the first series].

Hammond Peter
Guested as Bartholomew in the debut season **The Adventures of Robin Hood** episode *The Jongleur*.
Regular, as Lieutenant Beamish, in **The Buccaneers** [aka **Dan Tempest**]: *Blackbeard, The Raiders, Captain Dan Tempest, Dan Tempest's War with Spain, The Wasp, Slave Ship, Gunpowder Plot, Articles of War, Conquest of New Providence, Mother Doughty's Crew, Blood Will Tell, Hurricane, Dead Man's Rock, Dangerous Cargo, Hand of the Hawk, Gentleman Jack and the Lady, Mr. Beamish and the Hangman's Noose, Marooned, Before the Mast, Dan Tempest and The Amazons, The Ladies, The Surgeon of Sangre Rojo, The Return of Calico Jack, Conquistador* and *Cutlass Wedding*.
Played the Ambassador in the **Sword of Freedom** episode *The Ambassador*.
Regular in **William Tell** as Captain Hofmanstahl: *The Hostages, Secret Death, The Cuckoo, The Magic Powder, The Bear* and *The Young Widow*.

Hamnett Olivia
Played Anita in the **Department S** episode *The Treasure of the Costa del Sol*.
Played Anne Soames in the **Randall and Hopkirk [Deceased]** aka **My Partner the Ghost** episode *Just for the Record*.

Hampshire Susan
Played Lena in the second series **Danger Man** [aka **Secret Agent**] episode *You're Not in Any Trouble, Are You?* and Lesley Arden in *Are You Going to Be More Permanent?*
Played Celia in the **Sir Francis Drake** episode *King of America*.

Hampson Peter
Played Pedro in the **Sir Francis Drake** episode *The Prisoner*.

Hancock Prentis
Played William Arthur Mackay in the second season two part **The Protectors** episode *Wam*.
Played Vic in the **Return of the Saint** episode *Collision Course* [Part 1: 'The Brave Goose': also exists, combined with the second instalment as a movie entitled *The Saint and the Brave Goose*].
Starred as, first season regular, Paul Morrow in **Space 1999**.

Handl Irene
Played Polly in the second series of **The Adventures of Robin Hood** episode *The Shell Game*.
Played the woman in the lift in the **H. G. Wells' Invisible Man** episode *Shadow on the Screen*.

Handley Jenny
Played Julia Franklin in **The Adventurer** episode *The Case of the Poisoned Pawn*.

Hankins Brian
Played Whitmarsh in the **G.S.5** episode *The Goldfish Bowl*.

Hankinson Michael
Co-wrote the **Interpol Calling** episode *The Girl with Grey Hair* [with Leonard Fincham and Robert Stewart].

Hanley Jenny
Played Magda in **The Persuaders!** episode *Someone Waiting*.
Played Sandy in the **Return of the Saint** episode *The Poppy Chain*.

Hanlon Roy
Played the policeman in **The Baron** episode *The Man Outside*.
Played Machet in the **Department S** episode *Dead Men Die Twice*.
Played Jock in the **Gideon's Way** episode *The White Rat*.
Played Nero Jones in the fourth season **The Saint** two parter *The Fiction Makers*.

Hanny Kenneth
Played Sir Edwin in the **Gideon's Way** episode *Subway to Revenge*.

Hansard Paul
Played a number of roles in the second series of **The Adventures of Robin Hood**: Quentin in *A Village Wooing*, Gervaise in *The Scientist*, Lescaux in *Blackmail*, Constable in *A Year and a Day*, Ned in *The Goldmaker* & Rolf in *The Impostor*.
Returned in series three: as Troubadour in *Pepper* and as Augustine in *The Genius*.
Played Sir Lionel in **The Adventures of Sir Lancelot** episode *The Knight with the Red Plume* and Lionel in *The Queen's Knight*.
Played Alfie in **The Buccaneers** [aka **Dan Tempest**] episodes *Blackbeard, The Raiders* and *Captain Dan Tempest*. This was before becoming, series regular, Taffy: *Dan Tempest's War with Spain, Whale Gold, Gunpowder Plot, Articles of War, Ghost Ship, Conquest of New Providence, Mother Doughty's Crew, Hurricane, Dangerous Cargo, Hand of the Hawk, Gentleman Jack and the Lady, Mr. Beamish and the Hangman's Noose, Marooned, Before the Mast, Dan Tempest and The Amazons, The Ladies, The Surgeon of Sangre Rojo, The Return of Calico Jack, Conquistador, Aztec Treasure, Prize of Andalusia, Cutlass Wedding, Dan Tempest Holds an Auction, Flip and Jenny, To the Rescue, Indian Fighters, Mistress Higgins' Treasure, The Spy Aboard, The Decoy, Pirate Honour, Instrument of War* and *Printer's Devil*.
Played Emil Boder in **The Champions** episode *The Mission*.
Played Oberfeld in the **Man in a Suitcase** episode *Somebody Loses, Somebody ...Wins?*.
Played the guard in the **Sword of Freedom** episode *Serenade in Red* and Guidone in *The Marionettes*.

Hanson Bernard
Assistant Director on **The Adventures of Sir Lancelot** episodes *The Bridge, Maid of Somerset, The Ugly Duckling, Knight's Choice* and *The Missing Princess*.

Harbin Robert
Played Rolf in the first season **Danger Man** episode *The Lonely Chair*.

Harding Tony
Assistant Director on **The Secret Service**.

Harding Vincent
Played Standfast in the third season **Danger Man** [aka **Secret Agent**] episode *I'm Afraid you Have the Wrong Number*.
Played Hans in the season two **Ghost Squad** episode *Lost In Transit*.
Played PC Lashbrook in the **Gideon's Way** episode *The Tin God*.
Played the duty guard [1] in the fourth season **The Saint** two parter *The Fiction Makers*.

Hardtmuth Paul
Played Senor Paterno in the first season **Danger Man** episode *The Journey Ends Halfway.*

Hardwicke Edward
Played the frontier guard in the first season **Danger Man** episode *Time to Kill.*
Played Macbane in the **H. G. Wells' Invisible Man** episode *The Big Plot.*

Hardwicke Paul
Played Winters in **The Adventurer** episode *Make it a Million.*
Played the Priest in **The Count of Monte Cristo** episode *Majorca.*

Hardy Kim
Played Pam Plackett in the **Return of the Saint** episode *Signal Stop.*

Hardy Laurence
Played Sir William in the second series of **The Adventures of Robin Hood** episodes *The Haunted Mill* and *The Road in the Air.* Returned in season four as Sir Marmot in *Trapped.*
Played Professor Nesterenko in the season two **Ghost Squad** episode *A First Class Way to Die.*
Played Dr. Coles in the **Gideon's Way** episode *The Nightlifers.*

Hardy Lindsay
Wrote the first season **Man of the World** episodes *Masquerade in Spain* & *Specialist for the Kill.*
Wrote **The Sentimental Agent** episodes *Express Delivery* & *Meet my Son, Henry.*

Hardy Patricia
Played Cecile in **The Count of Monte Cristo** episode *The Golden Blade.*

Hardy Robert
Guested as Rupert in **The Adventures of Sir Lancelot** episode *Knight's Choice.*
Played Curt Hoffman in **The Baron** episode *A Memory of Evil.*
Played Lord Hinch in **The Buccaneers** episode *Flip and Jenny.*
Played Walter Faber in the fourth season **The Saint** episode *The Desperate Diplomat.*
Played Doctor Sanders in the **Strange Report** episode *Report 4407: HEART: 'No Choice for the Donor'.*

Hardy Tim
Played Andre in **The Zoo Gang** episode *The Twisted Cross.*

Hare Doris
Played Madame Hanska in the **Randall and Hopkirk [Deceased]** episode *But what a Sweet Little Room.*
Played Mrs. Barlow in the second season **The Saint** episode *The Crooked Ring.*

Hare Ernest
Played the English man in the second season **The Saint** episode *The Rhine Maiden.*

Hare Thomas
Played Stavro in **The Four Just Men** episode *The Deserter* and Pietro in *The Man in the Royal Suite.*
Played Aldo in the **Sword of Freedom** episode *The Duke.*

Hargreaves David
Played Russell in **The Adventurer** episode *Mr Calloway is a Very Cautious Man.*

Hargreaves Janet
Played Eirlys Brooks in the second series **Danger Man** [aka **Secret Agent**] episode *Parallel Lines Sometimes Meet.*

Harmer Juliet
Played Michelle in the second series **Danger Man** [aka **Secret Agent**] episode *Sting in the Tail* and Lady Kilrush in the third season's *The Man on the Beach.*
Played Trish in the **Department S** episode *The Man in the Elegant Room* and Paula in *A Ticket to Nowhere.*
Played Shelly Blackman in the **Jason King** episode *Uneasy Lies the Head.*
Played Prue in **The Persuaders!** episodes *The Old, the New and the Deadly* & *That's Me Over There.*
Played Miss Holliday in the **Randall and Hopkirk [Deceased]** aka **My Partner the Ghost** episode *You Can Always Find a Fall Guy.*

Harper Gerald
Guested as Croft in **The Champions** episode *The Fanatics.*
Played Deputy Commissioner Rae Cox in the **Gideon's Way** episode *State Visit.*
Played Freddie Maguire in the **G.S.5** episode *Hideout.*
Played Lieutenant Patrick in the **O.S.S.** episode *Operation Sardine.*

Harries Davyd
Played Logan in the **Department S** episode *The Bones of Byrom Blain.*

Harrington Victor
Played a passenger in the **Father Brown** episode *The Curse of the Golden Cross.*

Harris Allan
Art Director on **The Saint** and **Sir Francis Drake.**

Harris Anita
Make-up on season 3 and 4 of **Sapphire and Steel.**

Harris Bill
Directed the **Fireball XL5** episodes *Space Magnet, Flying Zodiac, Space Pirates, Convict in Space, Prisoner on the Lost Planet, Robert to the Rescue, 1875* and *Faster than Light.*
Directed the second season **Supercar** episodes *Hi-Jack, The Sky's the Limit, Jail Break* & *King Kool.*

Harris Joseph
Executive Producer on the series **O.S.S.**

Harris Len
Camera Operator on **The Prisoner** episodes *Do Not Forsake Me Oh My Darling, Living in Harmony, The Girl who Was Death* and, with Bob Kindred, on *Fall Out.*

Harris Leslie
Co-wrote **The Sentimental Agent** episode *Not Quite Fully Covered* [with Roger East].
Executive Producer on the **Man of the World** and **Sir Francis Drake** series.

Harris Paul
Played Wayne in **The Baron** episode *There's Someone Close Behind You.*

Harris Richard
Wrote the season two **Ghost Squad** episode *The Last Jump.*
Created the **Man in a Suitcase** series [with Dennis Spooner; devised by Stanley R. Greenberg].
Wrote the debut season **The Saint** episodes *The Loaded Tourist* & *The Pearls of Peace.*

Harris Stacy
Played Rolla in **The Count of Monte Cristo** episode *The Duel.*

Harrison Brian
Played the co-pilot in the **Department S** episode *A Ticket to Nowhere*.
Played the pilot in the third season **The Saint** episode *A Double in Diamonds* and the police doctor in the fourth season's *The Desperate Diplomat*.

Harrison Cathryn
Played Linda in the **Return of the Saint** episode *Duel in Venice*.

Harrison Felicity
Played Mother in *Adventure One* of **Sapphire and Steel**.

Harrison Gordon
Appeared as McCreery in the **White Hunter** episode *The Jackals*.

Harrison John
Played Daniels in the first season **Danger Man** episode *Deadline*.

Harrison Noel
Played Lord Allwood in the first series **Man of the World** episode *The Runaways*.

Harrison Norman
Directed the first series **Ghost Squad** episodes *Ticket for Blackmail & High Wire*.
Directed the **Interpol Calling** episode *A Foreign Body*.

Harron Donald
Featured in the **Espionage** episode *A Tiny Drop of Poison*.

Harrow Lisa
Played Anna in the first season **Space 1999** episode *The Testament of Arkadia*.

Hart David
Played the outlaw in the season three **The Adventures of Robin Hood** episode *Castle in the Air*.
Played Will in the third series **The Adventures of Robin Hood** episode *Elixir of Youth*.

Hart Jon
Starred as Hawkeye 'the Long Rifle' in the series **Hawkeye and the Last of the Mohicans**.

Hart Lewis
Wrote the **Sword of Freedom** episode *Francesca*.

Hart Ralph
Wrote the **Captain Scarlet and the Mysterons** episode *Renegade Rocket*.

Hartley Norman
Played P.C. Martin in the **Man in a Suitcase** episode *Why they Killed Nolan*.

Hartnell William
Played Fred Rice in the first series **Ghost Squad** episode *High Wire*.

Harvey Edward
Played the Sheriff in the fourth season **The Saint** episode *The Scales of Justice*.
Played Biotto in the **Sword of Freedom** episode *The Bracelet*.

Harvey Griselda
Played Lady Snatterthwaite in **The Scarlet Pimpernel** episode *The Imaginary Invalides*.

Harvey Jimmy
Second Unit Cameraman on **The Champions**.

Harvey John
Played the Lieutenant in the third series **The Adventures of Robin Hood** episodes *The Minstrel & The Lottery* and Sir George Woodley in *The Doctor*.
Played Dougal in **The Buccaneers** [aka **Dan Tempest**] episode *Instrument of War* and Lawyer Knox in *Dan Tempest Holds an Auction*.
Played Wade in the **H. G. Wells' Invisible Man** episode *Flight into Darkness*.
Played Toby in the **Man in a Suitcase** episode *Who's Mad Now?*.
Played the prosecuting counsel in the **Randall and Hopkirk [Deceased]** aka **My Partner the Ghost** episode *Could You Recognise the Man Again?*.

Hashfield Mark
Played the second soldier in the second series of **The Adventures of Robin Hood** episode *The Friar's Pilgrimage*.

Hassall Imogen
Played Cleo in **The Champions** episode *Reply Box No: 666*.
Played Gina in the **Jason King** episode *The Stones of Venice*.
Played Maria in **The Persuaders!** episode *Overture*.
Played Nikki in **The Sentimental Agent** episode *Not Quite Fully Covered*.
Played Sophia in the first season **The Saint** episode *Sophia*, Nadya in the third season's *Flight Plan* and Malia in the fourth's *The People Importers*.

Hasse Camilla
Played Ann in the season four **The Adventures of Robin Hood** episode *Bride for an Outlaw*.
Played the girl in the florists in the first season **Danger Man** episode *Hired Assassin*.
Played the Day Supervisor in **The Prisoner** episode *Dance of the Dead*.
Played Maria Naccaro in the second season **The Saint** episode *The Damsel in Distress*.

Hastings Charlotte
Wrote the **White Hunter** episode *Let My People Go* [with Gordon Wellesley].

Haswell James
Played the barman in the **Father Brown** episode *The Quick One*.

Hatch Tony
Composed the theme for **The Champions**.

Hatton John
Played the policeman in the season two **Ghost Squad** episode *Quarantine at Kavar*.
Played the Spanish soldier in the **Sir Francis Drake** episode *Visit to Spain*.

Haughton Brian
Played the telex operator in the **Return of the Saint** episode *The Armageddon Alternative*.

Hauser Philo
Guested as Carter in the **Interpol Calling** episode *You Can't Die Twice*.
Played the hotel manager in the second season **Man of the World** episode *Double Exposure*.
Played Suza in the second season **The Saint** episode *The Death Penalty* and Hans in the third season's *The Art Collectors*.
Played the official in the **Sentimental Agent** episode *Express Delivery*.

Havard Dafydd
Played the landlord in the series two **Danger Man** episode *Whatever Happened to George Foster?*.
Played the second local in the third season **The Saint** episode *The House on Dragon's Rock*.

Haward Ken
Played a warder in **The Baron** episode *You Can't Win Them All*; the third security man in the third season **Danger Man** [aka **Secret Agent**] episode *The Man who wouldn't Talk* and Peterson in the **Virgin of the Secret Service** episode *The Amazons*.

Hawdon Robin
Played Buckley in **The Adventurer** episode *Somebody Doesn't Like Me*.
Played Walter Pally in the **Department S** episode *A Cellar full of Silence*.
Played Grant in the **Randall and Hopkirk [Deceased]** aka **My Partner the Ghost** episode *The Smile Behind the Veil*.
Played the Skydiver's captain in the **UFO** episode *The Psychobombs*.

Hawk Jeremy
Played Addison Carshaw in the **Shirley's World** episode *Always Leave Them Laughing*.

Hawkins Brian
Played the guard in the first series **Man of the World** episode *The Sentimental Agent*.

Hawkins David
Editor on **The Adventures of Sir Lancelot** episodes *The Ferocious Fathers, The Outcast, Winged Victory, Sir Bliant, The Magic Sword, Lancelot's Banishment, Roman Wall, Caledon, Shepherd's War, The Pirates, The Black Castle, The Magic Book, Knight Errand* and *The Theft of Excalibur*.
Editor on **The Buccaneers** [aka **Dan Tempest**] episodes *Ghost Ship, Mother Doughty's Crew, Hurricane, Dangerous Cargo, Conquistador, Prize of Andalusia, Dan Tempest Holds an Auction, Flip and Jenny, Mistress Higgins' Treasure* and *The Decoy, Pirate Honour*.
Editor on the first series of **Danger Man**.

Hawkins Frank
Played the MI5 agent in the **O.S.S.** episodes *Operation Foulball* and *Operation Chopping Block*.
Played Inspector Dunlap in the **White Hunter** episode *Marked Man* and the Chief Air Controller in *Valley of the Dead*.

Hawkins Jack
Starred as Ben Manfred in the series **The Four Just Men** [The series was filmed in four separate blocks with the four stars actually appearing together in *The Battle of the Bridge* only. Dan Dailey & Richard Conte were each allocated ten episodes and Jack Hawkins & Vittorio de Sica each appeared in nine]: *Village of Shame, The Deserter, Their Man in London, National Treasure, The Survivor, Money to Burn, The Man Who Wasn't There, The Heritage* and *The Boy Without a Country*.

Hawkins John
Video Tape Editor on **Sapphire and Steel**.

Hawkins Mark
Played Tony Williams in the **Strange Report** episode *Report 4407: HEART: 'No Choice for the Donor'*.
Played an astronaut in the **UFO** episodes *Ordeal* & *The Responsibility Seat* and the Interceptor pilot in *Close up*.
Played Gerald in the **Virgin of the Secret Service** episode *Entente Cordiale*.

Hawkins Michael
Played Inspector Ralph Nelson in **The Baron** episode *The Island* [part 2 of a two-parter: also exists, edited together with part 1 - *Storm Warning*, as a feature entitled *Mystery Island*].

Played Detective Inspector Stoke in the **Man in a Suitcase** episode *Which Way did he Go, McGill?*.

Hawkins Peter
Played Gibbs in the **Father Brown** episode *The Hammer of God*.

Hawksley Brian
Played Inspector Greenwood in the **Father Brown** episode *The Quick One*.
Played Father General in the **Man in a Suitcase** episode *The Whisper*.

Hawthorne Nigel
Played the Assistant Director in the second season **Man of the World** episode *The Bandit*.

Hawtrey Nicholas
Played the waiter in the second series **Danger Man** [aka **Secret Agent**] episode *Don't Nail Him Yet*.

Hayden Jane
Played Aileen in the **Return of the Saint** episode *The Arrangement*.

Hayers Sidney
Directed **The Persuaders!** episodes *Take Seven* & *A Death in the Family*.
Directed the **Shirley's World** episode *Always Leave Them Laughing*.
Directed **The Zoo Gang** episodes *Revenge: Post-dated, African Misfire* & *The Lion Hunt*.

Hayes Brian
Played Benson in **The Persuaders!** episode *Read and Destroy*.

Hayes Malcolm
Played the intruder in the second season **The Protectors** episode *Goodbye George*.

Hayes Patricia
Played Miss Lee in **The Four Just Men** episode *National Treasure*.

Haygarth Anthony
Played the driver in the first series **The Protectors** episode *See No Evil*.

Hayles Kenneth
Wrote the **G.S.5** episode *An Eye for An Eye*.
Wrote the first season **The Saint** episode *The Invisible Millionaire*.

Hayman Cyd
Played Magda in **The Adventurer** episode *Love Always, Magda*.
Played Lyn in **The Persuaders!** episode *Anyone Can Play*.
Played Cynthia in the first season **Space 1999** episode *Alpha Child*.

Haymes Dick
Played Dunstan in the second season **The Saint** episode *The Contract*.

Hayne Murray
Played the policeman at the garage in the third season **Danger Man** [aka **Secret Agent**] episode *The Man who wouldn't Talk*.

Haystead Mercy
Played Teresa in **The Count of Monte Cristo** episode *The Portuguese Affair*.

Hayter James
Played Tom the Miller in the series two **The Adventures of Robin Hood** episodes *The Haunted Mill* & *The Road in the Air*.
Played Sir Aaron Armstrong in the **Father Brown** episode *Three Tools of Death*.
Played Jones in the **O.S.S.** episode *Operation Eel* and the music shop proprietor in *Operation Barbecue*.

Haythorne Joan
Played the wife in **The Four Just Men** episode *The Deadly Capsule*.

Haywood Alan
Played Sergeant Knox in the third season **The Saint** episodes *The Power Artist* & *A Double in Diamonds*.
Played the SHADO diver in the **UFO** episode *Sub-smash*.

Hayward Louise
Played Val Pearson in **The Four Just Men** episode *Panic Button*.

Head Murray
Played Pierre in the **Return of the Saint** episode *The Diplomat's Daughter*.
Played Ray King in the **Shirley's World** episode *Follow That Rickshaw*.

Head Sidney
Appeared as 'wooden leg' in **The Adventures of Sir Lancelot** episode *Thieves*.

Healy David
Played David Laver in **The Baron** episode *The Island* [part 2 of a two-parter: also exists, edited together with part 1 - *Storm Warning*, as a feature entitled *Mystery Island*].
Played Ramos in the **Department S** episode *The Soup of the Day*.
Played Norman Drage in the **Father Brown** episode *The Arrow of Heaven*.
Played Drakin in the **Jason King** episode *Flamingoes only Fly on Tuesdays*.
Voiced Shane Weston on the **Joe 90** series.
Played Colonel Adler in **The Persuaders!** episode *Element of Risk*.
Played Bugsy Spanio in the **Randall and Hopkirk [Deceased]** aka **My Partner the Ghost** episode *Murder ain't what it Used to Be!*.
Played Hal Ward in the third season **The Saint** episode *Simon and Delilah*.
Provided voices for **The Secret Service**.
Played Prentice in **The Sentimental Agent** episode *A Very Desirable Plot*.
Played Hansen in the **Return of the Saint** episode *The Arrangement*.
Played Mr Alsbury in the **Strange Report** episode *Report 3906: COVER GIRLS: 'Last Year's Model'*.
Played Joe Franklin in the **UFO** episode *Ordeal*.

Heard Brian
Assistant Director on **Joe 90**.
Directed **The Secret Service** episodes *To Catch a Spy* and *A Hole in One*.

Hearne Reginald
In **The Adventures of Sir Lancelot**, played Cedric in *Double Identity*, Sir Eustace in *The Bridge*, Hedrick in *The Witch's Brew*, Hugo in *Ruby of Radnor*, Rajah in *The Mortaise Fair*, Chamberlain in *Maid of Somerset*, the captain in *Sir Crustabread*, the blacksmith in *The Lady Lilith*, Sir Julian in *Knight's Choice* and Evanston in *The Missing Princess*.
Played Hawkes in the first season **Danger Man** episode *The Gallows Tree*.

Played the doctor in the **H. G. Wells' Invisible Man** episode *Strange Partners*.
Played Rawston in the **O.S.S.** episode *Operation Yodel*, the gendarme in *Operation Dagger* and the second Nazi patrol in *Operation Jingle Bells*.
Played Gomez in the **Sir Francis Drake** episode *The Flame Thrower*.

Heath Eira
Played Rosanna Lopez in **The Four Just Men** episode *Their Man in London*.

Heath Eric
Wrote **The Adventures of Robin Hood** episodes *The Coming of Robin Hood*, *The Moneylender* [with Ian Larkin], *Dead or Alive*, *Friar Tuck*, *A Guest for the Gallows*, *The Knight Who Came To Dinner*, *The Challenge*, *Queen Eleanor*, *The Ordeal*, *The Highlander*, *The Alchemist*, *The Brothers* and *The Deserted Castle*.

Heath Mark
Played Colonel M'Bota in the second series **Danger Man** [aka **Secret Agent**] episode *Loyalty Always Pays*.

Heathcote Humphrey
Played the male singer in the **Man in a Suitcase** episode *The Sitting Pigeon*.

Heathcote Thomas
Played Lt. Colonel Trent in the season two **Ghost Squad** episode *The Last Jump*.
Played Det. Chief Supt. Appleby in the **Gideon's Way** episode *The Prowler*.
Played the Lobo Man in **The Prisoner** episode *A Change of Mind*.
Played Chief Inspector Horner in the **Randall and Hopkirk [Deceased]** aka **My Partner the Ghost** episode *The Ghost Talks*.
Played Di Santi in the **Sword of Freedom** episode *The Slave*.

Hedges Natalie
Played the parasol girl in *Adventure Four* of **Sapphire and Steel**.

Hedison David
Played Bill Harvey in the first season **The Saint** episode *Luella*.

Hedley Bill
Wrote the **Captain Scarlet and the Mysterons** episode *Model Spy*.

Hedley Jack
Played Raikes in **The Buccaneers** [aka **Dan Tempest**] episode *The Spy Aboard*.
Played Bruce Carroway in the **Gideon's Way** episode *The Alibi Man*.
Played Colonel Dyson in the **Return of the Saint** episode *The Obono Affair*.
Played Duncan Rawl in the second season **The Saint** episode *The Old Treasure Story*.
Played Webb in the **UFO** episode *Court Martial*.
Played Steve Porter in the **White Hunter** episode *Marked Man*.

Hedley Maurice
Played Sir William Hallows in the season two **Ghost Squad** episode *The Magic Bullet*.
Played Colonel Alec Middleton in the **Gideon's Way** episode *The Big Fix*.
Played Colonel Chalmers in the **Randall and Hopkirk [Deceased]** aka **My Partner the Ghost** episode *Who Killed Cock Robin*.
Played Ivor North in the second season **The Saint** episode *The Inescapable Word*.

Heffer Richard
Played Hughes in the **Department S** episode *Spencer Bodily is 60 Years Old* and Ludwig in the **Jason King** episode *A Royal Flush*.

Hefferman Ann
Played Madame Lafleur in the second series **Danger Man** [aka **Secret Agent**] episode *Have a Glass of Wine*.

Heider Allen
Played the Guard Commander in the **Virgin of the Secret Service** episode *The Rajah and the Suffragette*.

Heilbron Lorna
Played Isla in the **Virgin of the Secret Service** episode *Wings Over Glencraig*.

Heinz Gerard
Played Count de Severne in the first series **The Adventures of Robin Hood** episode *The Coming of Robin Hood*.
Appeared as Eck in **The Adventures of Sir Lancelot** episode *The Lesser Breed*.
Played the Ambassador in **The Count of Monte Cristo** episode *A Toy for the Infanta*.
Played Dr Huber in the second series **Danger Man** [aka **Secret Agent**] episode *A Room in the Basement*.
Played Menger in **The Four Just Men** episode *The Man Who Wasn't There*.
Guested as Mr Dorner in the **Interpol Calling** episode *You Can't Die Twice*.
Played the hotel manager in the **Jason King** episode *If it's Got to Go - It's Got to Go*.
Played Kolonel in the **O.S.S.** episode *Operation Death Trap* and Schneider in *Operation Post Office*.
Played Professor Mueller in the first season **The Saint** episode *The Sporting Chance*, Joris Vanlinden in the second season's *The Saint Bids Diamonds* and Hortel in the third's *The Reluctant Revolution*.
Played Alva in the **Sir Francis Drake** episode *Beggars of the Sea*.

Held Karl
Played Major in **The Adventurer** episode *Action!*.
Played Shriver in the **Return of the Saint** episode *The Diplomat's Daughter*.
Played Travis in the second season **Space 1999** episode *The Immunity Syndrome*.
Played Drake in the **Strange Report** episode *Report 1553: RACIST: 'A Most Dangerous Proposal'*.

Heller Anthony
Camera Operator on **The Adventures of Sir Lancelot** episodes *The Outcast, Winged Victory, Sir Bliant, The Magic Sword, Lancelot's Banishment, Roman Wall, Caledon, Shepherd's War, The Pirates, The Black Castle, The Magic Book, Knight Errand* and *The Theft of Excalibur*.

Heller John
Played the German guard in the **O.S.S.** episode *Operation Powder Puff*.

Heller John G.
Appeared as the Czech policeman in the second season **Danger Man** [aka **Secret Agent**] episode *The Professionals* and as Joseph in *No Marks for Servility*. Played Manuel in the third season's *Someone is Liable to get Hurt*.
Played Joffe in the first series **Ghost Squad** episode *The Broken Doll*.
Played Jacques Boucher in the first season **The Saint** episode *The Lawless Lady* and the Major in the third season's *The Paper Chase*.

Helman Geoffrey
Production Manager on the series **The Zoo Gang**.

Hempel Anoushka
Played Milena Corri in **The Adventurer** episode *Has Anyone Here Seen Kelly?*.
Played the stewardess in the **Department S** episode *The Bones of Byrom Blain*.
Played Carla II in **The Persuaders!** episode *The Long Goodbye* and the stewardess in *The Ozerov Inheritance*.
Played Lynn Jackson in the **Return of the Saint** episode *The Armageddon Alternative*.
Played Annette in the second season **Space 1999** episode *The Metamorph*.

Hendel Kenneth
Played the Spanish Official in the first series **The Protectors** episode *The Quick Brown Fox*.

Henderson Betty
Played Mrs Cheavers in the season two **Ghost Squad** episode *The Big Time*.

Henderson Don
Played Walters in the first series **The Protectors** episode *Disappearing Trick*.

Henderson Robert
Played Albert in the second series **Danger Man** [aka **Secret Agent**] episode *Fish on the Hook*.
Played the doctor in **The Four Just Men** episode *Dead Man's Switch* and the Judge in *The Discovery*.
Played the General in the **O.S.S.** episodes *Operation Foulball* & *Operation Meatball*.
Appeared as General Walker in the **White Hunter** episode *The General*.
Played Henry Davis in **The Zoo Gang** episode *Revenge: Postdated*.

Henderson Russ
Played Sam in **The Persuaders!** episode *Someone Waiting*.

Hendry Ian
Played Wallace / Hagen in the third season **Danger Man** [aka **Secret Agent**] episode *Say it with Flowers*.
Played Lieutenant Daniels in the **H. G. Wells' Invisible Man** episode *Shadow Bomb*.
Played Lord Croxley in **The Persuaders!** episode *The Time and the Place*.
Played Inspector Wilson in the first series **The Protectors** episode *Thinkback*.
Played Roy Gates in the **Return of the Saint** episode *Yesterday's Hero*.
Played Destamio in the fourth season **The Saint** two parter *Vendetta for the Saint*.

Hendryx Shirl
Wrote the third series **The Adventures of Robin Hood** episode *The Angry Village*.

Heneghan Patricia
Played Anne Brown in the **G.S.5** episode *Death of a Cop*.

Henley Drewe
Played Bernard in the **Man in a Suitcase** episode *Three Blinks of the Eyes*.
Played Clarke in the second season **The Protectors** episode *The Tiger and the Goat*.
Played Tony in the **Randall and Hopkirk [Deceased]** aka **My Partner the Ghost** episode *A Sentimental Journey*.
Played Steve Maddox in the **UFO** episode *Conflict*.

Henney Del
Played the detective in the first series **The Protectors** episode *Triple Cross*.

Henry Gustav
Played the young boy in the **Department S** episode *The Ghost of Mary Burnham*.

Henry Kenneth
Played Ironside in the first season **The Saint** episode *The Well-Meaning Mayor*.

Henry Stuart
Played the technician in the **Timeslip** story *The Year of the Burn-Up* [series episode 16].

Henson Basil
Guested as Wolf Eisen in **The Champions** episode *The Final Countdown*.
Played Robert Trevor in the **Jason King** episode *It's Too Bad about Auntie*.

Henson Nicky
Played Beanie in the **Shirley's World** episode *To Dream the Improbable Dream*.

Hepton Bernard
Played Colonel Richards in the **Virgin of the Secret Service** episode *Dark Deeds on the Northwest Frontier*.

Herbert Percy
Played the innkeeper in the first season **Danger Man** episode *The Conspirators* and Sergeant Bates in the second series [now aka **Secret Agent**] episode *The Mercenaries*.
Played Brady in **The Four Just Men** episode *Riot*.
Played Hoppy in the first season **The Saint** episode *The Careful Terrorist* and Tom Kane in the second season's *The Frightened Inn-Keeper*.

Herbert Rachel
Played Verena in the third season **Danger Man** [aka **Secret Agent**] episode *Say it with Flowers*.
Played Vanessa Brading in **The Champions** episode *Autokill*.
Played Lady Carol Salt in the **Man in a Suitcase** episode *Castle in the Clouds*.
Appeared as Number 58, the Maid, in **The Prisoner** episode *Free for All*.

Herbert Ray
Directed the **Espionage** episode *Final Decision*.

Herder Laurence
Played the soldier in the second series **Danger Man** [aka **Secret Agent**] episode *Colony three*.
Played Lauber in the second season **The Saint** episode *The Saint Bids Diamonds* and Alexi in the third season's *The Helpful Pirate*.

Hermanny Ricardo
Played Ramon in the **Jason King** episode *A Kiss for a Beautiful Killer*.

Hermes Doug
Assistant Director on the second & third season of **Danger Man** [aka **Secret Agent**] and on the fourth series episode *Shinda Shima* which, edited together with the other season four episode *Koroshi*, also exists as a feature entitled *Koroshi*.
Assistant Director on **Man in a Suitcase**.

Herrick Roy
Played Holst in the third season **Danger Man** [aka **Secret Agent**} episode *Someone is Liable to get Hurt*.

Herries Yvette
Played Comere in the **Man in a Suitcase** episode *Three Blinks of the Eyes*.

Played Michelle in the third season **The Saint** episode *A Double in Diamonds*.

Herrington John
Played Korony in **The Adventurer** episode *Counterstrike*.
Played the night porter in the third season **Danger Man** [aka **Secret Agent**] episode *The Man who wouldn't Talk*.
Played the attendant/official in the second season two part **The Protectors** episode *Wam*.
Played the porter in the third season **The Saint** episode *The Paper Chase*.
Played the news vendor in the **Timeslip** story *The Day of the Clone* [series episode 22].

Herrington Julian
Played the police sergeant in the **Department S** episode *The Bones of Byrom Blain*.

Hersee Dorothy
Played Mrs Hardy in the first season **Danger Man** episode *The Lonely Chair*.

Hertner Walter
Played Hoffman in the **Jason King** episode *Variations on a Theme*.

Hesler Yvette
Played Lita in **The Four Just Men** episode *The Last Days of Nick Pompey*.

Heslop Charles
Played Prof. Harding in the first series **Man of the World** episode *The Mindreader*.
Played Withers in the **Sir Francis Drake** episode *Escape*.

Hess John D.
Wrote the **Espionage** episode *A Tiny Drop of Poison*.

Hesser Richard
Played Harry Druce in the **Father Brown** episode *The Oracle of the Dog*.

Hewitt Celia
Played Gretel in the **William Tell** episode *The Hostages*.

Hewitt Sean
Played Marco in **The Adventurer** episode *Poor Little Rich Girl*.

Hewitt-Jones Brian
Played Mr Pinter in **The Adventurer** episode *Return to Sender*.

Hewlett Arthur
Played Hargraves in **The Baron** episode *The Legions of Ammak*.
Played Admiral Makepeace in the **G.S.5** episode *Scorpion Rock*.
Played the gunsmith in the first season **The Saint** episode *The Elusive Ellshaw*.

Hewlett Donald
Played Chambers in the second season **The Protectors** episode *The Insider* and Howard in the second season **The Saint** episode *The Persistent Parasite*.

Hickin Brian
Sound Editor on **Thunderbirds**.

Hickson Joan
Played Mrs Curtis in the second series **Danger Man** [aka **Secret Agent**] episode *Yesterday's Enemies*.

Played Madame Dupont in the **H. G. Wells' Invisible Man** episode *The Mink Coat.*

Higgins Edward
Played doorman in the third season **The Saint** episode *The Power Artist.*

Higgins Jeremy
Played the barman in **The Adventurer** episode *Somebody Doesn't Like Me.*

High Bernard G.
Played radio man 1 in the fourth season **The Saint** episode *The World Beater.*

Hilary Jennifer
Played the Comtesse in the **Department S** episode *Death on Reflection.*
Played Myra Bergen in the **Jason King** episode *If it's Got to Go - It's Got to Go.*

Hill Charles
Played the Spanish Admiral in the **Sir Francis Drake** episode *King of America.*
Played Kovac in the first season **Danger Man** episode *Hired Assassin* and the tavern keeper in the second series [now aka **Secret Agent**] episode *A Date with Doris.*
Played Heinrich in the season two **Ghost Squad** episode *Lost In Transit.*
Played Arosa in the **H. G. Wells' Invisible Man** episode *The Gun Runners.*

Hill George
Construction Manager on **Strange Report**.

Hill James
Directed the **Gideon's Way** episode *The Big Fix.*
Directed **The Persuaders!** episode *A Home of One's Own.*
Directed **The Saint** episodes *Starring the Saint* & *The High Fence* [season 1] and *The Rhine Maiden* [2].

Hill Janna
Played the airline hostess in **The Baron** episode *Long Ago and Far Away.*
Provided the voice for Symphony Angel on **Captain Scarlet and the Mysterons**.

Hill Reg
Producer on **Captain Scarlet and the Mysterons**.
Associate Producer on **Fireball XL5**.
Executive Producer on **Joe 90** & **The Secret Service**.
Producer [with Gerry Anderson] on **The Protectors**.
Production Executive on **Space 1999**.
Special Effects [with Derek Meddings] and Associate Producer on **Stingray**.
Created [original idea with Gerry Anderson] the **Supercar** series.
Associate Producer on season one & produced season two of **Thunderbirds**.
Created the format and produced the series **UFO** [with Gerry Anderson & Sylvia Anderson].

Hill Steven
Featured in the **Espionage** episode *The Incurable One.*

Hilton Jasmina
Played the airport stewardess in the **Jason King** episode *Uneasy Lies the Head.*
Played Serena in **The Persuaders!** episode *The Old, the New and the Deadly.*

Hinchco Tamara
Played Sara Harvey in the **G.S.5** episode *Dr. Ayre.*

Hinde Madeline
Played Ingrid in the **Jason King** episode *A Page Before Dying.*
Played Mary Laroche in the first series **The Protectors** episode *It Could be Practically Anywhere on the Island.*

Hines Frazer
Played Carl in the **William Tell** episode *The Boy Slaves.*

Hines Ronald
Appeared in the second and fourth seasons of **The Adventures of Robin Hood**: Hereward in *The Path of True Love* [aka *Locksley Hall*], the seaman in *The Mystery of Ireland's Eye*, Edgar in *The Little People*, Ned Carter in *The Frightened Tailor*, the notary in *The Road in the Air*, & the outlaw in *Carlotta* [2] and the Lieutenant in *The Lady Killer*, Sir John Hanley in *A Touch of Fever*, the Lieutenant in *The Devil You Don't Know*, Dick in *Hue and Cry*, the Lieutenant in *Hostage for a Hangman* & Peter in *Trapped* [4].
Played Upton in **The Baron** episode *The Persuaders.*
Played Redman in the third season **The Saint** episode *The Paper Chase.*
Played Paolo in the **Sword of Freedom** episode *The Bracelet.*

Hinsliff Geoffrey
Played the hotel clerk in the **UFO** episode *Confetti Check A-O.K.*

Hinton Phillip
Played Mario in the first series **The Protectors** episode *See No Evil.*

Hird Thora
Guested in the first season **The Adventures of Robin Hood** episode *Husband for Marian* as Ada.

Hirsch Henrich
Directed the **Virgin of the Secret Service** episode *A Fate Worse Than Death.*

Hirschman Herbert
Executive Producer on **Espionage** and directed the episodes *A Tiny Drop of Poison* & *Some Other Kind of World.*
Produced the series **The Zoo Gang**.

Hitchcock Claude
Sound Recordist on **The Persuaders!**

Hitchman Michael
Played the barman in the first season **Danger Man** episode *An Affair of State.*
Played the assassin in **The Scarlet Pimpernel** episode *The Flower Woman.*

Ho Andy
Played Tang in **The Baron** episode *Storm Warning* [part 1 of a two-parter: also exists, edited together with part 2 - *The Island*, as a feature entitled *Mystery Island*].
Played Kai Min in **The Champions** episode *The Dark Island.*
Played General Chu Yee in the first season **Danger Man** episode *The Actor.*
Played Inspector Kee in the **Jason King** episode *Every Picture Tells a Story.*

Hobbs Carleton
Played Dean in the **Strange Report** episode *Report 8944: HAND: 'A Matter of Witchcraft?'.*
Played Professor Whitestone in the **Virgin of the Secret Service** episode *The Professor Goes West.*

Hobley Macdonald
Played the radio commentator in the second season **The Saint** episode *The Crooked Ring.*

Hockey Alan
Played the mechanic in the **Department S** episode *One of our Aircraft is Empty*.
Played Blacker in the **Father Brown** episode *The Dagger with Wings*.

Hodges Ken
Director of Photography on **The Adventures of Robin Hood**, **The Adventures of Sir Lancelot** episodes *The Knight with the Red Plume, The Ferocious Fathers, The Queen's Knight, Ruby of Radnor & The Lesser Breed* and **The Buccaneers** [aka **Dan Tempest**] episodes *Blackbeard & Gentleman Jack and the Lady*.

Hodgkins Peter C.
Wrote **The Buccaneers** [aka **Dan Tempest**] episodes *The Wasp, Ghost Ship, Dead Man's Rock, Hand of the Hawk* and *Marooned*.

Hodgson Charles
Played Charles Farson in the **Man in a Suitcase** episode *Property of a Gentleman*.

Hoffman David
Played Michaud in **The Count of Monte Cristo** episode *The Duel*.

Hogan Michael
Co-wrote **The Scarlet Pimpernel** episode *Thanksgiving Day* [with Angus McPhail and John Cousins].

Hogg Ian
Played Gregg in the first series **The Protectors** episode *Vocal*.

Holden Jan
Played Sara Knight in **The Baron** episode *The High Terrace*.
Played Miss Davies in **The Champions** episode *Project Zero*.
Played Marie in **The Count of Monte Cristo** episode *The Devil's Emissary*.
Guested as Jane Grant in the **Interpol Calling** episode *The Chinese Mask*.
Played Carla in the **O.S.S.** episode *Operation Lovebird*.
Played Vera in the second season **The Saint** episode *The Persistent Parasite* and Cynthia Quillen in the third season's *The Fast Women*.

Holden Katerina
Played the nurse in the third season **The Saint** episode *Locate and Destroy*.

Holden Michael
Played the messenger boy in the **Strange Report** episode *Report 1021: SHRAPNEL: 'The Wish in the Dream'*.

Holder Boscoe
Played Nero in the second series **Danger Man** [aka **Secret Agent**] episode *Parallel Lines Sometimes Meet* and appeared in *The Mercenaries*.
Played the male dancer in the second season **The Saint** episode *Sibao*.

Holder Christian
Played the bell boy in the season two **Ghost Squad** episode *The Man With the Delicate Hands*.
Played Sammy in the **G.S.5** episode *A Cast of Thousands*.

Holder Owen
Wrote the season four **The Adventures of Robin Hood** episode *The Devil You Don't Know*.
Teleplayed **The Four Just Men** episode *National Treasure* [from a story by Janet Green].

Holding Ernest
Production Supervisor on **Gideon's Way**.

Hollands Frank
Assistant Director on **The Buccaneers** [aka **Dan Tempest**] episodes *The Raiders, Captain Dan Tempest, Dan Tempest's War with Spain, The Wasp, Whale Gold, Slave Ship, Gunpowder Plot, Articles of War, Ghost Ship, Conquest of New Providence, Mother Doughty's Crew, Blood Will Tell, Hurricane, Dead Man's Rock, Dangerous Cargo, Hand of the Hawk, Gentleman Jack and the Lady, Mr. Beamish and the Hangman's Noose, Marooned, Before the Mast, Dan Tempest and The Amazons, The Ladies, The Surgeon of Sangre Rojo, The Return of Calico Jack, Conquistador, Aztec Treasure, Prize of Andalusia, Cutlass Wedding, Dan Tempest Holds an Auction, Flip and Jenny, To the Rescue, Indian Fighters, Mistress Higgins' Treasure, The Spy Aboard, The Decoy, Pirate Honour, Instrument of War* and *Printer's Devil*.
Assistant Director on **The Saint** and **UFO**.
Production Manager on **Joe 90** and **The Secret Service**.

Holliday David
Voiced Virgil Tracey - Pilot, Thunderbird 2 - in **The Thunderbirds** series [season one: Jeremy Wilkin did season two].

Hollis John
Played Lopez in the first series **Man of the World** episode *The Sentimental Agent* and Lt. Hang in the second season's *The Enemy*.
Played West in the first season **The Saint** episode *The Saint Plays with Fire* and Tordoff in the third season's *The Fast Women*.

Holloway Ann
Played Lavinia in the **Department S** episode *The Soup of the Day*.

Holloway Julian
Played Jim Richards in the **Gideon's Way** episode *State Visit*.
Played the waiter in the first season **The Saint** episode *Luella*.

Holman Vincent
Played Arthurson in the **H. G. Wells' Invisible Man** episode *Play to Kill*.

Holmes Alice
Hairdresser on **Jason King** and Chief Hairdresser on **UFO**.

Holmes Denis
Played the sturdy man in the season four **The Adventures of Robin Hood** episode *Goodbye, Little John*.
Played a variety of roles in **The Four Just Men**: the clerk in *The Judge*, the doctor in *National Treasure*, the M.I.5 man in *The Survivor*, Bianchi in *The Rietti Group*, the proprietor in *The Man in the Road* and the postman in *Money To Burn*.
Played the probation officer in the season two **Ghost Squad** episode *Polsky*.

Holmes John
Played the dog trainer in the **Father Brown** episode *The Oracle of the Dog*.
Trained 'Skipper' for the **Gideon's Way** episode *The Wall*.

Holmes Peter
Property Master on **Joe 90** & **The Secret Service**.

Holmes Robert
Wrote the first series **Ghost Squad** episode *The Green Shoes* [this episode was shot for the first series, but due to an actors' strike, was originally shown as a season two episode].
Wrote the fourth season **The Saint** episode *The Scales of Justice*.

Holmes William
Played Angus McGraw in the third season **The Saint** episode *The Convenient Monster*.

Holt Denis
Associate Producer on series one & two of **Ghost Squad**.

Holt Jonathan
Played Mark Harper in the **Strange Report** episode *Report 0846: LONELYHEARTS: 'Who Killed Dan Cupid?'*.

Holt Patrick
Played the District Attorney in **The Four Just Men** episode *The Bystanders*.
Played Bill in the **O.S.S.** episode *Operation Foulball*.
Played Barry Jones in the **Randall and Hopkirk [Deceased] aka My Partner the Ghost** episode *That's How Murder Snowballs*.
Played Herbert Wheeler in the third season **The Saint** episode *Simon and Delilah*.
Played Lord Westbrook in the **Sir Francis Drake** episode *Bold Enterprise*.
Appeared as Sandy Williams in the **White Hunter** episode *The Long Knife*.

Holt Seth
Directed the first season **Danger Man** episodes *The Key, The Sisters, Find and Return & Under the Lake*.
Directed the **Espionage** episode *The Liberators*.

Holy Ken
Special Effects Production Manager on **UFO**.

Homolka Oscar
Played Zoltan Kolas in the second series **The Protectors** episode *Border Line*.

Hong James
Starred as, series regular, Barry in **The New Adventures of Charlie Chan**.

Hood Morag
Played Suzanne in the first series **The Protectors** episode *The Big Hit*.

Hood Noel
Played the old woman in the second series of **The Adventures of Robin Hood** episode *Isabella*.
Played the Governor's wife in **The Buccaneers [aka Dan Tempest]** episode *Gunpowder Plot*.
Played the Duchess of Albany in the **Virgin of the Secret Service** episode *Entente Cordiale*.

Hoodekoff Larry
Played Charlie in **The Buccaneers [aka Dan Tempest]** episode *Conquistador*.

Hooley Joan
Played Susy in the second series **Danger Man [aka Secret Agent]** episode *Loyalty Always Pays*.
Appeared as Sister Agatha in the **White Hunter** episode *Sister My Spouse*.

Hooper Ewan
Played Eddy in the **Man in a Suitcase** episode *Night Flight to Andora*.
Played Caine in the **Strange Report** episode *Report 4821: X-RAY: 'Who Weeps For the Doctor?'*.

Hooper Terrance
Played the croupier in the second series **Danger Man [aka Secret Agent]** episode *The Ubiquitous Mr Lovegrove*.

Hope Gary
Played Colonel Torres in the second series **Danger Man [aka Secret Agent]** episode *English Lady Takes Lodgers* and Rafael in the third season's *The Man on the Beach*.
Played Major Aboukir in the third season **The Saint** episode *The Queen's Ransom*.

Hopkins Anthony
Played Greg Halliday in the **Department S** episode *A Small War of Nerves*.

Hopkins Julie
Played Medana in the first season **Danger Man** episode *The Deputy Coyannis Story*.

Hopper Dennis
Featured in the **Espionage** episode *The Weakling*.

Hordern Michael
Featured in the **Espionage** episode *The Gentle Spies*.

Horner Penelope
Played Krista in **The Adventurer** episode *Somebody Doesn't Like Me*.
Played Edith in the **Father Brown** episode *The Quick One*.
Played Janet Middleton in the **Gideon's Way** episode *The Big Fix*.
Played Princess Vania in the **Jason King** episode *A Royal Flush*.
Played Carrie in **The Persuaders!** episode *Someone Waiting*.
Played Oonagh O'Grady in the second season **The Saint** episode *The Set-Up*. In the third season played Irma Jorovitch in *The Russian Prisoner* & Hanya in *The Paper Chase*.

Hornery Bob
Played Shapes in *Adventure Four* of **Sapphire and Steel**.

Horsburgh Walter
Played the Bishop in the second series of **The Adventures of Robin Hood** episodes *Outlaw Money & The Blackbird* and the Abbot in *To Be a Student* [season 3] & *Tuck's Love Day* [4].
Played the English man in **The Baron** episode *Farewell to Yesterday*.
Played Magistrate in **The Buccaneers [aka Dan Tempest]** episode *Printer's Devil*.
Played Jerome in the **Gideon's Way** episode *Fall High, Fall Hard*.
Played the butler in **The Persuaders!** episode *The Morning After*.
Played the Judge in the third season **The Saint** episode *Escape Route*.
Played Baron de Rougement in **The Scarlet Pimpernel** episode *The Lady in Distress*.

Horsfall Bernard
Played Captain Carter in the **Department S** episode *Six Days*.
Played Christianson in **The Persuaders!** episode *The Morning After*.
Played Bill Bast in the third season **The Saint** episode *The Death Game*.

Horsley Bill
Played Philip Pearson in the season two **Ghost Squad** episode *The Heir Apparent*.

Horsley John
Played John Burdett in **The Adventurer** episode *Love Always, Magda*.
Played Bligh Denton in the fourth season **The Adventures of Robin Hood** episode *Bride for an Outlaw* and Sir Guy in *The Champion*.
Appeared as Athelred in **The Adventures of Sir Lancelot** episode *The Missing Princess*.

Guested as Chairman in **The Champions** episode *Project Zero*.
Played the detective in the **Department S** episode *The Shift that Never was*.
Played Supt. Hopkinson in the **Gideon's Way** episode *The White Rat*.
Played Montell in the **Interpol Calling** episode *In the Swim*.
Played the Governor of Akba in the **Virgin of the Secret Service** episode *The Great Ring of Akba*.
Played Jacques Brun in the **William Tell** episode *Secret Weapon* and Klaus in *The Spider*.

Hoskins Basil
Played Number 14 in **The Prisoner** episode *Hammer Into Anvil*.

Houen Erica
Played the air hostess in the second series **Ghost Squad** episode *Interrupted Requiem*.

Hough John
Second Unit Director on **The Champions**.

Hough Johnny
Second Unit Director on **The Baron**.
Directed the first season **The Protectors** episodes *2,000ft to Die, Triple Cross & For the Rest of your Natural ...* and the second's *Bagman & Shadbolt*.
Directed **The Zoo Gang** episodes *Mindless Murder, The Counterfeit Trap & The Twisted Cross*.

Houghton Barrie
Played Goran in the first series **The Protectors** episode *A Matter of Life and Death*.

Houston Charles
Played Shanks in the third series **The Adventures of Robin Hood** episode *Lincoln Green* and the Duke in *Little Mother*.
Played Hollins in **The Baron** episode *The Persuaders*.
Played David Ramsey in **The Buccaneers** [aka **Dan Tempest**] episode *Instrument of War*.
Played Orley in **The Champions** episode *The Gilded Cage*.
Played the cafe artist in the first season **Danger Man** episode *View from the Villa*. In the second series [now aka **Secret Agent**], played Bierce in *The Mirror's New*. Played Reever in the third season's *The Man with the Foot*.
Played Stevens in the **Department S** episode *Six Days*.
Guested as Graham in the **Interpol Calling** episode *Trial at Cranby's Creek*.
Played Jacoby in **The Persuaders!** episode *The Gold Napoleon*.
On **The Saint**: played Eddy Toscelli in *The Man who was Lucky* & Leghetti in *The King of the Beggars* [series 1]; Norton in *The Miracle Tea Party* [2]; Al Vitale in *Invitation to Danger* [3] the hotel reception clerk in *Vendetta for the Saint Part One* [4].
Played Guilio in the **Sword of Freedom** episode *The Eye of the Artist*.
Appeared as Vic Rader in the **White Hunter** episode *Decision* and as Parker in *The Fugitive*.
Played Weber in the **William Tell** episode *Landslide* and Paul in *The Young Widow*.

Houston Donald
Played Jan De Groot in **The Adventurer** episode *Double Exposure*.
Guested as Richter in **The Champions** episode *The Survivors*.
Played Bill Vincent in the third season **Danger Man** [aka **Secret Agent**] episode *To our Best Friend*.
Played John Burnham in the **Department S** episode *The Ghost of Mary Burnham*.
Played Tony Erickson in the **Gideon's Way** episode *Fall High, Fall Hard*.

Played Kenworthy in the **Jason King** episode *A Deadly Line in Digits*.
Played George Masters in the **Man in a Suitcase** episode *Essay in Evil*.
Played Lockier in the second season **The Protectors** episode *Dragon Chase*.
Played Commander Denning in the **Return of the Saint** episode *The Armageddon Alternative*.

Houston Glyn
Played Wykes in the third season **Danger Man** [aka **Secret Agent**] episode *The Man on the Beach*.
Played Bream in the first series **Ghost Squad** episode *The Green Shoes* [this episode was shot for the first series, but due to an actors' strike, was shown as a season two episode].
Played Detective Sergeant Carmichael in the **Gideon's Way** episodes *To Catch a Tiger* and *Fall High, Fall Hard*.
Played Dylan Williams in the third season **The Saint** episode *The House on Dragon's Rock*.

Houston Renee
Played the title role in the third series **The Adventures of Robin Hood** episode *Little Mother*.
Played Mrs Van Kempson in the first series **Man of the World** episode *The Runaways*.
Played Mrs McAlister in the first season **The Saint** episode *The Wonderful War* and Ida Warshed in *The Gentle Ladies*.

How Mrs
Played the native woman in the **White Hunter** episode *Voodoo Wedding*.

Howard Arthur
Played the Earl of Rochdale in **The Adventures of Robin Hood** episode *Too Many Earls* [second series] and Lord Eilmar in *The Flying Sorcerer* [season four].
Played the elderly member in the **Shirley's World** episode *The Berkeley Club Caper*.
Played Penhollow in the **Strange Report** episode *Report 4977: SWINDLE: 'Square Root of Evil'*.

Howard Ben
Played the delivery man in the **Department S** episode *The Bones of Byrom Blain*.
Played Vincenzo in the second season **The Protectors** episode *Fighting Fund*.

Howard Ronald
Appeared twice in the first series of **The Adventures of Robin Hood** as Will Scarlet [*Will Scarlet & The Deserted Castle*] the role eventually became a regular one for Paul Eddington.
Played Noel Goddard in the debut season **Danger Man** episode *The Traitor*. In series four [now aka **Secret Agent**] played Sanders in *Koroshi* [*Koroshi* was also merged with the only other surviving fourth season colour episode, *Shinda Shima*, to form a TVM entitled *Koroshi*].
Featured in the **Espionage** episode *The Light of the Friendly Star*.
Played Colonel Parkes in the **Four Just Men** episode *The Deserter*.

Howard Warren
Wrote the first series of **The Adventures of Robin Hood** episode *The Wager*.

Howe George
Played Brooks in the **Randall and Hopkirk [Deceased]** aka **My Partner the Ghost** episode *The Smile Behind the Veil*.

Howe Stephen
Played the second little boy in **The Prisoner** episode *The Girl who was Death*.

Howell Arthur
Played Moustache in the **Man in a Suitcase** episode *Man from the Dead* and the harrassed man in *Variation on a Million Bucks* [two parter: also a movie: *To Chase a Million*].
Played the Fencing Master in the first series **The Protectors** episode *The Big Hit*.

Howell George
Played Jean in the **O.S.S.** episode *Operation Jingle Bells*.

Howell Peter
Played Admiral Cox in **The Champions** episode *Twelve Hours* and the Professor in **The Prisoner** episode *The General*.

Howells Ursula
Played Miki in the **Interpol Calling** episode *Ascent to Murder*.
Played Mrs Arnoldson in the **Man in a Suitcase** episode *Why they Killed Nolan*.

Howes Basil
Played the Judge in the first season **The Saint** episode *The Element of Doubt*.

Howlett Noel
Played Phillipe in **The Count of Monte Cristo** episode *The Grecian Gift* [aka *The Brothers*].
Played Dr McKenna in the second series **Danger Man** [aka **Secret Agent**] episode *Fair Exchange*.
Played the President in **The Four Just Men** episode *The Deserter*.
Played Reverend J. Crichton in the season two **Ghost Squad** episode *Death of a Sportsman*.
Played Reverend Simon Blanding in the **Man in a Suitcase** episode *Dead Man's Shoes*.
Played Mr Giddy in **The Sentimental Agent** episode *The Height of Fashion*.

Hoyle Geoffrey
Scientific Adviser on the series **Timeslip**.

Hoyle Stuart
Played Kim in the **Randall and Hopkirk [Deceased]** aka **My Partner the Ghost** episode *That's How Murder Snowballs*.

Hoyt John
Played Cordot in **The Count of Monte Cristo** episode *First Train to Paris*.

Hu Kathy
Played Min-Lau in the **Shirley's World** episode *Evidence in Camera*.

Hubay Stephen
Played Klaus in the third season **The Saint** episode *The Gadget Lovers*.

Hudis Norman
Wrote the fourth season **Danger Man** [aka **Secret Agent**] episodes *Koroshi* & *Shinda Shima* [*Koroshi* and *Shinda Shima* are all that exist of a proposed fourth season and, uniquely for the series, were made in colour. A TVM, *Koroshi*, also exists being the two episodes edited together].
Wrote the **Gideon's Way** episodes *How to Retire without Really Working*, *Subway to Revenge*, *The Millionaire's Daughter* & *The Reluctant Witness*.
Wrote the second season **The Saint** episodes *The Imprudent Politician*, *The Frightened Inn-Keeper*, *The Chequered Flag*, *The Persistent Parasite* & *The Saint Bids Diamonds*.

Hug John
Starred as, second season regular, Bill Fraser in **Space 1999**.

Huggett Richard
Played Alonzo in the **Sir Francis Drake** episode *The Flame Thrower*.

Hughes Ann
Played the girl in the season three **The Adventures of Robin Hood** episode *The Charter*.
Played Maria in the **William Tell** episode *The General's Daughter*.

Hughes Bernard
Starred as Father Brown in the two-hour television feature film **Father Brown Detective**.

Hughes Billy
Played Sir Aaron's double in the **Father Brown** episode *Three Tools of Death*.

Hughes Geoffrey
Played Harper in the **Randall and Hopkirk [Deceased]** aka **My Partner the Ghost** episode *Somebody just Walked over my Grave*.

Hughes Hazel
Played Mere Lafond in the first season **The Saint** episode *The Work of Art* and Mrs Stewart in *The High Fence*.
Played Anita in **The Sentimental Agent** episode *The Height of Fashion*.
Played the landlady in the **Strange Report** episode *Report 4407: HEART: 'No Choice for the Donor'*.

Hughes Helena
Played Marie Trescal in **The Four Just Men** episode *The Discovery*.

Hughes John
Played the bank worker in the **Randall and Hopkirk [Deceased]** aka **My Partner the Ghost** episode *Money to Burn*.

Hughes Kenneth
Directed the **Espionage** episodes *We, the Hunted* and *Snow on Mount Kama* [also co-teleplayed with Allan Prior & Donald Jonson: from a story by Allan Prior].

Hughes Neville
Played Ibbett in the second season **The Protectors** episode *The Tiger and the Goat*.

Hughes Peter
Played Howes in the third season **Danger Man** [aka **Secret Agent**] episode *The Man on the Beach*.
Played Inspector Collins in the season two **Ghost Squad** episode *The Missing People*.
Played George Redmond in the **G.S.5** episode *It Won't be a Stylish Marriage*.
Played the butler in the **Randall and Hopkirk [Deceased]** aka **My Partner the Ghost** episode *Who Ever Heard of a Ghost Dying?*.

Hughes Robin
Played Dave Welford in the season two **Ghost Squad** episode *The Golden Silence*.
Played Harry Tiltman in the first season **The Saint** episode *The Pearls of Peace*.
Played Adam Forrester in the **Sir Francis Drake** episode *Court Intrigue*.

Hughes Vicki
Played Maria in the third season **The Saint** episode *Simon and Delilah* and Mirelle in *The Better Mousetrap*.

Hulke Malcolm

Wrote the second season **Danger Man** [aka **Secret Agent**] episode *Parallel Lines Sometimes Meet* [additional dialogue by Ralph Smart].
Wrote the **Gideon's Way** episode *Fall High, Fall Hard*.
Wrote the **G.S.5** episode *Hideout*.

Human Robert

Played Lieutenant in **The Count of Monte Cristo** episode *The De Berry Affair*.

Hume Roger

Played Inspector Palmer in the **Father Brown** episode *The Hammer of God*.

Humphrys Laraine

Played the co-star in **The Adventurer** episode *Has Anyone Here Seen Kelly?*.

Humpoletz Paul

Played Well in the **Jason King** two parter *All that Glisters*.
Played Graz in the **Timeslip** story *The Wrong End of Time* [series parts 1 - 6].

Hunnicutt Gayle

Played Annabel in the **Return of the Saint** two parter *Collision Course* [Part 1: *The Brave Goose* & part 2: *The Sixth Man*: also exists as a movie entitled *The Saint and the Brave Goose*].

Hunt Martita

Played the Duchess in the **Sword of Freedom** episode *The Tower* and Duchess Crespi in *The Besieged Duchess*.

Hunt Michael

Played Parsinski in the first season **Danger Man** episode *The Sisters*.

Hunt Peter

Directed **The Persuaders!** episode *Chain of Events*.
Directed the **Shirley's World** episode *The Rally*.

Hunter Alastair

Appeared as the armourer in the first season **The Adventures of Robin Hood** episode *Checkmate* and as a Monk in the second's *The Trap*.
Played Captain in **The Count of Monte Cristo** episode *The Art of Terror*.
Played Porter in the **Man in a Suitcase** episode *Burden of Proof*.
Played the doctor in the **O.S.S.** episode *Operation Yodel*.
Played the publican in the third season **The Saint** episode *The Convenient Monster*.

Hunter Bernard

Played the salesman in the first series **Ghost Squad** episode *The Green Shoes* [this episode was shot for the first series, but due to an actors' strike, was originally shown as a season two episode].
Played the Nazi officer in the **O.S.S.** episode *Operation Blue Eyes*.

Hunter Craig

Played the GSP 4 pilot in the **UFO** episode *The Sound of Silence* and Dale in *Mindbender*.

Hunter Ian

Played Sir Richard of Lea in **The Adventures of Robin Hood**: *The Knight Who Came to Dinner*, *The Challenge*, *The Betrothal* & *The Byzantine Treasure* [series one] and *Blackmail*, *The Goldmaker* & *Castle in the Air* [two].
Played Sir Walter Barling in **The Four Just Men** episode *Money To Burn*.

Hunter James

Played Tony King in the **Gideon's Way** episode *The Nightlifers*.

Hunter Robert

Played the villager in the season three **The Adventures of Robin Hood** episode *The Healing Hand*.
Guested as Capt. Fehr in the **Interpol Calling** episode *Eight Days Inclusive*.

Huntington Laurence

Directed **The Adventures of Sir Lancelot** episodes *Double Identity*, *Ruby of Radnor*, *The Mortaise Fair*, *Sir Crustabread*, *The Prince of Limerick* and *The Lady Lilith*.
Directed the **O.S.S.** episodes *Operation Big House*, *Operation Death Trap*, *Operation Orange Blossom*, *Operation Yodel*, *Operation Post Office*, *Operation Blackbird* & *Operation Newsboy*.

Huntley Raymond

Played Norman Sterling in **The Baron** episode *Samurai West*.
Played Reimer in **The Count of Monte Cristo** episode *Mecklenburg*.
Played Clements in the first season **Danger Man** episode *The Gallows Tree*.
Played Sir Percy Richmond in the **Gideon's Way** episode *To Catch a Tiger*.
Guested as Schroeder in the **Interpol Calling** episode *Payment in Advance*.
Played the title role in the **Sir Francis Drake** episode *Doctor Dee*.

Hurndall Richard

Played Father Superior in the **Father Brown** episode *The Arrow of Heaven*.
Played Mr King in the **Gideon's Way** episode *The Nightlifers*.
Played Collingwood in the **Jason King** episode *The Constance Missal*.
Played David Conron in **The Persuaders!** episode *Take Seven*.
Played Justice Cronin in the second season **The Protectors** episode *Trial*.

Hurndell William

Played the truck driver in the second series **Danger Man** [aka **Secret Agent**] episode *It's Up to the Lady*.

Hurst Veronica

Played Phyllis Thornton in **The Baron** episode *The High Terrace*.
Played Mrs Norman in the **Man in a Suitcase** episode *Which Way did he Go, McGill?*.
Played the secretary in **The Persuaders!** episode *Take Seven*.

Hurt John

Played Freddy Tinsdale in the **Gideon's Way** episode *The Tin God*.

Hutchenson David

Played Sir Richard in the **Jason King** episode *The Constance Missal*.

Hutcheson David

Played Sir Jeremy in the second series **Danger Man** [aka **Secret Agent**] episode *The Mirror's New* and Sir Alan Grose in the third season's *The Man on the Beach*.
Played Colonel McAlpine in the **Gideon's Way** episode *The Thin Red Line*.

Hutchins Peter

Played the bartender in **The Baron** episode *Long Ago and Far Away*.

Hutchinson Harry
Played the butler in the first series **The Protectors** episode *The Bodyguards*.
Played the second ghost in the **Randall and Hopkirk [Deceased]** episode *The Trouble with Women*.

Hutchinson Jeannette
Played Bess in the second series of **The Adventures of Robin Hood** episode *The Dowry*.
Played Amora in **The Adventures of Sir Lancelot** episode *The Ugly Duckling* and the second woman in *The Missing Princess*.

Hutchinson Ross
Played Owen in the season two **Ghost Squad** episode *P.G. 7*.

Hutchinson Tom
Co-wrote the story for the **Interpol Calling** episode *Fingers of Guilt* [with Ernie Player: teleplayed by Robert Stewart].

Hutchinson Wendy
Played Mrs Jonathan P. Hacket in the first series **The Protectors** episode *It Could be Practically Anywhere on the Island*.

Hutchison Stuart
Played Marco in the first season **Danger Man** episode *The Deputy Coyannis Story* and Sanderson in the second season **Space 1999** episode *The Seance Spectre*.

Hutchison Ken
Played Mark Jenner in the second season **The Protectors** episode *Burning Bush*.

Hutton Peter
Played Det. Sgt. Davis in the first season **Danger Man** episode *Name, Date and Place*.

Hutton Robert
Played Jason in the **Man in a Suitcase** episode *Who's Mad Now?*.
Played Frank Rocco in **The Persuaders!** episode *Five Miles to Midnight*.
Played Farnberg in the second season **The Saint** episode *The Contract*, Jack Forrest in *The Old Treasure Story* and Brett Sunley in the third season's *Invitation to Danger*.

Huxstable Judy
Played one of the girls in the second series **Danger Man** [aka **Secret Agent**] episode *Such Men are Dangerous* and Rosalind Fielding in *English Lady Takes Lodgers*.

Hyatt Charles
Played the hotel Maitre D' in the third season **The Saint** episode *Island of Chance*.

Hyde Jemma
Played Caroline in the third season **Danger Man** [aka **Secret Agent**] episode *Say it with Flowers*.
Played Barbara Sinclair in the first season **The Saint** episode *The Rough Diamonds*.

Hyde Kenneth
Starred as, series regular [episodes 1 - 32], Machiavelli in the series **Sword of Freedom**.

Hyde-Chambers Derek
Editor on the first series of **Danger Man**, and on **The Champions & The Persuaders!**

Hylton Jane
Regular in **The Adventures of Sir Lancelot** as Queen Guinevere: *The Knight with the Red Plume, The Queen's Knight, The Outcast, Lancelot's Banishment, Caledon, The Pirates, The Black Castle, The Bridge, Ruby of Radnor, The Theft of Excalibur* and *The Mortaise Fair*.
Played Suzy in the **Interpol Calling** episode *Dead on Arrival*.

****

Ibbs Ronald
Played the Lieutenant in the season three **The Adventures of Robin Hood** episode *The Challenge of the Black Knight*.
Played Sanders in the first season **The Saint** episode *The Lawless Lady*, Professor Walter Rand in the second season's *The Inescapable Word* and Professor Quell in *The Abductors*.

Ilinares Juan
Played the first assassin in the second series **Danger Man** [aka **Secret Agent**] episode *A Date with Doris*.

Illing Peter
Played Avraam in the second series **Danger Man** [aka **Secret Agent**] episode *No Marks for Servility*.
Played Mozek in **The Four Just Men** episode *The Prime Minister*, Gathis in *Mava* and Dr Cramer in *The Boy Without a Country*.
Played Inspector Strang in the **H. G. Wells' Invisible Man** episode *The Vanishing Evidence*.
Played Captain Omar in the **Interpol Calling** episode *The Thirteen Innocents*.
Played Inspector Buono in the first season **The Saint** episode *The Latin Touch*, Captain Garcia in the second season's *The Saint Bids Diamonds* and President Alverez in the third's *The Reluctant Revolution*.
Played Doctor Elvin in the **White Hunter** episode *Web of Death*.

Impey Betty
Guested in the second series of **The Adventures of Robin Hood** episode *A Village Wooing* as Widow Winifred.

Incorporated Television Programme Company Ltd
The New Adventures of Charlie Chan was 'a Television Programs of America Presentation, in association with the Incorporated Television Programme Company Limited'.
Produced **William Tell**.

Inescourt Elaine
Played Duchess in **The Count of Monte Cristo** episode *Flight to Calais*.

Ingalis Don
Co-wrote, with Ralph Smart the first season **Danger Man** episode *The Blue Veil*.

Ingham Barrie
Played Roland Haswell in **The Baron** episode *Long Ago and Far Away*.
Played Georges in the first season **Danger Man** episode *Vacation*.
Played Emil Cavallo-Smith in the **Randall and Hopkirk [Deceased]** aka **My Partner the Ghost** episode *Vendetta for a Dead Man*.

Inglis Margaret
Played Mirella in the second season **Space 1999** episode *The Exiles*.

Ingram Joan
Played Mrs Hendricks in the second season **The Saint** episode *The Unkind Philanthropist*.

Ingram William
Played Coleman in the third season **Danger Man** [aka **Secret Agent**] episode *The Hunting Party*.

Innes George
Played Gerard in the **Jason King** episode *Wanna Buy a Television Series* aka *A Face I Used to Know*.
Played Luigi in the first series **The Protectors** episode *The Numbers Game* and Marcus in the second season's episode *Decoy*.

Played Domino in the **Virgin of the Secret Service** episode *Pride of Assassins*.

Innocent Harold
Played Doctor Amis in **The Champions** episode *Autokill*.
Played Coady in **The Persuaders!** episode *To the Death, Baby*.
Played the assassin in the **Randall and Hopkirk [Deceased]** aka **My Partner the Ghost** episode *My Late Lamented Friend and Partner*.

International Tribune
With Television Reporters International, produced **The Persuaders!** for ITC World Wide Distribution.

Ipale Aharon
Played the driver in **The Adventurer** episode *Poor Little Rich Girl*.
Played Pedro in the **Jason King** episode *A Kiss for a Beautiful Killer*.
Played Paul in **The Zoo Gang** episode *Mindless Murder*.

Ireland Jill
Played Anna in the first series **Ghost Squad** episode *Assassin*.

Ireland John
Editor on **Randall and Hopkirk [Deceased]** aka **My Partner the Ghost**.

Irving Olivia
Played The Nurse in **The Count of Monte Cristo** episode *A Toy for the Infanta*.

Irwin Charles
Played the airport official in the first season **Danger Man** episode *The Island*.
Played Gus in **The Four Just Men** episode *Dead Man's Switch* and Flynn in *Crack-Up*.
Played Oliver in the **O.S.S.** episode *Operation Sweet Talk*.
Played Eddie Harmer in the first season **The Saint** episode *The Latin Touch*.

Irwin Margaret
Wrote the **Sir Francis Drake** episode *The Doughty Plot* [with David Greene].

ITP
White Hunter was 'a Bernard L. Schubert Production, for ITP, for ITC World Wide Distribution'.

Iveria Miki
Played Mama in the first season **Danger Man** episode *The Trap*.
Played Helene Morleiter in the second series **The Protectors** episode *Lena*.
Played Maria in the first season **The Saint** episode *The Work of Art*.

Ives Kenneth
Played the first detective in the **Strange Report** episode *Report 4407: HEART: 'No Choice for the Donor'*.

****

Jaber Zara
Played the nurse in the **Father Brown** episode *The Dagger With Wings*.

Jack Stephen
Played Dr Hutchins in the second series **Danger Man** [aka **Secret Agent**] episode *That's Two of Us Sorry*.

Jackson Brian
Played the policeman in the first season **Danger Man** episode *Colonel Rodriguez*; Jenson in **The Persuaders!** episode *The Long Goodbye* and the Turf Accountant in the first series **The Protectors** episode *A Kind of Wild Justice*.

Jackson Dan
Played the doorman in the second series **Danger Man** [aka **Secret Agent**] episode *Loyalty Always Pays*.
Played Dr Sanchez in the season two **Ghost Squad** episode *The Magic Bullet*.
Appeared as Chato in the **White Hunter** episode *Decision*.

Jackson David
Played the husky undergraduate in the second season **The Saint** episode *The Saint Steps In* and Chico in *The Spanish Cow*.
Played alien 1 in the second season **Space 1999** episode *The Rules of Luton*.

Jackson Freda
Played Mrs Evans in the **Randall and Hopkirk [Deceased]** aka **My Partner the Ghost** episode *The Smile Behind the Veil*.

Jackson Gordon
Played Andrew in the season three **The Adventures of Robin Hood** episode *The Profiteer*.
Played Mike Ferrers in the season two **Ghost Squad** episode *The Golden Silence*.
Played Sergeant McKinnon in the **Gideon's Way** episode *The Thin Red Line*.

Jackson Inigo
Played Bray in the **Department S** episode *Last Train to Redbridge*.
Played Leo Samson in the **Gideon's Way** episode *The 'V' Men*.
Played Corso in the **Jason King** episode *A Royal Flush*.
Played Stephane in the **Man in a Suitcase** episode *Blind Spot*.
Played Albert Costello in the second season **The Saint** episode *The Man who Liked Toys*.

Jackson Pat
Directed the third season **Danger Man** [aka **Secret Agent**] episode *The Hunting Party*.
Directed the **Man in a Suitcase** episodes *Man from the Dead*, *Variation on a Million Bucks* [part 1: also combined with part 2 to form a movie: *To Chase a Million*] and *The Bridge*.
Directed **The Prisoner** episodes *The Schizoid Man*, *A. B. and C.*, *Hammer into Anvil* & *Do Not Forsake Me Oh My Darling*.
Directed the second season **The Saint** episode *The Revolution Racket*.

Jackson Penny
Played the nurse in the **UFO** episode *Confetti Check A-O.K.*

Jackson Ron
Assistant Director on the series **Man of the World** and Production Manager on **Strange Report**.

Jacques Michael
Played Glazanov in the first season **Danger Man** episode *The Sisters*.
Played Juan in the **H. G. Wells' Invisible Man** episode *Behind the Mask*.

Jacobs Anthony
Played Lord Giles in the season four **The Adventures of Robin Hood** episode *The Flying Sorcerer*.
Played the waiter in the first season **Danger Man** episode *Time to Kill*.
Played Menardi in **The Four Just Men** episode *The Slaver*.
Played Van Tempel in the season two **Ghost Squad** episode *Lost in Transit*.
Played Artigas in the **Interpol Calling** episode *The Three Keys*.
Played Enrico Vespa in the first season **The Saint** episode *The Charitable Countess*.

Jaegar Frederick
Appeared as Sir Christopher in **The Adventures of Sir Lancelot** episode *Sir Crustabread*.
Played Major Harwood in the **Department S** episode *A Small War of Nerves*.
Played Bernarde in the **Interpol Calling** episode *Dressed to Kill*.
Played Dacre in the **Jason King** episode *Buried in the Cold, Cold Ground*.
Played Luther in **The Persuaders!** episode *The Old, the New and the Deadly*.
Played Bergen in the second season **The Protectors** episode *Baubles, Bangles and Beads*.
Played Inspector Grant in the **Return of the Saint** episode *Signal Stop*.
Played Vicary in the **Sir Francis Drake** episode *The Doughty Plot*.

Jaffe Carl
Played Professor Barkoff in the first season **Danger Man** episode *Time to Kill*.
Played Haddi in the first series **Man of the World** episode *Death of a Conference*.
Played the Kommandant in the **O.S.S.** episode *Operation Powder Puff* and General Kroll in *Operation Firefly*.
Played Martin in the **White Hunter** episode *Marked Man*.

Jaffrey Saeed
Played the President's Aide in the first series **The Protectors** episode *.....With a Little Help from my Friends*.
Played Ameen in the **Strange Report** episode *Report 3424: EPIDEMIC: 'A Most Curious Crime'*.

Jago Jo
Director of Photography on **The Buccaneers** [aka **Dan Tempest**]: *Ghost Ship*, *Conquest of New Providence*, *Mother Doughty's Crew*, *Blood Will Tell*, *Hurricane*, *Dead Man's Rock*, *Dangerous Cargo*, *Hand of the Hawk*, *The Return of Calico Jack*, *Conquistador*, *Aztec Treasure*, *Prize of Andalusia*, *Cutlass Wedding*, *Dan Tempest Holds an Auction*, *Flip and Jenny*, *To the Rescue*, *Indian Fighters*, *Mistress Higgins' Treasure*, *The Spy Aboard*, *The Decoy*, *Pirate Honour*, *Instrument of War* & *Printer's Devil*.

James Charles
Helicopter pilot for the scenes used in **The Prisoner**.

James Dick
Wrote & sang the theme for **The Adventures of Robin Hood**.

James Donald
Wrote **The Adventurer** episodes *Poor Little Rich Girl*, *Deadlock*, *Skeleton in the Cupboard*, *To the Lowest Bidder*, *Full Fathom Five*, *Mr Calloway is a Very Cautious Man* & *Somebody Doesn't Like Me*.
Wrote **The Champions** episodes *The Invisible Man*, *The Survivors*, *The Ghost Plane*, *Twelve Hours*, *The Mission*, *The Silent Enemy*, *The Night People* and *Full Circle*.
Wrote the **Department S** episodes *The Shift that Never was* & *The Pied Piper of Hambledown*.

Wrote the **Jason King** episodes *A Red, Red Rose Forever, Uneasy Lies the Head, The Stones of Venice & Chapter One: the Company I Keep.*
Wrote the **Joe 90** episodes *Test Flight* and *Trial at Sea.*
Wrote **The Persuaders!** episodes *The Man in the Middle & To the Death, Baby.*
Wrote the first season **The Protectors** episodes *Ceremony for the Dead, It was All Over in Leipzig, The Quick Brown Fox, A Kind of Wild Justice, A Matter of Life and Death, The Big Hit & Your Witness.*
Wrote the **Randall and Hopkirk [Deceased]** aka **My Partner the Ghost** episodes *Just for the Record, For the Girl who has Everything, You Can Always find a Fall Guy, A Sentimental Journey, It's Supposed to be Thicker than Water, The Man from Nowhere, Could You Recognise the Man Again?, Vendetta for a Dead Man, Money to Burn, All Work and No Pay & Somebody Just Walked over my Grave.*
Wrote the fourth series **The Saint** episodes *The Organisation Man, The People Importers & The World Beater.*
Wrote **The Secret Service** episodes *A Question of Miracles, The Deadly Whisper* and *School for Spies.*
Wrote the second season **Space 1999** episodes *The Exiles, Journey to Where & The Seance Spectre.*
Wrote the **UFO** episode *Kill Straker!.*

James Gerald
Played Tully in *Adventure Two* of **Sapphire and Steel**.

James Godfrey
Played Danvers in the **Department S** episode *The Man from X.*
Played Inspector Lebeau in the **Return of the Saint** episode *The Imprudent Professor.*
Played alien 2 in the second season **Space 1999** episode *The Rules of Luton.*
Played the Foreman in the **Strange Report** episode *Report 5055: CULT: 'Murder Shrieks Out'.*
Played a gamekeeper in the **UFO** episode *The Square Triangle.*

James Horace
Played the second African in the **Man in a Suitcase** episode *No Friend of Mine.*

James Juliette
Played Margarita Di Vallesi in the **Return of the Saint** episode *The Nightmare Man.*

James Keith
Played the milkman in the **Father Brown** episode *Three Tools of Death.*

James Lawrence
Played the first Man-at-Arms in the third series **The Adventures of Robin Hood** episode *Little Mother.*
Played Sergeant Fairfax in **The Champions** episode *Full Circle.*
Played Lew Geraghty in the **Man in a Suitcase** episode *Web with Four Spiders.*

James Oscar
Played Mombasa in the **Return of the Saint** episode *The Obono Affair* and the plain clothed officer in the **UFO** episode *The Psychobombs.*

James Philip
Played Holly in the **Randall and Hopkirk [Deceased]** aka **My Partner the Ghost** episode *When Did you Start to Stop Seeing Things?.*
Played Major Domo in the **Sword of Freedom** episode *The Bell.*

James Richard
Played, semi-regular, Mathew Gideon in **Gideon's Way**: *State Visit, The Firebug, The Housekeeper, How to Retire without Really Working, Subway to Revenge, The Prowler, The Millionaire's Daughter, Morna & The Rhyme and the Reason.*
Played the messenger boy in the **Man in a Suitcase** episode *Day of Execution.*

James Robert
Played the auctioneer in **The Adventurer** episode *Going, Going....*
Played Doctor Wynn in the **Father Brown** episode *The Hammer of God.*

James Sally
Played the secretary in the second season **The Protectors** episode *Trial.*

James Sidney 'Sid'
Appeared as Master Henry in the second series of **The Adventures of Robin Hood** episode *Outlaw Money.*
Played Chantey Jack in **The Buccaneers [aka Dan Tempest]** episode *Hand of the Hawk.*
Played Schaffner in the **William Tell** episode *Secret Death.*

James Sumner
Played Culliford in **The Champions** episode *The Invisible Man.*

Jameson Susan
Played Moira in the **Strange Report** episode *Report 8319: GRENADE: 'What Price Change?'.*
Played Anne Stone in the **UFO** episode *The Sound of Silence.*

Janson David
Played Pietro in the **Jason King** episode *A Royal Flush.*

Jarman Reginald
Played the General in the second season **Man of the World** episode *The Bullfighter* and Lord Loudon in the **Sir Francis Drake** episode *The Garrison.*

Jarvis Frank
Played Johnny Maxwell in the first season **The Saint** episode *The Rough Diamonds.*

Jarvis John
Set Dresser on **The Champions**.

Jason David
Played Abel in the **Randall and Hopkirk [Deceased]** aka **My Partner the Ghost** episode *That's How Murder Snowballs.*

Jason Neville
Played Paolo in the **Sword of Freedom** episode *Caterina.*
Played the reporter in **The Zoo Gang** episode *The Lion Hunt.*

Jason Tony
Played the police Sergeant in the third season **Danger Man [aka Secret Agent]** episode *I can only Offer you Sherry.*

Jay Stan
Played the night watchman in the third season **The Saint** episode *The Fast Women.*

Jayne Jennifer
Appeared in **The Adventures of Robin Hood** first season episode *The Betrothal* as Gladys & as Olivia in *Will Scarlet.*
Played the title role in the second season's *Carlotta.*
Played Elsa in **The Adventures of Sir Lancelot** episode *Shepherd's War.*
Played Rosa in the season one **Danger Man** episode *The Contessa.*
Played Pat Miller in the first series **Ghost Squad** episode *Million Dollar Ransom.*

Played Betty in the **H. G. Wells' Invisible Man** episode *Shadow Bomb*.

Played Joy in the **Man in a Suitcase** episode *Which Way did He Go, McGill?*.

Played Olga in the season two **The Saint** episode *The Abductors*.

Played Lisa in the **Sword of Freedom** episode *The Value of Paper*.

Appeared as Barbara in the **White Hunter** episode *A Moment of Truth* and as Irene Holmby in *The Plague*.

Regular in **William Tell** as Hedda Tell: *The Emperor's Hat, The Assassins, The Hostages, Landslide, The Baroness, Secret Death, Voice in the Night, The Gauntlet of St. Gerhardt, The Cuckoo, The Elixir, The Magic Powder, Gessler's Daughter, The Prisoner, The Young Widow, The Shrew, The Trap, The Surgeon* and *The Black Brothers*.

Jayston Michael
Played Russ Stone in the **UFO** episode *The Sound of Silence*.

J. Coales & Son [Hammersmith]
Provided the lorry for **The Prisoner** episode *Fall Out*.

Jeavons Colin
Played Tom Sterling in **The Baron** episode *Samurai West*, the gaoler in the **Man in a Suitcase** episode *Three Blinks of the Eyes* and the officer in **Sir Francis Drake**'s *Court Intrigue*.

Jeayes Alan
Played Jellybrand in **The Scarlet Pimpernel** episode *A Tale of Two Pigtails* and the landlord in *The Ambassador's Lady*.

Jeffrey Peter
Played Rymans in **The Adventurer** episode *Full Fathom Five*.

Played the Police Inspector in the second season **The Protectors** episode *Blockbuster*.

Played Quincy in the first season **The Saint** episode *The High Fence* and Gregory Marring in the second season's *The Crime of the Century*.

Played Superintendent Shaw in the **Strange Report** episode *Report 8319: GRENADE: 'What Price Change?'*.

Jeffries Lionel
Played Sir Charles in the second series of **The Adventures of Robin Hood** episode *The Path of True Love* aka *Locksley Hall*.

Played Arkwright in **The Four Just Men** episode *The Man Who Wasn't There*.

Jeffries Peter
Directed the **Father Brown** episodes *The Mirror of the Magistrate, The Dagger With Wings, The Eye of Apollo, The Secret Garden, The Man with Two Beards* & *The Oracle of the Dog*.

Directed the **Timeslip** story *The Time of the Ice Box* [series parts 7 - 12] and episodes 14-19 of *The Year of the Burn-Up* [Ron Francis directed 13-20].

Jeffs Ryan
Played Martier in the **Sir Francis Drake** episode *Mission to Paris*.

Jellinek Tristam
Played Finlay Thorp-Jones in the third season **The Saint** episode *The Power Artist*.

Jelly John
Visual Effects Production Manager on **Joe 90**.

Jenkins Clare
Played the girl hiker in the **Randall and Hopkirk [Deceased]** aka **My Partner the Ghost** episode *The Smile Behind the Veil*.

Jenkins Megs
Played Mrs Banks in the **Father Brown** episode *The Man with Two Beards*.

Played Liz Rikker in the **Gideon's Way** episode *The Wall*.

Jenkinson Roger
Played the clerk in the season two **Ghost Squad** episode *P.G. 7*.

Jenn Myvanny
Played the librarian in the **Man in a Suitcase** episode *Why they Killed Nolan*.

Jepson Selwyn
Co-wrote **The Adventures of Sir Lancelot** episode *Knight Errant* [with Peggy Phillips].

Jessel Patricia
Played Katrina in the **H. G. Wells' Invisible Man** episode *Point of Destruction*.

Played the Psychiatrist in **The Prisoner** episode *Checkmate*.

Jesson Peter
Played Fuller in the second series **Danger Man [aka Secret Agent]** episode *Colony Three*.

Played Jack in the **Gideon's Way** episode *The Prowler*.

Played Hooper in the **Randall and Hopkirk [Deceased]** aka **My Partner the Ghost** episode *The Smile Behind the Veil*.

Jessup Reginald
Played Markham in **The Baron** episode *The Persuaders*.

Guested as Grayson in **The Champions** episode *Project Zero*.

Played Demetrios in **The Count of Monte Cristo** episode *Athens*.

Played the cable car attendant in the first season **Danger Man** episode *Under the Lake*.

Played Gerald in the **Department S** episode *Spencer Bodily is 60 Years Old*.

Played Detective Superintendent Lemaitre in the **Gideon's Way** episodes *Subway to Revenge, The Alibi Man, The Prowler, The Thin Red Line, A Perfect Crime, The Millionaire's Daughter* & *The Reluctant Witness*.

Played the Headmaster in the **Return of the Saint** episode *Yesterday's Hero*.

Played Francisco in the second season **The Saint** episode *The Revolution Racket*.

Played the Sergeant in the **Sir Francis Drake** episode *Mary, Queen of Scots*.

Jewesbury Edward
Played Vickers in the second series **Danger Man [aka Secret Agent]** episode *Loyalty Always Pays*.

Guested as Slater in the **Interpol Calling** episode *No Flowers for Onno*.

Played Franklin in the second season **The Saint** episode *The Miracle Tea Party*.

John Alexander
Played a Constable in the **Father Brown** episode *The Quick One*.

John Errol
Played Col. Nyboto in the series two **Danger Man [aka Secret Agent]** episode *The Galloping Major*, Dessiles in *Parallel Lines Sometimes Meet* and Enugu in *Loyalty Always Pays*.

Played Sgt. Hamid in the **Interpol Calling** episode *Slave Ship*.

Played Masuto in the **Man in a Suitcase** episode *No Friend of Mine*.

John Ram
Played Rick in the **Strange Report** episode *Report 1553: RACIST: 'A Most Dangerous Proposal'*.

John Margaret
Played Miss Carew in the second season **Ghost Squad** episode *The Thirteenth Girl* and the nurse in the second season **The Protectors** episode *Trial*.

John Robin
Played the boy in the car in the **Department S** episode *The Man from X*.
Played the Constable in the **Randall and Hopkirk [Deceased]** aka **My Partner the Ghost** episode *Who Ever Heard of a Ghost Dying?*.

Johncock Brian
Director [special effects second unit] on **Thunderbirds**.

Johns Clay
Played the Floor Manager in the first season **The Saint** episode *The Careful Terrorist*.

Johns Harriette
Played The Countess in the debut season **The Adventures of Robin Hood** episode *The Alchemist*.
Played Honore in **The Count of Monte Cristo** episode *The Experiment*.
Played Julia Wilson in the season two **Ghost Squad** episode *Escape Route*.
Played Mrs Cuggen in the **Man in a Suitcase** episode *Who's Mad Now?*.
Played Gertrude in the **William Tell** episode *The Shrew*.

Johns Margo
Played Sister Rousseau in the second series **Danger Man** [aka **Secret Agent**] episode *A Room in the Basement*.
Played Ellen Northwade in the first season **The Saint** episode *Judith*.

Johns Mervyn
Played Franz Kolmar in **The Adventurer** episode *Deadlock*.
Played Armstrong in the second series **Danger Man** [aka **Secret Agent**] episode *No Marks for Servility*.
Played Dr. Davis in the third season **The Saint** episode *The House on Dragon's Rock*.
Appeared as Mr Doak in the **White Hunter** episodes *One Fatal Weakness* and *No Survivors*.

Johns Milton
Played Alex in **The Adventurer** episode *Nearly the End of the Picture*.
Played Conway in the second season **The Protectors** episode *Petard*.
Played Vargas in the third season **The Saint** episode *Island of Chance*.

Johns Norman
Played the airline Captain in the first series **Ghost Squad** episode *Hong Kong Story*.

Johns Peter
Puppet Operator on **Joe 90**.

Johns Stratford
Played the gendarme in **The Count of Monte Cristo** episode *Monaco*.
Played Paul Trenton in the **Department S** episode *The Man in the Elegant Room*.
Played Captain Starr in the first series **Ghost Squad** episode *Still Waters*.
Played Chaublin in the **Interpol Calling** episode *A Foreign Body*.
Played Georges Duchamps in the **Return of the Saint** two parter *Collision Course* [Part 1: *The Brave Goose* & part 2: *The Sixth Man*: also exists as a movie entitled *The Saint and the Brave Goose*].

Johnson Brian
Designed and directed the special effects on **Space 1999**.

Johnson Donald
Wrote the **Man in a Suitcase** episodes *The Girl who Never was* & *Why they Killed Nolan*.
Wrote the first season **The Protectors** episode *See No Evil*.

Johnson Fred
Played Parson Maine in the **Sir Francis Drake** episode *Lost Colony of Virginia* and Father in the **William Tell** episode *The Mountain People*.

Johnson Laurie
Music on **Jason King** and **Shirley's World**.

Johnson Malcolm
Assistant Director on **Strange Report**.

Johnson Noel
Played the Ambassador in the second series **Danger Man** [aka **Secret Agent**] episode *The Professionals*.

Johnson Oliver
Played Percy Whitehead in the **Gideon's Way** episode *The Housekeeper*.
Played Sir Hugo Kempson in the first series **Man of the World** episode *Portrait of a Girl*.

Johnson Peter
Played the Sheriff's captain in **The Adventures of Robin Hood** episode *Too Many Earls* [second series].
Played the first Bravo in the **Sword of Freedom** episode *Francesca*.

Johnson Peter Rolfe
Editor on **The Adventures of Robin Hood**.

Johnson Richard
Played Pegleg in **The Buccaneers** [aka **Dan Tempest**] episode *The Spy Aboard*.
Played Captain Bannion in **The Four Just Men** episode *The Deserter*.
Played Lee Russell in the first season **Space 1999** episode *Matter of Life and Death*.

Johnston Oliver
Played Peer in the third season **Danger Man** [aka **Secret Agent**] episode *The Hunting Party*.

Joint Alf
Stunt Co-ordinator on **The Adventurer**.
Played Carl in the third season **Danger Man** [aka **Secret Agent**] episode *Dangerous Secret*.
Played the second mechanic in **The Prisoner's** *Free for All*.
Played the taxi driver in the second season **The Protectors** episode *The Insider*.
Played Phillipe in **The Zoo Gang** episode *The Twisted Cross*.

Jonah Willie
Played the assistant in the **Jason King** episode *Wanna Buy a Television Series* aka *A Face I Used to Know*.
Played the assassin in the **Return of the Saint** episode *The Obono Affair*.

Jonic Bettina
Played the singer in the **Man in a Suitcase** episode *Somebody Loses, Somebody ...Wins?*.

Jones Barry
Played Otis Q. Fennick in the first season **The Saint** episode *The Ever-loving Spouse*.

Jones Carolyn
Played Sunshine in the **Virgin of the Secret Service** episode *The Professor Goes West.*

Jones Clifton
Played Lieutenant Labaste in the second series **Danger Man** [aka **Secret Agent**] episode *Parallel Lines Sometimes Meet* and Lyle in the third season's *The Man on the Beach.*
Played Sebastian in the **Jason King** episode *Flamingos only Fly on Tuesdays.*
Played Corporal Salinge in the **Man in a Suitcase** episode *The Whisper.*
Played Dr. Kibu in **The Persuaders!** episode *Greensleeves.*
Starred as, first season regular, David Kano in **Space 1999**.

Jones Douglas
Played the pageboy in the **Man in a Suitcase** episode *Web with Four Spiders* and the horse dealer in **The Prisoner** episode *Living in Harmony.*

Jones Dudley
Played Thurston in the **Father Brown** episode *The Eye of Apollo.*
Played Ben Craddock in the **Randall and Hopkirk [Deceased]** aka **My Partner the Ghost** episode *Could You Recognise the Man Again?.*

Jones Elwyn Brook
Played Palamas in **The Count of Monte Cristo** episode *Athens.*
Played Scheye in **The Four Just Men** episode *The Deadly Capsule.*

Jones Emrys
Played Leslie Dawson in the **G.S.5** episode *Hideout.*

Jones Freddie
Played Calloway in **The Adventurer** episode *Mr Calloway is a Very Cautious Man.*
Played the landlord in **The Baron** episode *So Dark the Night.*
Played Mr Quirly in the **Jason King** episode *A Deadly Line in Digits.*
Played Robard in the first series **The Protectors** episode *The Bodyguards.*
Played James McAllister in the **Randall and Hopkirk [Deceased]** aka **My Partner the Ghost** episode *For the Girl who has Everything.*
Played Martin Graves in the fourth season **The Saint** episode *The Time to Die.*
Played Dr Logan in the second season **Space 1999** episode *Journey to Where.*

Jones Glyn
Played Carter in the **Strange Report** episode *Report 0846: LONELYHEARTS: 'Who Killed Dan Cupid?'.*

Jones Griffith
Played Sir Noel Blanchard in the second series **Danger Man** [aka **Secret Agent**] episode *The Black Book.*
Played Lucian Currie in the **H. G. Wells' Invisible Man** episode *Strange Partners.*
Played Arnoldson in the **Man in a Suitcase** episode *Why they Killed Nolan.*
Played Lars Seelman in **The Persuaders!** episode *The Morning After.*
Played Sir George Davies in the **Strange Report** episode *Report 1553: RACIST: 'A Most Dangerous Proposal'.*

Jones Joanna
Played Julia in **The Adventurer** episode *Make it a Million*; Gina in the **Department S** episode *Les Fleurs du Mal* and Julia Marsh in the **Jason King** episode *A Deadly Line in Digits.*

Jones John Glyn
Played Vicar Stone in the first season **The Saint** episode *The Bunco Artists.*

Jones John Wynn
Played the official in the **H. G. Wells' Invisible Man** episode *Behind the Mask.*

Jones Jonathan
Recruited extras for **The Prisoner** at Portmeirion.

Jones Kenneth V.
Wrote the music for **The Buccaneers** [aka **Dan Tempest**] episode *Slave Ship.*

Jones Len
Voiced Joe 90 on the **Joe 90** series.

Jones Lewis
Played the Health Clinic Proprietor in the first series **The Protectors** episode *A Kind of Wild Justice.*

Jones Mark
Played Alden in **The Adventurer** episode *Nearly the End of the Picture.*
Played Scudder in the second season **The Protectors** episode *Petard.*

Jones Marshall
Played the Communist officer in the second season **Man of the World** episode *Double Exposure.*
Played Cooper in the **Sir Francis Drake** episode *The Doughty Plot* and Garrett in *The Slaves of Spain.*

Jones Mary
Played Mrs. Pugh in the second season **The Saint** episode *The Man who could not Die*, Mrs. Evans in *The Contract* and the nursing sister in the third season's *Flight Plan.*

Jones Michael
Hairdresser on **The Adventurer** & **The Champions**.

Jones Mike
Hairdresser on **Department S** & **The Persuaders!**.

Jones Nicholas
Played Ransome in the first series **The Protectors** episode *2,000ft to Die.*

Jones Norman
Played Helden in **The Champions** episode *The Final Countdown.*
Played Pete in the third season **The Saint** episode *Island of Chance.*

Jones Paul
Played Caspar in the second season **The Protectors** episode *Goodbye George.*
Played Ryan in the first season **Space 1999** episode *Black Sun.*

Jones Peter
Played the Minister in the first series **Man of the World** episode *The Sentimental Agent.*
Played Frederick P. Waller in the **Randall and Hopkirk [Deceased]** aka **My Partner the Ghost** episode *The House on Haunted Hill.*
Played George Lucas in the **Strange Report** episode *Report 2493: KIDNAP: 'Whose Pretty Girl Are You?'.*

Jones Rick
Played John Garton in the third season **The Saint** episode *The Death Game.*

Jones Robert
Art Director on **Department S**.

Jones Roderick
Played the farmer in the second series **Danger Man** [aka **Secret Agent**] episode *Whatever Happened to George Foster?*.

Jonson Bari
Played Lieutenant Kankana in the second series **Danger Man** [aka **Secret Agent**] episode *Loyalty Always Pays*.
Played Floyd in the **G.S.5** episode *Seven Sisters of Wong*.

Jonson Donald
Wrote the second season **Danger Man** [aka **Secret Agent**] episodes *Yesterday's Enemies, Colony Three, Judgement Day* [teleplayed from a story by Michael Bird] & *The Outcast* and the third's *The Man who wouldn't Talk* [with Ralph Smart] & *Dangerous Secret* [with Ralph Smart].
Wrote the **Espionage** episode *Final Decision* and co-teleplayed [with Allan Prior & Kenneth Hughes: from a story by Allan Prior] *Snow on Mount Kama*.

Jordan Desmond
Played the first soldier in the season three **The Adventures of Robin Hood** episode *The Healing Hand*.
Played the airline man in the **The Four Just Men** episode *The Prime Minister* and Shamus in *The Heritage*.
Played the Doctor in the first series **The Protectors** episode *.....With a Little Help from my Friends*.
Played a soldier in the **Sword of Freedom** episode *The Duke*.

Jordan Patrick
Played Ryker in **The Adventurer** episode *I'll Get There Sometime*.
Played Jamie in **The Buccaneers** [aka **Dan Tempest**] episode *The Raiders* and Morgan in *Blackbeard*].
Played Lackey in **The Count of Monte Cristo** episode *Naples*.
Played Brewster in the second series **Danger Man** [aka **Secret Agent**] episode *The Mercenaries*.
Played Corporal Kahn in the **Interpol Calling** episode *Desert Hi-Jack*.
Played Major Anderson in the **Man in a Suitcase** episode *The Whisper*.
Played Raoul in the **O.S.S.** episode *Operation Death Trap* and Max in *Operation Powder Puff*.
Played Pelli in **The Persuaders!** episode *Anyone can Play*.
Played Danvers in **The Prisoner** episode *Do Not Forsake Me Oh My Darling*.
Played Smart in the **Randall and Hopkirk [Deceased]** aka **My Partner the Ghost** episode *A Disturbing Case*.
Played Inspector Sullivan in the **Return of the Saint** episode *The Poppy Chain*.
Played the Russian base commander in the **UFO** episode *The Responsibility Seat*.

Jordine Merdel
Played Vera in the **Timeslip** story *The Year of the Burn-Up* [series episodes 13-17].

Josephs Wilfred
Incidental music on **The Prisoner**'s *Arrival*. His **Prisoner** theme was used in the alternate version of *Chimes of Big Ben*.

Jourd Judith
Casting on **The Champions** & **Department S**.

Joyce John
Played the Air Traffic Controller in the first series **The Protectors** episode *Talkdown*.

Joyce Paddy
Played the peasant in the season four **The Adventures of Robin Hood** episode *A Bushel of Apples*.

Played Shill in the **Return of the Saint** episode *Tower Bridge is Falling Down*.

Joyce Yootha
Played Sister Dryker in the **Jason King** episode *If it's Got to Go - It's Got to Go* and Milanov in the third season **The Saint** episode *The Russian Prisoner*.

Judd Alan
Played Sir Walter Battersley in **The Adventurer** episode *The Not-So-Merry Widow*.

Judd Edward
Played the Lieutenant in the third series **The Adventures of Robin Hood** episode *Too Many Robins*.
Played the Priest in **The Adventures of Sir Lancelot** episode *Double Identity*, Sir Grint in *The Bridge*, a soldier in *The Witch's Brew*, Garth in *Ruby of Radnor*, the auctioneer in *The Lesser Breed*, Ronk in *The Mortaise Fair*, James in *Maid of Somerset*, Sir Christopher in *The Ugly Duckling*, Abel in *The Lady Lilith*, a sentry in *Knight's Choice* and the leader of the King's men in *Thieves*.
Played Stephen Vasa in the **H. G. Wells' Invisible Man** episode *Shadow on the Screen*.
Played the first Nazi in the **O.S.S.** episode *Operation Firefly*.
Played Fred Langton in the **White Hunter** episode *Voodoo Wedding*.
Played the Austrian Officer in the **William Tell** episode *The Suspect* and Trooper Strauss in *The Gauntlet of St. Gerhardt*.

Junkin Harry W.
Wrote **The Baron** episode *Farewell to Yesterday*.
Wrote the **Department S** episodes *The Duplicated Man, A Small War of Nerves, Spencer Bodily is 60 Years Old, & The Ghost of Mary Burnham*.
Script Supervisor on **Gideon's Way** and wrote the episodes *The White Rat, The Tin God & The Prowler*.
Wrote the **Jason King** episodes *The Constance Missal, A Thin Band of Air & It's Too Bad about Auntie*.
Wrote **The Persuaders!** episode *The Ozerov Inheritance*.
Script Supervisor throughout **The Saint** series. Wrote the episodes: *The Fellow Traveller, Marcia, The Work of Art, The Elusive Ellshaw* - teleplayed from a story by John Kruse, *Starring The Saint, Luella* - with Kruse, *The Lawless Lady & The High Fence* [series 1]; *The Revolution Racket* - story: teleplayed by Terry Nation, *Jeannine, The Crooked Ring & The Abductors* - story: teleplayed by Brian Degas [2]; *The Russian Prisoner, The Paper Chase* - story: teleplayed by Michael Cramoy, *The Death Game* - telplayed from a story by Kruse & *A Double in Diamonds* - with Donald & Derek Ford [3] and *The Master Plan, The Fiction Makers* - parts 1 &2: additional scenes & dialogue: teleplayed by Kruse, *The Man Who Gambled with Life* - teleplayed from a story by Cramoy, *Vendetta for the Saint* - 2 parter: with Kruse: adapted from the original story by Leslie Charteris] & *Portrait of Brenda* [4].

Junkin John
Played Johnson in the season two **Ghost Squad** episode *Escape Route*.
Played Leonard Bright in the **Gideon's Way** episode *Morna*.
Played Jaseheroni in the **Jason King** episode *That isn't Me, It's Somebody Else*.

Justin George
Producer on **Espionage**.

****

Kalipha Stefan
Played Maurice in **The Adventurer** episode *Love Always, Magda.*

Kaminos Nicholas
Played the cafe owner in the **Jason King** episode *Wanna Buy a Television Series* aka *A Face I Used to Know.*

Kane John
Played Ludo Jones in the second season **The Protectors** episode *Petard* and Tom in the **Virgin of the Secret Service** episode *Wings Over Glencraig.*

Kann Lily
Played Mrs Weiss in **The Four Just Men** episode *The Deadly Capsule.*

Kanner Alexis
Appeared thrice in **The Prisoner**: debuted as the, non-speaking, Kid in *Living in Harmony*, featured in *The Girl Who Was Death* in an uncredited role as the photographer and guest starred as Number 48 in *Fall Out.*
Played Alec Misner in the first season **The Saint** episode *The Ever-loving Spouse.*
Played Jim Regan in the **UFO** episode *The Cat with Ten Lives.*

Kanter Bob
Played Brad Ryan in the first season **The Saint** episode *The Pearls of Peace.*

Karam Mia
Played Siegfried in the season two **Ghost Squad** episode *The Retirement of Gentle Dove.*

Karay Selan
Played Enrico in the **Return of the Saint** episode *The Roman Touch.*

Karlatos Olga
Played Vlora in the **Return of the Saint** episode *The Judas Game.*

Karli Michelle
Played the nurse in the **Department S** episode *The Ghost of Mary Burnham.*

Karlsen John
Played the second sentry in **The Four Just Men** episode *The Battle of the Bridge.*

Karnon Ted
Dubbing Mixer on **The Persuaders!** & **The Zoo Gang.**
Sound Recordist on **UFO.**

Karoubi Jimmy
Played Schneider in the **O.S.S.** episode *Operation Yodel.*

Karpf Eve
Played the desk clerk in the **Return of the Saint** episode *The Nightmare Man.*

Kash Murray
Played Sentry in **The Count of Monte Cristo** episode *Albania.*
Played Marcel in the **H. G. Wells' Invisible Man** episode *The Mink Coat.*
Played Kolinski in the **O.S.S.** episode *Operation Blackbird.*

Kasket Harold
Played Jacques in the second series of **The Adventures of Robin Hood** episode *The Bandit of Brittany.*

Played Moukta in the first season **Danger Man** episode *The Nurse* and Krummenacher in the third season [now aka **Secret Agent**] episode *Say it with Flowers.*
Played Korlandt in the **Department S** episode *The Perfect Operation.*
Played Michaelis in the first series **Ghost Squad** episode *Death from a Distance.*
Guested as Leooir in the **Interpol Calling** episode *Slave Ship* and as Thibault in *Slow Boat to Amsterdam.*
Played Colonel Davat in the **Jason King** episode *Uneasy Lies the Head.*
Played Guiseppe Rolfieri in the second season **The Saint** episode *The Damsel in Distress.*

Kasket Madeleine
Played Mrs Fawzi in the first season **Danger Man** episode *Position of Trust.*

Kath Katherine
Played Engadine in the **The Prisoner** episode *A. B. and C.*

Katzin Lee
Directed the first series **Space 1999** episodes *Black Sun* & *Breakaway.*

Kaufmann Maurice
Played Geoffrey Gains in **The Adventurer** episode *The Not-So-Merry Widow.*
Played Sir Loren in the season three **The Adventures of Robin Hood** episode *My Brother's Keeper* and William in the season four episode *Trapped.*
Played Savini in **The Count of Monte Cristo** episode *Naples* and Alfredo in *Sicily.*
Appeared as the pilot in the second season **Danger Man** [aka **Secret Agent**] episode *Judgement Day.*
Played Alem in **The Four Just Men** episode *The Prime Minister* and Hernandez in *Their Man in London.*
Played Dr Hussein Rasul in the season two **Ghost Squad** episode *Quarantine at Kavar.*
Played Robson in the **H. G. Wells' Invisible Man** episode *Jailbreak.*
Played Ronald Millais in the **Interpol Calling** episode *The Heiress.*
Played Ugo in the **Man in a Suitcase** episode *Jigsaw Man.*
Played Lecha in the second season **Man of the World** episode *In the Picture.*
Played George Fowler in the second season **The Saint** episode *The Man who Liked Toys* and Nathan in the third season's *Locate and Destroy.*
Played Sigismondo in the **Sword of Freedom** episode *Marriage of Convenience.*
Played Farley in the **White Hunter** episode *Second Dealer.*
Played Carl in the **William Tell** episode *The Bandit.*

Kavana Darryl
Played the naval guard in the **Man in a Suitcase** episode *Essay in Evil.*

Kavanaugh Paul
Played Du Chablon in **The Count of Monte Cristo** episode *Victor Hugo.*

Kay Bernard
Played Micholos Zentner in **The Adventurer** episode *Miss Me Once, Miss Me Twice and Miss Me Once Again.*
Played Kruger in **The Baron** episode *And Suddenly You're Dead.*
Guested as Emil in **The Champions** episode *The Survivors.*
Played Philip Bentley in the second season **The Protectors** episode *A Pocketful of Posies.*
Played Dighton in the **Randall and Hopkirk [Deceased]** episode *Somebody just Walked over my Grave.*

Played Schroeder in **The Zoo Gang** episode *The Twisted Cross*.

Kay Charles
Played Inspector Chilton in **The Adventurer** episode *The Not-So-Merry Widow*.

Kay Mary Ellen
Played Charmaine in **The Count of Monte Cristo** episode *The Pen and the Sword*.

Kay Elster
Played the Marketmaster in the second series of **The Adventures of Robin Hood** episode *Outlaw Money*.

Kay Henry
Played the butler in the season two **Ghost Squad** episode *Polsky*.
Played the Inspector in the second series **Danger Man** [aka **Secret Agent**] episode *Such Men are Dangerous*.

Kay Sydney John
Music on the series **H. G. Wells' Invisible Man**.
Musical Director on **William Tell**.

Kay Sylvia
Played the barmaid in the second series of **The Adventures of Robin Hood** episode *The Shell Game* and Alison in *The Borrowed Baby*.

Kaye David
Played Lord Mullrine in *Adventure Five* of **Sapphire and Steel**.

Kaye Kaplan
Played Chico in the first season **The Saint** episode *The Romantic Matron*.

Kaye Lila
Played Ma in the fourth season **The Saint** two parter *The Fiction Makers*.

Kaye Sylvia
Played Mrs Llwellyn in the **Strange Report** episode *Report 0649: SKELETON: 'Let Sleeping Heroes Lie'*.

Kayne Leo
Played the barman in **The Baron** episode *Portrait of Louisa*.

Keane Charlotte
Starred as Nikki, Ellery Queen's secretary, in the series **Mystery is My Business**.

Kearey Anthony
Producer on the second series of **Ghost Squad** and directed the episodes *The Missing People, Escape Route & Gertrude*.

Kearns William
Played Lyman in the **Jason King** episode *All that Glisters* [1].

Keats Viola
Played Madame Drobnic in **The Champions** episode *Twelve Hours*.
Played Mrs King in the **Gideon's Way** episode *The Nightlifers*.

Keegan Barry
Played Patrick Nolan in the season two **The Adventures of Robin Hood** episode *The Little People*.
Played Ruiz in **The Count of Monte Cristo** episode *The Portuguese Affair*.
Played Liamond in the first season **Danger Man** episode *The Sanctuary*.

Played Kevan Malone in **The Four Just Men** episode *The Heritage*.
Played Colonel Karlen in the first series **Ghost Squad** episode *Million Dollar Ransom*.
Played Colonel Williams in the **O.S.S.** episode *Operation Flint Axe*.
Played Barney Mailer in the second season **The Protectors** episode *Goodbye George*.
Played Martin Grahame in the first season **The Saint** episode *The Benevolent Burglary* and Bosun in season two's *Lida*.
Played Gomez in the **Sir Francis Drake** episode *Escape*.
Played Peter Renard in the **White Hunter** episode *Day of Reckoning*.

Keen Diane
Played Christine in the **Return of the Saint** episode *The Debt Collectors*.

Keen Geoffrey
Guested as the Blind Beggar in the first series of **The Adventures of Robin Hood** episode *The Wager*.
Played Commissioner Winlow in the third season **Danger Man** [aka **Secret Agent**] episode *Two Birds with One Bullet*.
Played Count Montesco in **The Four Just Men** episode *The Rietti Group*.
Played Dr. Stephens in the **H. G. Wells' Invisible Man** episode *Flight into Darkness*.
Played Count Maximillian Korvin in the second season **Man of the World** episode *The Prince*.
Played Thaddeus Krane in **The Persuaders!** episode *That's Me Over There*.
Played Charles Medley in the **Return of the Saint** episode *The Debt Collectors*.
Played Hobart Quennel in the second season **The Saint** episode *The Saint Steps In*.

Keen Malcolm
Played Talleyrand in **The Count of Monte Cristo** episode *The Talleyrand Affair*.

Keen Pat
Played the nurse in **The Prisoner** episode *The Schizoid Man*.

Keir Andre
Played Hassan in the **H. G. Wells' Invisible Man** episode *Man in Power*.

Keir Andrew
Played Laird in **The Buccaneers** [aka **Dan Tempest**] episode *Instrument of War*.
Played Dr. John Newman in **The Champions** episode *The Ghost Plane*.
Featured in the **Espionage** episode *He Rises On Sunday, and We On Monday*.
Starred as, series regular, Jock in **The Four Just Men**: *Village of Shame, Their Man in London, National Treasure, The Survivor, Money to Burn, The Man who wasn't There & The Boy without a Country*.
Played Sir John Hassocks in **The Persuaders!** episode *Greensleeves*.
Played Gilbert Kirby in the fourth season **The Saint** episode *The Scales of Justice*.
Played Flavel in the **Sir Francis Drake** episode *King of America*.
Played Leonardo de Vinci in the **Sword of Freedom** episode *Forgery in Red Chalk* and Sebastiano in *Who is Felicia?*.

Keith Brian
Starred as Stephen Halliday, codename The Fox, in the series **The Zoo Gang**.

Keith Sheila
Played Mrs Sands in the **Father Brown** episode *The Actor and the Alibi*.

Played Cynthia Ffouldes in the fourth season **The Saint** episode *Legacy for the Saint.*

Kelland John
Played the young doctor in the **Department S** episode *The Pied Piper of Hambledown.*
Played Harvester in **The Persuaders!** episode *Take Seven.*
Played Gilbert in the first season **The Saint** episode *The Talented Husband* and Ralph Windlay in *The Saint Plays with Fire.*

Kellerman Barbara
Played Gina in the first season **Space 1999** episode *Dragon's Domain.*

Kellett Bob
Directed the first series **Space 1999** episodes *Voyager's Return, The Last Enemy* [also wrote] and *The Full Circle.*

Kelley John
Played the Skydiver's navigator in the **UFO** episode *Destruction* and Masters in *Close up & Court Martial.*

Kellner William
Production Designer on **The Adventures of Sir Lancelot** episodes *The Outcast, Winged Victory, Sir Bliant, The Magic Sword, Roman Wall, Shepherd's War* and *The Theft of Excalibur* and on **Man in a Suitcase.**

Kelly Barbara
Was a series regular, providing the voice for the Moonbase computer, in **Space 1999.**

Kelly Clare
Played Lady Caroline Andrews in the season two **Ghost Squad** episode *The Magic Bullet.*
Played Mrs Norton in the **Gideon's Way** episode *The Rhyme and the Reason.*
Played Mary in the first season **The Saint** episode *The High Fence.*

Kelly David
Played Carlson in **The Adventurer** episode *To the Lowest Bidder.*

Kelly David Blake
Guested as the Lighthouse Keeper in **The Champions** episode *The Silent Enemy.*
Played Gavin Riordan in the season two **Ghost Squad** episode *The Heir Apparent.*
Played Harry Simpson in the **G.S.5** episode *Hideout.*
Played Insp. Shaunnesy in **The Sentimental Agent** episode *All that Jazz.*
Played Von Eckenburg in the **William Tell** episode *The Surgeon.*

Kelly Dermot
Guested as Hogan in **The Champions** episode *The Mission.*
Played Fingers in the **Gideon's Way** episode *The White Rat.*
Played Shorty in the first series **Man of the World** episode *Blaze of Glory.*
Played Henry Mace Horsfall in the **Randall and Hopkirk [Deceased]** episode *The House on Haunted Hill.*

Kelly Diarmuid
Played Malloy in the season two **The Adventures of Robin Hood** episode *The Mystery of Ireland's Eye* and Constantine in **The Count of Monte Cristo** episode *Athens.*

Kelly John
Directed the **Fireball XL5** episodes *Plant Man from Space, The Sun Temple, Space Monster, XL5 to H₂O, Space Pen,*

Sabotage, Mystery of The TA2, Dangerous Cargo, Whistle for Danger, Ghosts of Space and *The Fire Fighters.*
Directed the **Stingray** episodes *Sea of Oil, The Golden Sea, Emergency Marineville, Secret of the Giant Oyster, Man from the Navy, The Master Plan, Deep Heat, Tune of Danger* and *Trapped in the Depths.*

Kelly Mark
Played the reporter in the season two **Ghost Squad** episode *The Menacing Mazurka.*

Kelly Michael
Played a seaman in the **O.S.S.** episode *Operation Barbecue.*
Appeared as Arthur Korvin in the **White Hunter** episode *Operation Transfer.*

Kelly Pat
Assistant Director on **The Baron** and **The Champions.**

Kelly Paul
Played John Gordon in the second season **The Protectors** episode *Trial.*

Kelly Sean
Played the first man in **The Four Just Men** episode *Justice For Gino.*
Played Collins in the first series **Man of the World** episode *Specialist for the Kill.*

Kelly Tom
Played the soldier [Pearce] in *Adventure Two* of **Sapphire and Steel.**

Kelly Yvonne
Vision Mixer on **Sapphire and Steel.**

Kelsall Moultrie
Played Sir Angus in **The Persuaders!** episode *A Death in the Family.*
Played Calvin Gray in the second season **The Saint** episode *The Saint Steps In* and Fergus Clanraith in the third season's *The Convenient Monster.*

Kelsey David
Guested as Travers in **The Champions** episode *Nutcracker.*
Played the film director in the **Department S** episode *The Man who got a New Face.*
Played Miles in the third season **The Saint** episode *The Counterfeit Countess* and Dennis in the fourth season's *The Man who Gambled with Life.*

Kelsey Edward
Played Williams in the fourth season **The Saint** episode *Legacy for the Saint.*

Kelsey Gerald
Wrote **The Adventurer** episodes *The Bradley Way & Going, Going....*
Wrote **The Champions** episodes *Operation Deep-freeze* and *The Final Countdown.*
Wrote the **Department S** episodes *Six Days & Last Train to Redbridge.*
Wrote, with Dick Sharples, the first series **Ghost Squad** episodes *Assassin, Million Dollar Ransom & Princess* [*Princess* was shot for the first series, but due to an actors' strike, was shown in season two].
Wrote the **Jason King** episode *A Kiss for a Beautiful Killer.*
Wrote **The Prisoner** episode *Checkmate.*
Wrote the **Randall and Hopkirk [Deceased]** *The Smile Behind the Veil & The Ghost Talks.*
Co-wrote [with Dick Sharples] the first season **The Saint** episodes *The Latin Touch & The Charitable Countess.*

Kelson Bob
Wrote **The Secret Service** episode *May-day, May-day*.

Kemp Jeremy
Played Dr Linden in the first season **Space 1999** episode *Voyager's Return*.

Kemp Tony
Appeared as one of the dancers in the **Man in a Suitcase** episode *Three Blinks of the Eyes*.

Kempinski Thomas 'Tom'
Played the Spanish officer in the **Sir Francis Drake** episode *The Reluctant Duchess*.
Played Atahualpa in the **Virgin of the Secret Service** episode *The Amazons*.

Kempner Brenda
Played the nurse in the fourth season **The Saint** episode *The Master Plan*.

Kempson Juliet
Played the first fan in the **Jason King** episode *That isn't Me, It's Somebody Else*.

Kendall Felicity
Played the title role in the **Jason King** episode *Toki*.
Played Marcelle in the **Man in a Suitcase** episode *Blind Spot*.

Kendall Suzy
Played Kay in **The Persuaders!** episode *The Man in the Middle*.

Kendall William
Played Sir Wilfred in the **Department S** episode *Who Plays the Dummy?*.
Played Colonel Jarrett in the **Randall and Hopkirk [Deceased]** aka **My Partner the Ghost** episode *The House on Haunted Hill*.
Played Lord Merrion in the **Virgin of the Secret Service** episode *The Pyramid Plot*.

Kendrick Bryan
Played Bernard in the third season **The Saint** episode *The Art Collectors*.

Kennedy Arthur
Featured in the **Espionage** episode *The Whistling Shrimp*.

Kennedy Cheryl
Played the stewardess in the **Jason King** episode *Every Picture Tells a Story*.

Kent Faith
Played the saleslady in the **Man in a Suitcase** episode *Castle in the Clouds*.
Played Mrs. Donaldson in the second season **The Saint** episode *The Set-Up*.

Kent Harold
Wrote **The Adventures of Sir Lancelot** episodes *Roman Wall* and *Double Identity*.

Kent Jean
Starred in the series **Sir Francis Drake** as Queen Elizabeth I.
Played Valeska in the **Sword of Freedom** episode *The Lion and the Mouse*.

Kenton Mary
Played Mrs Peterson in **The Four Just Men** episode *The Bystanders*.

Played Alice Purdell in the first season **The Saint** episode *The Well-Meaning Mayor*.

Kenwright Bill
Played Mercier in **The Zoo Gang** episode *The Lion Hunt*.

Kerba Raymond
Production Manager on the series **Man of the World**.

Kerima
Played the belly dancer in **The Adventurer** episode *Love Always, Magda*.

Kerley Richard
Played the plain clothes Police Sergeant in the **Randall and Hopkirk [Deceased]** aka **My Partner the Ghost** episode *When the Spirit Moves You* and Sergeant Hinds in *Could You Recognise the Man Again?* & *Money to Burn*.

Kerr Annette
Played the nurse in the **UFO** episode *Identified*.

Kerr Bill
Played Wacker Dawson in the first series **Ghost Squad** episode *Hong Kong Story*.

Kerr Peter
Played Edwin in the third series **The Adventures of Robin Hood** episode *The Youthful Menace*.

Kerry James
Played Johnny in the **Department S** episode *The Shift that Never was*.
Played George Hapgood in the fourth season **The Saint** episode *The World Beater*.

Kessey Karen
Played Joan in **The Persuaders!** episode *Element of Risk*.

Kessey Katherine
Played Jean in **The Persuaders!** episode *Element of Risk*.

Keston John
Played Nazib in the **Department S** episode *A Fish out of Water*.

Key Alison
Played Pauline Stacey in the **Father Brown** episode *The Eye of Apollo*.

Key Janet
Played Jean in the **Department S** episode *One of our Aircraft is Empty*.
Played Elaine in the **Jason King** episode *The Constance Missal*.

Key Janey
Played Virginia Douglas in **The Adventurer** episode *The Bradley Way*.

Key Peter
Wrote the second series of **The Adventures of Robin Hood** episode *The Friar's Pilgrimage*.
Wrote **The Adventures of Sir Lancelot** episode *The Bridge*.

Keyes Karol
Played the ward nurse in the **Strange Report** episode *Report 3424: EPIDEMIC: 'A Most Curious Crime'*.

Keyes Thom
Wrote the second series **Space 1999** episode *The Taybor*.

Kidd Delena
Played Franky in the first season **Danger Man** episode *Name, Date and Place*.
Played Ingrid Brandt in **The Four Just Men** episode *Crack-Up*.

Kidd John
Played Simpson in the **Randall and Hopkirk [Deceased]** aka **My Partner the Ghost** episode *The House on Haunted Hill*.
Played the second professor in the **Return of the Saint** episode *The Imprudent Professor*.
Played Bateman in the second season **The Saint** episode *The Chequered Flag*.

Kilburn Richard
Assistant Director on the **Man in a Suitcase** series.

Killick Alan
Music Editor on season two & three of **Danger Man** [aka **Secret Agent**] and on **Randall and Hopkirk [Deceased]** aka **My Partner the Ghost**.
Supervising Editor on **The Secret Service**.
Editor on **Space 1999**.

Kilpinen Anna
Played the waitress in **The Adventurer** episode *Counterstrike*.
Played the hotel maid in the **Jason King** episode *To Russia With ....Panache* .

Kimberley Maggie
Played Jason King's companion in the **Department S** episode *The Man in the Elegant Room*.

Kinberg Jud
Producer on the Dailey / Conte episodes of **The Four Just Men** [Sidney Cole was Producer on the pilot - *The Battle of the Bridge* - and the Hawkins / de Sica episodes. The series was filmed in four separate blocks with the four stars actually appearing together in the pilot only. Dan Dailey & Richard Conte were each allocated ten episodes and Jack Hawkins & Vittorio de Sica each appeared in nine]: *The Prime Minister, The Beatniques, The Deadly Capsule, Marie, The Man in the Road, The Miracle of St. Philippe, The Princess, The Grandmother, The Godfather & The Moment of Truth* and *The Judge, Dead Man's Switch, Panic Button, The Discovery, Crack-Up, The Protector, The Bystanders, Riot, The Last Days of Nick Pompey & Justice for Gino*.

Kindred Bob
Camera operator, with Len Harris, on **The Prisoner** episode *Fall Out*.

King David
Played Damas in **The Adventures of Sir Lancelot** episode *The Magic Sword*.
Played the police Inspector in **The Baron** episode *Countdown*.
Played Sir Wilfred Underhill KC in the **Father Brown** episode *The Mirror of the Magistrate*.
Played Clive Jessell-Cave/Lawton V/O in the season two **Ghost Squad** episode *Quarantine at Kavar* and the doctor in *The Magic Bullet*.
Played Thompson in the **G.S.5** episode *It Won't be a Stylish Marriage*.

King Geoffrey
Played Sir Basil Duggan in the **Randall and Hopkirk [Deceased]** aka **My Partner the Ghost** episode *The Ghost Talks*.

King Louise
Played Joyce Eade in the first season **The Saint** episode *The Bunco Artists*.

Played Miss Ryman in **The Sentimental Agent** episode *Box of Tricks*.

King Peter
Played the man in the saloon car in the **Jason King** episode *Buried in the Cold, Cold Ground*.

King Sydney
Played Williams in the **White Hunter** episode *Marked Man*.

Kingsford Walter
Played Louis in **The Count of Monte Cristo** episode *The De Berry Affair*.

Kingsley Ben
Played Pierre in **The Adventurer** episode *The Good Book*.

Kingsley Ian
Played a reporter in the fourth season **The Saint** two parter *The Fiction Makers*.

Kingston Claude
Played Tim in the season two **The Adventures of Robin Hood** episode *The Little People* and Mark in the season three episode *Brother Battle*.
Played the second boy in **The Buccaneers** [aka **Dan Tempest**] episode *Mistress Higgins' Treasure*.

Kingston Mark
Played Inspector James Bagshaw in the **Father Brown** episode *The Mirror of the Magistrate*.

Kinkead Randall
Played the Attendant in **The Count of Monte Cristo** episode *The Experiment*.
Played Olot in the first season **Danger Man** episode *Josetta*.

Kinnear Roy
Played Marks in **The Adventurer** episode *Skeleton in the Cupboard*.
Played Robbins in the **Jason King** episode *An Author in Search of Two Characters*.

Kinoy Ernest
Wrote the **Espionage** episodes *The Frantic Rebel & The Gentle Spies*.

Kirby Audrey
Played an auction client in the **Father Brown** episode *The Arrow of Heaven*.

Kirby Johanna
Played the woman in *Adventure Six* of **Sapphire and Steel**.

Kirby John
Played the German guard in the second series **Danger Man** [aka **Secret Agent**] episode *Fair Exchange*.

Kirby Steve
Played Afredo in the season two **Ghost Squad** episode *Mr Five Per Cent*.

Kirek Milos
Played the Russian Delegate in the first series **The Protectors** episode *Balance of Terror*.

Kirshner Don
Musical Supervision on **The Adventurer** & **The Persuaders!**.

Kissoon Jeffrey
Starred as, season two regular, Dr Ben Vincent in **Space 1999**.

Kitchen Fred
Played Colonel de Seiberd in **The Four Just Men** episode *The Grandmother*.

Kitt Eartha
Played Carrie Blaine in the second season **The Protectors** episode *A Pocketful of Posies*.

Klauber Gertan
Played Hencke in the third season **Danger Man** [aka **Secret Agent**] episode *The Man with the Foot*.
Played Antonio Mardi in the **Department S** episode *The Double Death of Charlie Crippen*.
Played Arturo in the second season **Man of the World** episode *The Bandit*.
Played the cafe waiter in **The Prisoner** episode *Do Not Forsake Me Oh My Darling*.
Played Gromeld in the first series **The Protectors** episode *Chase*.
Played the Barman in the third season **The Saint** episode *The Counterfeit Countess* and Renato in the fourth season's *Vendetta for the Saint* [part 2].

Klee Richard
Played the waiter in the season two **Ghost Squad** episode *The Golden Silence* and the second clerk in *P.G. 7*.

Knapp Bud
Played Dr Hart in **The Four Just Men** episode *The Discovery*.

Kneale Patricia
Played Ellen in **The Adventures of Sir Lancelot** episode *Maid of Somerset*.

Knight David
Played Harry in the **Interpol Calling** episode *Dressed To Kill*.

Knight Eddie
Make-up on season two & three of **Danger Man** [aka **Secret Agent**], on **Jason King** and on **The Protectors**.
Makeup Artist on **The Prisoner** episodes *Arrival, The Chimes of Big Ben, A. B. and C., Free for All, The Schizoid Man, The General, Many Happy Returns, Dance of the Dead, Checkmate, Hammer into Anvil, It's Your Funeral, A Change of Mind* and *Once Upon a Time*.

Knight Esmond
Played the Minister in **The Champions** episode *The Silent Enemy*.
Played Gustav in **The Count of Monte Cristo** episode *Lichtenburg*.
Played the Baron in the first season **Danger Man** episode *Vacation*.
Played Robson in the **Gideon's Way** episode *Subway to Revenge*.
Played Wilson in the **H. G. Wells' Invisible Man** episode *Flight into Darkness*.
Guested as Von Schriber in the **Interpol Calling** episode *The Sleeping Giant*.
Played General Latour in the **O.S.S.** episode *Operation Dagger* and Emil in *Operation Firefly*.
Played Paul Hanson in the **Return of the Saint** episode *The Debt Collectors*.
Played Antoine Louvois in the first season **The Saint** episode *The Covetous Headman*.

Knight Howard
Played Chris Kirk in the **Gideon's Way** episode *Boy with a Gun*.

Knight Malcolm
Played the boy in **The Scarlet Pimpernel** episode *The Flower Woman*.

Knightly Will
Played the waiter in the **Jason King** episode *Variations on a Theme*.

Knorr Frieda
Played Josefina in **The Baron** episode *Time to Kill*.

Knowles Bernard
Directed **The Adventures of Robin Hood** episodes: *Husband for Marian, The Youngest Outlaw, The Jongleur, The Brothers, Richard The Lionheart, The Deserted Castle, The Miser, The May Queen, The Wanderer, Table's Turned, The Wager & The Prisoner* [series 1]; *A Village Wooing, Blackmail & A Year and a Day* [2]; *The Healing Hand* [3] and *The Flying Sorcerer* [4].
Producer on **The Adventures of Sir Lancelot** episodes *Double Identity, The Bridge, The Witch's Brew, Ruby of Radnor, The Lesser Breed, The Mortaise Fair, Maid of Somerset, Sir Crustabread, The Ugly Duckling, The Prince of Limerick, The Lady Lilith, Knight's Choice, The Missing Princess* and *The Thieves*. Directed the episodes *The Outcast, Sir Bliant, Shepherd's War, The Pirates, Knight Errant, The Theft of Excalibur* and *Thieves*.
Directed **The Buccaneers** [aka **Dan Tempest**] episodes *Instrument of War* and *Printer's Devil*.
Directed the **Sword of Freedom** episodes *Caterina, The Hero, Portrait in Emerald Green & The Ship*.

Knox Alexander
Played Hudson Inverest in the first season **The Saint** episode *The Latin Touch*.

Kochansky Hanja
Played Paula in the third season **Danger Man** [aka **Secret Agent**] episode *The Paper Chase*.

Koeppler Gerda
Played the old crone in the **Man in a Suitcase** episode *Somebody Loses, Somebody ...Wins?*.

Konopka Magda
Played Conchita in the second series **Danger Man** [aka **Secret Agent**] episode *A Date with Doris*.
Played Greta Weiss in the **Jason King** episode *Variations on a Theme*.
Played Ingrid in **The Persuaders!** episode *Read and Destroy*.
Played Michele Duplay in the **Department S** episode *A Fish out of Water*.

Korvin Charles
Starred in the series **Interpol Calling** as Inspector Paul Duval.

Kossoff David
Featured in the **Espionage** episode *Covenant with Death*.
Guested as Professor Renee in the **Interpol Calling** episode *The Long Weekend*.
Played Herman in the first season **The Saint** episode *The Careful Terrorist*.

Kotcheff William T.
Directed the **Espionage** episode *The Dragon Slayer*.

Kouri Thalia
Played Mai Lung in the **Virgin of the Secret Service** episode *Across the Silver Pass of Gusri Song*.

Krish John
Directed the first season **The Saint** episode *Marcia*.

Kriss Peter
Played Tonio in the second season **Man of the World** episode *The Bandit*.

Played Niko in the first season **The Saint** episode *Sophia*.

Kristof Peter
Played Giorgio in the fourth season **The Saint** two parter *Vendetta for the Saint*.

Kruschen Jack
Played Madroff in **The Count of Monte Cristo** episode *The Sardinia Affair*.

Kruse John
Writer on **Interpol Calling**: teleplayed *The Thousand Mile Alibi* [from a story by Leonard Fincham] and wrote the story for *Act of Piracy* [teleplayed by Edwin Richfield].
Wrote **The Persuaders!** episode *Powerswitch*.
Wrote the second season **The Protectors** episodes *Fighting Fund & Dragon Chase*.
Wrote the **Return of the Saint** episodes *The Nightmare Man*, *Yesterday's Hero* [teleplayed from a story by Roger Parkes], *The Poppy Chain*, *Signal Stop*, *Collision Course* [2 parter: part one:*The Brave Goose* & part 2: *The Sixth Man*: also exists as a feature entitled *The Saint and the Brave Goose*], *Vicious Circle* [co-wrote story with Michael Armstrong: teleplayed by John Goldsmith], *The Murder Cartel* [co-wrote story with Moris Farhi: teleplayed by John Goldsmith] and *Dragonseed*.
Wrote **The Saint** episodes *The Elusive Ellshaw* [story: teleplayed by Harry W. Junkin], *Teresa*, *The Saint Plays with Fire*, *The Sporting Chance* & *Luella* [with Harry W. Junkin] - season 1; *The Saint Steps In* - season 2; *The House on Dragon's Rock*, *The Death Game* [story: teleplayed by Harry W. Junkin], *The Gadget Lovers* & *The Power Artist* - season 3 and *The Double Take*, *The Fiction Makers* [parts 1 &2: additional scenes and dialogue by Harry W. Junkin], *The Ex-King of Diamonds* & *Vendetta for the Saint* [2 parter: Harry W. Junkin: adapted from the original story by Leslie Charteris] - season 4.
Wrote the **Strange Report** episode *Report 2641: HOSTAGE: 'If You won't Learn, Die!*.
Wrote the **William Tell** episodes *Landslide*, *The Boy Slaves* and *The Prisoner*, teleplayed *The Baroness* [original story by Ralph Smart]; wrote the original story for *The Bride* [teleplayed by Doreen Montgomery] and wrote the original story for *The Mountain People* [teleplayed by Doreen Montgomery].
Wrote **The Zoo Gang** episode *The Counterfeit Trap*.

Kum Kristopher
Played the passport official in the fourth season **Danger Man** [aka **Secret Agent**] episode *Shinda Shima* [*Shinda Shima* was also merged with the only other surviving fourth season colour episode, *Koroshi*, to form a TVM entitled *Koroshi*].
Played Harlun in the second season **The Saint** episode *The Sign of the Claw*.

Kumari Surya
Played Doctor Kaul in the **Interpol Calling** episode *Cargo of Death*.

Kurucz Janos
Played Riener in **The Adventurer** episode *The Solid Gold Hearse*.
Played Balenkov in the **Jason King** episode *Variations on a Theme*.
Played the KGB man in the first series **The Protectors** episode *Balance of Terror*.
Played a Russian astronaut in the **UFO** episode *The Responsibility Seat*.

Kwouk Burt
Played Johnny Morrison in **The Adventurer** episode *Deadlock* and Taiho in *Going, Going...*.
Played the Chinese Major in **The Champions** episode *The Beginning* [this episode was combined with *The Interrogation* to form a 'feature' entitled *Legend of The Champions*].

Played Tai in the debut season **Danger Man** episode *The Journey Ends Halfway*. In series two [now aka **Secret Agent**] played Chen Tung in *The Actor*, Masan in *You're Not in Any Trouble, Are You?* and Khim in *A Very Dangerous Game*.
Played Tanaka in the fourth season's *Koroshi* [*Koroshi* was also merged with the only other surviving fourth season colour episode, *Shinda Shima*, to form a TVM entitled *Koroshi*].
Played Lee Chung in the **Jason King** episode *Every Picture Tells a Story*.
Played Liu in the first series **Man of the World** episode *The Frontier*.
Played Chula in the **Return of the Saint** episode *Assault Force*.
Played Tawau in the second season **The Saint** episode *The Sign of the Claw*, Col. Wing in the third season's *The Gadget Lovers* and Mr. Ching in the fourth's *The Master Plan*.
Played Shunji in the **Shirley's World** episode *A Hell of an Engineer*.

Kydd Sam
Played Pick in the second series of **The Adventures of Robin Hood** episode *The Shell Game*.
Played Nolan in the **Man in a Suitcase** episode *Why they Killed Nolan*.
Played Dwyer in **The Persuaders!** episode *Someone Waiting*.
Played Charlie Steward in the **Return of the Saint** episode *Tower Bridge is Falling Down*.

Kyle Leslie
Played the landlord in **The Count of Monte Cristo** episode *Albania*.

****

La Touche Pat
Played the patron in the second season **The Protectors** episode *Implicado*.

La Trobe Peter
Appeared in **The Four Just Men** episode *The Last Days of Nick Pompey* and played Joubert in **The Scarlet Pimpernel** episodes *Antoine and Antoinette* & *A Tale of Two Pigtails*.

Lacey Catharine
Played Sarah Fischer in the **Gideon's Way** episode *State Visit*.

Lacey Denis
Played a variety of roles in **The Buccaneers** [aka **Dan Tempest**]: Lieut. Mendez in *Dan Tempest's War with Spain*, a guard in *Slave Ship*, Count Pedro Alfonso in *Articles of War*, one of the sons in *Mother Doughty's Crew*, the Spanish Mate in *Dangerous Cargo*, the Spanish Captain in *Gentleman Jack and the Lady*, Cunningham in *Marooned*, Jose in *Before the Mast*, Bo'sun in *Dan Tempest and The Amazons*, Posford in *The Ladies*, the first Spanish sailor in *The Surgeon of Sangre Rojo*, a Spanish sailor in *Prize of Andalusia*, the Captain in *Indian Fighters*, Jordan in *The Spy Aboard*, the pirate in *The Decoy* and Constable in *Printer's Devil*.

Lacey Ronald
Played Jeremy Standish in the **Department S** episode *The Soup of the Day*.
Played Jerry Blake in the **Gideon's Way** episode *Gang War*.
Starred as, series regular, Ryland in the series **Jason King**: *A Page Before Dying, A Red, Red Rose Forever* & *Uneasy Lies the Head*.
Played Cribbs in the first series **The Protectors** episode *King Con*.
Played the beatnik in the **Randall and Hopkirk [Deceased]** aka **My Partner the Ghost** episode *My Late Lamented Friend and Partner*.

Lack Simon
Played Colonel Andreyev in **The Adventurer** episode *Thrust and Counter Thrust*.
Played Gordon Symonds in the third season **Danger Man** [aka **Secret Agent**] episode *The Paper Chase*.
Played Jim in **The Four Just Men** episode *The Rietti Group*.
Played Federoff in the first series **Ghost Squad** episode *The Broken Doll*.
Played Inspector Maziol in the **Jason King** episodes *Buried in the Cold, Cold Ground* & *Toki*.
Played Salter in the third season **The Saint** episode *Locate and Destroy* and Craddock in the fourth's *The Organisation Man*.

Lafbery Roy
Sound Editor on **The Champions** & **Department S** and Dialogue Editor on **Thunderbirds**.

Laffan Kevin B.
Wrote the **Man in a Suitcase** episode *Essay in Evil* and the story for *The Revolutionaries* [teleplayed by Jan Read and Peter Duffell].

Laffan Patricia
Played Duchess of Maastricht in **The Count of Monte Cristo** episode *The Talleyrand Affair*, the Duchess in *The Island* and Mdme. Sablon in *Monaco*.

Lageu John
Set Dresser on **The Prisoner** episodes *Living in Harmony, The Girl who was Death* and *Fall Out*.

Lahee Sally
Played Mrs Steward in the **Return of the Saint** episode *Tower Bridge is Falling Down*.

Laird Jenny
Played Mrs Cookson in the first series **Ghost Squad** episode *Million Dollar Ransom*.

Laird Peter
Played Greville in *Adventure Five* of **Sapphire and Steel**.

Lake Alan
Played Carlo in **The Adventurer** episode *Icons are Forever*.
Played The Dandy in the **Department S** episode *Dead Men Die Twice* and Jacob in the third season **The Saint** episode *Locate and Destroy*.

Lamb Charles
Appeared in **The Adventures of Robin Hood** first season episode *The Jongleur* as the informer and as Ben Bradley in the third season's *An Apple for the Archer*.
Played Menard in **The Count of Monte Cristo** episode *Monaco*.
Played the porter in the **Department S** episode *A Small War of Nerves*.
Played the hotel porter in the **Randall and Hopkirk [Deceased]** aka **My Partner the Ghost** episode *Murder ain't what it Used to Be!*.
Played Tacco in the **Sword of Freedom** episode *The Sicilian* and Poggio in *The Marionettes*.

Lamb Irene
Casting Director on the series **Man of the World**.

Lambda Betty
Co-wrote **The Sentimental Agent** episodes *The Height of Fashion* & *Finishing School* [with Peter Lambda].
Wrote the **Virgin of the Secret Service** episode *Entente Cordiale*.

Lambda Peter
Wrote the first season **The Adventures of Robin Hood** episode *Checkmate*.
Co-wrote **The Sentimental Agent** episodes *The Height of Fashion* & *Finishing School* [with Betty Lambda].

Lambert Diana
Played Anna in the **William Tell** episode *The Avenger*.

Lambert Georges
Played Bayard in the first series **The Protectors** episode *Your Witness*.

Lambert Jack
Played Bart in the season three **The Adventures of Robin Hood** episode *Too Many Robins*.
Played the prison governor in the **H. G. Wells' Invisible Man** episode *Death Cell*.
Guested as Commander Smith in the **Interpol Calling** episode *In the Swim*.
Played the second man in the steam room in the **Randall and Hopkirk [Deceased]** aka **My Partner the Ghost** episode *The Ghost Talks*.
Played John McAndrew in the first season **The Saint** episode *The Wonderful War*.
Played Sir Robert Fenton in the **Virgin of the Secret Service** episode *The Professor Goes West*.
Appeared as Banstead in the **White Hunter** episode *Run to Earth*, as Dr. Mackenzie in *The Long Knife*, as Dr Waring in *Voodoo Wedding* and as Dr. Julian in *Let My People Go*.
Played Judge Furst in the **William Tell** episodes *Secret Death, Voice in the Night* and *The Lost Letter*.

Lambert Nigel
Played a Moonbase operative in the **UFO** episode *Computer Affair*.

Lamble Lloyd

Played General Ludovic in **The Count of Monte Cristo** episode *The Luxembourg Affair* and Armand in *Monaco*.
Played Granger in the season two **Ghost Squad** episode *Hot Money*.
Played Roo in the **G.S.5** episode *An Eye for An Eye*.
Played Dr Hanning in the **H. G. Wells' Invisible Man** episodes *Secret Experiment* & *The Locked Room*.
Guested as Capt. Merrick in the **Interpol Calling** episode *Air Switch*.
Played Loder in the **O.S.S.** episode *Operation Orange Blossom* and the editor in *Operation Newsboy*.
Played Stapleton in **The Prisoner** episode *Do Not Forsake Me Oh My Darling*.
Played the Assistant Superintendent in the **White Hunter** episode *Let My People Go*, the Superintendent in *Sickness of Kilimanjaro* and Inspector Burke in *Dead Man's Tale*.
Played the Colonel in the **William Tell** episode *The Bride*.

Lamont Duncan

Played Sir Dunstan in the second series of **The Adventures of Robin Hood** episode *The Black Patch* and Tom Barker in *Food for Thought*.
Played Joseph Brenner in the first season **Danger Man** episode *The Relaxed Informer*. In the second series [now aka **Secret Agent**], played Angus McKinnon in *That's Two of Us Sorry*.
Played Lowery in the **Department S** episode *The Man from X*.
Played Divisional Supt. Smedd in the **Gideon's Way** episode *The Rhyme and the Reason*.
Played Tommy in the **Man in a Suitcase** episode *All that Glitters* and the chauffer in *Why they Killed Nolan*.
Played Benton in **The Persuaders!** episode *The Time and the Place*.
Played Langford in the **Randall and Hopkirk [Deceased]** aka **My Partner the Ghost** episode *The House on Haunted Hill*.

Lampson David

Played Carl Bruner in **The Adventurer** episode *Action!*.

Lanchbury Liz

Played Sally in the first season **Danger Man** episode *The Lonely Chair*.

Landau Martin

Starred as Commander John Koenig throughout **Space 1999**.

Landen Dinsdale

Played Detective Sergeant Roddick in the **Jason King** episode *It's Too Bad about Auntie*.
Played Manning in the second season **The Protectors** episode *Wheels*.

Lander David

Played the taxi driver in **The Baron** episode *Time to Kill*.
Played Jailer in **The Count of Monte Cristo** episode *Albania*.
Played the chemist in the second series **Danger Man** [aka **Secret Agent**] episode *A Date with Doris* and the police officer in *The Mercenaries*.
Played Lorio in the **Department S** episode *Who Plays the Dummy?*.
Played the barman in the **G.S.5** episode *Dr. Ayre*.
Guested as Luis in the **Interpol Calling** episode *Checkmate*.

Lander Eric

Guested as Hedges in **The Champions** episode *Project Zero*.
Played Douglas Stayte in the **Department S** episode *The Shift that Never was*.

Landi Marla

Played Sita Shapadi in the first season **Danger Man** episode *Dead Man Walks*.
Played Suzanne Dumasse in the **H. G. Wells' Invisible Man** episode *The White Rabbit*.

Played Maria in the **Interpol Calling** episode *The Two-Headed Monster*.
Played Carmen in the second season **Man of the World** episode *The Bullfighter*.

Landis Harry

Guested as the Second Lieutenant in the **Interpol Calling** episode *Dead On Arrival*.
Played Versch in the **Jason King** episode *A Page Before Dying*.
Played Ryan in the **Man in a Suitcase** episode *Variation on a Million Bucks* [part 2: also combined with part 1 to form a movie: *To Chase a Million*].
Played Bloom in the third season **The Saint** episode *Locate and Destroy*.

Landone Avice

Appeared as Lady Lamorak in **The Adventures of Sir Lancelot** episode *The Ugly Duckling*.
Played Florence Warshed in the first season **The Saint** episode *The Gentle Ladies*.

Landry John F.

Played Tom Jenkins in the **Gideon's Way** episode *The Wall*.
Appeared as the morgue assistant in the **Strange Report** episode *Report 3424: EPIDEMIC: 'A Most Curious Crime'*.

Lane David

Directed the **Captain Scarlet and the Mysterons** episode *Winged Assassin*.
Editor on **Fireball XL5**.
Producer on the **Joe 90** series and co-wrote *Operation McClaine* [with Gerry Anderson].
Producer on **The Secret Service** series.
Supervising Editor & Technical Director on **Space 1999**.
Supervising Editor on **Strange Report**.
Directed the first season **Thunderbirds** episodes *Terror in New York City* [with David Elliott], *Desperate Intruder*, *End of the Road*, *Sun Probe*, *The Mighty Atom*, *The Man from MI5*, *Brink of Disaster* and *Attack of the Alligators!*.
Directed the **UFO** episodes *Exposed*, *A Question of Priorities*, *Sub-smash*, *The Square Triangle*, *The Man who Came Back*, *Computer Affair*, *Confetti Check A-O.K.* & *The Sound of Silence* [also co-wrote with Bob Bell].

Lane Martin

Played a variety of roles in the second series of **The Adventures of Robin Hood**: Lord Quincy in *A Year and a Day*, Tom in *The Impostor*, Senechal in *Ransom*, Sir Damon in *Isabella*, the second Man-at-Arms in *The Hero*, a page in *The Haunted Mill*, the Sheriff's Lieutenant in *Outlaw Money*, the Sheriff's Captain in *The Black Patch*, Seneschal in *Hubert* & the spy in *Ambush*.

Lane Silvia

Played an art student in the **Father Brown** episode *The Head of Caesar*.

Lang Howard

Appeared as the Landlord in the second series of **The Adventures of Robin Hood** episode *Isabella*.
Played Stanley White in **The Baron** episode *Countdown*.
Played Sergeant Fowler in the **Gideon's Way** episode *The Lady Killer*.
Guested as Commander Siddons in the **Interpol Calling** episode *Slave Ship*.
Played Bruehl in the **O.S.S.** episode *Operation Tulip* and Jean in *Operation Powder Puff* and the first farmer in *Operation Firefly*.
Starred as, series regular, Grenville in **Sir Francis Drake** [episodes 10 -26].
Played Majo Domo in the **Sword of Freedom** episode *Caterina*.

Played Hean Eunuch in the **Virgin of the Secret Service** episode *The Great Ring of Akba*.
Played Burrows in the **White Hunter** episode *The No-Account*.
Played Schmidt in the **William Tell** episode *Secret Death*.

Lang Tony
Played the Priest in the **Father Brown** episode *The Head of Caesar*.

Langan Glenn
Played Lassino in **The Count of Monte Cristo** episode *The Golden Blade*.

Langdon Anthony
Played Leeds in the **Father Brown** episode *The Quick One*.
Played Garcia in the season two **The Protectors** episode *Quin*.

Langova Sylva
Played Anna in the second season **Man of the World** episode *The Prince*.

Langton David
Played Lord Mauncey in **The Champions** episode *Nutcracker*.

Lapedus Norman
Played the servant in the **Danger Man** episode *The Trap*.

Lapotaire Jane
Played the French maid in the **Jason King** episode *Buried in the Cold, Cold Ground*.

Larkin Ian
Wrote **The Adventures of Robin Hood** episode *The Moneylender* [with Eric Heath].

Larkin Mary
Played the student, Jenny, in the second season **The Protectors** episode *Dragon Chase*.
Played Maria in the **Timeslip** story *The Day of the Clone* [series parts 21 - 26].

Lasky Jesse
Co-wrote, with Pat Lasky, the season one **The Protectors** episodes *One and One Makes One*, *Talkdown* & *A Case for the Right*.

Lasky Jesse Jr
Co-wrote, with Pat Silver, the third season **Danger Man** [aka **Secret Agent**] episode *Two Birds with One Bullet* & the first series **Space 1999** episode *The Full Circle*.

Lasky Pat
Co-wrote [with Jesse Lasky] the first season **The Protectors** episodes *One and One Makes One*, *Talkdown* & *A Case for the Right*.

Laszlo Charles
Played the police motorcyclist in the second series **Danger Man** [aka **Secret Agent**] episode *The Professionals* and the agent in *Colony Three*.

Latham Philip
Played Father Ignatius in the season four **The Adventures of Robin Hood** episode *A Bushel of Apples*.
Played Delroy in the first season **Danger Man** episode *View from the Villa*.
Played Valio in **The Four Just Men** episode *The Man with the Golden Touch*.
Played Ellshaw in the first season **The Saint** episode *The Elusive Ellshaw* and Long Harry in season two's *The Scorpion*.
Played Blake in the **UFO** episode *The Dalotek Affair*.

Latimer Hugh
Played Westmorland in the first series of **The Adventures of Robin Hood** episode *The Traitor*.

Latimer Max
Played Max in **The Adventurer** episode *The Case of the Poisoned Pawn*.

Laurence Andrew
Played Sir Alan in the second series **Danger Man** [aka **Secret Agent**] episode *Sting in the Tail*.

Laurence Charles
Played the van driver in the **Man in a Suitcase** episode *Night Flight to Andora*.

Laurence Oswald
Played a reporter in the fourth season **The Saint** two parter *The Fiction Makers*.

Laurenson James
Played Osgood in the second season **Space 1999** episode *Catacombs of the Moon*.

Laurenzi Silvio
Played Fabio in the **Return of the Saint** episode *Vicious Circle*.

Laurie E.S.
Production Manager on **The Adventures of Sir Lancelot** episodes *The Outcast*, *Winged Victory*, *Sir Bliant*, *The Magic Sword*, *Lancelot's Banishment*, *Roman Wall*, *Caledon*, *Shepherd's War*, *The Pirates*, *The Black Castle*, *The Bridge*, *The Witch's Brew*, *Ruby of Radnor*, *Double Identity*, *The Lesser Breed*, *The Magic Book*, *Knight Errand*, *The Theft of Excalibur*, *The Mortaise Fair*, *Maid of Somerset*, *Sir Crustabread*, *The Ugly Duckling*, *The Prince of Limerick*, *The Lady Lilith*, *Knight's Choice*, *The Missing Princess* and *The Thieves*.

Laurie John
Played The MacGillie in the first series **Man of the World** episode *The Highland Story*.
Played Dr Dufay in **The Scarlet Pimpernel** episode *The Imaginary Invalides*.
Played Doctor Hornsey in the **Strange Report** episode *Report 4821: X-RAY: 'Who Weeps for the Doctor?'*.

Laurimore Jon
Appeared as Ernst in **The Prisoner** episode *Many Happy Returns*.
Played the press reporter in the second series **The Protectors** episode *Border Line*.
Played Smithy in the season one **Space 1999** episode *Black Sun*.

Lauter Harry
Played Bouchet in **The Count of Monte Cristo** episode *Andorra*.

Lavelly Marjorie
Continuity on **The Protectors**.

Law John
Played the theatre doctor in the second season **The Protectors** episode *A Pocketful of Posies*.

Lawrence Arthur
Played the Judge in **The Adventures of Robin Hood** episode *Too Many Earls* [second series], the Herald in the third series episode *Marian's Prize* & Dyer in *Lincoln Green*. Played Sir Nedrick in the season four episode *Race Against Time*.

Played the hotel manager in the **Interpol Calling** episode *In the Swim.*
Played the Kommandant in the **O.S.S.** episode *Operation Sardine.*
Played Doctor Sheldon in the **White Hunter** episode *Pegasus* and as Doctor Larau in *Sister My Spouse.*

Lawrence Brenda
Played the announcer in the **Man in a Suitcase** episode *Day of Execution* and Marcia in *Jigsaw Man.*

Lawrence Charles
Played Martin in the **Man in a Suitcase** episode *The Girl who Never was.*

Lawrence Delphi
Played Stella Delroym in the first season **Danger Man** episode *View from the Villa.*
Played Nedra in **The Four Just Men** episode *The Beatniques.*
Played Lise in the season two **Ghost Squad** episode *Lost In Transit.*
Played Jane Kennet in the **Gideon's Way** episode *To Catch a Tiger.*
Guested as Marie Webber in the **Interpol Calling** episode *The Money Game.*
Played Cora in the first season **The Saint** episode *The Man who was Lucky.*
Played the Countess in the **Sir Francis Drake** episode *The English Dragon.*
Played Baroness Ulbricht in the **William Tell** episode *The Baroness.*

Lawrence John
Played the Gypsy violinist in the **Virgin of the Secret Service** episode *The Persuasion of a Million Drops.*

Lawrence Marjie
Played Della Maricut in the **Gideon's Way** episode *The Housekeeper.*
Played Diane in the season two **Ghost Squad** episode *The Missing People.*
Played Rose in the **Return of the Saint** episode *The Obono Affair.*
Played Mrs Cherry White in the **Virgin of the Secret Service** episode *The Persuasion of a Million Drops.*

Lawrence Peter
Played Harry Lewis in the **Department S** episode *The Pied Piper of Hambledown.*
Played the policeman in the **Randall and Hopkirk [Deceased]** aka **My Partner the Ghost** episode *The Smile Behind the Veil.*
Played the bartender in the first season **The Saint** episode *The Invisible Millionaire* and the third local in the third season's *The House on Dragon's Rock.*

Lawrence Quentin
Directed **The Baron** episode *The Edge of Fear.*
Directed the second season **Danger Man [aka Secret Agent]** episodes *A Date with Doris, That's Two of Us Sorry* & *The Affair at Castelevara.*
Directed the **Gideon's Way** episode *Gang War.*
Directed the **H. G. Wells' Invisible Man** episodes *Point of Destruction, The Prize, The Decoy, The White Rabbit, Man in Disguise* [with Peter Maxwell] & *The Rocket.*
Directed the **William Tell** episodes *The Suspect, The Bride, The Shrew, The Trap, The Mountain People, The Ensign* and *The Black Brothers.*

Lawrence Sheldon
Played Williams in the first season **Danger Man** episode *The Honeymooners.*
Played Whiting in **The Four Just Men** episode *Riot.*

Played Tony in the first series **Ghost Squad** episode *Bullet with My Name on it.*
Played Olson in the **O.S.S.** episode *Operation Blackbird.*
Played Winfield in the **White Hunter** episode *The General.*

Lawrence Tony
Played the first guard in the season two **Ghost Squad** episode *Gertrude.*

Lawson Anne
Featured in the **Espionage** episode *Castles In Spain.*
Played Ellen Winters in the **Gideon's Way** episode *Subway to Revenge.*
Played Janice Dixon in the second season **The Saint** episode *The Smart Detective.*

Lawson Gerald
Played Doctor Morrow in the season two **Ghost Squad** episode *Quarantine at Kavar.*

Lawson Leigh
Played Zarl in the second season **Space 1999** episode *One Moment of Humanity.*

Lawson Sarah
Played Lady Hilary Winrod in **The Buccaneers [aka Dan Tempest]** episode *Dangerous Cargo.*
Played Lisa Orin in the first season **Danger Man** episode *Time to Kill.*
Played Miss Wexler in the **Department S** episode *The Duplicated Man.*
Played Lady Diana Wales in the **Father Brown** episode *The Curse of the Golden Cross.*
Played Joan Erickson in the **Gideon's Way** episode *Fall High, Fall Hard.*
Played Mary Trevor in the **Jason King** episode *It's Too Bad About Auntie.*
Played Ella in the **O.S.S.** episode *Operation Newsboy.*
Played Mary in **The Persuaders!** episode *Nuisance Value.*
Played Betty Tregarth in the second season **The Saint** episode *The Crime of the Century.*
Played Hannah Elsom in the **White Hunter** episode *The Jackals.*

Lawson Wilfred
Played Corrigan in the third season **Danger Man [aka Secret Agent]** episode *Not So Jolly Roger.*

Lawton David
Played Anton Juryck in **The Adventurer** episode *Thrust and Counter Thrust.*
Played Guardia Civile in the first season **The Saint** episode *The Golden Journey.*

Lawton Mark
Played Dr Maurois in **The Scarlet Pimpernel** episode *The Christmas Present.*

Lay Me Me
Played Xanthe in the **Jason King** two parter *All that Glisters.*

Lay Raymond
Played Andrea in **The Sentimental Agent** episode *A Little Sweetness and Light.*

Laye Dilys
Played Laura Adams in the **G.S.5** episode *An Eye for An Eye.*

Layode Joseph
Played the affluent man in the second series **Danger Man [aka Secret Agent]** episode *Loyalty Always Pays* and the anarchist in *Parallel Lines Sometimes Meet.*

Layton Paul
Played the bell boy in the second series **Danger Man** [aka **Secret Agent**] episode *You're Not in Any Trouble, Are You?*

Leach Rosemary
Played Marion Grove in the **Gideon's Way** episode *The Lady Killer.*
Played Mary Hanson in the **Strange Report** episode *Report 2475: REVENGE: 'When a Man Hates'.*

Leacock Philip
Directed the second season **Danger Man** [aka **Secret Agent**] episode *The Colonel's Daughter.*

Leader Anton M.
Directed the **Espionage** episode *Castles In Spain.*

Leake Barbara
Played Mrs Foster in the second series **Danger Man** [aka **Secret Agent**] episode *Whatever Happened to George Foster?.*

Leakey Philip
Make-up on the series **The Zoo Gang.**

Leaman Graham
Played Colonel Carstairs in the **Father Brown** episode *The Head of Caesar.*

Leapman Jackie
Played Fred in the second series **The Protectors** episode *Zeke's Blues.*

Leary Nolan
Played Porello in **The Count of Monte Cristo** episode *Andorra.*

Leaver Don
Directed the second season **The Protectors** episodes *Quin, Lena, Burning Bush, Route 27* & *The Insider.*

Leaver Phillip
Played Brosa in **The Count of Monte Cristo** episode *Naples* [also, in the same episode, played Questore].
Played Starvos in the **H. G. Wells' Invisible Man** episode *The Decoy.*

Leavitt Sam, A.S.C.
Director of Photography on **The Count of Monte Cristo.**

Lebor Stanley
Played the guard in **The Adventurer** episode *Thrust and Counter Thrust.*
Played Fraser in the **Department S** episode *The Man from X.*
Played Boon in the **Father Brown** episode *The Curse of the Golden Cross.*
Played Miguel in the **Jason King** episode *A Kiss for a Beautiful Killer.*
Played Medina in the first series **The Protectors** episode *Ceremony for the Dead.*
Played Dalby in the **Return of the Saint** episode *The Nightmare Man.*

Le Beau Bettine 'Betty'
Played the receptionist in the first season **Danger Man** episode *The Girl who Liked GIs.*
Played the party maid in **The Prisoner** episode *A. B. and C.*

Le Mesurier John
Played Alvarado in the first season **Danger Man** episode *An Affair of State.*
Played Volgu in the first series **Ghost Squad** episode *Death from a Distance.*

Played Monsieur Lamprou in the **Interpol Calling** episode *The Long Weekend.*
Played Doctor Litz in the **Jason King** episode *If it's Got to Go - It's Got to Go.*
Played Guilio Basti in the **Sword of Freedom** episode *Portrait in Emerald Green.*
Played the Duke of Burgundy in the **William Tell** episode *The Avenger.*

Lee Annabelle
Played Miss Blake in the **Strange Report** episode *Report 4821: X-RAY: 'Who Weeps for the Doctor?'.*

Lee Barbara
Played the maid in the first season **Danger Man** episode *The Honeymooners.*

Lee Bernard
Played Morgan Travis in **The Baron** two parter *Masquerade* [*Masquerade* & *The Killing*: also edited together, to form a feature entitled *Man In a Looking Glass*].
Played Squires in **The Champions** episode *The Bodysnatchers.*
Played Lord Ammanford in the second series **Danger Man** [aka **Secret Agent**] episode *Whatever Happened to George Foster?* and Derringham in the third season's *The Man with the Foot.*
Featured in the **Espionage** episode *Snow on Mount Kama.*
Played Raggley in the **Father Brown** episode *The Quick One.*
Played Kershaw in the **Man in a Suitcase** episode *The Girl who Never was.*
Played Sam Milford in **The Persuaders!** episode *Someone Like Me.*
Played Arthur Pater in the **Strange Report** episode *Report 8319: GRENADE: 'What Price Change?'.*

Lee Christopher
Played Dessinger in the **O.S.S.** episode *Operation Firefly.*
Played Louis in **The Scarlet Pimpernel** episode *The Elusive Chauvelin.*
Played Zandor in the first season **Space 1999** episode *Earthbound.*
Played Mark Caldwell in the **White Hunter** episode *The Hungry Hell.*
Played Prince Erik in the **William Tell** episode *Manhunt.*

Lee David
Wrote the **Captain Scarlet and the Mysterons** episode *Codename Europa.*

Lee George
Played the police sergeant in the **Randall and Hopkirk** [**Deceased**] aka **My Partner the Ghost** episode *For the Girl who has Everything.*

Lee Gerry
Played the police officer in the first season **Danger Man** episode *The Journey Ends Halfway.*

Lee John
Played the Ambulance Doctor in **The Champions** episode *To Trap a Rat.*
Played Mayne in the first season **Danger Man** episode *View from the Villa.*
Played the killer in the **Man in a Suitcase** episode *Variation on a Million Bucks* [part 1: also combined with part 2 to form a movie: *To Chase a Million*] and Inspector Glenn in *Why they Killed Nolan.*

Lee Margareta
Played Susan in the first series **The Protectors** episode *The Numbers Game.*

Lee Robert
Played Tsi Chang in **The Champions** episode *The Dark Island*.
Played Chin Lee in the second series **Danger Man [aka Secret Agent]** episode *Loyalty Always Pays* and the manager of the Two-Tailed Dragon in the fourth season's *Shinda Shima* [*Shinda Shima* was also merged with the other surviving fourth season episode, *Koroshi*, to form a movie entitled *Koroshi*].
Played F. J. Wing in the **Jason King** episode *Every Picture Tells a Story*.
Played Ling in **The Sentimental Agent** episode *Finishing School*.
Played Ho-Chai in the **Strange Report** episode *Report 2641: HOSTAGE: 'If You Won't Learn, Die!*.

Lee Soo-Bee
Played the secretary in the first season **Danger Man** episode *The Actor*.

Lee Tony
Played Ramon in the second series **Danger Man [aka Secret Agent]** episode *The Outcast*.

Lee Waverly
Played Lisa in the **Interpol Calling** episode *The Man's Clown*.
Played Olwen in the **Sir Francis Drake** episode *Gentlemen of Spain*.

Lee-Wright Jennie
Played the first girl in the **Jason King** episode *A Page Before Dying*.

Leech George
Played the second guard in the **Man in a Suitcase** episode *Brainwash*.
Appeared as the first corridor guard in **The Prisoner** episode *The General* and as the fourth guardian in *Hammer into Anvil*.

Leech Richard
Played Sir Liones in **The Adventures of Sir Lancelot** episode *The Lady Lilith*.
Played Colonel Montes in the second series **Danger Man [aka Secret Agent]** episode *The Affair at Castelevara*.
Played Duclos in the first series **Ghost Squad** episode *The Broken Doll*.
Guested as Hanson in the **Interpol Calling** episode *Mr George* and as Garetta in *Pipeline* and as Finn in *The Collector*.
Played Duval in the first series **Man of the World** episode *A Family Affair*.
Played Stewart in the third season **The Saint** episode *The Persistent Patriots*.
Played Cosimo in the **Sword of Freedom** episode *Chart of Gold*.

Lees Michael
Played Tom Brooks in **The Champions** episode *The Final Countdown*.
Played the consultant in the second season **The Protectors** episode *A Pocketful of Posies*.
Played Professor Lemaire in the **Virgin of the Secret Service** episode *The Persuasion of a Million Drops*.

Leggatt Alison
Played Morgana le Fay in **The Adventures of Sir Lancelot** episode *Knight's Choice*.

Leigh Benedicta
Played Captain Wells in the first series **Man of the World** episode *Shadow of the Wall*.

Leigh Caroline
Played Monique in the **Interpol Calling** episode *Dressed To Kill*.

Leigh Suzanna
Played Emily in **The Persuaders!** episode *Chain of Events*
Played Lilla McAndrew in the first season **The Saint** episode *The Wonderful War*.
Played Jean in **The Sentimental Agent** episode *Never Play Cards with Strangers*.

Leigh-Hunt Ronald
Took over from Bruce Seton to become a regular in **The Adventures of Sir Lancelot** as King Arthur: *The Outcast, Winged Victory, Sir Bliant, Lancelot's Banishment, Caledon, Shepherd's War, The Pirates, The Black Castle, Double Identity, The Bridge, The Witch's Brew, Ruby of Radnor, The Lesser Breed, The Magic Book, Knight Errant, The Theft of Excalibur, Sir Crustabread, The Ugly Duckling, The Lady Lilith, Knight's Choice, The Missing Princess* and *Thieves*.
Played Commander Ford in the first season **Danger Man** episode *Find and Destroy*.
Played Haslet-Wood in the **Department S** episode *The Perfect Operation*.
Played Captain Davies in **The Four Just Men** episode *The Heritage*.
Played Joe Tobias in the first series **Ghost Squad** episode *Ticket for Blackmail* and Paul in the season two episode *Sentences of Death*.
Played Hart in the **G.S.5** episode *Dead Men Don't Drive*.
Played Hugo in the **Interpol Calling** episode *The Girl with Grey Hair*.
Played Gunther in the **O.S.S.** episode *Operation Newsboy*.
Played Herbert Wexall in the season one **The Saint** episode *The Arrow of God*, Mark Deverest in the second season's *The Scorpion* & John Ramsey in the fourth's *The Scales of Justice*.
Played Hawkins in the **Sir Francis Drake** episode *The Governor's Revenge*.
Played Carlo in the **Sword of Freedom** episode *The Bracelet*.
Played Jules Gunther in the **William Tell** episode *Voice in the Night*.
Played Slater in the **White Hunter** episode *The No-Account*.

Leighton Frank
Played Bartley Kern in the **White Hunter** episode *The Trophy*.

Leighton Margaret
Played Arra in the first season **Space 1999** episode *Collision Course*.

Leister Frederick
Played Sir Isaac Spendler in the **Interpol Calling** episode *Private View*.

Leith Audine
Played Joan in the **Man in a Suitcase** episode *Who's Mad Now?*.

Lemince Serge
Played Pym's Slave in **The Buccaneers [aka Dan Tempest]** episode *Blood Will Tell*.

Lemkow Tutte
Played Dutch in the **G.S.5** episode *Rich Ruby Wine*.
Played Kivich in the **Jason King** episode *To Russia With ....Panache*.
Played Singleton in the **UFO** episode *Court Martial*.

Lemming Arthur
Camera Assistant on **The Saint**.

Lemont John
Directed the **Sir Francis Drake** episodes *Drake on Trial, Gentlemen of Spain* & *The Gypsies*.

Lennard Peter
Dubbing Editor on **The Zoo Gang**.

Lennard Philip
Played the Lord Mayor in **The Adventures of Sir Lancelot** episode *Double Identity*.
Played Lopes in **The Count of Monte Cristo** episode *The Portuguese Affair*.
Played Johns in the **Randall and Hopkirk [Deceased]** aka **My Partner the Ghost** episode *Who Killed Cock Robin*.

Lennie Angus
Played Grodny in the first series **The Protectors** episode *Balance of Terror*.
Played Mactavish in the first season **The Saint** episode *The Fellow Traveller*.
Played Maclean in the **Virgin of the Secret Service** episode *Wings Over Glencraig*.

Lenny Bill
Editor on the third season of **Danger Man [aka Secret Agent]**.

Lenska Rula
Played Diana in the **Return of the Saint** episode *Hot Run*.

Leon Madeleine
Played the maid in **The Four Just Men** episode *The Rietti Group*, the Lady-in-Waiting in *The Princess* and the stewardess in *The Last Days of Nick Pompey*.

Leon Valerie
Played the film actress in **The Baron** episode *Countdown*.
Played the Space Queen in **The Persuaders!** episode *The Long Goodbye*.
Played Kay in the **Randall and Hopkirk [Deceased]** aka **My Partner the Ghost** episode *That's How Murder Snowballs*.
Played Therese in the third season **The Saint** episode *To Kill a Saint*.

Leonard David
Played Gautier in **The Count of Monte Cristo** episode *The Black Death*.

Leonard Hugh
Adapted G. K. Chesterton's *Father Brown* stories for the **Father Brown** series.

Leonard Sheldon
Executive Producer on the series **Shirley's World** [in association with Ronald Rubin].

Leslie Nan
Starred as Harriet [Jim's sister] in the **Fury** series.

Leslie Vilma Ann
Played the barmaid in the third season **The Saint** episode *The Fast Women*.

Lester Mark
Appeared in the third season **Danger Man [aka Secret Agent]** episode *Dangerous Secret*.

Lestocq Humphrey
Played Sir Gerald Fullerton in the fourth series **The Adventures of Robin Hood** episode *A Touch of Fever* and Lord Orford in *Hostage for a Hangman*.

L'Esty Jeanna
Played Leocadia in the **Man in a Suitcase** episode *The Man who Stood Still* and the Greek airline hostess in *The Boston Square*.

Letts Barry
Played Graves in the **G.S.5** episode *Party for Murder*.

Letts Pauline
Played Greta in the first season **Danger Man** episode *The Relaxed Informer*.
Played Dona Clara in the **Sir Francis Drake** episode *The Governor's Revenge*.

Leuenberger George
Special effects on season 2 & 3 of **Sapphire and Steel**.

Levene John
Played Tony in **The Adventurer** episode *I'll Get There Sometime*.

Levene Philip
Wrote the season two **Ghost Squad** episodes *The Retirement of Gentle Dove* & *The Man With the Delicate Hands*.
Co-wrote the story, with Ralph Smart, for the **H. G. Wells' Invisible Man** episode *Shadow on the Screen* [teleplayed by Ian Stuart Black].

Levitt Gene
Wrote, with Louis Marks, **The Four Just Men** episode *Marie*.

Levitt John
Played Aubrey Vernon in the **Father Brown** episode *The Actor and the Alibi*.

Levy Ralph
Directed the **Shirley's World** episodes *The Berkeley Club Caper*, *To Dream the Improbable Dream*, *Follow That Rickshaw*, *Evidence in Camera* & *Figuratively Speaking*.

Le-White Jack
Played the first Judge in **The Prisoner** episode *The Chimes of Big Ben*.

Lewin Mike
Played the second guard in the **Father Brown** episode *The Arrow of Heaven*.

Lewis Bernard
African Location Director on **White Hunter** and directed the episode *Forest of the Night*.

Lewis Dennis
Assistant Director on **The Champions**.

Lewis Duncan
Appeared as King Meliot in **The Adventures of Sir Lancelot** episode *Maid of Somerset*.

Lewis Ernie
With Gino Marotta, Assistant Director on **The Prisoner** episode *Do Not Forsake Me Oh My Darling*.
Assistant Director on **The Saint**.

Lewis Fiona
Played Clarissa De Vere Allan in **The Adventurer** episode *Nearly the End of the Picture*.
Played Lisa Crane in the **Department S** episode *A Ticket to Nowhere*.
Played Lady Pamela Radfield in the **Jason King** episode *It's Too Bad about Auntie*.
Played Diana in the third season **The Saint** episode *Flight Plan*.

Lewis Gillian
Played Joyce Grant in **The Baron** episode *So Dark the Night*.
Played Julia Howarth in the **Department S** episode *One of our Aircraft is Empty*.
Played Marjorie Hayling in the **Gideon's Way** episode *The Prowler*.

Lewis Michael
Played the boy in the fourth series **The Adventures of Robin Hood** episode *The Loaf*.
Played Joshua in **The Four Just Men** episode *The Godfather*.

Lewis Ray
Played Galvano in the first series **Man of the World** episode *The Mindreader*.

Lewis Rhoda
Featured in the **Espionage** episode *Do You Remember Leo Winters?*.

Lewthwaite Bill
Directed the **Interpol Calling** episodes *Checkmate* and *Slow Boat to Amsterdam*.

Leyden Leo
Played Dr. Julias in the season two **The Saint** episode *The Sign of the Claw* and Blaney in the third season's *Little Girl Lost*.

Leyshon Emrys
Played Master Weylin in the second series **The Adventures of Robin Hood** episode *Food for Thought* and Alfred in *The York Treasure*.
Played Clerk in the **H. G. Wells' Invisible Man** episode *The Locked Room*.
Played the records officer in the **Return of the Saint** episode *The Obono Affair*.
Played Major Domo in the **Sir Francis Drake** episode *Visit to Spain*.

Li Shiu Paula
Played the second girl islander in the fourth season **Danger Man** [aka **Secret Agent**] episode *Shinda Shima* [*Shinda Shima* was also merged with the only other surviving fourth season episode, *Koroshi*, to form a TVM entitled *Koroshi*].
Played a nurse in the **UFO** episode *Exposed*.

Libbott Robert Yale
Wrote the **White Hunter** episodes *Run to Earth* and *Forest of the Night*.

Licudi Gabriella
Played Emma in the second series **Danger Man** [aka **Secret Agent**] episode *English Lady Takes Lodgers*.
Played Hortense in the first series **Ghost Squad** episode *The Broken Doll*.
Played the Lady-in-Waiting in the **Sir Francis Drake** episode *The Garrison*.

Liddell Hilary
Played the Ward Sister in the **Timeslip** story *The Day of the Clone* [series episode 23].

Lieberman Frank
Played Jodie in the **G.S.5** episode *A Cast of Thousands*.

Lieven Albert
Played Troyan in the second season **Man of the World** episode *In the Picture*.

Liles Ronald
Production Manager on **The Prisoner** episodes *Do Not Forsake Me Oh My Darling*, *Living in Harmony*, *The Girl who was Death* and *Fall Out*.
Production Supervisor on **Department S**, **Jason King** & **Randall and Hopkirk [Deceased]** aka **My Partner the Ghost**.

Lilian Mona
Played the woodman's wife in the second series of **The Adventures of Robin Hood** episode *The Hero*.

Lilley Jack
Sound on **The Count of Monte Cristo**.

Lind Gillian
Played Madame Robart in the **Man in a Suitcase** episode *Blind Spot*.
Played Mrs Stratton in the fourth season **The Saint** episode *The Scales of Justice*.

Lindall Vanessa
Played Hilary in **The Champions** episode *The Ghost Plane*.

Linden Jennie
Played Kay Masterson in **The Adventurer** episode *Deadlock*.
Played Samantha in **The Champions** episode *The Gilded Cage*.
Played Shelley Masterson in **The Persuaders!** episode *To the Death, Baby*.
Played Moyna Stanford in the second season **The Saint** episode *The Man who could not Die* and Diane in the third season's *The Reluctant Revolution*.
Played The Hon. Maud la Moote in the **Virgin of the Secret Service** episode *The Rajah and the Suffragette*.

Linder Cec
Played General McCready in **The Adventurer** episode *Action!*.
Played Bannon in **The Four Just Men** episode *The Beatniques*.
Played Captain Tully in the **Interpol Calling** episode *You Can't Die Twice*.
Played Waldo in the second season **The Saint** episode *The Persistent Parasite*.

Lindholm Kirsten
Played Marissa in **The Persuaders!** episode *Angie. . . Angie*.
Played the actress in the **UFO** episode *Timelash*.

Lindop W.
Sound on **The Adventures of Sir Lancelot** episodes *The Mortaise Fair*, *The Ugly Duckling*, *The Prince of Limerick*, *The Lady Lilith*, *Knight's Choice* and *The Missing Princess*.

Lindsay Eric
Played Antoine in **The Scarlet Pimpernel** episode *Antoine and Antoinette*.

Lindsay Ernest
Played Pohlman in the second series **Danger Man** [aka **Secret Agent**] episode *Fair Exchange*.

Lindsay Helen
Played Mrs Brearley in the **Strange Report** episode *Report 8944: HAND: 'A Matter of Witchcraft?'*.

Lindsay-Hogg Michael
Directed the first season **The Protectors** episode *A Case for the Right* and the second season's *Goodbye George & Deccy*.

Lindup David
Composed and conducted the music on **The Persuaders!** [theme composed by John Barry].

Linehan Barry
Played the gambler in the El Hamra Bar in **The Baron** episode *Long Ago and Far Away*.
Played Foster in the second series **Danger Man** [aka **Secret Agent**] episode *Fair Exchange*.
Played an Australian in the first series **Man of the World** episode *The Highland Story*.
Played Thatcher in the first season **The Saint** episode *Iris* and Max in the second season's *The Crooked Ring*.

Lintern Brian
Music Editor on **Return of The Saint**.

Liss Joseph
Wrote the **Espionage** episode *Some Other Kind of World*.

Lissek Leon
Played Pannides in the first series **The Protectors** episode *Brother Hood*.
Played Pancho in the **Return of the Saint** two parter *Collision Course* [Part 1: *The Brave Goose* & part 2: *The Sixth Man*: also exists as a movie entitled *The Saint and the Brave Goose*].
Played Pierre in **The Zoo Gang** episode *The Counterfeit Trap*.

Lister Eve
Played Cynthia Deverest in the second season **The Saint** episode *The Scorpion*.

Lister Moira
Played Vanessa in the first season **Danger Man** episode *Find and Return* and Claudia Jordan in the third season [now aka **Secret Agent**] episode *The Hunting Party*.

Little George
Played Rostov in **The Adventurer** episode *Going, Going....*
Played the Indian Sergeant in the first series **Man of the World** episode *The Frontier*.
Played the desk clerk in the second season **The Protectors** episode *Decoy*.
Played the police Lieutenant in the first season **The Saint** episode *Teresa*.
Played the Lieutenant in the **Sir Francis Drake** episode *Beggars of the Sea*.

Littlewood Harry
Played the landlord in **The Baron** episode *The Man Outside*.
Played the second reporter in the third season **The Saint** episode *The Convenient Monster* and the postman in the fourth season's *Portrait of Brenda*.

Livesey Roger
Featured in the **Espionage** episode *The Frantic Rebel*.

Livingstone Douglas
Played Sergeant Copley in **The Baron** episode *You Can't Win Them All*.
Played Watters in the third season **The Saint** episode *When Spring is Sprung*.

Llewelyn Desmond
Played 'Two Fingers' in the third series **The Adventures of Robin Hood** episode *Little Mother*,
Played the doorman in the second series **Danger Man** [aka **Secret Agent**] episode *The Ubiquitous Mr Lovegrove*.
Played Count Kolinsky in the **Virgin of the Secret Service** episode *Russian Roundabout*.

Lloyd Diana
Played the Princess in **The Sentimental Agent** episode *The Height of Fashion*.

Lloyd Dora
Wardrobe on **The Prisoner** episodes *Do Not Forsake Me Oh My Darling, Living in Harmony, The Girl who was Death, Once Upon a Time* and *Fall Out*.

Lloyd Jeremy
Played Henry in the **Shirley's World** episode *Thou Shall Not Be Found Out*.

Lloyd Lala
Played Fisher in the **Father Brown** episode *The Head of Caesar*.

Lloyd Robert
Played the radar officer in the **UFO** episode *Destruction*.

Lloyd Sue
Starred as Cordelia Winfield in **The Baron**: *Diplomatic Immunity, Epitath for a Hero, Something for a Rainy Day, Enemy of the State, And Suddenly You're Dead, Masquerade* [two parter: *Masquerade* - part 1 and *The Killing* - part 2: edited together, also exists as a feature entitled *Man In a Looking Glass*], *The Maze, There's Someone Close Behind You, Storm Warning* [two parter: *Storm Warning* - part 1 and *The Island* - part 2: also exists as a feature called *Mystery Island*], *Time to Kill, A Memory of Evil, You Can't Win Them All, The High Terrace, The Seven Eyes of Night, Night of the Hunter, The Edge of Fear, Long Ago and Far Away, So Dark the Night, The Long, Long Day, The Man Outside* & *Countdown*.
Played Brigitte in the **Department S** episode *Black Out*.
Played Eve in the **Jason King** episode *An Author in Search of Two Characters*.
Played Maggie in **The Persuaders!** episode *Take Seven*.
Played Elizabeth Saxon in the **Randall and Hopkirk [Deceased]** aka **My Partner the Ghost** episode *Money to Burn*.
Played Marla Clayton in the third season **The Saint** episode *Island of Chance*.
Played Jackie in **The Sentimental Agent** episode *The Height of Fashion*.

Lloyd Susan
Played Mary Henderson in the **Gideon's Way** episode *The White Rat*.
Played Luella in the first season **The Saint** episode *Luella*.

Lloyd Suzanne
Appeared in a number of roles in **The Saint**: as Doris Harvey in *Luella* & as Gabby in *The High Fence* [season 1]; as Doris Inkler in *The Revolution Racket* [2]; as Claudia Molinelli in *The Man who Liked Lions* [3] and as Serena in *Simon and Delilah* & as Mary Ellen Brent in *The Time to Die* [4].

Lloyd Ted
Production supervisor on the series **O.S.S.**

Lloyd Pack Charles
Played Hugh in **The Adventures of Robin Hood** first series episode *The Betrothal*, the Abbot in *The Scientist* & Maurice in *Food for Thought* [series 2], the Abbot in *The Genius* [3] and the Bishop in *Double Trouble* [4].
Played Borner in **The Count of Monte Cristo** episode *Burgundy*.
Played the police Superintendent in the debut season **Danger Man** episode *The Key* and the gunsmith in *Vacation*. In series three [now aka **Secret Agent**] played the First Secretary in *To our Best Friend*.
Played Mr Hunter in the **Gideon's Way** episode *How to Retire without Really Working*.
Played Howard in the **Jason King** episode *The Constance Missal*.
Played Sir Charles Grainger in the **Man in a Suitcase** episode *Burden of Proof* and the Examining Magistrate in *Three Blinks of the Eyes*.
Played Jorgens in the first series **Man of the World** episode *Shadow of the Wall*.
Played the artist in **The Prisoner** episode *It's Your Funeral*.
Played Cecil Purley in the **Randall and Hopkirk [Deceased]** aka **My Partner the Ghost** episode *Who Ever Heard of a Ghost Dying?*.
Played Pettygrew in **The Sentimental Agent** episode *Not Quite Fully Covered*.

Played Sir Harold in the **Shirley's World** episode *The Berkeley Club Caper*.

Played Daniel Peters in the **Sir Francis Drake** episode *Lost Colony of Virginia*.

Was a semi regular in the **Strange Report** series as Professor Marks: *Report 0649: SKELETON: 'Let Sleeping Heroes Lie', Report 0846: LONELYHEARTS: 'Who Killed Dan Cupid?', Report 3424: EPIDEMIC: 'A Most Curious Crime', Report 1021: SHRAPNEL: 'The Wish in the Dream', Report 8944: HAND: 'A Matter of Witchcraft?', Report 4821: X-RAY: 'Who Weeps for the Doctor?' & Report 4407: HEART: 'No Choice for the Donor'*.

Played Herr Specker in the **William Tell** episode *Landslide*.

Lloyd Pack Roger
Played the radio operator in the **Jason King** episode *A Kiss for a Beautiful Killer*.

Played Russi in the second series **The Protectors** episode *Lena*.

Played Cuthbert in the **Virgin of the Secret Service** episode *Entente Cordiale*.

Locke Harry
Played Greg in the first series **Ghost Squad** episode *The Broken Doll*.

Played Joe Moss in the **Gideon's Way** episode *The Nightlifers*.

Played the night porter in the **Randall and Hopkirk [Deceased]** aka **My Partner the Ghost** episode *My Late Lamented Friend and Partner*.

Locke Philip
Played Compton in **The Baron** episode *Countdown*.

Played Yeats in **The Champions** episode *The Bodysnatchers*.

Played Topek in the **Department S** episode *The Perfect Operation*.

Played Frug in the fourth season **The Saint** two parter *The Fiction Makers*.

Locker James
Played Dr. King in the fourth season **The Saint** episode *The Master Plan*.

Lockhart Araby
Played the American lady in the fourth season **The Saint** episode *The Ex-King of Diamonds*.

Lockhart Harry
Played Pietro in the first season **Danger Man** episode *Hired Assassin* and Idris in *The Nurse*.

Played Rafael in the **Sir Francis Drake** episode *The Gypsies*.

Played Guiseppe in the **William Tell** episode *The Black Brothers*.

Lockwood Julia
Guested as Louisa in the **Interpol Calling** episode *The Heiress*.

Loder John
Played Danglers in **The Count of Monte Cristo** episode *Point Counter Point*.

Appeared as Steve Anderson in the **White Hunter** episode *The Treasure of Tippu Tib*.

Lodge Bill
Make-up Supervisor on **Gideon's Way** and Chief Make-up Artist on **Sir Francis Drake**.

Lodge David
Guested as Filmer in **The Champions** episode *The Gun-Runners* and as Porth in *The Night People*.

Played Mr Banks in the **Father Brown** episode *The Man with Two Beards*.

Played Max Leach in the season two **Ghost Squad** episode *The Golden Silence*.

Played Morris in the **Gideon's Way** episode *State Visit*.

Played Beeches in the **Randall and Hopkirk [Deceased]** aka **My Partner the Ghost** episode *Who Killed Cock Robin*.

Played Harry Duggan in the second season **The Saint** episode *The Man who Liked Toys*.

Lodge Ruth
Played Mrs Marquand-Forster in the season two **Ghost Squad** episode *The Menacing Mazurka*.

I the first series of **Man of the World**, played Directrice in *A Family Affair* and Elspeth in *The Highland Story*.

Played Mistress Seaton in the **Sir Francis Drake** episode *Lost Colony of Virginia*.

Lodge Terence
Played Heinman in **The Baron** episode *Enemy of the State*.

Played Boris in the **Jason King** episode *A Royal Flush*.

Loeb Lee
Wrote the story for **The Four Just Men** episode *Crack-Up* [teleplayed by Louis Marks].

Wrote the **White Hunter** episodes *A Moment of Truth, Marked Man, The Treasure of Tippu Tib, Deadfall, Voodoo Wedding, The No-Account, The Prisoner* and *Pegasus* [with Donn Mullally].

Loegering Stephen
Played Henry Peabody Jr. in **The Sentimental Agent** episode *Meet my Son, Henry*.

Logan Michael
Played Sir Matthew Blake KC in the **Father Brown** episode *The Mirror of the Magistrate*.

Logie Seymour
Dubbing editor on **The Buccaneers** [aka **Dan Tempest**] episode *Blackbeard* and editor on *The Raiders, Captain Dan Tempest, Dan Tempest's War with Spain, The Wasp, Whale Gold, Slave Ship, Mr. Beamish and the Hangman's Noose, Dan Tempest and The Amazons, The Ladies* and *The Surgeon of Sangre Rojo*.

Lomand Britt
Played De Crissac in **The Count of Monte Cristo** episode *Victor Hugo*.

Lomas Jimmy
Played the gambler in the first season **Danger Man** episode *Name, Date and Place*.

London Maggie
Played the nurse in the **Randall and Hopkirk [Deceased]** aka **My Partner the Ghost** episode *You Can Always find a Fall Guy*.

Played Julie in the fourth season **The Saint** episode *The Desperate Diplomat*.

Long Pauline
Played one of the models in the **Strange Report** episode *Report 3906: COVER GIRLS: 'Last year's Model'*.

Long Sue
Set Dresser on **Randall and Hopkirk [Deceased]** aka **My Partner the Ghost**.

Longden John
Played a range of roles in the first season of **The Adventures of Robin Hood**: the Abbot in *The Intruders*, Chamberlin in *The Deserted Castle*, Sir Gyles in *Trial by Battle*, Walter Fitzurse in *Children of the Greenwood*, Blackstone in *The May Queen*, Sir Walter in *The Wanderer*, the Archbishop in *The Byzantine Treasure*, Wulfrie in *Secret Mission*, Count Leger in *Table's Turned*, the tailor in *The Traitor* and Ned in *The Thorkill Ghost*. Returned in series three to play Hodges in *The Profiteer*.

Played Marat in **The Count of Monte Cristo** episode *Point Counter Point*.

Played Spencer Deeds in the season two **Ghost Squad** episode *Death of a Sportsman*.

Guested as Lord Ruskington in the **Interpol Calling** episode *The Absent Assassin*.

Played Umberto in the **Sword of Freedom** episode *The Value of Paper*.

Appeared as Davidson in the **White Hunter** episode *Rogue Man* and as Brad Holt in *Girl Hunt*.

Played Reinhardt in the **William Tell** episode *Undercover*.

Longden Terence
Played Supt. Finder in the **G.S.5** episodes *Pay Up or Else & Dr. Ayre*.

Longdon Terence
Played Saunders in the first season **Danger Man** episode *The Conspirators* and Rowland in the second series [now aka Secret Agent] episode *Fish on the Hook*.

Longhurst Henry
Played the security officer in the second series **Ghost Squad** episode *Interrupted Requiem*.

Played the old guest, Charlie, in **The Prisoner** episode *Do Not Forsake Me Oh My Darling*.

Appeared as Edward Storm in the **White Hunter** episode *Operation Transfer*.

Longhurst Jeremy
Played Fortune in the fourth season **Danger Man** [aka **Secret Agent**] episode *Koroshi* [*Koroshi* was also merged with the only other surviving fourth season colour episode, *Shinda Shima*, to form a TVM entitled *Koroshi*].

Played George McGeorge in the second season **The Saint** episode *The Persistent Parasite*.

Longworth Eric
Played Barnard in the **Father Brown** episode *The Man with Two Beards*.

Played Dr. Eutcher in the third season **The Saint** episode *The Persistent Patriots*.

Lonnen Ray
Played Patrick in the second series **The Protectors** episode *Zeke's Blues*.

Played Cpl. Buller in the third season **The Saint** episode *Flight Plan* and Jackson in the fourth season's *The People Importers*.

Lorane John
Played Tomasi in the **Jason King** episode *The Stones of Venice*.

Lord Justine
Played Rina in the **Gideon's Way** episode *The Lady Killer*.

Played Jane Farson in the **Man in a Suitcase** episode *Property of a Gentleman*.

Guest starred as Sonia in **The Prisoner** episode *The Girl who was Death*.

Played Jean Yarmouth in the first season **The Saint** episode *The Bunco Artist* and Lady Valerie in *The Saint Plays with Fire*. In season two played Andrea Quennel in *The Saint Steps In*, Denise Grant in *The Imprudent Politician* and Mandy Ellington in *The Chequered Flag*. Played Galaxy Rose in the fourth season two parter *The Fiction Makers*.

Lorimer Carole
Played Deidre in the season two **The Adventures of Robin Hood** episode *The Little People*.

Lorimer Enid
Played Miss Bentley in the second season **Man of the World** episode *The Prince*.

Played Madam Mureax in the **O.S.S.** episode *Operation Powder Puff*.

Played the Matron in the **White Hunter** episode *Forest of the Night*.

Lorraine Nita
Guested as Susan in **The Champions** episode *The Experiment*.

Played Radek's girl friend in the **Man in a Suitcase** episode *Night Flight to Andora*.

Played Celeste in the third season **The Saint** episode *To Kill a Saint*.

Lott Barbara
Played Jenny in the season three **The Adventures of Robin Hood** episode *The Ghost that Failed*.

Played Mrs Braithwaite in the second series **Danger Man** [aka **Secret Agent**] episode *That's Two of Us Sorry*.

Love Bessie
Played Mrs Trotter in the **Randall and Hopkirk [Deceased]** aka **My Partner the Ghost** episode *When Did you Start to Stop Seeing Things?*.

Played Mamie in **The Sentimental Agent** episode *Never Play Cards with Strangers*.

Lovegrove Arthur
Played Uncle Charley in the **Gideon's Way** episode *The Tin God*.

Played the Harbour Master in the **Strange Report** episode *Report 4977: SWINDLE: 'Square Root of Evil'*.

Lovell Angela
Played Betty Francis in **The Baron** episode *The Legions of Ammak*.

Played the girl in the bath in the third season **Danger Man** [aka **Secret Agent**] episode *The Man who wouldn't Talk*.

Played Jane Kilverton in the **Department S** episode *One of our Aircraft is Empty* and the French cabaret artiste in *The Man who got a New Face*.

Played the receptionist in the **Man in a Suitcase** episode *Essay in Evil*.

Lovell Dyson
Played Peter Bennett in the **Gideon's Way** episode *The 'V' Men*.

Played Jim Fasson in the first season **The Saint** episode *The High Fence*.

Lovell Roderick
Played Franz in **The Count of Monte Cristo** episode *Lichtenburg*.

Played Betrand in the third season **Danger Man** [aka **Secret Agent**] episode *To our Best Friend*.

Lovell Simone
Starred as, regular, Joan in **The Adventures of Robin Hood**: *Dead or Alive, Friar Tuck, The Youngest Outlaw, Ladies of Sherwood, Will Scarlet & The Deserted Castle* [season 1]; *Ransom, The Blackbird & Carlotta* [2]; *The Bride of Robin Hood, The Profiteer & The Healing Hand* [3] and *Six Strings to his bow, Goodbye, Little John, The Oath & Race Against Time* [4].

Played Yvonne in **The Count of Monte Cristo** episode *Marseilles* and Josette in *Burgundy*.

Played Marcia Richmond in **The Four Just Men** episode *The Man in the Road*.

Played Renee in **The Scarlet Pimpernel** episode *The Ambassador's Lady*.

Played Eva in the **William Tell** episode *The Bandit*.

Lowdell George
Played the third sailor in the second season **The Saint** episode *The Old Treasure Story*.

Lowe Barry
Played Keston in the **Gideon's Way** episode *Morna*.
Played Lemmy in the **Jason King** episode *A Deadly Line in Digits*.

Lowe Olga
Played the traffic warden in **The Persuaders!** episode *The Time and the Place*.
Played Angela Kendon in the **Randall and Hopkirk [Deceased] aka My Partner the Ghost** episode *Money to Burn*.
Played the Concierge in the **Return of the Saint** episode *The Nightmare Man*.

Lowin Jack
Camera Operator on **Jason King, The Prisoner** [*Arrival, The Chimes of Big Ben, A. B. and C., Free for All, The Schizoid Man, The General, Many Happy Returns, Dance of the Dead, Checkmate, Hammer into Anvil, It's Your Funeral, A Change of Mind & Once Upon a Time*] and **UFO**.
Second Unit Director on **Department S & Randall and Hopkirk [Deceased] aka My Partner the Ghost**.

Lowry Morton
Played the Lieutenant in the fourth season **The Adventures of Robin Hood** episodes *Tuck's Love Day, The Flying Sorcerer, Six Strings to his bow, Goodbye, Little John, The Oath, The Charm Pedlar, Bride for an Outlaw, The Pharaoh Stones, Double Trouble, The Edge and the Point* and *The Truce*.
Played Watkins in **The Four Just Men** episode *The Night of the Precious Stones*, Harry Green in *The Crying Jester* and the captain in *Riot*.
Played Orlando in the **Sword of Freedom** episode *A Game of Chance*.

LSQ
Produced, in association with Robert Siodmak, the series **O.S.S.** [an ITC and Buckeye Enterprises Production].

Lucarotti John
Wrote the season two **Ghost Squad** episodes *The Golden Silence, A First Class Way to Die & The Menacing Mazurka*.
Wrote the **Joe 90** episode *Child of the Sun God*.

Lucas Henri - aka/see Alexis **Kanner**.

Lucas Victor
Played Inspector Tribe in **The Adventurer** episode *Mr Calloway is a Very Cautious Man*.

Lucas William
Played Sir Jack in the season three **The Adventures of Robin Hood** episode *Knight Errant*.
Played Colonel Vasco in the first season **Danger Man** episode *The Prisoner* and Bernhard in the second series [now aka **Secret Agent**] episode *A Room in the Basement*.
Featured in the **Espionage** episode *Once a Spy*.
Played Paul in **The Four Just Men** episode *National Treasure*.
Played Ambrose Jerome in the first series **Ghost Squad** episode *Eyes of the Bat*.
Guested as Cliff McGrath in the **Interpol Calling** episode *The Thousand Mile Alibi*.
Played Eastbrook in the second season **The Protectors** episode *The Last Frontier*.
Played Crantor in the second season **The Saint** episode *The Crime of the Century*.
Played Count Julio in the **Sir Francis Drake** episodes *Beggars of the Sea & The Flame Thrower*.
Played Tortini in the **Sword of Freedom** episode *Caterina*.
Played Claude Holmby in the **White Hunter** episode *The Plague*.
Played Kramer in the **William Tell** episode *The Traitor*.

Lucette Eve
Played Katharine in the **Sir Francis Drake** episode *Doctor Dee* and the Lady-in-Waiting in *The English Dragon*.

Lucius Olive
Played the chic woman in the second season **The Saint** episode *The Unkind Philanthropist*.

Luck James
Played Mr Wilson in **The Sentimental Agent** episode *All that Jazz*.

Luckenbill Larry
Played Bruno in the **Return of the Saint** episode *The Roman Touch*.

Luckham Cyril
Played Lord Franklin in **The Adventurer** episode *The Case of the Poisoned Pawn*.
Played Walker in the **Department S** episode *The Perfect Operation*.
Played Lord Galloway in the **Father Brown** episode *The Secret Garden*.
Played Alec Weston in the second season **The Protectors** episode *Petard*.
Played Laverick in the **Randall and Hopkirk [Deceased] aka My Partner the Ghost** episode *Who Killed Cock Robin*.
Played the Coroner in the **Return of the Saint** episode *Collision Course* [Part 1: *'The Brave Goose'*: also exists, combined with the second instalment as a movie entitled *The Saint and the Brave Goose*].
Played Jack Hardy in the first season **The Saint** episode *Iris*.
Played Theodore Green in the **Virgin of the Secret Service** episode *Dark Deeds on the Northwest Frontier*.

Luckman Kenneth
Appeared as the Welshman in **The Adventures of Sir Lancelot** episode *The Black Castle*.

Lugrin Julian
Camera Operator on **Fireball XL5** and Lighting Cameraman on **The Secret Service & Thunderbirds**.

Lui-Wan Hao
Played Chi-Kwan in the **Shirley's World** episode *Evidence in Camera*.

Lulham Raymond
Played the vice in the **O.S.S.** episode *Operation Sardine*.

Lumley Joanna
Starred as Sapphire in the **Sapphire and Steel** series.

Lumsden Geoffrey
Played General Powers in the second series **Danger Man** [aka **Secret Agent**] episode *The Galloping Major*.
Played the Coroner in the third season **The Saint** episode *The Best Laid Schemes* and Dr. Williams in the fourth season's *The Man who Gambled with Life*.

Luscombe Doel
Played the customs man in the season two **Ghost Squad** episode *The Golden Silence*.
Played the police officer witness in the third season **The Saint** episode *When Spring is Sprung*.

Lyall Jock
Construction Manager on **Jason King**.

Lyden Pierce
Played gendarme in **The Count of Monte Cristo** episode *Victor Hugo*.

Lye Reg
Guested as Curtis in **The Champions** episode *Desert Journey*.
Played the night watchman in the season two **Ghost Squad** episode *Sentences of Death*.
Played Doctor Hill in the **Gideon's Way** episode *The Great Plane Robbery*.
Played Mistral in the **Jason King** episode *Buried in the Cold, Cold Ground*.
Played Manny in the **Randall and Hopkirk [Deceased]** aka **My Partner the Ghost** episode *When the Spirit Moves You*.
Played Lou in the **Return of the Saint** episode *The Arrangement*.
Played Captain Bill Williams in the second season **The Saint** episode *The Old Treasure Story*, George in the *The Smart Detective* and Pop Kinsall in *The Loving Brothers*.

Lyle Sandy
Guested as Page in the first series of **The Adventures of Robin Hood** episode *The Thorkill Ghost*.

Lynch Joe
Played Captain Finnigan in the **Return of the Saint** two parter *Collision Course* [Part 1: *The Brave Goose* & part 2: *The Sixth Man*: also exists as a movie entitled *The Saint and the Brave Goose*].

Lynch Michael
Played Rainer in the second season **The Saint** episode *The Revolution Racket*.

Lynch Sean
Played the Squire in the season three **The Adventures of Robin Hood** episode *The Charter*.
Played Renzino in **The Four Just Men** episode *The Night of the Precious Stones*.
Played Yates in **The Persuaders!** episode *Someone Waiting*.
Played Geordie in the **Man in a Suitcase** episode *The Sitting Pigeon*.
Played Stikow in the **Virgin of the Secret Service** episode *A Fate Worse Than Death* and Manoel in *The Amazons*.

Lynd Moira
Played Eugenia in **The Count of Monte Cristo** episode *The Barefoot Empress*.
Played Mrs McAfee in the **White Hunter** episode *A Moment of Truth* and Anne in *The Fugitive*.

Lyndon-Hayes T. S.
Production Supervisor on **White Hunter**.

Lynn Ann
Played Ann Seldon in **The Baron** episode *Something for a Rainy Day*.
Played Marianne in **The Count of Monte Cristo** episode *The Luxembourg Affair*.
Guested as Inge Kalmutt in **The Champions** episode *The Bodysnatchers*.
Played Suzanne in the second series **Danger Man** [aka **Secret Agent**] episode *Have a Glass of Wine*.
Featured in the **Espionage** episode *Final Decision*.
Played Philippa in the season two **Ghost Squad** episode *Sentences of Death*.
Played Ann Beaumont in the **Gideon's Way** episode *A Perfect Crime*.
Played Marie Spring in the third season **The Saint** episode *When Spring is Sprung*.
Played Helene Schroeder in **The Zoo Gang** episode *The Twisted Cross*.

Lynn Bob
Directed the **Captain Scarlet and the Mysterons** episodes *Special Assignment, Lunarville 7, Point 783, Shadow of Fear* and *Flight 104*.

Lynn Jack
Played Professor Williams in the second season **The Protectors** episode *Fighting Fund*.

Lynn Robert
Directed the **Captain Scarlet and the Mysterons** episode *White as Snow*.
Directed the first series **Ghost Squad** episodes *Still Waters, Assassin, Death from a Distance, Catspaw & Princess* [*Catspaw & Princess* were shot for the first series, but due to an actors' strike, were originally shown as season two episodes].
Directed the **Interpol Calling** episodes *Fingers of Guilt, Eight Days Inclusive, White Blackmail, Ascent to Murder, Dressed To Kill, The Absent Assassin, In the Swim* and *The Three Keys*.
Directed the first season **The Saint** episode *Judith*.
Directed the second season **Space 1999** episodes *The Beta Cloud & Catacombs of the Moon*.

Lynne Betty
Played Mrs Darbot in **The Zoo Gang** episode *Revenge: Post-dated*.

Lyon Edward
Played the police officer in the **Return of the Saint** episode *The Armageddon Alternative*.

Lyons John
Played the studio guard in the **UFO** episode *Timelash* and a SHADO guard in *Mindbender*.

Lysandrou Andreas
Played the Greek policeman in the second series **Danger Man** [aka **Secret Agent**] episode *It's Up to the Lady*.
Played the pharmacist's mate in the **Man in a Suitcase** episode *Variation on a Million Bucks* [part 2: also combined with part 1 to form a movie: *To Chase a Million*].

****

Macaulay Tom
Played the banker in the third season **The Saint** episode *The Better Mousetrap.*

MacCarthy John
Played Polo in the second season **Man of the World** episode *The Bandit.*

Macchi Annamaria
Played Carla in the **Return of the Saint** episode *Dragonseed.*

MacCormick Iain
Wrote the **Gideon's Way** episodes *To Catch a Tiger, The Alibi Man, The Thin Red Line, Boy with a Gun & The Nightlifers.*

MacDermot Rory
Played Clements in the second season **The Saint** episode *The Death Penalty.*

MacDermott Brian
Played Pierre in the second season **The Saint** episode *The Persistent Parasite.*

MacDonald Aimi
Played Lily in the fourth season **The Saint** two parter *Vendetta for the Saint.*
Played Sandra in the **Shirley's World** episode *The Rally.*

MacDonald David
Director on **The Count of Monte Cristo.**
Directed the **Interpol Calling** episode *Pipeline.*
Producer on **The Scarlet Pimpernel.** Directed *The Farmer's Boy, Gentlemen of the Road, Antoine and Antoinette, The Imaginary Invalides, The Flower Woman, The Christmas Present, The Ambassador's Lady, Thanksgiving Day, Something Remembered, A Tale of Two Pigtails & The Princess.*

MacDonald Harry
Editor on **Thunderbirds.**

MacDonald Ian
Played Borden in **The Count of Monte Cristo** episode *Return to the Chateau d'If.*

Macdonald Stephen
Played George McDee in *Adventure Five* of **Sapphire and Steel** [part 2].

MacDougall Roger
Wrote **The Buccaneers** [aka **Dan Tempest**] episodes *Before the Mast* and *The Ladies.*

Macduff Ewen
Played Hamish in the first season **Danger Man** episode *The Sanctuary.*
Played Sir Charles in the **H. G. Wells' Invisible Man** episode *The Big Plot.*
Played Roberts in the **Interpol Calling** episode *Last Man Lucky.*

MacGinnis Niall
Played Donovan in the second series **Danger Man** [aka **Secret Agent**] episode *Colony Three* and Kent in *The Battle of the Cameras.*
Played Colonel Probst in the third season **The Saint** episode *The Paper Chase.*

MacGowran Jack
Guested as Banner in **The Champions** episode *Happening.*
Played Prior in the first season **Danger Man** episode *The Nurse* and Shorty Pratt in the second series [now aka **Secret Agent**] episode *Such Men are Dangerous.*

Played Joe Hudson in the **Randall and Hopkirk [Deceased]** aka **My Partner the Ghost** episode *The Ghost Talks.*

MacGreevy Oliver
also spelled as Oliver MacGreevey
Played Noll in **The Buccaneers** [aka **Dan Tempest**] episode *The Spy Aboard.*
Played Sam in the third season **Danger Man** [aka **Secret Agent**] episode *The Paper Chase.*
Played Karnack in the **Department S** episode *The Duplicated Man.*
Played Max in **The Four Just Men** episode *The Man in the Royal Suite* and the policeman in *The Last Days of Nick Pompey.*
Played the contact man in the **Gideon's Way** episode *How to Retire without Really Working.*
Played Jules in the **Jason King** episode *Toki.*
Played the gardener/electrician in **The Prisoner** episode *Arrival.*

Macilraith Bill
Production Buyer on **UFO.**

MacIllwraith Bill
Wrote the season two **Ghost Squad** episode *Gertrude.*

MacIntosh Ellen
Played Fiona in **The Four Just Men** episode *The Man Who Wasn't There.*

Mackay Fulton
Played Willie in **The Saint** episode *The Convenient Monster* and John Everett in *The Best Laid Schemes* [season three]. Returned in season four to play Euston in *Vendetta for the Saint* [part 1].

Mackay Kenneth
Make-up on **The Saint.**

Mackenzie Mary
Played the title role in the season two **Ghost Squad** episode *Gertrude.*

Mackey John
Special Effects Photography on **The Champions.**

Mackintosh Kenneth
Played Mike Sentinal in **The Saint** episode *Marcia* [season 1].

MacLaine Shirley
Starred as Shirley Logan in the series **Shirley's World.**

MacLeod Robert
Played Jamieson in the **Man in a Suitcase** episode *Web with Four Spiders.*
Played Hal Sinfield in the first season **The Saint** episode *Judith.*

MacNaughtan Alan
Played Larry Holmes in **The Baron** episode *And Suddenly You're Dead* and Gaydon in *The Maze.*
Played Von Splitz in **The Champions** episode *The Final Countdown.*
Played Gilford in the **Department S** episode *Who Plays the Dummy?.*
Played Dr Claudel in the **Jason King** episode *A Red, Red Rose Forever.*
Played Colonel Vajda in the **Strange Report** episode *Report 7931: SNIPER: 'When is Your Cousin Not?'.*
Played Major Brenan in the **Randall and Hopkirk [Deceased]** aka **My Partner the Ghost** episode *The Ghost Talks.*
Played Dr. Manders **The Saint** episode *The Death Game* [season three] and Charlie Lewis in *Legacy for the Saint* [four].

MacOwen Norman
Played the gate keeper in the first season **The Adventures of Robin Hood** episode *The Coming of Robin Hood.*
Played Andreas in the **William Tell** episode *The Unwelcome Stranger.*

MacRae Duncan
Appeared as the Doctor in **The Prisoner** episode *Dance of the Dead.*

Madden Ciaran
Played Janie Lennox in the **Return of the Saint** episode *Signal Stop.*

Madden Donald
Featured in the **Espionage** episode *Never Turn Your Back On a Friend.*

Madden Peter
Played the Sheikh in **The Champions** episode *Desert Journey.*
Played Hobbs/Admiral Hobbs in the second season **Danger Man [aka Secret Agent]** episodes *Yesterday's Enemies, Colony three, The Battle of the Cameras, No Marks for Servility, Such Men are Dangerous & It's Up to the Lady.*
Featured in the **Espionage** episode *Do You Remember Leo Winters?.*
Played Debar in the second season **Man of the World** episode *In the Picture.*
Played Farid in the third season **The Saint** episode *The Queen's Ransom* and Lo Zio in the fourth season two parter *Vendetta for the Saint .*
Played Sheikh Abdul Amir in the **Virgin of the Secret Service** episode *The Pyramid Plot.*

Maddern Victor
Played Hugo in the fourth series of **The Adventures of Robin Hood** episode *The Charm Pedlar.*
Played Dino in **The Baron** episode *Farewell to Yesterday.*
Played Charles Randle in the **Gideon's Way** episode *Fall High, Fall Hard.*
Played the Band Master in **The Prisoner** episode *Hammer into Anvil.*
Played Detective Sergeant Watts in the **Randall and Hopkirk [Deceased]** aka **My Partner the Ghost** episode *A Sentimental Journey.*
Played Errico Montesino in the third season **The Saint** episode *The Fast Women* and Jim Cowdry in the fourth season episode *The Scales of Justice.*
Played the ship's cook in the **Sir Francis Drake** episode *Boy Jack* and Brewer in *The Doughty Plot*].

Madison Leigh
Played Madeleine in the **H. G. Wells' Invisible Man** episode *Man in Disguise.*
Played Emmy in the **Interpol Calling** episode *No Flowers for Onno.*

Madoc Philip
Played Frank Oddy in **The Baron** episode *There's Someone Close Behind You.*
Played Angel Martes in **The Champions** episode *Get Me Out of Here!.*
Played Hoffman in the **Jason King** episode *A Page Before Dying.*
Played the Kommandant in the **Man in a Suitcase** episode *Somebody Loses, Somebody ...Wins?* and Doctor Forsythe in *Who's Mad Now?.*
Played Rawlins in the **Randall and Hopkirk [Deceased]** aka **My Partner the Ghost** episode *Never Trust a Ghost.*
Played Alzon in the third season **The Saint** episode *The Counterfeit Countess.*
Played Rutland in the **UFO** episodes *A Question of Priorities & Mindbender* and the ship's captain in *Destruction.*

Magee Patrick
Played Paul Sabot in **The Zoo Gang** episode *The Counterfeit Trap.*
Guested as Pedraza in **The Champions** episode *The Iron Man.*
Played Garder in the first series **The Protectors** episode *Chase.*
Played the Major in **The Sentimental Agent** episode *Express Delivery.*

Magna-Tech
Post Production Sound on **Jason King**.

Maguire Oliver
Played Ashton Jarvis in the **Father Brown** episode *The Actor and the Alibi.*

Maher Frank
Played the first pursuer in the second series **Danger Man [aka Secret Agent]** episode *The Mirror's New*, the second agent in *Are You Going to Be More Permanent?* and **Carl** in the third season's *Say it with Flowers.*
Stunt Co-ordinator on **Department S**.
Played the first thug in the **Man in a Suitcase** episode *Blind Spot.*
Played Jones in **The Persuaders!** episode *The Man in the Middle.*
Stuntman and double on **The Prisoner**. Played the other Number Six in *The Schizoid Man* and the third gunman in *Living in Harmony.*
Stunt Co-ordinator on **Randall and Hopkirk [Deceased]** aka **My Partner the Ghost**.
Played Kraft in the third season **The Saint** episode *The Paper Chase* and Rip Savage in the fourth season two parter *The Fiction Makers.*

Mahoney Louis
Played the guard in the second series **Danger Man [aka Secret Agent]** episode *Parallel Lines Sometimes Meet.*
Played Hector in the **Jason King** episode *Flamingos only Fly on Tuesdays.*

Mai Anna
Played the airline clerk in the **Danger Man [aka Secret Agent]** episode *Shinda Shima* which was also merged with the other fourth season episode, *Koroshi*, to form a TVM called *Koroshi*.

Maine Laurence
Played Cook in **The Adventures of Robin Hood** first season episode *Ladies of Sherwood.*

Maiolini Alba
Played Signora Streso in the **Return of the Saint** episode *The Village that Sold its Soul.*

Maitland Marne
Played Turk in **The Buccaneers [aka Dan Tempest]** episode *The Decoy.*
Played Minoes in **The Champions** episode *The Silent Enemy.*
Played Sheik Ahmed in the first season **Danger Man** episode *The Leak.* In the second series [now aka **Secret Agent**], played the plain clothes man in *A Date with Doris.*
Played the Turkish caretaker in the **Department S** episode *The Perfect Operation.*
Featured in the **Espionage** episode *A Camel to Ride.*
Played Sabri in the first series **Ghost Squad** episode *Princess* [this episode was shot for the first series, but due to an actors' strike, was originally shown as a season two episode].
Played Bhandari in the **Interpol Calling** episode *Cargo of Death.*
Played Capt. Rashid in the **Randall and Hopkirk [Deceased]** aka **My Partner the Ghost** episode *The Ghost Talks.*
Played Kemal in the **Return of the Saint** episode *The Murder Cartel.*

Played Borota in **The Saint** episode *Teresa* [season one], Esteban in *Lida* [two], Hassan in *Flight Plan* [three] and the Guru in *Portrait of Brenda* [four].
Played Dr Abu in **The Sentimental Agent** episode *The Height of Fashion*.
Played Uluch Ali in the **Sir Francis Drake** episode *Gentlemen of Spain*.

Makino Marie
Played the old lady in the **Randall and Hopkirk [Deceased] aka My Partner the Ghost** episode *That's How Murder Snowballs*.
Played Miss Emmar in the first season **The Saint** episode *The Bunco Artists*.

Malandrinos Andreas
Played the waiter in the first season **Danger Man** episode *View from the Villa*, the old man in the second series [now aka **Secret Agent**] episode *You're Not in Any Trouble, Are You?* and the waiter in the third season's *The Paper Chase*.
Played del Piazzo in the season two **Ghost Squad** episode *Hot Money*.
Played Miguel in the first series **Man of the World** episode *Masquerade in Spain*.
Played a villager in the first season **The Saint** episode *Sophia*, the old man in the third season's *The Gadic Collection* and Gonzales in *Locate and Destroy*.

Malco Paolo
Played Gabriel in the **Return of the Saint** episode *Dragonseed*.

Malcolm Chris
Played Malloy in the first series **The Protectors** episode *Disappearing Trick*.

Malcolm Christopher
Played Sloan in the **Strange Report** episode *Report 3906: COVER GIRLS: 'Last Year's Model'*.

Malcolm John
Played Jansen in **The Adventurer** episode *Counterstrike*.
Played Colonel Kelkov in the **Jason King** episode *To Russia With ....Panache* .
Played Senor Curacha in the **Virgin of the Secret Service** episode *Entente Cordiale*.

Malicz Mark
Played Osuna in the first series **The Protectors** episode *The Quick Brown Fox*.

Malikyan Kevork
Played Kemal in the **Jason King** episode *Uneasy Lies the Head*.
Played Hima Dri in the fourth season **The Saint** episode *The People Importers*.
Played the Corporal in the **Virgin of the Secret Service** episode *The Great Ring of Akba*.

Malin Eddie
Appeared as Father Till in **The Adventures of Sir Lancelot** episode *The Magic Book* and as Paul in *Maid of Somerset*.
Played Jenkins in **The Buccaneers [aka Dan Tempest]** episode *Ghost Ship* and Dawson in *The Ladies*.

Malioz Mark
Played Danik in the **Jason King** episode *To Russia With ....Panache* .

Mallard Graham
Played the second tracker in the first series **The Protectors** episode *Chase*.

Malleson Miles
Appeared as Albertus in the second series of **The Adventures of Robin Hood** episode *The Scientist*.
Played Josiah Parkerhouse in **The Buccaneers [aka Dan Tempest]** episode *Printer's Devil*.

Mancini Al
Played Durres in the **Department S** episode *Six Days*.
Played Placide in the **Jason King** episode *Nadine*.
Played the announcer in **The Prisoner** episode *The General*.
Played the second astronaut in the **UFO** episode *The Cat with Ten Lives* and Andy Conroy in *Mindbender*.
Played Jesse in the **Virgin of the Secret Service** episode *The Professor Goes West*.

Mancini Henry
Wrote the theme music for the series **Man of the World**.

Mander Tony
Film Cameraman on **Father Brown**.

Mandlova Adlina
Played Anna in the **G.S.5** episode *Rich Ruby Wine*.
Played Helga in the second season **The Saint** episode *The Rhine Maiden*.

Mango Alec 'Alex'
Appeared as Duc de Mirancy in the second series of **The Adventures of Robin Hood** episode *Flight from France*.
Regular, as Van Brugh, in **The Buccaneers [aka Dan Tempest]**: *The Raiders, Dan Tempest's War with Spain, Slave Ship, Mr. Beamish and the Hangman's Noose, Blood Will Tell, Hurricane, The Surgeon of Sangre Rojo, The Return of Calico Jack* & *Conquistador*.
Played Enrico in the first season **Danger Man** episode *Find and Destroy*.
Played Dr Fawzil in **The Four Just Men** episode *Marie*.
Played Badillo in the first series **Ghost Squad** episode *Catspaw* [this episode was shot for the first series, but due to an actors' strike, was originally shown as a season two episode].
Played Hartz in the **Gideon's Way** episode *A Perfect Crime*.
Played Gomiero in the **Interpol Calling** episode *Act of Piracy*.
Played Dr. Rahn in the first season **The Saint** episode *The Arrow of God* & Abdul Aziz in *The Wonderful War*. Played Jose Jalisco in the second season's *The Revolution Racket*.
Played Arno in the **Sword of Freedom** episode *Serenade in Red*.
Played Maharaja in the **White Hunter** episode *Valley of the Dead*.

Manley Peter
Production Supervisor on season three & four of **The Saint**.

Mann Frank
Played the rocket launch controller in the **UFO** episode *Close Up*.

Mann Stanley
Wrote the **H. G. Wells' Invisible Man** episodes *Behind the Mask* [co-teleplayed with Leslie Arliss: from a story by Stanley Mann] and *Odds Against Death* [story idea: teleplayed by Ian Stuart Black].

Mannari Guido
Played Franco in the **Return of the Saint** episode *Vicious Circle*.

Mannheim Lucie
Starred as, series regular, The Countess de la Valliere in **The Scarlet Pimpernel**: *The Hostage, The Flower Woman, The Ambassador's Lady, The Sword of Justice, The Elusive Chauvelin, The Lady in Distress* & *Sir Percy's Wager*.

Manning Hugh
Played Albert in **The Four Just Men** episode *Village of Shame*.
Played the Chief of Police in **The Persuaders!** episode *The Gold Napoleon*.

Mansaray Samuel
Played the Chief in the **White Hunter** episode *Squire of the Serengeti*.

Mansell Charles
Played the neighbour in the first season **Danger Man** episode *The Trap*.

Mansell Ronald
Played Major in the **Virgin of the Secret Service** episode *The Persuasion of a Million Drops*.

Mansi John Louis
Played Maxime in the **Department S** episode *The Treasure of the Costa del Sol*.

Mansi Louis
Played Weasel in the **Gideon's Way** episode *Gang War*.

Manson Mary
Played Judith Denton in the season four **The Adventures of Robin Hood** episode *Bride for an Outlaw*.
Played Helga in **The Adventures of Sir Lancelot** episode *The Missing Princess*.

Mantez Dolores
Played Miss Sefadu in the second series **Danger Man** [aka **Secret Agent**] episode *Loyalty Always Pays* and Mary Ann in the third season's *The Man on the Beach*.
Played Happy Lee in the **Randall and Hopkirk [Deceased]** aka **My Partner the Ghost** episode *My Late Lamented Friend and Partner*.
Starred in the series UFO as, regular, Nina Barry.

Mantle Doreen
Played Mrs Olgilvie in the **Strange Report** episode *Report 3906: COVER GIRLS: 'Last Year's Model'*.

Manzi Louis
Played the waiter in **The Sentimental Agent** episode *A Little Sweetness and Light*.

Maples Terence
Writer on **The New Adventures of Charlie Chan**.
Wrote the **Strange Report** episode *Report 3906: COVER GIRLS: 'Last Year's Model'*.

Maranne Andre
Played Desmoulins in the season two **Ghost Squad** episode *Lost in Transit*.
Played Georges in the **Interpol Calling** episode *The Long Weekend*.
Played Inspector Rosseau in the **Jason King** episode *Wanna Buy a Television Series* aka *A Face I Used to Know*.
Played Sphela in the second season **Man of the World** episode *In the Picture*.
Played Louis in the first season **The Saint** episode *The Bunco Artists* and the radio operator in *The Benevolent Burglary*.

Maranzana Cesare
Played the Italian policeman in the first season **The Saint** episode *The King of the Beggars*.

March Elspeth
Played Lucy Wexall in the first season **The Saint** episode *The Arrow of God* and Tante Ada in *The Saint Sees it Through*.

Played Grace O'Malley in the **Sir Francis Drake** episode *The Irish Pirate*.

Marcus Ellis
Wrote the **White Hunter** episodes *Inside Story* and *The Jackals*.

Marcus James
Appeared as a SHADO operative in the **UFO** episode *Mindbender*.

Marden Adrienne
Played Elise in **The Count of Monte Cristo** episode *First Train to Paris*.

Marden Richard
Dubbing editor on **The Buccaneers** [aka **Dan Tempest**].

Margo George
Played Blackbeard in **The Buccaneers** [aka **Dan Tempest**] episodes *Blackbeard* and *Captain Dan Tempest*.
Played Creedy in the **Interpol Calling** episode *You Can't Die Twice*.
Played Malazza in the **Jason King** episode *That isn't Me, It's Somebody Else*.

Marguerite
Played Priestess Shiao in the **Virgin of the Secret Service** episode *Across the Silver Pass of Gusri Song*.

Marion-Crowford Howard
Played Portmore in the second season **The Saint** episode *The Frightened Inn-Keeper*.

Marioni Ray
Played Dino in the **Jason King** episode *As Easy as A B C*.

Markham David
Played Professor Baker in the season two **Ghost Squad** episode *The Magic Bullet*.

Markham Kika
Played Olenka in the **Strange Report** episode *Report 7931: SNIPER: 'When is Your Cousin Not?'*.

Marks Alfred
Played Darron in **The Adventurer** episode *Icons Are Forever*.
Played Ringo in the **Jason King** episode *Nadine*.
Played Pullicino in **The Persuaders!** episode *The Gold Napoleon*.

Marks Leo
Wrote the **Espionage** episode *A Free Agent*.

Marks Louis
Wrote the third series **The Adventures of Robin Hood** episode *Marian's Prize* and the fourth's *The Parting Guest, Bride for an Outlaw* & *Double Trouble*.
Wrote the second season **Danger Man** [aka **Secret Agent**] episode *The Professionals* [with Wilfred Greatorex].
Script Supervisor on **The Four Just Men** and wrote the episodes: *The Man with the Golden Touch* [teleplayed from a story by Jan Read], *Marie* [with Gene Levitt], *Crack-Up* [from a story by Lee Loeb], *The Miracle of St. Philippe* [with Jan Read: from a story by Barbara Hammer], *The Princess* [with Frank Tarloff: from a story by Marks], *Riot* [story: teleplayed by Leon Griffiths] and *The Heritage*.
Wrote the season two **Ghost Squad** episodes *Hot Money* & *Mr Five Per Cent*.

Marinelli Yole
Played Sonia in **The Champions** episode *Desert Journey*.

Mariner Marcus
Played the strong-arm man in the **Jason King** episode *To Russia With ....Panache* .

Marioni Ray
Played the Spanish mechanic in the **Department S** episode *Who Plays the Dummy?*.

Markos Andreas
Played Martis in **The Sentimental Agent** episode *A Little Sweetness and Light*.

Markstein George
Story Consultant on season three of **Danger Man** [aka **Secret Agent**] and Script Editor on season four.
Wrote the *Writers Guide* for **The Prisoner** and was Script Editor throughout [not *Do Not Forsake Me Oh My Darling*, *Living in Harmony*, *The Girl Who Was Death* or *Fall Out*]. Co-wrote *Arrival* [with David Tomblin]. Appears in the opening resignation sequence as the man behind the desk with a pen. Wrote the **Return of the Saint** episode *The Debt Collectors*.

Marle Arnold
Played Oregin in the season two **Ghost Squad** episode *The Grand Duchess*.
Played Gross in the **G.S.5** episode *The Goldfish Bowl*.
Played Valois Played Hugo in the **H. G. Wells' Invisible Man** episode *The White Rabbit*.

Marlow Hugh
Starred as Ellery Queen in the series **Mystery is My Business**.

Marlowe Anthony
Starred as, series regular, Geoffrey Stock in season two of **Ghost Squad**: *Interrupted Requiem, Sentences of Death, The Missing People, Lost In Transit, Hot Money, The Grand Duchess, A First Class Way to Die, The Desperate Diplomat, The Big Time, The Heir Apparent, Death of a Sportsman, Polsky, The Thirteenth Girl* & *Sabotage*.
Returned as Geoffrey Stock to star throughout **G.S.5**.
Played Cranley in the **Randall and Hopkirk [Deceased]** aka **My Partner the Ghost** episode *When the Spirit Moves You*.

Marlowe Fernanda
Played the girl in the phone box in the season two **Ghost Squad** episode *Polsky*.

Marlowe Linda
Played Laura Carlton in the fourth season **The Saint** episode *The Time to Die*.
Played Babette Lemaire in the **Virgin of the Secret Service** episode *The Persuasion of a Million Drops*.

Marlow William
Played Carlo in the season two **Ghost Squad** episode *Mr Five Per Cent*.
Played McKay in the **G.S.5** episode *An Eye for An Eye*.
Played Carl in **The Persuaders!** episode *Element of Risk*.
Played Smith in the season two **The Saint** episode *The Death Penalty*.

Marmont Patricia
Played Lady de Courcier in the debut season of **The Adventures of Robin Hood** episode *The Miser* and Duchess Constance in the fourth series episode *Race Against Time*.
Played Annette Fauntello in **The Count of Monte Cristo** episode *The Carbonari*.
Played Rosemary in the first season **Danger Man** episode *Name, Date and Place*.
Played Doctor Smits in the first series **Ghost Squad** episode *Still Waters*.
Played the headmistress in the **H. G. Wells' Invisible Man** episode *Bank Raid*.

Marmont Percy
Played Henri Fauntello in **The Count of Monte Cristo** episode *The Carbonari*.

Marner Richard
Played Werner Von Beck in **The Adventurer** episode *The Bradley Way*.
Played the anaesthetist in the first season **Danger Man** episode *The Girl in Pink Pyjamas*.
Played Cannack in the **Ghost Squad** episode *Princess* [shot for the first series but shown as a season two episode].
Played Signor Cabor in the **Jason King** episode *A Deadly Line in Digits* and Markevitch in *To Russia With ....Panache*.
Played the first Russian in the second season **The Protectors** episode *Dragon Chase*.

Marotta Gino
Assistant Director on the second series of **Danger Man** [aka **Secret Agent**], **Jason King**, **The Prisoner** [not *Many Happy Returns* or *Do Not Forsake Me Oh My Darling*], **The Protectors**, **Return of The Saint** & **Sir Francis Drake**.

Marquand Yvonne
Played Diana in the second series **Danger Man** [aka **Secret Agent**] episode *The Mirror's New*.

Marquis Max
Wrote the first series **Ghost Squad** episode *Still Waters*.
Writer on **Interpol Calling**: *Dead On Arrival* [with Philip Chambers: from a story by Leonard Fincham] and *The Heiress* [with Leonard Fincham: from a story by Philip Chambers].

Marrian Stephanie
Played the girl pupil in the fourth season **The Saint** episode *The Ex-King of Diamonds*.

Marriott Anthony
Wrote the **Fireball XL5** episodes *Space Magnet, Plant Man from Space, The Sun Temple, Space Immigrants, Flying Zodiac, Space Pirates, The Last of the Zanadus, Prisoner on the Lost Planet, Sabotage, The Forbidden Planet, 1875, Drama at Space City* and *Faster than Light*.
Wrote the first series **Ghost Squad** episode *Hong Kong Story* [with Connery Chappell].

Marriot-Watson Nan
Played Mrs Whicker in the first season **The Saint** episode *The Sporting Chance*.

Marryott Susan
Played Zizi in **The Four Just Men** episode *The Man in the Royal Suite*.

Marsden Roy
Played the HQ policeman in the third season **Danger Man** [aka **Secret Agent**] episode *The Man who wouldn't Talk*.
Played alien 3 in the second season **Space 1999** episode *The Rules of Luton*.

Marseilles Mikki
Played the gendarme in the **Department S** episode *The Mysterious Man in the Flying Machine*.
Played the third seaman in the **Man in a Suitcase** episode *Variation on a Million Bucks* [part 2: also combined with part 1 to form a movie: *To Chase a Million*].
Played the manservant in the **Randall and Hopkirk [Deceased]** episode *My Late Lamented Friend and Partner*.
Played Popescu in the **Strange Report** episode *Report 5055: CULT: 'Murder Shrieks Out'*.

Marsh Carol
Appeared as Sybil in **The Adventures of Sir Lancelot** episode *The Ugly Duckling*.

Marsh Gary
Played Johnson in the first series **Man of the World** episode *The Runaways*.

Marsh Jean
Played Kim Russell in the first season **Danger Man** episode *Name, Date and Place*.
Played Agatha Pollen in the **Department S** episode *The Perfect Operation*.
Played Sandra Casey in the **Gideon's Way** episode *A Perfect Crime* and Elspeth McRae in *The Nightlifers*.
Played Nicola in **The Persuaders!** episode *Five Miles to Midnight*.
In **The Saint**: played Marie in *The Good Medicine* [series 1], Helen Phillips in *The Imprudent Politician* [2], Ann in *Escape Route* [3] and Anne Kirby in *The Scales of Justice* [4].
Played Janna in the **UFO** episode *Exposed*.

Marsh Keith
Played the hotel porter in the season two **Ghost Squad** episode *The Man with the Delicate Hands*.
Played Leon in the **Man in a Suitcase** episode *Blind Spot*.

Marsh Kerry
Played Katherine Vale in **The Baron** episode *The Legions of Ammak*.

Marsh Reginald
Played Sorenson in **The Adventurer** episode *Somebody doesn't Like Me*.
Played Captain Brenner in **The Baron** two parter *Storm Warning* [*Storm Warning* - part 1 and *The Island* - part 2: also exists as a feature called *Mystery Island*]. Also played Chief Inspector Filmer in *You Can't Win Them All*.
Played Conrad Schultz in **The Champions** episode *The Search*.
Played Doctor Fowler in **The Persuaders!** episode *Someone Like Me*.
Played James Laker in the **Randall and Hopkirk [Deceased]** aka **My Partner the Ghost** episode *When Did you Start to Stop Seeing Things?*
Played Ed Brown in the fourth season **The Saint** episode *Legacy for the Saint*.

Marsh Sheena
Played the barmaid in **The Prisoner** episode *The Girl who was Death*.

Marsh Stephen
Played Hector in the **Father Brown** episode *The Head of Caesar*.

Marshall Bryan
Played O'Hara in the **Return of the Saint** episode *Assault Force*.
Played PC Burns in the first season **The Saint** episode *Starring the Saint* and Moreno in season three's *Invitation to Danger*.
Played Inspector Purcell in the **Strange Report** episode *Report 1021: SHRAPNEL: 'The Wish in the Dream'*.

Marshall Peggy
Played Maeve Nolan in the season two **The Adventures of Robin Hood** episode *The Little People*.
Played Connie Amherst in the second season **Ghost Squad** episode *The Thirteenth Girl*.
Played Mrs Maloney in the **Sentimental Agent** episode *May the Saints Preserve Us*.

Marshall Roger
Wrote the **G.S.5** episode *Death of a Cop*.
Wrote the **William Tell** episode *The Traitor* [with Leslie Arliss], teleplayed *Castle of Fear* [original story by Max Savage] and teleplayed *The Spider* [story by Ralph Smart].

Marshall Sarah
Played Barbara in the **Strange Report** episode *Report 1553: RACIST: 'A Most Dangerous Proposal'*.

Marshall Sidney
Producer & writer on **The Count of Monte Cristo**.
Producer on **The New Adventures of Charlie Chan**.

Marshall William
Played Khano in the first season **Danger Man** episode *Deadline* and the Prime Minister in the second series [now aka **Secret Agent**] episode *The Galloping Major*.

Marshall Zena
Played Mrs Ramfi in the first season **Danger Man** episode *Find and Return*, Doctor Leclair in *The Leak* and in the second series [aka **Secret Agent**] played Nadia in *Fish on the Hook*.
Played Yvonne Marsden in the **G.S.5** episode *Dead Men Don't Drive*.
Played Tania in the **H. G. Wells' Invisible Man** episode *The Locked Room*.
Played Madame Thiboeuf in the first series **Man of the World** episode *Death of a Conference*.
Played Lucille in the **O.S.S.** episode *Operation Flint Axe*.
Played Rita in **The Sentimental Agent** episode *Box of Tricks* and Melina in *A Little Sweetness and Light*.
Played Maria in the **Sir Francis Drake** episode *The Bridge*.

Martelli Angel
Continuity on **The Adventures of Sir Lancelot** episodes *The Knight with the Red Plume, The Ferocious Fathers* & *The Queen's Knight* and on **The Buccaneers [aka Dan Tempest]** episode *Blackbeard*.

Martin Doris
Continuity on **The Adventures of Sir Lancelot** episodes *The Outcast, Sir Bliant, The Magic Sword, Roman Wall, Caledon, Shepherd's War, The Pirates, The Black Castle, Double Identity, The Bridge, The Witch's Brew, Ruby of Radnor, The Lesser Breed, The Magic Book, Knight Errand, The Theft of Excalibur, The Mortaise Fair, Maid of Somerset, The Prince of Limerick, Sir Crustabread, The Lady Lilith, Knight's Choice, The Missing Princess* and *The Thieves*.
Continuity on **The Prisoner** episodes *Arrival, The Chimes of Big Ben, A. B. and C., Free for All, The Schizoid Man, The General, Dance of the Dead, Checkmate, It's Your Funeral, A Change of Mind* and *Once Upon a Time*.
Continuity on **The Persuaders!** & **Strange Report**.

Martin Ian Kennedy
Wrote the first season **The Saint** episode *The Saint Sees it Through*.

Martin Irving
Composed, with Brian Dee, the theme for **Return of The Saint** [original *Saint* theme by Leslie Charteris]. Also served as the Music Supervisor on the series.

Martin John
Played Det. Insp. Marsham in the **Gideon's Way** episode *The Housekeeper*.
Played the medical examiner in the first season **The Saint** episode *Starring the Saint*.

Martin John Scott
Played the mortuary attendant in the season two **Ghost Squad** episode *Lost in Transit*.

Martin Larry
Played the mechanic in the **Department S** episode *A Small War of Nerves*.
Played Harry in the **Man in a Suitcase** episode *Dead Man's Shoes*.

Martin Lewis
Played Perrier in **The Count of Monte Cristo** episode *The Black Death*.

Martin Mel
Played Janet Druce in the **Father Brown** episode *The Oracle of the Dog*.

Martin Michael
Played the bank official in **The Adventurer** episode *The Case of the Poisoned Pawn*.
Played the second assassin in the second series **Danger Man** [aka **Secret Agent**] episode *A Date with Doris*.
Played Jackson in **The Persuaders!** episode *Greensleeves*.
Played Doctor Lambrus in the **Strange Report** episode *Report 4407: HEART: 'No Choice for the Donor'*.

Martin Millicent
Featured in the **Espionage** episode *Once a Spy*.

Martin Paul
Played the technician in **The Four Just Men** episode *The Deadly Capsule*.

Martin Skip
Played Mr Brown in the **Shirley's World** episode *Always Leave Them Laughing*.

Martinelli Elsa
Played Renata in the **Return of the Saint** episode *Vicious Circle*.

Martins Orlando
Played the elderly man in **The Four Just Men** episode *The Slaver*.
Appeared as the Chief in the **White Hunter** episode *Day of Reckoning* and as Kruma in *Let My People Go*.

Mase Marino
Played Quirko in the **Return of the Saint** episode *The Judas Game*.

Maskell Virginia
Played Eve in the third series of **The Adventures of Robin Hood** episode *My Brother's Keeper*.
Played Rebecca in **The Buccaneers** [aka **Dan Tempest**] episode *The Decoy*.
Played Joanna in the second series **Danger Man** [aka **Secret Agent**] episode *The Colonel's Daughter*.
Played Rose Lenman in the **Gideon's Way** episode *The White Rat*.
Guest starred as the woman in **The Prisoner**'s first episode *Arrival*.

Mason Alan
Played the soldier in the **Strange Report** episode *Report 7931: SNIPER: 'When is Your Cousin Not?'*.

Mason Brewster
Played Clemente in **The Four Just Men** episode *The Man With the Golden Touch*.
Played Galbraith Stride in the second season **The Saint** episode *The Death Penalty*.

Mason Cecil
Recordist on **The Saint**.

Mason Don
Starred as, Junior Ranger, Steve in **The Forest Rangers**.
Played the co-pilot in the **O.S.S.** episode *Operation Yo Yo*.
Provided the voice for Troy Tempest for the series **Stingray**.

Mason Eric
Played the seaman in **The Baron** episode *Night of the Hunter*.
Played Hal in the third season **The Saint** episode *Escape Route* and a sailor in *The Best Laid Schemes*.

Mason Margery
Played Mabel Short in the **Gideon's Way** episode *The Big Fix*.

Masters Christopher
Played the doctor in the second season **The Protectors** episode *Route 27*.

Masters Donald
Played Favermann in the **O.S.S.** episode *Operation Tulip*.

Mastrogiacomo Guido
Played the Non-Com in the **Return of the Saint** episode *The Judas Game*.

Matalon Vivian
Played Victor Gaulte in **The Count of Monte Cristo** episode *The Art of Terror*.
Played Guido [as a man] in **The Four Just Men** episode *The Battle of the Bridge* and Arthur Vivian in *Justice For Gino*.
Played King Rashid in the **H. G. Wells' Invisible Man** episode *Man in Power*.
Played McGaffery in the **O.S.S.** episode *Operation Jingle Bells*.

Matania Clelia
Played Signora Manelli in the **Return of the Saint** episode *The Village that Sold its Soul*.

Maten Michael
Played the policeman in the second series **Danger Man** [aka **Secret Agent**] episode *A Date with Doris*.

Matheson Judy
Played Claire Adams in **The Adventurer** episode *Full Fathom Five*.

Mathews Richard
Played Mark Prentice in **The Baron** episode *The Maze*.

Mathie Marion
Played Lady Hallett in the **Department S** episode *Six Days* and Sheila Sentinal in the first season **The Saint** episode *Marcia*.

Matisse Anna
Appeared as the brunette in the **Department S** episode *Dead Men Die Twice*.
Played Helga in the first series **The Protectors** episode *The Quick Brown Fox*.

Matthews Eileen
Played a passenger in the **Father Brown** episode *The Curse of the Golden Cross*.

Matthews Francis
Played Ali in **The Adventures of Robin Hood** episode *The Little People* [season 2] and Roland in *The Minstrel* [3].
Provided the voice for Captain Scarlet for **Captain Scarlet and the Mysterons**.
Played Fawley in the **Interpol Calling** episode *White Blackmail*.
Played Peter Fox in the **O.S.S.** episode *Operation Powder Puff*.
Played Paula Farley in **The Saint** episode *The Noble Sportsman* [season one] and Andre in *To Kill a Saint* [three].

Mattick Stephen
Wrote the **Captain Scarlet and the Mysterons** episode *Operation Time* [with Richard Conway].

Maude Jean
Played The Duchess of Northumberland in **The Scarlet Pimpernel** episode *The Imaginary Invalides*.

Maude Mary
Played the helper in the stables in the **Man in a Suitcase** episode *Which Way did he Go, McGill?*.

Maughan Sharon
Played Carmela in the **Return of the Saint** episode *The Nightmare Man*.

Maule Annabel
Played Amy in the **Interpol Calling** episode *Last Man Lucky*.

Mauray Carol
Played a policewoman in the **G.S.5** episodes *Death of a Cop, An Eye for An Eye* & *It Won't be a Stylish Marriage*.

Maxim John
Played the second Judge in **The Prisoner** episode *The Chimes of Big Ben* and Number 86 in *Once Upon a Time*.
Played Trooper Strauss in the **William Tell** episode *The Ensign* and Captain Markheim in *The Unwelcome Stranger*.

Maxwell James
Played Stanton in **The Champions** episode *The Silent Enemy*.
Played Pieter in the second series **Danger Man** [aka **Secret Agent**] episode *Fair Exchange* and Peter Miller in *A Date with Doris*.
Featured in the **Espionage** episode *Final Decision*.
Played Professor Gerald Smaill in the **Father Brown** episode *The Curse of the Golden Cross*.
Played Mitchell in the second season **The Protectors** episode *The Bridge*.
Played Jock Ingram in the second season **The Saint** episode *The Inescapable Word* and Joseph in the third season's *The Art Collectors*.

Maxwell Lois
Played Charlotte Russell in **The Baron** episode *Something for a Rainy Day*.
Played Sandi Lewis in the first season **Danger Man** episode *Position of Trust*.
Played Mary Burnham in the **Department S** episode *The Ghost of Mary Burnham*.
Played Felissa Henderson in the **Gideon's Way** episode *The Millionaire's Daughter*.
Played Elisabeth Creasey in the **G.S.5** episode *Party for Murder*.
Played Virginia in the **O.S.S.** episode *Operation Orange Blossom*.
Played Louise in **The Persuaders!** episode *Someone Waiting*.
Played Kim Wentworth in the **Randall and Hopkirk [Deceased]** aka **My Partner the Ghost** episode *For the Girl who has Everything*.
Played Beth in the third season **The Saint** episode *Simon and Delilah* and Helen in *Interlude in Venice*.
Provided the voice for Atlanta on the series **Stingray**.
Played Miss Holland in the **UFO** episodes *The Cat with Ten Lives* & *The Man who Came Back*.

Maxwell Paul
Played Don Fleming in **The Adventurer** episode *Love Always, Magda*.
Played Jim Carey in **The Baron** episode *Epitath for a Hero* and Dino Rossi in *The Man Outside*.
Voiced Captain Grey in **Captain Scarlet and the Mysterons**.
Played Captain Baxter in **The Champions** episode *The Silent Enemy*.
Played Doyle in the first season **Danger Man** episode *The Girl who Liked GIs* and Colonel Doyle in *The Relaxed Informer*.
Voiced Colonel Steve Zodiac in **Fireball XL5**.

Played Frank Maine in the first series **Ghost Squad** episode *Assassin*.
Played Colonel Cutler in the first series **Man of the World** episodes *Specialist for the Kill* & *Shadow of the Wall*. Returned in season two as Perez in *Jungle Mission*.
Played Alan Corder in the **Randall and Hopkirk [Deceased]** aka **My Partner the Ghost** episode *The Trouble with Women*.
Played Buzz Wepner in the **Return of the Saint** episode *Tower Bridge is Falling Down*.
Played Kolben in **The Saint** episode *The Helpful Pirate* [season three].
Played Lamont in **The Sentimental Agent** episode *A Very Desirable Plot*.
Played Lieutenant Lewis in the **UFO** episode *Sub-smash*.

Maxwell Peter
Directed the third season **The Adventures of Robin Hood** episodes *Castle in the Air, The Ghost that Failed* & *Roman Gold*.
Directed **The Adventures of Sir Lancelot** episodes *The Bridge, Maid of Somerset* & *Knight's Choice*.
Directed **The Buccaneers** [aka **Dan Tempest**] episodes *Prize of Andalusia, Dan Tempest Holds an Auction, Flip and Jenny, To the Rescue, Indian Fighters* and *Pirate Honour*.
Directed the second season **Danger Man** [aka **Secret Agent**] episodes *The Galloping Major, A Man to be Trusted* & *Have a Glass of Wine*.
Directed the **H. G. Wells' Invisible Man** episodes *Play to Kill, The Gun Runners, Death Cell, The Vanishing Evidence, Flight into Darkness, Man in Disguise* [with Quentin Lawrence], *Man in Power, Shadow Bomb* & *The Big Plot*.
Directed the **O.S.S.** episodes *Operation Tulip, Operation Meatball* [with Peter Wrestler] and *Operation Fracture*.
Directed the **Sir Francis Drake** episode *The Prisoner*.
Directed the **Sword of Freedom** episodes *The Ambassador, The Strange Intruder, The Primavera, The Marionettes, Vendetta, Who is Felicia?* & *Violetta*.
Directed the **White Hunter** episodes *A Moment of Truth, Deadfall, The Fugitive* and *Rogue Man*.
Directed the **William Tell** episodes *The Hostages, The Baroness, Secret Death, The Gauntlet of St. Gerhardt, The Cuckoo, The Magic Powder, The Prisoner, Manhunt, Golden Wheel, The Young Widow, The Shrew, The Killer, The Surgeon, The Unwelcome Stranger, The General's Daughter, The Traitor* and *Castle of Fear*.

Maxwell Roger
Played the tweedy gentleman in the second series **Danger Man** episode *Such Men are Dangerous* and the club member in the season two **Ghost Squad** episode *Escape Route*.

May Jack
Played Caradoc in **The Adventures of Sir Lancelot** episode *The Bridge*.
Played the third secretary in the second series **Danger Man** [aka **Secret Agent**] episode *A Room in the Basement*.
Played the Priest in **The Four Just Men** episode *The Battle of the Bridge*.
Played the English delegate in the **UFO** episode *Confetti Check A-O.K.*.

May Jock
Sound Mixer on **Strange Report**.

May Julie
Played Mrs. Tompkin in the **Strange Report** episode *Report 0649: SKELETON: 'Let Sleeping Heroes Lie'*.

Mayberry David
Played Carlos in the second season **The Protectors** episode *The Bridge*.
Played the boy pupil in the fourth season **The Saint** episode *The Ex-King of Diamonds*.

Maycock Peter
Played the Egyptian Sergeant in the **Virgin of the Secret Service** episode *The Pyramid Plot*.

Mayer Gerald
Directed **The Persuaders!** episode *Element of Risk*.

Mayer Mandy
Played Glenda in the third season **The Saint** episode *The Fast Women*.

Mayer Ronald
Played the landlord in the **Father Brown** episode *The Curse of the Golden Cross*.
Played the Sergeant in the **Virgin of the Secret Service** episode *Dark Deeds on the Northwest Frontier*.

Mayeska Irena
Played Marie Mercier in the **Jason King** episode *Buried in the Cold, Cold Ground*.

Maynard Bill
Played Carver in the **Father Brown** episode *The Man with Two Beards*.

Maynard Patrick
Played the officer in the **Danger Man** episode *The Trap*.

Mayne Ferdy
Played El Supremo in The **Buccaneers** [aka **Dan Tempest**] episode *Before the Mast*.
Played Baron Garonne in **The Count of Monte Cristo** episode *The Talleyrand Affair*.
Played the Moukta in the debut season **Danger Man** episode *The Blue Veil*. In season three [now aka **Secret Agent**] played Laprade in *The Paper Chase*.
Played Aristide Valentin in the **Father Brown** episode *The Secret Garden*.
Played Bannerman in **The Four Just Men** episode *The Protector*.
Played Neville Shand in the season two **Ghost Squad** episode *The Desperate Diplomat*.
Played Castillon in the **Interpol Calling** episode *The Money Game*.
Played Haider in the **Man in a Suitcase** episode *The Revolutionaries*.
Played Ramos in the second season **Man of the World** episode *The Bullfighter*.
Played Abwehr Oberst von Bloch in the **O.S.S.** episode *Operation Dagger*.
Played Sangallo in **The Persuaders!** episode *Five Miles to Midnight*.
Played The Iman in the first season **The Saint** episode *The Wonderful War* and Stratford Keene in *Iris*. In season three, played Landek in *Flight Plan* & Nicholas in *A Double in Diamonds*.
Played Count de Rici in **The Sentimental Agent** episode *Box of Tricks*.
Played Joos in the **Sir Francis Drake** episode *The Reluctant Duchess*.
Played the Spanish Ambassador in the **Sword of Freedom** episode *Francesca*.
Played Dubois in the **White Hunter** episode *The General*.
Played Gustaf in the **William Tell** episode *Castle of Fear*.
Played De Broux in **The Zoo Gang** episode *The Lion Hunt*.

Mayne Margo
Played Lena in the **Danger Man** episode *The Sisters*.

Mayne Murray
Played Ludovico in the **Sword of Freedom** episode *The Reluctant Duke*.

McAlinney Patrick
Played Patsy O'Kevin in the first season **The Saint** episode *The Effete Angler*.
Appeared as Burke in **The Sentimental Agent** episode *May the Saints Preserve Us*.
Played Skipper Staunton in the **Sir Francis Drake** episode *The Irish Pirate*.

McAnally Ray
Played Mickey Keston in the **Gideon's Way** episode *The White Rat*.
Played Doctor James Norbet in the **Man in a Suitcase** episode *Web with Four Spiders*.
Played Lars in the **Strange Report** episode *Report 5055: CULT: 'Murder Shrieks Out'*.

McCallin Clement
Played the Inspector in the season two **Ghost Squad** episode *The Menacing Mazurka*.

McCallum David
Starred as Steel in the **Sapphire and Steel** series.
Played Lord Oakeshot in the **Sir Francis Drake** episode *The English Dragon*.

McCallum Neil
Played Eddie Curtis in the **Department S** episode *Handicap Dead*.
Featured in the **Espionage** episode *Castles in Spain*.
Played Finnigan in the **Jason King** episode *Every Picture Tells a Story*.
Played Bennett in the first series **The Protectors** episode *One and One Makes One*.
Played Rev. Henry Crackan in the **Randall and Hopkirk [Deceased]** aka **My Partner the Ghost** episode *It's Supposed to be Thicker than Water*.
Played Carl Mason in the **UFO** episode *Court Martial*.

McCallum Tait Kenneth
Set Dresser on **Department S**.

McCarthy Dennis
Played Porter in **The Adventurer** episode *Target!*.

McCarthy Henry
Played the American in the season two **The Saint** episode *Lida*.
Played Calvin Smith in **The Zoo Gang** episode *Revenge: Post-dated*.

McCarthy John
Played Richard Burke in the **Sir Francis Drake** episode *The Irish Pirate*.
Played Brother Jules in the **William Tell** episode *The Elixir* and Emil in *The Suspect* and Heinz in *The Unwelcome Stranger*.

McCarthy Michael
Directed **The Scarlet Pimpernel** episodes *The Hostage* & *The Elusive Chauvelin*.

McCarthy Neil
Played the skipper in the first season **Danger Man** episode *The Conspirators*.
Played Quince in the **Department S** episode *A Ticket to Nowhere*.
Played Tredgett in the **Jason King** episode *An Author in Search of Two Characters*.
Played Casey in the first series **Man of the World** episode *Portrait of a Girl*.
Played Griggs in the **Randall and Hopkirk [Deceased]** aka **My Partner the Ghost** episode *The Man from Nowhere*.
Played Bradley in the **Return of the Saint** episode *The Debt Collectors*.

Played Morgen in the second season **The Saint** episode *The Saint Steps In* and Alec Hunter in *The Chequered Flag*.

McCartney Paul
With Linda McCartney, composed **The Zoo Gang**'s theme.

McCartney Linda
With Paul McCartney, composed **The Zoo Gang**'s theme.

McClaren John
Played Brinkley in the second season **The Saint** episode *Sibao*.

McClelland Allan
Played Morgan Dean in the first season **The Saint** episode *The Benevolent Burglary*.
Played the Chief Inspector in the **Strange Report** episode *Report 0649: SKELETON: 'Let Sleeping Heroes Lie'*.

McCormick Miriam
Played Lady Jane in **The Adventures of Robin Hood** first season episode *The Vandals*.

McCourt Margaret
Played Linda Norton in the **H. G. Wells' Invisible Man** episode *Picnic with Death*.

McCrindle Alex
Played Fergus Maclish in the second season **The Saint** episode *The Golden Frog*.

McCulloch Ian
Played Kemp in the **Man in a Suitcase** episode *Sweet Sue*.
Played Inspector Stone in the **Return of the Saint** episode *The Arrangement*.

McCullum Neil
Played Nelson in **The Four Just Men** episode *Riot*.
Played Sam Finnigin in the **Jason King** episode *Every Picture Tells a Story*.
Played Nick Vashetti in the first season **The Saint** episode *The Fellow Traveller* and Ed Jopley in the second season's *The Hi-Jackers*.
Played Sir Martin Amyas in the **Sir Francis Drake** episode *The Flame Thrower*.

McDermot Pat
Hairdresser on season two of **Danger Man** [aka **Secret Agent**].
Hairdresser on **The Prisoner** episodes *Arrival, The Chimes of Big Ben, A. B. and C., Free for All, The Schizoid Man, The General, Many Happy Returns, Dance of the Dead, Checkmate, Hammer into Anvil, It's your Funeral, A Change of Mind* and *Once Upon a Time*.

McDermott Brian
Played Don in the **Department S** episode *Handicap Dead*.
Played Carlo in **The Four Just Men** episode *Treviso Dam*.

McDermott Hugh
Played Duncan in **The Adventures of Robin Hood**: *The Highlander* [series 1], *Highland Fling* [2] and *The Bagpiper & The Parting Guest* [4].
Played Andrew Amory in the first season **Danger Man** episode *Vacation*. In the third series [now aka **Secret Agent**], played Soleby in *The Man with the Foot*.
Played Pelli in the **Jason King** episode *Flamingos only Fly on Tuesdays*.
Played Soames in the **Man in a Suitcase** episode *Which Way did he Go, McGill?*.
Played Nestor in the second season **The Saint** episode *The Golden Frog*.
Played Lyons in **The Sentimental Agent** episode *Never Play Cards with Strangers*.

McDermott Rory
Played Burke in the first season **Danger Man** episode *The Conspirators*. In the second series [now aka **Secret Agent**], played the security man in *That's Two of Us Sorry*.
Played the mortuary attendant in the **G.S.5** episode *The Goldfish Bowl*.
Played Fletcher in the **Sir Francis Drake** episode *The Doughty Plot*.

McDowall Betty
Played Simone in **The Count of Monte Cristo** episode *Point Counter Point* and Mercedes in *Bordeaux*.
Played Betty Green in **The Four Just Men** episode *The Crying Jester* and Maria in *The Last Days of Nick Pompey*.
Played Betty Asher in the **G.S.5** episode *Death of a Cop*.
Played Carlotta in the **Interpol Calling** episode *The Heiress*.
Played the Professor's wife in **The Prisoner** episode *The General*.
Played Edna Kinsall in the second season **The Saint** episode *The Loving Brothers*.
Played Kay Gibson in the **White Hunter** episode *Dead Man's Tale*.

McDowell Paul
Played the bank teller in the second season **The Protectors** episode *Goodbye George*.

McFarland Olive
Played Madame Carnot in **The Champions** episode *A Case of Lemmings*.
Played the chambermaid in the first season **Danger Man** episode *Name, Date and Place*.
Played Jenny in the **Sir Francis Drake** episode *Lost Colony of Virginia*.
Played Vera in the **William Tell** episode *The Lost Letter* and Hilde in *The Baroness*.

McGeagh Stanley
Played the hero in the **Jason King** episode *An Author in Search of Two Characters*; the second customs officer in the **Return of the Saint** episode *The Diplomat's Daughter* and a SHADO guard in the **UFO** episodes *Mindbender & E.S.P.*.

McGee Henry
Played Mack Martinson in the **Gideon's Way** episode *How to Retire without Really Working*.
Played the floor walker in the season two **Ghost Squad** episode *The Big Time*.
Played Frank in the first series **The Protectors** episode *The Numbers Game*.
Played Reeves in the season three **The Saint** episode *Flight Plan*.

McGoohan Patrick
Played Sir Glavin in **The Adventures of Sir Lancelot** episode *The Outcast*.
Was the series star, playing John Drake, throughout **Danger Man** [known in the USA as **Secret Agent** after series one]. Directed the first series episode *Vacation* and the third's *To Our Best Friend & The Paper Chase*.
Starred throughout **The Prisoner** as Number 6 and served as Executive Producer. Directed *Many Happy Returns, A Change of Mind* [using the pseudonym Joseph Serf], *Free for All* [and wrote, using the pseudonym Paddy Fitz], *Once Upon a Time* [also wrote] and *Fall Out*.

McGowran Jack
Played 'Happy' Roden in the **Gideon's Way** episode *Big Fish, Little Fish*.

McGregor Ken
Played Anatole in the **White Hunter** episode *Forest of the Night*.

McGuire Tucker
Played Norma Willett in **The Four Just Men** episode *Panic Button*.

McIntosh Ellen
Played Jessie in the season four **The Adventures of Robin Hood** episode *The Parting Guest*; Kristyna in the second series **Ghost Squad** episode *Interrupted Requiem* and Mrs Ellshaw in the first season **The Saint** episode *The Elusive Ellshaw*.

McIntyre Duncan
Played King William in the season two **The Adventures of Robin Hood** episode *Highland Fling* and Mackay in the second series **Danger Man** episode *That's Two of Us Sorry*.

McKay Jock
Played the treasurer in the season two **The Adventures of Robin Hood** episode *Highland Fling*.

McKeag Michael
Played Jules in **The Adventures of Robin Hood** first season episode *The Intruders* and Noel in *The Thorkill Ghost*.

McKenna T. P.
Played Ivan in the third season **Danger Man** [aka **Secret Agent**] episode *To our Best Friend*.
Played Inspector Boyne in the **Father Brown** episode *The Dagger with Wings*.
Played Rene Chenard in the **Jason King** episode *A Thin Band of Air*.
Played Peter in the **Man in a Suitcase** episode *Day of Execution*.
Played Malone in the third season **The Saint** episode *The Angel's Eye* and Tony in the fourth season's *Legacy for the Saint*.

McKenzie Edna
Appeared as the hospital assistant in the **White Hunter** episode *Let my People Go*.

McKenzie Jack
Played Marek in the **Return of the Saint** episode *Assault Force*.

McKenzie Robert
Guested as Johnny in the **Interpol Calling** episode *In the Swim*.

McKern Leo
Guested twice in the first series of **The Adventures of Robin Hood**: as Sir Roger de Lisle in *The Coming of Robin Hood* and as Herbert of Doncaster in *The Moneylender*.
Played Number 2 in **The Prisoner** episode *The Chimes of Big Ben*. Returned to the role in *Once Upon a Time* & *Fall Out*.
Played Companion in the first season **Space 1999** episode *The Infernal Machine*.

McKevitt Michael
Played the waiter in the first season **The Saint** episode *The Invisible Millionaire*.

McKillop Donald
Played the Foreman in the **Gideon's Way** episode *Subway to Revenge*.
Played the policeman in the **G.S.5** episode *The Goldfish Bowl*.

McKinnon Errol
Played Frank Kleng in **The Four Just Men** episode *The Bystanders*.

McLaren John
Played Andy in **The Four Just Men** episodes *Dead Man's Switch* and *Justice For Gino*.

Played Doctor Cookson in the first series **Ghost Squad** episode *Million Dollar Ransom*.
Played Doctor Northwade in the first season **The Saint** episode *Judith* and Stephen Elliot in *The King of the Beggars*.
Played Harris in the **White Hunter** episode *Second Dealer*.

McLeod Robert
Played Professor Oakridge in the season two **The Saint** episode *The Inescapable Word*.

McLoughlin Patrick
Starred as Trevelyan in **Sir Francis Drake** [episodes 4 -8].

McMahon Dermot
Played one of the sons in **The Buccaneers** [aka **Dan Tempest**] episode *Mother Doughty's Crew*.

McMillan Roddy
Played Detective Inspector Caldwell in the **Gideon's Way** episode *The Nightlifers*.
Played Angus McRuddy in the **Shirley's World** episode *The Islanders*.

McNaughton Alan
Played Dr Claudel in the **Jason King** episode *A Red, Red Rose Forever*.

McNaughton Fred
Played the gardener in the second season **The Protectors** episode *Trial*.
Played the landlord in the **Sword of Freedom** episode *The Duke*.

McNaughton Ian
Played Sgt. Greenwood in the **Gideon's Way** episode *The Wall*.

McNeff Richard
Played the guard in the first season **The Saint** episode *The Fellow Traveller*.

McPhail Angus
Wrote **The Scarlet Pimpernel** episodes *Antoine and Antoinette* [with Diana Morgan], *Thanksgiving Day* [with Michael Hogan and John Cousins] and *A Tale of Two Pigtails* [with Diana Morgan].

McQueen Simone
Played Mary in **The Adventures of Sir Lancelot** episode *The Outcast*.

McShane Ian
Played Anton Zoref in the first season **Space 1999** episode *Force of Life*.

McSharry Carmel
Played Mrs Wray in the **Gideon's Way** episode *Big Fish, Little Fish*.
Played the cleaner in the second season **The Protectors** episode *Petard*.

McStay Michael
Played the Gendarme in the **Jason King** episode *Buried in the Cold, Cold Ground*.
Played Vernier in **The Persuaders!** episode *The Gold Napoleon*.

Meacham Michael
Played Captain James Murray in the **Gideon's Way** episode *The Thin Red Line*.
Played George Stanton in the first season **The Saint** episode *The Rough Diamonds*.

Meaden Dan
Played Lendrop in the second season **The Protectors** episode *Route 27*.

Meadows Stanley
Played David Price in **The Persuaders!** episode *The Man in the Middle*.
Played Birch in the second season **The Protectors** episode *Blockbuster*.
Played George Roden in the **Randall and Hopkirk [Deceased] aka My Partner the Ghost** episode *Could You Recognise the Man Again?*
Played Inspector Ashton in the **Return of the Saint** episode *Tower Bridge is Falling Down*.
Played Frank Landon in the first season **The Saint** episode *Marcia*, Bob Stryker in the first season's *The High Fence* and Georges in the third season's *The Queen's Ransom*.

Medak Peter
Directed **The Persuaders!** episode *Someone Waiting*.
Directed the **Return of the Saint** episode *The Arrangement*.
Directed the second season **Space 1999** episodes *Space Warp* & *The Seance Spectre*.
Directed the **Strange Report** episodes *Report 0649: SKELETON: 'Let Sleeping Heroes Lie'* & *Report 7931: SNIPER: 'When is Your Cousin Not?'*.

Medalie Mervyn
Hairdresser on **The Baron**.

Meddings Derek
Supervising Visual Effects Director / Visual Effects on **Joe 90**; Visual Effects Supervisor on **The Secret Service**; Supervising Special Effects Director on **Thunderbirds**; Special Effects [with Reg Hill] on **Stingray**; Special Effects on **Captain Scarlet and the Mysterons, Fireball XL5** & **Supercar** and Special Effects Director on **UFO**.

Medford Jill
Played Certhia in the second series **Danger Man [aka Secret Agent]** episode *Whatever Happened to George Foster?*.
Played Nancy Rand-Fuller in the season two **Ghost Squad** episode *Sabotage*.

Medford Paul
Played Joey in the **Return of the Saint** episode *The Obono Affair*.

Medwin Michael
Played Guy Northcott in the **Return of the Saint** episode *The Arrangement*.

Megahy Frances
Co-wrote, with Bernie Cooper, the **Man in a Suitcase** episodes *Brainwash* and *Which Way did he Go, McGill?*.

Meighan Michael
Assistant Director on **The Champions, Department S** & **Randall and Hopkirk [Deceased]** aka My Partner the Ghost.

Meillon John
Played Major Teong in the second season **Man of the World** episode *The Enemy*.

Melbourne David
Played a guard/auction client in the **Father Brown** episode *The Arrow of Heaven*.

Meldazzi Gino
Played Electrician in the third season **The Saint** episode *Simon and Delilah*.

Meldrum Geoff
Camera Operator on **Thunderbirds**.

Melek Angel
Played the dancer in the **Department S** episode *A Fish out of Water*.

Melford Jack
Guested once per series in **The Adventures of Robin Hood**: as the Archbishop in *The Prisoner* [season 1], as Lord Pomfret in *The Impostor* [2], as Lord Northeave in *Marian's Prize* [3] and as Lord Beaumont in *Hostage for a Hangman* [4].
Played Norrin in **The Adventures of Sir Lancelot** episode *Thieves*.
Played Caldwell in the first season **Danger Man** episode *The Lonely Chair*.
Played Plomer MP in **The Four Just Men** episode *The Heritage*.
Played Collins in the **H. G. Wells' Invisible Man** episode *Strange Partners*.
Played Colonel Dewar in **The Sentimental Agent** episode *Never Play Cards with Strangers*.
Played Sir Owen in the **Sir Francis Drake** episode *Gentlemen of Spain*.

Melford Jill
Played Suzanne in the second series **Danger Man [aka Secret Agent]** episode *The Galloping Major*.
Played Irene Cromwell in the first season **The Saint** episode *Marcia*.
Appeared as Carol in the **White Hunter** episode *A Moment of Truth* and as Laura West in *The Trophy*.

Melia Joe
Played Olsen in the **Man in a Suitcase** episode *The Sitting Pigeon*.

Mellinger Michael
Played Gen. Tornes in **The Champions** episode *The Iron Man*.
Played Bonaparte in **The Count of Monte Cristo** episode *The Island*.
Played Strobel in the **Department S** episode *Black Out*.
Played Jose in the **G.S.5** episode *Party for Murder*.
Played Ali in the first series **Man of the World** episode *The Nature of Justice*.
Played the hotel clerk in the fourth season **The Saint** episode *The Double Take*.
Played the servant in the **Sir Francis Drake** episode *Court Intrigue*.
Played Ral Guparji in the **White Hunter** episode *Run to Earth*.

Mellor James
Played Gervais in the **Jason King** episode *A Thin Band of Air*.

Melvazzi Gino
Played the policeman in the first season **Danger Man** episode *The Brothers*.
Played the police Captain in the second season **The Protectors** episode *Fighting Fund*.

Mendez Julie
Played the belly dancer in the **Virgin of the Secret Service** episode *The Great Ring of Akba*, a dancer in *The Pyramid Plot* and Paola in *Pride of Assassins*.

Merant Philip
Played the Captain in **The Scarlet Pimpernel** episode *Something Remembered*.

Mercer Diane
Played Maria in the first series **The Protectors** episode *It was All Over in Leipzig*.

Meredith Robin
Played Mr. Truslove in the **Father Brown** episode *The Head of Caesar.*

Meredity Charles
Played Von Humbolt in **The Count of Monte Cristo** episode *Affair of Honour.*

Meredyth-Lucas John
Associate Producer on the **Whiplash** series.

Merlin June
Appeared as Frankie in the **Interpol Calling** episode *Fingers of Guilt.*

Merrall Mary
Played Clara Faringham in the **Randall and Hopkirk [Deceased] aka My Partner the Ghost** episode *The Ghost who Saved the Bank at Monte Carlo.*
Played Sophie Yarmouth in the first season **The Saint** episode *The Bunco Artists.*
Played the Duchess in the **Sir Francis Drake** episode *The Reluctant Duchess.*
Played Mrs O'Connor in the **UFO** episode *A Question of Priorities.*

Merritt George
Played Lloyd in **The Adventures of Sir Lancelot** episode *Shepherd's War.*
Played the janitor in the **Gideon's Way** episode *A Perfect Crime.*
Played Chivers in **The Persuaders!** episode *Read and Destroy.*
Played the postman in **The Prisoner** episode *Dance of the Dead.*

Merrow Jane
Played Savannah in **The Baron** episode *Red Horse, Red Rider.*
Played Juana Romero in the second season **Danger Man [aka Secret Agent]** episode *A Date with Doris* and Susan in *A Room in the Basement.* In series three played Lydia Greshnova in *The Man who wouldn't Talk.*
Played Lollo Romano in the **Gideon's Way** episode *Gang War.*
Played Annabelle Fenchurch in the **Man in a Suitcase** episode *The Bridge.*
Played the nurse in the first series **Man of the World** episode *Blaze of Glory.*
Played Alison, Number 24, in **The Prisoner** episode *The Schizoid Man.*
Played Sandra Joyce in the **Randall and Hopkirk [Deceased] aka My Partner the Ghost** episode *Who Killed Cock Robin.*
Played Lois Norroy in **The Saint** episode *The Happy Suicide* [season two] and Mabel in *The Angel's Eye* [three].
Played Jill in the **Strange Report** episode *Report 1553: RACIST: 'A Most Dangerous Proposal'.*
Played Jo Fraser in the **UFO** episode *The Responsibility Seat.*

Merry Susanna
Continuity on **Man in a Suitcase**.

Merton Zienia
Played Zenia in the **Jason King** episode *Zenia.*
Played Mila in the **Return of the Saint** episode *The Nightmare Man.*
Starred as, series regular, Sandra Benes in **Space 1999**.
Played Zeba in the **Strange Report** episode *Report 3424: EPIDEMIC: 'A Most Curious Crime'.*

Mervyn William
Appeared as Thomas in the second series of **The Adventures of Robin Hood** episode *Hubert.*
Played Judd in the second series of **The Adventures of Robin Hood** episode *The Dowry.*

Played the Under Secretary in **The Four Just Men** episode *The Man who wasn't There.*
Played Mr Pater in the **Gideon's Way** episode *How to Retire without Really Working.*
Played Sir Charles Worthington in **The Persuaders!** episode *Read and Destroy.*
Played Whitty in the **Randall and Hopkirk [Deceased] aka My Partner the Ghost** episode *A Disturbing Case.*
Played Colonel Wilde in **The Sentimental Agent** episode *A Very Desirable Plot.*

Messina Roberto
Played Mario in the **Return of the Saint** episode *The Murder Cartel.*

Metliss Isabel
Played the clerk in the **Strange Report** episode *Report 4821: X-RAY: 'Who Weeps for the Doctor?'.*

Metro-Goldwyn-Mayer, Borehamwood
Studio used for the filming of **Danger Man** [first series & episodes 1 - 26 of season two], **UFO** [also filmed at Pinewood Studios] and **The Prisoner**.

Meyer Hans
Played Lucky Le Beau in the **Department S** episode *The Mysterious Man in the Flying Machine* and Angelo in the **Jason King** episode *All that Glisters* [part 2].

Meyer Otto
Film Editor on **The Count of Monte Cristo**.

Michael Ralph
Played Montfichet in the second series of **The Adventures of Robin Hood** episode *The Hero.*
Played Bogus Cristo in **The Count of Monte Cristo** episode *Albania.*
Played Dorset in the second series **Danger Man [aka Secret Agent]** episode *A Man to be Trusted* and the interrogator in the third season's *The Man who wouldn't Talk.*
Played the governor in the **H. G. Wells' Invisible Man** episode *Jailbreak.*
Played Sir Giles Watkins in the **Man in a Suitcase** episode *Web with Four Spiders* and the Governor in *No Friend of Mine.*
Played Quirini in the **William Tell** episode *The Avenger.*

Michaels Wally
Played Joseph in the **Jason King** episode *To Russia With ....Panache .*

Michelle Ruda
Played Joann in **The Four Just Men** episode *The Judge.*

Michelson Andre
Played the Ambassador in **The Four Just Men** episode *Money to Burn.*

Michon Pat
Played Dolores Gamma in the second season **The Saint** episode *The Unkind Philanthropist.*

Middlemas Frank
Played the Commander in the season two **Ghost Squad** episode *The Heir Apparent.*

Middleton Noelle
Played Fiona in the **Man of the World** episode *The Highland Story* [season one] and the Mother Superior in *Jungle Mission* [season two].
Played Mary in the **Sir Francis Drake** episode *Mary, Queen of Scots.*

Midwood Kenneth
Played the intruder in the **O.S.S.** episode *Operation Blackbird*.

Mike Sammes Singers, The
Vocal title music on **The Secret Service** series.

Mikell George
Played Lanik in **The Adventurer** episode *Counterstrike*.
Played the student in the second series **Danger Man** [aka **Secret Agent**] episode *Colony Three* and Wilhelm Berg in *Fair Exchange*.
Played the first sentry in **The Four Just Men** episode *The Battle of the Bridge*.
Played Jensen in the **G.S.5** episode *A Cast of Thousands*.
Played an officer in the **O.S.S.** episode *Operation Post Office*.
Played Pato in the **Strange Report** episode *Report 5055: CULT: 'Murder Shrieks Out'*.

Mikhelson Andre
Played Rousse in **The Count of Monte Cristo** episode *Marseilles*.
Played the Captain in the **H. G. Wells' Invisible Man** episode *Shadow on the Screen*.
Played Ruysman in the **White Hunter** episode *The General*.

Milan Lita
Played Teresa in **The Count of Monte Cristo** episode *The Sardinia Affair*.

Milbourne Olive
Played Mrs Haggerty in the third season **The Saint** episode *The Best Laid Schemes*.
Played Mrs Dewar in **The Sentimental Agent** episode *Never Play Cards with Strangers*.

Miles Keith
Wrote the second series **Space 1999** episode *All That Glisters*.

Miles Pamela
Played Lady Pamela in the **Virgin of the Secret Service** episode *The Amazons*.

Mill Robert
Played the assistant in **The Champions** episode *Nutcracker*.
Played Cranmore in the **Department S** episode *The Duplicated Man*.

Millan Victor
Starred as Zahir in the series **Ramar of the Jungle**.

Miller Cameron
Played the French customer in the second series **Danger Man** [aka **Secret Agent**] episode *Are you Going to be More Permanent?*

Miller Gary
Played Len in the **Gideon's Way** episode *The Great Plane Robbery* and Slater in the fourth season **The Saint** episode *The People Importers*.

Miller Gary
Sang the title for the **Stingray** series.

Miller Jan
Played the lass in the first series **The Adventures of Robin Hood** episode *A Guest for the Gallows*.
Played Racquel in **The Buccaneers** [aka **Dan Tempest**] episode *The Return of Calico Jack*.

Miller John
Played Colonel Salmson in the second series **Danger Man** [aka **Secret Agent**] episode *Are you Going to be More Permanent?*

Miller Mandy
Played Molly in the first season **The Saint** episode *The Well-Meaning Mayor*.

Miller Martin
Played Stavros in the first season **Danger Man** episode *The Lovers* and in the second series [aka **Secret Agent**] played Dr Zoren in *Fish on the Hook*.
Played Dutrov in the **Department S** episode *The Perfect Operation*.
Played Braune in the **Ghost Squad** episode *The Green Shoes* [shot for season one but, due to a strike, shown in season two].
Played Dr Stelitz in the first series **Man of the World** episode *Blaze of Glory*.
Played the Watchmaker in **The Prisoner** episode *It's Your Funeral*.
Played Jerome in the second season **The Saint** episode *Jeannine* and Mr Justin in *The Smart Detective*.
Played Astolat in **The Sentimental Agent** episode *A Little Sweetness and Light*.

Miller Mary
Played Freda in the first season **Space 1999** episode *Death's Other Dominion*.

Miller Michael
Appeared as the man in the buggy in **The Prisoner** episode *The General*, as Number 93 in *A Change of Mind* and as the Delegate in *Fall Out*.

Miller Peter
Wrote the **Shirley's World** episodes *Thou Shall Not Be Found Out, The Lovers, The Colonel, The Reunion & The Rally*.

Miller Phillis
Wrote **The Buccaneers** episode *To the Rescue*.

Miller Rachelle
Played the model in the **Man in a Suitcase** episode *Which Way did he Go, McGill?*.

Miller Stanley
Wrote the **White Hunter** episode *Killer Leopard*.

Mills George
Production Supervisor on the first season of **The Adventures of Robin Hood**, **The Adventures of Sir Lancelot** episodes *The Knight with the Red Plume, The Ferocious Fathers & The Queen's Knight* and on **The Buccaneers** [aka **Dan Tempest**] episode *Blackbeard*.

Mills John
Starred as Captain Tommy Devon, codename the Elephant, in the series **The Zoo Gang**.

Mills Juliet
Played Carla in the first series **Man of the World** episode *The Mindreader*.

Mills Lynette
Played the chambermaid in the second series of **The Adventures of Robin Hood** episode *Isabella*.
Played the serving girl in the **Sword of Freedom** episode *Chart of Gold*.

Mills Olive
Hairdresser on **The Prisoner** episodes *Living in Harmony, Do Not Forsake Me Oh My Darling, The Girl who was Death & Fall Out*.

Mills Stanley
Designer on the **Sapphire and Steel** series [not *Adventure 5*].

Milton Beaufoy
Played the butler in the first season **Danger Man** episode *Name, Date and Place*.

Milton Billy
Played Benson in **The Baron** episode *Something for a Rainy Day*.
Played the jeweller in **The Count of Monte Cristo** episode *Bordeaux*.
Played Papa in the **O.S.S.** episode *Operation Jingle Bells*.
Played Loftus in the **Randall and Hopkirk [Deceased]** episode *Could You Recognise the Man Again?*.
Played the gunsmith in the **White Hunter** episode *Valley of the Dead*.

Milton Ernest
Appeared as Furst in the **William Tell** episode *The Emperor's Hat*.

Minster Hilary
Played the German sailor [Fritz] in the **Timeslip** story *The Wrong End of Time* [series parts 1 - 6].

Miranda Isa
Played Mira Cossackian in **The Baron** episode *The Legions of Ammak*.
Played Teresa Pantera in the **G.S.5** episode *A Cast of Thousands*.
Played Lillian in the **Shirley's World** episode *Always Leave them Laughing*.

Mishkin Philip
Co-wrote the **Shirley's World** episode *To Dream the Improbable Dream* [with Bob Reiner].

Mitchell Bill
Played Farell in **The Sentimental Agent** episode *The Beneficiary*.

Mitchell Charlotte
Played Miss Parvant in the **Father Brown** episode *The Quick One*.

Mitchell Christopher
Played Juan in the second season **The Protectors** episode *The Bridge*.
Played Brand in the **Strange Report** episode *Report 5055: CULT: 'Murder Shrieks Out'*.

Mitchell Mary
Played the hotel receptionist in the **Department S** episode *Dead Men Die Twice*.

Mitchell Melan
Played the native policeman in the season two **Ghost Squad** episode *East of Mandalay*.
Played the Indian Medical Officer in the first series **Man of the World** episode *The Frontier*.

Mitchell Norman
Played the Earl of Steyne in the fourth series of **The Adventures of Robin Hood** episode *Sybella*.
Played Telmah in **The Adventures of Sir Lancelot** episode *The Magic Book*.
Played Roberts in the **Man in a Suitcase** episode *Dead Man's Shoes*.
Appeared as the mechanic in **The Prisoner** episode *The General*.
Played Mr Smith in the first season **The Saint** episode *The Talented Husband*.
Played Frederick in the **William Tell** episode *The Emperor's Hat*.

Mitchell Stuart
Played Renault in **The Count of Monte Cristo** episode *Point Counter Point*.
Played the labourer in **The Scarlet Pimpernel** episode *The Farmer's Boy*.

Mitchell Warren
Played Jose Santiago in the debut season **Danger Man** episode *An Affair of State*, Banarji in *The Traitor* and Shashig in *Find and Return*. In series two [now aka **Secret Agent**], played Chopra in *The Colonel's Daughter* and Lamaze in *Have a Glass of Wine*. Returned in season three to play the military attache / fortune teller in *I can only Offer you Sherry*.
Played George Rudley in **The Four Just Men** episode *Panic Button*.
Played Affiat in the first series **Ghost Squad** episode *Princess* and Major Mahmoud in the second season's *Death of a Sportsman* [*Princess* was shot for the first series, but due to an actors' strike, was originally shown as a season two episode].
Played Willi in the **Interpol Calling** episode *The Man's Clown*.
Played Alex in the first series **Man of the World** episode *Death of a Conference*.
Played Marco / Marco De Cesari in the first season **The Saint** episodes *The King of the Beggars, The Charitable Countess & The Latin Touch*.
Played Pugh in **The Sentimental Agent** episode *The Height of Fashion*.
Played Roberto in the **Sir Francis Drake** episode *The Prisoner*.
Played Carlo in the **William Tell** episode *The Black Brothers*.

Mival Eric
Music Editor on **The Prisoner** episodes *A. B. and C., Free for All, The Schizoid Man, The General, Many Happy Returns, Dance of the Dead, Hammer into Anvil, A Change of Mind, Do Not Forsake Me Oh My Darling, Living in Harmony, The Girl who was Death, Once Upon a Time* and *Fall Out*.

Modisane Bloke
Played the waiter in the cafe in the **Jason King** episode *Flamingos only Fly on Tuesdays*.

Moffatt Geraldine
Played Christina Vitale in **The Baron** episode *Time to Kill*.
Played Magda Kallai in the third season **Danger Man** [aka **Secret Agent**] episode *Someone is Liable to Get Hurt*.
Played Janet in the **Department S** episode *Six Days*.
Played Elizabeth Barnes in the **Father Brown** episode *The Hammer of God*.
Played Claudia in the **Jason King** episode *The Constance Missal*.
Played Senka in **The Persuaders!** episode *The Man in the Middle*.
Played Maria in the second season **The Protectors** episode *Goodbye George*.
Played Tessa O'Neill in the **Strange Report** episode *Report 0846: LONELYHEARTS: 'Who Killed Dan Cupid?'*.
Played Jean Regan in the **UFO** episode *The Cat with Ten Lives*.

Moffatt John
Played Armand in **The Adventurer** episode *The Good Book*.
Played the Spanish Captain in the **Sir Francis Drake** episode *Boy Jack*.

Mohyeddin Zia
Played Prengo in **The Champions** episode *Shadow of the Panther*.
Played Wasing in the first season **Danger Man** episode *Dead Man Walks*. In the second series [now aka **Secret Agent**], played Khan in *The Colonel's Daughter*, Mr Sen in *Such Men are Dangerous* and Sinclair Jones in *The Mercenaries*. Played Dr Sawari in the third season's *Someone is Liable to Get Hurt*.

Played Rafael in the **Man in a Suitcase** episode *Night Flight to Andora*.
Played King Phillip in the **Sir Francis Drake** episode *Visit to Spain*.

Mokadi Amos
Played Col. Leon Garvi in the **Return of the Saint** episode *One Black September*.

Mokae Zakes
Played the personal assistant in the second series **Danger Man** [aka **Secret Agent**] episode *The Galloping Major*.

Molinas Richard
Played Pillette in the **O.S.S.** episode *Operation Death Trap*.

Monaghan Leonard
Played Lennie in the second series **Danger Man** [aka **Secret Agent**] episode *Don't Nail Him Yet*.

Monk Conrad
Played the garage attendant in **The Baron** episode *And Suddenly You're Dead* and the first policeman in *Long Ago and Far Away*.
Guested as the mechanic in **The Champions** episode *Autokill*.

Monks Robert
Second Unit Cameraman on **The Prisoner** episodes *Arrival*, *The Chimes of Big Ben*, *Free for All*, *Many Happy Returns*, *Dance of the Dead*, *Checkmate* and *Hammer into Anvil*.

Montague Bruce
Played Verdon in **The Baron** episode *Red Horse, Red Rider*.
Played the police Captain in the second season **The Protectors** episode *Decoy*.
Played Jacques in the first season **The Saint** episode *The Good Medicine*.

Montague Lee
Played Asano in **The Baron** episode *Samurai West*.
Played Villon in **The Count of Monte Cristo** episode *Monaco* and the assassin in *Albania*.
Played Mr Chung Sun, Minister of Justice, in the first season **Danger Man** episode *The Honeymooners*. In the second series [now aka **Secret Agent**], played Major Latour in *Such Men are Dangerous*.
Played Rafic in the **Department S** episode *A Fish out of Water*.
Featured in the **Espionage** episode *The Dragon Slayer*.
Played Berto in **The Four Just Men** episode *The Crying Jester* and Mendri in *The Princess*.
Played Matt in the **H. G. Wells' Invisible Man** episode *Man in Disguise*.
Played Dikalos in the **Interpol Calling** episode *Dead On Arrival*.
Played Dorzac in the season two **Space 1999** episode *Dorzak*.
Played Sgt. Johann in the **William Tell** episode *The Mountain People*.

Montash Henry
Hairdresser on **Randall and Hopkirk [Deceased]** aka **My Partner the Ghost**.

Montee Richard
Played the Teneriffe policeman in the second season **The Saint** episode *The Saint Bids Diamonds*.

Montefiore Phyllis
Played Madame Bregonzi in **The Baron** episode *The High Terrace*.
Played Princess Alexandra in the third season **The Saint** episode *The Man Who Liked Lions*.

Montez Ricardo
Played Inspector Santos in **The Persuaders!** episode *Nuisance Value*.

Montez Richard
Played the detective in **The Champions** episode *Get Me Out of Here!*
Played Garcia in the **Jason King** episode *A Kiss for a Beautiful Killer*.
Played the guard in the **Man in a Suitcase** episode *Variation on a Million Bucks* [2 parter: also a movie: *To Chase a Million*], the police officer in *Night Flight to Andora* and the Spanish taxi driver in *The Man who Stood Still*.
Played the driver in the **Man of the World** episode *The Sentimental Agent* [season one] and Garcia in *The Bullfighter* [two].
Played the head waiter in the first season **The Saint** episode *The Golden Journey*, Carlos Segoia in *Teresa*, the immigration officer in the second season's *The Revolution* Racket, Peon in the third's *Locate and Destroy* and Nino in the fourth's *Vendetta for the Saint* [part 2].
Played a Mexican bandit in the **UFO** episode *Mindbender*.

Montgomerie Elaine
Played the female delegate in **The Adventurer** episode *Miss Me Once, Miss Me Twice and Miss Me Once Again*.

Montgomery Cec
Played Rocco in the season two **Ghost Squad** episode *P.G. 7*.

Montgomery Doreen
Wrote, with Jo Eisinger, the first season **Danger Man** episode *The Lovers*.
Wrote the **H. G. Wells' Invisible Man** episode *Bank Raid* [with Ralph Smart].
Wrote the **Sir Francis Drake** episodes *Doctor Dee*, *The Flame Thrower* & *Visit to Spain*.
Scenario Editor on **William Tell**. Wrote the episodes *The Surgeon* and *The Master Spy*. Teleplayed the episodes: *The Hostages* [from an original story by Ralph Smart], *Secret Death* [original story by Smart], *The Gauntlet of St. Gerhardt* [original story by Smart], *Manhunt* [original story by Smart], *The Bandit* [original story by Smart], *The Bear* [original story by Michael Connor], *The Suspect* [original story by Larry Forrester], *The Bride* [original story by John Kruse], *The Mountain People* [original story by Kruse] and *Secret Weapon* [story by Arnold Abbott].

Montgomery Ray
Starred as Ogden in the series **Ramar of the Jungle**.

Montinaro Brizio
Played Benito in the **Return of the Saint** episode *Vicious Circle*.

Moody Jeanne
Played Beth in the first season **Danger Man** episode *The Trap* and Leanka in the third season [now aka **Secret Agent**] episode *I'm Afraid you Have the Wrong Number*.
Played Liane Fennick in the first season **The Saint** episode *The Ever-loving Spouse*, Marjorie Enstone in the second season's *The Man who Liked Toys* and Lida Verity in *Lida*.

Moody Ron
Played Matthew Quick in the **Shirley's World** episode *To Dream the Improbable Dream*.

Moon Georgina
Featured in the series **UFO** as, regular, the Skydiver operative.

Moor Harry
Played the radio officer in the **O.S.S.** episode *Operation Blackbird*.

Moore Deborah
Played the girl in **The Persuaders!** episode *The Long Goodbye*.

Moore Eileen
Played Mary MacPherson in the first season **Danger Man** episode *The Nurse*.

Moore Gar
Played Marnet in **The Count of Monte Cristo** episode *The Duel*.

Moore John
Guested as Travis in **The Champions** episode *Project Zero*.
Played Prof. Edmond Gailbraith in the **Father Brown** episode *Three Tools of Death*.
Played Castellani in the **Sword of Freedom** episode *Choice of Weapons*.
Played the Priest in the **Virgin of the Secret Service** episode *Across the Silver Pass of Gusri Song*.

Moore John
Wrote **The Scarlet Pimpernel** episode *The Farmer's Boy*.

Moore Kenton
Played the bank guard in the **Jason King** episode *A Red, Red Rose Forever*.

Moore Kieron
Appeared as Nessim in **The Adventurer** episode *Love Always, Magda*.
Played Crawford in the first season **Danger Man** episode *The Sanctuary*.
Played Lomax/Reeves in the **Department S** episode *Dead Men Die Twice*.
Played Jean Le Grand in the **Jason King** episode *Toki*.
Played Mario Toza in the second season **The Protectors** episode *A Pocketful of Posies*.
Played Miklos Corri in the **Randall and Hopkirk [Deceased]** aka **My Partner the Ghost** episode *When the Spirit Moves You*.
Played Thomas Stukeley in the **Sir Francis Drake** episode *King of America*.
Played Jacques Picard in **The Zoo Gang** episode *African Misfire*.

Moore Maureen
Played Isabel in the **Sir Francis Drake** episode *The Governor's Revenge*.

Moore Roger
Starred as Lord Brett Sinclair throughout **The Persuaders!** series, designed the clothes for his character Lord Sinclair, directed *The Time and the Place* & *The Long Goodbye* and appeared as The General, The Admiral & Lady Agatha in *A Death in the Family*.
Starred as Simon Templar - aka The Saint - in **The Saint** series. Directed the episodes *Sophia* [season 1]; *The Miracle Tea Party, The Contract, The Man who could not Die* & *The Old Treasure Story* [2]; *The House on Dragon's Rock, Escape Route* & *Invitation to Danger* [3] and *Where the Money Is* [4].

Moore Terence
Wrote **The Buccaneers** [aka **Dan Tempest**] episodes *The Raiders, Captain Dan Tempest, Gunpowder Plot, Conquest of New Providence, Hurricane* [with Peggy Phillips], *Mr. Beamish and the Hangman's Noose, Conquistador* [with Basil Dawson], *Aztec Treasure* and *Printer's Devil*.

Moore William
Played the rifle range supervisor in the first series **The Protectors** episode *Talkdown*.

Moorehead Brian
Played a guard in **The Adventures of Sir Lancelot** episode *The Lesser Breed*.

Morahan Christopher
Directed the second season **Ghost Squad** episode *The Grand Duchess*.

Morand Timothy
Played Francois in the **Return of the Saint** episode *Assault Force*.

Morant Phillip
Played the Captain in **The Scarlet Pimpernel** episode *The Princess*.

Morant Richard
Played David Mitchell in the second season **The Protectors** episode *The Bridge*.

More Kenneth
Starred in the title role in the **Father Brown** series.

Moreland Alan
Wrote the second series of **The Adventures of Robin Hood** episodes *The Path of True Love* aka *Locksley Hall* with [Basil Dawson] and *The Goldmaker's Return*.
Wrote **The Buccaneers** [aka **Dan Tempest**] episodes *Articles of War* [with Peggy Phillips] and *Dan Tempest Holds an Auction*.
Teleplayed **The Four Just Men** episode *The Protector* [with Leon Griffiths: from a story by himself & Samuel B. West].

Morell Andre
Played Father Antonius in **The Adventurer** episode *Full Fathom Five*.
Played the Governor in **The Buccaneers** [aka **Dan Tempest**] episode *Gunpowder Plot*.
Played Sir Duncan in the second series **Danger Man** [aka **Secret Agent**] episode *The Affair at Castelevara*.
Played General Shafari in the **H. G. Wells' Invisible Man** episode *Man in Power*.
Played Bernhard Raxel in the second season **The Saint** episode *The Crime of the Century*.
Appeared as Manderley in the **White Hunter** episode *Run to Earth* and as Rankin in *The Lonely Place*.

Moreno John
Played Pierre in the **Return of the Saint** episode *The Imprudent Professor*.

Moreno Juan
Played the waiter in **The Persuaders!** episode *To the Death, Baby*.
Played Helmut in the **Virgin of the Secret Service** episode *Entente Cordiale*.

Morgan Bill
Played a Mexican bandit in the **UFO** episode *Mindbender*.

Morgan Charles
Played the Captain in the season two **Ghost Squad** episode *A First Class Way to Die*.
Played Arthur Phillips in the **Randall and Hopkirk [Deceased]** episode *A Disturbing Case*.
Played Inspector Welland in the first season **The Saint** episode *The Invisible Millionaire*.

Morgan Diana
Co-wrote, with Angus McPhail, **The Scarlet Pimpernel** episodes *Antoine and Antoinette* & *A Tale of Two Pigtails*.

Morgan Garfield

Played Stavaros in **The Baron** episode *Night of the Hunter*.

Played Mendham in the **Department S** episode *Spencer Bodily is 60 Years Old*.

Played Downs in the season two **Ghost Squad** episode *The Grand Duchess*.

Played Paul Morris in the **G.S.5** episode *Dr. Ayre*.

Played Gilley in the **Man in a Suitcase** episode *The Sitting Pigeon*.

Played Peter Hayward in **The Persuaders!** episode *Take Seven*.

Played Carlson in the **Randall and Hopkirk [Deceased]** aka **My Partner the Ghost** episode *The House on Haunted Hill* and Edwards in *You Can Always find a Fall Guy*.

Played Mundt in the third season **The Saint** episode *The Art Collectors*.

Morgan Guy

Wrote **The Four Just Men** episode *The Night of the Precious Stones* and the **G.S.5** episode *Scorpion Rock*.

Morgan Liz

Provided the voices for Rhapsody/Destiny Angel on **Captain Scarlet and the Mysterons**.

Morgan Patrick

Played Paul in **The Count of Monte Cristo** episode *The Talleyrand Affair*.

Morgan Priscilla

Played Mavis in the **Man in a Suitcase** episode *The Girl who Never was*.

Morgan Richardson

Played the security man in **The Adventurer** episode *Icons are Forever*.

Morgan Stanley

Played the Lieutenant in the **Sir Francis Drake** episode *Drake on Trial*.

Morgan Terence

Played Foster in **The Persuaders!** episode *To the Death, Baby*. Starred in the title role throughout the series **Sir Francis Drake**. Also played Hugh Graveney in *Drake on Trial*.

Morhain Joseph

Co-wrote the third season **The Saint** episode *The Best Laid Schemes* [with A. Sandford Wolfe].

Morko

Played Riko Miura in the **Shirley's World** episode *The Lovers*.

Morley Donald

Guest starred as Sloane in **The Champions** episode *Project Zero*.

Played Charley in the first series **Ghost Squad** episode *Ticket for Blackmail*.

Played Superintendent Browning in the **Gideon's Way** episode *Gang War*.

Played Freddie Moran in the **G.S.5** episode *Seven Sisters of Wong*.

Played Lebrun in the **Interpol Calling** episode *The Heiress*.

Played Inspector Clayton in the **Randall and Hopkirk [Deceased]** aka **My Partner the Ghost** episode *Never Trust a Ghost*.

Played Inspector Daws in the third season **The Saint** episode *The Fast Women*.

Played the Priest in **The Sentimental Agent** episode *Express Delivery*.

Played the clown in the **Sword of Freedom** episode *The Reluctant Duke*.

Morrell David

Played several roles in **The Adventures of Sir Lancelot** before becoming a regular as Sir Kay: Clodion in *The Ferocious Fathers*, Boltan in *Roman Wall*, Sir Claud in *Winged Victory*, Bartelot in *Sir Bliant* and Porter in *The Black Castle*; was Sir Kay in *The Outcast*, *The Magic Sword*, *Caledon*, *Shepherd's War*, *The Pirates*, *Ruby of Radnor*, *The Lesser Breed*, *The Magic Book*, *Knight Errant*, *The Theft of Excalibur*, *Sir Crustabread*, *The Ugly Duckling*, *The Lady Lilith*, *Knight's Choice* & *Thieves*.

Played Det. Sgt. Miller in **The Baron** episode *The Maze*.

Guested as Krasner in **The Champions** episode *The Fanatics*.

Played the driver in the **Department S** episode *The Soup of the Day*.

Played Maxin in the first season **The Saint** episode *The Well-Meaning Mayor*.

Morris Artro

Played Owen Davies in **The Baron** episode *Epitath for a Hero*.

Played Green in the **Father Brown** episode *The Mirror of the Magistrate*.

Played Louis in the **Return of the Saint** episode *The Diplomat's Daughter*.

Played the hotel clerk in **The Sentimental Agent** episode *The Beneficiary*.

Morris Aubrey

Guest starred as Van Velden in **The Champions** *The Invisible Man*.

Played Harris in the second season **Danger Man [aka Secret Agent]** episode *Yesterday's Enemies* & Fortunato Santos in *The Affair at Castelevara*. In series three played Tamasio in *The Paper Chase*.

Played Kenneth in the **Man in a Suitcase** episode *Variation on a Million Bucks* [two parter: also a movie: *To Chase a Million*].

Played the Town Crier in **The Prisoner** episode *Dance of the Dead*.

Played Garton in the **Return of the Saint** episode *One Black September*.

Played Pebbles in the second season **The Saint** episode *Lida*.

Played Rattan in **The Sentimental Agent** episode *The Beneficiary*.

Played the High Priest in the first season **Space 1999** episode *Mission of the Darians*.

Morris Chester

Featured in the **Espionage** episode *Castles In Spain*.

Morris Ernest

Directed the first season **The Saint** episode *The Ever-loving Spouse*.

Directed the **White Hunter** episodes *The General*, *The Treasure of Tippu Tib*, *The Stepfathers*, *The No-Account*, *The Prisoner*, *Squire of the Serengeti*, *Sister my Spouse*, *The Trophy*, *Pegasus*, *The Plague*, *The Lonely Place*, *The Long Knife*, *Dead Man's Tale*, *Gun Duel*, *Second Dealer*, *Voodoo Wedding* & *Valley of the Dead*.

Directed the **William Tell** episodes *Gessler's Daughter*, *Undercover*, *The Bear*, *Secret Weapon*, *The Spider* and *The Master Spy*.

Morris Ernie

Assistant Director on **The Prisoner** episode *Many Happy Returns*.

Morris Geoffrey

Played Dilling in **The Protectors** episode *Thinkback*.

Played the second man at the party in fourth season **The Saint** episode *The Double Take*.

Morris Joseph

Played the medic in the **UFO** episode *Ordeal*.

Morris Lana
Played Ellen Summers in the **H. G. Wells' Invisible Man** episode *Death Cell*.
Played Teresa in the first season **The Saint** episode *Teresa*.

Morris Mary
Played Dr Ibanez in the season two **Ghost Squad** episode *The Magic Bullet*.
Played Ingrid Hoffman in the **Interpol Calling** episode *White Blackmail*.
Played the New Number Two in **The Prisoner** episode *Dance of the Dead*.

Morris Michael
Make-up on **The Baron**.

Morris Robert
Played Max in the season four **The Saint** episode *The Master Plan*.

Morris Wolfe
Played Sakuma in **The Adventurer** episode *Deadlock*.
Played the chef in the first series **The Adventures of Robin Hood** episode *The Inquisitor*.
Played Nadkarni in **The Champions** episode *The Gun-Runners*.
Played Takla in the **Department S** episode *A Fish out of Water*.
Played Hoyoto in the season two **Ghost Squad** episode *East of Mandalay*.
Played Andraes in the **H. G. Wells' Invisible Man** episode *The Decoy*.
Played Vitorio in the **Jason King** episode *A Royal Flush*.
Played Colonel Filipe Garcia in the **Man in a Suitcase** episode *Burden of Proof*.
Played Gorgo in the first season **The Saint** episode *Sophia* and Dr. Lopez in the third season's *Locate and Destroy*.

Morse Barry
Starred as Mr Parminter in the series **The Adventurer** and directed the episodes *Action!*, *Mr Calloway is a Very Cautious Man* & *Make it a Million*.
Played Victor Lawrence in the third season **The Saint** episode *The Reluctant Revolution*.
Played the Governor in the **Sir Francis Drake** episode *Escape*.
Starred in season one of **Space 1999** as Prof. Victor Bergman.
Starred as ex-Canadian Air Force Lieutenant Alec Marlowe, codename the Tiger, in the series **The Zoo Gang**.

Mort Patricia
Starred as Sally Lomax in the series **Ghost Squad** & **G.S.5** [played Rose in the season two **Ghost Squad** episode *The Missing People*].

Mortimer Caroline
Played Kate Barnaby in the fourth season **The Saint** episode *The Organisation Man*.
Played Dione in the first season **Space 1999** episode *The Last Enemy*.

Mortimer Trisha
Played Peggy Gale in the **Strange Report** episode *Report 4821: X-RAY: 'Who Weeps For the Doctor?'*.
Played Lily Jones in the **Virgin of the Secret Service** episode *The Persuasion of a Million Drops*.

Morton Anthony
aka/see John Creasey

Morton Anthony
Played Wolkowsky in the season two **Ghost Squad** episode *The Missing People*.

Played Portagee in the second season **The Saint** episode *The Unkind Philanthropist*.

Morton Clive
Played Garfield Cameron in the **Man in a Suitcase** episode *No Friend of Mine*.
Played The Ambassador in the **Sir Francis Drake** episode *Boy Jack*.
Played Colonel Devereaux in the **Virgin of the Secret Service** episode *The Rajah and the Suffragette*.

Morton David
Played Detective Sergeant Merton in the **Father Brown** episode *Three Tools of Death*.

Morton Helen
Played Helen in the first season **Danger Man** episode *Find and Destroy*.

Morton Hugh
Played Parker in the **Interpol Calling** episode *Diamond S.O.S.*.
Played Bishop in the second season **The Protectors** episode *Fighting Fund*.
Played the manservant in the third season **The Saint** episode *The Persistent Patriots* and the attendant in the fourth season's *The Ex-King of Diamonds*.

Morton Judee
Played Jenny Kersh in the fourth season **The Saint** episode *Where the Money Is*.

Moruzzi Franco
Played Carlo in the **Return of the Saint** episode *The Murder Cartel*.

Mosley Bryan
Played the first sleuth in the third season **The Saint** episode *When Spring is Sprung*.

Moss Basil
Played Doctor Frazer in the **UFO** episode *Exposed*, Doctor Harris in *Ordeal* and the doctor in *The Dalotek Affair* & *The Sound of Silence*.

Moss Frank L.
Wrote the **White Hunter** episodes *The General* & *Operation Transfer*.

Moss Gerald
Second Unit Cameraman on the series **Department S** and **Randall and Hopkirk [Deceased]** aka **My Partner the Ghost**.

Mountain Terry
Played Peters in **The Baron** two parter *Storm Warning* [*Storm Warning* - part 1 and *The Island* - part 2: also exists as a feature called *Mystery Island*].
Played the gendarme in the third season **The Saint** episode *The Counterfeit Countess*.

Mower Patrick
Appeared as Fleming in **The Adventurer** episode *Return to Sender*.
Played Greene in the **Department S** episode *The Soup of the Day*.
Played Achille in the **Jason King** episode *Nadine*.
Played Raphael Santana in the second season **The Protectors** episode *Implicado*.
Played Reilly in the second season **Space 1999** episode *All That Glisters*.
Played Cass Fowler in the **UFO** episode *The Square Triangle*.

Moxey Hugh
Played Bement in the season three **The Adventures of Robin Hood** episode *To Be a Student*.
Played Sir Arthur Lindsay in the first season **Danger Man** episode *The Conspirators*.
Played James Purley in the **White Hunter** episodes *Rogue Man & Run to Earth*. Played Captain Hagen in *No Survivors*, the A.D.C. in *The No-Account* and the Commissioner in *Voodoo Wedding*.

Moxey John
Directed **The Baron** episodes *Red Horse, Red Rider, Epitath for a Hero, The Legions of Ammak, Samurai West & Portrait of Louisa*.
Directed **The Champions** episode *The Iron Man*.
Directed the **Gideon's Way** episodes *The Nightlifers* and *State Visit*.
Directed the second season **Man of the World** episodes *The Enemy & In the Picture*.
Directed **The Saint** episodes *The Elusive Ellshaw* [season 1]; *Jeannine, The Golden Frog, The Smart Detective & The Imprudent Politician* [2] and *The Russian Prisoner & The Best Laid Schemes* [3].

Moynihan Daniel
Played Bert in the **Strange Report** episode *Report 3906: COVER GIRLS: 'Last Year's Model'*.

Mudie Leonard
Played Cambrai in **The Count of Monte Cristo** episode *Victor Hugo*.

Muir Douglas
Played Doctor Jerome in the season two **The Saint** episode *The Contract*.

Muir James
Played a guard/auction client in the **Father Brown** episode *The Arrow of Heaven*.

Muir John
Wrote, with Brian Degas, the **Shirley's World** episode *The Defective Defector*.

Mulhare Edward
Played a number of roles in the second series of **The Adventures of Robin Hood**: the first soldier in *The Scientist*, Ulf in *Blackmail*, the Man-at-Arms in *The Goldmaker*, Le Blond in *The Impostor*, the Lieutenant in *Ransom*, Baron Mornay in *The Haunted Mill*, the steward in *The Black Patch*, the foppish Lord in *The Trap* & the courtier in *Ambush*.

Mullally Donn
Script Consultant on **White Hunter** and wrote the episodes *The Stepfathers, Squire of the Serengeti, Day of Reckoning, Sister my Spouse, Pegasus* [with Lee Loeb], *The Plague, The Lonely Place* [with Alan Cillou] and *The Hungry Hell*.

Mullen Barbara
Played Elsbeth in the first series of **The Adventures of Robin Hood** episode *The Thorkill Ghost*.
Played Violet Warshed in the first season **The Saint** episode *The Gentle Ladies*.
Played the Mother Superior in the **White Hunter** episode *Sister my Spouse*.

Muller Endre
Played the patrolman in the first season **Danger Man** episode *Time to Kill*.
Played Shultz in the season two **Ghost Squad** episode *The Man with the Delicate Hands*.
Played the chauffeur Played Hugo in the **H. G. Wells' Invisible Man** episode *The White Rabbit*.

Played Black Eagle in the **Sir Francis Drake** episode *The Fountain of Youth*.

Muller Robert
Wrote the **Man in a Suitcase** episode *The Bridge*.

Mullins Bartlett
Played Acardi in the first season **Danger Man** episode *The Deputy Coyannis Story*.
Played Chamacy in the second season **Man of the World** episode *In the Picture*.
Played the Committee Chairman in **The Prisoner** episode *A Change of Mind*.
Played the bald man in the first season **The Saint** episode *The Ever-loving Spouse*.
Played Josep in the **Virgin of the Secret Service** episode *Russian Roundabout*.

Mullins Peter
Art Director on **William Tell**.

Mulock Al
Featured in the **Espionage** episode *We, the Hunted*.
Played the Lieutenant in **The Four Just Men** episode *Justice For Gino*.
Played Dwight Sherman in the season two **Ghost Squad** episode *Quarantine at Kavar*.
Played Vincent in **The Sentimental Agent** episode *A Very Desirable Plot*.

Mundell Michael
Played Ken Matthews in the **UFO** episodes *Identified & Computer Affair*.

Munro Nan
Played Felicity McDee in *Adventure Five* of **Sapphire and Steel**.

Munro Pauline
Played Alison Clifton in the **Gideon's Way** episode *The Nightlifers*.
Played Cassie in the third season **The Saint** episode *The Power Artist*.

Munroe Carmen
Played Carmen Congoto in **The Persuaders!** episode *Greensleeves*.

Munroe Gregory
Played Otis in the **Return of the Saint** episode *The Arrangement*.

Murcell George
Played the Sheriff's guard in the second series of **The Adventures of Robin Hood** episode *The Trap*.
Played Jaggyd in **The Adventures of Sir Lancelot** episode *Caledon*.
Played Ofeg Cossackian in **The Baron** episode *The Legions of Ammak* and Captain Sereda in *Time to Kill*.
Guested as Nikko in **The Champions** episode *Reply Box No: 666* and as El Caudillo in *The Iron Man*.
Played Bruno in the first season **Danger Man** episode *Bury the Dead*.
Played Ernst Frenke in **The Four Just Men** episode *The Godfather*.
Played Slattery in the season two **Ghost Squad** episode *The Big Time*.
Played Kautsky in the **Gideon's Way** episode *The Great Plane Robbery*.
Played Bonisalvi in the **Jason King** episode *That isn't Me, It's Somebody Else*.
Played Zorakin in **The Persuaders!** episode *Nuisance Value*.

Played Mandrake in the **Randall and Hopkirk [Deceased]** aka **My Partner the Ghost** episode *Somebody just Walked over my Grave*.

Played Abdul Graner in the second season **The Saint** episode *The Saint Bids Diamonds*. In the third season played Vogler in *The Death Game* & *The Power Artist*.

Voiced Professor Popkiss and Masterspy in the first season of **Supercar** [Cyril Shaps took over for the second season].

Played Baglione in the **Sword of Freedom** episode *Caterina* and Duiseppe in *Cristina*.

Murcott Derek
Played the Admiral in **The Champions** episode *The Ghost Plane*.

Murcott Joel
Co-wrote, with Ralph Gilbert Bettinson, **The Scarlet Pimpernel** episodes *The Winged Madonna, The Ambassador's Lady, Something Remembered* & *Sir Percy's Wager*.

Murphy Aidan
Played the Room 22 guard in the **UFO** episode *The Psychobombs*.

Murphy Ann
Stage Manager on **Sapphire and Steel**.

Murphy Wesley
Played the second airman in the first season **Danger Man** episode *The Brothers*.

Played the Sergeant in the **Sir Francis Drake** episode *The Irish Pirate*.

Murray Anne
Played the nurse in the **G.S.5** episode *Seven Sisters of Wong*.

Murray Barbara
Played Lady Diana Battersley in **The Adventurer** episode *The Not-So-Merry Widow*.

Played Gerda in the first season **Danger Man** episode *The Sisters*.

Played Tania in the **Department S** episode *Dead Men Die Twice*.

Played Simone in the **Jason King** episode *A Red, Red Rose Forever*.

Played Iris Lansing in the first season **The Saint** episode *Iris* and Denise in *The Good Medicine*.

Played Mrs Sanders in the **Strange Report** episode *Report 4407: HEART: 'No Choice for the Donor'*.

Murray Elisabeth
Played Sheila O'Rourke in the **Virgin of the Secret Service** episode *The Amazons*.

Murray Mitch
Composed the music for **The Protectors** theme *Avenues and Alleyways* [lyrics by Peter Callander].

Murray Peter
Played Mullins in the first season **Danger Man** episode *The Sanctuary*.

Murton Lionel
Played Chris Jefford in **The Adventurer** episode *Has Anyone Here Seen Kelly?*.

Starred as, regular, Colonel Keller in the debut season of **Danger Man**: *Time to Kill, The Contessa* and *Under the Lake*.

Played the District Attorney in **The Four Just Men** episode *The Discovery*.

Played Birdie in the first series **Ghost Squad** episode *Eyes of the Bat*.

Played the General in the **H. G. Wells' Invisible Man** episode *The Decoy*.

Played Thackeray in the **Interpol Calling** episode *The Three Keys*.

Played Coughlin in the **Man in a Suitcase** episode *Man from the Dead*.

Played Ben in **The Persuaders!** episode *Angie. . . Angie*.

Played Cedric Parton in the second season **The Protectors** episode *Goodbye George*.

Played the Registrar in the **Strange Report** episode *Report 8319: GRENADE: 'What Price Change?'*.

Starred as the Chief throughout the series **O.S.S.**

Muscat Angelo
Regular, as the Butler, in **The Prisoner**: *Arrival, The Chimes of Big Ben, A. B. and C., Free for All, The Schizoid Man, The General, Dance of the Dead, Checkmate, Hammer into Anvil, It's Your Funeral, A Change of Mind, Do Not Forsake Me Oh My Darling, Once Upon A Time* & *Fall Out*.

Musgrave Michael
Played a passenger in the **Father Brown** episode *The Curse of the Golden Cross*.

Musgrove Ron
Played the police Sergeant in the **Father Brown** episode *The Head of Caesar* and a commercial traveller in *The Quick One*.

Myers Gary
Featured in the series **UFO** as, regular, Lew Waterman.

Myers Marion
Wrote **The Buccaneers** [aka **Dan Tempest**] episode *Pirate Honour*.

Myers Peter
Played Colonel Barfield in the **Department S** episode *Who Plays the Dummy?*.

Myers Stuart
Played the priest in the **Father Brown** episode *The Head of Caesar*.

****

Nadia Katya
Appeared as a dancer in the **Virgin of the Secret Service** episode *The Pyramid Plot*.

Nagazumi Yasuko
Played Moriko in the **Shirley's World** episode *A Hell of an Engineer*.
Played, second season regular, Yasko in **Space 1999**.

Nagy Bill
Played Controller in **The Champions** episode *The Dark Island*.
Played Cuevos in **The Count of Monte Cristo** episode *The Portuguese Affair*.
Played Mario in the debut season **Danger Man** episode *The Contessa* and Col. Fernandez in *Hired Assassin*. In series two [now aka **Secret Agent**] played George Murgia in *The Mirror's New*.
Played Paolo Cortoli in the **Department S** episode *The Trojan Tanker*.
Played Garnes in **The Four Just Men** episode *Dead Man's Switch*.
Played Roblez in the first series **Ghost Squad** episode *Catspaw* [this episode was shot for the first series, but due to an actors' strike, was originally shown as a season two episode].
Guested as Bill Grant in the **Interpol Calling** episode *The Chinese Mask* and as Sash in *Fingers of Guilt*.
Played Joe Sholto in the first season **The Saint** episode *The Element of Doubt*, David Stern in *The Good Medicine* and Tony Unciello in *The Latin Touch*.
Played the agent in the **Shirley's World** episode *The Defective Defector*.
Played Corsia in the **Sir Francis Drake** episode *The Bridge*.

Naidoo Bobby
Played the Headman in the first series **Man of the World** episode *The Frontier*.

Naidoo R. Bobby
Played the police sergeant in the first season **Danger Man** episode *The Journey Ends Halfway* and Chin Lee in *Sabotage*.

Naidu Leela
Played Dr Bahandi in the first series **Man of the World** episode *The Frontier*.

Naish J. Carrol
Starred as Charlie Chan in **The New Adventures of Charlie Chan**.

Naismith Laurence
Guested as Sir William de Courcier in the debut season of **The Adventures of Robin Hood** episode *The Miser*.
Played Spooner in the first season **Danger Man** episode *The Blue Veil*.
Starred as, series regular, Judge Fulton in **The Persuaders!**: *Overture, The Gold Napoleon, Take Seven, Powerswitch, Angie. . . Angie, That's Me Over There, The Long Goodbye, Element of Risk, Five Miles to Midnight* & *The Morning After*.
Played Schelpin in the first series **The Protectors** episode *Balance of Terror*.
Played General Platt in the **Return of the Saint** episode *The Poppy Chain*.
Played Sir Miles in the **Sir Francis Drake** episode *The Garrison*.

Namkos Peter
Played Victor in **The Count of Monte Cristo** episode *Andorra*.

Napier Russell
Played Inspector George in the **Man in a Suitcase** episode *Why they Killed Nolan* and Doctor Green in the **UFO** episode *A Question of Priorities*.

Nappi Malya
Played the bank clerk in the fourth season **The Saint** episode *Vendetta for the Saint* [part 1].

Nasagumi Yasuko
Starred in the first series of **The Protectors** as, regular, Harry Rule's au pair Suki.

Nash Brian
Guested as Johnny in the **Interpol Calling** episode *Mr George*.

Nash Charles
Make-up on **The Buccaneers** [aka **Dan Tempest**] episodes *The Raiders, Captain Dan Tempest, Dan Tempest's War with Spain, The Wasp, Whale Gold, Slave Ship, Gunpowder Plot, Articles of War, Ghost Ship, Conquest of New Providence, Mother Doughty's Crew, Blood Will Tell, Hurricane, Dead Man's Rock, Dangerous Cargo, Hand of the Hawk, Gentleman Jack and the Lady, Mr. Beamish and the Hangman's Noose, Marooned, Before the Mast, Dan Tempest and The Amazons, The Ladies, The Surgeon of Sangre Rojo, The Return of Calico Jack, Conquistador, Aztec Treasure, Prize of Andalusia, Cutlass Wedding, Dan Tempest Holds an Auction, Flip and Jenny, To the Rescue, Indian Fighters, Mistress Higgins' Treasure, The Spy Aboard, The Decoy, Pirate Honour, Instrument of War* and *Printer's Devil*.

Nasti Gustavo
Played the third reporter in the **Return of the Saint** episode *The Roman Touch*.

Nation Terry
Script Editor on **The Baron** and wrote the episodes: *Red Horse, Red Rider, Epitath for a Hero, Something for a Rainy Day, And Suddenly You're Dead* [with Dennis Spooner], *Masquerade* [with Dennis Spooner: two parter: *Masquerade* - part 1 and *The Killing* - part 2: edited together, also exists as a feature entitled *Man In a Looking Glass*], *Portrait of Louisa, There's Someone Close Behind You* [with Dennis Spooner], *Storm Warning* [two parter: *Storm Warning* - part 1 and *The Island* - part 2: also exists as a feature entitled *Mystery Island*], *A Memory of Evil* [with Dennis Spooner], *The Seven Eyes of Night, Night of the Hunter, So Dark the Night* [with Dennis Spooner], *Roundabout, The Man Outside* & *Countdown*.
Wrote **The Champions** episodes *The Fanatics* & *The Bodysnatchers*.
Wrote the **Department S** episodes *A Cellar Full of Silence* & *The Man in the Elegant Room*.
Seved as Story Consultant and Associate Producer on **The Persuaders!** Wrote the episodes *Take Seven, Someone Like Me, Chain of Events, A Home of One's Own, Five Miles to Midnight, A Death in the Family* & *Someone Waiting*.
Wrote the second season **The Protectors** episodes *Bagman, Baubles, Bangles and Beads, Route 27* and *A Pocketful of Posies*.
Wrote the **The Saint** episodes *The Revolution Racket* [teleplayed from a story by Harry W. Junkin], *Sibao, The Contract, The Inescapable Word, The Crime of the Century, The Sign of the Claw* & *The Man who could not Die* [series 2]; *Invitation to Danger* [3] and *The Desperate Diplomat, The Time to Die* & *Where the Money Is* [4].

National Studios, Elstree
Studio used for the filming of the series **H. G. Wells' Invisible Man, The Scarlet Pimpernel** and **William Tell**.

Naughton Alita
Played Lydia Merritt in the **Gideon's Way** episode *Morna*.

Naughton David
Second Assistant Editor on **The Prisoner**.

Naylor Tom
Played the German officer in the **O.S.S.** episode *Operation Dagger* and Paul Fouchet in the first season **The Saint** episode *The Work of Art*.

Nazarin Ken
Played the fisherman in the **Jason King** episode *Every Picture Tells a Story*.

Neal David
Played Jerry Sandford in **The Persuaders!** episode *Someone Waiting*.

Neal Patricia
Featured in the **Espionage** episode *The Weakling*.

Neame Christopher
Played Bailey in the second season **The Protectors** episode *Blockbuster*.

Nearn Graham
Managing Director of Caterham Cars. Supplied the Lotus Seven for **The Prisoner** episode *Fall Out*, the original having been exported. Can be seen in *Fall Out* polishing his charge.

Needs Philip
Played Franco in the first season **The Saint** episode *The Charitable Countess*.

Neep Rebecca
Casting secretary on **The Prisoner**.

Negin Louis
Played Amin in the **Man in a Suitcase** episode *The Revolutionaries*.
Played Claude in **The Zoo Gang** episode *Mindless Murder*.

Neil Hildegard
Played Lyra Delon in the **Jason King** episode *Flamingos only Fly on Tuesdays*.
Played Irina Gayevska in the second season **The Protectors** episode *The Last Frontier*.
Played the Catwoman in the second season **Space 1999** episode *Devil's Planet*.

Neilsen Trudi
Played Gretchen in the third season **The Saint** episode *The Gadget Lovers*.

Neilson Perlita
Played the title role in **The Four Just Men** episode *Marie*.
Played Anna in the **William Tell** episode *Gessler's Daughter*.

Neilson Richard
Played Lloyd Elsom in the **White Hunter** episode *The Jackals*.

Nelson Gwen
Played Mrs. Halloway in the **Randall and Hopkirk [Deceased]** aka **My Partner the Ghost** episode *The Trouble with Women*.

Nennett Richard
Played Hobson in **The Scarlet Pimpernel** episode *The Elusive Chauvelin*.

Nesbitt Derren
Played a variety of roles in **The Adventures of Sir Lancelot**: Andred in *The Ferocious Fathers*, the guard in *The Outcast*, Sir Tristran in *Winged Victory*, Breuse in *Sir Bliant*, Dion in *The Magic Sword*, Firth in *Lancelot's Banishment*, Gogus in *Roman Wall*, the first brigante in *Caledon*, Chad in *Shepherd's War*, Mac Kevin in *The Pirates*, Magnu in *The Black Castle*,

the cook-monk in *The Magic Book*, Sir Oringle in *Knight Errant* and Tristram in *The Theft of Excalibur*.
Played Hans Vogeler in the first season **Danger Man** episode *Time to Kill* and Hugo in *The Brothers*. In the second series [now aka **Secret Agent**] played Noureddine in *Sting in the Tail*.
Played John 'Benny' Benson in the **Gideon's Way** episode *The Tin God*.
Played the corporal in the **H. G. Wells' Invisible Man** episode *Crisis in the Desert* and Stephan in *Point of Destruction*.
Played Lucas Guardino in the **Man in a Suitcase** episode *Dead Man's Shoes*.
Played Polikoff in the first series **Man of the World** episode *Specialist for the Kill*.
Played Groski in **The Persuaders!** episode *The Old, the New and the Deadly*.
Guest starred as the New Number Two in **The Prisoner** episode *It's Your Funeral*.
Made two appearances in the first series of **The Protectors**: as Brad Huron in *Disappearing Trick* and as Foster in *Talkdown*.
Played Inspector Lebec in the **Return of the Saint** two parter *Collision Course* [Part 1: *The Brave Goose* & part 2: *The Sixth Man*: also exists as a movie entitled *The Saint and the Brave Goose*].
Played Netchideff in the first season **The Saint** episode *The Sporting Chance*.
Played Lewis in **The Sentimental Agent** episode *Meet my Son, Henry*.
Played Di Lucca in the **Sword of Freedom** episode *The Marionettes*.
Played Craig Collins in the **UFO** episode *The Man who Came Back*.
Appeared in several roles in **William Tell**: *The Emperor's Hat* - as the sentry, *The Traitor* - as the Sergeant, *The Boy Slaves* - as Schulemburg, *Voice in the Night* - as Frederick, *The Lost Letter* - as Frederick and *The Gauntlet of St. Gerhardt* - as Captain Werner.

Nesbitt Derry - aka/see Derren **Nesbitt**

Nesbitt Francis
Wrote the second series of The **Adventures of Robin Hood** episode *The Blackbird*.

Nethercott Geoffrey
Directed the season two **Ghost Squad** episode *Quarantine at Kavar*.

Nettheim David
Played Cravos in **The Baron** episode *Night of the Hunter*, the Doctor in **The Prisoner** episode *The Schizoid Man*, Leader in the **Man in a Suitcase** episode *Man from the Dead*, Inspector Crepi in the third season **The Saint** episode *Simon and Delilah*. and Kontell in the **Virgin of the Secret Service** episode *The Persuasion of a Million Drops*.

Nettlefold Studios, Walton-on-Thames
Studio used for the filming of **The Adventures of Robin Hood** [first two seasons: Walton Studios was used for seasons three & four] and **The Adventures of Sir Lancelot**.

Nettleton John
Guested as Booker in **The Champions** episode *Full Circle*.
Played Carter in the **Department S** episode *The Man from X*.
Played Inspector Hill in the first series **The Protectors** episode *Talkdown*.

Neuman Sam
Writer on **The New Adventures of Charlie Chan**.

Neve Suzanne
Played Linda in the first series **Man of the World** episode *Shadow of the Wall*.

Played Meryl Vascoe in the first season **The Saint** episode *The Benevolent Burglary* and Julia Jeffroll in the second season's *The Frightened Inn-Keeper*.
Played Mary Rutland in the **UFO** episodes *A Question of Priorities, Mindbender & Confetti Check A-O.K.*

Neves Vivien
Played Danny's girl in **The Persuaders!** episode *Someone Like Me.*

Neville John
Played Charlie in the first series **The Protectors** episode *Triple Cross.*
Played Sir Everard in the **Shirley's World** episode *Knightmare.*

Nevinson Nancy
Played the Director in the first series **Man of the World** episode *Shadow of the Wall.*
Played Dona Luisa Arroyo in the second season **The Saint** episode *The Spanish Cow.*
Played Madame Cassis in **The Scarlet Pimpernel** episode *Antoine and Antoinette.*
Played the housekeeper in the **UFO** episode *The Man who Came Back.*

New World Productions
Produced **Gideon's Way** for ITC World Wide Distribution.
Produced the first two seasons of **The Saint** for ITC World Wide Distribution [Bamore produced the third and fourth].

Newall Basil
Make-up on **Jason King**.

Newark Derek
Played Lucas in **The Baron** episode *Something for a Rainy Day* and Calvin Baggio in the two parter *Storm Warning* [*Storm Warning* - part 1 and *The Island* - part 2: also exists as a feature called *Mystery Island*].
Played Kruger in **The Champions** episode *The Final Countdown.*
Played Clark in the **Department S** episode *Last Train to Redbridge.*
Played Hartman in the **Jason King** episode *A Red, Red Rose Forever.*
Played Rudy in the **Man in a Suitcase** episode *All that Glitters* and Maurice in *Blind Spot.*
Played Lloyd in **The Persuaders!** episode *That's Me Over There.*
Played Reece in the second season **The Protectors** episode *The Tiger and the Goat.*
Played Wright in the **Return of the Saint** episode *The Obono Affair.*
Played Carl in the third season **The Saint** episode *The Counterfeit Countess* and German in the fourth season's *Where the Money Is.*

Newby Valli
Played Sirocco in **The Baron** episode *The Legions of Ammak.*

Newell Joan
Played Mrs Barrington in the second series **Danger Man** [aka **Secret Agent**] episode *Loyalty Always Pays.*
Played Mrs Reynold in the fourth season **The Saint** episode *The People Importers.*
Played the hotel proprietress in the **Strange Report** episode *Report 7931: SNIPER: 'When is Your Cousin Not?'.*

Newell Michelle
Played Madge in the **Father Brown** episode *The Head of Caesar.*
Played Genevieve in the **Return of the Saint** episode *Collision Course* [Part 1: 'The Brave Goose': also exists, combined with

the second instalment as a movie entitled *The Saint and the Brave Goose*].

Newell Patrick
Played Alex in the second series **Danger Man** [aka **Secret Agent**] episode *The Battle of the Cameras.*
Played the fat man in **The Persuaders!** episode *That's Me Over There.*
Played Mannering in the **Randall and Hopkirk [Deceased]** aka **My Partner the Ghost** episode *The Man from Nowhere.*
Played Ridou in **The Sentimental Agent** episode *A Little Sweetness and Light.*
Played Chen in the **Shirley's World** episode *Figuratively Speaking.*

Newlands Anthony
Played the Commissar in the **H. G. Wells' Invisible Man** episode *Shadow on the Screen.*
Played Cuevos in **The Champions** episode *Get Me Out of Here!.*
Played Frederick in **The Count of Monte Cristo** episode *Mecklenburg.*
Played Ma'Suud in the third season **Danger Man** [aka **Secret Agent**] episode *I can only Offer you Sherry.*
Played Phillipe in the first season **The Saint** episode *The Good Medicine*, the doctor in the fourth season's *Vendetta for the Saint* [part 2] and Father Bellini in *The Charitable Countess.*
Starred as, series regular, Lord Richard Hastings in **The Scarlet Pimpernel**: *The Farmer's Boy, Gentlemen of the Road, The Winged Madonna, Antoine and Antoinette, The Imaginary Invalides, The Flower Woman, The Christmas Present, The Ambassador's Lady, Sir Andrew's Fate, Something Remembered, A Tale of Two Pigtails, The Princess & Sir Percy's Wager.*

Newling Desmond
Played Bolton in the **Sir Francis Drake** episode *The Garrison* and Rietti in *Mission to Paris.*

Newman Nanette
Played Hannah in the **Interpol Calling** episode *White Blackmail.*
Played Geraldine McLeod in the second season **The Saint** episode *The Miracle Tea Party.*
Played Yana in the **Sir Francis Drake** episode *The Slaves of Spain.*

Newman Robert
Wrote the third series **The Adventures of Robin Hood** episode *The Mark.*

Newman Sam
Wrote the **Interpol Calling** episode *Checkmate.*

Newmark Rayner
Played Lord Arthur in the **Shirley's World** episode *The Berkeley Club Caper.*

Newney Raul
Played a policeman in the **Return of the Saint** episode *The Nightmare Man.*

Newth Jonathan
Played Captain Arapoff in the **Virgin of the Secret Service** episode *Russian Roundabout.*

Newton-John Rona
Played the nurse in **The Adventurer** episode *Full Fathom Five.*
Also played a nurse in the **UFO** episode *The Man who Came Back.*

Ney Marie
Played Madame de Seiberd in **The Four Just Men** episode *The Grandmother*.

Ngakane Lionel
Played Moses Amadu in the first season **Danger Man** episode *Deadline*.
Played Sam in the **O.S.S.** episode *Operation Barbecue*.

Nichol Madelena
Appeared as Chrissie in **The Champions** episode *The Experiment*.

Nichol Stuart
Played the man in the corridor in **The Adventurer** episode *Miss Me Once, Miss Me Twice and Miss Me Once Again*.
Played Pete in the first season **The Saint** episode *The Everloving Spouse*.

Nicholls Anthony
Played Samuel Cookson in **The Adventurer** episode *To the Lowest Bidder*.
Starred in **The Champions** as Tremayne.
Played Sir Walter Fenchurch in the **Man in a Suitcase** episode *The Bridge*.
Played George Marsh in the first season **The Saint** episode *The Gentle Ladies* and Lord Cranmore in the third season's *The Angel's Eye*.
Played Dr Warren in the first season **Space 1999** episode *The Troubled Spirit*.
Played Zanobi in the **Sword of Freedom** episode *Marriage of Convenience*.
Played Doctor Grant in the **Department S** episode *The Ghost of Mary Burnham*.

Nichols Dandy
Played the landlady in the **Man in a Suitcase** episode *Man from the Dead*.
Played Mina Remberg in the **Shirley's World** episode *A Mother's Touch*.

Nichols Robert
Played Robert Pargo in the second season **The Saint** episode *The Hi-Jackers*.

Nicholson Audrey
Played Rachel Gully in the **Gideon's Way** episode *The Reluctant Witness*.

Nicholson Nora
Played Mrs Manningham in the second series **Danger Man** [aka **Secret Agent**] episode *The Galloping Major*.
Played Hortense in the third season **The Saint** episode *The Queen's Ransom*.

Nick Bill
Played the first gunman in **The Prisoner** episode *Living in Harmony*.

Nicols Rosemary
Starred throughout the series **Department S** as Annabelle Hurst.
Played Moria in the **Man in a Suitcase** episode *Day of Execution*.
Played Melanie Sadler in **The Persuaders!** episode *Greensleeves*.

Nielson Claire
Starred as, series regular, Jean Carter in season two of **Ghost Squad**: *Interrupted Requiem, Sentences of Death, The Golden Silence, The Missing People, Lost In Transit, The Man With the Delicate Hands, Hot Money, The Grand Duchess, A First*

Class Way to Die, The Desperate Diplomat, The Last Jump, The Heir Apparent, Polsky, The Magic Bullet & The Menacing Mazurka.
Returned as Jean Carter to star throughout **G.S.5**.

Nightingale Benny
Played the second removal man in the second series **Danger Man** [aka **Secret Agent**] episode *Loyalty Always Pays*.

Nightingale Laura
Wardrobe Supervisor on **The Adventurer, The Baron, The Champions, Department S** and **Gideon's Way**.
Costume Supervisor on **Jason King** & **Randall and Hopkirk [Deceased]** aka **My Partner the Ghost**.

Nightingale Michael
Played Picton Jones in the second series **Danger Man** [aka **Secret Agent**] episode *The Colonel's Daughter*.
Appeared as the night supervisor in **The Prisoner** episode *Dance of the Dead*.
Played Mary's father in the **UFO** episode *Confetti Check A-O.K.*

Nimmo Derek
Played Lord Winrod in **The Buccaneers** [aka **Dan Tempest**] episode *Dangerous Cargo*.
Played Prior in the second series **Ghost Squad** episode *Interrupted Requiem*.

Ninchy Kate
Played Bridget O'Rourke in the **Virgin of the Secret Service** episode *The Amazons*.

Nissen Brian
Appeared as Sir Gawaine in **The Adventures of Sir Lancelot** episode *Sir Crustabread*.
Played Paul Lambert in the season two **Ghost Squad** episode *The Man with the Delicate Hands*.
Played Carlo Orsini in the **Sword of Freedom** episode *The Eye of the Artist*.
Played Jerry Douglas in the **White Hunter** episode *The Jackals*.

Noble Patsy Ann
Played Susan Wade in the third season **Danger Man** [aka **Secret Agent**] episode *Not So Jolly Roger*.

Noble Christopher
Assistant Director on the first season of **The Adventures of Robin Hood**.
Assistant Director on **The Adventures of Sir Lancelot** episodes *The Knight with the Red Plume, The Ferocious Fathers* and *The Queen's Knight*.
Assistant Director on **The Buccaneers** [aka **Dan Tempest**] episode *Blackbeard*.

Noble Larry
Played Michael Smith in the **Father Brown** episode *The Man with Two Beards*.

Noble Shaun
Appeared in the first season of **The Adventures of Robin Hood**.

Nolan Doris
Played Prince John's wife in the first series of **The Adventures of Robin Hood** episode *The Prisoner*.
Played Maude Inverest in the first season **The Saint** episode *The Latin Touch*.
Played Miss Gray in the **Strange Report** episode *Report 3906: COVER GIRLS: 'Last Year's Model'*.

Nolan John
Appeared as the young guest in **The Prisoner** episode *Do Not Forsake Me Oh My Darling*.
Played Korvis in the **Return of the Saint** episode *Hot Run*.
Played Cliff Hunt in the **Strange Report** episode *Report 8319: GRENADE: 'What Price Change?'*.

Nolan Margaret
Played Mrs Elliot in the second series **Danger Man** [aka Secret Agent] episode *Parallel Lines Sometimes Meet*.
Played Sophie in **The Persuaders!** episode *Element of Risk*.

Norman Gerard
Played the spaceship pilot in the **UFO** episode *Conflict*.

Norman Leslie
Directed **The Baron** episodes *Diplomatic Immunity, The Persuaders & Farewell to Yesterday*.
Directed **The Champions** episode *The Search*.
Directed the **Department S** episodes *A Small War of Nerves, Spencer Bodily is 60 Years Old & The Soup of the Day*.
Directed the **Gideon's Way** episodes *The Housekeeper, The Lady Killer, To Catch a Tiger, The Great Plane Robbery, Fall High, Fall Hard, The Wall & A Perfect Crime*.
Directed **The Persuaders!** episodes *Anyone Can Play, The Old, the New and the Deadly, That's Me Over There, The Man in the Middle, Nuisance Value & The Morning After*.
Directed the **Randall and Hopkirk [Deceased]** aka **My Partner the Ghost** episodes *Never Trust a Ghost, A Sentimental Journey & It's Supposed to be Thicker than Water*.
Directed the **Return of the Saint** episodes *One Black September, The Village that Sold its Soul, The Armageddon Alternative, The Debt Collectors & Dragonseed*.
Directed **The Saint** episodes: *Lida, The Loving Brothers, The Sign of the Claw, The Crooked Ring, The Chequered Flag & The Saint Bids Diamonds* [series 2]; *The Convenient Monster, The Angel's Eye, Interlude in Venice, Locate and Destroy, The Reluctant Revolution, The Paper Chase, The Fast Women, The Death Game, The Counterfeit Countess, Island of Chance & The Power Artist* [3] and *The Organisation Man, The Double Take, The Master Plan & The World Beater* [4].
Directed the **Shirley's World** episode *A Mother's Touch*.

Norman Valerie
Continuity on **The Champions**.

Normington John
Played Arthur Carstairs in the **Father Brown** episode *The Head of Caesar*.
Played Brian Dukes in the second season **The Protectors** episode *Sugar and Spice*.

North Virginia
Played Francoise in the **Department S** episode *The Mysterious Man in the Flying Machine*.

Norton Jim
Appeared as Morgan in **The Adventurer** episode *Somebody Doesn't Like Me*.

Nossek Ralph
Played Beni in the season two **Ghost Squad** episode *Quarantine at Kavar*.
Played Grand Duke Pavlacek-Falkenberg in the **Virgin of the Secret Service** episode *Pride of Assassins*.

Nott Grenville 'Gren'
Art Director on **Joe 90**; Camera Operator Manager on **The Secret Service** and Assistant Art Director on **Thunderbirds**.

Nottage Douglas
Played the SHADO maintenance engineer in the **UFO** episode *Timelash*.

Novelli Mario
Played gunman number two in the **Return of the Saint** episode *The Murder Cartel*.

****

Oakes Harry
Lighting Cameraman [Visual Effects Main Unit] on **Joe 90**, Special Effects Lighting Cameraman on **Space 1999**, Lighting Cameraman [Special Effects Second Unit] on **Thunderbirds** and Special Effects Lighting Cameraman on **UFO**.

Oates Robert
Played Larry in the **Timeslip** story *The Time of the Ice Box* [series parts 7 - 12].

Oates Simon
Played Mike Taylor in the **Department S** episode *The Trojan Tanker*.
Played Johnny De Souza in the second season **Ghost Squad** episode *The Thirteenth Girl*.
Played Broggi in the **Jason King** episode *That isn't Me, It's Somebody Else*.
Played Simon Croft in the **Man in a Suitcase** episode *Web with Four Spiders*.

O'Brine Paddy Manning
Co-wrote the **O.S.S.** episode *Operation Big House* [with Paul Dudley].
Wrote the **The Saint** episodes *The Miracle Tea Party* & *The Set-Up* [season 2] and *Interlude in Venice* [3].

O'Casey Ronan
Played Perkins in **The Buccaneers** [aka **Dan Tempest**] episode *Indian Fighters*.
Played the pilot in the first season **Danger Man** episode *The Island*.
Played Joe in **The Four Just Men** episode *The Rietti Group* and Dexter in *The Slaver*.
Appeared as Dick Goodwyn in the **White Hunter** episode *Out of the Wind* and as Harvey Benson in *Deadfall*.

O'Casey Shivaun
Played Francine in the **Man in a Suitcase** episode *Jigsaw Man*.
Appeared as the nurse in **The Prisoner** episode *Checkmate*.

Occhipinti Andrea
Played Leo in the **Return of the Saint** episode *Dragonseed*.

O'Connell Maurice
Played Slater in the second season **The Protectors** episode *Blockbuster*.

O'Connell Patrick
Played Ryder in **The Persuaders!** episode *The Time and the Place*.
Played Reagan in the first series **The Protectors** episode *A Kind of Wild Justice*.
Played Rogers in the third season **The Saint** episode *The Persistent Patriots*.
Played Jago in the **Strange Report** episode *Report 4977: SWINDLE: 'Square Root of Evil'*.

O'Connolly Jim
Wrote the **Gideon's Way** episode *State Visit*.
Directed the third series **The Saint** episodes *The Gadget Lovers* & *When Spring is Sprung* and the fourth season season two parter *Vendetta for the Saint*.

O'Connor John
Second Assistant Director on **The Prisoner**. Appeared in crowd scenes, as a gardener in *Arrival* and as a Pawn in *Checkmate*.

O'Connor Joseph
Played Stephano in the **Sword of Freedom** episode *The Ship*.

O'Dell Etain
Played Miss Fowler in the **Virgin of the Secret Service** episode *The Great Ring of Akba*.

Odengo Chief
Appeared as the Witch Doctor in the **White Hunter** episode *Killer Leopard*.

Odunton Muriel
Played Mora in the **Return of the Saint** episode *The Obono Affair*.

O'Farrell Bernadette
Starred as, series regular, Lady Marian Fitzwalter aka Maid Marian in the first two seasons of **The Adventures of Robin Hood** [Paricia Driscoll took over]: *Maid Marian, The Inquisitor, The Knight who Came to Dinner, The Challenge, Queen Eleanor, Checkmate, The Ordeal, Husband for Marian, The Highlander, The Youngest Outlaw, The Betrothal, The Brothers, The Intruders, The Sheriff's Boots, Richard the Lionheart, The Deserted Castle, Trial by Battle, Children of the Greenwood, The Byzantine Treasure, Table's Turned, The Traitor, The Thorkill Ghost & The Prisoner* [season one] and *A Village Wooing, Blackmail, A Year and a Day, The Goldmaker, The Impostor, Isabella, The Haunted Mill, The Black Patch, The Dream, The Blackbird, Ambush, The Goldmaker's Return, The Secret Pool, The Path of True Love* aka *Locksley Hall, Too Many Earls, The Mystery of Ireland's Eye, The Little People, The Infidel, The Frightened Tailor, The Black Five, The Road in the Air* & *Carlotta* [season two].

O'Ferrall George More
Directed **The Adventures of Sir Lancelot** episode *The Ugly Duckling*.

Offenbach Rudolf
Played the manservant in the first season **Danger Man** episode *The Girl who Liked GIs*.
Played Dr. Weltmann in the season two **Ghost Squad** episode *The Last Jump*.
Played Labourdet in the **O.S.S.** episode *Operation Death Trap*.

Official Films Incorporated
The Buccaneers [aka **Dan Tempest**] was "An Official Films Incorporated Presentation".

Offor Dick
Played Memba in the **Man in a Suitcase** episode *The Whisper*.

O'Flynn Philip
Played Alfred Powls in the first season **The Saint** episode *The Gentle Ladies*.

Ogden Edward
Played Edward Sharp in the fourth season **Danger Man** [aka **Secret Agent**] episode *Shinda Shima* [*Shinda Shima* was also merged with the only other surviving fourth season colour episode, *Koroshi*, to form a TVM entitled *Koroshi*].
Played the Sergeant in the season two **Ghost Squad** episode *Escape Route*.

Ogilvie Barbara
Played Mrs Rance in the first season **The Saint** episode *The Bunco Artists*.

Ogilvy Ian
Played Toby in the **Strange Report** episode *Report 2493: KIDNAP: 'Whose Pretty Girl Are You?'*.
Starred as Simon Templar, The Saint, throughout the **Return of the Saint** series.

O'Grady Tony - pen name of/see Brian **Clemens**

O'Hagan Michael
Played Michael Flood in the **Father Brown** episode *The Mirror of the Magistrate*.

O'Hara Gerry
Directed the **Man in a Suitcase** episode *The Sitting Pigeon*.

O'Hara Quinn
Played Cathy in the third season **The Saint** episode *Interlude in Venice*.
Played Sylvia Graham in the **UFO** episode *Ordeal*.

O'Hara Riggs
Played Bill in **The Sentimental Agent** episode *All that Jazz*.

Olegario Frank
Played the old Indian in **The Buccaneers** [aka **Dan Tempest**] episode *The Surgeon of Sangre Rojo*.
Played the plainclothes man in the second series **Danger Man** [aka **Secret Agent**] episode *The Colonel's Daughter*.
Played Khan in the first series **Ghost Squad** episode *Hong Kong Story* and Akbar in the season two episode *Death of a Sportsman*.
Played Guzik in the first series **Man of the World** episode *Specialist for the Kill*.
Played Padron in the first season **The Saint** episode *Teresa* and the Bartender in *The Pearls of Peace*.

Oliver Donald
Played Jim in the season two **Ghost Squad** episode *The Heir Apparent*.
Appeared as the policeman in the third season **The Saint** episode *Flight Plan*.

Oliver Tom
Played the first technician in the **UFO** episode *The Sound of Silence* and the doctor in *Confetti Check A-O.K.*

Olsen Pauline
Played Enid in **The Adventures of Sir Lancelot** episode *The Ferocious Fathers*.

O'Mara Kate
Played Jane Purcell in **The Champions** episode *To Trap a Rat*.
Played Annette in the second series **Danger Man** [aka **Secret Agent**] episode *A Room in the Basement*.
Played Pietra in the **Department S** episode *Who Plays the Dummy?*.
Played Delphi in the **Jason King** episode *A Kiss for a Beautiful Killer*.
Played Heidi in **The Persuaders!** episode *Read and Destroy*.
Played Sara Trent in the second season **The Protectors** episode *A Pocketful of Posies*.
Played Teresa Montesino in the third season **The Saint** episode *The Fast Women* & Nadine/Yvette in *The Counterfeit Countess*. Played Annabel II in the fourth season's *The Double Take*.

O'Neal Bob
Appeared as the co-pilot in the **O.S.S.** episode *Operation Fracture*.

O'Neil Robert
Played Red Johnson in the second series **Danger Man** [aka **Secret Agent**] episode *Such Men are Dangerous*.
Played Willis Burnham in the first season **The Saint** episode *The Element of Doubt*.

O'Neons Doug
Camera Operator on **The Zoo Gang**.

Orchard David
Played the second security man in the third season **Danger Man** [aka **Secret Agent**] episode *The Man who wouldn't Talk*.
Played Ace in the **Gideon's Way** episode *The Great Plane Robbery*.

Orchard John
Played Marvin in **The Baron** episode *The Maze*.
Played Gregor in **The Persuaders!** episode *The Man in the Middle*.

O'Regan Terence
Played the assassin in **The Count of Monte Cristo** episode *Naples*.

O'Reilly Maureen
Played Duchess Therese in **The Count of Monte Cristo** episode *The Luxembourg Affair*.

O'Riordan Shaun
Played a number of roles in the second series of **The Adventures of Robin Hood**: the guard in *Blackmail*, Surgeon Calend in *A Year and a Day*, Will in *The Goldmaker*, Quentin in *The Impostor*, the Page in *Isabella*, Jack in *The Hero*, the Seneschal in *The Haunted Mill*, Quentin in *Outlaw Money*, the Lieutenant in *The Black Patch*, Edward in *The Friar's Pilgrimage*, Archer in *The Trap*, the first groom in *Hubert*, the sailor in *The Dream*, Quentin in *The Blackbird*, Wall Eye in *The Shell Game*, Prince John's Captain in *Ambush* and the blind man in *The Bandit of Brittany*.
Played Sir Cebus in **The Adventures of Sir Lancelot** episode *The Queen's Knight*.
Producer on the **Sapphire and Steel** series. Also directed *Adventure One*, *Two* - with David Foster, *Three* and *Five*.

Orloff Oreste
Played Le Bon in **The Four Just Men** episode *The Night of the Precious Stones*.

Orme Geoffrey
Co-wrote the **Interpol Calling** episode *Slave Ship* [with Gil Winfield and Edwin Richfield].

Ornadel Cyril
Music on the **Sapphire and Steel** series.

Orton Harold
Co-wrote the **Interpol Calling** episode *Desert Hi-Jack* [with Robert Stewart].

Oryff Stefan
Played Krosnic in the **Jason King** episode *To Russia With ....Panache*.

Osborne Zorenia
Played the receptionist in the second series **Danger Man** [aka **Secret Agent**] episode *The Mercenaries*.
Played M'Kame in the **White Hunter** episode *Killer Leopard*.

Oscar Henry
Played Henri Mate in **The Count of Monte Cristo** episode *The Texas Affair*.
Played The Ruler in the season two **Ghost Squad** episode *The Heir Apparent*.
Played Renoir in the **Interpol Calling** episode *Desert Hi-Jack*
Played Doctor Kleine in the **William Tell** episode *The Magic Powder*.

O'Shea Milo
Played Carpiano in the first series **The Protectors** episode *A Case for the Right*.

O'Shea Steven
Played Rob in *Adventure One* of **Sapphire and Steel**.

Osmond Hal
Played Anselem in the first series **The Adventures of Robin Hood** episode *Errand of Mercy* & the King's Commissioner in

Trial by Battle. In season two he featured as Master Ricardo in *The Path of True Love* [aka *Locksley Hall*] and as Spinner in the third series episode *Lincoln Green*.

O'Sullivan Richard
Played Prince Arthur in **The Adventures of Robin Hood** episode *The Double* [Peter Asher & Jonathan Bailey also appeared in the role] and as Will in *The Challenge of the Black Knight* - both season three episodes.
Played Aldo Shargis in the third season **Danger Man** [aka **Secret Agent**] episode *Two Birds with One Bullet*.
Played Pietro in **The Four Just Men** episode *The Man With the Golden Touch*.
Played Perk in the **Strange Report** episode *Report 2493: KIDNAP: 'Whose Pretty Girl Are You?'*.
Played Alberto in the **Sword of Freedom** episode *Chart of Gold*.

Oswald Bobbie
Played Mimi in the **Strange Report** episode *Report 3906: COVER GIRLS: 'Last year's Model'*.

O'Toole Mickey
Chargehand Propsman on **The Prisoner**.

O'Toole Peter
Played the first soldier in **The Scarlet Pimpernel** episode *A Tale of Two Pigtails*.

Ottaway James
Played Sideman in the **Gideon's Way** episode *Gang War*.
Played Bradley in the second series **The Protectors** episode *Zeke's Blues*.
Played Dr. Cranston in the first season **The Saint** episode *The Elusive Ellshaw*.

Otway John
Played a police Inspector in the **G.S.5** episode *It Won't be a Stylish Marriage*.

Oulton Brian
Played Sir John in the third series **The Adventures of Robin Hood** episode *Quickness of the Hand*.
Played Major Langley in **The Buccaneers** [aka **Dan Tempest**] episode *Pirate Honour*.
Played Doctor Davis in the **Department S** episode *A Cellar full of Silence*.
Played Dixon in the **G.S.5** episode *An Eye for An Eye*.
Played Griffin in the **Jason King** episode *An Author in Search of Two Characters*.
Played Dr. Plevitt in the **Randall and Hopkirk [Deceased]** aka **My Partner the Ghost** episode *Never Trust a Ghost*.
Played Joe in the first season **The Saint** episode *The Fellow Traveller*.

Owen Bill
Played Mark in the second series **The Adventures of Robin Hood** episode *The Hero*.
Played Clip West in **The Buccaneers** [aka **Dan Tempest**] episode *Marooned*.
Played Lord Gormond in the **Man in a Suitcase** episode *The Bridge*.
Played Joe Burns in the **Shirley's World** episode *The Colonel*.
Played Otello in the **Sword of Freedom** episode *The Assassin*.

Owen Clare
Played the secretary in the **G.S.5** episode *The Goldfish Bowl*.

Owen Dickie
Played Sergeant Jones in the **Man in a Suitcase** episode *All that Glitters*.
Played the cab driver in the first season **The Saint** episode *The Man who was Lucky*.

Owen Gillian
Played Katherine in **The Adventures of Sir Lancelot** episode *Sir Bliant*.
Played Maria in **The Buccaneers** [aka **Dan Tempest**] episodes *Conquest of New Providence*, *Hurricane* and *Conquistador*.
Played the mother in **The Four Just Men** episode *The Man With the Golden Touch*.

Owen Glen
Played Randall in the second series **Danger Man** [aka **Secret Agent**] episode *Colony three*.

Owen Glyn
Played Smith in the **H. G. Wells' Invisible Man** episode *The Rocket*.
Played Gill in the **Interpol Calling** episode *Eight Days Inclusive*.
Played Superintendent Kinglake in the first season **The Saint** episode *The Fellow Traveller*.
Played Anton in the **William Tell** episodes *The Bride* and *The Master Spy*.

Owen John
Casting on **Randall and Hopkirk [Deceased]** aka **My Partner the Ghost**.

Owen Joy
Played Betty McQuaig in the **G.S.5** episode *A Cast of Thousands*.

Owens Richard
Played Sgt. Richards in **The Baron** episode *Portrait of Louisa*.
Played George Brading in **The Champions** episode *Autokill*.
Played the Naval Lieutenant in the second series **Danger Man** [aka **Secret Agent**] episode *A Date with Doris* and James in *The Black Book*.
Played the lorry driver's Mate in the **Man in a Suitcase** episode *Essay in Evil*.
Played the police Sgt. bodyguard in the **Randall and Hopkirk [Deceased]** aka **My Partner the Ghost** episode *Vendetta for a Dead Man*.
Played Shoni Morgan in the third season **The Saint** episode *The House on Dragon's Rock* and Cody in *Island of Chance*.

Oxley David
Played Sir Adrian in the season three **The Adventures of Robin Hood** episode *Castle in the Air*.
Played Ahmed in the first season **Danger Man** episode *The Nurse*.
Played Terry Flynn in the **White Hunter** episode *The Prisoner*.

Oxley Michael
Played the passport officer in the season two **Ghost Squad** episode *Lost in Transit* and the hotel clerk in *The Magic Bullet*.

Oxman Philip
Played the first American in the season two **Ghost Squad** episode *Mr Five Per Cent*.

****

Padwick Anne
Played the woman with the baby in **The Buccaneers** [aka **Dan Tempest**] episode *Dead Man's Rock*.
Played the woman in **The Four Just Men** episode *The Deserter*.
Played Marie in **The Scarlet Pimpernel** episode *The Christmas Present*.
Played Beatrice in the **Sword of Freedom** episode *The Lion and the Mouse*, Isabella in *The Reluctant Duke* and Lady Adrianna in *Adrianna*.

Page Lisa
Played Hele in the first series **Man of the World** episode *A Family Affair*.

Page Veronica
Played the first girl in the **Virgin of the Secret Service** episode *The Great Ring of Akba*.

Paget-Bowman Cicely
Played Lady Denby in the second series **Danger Man** [aka **Secret Agent**] episode *Colony Three*.
Played the Headmistress in the second season **The Protectors** episode *Sugar and Spice*.

Pagett Nicola
Played Nicola in the second series **Danger Man** [aka **Secret Agent**] episode *The Mirror's New*.
Played Cathy Bellman in the **Gideon's Way** episode *The Alibi Man*.
Played Carla Faversham in the **Man in a Suitcase** episode *Burden of Proof*.
Played Carla Wilks in **The Persuaders!** episode *The Long Goodbye*.

Paisner Dina
Played Consuelo in the first season **The Saint** episode *The Pearls of Peace*.

Paiva Nestor
Played Louis in **The Count of Monte Cristo** episode *Andorra*.

Pajo Louise
Played Marla in the **Strange Report** episode *Report 4977: SWINDLE: 'Square Root of Evil'*.
Played the nurse in the **UFO** episode *Kill Straker!* and Miss Scott in *Court Martial*.

Palermini Piero
Played the bartender in the **Return of the Saint** episode *The Murder Cartel*.

Palk Anna
Played Michelle Andre in the **Jason King** episode *Wanna Buy a Television Series aka A Face I Used to Know*.
Played Marie in **The Persuaders!** episode *The Time and the Place*.
Played Kate in the first series **The Protectors** episode *A Kind of Wild Justice*.

Pallo Jackie
Played Terry in the **Return of the Saint** episode *Tower Bridge is Falling Down*.

Palmer Donald
Played the estate agent in the **UFO** episode *Confetti Check A-O.K.*.

Palmer Ernest
Director of Photography on **The Adventures of Sir Lancelot** episodes *The Outcast, Winged Victory, Sir Bliant, The Magic Sword, Lancelot's Banishment, Roman Wall, Caledon, Shep-*

herd's War, The Pirates, The Black Castle, Double Identity, The Bridge, The Witch's Brew, The Magic Book, Knight Errand, The Theft of Excalibur, The Mortaise Fair, Maid of Somerset, Sir Crustabread, The Ugly Duckling, The Prince of Limerick, The Lady Lilith, Knight's Choice, The Missing Princess & The Thieves.

Palmer Geoffrey
Played Anstruther in **The Baron** two parter *Masquerade* [*Masquerade* - part 1 and *The Killing* - part 2: edited together, also exists as a feature entitled *Man In a Looking Glass*].
Played Jeff Grant in the **Gideon's Way** episode *The Alibi Man*.
Played Pete Ferguson in the first season **The Saint** episode *The Rough Diamonds*.

Palmer Greg
Played the Swiss policeman in the **Jason King** episode *A Red, Red Rose Forever*.

Palmer John
Focus puller [second unit] on **The Prisoner**.

Palmer Keith
Editor on **Strange Report**.

Palmer Lilli
Starred as Madame Manouche Roget, codename the Leopard, in the series **The Zoo Gang**.

Palmer Nicholas
Wrote the **G.S.5** episode *Party for Murder*.
Wrote the **Strange Report** episode *Report 7931: SNIPER: 'When is your Cousin Not?'*.
Editor on the series **Virgin of the Secret Service** and wrote the episodes *Dark Deeds on the Northwest Frontier* and *The Professor Goes West*.

Palmer Sidney 'Sid'
Property Buyer on **The Champions, Department S & The Prisoner**.

Palmer Toni
Played Sally in the **Gideon's Way** episode *The Wall*.

Palmer Valentine
Played Ronald in the fourth season **The Saint** episode *The Man Who Gambled with Life*.

Panczak Hugo
Played Heinz in **The Champions** episode *The Survivors*.
Played the SHADO mobile operator in the **UFO** episode *The Square Triangle*.

Pantelone Sal
Played the Bank Manager in the second season **The Protectors** episode *Fighting Fund*.

Pantera Malou
Played Janine in **The Four Just Men** episode *Village of Shame* and Mouche in *The Beatniques*.
Played the beauty shop girl in the first series **Man of the World** episode *Masquerade in Spain*.

Paoluzzi Luciana
Played Little Fawn in the **Sword of Freedom** episode *Vespucci*.

Paquis Garard
Played Henri Valentine in the **Father Brown** episode *The Oracle of the Dog*.

Parfitt Judy
Played the title role in the second series **The Protectors** episode *Lena*.
Played Anne Liskard in the third season **The Saint** episode *The Persistent Patriots*.
Played Sally Clare in **The Sentimental Agent** episode *The Height of Fashion*.

Parke Macdonald
Played John Crane in **The Count of Monte Cristo** episode *The Texas Affair*.

Parker Anthony
Played a soldier in the **William Tell** episode *The Magic Powder*.

Parker Cecil
Played Lord Gillingham in the third season **The Saint** episode *A Double in Diamonds*.

Parker Mibs
Hairdresser on **Jason King**.

Parker Ross
Played Sgt. Soustelle in the first season **The Saint** episode *Judith*.

Parkes Roger
Wrote **Man in a Suitcase** episode *Who's Mad Now?*.
Wrote **The Prisoner** episode *A Change of Mind*.
Wrote the story for the **Return of the Saint** episode *Yesterday's Hero* [teleplayed by John Kruse].
Wrote the **Strange Report** episodes *Report 0846: LONELYHEARTS: 'Who Killed Dan Cupid?'* & *Report 4821: X-RAY: 'Who Weeps For the Doctor?'*.

Parkes Timothy
Played Walther in **The Persuaders!** episode *The Ozerov Inheritance*.

Parkinson Roy
Production Manager on **The Buccaneers** [aka **Dan Tempest**] episodes *The Raiders, Captain Dan Tempest, Dan Tempest's War with Spain, The Wasp, Whale Gold, Slave Ship, Gunpowder Plot, Before the Mast, Dan Tempest Holds an Auction, The Ladies, The Surgeon of Sangre Rojo, Prize of Andalusia, Cutlass Wedding, Flip and Jenny, To the Rescue, Indian Fighters, Mistress Higgins' Treasure, The Spy Aboard, The Decoy, Pirate Honour, Instrument of War* & *Printer's Devil*.

Parmentier Richard
Played Demmell in the **Return of the Saint** episode *The Imprudent Professor*.

Parnell Jack
Music and theme on the **Father Brown** series.

Parnell Norma
Played Chloe in the season three **The Adventures of Robin Hood** episode *Pepper*.
Played Sarah Brion in **The Buccaneers** [aka **Dan Tempest**] episode *To the Rescue*.
Played the salesgirl in **The Four Just Men** episode *The Last Days of Nick Pompey*.
Played Lisa Orsini in the **Sword of Freedom** episode *The Eye of the Artist* and Prospera in *The Reluctant Duke*.
Played Maria in the **William Tell** episode *The Baroness* and Tina in *The Young Widow*.

Parr Derek
Assistant Director on **Gideon's Way**.

Parrish Clifford
Played Mister Roach in the fourth season **The Saint** episode *The Scales of Justice*.

Parritt Clive
Played Davey in the season three **The Adventures of Robin Hood** episode *The Angry Village*.

Parry Gordon
Directed the final series of **The Adventures of Robin Hood** episodes *Bride for an Outlaw, The Pharaoh Stones, The Champion, The Edge and the Point* and *The Truce*.

Parry Ken
Played Marty Cranwell in **The Baron** episode *There's Someone Close Behind You*.
Played Grant in the **G.S.5** episode *An Eye for An Eye*.

Parry Lesley
Played Iris in the season three **The Adventures of Robin Hood** episode *Pepper*.

Parry Loretta
Featured in the **Espionage** episode *The Light of the Friendly Star*.
Played Angelina in the first season **The Saint** episode *The Charitable Countess*.

Parry Lynne
Played Consuelo in the **Sir Francis Drake** episode *The Prisoner*.

Parry Natasha
Played Maria in the second season **Man of the World** episode *The Bandit*.
Played Countess Inez in the **Sir Francis Drake** episode *The Prisoner*.

Parsons Alibe
Starred as, second season regular, Alibe in **Space 1999**.

Parsons Derek
Dubbing editor on **The Buccaneers** [aka **Dan Tempest**] episode *Articles of War*.

Parsons Ian
Played Henri in the first season **The Saint** episode *The Benevolent Burglary*.

Parsons Nicholas
Guested as Sir Walter in the debut season of **The Adventures of Robin Hood** episode *Trial by Battle*.

Pasco Richard
Played De Vere in the second series of **The Adventures of Robin Hood** episode *Hubert*, Rufus in *Outlaw Money* and Sir Laurence in the third season's *Quickness of the Hand*.
Played Rodrigues in **The Buccaneers** [aka **Dan Tempest**] episode *Dead Man's Rock*.
Played Rivera in **The Four Just Men** episode *Dead Man's Switch* and Enrico Baldini in *Rogue's Harvest*.
Played the Duke of Ferrara in the **Sword of Freedom** episode *The Duke*.

Pastell George
Played Colonel Santos in **The Champions** episode *Operation Deep-freeze*.
Played Petel in the second series **Danger Man** [aka **Secret Agent**] episode *The Colonel's Daughter*.
Played Camilo Garria in the **Department S** episode *The Treasure of the Costa del Sol* and Sarrat in *Who Plays the Dummy?*

Played Cesar in **The Four Just Men** episode *Village of Shame*, Berto Fellini in *Rogue's Harvest* and Mazza in *Treviso Dam*.
Played Wang in the first series **Ghost Squad** episode *Hong Kong Story* and Mendoza in *Catspaw* [Catspaw was shot for the first series, but due to an actors' strike, was originally shown in season two]. Played Faria in the season two episode *P.G. 7*.
Guested as Captain Pagano in the **Interpol Calling** episodes *The Two-Headed Monster*, *The Man's Clown*, *The Thousand Mile Alibi* and *The Girl with Grey Hair*.
Played Sebastian in the first series **Man of the World** episode *Masquerade in Spain*.
Played Georges Olivant in the first season **The Saint** episode *The Covetous Headman*, King Fallouda in the third season's *The Queen's Ransom*, Vulanin in the third season's *When Spring is Sprung* and Marco Ponti in the fourth season two parter *Vendetta for the Saint*.
Played Dali in **The Sentimental Agent** episode *Box of Tricks*.

Patel Balu
Played the personal assistant to the Minister in the second series **Danger Man** [aka **Secret Agent**] episode *The Colonel's Daughter*.

Paterson Ann M.
Production Secretary on **The Persuaders!**

Paterson Hilary
Played Meg in the season two **The Adventures of Robin Hood** episode *Highland Fling*.

Patrick Ray
Played the officer in the first series **Man of the World** episode *The Sentimental Agent*.

Patrick Roy
Played the German police officer in the **Jason King** episode *A Page Before Dying*.
Played Georgio in the first season **The Saint** episode *The Latin Touch* and Big Tom in the second season's *The Old Treasure Story*.

Patterson Lee
Played Frankie Luca in the **Jason King** two parter *All that Glisters*.

Patterson Paula
Played Miss Hansen in the second season **The Protectors** episode *Baubles, Bangles and Beads*.

Pattillo Alan
Wrote the **Captain Scarlet and the Mysterons** episode *The Trap*.
Directed the **Fireball XL5** episodes *Hypnotic Sphere*, *The Doomed Planet*, *Space Immigrants*, *Spies in Space*, *The Last of the Zanadus*, *Space Vacation*, *The Granatoid Tanks*, *Drama at Space City*, *Invasion Earth*, *Trial by Robot* and *Space City Special*.
Directed the **Stingray** episodes *The Pilot* [aka *Stingray*], *Treasure Down Below*, *Countdown*, *Loch Ness Monster*, *Stand by for Action*, *Tom Thumb Tempest*, *An Echo of Danger*, *Titan goes Pop*, *The Cool Caveman*, *A Christmas to Remember* and *Aquanaut of the Year*.
Directed the first season **Supercar** episodes *Amazonian Adventure*, *False Alarm*, *Keep it Cool*, *Jungle Hazard*, *A Little Art*, *The Phantom Piper*, *Pirate Plunder*, *Flight of Fancy*, *Trapped in the Depths*, *The Lost City* & *The White Line* and the second season's *Precious Cargo*, *Calling Charlie Queen*, *70-B-Low* & *The Day Time Stood Still*.
Script Editor on **Thunderbirds**. Directed the first season episodes *Trapped in the Sky* [pilot], *The Perils of Penelope* [with Desmond Saunders], *Move and You're Dead* & *The Cham - Cham* and wrote *The Perils of Penelope*, *Move and You're Dead*, *Attack of the Alligators!*, *The Cham - Cham* & *Security*

Hazard [series 1] and *Alias Mr Hackenbacker* & *Give or Take a Million* [2].
Wrote the **UFO** episode *The Square Triangle*.

Paul Gloria
Played Lucy Sansetti in the **Gideon's Way** episode *The Reluctant Witness*.

Paul John
Played Edmund Wilson in the season two **Ghost Squad** episode *Sabotage*.
Played John Hammel in the second season **The Saint** episode *The Man who Liked Toys*.

Paulsen Carl
Played Raskolnikov in the **Virgin of the Secret Service** episode *Russian Roundabout*.

Pavey Vera
Continuity on **The Buccaneers** [aka **Dan Tempest**] episode *The Surgeon of Sangre Rojo*.

Payne Laurence
Played Skovic in **The Four Just Men** episode *The Godfather*.
Played Porton in the **Interpol Calling** episode *Cargo of Death*.
Played Noel Bastion in the third season **The Saint** episode *The Convenient Monster*.

Payne Sandra
Played Alice Short in the **Gideon's Way** episode *The Big Fix*.

Payne Tom
Played Joe Baker in the season two **Ghost Squad** episode *The Big Time*.

Payne Willie
Played the sergeant in the second series **Danger Man** [aka **Secret Agent**] episode *The Galloping Major*.
Played Sullivan in the second season **Ghost Squad** episode *The Thirteenth Girl*.

Paynter Robert, B.S.C
Director of Photography on **The Zoo Gang**.

Pays Howard
Played Richard/Alfred in **The Adventures of Sir Lancelot** episode *Double Identity*.
Played Pennington in **The Buccaneers** [aka **Dan Tempest**] episode *Mistress Higgins' Treasure*.
Played Holst in the first season **Danger Man** episode *The Lonely Chair*.
Played Jack Howard in the **H. G. Wells' Invisible Man** episode *Crisis in the Desert* and Sgt. Day in *Man in Disguise*.
Played Major Augustin in the **William Tell** episode *The Gauntlet of St. Gerhardt*, Vogler in *Gessler's Daughter* and Johan in *The Spider*.

Peach Mary
Played Smolenko in the third season **The Saint** episode *The Gadget Lovers*.

Peacock Keith
Appeared as the second guardian/croquet player in **The Prisoner** episode *Arrival*.

Peacock Trevor
Played the lodger in the **Man in a Suitcase** episode *Why they Killed Nolan*.

Peacock William
Played the secretary in the first season **Danger Man** episode *The Leak* and Azad in *Dead Man Walks*.

Played Girgio Rizzi in **The Four Just Men** episode *Rogue's Harvest*.
Played Lambert in the **Sir Francis Drake** episodes *The Flame Thrower & Lost Colony of Virginia*.
Played Klaus in the **William Tell** episode *Castle of Fear*.

Peake Lisa
Played the dancer in **The Sentimental Agent** episode *The Scroll of Islam*.

Peake Michael
Played the Seneschal in the second series of **The Adventures of Robin Hood** episode *The Frightened Tailor* and the Juggler in the fourth season's *Sybella*.
Played the President in the first season **Danger Man** episodes *The Honeymooners & The Prisoner*. In the third season [now aka **Secret Agent**] played Zepos in *The Hunting Party*.
Played Zolta in **The Four Just Men** episode *Mava* and Phillipe in *Marie*.
Played Dr Sanchez in the second season **Man of the World** episode *The Bullfighter*.
Played Hans Blatt in the first season **The Saint** episode *The Fellow Traveller* and Friste in the second season's *The Contract*.
Played the Governor in the **Sir Francis Drake** episode *Bold Enterprise*.
Played Malchus in the **Sword of Freedom** episode *Choice of Weapons* and the magistrate in *The Value of Paper & Violetta*.
Played the Landlord in the **William Tell** episode *The Bandit*.

Pearce Jackie
Played Jeannie in the second series **Danger Man** [aka **Secret Agent**] episode *Don't Nail Him Yet*.

Pearce Jacqueline
Played Ruth in the **Man in a Suitcase** episode *Somebody Loses, Somebody ...Wins?* and Miss Brown in *Sweet Sue*.
Played Brigitte Gautier in **The Zoo Gang** episode *The Counterfeit Trap*.

Pearce Sally
Played the barmaid in **The Buccaneers** [aka **Dan Tempest**] episode *Aztec Treasure*.

Pearce Tim
Played the editor in the second season **The Protectors** episode *The Insider*.

Pearce Timothy
Played the Spanish soldier in the **Sir Francis Drake** episode *Boy Jack*.

Pearl Arnold
Wrote the **Espionage** episode *The Weakling*.

Pearl Bert
Production Manager on **Man in a Suitcase**.

Pearson Donna
Played the American tourist in the first season **The Saint** episode *Sophia*.

Pearson Freda
Set Dresser on **Man in a Suitcase**.

Pearson H.C.
Sound on **The Adventures of Robin Hood**; **The Adventures of Sir Lancelot** episodes *The Knight with the Red Plume, The Ferocious Fathers & The Queen's Knight* and **The Buccaneers** [aka **Dan Tempest**] episode *Blackbeard*.

Pearson Lloyd
Played Doctor Wren in the **Gideon's Way** episode *The Housekeeper*.

Pearson Richard
Played Keith Smith in the first season **Danger Man** episode *Dead Man Walks*.
Played Bosanquet in the **Sir Francis Drake** episode *Bold Enterprise*.

Pearson Sid
Special Effects on **The Champions**.

Peck Brian
Played Carman in the **Man in a Suitcase** episode *Day of Execution*.

Peek Denys
Played Dante in **The Persuaders!** episode *The Ozerov Inheritance*.

Peel David
Played Sebastian in the **William Tell** episode *Undercover*.

Peel Richard
Played Richard Hyde in the **White Hunter** episode *The Lonely Place*.

Peer Salmaan
Played Ahmed in the third season **The Saint** episode *Flight Plan*. Played Suresh in the fourth season's *The People Importers* and the airline clerk in *Vendetta for the Saint* [part 1].
Played the Bus Boy in the **Strange Report** episode *Report 3424: EPIDEMIC: 'A Most Curious Crime'*.

Peers Leon
Played Martin in the first series **Man of the World** episode *The Runaways*.

Pegge Edmund
Played the policeman officer in the **Return of the Saint** episode *The Arrangement*.

Peisley Frederick
Played Doctor Winter in the second series **Danger Man** [aka **Secret Agent**] episode *The Mercenaries*.
Played Bowles in the second series **Ghost Squad** episode *Interrupted Requiem*.
Played Tiny Bray in the **Gideon's Way** episode *The Reluctant Witness*.
Played Paolo Morleiter in the second series **The Protectors** episode *Lena*.
Played Duke of Albany in the **Virgin of the Secret Service** episode *Entente Cordiale*.

Pellatt John
Associated Producer on the series **The Zoo Gang**.

Pember Ron
Played the taxi driver in the **Department S** episode *The Ghost of Mary Burnham*.
Played the workman in the second season **The Protectors** episode *Blockbuster*.
Played the fairground concessionaire in the **Randall and Hopkirk [Deceased]** aka **My Partner the Ghost** episode *Vendetta for a Dead Man*.
Played Sam in the fourth season **The Saint** episode *The People Importers*.
Played the shop manager in the **Strange Report** episode *Report 3906: COVER GIRLS: 'Last Year's Model'*.
Played the casting agent in the **UFO** episode *Timelash*.

Pemberton Charles
Played the security man in the **Return of the Saint** episode *Yesterday's Hero*.
Played the policeman in *Adventure One* of **Sapphire and Steel** [part 2].

Pemberton Frank
Played Woodcutter in **The Count of Monte Cristo** episode *The Grecian Gift* [aka *The Brothers*].

Pemberton Michael
Played the policeman in the third season **The Saint** episode *The Power Artist* and Egan the footman in the fourth season's *The Double Take*.

Pemberton Victor
Wrote the final instalment of the **Timeslip** story *The Year of the Burn-Up* [series parts 13 - 20: Bruce Stewart wrote episodes 13-19] and wrote *The Day of the Clone* [series parts 21 - 26].

Pendlebury Frank
Played the servant in **The Buccaneers** [aka **Dan Tempest**] episode *Prize of Andalusia*.

Pendry Richard
Played the American assistant in the **Jason King** episode *Wanna Buy a Television Series* aka *A Face I Used to Know*.

Penfold Christopher
First series Story Consultant on **Space 1999**. Wrote the first series episodes *War Games, Alpha Child, Dragon's Domain, Guardian of Piri, The Last Sunset* & *Space Brain* and the second season's *Dorzak*.

Penfold Helen
Hairdresser on **The Adventures of Sir Lancelot** episodes *Identity, The Bridge, The Witch's Brew, Ruby of Radnor, The Mortaise Fair, Maid of Somerset, Sir Crustabread, The Ugly Duckling, The Prince of Limerick, The Lady Lilith, Knight's Choice, The Missing Princess* and *The Thieves*.
Hairdresser on **The Baron** and **The Saint**.
Hairdressing Supervisor on **Gideon's Way**.

Penfold Len
Sound on **Sapphire and Steel**.

Penhaligon Susan
Played Emma in the **Return of the Saint** episode *The Imprudent Professor*.

Penn Dalia
Played Maria Pullerno in **The Baron** episode *The Long, Long Day*.
Played Juanita in **The Buccaneers** [aka **Dan Tempest**] episode *The Ladies*.

Pennell Nicholas
Played the young cop in the first season **The Saint** episode *The Elusive Ellshaw* and the intelligent undergraduate in the second season's *The Saint Steps In*.

Pennell Peter
Sound Editor on **Joe 90, The Protectors, Space 1999** & **UFO**.
Supervising Sound Editor on **The Secret Service**.

Penry-Jones Peter
Played John Godfrey in the **Father Brown** episode *The Curse of the Golden Cross*.

Pentelow Arthur
Played the landlord in **The Baron** episode *The Maze*.
Played Mr Lewis in the **Gideon's Way** episode *The Prowler*.

Penwarden Hazel
Appeared as Lady Bragwaine in **The Adventures of Sir Lancelot** episode *Knight Errant*.

Perceval Robert
Played Sir Charles Johnson in **The Buccaneers** [aka **Dan Tempest**] episode *Dan Tempest Holds an Auction* and Johnson in *Indian Fighters*.
Played Dan Reeves in **The Four Just Men** episode *The Bystanders*.
Played the American official in the **Man in a Suitcase** episode *The Boston Square*.
Played the General in the **O.S.S.** episode *Operation Sweet Talk* and the American General in *Operation Jingle Bells*.
Played Doctor Redfern in the **White Hunter** episode *The Plague*.

Percival Lance
Played Carl Gardner in **The Adventurer** episode *Skeleton in the Cupboard*.
Played Alfred Trim in the **Jason King** episode *Uneasy Lies the Head*.

Percy Esme
Played the blind man in **The Scarlet Pimpernel** episode *Something Remembered*.

Perkins Peter
Played Otto in the first season **The Saint** episode *The Saint Sees it Through*.

Perrins Leslie
Played Cavalo in **The Count of Monte Cristo** episode *The Portuguese Affair*.
Appeared as Harvey Baker in the **White Hunter** episode *The Treasure of Tippu Tib*.
Played Count Hegel in the **William Tell** episode *Manhunt*.

Perry Alan
Directed the **Captain Scarlet and the Mysterons** episodes *Manhunt, The Trap, The Heart of New York, Seek and Destroy, The Traitor, Treble Cross, Codename Europa* & *Inferno*.
Directed the **Joe 90** episodes *Hi-jacked, International Concerto, Big Fish, Business Holiday, Arctic Adventure, The Race* & *Talkdown*.
Directed **The Secret Service** episodes *A Case for the Bishop, Last Train to Bufflers Halt* and *May-day, May-day*.
Directed the **UFO** episodes *Kill Straker!, Close up, Survival, The Dalotek Affair* & *The Responsibility Seat*.

Perry Alan
Special Effects Camera Operator on **UFO**.

Perry Anthony
Producer on the series **Interpol Calling**.

Perry Desmond
Played the Northern Ireland Sergeant in **The Sentimental Agent** episode *May the Saints Preserve Us*.

Perry Morris
Played Schultz in **The Champions** episode *The Final Countdown*.
Played Beecham-Bennett in **The Persuaders!** episode *Chain of Events*.
Played Herbault in **The Zoo Gang** episode *Mindless Murder*.

Persica Giuliano
Played the first reporter in the **Return of the Saint** episode *The Roman Touch*.

Pertwee Carolyn
Played Sarah Pearson in the season two **Ghost Squad** episode *The Heir Apparent*.

Pertwee Michael
Wrote the first season **Danger Man** episode *Sabotage* [with Ian Stuart Black] and on series two - now aka **Secret Agent** - wrote *Fish on the Hook* [with John Roddick].
Wrote the **H. G. Wells' Invisible Man** episode *The Rocket*.
Wrote the first season **Man of the World** episode *The Runaways*.
Wrote **The Persuaders!** episodes *The Time and the Place* & *The Long Goodbye*.
Wrote the **Return of the Saint** episodes *The Obono Affair* & *The Diplomat's Daughter*.
Wrote the third series **The Saint** episodes *The Persistent Patriots, The Art Collectors* & *When Spring is Sprung*.

Pescud Richard
Played the hotel receptionist in the **Randall and Hopkirk [Deceased]** aka **My Partner the Ghost** episode *The Ghost who Saved the Bank at Monte Carlo*.

Peters Anet
Played a passenger in the **Father Brown** episode *The Curse of the Golden Cross*.

Peters Dennis Alaba
Starred in the series **Department S** as Sir Curtis Seretse.

Peters Leon
Played Alencon in the **Sir Francis Drake** episode *Mission to Paris* and Eastwood in *Bold Enterprise*.

Peters Reginald
Played the waiter in the **Jason King** episode *All that Glisters* [part 2].

Peterson Mark
Played Hein in **The Baron** episode *A Memory of Evil*.
Played the pilot in the **Man in a Suitcase** episode *The Revolutionaries*.

Petrie Daniel
Directed the **Strange Report** episodes *Report 3424: EPIDEMIC: 'A Most Curious Crime'* and *Report 2493: KIDNAP: 'Whose Pretty Girl Are You?'*.

Petrovitch Michael
Played Emilie in the **Jason King** episode *All that Glisters* [part one].
Starred as Lieutenant Georges Roget in the series **The Zoo Gang**.

Pettifer Brian
Played the bartender in the **Return of the Saint** episode *The Arrangement*.
Played Paul in the **Timeslip** story *The Year of the Burn-Up* [series episodes 14-19].

Petty Morris
Played Keller in the first series **The Protectors** episode *The Quick Brown Fox*.

Peverill John
Sound Editor on **Fireball XL5** and **UFO**.
Supervising Sound Editor on **Joe 90** and **Thunderbirds**.

Phelan Brian
Played Ernst Rishner in **The Baron** episode *Enemy of the State*.

Played Donald McKinnon in the second series **Danger Man** [aka **Secret Agent**] episode *That's Two of Us Sorry*.
Played Dandy Johnson in the **Gideon's Way** episode *The Big Fix*.
Played Sylvester O'Toole in **The Sentimental Agent** episode *May the Saints Preserve Us*.

Philips Jack
Played Scarb in the **G.S.5** episode *Party for Murder*.

Phillips Anton
Played the doctor in the **Return of the Saint** episode *The Poppy Chain*.
Starred as, series regular, Dr Mathias in **Space 1999**.

Phillips Conrad
Played the soldier in the second series of **The Adventures of Robin Hood** episode *The Shell Game*.
Played Sebastian in **The Buccaneers** [aka **Dan Tempest**] episode *Prize of Andalusia*.
Played Albert in **The Count of Monte Cristo** episode *Marseilles*, Pierre in *The Experiment* and Antoine/Francois in *The Grecian Gift* [aka *The Brothers*].
Played Mireaux in the **O.S.S.** episode *Operation Post Office*.
Appeared as the Doctor in **The Prisoner** episode *The General*.
Played Doctor Sandberg in the second season **The Saint** episode *The Miracle Tea Party*.
Played the skipper in the **UFO** episode *Reflections in the Water*.
Starred in the title role throughout the **William Tell** series.
Appeared as Westcott in the **White Hunter** episode *Deadfall*.

Phillips Dorothea
Played Miss Jones in the second series **Danger Man** [aka **Secret Agent**] episode *Whatever Happened to George Foster?*.
Played Mrs Edwards in the **Jason King** episode *It's Too Bad about Auntie*.
Played Karinski in the second season **Man of the World** episode *Double Exposure*.
Played Mrs Barnes in the fourth season **The Saint** episode *The Scales of Justice*.
Played Betty in **The Sentimental Agent** episode *A Very Desirable Plot*.

Phillips Joan
Played Mrs Benning in the **G.S.5** episode *Dead Men Don't Drive*.

Phillips Gregory
Played David Fenton in **The Champions** episode *The Bodysnatchers*.

Phillips John
Played Major Du Valle in **The Count of Monte Cristo** episode *A Matter of Justice*.
Played Paul in the first season **Danger Man** episode *Position of Trust*, Coyannis in *The Deputy Coyannis Story* and, in the third season [now aka **Secret Agent**], played Dr Brajanska in *Say it with Flowers*.
Played Brander Merton in the **Father Brown** episode *The Arrow of Heaven*.
Played General Montreaux in the first series **Man of the World** episode *Death of a Conference*.
Played Koestler in **The Persuaders!** episode *Powerswitch*.
Played Henry Peabody Sr. in **The Sentimental Agent** episode *Meet my Son, Henry*.

Phillips Leslie
Guested in the first season **The Adventures of Robin Hood** episodes *Friar Tuck* as Sir William & *Checkmate* as Count de Waldern; as Wat Longfellow in *A Village Wooing* [series two] and as Herbert in *The Reluctant Rebel* [four].

Played Sparrow in the **H. G. Wells' Invisible Man** episode *Blind Justice*.

Played Foxie in the **O.S.S.** episode *Operation Chopping Block*.

Phillips Peggy

Wrote **The Adventures of Sir Lancelot** episodes *Lancelot's Banishment, The Black Castle, The Witch's Brew, The Lesser Breed, Knight Errant* [with Selwyn Jepson], *The Theft of Excalibur* [with Hamish Hamilton Burns], *Maid of Somerset* and *Knight's Choice*.

Wrote additional dialogue for **The Buccaneers** [aka **Dan Tempest**] episodes *The Raiders, Captain Dan Tempest, Dan Tempest's War with Spain, The Wasp, Whale Gold, Marooned, Dan Tempest and The Amazons & The Ladies* and wrote *Articles of War* [with Alan Morland] & *Hurricane* [with Terence Moore].

Phillips Redmond

Played the secretary in the series two **Danger Man** [aka **Secret Agent**] episode *Whatever Happened to George Foster?*.

Played the little man in **The Four Just Men** episode *Justice for Gino*.

Played Bratski in the **H. G. Wells' Invisible Man** episode *Shadow on the Screen*.

Played Nilder in the second season **The Saint** episode *The Set-Up* and Professor Roeding in the third season's *The Helpful Pirate*.

Phillips Robin

Played Nigel Perry in the second season **The Saint** episode *The Man who could not Die*.

Phillips Sian

Featured in the **Espionage** episode *A Free Agent*.

Phillpott Gordon

Played the Abbot in the **Sir Francis Drake** episode *The Irish Pirate*.

Phipps C. Douglas

Wrote the first season **The Adventures of Robin Hood** episode *The Vandals*.

Picerni Paul

Played Patrini in **The Count of Monte Cristo** episode *The Sardinia Affair*.

Pickard Helena

Played Lady Barling in **The Four Just Men** episode *Money to Burn*.

Pickering Donald

Played Colonel Banks in **The Champions** episode *The Fanatics*.

Played 'Bookie' Barton-Smith in the **Gideon's Way** episode *The Thin Red Line*.

Played Lyndon in **The Persuaders!** episode *Someone Waiting*.

Played Sir Trevor Stevens in the **Return of the Saint** episode *The Arrangement*.

Played Jeremy in the third season **The Saint** episode *The Angel's Eye*.

Pickup Ronald

Played Kalon in the **Father Brown** episode *The Eye of Apollo*.

Pierce Barbara

Starred as, Junior Ranger, Denise in the series **The Forest Rangers**.

Pieroni Leonardo

Played Guido Volponi in the **Department S** episode *Spencer Bodily is 60 Years Old*.

Pierre Carlos

Played Tomas in the **Man in a Suitcase** episode *Night Flight to Andora*.

Pierres Thor

Played the hotel clerk in the season two **Ghost Squad** episode *Death of a Sportsman*.

Pigozzi Luciano

Appeared as Rotti in the **Return of the Saint** episode *Vicious Circle*.

Pik Robert

Associate Producer on the series **O.S.S.**

Pike Eddie

Production Manager on **The Four Just Men**.

Pike John

Played Martin in the **G.S.5** episode *The Goldfish Bowl*.

Pilavin Barbara

Played Lucia in the **Return of the Saint** episode *Dragonseed*.

Pilcher Martin

Played Corporal Reade in the **Virgin of the Secret Service** episode *Across the Silver Pass of Gusri Song*.

Pilkington Gordon

Editor on the second season of **Danger Man** [aka **Secret Agent**].

Pinero Bryan

Played Christian in the **Return of the Saint** episode *Appointment in Florence*.

Pinewood Studios

Studio used for the filming of **Man in a Suitcase, The Persuaders!**, **Space 1999** [also shot at Bray Studios], **Strange Report**, **UFO** [also at MGM Borehamwood Studios] and **The Zoo Gang**.

Pinkney Lyn

Played Helga Bauer in the **Strange Report** episode *Report 0846: LONELYHEARTS: 'Who Killed Dan Cupid?'*.

Pinn John A.

Played Jimmy Foy in the **Jason King** episode *Every Picture Tells a Story*.

Pinner David

Played Osric Orm in the **Father Brown** episode *The Mirror of the Magistrate*.

Pinson Allen

Played Lantini in **The Count of Monte Cristo** episode *Return to the Chateau d'If*.

Piper Frederick

Played the small man in the first season **Danger Man** episode *Name, Date and Place* and Sir Charles Fielding in the second series [now aka **Secret Agent**] episode *No Marks for Servility*.

Played Inspector Malcolm in the **Interpol Calling** episode *The Absent Assassin*.

Played Kimmel in the **O.S.S.** episode *Operation Tulip*.

Played the ex-Admiral, Number 66, in **The Prisoner** episode *Arrival*.

Piper Jack

Played Sally in the **Return of the Saint** episode *Tower Bridge is Falling Down*.

Pisdent Gordon
Starred as Sergeant Scott in the series **The Forest Rangers**.

Pithey Wensley
Played Nicholas in **The Adventurer** episode *Thrust and Counter Thrust*.
Played Senor Lazar in the first season **Danger Man** episode *Hired Assassin*.
Played Supt. Bill Hemmingway in the **Gideon's Way** episode *Big Fish, Little Fish*.
Played President in the second season **Man of the World** episode *In the Picture*.
Played Franklyn in the **Return of the Saint** episode *Collision Course* [Part 1: *'The Brave Goose'*: also exists, combined with the second instalment as a movie entitled *The Saint and the Brave Goose*].
Played Teal in the first season **The Saint** episode *Starring the Saint*.
Played Davey Preston in the **Sir Francis Drake** episode *Lost Colony of Virginia*.

Pitt Ingrid
Played Elayna in **The Adventurer** episode *Double Exposure*.
Played the title role in the **Jason King** episode *Nadine*.
Played Lynn Martin in **The Zoo Gang** episode *Mindless Murder*.

Pitt Norman
Played Charles Swinburne in the **G.S.5** episode *Scorpion Rock*.
Played Teal in the first season **The Saint** episode *The Elusive Ellshaw*.

Pitt Peter
Editor on **The Champions** and the first series of **Danger Man**.

Pitt Robert
Played the plainclothes man in the **Man in a Suitcase** episode *Which Way did he Go, McGill?*.

Pittel Michael
Set Dresser on **The Saint**.

Platt Victor
Played the Earl of Northgate in the second series **The Adventures of Robin Hood** episode *Too Many Earls*.
Played the jailer in **The Count of Monte Cristo** episode *Sicily*.
Played Chief Inspector Budd in the **Gideon's Way** episode *Morna*.
Played Inspector Quillan in the **H. G. Wells' Invisible Man** episode *Strange Partners*.
Played the farmer in **The Persuaders!** episode *Take Seven*.
Appeared as the assistant supervisor in **The Prisoner** episode *Checkmate*.
Played Charlie in the first season **The Saint** episode *The Bunco Artists*.
Played the Coroner in the **Strange Report** episode *Report 0649: SKELETON: 'Let Sleeping Heroes Lie'*.

Player Ernie
Co-wrote the story for the **Interpol Calling** episode *Fingers of Guilt* [with Tom Hutchinson: teleplayed by Robert Stewart].

Pleasence Donald
Starred as, series regular, Prince John in **The Adventures of Robin Hood** [the role was also played by Hubert Gregg & Brian Haines]: *The Prisoner* [first series], *Isabella* & *Ambush* [second] and *Marian's Prize* [third]. Also appeared in the second season as Bailiff Baldwin in *A Village Wooing*.
Played Captain Aldrich in the first season **Danger Man** episode *Position of Trust* and Nikolides in *Find and Return*.
A special guest star in the **Espionage** episode *The Liberators*.
Played Paul Koster in **The Four Just Men** episode *The Survivor*.

Played Haussman in the **Interpol Calling** episode *The Absent Assassin*.
Starred as The Spider in the **William Tell** episode *The Spider*.

Plenty Dennis
Played a SHADO Mobile 1 crew member in the **UFO** episode *Computer Affair*.

Plummer Terry
Played the gunman in the season two **The Protectors** episode *Lena*.
Played Pete in the **Randall and Hopkirk [Deceased]** episode *Who Ever Heard of a Ghost Dying?*
Played Healey in the fourth season **The Saint** episode *The Desperate Diplomat*.

Plunkett Patricia
Played Ann Hinds in the **O.S.S.** episode *Operation Flint Axe*.

Plytas Steve
Played Bowsin in **The Champions** episode *The Invisible Man*.
Played the interrogator in the second series **Danger Man** [aka **Secret Agent**] episode *The Professionals* and Constantine in the third season's *The Paper Chase*.
Played Lizardos in the **Department S** episode *Dead Men Die Twice*.
Played the Arab father in the season two **Ghost Squad** episode *Gertrude*.
Played Gonzales in the **Interpol Calling** episode *Act of Piracy*.
Played the Russian Delegate in the **Jason King** episode *Uneasy Lies the Head*.
Played Customs officer in the first series **Man of the World** episode *The Sentimental Agent*.
Played Ernst Schwerin in the third season **The Saint** episode *The Paper Chase* and Cirano in the fourth season's *Vendetta for the Saint* [part 2].
Played Gruber in the **White Hunter** episode *No Survivors*.

Pohlmann Eric
Played Luigi in **The Adventurer** episode *Has Anyone Here Seen Kelly?*.
Played Captain Heifetz in **The Baron** episode *Long Ago and Far Away*.
Played Hernandez in **The Buccaneers** [aka **Dan Tempest**] episode *Articles of War*.
Guested as Barkar in **The Champions** episode *Autokill* and as the Minister in *Get Me Out of Here!*.
Played Moham in the first season **Danger Man** episode *The Leak* & the innkeeper in *The Nurse*. In the second series [aka **Secret Agent**] played Eduardo in *A Date with Doris* and Carlos Bisbal in *The Affair at Castelevara*.
Played Emilio Andre in the **Department S** episode *The Man who got a New Face*.
Played Ponta in **The Four Just Men** episode *The Man in the Royal Suite* and Trenet in *The Godfather*.
Played Emil Zadeck in the season two **Ghost Squad** episode *Sabotage*.
Played Hassan in the **H. G. Wells' Invisible Man** episode *Crisis in the Desert*.
Played Kelkov in the **Jason King** episode *Variations on a Theme*.
Played Mario Cirrano in the first series **Man of the World** episode *Blaze of Glory*.
Played Casemegas in the first season **The Saint** episode *Teresa* and Carlos Xavier in the second season's *The Revolution Racket*.

Pollard George
Assistant Director on **The Four Just Men**.

Pollock Clair
Played Georgette in **The Scarlet Pimpernel** episode *The Sword of Justice*.

Pollock George
Directed the third season **Danger Man** [aka **Secret Agent**] episodes *I can only Offer you Sherry* & *I'm Afraid you Have the Wrong Number*.
Directed the **Gideon's Way** episode *How to Retire without Really Working*.
Directed the **Interpol Calling** episode *The Thousand Mile Alibi*.

PolyGram
Record and film production company owned largely by Philips electronics. Bought the ITC Entertainment Group for $156 million together with its catalogue of 10,000 hours of TV library and 350 movies. Made Lord Grade Chairman for life.

Poole Michael
Played Stavalov in the **Jason King** episode *To Russia With ....Panache* .

Pooley Olaf
Played Lorenzo in **The Four Just Men** episode *The Rietti Group*.
Played Dr. Lundquist in the first series **Ghost Squad** episode *Million Dollar Ransom* and Kobelik in season two's *The Menacing Mazurka*.
Played the manager in the **H. G. Wells' Invisible Man** episode *Odds Against Death*.
Played Gorini in the **Jason King** episode *A Page Before Dying*.
Played Commissioner Braun in the second season **The Protectors** episode *Wam* [part two].
Played the Inspector in **The Zoo Gang** episode *The Twisted Cross*.

Poore Richard
Played Robbins in the first season **The Saint** episode *The High Fence* and the Moonmobile Lieutenant in the **UFO** episode *The Dalotek Affair*.

Porteous Peter
Played a gang member in the second season **The Protectors** episode *Baubles, Bangles and Beads*.

Porter Dennis
Sound Recordist on **Randall and Hopkirk [Deceased]** aka **My Partner the Ghost**.

Porter John
Played Hans Davison in **The Champions** episode *The Survivors*.

Porter Nyree Dawn
Played the stewardess in the first season **Danger Man** episode *The Island*.
Played Yvette in the **G.S.5** episode *It Won't be a Stylish Marriage*.
Starred in the series **The Protectors** as Contessa di Contini.
Played Patsy Butler in the second season **The Saint** episode *The Scorpion*.

Porter-Davison John
Played Johnnie in the **Department S** episode *Les Fleurs du Mal*.

Portman Eric
Played Number Two in **The Prisoner** episode *Free for All*.
Played Elleston in the **Strange Report** episode *Report 0649: SKELETON: 'Let Sleeping Heroes Lie'*.

Portmeirion
The Prisoner was shot largely on location in the grounds of the Hotel Portmeirion, Penrhyndeudraeth, North Wales: by courtesy of Clough Williams-Ellis.

Potter Diana
Played Bessie in **The Buccaneers** [aka **Dan Tempest**] episode *Conquest of New Providence* and the second woman in *Dan Tempest and The Amazons*.

Pottle Harry
Art Director on **The Persuaders!** series.

Poulton Terry
Dubbing Editor on **The Adventures of Sir Lancelot** episodes *Identity, The Bridge, The Witch's Brew, Ruby of Radnor, The Lesser Breed, The Mortaise Fair, Maid of Somerset, Sir Crustabread, The Ugly Duckling, The Prince of Limerick, The Lady Lilith, Knight's Choice, The Missing Princess* and *The Thieves*.

Powell Dinny
Stuntman & double. Worked on **The Adventurer, The Baron, The Champions, Department S, The Four Just Men, Jason King, The Persuaders, The Prisoner** [appeared as the second guardian in *The Schizoid Man*], **Randall and Hopkirk [Deceased]** aka **My Partner the Ghost, The Saint** and **Space 1999**.

Powell Don
Played Lomax in the **Return of the Saint** episode *The Murder Cartel*.

Powell Eddie
Played the second thug in the third season **Danger Man** [aka **Secret Agent**] episode *I can only Offer you Sherry*.
Played the third guardian in **The Prisoner** episode *Hammer into Anvil*.

Powell Gwyneth
Played Helen Smaill in the **Father Brown** episode *The Curse of the Golden Cross*.

Powell Mark
Played P.C. Farley in the **Gideon's Way** episode *The Housekeeper*.

Powell Michael
Directed the **Espionage** episodes *Never Turn Your Back On a Friend, The Frantic Rebel* & *A Free Agent*.

Powell Nosher
Played Charlie in **The Baron** episode *Epitath for a Hero*.
Played Carl Young in the **Department S** episode *A Small War of Nerves*.
Played Lord Dorking in the **Randall and Hopkirk [Deceased]** aka **My Partner the Ghost** episode *Just for the Record*.
Played The Angel in the second season **The Saint** episode *The Crooked Ring* and Benson in the third season's *The Persistent Patriots*.
Played Ivan in the **Virgin of the Secret Service** episode *The Persuasion of a Million Drops*.

Powell Ruric
Wrote the **UFO** episodes *Conflict* & *The Dalotek Affair*.

Poynter Guy Kingsley
Played Martin in the first series **Man of the World** episode *Masquerade in Spain*.

Poynton Leslie
Wrote the season three **The Adventures of Robin Hood** episodes *Brother Battle, The Rivals, The Minstrel* & *The Doctor*.
Wrote **The Adventures of Sir Lancelot** episodes *The Outcast, Shepherd's War, The Magic Book, The Mortaise Fair, Sir*

406

Crustabread, The Ugly Duckling, The Prince of Limerick, The Lady Lilith and *The Missing Princess.*

Prador Irene
Played Maria in the first season **Danger Man** episode *The Contessa* and Mrs Aldrich in *Position of Trust.*
Played Anna in the **Jason King** episode *The Stones of Venice.*
Played Marina in the **O.S.S.** episode *Operation Orange Blossom.*
Played Signora Vespa in the first season **The Saint** episode *The Charitable Countess.*

Pratt Mike
Played Sheldon in **The Baron** episode *There's Someone Close Behind You.*
Guested as Raven in **The Champions** episode *Twelve Hours.*
Appeared as 'Briefcase' in the second season **Danger Man** [aka **Secret Agent**] episode *The Ubiquitous Mr Lovegrove,* as Serge in *The Black Book* and as the British Controller in *A Very Dangerous Game.* Played the garage manager in the third season's *The Man who wouldn't Talk.*
Played Colonel Hector Merton in the **Father Brown** episode *The Arrow of Heaven.*
Played Jenson in the **Gideon's Way** episode *Fall High, Fall Hard* and Red Carter in *The Reluctant Witness.*
Played Carson in the **Jason King** episode *A Red, Red Rose Forever.*
Played Detective Sergeant Peters in the **Man in a Suitcase** episode *Variation on a Million Bucks* [part 1: also combined with part 2 to form a movie: *To Chase a Million*].
Starred as Jeff Randall throughout the series **Randall and Hopkirk [Deceased]** aka **My Partner the Ghost**. Also, co-wrote, with Ian Wilson, the episode *A Disturbing Case.*
Played Alex Morgan in the second season **The Saint** episode *The Imprudent Politician* and Jeff Peterson in the third's *The Persistent Patriots.*
Played Clem Mason in the **UFO** episode *The Psychobombs.*

Pravda George
Played Newburg in **The Adventurer** episode *Make it a Million.*
Played Insp. Strauss in **The Baron** episode *And Suddenly You're Dead.*
Played Count Von Streicher in the **Department S** episode *The Double Death of Charlie Crippen.*
Played Rapelli in **The Four Just Men** episode *The Crying Jester.*
Played Laslo Radiv in the season two **Ghost Squad** episode *The Menacing Mazurka.*
Played Josef Farago in the **G.S.5** episode *A Cast of Thousands.*
Played President Majcek in the first series **Man of the World** episode *Specialist for the Kill.*
Played the Doctor in **The Prisoner** episode *A Change of Mind.*
Played Sneider in the second season **The Protectors** episode *Wheels.*
Played Clinton Uckrose in the first season **The Saint** episode *The Effete Angler,* Inspector Glessen in the second season's *The Rhine Maiden* and Uhrmeister in the third season's *The Helpful Pirate.*

Pravda Hana
Played the Czech receptionist in the second series **Danger Man** [aka **Secret Agent**] episode *The Professionals.*
Played Mrs Weisnevsky in the season two **Ghost Squad** episode *The Missing People.*

Prem Bakshi
Played the bookseller in the second series **Danger Man** [aka **Secret Agent**] episode *Judgement Day.*
Played the waiter in the third season **The Saint** episode *The Gadic Collection.*

Prentice Derek
Played the doorkeeper in the **Man in a Suitcase** episode *Somebody Loses, Somebody ...Wins?.*
Played Shelley in the **O.S.S.** episode *Operation Orange Blossom.*

Prescod Pearl
Played Nan Y Macao in **The Buccaneers** [aka **Dan Tempest**] episode *Blood Will Tell.*
Played the native woman in the first season **Danger Man** episode *Deadline* and Chloe in *Colonel Rodriguez.* Played Madame Celeste in the second series [now aka **Secret Agent**] episode *Parallel Lines Sometimes Meet* and Millie in the third season's *The Man on the Beach.*
Played the hotel maid in the first season **The Saint** episode *The Arrow of God.*

Prescott Kerrigan
Played the reporter in the first season **Danger Man** episode *The Honeymooners.*
Played Tex Norton in the **O.S.S.** episode *Operation Blackbird.*

Preston Mary
Starred as, series regular, Beth Skinner [Liz in the future] in the **Timeslip** series: *The Time of the Ice Box* & *The Year of the Burn-Up.*

Preston Trevor
Wrote the second season **The Protectors** episodes *Quin, Lena, Burning Bush, The Tiger and the Goat* & *The Insider.*

Prete Giancarlo
Played Boldini in the **Return of the Saint** episode *The Village that Sold its Soul.*
Played Mateo in the first season **Space 1999** episode *The Troubled Spirit.*

Price Dennis
Starred as Brandon in the series **The Adventurer:** *Nearly the End of the Picture, The Not-So-Merry Widow* & *The Case of the Poisoned Pawn.*
Played Constantine in the **H. G. Wells' Invisible Man** episode *Behind the Mask.*
Starred as Sir Brian in the series **Jason King:** *A Page Before Dying* & *A Deadly Line in Digits.*
Played Victor Frey in **The Sentimental Agent** episode *The Height of Fashion.*

Price Eric
Directed the **G.S.5** episodes *An Eye for An Eye, Pay Up or Else, Rich Ruby Wine* & *Dr. Ayre.*

Price Peter
Assistant Director on the second & third season of **Danger Man** [aka **Secret Agent**]. Assistant Director on the fourth series episode *Koroshi* which, edited together with the other season four episode *Shinda Shima,* also exists as a feature entitled *Koroshi.*
Assistant Director on **The Persuaders!**

Price Sherwood
Executive in Charge of Ferdorqui Productions on **The Protectors**. Appeared as Felix Costa in the first series episode *It Could be Practically Anywhere on the Island.*

Pringle Bryan
Played John Stewart in the **Gideon's Way** episode *Subway to Revenge.*

Pringle Val
Played Lead in *Adventure One* of **Sapphire and Steel** [part 4].

Prior Allan
Wrote the original story for the **Espionage** episode *Snow on Mount Kama* [and co-teleplayed with Donald Jonson & Kenneth Hughes].

Pritchard Hilary
Played Lydia in the **Department S** episode *Spencer Bodily is 60 Years Old*.
Played one of the models in the **Strange Report** episode *Report 3906: COVER GIRLS: 'Last year's Model'*.

Pritchard Reg
Played the fourth local in the third season **The Saint** episode *The House on Dragon's Rock*.

Proud Peter
Art Director on **The Adventures of Sir Lancelot** episodes *The Knight with the Red Plume, The Ferocious Fathers* and *The Queen's Knight*. Production Designer on *Lancelot's Banishment, Caledon, The Pirates, The Black Castle, The Magic Book, Knight Errand* and *The Mortaise Fair*.
Art Director on **The Buccaneers** [aka **Dan Tempest**] episodes *Blackbeard, Slave Ship, Before the Mast*, Production Designer on *The Raiders, Captain Dan Tempest, Dan Tempest's War with Spain, The Wasp, Whale Gold, Gunpowder Plot, Articles of War, Ghost Ship, Conquest of New Providence, Mother Doughty's Crew, Blood Will Tell, Hurricane, Dead Man's Rock, Dangerous Cargo, Hand of the Hawk, Gentleman Jack and the Lady, Mr. Beamish and the Hangman's Noose, Marooned, Dan Tempest and The Amazons, The Ladies, The Surgeon of Sangre Rojo, The Return of Calico Jack, Conquistador, Aztec Treasure, Prize of Andalusia, Cutlass Wedding, Dan Tempest Holds an Auction, Flip and Jenny, To the Rescue, Indian Fighters, Mistress Higgins' Treasure, The Spy Aboard, The Decoy, Pirate Honour, Instrument of War* & *Printer's Devil*.

Prowse David 'Dave'
Stuntman/actor & double. Worked on **The Champions, Department S** [played Adolfo in *The Treasure of the Costa del Sol*, **Jason King**, **The Saint** [played Tony in *Portrait of Brenda*] and **Space 1999**.

Pryor Christine
Played the blonde in the **Department S** episode *The Ghost of Mary Burnham*.

Pryor Maureen
Played Janet Norton in the **H. G. Wells' Invisible Man** episode *Picnic with Death*.
Played Lady Gormond in the **Man in a Suitcase** episode *The Bridge*.

Pudney John
Wrote the second season **Man of the World** episode *The Bandit*.

Pugh David
Played the milkman in **The Adventurer** episode *To the Lowest Bidder*.

Pugnalini Piero
Played the second reporter in the **Return of the Saint** episode *The Roman Touch*.

Purcell Harold
Wrote the lyrics for the **William Tell** song.

Purcell Noel
Played Llian in **The Adventures of Sir Lancelot** episode *The Pirates*.
Played Pat in **The Buccaneers** [aka **Dan Tempest**] episode *Whale Gold*.

Played Mike Kelly in the first season **The Saint** episode *The Wonderful War* and Brendan Cullin in the third season's *Little Girl Lost*.

Purcell Roy
Played the Lieutenant in the third series **The Adventures of Robin Hood** episode *The Crusaders* and the courier in the fourth's *The Oath*.
Played a variety of roles in **The Buccaneers** [aka **Dan Tempest**]: the Petty Officer in *Dan Tempest's War with Spain*, Trevallion in *Slave Ship*, Thompson in *Conquest of New Providence*, one of the sons in *Mother Doughty's Crew*, a Spanish soldier in *Dead Man's Rock*, the Merchant Skipper in *Dangerous Cargo*, a sailor in *Hand of the Hawk*, Captain Harding in *Mr. Beamish and the Hangman's Noose*, a sentry in *Marooned*, Captain Delacour in *Dan Tempest and The Amazons*, Captain Hawkins in *The Ladies*, the first Spanish guard in *The Surgeon of Sangre Rojo*, a pirate in *Cutlass Wedding*, Hicks in *Dan Tempest Holds an Auction*, a guard in *Flip and Jenny*, Constable in *Indian Fighters*, Bowles in *To the Rescue*, Mingo in *Mistress Higgins' Treasure*, the Landlord in *The Spy Aboard*, the Mate in *The Decoy*, the first Guard in *Instrument of War* an officer in *Pirate Honour* and Harkness in *Printer's Devil*.
Played Fritz in the **William Tell** episodes *The Assassins* and *The Hostages*.

Purdom Edmund
Starred in the series **Sword of Freedom** as Marco del Monte.

Purdom Herb
Wrote the **White Hunter** episodes *Sickness of Kilimanjaro, Decision* and *Rogue Man*.

Purkis Maureen
Played an auction client in the **Father Brown** episode *The Arrow of Heaven*.

Pursall David
Wrote the **Shirley's World** episode *Always Leave Them Laughing* [with Jack Seddon].

Pyne Natasha
Played Ann Somerby in **The Adventurer** episode *Action!*.
Played Nylene in the **Jason King** episode *If it's Got to Go - It's Got to Go*.

Pyott Keith
Played Carlsen in the first series **Ghost Squad** episode *Million Dollar Ransom*.
Played Dr. Dumasse Played Hugo in the **H. G. Wells' Invisible Man** episode *The White Rabbit*.
Played Baron De Charlot in the first series **Man of the World** episode *A Family Affair*.
Appeared as the waiter in **The Prisoner** episode *The General*.
Played Erlanger in the **William Tell** episode *The Prisoner* and Hans in the *The Shrew*.

****

Quashie Harry
Played Napi in the **White Hunter** episode *Voodoo Wedding*.

Quayle Anthony
Featured in the **Espionage** episode *A Free Agent*.
Played Dr Moetti in the second season **Man of the World** episode *The Enemy*.
Played Lord Yearley in the first season **The Saint** episode *The Noble Sportsman*.
Starred as Adam Strange in the **Strange Report** series.

Quick Diana
Played Anna De Santos in the second season **The Protectors** episode *The Bridge*.

Quick Jean
Played Maritza in **The Count of Monte Cristo** episode *Albania*.

Quigley Geoffrey
Played Sergeant Dooley in **The Sentimental Agent** episode *May the Saints Preserve Us*.

Quigley Godfrey
Played Josef in **The Champions** episode *Get Me Out of Here!*.
Played Johann Liebkind in the **Man in a Suitcase** episode *Somebody Loses, Somebody ...Wins?*.
Played Pavan in the first season **The Saint** episode *The Sporting Chance*, Max Valmon in the second season's *The Sign of the Claw*, Kirill in the third season's *The Russian Prisoner* and Ballard in *The Best Laid Schemes*.

Quilley Dennis
Starred as, series regular, Commander Traynor in **Timeslip**.

Quin Mary
Played Mary Murphy in the **Gideon's Way** episode *Boy with a Gun*.

Quince Peter
Played the bomb squad officer in the **Return of the Saint** episode *The Armageddon Alternative*.

Quinlan Siobhan
Played Karen in the **Jason King** episode *Flamingos only Fly on Tuesdays*.

Quinn Michael
Starred as Nick Craig in the series **Ghost Squad**.

Quinn Tony
Played King Anguish in **The Adventures of Sir Lancelot** episode *The Prince of Limerick*.
Played the piano tuner in **The Sentimental Agent** episode *All that Jazz*.

Quitak Oscar
Played Amant in **The Four Just Men** episode *The Beatniques*.
Guested as Abdul in the **Interpol Calling** episode *Slave Ship*.
Played Captain Roman Guzman in the **Man in a Suitcase** episode *Burden of Proof*.
Played Stoll in the first series **Man of the World** episode *Specialist for the Kill*.
Played the batman in the **O.S.S.** episode *Operation Fracture*.
Played Pell in the **Virgin of the Secret Service** episode *A Fate Worse Than Death*.

****

Rachelle Carol
Played Miss James in the **Randall and Hopkirk [Deceased]** aka **My Partner the Ghost** episode *The House on Haunted Hill*.

Radd Ronald
Played Hilverston in **The Adventurer** episode *Make it a Million*.
Played the Commandante in **The Champions** episode *Get Me Out of Here!*.
Played Joaquin Paratore in the second season **Danger Man [aka Secret Agent]** episode *A Date with Doris* and Alexandros in *Sting in the Tail*.
Played Allison in the **Department S** episode *The Perfect Operation*.
Played Alfred Thistle in the **Jason King** episode *Chapter One: the Company I Keep*.
Played Pargiter in the **Randall and Hopkirk [Deceased]** aka **My Partner the Ghost** episode *Just for the Record*.
Guest starred as the Rook in **The Prisoner** episode *Checkmate*.
Played Jerry Butler in the second season **The Protectors** episode *Decoy*.
Played Byron Ufferlitz in the first season **The Saint** episode *Starring the Saint*, Roberto Vittorini in the third season episode *Simon and Delilah* and Henri Flambeau in the fourth season's *The Ex-King of Diamonds*.

Radford Michael
Played the male hiker in the **Randall and Hopkirk [Deceased]** aka **My Partner the Ghost** episode *The Smile Behind the Veil*.

Radley Frederick
Played Sam the Stage Doorkeeper in the **Father Brown** episode *The Actor and the Alibi*.

Rae John
Played Shepherd in the first season **Danger Man** episode *The Gallows Tree* and Neil in *The Sanctuary*.
Played Dr Roach in the season two **Ghost Squad** episode *Sentences of Death*.
Played the Pathologist in the **Gideon's Way** episode *The Alibi Man*.
Played Lachy in the first series **Man of the World** episode *The Highland Story*.
Played Alexander in the **Randall and Hopkirk [Deceased]** aka **My Partner the Ghost** episode *A Sentimental Journey*.
Played Peter McLeod in the **White Hunter** episode *Forest of the Night*, Pete McAfee in *A Moment of Truth* and Bailey Deadfall.

Rafat Soraya
Played Sybella in the fourth series **The Adventures of Robin Hood** episode *Sybella*.

Raglan James
Played Professor Harper in the **H. G. Wells' Invisible Man** episode *The Vanishing Evidence*.

Raglan Robert
Played Beavis in **The Adventurer** episode *Has Anyone Here Seen Kelly?*.
Played Count Beaumont in the second series of **The Adventures of Robin Hood** episode *Ransom*.
Played Storch in the first season **Danger Man** episode *The Deputy Coyannis Story* and Doctor Stanifors in *The Girl in Pink Pyjamas*.
Played a police Inspector in the **G.S.5** episode *It Won't be a Stylish Marriage*.
Played Detective Inspector Heath in the **H. G. Wells' Invisible Man** episodes *Blind Justice*, *Man in Disguise* & *The Rocket*.
Played Inspector Maxwell in the second season **The Saint** episode *Lida*.
Played Hans in the **William Tell** episode *The Bandit*.

RAI
Return of The Saint was credited: 'a Robert S. Baker Tribune Films, a RAI/ITC Co-Production for ITC World Wide Distribution'. **Space 1999** was an ITC/RAI co-production, produced by Group Three for world-wide distribution.

Raikes Robert
Played Harry in the second series of **The Adventures of Robin Hood** episode *Fair Play*.
Played the Captain in the **Sword of Freedom** episode *The Duke*.

Railton John
Played Les in the **Man in a Suitcase** episode *Burden of Proof*.

Rainer Mike
Visual Effects Unit Camera Operator on **The Secret Service**.

Raki Lava
Played Kyro Caro in the **O.S.S.** episode *Operation Sweet Talk*.

Rakoff Alvin
Director on **The New Adventures of Charlie Chan**.
Directed the fourth season **The Saint** episode *The Ex-King of Diamonds*.

Rakoff Ian L.
Wrote the story [with David Tomblin] for **The Prisoner** episode *Living in Harmony* [the episode itself was written by David Tomblin].

Ramford Freda
Played Mrs Kautsky in the **Gideon's Way** episode *The Great Plane Robbery*.

Ramirez Pepita
Played Flamenco Dancer in the **G.S.5** episode *Scorpion Rock*.

Ramsay Jimmy
Played Kenduyu in the **White Hunter** episode *Inside Story*.

Ramsden Dennis
Played Comdr Corbett in the second series **Danger Man [aka Secret Agent]** episode *A Very Dangerous Game*.

Ranchev Jeremy
Played Ginger in the second series **Danger Man [aka Secret Agent]** episode *Whatever Happened to George Foster?*.

Randall George
Music Editor on **Joe 90**, **The Secret Service** & **UFO**.

Randall June
Continuity on **The Saint**.

Randall Stephanie
Played the Maid in **The Prisoner** episode *Arrival*.
Played Julia Harrison in the second season **The Saint** episode *The Rhine Maiden*.

Randall Walter
Played the Cockney soldier in the second series **Danger Man [aka Secret Agent]** episode *Fish on the Hook*.
Played Meeker in the season two **Ghost Squad** episode *Lost In Transit*.
Played Pepe in the **G.S.5** episode *Scorpion Rock*.
Played the male secretary in the **Jason King** episode *Nadine*.
Played Juan in the second season **The Saint** episode *The Revolution Racket* and the head waiter in the third season's *The Reluctant Revolution*.
Played the Spanish Captain in the **Sir Francis Drake** episode *King of America*.

Randell Ron
Featured as a special guest star in the **Espionage** episode *Some Other Kind of World*.
Starred as Major Frank Hawthorne throughout the series **O.S.S.**
Played Michaels in the **Man in a Suitcase** episode *Variation on a Million Bucks* [2 parter: also a movie: *To Chase a Million*].
Played Jim Palmer in the first series **The Protectors** episode *It was All Over in Leipzig*.

Randolph Elsie
Played Miss Oliphant in the **Father Brown** episode *The Head of Caesar*.

Rangel Germinal
Designed Miss Dawn Porter's Wardrobe on **Strange Report**.

Ranji Kumar
Played Gumta in the second series **Danger Man** [aka **Secret Agent**] episode *The Colonel's Daughter*.

Rank
Produced the series **Interpol Calling** [with Wrather].

Rank Film Laboratories
Film processing for **The Protectors, Space 1999, UFO & The Zoo Gang**.

Rank Organisation
Season two of **Ghost Squad** was a Rank Organisation Television Film in Association with Associated Television Ltd. for ITC World Wide Distribution, as was **G.S.5**.

Ransome Prunella
Played Maria Gustave in **The Adventurer** episode *Full Fathom Five*.
Played Princess Alexandra in **The Persuaders!** episode *The Ozerov Inheritance*.

Rathbone Michael
Played the man in the laundromat in the **Randall and Hopkirk [Deceased]** aka **My Partner the Ghost** episode *All Work and No Pay*.

Rathborne Michael
Played the look-out in **The Buccaneers** [aka **Dan Tempest**] episode *Marooned*.

Rawlings Frederick
Played the Indian Chief in the **Sir Francis Drake** episode *King of America*.

Rawlings Keith
Appeared in the fourth series of **The Adventures of Robin Hood**: as the first forester in *The Lady Killer*, the first soldier in *The Loaf*, Bault in *The Devil You Don't Know*, the first villager in *The Charm Pedlar* and the surveyor in *The Champion*.
Played the detective in the first season **Danger Man** episode *Find and Return*.
Played a gendarme in **The Four Just Men** episode *The Beatniques* and the plainclothes man in episode *Marie*.
Played the customs officer in the **H. G. Wells' Invisible Man** episode *The Mink Coat*.
Played Hans in the **William Tell** episode *Castle of Fear*.

Rawlinson Brian
Played Martin in the season four **The Adventures of Robin Hood** episode *The Debt*.
Played Bruno Navini in **The Baron** episode *The Long, Long Day*.
Regular, as Gaff Guernsey, in **The Buccaneers** [aka **Dan Tempest**]: *Dan Tempest's War with Spain, The Wasp, Whale Gold, Slave Ship* [as Davies], *Gunpowder Plot, Articles of War, Ghost Ship, Conquest of New Providence, Mother Doughty's Crew, Blood Will Tell, Hurricane, Dead Man's Rock, Dangerous Cargo, Hand of the Hawk, Gentleman Jack and the Lady, Mr. Beamish and the Hangman's Noose, Marooned, Before the Mast, Dan Tempest and The Amazons, The Ladies, The Surgeon of Sangre Rojo, The Return of Calico Jack, Conquistador, Aztec Treasure, Prize of Andalusia, Cutlass Wedding, Dan Tempest Holds an Auction, Flip and Jenny, To the Rescue, Indian Fighters, Mistress Higgins' Treasure, The Spy Aboard, The Decoy, Pirate Honour* and *Instrument of War*.
Played Equerry in **The Count of Monte Cristo** episode *The Barefoot Empress*.
Played Frederick in the first season **Danger Man** episode *The Relaxed Informer*.
Played the Duty Sergeant in the **Gideon's Way** episode *Subway to Revenge*.
Played Williams in the **H. G. Wells' Invisible Man** episode *Bank Raid*.
Played Rinaldo in the **William Tell** episode *The Bandit*.

Rawnsley David
Art Director on **The Adventures of Sir Lancelot** episodes *Ruby of Radnor* and *The Lesser Breed*.

Ray Andrew
Played Chips in **The Sentimental Agent** episode *Finishing School*.

Ray J. M.
Played the American Delegate in the **Jason King** episode *Uneasy Lies the Head*.

Ray Jimmy
Played Jean in **The Scarlet Pimpernel** episode *The Winged Madonna*.

Ray Philip
Played Hulm in the season three **The Adventures of Robin Hood** episode *The Charter* and Walter in *The Mark*.
Played Mr Tresilian in the season two **Ghost Squad** episode *The Retirement of Gentle Dove*.
Played Langley in the **Gideon's Way** episode *The Wall*.
Played Meyer in the **Interpol Calling** episode *The Angola Brights*.

Ray Raymond
Played the hermit in the season two **The Adventures of Robin Hood** episode *Highland Fling*.
Played Old Tom in **The Buccaneers** [aka **Dan Tempest**] episode *Cutlass Wedding*.
Played the peasant in the second season **Man of the World** episode *The Bandit*.
Played the butler in the first season **The Saint** episode *The Loaded Tourist* and the photographer in *Sophia*.

Rayant Pictures
Produced **The Scarlet Pimpernel** [with Towers of London] for the Incorporated Television Programme Co.

Raymond Cyril
Played Nash in the first season **Danger Man** episode *Name, Date and Place*.

Raymond Gary
Played Henry in the season three **The Adventures of Robin Hood** episode *One Man's Meat*.
Played Prince Jonetta in the **H. G. Wells' Invisible Man** episode *Man in Power*.
Played Sandro in the **Jason King** episode *Buried in the Cold, Cold Ground*.
Played Hossari in the first series **Man of the World** episode *The Frontier*.

Played Sergei in **The Persuaders!** episode *The Ozerov Inheritance*.

Played Gilberto Arroyo in the second season **The Saint** episode *The Spanish Cow*.

Played Mateo in **The Sentimental Agent** episode *Box of Tricks*.

Played Colonel John Grey in the **UFO** episode *The Man who Came Back*.

Rayner Bob
Assistant wardrobe on **The Prisoner**.

Rayner David
Played the reporter in **The Adventurer** episode *The Not-So-Merry Widow*.

Raynes Louis
Played the landlord in the season two **Ghost Squad** episode *Gertrude* and Luigi in the **Jason King** episode *That isn't Me, It's Somebody Else*.

Raynor Desmond
Appeared as the jailer in **The Adventures of Sir Lancelot** episode *Ruby of Radnor*.

Raynor Louis
Played Karim in the first season **The Saint** episode *The Wonderful War* and Pablo in the third season's *The Reluctant Revolution*.

Raynor Sheila
Played Bertha in the first series **Man of the World** episode *Shadow of the Wall*.

Played Josephine in the **William Tell** episode *The Suspect*.

RCA Sound Recording
Sound Recording on **The Buccaneers** [aka **Dan Tempest**], **Department S**, **Randall and Hopkirk [Deceased]** aka My **Partner the Ghost** & **William Tell**.

Rea Charles
Played Jack in the third season **The Saint** episode *The Power Artist*.

Read Darryl
Played the boy pupil II in the fourth season **The Saint** episode *The Ex-King of Diamonds*.

Read Jan
Wrote the season four **The Adventures of Robin Hood** episodes *The Lady Killer*, *The Bagpiper* & *A Bushel of Apples*.

Wrote the second season **Danger Man** [aka **Secret Agent**] episode *That's Two of Us Sorry*.

Wrote **The Four Just Men** episodes *The Deadly Capsule* [teleplayed from a story by Oliver Skene & Samuel B. West], *The Man with the Golden Touch* [story: teleplayed by Louis Marks], *Money to Burn* and *The Miracle of St. Philippe* [teleplayed with Louis Marks: story by Barbara Hammer].

Script Editor on the **Man in a Suitcase** series and wrote the episodes *Somebody Loses, Somebody ...Wins?*, *The Revolutionaries* [teleplayed, with Peter Duffell, from a story by Kevin B. Laffan], *Castle in the Clouds* & *Night Flight to Andora* [with Reed de Rouen].

Associate Script Editor on **Strange Report** and wrote the episode *Report 1021: SHRAPNEL: 'The Wish in the Dream'*.

Read John
Associate Producer on **Captain Scarlet and the Mysterons** and on season two of **Thunderbirds**.

Director of Photography on on **Fireball XL5** & **Thunderbirds**.

Reading Donna
Played Teresa in the **Jason King** episode *A Royal Flush*.

Real Fred
Played the porter in the **UFO** episode *The Man who Came Back*.

Reason Rhodes
Starred as John Hunter in the **White Hunter** series.

Reckord Lloyd
Played the barman in the first season **Danger Man** episodes *Deadline* & *Colonel Rodriguez*. In series two [now aka **Secret Agent**], again, played a barman in *The Galloping Major* but played Kanda in *Loyalty Always Pays*.

Reder Gigi
Played Valerio in the **Return of the Saint** episode *The Murder Cartel*.

Redmond Liam
Played Tom Upwater in the third season **The Saint** episode *The Angel's Eye*.

Redmond Moira
Played Louisa Trenton in **The Baron** episode *Portrait of Louisa*.

Played Mitzi in the first season **Danger Man** episode *Under the Lake*, Ruth in *The Relaxed Informer* and Nicola Tarasova in the second series [now aka **Secret Agent**] episode *Parallel Lines Sometimes Meet*.

Played Susie in the first series **Ghost Squad** episode *Death from a Distance* and Anita in *Catspaw* [*Catspaw* was shot for the first series, but due to an actors' strike, was originally shown as a season two episode].

Played Nina in the **Interpol Calling** episode *Private View*.

Played Linda in the first series **Man of the World** episode *The Mindreader*.

Played Livia Moreno in the **Return of the Saint** episode *The Nightmare Man*.

Redwood Manning
Played Mason in the first series **The Protectors** episode *The Bodyguards*.

Reed Bill
Appeared as Parkin in the **Randall and Hopkirk [Deceased]** aka My **Partner the Ghost** episode *When the Spirit Moves You*.

Reed Geoffrey
Played Butler in **The Adventurer** episode *Make it a Million*.

Played the taxi driver in the **Man in a Suitcase** episode *Web with Four Spiders*.

Appeared as the Skipper in **The Prisoner** episode *Checkmate*.

Played the first male nurse in the **Randall and Hopkirk [Deceased]** aka My **Partner the Ghost** episode *A Disturbing Case*.

Reed Myrtle
Played April in the second series of **The Adventures of Robin Hood** episode *The Shell Game*.

Played the second tart in **The Four Just Men** episode *The Boy Without a Country*.

Played Midge Carberry in the season two **Ghost Squad** episode *The Golden Silence*.

Played Louise in the **H. G. Wells' Invisible Man** episode *The White Rabbit*.

Reed Oliver
Played Joe Catelli in the first season **The Saint** episode *The King of the Beggars* and Aristides in *Sophia*.

Reed Tracey
Starred as, series regular, Maggie in **Man of the World**: *Death of a Conference*, *Masquerade in Spain*, *Blaze of Glory*, *The*

*Runaways, The Sentimental Agent, The Highland Story &
Specialist for the Kill.*
Played Jane Carson in the **UFO** episode *The Dalotek Affair.*

Reede Rosemary
Played Claire Wheeler in the second season **The Saint** episode
The Man who Liked Toys.

Rees Angharad
Played Charlie's girlfriend in the first series **The Protectors**
episode *Triple Cross.*

Rees David
Played the TV interviewer in **The Persuaders!** episode *The
Time and the Place.*

Rees John
Played the Welsh Napoleon/Marshall in **The Prisoner** episode
The Girl Who Was Death.
Played Gale in the second season **The Saint** episode *The Sign
of the Claw.*
Played Lou Oliver in the **Strange Report** episode *Report
3906: COVER GIRLS: 'Last Year's Model'.*

Rees Llewellyn
Played the Bishop in the season three **The Adventures of
Robin Hood** episode *The Mark.*
Played Antrobus in the **Strange Report** episode *Report 2475:
REVENGE: 'When a Man Hates'.*
Played Count Origi in the **Sword of Freedom** episode *Violetta.*

Reeve Spencer
Editor on **The Prisoner** episode *The Chimes of Big Ben.*
Editor on **The Saint.**

Reeves Kynaston
Played the Minister in **The Prisoner** episode *Do Not Forsake
Me, Oh My Darling.*

Reeves Peter
Played the scooter salesman in the **Gideon's Way** episode *The
Firebug.*

Regin Nadja
Played Melina in the debut season **Danger Man** episode *Find
and Destroy.* In series two [now aka **Secret Agent**] played Ira
in *The Professionals.*
Played Princess Taima in the **H. G. Wells' Invisible Man**
episode *Man in Power.*
Played Maria in the second season **Man of the World** episode
In the Picture.
Played Lucille in the third season **The Saint** episode *The Art
Collectors.*
Played Maddelena in the **William Tell** episode *The Bride.*

Reid Ann
Played Betsey in the season three **The Adventures of Robin
Hood** episode *One Man's Meat*, Melissa in *Elixir of Youth* and
Alison in *Farewell to Tuck & At the Sign of the Blue Boar.*

Reid David
Executive Producer on the **Sapphire and Steel** series.

Reid Milton
Played the Arab in the **Department S** episode *Spencer Bodily
is 60 Years Old.*
Played Jania in the **Jason King** episode *To Russia With
....Panache .*
Starred in the series **Sir Francis Drake** as Diego.
Played Taro in the **Virgin of the Secret Service** episode *Wings
Over Glencraig.*

Reid Trevor
Played Insp. Holt in the **Interpol Calling** episode *Air Switch*
and as Cummings in *In the Swim.*
Played Harrison in the **White Hunter** episodes *Pegasus* and
Out of the Wind.
Played Von Brenen in the **William Tell** episode *The Spider.*

Reiner Bob
Co-wrote the **Shirley's World** episode *To Dream the Improbable Dream* [with Philip Mishkin].

Reisser Dora
Played Eva Dumel in **The Baron** episode *Diplomatic Immu-
nity.*
Featured in the **Espionage** episode *Some Other Kind of World.*
Played Janine in the **Man in a Suitcase** episode *Three Blinks of
the Eyes.*
Played Tania in **The Sentimental Agent's** *All that Jazz.*

Remberg Erika
Played Trina in the second season **Man of the World** episode
Double Exposure.
Played Eva in the third season **The Saint** episode *The Helpful
Pirate.*

Renard Manuela
Played the girl at Anif in the second season **The Protectors**
episode *The Last Frontier.*

Rendell David
Played a reporter in the fourth season **The Saint** two parter *The
Fiction Makers.*

Renison Cyril
Played Andrews in the **Randall and Hopkirk [Deceased]** aka
My Partner the Ghost episode *But what a Sweet Little Room.*

Rennie Hugh
Directed the season two **Ghost Squad** episodes *The Menacing
Mazurka & Sabotage.*

Renwick Linda
Appeared as Jennie in the **Strange Report** episode *Report
4821: X-RAY: 'Who Weeps For the Doctor?'.*

Retey Peter
Played the first soldier in the second season **The Adventures of
Robin Hood** episode *The Friar's Pilgrimage* and the Sheriff's
Lieutenant in *The Black Five.*

Revill Clive
Appeared as Horatio in the second series of **The Adventures of
Robin Hood** episode *Too Many Earls.*
Played Lord Barnes in the **Jason King** episode *The Constance
Missal.*

Reynolds David
Played the policeman in the **Department S** episode *A Small
War of Nerves.*

Reynolds Leighton
Wrote the season two **The Adventures of Robin Hood** epi-
sode *Highland Fling.*
Wrote **The Adventures of Sir Lancelot** episodes *The Knight
with the Red Plume, The Ferocious Fathers, The Queen's
Knight, The Magic Sword, Caledon* and *The Pirates.*
Wrote the **Sword of Freedom** episodes *Portrait in Emerald
Green, Serenade in Red, Forgery in Red Chalk & Chart of
Gold.*

Reynolds Malcolm
Played a technician in the **UFO** episode *The Sound of Silence.*

Reynolds Peter
Played Steven Radlett in the **Department S** episode *The Man in the Elegant Room.*
Played the Ober-Lieutenant in the **O.S.S.** episode *Operation Blue Eyes.*
Played Jack Palmer in the **White Hunter** episode *Web of Death.*
Played Hilaire in the **William Tell** episode *The Avenger.*

Rhodes Christopher
Played Gunther Klaus in the first season **Danger Man** episode *Under the Lake.*
Played Whitey Svensson in the **O.S.S.** episode *Operation Barbecue.*
Played Howard in the **Interpol Calling** episode *The Heiress.*
Played Bernabe in the first season **The Saint** episode *The Romantic Matron.*

Rhodes Edward
Played Digby Haynes in the **Man in a Suitcase** episode *Web with Four Spiders.*

Rhodes Marjorie
Played Mrs Pleasance in the **Randall and Hopkirk [Deceased]** aka **My Partner the Ghost** episode *For the Girl who has Everything* and Aunt Maria in the **William Tell** episodes *Landslide & The Boy Slaves.*

Rhue Madlyn
Featured in the **Espionage** episode *We, the Hunted.*

Richard Emily
Played Joan Stacey in the **Father Brown** episode *The Eye of Apollo.*

Richard Wendy
Played Sue in the second series **Danger Man** [aka **Secret Agent**] episode *Don't Nail Him Yet.*

Richards Angela
Played the receptionist in the **Jason King** episode *A Red, Red Rose Forever.*

Richards Aubrey
Played Det. Sgt. Steve Brady in the **Gideon's Way** episode *The Firebug.*

Richards Keith
Played Victor Hugo in **The Count of Monte Cristo** episode *Victor Hugo.*

Richards Pennington
Producer and Director on **The Buccaneers** [aka **Dan Tempest**]: produced *Ghost Ship, Mother Doughty's Crew, Blood Will Tell, Dead Man's Rock, Dangerous Cargo, Hand of the Hawk & Gentleman Jack and the Lady* and directed *Mr. Beamish and the Hangman's Noose, Mother Doughty's Crew, Dan Tempest and The Amazons, The Ladies, The Surgeon of Sangre Rojo, The Return of Calico Jack, Aztec Treasure, Mistress Higgins' Treasure & The Decoy.*
Directed the **H. G. Wells' Invisible Man** episodes *Secret Experiment, The Locked Room, Behind the Mask, Crisis in the Desert, The Mink Coat, Picnic with Death, Blind Justice, Strange Partners, Odds Against Death, Jailbreak & Shadow on the Screen.*
Directed the **Interpol Calling** episodes *The Angola Brights, You Can't Die Twice, The Money Game, No Flowers for Onno, Private View, Air Switch, The Sleeping Giant, The Chinese Mask, Slave Ship, The Thirteen Innocents, The Two-Headed Monster, Last Man Lucky, The Heiress, Game for Three Hands, Act of Piracy, The Collector, Payment in Advance, Trial at Cranby's Creek and Cargo of Death.*

Directed the **O.S.S.** episodes *Operation Lovebird, Operation Sweet Talk, Operation Payday, Operation Blue Eyes, Operation Dagger, Operation Yo Yo & Operation Firefly.*

Richards R. Pennington
Directed the first season **Danger Man** episodes *The Island & The Trap.*

Richards Susan
Played the gate keeper's wife in the first season **The Adventures of Robin Hood** episode *The Coming of Robin Hood.*

Richards Terry
Played Smart in the **G.S.5** episode *Death of a Cop.*
Played the detective in the second season **The Protectors** episode *Route 27.*

Richards Vikki
Played Nina in the **Return of the Saint**'s *The Arrangement.*

Richardson Charles
Played the doctor in the **Interpol Calling** episode *Game for Three Hands.*

Richardson Lee
Played Jan in the season two **Ghost Squad** episode *The Man With the Delicate Hands.*
Played Pablo in the **G.S.5** episode *Scorpion Rock* and Jim Johnson in *Hideout.*

Richens Iris
Wardrobe on **Joe 90 & The Secret Service.**

Richfield Edwin
Played Sir Christopher in **The Adventures of Sir Lancelot** episode *The Knight with the Red Plume* and Sir Tor in *The Queen's Knight.*
Played Heller in **The Baron** episode *A Memory of Evil* and Georges Delair in *Roundabout.*
Starred throughout **The Buccaneers** [aka **Dan Tempest**] as Armando.
Played Marco Janson in the third season **Danger Man** [aka **Secret Agent**] episode *Not So Jolly Roger.*
Played Degrange in the first series **Ghost Squad** episode *Ticket for Blackmail* and Tony Esposito in the season two episode *Mr Five Per Cent.*
Played Frank Dobson in the **Gideon's Way** episode *The Great Plane Robbery.*
Played Royston Lambert in the **G.S.5** episode *A Cast of Thousands.*
Starred in the series **Interpol Calling** as Inspector Mornay. Also wrote for the show: co-wrote *Slave Ship* [with Gil Winfield and Geoffrey Orme] and teleplayed *Act of Piracy* [from a story by John Kruse].
Played Fischer in the **O.S.S.** episode *Operation Sweet Talk* and Van Kuhl in *Operation Lovebird.*
Played Melozzo in the **Sword of Freedom** episode *Marriage of Convenience.*
Played Admiral Sheringham in the **UFO** episode *Destruction.*
Played Joe Kells in the **White Hunter** episode *Rogue Man.*
Played Maddeaux in the **William Tell** episode *The Assassins* and Eric in *Castle of Fear.*

Richmond John
Played Lord Manning in the **Randall and Hopkirk [Deceased]** aka **My Partner the Ghost** episode *Who Ever Heard of a Ghost Dying?.*

Richmond Susan
Played Mother Agnes in the second series of **The Adventures of Robin Hood** episode *The Hero.*
Played Madame Tussaud in **The Scarlet Pimpernel** episode *Sir Andrew's Fate.*

Rickard David
Played Private Watney in the **Virgin of the Secret Service** episode *Across the Silver Pass of Gusri Song.*

Rickford Allen
Played Andrew Bishop in the **Jason King** episode *It's Too Bad about Auntie.*

Rider Brian
Set Dresser on **The Champions.**

Ridgely John
Wrote **The Adventures of Sir Lancelot** episodes *Winged Victory* and *Sir Bliant.*

Ridley Arnold
Played Uncle Rodney in **The Persuaders!** episode *The Ozerov Inheritance.*
Appeared as Prof. Rosehill in the **White Hunter** episode *Run to Earth.*

Riettey Peter
Played Auctioneer in **The Buccaneers** [aka **Dan Tempest**] episode *Dan Tempest Holds an Auction.*

Rietty Robert
Played the bank director in **The Adventurer** episode *Deadlock.*
Played Captain Catalan in **The Buccaneers** [aka **Dan Tempest**] episode *Dan Tempest's War with Spain.*
Played the receptionist in the second season **Danger Man** [aka **Secret Agent**] episode *You're Not in Any Trouble, Are You?* and as the translator in the third season's *To our Best Friend.*
Played Francesco in **The Four Just Men** episodes *The Rietti Group & The Man in the Royal Suite.*
Played Decker in the first series **Ghost Squad** episode *Princess* [this episode was shot for the first series, but due to an actors' strike, was originally shown as a season two episode].
Played Victor in the **H. G. Wells' Invisible Man** episode *Man in Disguise.*
Played Pinelli in the **Interpol Calling** episode *Diamond S.O.S.*
Played the insurance executive in the **Man in a Suitcase** episode *Find the Lady.*
Played Chivaro in the second season **Man of the World** episode *The Bandit.*
Played Joe Hinds in the **O.S.S.** episode *Operation Flint Axe.*
Played Torino in **The Persuaders!** episode *Five Miles to Midnight.*
Voiced Number Two for the intro to **The Prisoner** episode *Many Happy Returns.*
Played the bank manager in **The Sentimental Agent** episode *The Beneficiary & Torta in Box of Tricks.*
Played Captain Riccardo in the **Sir Francis Drake** episode *Beggars of the Sea.*

Rietty Victor
Played Papa in the first season **Danger Man** episode *The Trap.*
Played Count Alzerno in the first season **The Saint** episode *The Charitable Countess.*

Rigby Terence
Played Zuilen in the third season **The Saint** episode *The Angel's Eye* and Charlie Mason in the fourth season's *The Time to Die.*
Played Sergeant Boyko in the **Virgin of the Secret Service** episode *Russian Roundabout.*

Rigg Carl
Played Forrester in **The Adventurer** episode *To the Lowest Bidder.*
Played Howard's henchman in the first series **The Protectors** episode *The Big Hit.*

Rigg Diana
Played Francy in **The Sentimental Agent** episode *A Very Desirable Plot.*

Rilla Walter
Played The Baron in the **Interpol Calling** episode *The Money Game.*

Rilla Wolf
Directed **The Scarlet Pimpernel** episodes *The Winged Madonna & Sir Andrew's Fate.*

Rimmer Shane
Co-starred in the **Cannonball** episode *Sights on Safety.*
Wrote the **Captain Scarlet and the Mysterons** episodes *Avalanche, Expo 2068* and *Inferno* [with Tony Barwick].
Played Buchanan in the second series **Danger Man** [aka **Secret Agent**] episode *The Mercenaries.*
Played the doctor in the **G.S.5** episode *Seven Sisters of Wong.*
Co-starred in the **Hawkeye and the Last of the Mohicans** episode *The Prisoner.*
Wrote the **Joe 90** episodes *The Fortress, King for a Day, Big Fish, Relative Danger* and *Breakout.*
Played Lomax in **The Persuaders!** episode *Element of Risk.*
On **The Protectors**: Played Vickers in the first series episode *Vocal* and Zeke in the second series episode *Zeke's Blues.* Wrote the second season episodes *Zeke's Blues & Blockbuster.*
Played Falco in the **Return of the Saint** episode *Dragonseed.*
Played Major Smith in the second season **The Saint** episode *The Hi-Jackers.*
Wrote **The Secret Service** episode *A Hole in One.*
Played Kelly in the first season **Space 1999** episode *Space Brain.*
Voiced Scott Tracy - Pilot, Thunderbird 1 - on **Thunderbirds.**
Played the CIA man in the **UFO** episode *Confetti Check A-O.K.*

Ringham John
Played Inspector Duncan in **The Baron** episode *The Man Outside.*
Played Farley in the season two **Ghost Squad** episode *The Grand Duchess.*
Played Prosecuting Counsel in the second season **The Protectors** episode *Trial.*
Played Dr. Russell in the third season **The Saint** episode *The Best Laid Schemes.*

Ripper Michael
Played Brack in the third series of **The Adventures of Robin Hood** episodes *Change of Heart* & Oswald in *The Healing Hand.* In season four, played Wilfred in *Race Against Time.*
Played Rangit Pal in the first season **Danger Man** episode *Dead Man Walks*, Kane in *The Island* and Miguel Torres in *The Lovers.*
Played Barker in **The Four Just Men** episode *The Man Who Wasn't There.*
Played Joe Short in the **Gideon's Way** episode *The Big Fix.*
Played the stableman in the **H. G. Wells' Invisible Man** episode *Picnic with Death* and Porter in *The Vanishing Evidence.*
Played Le Couteau in the **O.S.S.** episode *Operation Dagger.*
Played Punter in the **Randall and Hopkirk [Deceased]** aka **My Partner the Ghost** episode *It's Supposed to be Thicker than Water.*
Played Sukan in the third season **The Saint** episode *The Gadic Collection.*
Played Elbeuf in **The Scarlet Pimpernel** episode *The Farmer's Boy.*
Played Caylus in the **Sir Francis Drake** episode *Mission to Paris* and Almighty Jones in *The Slaves of Spain.*
Played Schwartz in the **William Tell** episode *Voice in the Night.*

Riscoe Maureen
Casting on **Sapphire and Steel.**

Ritch David
Played the Spanish Aide in **The Buccaneers** [aka **Dan Tempest**] episode *Hurricane* and Blasco in *Prize of Andalusia*.
Played the taxi driver in the first season **Danger Man** episode *View from the Villa* and the immigration officer in the second season's [now aka **Secret Agent**] *The Affair at Castelevara*.
Played Akbal in **The Four Just Men** episode *The Prime Minister* and the youth in *The Beatniques*.
Played Josef in the **H. G. Wells' Invisible Man** episode *Behind the Mask*.
Played the attendant in the **Sword of Freedom** episode *Francesca*.

Ritchie Barbara
Hairdresser on **The Zoo Gang**.

Ritchie Joe
Played the porter in **The Baron** episode *The High Terrace*.
Played Wally in the **G.S.5** episode *Rich Ruby Wine*.

Ritchie June
Played Jeanne Varda in **The Baron** episode *Roundabout*.
Played Charlie in **The Persuaders!** episode *Element of Risk*.
Played Mildred in the third season **The Saint** episode *Little Girl Lost*.

Ritt Peter
Editor on **The Champions**.

Ritterman Michael
Played Tazco in **The Buccaneers** [aka **Dan Tempest**] episode *Aztec Treasure*.
Played the Middle East Delegate in **The Four Just Men** episode *The Prime Minister* and Kubek in *The Night of the Precious Stones*.
Played Tadeusz in the season two **Ghost Squad** episode *The Missing People* and the Ambassador in *The Menacing Mazurka*.
Played the Captain in the second season **Man of the World** episode *The Bandit*.
Appeared as the hotel manager in the first season **The Saint** episode *The Romantic Matron* and as Galen in *The Loaded Tourist*.

Rivera Marika
Played the receptionist in the third season **The Saint** episode *The Better Mousetrap*.

Rivers Johnny
Sang the theme song, *Secret Agent Man*, for the US title sequence of **Secret Agent** [aka **Danger Man**].

Rix Colin
Played the policeman in **The Baron** episode *So Dark the Night*.
Appeared as the airport official in the **G.S.5** episode *Dr. Ayre*.
Played the police driver in the **Randall and Hopkirk [Deceased]** aka **My Partner the Ghost** episode *Vendetta for a Dead Man*.
Played the radio expert in the third season **The Saint** episode *When Spring is Sprung*.
Played the prisoner in the **Sir Francis Drake** episode *The Slaves of Spain*.

Robbie Christopher
Played the bomb disposal expert in the **UFO** episode *The Long Sleep*.

Robbins Michael
Played Alan Jordan in **The Baron** episode *There's Someone Close Behind You*.
Played Burton in the **Department S** episode *The Man in the Elegant Room*.

Played the waiter in the season two **Ghost Squad** episode *The Grand Duchess*.
Played Smith in the **Gideon's Way** episode *Fall High, Fall Hard*.
Played Stripey Hoskins in the **G.S.5** episode *Scorpion Rock*.
Played Beeky in the **Return of the Saint** episode *Collision Course* [Part 1: 'The Brave Goose': also exists, combined with the second instalment as a movie entitled *The Saint and the Brave Goose*].
Played Smith in the second season **The Saint** episode *The Saint Steps In*. Played Pat Hurst in the fourth season episode *The Double Take* and Harry in *The People Importers*.

Roberton Matthew
Played Doctor Harris in the **UFO** episode *Identified*.

Roberts Christian
Played Mark Lindley in **The Persuaders!** episode *Take Seven*.
Played Tim in the **UFO** episode *The Long Sleep*.

Roberts Desmond
Played the Large Man in the second series of **The Adventures of Robin Hood** episode *The York Treasure*.
Played Marne in **The Count of Monte Cristo** episode *The Experiment*.
Played Atherton in the **White Hunter** episode *Marked Man*.

Roberts Ewan
Played Richard Bates in **The Baron** episode *Roundabout*.
Played Craig in the first season **Danger Man** episode *The Gallows Tree*.
Played Inspector Mackenzie in the third season **The Saint** episode *The Convenient Monster*.
Played Munroe in the **Sir Francis Drake** episodes *Mary, Queen of Scots, Boy Jack, Bold Enterprise, Mission to Paris, The Flame Thrower, The Reluctant Duchess & Court Intrigue*.
Played Baiteson in the **Strange Report** episode *Report 0846: LONELYHEARTS: 'Who Killed Dan Cupid?'*.

Roberts Gerry
Designer on the series **Timeslip**.

Roberts John
Wrote the **Virgin of the Secret Service** episode *Wings Over Glencraig*.

Roberts Ray
Played the second counter agent in the second series **Danger Man** [aka **Secret Agent**] episode *The Black Book*.

Robertson Dennis
Assistant Director on **Gideon's Way**.

Robertson Donald
Wrote the first season **Thunderbirds** episodes *Edge of Impact, Desperate Intruder & Danger at Ocean Deep* and the second season's *Path of Destruction*.

Robin Georges
Played a guard in the first season **The Saint** episode *The Romantic Matron* and the French waiter in *Judith*.

Robins Jessie
Played Maria Calvetti in the first season **The Saint** episode *The King of the Beggars*.
Played the woman in the plane in **The Sentimental Agent** episode *A Very Desirable Plot*.

Robins Toby
Played Ingrid Shore in **The Adventurer** episode *Mr Calloway is a Very Cautious Man*.

Played Selina Trenton in the **Department S** episode *The Man in the Elegant Room.*

Played Madame Rue in the first series **The Protectors** episode *Ceremony for the Dead.*

Played Joanne Dell in the third season **The Saint** episode *When Spring is Sprung.*

Robins Tony
Played Contessa Di Magiere in the **Jason King** episode *Chapter One: The Company I Keep* and Martine in *That isn't Me, It's Somebody Else.*

Robinson Ann
Starred as Helen [Joey's schoolteacher] in the **Fury** series.

Robinson Bruce
Appeared as Peter in the second season **The Protectors** episode *Dragon Chase.*

Robinson Joe
Played Austin in the first season **The Saint** episode *The Saint Plays with Fire.*

Robinson John
Guested as Collings in **The Champions** episode *The Fanatics.*
Played Creasey in the GS5 episode *Party for Murder.*
Played Sidney Fairweather in the first season **The Saint** episode *The Saint Plays with Fire* and Jason Douglas in the fourth season's *The Desperate Diplomat.*
Played Ferrucci in the **Sword of Freedom** episode *The Hero.*

Robinson Neil
Played Pantoni in **The Baron** episode *The Long, Long Day.*

Robinson Rex
Played the police Sergeant in the season two **Ghost Squad** episode *The Menacing Mazurka.*

Robinson Richard 'Dickie'
Focus puller on **The Prisoner.**

Robinson Robert
Appeared as the merchant in **The Adventures of Sir Lancelot** episode *The Mortaise Fair.*
Played the gendarme in **The Four Just Men** episode *The Prime Minister* and Hill in *The Judge.*

Robson Zuleika
Played the gent's wife in the **Return of the Saint** episode *The Poppy Chain.*

Roc Patricia
Played Madge Clarron in the first season **The Saint** episode *The Talented Husband.*
Played Marge Wilson in the **White Hunter** episode *Pegasus.*

Roche Marga
Played Tonia Colsen in the **Man in a Suitcase** episode *The Revolutionaries.*

Rochelle Carol
Played the girl in the discotheque in the **Department S** episode *The Man from X.*

Roddenberry Gene
Wrote the **Whiplash** episodes *Episode in Bathurst, Sarong, The Actress* & *Act of Courage.*

Roddick John
Co-wrote, with Ralph Smart, the first season **Danger Man** episodes *The Lonely Chair, The Sanctuary, Name, Date and Place, The Conspirators, The Contessa, The Trap, Hired*

Assassin & *Find and Destroy.* Wrote *The Blue Veil* & *The Traitor* alone. On series two [now aka **Secret Agent**] wrote *Fish on the Hook* [with Michael Pertwee] and the original story for *It's Up to the Lady* [teleplayed by Philip Broadley].
Wrote the first season **Man of the World** episode *Blaze of Glory.*
Wrote the season one **The Saint** episode *The Covetous Headman.*
Wrote the **Sir Francis Drake** episode *Bold Enterprise.*

Roderick George
Played Pettorosso in the season two **Ghost Squad** episode *Mr Five Per Cent.*
Played Bodega Landlord in **The Persuaders!** episode *Nuisance Value.*
Played Mario in the first season **The Saint** episode *The Talented Husband.*

Rodger Struan
Appeared as Erhart in the **Return of the Saint** episode *Hot Run.*

Rodgers Anton
Played Jules in **The Champions** episode *Reply Box No: 666.*
Played Attala in the second series **Danger Man** [aka **Secret Agent**] episode *Yesterday's Enemies.*
Played Terrell in the **Department S** episode *One of our Aircraft is Empty.*
Played Peta Sloane in the **Gideon's Way** episode *The Nightlifers.*
Played Phillipe de Brion in the **Jason King** two parter *All that Glisters.*
Played Max Stein in the **Man in a Suitcase** episode *Variation on a Million Bucks* [two parter: also a movie: *To Chase a Million*].
Guest starred as the New Number Two in **The Prisoner** episode *The Schizoid Man.*
Played Sutherland in the first series **The Protectors** episode *King Con.*
Played Calvin P. Bream in the **Randall and Hopkirk [Deceased]** aka **My Partner the Ghost** episode *When the Spirit Moves You.*
Played Geoffrey Connaught in the **Return of the Saint** episode *The Debt Collectors.*
Played Pierre in the third season **The Saint** episode *A Double in Diamonds.*
Played Mr Fripp in **The Sentimental Agent** episode *The Height of Fashion.*

Rodgers Ilona
Played Mary in the third season **The Saint** episode *A Double in Diamonds* and Beth in the **Strange Report** episode *Report 4977: SWINDLE: 'Square Root of Evil'.*

Anne Rodney
Writer on **The Adventures of Robin Hood**: *Maid Marian, The Inquisitor, Table's Turned* & *The Prisoner* [season 1] and *Hubert* - with Ralph Smart, *The Dream* & *The Shell Game* [season 2].

Rodney Jack
Played Shorty Fleming in the **Gideon's Way** episode *How to Retire without Really Working* and 'Taffy' Jones in *The Tin God.*

Rodney June
Played Eugentia in **The Count of Monte Cristo** episode *Sicily.*
Played the maid in the first season **Danger Man** episode *View from the Villa.*
Played Rosalina in **The Four Just Men** episode *The Slaver.*
Played Lucrezia in the **Sword of Freedom** episode *Portrait in Emerald Green.*

Rodska Christian
Played Giles Carstairs in the **Father Brown** episode *The Head of Caesar*.

Rodway Norman
Played Meredith in the third season **Danger Man** [aka **Secret Agent**] episode *The Man who wouldn't Talk*.
Played Colin Grant in the first series **The Protectors** episode *For the Rest of your Natural ....*

Roeves Maurice
Played Rigmera in the **Jason King** episode *A Kiss for a Beautiful Killer*.
Played Wilcox in the **Return of the Saint** episode *The Judas Game*.

Rogan Beth
Appeared as Lee Holt in the **White Hunter** episode *Girl Hunt*.

Rogers Clive
Played a guard/auction client in the **Father Brown** episode *The Arrow of Heaven*.

Rogers Erica
Played Clare Selby in the **Gideon's Way** episode *To Catch a Tiger*.
Played Joanne in the first series **Man of the World** episodes *The Runaways* & *Portrait of a Girl*.
Played Belinda in the first season **The Saint** episode *The Golden Journey* & Joss Hendry in *The Pearls of Peace*. Played April Mallory in the second season's *The Old Treasure Story* & Joan Wingate in *Lida*.

Rogers Maclean
Directed the **White Hunter** episode *Decision*.

Rogers Malcolm
Played the police officer in the third season **Danger Man** [aka **Secret Agent**] episode *Two Birds with One Bullet*.

Rogers Mitzi
Played the girl in the season two **Ghost Squad** episode *A First Class Way to Die*.

Rogers Paul
Played Laing in the first season **Danger Man** episode *The Gallows Tree*.

Rogers Richard
Played Charles in **The Scarlet Pimpernel** episode *The Christmas Present*.
Regular in **William Tell** as Walter Tell: *The Emperor's Hat*, *The Raid*, *The Assassins*, *The Hostages*, *The Boy Slaves*, *Voice in the Night*, *The Gauntlet of St. Gerhardt*, *The Cuckoo* and *The Elixir*.

Rogers Tristan
Played Dieter in **The Adventurer** episode *Target!*.
Played Maxwell in the second season **The Protectors** episode *Quin*.

Roland Jeanne
Played Samantha in **The Baron** episode *Samurai West*.
Played Claudine in **The Champions** episode *A Case of Lemmings*.
Played Marie Valedon in the second series **Danger Man** [aka **Secret Agent**] episode *Sting in the Tail*.
Played Francesca in the **Man in a Suitcase** episode *Find the Lady*.
Played the title role in the second season **The Saint** episode *Sibao*.

Rolfe Alan
Played the prison guard in the **O.S.S.** episode *Operation Big House*.

Rolfe David
Co-wrote **The Persuaders!** episode *Nuisance Value* [with Tony Barwick].

Rolfe Guy
Played Walter Pelham in **The Champions** episode *To Trap a Rat*, Yves in the **Department S** episode *Death on Reflection*, David Bradley in the third season **The Saint** episode *Simon and Delilah* and Magus in the second season **Space 1999** episode *New Adam, New Eve*.

Rolfe John
Played Doland in the **Return of the Saint** episode *Yesterday's Hero*.

Rollason Jon
Played Oscar Dancer in **The Baron** episode *A Memory of Evil*.
Played Summers in the third season **Danger Man** [aka **Secret Agent**] episode *Not So Jolly Roger*.

Rollet Raymond
Played the prison Sergeant in **The Scarlet Pimpernel** episode *The Flower Woman*.

Rollins Jean
Played the gallery assistant in the second season **Man of the World** episode *In the Picture*.

Rolls Ken
Sound editor on **The Prisoner** episodes *The General*, *Hammer into Anvil* and *It's Your Funeral*.

Romain Yvonne
Played Giselle in the season one **Danger Man** episode *Sabotage*.
Played Theresa Mantania in the first season **The Saint** episode *The King of the Beggars*.

Romanelli Carla
Played Lea in the **Return of the Saint** episode *Appointment in Florence* and Melita in the first season **Space 1999** episode *Space Brain*.

Romanoff Elizabeth
Make-up on **Randall and Hopkirk [Deceased]** aka **My Partner the Ghost**.

Romoli Alessandro
Played Gabriel's driver in the **Return of the Saint** episode *Dragonseed*.

Ronald Norma
Featured in the series **UFO** as, regular, Miss Ealand.

Ronane John
Played Villiers in the **Department S** episode *The Soup of the Day*.
Played Ray Evans in the second season **Ghost Squad** episode *The Thirteenth Girl*.
Played Rupert Hathaway in **The Persuaders!** episode *A Home of One's Own*.
Played Mark Belden in the first season **The Saint** episode *Iris* and Justine Pritchard in the fourth season's *The World Beater*.
Played the Spanish officer in the **Sir Francis Drake** episode *The Bridge*.
Played Newcome in the **Strange Report** episode *Report 5055: CULT: 'Murder Shrieks Out'*.

Ronay Edina
Guested as Sandra in **The Champions** episode *To Trap a Rat*.
Played Miss Simms in the **Department S** episode *One of our Aircraft is Empty* and Danielle in *Les Fleurs du Mal*.
Played Bodil Henderson in the second season **Ghost Squad** episode *The Thirteenth Girl*.
Played Irene Culver in the **Jason King** episode *A Thin Band of Air*.
Played Sandra in the **Randall and Hopkirk [Deceased]** aka **My Partner the Ghost** episode *Never Trust a Ghost*.

Ronder Jack
Wrote the second series **Space 1999** episode *Brian the Brain*.

Rootes Maurice
Supervising Editor on **The Adventures of Sir Lancelot** episodes *Double Identity, The Bridge, The Mortaise Fair, Maid of Somerset, The Ugly Duckling, The Prince of Limerick, The Lady Lilith, Knight's Choice, The Missing Princess & The Thieves*.

Roper Brian
Played Alan in **The Adventures of Sir Lancelot** episode *The Witch's Brew*.

Roper Tony
Sound Editor on **The Secret Service**.

Ropes Adrian
Played the Sergeant in the **Randall and Hopkirk [Deceased]** aka **My Partner the Ghost** episode *A Disturbing Case*.

Roscoe Barbara
Played Air Hostess in the first season **The Saint** episode *The Covetous Headman*.

Rose Alec
Played the policeman in the first series **Man of the World** episode *The Mindreader*.

Rose George
Guested as the Beggar in the first series of **The Adventures of Robin Hood** episode *The Wager*.

Rose Jason
Played the publican in the **Return of the Saint** episode *The Obono Affair*.

Rose Phillip
Appeared as M'Kimba in the **White Hunter** episode *Squire of the Serengeti*.

Rose Reginald
Developed the series **The Zoo Gang** for television and wrote the episode *Revenge: Post-dated*.

Rose Tommy
Played Abelard in the third series **The Adventures of Robin Hood** episode *The Genius*.

Rosenberg Stuart
Directed the **Espionage** episodes *The Incurable One, The Weakling, Covenant With Death & The Whistling Shrimp*.

Rosenwald Francis
Wrote **The Four Just Men** episodes *The Bystanders & The Moment of Truth*.

Rosington Norman
Played Captain in the **Man in a Suitcase** episode *Variation on a Million Bucks* [part 2: also combined with part 1 to form a movie: *To Chase a Million*].

Rosmer Milton
Played Father Pietro in **The Count of Monte Cristo** episode *The Mazzini Affair* and Rothstein in **The Scarlet Pimpernel** episode *The Imaginary Invalides*.

Ross Alec
Played the constable in the season two **Ghost Squad** episode *Polsky* and Frank Simmons in the **Gideon's Way** episode *The Millionaire's Daughter*.

Ross Annie
Appeared in the second season **The Saint** episode *The Happy Suicide*.

Ross Arnold
Location Manager on **The Persuaders!**

Ross Charles
Played Fritz in the **William Tell** episode *Golden Wheel* and the major in *The Traitor*.

Ross Harry
Played Marks in the season two **Ghost Squad** episode *The Last Jump*.

Ross Hector
Played Sir Egbert in **The Adventures of Sir Lancelot** episode *The Ugly Duckling* and Baron Braynor in *Sir Crustabread*. Played the doctor in the **Father Brown** episode *The Curse of the Golden Cross*.

Ross Helena
Played Joe in **The Persuaders!** episode *Someone Waiting*.

Ross Phillip
Played Canon Lewis in the **Strange Report** episode *Report 1553: RACIST: 'A Most Dangerous Proposal'*.

Rossano Peter
Wrote **The Buccaneers** [aka **Dan Tempest**] episode *Instrument of War*.

Rosser Dilys
Played Sylvia in the **Gideon's Way** episode *Fall High, Fall Hard*.

Rossini Jan
Played Miss Moscow in the **Randall and Hopkirk [Deceased]** aka **My Partner the Ghost** episode *Just for the Record*.

Rossiter Ian
Played Detective Chief Superintendent Joe Bell in **Gideon's Way**: *State Visit, The 'V' Men, The Firebug, The White Rat & The Tin God*.

Rossotti Roy
The original director of **The Prisoner** episode *A Change of Mind*, taken over by Patrick McGoohan.

Roth Marty
Story Consultant on **The Adventurer** and wrote the episodes *Return to Sender, Double Exposure, Miss Me Once, Miss Me Twice and Miss Me Once Again & The Not-So-Merry Widow*.

Rothman Robert
Played Hank in the **Shirley's World** episode *Figuratively Speaking*.

Rothwell Alan
Played Bill Rose in the **Gideon's Way** episode *The Rhyme and the Reason*.

Rothwell Michael
Played Tanner in the **Strange Report** episode *Report 5055: CULT: 'Murder Shrieks Out'*.

Roubicek George
Played Semenkin in **The Champions** episode *Reply Box No: 666*.
Played Balik in the **Department S** episode *The Perfect Operation*.
Played John Wilton in the **Father Brown** episode *The Arrow of Heaven*.
Played the policeman in the first series **The Protectors** episode *The First Circle*.
Played Carter in the third season **The Saint** episode *The Power Artist*.

Roughhead James
Played Rodrigo in the **Sword of Freedom** episode *Portrait in Emerald Green*.

Roumanov George
Played Butler in the **Virgin of the Secret Service** episode *Russian Roundabout*.

Rousseau Carolle
Played Colonel Dibha in the **Return of the Saint** episode *Assault Force*.

Rowbottom Jo
Played Jane Benson in **The Baron** episode *Portrait of Louisa*.
Played Mary Rose in the **Gideon's Way** episode *The Rhyme and the Reason*.

Rowe Alan
Played Sir William in the season three **The Adventures of Robin Hood** episode *To Be a Student*.
Played the guard captain in the first series **Man of the World** episode *Death of a Conference* and Garcia in the second season's *Jungle Mission*.
Played Lafitro in the fourth season **The Saint** episode *The Ex-King of Diamonds*.
Played Merula in the **Sword of Freedom** episode *The Pagan Venus* and Antonio in *Violetta*.
Played Anton in the **William Tell** episode *Castle of Fear*.

Rowe Bill
Sound Recordist on **Randall and Hopkirk [Deceased]**.

Rowe Douglas
Played the barman in the **Father Brown** episode *The Curse of the Golden Cross*.

Rowe Fanny
Played Lady Campbell-Gore in the **Gideon's Way** episode *The Prowler*.

Rowe Royston
Played the stuntman in the **UFO** episode *The Responsibility Seat*.

Rowland Noel
Camera operator on **The Adventures of Robin Hood**, **The Adventures of Sir Lancelot** episodes *The Knight with the Red Plume, The Ferocious Fathers* & *The Queen's Knight* and **The Buccaneers** [aka **Dan Tempest**] episode *Blackbeard*.

Rowland Roger
Played Carstairs K.C. in the **Father Brown** episode *The Mirror of the Magistrate*.

Rowlands Anthony
Played Soames in **The Adventurer** episode *Mr Calloway is a Very Cautious Man*.

Rowlands Noel
Camera Operator [Visual Effects Second Unit] on **Joe 90**.
Location Unit Camera Operator on **The Secret Service**.

Rowlands Patsy
Appeared as Mrs Harkness in the first season **Danger Man** episode *The Actor* and, in the second series [now aka **Secret Agent**] played Mrs Fairbrother in *The Ubiquitous Mr Lovegrove*.

Royd Frank
Played the Abbot in the first series **The Adventures of Robin Hood** episode *The Knight Who Came To Dinner*.

Roza Maria
Played Consuela in the third season **The Saint** episode *The Reluctant Revolution*.

Ruben Albert
Co-wrote the **Espionage** episode *The Dragon Slayer* [with Halstead Welles].

Ruben Albert G.
Script Supervisor on seasons one to three of **The Adventures of Robin Hood**.
Script Supervision throughout **The Adventures of Sir Lancelot** and wrote the first series episode *The Wanderer*.
Script Supervision on **The Buccaneers** [aka **Dan Tempest**] episodes *Blackbeard, Prize of Andalusia, Cutlass Wedding, Dan Tempest Holds an Auction, Flip and Jenny, To the Rescue, Indian Fighters, Mistress Higgins' Treasure, The Spy Aboard, Pirate Honour, Instrument of War* & *Printer's Devil* and wrote *The Decoy*.
Wrote the **Sword of Freedom** episode *The Assassin* [with Sidney Cole].

Rubin Ronald
Executive Producer on the series **Shirley's World** [in association with Sheldon Leonard].

Ruddock John
Played Photographer in the **H. G. Wells' Invisible Man** episode *The Mink Coat*.

Rudling John
Played Dr. Court in the **H. G. Wells' Invisible Man** episode *Point of Destruction*.

Rule Bert
Sound editor on **The Champions**.

Rumney John
Played Risk in the **Jason King** episode *All that Glisters* [part one].

Rushton William
Played Lance in **The Persuaders!** episode *A Death in the Family*.

Ruskin Coby
Directed the **Sword of Freedom** episodes *Angelica's Past, Cristina, A Game of Chance* & *The Reluctant Duke*.

Russ Debbie
Played Debbie in **The Adventurer** episode *Return to Sender*.
Played Vicky Standish in the second season **The Protectors** episode *Sugar and Spice*.

Russell Billy
Played the old man in the **Strange Report** episode *Report 0649: SKELETON: 'Let Sleeping Heroes Lie'*.

Russell Clive
Played G's secretary in the second series **Danger Man** [aka **Secret Agent**] episode *Fish on the Hook*.

Russell Geoffrey
Played the hotel manager in **The Adventurer** episode *The Not-So-Merry Widow*.
Played Wills in the **Father Brown** episode *The Quick One*.
Played Dmitri in the **Virgin of the Secret Service** episode *Russian Roundabout*.

Russell Iris
Played the doctor in the first series **Ghost Squad** episode *Eyes of the Bat*.
Starred as, series regular, Jean Skinner [Cheryl's mum] in the **Timeslip** series.

Russell Leonard
Played the little man in the **G.S.5** episode *Dr. Ayre*.

Russell Peter
Played John Hamilton in the **Gideon's Way** episode *The 'V' Men*.

Russell Robert
Guested as Maltman in **The Champions** episode *The Mission*.
Played Chalmers in the **Department S** episode *One of our Aircraft is Empty*.
Played Ramon in **The Persuaders!** episode *To the Death, Baby*.
Played a gang member in the second season **The Protectors** episode *Baubles, Bangles and Beads*.
Played Harry in the **Randall and Hopkirk [Deceased]** aka **My Partner the Ghost** episode *The Trouble with Women*.
Played Guido in the third season **The Saint** episode *The Man Who Liked Lions*.

Russell Roy
Wrote the third season **The Saint** episode *The Helpful Pirate*.

Russell Roy
Appeared as the old Duke in the second series of **The Adventures of Robin Hood** episode *Flight from France*.

Russell William
Starred in the title role in **The Adventures of Sir Lancelot**.
Played Rev. Wilfred Bohun in the **Father Brown** episode *The Hammer of God*.
Played the title role in the **Sir Lancelot** episode *Sir Bliant*.
Played Count Rene D'Albert in the **Sword of Freedom** episode *The Strange Intruder*.

Ruta Tina
Played the opera singer in the fourth season **The Saint** episode *Portrait of Brenda*.

Rutland John
Guested in the season one **The Adventures of Robin Hood** episode *Dead or Alive* as the Earl & in *Maid Marian* as Edgar.
Played Max in the **Father Brown** episode *The Head of Caesar*.

Ryan Fred
Sound on **The Adventures of Sir Lancelot** episodes *The Outcast, Winged Victory, Sir Bliant, The Magic Sword, Lancelot's Banishment, Roman Wall, Caledon,The Pirates, The Black Castle, Identity, The Bridge, The Witch's Brew, Ruby of Radnor, The Lesser Breed, The Magic Book, Knight Errand, The Theft of Excalibur, Maid of Somerset* and *Sir Crustabread*.

Ryan Joseph
Played Captain of the Guard in **The Count of Monte Cristo** episode *The Luxembourg Affair*.
Played Bonar in **The Count of Monte Cristo** episode *The Experiment*.

Ryan Ken
Assistant art director on **The Prisoner**.

Ryan Madge
Played Mrs Apsimon in the second season **The Protectors** episode *Burning Bush*.
Played Mrs Roden in the **Randall and Hopkirk [Deceased]** aka **My Partner the Ghost** episode *Could You Recognise the Man Again?*.
Played Bertha Noversham in the third season **The Saint** episode *The Better Mousetrap*.

Ryan Matthew
Played Michael in the **Return of the Saint** episode *Yesterday's Hero*.

Ryan Paddy
Played Zenn in **The Adventurer** episode *Action!*.
Played Larry in the **Randall and Hopkirk [Deceased]** aka **My Partner the Ghost** episode *Who Ever Heard of a Ghost Dying?*.

Ryan Phil
Played the patron in the **Jason King** episode *Zenia*.

Ryan Rhonda
Played the girl in the phone box in the third season **Danger Man** [aka **Secret Agent**] episode *To our Best Friend*.

Rydon Ryck
Played the corporal in the **O.S.S.** episode *Operation Fracture*, the Sergeant in *Operation Yo Yo* and Mike in the **O.S.S.** episode *Operation Meatball*.

****

Saad Margit
Played Lili in the first season **The Saint** episode *The Saint Sees it Through.*

Sachs Andrew
Played the commentator in the **Randall and Hopkirk [Deceased]** aka **My Partner the Ghost** episode *Somebody just Walked over my Grave.*
Played Jacques in the first season **The Saint** episode *The Loaded Tourist.*

Sachs Leonard
Appeared as Minter in the second series of **The Adventures of Robin Hood** episode *Outlaw Money.*
Played King Rolf in **The Adventures of Sir Lancelot** episode *The Witch's Brew.*
Played the Finance Minister in the first season **Danger Man** episode *The Deputy Coyannis Story.*
Played the art dealer in **The Four Just Men** episode *The Crying Jester* and Amishar in *The Princess.*
Played Doctor Siligi in the first series **Ghost Squad** episode *Hong Kong Story* and Anton Brissac in the second season's *Interrupted Requiem.*
Played Deprae in the **G.S.5** episode *Seven Sisters of Wong.*
Guested as Muller in the **Interpol Calling** episode *You Can't Die Twice* and as Carlo in *The Collector.*
Played the Senator in the first series **The Protectors** episode *See No Evil.*
Played Deigo Ramiriz in the second season **The Saint** episode *The Spanish Cow.*
Played Grillo in the **Sword of Freedom** episode *The Pagan Venus* and Bosti in *The Suspects.*
Played Mortimer in the **White Hunter** episode *Killer Leopard.*

Sackheim Jerry
Story Editor on **The New Adventures of Charlie Chan.**

Sadoff Fred
Played Captain Williams in the second season **The Saint** episode *The Happy Suicide.*

Sagar Anthony
Played Nils in the season two **Ghost Squad** episode *A First Class Way toDie.*
Played the hotel proprietor in the **Randall and Hopkirk [Deceased]** aka **My Partner the Ghost** episode *My Late Lamented Friend and Partner.*

St.Clair Cheryl
Appeared as one of the dancers in the **Man in a Suitcase** episode *Three Blinks of the Eyes.*

St.Clair Jean
Played Miss Hill in the first season **The Saint** episode *Luella* and Madame Calliope in the second season's *The Saint Bids Diamonds.*

St.John Betta
Guested as Martha Crane in **The Count of Monte Cristo** episode *The Texas Affair.*
Played Princess Toma in **The Four Just Men** episode *The Princess.*
Played Toni Trent & Terry Trent in the **H. G. Wells' Invisible Man** episode *The Decoy.*

St.John Kathleen
Played Dowager in the **Man in a Suitcase** episode *All that Glitters.*

Saire David
Played Manual in the second series **Danger Man [aka Secret Agent]** episode *The Affair at Castelevara* and Ygal in *Judgement Day.*

Played Joe Mason in the **Man in a Suitcase** episode *Dead Man's Shoes.*
Played David Tregarth in the second season **The Saint** episode *The Crime of the Century.*

Salem Pamela
Played Michele in **The Adventurer** episode *Return to Sender.*
Played Alexandra Lamova in the **Jason King** episode *To Russia With ....Panache .*

Salew John
Played Cookie in **The Buccaneers** episode *The Spy Aboard.*
Played Jacobi in the first series **Ghost Squad** episode *Assassin.*
Guested as Moltz in the **Interpol Calling** episode *Fingers of Guilt* and as the fake professor in *Desert Hi-Jack.*
Played Col. Wentzel in the **William Tell** episode *The Shrew.*

Salkow Sidney
Director on **The Count of Monte Cristo.**

Sallis Peter
Played John Gordon in the first season **Danger Man** episode *Find and Destroy.*
Played Nesib in the **H. G. Wells' Invisible Man** episode *Crisis in the Desert.*
Played Piper in **The Persuaders!** episode *The Long Goodbye.*

Salter Ivor
Played Bertrand in the second series **Danger Man [aka Secret Agent]** episode *Yesterday's Enemies* and Williams in *Such Men are Dangerous.*
Played Joe in the season two **Ghost Squad** episode *The Desperate Diplomat.*
Played Lerik in the **Jason King** episode *If it's Got to Go - It's Got to Go.*
Played Germaine in the first season **The Saint** episode *The Benevolent Burglary.*
Played Karl Dekker in the **White Hunter** episode *Day of Reckoning.*

Samuel Julie
Played Shirley Simpson in the **G.S.5** episode *Hideout.*
Played the girl friend in the **Strange Report** episode *Report 4407: HEART: 'No Choice for the Donor'.*

Sanbrell Aldo
Played Jacques in the second season **The Protectors** episode *Implicado.*

Sandall Cliff
Sound on **The Adventures of Sir Lancelot** episode *The Thieves.*

Sanders Jack
Wrote the first season **The Saint** episode *The Talented Husband.*

Sandford Christopher
Played Lanik in **The Adventurer** episode *Has Anyone Here Seen Kelly?.*
Played Arthur in the second series **Danger Man [aka Secret Agent]** episode *A Very Dangerous Game.* Played Phelps in the third season episode *To our Best Friend* and Andrews in *Not So Jolly Roger.*
Played Onslow in **The Persuaders!** episode *A Death in the Family.*
Played the photographer in the fourth season **The Saint** episode *The People Importers.*

Sands Leslie
Played Draper in the **Department S** episode *Last Train to Redbridge.*

Played Sam Purdell in the first season **The Saint** episode *The Well-Meaning Mayor*.

Sands Michael
Played George in the first season **Danger Man** episode *The Conspirators*.

Sands Mike
Played Pip Jago in the **G.S.5** episode *Scorpion Rock*.

Sansom Robert
Played the Magistrate in the **Gideon's Way** episode *A Perfect Crime*.
Played the Coroner in the first season **The Saint** episode *The Well-Meaning Mayor*.

Santana Gito
Played an alien in the **UFO** episodes *The Sound of Silence*, *Identified* & *Survival*.

Sapinsley Alvin
Wrote the **Espionage** episode *He Rises On Sunday, and We On Monday*.

Sapphire Films
Produced the first two seasons of **The Adventures of Robin Hood** for the Incorporated Television Programme Co. Season three was billed as 'a Weinstein Production for Sapphire Films, for the Incorporated Television Programme Co.' and season four as 'a Hannah Fisher Production for Sapphire Films, for the Incorporated Television Programme Co.'
The Adventures of Sir Lancelot was 'a Weinstein Production for Sapphire Films Limited., for the Independent Television Programme Co. Ltd.'
The Buccaneers [aka **Dan Tempest**] series was 'a Weinstein Production for Sapphire Films Limited., for the Incorporated Television Programme Co. Ltd.'
The Four Just Men was a 'Hannah Fisher Production for Sapphire Films Ltd., for Associated TeleVision: an ITC Presentation'.
Made **Sword of Freedom** [for ITC World Wide Distribution].

Sarchielli Massimo
Played Marcello in the **Return of the Saint** episode *The Roman Touch*.

Sargent Gundel
Played the girl in the cafe in the **Man in a Suitcase** episode *Variation on a Million Bucks* [part 1: also combined with part 2 to form a movie: *To Chase a Million*].

Sarne Michael
Played Tony in the **Man in a Suitcase** episode *Jigsaw Man*.

Sarony Leslie
Played the ticket collector in the **Strange Report** episode *Report 0649: SKELETON: 'Let Sleeping Heroes Lie'*.

Sasdy Peter
Directed the season two **Ghost Squad** episodes *Sentences of Death, The Man with the Delicate Hands, A First Class Way to Die, The Desperate Diplomat, The Big Time* & *The Thirteenth Girl*.
Directed the **G.S.5** episodes *A Cast of Thousands* & *Dead Men Don't Drive* & *Hideout*.
Directed the **Return of the Saint** episodes *The Nightmare Man, Assault Force Hot Run, The Obono Affair* & *Appointment in Florence*.
Directed the **Shirley's World** episode *Knightmare*.

Satoris Rene
Appeared as one of the dancers in the **Man in a Suitcase** episode *Three Blinks of the Eyes*.

Saunders Desmond 'Des'
Visual Effects Supervisor on **Captain Scarlet and the Mysterons** and directed the Pilot: *The Mysterons*.
Production Controller on **Joe 90**, wrote the episode *Lone Handed 90* [with Keith Wilson] and directed the episodes *The Most Special Agent* and *The Professional*.
Associate Producer on **The Protectors**.
Production Supervisor on **The Secret Service** series.
Directed the **Stingray** episodes *Hostages of the Deep, The Ghost Ship, Subterranean Sea, Raptures of the Deep, Marineville Traitor, Star of the East, In Search of the Tajmanon, Rescue from the Skies* and *Eastern Eclipse*.
Directed the first season **Supercar** episodes *Ice-Fall, Deep Seven, Hostage, Crash Landing, Magic Carpet* & *Supercar Take One* and the second season's *Operation Superstork, Space for Mitch, Atomic Witch Hunt* & *Transatlantic Cable*.
Directed the first season **Thunderbirds** episodes *The Perils of Penelope* [with Alan Pattillo], *Pit of Peril, Edge of Impact, The Uninvited, Operation Crash Dive, The Imposters, Danger at Ocean Deep* & *Security Hazard* and season two's *Atlantic Inferno, Alias Mr Hackenbacker* & *Give or Take a Million*.
Post Production Executive & Assistant to the Producer on the series **UFO**.

Saunders George A.
Played the secretary in the second series **Danger Man** [aka **Secret Agent**] episode *Loyalty Always Pays*.

Saunders Stuart
Played Beavis in the season two **Ghost Squad** episode *Sentences of Death* and George Ulrig in the first season **The Saint** episode *The Lawless Lady*.

Savage Max
Wrote the **William Tell** episodes *The Shrew, The Ensign* [with Leslie Arliss], *The Trap* [original story: teleplayed by Doreen Montgomery] and *Castle of Fear* [original story: teleplayed by Roger Marshall].

Savage Mike
Played Falkner in the **Return of the Saint** episode *The Poppy Chain*.

Savident John
Played the Consul in **The Adventurer** episode *Poor Little Rich Girl*.
Played Captain Svenoski in the **Department S** episode *The Double Death of Charlie Crippen*.
Played Joe Gulliver in the **Man in a Suitcase** episode *Web with Four Spiders*.
Played Frank Lomax in the fourth season **The Saint** episode *Where the Money Is*.

Savile David
Played Norman Knight in the **Father Brown** episode *The Actor and the Alibi*.
Played the hospital doctor in the **UFO** episode *The Man who Came Back*.

Saville Edith
Played Lady Levy in the first season **The Saint** episode *The Lawless Lady*.

Sawalha Nadim
Played Nickolaou in the second series **Danger Man** [aka **Secret Agent**] episode *Yesterday's Enemies*.
Played Rahman in the **Return of the Saint** episode *One Black September*.
Played Zoran in the second season **Space 1999** episode *The Immunity Syndrome*.

Sawyer Bill
Stunt Arranger on **The Champions**.

Scace Norman
Played Stanley Merrick in **The Baron** episode *There's Someone Close Behind You*.
Played the Judge in the **Father Brown** episode *The Dagger with Wings*.
Played Beyla in the second series **Ghost Squad** episode *Interrupted Requiem*.
Played Warner in the **Gideon's Way** episode *State Visit*.
Appeared as the Psychiatric Director in **The Prisoner** episode *Hammer into Anvil*.
Played Stephens in the **Sir Francis Drake** episode *Gentlemen of Spain*.
Played Chu Chen Yu in the **Virgin of the Secret Service** episode *The Persuasion of a Million Drops*.

Schell Carl
Featured in the **Espionage** episode *The Light of the Friendly Star*.

Schell Catherine
Starred as Diane [Bradley's contact] in the series **The Adventurer**: *The Good Book, Poor Little Rich Girl, Double Exposure, Thrust and Counter Thrust, Miss Me Once, Miss Me Twice and Miss Me Once Again, Counterstrike, The Bradley Way, I'll Get There Sometime, The Solid Gold Hearse, Full Fathom Five & Going, Going....*
Played Kristin in **The Persuaders!** episode *The Morning After*.
Played Samantha in the **Return of the Saint** episode *The Imprudent Professor*.
Debuted in **Space 1999** as the Guardian of Piri in the first series episode *Guardian of Piri*. Went on to star as, second season regular, Maya.

Scheur David
Played Lionel in the **Man in a Suitcase** episode *Variation on a Million Bucks* [part 1: also combined with part 2 to form a movie: *To Chase a Million*] and the airport official in *Somebody Loses, Somebody ...Wins?*

Schiller Frederick
Played the woodsman in **The Adventurer** episode *Counterstrike*.
Played the mine attendant in **The Champions** episode *The Survivors*.
Played the country doctor in the first season **Danger Man** episode *The Girl in Pink Pyjamas*.
Played Nyziad Senior in the season two **Ghost Squad** episode *Polsky*.
Played Otto in the second season **The Saint** episode *The Rhine Maiden*.
Played the police sergeant in **The Sentimental Agent** episode *Express Delivery*.

Schiller Frederick
Writer on **The New Adventures of Charlie Chan**.

Schiller Wilton
Wrote the season four **The Adventures of Robin Hood** episode *Trapped*.
Writer on **The Four Just Men**: *The Beatniques* [teleplayed from a story by Alec Coppel], *The Godfather* [teleplayed from a story by himself & William Fairchild] and *Dead Man's Switch*.
Co-wrote the **Interpol Calling** episode *The Collector* [with David Chantler].

Schjelderup Gerik
Played Dr. Henri in the **O.S.S.** episode *Operation Sardine*.

Schlesinger John
Played Hale in the second series of **The Adventures of Robin Hood** episode *The Haunted Mill* and Alan-a-Dale in *The Dowry*.

Played Pigtail in **The Buccaneers** [aka **Dan Tempest**] episode *The Surgeon of Sangre Rojo*.
Second Unit Director on the first season **Danger Man** episodes *View from the Villa, Time to Kill, Under the Lake & The Journey Ends Halfway*.

Schlesinger Milton S.
Wrote the second series of **The Adventures of Robin Hood** episodes *The Bandit of Brittany, Flight from France & Too Many Earls*.

Schneiderman Walter
Make-up Supervisor on **The Adventures of Robin Hood, The Adventures of Sir Lancelot & The Four Just Men**.
Make-up Supervisor on **The Buccaneers** [aka **Dan Tempest**] episode *Blackbeard*.

Schoeller Ingrid
Played Mathilde Baum in the second season **The Saint** episode *The Hi-Jackers*.

Schoenbrun Herman
Set Decorator on **The Count of Monte Cristo**.

Schofield Katharine
Played Gretl in the third season **The Saint** episode *The Death Game*.
Played the receptionist in the third season **The Saint** episode *The Angel's Eye*.
Played Miss Garwood in the **Department S** episode *The Bones of Byrom Blain*.
Played Cigarette in the **Virgin of the Secret Service** episode *Entente Cordiale*.

Schofield Leslie
Played Sam in the **Department S** episode *The Shift that Never was*.
Played Peter in the **Randall and Hopkirk [Deceased]** aka **My Partner the Ghost** episode *Who Killed Cock Robin*.

Schrecker Frederick
Played Weiss in **The Four Just Men** episode *The Deadly Capsule*.

Schubert Bernard L.
Executive Producer [with Sydney Box] on **White Hunter** the series was billed as 'A Bernard L. Schubert Production, for ITP, for ITC World Wide Distribution'.

Schuster Hugo
Played Seltzman in **The Prisoner** episode *Do Not Forsake Me Oh My Darling*.

Schwartz Lew
Wrote the **Shirley's World** episodes *A Hell of an Engineer & The Islanders*.
Wrote the series two **Space 1999** episode *The Mark of Archanon*.

Scoble Lesley
Played Alpha 17 in the **Timeslip** story *The Year of the Burn-Up* [series episodes 14-18].

Scoble Teresa
Played Alpha 16 the **Timeslip** story *The Year of the Burn-Up* [episodes 14-18] and Miss Stebbins in *The Day of the Clone* [series parts 21 - 26].

Scoton
Produced **The Adventurer** & **Jason King** for ITC World Wide Distribution.

Scott Alex
Played Gregory Varna in **The Adventurer** episode *Miss Me Once, Miss Me Twice and Miss Me Once Again.*
Played Lucas in the season two **The Adventures of Robin Hood** episode *The Little People* and a Lieutenant in the third season's *The Genius.*
Played Ramon Petrarca in **The Baron** episode *Long Ago and Far Away.*
Played Black Bart in **The Buccaneers** [aka **Dan Tempest**] episode *Pirate Honour.*
Played Benson in the first season **Danger Man** episode *Sabotage* and Milos Kaldor in the second season's [now aka **Secret Agent**] *The Professionals.*
Played Enzo Brandini in the **Department S** episode *Les Fleurs du Mal.*
Played Graham Tobias in the first series **Ghost Squad** episode *Ticket for Blackmail.*
Played Fisher in the **H. G. Wells' Invisible Man** episode *Flight into Darkness.*
Played Rodriguez in the **Jason King** episode *A Kiss for a Beautiful Killer.*
Played Teniente in the **Man in a Suitcase** episode *The Man who Stood Still.*
Played Coley in **The Persuaders!** episode *Overture.*
Played Seaton in the **Randall and Hopkirk [Deceased]** aka **My Partner the Ghost** episode *The Smile Behind the Veil.*
Played Andre Grillot in the first season **The Saint** episode *The Work of Art*, Jan Vanderfelt in the third season's *Island of Chance*, Armstrong in *The House on Dragon's Rock* and the Major in the fourth's *Vendetta for the Saint* [part 2].
Played the soldier in **The Scarlet Pimpernel** episode *Thanksgiving Day.*
Played Don Petro in the **Sir Francis Drake** episodes *Doctor Dee* and *The English Dragon.*
Played Aarchon in the first season **Space 1999** episode *Voyager's Return.*
Played Voss in the **Strange Report** episode *Report 8319: GRENADE: 'What Price Change?'.*
Played Julius in the **Sword of Freedom** episode *The Eye of the Artist.*
Played Franz in the **William Tell** episode *The Lost Letter* and Klaus in *The Killer.*
Played Jean in **The Zoo Gang** episode *Mindless Murder.*

Scott Anthony
Played Carl in the **Department S** episode *The Mysterious Man in the Flying Machine.*
Played Harris in the **Father Brown** episode *The Arrow of Heaven.*

Scott Donald
Played Stevan Milner in the **Strange Report** episode *Report 0846: LONELYHEARTS: 'Who Killed Dan Cupid?'.*

Scott Harold
Played Gaston in the **William Tell** episode *The Suspect.*

Scott John
Played the police Inspector in the season two **Ghost Squad** episode *Hot Money* and Inspector Munroe in *Escape Route.*
Played the Civil Servant in the first series **The Protectors** epiosde *2,000ft to Die.*
Played the Prime Minister in the **Virgin of the Secret Service** episode *A Fate Worse than Death.*

Scott Johnny
Music on the **Return of the Saint** series.

Scott Kathryn Leigh
Played Gayle in the **Return of the Saint** episode *The Nightmare Man.*

Scott Kevin
Played Des in the first season **The Saint** episode *The Effete Angler* and Sergeant Henry Johns in the second season's *The Hi-Jackers.*

Scott Margaretta
Played Lady Hargrom in **The Adventurer** episode *Miss Me Once, Miss Me Twice and Miss Me Once Again.*
Played The Queen in **The Count of Monte Cristo** episode *Mecklenburg.*
Played Lady Sangore in the first season **The Saint** episode *The Saint Plays with Fire.*

Scott Michael
Played the third Knight in **The Adventures of Sir Lancelot** episode *The Magic Sword.*

Scott Peter Graham
Directed the first season **Danger Man** episodes *The Lovers, The Girl in Pink Pyjamas, An Affair of State, Deadline, Sabotage, The Deputy Coyannis Story* & *The Nurse.*
Directed **The Prisoner** episode *The General.*
Directed the **Sir Francis Drake** episodes *Johnnie Factotum* & *The Irish Pirate.*

Scott Steven
Played Gardo in **The Baron** episode *Time to Kill.*
Played Swede in the season two **Ghost Squad** episode *Escape Route.*
Played the policeman in the first series **Man of the World** episode *Shadow of the Wall.*
Played the hotel clerk in the first season **The Saint** episode *The Pearls of Peace* and Frascatto in the third season's *The Man who Liked Lions.*

Scoular Angela
Played Dorinda in **The Adventurer** episode *Nearly the End of the Picture.*

Scroggins Robert
Regular in **The Adventures of Sir Lancelot** as Brian: *The Ferocious Fathers, The Queen's Knight, The Outcast, Winged Victory, Sir Bliant, The Magic Sword, Roman Wall, The Black Castle, Double Identity, The Bridge, The Witch's Brew, Ruby of Radnor, The Lesser Breed, The Magic Book, The Theft of Excalibur, The Mortaise Fair, Maid of Somerset, The Prince of Limerick* and *The Lady Lilith.*

Seabourne Peter
Directed the third series **The Adventures of Robin Hood** episodes *The Minstrel, The Doctor, The Genius, The Lottery, Woman's War* & *Marian's Prize* and the fourth's *A Touch of Fever, The Loaf, The Devil You Don't Know, Hostage for a Hangman, The Reluctant Rebel* & *The Charm Pedlar.*

Seabrooke Nancy
Played Mrs Nikolides in the first season **Danger Man** episode *Find and Return.*
Played the woman in the bookshop in **The Sentimental Agent** episode *Meet my Son, Henry.*

Seaforth Susan
Played Renee in **The Count of Monte Cristo** episode *Andorra.*

Seale Paddy
Special Effects Camera Operator on **Fireball XL5**.
Lighting Cameraman on **Joe 90**.

Sealy James
Starred as the Sheriff in the **Fury** series.

Searle Audrey
Played an art student in the **Father Brown** episode *The Head of Caesar*.

Seddon Jack
Wrote the **Shirley's World** episode *Always Leave Them Laughing* [with David Pursall].

Seebohm Alison
Played Frances in the second series **Danger Man** [aka **Secret Agent**] episode *The Mirror's New*.

Seeley Tim
Played Lorenzo in the **Sword of Freedom** episode *Vendetta*.

Segal Jeffrey
Played the extremist officer in the first series **The Protectors** episode *A Case for the Right*.
Played the French delegate in the **UFO** episode *Confetti Check A-O.K.*

Segal Michael
Played Carre in **The Baron** episode *The Seven Eyes of Night*.
Played the Austrian officer in the second season **Man of the World** episode *Double Exposure*.
Played Denton in **The Persuaders!** episode *The Old, the New and the Deadly*.
Played the laboratory technician in **The Prisoner** episode *Hammer into Anvil*.
Played the train guard in the **Return of the Saint** episode *Signal Stop*.

Sekka Johnny
Played Beyla in the second series **Danger Man** [aka **Secret Agent**] episode *Loyalty Always Pays*.
Played Chay in the **Gideon's Way** episode *Morna*.

Selby Nicholas
Played Bailey in the first season **The Saint** episode *The Man who was Lucky*.
Played Inspector Franklin in the **Strange Report** episode *Report 4821: X-RAY: 'Who Weeps for the Doctor?'*.

Selby Tony
Played Mallin in the **Department S** episode *The Man from X*.

Selway George
Played Sven in the **Jason King** episode *Chapter One: The Company I Keep*.

Selway Kevin
Played Smiler in the **Return of the Saint** episode *Signal Stop*.

Selway Mary
Casting Director on **Strange Report**.

Selwyn Charlotte
Played the Dolly Girl in the third season **The Saint** episode *The Power Artist*.
Played the shop assistant in the fourth season **The Saint** episode *The Desperate Diplomat*.

Selwyn Lorna
Continuity on **The Buccaneers** [aka **Dan Tempest**] episodes *Before the Mast*, *Prize of Andalusia*, *Cutlass Wedding* & *Dan Tempest Holds an Auction*.

Serf Joseph - Pseudonym of/see Patrick **McGoohan**.

Sernas Jacques
Played Fabrizzio in the first series **The Protectors** episode *A Case for the Right*.

Serret Jean
Played the bank manager in the third season **The Saint** episode *The Queen's Ransom*.

Serret John
Played the cafe proprietor in **The Adventurer** episode *Poor Little Rich Girl*.
Played the senior executive in the second series **Danger Man** [aka **Secret Agent**] episode *The Battle of the Cameras*.
Played the croupier in the **Department S** episode *The Trojan Tanker* and the mortuary attendant in *Dead Men Die Twice*.
Played Antoine Dubec in the **Gideon's Way** episode *The Thin Red Line*.
Played Doctor Lucenet in the **Jason King** episode *A Thin Band of Air*.
Played Inspector Lavin in the first season **The Saint** episode *Judith* and Inspector Quercy in the second season's *The Abductors* & the third's *To Kill a Saint*.

Service Penny
Played the waitress in the **Strange Report** episode *Report 3424: EPIDEMIC: 'A Most Curious Crime'*.

Sessions Helen
Played Mrs Mason in the season two **Ghost Squad** episode *Death of a Sportsman*.

Sessions Robert
Played Martin in the **Department S** episode *Spencer Bodily is 60 Years Old*.
Played Skipper in the first series **The Protectors** episode *Ceremony for the Dead*.

Seth Roshan
Played the pursuer in the first series **The Protectors** episode *.....With a Little Help from my Friends*.
Played Jamal in the **Strange Report** episode *Report 3424: EPIDEMIC: 'A Most Curious Crime'*.

Setna Renu
Played the shopkeeper in the **Return of the Saint** episode *Signal Stop*.
Played Vizier's servant in the **Virgin of the Secret Service** episode *The Rajah and the Suffragette*.

Seton Alex
Played Arnulf in the third series **The Adventures of Robin Hood** episode *Elixir of Youth*.

Seton Bruce
Played Lord Terrence in the first series **The Adventures of Robin Hood** episode *The Youngest Outlaw*. Also appeared [uncredited] as Will Scatlock in *The Coming of Robin Hood* & *The Moneylender*.
Starred as King Arthur in **The Adventures of Sir Lancelot** episodes *The Knight with the Red Plume* and *The Queen's Knight*.
Played Kemp in the **H. G. Wells' Invisible Man** episode *Secret Experiment*, Col. Grahame in *The Gun Runners* and Sir Charles in *Death Cell*.
Played Colonel Bullinger in the **William Tell** episode *The Baroness*, Bullinger in *The Prisoner* & *The Traitor* and the General in *The General's Daughter*.

Seton Frank
Played the mechanic in the season two **Ghost Squad** episode *The Golden Silence*.
In **G.S.5**, played Harris in *Seven Sisters of Wong*.
Played the Afghan in the **Virgin of the Secret Service** episode *Dark Deeds on the Northwest Frontier*.

Severn Bernard
Played the first businessman in **The Adventurer** episode *Make it a Million.*

Severne Mary Ann
Played Beatrice in the **Father Brown** episode *The Quick One.*

Sewards Terence
Played Marsden in **The Persuaders!** episode *The Time and the Place.*

Sewell George
Appeared as Harry Venner in **The Adventurer** episode *Target!.*
Played Tim Murphy in the **Gideon's Way** episode *Boy with a Gun.*
Played Rufus Blake in the **Man in a Suitcase** episode *The Sitting Pigeon.*
Played Jansen in the **Randall and Hopkirk [Deceased]** aka **My Partner the Ghost** episode *Vendetta for a Dead Man.*
Starred in the series **UFO** as, regular, Colonel Alec Freeman.

Seymour Carolyn
Played Lady Greer Stevens in the **Return of the Saint** episode *The Arrangement.*
Played Eva in the second season **Space 1999** episode *The Seance Spectre.*

Seymour Heather
Played Mary in the third season **The Saint** episode *The House on Dragon's Rock.*

Seymour Jane
Hairdresser on **The Buccaneers** [aka **Dan Tempest**] episodes *The Raiders, Captain Dan Tempest, Dan Tempest's War with Spain, The Wasp, Whale Gold, Slave Ship, Gunpowder Plot, Articles of War, Ghost Ship, Conquest of New Providence, Mother Doughty's Crew, Blood Will Tell, Hurricane, Dead Man's Rock, Dangerous Cargo, Hand of the Hawk, Gentleman Jack and the Lady, Mr. Beamish and the Hangman's Noose, Marooned, Before the Mast, Dan Tempest and The Amazons, The Ladies, The Surgeon of Sangre Rojo, The Return of Calico Jack, Conquistador, Aztec Treasure, Prize of Andalusia, Cutlass Wedding, Dan Tempest Holds an Auction, Flip and Jenny, To the Rescue, Indian Fighters, Mistress Higgins' Treasure, The Spy Aboard, The Decoy, Pirate Honour, Instrument of War* and *Printer's Devil.*

Shakesby Patricia
Played Anne Shaw in *Adventure Five* of **Sapphire and Steel**.

Shampan Jack
Art Director on the season two **Danger Man** [aka *Secret Agent*] episodes: *Fish on the Hook, Don't Nail Him Yet, Fair Exchange , The Professionals, The Colonel's Daughter, It's Up to the Lady, That's Two of us Sorry, The Galloping Major, Yesterday's Enemies, Colony Three, A Man to be Trusted, The Battle of the Cameras, No Marks for Servility, The Ubiquitous Mr Lovergrove, A Date with Doris, Such Men are Dangerous, Have a Glass of Wine, The Mirror's New, Parallel Lines Sometimes Meet, You Are Not In Any Trouble Are You, The Outcast, The Mercenaries* and *Sting in the Tail.*
Art Director on all of **The Prisoner**'s episodes.

Shamsi Mohhammad Moosa
Played the carrier in the second series **Danger Man** [aka *Secret Agent*] episode *Judgement Day.*

Shannon Norma
Wrote the first series of **The Adventures of Robin Hood** episode *The Traitor* [with Ralph Smart].

Shaps Cyril
Played Zorba in **The Count of Monte Cristo** episode *Athens.*
Played Luis in the first season **Danger Man** episode *Hired Assassin* and Pietro in episode *Colonel Rodriguez.*
Played Esplin in the **Department S** episode *A Fish out of Water.*
Played Gamel in the **Interpol Calling** episode *Slave Ship* and Slade in *The Three Keys.*
Played Jean Cazette in the **Jason King** episode *A Thin Band of Air.*
Played Palma in the **Man in a Suitcase** episode *The Man who Stood Still.*
Played Zapata in the first series **Man of the World** episode *The Sentimental Agent.*
Played Professor Ganguin in **The Persuaders!** episode *The Ozerov Inheritance.*
Played the Doctor in the first series **The Protectors** episode *A Matter of Life and Death.*
Played Dr. Cholmond in the **Randall and Hopkirk [Deceased]** aka **My Partner the Ghost** episode *Somebody just Walked over my Grave.*
Played Jonkheer in the third season **The Saint** episode *The Angel's Eye.*
Played Bibot in **The Scarlet Pimpernel** episodes *The Lady in Distress, Sir Percy's Wager* & *Gentlemen of the Road.*
Played Saphodes in **The Sentimental Agent** episode *Not Quite Fully Covered.*
Took over from George Murcell to voice Professor Popkiss and Masterspy in the second season of the **Supercar** series.

Sharman Bruce
Played Scullion in the second series **The Adventures of Robin Hood** episode *Food for Thought.*
Assistant Director on **The Saint**.
Played Angelo in the **Sword of Freedom** episode *The School.*

Sharp Anne
Played Laura Darnley in **The Adventurer** episode *Mr Calloway is a Very Cautious Man.*
Played Jean Henderson in **The Baron** episode *The Man Outside.*
Starred as, series regular, Nicola Harvester in **Jason King**: *Toki, The Constance Missal, Uneasy Lies the Head, Nadine, Every Picture Tells a Story, Chapter One: The Company I Keep* & *That isn't Me, It's Somebody Else.*
Played Fay Sorrensen in the **Randall and Hopkirk [Deceased]** aka **My Partner the Ghost** episode *My Late Lamented Friend and Partner.*
Played Jane Soames in **The Champions** episode *The Night People.*
Played the receptionist in the first season **The Saint** episode *The Work of Art*, Janet Blaise in *The Arrow of God* and May Ulrig in *The Lawless Lady.*

Sharp Anthony
Played the Earl in the debut season **The Adventures of Robin Hood** episode *The Alchemist.*
Played Rice in **The Four Just Men** episode *The Man who wasn't There.*

Sharp Don
Directed **The Champions** episode *Project Zero.*
Directed the first series **Ghost Squad** episodes *Bullet With My Name on it, Hong Kong Story, The Broken Doll, Eyes of the Bat, Million Dollar Ransom* & *The Green Shoes* [*The Green Shoes* was shot for the first series, but due to an actors' strike, was originally shown as a season two episode].

Sharp John
Played Number 2 in **The Prisoner** episode *A Change of Mind.*
Played Sagran in the **Randall and Hopkirk [Deceased]** aka **My Partner the Ghost** episode *The Ghost who Saved the Bank at Monte Carlo.*

Sharp Leonard

Played the Dumb Beggar in the first series of **The Adventures of Robin Hood** episode *The Wager* and, in the third series, played the older man in *The Angry Village*, the Village Elder in *The Profiteer* & the weaver in *Lincoln Green*.

Played Rafferty in the **O.S.S.** episode *Operation Big House*.

Played the dealer in the **Sword of Freedom** episode *The Pagan Venus*.

Sharpe-Bolster Anita

Played the old lady in the second season **Danger Man** [aka **Secret Agent**] episode *Have a Glass of Wine*.

Played Zero's sister in the **O.S.S.** episode *Operation Chopping Block*.

Played Ada Harmer in the first season **The Saint** episode *The Latin Touch*.

Sharples Dick

Wrote, with Gerald Kelsey, the first series **Ghost Squad** episodes *Assassin, Million Dollar Ransom & Princess* [*Princess* was shot for the first series, but due to an actors' strike, was originally shown as a season two episode].

Wrote, with Gerald Kelsey, the first season **The Saint** episodes *The Latin Touch & The Charitable Countess*.

Sharplin John

Played Count Olivier in the second series **The Adventures of Robin Hood** episode *Food for Thought*.

Shaughnessy Alfred

Teleplayed the third season **The Saint** episode *Flight Plan* [from a story by Anthony Squire].

Shavelson Melville

Created the series **Shirley's World** [with Frank Tarloff].

Shaw Barnaby

Played John Rutland in the **UFO** episodes *Mindbender* and *A Question of Priorities*.

Shaw Denis

Appeared as the butcher in **The Adventures of Robin Hood** first series episode *A Guest for the Gallows*.

Played the estate agent in the second series **Danger Man** [aka **Secret Agent**] episode *Are You Going to Be More Permanent?*

Played U Toke in the season two **Ghost Squad** episode *East of Mandalay*.

Played the Ambassador in the **G.S.5** episode *Death of a Cop*.

Played the club manager in the **H. G. Wells' Invisible Man** episode *Man in Disguise*.

Played the shopkeeper in **The Prisoner** episode *Arrival* and reprised the role in *Checkmate*.

Played Karger in the **O.S.S.** episode *Operation Tulip*.

Played Wazir in the **Virgin of the Secret Service** episode *Dark Deeds on the Northwest Frontier*.

Appeared as Peter Carr in the **White Hunter** episode *Squire of the Serengeti*.

Shaw Jean

Played Annette in the third season **Danger Man** [aka **Secret Agent**] episode *The Hunting Party*.

Shaw June

Played the secretary in the season two **Ghost Squad** episode *The Golden Silence*.

Shaw Lou

Wrote **The Adventurer** episode *The Good Book*.

Shaw Martin

Played Savi in the **Strange Report** episode *Report 7931: SNIPER: 'When is Your Cousin Not?'*.

Shaw Maxwell

Played Sharp in **The Buccaneers** [aka **Dan Tempest**] episode and *Printer's Devil*.

Played Ghazi in the first season **Danger Man** episode *The Nurse*. In the second series [now aka **Secret Agent**] played Nicos in *It's Up to the Lady* and Kronenberg in *Are You Going to Be More Permanent?*

Featured in the **Espionage** episode *Festival of Pawns*.

Played Ashley in the **Father Brown** episode *The Quick One*.

Played Leeser in the first series **Ghost Squad** episode *Princess* [this episode was shot for the first series, but due to an actors' strike, was originally shown as a season two episode].

Played Mark 'Frisky' Lee in the **Gideon's Way** episode *Big Fish, Little Fish*.

Played Guilio in the **Man in a Suitcase** episode *Find the Lady*.

Played Vine in **The Persuaders!** episode *Someone Waiting*.

Played Baruna in the first series **The Protectors** episode *A Matter of Life and Death*.

Played Spencer Vallance in the second season **The Saint** episode *The Imprudent Politician*.

Played Grifone in the **Sword of Freedom** episode *The Ship* and Ginori in *Vespucci*.

Played Doctor Schroeder in the **UFO** episodes *E.S.P., Flight Path & Computer Affair*.

Shaw Michael

Played Klos in the second season **Man of the World** episode *In the Picture*.

Shaw Richard

Played the Kommandant in the **O.S.S.** episode *Operation Meatball*.

Played Schultz in the second season **The Saint** episode *The Hi-Jackers* and Gunter in the third season's *The Art Collectors*.

Played Vanderhof in the **Sir Francis Drake** episode *Drake on Trial*.

Played Tasker in the **William Tell** episode *The Prisoner*.

Shaw Robert

Starred, as from the third episode, as Dan Tempest in the series **The Buccaneers** [aka **Dan Tempest**].

Played Tony Costello in the first season **Danger Man** episode *Bury the Dead*.

Played Stuart in **The Four Just Men** episode *Crack-Up*.

Played Lord Anthony Dewhurst in **The Scarlet Pimpernel** episode *The Hostage*.

Played Bob Gordon in the **White Hunter** episode *Voodoo Wedding*.

Guest starred as Peter in the **William Tell** episode *The Trap*.

Shaw-Vance Denise

Stage Manager on **Sapphire and Steel**.

Shawzin Barry

Guested as Sir Hubert in the debut season of **The Adventures of Robin Hood** episode *Trial by Battle*.

Played Marko in **The Baron** episode *Farewell to Yesterday*.

Played Salah in the first season **Danger Man** episode *The Leak*.

Played Tony in **The Four Just Men** episode *The Man in the Royal Suite*.

Played Suratmo in the season two **Ghost Squad** episode *East of Mandalay*.

Played Giorgio in the **H. G. Wells' Invisible Man** episode *The Decoy*.

Played Malouf in the **Man in a Suitcase** episode *The Revolutionaries*.

Played Nick Nigkoma in the second season **The Saint** episode *The Smart Detective* and Paco in *The Golden Frog*.

Played Uncle Georgi in **The Sentimental Agent** episode *Not Quite Fully Covered*.

Played Chamberlain in the **Sir Francis Drake** episode *Johnnie Factotum*.

Played Marezza in the **Sword of Freedom** episode *Angelica's Past*.

Sheard Michael
Played Philip Aylmer in the **Father Brown** episode *The Dagger with Wings*.
Played the electrician in the **Jason King** episode *A Page Before Dying*.
Played Walden in **The Persuaders!** episode *A Home of One's Own*.
Played Inspector Luhrs in the second season **The Protectors** episode *Wam* [part two].
Played the German commentator in the **Randall and Hopkirk [Deceased]** aka **My Partner the Ghost** episode *Somebody just Walked over my Grave*.
Played the T.V. manager in the **Strange Report** episode *Report 7931: SNIPER: 'When is Your Cousin Not?'*.

Sheean Ellen
Played Lady Miriam Marden in the **Father Brown** episode *The Actor and the Alibi*.

Sheeny Brian
Played Neilson in the **O.S.S.** episode *Operation Sardine*.

Sheers Susan
Played the female code expert in **The Prisoner** episode *Hammer into Anvil*.

Sheerwin Derrick
Played the second officer in the **H. G. Wells' Invisible Man** episode *The Big Plot*.

Shelby Nicole
Played the receptionist in the third season **Danger Man [aka Secret Agent]** episode *Dangerous Secret*.
Played Ayesha in the third season **The Saint** episode *The Gadic Collection*.

Sheldon James
Directed the **Espionage** episodes *The Light of the Friendly Star* & *Festival of Pawns*.

Shelley Barbara
Played Margaret Errington in the season two **Ghost Squad** episode *The Desperate Diplomat*.
Guested as Diane in the **Interpol Calling** episode *Checkmate*.
Played Dolores Hornsby in the **Man in a Suitcase** episode *All that Glitters*.
Played Valerie North in the first season **The Saint** episode *The Covetous Headman*.
Appeared as Martha in the **White Hunter** episode *Inside Story* and as Anna Williams in *The Long Knife*.
Played Louise Goddard in the first season **Danger Man** episode *The Traitor* and Gina Scarlotti in *View from the Villa*.

Shelton Shane
Played Kruger in the second season **The Protectors** episode *Sugar and Spice*.

Shepherd Albert
Played the first prison guard in the third season **Danger Man [aka Secret Agent]** episode *Two Birds with One Bullet*.
Played Lomax in the **Department S** episode *The Bones of Byrom Blain*.
Played Hayes in the **Strange Report** episode *Report 3906: COVER GIRLS: 'Last year's Model'*.

Shepherd Elizabeth
Played Louise Carron in the third season **Danger Man [aka Secret Agent]** episode *Dangerous Secret*.

Shepherd Paul
Played Verdis in **The Count of Monte Cristo** episode *First Train to Paris*.

Shepherd Tony
Played the first Nazi in the **O.S.S.** episode *Operation Jingle Bells*.

Shepley Michael
Played Sir Jasper in the **H. G. Wells' Invisible Man** episode *Flight into Darkness*.

Sheppard Antony
Played the peasant in the **O.S.S.** episode *Operation Firefly*.
Played a rally official in the fourth season **The Saint** episode *The World Beater*.

Sheppard Stephen
Played Stephen in **The Adventurer** episode *Thrust and Counter Thrust*.
Played Conyapepi in the second season **The Protectors** episode *Decoy*.

Sheppard Tony
Appeared as Henry Zender in the **White Hunter** episode *Operation Transfer*.

Shepperton Studios
As from episode 27 of series two, where **Danger Man [aka Secret Agent]** was filmed.
Where the series **Man of the World** was filmed.

Sherman Bob
Played Patrick Floyd in the **Father Brown** episode *The Oracle of the Dog*.
Played the Lieutenant in **The Persuaders!** episode *Element of Risk*.
Played Jimmy in the **Return of the Saint** episode *The Debt Collectors*.

Sherman Geraldine
Played the secretary in the **Strange Report** episode *Report 2475: REVENGE: 'When a Man Hates'*.

Sherman John
Played Diabolo in **The Count of Monte Cristo** episode *The Devil's Emissary*.

Sherriff Betty
Hairdresser on **The Adventures of Sir Lancelot** episodes *The Outcast, Winged Victory, Sir Bliant, The Magic Sword, Lancelot's Banishment, Roman Wall, Caledon, Shepherd's War* and *The Theft of Excalibur*.
Hairdressing on season three of **Danger Man [aka Secret Agent]**.
Hairdressing on **The Protectors**.

Sherrier Julian
Played the French truck driver in **The Baron** episode *Something for a Rainy Day*.
Played Sayyed in the third season **Danger Man [aka Secret Agent]** episode *To our Best Friend*.
Played Rene in **The Four Just Men** episode *Marie*.
Played the telephone operator in the season two **Ghost Squad** episode *Quarantine at Kavar* and Karim in *The Heir Apparent*.
Guested as Baratopi in the **Interpol Calling** episode *Ascent to Murder* and as De Silva in *The Angola Brights*.
Played Kahan's henchman in the first series **The Protectors** episode *.....With a Little Help from my Friends*.
Played Mr. Sen in the fourth season **The Saint** episode *The People Importers*.

Sherwin Derrich
Played Vee in **The Baron** episode *The Long, Long Day*.
Played Aly in the first season **Danger Man** episode *Position of Trust*.
Played Hans in the **William Tell** episode *Secret Weapon*.

Sherwin Stuart
Played the driver in **The Adventurer** episode *Action!*.

Sheybal Vladek
Played Reiner in **The Baron** episode *And Suddenly You're Dead*.
Played Kellor in **The Champions** episode *The Dark Island*.
Played Tewflick in the second series **Danger Man** [aka **Secret Agent**] episode *Fish on the Hook*.
Played Sandor Karoleon in the first series **The Protectors** episode *Brother Hood*.
Played Nikita Roskin in the third season **The Saint** episode *The Helpful Pirate*.
Played Arva in **The Sentimental Agent** episode *Meet my Son, Henry*.
Played Kulik in the **Strange Report** episode *Report 7931: SNIPER: 'When is Your Cousin Not?'*.
Starred in the series **UFO** as, regular, Dr Jackson.

Shin Lian
Voiced Harmony Angel in **Captain Scarlet and the Mysterons**.

Shine Bill
Played Mr Hathwin in the season two **Ghost Squad** episode *Escape Route*.

Shingleton Wilfrid
Production Designer on **Strange Report**.

Shrapnel John
Played Jack Turner in the first season **Space 1999** episode *Death's Other Dominion*.

Shrubshawe Michael
Played the Colonel in the **Shirley's World** episode *The Colonel*.

Shutt Ernest
Puppet Operator on **Thunderbirds**.

Shutt Judith
Puppet Operator on **Thunderbirds**.

Shutt Plugg
Puppet Sculptor on **Joe 90** and **The Secret Service**.

Sibley Jim
Sound Editor on **The Champions**.
Dubbing Editor on **The Persuaders!**
Dubbing Editor on **The Saint**.

Sichel John
Directed the **Virgin of the Secret Service** episodes *Russian Roundabout* & *The Rajah and the Suffragette*.

Siddons Harold
Played the pilot in the season one **Danger Man** episode *The Nurse*.

Sidwell Richard
Editor on **The Adventures of Robin Hood**.
Editor on **The Buccaneers** [aka **Dan Tempest**] episodes *Gunpowder Plot, Articles of War, Conquest of New Providence, Mother Doughty's Crew, Blood Will Tell, Dead Man's Rock, Hand of the Hawk, Gentleman Jack and the Lady, Marooned,*

Before the Mast, The Return of Calico Jack, Aztec Treasure, Cutlass Wedding, To the Rescue, Indian Fighters, The Spy Aboard, Instrument of War and *Printer's Devil*.

Siegenberg Kurt
Played the boy in **The Four Just Men** episode *Village of Shame* and Pierre in *The Deadly Capsule*.

Sieman Frank
Played Detective Inspector Marks in the first season **Danger Man** episode *Name, Date and Place*.
Played the doctor in the **O.S.S.** episode *Operation Eel*.
Played Joe Tracey in the first season **The Saint** episode *The Gentle Ladies*.

Silver Pat
With Jesse Lasky Jr, wrote the third season **Danger Man** [aka **Secret Agent**] episode *Two Birds with One Bullet* and the first series **Space 1999** episode *The Full Circle*.

Sim Gerald
Played Foster in **The Baron** episode *The Edge of Fear*.
Played Crawford in the **G.S.5** episode *The Goldfish Bowl*.
Played James Hedley in the **Man in a Suitcase** episode *Dead Man's Shoes* and Detective Inspector Hedley in *Burden of Proof*.
Played Dr. Gordon in **The Persuaders!** episode *Someone Like Me*.
Played Chief Superintendent Cavanagh in the **Strange Report** episodes *Report 2641: HOSTAGE: 'If You Won't Learn, Die!* & *Report 0846: LONELYHEARTS: 'Who Killed Dan Cupid?'*.

Simon Charles
Played Gower in the first season **The Saint** episode *The Fellow Traveller*.

Simpson Bill
Played Professor Bartlett in the **Return of the Saint** episode *The Imprudent Professor*.

Simpson Carroll
Played Maria in the first season **The Saint** episode *The Latin Touch*.

Simpson Georgina
Played the nurse in the **Jason King** episode *A Royal Flush*.
Played Magda in **The Persuaders!** episode *The Ozerov Inheritance*.

Simpson John
Played the second bank teller in the season two **Ghost Squad** episode *Hot Money*.

Sims Joan
Played Nell in the debut series **The Adventures of Robin Hood** episode *The Sheriff's Boots*.
Played Abigail in **The Buccaneers** [aka **Dan Tempest**] episodes *Dan Tempest and The Amazons* and *Cutlass Wedding*.

Sinclair David
Played Smith in the **Randall and Hopkirk [Deceased]** aka **My Partner the Ghost** episode *The House on Haunted Hill*.

Sinclair Edward
Played the business man in the second series **Danger Man** [aka **Secret Agent**] episode *The Black Book*.

Sinclair Peter
Played Archie, the piper in the first series **Man of the World** episode *The Highland Story*.
Appeared as Harajo Sam [Fergus] in the **White Hunter** episodes *The Treasure of Tippu Tib* & *The Prisoner*.

Sinden Donald
Played The Colonel in **The Prisoner** episode *Many Happy Returns*.

Singer Campbell
Played Colonel Segur in the first season **Danger Man** episode *Josetta* and General Abeijon in *Colonel Rodriguez*.
Played Porter in **The Persuaders!** episode *The Time and the Place*.
Played Inspector Teal in the first season **The Saint** episode *The Man who was Lucky* and Fenton in the third season's *The Gadget Lovers*.

Singh Mohan
Played Jam Singh in the **Virgin of the Secret Service** episode *The Rajah and the Suffragette*.

Singleton Mark
Played the psychiatrist in the **Department S** episode *Black Out*.

Singuineau Frank
Played the Chief in **The Buccaneers** [aka **Dan Tempest**] episode *Hurricane*.
Played Simon in the second season **Man of the World** episode *Jungle Mission*.
Played Karakaan in the **Virgin of the Secret Service** episode *The Amazons*.
Played Kilmani in the **White Hunter** episode *Out of the Wind* and Dr. Hudia in *Let My People Go*.

Sinha Shivendra
Played Kumar in the fourth season **The Saint** episode *The People Importers*.
Played Mehdi in the **Strange Report** episode *Report 3424: EPIDEMIC: 'A Most Curious Crime'*.

Siodmak Robert
Directed the **O.S.S.** episodes *Operation Foulball, Operation Flint Axe, Operation Powder Puff* & *Operation Eel*. The series was a 'Robert Siodmak Production in association with LSQ: an ITC and Buckeye Enterprises Production'.

Sirr Michael
Played Tulan in the second season **Man of the World** episode *The Prince*.

Skarreso Karin
Played the hotel clerk in the **Return of the Saint** episode *The Murder Cartel*.

Skene Anthony
Wrote **The Prisoner** episodes *A. B. and C., Many Happy Returns* and *Dance of the Dead*.
Wrote the **Shirley's World** episode *A Girl Like You*.

Skene Oliver
Wrote the season three **The Adventures of Robin Hood** episodes *The Bride of Robin Hood, The Christmas Goose, Castle in the Air* & *The Genius*.
Teleplayed **The Four Just Men** episode *The Prime Minister* [from a story by Alec Coppel] and co-wrote the story for *The Deadly Capsule* [with Samuel B. West: teleplayed by Jan Read].

Skillan George
Played Bergere in **The Count of Monte Cristo** episode *The Art of Terror*.

Skinner Arthur
Appeared in a range of roles in **The Adventures of Robin Hood**: Will in *The Sheriff's Boots*, the Sergeant in *Errand of Mercy*, Skinner in *The Miser*, Arthur a Bland in *Children of the*

Greenwood, the reveller in *The Wanderer*, the Vintner in *The Byzantine Treasure*, Much in *Table's Turned*, Rolf in *The Traitor*, Quentin in *The Thorkill Ghost* & the Captain of the Guard in *The Prisoner* [series 1]; Hugh in *The Road in the Air* [2]; the first Man-at-Arms in *The Fire*, the first Sentry in *The Genius* & the second Man-at-Arms in *Little Mother* [3] and the tradesman in *The Flying Sorcerer* [4].
Played Johann in the **William Tell** episode *The Baroness*.

Skipp Raymond
Played Barney in the second season **The Protectors** episode *Blockbuster*.

Skriver Ina
Played A in the second season **Space 1999** episode *The A B Chrysalis*.

Slaney Ivor
Director of Music on the series **Man of the World**.
Music on the **Sir Francis Drake & The Sentimental Agent** series.

Slater Guy
Played Donald Druce in the **Father Brown** episode *The Oracle of the Dog*.

Slater John
Played the Prime Minister in the second series **Danger Man** [aka **Secret Agent**] episode *The Mercenaries*.

Slater Michael
Played Pillet in **The Champions** episode *A Case of Lemmings*.

Slavid John
Played the policeman in the first season **Danger Man** episode *The Prisoner*.

Slavin George
Co-wrote **The Four Just Men** episode *The Man in the Road* [with Samuel B. West].

Sloan Michael
Played the radio operator in **The Persuaders!** episode *Element of Risk*.

Smart Patsy
Played Mrs Parkes in the first season **Danger Man** episode *The Leak* and in the second series [now aka **Secret Agent**] played the nanny in *Whatever Happened to George Foster?*.
Played Mrs Samuels in the **Gideon's Way** episode *To Catch a Tiger*.
Played the Australian's wife in the first series **Man of the World** episode *The Highland Story*.
Played the waitress in **The Prisoner** episode *Arrival* and the night maid in *Dance of the Dead*.
Played the nurse in the **William Tell** episode *Gessler's Daughter*.

Smart Ralph
Directed the first season **The Adventures of Robin Hood** episodes *The Coming of Robin Hood, The Moneylender, Friar Tuck, Maid Marian, A Guest for the Gallows, The Inquisitor, The Knight Who Came To Dinner, The Challenge, Checkmate, The Highlander, The Betrothal, The Alchemist, The Intruders, The Sheriff's Boots, Errand of Mercy, Ladies of Sherwood, Will Scarlet* and *Children of the Greenwood*. Wrote the first series episodes *The Sheriff's Boots* [with James Aldridge], *Ladies of Sherwood, The Miser, The May Queen, Secret Mission* & *The Traitor* [with Norma Shannon] and the second season's *Hubert* [with Anne Rodney] & *The Final Tax* [with Ernest Borneman].

Directed **The Adventures of Sir Lancelot** episodes *The Knight with the Red Plume, The Ferocious Fathers* and *The Queen's Knight*.

Producer and director on **The Buccaneers** [aka **Dan Tempest**]: directed *Blackbeard, The Raiders, Captain Dan Tempest & Before the Mast* and produced *Dan Tempest's War with Spain, The Wasp, Whale Gold, Slave Ship, Gunpowder Plot, Articles of War, Mr. Beamish and the Hangman's Noose, Marooned, Before the Mast, Dan Tempest and The Amazons, The Ladies & The Surgeon of Sangre Rojo*.

Wrote **The Champions** episodes *To Trap a Rat* and *Get Me Out of Here!*.

Created the **Danger Man** [aka **Secret Agent**] series. Produced series one and executive produced season two & three. Directed the first season episodes *Time to Kill & Position of Trust*. Wrote the first season episodes: *View from the Villa* [with Brian Clemens], *Josetta, The Blue Veil* [with Don Ingalis], *The Girl in Pink Pyjamas* [with Ian Stuart Black: teleplayed from a story by Brian Clemens], *Position of Trust* [original story: teleplayed by Jo Eisinger], *The Lonely Chair* [with John Roddick], *The Sanctuary* [with John Roddick], *The Key* [original story: teleplayed by Jack Whittingham], *The Prisoner* [with Robert Stewart], *Colonel Rodriguez, The Island* [with Brian Clemens], *The Girl who Liked GIs* [with Marc Brandel], *Name, Date and Place* [with John Roddick], *The Conspirators* [with John Roddick], *Vacation, The Honeymooners* [with Lewis Davidson], *The Gallows Tree* [with Marc Brandel], *The Relaxed Informer* [with Robert Stewart], *The Brothers, Bury the Dead* [teleplayed from a story by Brian Clemens], *The Contessa* [with John Roddick], *The Leak* [with Brian Clemens], *The Trap* [with John Roddick], *Hired Assassin* [with John Roddick], *Find and Destroy* [with John Roddick], *The Nurse* [with Brian Clemens] & *Dead Man Walks* [with Brian Clemens]; the second season's: *No Marks for Servility, Such Men are Dangerous, A Room in the Basement, Parallel Lines Sometimes Meet* [additional dialogue: written by Malcolm Hulke], *A Very Dangerous Game* [with David Stone] & *The Mercenaries* and the third's *To our Best Friend, Say it with Flowers* [with Jacques Gilles], *The Man who wouldn't Talk* [with Donald Johnson], *Someone is Liable to get Hurt* [with Philip Broadley], *Dangerous Secret* [with Donald Johnson], *I can only Offer you Sherry, I'm Afraid you Have the Wrong Number* & *The Paper Chase* [with Philip Broadley].

Producer on the series **H. G. Wells' Invisible Man**. Wrote the episodes: *Crisis in the Desert, The Locked Room* [story: teleplayed by Lindsay Galloway], *Blind Justice, Bank Raid* [with Doreen Montgomery], *The Big Plot* [co-wrote the story with Tony O'Grady - aka Brian Clemens: teleplayed by Ian Stuart Black] and *Shadow on the Screen* [co-wrote the story with Philip Levene: teleplayed by Ian Stuart Black]. Directed *Bank Raid*.

Wrote the first season **The Protectors** episode *The Numbers Game*.

Wrote the **Randall and Hopkirk** [**Deceased**] aka **My Partner the Ghost** episodes *My Late Lamented Friend and Partner & But what a Sweet Little Room*.

Worked extensively on the **William Tell** series: directed *The Emperor's Hat*; produced *The Emperor's Hat, The Raid, The Assassins, The Hostages, Landslide, The Boy Slaves, The Baroness, Secret Death, Voice in the Night, The Lost Letter, The Gauntlet of St. Gerhardt, The Cuckoo, The Elixir* and *The Magic Powder*; executive produced *The Prisoner, Gessler's Daughter, Manhunt, The Bandit, Undercover, The Suspect, Golden Wheel, The Bride, The Avenger, The Young Widow, The Trap, The Killer, The Mountain People, The Surgeon, The Ensign, The Unwelcome Stranger, The Black Brothers, The General's Daughter, Secret Weapon, Castle of Fear, The Spider* and *The Master Spy*; teleplayed *The Assassins* [original story by Rene Wilde]; wrote the original story for *The Hostages* [teleplayed by Doreen Montgomery]; wrote the original story for *The Baroness* [teleplayed by John Kruse]; wrote the original story for *Secret Death* [teleplayed by Doreen Montgomery]; wrote *Voice in the Night*; wrote the original story for *The Gauntlet of St. Gerhardt* [teleplayed by Doreen Montgomery];

wrote *The Cuckoo*; wrote the original story for *The Elixir* [teleplayed by Lindsay Galloway]; wrote the original story for *The Magic Powder* [teleplayed by Martin Worth]; wrote the original story for *Manhunt* [teleplayed by Doreen Montgomery]; wrote the original story for *The Bandit* [teleplayed by Doreen Montgomery] and wrote the story for *The Spider* [teleplayed by Roger Marshall].

Smedley-Aston Brian
Second Unit Director on **Strange Report** and directed the episodes *Report 4977: SWINDLE: 'Square Root of Evil'* and *Report 1021: SHRAPNEL: 'The Wish in the Dream'*.

Smee Derek
Played the manager of Aladdin's Cave in the **Man in a Suitcase** episode *The Girl who Never was*.
Played the young man at the airport in the fourth season **The Saint** episode *The Ex-King of Diamonds*.

Smilie Jim
Played Baxter in the first season **Space 1999** episode *End of Eternity*.

Smith Andrea
Played the nurse in the **Return of the Saint** episode *The Roman Touch*.

Smith Clive
Sound Editor on **The Prisoner** episode *Checkmate*.

Smith Cyril
Regular in **The Adventures of Sir Lancelot** as Merlin: *The Knight with the Red Plume, The Queen's Knight, The Outcast, Winged Victory, Sir Bliant, The Magic Sword, Lancelot's Banishment, Caledon, Shepherd's War, The Pirates, Double Identity, The Witch's Brew, Ruby of Radnor, The Lesser Breed, The Magic Book, Knight Errant, The Theft of Excalibur, Maid of Somerset, Sir Crustabread, The Ugly Duckling, The Lady Lilith, Knight's Choice* and *Thieves*.

Smith Derek
Played Jason Howard in the first series **The Protectors** episode *The Big Hit*.

Smith J. B.
Sound Recordist on **The Protectors** and **UFO**.

Smith James
Wardrobe on **The Protectors**.

Smith John S.
Music Editor on **The Prisoner** episodes *The General, Dance of the Dead* and *It's Your Funeral*.

Smith June
Played Annette Dosterd in the first season **The Saint** episode *The Work of Art*.

Smith Keith
Played the thin man in **The Four Just Men** episode *The Crying Jester*.
Played Latignant's Assistant in the second season **The Saint** episode *The Persistent Parasite*.

Smith Kevin
Played the photographer in the **Randall and Hopkirk** [**Deceased**] aka **My Partner the Ghost** episode *Just for the Record*.

Smith Kim
Played the office boy in the **Shirley's World** episode *To Dream the Improbable Dream*.

Smith Madeline
Played Jonquil in the **Jason King** two parter *All that Glisters*.
Played Carla I in **The Persuaders!** episode *The Long Good-bye*.

Smith Nicholas
Played the Postmaster in **The Champions** episode *Project Zero*.
Played the Bishop in the fourth season **The Saint** two parter *The Fiction Makers*.

Smith Raymond
Played Henry in the **Man in a Suitcase** episode *The Girl who Never was*.

Smith Stanley
Sound Editor on **The Prisoner** episodes *The Schizoid Man* and *Dance of the Dead*.

Smithers William
Featured in the **Espionage** episode *A Tiny Drop of Poison*.

Smythe Rita
Played the telephonist in **The Sentimental Agent** episode *The Height of Fashion*.

Snaith Bill
Assistant Director on **Gideon's Way**.

Snell Tony
Played a passenger in the **Father Brown** episode *The Curse of the Golden Cross*.

Snowden Roger
Played Rodriguez in **The Buccaneers** [aka **Dan Tempest**] episode *Before the Mast*.

Soall Terence
Played Mears in the **G.S.5** episode *Rich Ruby Wine*.

Soan Doreen
Continuity on **UFO**.

Soblosky Perry
Played Gigilo in **The Adventurer** episode *The Good Book*.

Sofiano Jayne
Played Juliet Crowther in the **Man in a Suitcase** episode *Dead Man's Shoes*.
Played Stella Longman in the fourth season **The Saint** episode *The Man who Gambled with Life*.

Softley Ken
Assistant Director on **The Champions**.

Soiron Elma
Played the bridge player in the **Department S** episode *A Fish out of Water*.

Sokoloff Harvey
Played Terry Mitchell in the **Department S** episode *Death on Reflection*.

Solon Ewan
Played Major Percy in **The Buccaneers** [aka **Dan Tempest**] episode *To the Rescue* and the Spanish Admiral in *Hurricane*.
Played the tall man in **The Count of Monte Cristo** episode *The Barefoot Empress*.
Played President Pablo Gomez in the first season **Danger Man** episode *The Lovers*.
Played the Sheriff in **The Four Just Men** episode *Panic Button* and the Inspector in *The Man with the Golden Touch*.

Played Rev. Anthony Felling in the first series **Ghost Squad** episode *The Green Shoes* [this episode was shot for the first series, but due to an actors' strike, was originally shown as a season two episode].
Played the Superintendent in the **H. G. Wells' Invisible Man** episode *The Vanishing Evidence*.
Played Gault in the first series **Man of the World** episode *The Nature of Justice*.
Played The Oracle in the **Virgin of the Secret Service** episode *Across the Silver Pass of Gusri Song*.

Somers Julian
Played Sir Paul in the season three **The Adventures of Robin Hood** episode *The Crusaders*.
Appeared as Kafan in **The Adventures of Sir Lancelot** episode *Knight Errant*.
Played Pierre Duval in **The Count of Monte Cristo** episode *The Art of Terror*.
Played the police Inspector in the second series **Danger Man** [aka **Secret Agent**] episode *Sting in the Tail*.
Played Bernard Blake in the **Father Brown** episode *The Arrow of Heaven*.
Played Cameron in the **Gideon's Way** episode *The Great Plane Robbery*.
Played Simmons in the **H. G. Wells' Invisible Man** episode *Blind Justice*.
Played the Sergeant in **The Scarlet Pimpernel** episode *The Princess*.
Played Hugo in the **William Tell** episode *The Ensign* and Kurt in *The Young Widow*.

Sommers Julie
Played Julia in **The Count of Monte Cristo** episode *Mecklenburg*.

Soong Lucille
Played the hotel barmaid in the season two **Ghost Squad** episode *Sabotage*.
Appeared as the flower girl in **The Prisoner** episode *A. B. and C.*

Sorell Maya
Played Barbara Keogh in the season two **Ghost Squad** episode *The Big Time*.

Soskin Henry
Played Branco in **The Champions** episode *Desert Journey*.
Played Abdul in the season two **Ghost Squad** episode *Gertrude*.
Played Douglas in the **Man in a Suitcase** episode *Which Way did he Go, McGill?*.
Played Kemal in the third season **The Saint** episode *The Gadic Collection* and Warburg in *The Counterfeit Countess*.

Soule Peter
Played Flip in **The Buccaneers** [aka **Dan Tempest**] episode *Flip and Jenny*.

Southcott Colin
Set Dresser on **The Prisoner** episode *Do Not Forsake Me Oh My Darling*.

Southgate Mary
Make-up on season one and two of **Sapphire and Steel**.

Southworth John
Played Todd in the second series **Danger Man** [aka **Secret Agent**] episode *That's Two of Us Sorry*.

Spafford Robert
Co-wrote the **O.S.S.** episode *Operation Death Trap* [with Paul Dudley].

Spalding Kim
Played Esco in **The Count of Monte Cristo** episode *The Golden Blade*.

Sparks Fay
Played Roshan Cooch Benares in the **Virgin of the Secret Service** episode *The Rajah and the Suffragette*.

Sparrow Walter
Played George Whetlor in **The Champions** episode *The Night People*.
Played the tramp in the **Randall and Hopkirk [Deceased]** aka **My Partner the Ghost** episode *Could You Recognise the Man Again?*.

Spear Bernard
Played the barman in the season two **Ghost Squad** episode *Sentences of Death*.

Spear Michael
Played Kaplan in the first season **The Saint** episode *The Covetous Headman*.

Spencer Don
Title music vocals for **Fireball XL5**.

Spencer Gladys
Played Principessa Lilli in the second season **The Protectors** episode *Fighting Fund*.

Spencer Linbert
Played Clive in **The Champions** episode *Reply Box No: 666*.

Spencer Penny
Played a SHADO operative in the **UFO** episode *A Question of Priorities*.

Spencer Sally-Jane
Played the young girl in the car in the **Department S** episode *The Man from X*.

Spenser David
Appeared as Atar in the third season **The Saint** episode *Flight Plan*.

Spenser Jeremy
Played Shah of Assini in the second series **Danger Man** [aka **Secret Agent**] episode *Sting in the Tail*.
Played Cesarito in **The Four Just Men** episode *The Moment of Truth*.
Played Bradshaw in the **Man in a Suitcase** episode *Day of Execution*.

Sperdakos George
Played Ricci in the first season **The Saint** episode *The Careful Terrorist*.

Spicer Penny
Played the second model in the **Man in a Suitcase** episode *Variation on a Million Bucks* [part 1: also combined with part 2 to form a movie: *To Chase a Million*].

Spinetti Victor
Played the Commissionaire in the first season **The Saint** episode *The Romantic Matron*.

Spinner Anthony
Producer on the **Return of the Saint** series.

Spiro Alyson
Played Liz in *Adventure Four* of **Sapphire and Steel**.

Spooner Dennis
Created the series **The Adventurer** [with Monty Berman] and served as Executive Story Consultant.
Wrote **The Baron** episodes *Diplomatic Immunity*, *The Persuaders*, *Enemy of the State*, *And Suddenly You're Dead* [with Terry Nation], *Masquerade* [with Terry Nation: two parter: *Masquerade - part 1* and *The Killing - part 2*: edited together, also exists as a feature entitled *Man In a Looking Glass*], *There's Someone Close Behind You* [with Terry Nation], *Time to Kill*, *A Memory of Evil* [with Terry Nation], *You Can't Win Them All*, *The High Terrace*, *The Edge of Fear*, *Long Ago and Far Away* & *So Dark the Night* [with Terry Nation].
Created **The Champions** [with Monty Berman], served as Script Supervisor and wrote *The Beginning*, *The Search*, *The Interrogation* & *The Gun-Runners* [*The Beginning* & *The Interrogation* were combined to form a 'feature' entitled *Legend of The Champions*].
Created the series **Department S** [with Monty Berman] and served as Executive Story Consultant.
Wrote the **Fireball XL5** episodes *Space Pen*, *Space Vacation*, *Robert to the Rescue*, *Mystery of The TA2*, *Dangerous Cargo*, *Whistle for Danger*, *Invasion Earth* and *Space City Special*.
Created the series **Jason King** [with Monty Berman] and served as Executive Story Consultant. Wrote the episodes *Wanna Buy a Television Series* aka *A Face I Used to Know*, *An Author in Search of Two Characters* & *That isn't Me, It's Somebody Else*.
Created the **Man in a Suitcase** series [with Richard Harris: devised by Stanley R. Greenberg].
Wrote the first season **The Protectors** episode *The Bodyguards*.
Created the series **Randall and Hopkirk [Deceased]** aka **My Partner the Ghost** and served as Executive Story Consultant.
Wrote the **Stingray** episodes *Sea of Oil*, *Treasure Down Below*, *The Golden Sea*, *Countdown*, *Loch Ness Monster*, *The Invaders*, *Stand by for Action*, *An Echo of Danger*, *In Search of the Tajmanon*, *Set Sail for Adventure*, *Rescue from the Skies* and *A Christmas to Remember*.
Wrote the first season **Thunderbirds** episodes *Day of Disaster*, *End of the Road*, *Vault of Death*, *The Mighty Atom*, *The Imposters* & *Cry Wolf*.
Wrote the **UFO** episode *Destruction*.

Spratling Tony
Director of Photography on **The Persuaders!**

Sproule Peter
Played Ferris in the **Timeslip** story *The Wrong End of Time* [episode 1].

Spyrou Maxine
Played Hedi in the first series **Man of the World** episode *Specialist for the Kill*.

Squire Anthony
Wrote the story for the third season **The Saint** episode *Flight Plan* [teleplayed by Alfred Shaughnessy].

Squire Anthony
Director on **The Adventures of Robin Hood**: *The Dowry*, *The Frightened Tailor*, *The Black Five* & *Carlotta* [series 2]; *The Bride of Robin Hood*, *The Challenge of the Black Knight* & *Knight Errant* [3] and *The Debt* [4].
Directed **The Adventures of Sir Lancelot** episodes *Lancelot's Banishment* and *The Black Castle*.
Directed the **Sword of Freedom** episodes *The Pagan Venus*, *Vespucci*, *Chart of Gold* & *The Lion and the Mouse*.
Directed the **William Tell** episodes *The Bandit* & *The Avenger*.

Squire William
Guested as Vef in the first series of **The Adventures of Robin Hood** episode *The Byzantine Treasure*.
Guested as Duncan in **The Champions** episode *Nutcracker*.

Played Waring in the **H. G. Wells' Invisible Man** episode *The Big Plot*.
Played Colonel Gardner in the **Jason King** episode *The Stones of Venice*.
Played Sam Seymour in the **Randall and Hopkirk [Deceased] aka My Partner the Ghost** episode *A Sentimental Journey*.

Staab Linda
Played Linda McCall in the first series **The Protectors** episode *It Could be Practically Anywhere on the Island*.

Stacy Neil
Played Randolph Smith in the **Return of the Saint** episode *Assault Force*.

Staffe Stanley
Film Editor on **Father Brown**.

Stafford Brendan J, B.S.C.
Director of Photography on **Danger Man I, Danger Man [aka Secret Agent], The Prisoner, The Protectors, The Saint, Sir Francis Drake** and **UFO**.

Stafford Brendon
Lighting cameraman on the series **UFO**.

Stamboulieh Antony
Played the Lieutenant in the **Jason King** episode *Uneasy Lies the Head*.
Played Yanos in the first series **The Protectors** episodes *Brother Hood* & *One and One Makes One*.
Played Franco in the fourth season **The Saint** episode *The Ex-King of Diamonds*.
Played Challon in **The Zoo Gang** episode *The Counterfeit Trap*.

Stampe Will
Played Tony Mazzo in the **Gideon's Way** episode *Gang War*.
Played the porter in the **Man in a Suitcase** episode *Castle in the Clouds*.
Played Don Gonzalo in the **Sir Francis Drake** episode *The Governor's Revenge*.
Played Sgt. Polkinghorne in the **Virgin of the Secret Service** episode *The Rajah and the Suffragette*.

Stanbury Jacqueline
Played Susan in the first series **The Protectors** epiosde *2,000ft to Die* and the car hire receptionist in the second season's *Baubles, Bangles and Beads*.

Standing John
Played James in the second series **Danger Man [aka Secret Agent]** episode *Sting in the Tail*.
Played gendarme in the first season **The Saint** episode *The Bunco Artists*.
Played Pasc in the second season **Space 1999** episode *The Mark of Archanon*.

Standing Michael
Played Edwards in **The Champions** episode *To Trap a Rat*.
Played Chez Kelly in the **Gideon's Way** episode *Boy with a Gun*.
Played Barlow in the second season **The Saint** episode *The Miracle Tea Party*.

Stanford Deborah
Played Stella Croxley in the **UFO** episode *E.S.P.*

Stanhope Warren
Played Brett in **The Adventurer** episode *The Bradley Way*.

Played Willis in **The Baron** episode *The Island* [part 2 of a two-parter: also exists, edited together with part 1 - *Storm Warning*, as a feature entitled *Mystery Island*].
Played Admiral Parker in **The Champions** episode *The Silent Enemy*.
Played Graves in the **Department S** episode *Spencer Bodily is 60 Years Old*.
Played Johnson in the **Man in a Suitcase** episodes *Variation on a Million Bucks* [two parter: also a movie: *To Chase a Million*] and *Web with Four Spiders*.
Played Forrester in the second season **Man of the World** episode *The Prince*.
Played Mike Harris in the first season **The Saint** episode *The Pearls of Peace* and Tom Mackinnon in *Judith*. Played Marty Bressett in the third season's *Invitation to Danger* and Arnie Garnett in the fourth's *Where the Money Is*.

Stannard Roy
Art Director on **The Zoo Gang**.

Stanton Barry
Played Faber in **The Champions** episode *The Fanatics*.
Played Soaper in the first series **The Protectors** episode *A Kind of Wild Justice*.
Played Pete in the fourth season **The Saint** episode *The Man who Gambled with Life*.

Stanton John
Wrote the **Man in a Suitcase** episode *No Friend of Mine*.
Wrote the third series **The Saint** episodes *The Reluctant Revolution, Locate and Destroy* & *Island of Chance* [from a story by Leigh Vance].

Stanton Valerie
Played Mia in the **Jason King** episode *All that Glisters* [part 2].

Stapley Charles
Played a variety of roles in the debut season of **The Adventures of Robin Hood**: Sir Miles in *The Betrothal*, Rolf in *The Alchemist*, Blackbeard in *The Sheriff's Boots*, the Lieutenant in *Errand of Mercy*, Charles the Hunter in *The Vandals*, the Captain in *Ladies of Sherwood*, Sir Gaillard in *The Deserted Castle*, Seneschal in *The Miser*, Dick the Smith in *Children of the Greenwood*, the stranger in *The May Queen*, Spicer in *The Byzantine Treasure*, Will in *Secret Mission*, William in *Table's Turned*, Exeter in *The Traitor*, Edmund in *The Thorkill Ghost* and Lt. Howard in *The Wager*.
Played the doctor in the **O.S.S.** episode *Operation Post Office* and a German in *Operation Sardine*.
Played Bill West in the **White Hunter** episode *The Trophy*.

Stark Graham
Starred as, series regular, Hank in **Man of the World**.

Stark John
Played the Sergeant in **The Sentimental Agent** episode *Express Delivery*.

Stassino Paul
Played Joaquin Salvador in **The Baron** episode *Long Ago and Far Away*.
Played Selvameni in **The Champions** episode *The Gun-Runners*.
Played Ramfi in the first season **Danger Man** episode *Find and Return* and the police Captain in *Bury the Dead*.
Played Flores in the **Department S** episode *Black Out*.
Played Edmond in **The Four Just Men** episode *Village of Shame* and Jose Pereza *Their Man in London*.
Played Karolides in the first series **Ghost Squad** episode *Ticket for Blackmail* and Torres in *Catspaw* [*Catspaw* was shot for the first series, but was shown in season two].

Played Sardi in the **H. G. Wells' Invisible Man** episode *The Gun Runners*.

Played Pavone in the **Interpol Calling** episode *The Collector*.

Played Capitano Rizio in the **Jason King** episodes *As Easy as A B C* & *Chapter One: The Company I Keep*.

Played Carozza in the first series **The Protectors** episode *2,000ft to Die*.

Played several roles in **The Saint**: Ricco in *The Rough Diamonds* & Vincent Innutio in *The Effete Angler* [series 1]; Abdul Osman in *The Death Penalty* [2]; Prince Ubaldo in *Interlude in Venice* [3] and Col. Rakos in *The Ex-King of Diamonds* [4].

Played Hassan Bey in the **Sir Francis Drake** episode *Gentlemen of Spain*.

Played Pietro in the **William Tell** episode *The Black Brothers*.

Steafel Sheila
Played Jill Preston in the third season **Danger Man** [aka **Secret Agent**] episode *Dangerous Secret*.

Steedman Tony
Played Hardwick in **The Champions** episode *The Ghost Plane*.

Played Hallet in the **Department S** episode *Six Days*.

Played Professor D'Arblay in the **Jason King** episode *A Red, Red Rose Forever*.

Played the surgeon in the **Randall and Hopkirk [Deceased]** aka **My Partner the Ghost** episode *You Can Always find a Fall Guy*.

Played Brig. Danvers in the **Return of the Saint** episode *Yesterday's Hero*.

Played Inspector Morrell in the **Strange Report** episode *Report 5055: CULT: 'Murder Shrieks Out'*.

Steel Anthony
Played Adam Ferris in the second season **The Protectors** episode *Burning Bush*.

Played Max Boothroyd in the **Return of the Saint** episode *The Imprudent Professor*.

Steel Pippa
Played Karen Dorron in **The Adventurer** episode *I'll Get There Sometime*.

Played Trish in the **Department S** episode *The Soup of the Day*.

Played Diane in the **UFO** episode *Court Martial*.

Steele Anna
Played Mrs Bohun in the **Father Brown** episode *The Hammer of God*.

Steele Barbara
Played Cleo in the third season **Danger Man** [aka **Secret Agent**] episode *The Man on the Beach*.

Steele Christopher
Played Gabrier in **The Count of Monte Cristo** episode *Albania*.

Played Count Latour in **The Scarlet Pimpernel** episode *The Sword of Justice*.

Steele Mary
Played Anne in **The Adventures of Sir Lancelot** episode *The Missing Princess*.

Played Helena in **The Count of Monte Cristo** episode *Mecklenburg* and Suzanne in *The Grecian Gift* [aka *The Brothers*].

Steen Derek
Played a tracking station guard in the **UFO** episode *The Psychobombs*.

Stefanelli Marco
Played Pietro in the **Return of the Saint** episode *The Murder Cartel*.

Steiger Frieda
Hairdresser on **Man in a Suitcase** and **Strange Report**.

Steiner John
Played Hershall in the **Department S** episode *A Ticket to Nowhere*.

Played Grey Wyler in the third season **The Saint** episode *The Death Game*.

Stensgaard Yutte
Played Arlene in the **Jason King** episode *As Easy as A B C*.

Played Bibi in **The Persuaders!** episode *The Morning After*.

Played the telephone operator in the fourth season **The Saint** episode *The Desperate Diplomat*.

Stepanek Karel
Played Joseph in the first series of **The Adventures of Robin Hood** episode *The Wanderer* and Joseph of Cordoba in the second season's *The York Treasure*.

Stephen Susan
Played Alma in the season three **The Adventures of Robin Hood** episode *Too Many Robins*.

Stephens Ann
Appeared as Sella in **The Adventures of Sir Lancelot** episode *The Lesser Breed*.

Played Anne in **The Count of Monte Cristo** episode *Flight to Calais*.

Stephens P. G.
Played Paddy in the third season **The Saint** episode *The Fast Women*.

Stephens Peter
Played Hassan Ben Ali in **The Count of Monte Cristo** episode *Albania*.

Played Mr Jones in the first season **Danger Man** episode *The Island* and Frankie in the third season [now aka **Secret Agent**] episode *The Paper Chase*.

Played Sir Timothy Grange in the **Randall and Hopkirk [Deceased]** aka **My Partner the Ghost** episode *When Did you Start to Stop Seeing Things?*.

Played Phillips in **The Sentimental Agent** episode *Never Play Cards with Strangers*.

Stephens Roy
Played P.F.C. Kirk in the second season **The Saint** episode *The Hi-Jackers*.

Stephenson Pamela
Played Michelle Osgood in the second season **Space 1999** episode *Catacombs of the Moon*.

Stephenson Shelagh
Played Ruth in *Adventure Four* of **Sapphire and Steel** [part 3].

Sterke Jeanette
Played Sgt. Winter in the **H. G. Wells' Invisible Man** episode *Man in Disguise*.

Played Josette in the **O.S.S.** episode *Operation Death Trap*.

Played Maria Conti in the **White Hunter** episode *Web of Death*.

Sterland John
Played a pilot in the season one **Danger Man** episode *Sabotage*.

Sterling John
Played Phillipe in **The Four Just Men** episode *The Deadly Capsule*.

Sterling Joseph
Directed the **White Hunter** episodes *No Survivors, Inside Story, Big Bwana Brady, Killer Leopard, Sickness of Kilimanjaro, The Hungry Hell* and *Out of the Wind.*

Stern Tom
Featured in the **Espionage** episode *Some Other Kind of World.*

Sterndale Martin
Played the detective in the first season **Danger Man** episode *The Key.*

Sterne Gordon
Played Franconi in **The Four Just Men** episode *The Night of the Precious Stones* and Dr. Wayne in *The Discovery.*
Played Ernst Liebkind in the **Man in a Suitcase** episode *Somebody Loses, Somebody ...Wins?.*
Played the flight medic in the **O.S.S.** episode *Operation Blackbird.*
Played a bystander in **The Prisoner** episode *Living in Harmony.*
Played the barman in the first series **The Protectors** episode *Your Witness.*
Played Fritz Kapel in the first season **The Saint** episode *The Saint Sees it Through* and Vopos in the third season's *The Paper Chase.*
Played the helmsman in the **UFO** episode *Reflections in the Water* and the German delegate *Confetti Check A-O.K.*
Played Richardson in the **White Hunter** episode *Marked Man.*

Sterrett Gillian
Guested as Genevieve in the debut season of **The Adventures of Robin Hood** episode *The May Queen.*

Steven Anthony
Wrote the **Virgin of the Secret Service** episodes *The Rajah and the Suffragette* [with Vincent Tilsley] and *Pride of Assassins.*

Stevens Craig
Starred as Mike Strait in the series **Man of the World.**

Stevens Dorinda
Played Miss Jackson in the second series **Danger Man** [aka **Secret Agent**] episode *Such Men are Dangerous.*
Guested as Helen in the **Interpol Calling** episode *Air Switch* and as Millicent in *In the Swim.*
Played Verna in the first season **The Saint** episode *The Careful Terrorist.*

Stevens Mike
Played the chauffeur in the **UFO** episode *The Man who Came Back.*

Stevens Peter
Played the Consellor in the **Sir Francis Drake** episode *Drake on Trial.*

Stevens Vi
Played the cleaner in the **G.S.5** episode *Hideout.*

Stevenson Alexandra
Played Miss Lamb in the **Man in a Suitcase** episode *The Boston Square.*

Stevenson Jean
Production Assistant on **Sapphire and Steel.**

Stevenson Monica
Played Princess Irene in the season three **The Adventures of Robin Hood** episode *Pepper.*

Played Peggy Warden in the first season **The Saint** episode *Starring the Saint.*
Played Francesca the **Sword of Freedom** episodes *Francesca, The Bracelet, The Bell, The Ambassador, The Strange Intruder, The Primavera, A Game of Chance & Adrianna.*

Steward Gaynor
Played the little girl in **The Prisoner** episode *The Girl who was Death.*

Steward Graham
Played the first little boy in **The Prisoner** episode *The Girl who was Death.*

Stewart Alexandra
Played Jessica in the second series **Danger Man** [aka **Secret Agent**] episode *Judgement Day.*
Played Natalie Sheridan in the third season **The Saint** episode *The Better Mousetrap.*

Stewart Bill
Played the garage attendant in the first series **The Protectors** episode *Triple Cross.*

Stewart Bill
Directed the **G.S.5** episodes *Scorpion Rock, The Goldfish Bowl, Seven Sisters of Wong & It Won't be a Stylish Marriage.*

Stewart Bruce
Wrote the **Timeslip** stories: *The Wrong End of Time* [series parts 1 - 6], *The Time of the Ice Box* [series parts 7 - 12], *The Year of the Burn-Up* [series parts 13 - 20: Victor Pemberton wrote episode 20].

Stewart David J.
Featured in the **Espionage** episode *The Whistling Shrimp.*

Stewart Donald
Guested as Steve Taylor in the **Interpol Calling** episode *Last Man Lucky.*
Played Van Kempson in the first series **Man of the World** episodes *Portrait of a Girl & The Runaways.*
Played the doctor in the **O.S.S.** episode *Operation Flint Axe.*
Played Elmer in **The Sentimental Agent** episode *Never Play Cards with Strangers.*

Stewart Graham
Appeared in a number of roles in **The Adventures of Robin Hood**: the Town Crier in *The Path of True Love* [aka *Locksley Hall*], Giles in *The Borrowed Baby*, Malcolm in *Highland Fling*, the serf in *The Mystery of Ireland's Eye*, William in *The Little People*, Waldo in *The Frightened Tailor*, the messenger in *The Black Five* & Andrew in *The Road in the Air* [series two]; the prison guard in *The Minstrel*, the guard in *The Youthful Menace*, the second guard in *Woman's War* & Stephen in *Marian's Prize* [three] and the attendant in *Sybella*, Bault in *Goodbye, Little John* & the Lieutenant in *Hue and Cry* [four].
Appeared as Damien in **The Adventures of Sir Lancelot** episode *The Witch's Brew.*
Played the pilot in the first season **Danger Man** episode *The Trap.*
Played the helper in **The Four Just Men** episode *The Boy Without a Country.*
Played Franz in the **O.S.S.** episode *Operation Fracture.*
Played Hans in the **William Tell** episode *The Bear.*

Stewart Ian Scott
Wrote the **UFO** episode *Flight Path.*

Stewart Jack
Guested as MacLelland in the **Interpol Calling** episode *The Sleeping Giant.*

Stewart Joy
Appeared as Maisie in the **G.S.5** episode *An Eye for An Eye*.

Stewart Larry
Wardrobe on the series **Man of the World**.

Stewart Robert
Co-wrote, with Ralph Smart the first season **Danger Man** episodes *The Prisoner* & *The Relaxed Informer*.
Wrote the first series **Ghost Squad** episode *Eyes of the Bat*.
Writer on **Interpol Calling**: teleplayed *Fingers of Guilt* [from a story by Tom Hutchinson and Ernie Player] & *The Three Keys* [with Connery Chappell: from a story by Paul Erickson] and wrote: *No Flowers for Onno, Private View, The Man's Clown, The Girl with Grey Hair* [with Leonard Fincham and Michael Hankinson], *Game for Three Hands, Eight Days Inclusive, White Blackmail, Desert Hi-Jack* [with Harold Orton], *Dressed To Kill* [with David Chantler], *A Foreign Body* & *In the Swim* [with Connery Chappell].
Wrote the first season **The Saint** episodes *Sophia* & *The Well-Meaning Mayor*.

Stewart Robert Banks
Wrote the **Jason King** episode *Every Picture Tells a Story*.
Wrote the second season **The Protectors** episode *Trial*.

Stewart Roy
Played a guard in the **Virgin of the Secret Service** episodes *Dark Deeds on the Northwest Frontier* & *The Great Ring of Akba*.

Stewart Salvin
Played One Eye in **The Buccaneers** [aka **Dan Tempest**] episode *Before the Mast* and Commander Byng Howard in the **Virgin of the Secret Service** episode *Russian Roundabout*.

Stewart Stanley
Played the Police Inspector in the second season **The Protectors** episode *Shadbolt*.

Stewart Val
Camera Operator on **Randall and Hopkirk [Deceased]** aka **My Partner the Ghost**.

Stock Michael
Played the police Constable in the **Father Brown** episode *The Oracle of the Dog*.

Stock Nigel
Played Major Barrington in the second series **Danger Man** [aka **Secret Agent**] episode *Loyalty Always Pays*.
Featured in the **Espionage** episode *Medal for a Turned Coat*.
Stood in for Patrick McGoohan - who was filming *Ice Station Zebra* - to play The Colonel/Number 6 in **The Prisoner** episode *Do Not Forsake Me Oh My Darling*.
Played Jim Chase in the first season **The Saint** episode *The Invisible Millionaire*.

Stockwell Thomas A.
Wrote **The Buccaneers** [aka **Dan Tempest**] episodes *Blackbeard, The Surgeon of Sangre Rojo, Cutlass Wedding* and *Mistress Higgins' Treasure*.

Stokes Barry
Played Haines in the first season **Space 1999** episode *Voyager's Return*.
Played the Skydiver's engineer in the **UFO** episode *Destruction* & the Skydiver's navigator in *Reflections in the Water*.

Stoliaroff Nicole
Played Gaby in the **Return of the Saint** episode *Appointment in Florence*.

Stoll David
Played Tilvers in the **Randall and Hopkirk [Deceased]** aka **My Partner the Ghost** episode *When Did you Start to Stop Seeing Things?*.

Stoll John
Production designer on the **Return of the Saint** series.

Stoller Jennie
Played Annabelle Harborough in *Adventure Five* of **Sapphire and Steel**.

Stone David
Wrote the second season **Danger Man** [aka **Secret Agent**] episodes *The Galloping Major, Whatever Happened to George Foster?, The Ubiquitous Mr Lovegrove, Have a Glass of Wine, A Very Dangerous Game* [with Ralph Smart], *English Lady Takes Lodgers* & *Loyalty Always Pays*.

Stone John
Played the Naval Captain in **The Champions** episode *Twelve Hours*.
Played the auctioneer in **The Persuaders!** episode *That's Me Over There*.
Played Ted Orping in the second season **The Saint** episode *The Set-Up*.
Appeared as Robert Storm in the **White Hunter** episode *Operation Transfer*.

Stone Marianne
Played the hairdresser in the **Man in a Suitcase** episode *Essay in Evil*.
Played the chambermaid in **The Persuaders!** episode *The Morning After*.
Played the wardress in the **Return of the Saint** episode *The Debt Collectors*.

Stone Peter
Wrote the **Espionage** episode *Covenant With Death*.

Stone Phillip
Played Sir Arthur Travers KC in the **Father Brown** episode *The Mirror of the Magistrate*.
Played Supt Landon in the **Jason King** episode *A Deadly Line in Digits*.
Played Inspector Carlton in the first season **The Saint** episode *Marcia*.

Stoneman Joyce
Wardrobe on **The Saint**.

Stoney Kevin
Played Miesner in **The Adventurer** episode *The Solid Gold Hearse*.
Played Thaddeus Goldfinch in the third series of **The Adventures of Robin Hood** episode *One Man's Meat* and Ralph in *The Ghost that Failed*. In the final season he appeared as Smith in *Hue and Cry* and as Marshall in *The Truce*.
Played Buchler in the third season **Danger Man** [aka **Secret Agent**] episode *Say it with Flowers*.
Played Sir Harold Tyler in **The Four Just Men** episode *The Survivor*.
Played Onno in the **Interpol Calling** episode *No Flowers for Onno*.
Played the barman in the **Man in a Suitcase** episode *All that Glitters*.
Played Colonel J. in **The Prisoner** episode *The Chimes of Big Ben*.
Played Dr. Farrere in the second season **The Saint** episode *Sibao*.
Played Talos in the first season **Space 1999** episode *The Last Enemy*.

Played Niccolo in the **Sword of Freedom** episodes *Vendetta & Who is Felicia?*.
Played Heinrich in the **William Tell** episode *Manhunt* and Strauss in *The Killer*.

Storch Larry
Played Angie in **The Persuaders!** episode *Angie. . . Angie*.

Stovin Jerry
Played Al Graham in **The Adventurer** episode *Love Always, Magda*.
Played Peter Franklin in **The Baron** episode *And Suddenly You're Dead*.
Played Desmond Pearson in the second series **Danger Man** [aka **Secret Agent**] episode *The Professionals*.
Played Clavik in the season two **Ghost Squad** episode *A First Class Way toDie*.
Played a pilot in the **O.S.S.** episode *Operation Blackbird*.
Played Bob Kendricks in the first season **The Saint** episode *Starring the Saint*. Appeared as Ted Coblin in the second season's *The Happy Suicide* and Tony Kreiger in *Sibao*.
Played Henry in the **Virgin of the Secret Service** episode *The Professor Goes West*.

Strait Bud
Played the second detective in the season two **Ghost Squad** episode *Mr Five Per Cent*.

Strange Julian
Appeared as the Mate in **The Buccaneers** [aka **Dan Tempest**] episode *Hand of the Hawk*.

Stratford Donald
Played an auction client in the **Father Brown** episode *The Arrow of Heaven*.

Stratton John
Played Mundon Mandeville in the **Father Brown** episode *The Actor and the Alibi*.
Played John Croxley in the **UFO** episode *E.S.P.*

Street George
Played Rodriguez in the second season **Man of the World** episode *The Bullfighter*.
Played the Commissionaire in **The Sentimental Agent** episode *The Height of Fashion*.

Stribling Melissa
Played Mrs Bannon in **The Four Just Men** episode *The Deserter*.
Played Lisa in **The Persuaders!** episode *Powerswitch*.
Played Countess Von Markheim in the **William Tell** episode *The Young Widow*.

Stride Virginia
Played Sara in **The Baron** episode *The Persuaders*.

Strong Veronica
Played Claire Bradfield in **The Baron** episode *Enemy of the State*.
Starred as Mrs Virginia Cortez [a British Agent] in **Virgin of the Secret Service**.

Stroud Pauline
Played Jane Sinclair-Morley in the season two **Ghost Squad** episode *The Big Time*.

Strutton Bill
Wrote the first season **The Saint** episodes *Iris & The Rough Diamonds*.
Wrote the **Strange Report** episode *Report 8319: GRENADE: 'What Price Change?'*.

Stuart Giacomo Rossi
Played Sheffer in the **Return of the Saint** episode *Appointment in Florence*.

Stuart John
Played the records clerk in **The Adventurer** episode *Mr Calloway is a Very Cautious Man*.
Played Pinot in the debut season of **The Adventures of Robin Hood** episode *The Deserted Castle* and Stationarius in *The Byzantine Treasure*.
Played Colonel Havis in the **G.S.5** episode *The Goldfish Bowl*.
Played the Prison Governor in the **O.S.S.** episode *Operation Big House*.
Played Paul Haggis in the **White Hunter** episode *Decision*.

Stuart Nicholas
Played Inspector Hackett in the first season **The Saint** episode *The Sporting Chance*, Doctor Grant in *The Careful Terrorist* and Atherton Lee in the second season's *Sibao*.

Stubbs Una
Played Marion in the **Shirley's World** episode *A Girl Like You*.

Sturgess Ray
Camera Operator on **The Saint**.

Styles John
Played the ventriloquist in the **Randall and Hopkirk [Deceased]** aka **My Partner the Ghost** episode *That's How Murder Snowballs*.

Suchet David
Played Leo in the second season **The Protectors** episode *Fighting Fund*.

Sugg Fanny
Played the nurse in the **Jason King** episode *A Red, Red Rose Forever*.

Sugg Penny
Appeared as Liv in **The Persuaders!** episode *The Morning After*.
Played the nurse in the series one **The Protectors** episode *Thinkback*.

Sullivan Didi
Played Alex in the **Man in a Suitcase** episode *The Whisper*.
Played Nina in the first series **Man of the World** episode *Specialist for the Kill*.

Sullivan Eileen
Wardrobe on **Space 1999**.

Sullivan Elliott
Played Pfeiffer in **The Persuaders!** episode *Read and Destroy*.

Sullivan Jerry
Played the civic guard in **The Sentimental Agent** episode *May the Saints Preserve Us*.

Sullivan John
Stunt Co-ordinator on **The Adventurer**.
Played one of the sons in **The Buccaneers** [aka **Dan Tempest**] episode *Mother Doughty's Crew*.
Stunt Co-ordinator on **Jason King** and appeared as the attendant in *If it's Got to Go - It's Got to Go* and as Reynolds in *An Author in Search of Two Characters*.
Played Harry in the first season **The Saint** episode *The Man who was Lucky*.

Sullivan Lian
Played Renoldi in **The Count of Monte Cristo** episode *Return to the Chateau d'If*.

Summer David
Played Frank Craig in the **UFO** episode *Kill Straker!*.

Summerfield Eleanor
Played Mrs Evans in the **Department S** episode *A Small War of Nerves*.
Played Muriel Thompson in the **UFO** episode *The Cat with Ten Lives*.

Summerford Barry
Played the Reading police constable in the **Father Brown** episode *The Quick One*.

Summers Jeremy
Directed **The Baron** episodes *Enemy of the State* & *The Maze*.
Directed the third season **Danger Man** [aka **Secret Agent**] episode *The Man with the Foot*.
Directed the **Gideon's Way** episodes *Boy with a Gun* & *The Reluctant Witness*.
Directed the **Interpol Calling** episode *Desert Hi-Jack*.
Directed the **Jason King** episodes *A Page Before Dying, Buried in the Cold, Cold Ground, A Deadly Line in Digits, As Easy as A B C, Flamingoes only Fly on Tuesdays, Toki, The Constance Missal, It's Too Bad about Auntie* & *The Stones of Venice*.
Directed the **Man in a Suitcase** episode *Blind Spot*.
Directed the first season **Man of the World** episode *Specialist for the Kill* and the second season's *Double Exposure*.
Directed the first season **The Protectors** episodes *See No Evil, Disappearing Trick, Ceremony for the Dead, King Con, A Kind of Wild Justice, Talkdown, ...With a Little Help from my Friends* & *Your Witness* and the second's *Fighting Fund, Baubles, Bangles and Beads, Wam* [2 parter], *Implicado, The Bridge, Zeke's Blues, The Tiger and the Goat* & *Blockbuster*.
Directed the **Randall and Hopkirk [Deceased]** aka **My Partner the Ghost** episodes *When Did you Start to Stop Seeing Things?, Just for the Record, Murder ain't what it Used to Be!, The Ghost who Saved the Bank at Monte Carlo, The Smile Behind the Veil, Could You Recognise the Man Again?* & *All Work and No Pay*.
Directed the **Return of the Saint** episodes *The Judas Game, Duel in Venice* & *The Roman Touch*.
Directed **The Saint** episodes *The Loaded Tourist, The Charitable Countess, The Invisible Millionaire, The Gentle Ladies, The Benevolent Burglary, The Well-Meaning Mayor, The Sporting Chance* & *The Lawless Lady* [season 1]; *The Death Penalty, The Unkind Philanthropist* & *The Abductors* [2] and *The Man Who Liked Lions* [4].
Directed the **UFO** episodes *The Psychobombs* & *The Long Sleep*.

Sumner David
Played Wolf in the **Department S** episode *Black Out*.
Played Nuri in the **Man in a Suitcase** episode *The Revolutionaries*.
Played Paul in the first series **Man of the World** episode *The Mindreader*.
Played Dickie Tremaine in the first season **The Saint** episode *The Lawless Lady*.

Sundquist Gerry
Played Malik in the second season **Space 1999** episode *The Dorcans*.

Supermarionation
Technique used for the filming of **Fireball XL5, Joe 90, The Secret Service** and **Thunderbirds** [with Videocolor] series.

Sutherland Donald
Guested as David Crayley in **The Champions** episode *Shadow of the Panther*.
Played Philip Guest in the **Gideon's Way** episode *The Millionaire's Daughter*.

Played Willard in the **Man in a Suitcase** episode *Day of Execution* and Earle in *Which Way did he Go, McGill?*.
Played McCleery in the second season **The Saint** episode *The Happy Suicide* and John Wood in the third season's *Escape Route*.
Played the hotel clerk in **The Sentimental Agent** episode *A Very Desirable Plot*.

Sutherland Gil
Played the young boatman in the third season **The Saint** episode *The Persistent Patriots*.

Sutton Dudley
Played Brian Carlton in **The Baron** two parter *Storm Warning* [*Storm Warning* - part 1 and *The Island* - part 2: also exists as a feature called *Mystery Island*].
Played Sonny in the **Department S** episode *Handicap Dead*.
Played Mort Roden in the **Randall and Hopkirk [Deceased]** aka **My Partner the Ghost** episode *Could You Recognise the Man Again?*.
Played Eddy in the second season **The Saint** episode *The Scorpion*.

Sutton John
Played De Villefort in **The Count of Monte Cristo** episode *The Affair of the Three Napoleons*.

Sutton Julia
Played Miss Theresa Talbot in the **Father Brown** episode *The Actor and the Alibi*.

Suzman Jesus
Played the waiter in the second season **The Protectors** episode *Quin*.

Swann Robert
Played Bill Grant in the **UFO** episode *Survival*.

Swanson Ruth
Played Madame Rousse in **The Count of Monte Cristo** episode *The Black Death*.

Swanwick Peter
Played Joe in the debut season **Danger Man** episode *The Key*. In season three [now aka **Secret Agent**] played Joe in *The Paper Chase*.
Played the butler in the **Man in a Suitcase** episode *Night Flight to Andora*.
Played Hendrick in the **O.S.S.** episode *Operation Tulip*.
Regular, as the Supervisor, in **The Prisoner**: *Arrival, The Chimes of Big Ben, Free for All, The General, Hammer into Anvil, It's Your Funeral, A Change of Mind, Once Upon a Time* & *Fall Out*.
Played Klaus Striebeck in the **Virgin of the Secret Service** episodes *The Great Ring of Akba, The Persuasion of a Million Drops* & *A Fate Worse Than Death*.
Played Ezra McGivney in the **White Hunter** episode *The General*.
Played Hofer in the **William Tell** episode *The Unwelcome Stranger*.

Swash Walter
Played Mr Bigley in the **G.S.5** episode *The Goldfish Bowl*.

Sweden Morris
Played the airport clerk in the **H. G. Wells' Invisible Man** episode *The Gun Runners*.
Played Zero in the **O.S.S.** episode *Operation Chopping Block* and Matthews in *Operation Orange Blossom*.

Sweeney George
Played Tad in the **Return of the Saint** episode *Signal Stop*.

Swern Cyril
Sound Recordist on **The Prisoner** episodes *Living in Harmony, The Girl who was Death* and *Fall Out.*

Swift David
Played Phillips in **The Baron** episode *Long Ago and Far Away.*
Played Stephen Aylmer in the **Father Brown** episode *The Dagger With Wings.*

Swinburne Nora
Played Madame Latour in the **O.S.S.** episode *Operation Dagger.*

Swindells John
Played Pitman in the **Timeslip** story *The Day of the Clone* [series parts 21 - 26].

Sydney Derek
Played the Spanish Lieutenant in **The Buccaneers** [aka **Dan Tempest**] episode *Hurricane.*
Played Zerrilli in **The Champions** episode *Operation Deepfreeze.*
Played Panah in the first season **Danger Man** episode *The Traitor.*
Played Silva in the season two **Ghost Squad** episode *P.G. 7.*
Played the surgeon in the **H. G. Wells' Invisible Man** episode *Crisis in the Desert* and Colonel Fayid in *Man in Power.*
Played the fascist in the **O.S.S.** episode *Operation Big House.*
Played O'Mallamo in the third season **The Saint** episode *Interlude in Venice* and the Maitre 'D in the fourth season's *Vendetta for the Saint* [part 1].
Played the Governor in the **Sir Francis Drake** episode *The Slaves of Spain.*
Played Rodrigo in the **Sword of Freedom** episodes *Francesca, The Bracelet, The Bell, The Suspects, Serenade in Red, Forgery in Red Chalk, Chart of Gold, The Lion and the Mouse, The Besieged Duchess, The Primavera, A Game of Chance, The Marionettes, Vendetta, Adrianna* & *The Assassin.*
Played De Saram in the **Timeslip** story *The Day of the Clone* [series episodes 22-24].

Sykes Allen
Played Albert Smith in the **Virgin of the Secret Service** episode *The Great Ring of Akba.*

Sylvaine June
Played Gloria in **The Adventures of Sir Lancelot** episode *Double Identity.*

Sylvester Ingrid
Played the receptionist in the **Randall and Hopkirk [Deceased]** episode *You Can Always find a Fall Guy.*

Sylvester William
Played Nick in **The Baron** episode *Farewell to Yesterday.*
Played James Carpenter and Oscar Schumak in the first season **Danger Man** episode *The Prisoner.*
Played Stephen Brett in the first series **Ghost Squad** episode *Death from a Distance.*
Played Ralph Damian in the second season **The Saint** episode *The Happy Suicide* and Foots Fortunati in the third season's *Interlude in Venice.*
Played Shaw in **The Sentimental Agent** episode *The Scroll of Islam.*

Sylvestre Cleo
Played Margaret in the **Strange Report** episode *Report 1553: RACIST: 'A Most Dangerous Proposal'.*

Symonds Paul
Writer on **The Adventures of Robin Hood**: *The Betrothal, The Intruders, Richard the Lionheart & The Byzantine Treasure* [series 1] and *Blackmail, The Goldmaker, The Haunted Mill & The Final Tax* [2].

Sympson Tony
Played the news vendor in **The Count of Monte Cristo** episode *Majorca.*
Played the fisherman in the season two **Ghost Squad** episode *Mr Five Per Cent.*

Syms Sylvia
Played Karen Ballard in **The Adventurer** episode *Skeleton in the Cupboard.*
Played Cathy Dorne in **The Baron** episode *Farewell to Yesterday.*
Played Paula in the second series **Danger Man** [aka **Secret Agent**] episode *It's Up to the Lady.*
Guested once per season in **The Saint**: as Lady Anne Yearley in the first season episode *The Noble Sportsman,* as Jeannine Roger in the second season's *Jeannine,* as Arlene in the third season's *The Best Laid Schemes* and as Amos Klein in the fourth season two parter *The Fiction Makers.*
Played Carol Webber in the **Strange Report** episode *Report 1021: SHRAPNEL: 'The Wish in the Dream'.*

****

Tabori Paul
Wrote the **Sir Francis Drake** episode *The Reluctant Duchess* [with Gordon Wellesley].

Tafler Sydney
Played Wyvern in **The Adventurer** episode *The Solid Gold Hearse*.
Played Radek in the first season **Danger Man** episode *The Sisters*.
Played Gabriel Lyon in the **Gideon's Way** episode *Big Fish, Little Fish*.
Played Reynolds in the **Man in a Suitcase** episode *Castle in the Clouds*.

Tait Ken
Set Dresser on **The Persuaders!**

Takaki Kenjin
Played Angkor in the second season **The Saint** episode *The Sign of the Claw*.

Talfrey Hira
Played Senora Gomez in the **Man in a Suitcase** episode *The Man who Stood Still*.
Played Madame Duclos in the first series **Man of the World** episode *A Family Affair*.

Tamarin Paul
Played Kazime in the **Department S** episode *A Fish out of Water*.
Played a Russian astronaut in the **UFO** episode *The Responsibility Seat*.

Tamm Mary
Played Jeri Hanson in the **Return of the Saint** episode *The Debt Collectors*.

Tandy Donald
Appeared as the doorman in the second season **Danger Man** [aka **Secret Agent**] episode *A Date with Doris*.
Played Detective Sergeant in the first season **The Saint** episode *The Gentle Ladies*.
Played the gateman in the **UFO** episode *E.S.P.*

Tandy Gareth
Played Duncan in the first season **Danger Man** episode *The Gallows Tree*.

Tani Yoko
Played Miho in the fourth season **Danger Man** [aka **Secret Agent**] episode *Shinda Shima* and Ako Nakamura in *Koroshi* [*Shinda Shima* was merged with *Koroshi* to form a TVM entitled *Koroshi*].
Played Taiko in the **Man in a Suitcase** episode *Variation on a Million Bucks* [two parter: also a movie: *To Chase a Million*].
Played Okiyo in the **Shirley's World** episode *A Girl Like You*.

Tania
Played the Girl in Red in **The Champions** episode *Shadow of the Panther*.

Tann Paul
Appeared as the gunman in the second series **Danger Man** [aka **Secret Agent**] episode *A Very Dangerous Game*.

Tanner Gordon
Played Flynn in **The Four Just Men** episode *Dead Man's Switch* and Sam Brady in *The Man in the Road*.
Played Sullivan in the season two **Ghost Squad** episode *P.G. 7*.
Played Clyde in the **Interpol Calling** episode *Ascent to Murder*.

Played General Oliver in the first series **Man of the World** episode *Specialist for the Kill*.
Played Ferry in the **O.S.S.** episode *Operation Firefly*.
Played the Town Elder in **The Prisoner** episode *Living in Harmony*.
Played Arthur Gresson in the first season **The Saint** episode *The Arrow of God*.
Played Harry Crane in **The Zoo Gang** episode *Revenge: Post-dated*.

Tansley Derek
Played Crispin in the fourth series **The Adventures of Robin Hood** episode *The Truce*.
Played Sylvester in **The Buccaneers** [aka **Dan Tempest**] episode *Flip and Jenny*.
Played Mr Burton in the **Interpol Calling** episode *Chinese Mask*.

Tapley Colin
Played Everard in **The Adventures of Sir Lancelot** episode *Ruby of Radnor* and Lord Vanton in *Thieves*.
Played Martinson in the **White Hunter** episode *Operation Transfer*.

Tardios Harry
Played Mimiko in the second series **Danger Man** [aka **Secret Agent**] episode *It's Up to the Lady* and the left luggage clerk in *You're Not in Any Trouble, Are You?*
Played the travel agent in **The Four Just Men** episode *Marie*.
Played Carlo in the season two **Ghost Squad** episode *Escape Route*.
Played the steward in the **Man in a Suitcase** episode *Variation on a Million Bucks* [part 2: also combined with part 1 to form a movie: *To Chase a Million*].

Tarimer Zeynep
Played the airport clerk in the second series **Danger Man** [aka **Secret Agent**] episode *Sting in the Tail*.

Tarloff Frank
Co-teleplayed **The Four Just Men** episode *The Princess* [with Louis Marks: from a story by Louis Marks].
Created the series **Shirley's World** [with Melville Shavelson]. Also, wrote the episode *The Berkeley Club Caper*.

Tarr Ron
Played the Gorilla in the **Return of the Saint** episode *One Black September*.

Tasto Charles
Sound for **The Adventures of Sir Lancelot** episode *Shepherd's War*.

Tate John
Played Josef Holz in **The Baron** episode *A Memory of Evil*.
Played Schmeltz in **The Champions** episode *The Survivors*.
Played the fisherman in the third season **Danger Man** [aka **Secret Agent**] episode *Not So Jolly Roger*.
Played Henri Rachou in the **Department S** episode *Les Fleurs du Mal*.
Played Bert Macey in the **Gideon's Way** episode *The Lady Killer*.
Played Washington official in the second season **Man of the World** episode *Double Exposure*.
Played the assayer in the second season **The Saint** episode *The Loving Brothers*, Dave Snyders in *The Crooked Ring* and Skinner in the third season's *The Best Laid Schemes*.
Played Wiglow in the **Strange Report** episode *Report 4977: SWINDLE: 'Square Root of Evil'*.

Tate Nick
Starred as, series regular, Alan Carter in **Space 1999**.

Tatimer Hugh
Played Tom in the **H. G. Wells' Invisible Man** episode *Play to Kill*.

Taylor Bill
Sound Editor on **Man in a Suitcase**.

Taylor Christina
Played Lee Rogers in **The Champions** episode *The Bodysnatchers*.

Taylor Davina
Played Constance in the **Jason King** episode *A Deadly Line in Digits*.

Taylor Elaine
Played Karen in the **Jason King** episode *A Royal Flush*.
Played Cricket in the **Strange Report** episode *Report 3906: COVER GIRLS: 'Last year's Model'*.

Taylor Geoffrey
Played Ralph in the fourth series **The Adventures of Robin Hood** episode *Sybella*.

Taylor Gill
Directed the **Department S** episode *The Man from X*.

Taylor Gladys
Played the housekeeper in the first season **The Saint** episode *The Effete Angler*.

Taylor Grant
Guested as Winters in **The Champions** episode *Happening*.
Played Peter Grove in the second season **The Saint** episode *The Loving Brothers*.
Featured in the series **UFO** as, regular, General Henderson.

Taylor Jack
Played the second Man-at-Arms in the third series **The Adventures of Robin Hood** episode *The Fire*.
Played Frank in the first season **The Saint** episode *The Man who was Lucky*.
Played the drunk in the **White Hunter** episode *One Fatal Weakness*.

Taylor John
Sound Recording on **Fireball XL5**.
Music Editor on **Strange Report**.
Sound on **Thunderbirds**.

Taylor Ken
Wrote the **White Hunter** episodes *Web of Death* and *Out of the Wind*.

Taylor Kit
Played the croupier in **The Persuaders!** episode *Anyone Can Play*.

Taylor Larry
aka Laurence Taylor.
Played Angelo in **The Adventurer** episode *Love Always, Magda*.
Played Yasugi in **The Baron** episode *Samurai West*.
Played Henri in the second series **Danger Man** [aka **Secret Agent**] episode *Have a Glass of Wine*.
Played the French driver in the **Department S** episode *The Trojan Tanker*.
Played Walter in the **G.S.5** episode *Party for Murder*.
Played Milia in the **H. G. Wells' Invisible Man** episode *The Gun Runners*.
Played Luigi in the **Jason King** episode *As Easy as A B C*.

Played Getulio in the **Man in a Suitcase** episode *Burden of Proof*.
Appeared as the Gypsy man in **The Prisoner** episode *Many Happy Returns* and as Mexican Sam in *Living in Harmony*.
Played the man in phone booth in the **Randall and Hopkirk [Deceased]** aka **My Partner the Ghost** episode *A Sentimental Journey*.
Played Juanito in the first season **The Saint** episode *The Romantic Matron*, Alicron in the second season's *The Unkind Philanthropist* & Swann in *The Smart Detective*. Was Mustafa in the third season episode *The Queen's Ransom* and Ashok in the fourth season's *Portrait of Brenda*.
Played the janitor in the **Sir Francis Drake** episode *Johnnie Factotum*.
Played a Mexican bandit in the **UFO** episode *Mindbender*.
Played Howard in the **White Hunter** episode *Valley of the Dead*.

Taylor Laurence
aka/see Larry **Taylor**.

Taylor Lynn
Played the stewardess in the second series **Danger Man** [aka **Secret Agent**] episode *Yesterday's Enemies*.

Taylor Peter
Played Bruno in the **H. G. Wells' Invisible Man** episode *Odds Against Death*.
Played the sentry in the **O.S.S.** episode *Operation Tulip*.

Taylor Totte Truman
Played the English woman in **The Baron** episode *Farewell to Yesterday*.
Played the English woman in the second season **The Saint** episode *The Rhine Maiden*.

Te Wiata Inia
Played Loro in the second season **The Saint** episode *The Golden Frog*.

Teague Guy
Starred as the Deputy Sheriff in the **Fury** series.

Teasdale Lewis
Played the waiter in the **Man in a Suitcase** episode *Sweet Sue*.

Television Programmes of America Incorporated
Made **The Count of Monte Cristo** for ITC World Wide Distribution.
The New Adventures of Charlie Chan was a 'Television Programmes of America presentation in association with the Incorporated Television Programme Company Limited'.

Television Reporters International
With International Tribune, produced **The Persuaders!** for ITC World Wide Distribution.

Telezynska Izabella
Played Garder's secretary in the first series **The Protectors** episode *Chase* and Irena in *King Con*.

Telford Frank
Wrote **The Adventurer** episode *Thrust and Counter Thrust*.

Templer Sally
Played Sarah in the **Timeslip** story *The Wrong End of Time* [episodes 1- 4].

Templeton William
Wrote the season four **The Adventures of Robin Hood** episode *The Pharaoh Stones*.

Wrote the **Sword of Freedom** episodes *The Eye of the Artist, The Ship, The School, The Ambassador, The Marionettes & The Reluctant Duke*.

Terpiloff Anthony
Wrote the second season **The Protectors** episode *Border Line*.
Wrote the **Return of the Saint** episode *The Arrangement*.
Wrote the first series **Space 1999** episodes *Collision Course, Death's Other Dominion* [with Elizabeth Barrows], *The Infernal Machine* [with Elizabeth Barrows], *Earthbound* and the second season's *Catacombs of the Moon*.

Terry Diana
Played Brett's girl in **The Persuaders!** episode *Someone Like Me*.

Terry Nigel
Played Harry in the **Randall and Hopkirk [Deceased]** episode *Somebody just Walked over my Grave*.

Tesdahl Don
Played the American journalist in the **Return of the Saint** episode *The Murder Cartel*.

Thake Charles
Played the police Inspector in the first series **The Protectors** episode *Ceremony for the Dead*.

Thamm Sylvia
Dialogue Director on the **Supercar** series and voiced Jimmy Gibson.

Thaw John
Played Mauro Carpiano in the second series **The Protectors** episode *Lena*.
Played Inspector Jenner in the **Strange Report** episode *Report 2475: REVENGE: 'When a Man Hates'*.

Thawnton Tony
Appeared in **The Adventures of Robin Hood**: played Cressy in *The Bandit of Brittany*, Will in *The Goldmaker's Return & Fair Play* [season two] and the Captain in *The Salt King & the guard in Woman's War* [three].
Played Lowery in **The Baron** episode *The Persuaders*.
Played the Spanish speaking Sailor in **The Buccaneers** [aka **Dan Tempest**] episode *Dan Tempest's War with Spain*, Sykes in *Whale Gold*, Captain Scobie in *Slave Ship*, Jamieson in *Articles of War*, Sam One-Eye in *Marooned*, the First Mate in *Dan Tempest and The Amazons*, Cranstone in *The Ladies* and the Fish Peddler in *The Surgeon of Sangre Rojo*.
Played Vladimir in the second series **Danger Man** [aka **Secret Agent**] episode *Are You Going to Be More Permanent?*
Played the official in the **Department S** episode *Handicap Dead*.
Played the photographer in **The Four Just Men** episode *The Beatniques* and the officer in *The Slaver*.
Played Detective Inspector Smith in the **Gideon's Way** episode *Boy with a Gun*.
Played the hotel clerk in the **Jason King** episode *Uneasy Lies the Head*.
Played the French officer in the **O.S.S.** episode *Operation Eel*.
Played Fernandez in the **Randall and Hopkirk [Deceased]** episode *That's How Murder Snowballs*.
Played the Captain in the **Sword of Freedom** episode *The Tower*.
Played Fritz in the **William Tell** episode *The Raid*.

Thomas Charles
Played Caron in **The Baron** episode *Roundabout*.

Thomas Colin
Played a commercial traveller in the **Father Brown** episode *The Quick One*.

Thomas Damien
Played Phillipe in the **Jason King** episode *A Kiss for a Beautiful Killer*.
Played the visitor in the first series **The Protectors** episode *For the Rest of your Natural ....*

Thomas Evan
Played the vicar in the second series **Danger Man** [aka **Secret Agent**] episode *Whatever Happened to George Foster?*.
Played Doctor Beamish in the first season **The Saint** episode *The Sporting Chance*.

Thomas Ewan
Played Detective Inspector Russell in the season two **Ghost Squad** episode *P.G. 7*.

Thomas Helen
Set Dresser on **Strange Report**.

Thomas Lisa
Played the receptionist in **The Baron** episode *Masquerade* [Part 1 of a 2 parter: also exists, edited together with part 2, *The Killing*, to form a feature *Man In a Looking Glass*], Beth in *Portrait of Louisa* and Claudine in *Roundabout*.

Thomas Madeline
Played Mrs Rosehill in the **White Hunter** episode *Run to Earth*.

Thomas Nina
Played Alice Armstrong in the **Father Brown** episode *Three Tools of Death*.

Thomas Peter
Played the chauffeur [Reynolds] in **The Baron** two parter *Masquerade* [*Masquerade* - part 1 and *The Killing* - part 2: also exists as a feature entitled *Man In a Looking Glass*].
Played Achille in the **Department S** episode *The Treasure of the Costa del Sol*.

Thomas Talfryn
Played Smart in the **G.S.5** episode *The Goldfish Bowl*.
Played the poacher in **The Persuaders!** episode *A Home of One's Own*.
Played Owen Thomas in the third season **The Saint** episode *The House on Dragon's Rock*.

Thomas Terry
Played Archie in **The Persuaders!** episode *The Man in the Middle*.

Thomas Trevor
Played Cornelius in the **Return of the Saint** episode *Assault Force*.

Thomas Wally
Played the police Sergeant in the **Father Brown** episode *The Actor and the Alibi*.

Thompson Carlos
Starred as Carlos Varela in **The Sentimental Agent**.
Originally appeared as *The Sentimental Agent* in the episode of that title in the first series of **Man of the World** although, at that time, his character was named Borella.

Thompson Eric
Played George Hornsby in the **Man in a Suitcase** episode *All that Glitters*.

Thompson Ian
Played Vasile in **The Persuaders!** episode *Five Miles to Midnight*.

Thompson Jimmy
Played the fisty coachman in **The Scarlet Pimpernel** episode *Sir Percy's Wager*.

Thompson Palmer
Wrote the season four **The Adventures of Robin Hood** episode *The Flying Sorcerer*.

Thompson Robert E.
Wrote the first season **Man of the World** episode *A Family Affair* [with Norman Borisoff] and *Death of a Conference* [with Tudor Gates].

Thompson Wilfred 'Wilf'
Sound Editor on **The Prisoner** episodes *Arrival, The Chimes of Big Ben, Free for All, Many Happy Returns, A Change of Mind, Do Not Forsake Me Oh My Darling, Living in Harmony, The Girl who was Death, Once Upon a Time & Fall Out*.

Thomsett Sally
Played Catriona Macdonald in the **Shirley's World** episode *The Islanders*.

Thorburn June
Played Sue Carpenter in the first season **Danger Man** episode *The Prisoner*.
Played, regular, Vicky in **The Four Just Men**: *The Discovery, Crack-Up, The Protector & Justice for Gino*. [First appeared in the series as Hilary Colson in *Their Man in London*].

Thorburn William
Appeared as Kemp in the **White Hunter** episode *No Survivors*.

Thorne Clare
Wrote the second series of **The Adventures of Robin Hood** episode *The York Treasure*.

Thorne Denis
Played Major Jack Naismith in the season two **Ghost Squad** episode *The Last Jump*.

Thorne Garry
Played Emissary in **The Adventures of Sir Lancelot** episode *Winged Victory*, the old retainer in *Sir Bliant*, the guard in *The Magic Sword*, the guard in *Caledon*, the Man-at-Arms in *The Pirates* and the Squire in *The Theft of Excalibur*.
Played First Corsican in **The Count of Monte Cristo** episode *The Island*.
Played Linden in **The Four Just Men** episode *The Discovery*.
Played Simon in the **H. G. Wells' Invisible Man** episode *Play to Kill*.

Thorne Ken
Music on **The Persuaders!** series [theme by John Barry].
Composed and conducted music for the series **The Zoo Gang** [the theme was by Paul & Linda McCartney].

Thornton Frank
Played the Clerk in **The Champions** episode *The Night People*.
Played the airport official in the first season **Danger Man** episode *Find and Return* and Pepe in *Hired Assassin*.
Played a variety of roles in **The Four Just Men**: the Coroner in *The Crying Jester*, the clerk in *The Beatniques*, the auctioneer in *National Treasure*, Azin in *Marie*, the auctioneer in *The Man with the Golden Touch*, the announcer in *The Survivor*, the gendarme in *The Man in the Road*, Enrique Vidal in *Money To Burn* and the policeman in *The Boy without a Country*.
Played the tailor in **The Sentimental Agent** episode *The Scroll of Islam*.
Played the tax collector in the **William Tell** episode *Landslide* and Heinburgher in *The Surgeon*.

Thornton Peter
Played the pilot in the first season **Danger Man** episode *The Blue Veil*.

Thorp Richard
Played Sir Humphrey in the season three **The Adventures of Robin Hood** episode *The Double*.
Played Bobby in the first season **Danger Man** episode *The Island*.
Played the officer in **The Four Just Men** episode *The Man Who Wasn't There*.
Played George Pointer in the **Timeslip** story *The Day of the Clone* [series episode 24].

Thorpe-Bates Peggy
Played Mrs Cloonan in the **Return of the Saint** episode *Collision Course* [Part 1: 'The Brave Goose': also exists, combined with the second installment as a movie entitled *The Saint and the Brave Goose*].
Played Lady Caroline in **The Scarlet Pimpernel** episode *Sir Percy's Wager*.
Played Mrs Deeds in the **Strange Report** episode *Report 2641: HOSTAGE: 'If You Won't Learn, Die!*.
Played Doctor Joynton in the **Timeslip** story *The Time of the Ice Box* [series episodes 7-11].

Thorson Linda
Played Diamond in the **Return of the Saint** episode *The Roman Touch*.

Thulin Ingrid
Featured in the **Espionage** episode *The Incurable One*.

Thynov Gert
Played the waiter in the second season **The Protectors** episode *Bagman*.

Tickner Royston
Played Simpson in **The Baron** episode *Samurai West* and Griffiths in *The Maze*.
Played Charlie Berry in the **Gideon's Way** episode *Boy with a Gun*.
Played Billy Bradshaw in the **Return of the Saint** episode *Signal Stop*.
Played George Bradley in the **Timeslip** story *The Wrong End of Time* [series parts 1 - 6].

Tighe Gwynneth
Played Jennifer in the second season **The Saint** episode *The Damsel in Distress*.

Tilbern Alan
Played Colonel Gomez in **The Four Just Men** episode *Money to Burn*.

Tillar Ramon
Played one of the Flamenco dancers in the second season **Man of the World** episode *The Bullfighter*.

Tilsley Vincent
Wrote the **Man in a Suitcase** episode *Three Blinks of the Eyes*.
Wrote **The Prisoner** episodes *The Chimes of Big Ben & Do Not Forsake Me Oh My Darling*. Also wrote the unused segment *Don't Get Yourself Killed*.
Co-wrote the **Virgin of the Secret Service** episode *The Rajah and the Suffragette* [with Anthony Steven].

Tilvern Alan
Featured in the **Espionage** episode *Some Other Kind of World*.
Played Zoldi in **The Four Just Men** episode *Justice for Gino*.
Played Major Minos in the first season **Danger Man** episode *The Girl in Pink Pyjamas*.

Played Caletta in the **H. G. Wells' Invisible Man** episode *Odds Against Death*.

Played Stefano in the **Interpol Calling** episode *The Two-Headed Monster*.

Played Captain Quintana in the second season **The Saint** episode *The Golden Frog*.

Played the US delegate in the **UFO** episode *Confetti Check A-O.K.*

Timothy Christopher

Played the Gent in the **Return of the Saint** episode *The Poppy Chain*.

Played the Skydiver's Navigator in the **UFO** episode *The Psychobombs*.

Tindall Hilary

Played Nancy Cummings in **The Baron** episode *The Seven Eyes of Night*.

Played Cynthia in the **Randall and Hopkirk [Deceased]** aka **My Partner the Ghost** episode *The Smile Behind the Veil*.

Tingwell Charles

Voiced Dr Fawn in **Captain Scarlet and the Mysterons**.

Played Kemp in the second series **Danger Man** [aka **Secret Agent**] episode *The Affair at Castelevara*.

Played Beaver James in the **UFO** episode *Mindbender*.

Tinn John A.

Played Sung Lee Crackan in the **Randall and Hopkirk [Deceased]** aka **My Partner the Ghost** episode *It's Supposed to be Thicker than Water*.

Tipaldi Pearl

Hairdresser on **The Adventures of Sir Lancelot** episodes *The Knight with the Red Plume*, *The Ferocious Fathers* and *The Queen's Knight*.

Hairdresser on **The Buccaneers** [aka **Dan Tempest**] episode *Blackbeard*.

Tirard Ann

Played the old woman in the third season **The Saint** episode *The Gadic Collection*.

TLH 858

The hearse seen in **The Prisoner** episode *Arrival*.

Tobias-Shaw Rose

Casting Director on **Danger Man I**, **Danger Man** [aka **Secret Agent**], **Man in a Suitcase**, **The Prisoner** and **UFO**.

Todd Diane

Played the singer in the **O.S.S.** episode *Operation Barbecue*.

Toguri David

Played Commander Yamada in the fourth season **Danger Man** [aka **Secret Agent**] episode *Shinda Shima* [*Shinda Shima* was also merged with the only other surviving fourth season colour episode, *Koroshi*, to form a TVM entitled *Koroshi*].

Tokatyan Leon

Wrote the **Espionage** episode *The Whistling Shrimp*.

Tolan Michael

Featured in the **Espionage** episode *The Liberators*.

Toller Anthony

Played the first boy in **The Adventures of Sir Lancelot** episode *The Outcast*.

Tomb Harry

Played Tod Cowan in the **Gideon's Way** episode *Big Fish, Little Fish*.

Tomblin David

Assistant Director on the first and second series of **Danger Man** [aka **Secret Agent**].

Assistant Director on the series **H. G. Wells' Invisible Man**.

Assistant Director on **The New Adventures of Charlie Chan**.

Producer throughout **The Prisoner**. Co-wrote *Arrival* [with George Markstein], wrote [from a story by Ian L. Rakoff] & directed *Living in Harmony* and directed *The Girl who was Death* which was written by Terence Feely, based on Tomblin's original idea.

Directed the second season **The Protectors** episode *Wheels*.

Directed the first series **Space 1999** episodes *Force of Life*, *Another Time Another Place*, *The Infernal Machine* & *The Testament of Arkadia*.

Wrote & directed the **UFO** episodes *The Cat with Ten Lives* & *Reflections in the Water* and wrote *The Long Sleep*.

Assistant Director on **William Tell**.

Toms Donald

Production Manager on **Ghost Squad** [season one] & **Space 1999**.

Tondinelli Gianrico

Played Antonio in the **Return of the Saint** episode *Vicious Circle*.

Toon Nyo

Played the gate-keeper in the first season **Danger Man** episode *The Honeymooners*.

Toone Geoffrey

Played the General in **The Persuaders!** episode *The Time and the Place*.

Torquill Peter

Played Roger in the season four **The Adventures of Robin Hood** episode *Tuck's Love Day*.

Played Giorgio in the **Sword of Freedom** episode *A Game of Chance* and the captain in *Violetta*.

Played Corporal Muller in the **William Tell** episode *The General's Daughter* and Rudi in *The Trap*.

Total Look [of Debenhams]

Supplied the gowns for **The Persuaders!** series.

Tovey George

Played the cabbie in the **O.S.S.** episode *Operation Chopping Block*.

Tovey Roberta

Played Doris Jennings in the **Father Brown** episode *The Actor and the Alibi*.

Towb Harry

Guested as George in **The Champions** episode *The Mission*.

Played Feyer in the season two **Ghost Squad** episode *The Menacing Mazurka*.

Played Harry Mason in the **G.S.5** episode *Pay Up or Else*.

Played Marty O'Connor in the first season **The Saint** episode *The Man who was Lucky* & Johnny in *The High Fence*.

Towers of London

Produced **The Scarlet Pimpernel** [with Rayant Pictures Production] for the Incorporated Television Programme Co.

Towne Gillian

Played Elise in **The Scarlet Pimpernel** episode *Antoine and Antoinette*.

Townley Toke

Played the peanut vendor in **The Champions** episode *To Trap a Rat*.

Played Parsons in the **Department S** episode *The Shift that Never was*.
Played Seers in **The Four Just Men** episode *National Treasure*.
Played Mr Wheedon in the season two **Ghost Squad** episode *The Big Time*.

Townsend Jill
Played Monica Davies in the second season two part **The Protectors** episode *Wam*.
Played Sahala in the second season **Space 1999** episode *Dorzak*.

Townshend Phyllis
Continuity on **The Prisoner** episodes *Living in Harmony*, *The Girl who was Death* and *Fall Out*.
Continuity on **The Zoo Gang**.

Toyne Gabriel
Appeared in the first season **The Adventures of Robin Hood**: as the Sheriff's Clerk in *The Coming of Robin Hood*, as the old man driver in *The Moneylender*, as Eric in *Dead or Alive*, as Eric in *Maid Marian*, as the first citizen in *The Vandals* and as the deaf beggar in *The Wager*.
Played the magistrate in the season two **Ghost Squad** episode *Polsky*.

Tozer Geoffrey
Assistant Art Director on **Strange Report**.

TPA
aka/see **Television Programmes of America**

Tracey Melinda
Played an auction client in the **Father Brown** episode *The Arrow of Heaven*.

Tracy Ken
Played the technician in the **Father Brown** episode *Three Tools of Death*.

Tracy Kim
Played Zaharra in the **Sir Francis Drake** episode *Gentlemen of Spain*.

Travers Bill
Featured in the **Espionage** episode *A Camel to Ride*.

Travers Sally
Played Meg in the season three **The Adventures of Robin Hood** episode *Change of Heart*.
Played Frau Strauss in the **William Tell** episode *The Killer*.

Travers Susan
Played the serving girl in the season four **The Adventures of Robin Hood** episode *Race Against Time*.
Played Nita in the first season **Danger Man** episode *Name, Date and Place*.
Played the receptionist in **The Four Just Men** episode *Money To Burn*.
Guested as Carol in the **Interpol Calling** episode *Mr George*.
Played the girlfriend in the first series **The Protectors** episode *For the Rest of your Natural ...*.
Played Laura in the fourth season **The Saint** episode *The People Importers*.
Played the nurse in the **White Hunter** episode *Voodoo Wedding*.
Played Dina in the **William Tell** episode *The Unwelcome Stranger*.

Traverse Lans
Played Nina Henderson in the **Gideon's Way** episode *The Millionaire's Daughter*.

Tregear Frank
Played the first detective in the season two **Ghost Squad** episode *Mr Five Per Cent* and the porter in the **UFO** episode *Confetti Check A-O.K*.

Trent William
Sound Editor on **The Champions**.

Trevarthen Noel
Played Gino in the first season **Danger Man** episode *The Trap*.
Played Jack Bryant in the first season **The Saint** episode *The Well-Meaning Mayor* and Joe Casey in the second season's *The Loving Brothers*.
Played Nalo in **The Sentimental Agent** episode *Box of Tricks*.

Treves Frederick
Had a variety of parts in **The Adventures of Sir Lancelot**: Rolf in *The Ferocious Fathers*, the clerk in *The Outcast*, Sir Rolf in *Sir Bliant*, the first peasant in *The Magic Sword*, the first guard in *Lancelot's Banishment*, Colman in *Shepherd's War*, a villager in *The Pirates*, a bearer in *The Black Castle*, Sir Exeter in *The Magic Book* and the first thief in *The Theft of Excalibur*.
Played the doctor in **The Baron** episode *Roundabout*.
Played Quetzl in **The Buccaneers** [aka **Dan Tempest**] episode *Aztec Treasure*.
Played Rev. David Pryce-Jones in the **Father Brown** episode *The Quick One*.
Played Sir Walter in the first series **The Protectors** episode *The Numbers Game*.
Played the Inspector in the **Randall and Hopkirk [Deceased]** aka **My Partner the Ghost** episode *The Trouble with Women*.

Trevor Austin
Played Don Feliz in **The Count of Monte Cristo** episode *A Toy for the Infanta*.
Played Hugo in the **H. G. Wells' Invisible Man** episode *The White Rabbit*.
Played Doctor Martin in the **Interpol Calling** episode *The Heiress*.

Trevor John
Played Paul in **The Count of Monte Cristo** episode *Flight to Calais*.

Trewinnard Philip
Played the police Constable in the **Father Brown** episode *The Mirror of the Magistrate*.

Tribune Films
Return of The Saint was credited as 'a Robert S. Baker Tribune Films, a RAI/ITC Co-Production for ITC World Wide Distribution'.

Tribune Productions
Produced **The Persuaders!** series [with Television Reporters International] for ITC World Wide Distribution.

Triffez Tamara
Played Helga in the **Return of the Saint** episode *Appointment in Florence*.

Trigger John
Played Harry Crabb in the **Virgin of the Secret Service** episode *Dark Deeds on the Northwest Frontier*.

Trim Michael 'Mike'
Designer on **Joe 90**; Visual Effects Designer on **The Secret Service** and Special Effects Designer on **UFO**.

Trimble Lawrence
Played Paul Tarrant in the **Father Brown** episode *The Curse of the Golden Cross*.

Tripp Frederick
Played Groom in **The Count of Monte Cristo** episode *The Grecian Gift* [aka *The Brothers*].

Trolley Leonard
Played Charlie in the **Jason King** episode *A Deadly Line in Digits*.
Played Ferrand in **The Zoo Gang** episode *African Misfire*.

Tronson Robert
Directed **The Baron** episodes *Long Ago and Far Away, So Dark the Night* & *Roundabout*.
Directed the **Father Brown** episodes *The Hammer of God, The Actor and the Alibi, The Head of Caesar, The Curse of the Golden Cross, Three Tools of Death* & *The Arrow of Heaven*.
Directed the **Gideon's Way** episode *The Prowler*.
Directed the **Man in a Suitcase** episodes *Variation on a Million Bucks* [part 2: also combined with part 1 to form a movie: *To Chase a Million*], *The Girl who Never was, Sweet Sue, Find the Lady* & *Web with Four Spiders*.
Directed the **Randall and Hopkirk [Deceased]** aka **My Partner the Ghost** episode *The Man from Nowhere*.
Directed the second season **The Saint** episodes *The Happy Suicide* & *The Persistent Parasite* and the fourth season's *The Time to Die*.

Troughton Patrick
Played a range of parts in **The Adventures of Robin Hood**: Constable in *The Friar's Pilgrimage*, Sir William in *The Dream*, Seneschal in *The Blackbird*, Traveller in *The Shell Game*, Raoul in *The Bandit of Brittany* & Seneschal in *Food for Thought* [series 2]; Sir Boland in *Elixir of Youth* [3] and Sir Fulke in *The Bagpiper* [4].
Played Marcel in **The Count of Monte Cristo** episode *Marseilles*, Branza in *The Portuguese Affair* and The Ferret in *The Island*.
Played Brenner in the first season **Danger Man** [aka **Secret Agent**] episode *The Lonely Chair* and Bart in *Bury the Dead*.
Featured in the **Espionage** episode *He Rises On Sunday, and We On Monday*.
Played Inspector Nardi in **The Four Just Men** episode *The Night of the Precious Stones* and Vito in *The Moment of Truth*.
Played Vickers in the **H. G. Wells' Invisible Man** episode *Strange Partners*.
Played Sukru in the **Interpol Calling** episode *The Thirteen Innocents*.
Played Bennett in the **Jason King** episode *That isn't Me, It's Somebody Else*.
Played Thiboeuf in the first series **Man of the World** episode *Death of a Conference*.
Played Marceau in **The Persuaders!** episode *The Old, the New and the Deadly*.
Played Bela Karoleon in the first series **The Protectors** episode *Brother Hood*.
Played the police Inspector in the first season **The Saint** episode *The Romantic Matron* and Inspector Gambetti in the third season's *Interlude in Venice*.
Starred as, series regular, Sir Andrew Ffoulkes in **The Scarlet Pimpernel**: *Gentlemen of the Road, Antoine and Antoinette, The Imaginary Invalides, The Flower Woman, The Christmas Present, The Ambassador's Lady, Sir Andrew's Fate, Thanksgiving Day, The Sword of Justice, The Elusive Chauvelin* [as 'Sir Anthony Dewhurst'], *Something Remembered, The Lady in Distress, A Tale of Two Pigtails, The Princess* and *Sir Percy's Wager*.
Played the Shiekh in the **Sentimental Agent** episode *The Scroll of Islam*.
Played Gazio in the **Sir Francis Drake** episode *The Bridge*.
Played Archon in the second season **Space 1999** episode *The Dorcans*.
Played Duke Di Luca in the **Sword of Freedom** episode *The Tower*, Bastiano in *Vespucci*, Teofilo in *The School* and Cecci in *The Ambassador*.
Played Hanzler in the **William Tell** episode *Golden Wheel*.

Trouncer Ruth
Played Helen Kirk in the **Gideon's Way** episode *Boy with a Gun*.
Played Mrs Douglas in the second season **The Protectors** episode *Implicado*.
Played Barbara Coles in the **Strange Report** episode *Report 0846: LONELYHEARTS: 'Who Killed Dan Cupid?'*.

Trubshawe Michael
Appeared as Colonel Blakeley in the second series **Danger Man** [aka **Secret Agent**] episode *The Colonel's Daughter*.

Truman Michael
Directed episodes throughout the four seasons of **Danger Man** [aka **Secret Agent**]: *Josetta, The Girl who Liked GIs, The Conspirators, The Gallows Tree* & *The Actor* [series 1]; *The Professionals, Don't Nail Him Yet, It's Up to the Lady, The Mirror's New, The Black Book, English Lady Takes Lodgers* & *The Outcast* [2]; *The Man who wouldn't Talk* & *Someone is Liable to get Hurt* [3] and the fourth season episode *Koroshi* [*Koroshi* and *Shinda Shima* - directed by Peter Yates - are all that exist of a proposed fourth season and, uniquely for the series, were made in colour. A TVM, *Koroshi*, also exists being the two episodes edited together].
The original director of **The Prisoner** episode *Many Happy Returns*. Direction was taken over by Patrick McGoohan.
Directed the first series **The Saint** episodes *The Talented Husband* & *The Covetous Headman*.

Truman Ralph
Played the Minister in the first season **Danger Man** episode *The Contessa*.
Played Dos Petros in **The Four Just Men** episode *Their Man in London*.
Played Stevens in the **Jason King** episode *A Red, Red Rose Forever*.

Tu Francisca
Played the Turkish nurse in the **Department S** episode *The Perfect Operation* and Lee Bailey in the **Jason King** episode *A Thin Band of Air*.

Tu Poulet
Played Suzy in the second series **Danger Man** [aka **Secret Agent**] episode *A Very Dangerous Game*.

Tucker Alan
Played the lunar module pilot in the **UFO** episode *The Dalotek Affair*, the tracking station operative in *Close up* and the spaceship navigator in *Conflict*.

Tucker Burnell
Played the GSP 4 co-pilot in the **UFO** episode *The Sound of Silence* and the pilot in *Sub-smash*.

Tudley Herbert
Played Doctor Rousse in **The Count of Monte Cristo** episode *The Black Death*.

Tudor-Jones David
Played the Corporal in **The Scarlet Pimpernel** episode *Antoine and Antoinette*.

Tully Brian
Played Doctor Grange in the fourth season **The Saint** episode *The Man Who Gambled with Life*.

Tully Peter
Starred as, Junior Ranger, Mike in **The Forest Rangers**.

Tunnicliffe Jerry
Played the East German guard in the second series **Danger Man** [aka **Secret Agent**] episode *Fair Exchange*.

Turleigh Veronica
Played Madame Dumont in the first season **The Saint** episode *The Good Medicine.*

Turner Aidan
Played Matt Joyson in the first season **The Saint** episode *Luella.*

Turner Frank
Makeup artist on **The Prisoner** episodes *Do Not Forsake Me Oh My Darling, Living in Harmony, The Girl who was Death* and *Fall Out.*

Turner John
Played Lieutenant Commander Street in **The Champions** episode *Twelve Hours.*
Played Hill Billy in the **O.S.S.** episode *Operation Fracture.*
Played Cord Thrandel in the fourth season **The Saint** episode *The Master Plan.*
Starred as, series regular, Bill Randle in **The Sentimental Agent** series [episodes 6, 10 - 13].

Turner Ken
Directed the **Captain Scarlet and the Mysterons** episodes *Operation Time, Spectrum Strikes Back, Model Spy, Crater 101, Fire at Rig 15, Noose of Ice, Attack on Cloudbase* and *The Inquisition.*
Directed the **Joe 90** episodes *Colonel McClaine, Operation McClaine, The Unorthodox Shepherd, Double Agent, Lone Handed 90* and *Mission X-41.*
Location Unit Director on **The Secret Service** and directed the episodes *School for Spies* and *More Haste - Less Speed.*
Directed the **UFO** episodes *Conflict, E.S.P., Destruction, Mindbender, Flight Path* & *Ordeal.*

Turner Mary
Made and operated puppets on the **Supercar** series; Puppet Co-ordinator on **Joe 90** & **The Secret Service** and Puppetry Supervision on **Fireball XL5, Stingray** & **Thunderbirds.**

Turner Michael
Played Taran in the **Strange Report** episode *Report 7931: SNIPER: 'When is Your Cousin Not?'.*

Turner Tim
Voiced Peter Brady - the Invisible Man - in **H.G. Wells' Invisible Man.** Appeared as Nick in the episode *Man in Disguise.* Appeared as Leeds in the **White Hunter** episode *The Fugitive* and as Denny in *A Moment of Truth.*

Turner Yolande
Played Countess Von Streicher in the **Department S** episode *The Double Death of Charlie Crippen.*
Played Juliette in the first season **The Saint** episode *The Work of Art* and Kate in the third season's *A Double in Diamonds.*

Turtle Fred
Sound Supervisor on **William Tell.**

21 Television Productions
Co-produced, with ITC, **Captain Scarlet and the Mysterons.**

Twickenham Studios
Studio used for **The Buccaneers** [aka **Dan Tempest**] & **White Hunter.**

Twiddy Douglas
Production Manager on the first series of **Danger Man.**

289 ALW
The hearse seen in **The Prisoner** episode *Fall Out.*

Tye-Walker Micheal
Appeared as one of the dancers in the **Man in a Suitcase** episode *Three Blinks of the Eyes.*

Tyzack Margaret
Played the wife in **The Four Just Men** episode *The Miracle of St. Philippe.*

****

Ulman Ernst
Played Bulack in the second series **Danger Man** [aka **Secret Agent**] episode *Sting in the Tail*.
Played the Arab servant in the third season **The Saint** episode *The Queen's Ransom*.

Underdown Edward
Played Lord Denby in the second series **Danger Man** [aka **Secret Agent**] episode *Colony Three*, Morgan in *The Ubiquitous Mr Lovegrove* and Max Dell in the third season's *The Hunting Party*.
Played Rankin in the **Man in a Suitcase** episode *All that Glitters* and Maxted in *Night Flight to Andora*.
Played Jack Laurie in the second season **The Saint** episode *The Set-Up*.

Unicomb John
Played the Nazi officer in the **O.S.S.** episode *Operation Meatball*.

Unwin Stanley
Appeared & voiced Father Unwin in **The Secret Service** series.

Urquhart James
Played Bentall in the **G.S.5** episode *The Goldfish Bowl*.

Urquhart Robert
Guested as Hemmings in **The Champions** episode *Operation Deep-freeze*.
Played Pilkington in the second series **Danger Man** [aka **Secret Agent**] episode *English Lady Takes Lodgers*, Charles in *It's Up to the Lady* and Monckton in the third season's *The Man with the Foot*.
Played Anthony James Harvey / Andrew Heywood in the **Department S** episode *The Duplicated Man*.
Played Jarvis in the **Man in a Suitcase** episode *Day of Execution*.
Played Brian Quell in the second season **The Saint** episode *The Abductors*.

****

Valentine Anthony
Played Gregory in the **Department S** episode *The Soup of the Day*.
Played the alien man in the first season **Space 1999** episode *War Games*.

Valentine John
Played the radio Sergeant in the **O.S.S.** episode *Operation Blue Eyes*.

Vallin Rick
Played Tirelle in **The Count of Monte Cristo** episode *Victor Hugo*.

Vallon James
Played James in the fourth season **The Saint** episode *The Man who Gambled with Life*.

Van Beers Stanley
Played Steiger in **The Count of Monte Cristo** episode *Lichtenburg* & the French Prime Minister in *The Texas Affair*.
Played Benedict in the first season **Danger Man** episode *The Relaxed Informer*.
Played the Commissaire in the **Interpol Calling** episode *Slow Boat to Amsterdam* and Mario in *The Girl with Grey Hair*.
Played the doctor in the **O.S.S.** episode *Operation Death Trap*.
Starred as Chauvelin in **The Scarlet Pimpernel**: *The Hostage, The Farmer's Boy, The Winged Madonna, Antoine and Antoinette, The Imaginary Invalides, The Flower Woman, The Christmas Present, The Ambassador's Lady, Sir Andrew's Fate, Thanksgiving Day, The Sword of Justice, The Elusive Chauvelin, Something Remembered, The Lady in Distress, A Tale of Two Pigtails, The Princess & Sir Percy's Wager*.
Played Michael Bridges in the **White Hunter** episode *The Plague*.
Appeared as the Chancellor in the **William Tell** episode *Undercover* and as the Apothecary in *The Surgeon*.

Van Bunnens Jeremy
Floor Manager on **Sapphire and Steel**.

Van Eyssen John
Played Raoul in **The Four Just Men** episode *The Grandmother*.
Played Captain Flormann in the **Interpol Calling** episode *Air Switch*.
Played the secretary in **O.S.S.** episode *Operation Big House*.

Van Gyseghem Andre
Played Resson in **The Count of Monte Cristo** episode *The Experiment*.
Played Otto Berg in the second season **Danger Man** [aka Secret Agent] episode *Fair Exchange* and Enzo Bandone in *You're Not in Any Trouble, Are You?*
Starred as the retiring Number two in **The Prisoner** episode *It's Your Funeral*.
Played Ahmed Bayer in the third season **The Saint** episode *The Gadic Collection*.
Played Grand Duke in the **William Tell** episode *The Ensign*.

Van Montagu A. J.
Scenic Artist on **The Champions, Department S, Jason King & Randall and Hopkirk [Deceased]** aka **My Partner the Ghost**.

Van Norde Frans
Played the hotel clerk in the **Jason King** episode *A Page Before Dying*.

Van Ost Valerie
Played Estelle in the **Strange Report** episode *Report 4977: SWINDLE: 'Square Root of Evil'*.

Van Zandt Phil
Guested as the Prosecutor in **The Count of Monte Cristo** episode *The Golden Blade*.

Vancao Colin
Played the croupier in the **Jason King** episode *Variations on a Theme*.
Played the major in **The Persuaders!** episode *Take Seven*.
Played the French croupier in the **Randall and Hopkirk [Deceased]** aka **My Partner the Ghost** episode *The Ghost who Saved the Bank at Monte Carlo*.

Vance Charles
Played the Sergeant in the first season **Danger Man** episode *The Relaxed Informer*.

Vance Dennis
Director of episodes of **The Count of Monte Cristo**.
Directed the season two **Ghost Squad** episodes *East of Mandalay, The Retirement of Gentle Dove, The Last Jump, The Heir Apparent* & *Polsky*.
Producer on **G.S.5** and directed the episodes *Death of a Cop* & *Party for Murder*.
Producer on **The Scarlet Pimpernel** and directed the episodes *The Sword of Justice, The Lady in Distress* & *Sir Percy's Wager* and wrote *The Imaginary Invalides*.

Vance Leigh
Wrote the third series **The Saint** episodes *The Queen's Ransom, The Better Mousetrap, Little Girl Lost, The Fast Women* & *Island of Chance* [story: teleplayed by John Stanton].
Wrote the **Strange Report** episode *Report 4977: SWINDLE: 'Square Root of Evil'*.

Vanders Bill
Played Captain George in the **Return of the Saint** episode *Dragonseed*.

Vanstone Richard
Played Bruce in the **Strange Report** episode *Report 3906: COVER GIRLS: 'Last year's Model'*.

Vargas Daniele
Played Capo in the **Return of the Saint** episode *The Roman Touch*.

Varnel Max
Directed the **Interpol Calling** episode *Dead On Arrival*.
Directed the **White Hunter** episode *One Fatal Weakness*.

Vasey Suzanne
Played the telephone operator in the **Department S** episode *The Ghost of Mary Burnham*.

Vashti Talya
Played one of the Concubines in the **Virgin of the Secret Service** episode *The Persuasion of a Million Drops*.

Vasquez Marina
Played Flamenco Dancer in the second series **Danger Man** [aka **Secret Agent**] episode *The Outcast*.

Vaughan Brian
Played Haakman - the Dutch tough - in the season two **Ghost Squad** episode *Lost In Transit*.

Vaughan Gillian
Played Anna in the **William Tell** episode *The Black Brothers*.

Vaughan Peter
Played Roberts in **The Adventurer** episode *Somebody Doesn't Like Me*.

Featured in the **Espionage** episode *Once a Spy*.
Guested as Inspector Grimond in the **Interpol Calling** episode *Diamond S.O.S.*
Played Felix De Burg in the **Man in a Suitcase** episode *Essay in Evil*.
Played Schubert in **The Persuaders!** episode *Chain of Events*.
Played Quin in the second season **The Protectors** episode *Quin*.
Played James Howarth in the **Randall and Hopkirk [Deceased]** aka **My Partner the Ghost** episode *Never Trust a Ghost*.
Played Walter Devan in the second season **The Saint** episode *The Saint Steps In*.
Played Morrison in the **Strange Report** episode *Report 3424: EPIDEMIC: 'A Most Curious Crime'*.

Vaughan Robert
Starred in the series **The Protectors** as Harry Rule. Also directed the first season episode *It could be Practically Anywhere on the Island*.

Vaughan Sue
Played the blonde girl in car in the **Randall and Hopkirk [Deceased]** aka **My Partner the Ghost** episode *Vendetta for a Dead Man*.

Vayant Greta
Appeared as Inga in the **Return of the Saint** episode *Dragonseed*.

Vaz Dias Selma
Played Madame Zsa Zsa in the second series of **The Adventures of Robin Hood** episode *Fair Play*.

Venantini Venantino
Played Xexo in the **Return of the Saint** episode *The Judas Game*.

Ventham Wanda
Played Stella Dorset in the second season **Danger Man** [aka **Secret Agent**] episode *A Man to be Trusted* and Penny in *The Mirror's New*.
Played Leila in the **Department S** episode *The Man from X*.
Played the computer attendant in **The Prisoner** episode *It's Your Funeral*.
Played Laura Stride in the season two **The Saint** episode *The Death Penalty* and Penny in the third season's *Escape Route*.
Starred in the series **UFO** as, regular, Colonel Virginia Lake.

Ventura Micky
Played the bell boy in the second series **Danger Man** [aka **Secret Agent**] episode *A Date with Doris*.

Ventura Viviane
Played Lisa in **The Persuaders!** episode *Nuisance Value*.
Played Consuela Flores in the second season **The Saint** episode *The Spanish Cow*.

Verney Guy
Played the Count of Severne in **The Adventures of Robin Hood** episode *The Borrowed Baby* [second series].
Played Cavalcanti in **The Count of Monte Cristo** episode *Sicily*.

Verno Jerry
Played Petitpierre in the **William Tell** episode *The Prisoner*.

Vernon Don
Played the choreographer in the **Randall and Hopkirk [Deceased]** aka **My Partner the Ghost** episode *Money to Burn*.

Vernon Gabor
Played Skirnof in the **Jason King** episode *To Russia With ....Panache*.
Played one of the Hungarian border guards in the second series **The Protectors** episode *Border Line*.

Vernon Richard
Played Sir Richard McKenzie in **The Adventurer** episode *Skeleton in the Cupboard*.
Played Colonel Loring in the **Department S** episode *The Pied Piper of Hambledown*.
Played Sir Maxwell Dean in **The Persuaders!** episode *Anyone Can Play*.
Played Sir John Ripwell in the first season **The Saint** episode *The Elusive Ellshaw*.
Played Stone in the **UFO** episode *The Sound of Silence*.
Played the merchant in the **William Tell** episode *The Killer*.

Vernon Virginia
Appeared as Lynette in **The Adventures of Sir Lancelot** episode *Sir Crustabread*.

Vicars Anthony
Played the policeman in the first season **Danger Man** episode *Josetta* and the police sergeant in *An Affair of State*.
Played Marco in **The Sentimental Agent** episode *Box of Tricks*.

Vickers Philip
Played Rossi in **The Count of Monte Cristo** episode *Majorca*.

Victer Maggie
Appeared as one of the dancers in the **Man in a Suitcase** episode *Three Blinks of the Eyes*.

Videcolor
Technique used for the filming of **Thunderbirds**.

Vidon Henry
Played Benvolio in the third series **The Adventures of Robin Hood** episode *The Doctor*.
Played the French delegate in the first season **Danger Man** episode *The Relaxed Informer*.
Played Peter Davos in the first season **The Saint** episode *The Benevolent Burglary*.
Played the Prefect in the **Sir Francis Drake** episode *The English Dragon*.

Vidovic Petar
Played one of the Hungarian border guards in the second series **The Protectors** episode *Border Line*.

Viko Viktor
Played Inescue in the second season **The Saint** episode *The Miracle Tea Party*.

Viljoen Hein
Played a SHADO Mobile 1 crew member in the **UFO** episode *Computer Affair*.

Villiers James
Played Roddy Harrington in **The Baron** episode *The Persuaders*.
Played Peters in the **Man in a Suitcase** episode *Dead Man's Shoes*.
Played Inspector Pryor in the first season **The Saint** episode *The High Fence*.
Played Morgan in the **Shirley's World** episode *Knightmare*.

Villiers Mavis
Played Louise in **The Four Just Men** episode *Justice For Gino*.

Played Texas Mother in the second season **The Saint** episode *The Happy Suicide.*

Vinalli Frank
Wardrobe on **The Protectors**.

Vincente Roy
Played the soldier in the second series **Danger Man** [aka Secret Agent] episode *A Date with Doris.*
Stunt arranger on the **Man in a Suitcase** series and appeared as a German soldier in the episode *The Girl who Never was.*
Stunt Arranger on **Strange Report**.

Vines Margaret
Played Mrs Fennimore in **The Four Just Men** episode *The Bystanders.*
Played Mrs Every in the season two **Ghost Squad** episode *The Retirement of Gentle Dove.*
Played Agnes Yarrow in the first season **The Saint** episode *The Element of Doubt.*

Vinson Ian
Camera Operator on **Joe 90**.

Violetta
Played the Sister of Mercy in the **Jason King** episode *Buried in the Cold, Cold Ground.*

Vivian Sidney
Appeared as De Vere's cook in the second series of **The Adventures of Robin Hood** episode *Hubert.*
Played the baker in **The Adventures of Sir Lancelot** episode *Sir Crustabread.*
Played Inn Keeper in **The Count of Monte Cristo** episode *Flight to Calais.*
Played Danny in the **Gideon's Way** episode *The Tin God.*

Vladon Jean
Played the actor in the UFO episode *Timelash.*

Vogel Tony
Played Enzio in the **Jason King** two parter *All that Glisters.*
Played Diskett in the **Return of the Saint** episode *Yesterday's Hero.*

The Volants
Appeared as 'The Flying Four' in the second series of **The Adventures of Robin Hood** episode *Fair Play.*

Von Moos George
Played the airline steward in the second season **The Protectors** episode *Decoy.*

Von Salvesberg Heidy
Played Contessa Fardango in the **Return of the Saint** episode *The Murder Cartel.*

Voskovec George
Featured in the **Espionage** episode *Never Turn Your Back On a Friend.*

Voss Phillip
Played Capt. Nigel Bratby in the **Virgin of the Secret Service** episode *The Rajah and the Suffragette.*

Voysey Michael
Story Advisor on the **Father Brown** series.

****

Waddington Patrick
Played the N.A.T.O. General in the **Department S** episode *Who Plays the Dummy?*.
Played the German Ambassador in the **O.S.S.** episode *Operation Big House*.

Wade John
Played Johnson in **The Adventurer** episode *Skeleton in theCupboard*.
Played the card dealer in the **Return of the Saint** episode *Tower Bridge is Falling Down*.

Wadsworth Derek
Music on the second series of **Space 1999** [Barry Gray did season one].

Wager Anthony
Played Calder in the first season **The Saint** episode *Iris*, Corrigan in the second season's *The Set-Up* and the Lieutenant in the third's *The Paper Chase*.

Wagstaff Elsie
Appeared as the old woman in the first series **The Adventures of Robin Hood** episode *The Sheriff's Boots*.

Wain Gerry
Played Cap in the **Man in a Suitcase** episode *Man from the Dead*.
Played a guard in the **Virgin of the Secret Service** episode *The Persuasion of a Million Drops*, the torturer in *Across the Silver Pass of Gusri Song* and Ed in *The Professor Goes West*.

Wait Nancie
Played the secretary in **The Adventurer** episode *Mr Calloway is a Very Cautious Man*.

Wakabayashi Akiko
Appeared as Tamiko in the **Shirley's World** episode *The Lovers*.

Wakefield Anne
Appeared as Rita in the first series **Ghost Squad** episode *High Wire*.

Walder Ernst
Played Neuman in **The Baron** episode *And Suddenly You're Dead*.
Guested as Allbrecht in **The Champions** episode *The Search*.
Played Esser in the second series **Danger Man** [aka **Secret Agent**] episode *The Mirror's New*.
Played the German officer in **The Four Just Men** episode *The Battle of the Bridge*.
Played the train steward in the second season **The Saint** episode *The Rhine Maiden*.

Waldhorn Gary
Played Rickman in the **Return of the Saint** episode *The Poppy Chain*.

Walker April
Played Daphne Aylmer in the **Father Brown** episode *The Dagger With Wings*.

Walker Danvers
Played Rudi Gemmel in **The Baron** episode *A Memory of Evil*.
Appeared as the painter, Number 42, in **The Prisoner** episode *Checkmate* and as the first young man in *Do Not Forsake Me Oh My Darling*.

Walker G. B.
Casting Director on **The Saint**.

Walker Harry
Played Mallory in the **Father Brown** episode *The Hammer of God*.

Walker John
Played the mechanic in the **Randall and Hopkirk [Deceased]** aka **My Partner the Ghost** episode *You Can Always find a Fall Guy*.

Walker Robert
Played a constable in the **Father Brown** episode *The Quick One*.

Walker Zena
Played the title role in the second series of **The Adventures of Robin Hood** episode *Isabella* and returned as Ann de Brissac for the third season's *Woman's War*.
Played Lady Angela in **The Adventures of Sir Lancelot** episodes *Lancelot's Banishment* and *The Bridge*].
Guested as Janet in **The Prisoner** episode *Do Not Forsake Me Oh My Darling*.
Played Felicia in the **Sword of Freedom** episode *Who is Felicia?*.

Wall Tony
Played Riley in **The Champions** episode *Shadow of the Panther*.

Wallace Art
Wrote the **Espionage** episode *Do You Remember Leo Winters?*
Co-wrote the first series **Space 1999** episode *Matter of Life and Death* [with Johnny Byrne].

Wallace Edgar
The Four Just Men was based on his original novel.

Wallace Elizabeth
Played Maria in **The Four Just Men** episode *Rogue's Harvest*.

Wallace Hedger
Played Charters in **The Champions** episode *Shadow of the Panther*.
Played the Embassy secretary in the first season **Danger Man** episode *The Sisters*.
Played Norman in the **Man in a Suitcase** episode *Which Way did he Go, McGill?* and Williams in *Who's Mad Now?*.
Played Geoffrey Bane in the third season **The Saint** episode *The Gadic Collection* and Ian in the fourth season's *The Man who Gambled with Life*.

Wallace Ian
Played Dr. Trevor in the **H. G. Wells' Invisible Man** episode *Death Cell*.
Played Father Abbot in the **William Tell** episodes *The Gauntlet of St. Gerhardt* and *The Elixir*.

Wallace Julie
Played Mrs McKinnon in the second series **Danger Man** [aka **Secret Agent**] episode *That's Two of Us Sorry*.

Waller David
Played the gentleman in **The Four Just Men** episode *National Treasure*.

Wallis
Provided Sue Lloyd's wardrobe on **The Baron**.

Wallis Jackie
Played the stewardess in **The Sentimental Agent** episode *A Very Desirable Plot*.

Walmsley Anna
Played Betsy in **The Buccaneers** [aka **Dan Tempest**] episode *Mother Doughty's Crew* and Mollie in *Dan Tempest and The Amazons*.

Walsh Dermot
Played Hugo Delano in the first season **Danger Man** episode *Bury the Dead*.
Played Joe Green in the **H. G. Wells' Invisible Man** episode *Jailbreak*.

Walsh Kay
Played Ingar Sorenson in **The Baron** episode *And Suddenly You're Dead*.
Played Martha Maricut in the **Gideon's Way** episode *The Housekeeper* and Harriet Bright in *Morna*.

Walsh Stanley
Played the policeman in the season two **Ghost Squad** episode *The Big Time*.

Walsh Terry
Stuntman & double.
Worked on **The Baron, The Champions** [doubled William Gaunt on the Bill Sawyer episodes], **Danger Man, Gideon's Way, The Persuaders!, The Prisoner, Return of the Saint** [doubled Ian Ogilvy],**The Saint and Space 1999**.

Walter Len
Supervising Film Editor on **Joe 90 & Thunderbirds**.
Editor on **UFO**.

Walter Meg
Appeared as one of the models in the **Strange Report** episode *Report 3906: COVER GIRLS: 'Last Year's Model'*.

Walters Hugh
Played Pestrade in **The Adventurer** episode *Action!*.
Played Bernard in the **Jason King** episode *An Author in Search of Two Characters*.

Walters Russell
Played Kelly in the first season **The Saint** episode *The Noble Sportsman*.

Walters Thorley
Featured in the **Espionage** episode *The Dragon Slayer*.
Played Hatton in **The Persuaders!** episode *To the Death, Baby*.

Walton Studios, Walton-on-Thames
Studio used for the filming of seasons three & four of **The Adventures of Robin Hood** [Nettlefold Studios was used for seasons one & two], **The Four Just Men** and **Sword of Freedom**.

Wang Gene
Writer on **The New Adventures of Charlie Chan**.

Wannamaker Sam
Played Sefton Folkard in **The Baron** episode *You can't Win Them All*.
Directed **The Champions** episode *To Trap a Rat*.
Played Patrick Laurence in the first season **Danger Man** episode *The Lonely Chair*.
Featured in the **Espionage** episode *Festival of Pawns*.
Played Nicko in the second season **Man of the World** episode *The Bandit*.
Played Domenico in the **Return of the Saint** episode *Dragonseed* and directed *Vicious Circle*.

Warbeck David
Played the Skydiver's Captain in the **UFO** episodes *Destruction & Reflections in the Water*.

Warburg Maria
Played the young German woman in the **Man in a Suitcase** episode *Somebody Loses, Somebody ...Wins?*.

Warburton John
Played Debray in **The Count of Monte Cristo** episode *Affair of Honour*.

Ward Dervis
Appeared in **The Adventures of Robin Hood**: as Ben in *A Year and a Day*, as the Blacksmith in *The Friar's Pilgrimage*, as a villager in *Food for Thought* [all series 2] and as Ned in *The Challenge of the Black Knight* [3].
Appeared as a guard in **The Champions** episode *Nutcracker*.
Played Hawkinson in the second series **Danger Man** [aka **Secret Agent**] episode *The Mercenaries*.
Played Keith Smith in the **Gideon's Way** episode *The 'V' Men* and Larry Larkin in *The Reluctant Witness*.
Played the Colonel in the **Interpol Calling** episode *Pipeline*.
Played Jonathan P. Hacket in the first series **The Protectors** episode *It Could be Practically Anywhere on the Island*.

Ward Edmund
Wrote the **Man in a Suitcase** episodes *Dead Man's Shoes, The Sitting Pigeon, Burden of Proof & Web with Four Spiders*.

Ward Georgina
Played Verity Montand in **The Baron** episode *The Persuaders*.
Played Diana in the second series **Danger Man** [aka **Secret Agent**] episode *Such Men are Dangerous* and Simone in *The Black Book*.
Played Erica Townsend in the **Gideon's Way** episode *The Millionaire's Daughter*.

Ward Lalla
Played Evi Andersen in the second season **The Protectors** episode *Bagman*.

Ward Trevor
Played Victor in the **Return of the Saint** episode *The Nightmare Man*.

Ware James
Played Reynolds in **The Adventurer** episode *Somebody Doesn't Like Me*.

Waring Derek
Played Tom in the season three **The Adventures of Robin Hood** episode *Too Many Robins* and Peter Larkin in *To Be a Student*.
Played Balin in **The Adventures of Sir Lancelot** episode *Knight's Choice*.
Played George in **The Buccaneers** [aka **Dan Tempest**] episode *The Decoy*.
Played Peter Welcome in the season two **Ghost Squad** episode *The Big Time*.
Played Louis in the **William Tell** episode *The Avenger*.

Warner Richard
Played Vittoria Guardy in **The Baron** episode *The Long, Long Day*.
Played the hospital director in the first season **Danger Man** episode *The Girl in Pink Pyjamas*.
Played Detective Inspector Forbush in the **Father Brown** episode *The Actor and the Alibi*.
Played the first officer in the **H. G. Wells' Invisible Man** episode *The Big Plot*.
Played Inspector Sanglett in the first series **Man of the World** episode *A Family Affair*.

Played Don Battista in the third season **The Saint** episode *Interlude in Venice*.

Played the General in **The Sentimental Agent** episode *Box of Tricks*.

Played Walsingham in the **Sir Francis Drake** episodes *Mary, Queen of Scots*, *Lost Colony of Virginia* and *Mission to Paris*.

Played Headman of Dosten in the **William Tell** episode *Golden Wheel*.

Warren Barry
Played the hotel receptionist in the first series **The Protectors** episode *Balance of Terror*.

Warren Kenneth J.
Played Fox-Stuart in **The Baron** two parter *Masquerade* [*Masquerade* - part 1 and *The Killing* - part 2: edited together, also exists as a feature entitled *Man in a Looking Glass*].

Played Whittaker in **The Champions** episode *The Beginning* [this episode was combined with *The Interrogation* to form a 'feature' entitled *Legend of The Champions*].

Played Eddie Gelb in the third season **Danger Man** [aka Secret Agent] episode *The Paper Chase*.

Played Verner in **The Persuaders!** episode *The Old, the New and the Deadly*.

Played Warlock in the fourth season **The Saint** two parter *The Fiction Makers* and Ben Kersh in *Where the Money Is*.

Warren Yvonne
Played the second sister in **The Adventures of Sir Lancelot** episode *Sir Bliant* and Lady Iolta in *Roman Wall*.

Played Maria in **The Buccaneers** [aka **Dan Tempest**] episode *The Surgeon of Sangre Rojo*.

Played the French girl in the **O.S.S.** episode *Operation Orange Blossom*.

Warwick Edmund
Appeared in **The Adventures of Robin Hood**: as the servant in *Flight from France*, as the Man-at-Arms in *The Dowry*, as the drinker in *The York Treasure* & as Simon in *The Little People* [series 2]; as the landlord in *Roman Gold*, as the cook in *The Lottery* & as Michael in *Farewell to Tuck* [3] and as the old man in *Double Trouble* [4].

Played Matt in **The Adventures of Sir Lancelot** episode *Shepherd's War*.

Played Magistrate in **The Buccaneers** [aka **Dan Tempest**] episode *Indian Fighters*.

Warwick Gina
Played Susan Lewis in the **Department S** episode *The Pied Piper of Hambledown*.

Warwick James
Played Litchfield in the **Jason King** episode *Wanna Buy a Television Series* aka *A Face I Used to Know*.

Warwick Joan
Editor on **The Adventures of Robin Hood**.

Editor on **The Adventures of Sir Lancelot** episodes *Double Identity, The Bridge, The Witch's Brew, Ruby of Radnor, The Lesser Breed, The Mortaise Fair, Maid of Somerset, Sir Crustabread, The Ugly Duckling, The Prince of Limerick, The Lady Lilith, Knight's Choice, The Missing Princess* and *The Thieves*.

Waters Jan
Played Jan Rose in the **Jason King** episode *A Deadly Line in Digits*.

Played Mary Ford in the third season **The Saint** episode *The Persistent Patriots*.

Waters Russell
Played Thompson in the second season **The Saint** episode *The Inescapable Word*.

Played the barman in **The Champions** episode *The Experiment*.

Played Reitter in the **H. G. Wells' Invisible Man** episode *The Rocket*.

Guested as MacPherson in the **Interpol Calling** episode *Game for Three Hands* and as Zelnikov in *The Absent Assassin*.

Watford Gwen
Played Ruth Osterman in the **White Hunter** episode *Rogue Man*.

Watkin Pierre
Played Charcot in **The Count of Monte Cristo** episode *Return to the Chateau d'If*.

Watling Deborah
Starred as, series regular, Sally in the series **H. G. Wells' Invisible Man**: *Secret Experiment, The Locked Room, Picnic with Death, Strange Partners, Jailbreak, Bank Raid, Point of Destruction* & *Man in Disguise*.

Played the first child in the **William Tell** episode *The Spider*.

Watling Giles
Played, semi-regular, Malcolm Gideon in **Gideon's Way**: *State Visit, The Firebug, How to Retire without Really Working, Subway to Revenge, The Tin God, The Alibi Man* & *The Rhyme and the Reason*.

Watling Jack
Played Sir Leon in the season three **The Adventures of Robin Hood** episode *The Christmas Goose*.

Played Rollo Waters in the first season **Danger Man** episode *The Traitor*.

Played Captain Roly Horstead in the season two **Ghost Squad** episode *The Last Jump*.

Played Sandy Mason in the **H. G. Wells' Invisible Man** episode *Blind Justice*.

Played Geoffrey Winters in the **Jason King** episode *It's Too Bad about Auntie*.

Played Ferdinand in the **William Tell** episode *The Cuckoo*, Hofmanstahl in *The Master Spy*, the Captain of the fort in *Secret Weapon* and Ferdinand in *The Elixir*.

Watson Gary
Played Colin Bradfield in **The Baron** episode *Enemy of the State*.

Played Donald Seaton in the **Randall and Hopkirk [Deceased]** aka **My Partner the Ghost** episode *The Smile Behind the Veil*.

Played John Spring in the third season **The Saint** episode *When Spring is Sprung*.

Watson Greta
Played Antoinette in **The Scarlet Pimpernel** episode *Antoine and Antoinette*.

Watson Jack
Played Inspector Melton in the first series **Man of the World** episode *The Mindreader*.

Watson John
Played the lame beggar in the first series of **The Adventures of Robin Hood** episode *The Wager*.

Watson John H.
Played Count Eger in the season three **The Adventures of Robin Hood** episode *To Be a Student*.

Watson Ken
Played Inspector Newman in the first series **The Protectors** episode *The Bodyguards*.

Played the police Sergeant in the **Randall and Hopkirk [Deceased]** aka **My Partner the Ghost** episode *Just for the Record.*

Watson Kenneth
Played Sandy in the **G.S.5** episode *Dead Men Don't Drive.*
Played Willie in the first series **Man of the World** episode *The Highland Story.*
Played Dr Fordyce in the **Timeslip** story *The Wrong End of Time* [episodes 1& 2].

Watson Moray
Played Buckingham in the **Return of the Saint** episode *The Judas Game.*
Played Ken Shield in the second season **The Saint** episode *The Imprudent Politician.*

Watson Tom
Played the crewman in the **O.S.S.** episode *Operation Lovebird.*

Watt Harry
Directed **The Four Just Men** episodes *The Judge, Dead Man's Switch, The Slaver & Justice For Gino.*

Wattis Richard
Starred as, series regular, Hardy in the debut season of **Danger Man**: *The Lonely Chair, The Sisters, Find and Return, Name, Date and Place & Dead Man Walks.*
Guested as Fotheringay in **The Prisoner** episode *The Chimes of Big Ben.*

Watts Allan
Played the croupier in the **Man in a Suitcase** episode *Burden of Proof.*

Watts Frank, B.S.C.
Director of Photography on **The Champions, Department S, Jason King & Randall and Hopkirk [Deceased]** aka **My Partner the Ghost & Space 1999.**

Watts Jeanne
Played Mrs Matson in the first season **The Saint** episode *The Fellow Traveller.*

Waugh Eileen
Played Lady Margaret Graham in the **Father Brown** episode *The Secret Garden.*

Way Eileen
Played Catrina in the second season **Man of the World** episode *The Bullfighter.*
Played the maid in the fourth season **The Saint** two parter *Vendetta for the Saint.*
Played Miss Mithras in **The Sentimental Agent** episode *A Little Sweetness and Light.*
Played Pastora in the **Sir Francis Drake** episode *The Gypsies.*
Played Granny Rossi in the **William Tell** episode *The Black Brothers.*

Way Paul
Appeared as the Chinese dice player in **The Adventures of Sir Lancelot** episode *The Mortaise Fair.*

Way Tony
Assistant Director on the second season of **Danger Man** [aka **Secret Agent**].

Wayne Ken
Played the Director in **The Adventurer** episode *The Solid Gold Hearse.*
Played Gilroy in the first season **The Saint** episode *The Element of Doubt.*

Weaver Elizabeth
Played Eileen Ballinger in the second season **The Saint** episode *The Contract.*

Weaver Fritz
Featured in the **Espionage** episode *Medal For a Turned Coat.*

Webb Alan
Played the blind man in the first series **The Protectors** episode *See No Evil.*

Webb David
Played the police sergeant in the **Randall and Hopkirk [Deceased]** aka **My Partner the Ghost** episode *Who Killed Cock Robin.*

Webb Rita
Played the fishwoman in **The Count of Monte Cristo** episode *The Island.*

Webb Roger
Music on the **Strange Report** series.

Webb Wanda
Puppet Operator on the **Joe 90** series.

Webber Robert
Featured in the **Espionage** episode *The Liberators.*

Webster Donald
Played Johnny Haswell in **The Baron** episode *The High Terrace.*
Played George in the second series **The Protectors** episode *Zeke's Blues.*

Webster Harry
Played Beaver Johnson in the first season **The Saint** episode *The Sporting Chance.*

Webster Joy
Played the girl at the bar in the **O.S.S.** episode *Operation Eel.*

Webster Mary
Played Daphne Miller in the second series **Danger Man** [aka **Secret Agent**] episode *Sting in the Tail.*
Played Marthe in the **William Tell** episode *The Bride.*

Weingreen Peter
Assistant Director on **The Adventures of Sir Lancelot** episodes *The Outcast, Winged Victory, Sir Bliant The Magic Sword, Lancelot's Banishment, Roman Wall, Caledon, Shepherd's War, The Pirates, The Black Castle, The Lesser Breed, The Magic Book, Knight Errand* and *The Theft of Excalibur.*

Weinstein Productions - see Hannah **Weinstein**

Weinstein Hannah
Largely responsible for **The Adventures of Robin Hood**: Credited as Executive Producer on season one and two. Season one & two was credited as 'a Sapphire Films Production for the Incorporated Television Programme Co.', season three as 'a Weinstein Production for Sapphire Films, for the Incorporated Television Programme Co.' and season four as 'a Hannah Fisher Production for Sapphire Films, for the Incorporated Television Programme Co.'
Executive Producer on **The Adventures of Sir Lancelot**: *The Knight with the Red Plume, The Queen's Knight* and *Sir Bliant.* The series was billed as 'a Weinstein Production for Sapphire Films Limited, for the Independent Television Programme Co. Ltd.'
Executive Producer on **The Buccaneers** [aka **Dan Tempest**] episodes *Blackbeard, The Raiders, Captain Dan Tempest, Dan*

Tempest's War with Spain, The Wasp, Whale Gold, Slave Ship, Before the Mast and *The Decoy*. The series was billed as 'a Weinstein Production for Sapphire Films Limited, for the Incorporated Television Programme Co. Ltd.'
Executive Producer on Hannah Fisher **The Four Just Men** [a 'Hannah Fisher Production for Sapphire Films Ltd., for Associated TeleVision: an ITC Presentation'].
Executive Producer on the series **Sword of Freedom**.

Weir David
Wrote the second season **Danger Man** [aka **Secret Agent**] episode *The Colonel's Daughter*.
Wrote the first series **Space 1999** episode *Black Sun*.

Weir Ivor
Title sequence for **Sapphire and Steel**.

Weir Molly
Played Mrs Henderson in the second season **Ghost Squad** episode *The Thirteenth Girl*.

Weiss Zachary
Wrote **The Buccaneers** [aka **Dan Tempest**] episodes *Dan Tempest's War with Spain, Whale Gold, Mother Doughty's Crew, Blood Will Tell, Dangerous Cargo, Gentleman Jack and the Lady, Dan Tempest and The Amazons, The Return of Calico Jack* [with Basil Dawson] and *Prize of Andalusia* [with Basil Dawson].

Welch Peter
Played the Sheriff's servant in **The Adventures of Robin Hood** episode *Too Many Earls* & the wounded man in *The Black Five* [both second series]. Returned in series three as the Ambassador in *Pepper* and Howard in *Roman Gold*.
Played Salcito in the first season **Danger Man** episode *The Deputy Coyannis Story*.
Played the police Sergeant in the **Strange Report** episode *Report 8944: HAND: 'A Matter of Witchcraft?'*.
Played Johann in the **William Tell** episode *Undercover* and the first guard in *Secret Death*.

Welles Halstead
Co-wrote the **Espionage** episodes *The Incurable One* [with Sidney Carroll] and *The Dragon Slayer* [with Albert Ruben].

Wellesley Gordon
Wrote the **White Hunter** episode *Let My People Go* [with Charlotte Hastings].
Wrote the **Sir Francis Drake** episode *The Reluctant Duchess* [with Paul Tabori].

Welling Ron
Played the garage mechanic in the second season **The Saint** episode *The Smart Detective*.

Wells Alan
Played D'Avril in **The Count of Monte Cristo** episode *The Golden Blade*.

Wells Cedric
Wrote the **Sir Francis Drake** episode *Boy Jack* [with Ian Stuart Black].

Wells Ingeborg
Played Lady Irina in the debut season of **The Adventures of Robin Hood** episode *The Vandals* and Michele in season two's *Flight from France*.
Played Cecille in **The Scarlet Pimpernel** episode *The Lady in Distress*.

Wells Jerold
Played Hoad in **The Champions** episode *The Night People*.

Played Alfred Porter in the **Man in a Suitcase** episode *The Whisper*.

Wells Jerome
Played Klaus in the **O.S.S.** episode *Operation Sweet Talk*.

Wells Sidney
Wrote the second series of **The Adventures of Robin Hood** episodes *Fair Play & Food for Thought* and the third's *To Be a Student*.

Wells Sidney B.
Wrote the third series **The Adventures of Robin Hood** episode *At the Sign of the Blue Boar*.

Welsh John
Played the British First Secretary in the second series **Danger Man** [aka **Secret Agent**] episode *A Room in the Basement*, Emmerson in *You're Not in Any Trouble, Are You?*, Rhodes in *The Professionals* and Ross in the third season's *The Hunting Party*.
Played Moffat in **The Four Just Men** episode *The Protector*.
Played Professor Wallace in the first series **Ghost Squad** episode *The Green Shoes* [this episode was shot for the first series, but due to an actors' strike, was shown in season two].
Played Governor Walters in the **Sir Francis Drake** episode *Lost Colony of Virginia*.
Played Dermot O'Rourke in the **Virgin of the Secret Service** episode *The Amazons*.

Wentworth John
Played Mr Whitehead in the second season **Ghost Squad** episode *The Thirteenth Girl*.
Played Bovic in the **G.S.5** episode *A Cast of Thousands*.
Played Sir Charles in **The Prisoner** episode *Do Not Forsake Me Oh My Darling*.
Played Professor Grant in the first season **The Saint** episode *Sophia*.

Weske Brian
Played the Duty Officer in the second series **Danger Man** [aka **Secret Agent**] episode *Have a Glass of Wine* and Simpson in the third season's *To our Best Friend*.
Played the barrow boy in the **Gideon's Way** episode *How to Retire without Really Working* and Gerry Adams in *The Millionaire's Daughter*.
Played Kurnitz in the **G.S.5** episode *Pay Up or Else*.
Played the cabbie in the first season **The Saint** episode *Starring the Saint*.

West Anita
Played Sandra in the second series **Danger Man** [aka **Secret Agent**] episode *The Outcast*.
Played Mary Hammond in the first season **The Saint** episode *The Element of Doubt*.

West Lockwood
Played the camera shop manager in **The Prisoner** episode *Do Not Forsake Me Oh My Darling*.
Played Doctor Ward in the **Strange Report** episode *Report 2641: HOSTAGE: 'If You Won't Learn, Die!*.

West Norma
Played Pauline in the second series **Danger Man** [aka **Secret Agent**] episode *A Very Dangerous Game*.
Played Girl Bo-Peep in **The Prisoner** episode *Dance of the Dead*.
Played the receptionist in the third season **The Saint** episode *The Paper Chase*.

West Samuel B.
Wrote the season three **The Adventures of Robin Hood** episodes *The Profiteer, The Crusaders & Elixir of Youth*.

Writer on **The Four Just Men**: *The Deadly Capsule* [story with Oliver Skene: teleplayed by Jan Read], *Panic Button* [with Marianne Foster], *The Man in the Road* [with George Slavin], *The Protector* [story with Alan Moreland: teleplayed by Leon Griffiths & Alan Moreland] and *The Man in the Royal Suite* [with John Collier: from an idea by Alec Coppel].
Wrote the **Sword of Freedom** episodes *The Sicilian* & *Choice of Weapons*.

West Timothy
Played Sam Grimes in the **Randall and Hopkirk [Deceased]** aka **My Partner the Ghost** episode *Vendetta for a Dead Man*.

Westerby Robert
Wrote the story for the **H. G. Wells' Invisible Man** episode *Play to Kill* [teleplayed by Leslie Arliss].
Wrote the **Sword of Freedom** episodes *Caterina, The Hero, The Duke, The Bracelet, Marriage of Convenience* & *The Pagan Venus*.

Westerby Susan
Played the woman in the season three **The Adventures of Robin Hood** episode *The Angry Village*.

Weston David
Played Farley in **The Adventurer** episode *The Solid Gold Hearse*.
Played a rescuer in the **UFO** episode *Survival* and Phil Mitchell in *The Dalotek Affair*.

Weston Graham
Played the Northern agent in **The Persuaders!** episode *Anyone Can Play*.
Played Max in the second series **The Protectors** episode *Zeke's Blues*.

Weston Leslie
Played Moray in **The Count of Monte Cristo** episode *The Devil's Emissary*.
Guested as Doc Carson in the **Interpol Calling** episode *Trial at Cranby's Creek*.

Weston Paul
Played Lintar in the first series **The Protectors** episode *It was All Over in Leipzig*.

Weston Philip
Played the second constable in the **Randall and Hopkirk [Deceased]** aka **My Partner the Ghost** episode *Who Ever Heard of a Ghost Dying?*.

Westrex Sound Recording System
Recording System used **Danger Man** & **Fireball XL5**.

Westwood Patrick
Played Parkinson in the **Department S** episode *The Duplicated Man*.
Played Menendez in the **Jason King** episode *A Kiss for a Beautiful Killer*.
Played Major Hussein in the first season **The Saint** episode *The Wonderful War*, Osbett in the second season's *The Miracle Tea Party* and Saleb in the third's *The Queen's Ransom*.
Played Doctor Shaw in the second season **Space 1999** two parter *The Bringers of Wonder*.

Wetherell Virginia
Played the nurse in the second season **The Protectors** episode *Route 27*.

Whalen Michael
Played Balbec in **The Count of Monte Cristo** episode *The Duel*.

Wheatley Alan
Starred as the Sheriff in **The Adventures of Robin Hood**: *The Coming of Robin Hood, The Moneylender, Friar Tuck, Maid Marian, A Guest for the Gallows, The Knight Who Came To Dinner, The Miser, The Challenge, Queen Eleanor, The Ordeal, The Alchemist, The Jongleur, The Brothers, The Sheriff's Boots, Errand of Mercy, The Vandals, Richard the Lionheart, Ladies of Sherwood, Will Scarlet, The Deserted Castle, Trial by Battle, The May Queen, The Wanderer* & *Secret Mission* [season 1]; *The Scientist, Blackmail, A Year and a Day, The Goldmaker, Ransom, The Hero, The Haunted Mill, Outlaw Money, The Black Patch, The Trap, The Dream, The Blackbird, Ambush, The Goldmaker's Return, Fair Play, The Secret Pool, The Path of True Love* [aka *Locksley Hall*], *The Dowry, The York Treasure, The Borrowed Baby, The Frightened Tailor, The Black Five, The Road in the Air, Carlotta* & *Too Many Earls* [2]; *The Salt King, A Tuck in Time, The Charter, Brother Battle, My Brother's Keeper, The Challenge of the Black Knight, The Rivals, Knight Errant, The Crusaders, Castle in the Air, The Double, Roman Gold, The Minstrel, The Doctor, The Fire, At the Sign of the Blue Boar, Quickness of the Hand, The Lottery, Lincoln Green, Woman's War* & *Farewell to Tuck* [3] and *Sybella, The Lady Killer, A Touch of Fever, Tuck's Love Day, The Loaf, Six Strings to his Bow* & *The Devil You Don't Know* [4].
Played Lord Mountford in **The Baron** episode *The Edge of Fear*.
Played Col. Michelle in **The Count of Monte Cristo** episode *A Matter of Justice* and Bonnet in *Bordeaux*.
Played Alexis in the first season **Danger Man** episode *Hired Assassin* and the solicitor in the second series [now aka **Secret Agent**] episode *Such Men are Dangerous*.
Played Carter in the **Department S** episode *A Ticket to Nowhere*.

Wheatley Frank
Played Giovanni in the season two **Ghost Squad** episode *Mr Five Per Cent*.

Wheeler Cyril
Played the Nazi leader in the **O.S.S.** episode *Operation Jingle Bells*.

Wheeler Lionel
Played the police driver in the **Department S** episode *Last Train to Redbridge*.

Wickert Anthony
Starred as Dan Ledward in the **Whiplash** series.

Wickham Jeffrey
Played Paul Millett in **The Baron** episode *The Island* [part 2 of a two-parter: also exists, edited together with part 1 - *Storm Warning*, as a feature entitled *Mystery Island*].
Played Perekev in the **Jason King** episode *To Russia With ....Panache* .
Played Felix Harborough in *Adventure Five* of **Sapphire and Steel**.

Whightman Bruce
Played the English taxi driver in the second series **Danger Man** [aka **Secret Agent**] episode *Fair Exchange*.

Whitcutt Mike
Cameras on **Sapphire and Steel**.

White Alan
Played Heffner in **The Champions** episode *Operation Deepfreeze*.
Played Edwards in the third season **Danger Man** [aka **Secret Agent**] episode *The Hunting Party*.
Played the Captain in the season two **Ghost Squad** episode *Escape Route*.

Played Charles in the **Man in a Suitcase** episode *Variation on a Million Bucks* [part 1: also combined with part 2 to form a movie: *To Chase a Million*].
Played Roland Walter Dutton in **The Prisoner** episode *Dance of the Dead.*

White Angela
Played the girl in the fourth series **The Adventures of Robin Hood** episode *The Loaf.*
Played Sonia in the first series **Ghost Squad** episode *Death from a Distance.*

White Arthur
Played the stall-holder in **The Prisoner** episode *It's Your Funeral.*

White Carol
Played Winifred Norton in the **Gideon's Way** episode *The Rhyme and the Reason.*

White Dorothy
Played Raquel Vargas in the first season **Danger Man** episode *An Affair of State.*

White Frank
Art Director on the first series of **Danger Man**.

White Ian
Played Prince Luigi in the **Virgin of the Secret Service** episode *Wings Over Glencraig.*

White Jeremy
Played the third Man-at-Arms in the third series **The Adventures of Robin Hood** episode *The Fire.*

White Jonathan
Played the milkman in **The Four Just Men** episode *Panic Button.*

White Larry
Suggested and developed for television the series **H. G. Wells' Invisible Man**.

White Les
Played Wilhelm in the third season **Danger Man** [aka **Secret Agent**] episode *Say it with Flowers* and Corbu in *I'm Afraid you Have the Wrong Number.*
Played Hales in the **Randall and Hopkirk [Deceased]** aka **My Partner the Ghost** episode *A Disturbing Case.*
Played the frogman in the fourth season **The Saint** episode *The Ex-King of Diamonds.*

White Leslie
Played Yates in **The Baron** episode *Countdown.*

White Meadows
Appeared as Aidan in **The Adventures of Sir Lancelot** episode *Shepherd's War.*
Played Groggins in **The Buccaneers** [aka **Dan Tempest**] episode *The Return of Calico Jack.*
Played the customs man in the second series **Danger Man** [aka **Secret Agent**] episode *It's Up to the Lady.*
Played the stage door keeper in the first season **The Saint** episode *The Bunco Artists* and Harry Blundell in *Iris.*
Played Burgomaster in the **William Tell** episode *The Bear.*

White Rowena
Puppet Operator on **Joe 90** and **The Secret Service**.

White Rupert
Played Revel in **The Count of Monte Cristo** episode *The Devil's Emissary.*

White Tony
Camera Operator on **Department S**.

White Valarie
Played Mrs Lister in the season two **Ghost Squad** episode *The Retirement of Gentle Dove.*

Whitehead Reg
Played the microphone man in the fourth season **The Saint** episode *The World Beater.*

Whitelaw Billie
Played Brenda in the season three **The Adventures of Robin Hood** episode *The Bride of Robin Hood.*
Featured in the **Espionage** episode *He Rises On Sunday, and We On Monday.*
Played Zamara in the second season **Space 1999** episode *One Moment of Humanity.*

Whiteley Jon
Played Davy in the season three **The Adventures of Robin Hood** episode *The Christmas Goose.*

Whitfield David
Sang the **William Tell** song.

Whiting Gordon
Played the Man-at-Arms in the season two **The Adventures of Robin Hood** episode *The Black Five*. In series four he appeared twice as Harold in *The Lady Killer* & *The Flying Sorcerer.*
Played Dark Glasses in the third season **Danger Man** [aka **Secret Agent**] episode *Dangerous Secret.*
Played Doctor Cooper in the **Gideon's Way** episode *Fall High, Fall Hard.*
Played Doctor Pineda in the third season **The Saint** episode *Locate and Destroy.*
Played Harding in **The Scarlet Pimpernel** episode *The Elusive Chauvelin.*
Played Mohammed in the **Virgin of the Secret Service** episode *The Great Ring of Akba.*

Whiting Margaret
Played Queen Maria in **The Count of Monte Cristo** episode *A Toy for the Infanta* and Anna in *Lichtenburg.*

Whiting Neville
Played Wilson in the second season **The Saint** episode *The Miracle Tea Party.*

Whitlock Dennis
Sound Recordist on **Jason King** & **The Protectors**.

Whitney John
Co-wrote the season two **Ghost Squad** episode *Sentences of Death* [with Geoffrey Bellman].

Whitsun-Jones Paul
Played Martin Kyle in the **Department S** episode *A Cellar full of Silence* and Gresford in *Death on Reflection.*
Played Emilio Zafra in the **G.S.5** episode *Scorpion Rock.*
Played Giorgio in the **Jason King** episode *Chapter One: the Company I Keep.*
Played the Midwesterner in the first series **Man of the World** episode *A Family Affair.*
Played Inspector Blanchard in **The Persuaders!** episode *Powerswitch.*
Appeared in several roles in the first season of **The Saint**: as the woodcutter in *The Golden Journey*, as Vic Lazaroff in *Starring the Saint* and as Sebastian in *Teresa*. Played Domenick Naccaro in the second season episode *The Damsel in Distress.*

Whittaker Ian
Appeared as Gault in **The Adventures of Sir Lancelot** episode *The Ugly Duckling*.
Played Godric in the first series **The Adventures of Robin Hood** episode *The Intruders*, Harold in *The Thorkill Ghost* and Frisby in the third season's *The Lottery*.

Whittaker Stephen
Played the office boy in the **Strange Report** episode *Report 2475: REVENGE: 'When a Man Hates'*.

Whittacker-Cook Shaun
Director [Visual Effects Main Unit] on **Joe 90**.
Visual Effects Unit Director on **The Secret Service**.

Whittam Penny
Played Linka in the season two **Ghost Squad** episode *The Menacing Mazurka*.

Whitting Peter
Appeared as Stanislav in the **Jason King** episode *A Royal Flush*.

Whittingham Jack
Wrote the series one **Danger Man** episodes *The Key* [teleplayed from a story by Ralph Smart] & *Under the Lake*.
Wrote the **Gideon's Way** episodes *The Big Fix* & *The Rhyme and the Reason*.

Whyte Patrick
Played Bernie Kovar in the third season **The Saint** episode *The Better Mousetrap*.

Wilber Carey
Wrote the season three **The Adventures of Robin Hood** episode *The Salt King*.

Wilcock Sheelah
Played Gerda in the **William Tell** episode *The Spider*.

Wilcox Elizabeth
Continuity on **Department S**.

Wilcox Frank
Played Beaumont in **The Count of Monte Cristo** episode *Affair of Honour*.

Wilde Brian
Played Sutton in **The Baron** episode *Portrait of Louisa*.
Played Sir Thomas Landers in **The Scarlet Pimpernel** episode *The Sword of Justice*.

Wilde Colette
Played the farmer's wife in the first season **Danger Man** episode *The Girl in Pink Pyjamas*.
Played Pauline in the first series **Ghost Squad** episode *High Wire*.
Played Lucia in the **H. G. Wells' Invisible Man** episode *Odds Against Death*.
Guested as Shana in the **Interpol Calling** episode *Desert Hi-Jack* and as Anna Grauber in *You Can't Die Twice*.
Played Ingrid in the **William Tell** episode *The Trap*.

Wilde David
Played an art student in the **Father Brown** episode *The Head of Caesar*.

Wilde Lorna
Played Carla Lawrence in the fourth season **The Saint** episode *The Desperate Diplomat*.

Wilde Rene
Teleplayed the **William Tell** episode *The Emperor's Hat* [with Leslie Arliss: original story by Rene Wilde], teleplayed *The Raid* [with Leslie Arliss: original story by Rene Wilde] and wrote the original story for *The Assassins* [teleplayed by Ralph Smart].

Wilde Sammy
Played the Witch Doctor in the **White Hunter** episode *Voodoo Wedding*.

Wilde William
Played Gerhard in the **Department S** episode *The Man who got a New Face*.
Played Tom Stevens in the fourth season **The Saint** episode *The World Beater*.

Wilding April
Played Mary Wilson in the second series **Danger Man** [aka **Secret Agent**] episode *Yesterday's Enemies*.
Played Mary Hardy in the first season **The Saint** episode *Iris*.

Wilheim Theodore
Played the Czech official in the season two **Ghost Squad** episode *The Missing People*.
Played Strebel in the **Jason King** episode *All that Glisters* [part one].
Played the Nazi officer in the **O.S.S.** episode *Operation Lovebird*.

Wilkin Jeremy
Provided additional character's voices on **Captain Scarlet and the Mysterons**.
Played Manny in the **Man in a Suitcase** episode *Variation on a Million Bucks* [part 2: also combined with part 1 to form a movie: *To Chase a Million*].
Played Inspector Lars Bergen in the second season **The Protectors** episode *Route 27*.
Voiced the Bishop in **The Secret Service** series.
Voiced Virgil Tracey [season two] in **The Thunderbirds** series - David Holliday was Virgil for the first series.
Featured in **UFO** as, series regular, the Skydiver's navigator.

Willard Edmund
Played the concierge in **The Scarlet Pimpernel** episode *Sir Percy's Wager*.

William David
Played the Lieutenant in the season two **The Adventures of Robin Hood** episode *The Frightened Tailor*.

Williams Ben
Played the cobbler in **The Count of Monte Cristo** episode *The Portuguese Affair*.
Played the landlord in **The Scarlet Pimpernel** episode *The Imaginary Invalides*.

Williams Beresford
Played the politician in the second series **Danger Man** [aka **Secret Agent**] episode *The Black Book*.

Williams Bernard 'Bernie'
Production Manager on **The Prisoner** episodes *Arrival, The Chimes of Big Ben, A. B. and C., Free for All, The Schizoid Man, The General, Many Happy Returns, Dance of the Dead, Checkmate, Hammer into Anvil, It's Your Funeral, A Change of Mind* and *Once Upon a Time*.

Williams David
Co-wrote, with Peter Curran, the **Captain Scarlet and the Mysterons** episodes *White as Snow, Point 783, Seek and Destroy* and *The Launching*.

Williams David
Appears briefly as the little boy in the tower in **The Prisoner** episode *Arrival*.

Williams David
Played the soldier in the **O.S.S.** episode *Operation Death Trap*.

Williams Eric
Camera Operator **The Adventures of Robin Hood** and on **The Adventures of Sir Lancelot** episodes *Identity, The Bridge, The Witch's Brew, Ruby of Radnor, The Lesser Breed, The Mortaise Fair, Maid of Somerset, Sir Crustabread, The Ugly Duckling, The Prince of Limerick, The Lady Lilith, Knight's Choice, The Missing Princess* and *The Thieves*.

Williams Gwenda
Played Agnes in the second series of **The Adventures of Robin Hood** episode *The Black Patch*.

Williams Hugh
Played Milet in **The Count of Monte Cristo** episode *Flight to Calais*.
Starred as, series regular, Inspector Marlowe in **The New Adventures of Charlie Chan**.

Williams Jan
Played the girl cleaner in the **Man in a Suitcase** episode *Castle in the Clouds*.

Williams Kenneth
Appeared as Tizio in the **Sword of Freedom** episode *The School*.

Williams Leila
Played the secretary in the **White Hunter** episode *Out of the Wind*.

Williams Megan
Played Molly in the second series of **The Adventures of Robin Hood** episode *The Borrowed Baby*.

Williams Norman
Producer on the series **White Hunter** and wrote the episode *Valley of the Dead*.

Williams Peter
Played Chris Charles in the first series **Ghost Squad** episode *Bullet With My Name on it*.
Played the control tower supervisor in the **Gideon's Way** episode *The Great Plane Robbery*.

Williams Caroline Sheldon
Played Suzy in the **O.S.S.** episode *Operation Powder Puff*.

Williams Simon
Appeared as Lestrange in the **Man in a Suitcase** episode *The Bridge*.

Williams Wendy
Played Kathy in the first season **Danger Man** episode *The Sanctuary*.
Played Eva in the **Interpol Calling** episode *Payment in Advance*.

Williamson Alistair
Played Todd in the season two **Ghost Squad** episode *P.G. 7*.
Played Dibs Brown in the first season **The Saint** episode *The Element of Doubt*.

Williamson Hugh Ross
Wrote the **Sir Francis Drake** episode *Court Intrigue*.

Williamson Michael
Played Masekela in the **Man in a Suitcase** episode *The Whisper*.

Williamson Paul
Played the Superintendent in **The Adventurer** episode *The Case of the Poisoned Pawn*.
Appeared as Osbert in **The Adventures of Sir Lancelot** episode *The Outcast*, as the second knight in *The Magic Sword* and as Robert in *The Black Castle*. Played Sir Lionel in *Caledon, Shepherd's War, The Pirates* and *Knight Errant*.
Played Vance in the **Father Brown** episode *The Quick One*.
Played the London policeman in the third season **The Saint** episode *The Paper Chase*.
Played Chauvelin's agent in **The Scarlet Pimpernel** episode *The Christmas Present*.
Played Major Trangmere in the **Virgin of the Secret Service** episode *Entente Cordiale*.

Williamson Tony
Wrote **The Adventurer** episodes *Counterstrike, Has Anyone Here Seen Kelly?, I'll Get There Sometime, The Solid Gold Hearse, Icons Are Forever* & *Make it a Million*.
Wrote the third season **Danger Man** [aka **Secret Agent**] episode *Not So Jolly Roger*.
Wrote **The Champions** episodes *The Experiment, The Dark Island, Shadow of the Panther* and *Project Zero*.
Wrote the **Department S** episodes *One of our Aircraft is Empty, Who Plays the Dummy?, A Ticket to Nowhere, The Man from X* & *The Bones of Byrom Blain*.
Wrote the **Jason King** episodes *A Page Before Dying, A Deadly Line in Digits, As Easy as A B C, To Russia With ....Panache, Flamingoes only Fly on Tuesdays* & *If it's Got to Go - It's Got to Go*.
Wrote **The Persuaders!** episode *Anyone Can Play*.
Wrote the **Randall and Hopkirk [Deceased]** aka **My Partner the Ghost** episodes *Never Trust a Ghost, Who Ever Heard of a Ghost Dying?, The House on Haunted Hill, When Did you Start to Stop Seeing Things?, Murder ain't what it Used to Be!, Who Killed Cock Robin, The Ghost who Saved the Bank at Monte Carlo, When the Spirit Moves You* & *The Trouble with Women*.
Wrote the **Return of the Saint** episode *Hot Run*.

Willis Alan
Music Editor on **The Champions, Man in a Suitcase, The Protectors** & **Randall and Hopkirk [Deceased]** aka **My Partner the Ghost** and **Space 1999**.

Willis Austin
Starred as Admiral Fox in the **Seaway** series.

Willis Jerome
Played the title role in **The Adventures of Sir Lancelot** episode *The Prince of Limerick*.
Played Detective Inspector Thomson in **The Baron** episode *There's Someone Close Behind You*.
Played the second pursuer in the second series **Danger Man** [aka **Secret Agent**] episode *The Mirror's New*, the customs official *English Lady Takes Lodgers* and Colonel Maturin in the third season's *Someone is Liable to get Hurt*.
Played Inspector Thornton in the **Return of the Saint** episode *The Obono Affair*.

Willis Ted
Devised the series **Virgin of the Secret Service** and wrote the episodes *The Great Ring of Akba, The Persuasion of a Million Drops* & *Across the Silver Pass of Gusri Song*.

Willman Noel
Played Holvera in **The Adventurer** episode *Icons Are Forever*.

Played Don Carlos in **The Count of Monte Cristo** episode *A Toy for the Infanta* and Count de Morcef in *Bordeaux*.
Played the title role in the first season **Danger Man** episode *Colonel Rodriguez*.
Played Theopolos in **The Persuaders!** episode *The Long Goodbye*.

Wills Anneka
Played Fran Roeding in the third season **The Saint** episode *The Helpful Pirate*.
Played Sarah in **The Sentimental Agent** episode *All that Jazz*.
Starred as Evelyn McLean in the **Strange Report** series.

Wilmer Douglas
Played Lord Germain in the first series **The Adventures of Robin Hood** episode *Friar Tuck*.
Played Raphael Saumarez in **The Baron** episode *Long Ago and Far Away* and Rafael in *Long Ago and Far Away*.
Played Marrat in **The Count of Monte Cristo** episode *The Grecian Gift* [aka *The Brothers*].
Played Kartalis in the first series **Ghost Squad** episode *Death from a Distance* and the Inspector in the season two episode *Gertrude*.
Played Colonel Warren in the **H. G. Wells' Invisible Man** episode *Crisis in the Desert*.
Guested as Steinitz in the **Interpol Calling** episode *White Blackmail*.
Played Commander Whiting in the second season **The Protectors** episode *The Tiger and the Goat*.
Played Alan Uttershaw in the first season **The Saint** episode *The Rough Diamonds*.
Played Commissioner Dixon in the first season **Space 1999** episode *Dragon's Domain*.
Played Doctor Ward in the **UFO** episode *E.S.P.*

Wilmot Masada
Wardrobe on **Danger Man I, Danger Man** [aka **Secret Agent**], **The Prisoner** episodes *Arrival, The Chimes of Big Ben, A. B. and C., Free for All, The Schizoid Man, The General, Many Happy Returns, Dance of the Dead, Checkmate, Hammer into Anvil, It's Your Funeral, A Change of Mind* and *Once Upon a Time* and **The Saint**.

Wilsher Barry
Played PC Brown in the **G.S.5** episode *Death of a Cop*.
Played the waiter in the first season **The Saint** episode *The Gentle Ladies*.

Wilson Alan
Played the first Nazi patrol in the **O.S.S.** episode *Operation Jingle Bells*.

Wilson Audrey
Played Gretchen in the first series **Man of the World** episode *Specialist for the Kill*.

Wilson Elisabeth
Played Michelle in the **Interpol Calling** episode *The Girl with Grey Hair* and Vicenta in *Pipeline*.

Wilson Ian
Wrote, with Mike Pratt, the **Randall and Hopkirk [Deceased]** aka **My Partner the Ghost** episode *A Disturbing Case*.

Wilson Jennifer
Played Ruby Benson in the **Gideon's Way** episode *The Tin God*.
Played Jill Norman in the **G.S.5** episode *Dr. Ayre*.

Wilson Kara
Played Karen Voriska in **The Adventurer** episode *Counterstrike*.

Played Lucy Cameron in the **Jason King** episode *Every Picture Tells a Story* and Sonja in *Uneasy Lies the Head*.

Wilson Keith
Art Director on **Joe 90 & The Secret Service**, Production Designer on **Space 1999** and Assistant Art Director on **UFO**.
Wrote the **Joe 90** episode *Lone Handed 90* [with Des Saunders].

Wilson Lewis
Played the night security man in the second season **The Protectors** episode *Petard*.

Wilson Manning
Played de Moreville's Seneschal in the season two **The Adventures of Robin Hood** episode *The Black Five* and, in the third season, played Sir Charles in *The Crusaders* & Lord Guthrie in *The Salt King*.
Played the Captain in **The Four Just Men** episode *The Miracle of St. Philippe*, the hotel manager in *The Princess* and Doran in *The Godfather*.
Played Inspector Quercy in the first season **The Saint** episode *The Work of Art* & in the second season's *Jeannine*.
Played Federici in the **Sword of Freedom** episode *Alessandro*.

Wilson Michael
Special Effects Lighting Cameraman on **Thunderbirds**.

Wilson Neil
Played the police constable in the **The Persuaders!** episode *Chain of Events*.

Wilson Ronald
Played the hotel bartender in the first season **The Saint** episode *The Effete Angler* and the desk clerk in *Judith*.

Wilson Seretta
Starred as Jill Burton [Tommy's niece] in **The Zoo Gang**.

Wilson Stuart
Played Brian Hamilton in **The Adventurer** episode *The Case of the Poisoned Pawn*.
Played Marko in the **Jason King** episode *Zenia*.
Played Smith in the second season **The Protectors** episode *The Insider*.
Played Manfred in the **Return of the Saint** episode *Appointment in Florence*.
Played Vindrus in the second season **Space 1999** episode *A Matter of Balance*.

Wilson Thick
Played the American tourist in the **Return of the Saint** episode *Tower Bridge is Falling Down*.

Wiltshire Maurice
Wrote the season two **Ghost Squad** episode *The Magic Bullet*.

Winbolt Jack
Camera Operator on **The Protectors**.

Winbolt John
Camera Operator on **The Champions**.

Winder Michael
Wrote the third series **The Saint** episodes *Escape Route* & *To Kill a Saint* and the fourth's *Legacy for the Saint*.
Wrote the second series **Space 1999** episode *Devil's Planet*.

Winding Victor
Played Braddock in the third season **The Saint** episode *To Kill a Saint*.

Winfield Gilbert 'Gil'
Wrote the **Interpol Calling** episodes *Air Switch* [with Leonard Fincham] and *Slave Ship* [with Geoffrey Orme and Edwin Richfield].
Wrote the **White Hunter** episode *Second Dealer*.

Winfield Gilbert
Played Alison in the first season **Danger Man** episode *Position of Trust*.
Played the U.S.S. driver in the **O.S.S.** episode *Operation Big House*.

Windsor Frank
Played John Sorrensen in the **Randall and Hopkirk [Deceased] aka My Partner the Ghost** episode *My Late Lamented Friend and Partner*.

Wing Anna
Played Mrs Deveraux in the **Father Brown** episode *The Hammer of God*.

Winn Beverly
Played the girl in the **Department S** episode *A Fish out of Water*.
Played Valerie in the **Randall and Hopkirk [Deceased] aka My Partner the Ghost** episode *Somebody just Walked over my Grave*.

Winogradsky Louis
aka/see Lord Lew **Grade**

Winsor Juliet
Played Paula in the first series **Ghost Squad** episode *Still Waters*.

Winston Jimmy
Played the rating in the **UFO** episode *Destruction*.

Winter Donavan
Played the pilot in the **White Hunter** episode *Valley of the Dead*.

Winter Nicolas
Co-wrote, with James Carhartt, **The Adventures of Robin Hood** episodes *The Mystery of Ireland's Eye & The Little People* [season 2] and *A Tuck in Time* [3].

Winter Pauline
Played the waitress in the **O.S.S.** episode *Operation Jingle Bells*.

Winton Sheree
Played Shorty's friend in the first series **Man of the World** episode *Blaze of Glory*.
Played the fellow traveller in **The Sentimental Agent** episode *Box of Tricks*.

Wise Herbert
Directed the **Man in a Suitcase** episode *All that Glitters*.

Wise Joseph
Played the senior official in the **Man in a Suitcase** episode *Castle in the Clouds*.

Wise Sybil
Played Alice in **The Scarlet Pimpernel** episode *A Tale of Two Pigtails*.

Wise Vic
Played the fairground barker in the first series **Ghost Squad** episode *High Wire*.

Witherick Albert
Assistant Director on **The Adventurer**.
Art Director on the fourth season of **Danger Man [aka Secret Agent]** and on **Jason King**.

Witkin Jacob
Played Magnus in the **Father Brown** episode *Three Tools of Death*.

Witty Christopher
Played Ricci in the first series **Ghost Squad** episode *Assassin*.

Witty John
Played the MI5 man in the **O.S.S.** episode *Operation Barbecue*.
Played Denis Ashmore in the **White Hunter** episode *Squire of the Serengeti*.

Woddis Roger
Wrote **The Prisoner** episode *Hammer into Anvil*.

Wolfe A. Sandford
Co-wrote the third season **The Saint** episode *The Best Laid Schemes* [with Joseph Morhain].

Wolfe Ian
Played Polineaux in **The Count of Monte Cristo** episode *Victor Hugo*.

Wolf Michael
Played Kimitz in **The Baron** episode *Diplomatic Immunity* and Albrecht in *Enemy of the State*.
Played the barman in the second season **The Saint** episode *The Rhine Maiden* and the hotel receptionist in the third season's *The Helpful Pirate*.

Wolff Frank
Played Miros in **The Baron** episode *Red Horse, Red Rider* and Frank Martin in *The Killing* [Part 2 of a 2 parter: also exists, edited together with part 1, *Masquerade*, to form a feature *Man In a Looking Glass*].
Played Jim Reston in the second season **The Saint** episode *The Old Treasure Story*.

Wolfit Donald
Starred as Sir Andrew Wilson in the series **Ghost Squad**.

Wolfit Margaret
Played Maria in **The Four Just Men** episode *Dead Man's Switch*.

Wong Anna May
Played Miss Lee in the first season **Danger Man** episode *The Journey Ends Halfway*.

Wontner Hilary
Played the first man in the steamroom in the **Randall and Hopkirk [Deceased] aka My Partner the Ghost** episode *The Ghost Talks*.

Wood Charmaine
Puppet Operator on the **Joe 90** series.

Wood Mary Laura
Played Queen Isolt in **The Adventures of Sir Lancelot** episode *Winged Victory*.
Played Madeleine in **The Count of Monte Cristo** episode *The Luxembourg Affair*.
Played Anita in the **Interpol Calling** episode *The Girl with Grey Hair*.
Played Barbara in the **White Hunter** episode *The No-Account*.

Wood Peter M.

Technical Advisor on **The Buccaneers** [aka **Dan Tempest**] episodes *The Raiders, Captain Dan Tempest, Dan Tempest's War with Spain, The Wasp, Whale Gold, Gunpowder Plot, Articles of War, Ghost Ship, Conquest of New Providence, Mother Doughty's Crew, Blood Will Tell, Hurricane, Dead Man's Rock, Dangerous Cargo, Hand of the Hawk, Gentleman Jack and the Lady, Mr. Beamish and the Hangman's Noose, Marooned, Dan Tempest and The Amazons, The Ladies, The Surgeon of Sangre Rojo, The Return of Calico Jack, Conquistador, Aztec Treasure, Prize of Andalusia, Cutlass Wedding, Dan Tempest Holds an Auction, Flip and Jenny, To the Rescue, Indian Fighters, Mistress Higgins' Treasure, The Spy Aboard* [Master-at-Arms], *Pirate Honour, Instrument of War* and *Printer's Devil.*

Woodbridge George

Played Sir Melias in **The Adventures of Sir Lancelot** episode *The Ferocious Fathers* and Leonides in *The Magic Sword.*
Played Gregory Ward in **The Persuaders!** episode *Greensleeves.*

Woodburn Roger

Made and operated puppets on the **Supercar** series.

Woodcock David

Was the first voice in part 2 of *Adventure Two* of **Sapphire and Steel** and played the Submariner in part 4.

Woodford Jospehine

Played Miss Woodfall in **The Sentimental Agent** episode *Finishing School.*

Woodgrove Charles - pseudonym of/see Fred **Freiberger**

Woodhouse Hugh

Co-wrote [with Martin Woodhouse] the first season **Supercar** episodes *Rescue, Amazonian Adventure, Talisman of Sargon, False Alarm, What Goes Up, Keep it Cool, Grounded, Jungle Hazard, High Tension, A Little Art, Ice-Fall, Island Incident, The Tracking of Masterspy, The Phantom Piper, Deep Seven , Pirate Plunder, Hostage, The Sunken Temple, Trapped in the Depths, Dragon of Ho Meng, Magic Carpet & The White Line.*

Woodhouse Martin

Wrote [with Hugh Woodhouse] the first season **Supercar** episodes *Rescue, Amazonian Adventure, Talisman of Sargon, False Alarm, What Goes Up, Keep it Cool, Grounded, Jungle Hazard, High Tension, A Little Art, Ice-Fall, Island Incident, The Tracking of Masterspy, The Phantom Piper, Deep Seven , Pirate Plunder, Hostage, The Sunken Temple, Trapped in the Depths, Dragon of Ho Meng, Magic Carpet & The White Line.*

Woodnutt John

Played the head porter in the first season **The Saint** episode *Luella.*

Woods Middleton

Played the merchant in the season four **The Adventures of Robin Hood** episode *The Flying Sorcerer* and Geoffrey Carr in the **Gideon's Way** episode *The Housekeeper.*

Woods Phil

Played Howard's henchman in the first series **The Protectors** episode *The Big Hit* and Colson in the second season's *Sugar and Spice.*

Woodthorpe Peter

Played Radek in the **Man in a Suitcase** episode *Night Flight to Andora.*

Woodville Catherine

Played Janet in the second series **Danger Man** [aka **Secret Agent**] episode *Colony Three.*
Played Nicola Webb in the **G.S.5** episode *Scorpion Rock.*
Played Karen Bates in the second season **The Saint** episode *The Scorpion* and Barbara Astral in *The Damsel in Distress.*
Played Little Dove in the **Sir Francis Drake** episode *The Fountain of Youth* and Anne in *Visit to Spain.*

Woodvine John

Played John Garvey in **The Baron** episode *Storm Warning* [part 1 of a two-parter: also exists, edited together with part 2 - *The Island*, as a feature entitled *Mystery Island*].
Played Kruger Haller in **The Champions** episode *The Search.*
Played Luigi in the first season **Danger Man** episode *The Brothers*, Shimon in the second series [now aka **Secret Agent**] episode *Judgement Day* and Singri Rhamin in the third season's *Two Birds with One Bullet.*
Played Karl Epper in the season two **Ghost Squad** episode *Lost In Transit.*
Played Gioti in the second season **Man of the World** episode *The Bandit.*
Played Ray Dennis in the **Return of the Saint** episode *Tower Bridge is Falling Down.*
Played the pilot in the third season **The Saint** episode *The Queen's Ransom.*

Woodward Edward

Played Arkin Morley in **The Baron** episode *Countdown.*
Played Jack Liskard in the third season **The Saint** episode *The Persistent Patriots.*
Played the Spanish Captain in the **Sir Francis Drake** episode *Court Intrigue.*

Woodworth Richard

Played the guard in **The Zoo Gang** episode *The Lion Hunt.*

Woof Harry

Location Manager on **Strange Report**.

Wooldridge Ted

Special Effects Lighting on **Fireball XL5**.
Lighting Cameraman [Visual Effects Second Unit] on **Joe 90**.
Location Unit Lighting Cameraman on **The Secret Service**.

Woolf Gabriel

Played Anders in **The Sentimental Agent** episode *Express Delivery.*

Woolf Henry

Played Paco in the season two **The Protectors** episode *Quin.*

Woolf Malya

Played the Russian lady in the **Strange Report** episode *Report 8944: HAND: 'A Matter of Witchcraft?'.*

Woolf Vicki

Played Francis in the **Man in a Suitcase** episode *The Girl who Never was.*
Played the Rent-A-Car girl in **The Persuaders!** episode *Powerswitch.*
Played Maggie in the third season **The Saint** episode *Escape Route.*
Played the prisoner in the **Sir Francis Drake** episode *The Bridge* and the Lady-in-Waiting in the *Court Intrigue.*

Woolf Victor

Starred as, series regular, Derwent in **The Adventures of Robin Hood**: *Husband for Marian, The Highlander, Secret Mission, Table's Turned & The Thorkill Ghost* [season one]; *A Village Wooing, The Scientist, Blackmail, Ransom, Outlaw Money, The Trap, Hubert, The Dream, The Blackbird, The Shell Game, The Final Tax, Ambush, The Goldmaker's Re-*

turn, Fair Play, The Borrowed Baby, Food for Thought, Too Many Earls, The Black Five, The Road in the Air & Carlotta [two]; The Salt King, Pepper, Change of Heart, Brother Battle, My Brother's Keeper, An Apple for the Archer, The Angry Village, The Mark, The Bride of Robin Hood, The Christmas Goose, The Challenge of the Black Knight, The Rivals, Knight Errant, The Healing Hand, One Man's Meat, Too Many Robins, The Ghost that Failed, The Crusaders, Roman Gold, The Doctor, The Fire, At the Sign of the Blue Boar, The Youthful Menace, Woman's War, Little Mother & Marian's Prize [three] and The Lady Killer, A Touch of Fever, Sybella, Tuck's Love Day, The Loaf, Six Strings to his Bow, The Devil You Don't Know, Goodbye, Little John, The Parting Guest & The Pharaoh Stones [four].

Also played a variety of roles in the first and second series of **The Adventures of Robin Hood**: Alfred in *Dead or Alive* & *The Youngest Outlaw*, a monk in *The Inquisitor*, Cedric in *Maid Marian*,*The Knight Who Came To Dinner* & *Checkmate*, a clerk in *The Brothers*, the first pilgrim in *The Intruders*, Limpus in *The Vandals*, Lame Ned in *Ladies of Sherwood*, Edward in *The Wanderer*, the armourer in *The Byzantine Treasure* & the short monk in *The Wager* [season 1] and a clerk in *A Year and a Day*, the goldsmith in *The Goldmaker*, Notarius in *The Impostor*, the first villager in *The Hero*, the Abbot of Whitby in *The Haunted Mill*, Sir Henry Beaulieu in *The Black Patch*, the Warden in *The Secret Pool* & the Landlord in *Highland Fling* [2].

Played the shop assistant in **The Prisoner** episode *Hammer into Anvil*.

Woolfe Betty
Played Martha in the **Randall and Hopkirk [Deceased]** aka **My Partner the Ghost** episode *But what a Sweet Little Room*.

Woolgar Jack
Played the old man in the **Randall and Hopkirk [Deceased]** aka **My Partner the Ghost** episode *Just for the Record*.
Played Charlie Hallowes in the third season **The Saint** episode *A Double in Diamonds*.

Woottan Russell
Played the Changeling in *Adventure Three* of **Sapphire and Steel** [part 2].

Wordsworth Richard
Played the curator in **The Four Just Men** episode *National Treasure* and Walter in *Panic Button*.
Played Porcelli in the **Sword of Freedom** episode *The Suspects* and Coppa in *Angelica's Past*.

Worrod Roger
Played the porter in the second series **Danger Man** [aka **Secret Agent**] episode *English Lady Takes Lodgers*.

Worth Brian
Appeared as Sir Hubert in **The Adventures of Robin Hood** first series episode *Husband for Marian*.
Played Sir Kay in **The Adventures of Sir Lancelot** episode *The Knight with the Red Plume* and Sir Modred in *The Queen's Knight*.
Played Rackam in **The Buccaneers** [aka **Dan Tempest**] episode *Blackbeard*, Charles Vane in *The Raiders*, Rackam in *Captain Dan Tempest* and Calico Jack in *The Return of Calico Jack*.
Played Bourges in **The Champions** episode *Reply Box No: 666*.
Played El Ferro in the second series **Danger Man** [aka **Secret Agent**] episode *The Affair at Castelevara*, Xavier in *The Outcast* and Forbes in the third season's *The Man who wouldn't Talk*.
Played Crandall in **The Four Just Men** episode *The Night of the Precious Stones*.

Appeared as the Group Captain in **The Prisoner** episode *Many Happy Returns*.
Played the salesman in the first series **The Protectors** episode *King Con*.
Played Peter Corrio in the second season **The Saint** episode *The Smart Detective*.

Worth Martin
Teleplayed the **William Tell** episode *The Magic Powder* [original story by Ralph Smart].

Woxholt Egil
Shot the underwater sequences for the fourth series **Danger Man** [aka **Secret Agent**] episode *Shinda Shima* which, edited together with the other season four episode *Koroshi*, also exists as a feature entitled *Koroshi*.

Wragg Peter
Director [Visual Effects Second Unit] on **Joe 90**.

Wrather
Produced the series **Interpol Calling** [with Rank].

Wrestler Peter
Co-directed the **O.S.S.** episode *Operation Meatball* [with Peter Maxwell].

Wright Brian
Played the motorcyclist in the second season **Man of the World** episode *Double Exposure*.

Wright Heather
Played the third fan in the **Jason King** episode *That isn't Me, It's Somebody Else*.
Played Sally in the **Return of the Saint** episode *Signal Stop*.

Wright Jennifer
Played Mrs Smith in the **H. G. Wells' Invisible Man** episode *The Rocket*.
Played Janet Waites in the second season **The Saint** episode *The Imprudent Politician*.

Wright Jenny Lee
Played Julie in the first series **The Protectors** episode *Ceremony for the Dead*.

Wright Maggie
Played Latticia in **The Baron** episode *Diplomatic Immunity*.
Played Sandra in the **Department S** episode *A Fish out of Water*.
Played Jean in the **Gideon's Way** episode *The White Rat*.
Played Dana in the **Jason King** episode *Buried in the Cold, Cold Ground*.
Played Anita in the **Man in a Suitcase** episode *Day of Execution*.
Played Cleaver's P.A. in the **Return of the Saint** episode *Yesterday's Hero*.
Played the girl receptionist in the second season **The Saint** episode *Jeannine*, Mara in *Lida*, Madeline in *The Crime of the Century* and Jacqueline in the third season's *To Kill a Saint*.

Wright Pamela
Played the Governor's daughter in **The Buccaneers** [aka **Dan Tempest**] episode *Gunpowder Plot*.

Wright Pat
Played Henrietta in **The Count of Monte Cristo** episode *The Pen and the Sword*.

Wright Tony
Played David Alton in **The Persuaders!** episode *Someone Like Me*.

Played John Herrick in the first season **The Saint** episode *The Arrow of God*, Steve Nelson in the second season's *The Crooked Ring* and Largo in the fourth's *Where the Money Is*. Played Tonio in the **Sword of Freedom** episode *Serenade in Red*.

Wrubel Peter
Played the Swiss soldier in the **Sword of Freedom** episode *Francesca*.

Wyatt Peter
Played the airport security officer in the season two **Ghost Squad** episode *The Magic Bullet*.

Wyatt Tessa
Played Anna in the **Return of the Saint** episode *Vicious Circle*.
Played Catherine Fraser in the **UFO** episode *The Long Sleep*.

Wyeth Kathja
Played Miss Budapest in the **Randall and Hopkirk [Deceased]** aka **My Partner the Ghost** episode *Just for the Record*.

Wyldeck Martin
Played Prokov in **The Adventurer** episode *Counterstrike*.
Played Ulrich in the third series **The Adventures of Robin Hood** episode *At the Sign of the Blue Boar*.
Played Sir Robert Ellacott in **The Baron** episode *The Persuaders*.
Played Nagor in the first season **Danger Man** episode *The Sisters* and Kasser in the third season [now aka **Secret Agent**] episode *Say it with Flowers*.
Played The Emir of Kavar in the season two **Ghost Squad** episode *Quarantine at Kavar*.
Played Karl in the **Jason King** episode *Chapter One: The Company I Keep*.
Played Bates in the first season **The Saint** episode *The Noble Sportsman*, Mr Mason in the second season's *The Abductors*, Van Effen in the third's *The Angel's Eye* and the first man at the party in the fourth's *The Double Take*.

Wyler Judith
Played Lolita in **The Buccaneers** [aka **Dan Tempest**] episode *Captain Dan Tempest*.

Wyler Richard
Played Gregg Wilde in **The Baron** episode *There's Someone Close Behind You*.
Played Jenson in the **Jason King** episode *A Page Before Dying*.
Played Algernon in the **Return of the Saint** episode *The Judas Game*.
Played Allessandro Naccaro in the second season **The Saint** episode *The Damsel in Distress* and Roddy Morton in *The Man who could not Die*.

Wylton Tim
Played the waiter in the **Strange Report** episode *Report 3424: EPIDEMIC: 'A Most Curious Crime'*.

Wyman Bryan
Played Ruckert in the **Department S** episode *A Small War of Nerves*.

Wymark Patrick
Guested as General Gomez in **The Champions** episode *Operation Deep-freeze*.
Played Ortiz in the first season **Danger Man** episode *An Affair of State*.
Played Downing in the first series **Man of the World** episode *The Mindreader*.
Played Captain Williams in the **Sir Francis Drake** episode *The Garrison*.

Wyndham Anthea
Played Miss Williams in the first season **The Saint** episode *The Lawless Lady*.

Wyngarde Peter
Played King Ibrahim/Roland Noyes in **The Baron** episode *The Legions of Ammak*.
Played Hallam in **The Champions** episode *The Invisible Man*.
Starred as Jason King in the series **Department S** and **Jason King**.
Guest starred as The New Number 2 in **The Prisoner** episode *Checkmate*.
Played Tiberio in the third season **The Saint** episode *The Man Who Liked Lions* and Turin in *The Gadic Collection*.
Played Colonna in the **Sword of Freedom** episode *The Sicilian*.

Wynne Michael
Played "Fats" Logan in **The Baron** episode *Countdown*.
Played Coates in **The Champions** episode *The Ghost Plane*.
Played Alf in the **Gideon's Way** episode *The White Rat*.
Played the policeman in **The Persuaders!** episode *A Home of One's Own*.
Played Ted Kermein in the first season **The Saint** episode *Luella*,. Rene in the second season episode *The Spanish Cow* and Franco De Cesarie in the third season's *The Man Who Liked Lions*.
Played Vlakon in the **Virgin of the Secret Service** episode *A Fate Worse Than Death*.

Wynne Norman
Played Jones the Boat in the season two **Danger Man** [aka **Secret Agent**] episode *Whatever Happened to George Foster?*.
Played Mr Gilliat in the **Gideon's Way** episode *The Firebug*.
Played Mason in the **Man in a Suitcase** episode *All that Glitters*.

Wynyard John
Played the butler in the first season **Danger Man** episode *Vacation*.

Wyse John
Played Julio in the first season **Danger Man** episode *The Contessa*.

****

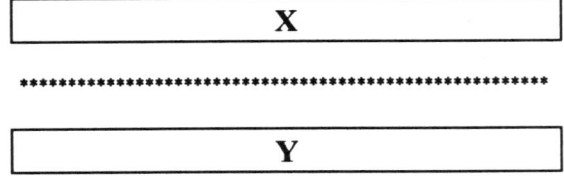

****

Y

Yaltan Jaron
Played Subra in the second series **Danger Man** [aka **Secret Agent**] episode *The Colonel's Daughter*.

Yang Lian-Shin
Played Miss Shoo in the first season **Danger Man** episode *The Journey Ends Halfway*.

Yang Marie
Played the Asian girl in the second season **Man of the World** episode *The Prince*.

Yapp Tommy
Played the barman in the second series **Danger Man** [aka **Secret Agent**] episode *A Very Dangerous Game* and the contact man in the fourth season's *Shinda Shima*.
Played the Chinese man in the **Virgin of the Secret Service** episode *Entente Cordiale*.

Yardley Stephen
Guested as Pieter in **The Champions** episode *The Survivors*.
Played the stranger in the second series **Danger Man** [aka **Secret Agent**] episode *The Outcast*.

Yarrow Arnold
Played Dr. Malik in the season two **Ghost Squad** episode *Death of a Sportsman*.

Yates Pauline
Played Diana Heeley in the season two **Ghost Squad** episode *P.G. 7*.
Played Mary Mason in the **Gideon's Way** episode *The Wall*.
Played Karen Rose in the **Strange Report** episode *Report 4977: SWINDLE: 'Square Root of Evil'*.

Yates Peter
Directed the **Danger Man** [aka **Secret Agent**] episodes *Sting in the Tail* & *Loyalty Always Pays* [series 2] *The Man on the Beach*, *Say it with Flowers* & *Two Birds with One Bullet* [3] and the fourth season episode *Shinda Shima* [*Shinda Shima* was combined with *Koroshi* - directed by Michael Truman - to form a TVM called *Koroshi*].
Directed **The Saint** episodes *The Fellow Traveller*, *The Bunco Artists*, *The Work of Art*, *The Rough Diamonds* & *The Noble Sportsman* [season 1] and *Sibao* & *The Damsel in Distress* [2].

Yeldham Peter
Wrote the third series **The Adventures of Robin Hood** episode *The Lottery*.
Wrote the **Espionage** episode *We, the Hunted*.
Wrote the season two **Ghost Squad** episodes *The Missing People* & *Escape Route*.
Wrote **The Persuaders!** episode *Read and Destroy*.
Wrote **The Zoo Gang** episode *African Misfire*.

Yeomans Mary
Played Virginia Bierce in the second series **Danger Man** [aka **Secret Agent**] episode *The Mirror's New*.
Played Ann Ross in the **Gideon's Way** episode *The Thin Red Line*.

York John
Played Johnny in **The Adventurer** episode *To The Lowest Bidder*.

York Mark
Played a Skydiver engineer in the **UFO** episode *The Psychobombs*.

Yorke Terry
aka Terence Yorke
Appeared in **The Adventures of Robin Hood**: as the guard in *The Goldmaker's Return* & the Man-at-Arms in *Carlotta* [series 2]; the Man-at-Arms in *Brother Battle*, the servant in *The Challenge of the Black Knight* & the Squire in *Quickness of the Hand* [3] and Mauger in *The Flying Sorcerer*, Bault in *Hostage for a Hangman*, John Dale in *The Debt* & the Sergeant in *The Edge and the Point* [4].
Played the Man-at-Arms in **The Adventures of Sir Lancelot** episode *The Mortaise Fair*.
Played a thug in the **Man in a Suitcase** episode *Blind Spot*.
Appeared as the thug in **The Prisoner** episode *A. B. and C.*
Played Sancho in the second season **The Saint** episode *The Spanish Cow* and Jim in the third season episode *Escape Route*.

Young Aida
Associate Producer on the first series of **Danger Man** [episodes 13 - 39] and Producer on the second series [episodes 1-7]; Production Supervisor on **H. G. Wells' Invisible Man** & **William Tell** and Production Manager on **The New Adventures of Charlie Chan**.

Young Arthur
Played Dukas in **The Count of Monte Cristo** episode *Monaco* and Jacques in **The Scarlet Pimpernel** episode *The Christmas Present*.

Young Carleton G.
Guested as D'Alba in **The Count of Monte Cristo** episode *The Sardinia Affair*.

Young Eric
Played Ho Ling in **The Champions** episode *The Beginning* and the Burmese Police Captain in *The Gun-Runners*. [*The Beginning* was combined with *The Interrogation* to form a 'feature' entitled *Legend of The Champions*].
Played Mr Toy in the first season **Danger Man** episode *The Actor*, the police Lieutenant in *The Honeymooners* and Ming in *The Journey Ends Halfway*.
Played Robert E. Lee in the first series **Ghost Squad** episode *Hong Kong Story* and the barman in season two's *East of Mandalay*.
Played the airport barman in the **Jason King** episode *Every Picture Tells a Story*.
Played Chou in the first series **Man of the World** episode *The Frontier*.
Played Surinit in the **Return of the Saint** episode *Assault Force*.
Played Lo Yung in the second season **The Saint** episode *Jeannine*.
Played Sung-Lee in the **Strange Report** episode *Report 2641: HOSTAGE: 'If You Won't Learn, Die!*.

Young Felicity
Played Ruth in the **Interpol Calling** episode *Trial at Cranby's Creek*.

Young Gerald
Played Sir Edras Levy in the first season **The Saint** episode *The Lawless Lady*.

Young Harold
Played Durand in **The Scarlet Pimpernel** episode *The Lady in Distress*.

Young Jeremy
Played Doctor Brogan in the **Department S** episode *The Pied Piper of Hambledown*.

Played Jimmy Rice in the season two **Ghost Squad** episode *Lost In Transit*.

Played Douglas Kershaw in the **Randall and Hopkirk [Deceased]** aka **My Partner the Ghost** episode *You Can Always find a Fall Guy*.

Played Inspector Galba in the third season **The Saint** episode *The Man Who Liked Lions* and Gregorio in the fourth season's *The Ex-King of Diamonds*.

Young Joan
Played Miss Burnham in the second series **Danger Man [aka Secret Agent]** episode *The Professionals*.

Young Karen
Played Alba in the fourth season **The Saint** episode *The Ex-King of Diamonds*.

Young Lilani
Appeared as the Japanese granddaughter in the fourth season **Danger Man [aka Secret Agent]** episode *Koroshi* [*Koroshi* was also merged with the only other surviving fourth season colour episode, *Shinda Shima*, to form a TVM entitled *Koroshi*].

Young Muriel
Played Lady Coulchaud in **The Adventures of Robin Hood** first season episode *Richard The Lionheart*.

Young Raymond
Played Armand in **The Count of Monte Cristo** episode *Point Counter Point*.

Played the marine officer in the first season **Danger Man** episode *View from the Villa*.

Played the Spanish Colonel in the **Department S** episode *Who Plays the Dummy?*.

Played Bruno in **The Four Just Men** episode *Mava*.

Played Inspector Mansour in **The Persuaders!** episode *The Ozerov Inheritance*.

Played Rawlings in the **Randall and Hopkirk [Deceased]** aka **My Partner the Ghost** episode *But what a Sweet Little Room*.

Played Aldo in the **William Tell** episode *The Avenger*.

Young Stephen
Starred as Nick King in the **Seaway** series.

Young Yee Wah
Played Priestess Chaeo in the **Virgin of the Secret Service** episode *Across the Silver Pass of Gusri Song*.

Yu Chin
Played Zuleika in **The Adventures of Sir Lancelot** episode *The Mortaise Fair*.

Played the receptionist in the first season **Danger Man** episode *The Actor*.

Yu Ling Barbara
Played the second hostess in the second series **Danger Man [aka Secret Agent]** episode *A Very Dangerous Game* and also appeared as a hostess in the fourth season episode *Shinda Shima* [*Shinda Shima* was also merged with the other surviving fourth season episode, *Koroshi*, to form a TVM entitled *Koroshi*].

Played the taxi driver in **The Prisoner** episode *Arrival*.

Played Choa Chun in the **Shirley's World** episode *Follow That Rickshaw*.

Yunus Tariq
Played Akbar in the **Father Brown** episode *The Quick One*.

Z

Zakari Zed
Played Ti Sung in the **Interpol Calling** episode *Chinese Mask*.

Zaran Nik
Played Charolais in **The Adventurer** episode *Poor Little Rich Girl*.

Guested as Said in **The Champions** episode *Desert Journey*.

Played Jean in the **Department S** episode *The Man who got a New Face*.

Played Mareen in the **Jason King** episode *Flamingos only Fly on Tuesdays*.

Played Casim in the **Man in a Suitcase** episode *The Revolutionaries*.

Played Brin in the **Randall and Hopkirk [Deceased]** aka **My Partner the Ghost** episode *The Trouble with Women*.

Played Chaudri in the fourth season **The Saint** episode *The People Importers*.

Zenios George
Played the second policeman in **The Baron** episode *Long Ago and Far Away*.

Played the barman in the second series **Danger Man [aka Secret Agent]** episode *Yesterday's Enemies* and the Greek boy in the *It's Up to the Lady*.

Played the first seaman in the **Man in a Suitcase** episode *Variation on a Million Bucks* [part 2: also combined with part 1 to form a movie: *To Chase a Million*].

Played Nicky in the third season **The Saint** episode *Escape Route*.

Played the Sheik in the **Virgin of the Secret Service** episode *The Great Ring of Akba*.

Zenon Mickael
Starred as Joe Two-Rivers in the series **The Forest Rangers**.

Zephyr Zoe
Played Margaret in the second series **Danger Man [aka Secret Agent]** episode *The Colonel's Daughter*.

Zetterling Mai
Played Nadia in the first season **Danger Man** episode *The Sisters*.

Played Maya in **The Four Just Men** episode *Mava*.

Played Tania in the **H. G. Wells' Invisible Man** episode *The Prize*.

Zimmerman Matt
Voiced Alan Tracey in **The Thunderbirds** series.

Played Jim Wade [co-pilot] in the **UFO** episode *Exposed*.

Zinn Elizabeth
Played Miss Brown in the season two **Ghost Squad** episode *Sabotage*.

Zoppellini Mario
Played the kitchen porter in the **Jason King** episode *The Stones of Venice*.

Zoremah
Played Lida in the **White Hunter** episode *Sister My Spouse*.

Zuber Marc
Played Kanarek in **The Adventurer** episode *Poor Little Rich Girl*.

Played the policeman in the **Jason King** episode *A Kiss for a Beautiful Killer*.

Played Kahan's henchman in the first series **The Protectors** episode *.....With a Little Help from my Friends*.

Played the French tough in the **Return of the Saint** episode *Collision Course* Part 1: *The Brave Goose* [also exists, combined with part 2, as a movie entitled *The Saint and the Brave Goose*].

****

Coming soon from SJG Communications Services:

The Rogers & Gillis Guide to The Avengers

From
Dave Rogers
The Complete Avengers [Boxtree ISBN 1 85283 244 4]
The Avengers and Me[Titan Books: Patrick Macnee with Dave Rogers]
The Ultimate Avengers
&
Stay Tuned ['*The Avengers* Magazine']
and
Steve Gillis
[*The Gillis Guide to The Prisoner* and *The Gillis Guide to Trek*]
comes the enormous and definitive guide to
The Avengers

This quintessential guide is timed to co-incide with the release of the spectacular new movie.

Covers every episode, every series & the new movie.

The Avengers
The New Avengers
The Avengers Movie

This landmark book details the participation of all the artistes and creative personnel who have made a legend.

◆ Over 300 Pages ◆ A4 Size ◆ A-Z Format of ALL THE PEOPLE ◆ Series & episode guide

◆ Actors ◆ Directors◆ Make-up artists ◆ Producers ◆ Special fx people ◆ Stunt persons ◆ Writers
◆ And More

Plus all their other important achievements:
◆ Books ◆ CD-Roms ◆ TV ◆ TV Movies ◆ Movies ◆ Miniseries ◆ And More

Next to the video, the best book to have.

All enquiries should be made to **SJG PO Box 44 Shrewsbury SY2 5WB UK**
Information herein is for trade and publicity purposes only. Copyright © S. J. Gillis 1997 All Rights Reserved. **Published by: SJG Communications Services Limited**

Also available from SJG Communications Services: *From the author of The Gillis Guide to Trek*

The Gillis Guide to The Prisoner *by S.J. Gillis*

ISBN: 0-9528441-1-7

A Gillis Guide: All you need to know

Patrick McGoohan's TV classic examined like never before

This quintessential guide details the participation of all of the artistes who have made a legend.

◆Every Star ◆Every Episode ◆Every Actor ◆Every Writer ◆Every Director

Essential to all TV and movie buffs
A must for all Prisoner fans.

It's A Gillis Guide!

◆ Actors ◆ Directors ◆ Producers ◆ Writers ◆ Stunt persons ◆ And More

Plus all their other important achievements:

◆ Books ◆ CD-Roms ◆ TV ◆ TV Movies ◆ Movies
◆ Miniseries ◆ And More
Next to the video, the best book to have.

Such a book on *The Prisoner* has never been done before.

All enquiries should be made to **SJG PO Box 44 Shrewsbury SY2 5WB UK**

The Rogers & Gillis
Guide
To
ITC

Also available from SJG Communications Services:

ISBN 0-9528441-0-9

The Gillis Guide to Trek by S.J. Gillis

A Gillis Guide: All you need to know
The Quintessential Guide
A must for all Sci-fi fans.
A colossal work.

Covering every episode, every series & every movie, this landmark book details the participation of over 4,000 artistes and creative personnel who have made a legend.
◆ A4 Size ◆ A-Z Format ◆ 320 Pages

◆ **Actors** ◆ **Directors** ◆ **Make-up artists** ◆ **Producers** ◆ **Special fx people** ◆ **Stunt persons** ◆ **Writers**
◆ **And More**
Plus all their other important achievements:
◆ **Books** ◆ **CD-Roms** ◆ **TV** ◆ **TV Movies** ◆ **Movies** ◆ **Miniseries** ◆ **And More**

Next to the video, the best book to have.

The Gillis Guide to Trek is <u>a must for all Trek fans.</u> This <u>colossal work</u> covering such an extensive amount of people from every corner of the globe who have been involved over a 30 year period in the most famous Sci-fi phenomenon in the universe has led to a <u>who is who in the Sci-fi genre.</u> Listing their other major achievements has given an invaluable reference book <u>essential to all TV and movie buffs.</u>

The A-Z Guide lists <u>over 4000</u> entries covering pages 4-307: The episode guide is in appendix form and covers pages 308-320
No wasted pages, superfluous graphics or large print.

The detailing of collaboration with fellow Trek crew gives a <u>new insight</u> to the careers of so many people.

This will certainly be a well thumbed and treasured book.

<u>All enquiries</u> should be made to **SJG PO Box 44 Shrewsbury SY2 5WB UK**